SOCIAL AND CULTURAL DYNAMICS

Volume One: Fluctuation of Forms of Art

*Volume Two: Fluctuation of Systems of Truth,
Ethics, and Law*

*Volume Three: Fluctuation of Social Relationships,
War, and Revolution*

Volume Four: Basic Problems, Principles, and Methods

AMERICAN SOCIOLOGY SERIES

KIMBALL YOUNG, *General Editor*

Social and Cultural Dynamics

VOLUME ONE

Fluctuation of Forms of Art

(PAINTING, SCULPTURE, ARCHITECTURE, MUSIC,
LITERATURE, AND CRITICISM)

BY PITIRIM A. SOROKIN

AMERICAN BOOK COMPANY

NEW YORK   CINCINNATI   CHICAGO

BOSTON   ATLANTA   DALLAS   SAN FRANCISCO

TO PETER AND SERGEI

and

Their Godfathers and Godmothers

SERGEI A. and NATALIA K. KOUSSEVITZKY

MICHAEL I. and SOPHIA M. ROSTOVTZEFF

ACKNOWLEDGMENTS

I wish, first of all, to thank the Harvard Committee for Research in the Social Sciences, without whose financial aid this work could not have been carried out on its present scale.

I am indebted also to a large number of older and younger scholars, whose names are mentioned in the various chapters, but particularly to N. O. Lossky, I. I. Lapshin, N. S. Timasheff, N. Okuneff, Peter Struve; to N. N. Golovine, A. A. Zaitzoff, S. S. Oldenburg, P. A. Ostrouchov, G. Mickwitz; to C. A. Anderson, P. N. Savitzki, S. Pushkareff, E. Maximovitch, R. K. Merton, H. Cross, R. H. Phelps, E. F. Parker; to John V. Boldyreff, K. B. Krishna, and C. Q. Berger. The spadework which they have so willingly done for me in their respective fields has gone far to provide the vast and systematic basis in facts on which the present work rests. Elizabeth Gilboy, Mrs. M. S. Butler, and Mrs. K. H. Bessell, of the Statistical Laboratory of the Harvard Committee for Research in the Social Sciences, have given statistical assistance. R. H. Williams, Miss B. Miller, and H. T. Silverstein have helped me with the writing, and Mrs. Marjorie Noble, secretary of the Department of Sociology, has prepared much of the typescript for the press. The staff of the Harvard College Library, by its unfailing service, has greatly hastened the completion of the work.

For many fruitful suggestions, I am grateful to Sergei Koussevitzky, M. I. Rostovtzeff, Wilbur C. Abbott, Charles J. Bullock, Edwin B. Wilson, E. F. Gay, O. L. Spaulding, V. V. Leontieff, C. C. Zimmerman, Kimball Young, C. A. Ellwood, S. G. Elisséeff, F. C. Frey, T. L. Smith, E. Y. Hartshorne, W. A. Lunden, and N. B. De Nood. Nor shall I leave unmentioned my former and present students, both graduates and undergraduates, many of whom have been among my severest and most stimulating critics. For kind permission to make quotations from the works of various authors my thanks are due to George Allen & Unwin Ltd., Librairie Armand Colin, Dodd, Mead & Company, E. P. Dutton & Co., Harper & Brothers, Harvard University Press, Henry Holt and Company, Alfred A. Knopf, Librairie H. Laurens, The Macmillan Company, Charles Scribner's Sons, and other publishers. I am indebted also to Otto Bettmann, The Valentine Gallery, and other art galleries and museums for photographs of several of the art works included.

To the University of Minnesota and to Harvard University I am most humbly and sincerely grateful for their making possible, by granting me a place on their teaching staffs, the continuation of my scientific investigations. I thank also, for their kindness to me and their appreciation of my labors, many of my colleagues, American, European, and Asiatic social scientists, and the scientific institutions and societies that have granted me honorary membership.

Finally, I am indebted to my wife for her inestimable help in this work and in my lifework.

This work has grown out of my efforts to understand something of what has been happening in the social and cultural world about me. I am not ashamed to confess that the World War and most of what took place after it were bewildering to one who, in conformity with the dominant currents of social thought of the earlier twentieth century, had believed in progress, revolution, socialism, democracy, scientific positivism, and many other "isms" of the same sort. For good or ill, I fought for these values and paid the penalty. I expected the progress of peace but not of war; the bloodless reconstruction of society but not bloody revolutions; humanitarianism in nobler guise but not mass murders; an even finer form of democracy but not autocratic dictatorships; the advance of science but not of propaganda and authoritarian *dicta* in lieu of truth; the many-sided improvement of man but not his relapse into barbarism. The war was the first blow to these conceptions. The grim realities of the Russian Revolution provided the second. If anybody had seriously predicted in 1913 a small fraction of what has actually taken place since, he would have been branded then as mad. And yet what then appeared to be absolutely impossible has indeed happened.

All this naturally gave rise to insistent questioning. What were the reasons, the causes, and the meaning of these surprises? The leading principles of the social science that I had learned did not help much in my attempt to understand. Quietly, sincerely, only for myself, I began to meditate, to study, and to look for the answer. This personal quest has continued for a number of years. For a long time I was groping in darkness. Various hypotheses were tried and found inadequate. After many trials and errors the central idea of this work emerged. Step by step it developed and crystallized. After preliminary tests of its truth, I undertook its systematic elaboration. At that stage it was my good fortune to receive financial aid from the Harvard Committee for Research in the Social Sciences, and this, together with the generous co-operation of many scholars, enabled me to proceed in a fashion hardly possible for an individual scholar working alone. The result is the present group of volumes.

In spite of its great size, the work deals with only one central problem, namely, the change and fluctuation of Ideational, Idealistic, and Sensate cultures. But it is one of those problems which embrace thousands of others that are fundamental. For an adequate understanding of it, the investigation and interpretation of countless subsidiary matters are necessary. In this respect the work follows the example provided by many great social thinkers. After all, G. B. Vico dealt only with one problem in his *Scienza nuova;* August Comte developed in all his writings only one idea, positivism in connection with the law of the three states; all the works of Herbert Spencer are but a development of his formula of evolution and progress.

Viewed psychologically, this work represents, as has already been observed, my attempt to understand the character of contemporary culture and society. To this extent it is the world as seen through the window of an individual temperament and a personal life experience. The standpoint assumed is Idealistic in the specific sense of the term as used in this work. It is the only point of view that permits us to see without serious distortion both extreme types of integrated culture — the Ideational and the Sensate.

Considered objectively, these volumes are an investigation of the nature and change, the dynamics of integrated culture: its types, its processes, its trends, fluctuations, rhythms, tempos. The main material with which this investigation deals is that provided by the Graeco-Roman and Western civilizations during the more than twenty-five hundred years of their history. In briefer fashion it touches also on the Egyptian, the Babylonian, the Hindu, the Chinese, and the Arabic cultures. It is not, however, a *history* of these cultures, but a *sociology of their change.* What the difference is between these two, the work itself should make clear. Nor has the work, in its choice of materials, its principles, methods, and aims anything to do with what is called Cultural History. Of the semi-historical disciplines which it resembles, it is nearest to what often is styled Philosophy of History. Since almost all great sociological systems are a brand of philosophy of history, and since most of the great philosophies of history are a sort of sociology of cultural change, I do not have any objection to the use of this name by anyone who fancies it to describe the present work.

The materials on which this study is based have been chosen for evident reasons: the Graeco-Roman and Western cultures provide us with fuller records than does any other culture. Primitive societies cannot furnish the material needed: they have no "history," no long-time records; they are little known to us, and that little, poorly understood. Moreover, to repeat Aristotle, one can study the life and properties of an oak better

in the fully developed tree than in the acorn. If we wish to investigate
the life processes of integrated culture, we can do it better with one fully
developed than with another as yet at its beginning. Here and there,
as problems demand, the primitive cultures are touched upon; but they
are of necessity not the center for a study of sociocultural fluctuations.

As to the method of the study, it follows what, in the subsequent pages,
I call the logico-meaningful, combined with the causal-functional. It
gives full freedom to logical thought — generalizing and analytical —
and, at the same time, it tests its deductions inductively by the relevant
empirical facts. Such a combination appears to me to be the only sound
approach in the social sciences. Without logical thought there cannot
be relevant "fact." Without the relevant facts we never know which
of several — and per se equally logical — theories fits the empirical
reality best, and most successfully orders its perceptional chaos into a
comprehensible system. Pure "fact finding" is thoughtless and rarely
fruitful of significant results. Pure logical speculation in the social
sciences is sterile.

Social and Cultural Dynamics is complete in four volumes, all of which
form a rounded treatment of the subject, but each of which presents the
fluctuation of different aspects of the cultures as a whole. In *Volume
One* the first section is introductory: it sets forth compactly and in
preliminary fashion the problem of integrated culture, in order to make
comprehensible the subsequent sections and the series of concepts used
in them. The second part deals with the fluctuations in the field of art:
painting, sculpture, architecture, music, literature, and criticism. In
Volume Two the first part is devoted to the fluctuation in science, philosophy, and religion. It is a *Wissenssoziologie*, even of the contemporary
Wissenssoziologie itself. Part Two examines the fluctuations in ethical
and juridical mentality on its highest and lowest planes. In *Volume
Three*, Part One treats of the types and fluctuations of social relationships,
including many fundamental associations in the sociopolitical and economic sphere. Part Two is an inquiry into the fluctuation of war; Part
Three, into that of internal disturbances. Part Four deals with the relationships between culture mentality and conduct and ends with a post-
script to the first three volumes. With this, the first three volumes are
complete. *Volume Four* will offer a summarized theory of sociocultural
change, and close with a treatise on the *règles de la méthode sociologique*.

This outline indicates that the work concerns itself not with surface
and trifles, but with the fundamental categories of cultural phenomena.
I believe that it deals with them thoughtfully and with due attention

to the data. It has certainly many shortcomings, but these have come about, I feel, not so much because of the incompetence of the author as because the problems are difficult and complete materials for their solution do not exist. Generally, the larger the problems and the wider the field studied, the greater the probability of error. As the problems and the field of this work are immense, any scholar who ventures to wrestle with them cannot escape failure to achieve entirely satisfactory results in every respect. The point is not the mere presence of shortcomings, but how great they are in comparison with those in other treatises of the kind and to what extent they affect the soundness of the major contentions. It is hoped that the answers to these considerations will not be entirely unfavorable to the present work. It should be remembered that the work attempts to delineate a continent and not a county; and what in a map of one would be a straight line would in a map of the second be twisted into curves and turns. Yet both maps would be accurate, each in its own way. I have avoided the psychologically impressive device of giving long rows of illustrative qualitative cases and have refused to parade intuitional dicta veiled in the cloak of seemingly deep thought. Throughout this work I have instead preferred the more adequate and more difficult methods. I have chosen to use systematically the numerically quantitative rather than the verbally quantitative method, and I have laid open to the reader all the data upon which my conclusions are based. At any rate, shortcomings, doubtful points, and uncertainties are not glossed over. On the contrary, they have, if anything, been unduly pointed to throughout; and no attempt has anywhere been made to mislead the reader or to impress him with various simulacra of thought and scholarship.

As to the conclusions, they certainly deviate greatly from the commonly accepted current opinions. Nor are they in complete agreement with any existing shade of opinion or thought. Hence they are not likely to be acceptable to any faction, but to be assailed by all factions. This, however, does not trouble me much. The fact is that many of these conclusions were surprising even to me. Yet, the logic of the situation and the data being considered, no others were at all possible. In this connection, it should be pointed out that the main body of materials were collected not by me, but by various scholars, each working independently without knowledge either of the objective for which the data were needed, or of my theories. Despite this, the materials in the different fields of culture exhibit a notable agreement with one another. Such a spontaneous agreement is of itself important evidence of the validity of the conclusions.

Particularly surprising will be the portrait in the following pages of our contemporary culture. But I believe it to be a good likeness. The original seems to be a typical Sensate culture in its postmature stage. As a child of this culture, I am fond of it, despite its imperfections; but, conscious of the symptoms of its overripeness, I am also resigned to the possibility of its decline. As an impartial observer, I can admire greatly all three kinds — Ideational, Idealistic, and Sensate — but each only in the period of its ascendancy and vigor. In their decline they deserve condolence, not admiration.

But the possible decline of our present-day Sensate phase does not necessarily mean the end of the Western culture, any more than did the decay of medieval Ideationalism. There was a shift from a withered Ideational to a resplendent Sensate phase, just as there may again be a turn from our superannuated Sensatism to a new and vigorous Ideationalism.

This explains why the possibility of the decline of the present cultural phase does not make me at all pessimistic. However profound the contemporary crisis may be — and it is infinitely deeper than most people recognize — after a trying transitory period, there looms not an abyss of death, but a mountain peak of life, with new horizons of creation and a fresh view of the eternal heavens.

PITIRIM A. SOROKIN

Cambridge — Winchester

CONTENTS

PART ONE

INTRODUCTORY

Chapter One. FORMS AND PROBLEMS OF CULTURE INTEGRATION AND METHODS OF THEIR STUDY 3

I. Culture integration and culture unity — a dark problem. Most of the works in the field do not distinguish fundamentally different forms of integration. II. Various meanings of culture integration. III. Classification of the main forms of the integration of culture elements. Four basic types of interrelations of culture elements: spatial or mechanical adjacency, association due to an external factor, causal or functional integration, internal or logico-meaningful unity. The causal and logico-meaningful unifications are the central forms of culture integration. IV. Logico-meaningful integration and the method of its study. Each of the four forms of culture integration demands and admits a respective method of their study: purely descriptive method in regard to the spatial congeries and external associations used abundantly in anthropological and historical works; the causal-functional method in application to the causal and functional unifications; logico-meaningful method in regard to the logico-meaningful unities. Logico-meaningful method is analogous to causal-functional in its cognitive functions, but differs from it in a series of fundamental characteristics. In the study of social and cultural phenomena it is as important as the causal-functional method and is the only method that grasps the logico-meaningful sociocultural unities. It is heuristically helpful for a discovery of causal relationships. V. Some results of the preceding analysis. Not every culture is wholly integrated. Integrated culture lives and changes in a way different from that of the unintegrated cultural congeries.

Chapter Two. IDEATIONAL, SENSATE, IDEALISTIC, AND MIXED SYSTEMS OF CULTURE 55

I. Internal and external aspects of culture and methods of reading them. Internal aspect of culture is its meaning or mentality. Psychological, causal, and logico-meaningful readings of culture. Importance of logico-meaningful reading. Its premises and assumptions. II. Ideational, Sensate, and Mixed systems of culture. Preliminary definitions. Four major premises of each type of culture: the nature of reality, the nature of the needs and ends to be satisfied, the extent of satisfaction and the method of satisfaction. In accordance with the character of the solution of these premises we have the main types of integrated culture: Ideational (active and passive), Sensate (active, passive, and cynical), Idealistic (harmonious synthesis of Ideational and Sensate types) and other Mixed forms. Each type has many satellites implied in its major premises. Enumeration of the satellites.

Chapter Three. CONCRETE ILLUSTRATIONS OF THE CHIEF TYPES OF CULTURE MENTALITY 103

I. Concrete examples of distribution of each type of culture mentality among the individuals and small groups. II. Hinduism, Buddhism, Jainism, Taoism, Sufism, Christianity, and other Ascetic and Mystic systems as examples of Ideational culture mentality given in vast sociocultural systems. Historical examples of Active Ideational, Sensate, Idealistic, and other Mixed culture mentalities.

Chapter Four. SOCIOCULTURAL FLUCTUATIONS: CONCEPT AND FORMS OF SOCIOCULTURAL PROCESS 153

I. Fundamental specifications of the concept process. Becoming versus Being, Change versus Permanency. Without specification of the unit of the process, its time relationship, its space relationship, and its direction, the term "process" remains indeterminate and ill defined. Four fundamental directions of process: space direction, time direction, quantitative and qualitative directions. Many-dimensionality of social space — time, quantity, and quality. Complexity of sociocultural "vector." II. Forms and degrees of uniqueness and recurrence. III. Are sociocultural processes unique or recurrent? Criticism of the unicist conception of sociocultural processes. Does history repeat itself? Historical and sociocultural processes as ever-new variations of ever-repeated themes. IV. Punctuation and pulsation of sociocultural processes. Change in the direction of sociocultural process as its punctuation. Cumulative change in two or more directions as particularly noticeable punctuation. The problem of periodization of continuous historical process. V. Linear, cyclical, and varyingly recurrent patterns of process from the standpoint of their direction. Criticism of linear and cyclical conceptions.

PART TWO

FLUCTUATION OF IDEATIONAL, IDEALISTIC, AND SENSATE FORMS OF ART

Chapter Five. IS THERE ANY UNIFORM SEQUENCE IN THE FLOURISHING OF VARIOUS ARTS IN THE HISTORY OF A GIVEN CULTURE? PRELIMINARY CRITICAL SURVEY OF THEORIES ON THE SUBJECT . 195

I. Introductory remarks. Purely descriptive histories of art rarely answer many important questions of a general nature in the field and rarely give us any formula of uniformity. The problems, however, exist and in some way have to be answered. II. Theories of the recurrence of art phenomena in space, in time, and in both together: of Petrie, Ligeti, Laprade, Hegel, Combarieu, and others. Criticism.

Chapter Six. IS THE CURVE OF ART DEVELOPMENT UNIFORMLY SIMILAR IN VARIOUS SOCIETIES AND CULTURES? PRELIMINARY CRITICAL SURVEY OF THEORIES ON THE SUBJECT (*Continued*) . . 223
Theories of Bayet, Deonna, Chambers, Bovet, Lalo, and others. Criticism.

Chapter Seven. IDEATIONAL, SENSATE (VISUAL), AND MIXED (IDEALISTIC, CUBISTIC, AND OTHER) STYLES IN ART: PAINTING AND SCULPTURE 243
I. Ideational and Sensate (Visual) styles. Definitions according to the content and form of painting and sculpture. II. Main subclasses of each type. The main characteristics of each style.

Chapter Eight. RECURRENCE IN SOCIAL SPACE AND FLUCTUATION IN TIME OF THE IDEATIONAL, VISUAL, AND MIXED STYLES IN PAINTING AND SCULPTURE (QUALITATIVE OUTLINE) 269
I. Is the style of primitive art Visual or Ideational? II. Brief notes on recurrence of the main styles in Egyptian, Assyrian, Chinese, and Hindu pictorial art. III. Fluctuation of the main styles in the Greek culture. IV. Fluctuation of the styles in Roman painting and sculpture.

Chapter Nine. FLUCTUATION OF THE MAIN STYLES IN THE PAINTING AND SCULPTURE OF WESTERN EUROPE (QUALITATIVE OUTLINE, *Continued*) 309
I. Rise and domination of Ideational Christian art from the sixth to the twelfth centuries. II. The thirteenth-century Idealistic art. III. Rise of Visualism from the fourteenth to the sixteenth centuries. IV. The end of the sixteenth and the seventeenth century. The baroque as a further growth of Sensate Visualism. V. The eighteenth century. VI. The end of the eighteenth century and the nineteenth century, as a climax of the triumph of Visual art. Antivisual reaction in the art of the twentieth century.

Chapter Ten. QUANTITATIVE DESCRIPTION OF THE FLUCTUATION OF THE MAIN STYLES AND THEIR SATELLITES IN THE PAINTING AND SCULPTURE OF WESTERN EUROPE 369
I. Preliminary methodological remarks. II. Fluctuation of the proportion of religious and secular topics in painting and sculpture of Christian medieval Europe, of Italy, France, Spain, The Netherlands, Central Europe, England, Russia, and Islamic countries, from the beginning of the Middle Ages up to the present time. III. Fluctuation of Ideational, Idealistic,

and Visual styles (impressionistic, naturalistic, expressionistic, ideational, and antivisual mixed — cubistic, etc.) in pictures and sculptures. IV. Fluctuation of the Spiritual and Sensual character of painting and sculpture. V. Fluctuation of quantitative and qualitative nudity. VI. Fluctuation of other satellites of the Ideational and Visual forms of art. "Thematic spectrum" of the secular art and its changes: fluctuation of the proportion of subjects of antiquity, portraiture, *genre*, *paysage*, fantastic subjects, animals, and *nature morte* in painting and sculpture. *Paysage* and its quantitative ups and downs. Change in the content of *paysage*: rural-urban, pure and impure, sunny and gloomy, sea, mountains, etc. Fluctuation of the proportion of animal and *nature morte* pictures and sculptures. Portraiture and fluctuation of its proportions in the total secular art. Fluctuation of the proportion of the social classes (royalty, nobility, clergy, bourgeoisie, intellectuals, artists, lower classes) depicted in portraiture. Male and female in portraiture. Caricature. *Genre.* Curve of its quantitative fluctuations. Qualitative changes of *genre*. Subjects of antiquity in painting and sculpture. VII. Summary.

Chapter Eleven. FLUCTUATION OF IDEATIONAL AND VISUAL FORMS OF ARCHI-
TECTURE 507

Definition of these forms of architecture. A concise outline of the main waves in the history of Egyptian, Graeco-Roman, and Western architecture.

Chapter Twelve. FLUCTUATION OF IDEATIONAL, SENSATE, AND MIXED FORMS
OF MUSIC 531

I. Definition of these forms of music. II. Fluctuation of the main styles in time and space: in preliterate societies; in Oriental, Graeco-Roman, and Western cultures. To what extent are the main waves in music contemporaneous with the respective waves in painting, sculpture, architecture, and literature?

Chapter Thirteen. FLUCTUATION OF IDEATIONAL AND SENSATE FORMS OF
LITERATURE AND CRITICISM 595

I. Literature of preliterary groups. II. Fluctuation of the main forms of literature and criticism in Graeco-Roman culture. III. Medieval Ideational literature and criticism, in their inner and external characteristics. IV. Idealistic literature and criticism of the thirteenth and fourteenth centuries. V. The period of the domination of Sensate literature and criticism. Change in the proportion of religious and secular literature, in its heroes (God, saints, human heroes, common man, pathological and subsocial types of human personality), in its styles, its forms, its topics, its mores and morals. VI. Related problems considered in the light of the present theory: "Purposeful" and "pure" art. Rhythm of separation of art from other cultural values (knowledge, religion, ethics, etc.) and of unifi-

cation with them. VII. General summary on art fluctuation. Present-
day revolt in art against its Sensate forms.

APPENDIXES 689
   APPENDIX TO CHAPTERS NINE AND TEN 691
   APPENDIX TO CHAPTER THIRTEEN 720

INDEXES 731
   INDEX OF AUTHORS 733
   INDEX OF SUBJECTS 738

LIST OF TABLES

1. Summary of the Main Traits and Satellites of the Discussed Types of Adaptation 97
2. Distribution of Ideational, Mixed, and Sensate Types among Popes and Kings 106
3. Summary: Main Forms of Uniqueness and Recurrence . . . 164
4. The Phenomena of Identity 165
5. Discoveries in the Natural Sciences 204
6. Mechanics and Technical Inventions 205
7. Discoveries and Inventions in Greece and Rome 206
8. Sequence of Blossoming of the Main Arts in Ten Great Cultures . 209
9. Culture Characteristics 217
10. Parallelism of Greek and European Art 240
11. Prague and Cambridge Studies Compared 373
12. Fluctuation of the Religious and Secular in Art 378
13. Fluctuation of the Main Styles in Art 389
14. Approximate Estimates of the Curves Data 407
15. Fluctuation of the Spiritual and the Sensual Character in Art . . 411
16. Fluctuation of Extremely Spiritual and Sensual Art 421
17. Fluctuation of Nudity in Art — Qualitative 423
18. Fluctuation of Ascetic, Neutral, and Erotic in Art 428
19. Fluctuation of Nudity in Art — Quantitative 432
20. Fluctuation of the Content of Secular Art 440
21. Fluctuation of *Paysage* in Art 455
22. Fluctuation of *Paysage* Types in Art 457
23. Urban and Rural *Paysage* in Art 461
24. Joyful and Sad *Paysage* in Art 463
25. Number and Per Cent of Animal Pictures and Sculptures in the Total Secular Art 466
26. Fluctuation of Portraiture 469

27. Fluctuation of Social Classes and Sexes in Portraiture 472
28. Social Classes in Portraiture for Europe 486
29. Male and Female in Portraiture 489
30. *Genre* in Secular and Religious Art 491
31. Fluctuation of Types of *Genre* 493
32. Proportion of Religious and Secular Composers by Centuries . . . 575
33. Proportion of Religious and Secular Compositions by Centuries . . 576
34. Fluctuation of Theatrical and Nontheatrical Compositions by Centuries . 580
35. Fluctuation of Compositions by Content 591

LIST OF FIGURES

1. Spatial Directions 160
2. Varieties of Linear Process 184
3. Religious and Secular Art by Countries 383
4. Main Styles in Art by Countries 394
5. The Visual and Ideational in Art by Countries 400
6. Long-Time Waves of the Main Styles in Art 404
7. The Spiritual and Sensual in Art by Countries 416
8. The Extremely Spiritual and Sensual in Art by Countries 417
9. The Covered, Ideational, Religious, and Spiritual in Art for Europe as a Whole 418
10. The Nude, Secular, Sensual, and Visual in Art for Europe as a Whole . 419
11. Ascetic, Sexual, and Neutral in Art by Countries 429
12. Fluctuation of Nudity in Art by Countries 437
13. Animals, *Nature Morte*, and *Paysage* in Art by Countries . . . 445
14. *Genre* and Portraiture in Art by Countries 446
15. The Fantastic and Antique in Art by Countries 447
16. Fluctuation of the Content of Art for Europe as a Whole 448
17. Joyful and Sad *Paysage* in Art by Countries 464
18. Aristocracy, Clergy, and Bourgeoisie in Art by Countries 481
19. Intellectuals, Military, and Lower Classes in Art by Countries . . . 482
20. The Social Classes in Portraiture for Europe as a Whole . . . 483
21. The Sexes in Portraiture by Countries 484
22. The Sexes in Portraiture for Europe as a Whole 485

LIST OF PLATES

PLATE	FACING PAGE
I	244
II	246
III	248
IV	250
V	252
VI	254
VII	256
VIII	258
IX	264
X	288
XI	300
XII	306
XIII	308
XIV	328
XV	334
XVI	342
XVII	362
XVIII	364
XIX	366
XX	510
XXI	512
XXII	514

PART ONE

Introductory

Chapter One

FORMS AND PROBLEMS OF CULTURE INTEGRATION AND METHODS OF THEIR STUDY

I. Culture Integration and Culture Unity — a Dark Problem

Is every culture an integrated whole, where no essential part is incidental but each is organically connected with the rest? Or is it a mere spatial congeries of cultural objects, values, traits, which have drifted fortuitously together and are united only by their spatial adjacency, just by the fact that they are thrown together, and by nothing more? If it is the first, then what is the principle of integration, the axis around which all the essential characteristics are centered and which explains why these characteristics are what they are and why they live and pulsate as they do? If the second, then how did it happen that in a given area one kind of conglomeration of cultural objects and values took place, while in another area a different kind occurred? How and why did it happen that in the course of time one conglomeration moved in one direction while another changed in a way that was wholly diverse?

These are the problems which I shall consider briefly in Part One of this volume before passing on to a more substantial study of the fundamental types of integrated cultures, their functioning and change.

For the moment it is unimportant how we define human culture. *In the broadest sense it may mean the sum total of everything which is created or modified by the conscious or unconscious activity of two or more individuals interacting with one another or conditioning one another's behavior.* According to this definition, not only science, philosophy, religion, art, technics, and all the physical paraphernalia of an advanced civilization are cultural phenomena; but the trace of a footstep on the sand left by a savage and seen by Robinson Crusoe, a heap of refuse and broken trees left by an exploring party in a virgin forest, the bones and shells and ashes left by some prehistoric tribe in the ground excavated by an archeologist — these and millions of other human creations and modifications are all a part of culture. Such a definition is the broadest possible, and these wide limits

3

are accepted by many anthropologists and sociologists.   Others give a narrower definition, meaning by culture not everything created and modified by man, but only collective and superindividual creations (E. Tylor), or only those that are marked by "exteriority and constraint" (E. Durkheim), or those that are due not to heredity but to invention-imitation-borrowing (G. Tarde), or those which represent a variety of the social thought (E. de Roberty), or finally only the finest and most magnificent creations of human genius in the form of the masterpieces of science, philosophy, religion, art, law, and technique.

Which of these definitions is right just now is unimportant for my purposes.   It is enough to say that each may be right if it is useful for the specific purpose to which it is applied, and wrong if it does not meet the requirements or is used inconsistently.   Most, however, are far from being clear and satisfactory, for they replace one unknown, x, by another factor not better known, y.[1]   But I am not going to press this point for the moment.   What I do mean to pursue further here is to what extent these definitions are used by their authors consistently in discussing the problem of integrated and nonintegrated culture, and how much they help toward a comprehension of all the numerous subsidiary questions connected with that basic problem.

Many of the cultural anthropologists, sociologists, historians, and other social scientists seem to assume unreservedly that each culture is an integrated whole, and that nonintegrated culture either does not exist or represents something rare and abnormal.   Here are several typical examples of this view:

A culture is a functioning dynamic unit and the various traits which compose it are interdependent.   A culture trait does not function in isolation nor independently of other traits of the culture, but each is influenced by a change in any phase of the culture. . . .   Since the traits which comprise a culture are interrelated, an innovation affects the entire culture.[2]

Can historical data be torn out of their full context?   Dare we assume when we begin an investigation that we can tear a closely woven tapestry apart, sew the fragments on a "timeless" background, and get anything but a crazy quilt for our labour? . . .   In order for separate characteristics . . . to have meaning, they must be considered with reference to the whole problem and to each

---

[1] For instance, what are the criteria which distinguish the peculiarly "individual" and "group" traits?   Likewise, there are enormous difficulties involved in separating clearly "inherited" from "acquired" traits, or the traits which are stamped by "exteriority" and "constraint" from those which are "free" and "internal."   In this, as well as in the subsequent points discussed, analytical thinking has been shallow.

[2] W. D. Wallis, *Culture and Progress* (New York, 1930), pp. 11-12, and chaps. i and ii.

other — they must be considered as a configuration united by the logic of internal relationships. . . . The configuration constitutes the parts just as the parts constitute the configuration; neither can be considered in isolation. . . . [Otherwise] we shall have nothing left but a scattered collection of *disjecta membra* that helps us to explain nothing.[3]

To a greater or less extent, every cultural element is inextricably interconnected with other cultural elements and with the general cultural milieu itself. A culture is more than the simple mathematical addition of its individual parts.[4]

Since the assumption here is that of complete integration, therefore no trait can be properly understood without a consideration of the whole of the culture in question. Almost all those who claim that culture is a unity, or organism, or living and functioning whole, from the promulgators of various organistic, organismic, and organic theories of society and culture, from the sociological realists and universalists, up to the Spenglerian type of philosophers of culture — all of these are either explicit or implicit partisans of this belief.[5] The same is to be said of all those who with one factor or variable — be it economic, racial, geographic, familistic, religious, or any other — try to explain the main characteristics of a given culture as mere functions of the selected variable or factor. The very essence of such theories consists in the assumption of the existence of a causal or functional relationship between the postulated main factor and all the other properties of a given culture, which makes those other properties simply the "superstructure" or "result" or "function" or "satellite" of it. Such a theory in its very nature means the assumption that the culture is functionally integrated.[6]

But the champions of the integrated character of culture do not agree all along the line. Some hold for an integration without any reservation whatsoever, as was illustrated in the passages from W. D. Wallis and S. Winston quoted above. Others make reservations similar to that which appears in the following statement: "A culture, like an individual, is a more or less *consistent* pattern of thought and action. . . . This integration of cultures is not in the least mythical." It is true, the author continues, that "some cultures, like some periods of art, fail of such integration. . . . But cultures at every level of complexity, even

[3] H. Becker, "Culture Case Study," in *Social Forces*, Vol. XII (1934), p. 399.

[4] S. Winston, *Culture and Human Behavior* (New York, 1933), p. 32.

[5] For a discussion of these theories see my *Contemporary Sociological Theories* (New York, 1928), chaps. ii, iv, and vii.

[6] For a discussion of these theories see *ibid.*, *passim*.

the simplest, have achieved it." And further we read, "This lack of integration seems to be as characteristic of certain cultures as extreme integration is of others."[7] Here the author introduces some reservation, but states it ambiguously and inconsistently.

Most of the recent anthropologists who are supposed to deal with this problem more intensively belong to one of the above varieties. Many of them, like R. Benedict, B. Malinowski, A. R. Radcliffe-Brown, M. Mead, E. Sapir, C. Wissler, R. B. Dixon, to mention but few names, virtually claim that a culture is a unity, a functional whole; that it has its own pattern; that it requires to be studied in its whole configuration if its separate traits are to be properly understood and interpreted.[8] Somewhat similar is the claim of the "statistical investigators" for the affinity or adhesion or correlation of various culture traits, a theory represented by such investigations, besides the early study of E. Tylor, as Hobhouse, Wheeler, and Ginsberg's *The Social Institutions and Material Culture of the Simpler Peoples*.[9]

On the other hand, many of these same investigators indicate that a combination of the culture traits and culture complexes as well as the whole given culture may in some cases be "logical," as Dixon puts it, in some cases merely "accidental,"[10] in some cases the "external associations" of the traits, and in others the "adhesions" or their intrinsic association (C. Wissler);[11] some cultures may be "genuine," while others are "spurious" (E. Sapir).[12] Such distinctions make the meaning of the unity or interdependence or integration of culture somewhat indefinite; in a sense they even contradict the very claim that all cultures are integrated. If some cultures are a purely "accidental" or "external" or "spurious" mass of objects, traits, and values, can such a congeries be regarded as an integrated whole, a unity? If so, does this not make the concept of unity and integration meaningless, since every congeries would now possess organic unity and nothing in the world would be unintegrated? If such an accidental agglomeration is not a unity, then is this not a

[7] R. Benedict, *Patterns of Culture* (Boston, 1934), pp. 46–48.

[8] See M. Mead, *Coming of Age in Samoa* (New York, 1928); C. Wissler, *Man and Culture* (New York, 1923); R. B. Dixon, *The Building of Cultures* (New York, 1928); E. Sapir, *Time Perspective in Aboriginal American Culture: A Study in Method* (Ottawa, 1916); B. Malinowski, *Crime and Custom in Savage Society* (New York, 1926) and "Culture," in *Encyclopedia of the Social Sciences* (New York, 1933–34), Vol. IV, pp. 621–646; A. R. Radcliffe-Brown, "On the Concept of Functional Social Science," in *American Anthropologist*, Vol. XXXVII (1935), pp. 394–402.

[9] London, 1915.   [10] Dixon, *op. cit.*, pp. 156 ff.   [11] Wissler, *op. cit.*, pp. 66 ff.

[12] E. Sapir, "Culture, Genuine and Spurious," in *American Journal of Sociology*, Vol. XXIX (1924), pp. 401–429.

contradiction of the claim that every culture is an integrated whole? These considerations show the state of confusion in the field of the problem. The reason for this confusion seems to be chiefly that most of the investigators fail to elucidate exactly what they mean by integration or unity or interdependence of parts or organic character as applied to a culture. As we shall see, they either mean nothing specific or include in one term several things so fundamentally different that the whole statement about the integrated character of culture becomes void of all clear meaning. As a result, many writers proffer contradictory statements, like those above. Until the investigators busy themselves with at least an elementary analysis of what they mean by these terms, no real understanding of either the structure and the nature of culture, or its traits, or its changes, is possible in any satisfactory degree. Hence the attempt on my part in the pages which follow to pause at this problem and explain what are the main forms of relationship between the various culture traits, characteristics, and complexes from the standpoint of integration, and consequently, what may be the main divergent meanings of culture integration. We shall see that an enormous number of important problems in the field of the nature and life of culture are dependent for their solution upon the clear treatment of this preliminary consideration.

II. Various Meanings of Culture Integration

Many of us are familiar with the fine living rooms of some of our well-to-do friends. I have in mind just such a room. It is spacious and is filled with exquisite furniture and rare art objects. There are a few pieces of antique New England furniture. The ceremonial costume of a Russian priest ("riza") is fastened on one of the walls. Side by side with it there is a picture of a famous Japanese school of painting. Then there are two works by a French Impressionist, and one by a prominent cubistic painter. There are also an Italian Primitive, two genuine statues of Buddha imported from Siam, two Chinese vases of the T'ang period, and several other treasures of different times and countries. On the floors antique Oriental rugs lie near a hooked rug of old New England. The living room is a "culture area." Now the question arises: Is the culture represented by the living room an integrated whole, or is it a mere spatial conglomeration of various things (each valuable separately), and is this adjacency the only bond which unites them into a single cultural complex?

Let us assume for a moment that spatial adjacency is the only bond of union. Shall we then style an array of this sort by the term "integrated culture"? Or shall we refuse the term to such accumulations?

Whether or not we grant the term is of little importance. What is important is that there do exist cultural conglomerations where the parts are bound together by different and additional ties. Suppose we take such a culture area as the Cathedral of Chartres. Most of its component details are not only spatially adjacent but are of the same style, and thus are comprehensive parts of the whole: the cathedral of the Christian religion as it was in the twelfth, thirteenth, and fourteenth centuries. When the essence of the religion is understood, the meaning of almost all of its important venerated objects and forms becomes comprehensible; the parts become inseparable from the whole and from one another. They are lines and phrases of one book, unified, consistent, devoted to the same topic, where every page is part of the whole and, to be properly understood, demands the reading of the rest of the book. The difference between this kind of integrated culture area and that which is based on mere spatial adjacency is evident without further comment. What this consists of in detail I shall discuss later. For the time being let us continue with our concrete cases.

Instead of a cathedral, let us take a modern garage or filling station or factory. Each of these culture areas is certainly unified. In each the individual components of the total mass of culture objects and traits bear a functional relationship to one another and to the whole, and the entire complex is thus integrated functionally. In the filling station you cannot eliminate either the automatic gasoline fillers, or the air pump, or the tanks, or any of the other parts without which the station could not function successfully. And this is true of the garage or factory. There are, of course, a few superficial details, mainly of an ornamental nature, as, for example, the architectural style of the building, the landscaping and planting of the surrounding grounds, the exact pattern or nature of which is, relatively, a matter of indifference. But subtract these and there still will remain a causal (functional) system of many objects, traits, and complexes which cannot be separated without destroying the essential nature of the station, garage, or factory. Even the basis of their architectural type (structural and functional aspects) often belongs to this integrated whole: one cannot build a filling station or factory like a medieval castle or a Gothic cathedral. Here again we sense a coalescence different from that of mere spatial adjacency.

Still another shade of difference in the integration of culture appears when one observes, say, a part of a city where within the area of a few blocks one sees a conglomeration of late Gothic, Renaissance, and baroque buildings surrounded by the usual flat, two- or three-story box houses.

Compare with this the medieval parts of some European cities where everything in sight is Gothic, or a few blocks in the City of New York occupied entirely by skyscrapers. The difference is immediately evident. In the first case all the divergent architectural types are united only by spatial adjacency. Nothing consistent is easily perceptible in their styles, not even that of the functional relationship of one building to another. They do not belong together. The styles are just accumulated in one area by the interplay of various accidental factors. They are not united either logically or functionally. The buildings of the medieval city and the skyscraper area display both an inner consistency of style (logico-aesthetic unity), at least in its essential details, and a functional connection of the parts with one another.

The preceding examples are taken from the realm of "material" culture. Let us turn for further instances to "immaterial" culture. Suppose we take, on the one hand, August Comte's *System of Positive Philosophy* and, on the other, one of the recent elementary texts in social problems. Putting aside the question as to whether or not this or that theory expounded in these works is true, throughout all the volumes of Comte there runs a unity of fundamental principles which binds all the chapters logically. Without Comte's law of the three states connected with his classification of sciences and principles of positive knowledge the chapters lose their chief meaning. The work is inwardly integrated by the logic of its main principles. In the text on social problems, however, usually one chapter treats of poverty, the next of crime, the third of fascism or communism, the next of case method, the next of religion, another of the city and the farmer. Something may be said on ecology; ecology is perhaps followed by a chapter on the negro and race problems; then all this farrago is further enriched by pages on the family and birth control, the League of Nations, and countless other subjects. When one tries to find out what unites all these topics, one often finds only the binding of the book. They are connected neither logically nor functionally. The book has become a dumping place for a miscellaneous heap of topics, theories, ideas, and facts; their only connection is that of spatial adjacency.

Take a further example from the field of music. Consider, say, the Gregorian chant or Mozart's *Concerto in G minor* on the one hand, and on the other, a musical composition of some Hollywood "composer," in which jazz is interspersed with phrases stolen from Tschaikovsky, Wagner, Bizet, Handel, Haydn, Berlioz, Bach, and Stravinsky. The contrast is similar to those already considered: one is a consistent, integrated whole; the other is the "dumping place" of opposite and unrelated fragments united on the pages of a manuscript or played in adjacent units of time.

Enough of illustration. It has already sufficiently shown that there are various forms of integration which differ from one another fundamentally. Now we can attempt to order them and to reduce their multiplicity to the simpler form of a few fundamental classes with an indication of the basis of integration in each class.

III. Classification of the Main Forms of the Integration of Culture Elements

All the numerous interrelations of the various elements [13] of culture can be reduced to four basic types: (1) *Spatial or Mechanical Adjacency*, ranging from a loose and accidental concurrence of two or more cultural objects to a mechanical union of the elements into one structural unity (say, glued or cemented or sewn or tied together); (2) *Association Due to an External Factor;* (3) *Causal or Functional Integration;* (4) *Internal or Logico-meaningful Unity.*

A. *Spatial or Mechanical Adjacency (Congeries)*. This means any conglomeration of cultural elements (objects, traits, values, ideas) in a given area of social and physical space, with spatial or mechanical concurrence as the only bond of union. A dump in which are fragments of a great variety of objects — pieces of paper, broken bottles, empty cans, fragments of clothing, discarded spoons, wire, garbage, furniture, ashes, coal, tools — offers an example of such a combination. All these objects just drifted or were thrown together, and this is the only bond that unites them. An attic with its miscellaneous array of articles, from the ancient family album to the broken chair, is another example. The drawing room mentioned above, with its valuable but functionally or logically unrelated furnishings, is still another. The same can be said of the cases of the spatial conglomeration of various architectural styles and of the logically unrelated discussions of various social problems within the limits of one book. Two pieces of paper (say, a page from Plato's *Republic* and

---

[13] The usual division of the elements of culture into "traits," "complexes," and unified "patterns" is quite relative: any element can be regarded in one case as a trait, in others as a complex or even a pattern. The same is true of the pattern and the complex. Therefore there is no need to follow this division here; especially since its bases are as yet unclear. It still must undergo a great deal of critical analysis before it can become a real tool for scientific study of cultural phenomena. The term "element" as used in the present context means a part of a given cultural conglomeration, no matter whether the part is a trait or complex or even a pattern.

the advertisement of an automobile company) glued together into one meaningless mechanical unity; a piece of wood nailed to a remnant of a shoe without any meaning or function as an instrument for anything; an Ionic or Corinthian column attached to a flat-roofed garage without architectural, aesthetic, or structural significance — these and hundreds of similar combinations are examples of the spatial and purely mechanical congeries of various cultural objects and values.[14]   As a matter of fact, what anthropologists call a culture area is often nothing more than a spatial adjacency of the traits and complexes of the area in question. The same is to be said of the culture complexes which Dixon calls accidental.   At least the anthropologists themselves, talking of culture areas, have not been able to point out any either functional or inherent and logical bond between various complexes and traits found together within the area.   This does not mean that, if proper search is made, such a bond will not in many cases be found.   It means that, owing to the lack of a preliminary analysis of various forms of integration, many anthropologists and sociologists pay attention only to spatial and mechanical distribution, to whether it is concentric or eccentric, and to the frequency of occurrence of its elements; they somehow forget to analyze carefully the further bonds — functional, logical — that may unite these traits.   Is there such a further liaison?   What is its nature?   Not only with reference to primitive culture but even to modern culture such a search is often lacking.   For instance, C. Wissler finds three dominant characteristics in our culture: mechanical invention, mass education, and universal suffrage.[15]   Let us grant that this is so.   If, however, we ask, "Is the coexistence of these three complexes within the area of the United States merely a spatial congeries or is it something functionally or internally determined, so that the elements are inseparable?" we have virtually no answer.   Even if a positive answer be hazarded, and we then ask, "What unites these three complexes into one functional or logical unity?" we can be sure now of a complete silence.   For when the problems themselves are ordinarily not raised, it is not strange that the answers should be passed by.   The same question can be asked — and with no better expectation

[14] It may be conceded that the components of such a congeries did not drift together entirely without cause.   But, as the "causes" are diverse and numerous, their total effect amounts to that of mere accident, as of an unforeseen crossing of two or more unrelated causal series. Such accidental relations are fundamentally different from the causal in a proper sense. A. Cournot, *Exposition de la théorie des chances et des probabilités* (Paris, 1843), p. 43.   See also Borel, *Le hasard* (Paris, 1914); A. Cournot, *Traité de l'enchaînement des idées fondamentales dans les sciences et dans l'histoire* (Paris, 1861); H. Poincaré, *Science et méthode* (Paris, 1920), pp. 64 ff.; A. A. Tschuproff, *Ocherki po teorii statistiki* (St. Petersburg, 1909), chap. iii.

[15] Wissler, *op. cit.*, pp. 5 ff.

I — 3

of results — about the other traits of American life which Wissler adds to these three: nationalism,[16] the veneration of the Bible (in connection with the whole problem of Euro-American culture), the sacred seventh day, the codification of law, militarism, and commercialism.[17] When, therefore, the author says that, as with any culture, that of the United States is "unique" and "typical" and represents a "unity," these statements mean almost nothing, because even a dump is unique, is a spatial unity; because, if all such accidental conglomerations are styled typical and unities, then everything in the world is typical and unified, and the terms become empty of meaning. To put the problem in another form, we may ask: Is the combination of traits — mechanical invention, mass education, universal suffrage, nationalism, militarism, the Bible, the sacred seventh day, commercialism — a mere accidental congeries, or is it a deeper unity, where one part cannot be taken from the others and cannot exist apart from them? If the first, then any accumulation of contiguous elements of culture will be a culture area, unique, typical, united, integrated. In that case the enormous difference between functional or logical unity and merely accidental, mechanical, or spatial unity is denied, and into one class are put phenomena of entirely different kinds. In that case, no difference will be recognized between a haphazard pile of bricks and, say, a house; between the parts of an automobile unassembled and the assembled automobile itself. Such an equalization of totally different classes of unity is evidently inadmissible.

If, however, the answer to the question is that the above complex is functionally or inwardly united, then the author has to show that we cannot find nationalism without the other traits; the Bible without mechanical inventions; commercialism without mass education; mass education without militarism; universal suffrage without the Bible and nationalism and militarism; and so on. Any attempt to prove all this will be a large order; neither Wissler nor anybody else is able to do it, because, as a matter of fact, each of these elements has existed and exists without many of the other elements of Wissler's Euro-American complex. The complex is such that its elements are separable functionally and logically. Therefore it is not a functional or logical unity in the form in which it is put before us. To sum up: the author, like a great many other anthropologists, ended his analysis where it should have begun. Thus many further statements of his about the unity, uniqueness, typicality, continuity, change, transformation, or span of life of cultural configurations become exceedingly vague and in part fallacious. Since different

[16] *Ibid.*, p. 11.   [17] *Ibid.*, pp. 25 ff.

sorts of unity are lumped together without distinction, it is natural that the derivative concepts are also a kind of "hash" made out of fundamentally different things.

What is said of Wissler's case can be said of many other similar studies. Most of them suffer from the lack of distinction between purely spatial adjacency and functional or logico-internal unity.

For the time being we can move to the other types of integration.

B. *Indirect Association through a Common External Factor.* A somewhat greater unification occurs in such cases where two or more culture elements, spatially adjacent but with no functional or logical connection, are also related to one another through the association of each with a common factor external to both or all of them. In the northern part of Vologda province in North Russia, for example, the following culture elements exist together : *vodka* as a beverage, skis used by the peasants in the winter time, houses built out of heavy timber, large stoves for heating, felt winter boots, the gathering together during the winter evenings of the boys and girls in each of their houses in turn, the performance of plays, singing, and love making. None of these elements requires the others either logically or functionally. *Vodka* as such does not require skis or felt boots; felt boots do not require a large stove or specific forms of winter-evening entertainment. But all of these traits are perceptibly connected with the climatic conditions of the area with its cold and its long winters. Each trait, through its connection with the climatic factor, is likewise affiliated indirectly with the other traits. As a result we have a unification of heterogeneous culture elements, not only spatially but also through their connection with one common external factor. That is the unification talked of by many sociological and anthropological integrators. When Wissler refers to the "tundra-mesa-jungle" cultures and the complexes and patterns of each of these types, he implies an integration of this kind.[18] When social geographers try to see the unity of the many cultural traits of a given area in terms of its geographic conditions, they are talking of the same type of integration. In fact all the theories which account either for the whole or for a part of the traits of a given culture through the geographic, the biological (heredity, race, selection), or any similar factor *outside* of the culture itself are attempting nothing other than an integration of this kind.[19]

[18] *Ibid.*, pp. 230 ff. See also Wissler, *The Relation of Nature to Man in Aboriginal America* (New York, 1926).

[19] See my discussion of these theories in *Contemporary Sociological Theories*, chaps. i, ii, iii, iv, v, and, to some extent, vi and vii.

This kind of unity has something more of real integration than that of mere spatial adjacency. But it is still a very low and loose form of integration. A group of heterogeneous traits united only by an external factor does not possess inward cohesion; it is not impossible to replace any single trait by another which is quite different, provided only that the new trait meet the requirement of connection with the unifying external factor. Instead of *vodka*, whisky or rum could serve; instead of skis, snowshoes could be used; instead of a large stove made of bricks, a different kind of stove capable of heating the house well and keeping the heat for a long time would serve. Instead of plays and games during the winter evenings, bridge or dominoes or some other pastimes would be suitable. The parts are easily removed and easily replaced. A change in one such element does not require a change in the others. The remaining configuration of the culture would suffer little modification, since no direct functional or logical unity exists to begin with.

C. *Causal or Functional Integration.* By this is meant a combination of cultural elements in which they compose one causal (functional) unity. Usually, where the elements are "material," functional unity is superimposed upon spatial adjacency and external association, but not every spatially adjacent or externally related combination will be a functionally integrated unity. The parts of an automobile spread over the floor of a factory or packed into one box before being assembled into one functional whole, the finished automobile, are a mere spatial array. When they are assembled into one whole, their combination becomes functional and operates so that every important part depends upon the others. The same can be said of the house in contradistinction to the sum of the materials of which it is built: stone, cement, bricks, timber, paint, nails, and so on. Dumped together in one yard these elements form a mere heap of contiguous parts. When the house is built, it is a structural and functional unity. The same situation is true of the essential elements of various other "logical" (in Dixon's terminology) culture complexes, like the "horse complex" or the "milk complex" or others.

Similarly, causal or functional unity is likewise of a far higher degree of integration than that of a number of elements spatially adjacent but also related through a common external factor. In a functional array as a rule the parts are related to one another directly, or, if indirectly, by several internal "centers" which are closer to them in essential nature than would be the case in a purely external integration. Not every cell of an organism or bolt in a car is adjacent or directly related to all the other cells or parts. But all the cells are directly connected through the nervous system, the blood circulation, and the organs, just as the bolts or other parts are united through the whole frame of the car, the electric system, and so on. And these unifying factors are all internal to the system itself.

But the simple cases we have been considering are far from exhausting the problems of the functional integration of cultural elements. The field is infinitely larger and more important. In order to make this clear, a few diagnostic criteria of the functional relationship between the parts of a cultural configuration should be pointed out. Simply stated, they consist chiefly of the *tangible, noticeable, testifiable,*[20] *direct interdependence (mutual or one-sided) of the variables or parts upon one another and upon the whole system.* If variation A is always followed by B (under the same conditions and in a large enough number of cases so that mere chance is eliminated), we say that they are functionally related. *This means that any cultural synthesis is to be regarded as functional, when, on the one hand, the elimination of one of its important elements perceptibly influences the rest of the synthesis in its functions (and usually in its structure); and when, on the other hand, the separate element, being transposed to a quite different combination, either cannot exist in it or has to undergo a profound modification to become a part of it.* Such is the symptomatic barometer of internal integration, a barometer which simply applies the principle of causality or functionalism to each case in question.

One can now see the profound difference between mere spatial adjacency, between external unification, and the deeper synthesis of functional unity. A bolt or spring taken from an unassembled pile of automobile parts does not modify the pile essentially; removed from an assembled car, it may completely impede the performance of the car. Moreover, the bolt or spring itself does not change in significance when removed from a miscellaneous heap, but if it be detached from a machine in which it performs an essential function, it loses that function entirely.[21] Similarly, the

---

[20] "Tangible, noticeable, testifiable" because theoretically everything in this world is connected. But in some cases, for instance in the case of the sneezing of a native of the Trobriand Islands and the monetary policy of the United States, the liaison is so negligible that we cannot discover any functional connection between them. In other cases, for instance a shot by one man and the wound of another following the shot, the connection is evident and testifiable.

[21] Already we note that statements like "the various traits of culture are interdependent," "an innovation affects the entire culture," "the interdependence of traits is a universal characteristic of culture," "when a new trait is added the entire culture is modified " (W. D. Wallis, *op. cit.*, pp. 11–21) — statements often repeated by anthropologists — overshoot the mark enormously. If there are purely spatial conglomerations of cultural elements — and we have seen and shall see that there are many — then the addition, subtraction, or modifica-

heart, lungs, head, or any other vital part of a biological organism cannot be removed without impairing the organism itself, nor can these organs be made to function outside of their organism as they functioned in it.[22]

Let us now pass on to more complex examples. Can we take, say, the stock-market system of Wall Street from the modern capitalistic type of economic organization and transpose it, say, to the society of the Trobriands? The answer is that as soon as this is done, the capitalist system of economy here fails to function normally for lack of the stock market, while among the Trobriands, Wall Street does not have any chance to exist or survive generally in the form which it has in the United States. This means that the stock market is essentially a functional part of the American economic system. Suppose we should take the parliamentary regime in its English form, together with the principles of contractual relations and of the equality of all citizens before the law, and the other democratic tenets of Victorian England, and transplant them in the Hindu caste society. The results would be similar; the democratic politico-juridical complex can hardly be grafted on the caste-society tree and yet retain the same form which it had; it would either die or be changed enormously. On the other hand, the rest of the Victorian democratic sociopolitical system could hardly function as it did without the aid of the transplanted parts of the complex. As a matter of fact, even in Continental European societies, where the configuration of cultural elements differs from that of England, though by less than does the Hindu, the parliamentary system has never functioned in the way in which it does in England. One has only to glance at the history of parliamentarism in Germany, Austria, Russia, or Italy to perceive the difference. The Gothic cathedral transplanted to the South Sea Islands would be an isolated monster there, devoid of its meaning as well as of its functions, though it was a necessary part of the medieval culture of the twelfth to the fifteenth centuries. The full evening dress of our society would seem grotesque to a native of the Fiji Islands; and if in-

---

tion of one or more elements may, and often does, not change anything in the rest of the array. The same is to be said, as we shall see, about a great many other fundamental statements of the cultural sociologists and anthropologists. With a proper modification this applies also to cases of external unification, though in a smaller degree.

[22] It is to be noted that in an inorganic mechanical system, like a machine, where one part may be replaced by another, for instance one bolt by another, the replacement must be *identical* in form with the replaced part. If it deviates essentially, it cannot be a substitute. In organic, psychosocial, or functional cultural systems even such a replacement is ordinarily impossible or extremely difficult; while in a purely spatial or even externally related combination the exchange of one part for another is ordinarily easy even when the new part is very different from the old.

troduced there, would lose its meaning and change its functions. The Civil Code of Napoleon or the English Common Law system could, of course, be imposed upon Chinese, Hindu, or Siamese society; but the result would be either a profound transformation of the meaning and functions of these systems or their failure, or, as the case of the Fiji Islanders shows, the destruction of the native population.

In brief, in any culture area there are always present in the totality of the traits, patterns, objects, and values of which it consists, complexes which represent a functional integration. A deep change in, or the disappearance of, one of the important components tends to modify the rest of the complex; while the components transplanted in a different configuration either do not survive or are profoundly changed or destroy the complex on which they are grafted.

There is no need to stress the fact that *the degree of functional unity or functional interdependence is everywhere not the same:* it fluctuates from unity to unity; in some cases it is exceedingly close, in others looser, until finally it imperceptibly passes into either a mere external unity or even a mere spatial adjacency.

In sociology and the social sciences there is a multitude of theories that attempt to describe and interpret culture generally along the lines of functional unity. All the theories that take some specific variable internal to a culture (whether it be modes of production, technique and invention, religion, morals, art and science, philosophy and forms of government) and try to "explain" all or the majority of the other characteristics of the culture in question as a "function" or "superstructure" or "effect" of this variable: all such theories, as I have already suggested, assume the existence of a causal-functional integration between the parts. In other words, their promulgators appear to be partisans of the view of the functional unity of all culture elements.[23] Thus, when Karl Marx and other supporters of the economic interpretation of history attempt to explain all of culture as a mere superstructure of the economic factor, which changes as the economic situation changes, they assume that culture is a functional unity where all the parts are hung upon the arc of economics, live one life with it, and change when it changes: property relations, social and political organization, art, religion, science,

[23] See the treatment of these ideas in my *Contemporary Sociological Theories*, especially the chapters devoted to the sociologistic and psychological schools. As a matter of fact the problem of the integration of culture, which some of the anthropologists have considered as only recently raised, has been since time immemorial one of the central problems of social science generally and sociology in particular. The subsequent pages of this work make this clear.

law, morals, and the whole class of ideologies.[24]   This is true of any other "main-factor" theory, whether religious, scientific, or otherwise.   Like Marxism it also assumes that culture is a functional unity; and that as soon as one discovers the leading factor through the study of its nature and changes, one is capable of understanding the entire culture, and of forecasting the changes and fluctuations in any of its compartments.[25]   More than this, almost all of the contemporary social scientists assume that culture is a functional unity.   Through experiments, through statistical correlation, through observation, through the comparative historical method, through "case studies," and through all the other possible methods, approaches, and techniques, they have been busy hunting for the causal-functional relationships, uniformities, and laws which supposedly exist between two or more culture variables.   If sometimes, to their regret, they do not find a high coefficient of correlation or some other patented guarantee of the existence of the functional relationship between various elements of culture, this means for most of them only that they started from a wrong end.   It does not shake in any way their strong belief in the soundness of their theory.

In view of the virtual unanimity of opinion it is unnecessary to insist upon the existence of the causal-functional sort of integration as a form *sui generis*.   But the application of the theory is to be somewhat moderated. We have seen and shall see that not all the components of any culture are linked together causally, but only a part of them.   In any culture there are also spatial and external unities where no causal association in the narrow sense can be found.   And in many cultural complexes there are "logico-meaningful" unities, different from the causal-functional.   Therefore it is fallacious to assume, as many causalists do, that every conglomeration of cultural objects is a functional unity and that there must be a functional connection between all of the components.   Such an exaggerated belief in causal-functional integration is unwarranted and calls for sharp limitation.

Let us now turn from these considerations to the fourth form of integration with which we are to deal.

D. *Logico-meaningful Integration of Culture.*   Having beclouded the true nature of functional integration by being unable to distinguish its elements from those of spatial adjacency and external association in highly heterogeneous conglomerations of cultural elements, many integrators have also failed to see that above functional integration proper

---

[24] See my *Contemporary Sociological Theories*, chap. x.
[25] For all these theories see *ibid., passim.*

there is an additional form of association quite different from it, and more different still from the spatial and external types of unification. For lack of a better term, I style this the Logico-meaningful Integration of Culture. This is integration in its supreme form. In what does it consist? What are its qualities? Suppose we have before us the scattered pages of a great poem, or of Kant's *Critique of Pure Reason*, or fragments of the statue of Venus of Milo, or the scattered pages of the score of Beethoven's *Third Symphony*. If we know the proper patterns of meaning and value, we can put these pages or parts together into a significant unity in which each page or fragment takes its proper place, acquires a meaning, and in which all together give the supremely integrated effect that was intended. I say "supremely integrated" because in such instances each part, when set in its designated position, is no longer noticeable as a part, but all the parts together form, as it were, a seamless garment. Their unification is far closer than that of mere functional association. The connection is similar in nature to that between the premises, "All human beings are mortal," and "Socrates is a human being," and the conclusion, "Ergo, Socrates is mortal." Is this connection functional? Hardly, unless we broaden the meaning of functional to such an extent that it loses distinct meaning altogether. To say that the chapters of Kant's *Critique*, or the head and the torso of the Venus of Milo, or the beginning and the end of the first movement of Beethoven's *Third Symphony*, or the foundation, flying buttresses, towers, and sculpture of the Cathedral of Chartres, or the first and the second parts of the *Iliad* — to say that the connection between these is functional or causal is to say something almost absurd and, at the same time, to omit the higher nature of their unity.

Operationally, to use Professor Bridgman's term, the procedure involved in this sort of integration is not unlike that of putting into logical order the numerous meaningless fragments of a jigsaw puzzle. The person attempting the solution has before him many variform pieces: triangles, squares, and others, of strange and fanciful design, all mixed together without significance. His task consists in putting them together in such a way that they will make a meaningful unity: a dog, a cow, a castle, a man, a landscape, or some other comprehensible whole. The fitting together of these fragments is not an integration by mere spatial adjacency: they were already adjacent when they lay in a heap on the table. Neither is it an integration through some external factor: one could hang the fragments on a single thread or put them into a box or glue them upon a sheet of paper or integrate them externally in many

different ways. The result would still be a senseless conglomeration.
Nor is the procedure of putting them together functional or causal. One
could proceed as much as one liked according to the inductive method of
observing identity or difference or concomitant changes, and still, as
long as one failed to seek and find the unifying meaning, one would not
arrive at the solution. As a matter of fact no functional method is useful
here. There is, strictly speaking, neither cause nor effect, neither variable
nor function. None of the parts rules the others causally or functionally.
The whole apparatus of the causal-functional procedure is simply inapplicable to the problem.

What must be used are the *logical* laws of identity, contradiction, consistency; and it is these laws of logic which must be employed to discover
whether any synthesis is or is not *logico-meaningful*. Side by side with
such logical laws, in the narrow sense, the broader principles of "keeping,"
of internal consistency, must also be used to determine the existence of
this higher unity, or the lack of it. These are the principles expressed in
the terms "consistent style," "consistent and harmonious whole," in
contradistinction to "inconsistent mingling of styles," "hodgepodge,"
"clashing" patterns or forms, and they apply especially to the examination of artistic creation.[26] Many such superlative unities cannot be
described in analytical verbal terms; they are just felt as such, but this
in no way makes their unity questionable. One cannot prove by mere
words — no matter what they are — the inner consistency and supreme
integration of the Cathedral of Chartres, or the Gregorian chant, or the
musical compositions of Bach or Mozart or Beethoven, or the tragedies
of Shakespeare, or the sculpture of Phidias, or the pictures of Dürer or
Raphael or Rembrandt, or many other logico-meaningful unities. But
not being completely describable in terms of language, their supreme
unity is felt by competent persons as certainly as if they could be analyzed

---

[26] If the psychologists would say that such a sense or feeling of consistency and unity is a
mere matter of association and the routine of perception, or is nothing but a conditioned
response, my answer is simple. In most cases it is not such a simple phenomenon, but,
granting for a moment that it is so, there still remains the fact that some creations, like those
of Phidias or Bach or Dante or Homer, have been felt for numbers of generations as "consistent unities," or "consistent associations," while millions of other sculptures, musical
compositions, or poems have never been considered so faultlessly unified but have been
sensed as styleless, senseless, discordant, disjointed concoctions of forms, colors, words, or
sounds. The difference between these two classes of "associations" still remains. Some
associations are sensed as the supreme unities, others as concoctions. Some chains of reasoning are "felt" as logical, others as inconsistent. And this is what is important for my purposes.
For the rest, I leave it to whosoever will to amuse himself "associationally," "reflexologically,"
"physiologically," "endocrinologically," "psychoanalytically," and in any other way in
which he pleases, according to his sense or non-sense. It does not concern my point.

with mathematical or logical exactness. All such unities are covered here by the term logico-meaningful, though many are not logical unities in the formal sense of the word logic.

A few concrete illustrations will make still clearer the nature of this sort of integration. Suppose we find side by side in some cultural conglomeration a highly developed ascetic-monastic life and a materialistic-Sensate philosophy. At once we feel that the two are inconsistent; they do not belong together; they do not make any sense; their combination is not integrated in a logico-meaningful unity. This conclusion will remain valid no matter how frequently such a coexistence of these two variables is found. Asceticism and a purely idealistic philosophy of life, on the contrary, do belong to each other logically. If we find together in a given cultural area the strictest caste system and the equalitarian ideology shared by all castes, it once again becomes evident that we are faced with inconsistency. These opposing elements, though they may form a spatial or some other form of congeries, cannot be integrated in a logico-meaningful unity. The case of the city, mentioned previously, with its conglomeration of Gothic, Renaissance, baroque, and "box" types, is a further example of inconsistency, illustrating the lack of the logical integration of architectural styles in a single area. Only if it is known that the planners of the city intended the styles to be as diverse as possible and so arranged them according to a definite principle of variety and diversity—only in such a case could the area in question pretend to some degree of logico-meaningful association. But even then it would remain a logico-meaningful integration of low order. When in a house fitted with gas and electric appliances for boiling water one finds, say, a Russian samovar regularly used for that purpose, the logical incompatibility of the two elements of the configuration is evident. A society of multimillionaires who are simultaneously sincere partisans of the sacred right of private property and of the communist creed exhibits an utter lack of logico-meaningful integration of economic-cultural ideals. If we have a culture complex in which the main ethical mentality is hedonistic, while its influential literature is Holy Scripture and the lives of the saints; or vice versa, if we have a sex literature predominant in a culture permeated with otherworldly, ascetic ideals and an absolutistic morality, we once again face a case of the lack of logical integration.

So much then, in a preliminary way, for the nature of logico-meaningful integration. But let us now go a little further in its analysis by confronting it directly with the functional type of association.

IV. Logico-meaningful Integration and the Method of Its Study

A. The causal-functional and the logico-meaningful methods of integration both act as the *means of ordering into comprehensible systems the infinitely numerous and complex phenomena of the sociocultural world.* What we style the sociocultural world consists of endless millions of individual objects, events, processes, fragments, having an infinite number of forms, properties, and relationships.[27] With a proper modification we can say of it what is said of the whole universe: "The universe is infinite: unbounded in space and time and infinitely complex. In its infinite complexity it cannot be known and understood through direct sensory perception."[28] "It is absolutely impossible for the human mind to know the universe through considering separately all its singular forms."[29] Not only the whole universe but any small part of it cannot be known and grasped in all the complexity of its infinitely numerous and diverse separate forms, events, and elements.[30] If we had not had some means of ordering this infinity or of any small part of it, we should have been lost in chaos, and no comprehensible understanding of it would have been possible.

The same is true of the sociocultural universe. To our perception it also is given as a complicated and inexhaustible chaos of infinitely numerous and diverse fragments. The investigator of cultural and social phenomena stands in a position not unlike that of the man with the jigsaw puzzle. He has before him millions of sociocultural fragments, from the daily round of birth, death, marriage, divorce, bridge playing, electioneering, lunch, friendship, quarreling, concerts, exhibitions of paintings, lectures on relativity, discussions in Congress, and acts of the Government, to religious movements, the Communist revolution, and the publication of the Pope's bull or the dictator's manifesto. Every copy of a newspaper gives us thousands of pieces of the most heterogeneous news — scattered pages, as it were, of the book of culture — as different from one another and as unrelated internally as they can be. Any large cultural configuration is made up of millions of such various fragments. None of us perceives directly the culture of any area as something whole which is bound compactly and comprehensively in a book, or packed in a box, or depicted upon a single canvas. At any moment, and even during the whole span of our life, we perceive mainly this infinity of individual fragments.

[27] See especially H. Rickert, *Die Grenzen der naturwissenschaftlichen Begriffsbildung* (Tübingen and Leipzig, 1902).

[28] Tschuproff, *op. cit.*, p. 1.   [29] Rickert, *op. cit.*, p. 33.   [30] Tschuproff, *op. cit.*, pp. 1 ff.

One of the main ways of ordering the chaos of the whole universe as well as of the cultural world is furnished by the causal-functional formulas of integration. They give us the *patterns of uniformity* that are to be found in the relationships of a vast number of individual components of this infinite chaos. By means of these formulas we can reduce the chaos to a series of comprehensive systems, in which we are more easily oriented and which permit us to distinguish more important from less important aspects. Causal-functional formulas like the Newtonian Law of Gravitation sum up briefly a prodigious number of separate relationships. They are like a beam of light that cuts across chaotic darkness through all its unlimited depths. This, with proper reservations, can be said of any causal formula. It achieves its purpose by establishing a *uniformity* of relationship between the variables under scrutiny. Through it a vast concurrence of fragmentary events, forms, objects, and relationships becomes a comprehensive whole. When the formula shows that the variables A and B — depression and birth rate, modes of production and ideological forms, isolation and suicide, urbanization and crime — are more or less uniformly associated with each other in the sense that B normally follows A or changes with A, this *uniformity* binds the variables together, introduces a readily understood causal order into disorder.

Different in nature, but similar in function, is the role of the *logico-meaningful method of ordering chaos*. Here, however, the ordering element is not uniformity of relationship between the fragmentary variables, but *identity of meaning* or *logical coalescence*. Hidden behind the empirically different, seemingly unrelated fragments of the cultural complex lies an identity of meaning, which brings them together into consistent *styles*, typical *forms*, and significant *patterns*. If, therefore, *uniformity of relationship is the common denominator of causally united phenomena, in the logico-meaningful union it is identity of central meaning or idea.*

The procedure involved in arranging the scattered pages of a treatise or putting into a comprehensible unity the individually meaningless fragments of a jigsaw puzzle is, as we have seen, a concrete example of such a logically meaningful ordering. Of course, if the sociocultural conglomeration — the scattered pages or the fragments of the puzzle — do not belong together, the procedure is impossible. But this means only that where there is no factual logical unity in the cultural conglomeration one cannot find it ; and if one tries to impose it upon the mass, one commits an error similar to that of finding or imposing a causal relationship where it does not exist.

We thus see that the ordering natures of the causal and of the logico-meaningful principle are different, but that their cognitive functions are similar : both serve the same purpose, each in its own way ; both sum up in their formulas large accumulations of events, objects, relationships ; both connect into a unity chaotic masses of fragments.   Both are necessary for a study of the sociocultural phenomena, each in its own field. Obviously, as we shall see in some detail, on the level of the logically integrated layers of culture the logico-meaningful method is much more important than the causal.

Let us, therefore, continue the comparison of both methods, further defining the type of cultural complexes to which each applies, and the character of their resultant unifications.

B. The causal method, especially in the natural sciences, obtains its formulas mainly through breaking up the complex phenomena into their simpler units ; and the more general the formula, the further the reduction of complex to simple, until ultimate simplicity — the atom, electron, proton — is reached.   Studying the relationships between these simplest and therefore universal units and discovering the nature of their uniformity, the causal method offers *eo ipso* formulas of uniformity which are also universal in their application.   For, since all the complex material systems are made up of the simple universal units, their uniformity becomes the pattern for all the more complex phenomena.   These units are, as it were, the common denominator of all functional integration in the natural world.   They are, so to speak, the "stuff" that permeates all complexes and makes them all causally related in the way in which the individual units are related to one another.

In the logico-meaningful method of formulating the unifying principles, such a procedure is impossible.   Despite the endless efforts of a legion of social scientists, simple social atoms or units have not been found, and cannot be found, so far as the logically integrated part of culture is concerned.[31]   One cannot indicate what is the cultural atom in literature, painting, music, science, philosophy, architecture, or in any other similar compartment of culture.   Instead, however, the logico-meaningful method has its own common denominator of all relevant phenomena : *it is the identity (or similarity) of central meaning, idea, or mental bias that permeates all the logically related fragments.*   Because of this all the fragments in question are identical or similar in their significance, all of them have the same common denominator, which binds them together, conditions their

---

[31] See my discussion of the various mechanical theories as well as "organismic" theories in my *Contemporary Sociological Theories*, chaps. i and iv *et passim*.

relationship, makes them a unity.   In this sense identity of central principle, idea, or norm plays in the cultural world a role analogous to that
of the atom, proton, electron, or other ultimate unit universally common
to all the material systems.

C. The functional or causal connection of separate units is almost
always inferential and external; it rarely gives us an intimate or internal
comprehension of the connection.   Through experimental or observa-
tional or statistical manipulations we find that two variables, A and B,
seem always to go together : they either coexist, or follow each other, or
vary together.   But why they do so — why, for instance, the force of
gravitation is in direct ratio to the mass and in inverse ratio to the square
of the distance; why the volume of gas varies in inverse ratio to the
pressure; why oxygen and ·hydrogen in certain conditions turn into
H_2O — we do not know.   All we know is that within the limits of our
perception they have usually done so, and that they will probably continue to do so in the future.   Beyond this externally observed connection,
we do not have any intimate understanding of such associations.   For
example, if somebody could properly prove that the rate of divorce and
the use of yellow leather shoes always go together, rise and fall together,
we should have to agree that they were connected functionally, though
we would not have the slightest understanding of why it is so.

Different is the feeling we have in regard to logically integrated unities.
The properly trained mind [32] apprehends, feels, perceives, senses, and
understands the supreme unity of Euclid's or Lobachevski's geometry of
perfect mathematical deduction; of Platonic metaphysics; of Phidias's
Athena; of a suite or concerto by Bach; of a Shakespeare drama; of
the architecture of the Parthenon or the Cathedral of Chartres.   Such a
mind comprehends their sublime unity internally, intimately; often
feels it immediately and directly, senses it without any experimental or
statistical manipulations and without indirect reasoning.   It is given to
such a mind axiomatically, so to speak, as the supreme certainty to
which no inference can add anything.   If by chance the torso of the
Venus of Milo were found in one place and its head in another, when
they were brought together their belonging to each other would be self-
evident; while if to the head of the Venus were added, say, the body of

[32] It is true that for their apprehension a talent and training are necessary, just as they are
necessary for the discovery and apprehension of causal or functional liaisons.   To an un-
trained mind the causal and incidental associations are about the same : such a mind does not
make causal discoveries.   So let this point not be invoked by the narrower-minded causalists
as an objection either to the existence of or to the objectivity of apprehension of the logico-
integrated unities.   *Cf.* M. Planck, *Where Is Science Going?* (New York, 1932), pp. 150-151.

the Egyptian Sphinx or of Bernini's St. Teresa, their heterogeneity would
also appear at once. They just do not belong to each other. If in a
manuscript of music supposedly by Bach there were found several bars
similar, say, to the music of Honegger or Gershwin, a competent person
would understand at once that they happened to be there by some mistake. If in a volume containing several chapters of Kant's *Critique of
Pure Reason* one found further chapters similar, say, to the writings of
Dorothy Dix, their incongruousness would be immediately perceptible.
In other words, the logico-meaningful unities are much more intimately
comprehensible, more readily perceived, than are causal-functional
unities.[33] Common speech strikingly marks out the difference between
the two types of integration. We employ the word "cause" for the
causal-functional relationships; but for the higher unity of logic and
meaning we use the word "reason" ("the cause of it," "the reason of
it," or the *raison d'être*). In this limited field we can say with Descartes,
causa sive ratio, or rather, *ratio sive causa*.[34]

D. The primary difference between the causal and logico-meaningful
connection leads to a further derivative difference between them. The
essentially external nature of the causal association in many cases precludes our grasping the relationship between discrete variables in time or
space. If variables A and B are not met with regularly, nor coexist,
nor follow each other in immediate sequence, nor vary uniformly, such
variables cannot be declared to be connected causally. Even if theoretically such a causal chain exists between them (as is possible from the
standpoint of "singularistic causality"), it cannot be discovered and
understood and, therefore, for the observer is practically nonexistent.
Considerably different is the situation in regard to logico-meaningful
connection. Theoretically (and not infrequently in fact) this sort of
association is comprehensible even when the interrelated fragments are

---

[33] It is to the credit of W. Dilthey that he stressed especially strongly, though mainly
psychologically, this difference. "Die Natur erklären wir, das Seelenleben verstehen wir."
The purpose of the causal-natural sciences is to find the relationship between objects and
variables (*zwischen den Gegenstanden*), while that of the *Geisteswissenschaft* is an understanding (*das Verstehen*) of the objectivizations of life through the personal life experience of
each who desires to understand. As such it gives direct and immediate comprehension.
See W. Dilthey, *Einleitung in die Geisteswissenschaften* (Leipzig, 1883), Bk. I; also *Der
Aufbau der geschichtlichen Welt in der Geisteswissenschaften*, in *Abhandlungen der Berliner
Akademie, philosophisch-historische Klasse* (1910), pp. 1–112. His world of the *Zweckzu-
sammenhänge* is close to (but not identical with) what I call the world of the logico-meaningful
integration of culture. In other respects there is a profound difference between Dilthey's
system and that developed in the present work.

[34] Descartes, *Œuvres*, ed. by Adam and Tannery (Paris, 1904), Vol. VII, p. 236.

met with at quite different periods, and in quite different places, and only once or a few times. Conversely, the mere fact of our regular observation of the variables A and B in causal association does not necessarily force us to recognize that they are logically and meaningfully integrated.

If one meets only once and only in one culture (say, the Egyptian) a belief in the hereafter, funeral rites, and the practice of mummifying the body, this one case is sufficient to establish the logical connection between these three elements. Or if one finds only once the association of a dominant philosophical materialism, the naturalistic style of painting, and the economic and mechanistic interpretation of history, this case is sufficient to make clear that they belong logically together, though on the basis of one case we cannot say anything of their causal connection. Contrariwise, a scientist could prove, on the basis of a large number of "cases," that the variables A and B — say, the number of yellow leather shoes in use and the divorce rate — always vary together. And yet such an exceptionless causal association in no way forces us to conclude that the elements are united also logically and meaningfully. A competent person could listen as many times as you like to a musical composition where jazz and crooning are interspersed with bars from Tschaikovsky, Stravinsky, or Wagner. Any number of repetitions of these bars would not oblige him in any way to declare that such musical compositions are logical and consistent unities. Suppose we find a large number of houses in the classical style upon which is superimposed a Gothic tower. This does not prevent our declaring such houses architectural "hash." For the same reason we would declare illogical the conclusion, "Socrates is immortal," from the premises which should establish his mortality; or the answer, "Six," to the question, "How much do two and two make?" There certainly must be *causes* for such illogicality; but no matter how frequent such answers are or how many people make them, they still remain illogical. This shows once again that the causal and logical forms of connection are governed by entirely different principles.

Now it frequently happens in fact, as will be shown in the subsequent parts of this work, that the presence of the logical connection between variables is accompanied by their causal cohesion. It thus comes about that the discovery of a logico-meaningful relationship is often one of the best heuristic symptoms of a probable causal link as well. But not every causal association is followed necessarily by a logical connection. All the causal-functional connections in the field of the natural sciences, for example, and many in the field of human culture are free from additional logical bonds. And this throws light on the mixture of different archi-

I—4

tectural forms, opposing musical styles, disparate premises and conclusions which were cited above as examples of alogical, nonlogical, and
illogical combinations which might yet be causally explicable.[35]

E. Causal-functional connections vary so greatly in *degree of intensity* that we not only have cases in which we can be reasonably certain of the causal nature of the association, but also others in which we
are not certain whether the association is really causal or merely incidental
(*post hoc propter hoc* and the like).   Similarly, the closeness of logico-
meaningful integration also varies from the sublime unity to one barely
perceptible and merging into the lower grades of association.   The greatest values in all the important compartments of culture represent, as a
rule, the logico-meaningful synthesis in its most intense form.   A mere
heaping-up of various bits of information, on the contrary, hardly ever
has acquired the distinction of being considered a great scientific or philosophical contribution ; nor has a mere hodgepodge of various styles made
great music, painting, or poetry.   It is not incidental that the very term
"eclectic" has a negative connotation, even in its application to supposedly impressive achievements in these fields of cultural creation.

F. Causal integration, being external and inferential, exists supposedly in the inorganic, organic, and superorganic worlds.   The logico-
meaningful unities can be looked for only in the field of the phenomena
that involve human thought and imagination ; that is, in the field of
human culture, and there only in that part which is a result of the activity
of the human mind, whether this activity is scientific, religious, artistic,
philosophical, moral, or technical.[36] *Meaningful and logical integration by
definition can only exist where there is mind and meaning.*   It cannot exist
outside of this realm, though elsewhere there may be causal, external, or
spatial unities.   This means that in the lower levels of culture, if culture
be understood in the broadest sense, that is, on the levels of the biosocial
layer of sociocultural phenomena, we can hardly look for unities of this

[35] This means that, with the exception of the logically integrated part, culture is not so
much nonlogical or illogical (as Pareto mistakenly claims) as alogical, being outside of the
category of the logical or nonlogical.   If the volume of gas is inversely proportional to the
pressure, this causal uniformity is neither logical nor nonlogical.   The same is to be said of
any causal relationship.   On the other hand, Pareto greatly underestimated the extent of the
logical aspects of the Graeco-Roman and Western cultures.   As we shall see, the highest
layer of these cultures — the logically integrated part of it — was in fact far more extensive
than he thought.

[36] If a thinker seeks this sort of integration for the entire cosmos, believing that it has an
intelligent plan and logico-meaningful unity, he assumes invariably the existence of a Supreme
Mind which was its creator.   But in this present work I am not concerned with such problems; my analysis is confined entirely to human culture.

kind, except in part where there is an indirect influence from the higher levels. In these inferior regions the causal and other looser relationships dominate.

G. As a corollary to this statement it is to be pointed out that, since the highest values and complexes of values in any great culture belong to the class of the logico-meaningful unities, *this level gives it its sociocultural* and *logico-meaningful individuality; its specific style; its physiognomy and personality.* When we talk of the Greek culture of the fifth century B.C. as something peculiar, we do not mean primarily the enormous layer of traits that lies below the highest level; it is of secondary importance that these Greeks performed their physiological needs : ate, slept, worked, loved, fought, and earned their means of subsistence. What we do mean first and most of all is the totality of the specific logico-meaningful systems created by their great men of genius — such men as Phidias, Praxiteles, Aeschylus, Pindar, Sophocles, Polygnotus, Socrates, and later, Plato. And this is true of any other culture or cultural period so far as its highest form of individuality is concerned.

H. Causal relationships and the formulas which describe their uniformities vary widely in the *extent of their applicability.* Some have a very limited range of pertinence; others are relevant to an infinitely great number of cases. Newton's Law of Gravitation is more general, covers a much larger class of phenomena, than Kepler's laws. As was previously pointed out, the greater the progressive reduction of phenomena from more complex to simpler, the broader will be the applicability of the causal formula which expresses their relationship.[37]

In a similar fashion the logico-meaningful principles of integration in the cultural world vary in range of applicability, beginning with the narrow principle which describes the coalescence of a few components of infrequent occurrence and in a limited cultural scheme — as, for example, the concurrence of images of anchor, dove, and olive branch in the frescoes of the Catacombs with the peculiar contents of the early Christian funeral prayer — and ending with the principle that explains and fits together

---

[37] Out of millions of facts science chooses those "which can serve us many times," says H. Poincaré; and such facts permit the formation of causal formulas with the largest general relevance. The same idea is expressed by E. Mach in the statement that science concentrates its attention on "those elements that are the same, and amidst all multiplicity are ever present." When the uniformities in their relationships are understood, the "laws" which result become applicable to similar associations throughout the universe. See H. Poincaré, *op. cit.*, pp. 8 ff. and his *Dernières pensées* (Paris, 1913), pp. 11 ff.; E. Mach, *The Science of Mechanics* (Chicago, 1902), pp. 5 ff. and 77–78; A. Comte, *System of Positive Polity* (London, 1875), Vol. I, pp. 18–21 and 343–345.

millions of cultural fragments of wide distribution in space and time. The hedonistic or utilitarian principle may give sense and unity to many scattered phenomena in a large cultural conglomeration, which includes such elements as large-scale kidnaping, "get-rich-quick" schemes, emphasis on the *useful* in arts and science, "wine, women, and song" morality, and the philosophy of pragmatism with its utilitarian tenet to the effect that if the belief in God is useful, God exists; if not, God does not exist. But there may be a still broader principle in which that of utilitarianism itself becomes only one of the small subordinate fragments. In this sense we may speak of a long gradation of logico-meaningful formulas from the very limited to the most general.

But the process of arriving at the broadest logico-meaningful formulas differs fundamentally from that which applies to causal-functional associations. As has already been explained, we cannot break up complicated sociocultural accumulations into "atoms" as we can in the sciences, which have a causal unity. Instead, we must reverse the procedure and seek an all-embracing meaning which includes every individual element of the vast complex.[38]

I. From everything that has thus far been said, it follows that the investigation of each type of culture integration requires its own special procedure and brings about its characteristic results. *A study of any purely spatial and mechanical congeries cannot give anything but a mere*

---

[38] Since most of the social scientists of the last few decades have believed that there exists nothing beyond causal unities and the causal method for the study of cultural phenomena, it is comprehensible why they have sought so assiduously for a single, ultimate social and cultural element; why even in the logically integrated part of culture they have attempted to distinguish the "simple" and the "complex," the "elementary" and the "compound," forms of relationship. The "atoms" of the mechanistic, and in part of the organismic, schools of sociology; the Spencerian and Durkheimian classifications of societies into the simple and compound (with the further complication of the double and triple compound); and hundreds of similar theories — these are the examples and products of this general line of attack. If the application of such a procedure to the causal layer of culture can be, at least theoretically, justified, it is a hopeless enterprise where the logico-meaningful layer is concerned. There is no "cultural atom," no "simple," no "elementary," no "complex," no "compound" form per se. The predominant opinion which assumes that the elementary is identical with "primitive," and the complex with "advanced," civilization is, in the main, an unsound belief. Only in a purely conditional way is it possible sometimes to use these categories. This explains why all such efforts, when applied to the higher level of culture, have not yielded anything but atrocities and, at the best, platitudes. A tool well fitted for causal analysis is being employed in a field for which it is not suitable at all. For this problem see P. Sorokin, "Remarks," in *Revue international de sociologie*, Vol. XLIII (March, 1935); G. L. Duprat, "*Introduction à l'étude des formes élémentaires de la vie social,*" *Archives de sociologie*, series B, no. 1, June, 1934; and the *Proceedings* of the *XIIe Congrès de l'Institut International de Sociologie*, 1935, where this question was the main topic of discussion; also H. Rickert's work quoted above.

descriptive catalogue of the parts. Since these are not united causally, no formula of causal uniformity, no causal or functional generalization, can be made for them. Where there is no causal relationship, there can be no causal law. This explains why most of the ethnographic and anthropological works dealing with primitive peoples are in fact — and must be — a mere cataloguelike description of religious, moral, family, economic, geographic, magical, and other fragments which represent the various aspects of such cultures. Since the culture complex of some of these tribes is at least in part a mere spatial congeries, or an accumulation based on some entirely external factor; and since the investigators have not been able to seek properly — let alone grasp — either the causal or the logico-meaningful integrating principles in the "primitive" cultures which are thus far only incompletely known, mere description — fanciful or accurate, as the case may be — has been and has had to be the only result of their study. Wherever we have to deal with purely spatial conglomerations, no other result is possible.[39] If an overenthusiastic explorer attempts to insinuate a causal or logical integrating principle into such accumulations, he is adding something that does not exist in, and therefore distorts, the reality studied.

In a study of cultural syntheses the parts of which are united causally or functionally, the causal-functional method with its more or less general causal formulas provides the proper procedure. If in a given group of cultural objects, A, B, C, D . . . N, A is united functionally with C, and B with D, the formulas that describe such causal unions, being suited to the nature of the association, would apply to other such associations of A and C, B and D, no matter where or when they occur.

Since social scientists, especially those of the nineteenth century, have believed that all the elements of culture are causally united, it has been consistent on their part to hold the discovery of a causal-functional uniformity of some kind, in the relationship of two or more sociocultural variables, to be the chief object of their study. They have therefore devoted the larger part of their energy to the discovery of the various formulas of causal or functional uniformity. The immense mass of

[39] It should be noted here that, since no broad culture is causally or logically integrated in its totality, historians who (*as historians*) attempt to deal with all its aspects are unable to provide a thoroughgoing formula of uniformity, whether causal or otherwise. Most historical works are merely catalogues of men, events, objects, values, organized mechanically on the principles of time or space adjacency; and their inferences rarely have bearing beyond the specific area or group which they study. As providing causal or logical formulas of generalization, their value is virtually nil. Fortunately, however, a number of great historians sometimes ceased to be historians and indulged in sociological and philosophical inquiries and in this way made great contributions to the field of causal and logical interpretation of culture.

theories of the existence of uniform relationships, whether positive or
negative, between two or more social variables, beginning with the most
minor — like that between the number of windows in a farmhouse and the
number of toilet rooms with and without running water — and ending
with the vast generalizations of the sociologistic, economic, racial, geographic, psychological, and other schools of sociology [40] and social science :
all these are the product of the causal or functional study of sociocultural
phenomena.   Wherever in a sociocultural synthesis some elements are
indeed united causally, and where such unifications are correctly discovered, the attempts to apply causal formulas have been appropriate
and have given valid results.[41]

Finally, in the study of logico-meaningful relationships, the proper
method is neither a mere concrete description nor a causal formula, but
the appropriate unification of the fragments into a whole according to
their logical significance or their logical cobelonging.   Such a statement
will naturally be questioned by all those who, champions of the causal-
functional methods, hold to the saying, *Vere scire id est per causam scire*,
and maintain that there is no means for the scientific study of anything
beyond the causal-functional analysis.   To many of them the claim that
there is such a higher means sounds like bad metaphysics.   And yet a
slight concentration of thought is sufficient to make clear the validity of,
even the logical necessity for, this claim.   It is not necessary here to do
more than recall briefly what has already been established about the
nature of the logico-meaningful type of unity in contradistinction to that
of the causal-functional form, or what was said of the supreme forms of
cultural creation to which this, and essentially only this, highest kind of
integration applies.   It is sufficient simply to state its existence and to
insist on its difference in significance.

*The essence of the logico-meaningful method of cognition is, as has already
been mentioned, in the finding of the central principle* (the "reason") *which
permeates all the components, gives sense and significance to each of them, and
in this way makes cosmos of a chaos of unintegrated fragments.*   If in a given

[40] See my *Contemporary Sociological Theories, passim.*
[41] Unfortunately many causalists did not realize that some sociocultural conglomerations
are purely spatial accumulations, and often looked for and "found" causalities where none
existed.   This explains why such formulas are often unsound and why sociology overflows
with quasi-causal uniformities which cannot stand the slightest test.   On the other hand, the
causalists have also not realized that in many cultures there exists a layer of logically integrated systems which cannot be studied fruitfully by the causal method.   We should not
wonder, then, that they have either missed the specific nature of this layer entirely or, by trying
to fit it into a causal formula, have produced something grotesquely unsound.

concurrence of cultural elements such unity exists, and if it is correctly discovered and the unifying principle accurately formulated, the formula is as important in its field from the cognitive standpoint as any causal formula in a case of causal coalescence. In one respect at least it is even more important : it is the only type of formula, and applies to the only sort of association, in which we catch a glimpse of the inward nature of phenomenal unity. As everything that follows in the subsequent chapters of this work will be a systematic realization of these statements, it is unnecessary to try to present extensive proof here. For the purposes of clarification a few examples will suffice. Suppose, of two given cultural complexes, we find one through which, among countless other elements, runs the predominant thought that the true or *ultimate reality is supersensory*, that the reality detected by our organs of perception is illusory. Suppose, further, that in the second culture the current of thought is just the opposite : that the only reality is that of our organs of sensory perception. We now begin a series of logical deductions which runs something like this : If each of the two cultures is logically integrated to a substantial degree, we shall find the following characteristic details representing the dominant current in it. (I have intentionally enumerated variables taken from the different compartments of culture.)

First Culture	Second Culture
Dominance of	Dominance of
Rationalism, Mysticism	Empiricism
Idealism	Materialism
Eternalism	Temporalism
Indeterminism	Determinism
Realism	Nominalism
Sociological Universalism	Sociological Singularism
The Conception of Corporation or Juridical Personality as a Primary Reality	The Conception of Corporation or Juridical Personality as an Expedient Fiction
Ethics of Absolute Principles	Ethics of Happiness (Hedonism, Utilitarianism, Eudaemonism)
Few Discoveries in the Natural Sciences and Few Inventions	Many Discoveries and Inventions
Static Character of Social Life with a Slow Rate of Change	Dynamic Character of Social Life with a Rapid Rate of Change
Ideational Style of Painting	Visual Style of Painting
"Scripture" as the Main Form of Literature	Secular Realism and Naturalism in Literature, with Sensualism and even Sexualism
Pure or Diluted Theocracy	Pure or Diluted Secular Power
"Expiation" as the Basic Principle of Punishment and of Criminal Law	"Adjustment," Re-education Mixed with Extermination of the "Unadjusted" and "Socially Dangerous" Persons.

We shall find these variables because each of them is connected logically with the dominant attitude toward the nature of ultimate reality. All the traits of the first culture follow logically from the principle that reality is supersensory; all the traits of the second culture follow from the belief that reality is sensory.

Thus, the distinguishing of one variable of a culture enables us to construct logically a large network of connections with many of its other variables; to forecast what will be the nature of each of these variables *if the culture is logically integrated;* and, in this way, to comprehend quickly the enormous diversity of its traits, qualities, quantities, in one united and all-embracing system. Each of the variables, including the most detailed elements of such a culture, becomes an orderly part of one logically meaningful treatise, so to speak, where each page contributes to the sense of the others. In this way the logico-meaningful method catches in its net countless sociocultural details which cannot be caught by the causal net: even the few variables listed above are so diverse, and their association, whether in positive or negative fashion, is met with so rarely, that there is almost no possibility even of guessing, and still less of judging, whether or not they are causally united. Since they cannot be studied under "experimental" conditions, that is, under conditions where all the factors except the variable under scrutiny remain constant, and since the number of the occurrences of these variables in association is so small that no statistical or any other causal technique can be applied to it, the causal method is not adequate as a test of the nature of their union. More than this, if we could not grasp their logical relationship by the logical method, we would not even be able to guess that all this seeming diversity could have any orderly pattern of relationship whatsoever, nor that such a pattern should be expected if the cultural configurations in which the variables occur are at all logical.[42]

Now, when the two sets of deductions have been made and the series of expected patterns formulated, there remains the second step, namely, the application of the proper set of formulas to a specific culture in order to find out whether or not it is logically integrated. If we discover that this culture does contain the appropriate body of traits and variables, by one stroke we obtain several important cognitive results: (1) a highly intimate and certain understanding of many of the impor-

---

[42] From this one can see that the logico-meaningful method is essentially similar to the mathematical, both being first of all logical reasoning but with the difference that mathematical reasoning operates with quantities and number, while logical reasoning has to deal here mainly with qualities.

tant aspects of the culture; (2) an insight into the nature and workings of most of its significant components; (3) a knowledge of the spectrum of its dominant mentality; (4) a comprehensive grasp of the very complex network of relationships between many of its traits which otherwise would escape us; and (5) an answer to the question as to whether or not, and to what extent and in what parts, the culture is indeed logically integrated.

If it happens that, in such a study, we find that the expected variables do not occur in the culture under consideration; that the nature of its combination of traits tends to take a direction quite opposite to or different from what it should be logically, we still gain information of the first importance. We know, for example: (1) that the given culture is not logically integrated; (2) that, if it is not integrated, it is mainly alogical or nonlogical (a diagnosis of not a little significance, considering all the fuss which many followers of Pareto are making of his "discovery," as old as history of human thought, that the beliefs and activities of man and that social systems are mainly nonlogical or illogical); (3) possibly to what extent and in what parts it is alogical and nonlogical; and (4) that we may now expect more fruitful results in our study of this culture if we give up entirely the logico-meaningful procedure and employ instead causal, external, or spatial formulas.

Such, in brief, are the nature and the possible results of the logico-meaningful method of study.[43]

J. If the fruitfulness of this method depends upon the discovery of the unifying principle that permeates a large or small portion of the components of a given cultural synthesis, the questions now arise: *How can such a principle be discovered? What are the guarantees that it is an adequate principle and not the mere phantasy of a "speculative" mind superimposed upon a reality in which it does not actually occur? If different investigators offer quite different principles, how can it be ascertained which of them is valid, which not, or which is more valid than the others?*

The first question is almost superfluous. As is true also of scientific or causal investigation, the principle may be suggested by observation, statistical study, meditation, logical analysis, even by dreaming and by what is called mere "chance," or "intuition." All of these ways, alone

[43] It should be noted that in this work the logico-meaningful method of study is applied in detail to the Greek, Graeco-Roman, and general Western cultures from approximately 600 B.C. to A.D. 1920, and, more cursorily, to the Egyptian, Hindu (Brahmanic), and Chinese (Confucian and Taoist). For the moment it must suffice to say that these cultures show logical integration to a large extent in their "higher" layers.

or in various combinations, have been operative in the first stages of most scientific discovery.

More important is the question : *How can it be ascertained that a given principle of logical integration is valid?*   Do we know that it is not imposed artificially upon the reality; but, like a law in the natural sciences, represents a formula which describes adequately and without distortion, and in process of description unifies or "explains," many separate phenomena which otherwise would remain *disjecta membra*, fragmentary and meaningless?   How, in brief, can we be certain that the principle corresponds to the reality?   The answer is that the criteria of validity are virtually the same as for any scientific law.   First of all, the principle must by nature be logical; and second, it must stand successfully the test of the "relevant facts," that is, it must fit and represent them.

The first standard is self-explanatory and needs no further discussion. The second calls for a few notes.   The point here is that in the field of sociocultural phenomena as in almost any other field, one can construct about the same set of phenomena not one but several theories, each of which may be logically impeccable.   Which of these rivals is the best is decided by the testimony of the relevant facts.   When we try with this evidence to check the validity of all the principles set up, some will show themselves to be unsound almost at once.   Others will be generally relevant.   But the more deeply and more carefully we probe them, the further will proceed the progressive separation of the more adequate from the less.

Suppose that the application of a theory to a given culture results in our finding that the combination of its components runs contrary in nature to the implications of the principle.   In that case there are two possibilities open to us : either to conclude that the culture is not integrated logically, with all the consequences that follow from this; or to suspend judgment and, asking whether perhaps the principle itself is wrongly chosen, to try to find another principle which may fit the facts better.   If we consider the enormous difficulty of finding the right principle — a difficulty which seems the greater by comparison with the same problem in the field of causal relationships [44] — the second course will appear the more reasonable.   Before declaring a given culture nonlogical

[44] For this, see especially A. A. Tschuproff's work, where he shows with great clarity how difficult it is to discover the real nature of a causal connection, and how great is the danger of our making the gross error of taking for a causal factor a variable, which is almost always present but which nevertheless has no causal relationship with the "function" or "effect" under investigation.   The history of the natural sciences, not to mention the social sciences, is full of cases of such "mistaken identity."

or alogical, one has to experiment with as many principles as will fit any of the relevant facts at all.[45]   At this stage we may have a number of such theories, all of them varying more or less from one another.   Now we must proceed with a progressive elimination of those among them which fit the fewest facts.   For example, we may have a principle, A, which fits the sets of phenomena, A, B, C, but does not fit D, E, F, and is contradicted by M.   We may have also a second principle, B, which fits A, B, C, D, E, does not fit F, and is contradicted by N.   A third principle, C, which we likewise formulate, may, on the other hand, fit all these sets of phenomena from A to F, and be contradicted neither by M nor by N, nor by any other set, and besides fit the additional groups, G, J, S, P, X, Y.   Evidently, of these theories the last, if logically as impeccable as the others, is the most valid.

Here the comparative value of the principles is decided by the same criteria as those used in the natural sciences.   *Of several rival theories, that theory is best which describes the field of the phenomena in question most accurately and embraces in its description the largest number of phenomena.*   For these reasons the Copernican system is better than the Ptolemaic, Newton's laws than Kepler's.   Similarly, in the realm of sociocultural phenomena, where several different principles of integration may be formulated, some may be more correct and more broadly applicable than others.   Some, for example, may fit only a limited set of phenomena, while others will apply to several sets.   But one will stand forth as giving the most satisfactory meaning to the larger part of the elements.   And this is the theory we must choose.

Thus we may have a gradation of various theories from the standpoint of their cognitive value.   The theory which would fit all the facts would be perfect.   But such a theory could hardly be formulated in fact, because it presupposes complete information about realms of which our knowledge can, at best, be only a more or less accurate approximation.

In explaining the process of "fitting the facts," we may draw again on the analogy of the jigsaw puzzle.   In attempting to solve the puzzle, one may make several guesses, each of which is logically irreproachable, as to what the figure is going to be.   When, however, one begins to test the guesses by the facts, that is, begins under the guidance of each guess in turn to put the fragments into order, one soon sees that they do not fit according to the principle.   Step by step several guesses are eliminated

[45] As a matter of fact, if no cultures are completely integrated logically, hardly any are absolutely alogical or nonlogical.   Therefore, with the proper efforts a principle can be found that unifies at least a small part of the components of any culture.

until the correct one appears and turns a confused heap of fragments into a comprehensive unity. The same procedure is used in testing each integrative principle by the facts which it attempts to unite. From this the most exacting thinker in the natural sciences can see that the nature of logical integration is in no way more metaphysical or speculative than the most rigorously controlled generalization in his field.

These remarks clarify sufficiently the nature of the logico-meaningful form of integration, the situations in which it is relevant, and the methods of its application.

It is hardly necessary to add that the method is not new : it has been used, and used effectively, by the great social thinkers of the remote, as well as the more recent, past. Only in the second part of the nineteenth century and at the beginning of the twentieth, when the social sciences began thoughtlessly to imitate the natural, and the natural became particularly "causal" (at least in their aspirations), was the method neglected and even branded by the less discerning among the causalists as "metaphysical," "subjective," and the like. Plato and Aristotle's method of analysis of the fundamental forms of political and social regimes, and of the mentality and psychosocial variables of each, is, first of all, logico-meaningful. And this is true of such other great social thinkers as St. Thomas Aquinas, Albertus Magnus, Ibn-Khaldun, J. B. Vico, Montesquieu, Machiavelli (in the *Discourses*), and, in modern times, the very high priests of scientific positivism and causalism, Spencer and August Comte. Most of their important contributions, often even contrary to their express declarations, have been the result not of a causal study but of the conscious or unconscious use of the logico-meaningful. Even such supposed empiricists, causalists, and functionalists as Durkheim (particularly in his *Division du travail social* and his *Elementary Forms of Religious Life*) and Pareto (whose works after some twenty-five years have finally reached America at the moment when their significance is definitely on the decline) use, contrary to their intention, not a causal method but first and foremost an imperfect form of the logico-meaningful method.[46]

---

[46] Especially curious is the case with Pareto. In spite of his indefatigable insistence on the logico-experimental as the only method in sociology, he uses in fact a method neither very logical nor especially experimental nor particularly causal or functional. All his main concepts and theories (equilibrium, residue, derivation, his classification of residues, the rentieri and speculatori types, and so on) are in all their aspects logico-meaningful through and through; only the corresponding method is applied by him in its poorest form, a weakness which results from his empiricist and positivistic obsession to create a scientific sociology by a mere aping of the methods, concepts, and framework of reference of the natural, and especially of physico-chemical, sciences.

The same can be said of other social scientists. Whenever the theoreticians in the various fields of the social sciences have discussed the branches with which they are concerned — whether it involves consideration of the monarchical and republican forms of government; totemic and national society; the natural, money, and credit economy; the theological, metaphysical, and positive types of social mentality; mechanistic and organic solidarity as the bases of society; *Gemeinschaft und Gesellschaft;* opposition of capitalist and communist; the culture of East and West; the Greek and "Faustian" forms of culture; the caste, feudal, city-state, and modern national and international society; or the extrovert and introvert types of personality — they have in fact attempted to apply, whether well or ill, what is styled here the principle of logico-meaningful integration. This is generally true of nearly every case where the procedure is based on the establishment of a type, norm, or ideal.[47]

K. In the light of all this it is peculiar that the cultural anthropologists, who have recently rather monopolized the study of culture, have failed, with few exceptions, to formulate clearly the principles of logical integration. Using the principles unconsciously (as they do when they talk of the totemic and other types of primitive society), in their deliberate efforts, they have concentrated mainly upon the purely spatial and external forms of integration (for example, a study of the cultural traits from the point of view of their area of occurrence and the frequency of their distribution), supplemented occasionally by the functional. Only rarely has the logical method been tried deliberately, and even then with not very great skill.

Two recent examples will serve to illustrate this unskillful use. The first is offered by Professor Sapir, the second by Dr. Benedict. Sapir tries to distinguish the "genuine" culture from the "spurious."

The genuine culture [he writes] is not of necessity high or low; it is merely inherently harmonious, balanced, self-satisfactory. . . . It is . . . a culture in which nothing is spiritually meaningless, in which no important part of the general functioning brings with it a sense of frustration, of misdirected or unsympathetic effort. It is not a spiritual hybrid of contradictory patches.[48]

In brief, it is a culture in which the parts are meaningfully unified. The "spurious" culture, on the contrary, is that which does not have this organic synthesis. From the characterization of the genuine culture one

[47] Most of these studies have, however, been badly done. See my *Contemporary Sociological Theories*, pp. 719–724, where this point is discussed more extensively.
[48] Sapir, *op. cit.*, Vol. XXIX, p. 410.

can easily see that by it Professor Sapir means neither a spatial nor an external accumulation, nor even a functionally united congeries, but something near to what I call logically integrated culture. Unfortunately, in his detailed characterization Sapir's concept of the logically integrated culture is marred by its partial identification with the idealized culture of the type which he finds most attractive.[49] We may disregard this defect and give credit to the author for his groping for something which is of the first importance, even though he has not as yet seen it clearly. Now, however, we ask the question : " What is the specific logical principle which Sapir applies to cultures in order to find out whether they are genuine or not? " We see at once the limits of his method. He does not have any really significant and systematically applied key principles. All his attempts to find such keys are virtual failures. We read that the supposed key of the French culture is "clarity, lucid systematization, balance, care in choice of means, and a good taste." [50] The key to the Russian culture is

the tendency of the Russian to see and think of human beings not as representatives of types, not as creatures that appear eternally clothed in the garments of civilization, but as stark human beings existing primarily in and for themselves, only secondarily for the sake of civilization.[51]

All this perhaps sounds "romantic" but it is neither clear nor united and is factually wrong. First of all, in the French case not one but several keys fit the same door; clarity is not the same thing as balance or systematization or good taste or care in choice of means. Such an array of traits is nothing but a hodgepodge. Second, the integration is superficial and journalistic; it does not give the slightest idea of the content of French culture, its meaning, its real physiognomy. The physiognomy of a dog, a bird, a fish, a man, may all be "lucid" and "clear "; nevertheless they are very different from one another. Sapir's characterization is just what one may expect to hear from the summer tourist. Even if the traits are accurate they integrate at the best the mere formal surface of the phenomena of the French culture. They do not give any "key" to its science and philosophy, religion and ethics, art and law, economics and politics.

[49] This mixture of logical integration with the idealization of the culture which meets one's taste is clear even from the brief passage quoted, with its partisan adjectives and phrases, "harmonious," "unsympathetic effort"; and this is true of the entire study. Sapir's "genuine" culture is the culture which he likes, and all the cultures which he dislikes are "spurious."

[50] Sapir, *op. cit.*, p. 407.

[51] *Ibid.*, pp. 407–408.

In the case of Russia only one, but that the most "significant," principle is indicated: the principle of the "stark human beings," of the famous and mysterious *âme Slave*, as all the janitresses in Paris call it. Evidence? Practically none, except indefinite references to Tolstoi, Dostoevsky, Gorki, Chekhov, Turgenev, with a little Moussorgsky and Tschaikovsky.

This is surely not a broad enough basis for generalization on the whole of Russian culture. If only the author had asked himself how this Russian was able to create one of the vastest of empires, occupying about one-sixth of the planet, he would probably never have set down the key principle which he offers as the open-sesame of the entire civilization. Moreover, Sapir's key really does not tell us anything about the character of Russian science, philosophy, religion, art, or literature, or of its forms of social, political, economic, and other organizations. The same is true even of his key to the culture of the "typical American Indian tribe," his great knowledge of which should have given his words special authority.[52]

To sum up: Professor Sapir is on the right track in his search for what I style the logical form of culture integration, but he fails, partly because he does not have a clear idea of the true nature of logical integration or of how to find a logico-meaningful key principle and apply it to and test it by the relevant facts.

With slight modification the same can be said of Dr. Benedict's effort. She also tries to integrate the cultures which she studies in a way which approaches logical integration. But when she seeks to unify in this

[52] Sapir's subsequent discussion of civilization and of culture, art, and so on is rather naïve. Here we find the usual error committed by modern anthropologists when they discuss "complex" civilizations. Accustomed to dealing with the "recordless" primitive societies and cultures, they consciously or unconsciously apply the "timeless" typology — which is wrong even in application to the primitive societies — to the cultures whose history and profound changes are known to us. To talk of them, regardless of time and period, as of something which remains the same throughout the centuries is unsound. But this is what is done almost all the time by the anthropologists who indulge in such characterizations of the "historical" cultures. For instance, we read in Wissler, *op. cit.*, pp. 233 ff.: "Oriental art is highly conventionalized and does not strive to be realistic, while Occidental work approaches exactness in reproduction." If the author had taken Occidental art, say, before the fifteenth century, he would have seen that it was highly conventionalized, as much as any Oriental art at any period. And vice versa, the art of some of the Oriental countries at some periods was as realistic as the Occidental art of the last four centuries. What Wissler says further about Occidental and Oriental music, the "flowing bowl," and so on, is still more fallacious. The main source of the error is, besides incomplete knowledge of these subjects, the application of the timeless categories to the historical and changing cultures of which we have records which show the change. In a less degree the same mistake is made by Sapir and others when they talk of the modern culture.

fashion a number of "preliterate" cultures (the Zuñi, the Dobu, and that
of the tribes of the northwest coast of America), she also fails. For
instance, we are shown that among the Zuñi there exist a distrust of
individualism, sobriety and inoffensiveness, ritualism, imitative magic,
a highly developed priesthood together with theocracy, the blood-relation-
ship group, property tabu, and certain specified forms of family relationship, marriage, household economy, and so on.[53] Granted that the
description is accurate, it is not sufficiently discriminating to enable us
to decide whether in these combinations we have logical or functional
unity, or purely spatial adjacency, or accumulation affected by an external
factor.[54] Even her invocation of the Nietzschean "key" to the Dionysian

[53] See R. Benedict, *op. cit.*, chap. iv.
[54] The same is true of the other two tribes described in the work. The author, as we shall
see, tries to show that these cultures are functionally integrated, but the procedure of the
integration which she follows is not so much functional as logical. The same is to be said
of Wissler's treatment of the main traits of the modern American culture mentioned before.
A similar failure to distinguish the spatial, external, functional, and the logico-meaningful
forms of culture integration, plus a lack of clear understanding of the necessity of some unifying principle in logico-meaningful integration, is quite noticeable, especially in the methodological formulation of functionalism by A. R. Radcliffe-Brown. Putting aside his unen-
lightening organismic analogies, we turn to his definition of functional relationships: "Function is the contribution which a partial activity makes to the total activity of which it is a part.
The function of a particular social usage is the contribution it makes to the total social system.
. . . Such a view implies that a social system (the total structure and the totality of
usages in which this structure appears and on which it depends for its continued existence) has
a certain kind of unity, which we may speak of as a functional unity. . . . We may define
it as a condition in which *all parts* of the social system work together with a sufficient degree
of harmony or internal consistency, *i.e.*, without producing persistent conflicts which can
neither be resolved nor regulated. . . ." Here, as well as in other similar statements of his,
there is present a mixture of all the main forms of integration, of the spatial, functional, and
logico-meaningful connections. If by functional he means the causal-functional connections
of the parts of a given cultural conglomeration, then it is hard to talk of such connections in
terms of harmony and disharmony, of inner consistency and inconsistency, because causal
relationships are neither harmonious nor disharmonious, neither consistent nor inconsistent.
They are simply either causal or not. The relationship between the volume of gas and the
pressure is neither harmonious nor disharmonious, consistent nor inconsistent. It is simply
causal. The terms harmonious and the like are suitable as indications of the existence of
a logico-meaningful relationship between the parts. But the author nowhere formulates
such relationships and talks of functionalism in the sense of causal functionalism. On the
other hand, taking his definition of functionalism, one cannot separate a mere spatial congeries
from causal-functional unity. Any part of any spatial congeries contributes something to
the whole of which it is a part. This, however, does not mean that it is functionally connected with the rest of the congeries. Though the distinguished author seems to admit the
existence of such accumulations, saying that "not everything in the life of community has
a function" (an awkward expression !), nevertheless, he nowhere attempts to give any inkling
as to how we are to distinguish a congeries from a causal-functional unity. In brief, in his
words "function" and "functionalism" he includes a great many different things, from the
biological meaning of the terms in the connotation function-organ, to the fusion of spatial,

and Apollonian types of culture (this actually refers to music in Nietzsche) does not help much. What she really gives us is not a key to the cultures studied but an empirical description of them, in which are put side by side traits and complexes the logical or causal relationship of which, one to the other, remains unilluminated by the juxtaposition. The application of Nietzsche's categories does not improve the situation — rather makes it worse, because the meaning given to the terms Apollonian and Dionysian is somewhat different from that which Nietzsche gave to them; because the categories are not naturally applicable to the situation, but represent an artificial imposition upon cultures which have little to do with them; and, finally, because some of the cultures with which Dr. Benedict deals in any case have a very small degree of logical integration.[55]

Thus, from these examples we perceive that some modern anthropologists have at last begun to search for logico-meaningful principles with which to explain certain cultures. Up to now their efforts have yielded few results, and for not unfathomable reasons. As we shall see, even in the comparatively highly integrated cultures logical synthesis takes place only among part of their elements. Therefore, so far as the primitive cultures are concerned, we must expect even a lesser degree of logical integration. At best, only a relatively small part of their traits would show such coalescence; yet, in order to understand even this portion of the culture we must discover a key which is neither haphazard nor based upon journalistic observations. Here, as anywhere in science, keys are not found by everybody, nor even by every serious specialist, without concentrated and systematic thought, meticulous labor, and — luck. These examples likewise offer further confirmation of the present writer's claim that the validity of the integrating principle can be tested as

---

external, functional-causal, and logico-meaningful forms of relationship. In such a setting he is likely to take as functional the connection discussed above of the elements, A, B, C, D . . . N, found empirically in association in a given locality, for he does not have any means of separating the really functional from the accidental. In this respect the criticism of functionalism in anthropology by A. Lesser — that functionalists are open to the error of confusing these connections, having virtually no ground on which to test which of the integrations are functional and which mere coexistences — is also valid.

What I have said here is not aimed at the very valuable contributions of Radcliffe-Brown and others in their actual field studies. All that is intended is to show that in this basic problem a great deal of confusion exists; that it exists even in the best works; and that some of the best investigators seem to sense the existence of what I style the logico-meaningful unities, but have hardly thought the problem through clearly.

See A. R. Radcliffe-Brown, op. cit., Vol. XXXVII, pp. 394–402; A. Lesser, "Functionalism in Social Anthropology," ibid., pp. 386–394; and A. L. Kroeber, "History and Science in Anthropology," ibid., pp. 539–570.

[55] See R. Benedict, op. cit., passim.

severely as that of any causal principle in the natural sciences: those
keys that are invalid fail to work or break easily under a test; those
that survive the test merit the name "scientific" until their shortcomings
are demonstrated.[56]

L. The logico-meaningful method cannot be avoided even by those
investigators who are most intent on the use of the causal-functional
formulas as long as they claim the totalitarian integration of culture.
Even when a culture is completely integrated, still it cannot be claimed,
as many sociologists and anthropologists wrongly claim, that the culture is
one sort of unity as a whole, namely, a causal unity. The reason is clear
and unquestionable. Any culture may consist of countless millions of
elements. The discovery of a perceptible functional relationship between
a few of these components does not entitle us in any way to assume that
this relationship extends to the rest. If it is shown that business conditions are definitely associated with the movement of the birth rate, it
does not as yet follow that either of these components is, or both together
are, united in functional synthesis with the art forms, beliefs, ideologies,
marriage conventions, funeral rites, festivals, conflicts, ways of fraterni-
zation, systems of kinship, political regimes, church architecture, sport,
or other elements. Only by having shown convincingly that these elements exhibit the marks of functional association with one another and
with business conditions and the birth rate are we in a position to claim
with more justice that culture is a dominantly functional unity. But
even then our claim is not entirely justified. Suppose a given culture
consists of 1000 diverse elements. Let us grant that we can show that
all of these variables are functionally integrated in groups of two, three,
or four each. In that case we reduce the number of separate components
from 1000 to 500, 333, or 250 diverse groups or complexes. Such a
reduction is, however, still very far from achieving a single unity which
embraces functionally all the 1000 elements. Instead, we still have
from 500 to 250 ununified or unintegrated separate complexes. If we
decrease it to 100, the result is the same: we do not have a totally unified
culture; we still have *disjecta membra* to the number of 100.

---

[56] In the subsequent sections of this work a definite key for the logical integration of the
Graeco-Roman, the Western, and other great cultures will be offered. It attempts to be
thoroughgoing and rigidly tested. I believe that it is a better key than any other hitherto
offered. Whether it is or not, the reader will judge for himself. In the meantime I can say
that the theory that will be there developed will show that, in making the charges and criticism
I have of the theories of others, I do not choose the easy and negative way simply of finding
fault, but assume also the responsibility of a positive offering which will thus expose me to the
criticism of others.

Under such conditions to talk of culture as a unity is obviously a gross blunder. The causal-functionalists have tried to overcome the difficulty in two different ways. First, they have taken a specific variable as the *main factor* (*i.e.*, the monists in sociology) and hung to its "arc" all the other culture variables as "functions" or dependents. Geographic theories, for example, make climate or erosion of the soil or sunspots such a main factor and try to interpret all the other variables of culture as dependent. Marxians take for such a factor the modes of production; other sociologists take race, density of population, the struggle for existence, religion, mores.[57] The second method in solving the difficulty used by the causalists has been through the claim that all the component variables of a given culture are in fact functionally connected with one another in a "decentralized" fashion: A with B, B with C, C with D . . . X with Y, Y with Z. Each element being functionally connected with at least one other, all compose a unified chain that links them together into what in a sense we have a right to call a single functional unity. Most of the work of the functional anthropologists, like Malinowski, Radcliffe-Brown, Benedict, and others, furnishes samples of this method.

That neither of these ways can bring functional unity to a whole culture needs no lengthy argument. Thus far no attempt to apply the *main factor method*, whether by functionalists or others, has succeeded. Without exception, all such theories based on this procedure have come to grief and exactly at the point where the main factor begins to be stretched beyond its limited possibilities.[58] The very fact that we have a vast number of diverse main factors in sociology is testimony against the soundness of such efforts. In addition, a few other considerations will be enough to show in general why the totalitarian and centralistic assumptions of the main-factor method cannot give us a true picture of the nature of the unity of all the components. If in a culture there are any purely spatial conglomerations, the attempt to view them and their elements as mere dependent variables of the functional main factor amounts to the imposition of a functional tie where it does not exist. If, moreover, the main factor taken happens to be *external* to the variables of the culture, it involves the assumption that all these variables are absolutely dependent upon it; that their dependence upon the external factor is closer than upon one another; and that culture as unity is in fact a passive system depending entirely upon an external agency and

---

[57] See my *Contemporary Sociological Theories, passim.*
[58] For their shortcomings see *ibid., passim.*

having no autonomy of its own and not even a narrow margin of immunity from external conditions.   This amounts virtually to a denial of the very claim that culture is a unity, a system, an organism.   Besides all this it should be noted further that, if the main factor taken is one of the variables within the culture to be explained, the procedure amounts to an attempt to explain the whole through its part (*pars pro toto*), which is unsound; or it leads to mere tautology, which is no better.   Thus, by claiming too much for a main factor, the functionalists distort and the externalists destroy the very thing they seek to integrate, and both besides are subject to the charge of employing false logic.

No better is the situation with the decentralized method of totalitarian integration suggested by the functionalists.   If it does not pass into the logico-meaningful method but stays strictly in the causal or functional position, it never can give us a complete integration of all the cultural components in question.   The point is that the mere linking of A with B, B with C, C with D, and so on, cannot give us either a true functional unity or any comprehension of the real nature of the connection between these A, B, C, D's or between these and the more remote elements of the chain.   In fact it results in a kind of externally descriptive characterization of the combination of the given cultural elements which furnishes us no idea of whether the combination is functional or a mere congeries of traits thrown incidentally together.   So far as the functional-causal relation means a uniform and regularly occurring connection between two or more variables, the mere statement that in a given culture area we find A and B together is not necessarily, and cannot pretend to be, a clue to the functional union of A and B.   Suppose we find in a group the coexistence of A (the kula trade) with B (certain forms of marriage) and C (sexual life) and these coexisting with D (certain forms of religion) [59] and M (certain forms of crime and punishment).   Unless it is shown that the concurrence of these elements in this fashion is found always or in many cases (a matter which would in fact be difficult at present since the material at hand is quite insufficient); or unless the elements are shown to be meaningfully and logically united (and this would mean the supplementary use of the logical method of integration); we cannot decide whether the combination is indeed a functional unity, or whether it is accidental, representing mere spatial adjacency or, at the best, external unification.   Such a method does not permit us to

[59] See, for instance, B. Malinowski's *The Argonauts of the Western Pacific* (London, 1922), *The Sexual Life of Savages* (New York, 1929), and *Crime and Custom in Savage Society* (New York, 1926).

claim even that A is causally connected with B, B is causally connected with C, and so on. All that we can claim on the basis of it is that in a given culture A and B and C . . . Z are found in coexistence. This means that it results in a cataloguing description of the conglomeration and nothing more.[60]

It is now clear why the causal-functional method pursued by many social scientists can give illuminating formulas for the relationship of two or more variables of a culture but can never produce a synthesis of all the variables. Too exclusive a preoccupation with this form of integration results not only in a distortion of the nature of a culture, but also in the neglect of the other methods of integration by which the essential nature of the culture might be discovered. I refer in particular to the failure to perceive the value of the logico-meaningful method, which applies to all culture at its highest level, and which therefore must supplement the causal whenever we suspect a high degree of culture integration. Thus, by using these two powerful beams together, we illuminate more widely and completely the chaotic darkness of the infinite multitude of the fragments of culture, and may then proceed to order them into systems which permit us to grasp the nature of the components which, beyond mere spatial and external accumulations, possess true unity.

Each of these methods, however, must be applied separately and in its proper field. But this does not preclude a further study of the relationship between the logically integrated and the functionally united layers of culture [61] with a view to throwing up a bridge between them. Thus, proceeding along these orderly lines, we get at least a part of the culture soundly integrated and therefore properly comprehended. But if we mix indiscriminately the different forms of culture integration and the different methods which apply to each, we are likely to be lost in chaos, and our results will be confused, unbalanced, unsound.

[60] For the sake of economy of space I do not mention many other reasons against the possibility of the wholesale integration of culture through the causal method, such as the fact that the larger the nature of the main factor, the more indefinite it becomes, and the greater becomes the difficulty of operating with it causally and testing its relationship to other variables, such as the "principle of limit" sometimes formulated in this book; such as the almost insuperable impediment to causal analysis offered by the incessant change and enormous complexity of the culture variables. In addition, when the causal association of variables is not frequently met with, we are practically helpless to discover it when it does occur.

[61] As the present work will show with full facts in its subsequent sections, the relationship between the two layers is peculiar in many respects, and its peculiarity throws an interesting light upon many compartments of culture as well as upon the nature and direction of sociocultural change.

V. Some Results of the Preceding Analysis

If it is valid that there are at least four different types of cultural integration — spatial, external, functional, and logical — each with the properties described, then one may draw a definite series of conclusions.

A. All the cultural conglomerations can be ranged theoretically upon a scale beginning with those which are a mere spatial congeries, that is, are unintegrated in the proper sense of the word, and ending with those which are completely integrated logically. We virtually never meet in fact with a perfect case of either an absolutely unintegrated or a completely integrated cultural complex. All the combinations which are now known occupy, however, different places upon the scale, some being nearer to the lowest, others to the highest, still others to the intermediate forms of integration.

B. If spatial adjacency and, in part, external unification are present in nearly every cultural complex, the same cannot be said of the functional and logical forms of synthesis. It is probable that at least some of the elements are bound either functionally or logically; but what they are, and how great a part of the whole they compose depends upon the culture and the period, and must be found by special study. No generalization equally applicable to all cultures is possible here. As will be shown in these chapters, so far as logical integration is concerned, there are some compartments of a given culture which display it more conspicuously than others.

C. If propositions A and B are valid, then the following theories widely accepted are fallacious:

(1) That every culture is an integrated unity (unless, of course, by integration is meant a mere spatial congeries, a meaning which in its turn not only destroys the significance of the term, but also leads to other errors and illogicalities).

(2) That any change in any component of a given cultural configuration functionally or logically affects all the other components and therefore the whole of the given culture. This would be so if any cultural conglomeration were either a functional or a logical unity throughout. But since every combination has among its elements some united only in a spatial congeries or by external association, then removing old or adding new elements may not tangibly influence the rest of the accumulation in any functional or logical way. Contrary to the prevalent opinion, this sort of change has actually been occurring on a relatively large scale and with comparative frequency.

D. The nature of the change of a spatial congeries differs from that of functionally or logically unified systems. In the congeries the change would mean mainly a mechanical addition or subtraction of elements, or their rearrangement chiefly through external forces. In the unified cultural systems the change would mean a transformation of the system as a whole or in its greater part. This transformation would involve not just a quantitative addition or subtraction or a mechanical rearrangement of some elements, but an inner or organic change produced in part perhaps by external forces, but primarily, as will be shown in the future chapters of the present work, generated by forces within the system itself. The change in the spatial congeries is almost always accidental. It does not have any inner logic and is the result of the interplay of various external factors. A wind can carry away some leaves from a dead pile or add some to it; a stone thrown into the pile may press some of the leaves more firmly to the ground; a dog playing in the leaves can rearrange their places as well as the general form of the pile. Such a congeries is passive: it does not have either an inner tendency to, or an inner selection of, change in a specific direction. Except for its purely mechanical inertia it is the plaything of external conditions.

Somewhat similar is the situation in a cultural congeries. A force external to the heap may dump into it some additional elements or carry away some of the objects which were there; it may change their mechanical order. The congeries remains passive through all these changes, does not have initiative, preferences, attraction and repulsion, selection and resistance. It is inert, like the "broad-minded" reader whose mind is filled now by *Trader Horn*, now by a psychoanalytical biography of Queen Victoria, now by Marco Polo's travels, now by contract bridge, now by a monograph on Hindu architecture, according to what is advertised and brought directly to him. The contents with which his mind is filled are determined, not so much by his own selective activity as by that of agencies external to him. He reads the "best sellers"; thinks in terms of the editorials of the latest edition of the newspaper; wears the latest fashions; approves now this, now the opposite, caring little about consistency or logic. He can "reconcile" the most contradictory things. His "cultural area" is open to almost anything which may be thrown in at random. It does not have any character of its own; it is passive, it is "rudderless." And all that may be said of such a mind can be said as readily of a haphazard collection of cultural objects.

The difference between the merely spatial accumulation and the genuinely integrated system is so profound that the nature and methods of their change are also profoundly different. What these differences are have in the main just been indicated. While it is useless to look for an inner logic of change in the accidental congeries, it is absolutely necessary to do so in the genuine cultural unity. There is little reason to talk of evolution or development or stages of change in the spatial congeries, but we can use these terms in the case of the functional and logical systems. The congeries is changed by mere chance; the systems change according to the course of life which is predetermined for them by their very nature. They are the "equilibrium systems," as the lovers of the mechanistic terms sometimes say.

E. So far as the logically and functionally integrated systems are concerned, because they are real systems, they possess several fundamental traits and give rise to a number of important considerations which are usually neglected.

(1) Any functional or logical system as a unity has a certain degree of autonomy and inherent self-regulation in its functioning and change ("equilibrium" of the imitators of mechanics). Any system, whether it be a mechanism like an automobile, an organism like even the paramecium, or a cultural system, has a certain degree of independence of, or immunity to, external conditions. In some cases this freedom may be large, in others narrow, but it is possessed to some extent by every system which pretends to integration. Thus, to a considerable degree an automobile is immune to the defects in the road, to change in temperature, and to many other circumstances; and the better the car the larger is its margin of immunity. A biological organism is also immune to a rather large number of external elements. Similarly the functional and, especially, the logical cultural systems have such an immunity to external circumstances — to weather, climate, seasonal change, various biological processes, including even such calamities as a poor harvest or an earthquake or an epidemic; and to external social conditions, such as the pressure of other societies and cultures. Even when these circumstances reach the scale of catastrophe (war, famine, plague), the systems, like a biological organism, may temporarily be shocked and fall ill, but often they recover in due time and resume their proper forms and functions.

(2) The autonomy of any system means further the existence of some margin of choice or selection on its part with regard to the infinitely great number of varying external agents and objects which may influence it. It will ingest some of these and not others. It has an affinity for some and a repulsion for others.

(3) Autonomy means further still that the functions, change, and destiny of the system are determined not only and not so much by the external circumstances (except in the case of catastrophic accidents), but by the nature of the system itself and by the relationship between its parts. An airplane can fly, but a cow cannot; a gun can fire, but a spade cannot. Whatever are the external circumstances, man cannot help passing from childhood to senility and sooner or later dying. Likewise, a cultural system has its own logic of functioning, change, and destiny, which is a result not only (and regularly not so much) of the external conditions, but of its own nature. This does not deny the influence of the external circumstances; neither does it deny the possibility of occurrence of the most decisive, catastrophic accidents caused by an external force; but it stresses what seems to have been forgotten for the last few decades, namely, that one of the most important "determinators" of the functioning and course of any system lies within the system itself, is inherent in it. In this sense any inwardly integrated system is an autonomous self-regulating, self-directing, or, if one prefers, "equilibrated" unity. Its life course is set down in its essentials when the system is born. This is one of the specific aspects of the larger principle which may be called "immanent self-regulation and self-direction."

(4) If this is true, then it is incorrect to "explain" any true system as the mere plaything of external conditions and reduce the explanation of the change in the system to this or that external factor.[62] Such an explanation, if it neglects the nature of the autonomy of the system, can only land the one who explains in a swamp of logical and factual error. It would hinder the understanding of the trends, recurrences, turns, oscillations, rhythms, tempos of change in almost any, and especially a cultural and social, system.

(5) Reliance upon one element of an integrated combination as a main factor in explaining changes within the combination, as many investigators in the field have done, is a serious error in procedure. The partisans of the economic interpretation of history make the economic

[62] This "external" standpoint has gone so far that, as a humorist has said, nowadays historians begin the history of any people and country with the indication that the people did not live where they live now but came from some other place, and the people who began the history of a given place were not the people who lived there before the beginning of its history. Similarly, if we must explain a change in the family, we take as a factor either an economic or religious or demographic or any other condition *external* to the family and in this way "explain" its change. The same procedure is often used with regard to other social systems in explanation of their change or workings. As we shall see, such a disposition to "externality" is not accidental, but represents one of the traits of the contemporary integrated culture.

factor the source of change in all the compartments of culture; partisans of religion, of race, of heredity, and of other factors, make each of these respectively the chief source. But, in the meantime, if a given culture . is a unity in which economic, religious, populational, and other compartments are but single elements, its change can be explained through such a main factor procedure with as little accuracy as, for instance, the change of the human organism as it passes from childhood to puberty could be explained through increase in stature or some other such "factor." Not just a single part is changing in such a passage, but the whole organism with many of its anatomical, physiological, and psychological properties. To say that the real factor of the change is the increase in stature, that this causes the growth of whiskers and of weight, muscular and glandular changes, and many others, is obviously absurd. Absurd also would be the selection of any other similar trait to serve as the controlling element. The truth is that no one of the parts, or the minute changes proper to it, exercises a major influence on the other parts, but all the parts together and the common movement of their transformation are controlled by the general inward nature of the organism as a whole. Or, if one prefers, the inwardly controlled change of the system as a whole is manifested in the special change of each of its parts. This is readily comprehensible where a biological organism is concerned; but with reference to a cultural system (not a mere spatial congeries) it is not often comprehended. Yet the situation is exactly the same as with the organism. There are purely compartmental changes, but they are limited to the compartment and therefore do not concern the other sections.

(6) Even accidental changes which, like infection in an organism, may start with one part and spread throughout the system, leading either to its permanent modification or even its destruction—even these do not permit us to take the compartment from which they happened to spread as the universal or invariable source of all change in similar systems. In cases of accident to the human organism, the infection may now start with the irritated membranes of the nose, now with a cut finger, now with a disease of the alimentary tract or the lungs. Similarly, in a cultural system there may be an accidental economic crisis, a military invasion, an epidemic of the Black Death, the evil effects of a pernicious ideology, and these may spread throughout the system. They are not, however, the changes which go on normally in such a system by virtue of its inherent nature and way of functioning.

When all this is understood, the futility will at once be apparent of the many heated disputes as to whether Protestantism was the result of capitalism or capitalism of Protestantism; whether the Renaissance of the sciences and arts was the result of the discovery of America and the overabundance of gold, or the gold and the discovery, as well as other related elements, were the results of the changed mentality of the fifteenth and the subsequent centuries; whether war and peace are the results of the demographic factors, or the demographic situation is in a considerable degree the result of war and peace. These and endless similar disputes (except as they involve relevant accidental changes) have in many cases been wrongly set forth, wrongly argued, and wrongly decided by both parties to the dispute. At a certain period the human organism has to pass from childhood to puberty and all its properties are transformed in the process regardless of any external factors, which at best may retard or accelerate, accentuate or smooth, it. It is useless to argue as to whether the increase of stature is a factor in the growth of whiskers and in the changes in the sexual glands, or vice versa. Similarly, at a certain point of its history (slightly accelerated or retarded by the external circumstances) the cultural system must undergo its inwardly ordained change. When this begins, all the main compartments of the culture change. It is therefore equally futile to argue that the transformation of one factor causes another, or all the others, to change, or vice versa.

From these conclusions it is apparent that the investigators of cultural phenomena who have sought to explain the transformations of an integrated system by means of a factor which is merely a symptom or result have failed to recognize the true nature of change in such a system. In addition if their main factor is dependent on something external and accidental, they are also guilty of failing to discriminate between a genuine integration of cultural elements and a mere spatial congeries. This point will be developed more fully in the subsequent parts of the present work.

Having elucidated the nature of our tools so far as the problem of integrated culture is concerned, we can turn now to a preliminary outline of the key principles of the logico-meaningful integration of culture.

Chapter Two

IDEATIONAL, SENSATE, IDEALISTIC, AND MIXED SYSTEMS OF CULTURE

I. INTERNAL AND EXTERNAL ASPECTS OF CULTURE AND METHODS OF READING THEM

The elements of thought and meaning which lie at the base of any logically integrated system of culture may be considered under two aspects: the *internal* and the *external*. The first belongs to the realm of inner experience, either in its unorganized form of unintegrated images, ideas, volitions, feelings, and emotions; or in its organized form of systems of thought woven out of these elements of the inner experience. This is the realm of mind, value, meaning. For the sake of brevity we shall refer to it by the term "mentality of culture" (or "culture mentality"). The second is composed of inorganic and organic phenomena: objects, events, and processes, which incarnate, or incorporate, or realize, or externalize, the internal experience. These external phenomena belong to a system of culture only as they are the manifestations of its internal aspect. Beyond this they cease to be a part of integrated culture. This means that for the investigator of an integrated system of culture the internal aspect is paramount. It determines which of the externally existing phenomena — and in what sense and to what extent — become a part of the system. In other words, it controls the external aspect of the culture.

Deprived of its inner meaning, the Venus of Milo becomes a mere piece of marble identical in its physicochemical qualities with the same variety of marble in the state of nature. A Beethoven symphony turns into a mere combination of sounds, or even into a vibration of air waves of certain lengths to be studied by the laws of physics. Aristotle's *Metaphysics* becomes a material paper object — a book similar to millions of other books. Deprived of this internal aspect, many phenomena fundamentally different in their cultural nature become similar. The action of a surgeon plunging his knife into the body of his patient and that of a murderer knifing his victim become indistinguishable, on account of the likeness of their external forms. In a series of books, alike in size, color, binding, and other external marks, Plato's *Republic* becomes identical in appearance with a volume of tales by De Maupassant. And, vice versa, phenomena which are profoundly different in their external qualities may be identical with regard to their inward cultural nature. Thus Plato's *Republic*, whether read orally, published in the form of a book (either in the original Greek or in translation), or recorded on a phonograph record, still remains Plato's *Republic*. Deprived of their internal significance, such external phenomena can be studied by the physicist, chemist, or biologist, as physical, chemical, or biological data; but they cannot be studied by an investigator of culture because they are not a part of culture.

As a mere inorganic or organic phenomenon the external vehicle of the mentality of a culture may be perceived by many animals. Even a mouse is capable of noticing Aristotle's *Metaphysics* as a corporeal paper object, and may nibble at it, as sometimes mice do. Many animals are able to hear the sounds of a Beethoven symphony, see the colors of a picture by Raphael, notice buildings of this or that kind; but they observe all these things purely as inorganic and organic objects. Only rarely can animals be "conditioned" to some vague understanding of internal significance, and then only when the highest species of animals are concerned, and the simplest forms of inner cultural meaning. The mentality of culture, to be properly grasped, demands a development of mind and a concentration of thought far above that of the ape. Many qualified meanings of culture cannot be understood even by an average human intellect. The point is that diverse cultural values require different degrees of intelligence for their understanding; they range from the easiest to the most difficult. Beginning with comparatively simple meanings — say, the rudiments of arithmetic in the field of mathematics, which can be understood by an average human intellect — they increase in their difficulty — for instance, calculus is accessible to a much smaller number of intellects — until they reach meanings which are comprehensible to only a few. And so it is with the values of most of the compartments of culture. The result of this is not only that human intellect is necessary for the comprehension of the internal aspect of culture, but that many levels or forms of this aspect are inaccessible even to the normal human mind, demand an intellect of a much superior refinement. The same is to be said of many specific meanings accessible only to either specially trained intelligence or minds endowed with the specific power of understanding such meanings.

Several questions now arise: Can we grasp the internal aspect of a given culture adequately? Since it is somewhat elusive, and often inferential — in the sense that in order to grasp it, one has to "read" it in external vehicles which differ from the internal meaning — how can we be sure that our reading is correct, that we do not superimpose on a given configuration of external cultural phenomena meanings which are not there? How can we ascertain that out of several different readings one is more correct than the others? Are there any means by which to test, and thus to validate, a given reading?

These questions are ages old, have always been — and still remain — a stumbling block for the humanistic and social sciences. It is not my purpose to analyze them in detail here. If I mention them, it is merely to indicate the fact that they are involved in a study of our problems and thus have to be answered in some way, at least to the extent of making clear the position of the investigator. The discussion which follows aims only to outline this position as a means of making comprehensible the character of the subsequent analysis.

The answer to the above questions depends upon what is meant by the true, or *real*, mentality incorporated in a given complex of external vehicles. Out of several possible kinds of real meanings the following may be mentioned.

The term *real* meaning can refer to the state of mind of the person or group of persons creating or using given external vehicles — for instance, the meanings which Beethoven had in mind in the composition of his music, or which Dante kept before him in writing the *Divine Comedy*, or which are intended by any other creator or modifier of a complex containing cultural value. Here we have the *psychological* interpretation of what is the *real* meaning of a given phenomenon. According to this point of view the correct reading of the internal aspect of culture is that which regards it *exactly in the same way as it was regarded by its creators or modifiers*. If an investigator can show that his interpretation is indeed identical with that of the persons or groups involved, then his is correct as a *psychological* reading. Hence it is the aim of any psychological reading to show how this or that value was understood by this or that man or group or generation.

But can this be done with any certainty? Can the reading of the creators, the modifiers, of any individual or group be correctly restored and restated? In many cases, yes. And for a simple reason: the meaning or purpose is often clearly and explicitly announced by the creator. We can grasp the essential meaning of Aristotle's *Politics* or

Dante's *Divine Comedy* or Newton's *Principia* or Lincoln's "Gettysburg Address" because it is there in their works, expressed explicitly. Similarly we can grasp and restore, at least approximately, the meaning of the artists who molded the sculpture of the Gothic cathedrals because it is unmistakably embodied in these sculptures and because we possess documents, like the treatise of Theophilus or the *Mirror of Nature*, where *expressis verbis* the meaning of the creators is given. And so with many other cases. The character of the cultural objects themselves — inscriptions, letters, chronicles, books, memoirs, and other "evidences" — often furnishes a sufficient basis for the restoration of the original meanings intended by the creators. If this were not so, the whole science of history would have to be discarded because such a psychological reading of culture is one of the main procedures of history.

In many other cases, however, we cannot verify our psychological reading, either because the given external vehicle admits the possibility of divers interpretations or because we lack the documentary evidences of the meaning and intention of the creator or for other similar reasons. But this does not nullify the possibility in a great many cases of the correct psychological reading of a given cultural value or of a vast cultural conglomeration. Whatever may be the differences in the interpretation of minor points of the Aristotelian philosophical position, its essentials are well known and similarly understood by all competent scholars. None of them would ascribe to him the position of a materialist in metaphysics, a pure empiricist in epistemology, an individualist in social and political theory. The same can be said of other individuals and groups. Whatever are the shortcomings of history as a science and an art, its severest critic cannot prove its results but a myth. In brief, the correct psychological reading of the inner aspect of a culture or a cultural value is often possible and can be supported with sufficient evidence to prove its accuracy.

This, then, is one way of reading the real mentality of cultural phenomena, and these are the means of testing the comparative correctness of its results. It will be used to some extent in the present work.

It is not, however, the only form of reading possible. There may also be a *sociologico-phenomenological* [1] reading of the inner aspect of cultural phenomena. This form of interpretation is perhaps more important for

---

[1] I use the term phenomenological in a sense congenial with E. Husserl's term, indicating by it the socially "objective" existence of a meaning, regardless of whether it coincides with the psychological meaning. See E. Husserl, *Ideas: General Introduction to Pure Phenomenology*, trans. by W. R. Gibson (New York, 1931), and *Logische Untersuchungen*, 3 vols. (Halle, 1922).

my purposes, and for sociologists in general, than that which is purely psychological.

What are the essentials of the sociologico-phenomenological reading? In order to introduce it in a simple way, let us begin with facts known to every reader. It is not a rare phenomenon that the objective results of an activity deviate greatly from the subjective aims of those who undertake it. Poets are legion who aim to write great verse but succeed only in writing trash. There are multitudes of scientists and scholars who aim to be Platos, Newtons, Darwins, but do not in fact achieve anything but mediocre results. There are crowds of statesmen and politicians who undertake reforms with the expectation of results which never occur in actuality. There are countless armies of persons who, aspiring to be multimillionaires, plan their careers with this in view, but only a few ever reach their aim. Finally, there are creators who, achieving greatness, have yet shaped a work the effect of which is different from, even perhaps opposite to, that intended. In brief, there are vast numbers of cultural complexes in which the meaning of the creator and the social meaning do not at all coincide.[2]

What shall we infer from such facts? Shall we say that there is no meaning outside of the psychological? Or shall we admit an additional and different form of meaning? To assume the first alternative would mean to deny an obvious fact: that the discrepancy between intention and effect does not necessarily make a cultural complex meaningless.

Suppose that we do not know anything about Beethoven's motives, related as they were to the French Revolution and Napoleon, in the creation of his *Eroica Symphony;* or about his superscription, "Fervent thanksgiving to the Godhead of one who had recovered," in the adagio of his great *Quartet in A minor* (op. 132), written after his recovery from abdominal inflammation in 1825. Neither the symphony nor the quartet becomes thereby meaningless. On the contrary, there are countless millions of people who are unaware of these aims and yet find significance in both pieces of music. The same can be said of any other cultural phenomena. We may know nothing about the psychological meaning, the purposes that lie behind them; yet they can continue to be meaningful. We know little, often nothing, of the intention and meaning of the creators of much of the Egyptian, the Babylonian, the Chinese,

---

[2] Since Pareto's theory of logical and nonlogical actions is now known, a mere reference to his work is sufficient to validate the point. Though the distinction which he establishes between logical and nonlogical actions varies considerably from that of the present work, his contention that nonlogical actions prevail has a bearing upon the problem under consideration here.

I — 6

the Greek, the Roman, or the medieval cultural complexes; yet this does not prevent our discovering the manifold significances which cluster about the surviving remnants of these cultures.

What does all this imply? It may imply, of course, that, not knowing the original intention or meaning of the creator, we substitute another subjective interpretation, namely, our own, or that of any other person or group, whether contemporary or not. But even this would involve merely a variety of psychological reading. The point, in other words, is this: Does there exist any sociologico-phenomenological reading of cultural phenomena which is fundamentally different from the psychological one? The answer is, "Yes."

First there is a causal-functional reading of culture which aims to discover the *causal-functional relationships* between the component parts of a cultural value or complex. Many persons may not be aware of the real causes of their actions and that there is a causal relationship between their activities and those of their contemporaries; they may not be aware of the causal connection between many of the variables in their cultural scheme; yet such causal relationships may exist. It is the privilege of the scientist to discover and to demonstrate their existence. As soon as this is done, the details of a cultural configuration, independently of any psychological meaning which may be given to them, become at once comprehensible as the elements of a causally bound unity. In other words, *the first form of the sociologico-phenomenological interpretation of the mentality of cultural phenomena is the causal-functional reading.* Theoretically at least it may be quite independent of the psychological reading. The significance of the relationship between density of population and crime, business cycles and the mortality rate, modes of production and forms of property, religion and the divorce rate, are examples of the sort of phenomena to which the causal reading may be applied.[3]

A second form of the sociologico-phenomenological interpretation of the internal aspect of culture is the *logical reading.* We may know nothing about the psychological meaning of cultural values or about their causal relationships; yet in regard to many cultural complexes we can legitimately put the following questions and expect to find satisfactory answers: Are the elements of a given culture logically united, or are they logically contradictory? Do they make a comprehensible and consistent system, or do they not? If they do, what is the nature

---

[3] Most sociological theories are built basically upon causal readings. See my *Contemporary Sociological Theories* (New York, 1928), *passim.*

of the system? Are there unifying principles that permeate all the components of a given configuration, or not? These and similar problems may arise and be answered regardless of any psychological reading of the cultural configuration in question. In many cases the psychological interpretation helps to discover the logical meaning; often they go together; sometimes we cannot say anything about the psychological meaning; sometimes it clashes with the logical reading. Whatever the situation is, the logical reading stands upon its own feet, theoretically independent of the psychological significance. The situation may be exactly the same in the reading of any work, beginning with the examination papers written by students whom we do not know, and ending with the masterpiece of a known or an anonymous author. We can judge all these writings with regard to the logicality or inner consistency of their ideas, regardless of their authorship or immediate purpose. The logical validity of the work stands, independent of the state of mind of the writer. The same can be said of all religious, moral, aesthetic, and other cultural values, and their complexes. This has been shown in the preceding chapter and will be demonstrated in much greater detail subsequently throughout these volumes.

The necessity for the logical interpretation follows also from the limitations of the psychological reading which, as we have seen, cannot be applied in cases where the evidence of the aims and meanings of the creator are not available. Even where such evidence is available, the psychological reading may not be quite sufficient. The point is that most of the cultural phenomena represent the results of the activities of many individuals and groups, whose purposes and meanings may be different from one another, often opposite. They all mix together, partly reinforcing, partly inhibiting, partly modifying one another, to such an extent that there is little likelihood of our distinguishing one from another. Whether we take the Parthenon or one of the great Christian cathedrals or a set of mores or laws or beliefs or any other cultural creations, they all are the manifestations of the activities, efforts, aims, volitions, ideas, feelings, of large masses of individuals and combinations of groups. It would be next to impossible to decipher or separate what in these complex cultural values manifests the aims and meanings of each of the participants in their creation, or what is the "psychological reading" of each. Meanwhile the Parthenon or the cathedral or the set of mores or beliefs or laws exists unquestionably in the cultural world and functions in it as a vehicle of the internal aspect of the culture. If it cannot be read psychologically, it can be understood either causally or logico-meaningfully. For readings of these sorts we need not know the documents necessary for a psychological reading; we can take the elements of a given culture as data and can inquire whether they logically fit one another.

We now have a preliminary notion of the nature of logical reading which is sufficient for the present. It is necessary in addition only to point out one or two of the implications of such reading.

The first of these implications is the necessary assumption, whether explicit or implicit, of certain *norms of logical validity*. Only with such norms in mind can one reasonably attempt to read the book of culture and to decide what part of it is logical and what is not. The canon assumed here will correspond to that assumed for any science, because no science is possible without a norm of what is valid and what is not. This will embrace the bases of deductive as well as of inductive logic, with all their varieties, beginning with mathematical logic and ending with the norms of causal study as a form of inductive logic. The assumption, therefore, of the present work, that any cultural complex may be logically interpreted, is simply the assumption made by any scientific study, no more and no less.

One special aspect of this assumption deserves, however, to be mentioned specifically. It is as follows: Euclid's and Lobachevski's systems of geometry are both logically unimpeachable; both follow the canons of the same mathematical logic in the most perfect way; yet their theorems and deductions differ. How are we to explain such a discrepancy? The answer is simple. Both are logically correct, both follow the same canons of mathematical logic, *but they start with different major premises:* one with the axiom that the straight line is the shortest distance between two points, the other with a different assumption. *This discrepancy at the roots of each system leads to a whole series of differences in subsequent deductions, despite the identity of the logico-mathematical canon being applied in both cases.* The major premise of each system once accepted, each is logically valid within its own limits. This principle is particularly important in the field of the logical readings of culture. Any interpretation of this kind must comply with the canons of logical validity in both its deductive and inductive aspects, but the investigator has to be aware that the major premises of various cultures may be different. If this be the case, then most of the other characteristic configurations of the cultures will differ also. Each, however, might be adjudged integrated from the standpoint of the same canons of logical validity.

Now this is a point of paramount importance. Its neglect has been the cause of numerous errors in the attempts that have been made to interpret the logical unity of culture complexes. The same oversight is responsible for the most biased theories of culture integration that have hitherto been advanced. The authors of these theories, desiring to apply the canon of logical norms to the characterization of cultural phenomena, often fail to grasp the perfectly logical nature of cultures different from their "favorites" simply because they do not notice that the major premises of these cultures differ from those which they (the theorists) happen to prefer. Thus, not seeing that two or more cultures can differ from one another throughout all their parts and yet each be logically integrated from the standpoint of its own assumptions, they declare illogical or nonlogical all cultures varying from that which is their choice. Such a procedure is equivalent to declaring the whole grammar and syntax of the German or Russian language illogical or non-logical just because their rules are different from those of English. When, however, such an investigator studies Russian and German properly, he finds that within their own major premises these languages are quite as logical as English. A sociologist, unaware of the roots of, say, the caste system, may find the prohibition of intercaste marriage ridiculous. When, however, he grasps the major premises of the system, he finds the prohibition to be the logical consequence of these basic assumptions.[4] We may sum up this discussion with the statement that a proper logical reading of cultural phenomena requires: first, the application of the canon of deductive and inductive logic; second, the realization of the possibility that the major premises of various cultures may differ; third, the assumption of an impartial position in regard to the validity or invalidity of the major premises. If the investigator grasps the characteristic premises of a culture accurately, his main task then is to show to

---

[4] Two conspicuous recent examples of this form of error are offered by Pareto and Lévy-Bruhl. Both, applying the yardstick of their own assumptions to systems of mentality with profoundly different major premises, naturally found most of these systems either nonlogical or illogical or prelogical. However, many of these systems are, within their own limits, quite as logical as Pareto's or Lévy-Bruhl's. See V. Pareto, *The Mind and Society* (New York, 1935), *passim*, and especially Vol. I, chap. i; L. Lévy-Bruhl, *Les fonctions mentales dans les sociétés inférieures* (Paris, 1910). As an example of the opposite, correct logical reading of a culture mentality different from our own, M. Granet's *La pensée chinoise* (Paris, 1934) may serve. Pointing out that the central principle (*"une sorte de formule maîtresse ou de recette centrale"*) of the Chinese thought and language was the aim not to convey abstract ideas, but rather to guide and stimulate action (*"Il prétend moins à informer clairement qu'à diriger la conduite"*), he shows systematically the logical consistency of all the fundamental categories of the Chinese thought — the Yin, the Yang, the Tao, the categories of time, space, number, order, totality, efficacy. Pages 15–16, 37, *et passim*.

what extent the culture is integrated from the standpoint of these premises, judged by the inflexible canons of logical validity. If he succeeds in solving this problem, his main task is ended. In defining the major premises of a given culture, he illuminates its soul, body, and its socio-cultural physiognomy; by indicating the extent and the character of its logical integration, he answers the question as to its integration or nonintegration.

In the logical interpretation of culture complexes this rigorously scientific and impartial attitude is preserved throughout the present work.[5] *The canon of logical norms remains the same in the study of all the different cultures, but the logicality or nonlogicality of each is judged always from the standpoint of its major premises (if it has any).* The acceptability or nonacceptability of such premises I leave to the taste of the reader. So far as the task of the logical reading of culture consists of an elucidation of the existence or nonexistence of forms and modes of logical relationship in a given culture, the above procedure serves this purpose. The praise or blame of the basic assumptions is the concern of the police, the moral educator, the physician, the missionary, the statesman, and all those sociocultural agencies that decide the choice of values, and defend and perpetuate them, once chosen.

This point must be stressed in order to prevent possible misunderstanding and to forestall all misdirected objections. An unattentive reader, observing in subsequent parts of this book remarks about the relativity and variability of the systems of truth, of ethics, of art, may conclude that the author belongs to the group of relativists, skeptics, and the like, since the work contends, for instance, that there are at least three fundamentally different systems of truth, of knowledge, of art, of morality; and admits that, within their major premises, they are all valid and that there is no decisive evidence which can show one of these systems to be valid or superior and the others to be invalid or inferior. To an insufficiently discriminating mind such a position may appear to be entirely sophistical. But if the distinction between the absolute character of the canon of logic as applied in the logical reading of cultures is properly considered, together with the relativity of the empirically given major premises of various cultures, the position of the author appears absolutistic, phenomenological, having little if anything to do with any genuine relativistic, agnostic, skeptic points of view.

---

[5] This does not mean that this work limits its task to the logical reading of culture within the above concisely outlined limits. As we shall see, reading involves a great many other problems which will be unfolded subsequently. Besides, the causal and the psychological readings also enter into the ground covered by this study.

These misdirected objections may consist of critical questions like the following: Granted that there is an internal aspect in any logically integrated culture which constitutes its meaning or mentality; since these are rarely directly given and have to be "read" inferentially, what are the guarantees that your reading, rather than any of a dozen others, is correct? What are the tests and evidences to decide this and similar questions? But if the reader has been attentive, he will have observed that these and other related questions have, in point of fact, already been answered. If the interpretation of a culture is purely descriptive, the tests of its accuracy are exactly the same as for any descriptive theory: Have all the elements been catalogued? Are their quantities and qualities accurately described? Are their relative positions in space and time correctly observed? If the reading is causal, the test is basically the same as for a theory in any field of observation which claims the existence of causal relationships between the phenomena involved. If the reading of culture is psychological, the methods of testing it are also psychological: They consist of an investigation of whether or not there are sufficient documentary and other evidences of the meanings and purposes of the persons and groups who created the culture; and if there are such evidences, of whether or not the theory accurately restores and describes the meaning to which they testify.[6] Finally, if the reading of culture is logical, the test must be logical, as this term is understood in the present chapter and that preceding.

As to the question, Which of several possible logical readings of a culture is the most correct and according to what evidence? this also has been answered in the preceding chapter. There the essentials of the procedure were outlined, by which the value of such theories as these might be examined and their comparative adequacy established. This bears equally upon the problem of how to discover whether the major premises ascribed to a given culture are its premises indeed, and not merely those superimposed by the bias of an investigator. And this answer must suffice for the moment. As to the details, the entire present work is a realization of these methodological principles.

A further point in regard to method suggests itself. *If the nature of the major premises of a culture plays such an important part in the qualification of its logical integration, it follows that the key principle by which the*

---

[6] All the important technical and methodological tests of historical studies are examples of such a test because history, as a scientific discipline, is mainly "psychological," and descriptive readings of culture are supplemented sometimes, in the works of great historians, by causal and logical readings.

*character of an integrated culture may be understood should be sought, first
of all, in these premises.* In any chain of logical judgments, whether in
regard to culture or otherwise, the entire series of deductions, and especially the conclusion, are conditioned by the statement with which the
chain begins. Thus in the syllogism, "All human beings are mortal;
Socrates is human; therefore Socrates is mortal," the choice of Socrates,
the statement that he is human, and the conclusion as to his mortality,
all were controlled in advance by the original premise, which therefore
embodies the key by which the nature of the entire unity, *i.e.*, the syllogism, is characterized. Thus, if we wish to discover the key to such a
unity aside from the logic by which it is shaped, we must turn, not to
second premise or conclusion, but to the major premise itself. A similar
method must be employed in dealing with a logically integrated culture
unity. It is for this reason that in the subsequent pages, which are
devoted to preliminary classification of the main types of integrated
culture, I shall follow the rule of arranging the types of culture not upon
the basis of their secondary characteristics but according to their major
premises.

To sum up: (1) Cultural phenomena have two aspects: *internal*
(mentality of culture) and *external* (the organic and inorganic phenomena
that manifest and externalize the internal aspect). (2) Of these two
aspects the first is of greater importance for an investigator of the nature
of culture. The external is also an inextricable part of the complex, but
only as it is the vehicle of the internal aspect. (3) Any "reading" of
culture involves the understanding of its internal aspect and is impossible
without such comprehension. (4) Several kinds of reading of culture
are possible: (*a*) the purely descriptive, (*b*) the psychological, and
(*c*) the sociologico-phenomenological. The last kind has two main
varieties: *causal-functional* and *logical*. (5) For a sociologist, the
causal and, especially, the logical readings are particularly important.
(6) The logical reading of cultures is based upon the inflexible canons of
inductive and deductive logic, but it must recognize the possibility of
wide divergences between different cultures in the nature of their major
premises.

II. IDEATIONAL, SENSATE, AND MIXED SYSTEMS OF INTEGRATED CULTURE. PRELIMINARY DEFINITIONS

Many systems of logically integrated culture are conceivable, each with
a different set of major premises but consistent within itself. Not all
those, however, are likely to be found in those cultural complexes which

have been in actual existence; and still fewer will serve as fruitful instruments for ordering the chaos of the cultural worlds which we can perceive into a limited number of completely comprehensible unities. Like stainless ideal virgins they remain in the realm of pure thought, without being married to any of the systems of culture that have had empirical being. We can admire such ideal classifications, but we cannot use them fruitfully for the purposes of becoming oriented in the apparently purposeless welter of fragments of which a specific cultural world happens to consist.

In the following sections there will be offered, not a survey of the enormously large number of classifications of culture that are possible, but that selection of classifications which is to be the main concern of this work. If a classification is set forth, this means that in my opinion it meets two of the above requirements. It is logically satisfactory; and it helps us to order the chaos of an empirically perceptible cultural world. In brief, it meets the requirements of any valid and fruitful classification.

This is sufficient by way of introduction. Let us now turn directly to the task of classification.

We can begin by distinguishing two profoundly different types of the integrated culture. Each has its own mentality; its own system of truth and knowledge; its own philosophy and *Weltanschauung;* its own type of religion and standards of "holiness"; its own system of right and wrong; its own forms of art and literature; its own mores, laws, code of conduct; its own predominant forms of social relationships; its own economic and political organization; and, finally, its own type of *human personality*, with a peculiar mentality and conduct. The values which correspond to one another throughout these cultures are irreconcilably at variance in their nature; but within each culture all the values fit closely together, belong to one another logically, often functionally.

Of these two systems one may be termed *Ideational* culture, the other *Sensate*. And as these names characterize the cultures as a whole, so do they indicate the nature of each of the component parts.

The probability is that neither the Ideational nor the Sensate type has ever existed in its pure form;[7] but all integrated cultures have in fact been composed of divers combinations of these two pure logico-meaningful forms. In some the first type predominates; in others, the second; in still others both mingle in equal proportions and on an equal basis. Accordingly, some cultures have been nearer to the Ideational,

---

[7] This should not bother us at all, since the categories of most science are rarely found existing empirically in pure form in the complexes from which they are abstracted.

others to the Sensate type; and some have contained a balanced synthesis of both pure types. This last I term the *Idealistic* type of culture. (It should not be confused with the Ideational.)

Viewed in time, the culture of a single area, say, the Greek or the Roman or the Western European culture,[8] exhibits periods when its integration is mainly Ideational, and other periods when the Sensate type dominates; while in the passage from the domination of one of these types to that of the other, several intermediary forms, among them the Idealistic, rise to positions of predominance. When such a shift happens, a corresponding change in all the main cultural values, as well as in the predominant types of personality, takes place. The body and soul of these kinds of culture are so profoundly different, and the difference goes so deep to the roots of the whole sociocultural life, that when one grasps the essentials of each, one grasps the nature of the bond between a multitude of seemingly unrelated processes, events, "facts," traits, that occur in its various compartments, as well as in the personality and conduct of its human members. If such a grasp does not eliminate the ultimate, unfathomable mystery of sociocultural life, it eliminates at least the smaller mysteries connected with isolated "facts," happenings, events, and forms, amidst which we live, often lost, as in darkness. This is truer still as regards the comprehension of human personality, not as a stimulus-response mechanism, not as a biological organism, but as the symbol and bearer of sociocultural values in all their quantitative-qualitative richness of form and content. When the essentials of each type of culture are understood, and the nature of an historical culture complex is diagnosed in terms of these types, then the peculiar personality of its members becomes comprehensible. Their multifarious traits, mores, mental patterns, and contents, hitherto unrelated and fragmentary, now appear intelligibly ordered into a single, meaningful *Gestalt*. For this reason, a study of these major culture types, their distribution in time and space, their alternation and change, is at the same time a genuine social psychology of human personality in its structural, as well as its dynamic, aspects.

[8] For the present the reader can choose either of two assumptions: first, that the Ideational and Sensate are merely opposite phases of a single culture, which may, therefore, be regarded as the "same" whichever phase happens to dominate; or second, that the change from Ideational to Sensate, or vice versa, must be regarded as changing the culture entirely, and that we therefore get an alternation of different cultures within the same culture area. For the moment it is unimportant for me which of these alternatives is preferred — the statements of the text are equally applicable to either when they are properly "translated" into the language of the chosen assumption. In the methodological part of this work, to appear in Volume Four, the problem will be discussed specifically.

Let us now turn to a closer scrutiny of the culture types we have named. *What specifically is meant by the Ideational, the Sensate, the Idealistic, and other intermediary categories? What are their major characteristics? How are these characteristics combined and how do they operate to give united or integrated systems of culture? And, finally, why should these types of culture be regarded as fundamental and capable of providing the best possible means of understanding how the millions of fragments of the perceptual sociocultural world have been integrated into ordered systems?* Such are the problems with which we shall start our study.

Since the character of any culture is determined by its internal aspect — by its *mentality,* as we agreed to call it [9] — the portraiture of the Idea-

[9] Those who are trained in the nominalistic-singularistic way of thinking — the way which is, as we shall see, predominant in the Sensate culture in which we live — will certainly object to the term "culture mentality" and all its derivatives. Their objections usually run along the line that only human beings with a developed nervous system can have mentality, that culture mentality is but a "nominal entity," and so on. As we shall see (in Chapters Six, Seven, and Eight of Volume Two of this work) the objection itself, as well as the manner of argumentation, is an excellent example of how the dominant mentality of a Sensate culture has conditioned the thinking processes of these persons. They demonstrate — what was logically inevitable — their inability to understand the realistic-universalistic language of the Idealistic-Ideational culture, and show themselves flesh and bone of the Sensate culture. Without entering here into a further analysis of this problem, I can easily appease the objectors by suggesting a very easy way of translating these terms into the nominalistic-singularistic language familiar to them. Instead of "culture mentality," they can use "the mentality of the bearers of the given culture"; instead of "the needs and ends of a given culture," "the needs and ends of its bearers"; and so forth. We can even go further. The whole subsequent text can easily be translated into the still more Sensate language of "adaptation," by which is meant the complex process which an individual goes through in maintaining his existence, that is, in the satisfaction of his indispensable needs through the interaction of himself with his milieu, and of his organs with each other. The whole business can be put in the following terms: the nature of the milieu as it is perceived by an individual in the process of adaptation; the nature of his needs, as a result of the satisfaction of which the adaptation takes place; the extent to which each of these needs must be satisfied; the methods of satisfaction, whether involving change in the individual himself, or in the milieu, or in both. In this fashion the meaning of my statements can easily be made understandable to thinkers of the nominalistic-singularistic type. As a matter of fact the present section of my work was first written in the language of "adaptation." Later I translated it into the language of those who think in terms of what I call the Idealistic culture. Thus I was able to see the problems from two opposite points of view and in two different languages. If the representatives of the Sensate nominalistic-singularistic thought wish to go still further, they can easily translate the terms of "adaptation" into the language of "equilibrium." In such a transcription the statement in question will read: "The process by which an individual maintains an equilibrium between himself and his milieu, and between his various parts." But I do not advise such a transcription. As will be shown in the methodological part of the present work to appear in Volume Four, this fashionable term, despite its extensive use in the social sciences, seems to have proved itself a liability rather than an asset. See P. Sorokin. *"Le concept d'équilibre est-il nécessaire aux sciences sociales."* *Revue international de sociologie,* September-October, 1936.

tional, Sensate, and Mixed types of culture begins properly with the delineation of the major premises of their mentality. As a starting point let us assume that these major premises concern the following four items: (1) *the nature of reality;* (2) *the nature of the needs and ends to be satisfied;* (3) *the extent to which these needs and ends are to be satisfied;* (4) *the methods of satisfaction.* Each of these points raises problems which can be, and have been, solved in different, often opposite, ways. A brief comment on each of them, the questions related to them, and the answers to these questions will thus provide us quickly with a useful preliminary notion of the character of the culture types with which we are dealing. For the benefit of the empiricists and nominalists let us translate the comments into nominalistic and at least half-empirical terminology.

A. *The Nature of Reality.* The same complex of material objects which compose one's milieu is not perceived and interpreted identically by various human individuals. Without entering here into the psychological, biological, and other reasons for this, let us simply state the fact that the heterogeneity of individual experiences, together with other factors, leads to a multiplicity of the modes of perception of the same phenomenon by different persons. On one extreme is a mentality for which reality is that which can be perceived by the organs of sense; it does not see anything beyond the sensate being of the milieu (cosmic and social). Those who possess this sort of mentality try to adapt themselves to those conditions which appear to the sense organs, or more exactly, to the exterior receptors of the nervous system. On the other extreme are persons who perceive and apprehend the same sensate phenomena in a very different way. For them they are mere appearance, a dream, or an illusion. True reality is not to be found here; it is something beyond, hidden by the appearance, different from this material and sensate veil which conceals it. Such persons do not try to adapt themselves to what now seems superficial, illusory, unreal. They strive to adapt themselves to the true reality which is beyond appearances. Whether it be styled God, Nirvana, Brahma, Om, Self, Tao, Eternal Spirit, *l'élan vital*, Unnamed, the City of God, Ultimate Reality, *Ding für und an sich*, or what not, is of little importance. What is important is that such mentality exists; that here the ultimate or true reality is usually considered supersensate, immaterial, spiritual. Consequently, this difference in the perception and interpretation of reality, to which one has to adapt oneself, must be taken into account at the very starting point of any inquiry into the nature of a culture type. Otherwise, the inquiry will suffer at its very inception from a failure to recognize properly what are the "facts" in the situation and what are not. This has happened with most of the studies in the field.

It is evident that the mentality which accepts the milieu in its sensate and material reality will stress the satisfaction of the sensual bodily needs. Those who see it as a mere appearance will seek the satisfaction mainly of spiritual needs through an interaction with the ultimate reality. Those who occupy an intermediate position will be sensitive to needs partly sensate and partly spiritual.

B. *The Nature of the Needs and Ends to Be Satisfied.* Needs may be viewed as purely *carnal* or *sensual*, like hunger and thirst, sex, shelter, and comforts of the body generally; as purely *spiritual*, like salvation of one's soul, the performance of sacred duty, service to God, categoric moral obligations, and other spiritual demands which exist for their own sake, regardless of any social approval or disapproval; or as *mixed* or *carnal-spiritual*, like the striving for superiority in scientific, artistic, moral, social, and other creative achievements, partly for their own sake and partly for the sake of human fame, glory, popularity, money, physical security and comfort, and other "earthly values" of an empirical character. Of course, in reality one class of needs passes gradually and imperceptibly into another, but, as in any classification, this does not mean that the gradual scale may not be divided into a few main categories for purposes of reference.

C. *The Extent to Which These Needs and Ends Are to Be Satisfied.* Each need may be regarded as requiring satisfaction to a different extent or on a different level, from the widest and most luxurious maximum to the narrowest and poorest minimum. One's need for food may range from a small amount of coarse bread and water, barely sufficient to maintain the physiological expenditures of the body, to the most extravagant gluttony, where all means are employed not only to supply luxurious and fine foods but also to stimulate the satiated appetite by various devices. The same is to be said of clothing, shelter, sex, self-protection, recreation, and amusement. This also holds true for the purely spiritual and for the mixed or carnal-spiritual needs. Like the purely carnal needs, they also seem to demand different levels and extents of satisfaction; from craving and seeking what is barely decent and barely reaches above the negative or zero line in a given activity — *i.e.*, something that is not quite criminal, or irreligious and positively sinful, something that approaches the mediocre standard of creativeness in a given society, and does not endanger the reputation of a "fairly decent fellow," and so on — up to consecration of oneself entirely to a specific carnal-spiritual or a purely spiritual purpose, with a maximal limit that is virtually infinite. Every need, therefore, regardless of its nature, can have minimum and maximum levels of satisfaction, whatever these levels may happen to be in the given circumstances.

D. *The Methods of Satisfaction of Needs*. These may be, or appear to be, different with various individuals. We can divide them roughly into three main classes :

(1) Modification of one's milieu in that manner which will yield the means of satisfying a given need : for instance, one suffering from cold can start a furnace, build a fire, put on a warm fur coat, etc.

(2) Modification of self, one's body and mind, and their parts — organs, wishes, convictions, or the whole personality — in such a way as to become virtually free from a given need, or to sublimate it through this "readjustment of self." In the above illustration of suffering from cold one can train oneself to become less sensitive to cold or to endure it within considerably broad limits. The same can be said of other needs.

(3) Modification partly of milieu and partly of self. In the case of cold, to return to our example, we often resort to both methods — we may light a fire, but also engage in vigorous physical activity to warm ourselves.

Combining in various ways these four major items (the nature of reality, the nature of human needs, the levels and extent of their satisfaction, and the method by which these needs are satisfied) and their subclasses, we can obtain a goodly number — as large as the mathematical formula of combinations will give — of various forms of culture mentality.

It is evident, however, that their total number will be too large to permit a careful analysis of each. For the sake of economy of effort and without any considerable loss of validity, we shall group these forms into fewer classes, in such a way as to include all the really important forms of mentality as separate classes, while the relatively less important forms are left out, since their characteristics are easily deducible from the knowledge of the more important forms. It will serve our purposes best, then, to single out the following main forms of culture mentality and, consequently, of culture systems.

I. IDEATIONAL CULTURE

In the terms of the above four items its major premises are these : (1) Reality is perceived as nonsensate and nonmaterial, everlasting

Being (*Sein*); (2) the needs and ends are mainly spiritual; (3) the extent of their satisfaction is the largest, and the level, highest; (4) the method of their fulfillment or realization is self-imposed minimization or elimination of most of the physical needs, and to the greatest possible extent. These major premises are common to all branches of the Ideational culture mentality. But, on the basis of variations under (4), it is possible to distinguish two fundamental subclasses of the Ideational culture mentality and the related culture system :

A. *Ascetic Ideationalism.* This seeks the consummation of the needs and ends through an excessive elimination and minimization of the carnal needs, supplemented by a complete detachment from the sensate world and even from oneself, viewing both as mere illusion, nonreal, nonexisting. The whole sensate milieu, and even the individual "self," are dissolved in the supersensate, ultimate reality.

B. *Active Ideationalism.* Identical with general Ideationalism in its major premises, it seeks the realization of the needs and ends, not only through minimization of the carnal needs of individuals, but also through the transformation of the sensate world, and especially of the sociocultural world, in such a way as to reform it along the lines of the spiritual reality and of the ends chosen as the main value. Its bearers do not "flee from the world of illusion" and do not entirely dissolve it and their own souls in the ultimate reality, but strive to bring it nearer to God, to save not only their own souls but the souls of all other human beings. The great spiritual reformers, like the early Christian Apostles and such popes as Gregory the Great and Leo the Great, may serve as examples of the Active Ideational mentality.

Such, then, are two main varieties of the Ideational mentality and system of culture, as far as their major premises are concerned.

II. SENSATE CULTURE

The Sensate mentality views reality as only that which is presented to the sense organs. It does not seek or believe in any supersensory reality ; at the most, in its diluted form, it assumes an agnostic attitude toward the entire world beyond the senses. The Sensate reality is thought of as a Becoming, Process, Change, Flux, Evolution, Progress, Transformation. Its needs and aims are mainly physical, and maximum satisfaction is sought of these needs. The method of realizing them is not that of a modification within the human individuals composing the culture, but of a modification or exploitation of the external world. In brief, the Sensate culture is the opposite of the Ideational in its major premises.

These traits are common to all varieties of the Sensate culture mentality. But on the basis of the variation in the fourth item (*i.e.*, method of adjustment) it is possible to distinguish three main varieties of this type.

A. *Active Sensate Culture Mentality* (Active "Epicureans"). Sharing with other forms of Sensate mentality all the above four premises, it seeks the consummation of its needs and ends mainly through the most "efficient" modification, adjustment, readjustment, reconstruction, of the external milieu. The transformation of the inorganic, organic (technology, medicine, and the applied disciplines), and the sociocultural world, viewed mainly externally, is the method of this variety. The great executives of history, the great conquerors, builders of empire, are its incarnation.

B. *Passive Sensate Mentality* (Passive "Epicureans"). This is characterized by the attempt to fulfill physical needs and aims, neither through the inner modification of "self," nor through efficient reconstruction of the external world, but through a parasitic exploitation and utilization of the external reality as it is, viewed as the mere means for enjoying sensual pleasures. - "Life is short"; "*Carpe diem*"; "Wine, women, and song"; "Eat, drink, and be merry" — these are the mottoes of this mentality.

C. *Cynical Sensate Mentality* (Cynical "Epicureans"). The civilization dominated by this type of mentality, in seeking to achieve the satisfaction of its needs, uses a specific technique of donning and doffing those Ideational masks which promise the greatest returns in physical profit. This mentality is exemplified by all the Tartufes of the world, those who are accustomed to change their psychosocial "colors" and to readjust their values in order to run along with the stream. They are enthusiastic monarchists under a monarchy; ardent communists when a communistic regime comes to power; and if, instead of communism, theocracy reigns supreme, they "adapt" themselves to this regime as well. In every case their main concern is bread and butter. In its premises the Cynical Sensate mentality clearly belongs to the Sensate class, resembling only superficially the Ideational type in its apparent modification of self rather than of environment.

III. THE MIXED TYPES OF MENTALITY AND CULTURE

All the other culture mentalities represent in their major premises a mixture of the Ideational and Sensate forms in various combinations and proportions. With one conspicuous exception they are, therefore, eclectic, self-contradictory, poorly integrated logically. Their Ideational and

Sensate elements remain adjacent and mechanically coexistent, without achieving genuine inner synthesis. Sometimes the coexistence is comparatively inconspicuous and does not lead to an active antagonism between opposites. Sometimes their latent antagonism flares up into open war; then we have a culture mentality divided against itself.

The Mixed culture type has many varieties, according to the mode of combination of the Ideational and Sensate elements, and the proportion of each in the mixture. Of these, two should be specifically mentioned.

A. *Idealistic Culture Mentality*. This is the only form of the Mixed class which is — or at least appears to be — logically integrated. Quantitatively it represents a more or less balanced unification of Ideational and Sensate, with, however, a predominance of the Ideational elements. Qualitatively it synthesizes the premises of both types into one inwardly consistent and harmonious unity. For it reality is many-sided, with the aspects of everlasting Being and ever-changing Becoming of the spiritual and the material. Its needs and ends are both spiritual and material, with the material, however, subordinated to the spiritual. The methods of their realization involve both the modification of self and the transformation of the external sensate world : in other words, it gives *suum cuique* to the Ideational and the Sensate. Each of them it views as real, as a mode or aspect of the supreme reality. Its face is simultaneously otherworldly and of this world. Recognizing the Ideational values as supreme, it does not declare the Sensate world a mere illusion or of negative value; on the contrary, as far as the Sensate is in harmony with the Ideational, it possesses positive value.

It would be inadvisable to attempt to demonstrate here that such a mentality does indeed succeed in integrating opposite elements logically and in achieving a real unity instead of an eclectic mixture. This will be done in the proper place subsequently with full and convincing detail, drawn from the systems of truth and knowledge, of ethics and law, from the arts, and from all the other main compartments of such cultures.[10]

B. *Pseudo-Ideational Culture Mentality*. Another specific form of the Mixed type is the unintegrated, Pseudo-Ideational mentality. One might style it "subcultural" if the term culture were used to designate

---

[10] In passing it is to be noted that the author of the present work intentionally takes the standpoint of this Idealistic form of mentality. This permits him to understand both of the opposite types of culture mentality, because it is congenial to both. Otherwise, the one-sidedness of each of the opposite types would preclude the use of a common language by which both could be fairly interpreted. For the Ideational mentality the Sensate is but an illusion and blasphemy; for the Sensate the Ideational is but prejudice, superstition, or "pathology."

only a logically integrated system.   This type has occupied a conspicuous place in the history of culture mentality.   Its characteristics are as follows.

The nature of reality is not clearly defined, but is felt largely as Sensate. Here needs and ends are predominantly of a physical nature.   They are only moderately satisfied, and the method of satisfaction is neither an active modification of the milieu to any appreciable degree, nor a free modification of self, nor a search for pleasure, nor successful hypocrisy. It is a dull and passive endurance of blows and privations, coming from the outside, as long as these can be borne physically.   This minimization of spiritual and carnal needs is not freely sought, it is imposed by some external agency (*vis absoluta*).   It is the result of helplessness to resist. The oppressive power is so overwhelming that, after several unsuccessful attempts to oppose it, there remains to those oppressed no energy to try to free themselves and to adapt themselves physically and spiritually to a better order.   Given an opportunity, a Pseudo-Ideationalist may easily plunge into Passive, Cynical, or even Active "Epicureanism."   The life processes of slaves under dire and cruel conditions, of many prisoners, of subjects under the cruel regime of their rulers, of some primitive people who live in a condition of misery and privation, of groups stricken by a great catastrophe bringing with it utter ruin, of sensate persons stricken by an incurable malady — these offer examples of this type of mentality. Life under such conditions is dull, painful, aimless ; no physical comfort mitigates its long agony ; nor does the inner light of the triumphant spirit brighten its unending darkness.

Many other subclasses of culture mentalities might be enumerated, but the seven which have just been described under the three headings, Ideational, Sensate, and Mixed, together are sufficiently broad and inclusive to serve for all the main and clearly defined special types with which we shall have to deal.   For this reason we can now turn from the preliminary definitions, which have established the types and marked them out, one from the other, to a fuller and closer analysis of the detailed characteristics of each.

It is obvious that an examination of the characteristics of the Ideational and Sensate culture types is a different problem from that of how these mentalities and their characteristics are distributed in various actual culture complexes and in the actual behavior of individuals and groups. Our investigation thus falls into two parts or has two aspects : (1) the elucidation of the meaning and content of each culture type, as these follow from the major premises; and (2) the discovery of the actual distribution of the characteristics of all types in time and space.

Now there is one point which it is very important to keep in mind. If we could look into the mind of every individual and every group or social organization, and if we should discover in every one the existence simultaneously and conjunctively of the characteristics of many culture mentalities, it would not follow from this that each of the culture types is not distinct and should not be treated as a separate category, or that its characteristics are not its distinct property. If the above types, especially those that are unmixed, were to be found separately in the human universe, isolated from one another and never coexistent in the same individual or group, then the problem of the classification of the types would coincide with that of their distribution. Such coincidence is rare, however, not only in the realms of social phenomena, but also in those of the biological and the inorganic. Thus, chemistry has its definite concept of elements in their "pure," isolated form, like hydrogen, oxygen, carbon, and others. Each of these, however, is found in the material world, perhaps more often than otherwise, in combination with other chemical elements. To give a few typical examples: Pure carbon occurs naturally only as the diamond and as graphite, whereas, mixed with other elements, it is a constituent of all organic compounds. Oxygen, even though it occurs in the free state in the air, of which it forms about twenty-one per cent by volume, is very active chemically and is best known for its property of mixing with other elements and combining to form various oxides. Hydrogen is principally encountered in its union with oxygen as water. Hence the analysis of the properties of the elements and their classification is one thing; the problem of their actual distribution and combination, another. But the fact that any of the chemical elements is found in the world in a considerable number of combinations neither renders fruitless the classification of the chemical world into "pure elements" nor proves the nonexistence of these elements in the free state. That the same holds true for any analytical science and any classification is quite obvious.

Historically, there has probably never existed in pure form in a single individual, group, or culture, any one of the unmixed types of culture mentality that have been described in the present work. There is perhaps not a single person alive who has one type of mentality exclusively, whether Ascetic or Active Ideational, or Active or Passive Sensate. Even the most ascetic, the most austere, mystic cannot help changing his empirical milieu or satisfying to some extent his bodily needs. Other-

wise he would die.   He must pick berries or ask for alms or accept gifts
of believers; he must build himself a hut or seek a cave.   And as far
as he is occupied with these matters, sensate reality, by implication,
becomes a part of his larger view of reality.[11]   Likewise, even the most
complete representative of the Active Sensate or the Passive Sensate
mentality cannot help occasionally forgoing the satisfaction of this or
that physical need (otherwise it would be necessary that he be endowed
with the sorcerer's magic power of procuring anything as soon as it is
asked for); at times he may even enter into a kind of "spiritual" meditation and limit to some extent his bodily appetites or that part of his
activity which is directed toward the modification of the external milieu.[12]
Man's power and efficiency, his desires and the means of their satisfaction are organically limited.   Therefore, sometimes even those of Sensate
mentality modify themselves, and not their milieu; satisfy their spiritual,
instead of their material, needs.   Thus it is that, at one time or other,
almost every individual experiences to some extent many types of culture
mentality.   Each of us may be now partly Ascetic, now partly Active
Ideational, now partly Active, and now partly Passive Sensate; occasionally we may be Cynically Sensate, Pseudo-Ideational, or Idealistic.
There are few, if any, persons who in the course of a lifetime do not
experience some vacillation among these forms; and what is true of any
individual is surely true of any group of individuals or any actual culture
complex.

Thus, in concrete social reality no one of the types designated above
is often found in pure form, unmixed with others, either in an individual
or in a group or culture.   On the other hand, these types and their
characteristics are not distributed identically among individuals, groups,
or cultures.   In some the Ascetic Ideational, in some the Active Ideational, in some the Passive or Active Sensate, in some the Idealistic,
predominates.   A close examination of the life history of an individual
or group would reveal the major current of the flow of its culture patterns.

[11] The above description of the ascetic person is, of course, couched in the terminology of
an "Idealistic" mind.   A true Ascetic (or mystic) Ideationalist would, naturally, not modify
the external milieu, which is for him nonexistent; nor would he repress his desires or minimize
his needs and refrain from satisfying them, for again, from his point of view, he is free from
desires and therefore has no needs.   Here it is essential to remember that to such an individual
his material and individual self becomes unreal, being but a part in the general scheme of the
illusory external milieu.

[12] Of course to a consistent and thoroughgoing bearer of the Sensate mentality, giving up
the satisfying of one need or another is generally a case of substituting a less desired need for
a more desired one, and in the strict sense is not a genuine renunciation of the sort that is
met in Ideational behavior.

In the present work we propose at first to deal with the characteristics of each form of culture mentality taken in pure form, regardless of whether or not it is ever found pure empirically. In other words, we are going to typify each, and thus set up criteria for later comparison and differentiation. The diagnostic value of this procedure is quite obvious. After this preliminary typification we shall turn to see how each form of mentality and its characteristics are distributed : in time, in the life of a single individual, group, organization, culture; and in space, among various individuals, groups, organizations, cultures.

Each of the seven forms described above and the combination of elements of which it is composed are associated, logically and functionally, with several additional characteristics. These are the satellites which are usually present if a given culture mentality is integrated logically according to its type. For the sake of brevity, it will perhaps be enough to describe the implicit elements, or "satellites," of only the Ascetic Ideational and the Active Sensate mentalities, which are direct opposites. The other five forms, as well as all the Mixed types thus far unnamed, represent combinations of the characteristics of these two. Therefore, such a simplified description should lay a foundation for the deduction of the nature of the satellites of all the types, both named and unnamed.

Differing as they do in their four major premises, the Active Sensate and the Ascetic Ideational mentality also vary from each other in the nature of their satellites, of which the following are the chief.

(1) Since the Ascetic Ideational mentality strives toward the ultimate, supersensory reality, lasting, eternal, unchangeable, and not toward the everchanging and ephemeral Sensate reality, it associates itself either with indifference to, and a detachment from, the physical environment ("What is the use of trying to adapt oneself to that which is merely illusory!"), or a reluctance to change it ("Only fools try to write on waves."), or with a contempt for it. Hence ataraxia, self-sufficiency, apathy, imperturbability, indifference, Nirvana, and insensibility to temporal existence, to its pains and pleasures, sorrows and joys, life and death, are traits common to all shades of such a mentality — from the Hindu, Buddhist, Taoist, Sufist, Jainist, Zoroastrian, Greek, Roman Ascetic "Primitive" Ideationalism, Cynicism, Skepticism, and, in part at least, Stoicism, to Ascetic Christianity, and to all other varieties of the Ascetic Ideational culture mentalities.

(2) The above attitude leads logically either to a repression of bodily needs, or to a detached indifference to them as if nonexistent.

(3) The attention is turned to the principle of Being, views reality as everlasting and unchangeable Being (*Sein*), in contradistinction to ever-changing Becoming (*Werden*);[13] the ultimate reality remains eternally the same, unchangeable even in its manifold modifications. Only illusions and appearances change. Empirically viewed this mentality is thus static in its essence: static in its philosophy, in its *Weltanschauung*, in its choice of values and behavior. If it is consistently carried through, it chooses and prefers the values which are everlasting and durable, and consequently unchangeable. Temporary and transient values are nonvalues for such a mentality. Therefore the empirical values, which all are transient, are pseudo values. In wisdom and in knowledge, in moral, social, aesthetic, and other compartments, this selection of the lasting is characteristic of the mentality of the Ascetic Ideational adaptation. The category of *Time*, in the sense "before and after," "past, present, and future," "long and short," measured by empirical units, either does not play any role in such a mentality, or it becomes identical with the eternal, ultimate reality and, as such, is "punctuated" only by the changes in the distance of the Ascetic Ideational mind from total engulfment by, or union with, this everlasting Being. In such a mind time, viewed empirically, lacks perspective of the past, the present, and the future, of the sequence of Sensate phenomena in the time flow, of their mutual relationship in the "before-after-simultaneous" associations. In its "punctuations" it is qualitative rather than quantitative. In this sense it is an antihistorical, or rather ahistorical, mentality.[14]

Quite contrary are the standpoint and satellites of the Active Sensate mentality. It sees only the empirical reality. Full of appetites and vigor, it wants to change the surrounding sensate environment to meet its needs. The empirical reality is ever changing, is ever in a flux; consequently, the adaptive activities must also vary incessantly. Nothing is static, nothing is everlasting; at any moment one must be ready to meet the change in environment by a necessary change in one's trans-

---

[13] In this connection it is important to stress again that this attitude is extended to self as a part of the general scheme of things. Thus, Sufi and Hindu mystics strive to annihilate mentally the transient appendage — their earthly vehicle, the body, and its needs — and join the One, Eternal Being. This is a mental and not a physical annihilation.

[14] As we shall see, it is not incidental that the time perspective of the medieval mind is so blurred; that the Hindu culture did not develop a sense of history and did not care to do it; that the Taoist time is "peculiar" in its nature; that the time apprehension and time concept of such a mentality, as it is given in its time system, time theories, time definitions are marked by the same characteristics. See Chapter Eleven of Volume Two.

forming activity. *Therefore, this mentality is inseparable from a dynamic, evolutionary, progressive principle.* This principle pierces it through and through, its philosophy, its choice of values, its practical activity. Its philosophy has always been the philosophy of Becoming, not Being. "All things are in incessant flux. Only Becoming is real. Unchangeable Being is an illusion." From the earlier representatives of this mentality, from Heraclitus [15] and Lucretius to the modern Evolutionists, devotees of Transformation, Progress, Dynamism, Movement, Mobility, Revolution, Incessant Change, and Adjustment, the dynamic principle has regularly been an integral part of the theories and practices of the followers of the Active Sensate mentality. Here the time category plays a most conspicuous part, and Time perspective is an indispensable trait of a mentality which is historical par excellence.

> *Mutat enim mundi naturam totius aetas*
> *ex alioque alius status excipere omnia debet,*
> *nec manet ulla sui similis res: omnia migrant*
> *omnia commutat natura et vertere cogit.*

(For time changes the nature of the whole world, and all things must pass from one condition to another, and nothing remains like itself; all things are in process, all things nature transforms and compels to alter; for one thing crumbles away and becomes faint and enfeebled with age, another in its turn springs up from and rises above despised things. So therefore time changes the nature of the whole world.)[16]

These lines give a sample of the all-important part played by Time in such a mentality.

Likewise, in their practical activity, when it is integrated consistently with the Active Sensate mentality, the eternal panacea of such theorists is "readjustment"; *readjustment by all means, at all times, at all cost.* Incessant change of the empirical reality forces them to do this endless work of Sisyphus; their incessant readjustment in turn changes incessantly their milieu, and thus compels them to the unceasing task of readjusting their preceding readjustments. As we shall see, it is not accidental that at the present time these theorists talk so much of the "adjustment," "maladjustment," "readjustment," of everything from the idiot and murderer to political machinery, religion, and science; and, what is more important, mean by this mainly an external modification of "conditioned reflexes," "social institutions," and even of "religion,"

---

[15] "And all things are born through opposition and all are in flux like a river." "Herakleitos," in Diogenes Laërtius, *Lives*, IX, 7-9.
[16] Lucretius, *De rerum natura*, V, 827-833.

trying to readjust this last through better furniture and more recreation
in the churches, better pay for ministers, and by similar "external"
means. In this way they run in an eternal circle like a squirrel on a
wheel. The same fact explains their preference for the short-time values
of the immediate present. Since there are no values which can be eternal, the only real values are those which meet the needs of the given
moment. One cannot reject them in favor of some remote future values,
merely because the changing values of the present may be depreciated
under the different conditions of the future; one cannot even be sure of
what will have value in these future conditions, and what will not.
Hence the preference is given to the immediate, short-time values, and
not to those which we guess to have qualities of eternal duration, or
which we think may possibly exist at some remote time beyond the
present.[17] Drunk with empirical reality, one who has an Active Sensate
mentality is full of a feeling of the actuality of the present, of dynamism,
of tireless activity, efficiency, doing. Instead of detachment from the
empirical milieu, he lives in it, breathes it, swims in it and with its current.

Active Ideationalism and the Idealistic mentalities occupy an intermediate position between the two extreme standpoints. Active Ideationalism, side by side with the philosophy of Being and Eternal Value,
or Eternalism, admits some, though subordinated, Becoming; some
interest in the affairs of this world; some empirical activities; and some
temporal values, subordinate to, and, as it were, a shadowy reflection of,
the Eternal. Similar is the position of the Idealistic mentality, but it
puts more emphasis on Becoming, on the empirical, temporal aspects of
things and values.

Passive Sensate mentality is imbued with a still more pointed, extreme
philosophy of Becoming ("The past is no more; the future may never
be; the present is all that we can be certain of."), with its *Carpe diem*,
with decisive preference for the values of the given moment rather than
any lasting, future values. Only Sensate, even sensual, values are true
values; all others are unreal. The environment is in an anarchic flux,
and as such it is never certain, never durable, never to be credited with
the possibility of a future.

Cynical Sensate mentality is somewhat similar to the Passive
Sensate. But, being obliged to exert themselves to get what Passive

---

[17] This does not exclude a short-time preference of the near future to the present, if the
sacrifice promises to be profitable and safe. An analysis from this standpoint of economic
theories of profit, especially those of sacrifice and postponement of immediate enjoyment,
gives an excellent example of how such a trait impregnates scientific thinking.

"Epicureans"[18] receive as gifts, the devotees of this type of mentality have to resort to hypocrisy as their technique, and in this lies their principal difference from Passive "Epicureans."

Finally, an enslaved Pseudo-Ideationalist is here, as in other points, a creature of the circumstances rather than their master. Therefore, he cannot have any clear conception of either Being or Becoming, lasting or momentary value; in his poverty and misery he must take any value given to him and be prepared for any Being or Becoming which falls upon him. Instead of a logically integrated mentality and a systematic philosophy of life he can have but incoherent fragments of each.

(4) The Ascetic Ideational mentality facilitates *man's control of himself*, especially of his bodily senses, of his emotions, feelings, wishes, lusts. The Active Sensate mentality leads to *man's control of the external world*, so far as its material and sensate aspects are concerned (since any externality is apprehended mainly as a material and sensate phenomenon or process). The reasons for this are evident and follow directly from the nature of each mentality. Historically, the character of the first type has been frequently demonstrated by the almost miraculous repression of vital needs in the asceticism of Hindus, Buddhists, Taoists, Christians, Jainists, Sufists, not to mention the numberless ascetics affiliated with smaller sects. On the other hand, full-blooded, energetic "Epicureans" always have been the main transformers of the external milieu, whether it involved pioneering in the wilderness, or the organization of business empires, metropolitan centers, political or other, less extensive, organizations.

As to the other forms of mentality, the Active Ideational and the Idealistic, each of these types logically combines in itself satellites of both opposite sorts. Each implies the development of self-control, as well as control of environments. The first is stressed more in the Active Ideational, the second in the Idealistic mentality, though in neither is there stress to such an extent as in each of the extreme types of Sensate and Ideational.

The Passive Sensate mentality does not imply either of these controls; it seeks only an uninhibited satisfaction of individual lusts from the given milieu.

[18] Henceforth, I shall sometimes use the term "Epicurean" and its derivatives, instead of "Sensate" and its derivatives, giving to it a meaning identical with "Sensate" (though the mentality of Epicurus was nearer to the balanced type). Likewise, sometimes the term "Stoic" is used instead of "Ideational" though the mentality and adaptation of some of the Stoics were nearer to the balanced than to the Ideational type. Such a substitution is required by my desire to avoid introducing new and cumbersome terms, like "sensatist," etc.

The same, but in a different sense, is true of Pseudo-Ideational adaptation. It requires mainly dull and aimless patience, stupefying endurance, but not a control in the proper sense of the word.

Finally, the Cynical Sensate mentality implies, not so much control of self or of environment, but rather skill in manipulation of, and masquerading in, various psychosocial "costumes"; Cynical "Epicureans" acquire a particular versatility in putting on and off various psychosocial masks — *i.e.*, convictions, ideas, beliefs, opinions, devotions, loyalties, attachments — which become less valuable the more often they are changed.

(5) The Ascetic Ideational mentality is mainly of an "introvert" nature (directed upon self and its analysis and modification). The Active Sensate mentality and its adaptational activities by definition are of an "extrovert" nature (pointed toward the transformation of the sensate milieu).[19] Whether in regard to himself or to others, an Ascetic

[19] The words "introvert" and "extrovert" are used here in a different sense from that which is generally met with in psychoanalytic writings, and in psychological literature generally, by Freud, Jung, Adler, and others, though in neither, nor in the literatures of related fields (philosophy, physiology, etc.), is there any unanimity as to the meaning of these terms. See, for example, various dichotomic theories related to the "introvert" and "extrovert" types of personality, subjective and objective, and so on, such as the distinctions set forth by Plato, Aristotle, Plutarch, Philo, or by various mystics, like Arabi (1165–1240; see M. Horten, *Mystische Texte aus dem Islam*, Bonn, 1912), J. B. von Helmont (1577–1644; J. Ennemoser, *Geschichte der Magie*, Leipzig, 1844, particularly pp. 906 and 914), Jacob Boehme (*De Vita Mentali*), and even Staudenmaier (*Die Magie als experimentelle Naturwissenschaft*). Likewise, the more recent theories in the field are also different in their meanings. Compare, for instance, the dichotomic theories of C. G. Jung in his *Collected Papers on Analytical Psychology* (New York, 1916), *Psychology of the Unconscious* (New York, 1916), and in *Psychological Types* (New York, 1923); W. Ostwald, *Grosse Männer* (Leipzig, 1910) (classics and romantics); F. Nietzsche (Apollo and Dionysian types); Worringer (sympathy-abstraction); Schiller (naïve-sentimental); William James, *Pragmatism* (New York, 1907), chap. i (toughminded-tenderminded); Otto Gross, *Die zerebrale Sekundärfunktion* (Leipzig, 1902) (deep-narrow and shallow-broad); G. Heyman and E. Wiersma, *Zeitschrift für Psychologie* (1906–1909), nos. 42, 43, 45, 46, 51; L. W. Stern, *Über Psychologie der individuellen Differenzen* (Leipzig, 1900) (objective and subjective); L. Klages, *Prinzipien der Charakterologie* (Leipzig, 1910); H. Kurella, *Die Intellektuellen und die Gesellschaft* (Würzburg, 1912); J. M. Baldwin, *The Story of Mind* (New York, 1902) (sensory-motor); B. J. Kempf, *The Autonomic Functions and the Personality*, in Nervous and Mental Disease Monograph Series No. 28 (Washington, 1918); L. R. Marston in *Iowa Studies in Child Welfare* (Iowa City, 1925), no. 3; W. McDougall, *Outline of Abnormal Psychology* (New York, 1926); R. Hunt, in *Journal of Abnormal and Social Psychology* (1929), no. 23, pp. 176–181; E. Spranger, *Lebensformen* (Halle, 1922); L. Klages, *Principien der Characterologie* (Leipzig, 1920); E. Kretschmer, *Körperbau und Character* (1922); G. W. Allport, "Attitudes," in *Handbook of Social Psychology* (Worcester, 1935); G. W. Allport and P. J. Vernon, "The Field of Personality," in *The Psychological Bulletin*, Vol. XXVII (1930). For a general survey see H. Klüver, "An Analysis of Recent Works on the Problem of Psychological Types," in *Journal of Nervous and Mental Disease*, Vol. LXII, pp. 561–596; F. L. Wells, "Social Maladjustments," in *Hand-*

Ideationalist in his introvert activity addresses mainly the needs of the "inner life" and uses its subtle, often intangible, technique, difficult of analysis in mechanical terms, and directed at self; [20] he rarely makes use of mechanical or overt technique based on purely material properties. Therefore, he rarely attempts to transform the external sensate world. If sometimes a transformation does take place as a result of his existence, it comes as a by-product, neither sought for nor welcomed by the mystic Ideationalist. An "Epicurean" in his extrovert activity is addressing himself to the external world, or to the "materialistic-behavioristic" aspect even of psychosocial phenomena and human individuals. His *modus operandi* and technique are mechanically rational, based upon and calculated by the physical, chemical, and other sensate properties of the means used and on their effect on the milieu involved. Sensate mentality tends to be scientific, and physically causative, and, in this sense, rational and calculated. Therefore his activity tends to, and frequently does, produce many a change in the sensate world.

The behavior of Active Ideational and of Idealistic mentalities will be, respectively, "introvert-extrovert" and "extrovert-introvert." The Passive Sensate mentality resolves itself mainly into parasitic extrovert activity. The Pseudo-Ideational activity is largely undifferentiated, dull introvert-extrovert. Here the extrovert activity is ordered by an outside agency and not chosen by the person engaged in it; and the introvert behavior is either imposed from without or resorted to *faut de mieux*. Finally, Cynical "Epicureanism" manifests itself primarily in extrovert behavior of a specified type, namely, of the type of *captatio benevolentiae* of the rich and mighty, combined with practiced skill in manipulation of the psychosocial masks according to the circumstances.

(6) The Ascetic Ideational mentality implies a close association with an introdetermination of self — attention, sensation, perception, ideas, volition, desires, entire personality — with the phenomena of the inner mental experience, and with nonmaterial and spiritual problems, accompanied by detachment from, and relative indifference to, the external world in its physical and sensate aspects. Such a mentality opens wide the mental eyes and ears to grasp, register, and understand the

---

book of Social Psychology, cited. Such a heterogeneity stresses the need for the reader to keep clearly in mind the meaning of these terms as given in my text for the subsequent discussion.

[20] The "dig within" of Marcus Aurelius; "retreat unto self" of the Taoist; the "deep meditation" of Buddhists, Hindus, and other mystics, are samples of this "introversion." If a specific technique is used to facilitate this state of mind — like the Yoga or Taoist or Sufist — it is again a technique aimed at and applied to "self."

essence of Soul, Mind, Ultimate Reality, God, the Devil, Good, Evil, Salvation, Eternal Value, Consciousness, Conscience, Justice, and so on. One is plunged into this intangible realm. The whole external world becomes secondary; it is a mere illusion or, at best, a mere "content of consciousness" or a visible sign of an invisible world. As such it is not to be paid much attention to and does not deserve to be studied with particular care for all its illusory details. In this way, an Ascetic Ideational mind makes the whole external cosmos a mere vehicle of the inner life and swallows it up into the "inner world." An Active Sensate mentality, on the contrary, dissolves the inner life and inner world into external.[21] In contrast to Ideationalists, "Epicureans" view the whole inner life, its processes, and all spiritual and immaterial phenomena, as either ignorant delusion or aberration or a peculiar by-product ("function," "effect," "resultant") of purely physiological processes in the

[21] From a purely "Sensate" standpoint it may be permissible to venture the hypothesis that perhaps each type of mentality is associated with the lowered sensibility of one type of receptors and the raised sensibility of another type within the nervous system. John Brown (*Elementa medicinae*, London, 1778) described the difference between external and internal stimulation of the human body; later Claude Bernard (*Les phénomènes de la vie*, Paris, 1878) brilliantly developed this idea in differentiating the concept of environment into environment external to the body and the inner environment of the body (*milieu interne*), the latter being the totality of the circulating fluids of the organism. The works of subsequent investigators, particularly of Sherrington (*Integrative Action of the Nervous System*, New Haven, 1926), Gaskell (*The Involuntary Nervous System*, London, 1916), Langley (*The Autonomic Nervous System*, Cambridge, England, 1921), and Herrick (*An Introduction to Neurology*, Philadelphia, 1924), permit us to distinguish between three fields of reception (which in reality are not separable but incessantly interacting): (1) The exteroceptive group, the sense organs of which are stimulated by objects outside the body and typically call forth reactions of the whole body, such as movement of the body or of its parts, so as to change the relation of the body to its environment. This field is coextensive with the so-called external surface of the animal (touch corpuscles, taste buds on the tongue, internal ear, eye). (2) The interoceptive group (also referred to as visceral). Here the sense organs fall into two well-defined groups: first, the general interoceptive systems without highly specialized end organs and innervated through the sympathetic nervous system, and their reactions chiefly unconsciously performed; second, the special interoceptive senses provided with highly developed end organs which are innervated directly from the brain without any connection with the sympathetic nervous system. (Herrick includes under interoceptive: organs of hunger, thirst, nausea, organs giving rise to respiratory sensations, to circulatory sensations, to sexual sensations, organs of sensations of distending cavities, of visceral pain, of obscure abdominal sensations associated with strong emotions of fright, anger, affection, organs of taste, and of smell.) (3) The proprioceptive group, whose sense organs are contained within the skeletal muscles, joints, etc., and are stimulated by the functioning of these organs. (Herrick includes here: end organs of muscular sensibility, end organs of tendon sensibility, end organs of joint sensibility, and organs of static and equilibratory sensation arising from stimulation of the semicircular canals of the internal ear.) Sherrington considered the proprioceptors to be largely secondary to the surface receptors. It is interesting to remember in this connection that the cerebellum is the main ganglion of the proprioceptive system,

nervous system or in any other part of the body. For consistent "Epicureans" the processes of the inner life are in essence nothing but a mere variety of the "stimulus-response" relationship, the effect of given physicochemical processes; and human mind itself is but an incorrect name for a *special mechanism of the nervous system.* Everything is a manifestation of the action-reaction, cause-effect relationship, which they have discovered from contact with the external material world. An Ideationalist spiritualizes the external, even the inorganic, world; an "Epicurean" mechanizes and materializes even the spiritual, immaterial self.

The position of the Active Ideational and Idealistic mentalities in this respect is intermediary. Both imply internal and external worlds, the Active Ideationalist paying more attention to internal and immaterial reality than the Idealist. The Passive Sensate mentality implies a generally narrow tendency to view everything in terms of sensual pleasure and its opposite. With such a view much of the content of reality is missed. Cynical "Epicureanism" also implies a limiting concentration of the attention on a specific part of the external world, *i.e.*, on the means of satisfying sensual needs and appetites and on the versatile technique of playing the hypocrite successfully. Finally, the Pseudo-Ideational mentality is rather "vegetative" or "animal" and essentially unintegrated, and is therefore not conducive to a proper concentration of the attention on either the external or the internal world and its processes. The alternation of hunger, fatigue, hardships, toil, with relatively better physiological conditions of living, occupies the Pseudo Ideationalist constantly, leaving little attention for the apprehension of much else beyond the most elementary psychophysiological processes.

---

and it is, according to Luciani (*Human Physiology*, New York, 1921), an organ which by unconscious processes exerts a continual reinforcing action on the activity of all other nerve centers.

It is permissible to venture a hypothesis based on the more recent data of Sherrington, Pavlov, Cannon, Carlson, and others. The interoceptive (and to some extent also proprioceptive) system controlling the inner reactions should seem to be playing a much more important role in the Ideational mentality than in the Sensate. In an Ideational nervous system the sensibility of the exteroceptive field is lessened and hence his indifference to the external world, whereas the interoceptive sense organs acquire a heightened sensibility. The reverse is true of the Sensate mentality and nervous system. The results of Langfeld ("On the Psychophysiology of a Prolonged Fast," in *Psychological Review Publications*, Vol. XIV, no. 5) seem to support the above hypothesis. He performed experiments on a fasting subject daily for thirty-one days and observed improvement in attention, perception, and association and decline in purely physical abilities. Whether the hypothesis is valid or not, its validity or invalidity does not concern the logical association of the Ideational mentality with "introversion," of Sensate with "extroversion."

(7) Each of the types of adaptation discussed implies logically a different conception of self, or the "ego," and its relationship to other forces and agencies. The Ascetic Ideational mentality tends to dissolve the self in the universe of impersonal and immaterial reality. In no way will an Ascetic Ideationalist identify self with the body or with any material value associated with himself (clothing, dwelling, children, relatives, etc.) The supreme task of the individual self is a union with ultimate reality, from which, like water in a cup separated from the ocean, it is temporarily isolated by the frame of material existence. The ultimate reality may be called God, Nirvana, Tao, Essence of Reality, Energy, Eternal Being, and so on. Such a mentality is naturally detached from the external world, does not care for it, is not afraid of nor moved by it. Therefore it will not fight for worldly interests and will not resist purely bodily and material injuries to itself, provided that its spiritual values are not assailed. On the other hand, it will resist to the utmost any attempts to violate its main values. Its liberty is spiritual. It regards the external world and all its forces, including those causing bodily pains and death, as a dream or an illusion. Hence, as we shall see in the next chapter, a denial of death and of fear of death is a normal trait in all systems based on this mentality.

The Active Sensate mentality implies a very different perception and conception of self. Here self appears as one of the foci, or knots, of material forces which make up the external world. This center of forces is one with the machinery of the body, inseparable from it. Since this knot, or focus, is capable of affecting powerfully many external forces, of rearranging and controlling them, this self is considered as a kind of dynamo, which does not need help from any mysterious supernatural forces or immaterial agencies. On the other hand, when the activities of environmental modification are successful, this power gives self-confidence and pride in dealing with external agencies. This means that the Active Sensate mentality implies a corporeal conception of self which makes it inseparable from the body; a skeptical or irreligious or disrespectful attitude toward nonmaterial forces and agencies; individual pride and self-reliance and a care of the body and its well-being, because it is looked upon as identical with self and personality. An Active "Epicurean's" liberty is sensate and physical. Sensate egotism, readiness to fight for physical integrity and the interests of self, color the Active Sensate type of adaptation.

Other mentalities, such as the Active Ideational and Idealistic, imply a perception and apprehension of self intermediate in nature between the two outlined above. The Passive Sensate as well as the Cynical Sensate mentalities have a kind of self nearly identical with the complex of the main organs of sensual pleasure and pain : the self of a glutton is almost identical with his stomach,[22] the self of a sexual profligate with his sex organs,[23] and so on. Take away from the bearers of such mentalities these pleasures, and they become most unhappy creatures with no objectives in their lives. Finally, we can hardly speak of any definite conception of self in the Pseudo-Ideational mentality. It has little opportunity to meditate upon and analyze such problems, and to differentiate self from the flux of unintegrated experiences and fragments of consciousness of which it consists. It is, probably, closely akin to the "mind" of some of the higher animals, like monkeys, in captivity.

(8) The above being true, it is logically inevitable that the Ascetic Ideational mentality will require and stimulate *cognition of inner, psychical, and mental processes* (not, however, in terms of physiology or chemistry) from the most elementary psychological processes of sensation, perception, recollection, representation, thinking, emotions, wishes, volitions, etc., to the most sublime and subtle experiences of ecstasy, trance, mysticism, suggestion, and hypnosis, and others like "reunion with the absolute," "revelation," "divine inspiration," etc.; from the simplest ideas about immaterial phenomena to the most difficult conceptions of ultimate reality, the human soul, immortality, God, truth, justice, value, and others which are the concern of the humanitarian sciences, *i.e.*, ethical systems, religions, law, aesthetics, philosophy, and education. Since an Ideationalist is, so to speak, everlastingly brooding over such matters, since the knowledge and the understanding of them are essential for him in his attempt to modify, control, or dissolve his inner self, it is obvious that all this should lead to an increase of the Ideationalist's direct experience in these fields of immaterial phenomena. Hence it will not be surprising later when we discover inductively that the periods of predominance of Ideational mentality in a given culture have been regularly marked by an exclusive concentration upon such noumenal or transcendental problems and, so far as we empiricists can judge, by an

---

[22] "Of what use to the country can be a man who is nothing but stomach?" said Cato of one of such persons (Cicero, *Against Catiline*, III). Hujwiri quotes Shafi'i to the same effect: "He who thinks about that which goes into his belly is worth only that which comes out of it." The *Kashf Al Mahjub* (London, 1911), p. 347.

[23] Eventually we shall see that it is not incidental to our culture that man has been reduced to the *libido* by psychoanalysts, to "stomach" by vulgar economic interpreters and other contemporary sensual interpretations of man and his "mind" and "psychology." Such an interpretation is logically implied in the Sensate mentality.

intimate, deep, and sublime experience of the mysteries of man's inner life; and always have led to a domination, in the field of human knowledge, of theological, philosophical, ethical, and other systems of thought which deal with these immaterial and sublime problems. On the other hand, such cultures and periods have regularly been marked by a stagnation and regress of the natural sciences and other disciplines dealing with the external, sensate, material phenomena.[24]

For the same reasons, the Active Sensate mentality is naturally associated with, logically requires, and stimulates man's knowledge of the external, material world. Such a knowledge is indispensable for a successful modification and control of natural phenomena. It results from an incessant contact with, manipulation of, and effort to control, the external milieu: physical, chemical, biological, and materialized psychosocial phenomena. Therefore, in a society or culture which at a given period is predominantly Sensate we must expect a successful development of natural sciences and a blossoming of man's knowledge of the material, external world and of the technical inventions for its control. The Active Ideational and the Idealistic mentalities should logically develop both types of knowledge, the former tending to emphasize more spiritual phenomena, the latter material. Cynical "Epicureanism" stimulates only a special cognition of how and when one has to vary his masquerading; Passive "Epicureanism," the technique of *savoir vivre*, or the refined (occasionally even perverted) art of sensual pleasure; Pseudo-Ideationalism, patience, submissiveness, almost fatalism, without any developed and integrated system of knowledge, with only fragments of it, woven in inconsistently, brokenly, and fantastically.

(9) For similar reasons the whole intellectual, moral, and psychosocial *Gestalt* of the Ideational mentality is profoundly different from the Active Sensate.

(a) *Ideational truth and its criteria cannot be identical with Sensate.* Even if it were true that *Nihil esse in intellectu quod non fuerit prius in sensu* (John Locke) from the Sensate standpoint, the material brought to the mind of an Ideationalist and to that of an "Epicurean" may be brought there by different agencies: by the autonomic system to an Ideationalist, and by the exteroceptive system to an "Epicurean"; by

[24] It is but logical that the Greek (philosophical) Cynics "hold that [in a system of education and knowledge] the subjects of logic and physical science may be dispensed with. . . . It is to ethics alone that they give any attention. They eliminate, likewise, geometry and music and all such studies. And so, when somebody showed Diogenes a clock, 'a useful thing,' he said, 'to save you from being late for dinner.'" Diogenes Laërtius, *Lives*, VI, 103. Diogenes and the Cynics were a variety of the Ideational group.

inner experience, meditation, revelation, and divine inspiration to the former, by exterior observation to the latter. Since the agencies of the accumulation of material for thought are different, and the regions from which the material is collected are different also (psycho-organic inner experiences and sensations and perception of external phenomena by the external sense organs), it would be miraculous if the concepts, theories, forms, and categories of thought could be identical in both cases. Such is the verdict of logic. And such, as we shall see, will be the result of any inductive study. The Ideationalist has eyes that do not see much in the external world. The "Epicurean's" inner experience passes unnoticed in his absorption in an external world. It is seldom realized that, in fact, truth has different meanings in Ideational and Sensate culture mentalities. What is truth or science for one is often prejudice, ignorance, error, heresy, blasphemy, for the other. (Compare, from this standpoint, the medieval mind and the modern mind; the logic of revelation and of factual observation; of primitive mentality and of modern natural science; the truth of mysticism and that of empiricism. Those who are acquainted with both can easily grasp the point I am making; later on we shall deal *in extenso* with these phenomena.)

If the criteria and the bases of truth are different for the Ideational and Sensate mentalities, it is to be expected that most of the *contents* of truth, its detailed manifestations in science, theology, philosophy, will be different. The first culture type builds its concepts, theories, arguments, evidence, mainly from the data supplied by the inner experience; the second, from the objects of external observation. Hence we can talk quite seriously of Ideational and of Sensate knowledge, science, logic, methodology, categories, systems of truth, as different from one another. "Vomit thy [empirical] knowledge" and "The wisdom of this world is foolishness with God": so an Ideationalist talks about the Sensate truth.[25] And vice versa, "superstition," "ignorance": so will an Epicurean express himself in regard to the Ideational truth. In a preliminary way, the essential differences in regard to truth can be listed as follows:

(i) Ideational mentality implies the acceptance of the validity of the inner experience — divine inspiration, mystical union, revelation,

---

[25] "That we may rather imitate Christ . . . so as to desire to be unlearned and a fool for Christ, Who was so reputed once, than to be esteemed wise and prudent in this world." St. Ignatius Loyola, *Spiritual Exercises*, note 3 to the Twelfth Day (London, 1870), pp. 3 and 71. Or Joachim de Flore: "Truths which remain sealed to the savants are disclosed to the children. The dialectic closes what was open; and renders obscure what was clear." Or "Vomit thy [empirical] knowledge" and "empty thy mind" [of it]. Lao-tse and Kwangtze.

pure meditation, ecstasy, trance — as the ultimate basis and source of truth. The Sensate mentality implies the validity of perception, rests entirely, or mainly, on man's external sense organs. Each is skeptical about the ultimate basis of truth of the other.

(ii) The Ideational wisdom, knowledge, mentality, seems to be marked by idealism, spiritualism, quietism, religiosity, organicism, mysticism, indeterminism, qualitativism. The Sensate mentality, knowledge, science, is characterized by materialism, empiricism, mechanisticism, determinism, quantitativism.

(iii) An Ideationalist is prone to interpret the whole external world according to the patterns and traits of his inner experience. As a result, he spiritualizes the material world, even in its inorganic part; he dissolves it in the inner experience.

An "Epicurean," on the contrary, is inclined to interpret all phenomena, including those of the inner psychical experience, as mere modifications of the material in its inorganic form. Therefore, he is prone to ascribe to all vital, mental, psychical, and other phenomena the properties of matter, determinism, mechanisticism. He tends to treat everything with the same method and technique that he uses for purely physicochemical and mechanical phenomena. He materializes and externalizes the inner experience.

(iv) The Ideational mentality is generally posited in everlasting Being. The Sensate is centered in Becoming and Change, in endless dynamic processes, progress, evolution.

(b) Similarly, and for similar reasons, *the moral, social, and other values should be different in these mentalities.* Since an Ideationalist is indifferent to the external world and is centered at the inner, always "immaterial," or supersensate world, and since his ideal is to repress his sensual and material needs as much as possible, the external values of material character which can give but a transient satisfaction of sensual needs have no, or little, value for him. He seeks to be independent of them and self-sufficient. He wants to live in the eternal, imperishable world. His values are of an inner and immaterial character. They are, therefore, of endless duration, free from the caprices of chance and external conditions. The reverse is the situation for the Sensate mentality. Its criteria of value are the fitness of a given external object, of the way of handling it, and of specific forms of extrovert activity to satisfy mainly sensual needs. These needs are never at rest: if one is temporarily appeased, another immediately arises and demands to be satisfied. Therefore, the life of an "Epicurean" is an incessant effort to acquire, modify, and use all possible external objects which can for a given moment appease his sensual appetite — be it hunger, thirst, sex, pleasure, ambition, fame, or any other similar need. He cannot be, and does not want to be, self-sufficient and cut off from the external world. He does not want to seek for imperishable and everlasting values. Such values are nonvalues to him, being almost useless for the satisfaction of his manifold needs. Life is short, and in this short life the sensual needs are transient — a good meal has its value only when one has an appetite and can enjoy it. Love and sex again are of value only when they can be enjoyed ; for an old or impotent man they are of no value at all. Therefore, why miss a chance when it comes and can be enjoyed, why seek for something eternally lasting, since such a thing either does not exist, or, if it exists at all, provides a much smaller measure of enjoyment than the incessant series of pleasures which follow from the satisfaction of all wishes at the moment of their greatest intensity? Such a life to an "Epicurean" is much happier, richer quantitatively and qualitatively in pleasure, thrill, variety, and experience, than the Ideational life of giving up all these pleasures, repressing lusts and denying their satisfaction. To an "Epicurean" the Ideational life would seem a flat and monotonous existence, and the achievement of problematic everlasting values could never compensate him for the lack of sensate pleasures and experiences.

In regard to *all values*, as has been pointed out, an Ideationalist places more emphasis on the long-time, permanent values than on those that are immediate, transient, short-lived. His standpoint gravitates to the philosophy of Being, everlasting, unchangeable, enduring.

After these considerations, the following typical traits implied in Ideational and Sensate mentalities will be comprehensible.

(c) In the field of moral values *the Ideational mentality tends to be associated with the values which are absolute, eternal, and everlasting*. As such values are almost exclusively "transcendental," and as almost all Sensate values are temporary and perishable, the Ideational moral systems are mainly transcendental, are of the type of the "categorical imperative," free from the Sensate and relativistic moral codes typical of the Sensate mentality. Ideational moral systems (*e.g.*, Hindu, Buddhist, and Taoist Nirvana), whatever their secondary traits, are marked, first, by indifference to, or contempt of, or a low evaluation of, the external empirical world and its material values. ("My kingdom is not of this world.") They are marked, second, by repression, limitation, and bridling of physical needs, wishes, lusts, desires, for any of the pleasures and values of the empiric and material world. Asceticism is one manifestation of this. The indifference of Nirvana to external phenomena is another manifestation, perhaps even still more completely Ideational than asceticism. Third, Ideational morals emphasize always the immaterial, inner, spiritual, supersensory values, whether bearing the aspect of God, the Eternal Life, the City of God, Eternal Transcendental Value, Ultimate Value, the Categorical Imperative, the Union with Brahma, Nirvana, Tao, or what not. Even in its moderate and "practical" forms the Ideational code always recommends a preference for the lasting spiritual values as against the transient sensate values.

The Sensate mentality implies and is associated with an opposite type of moral code. It chooses and emphasizes predominantly the sensate, empirical, material values. *Eudaemonism, hedonism, utilitarianism, sensualism; the morals of "Carpe diem," of "Wine, women, and song"* — these are the forms established by the Sensate mentality. Consequently, its moral systems are marked typically, first, by emphasis, in an extreme or moderate degree, on pleasure and pain, enjoyment and suffering, happiness and unhappiness, utility and disutility, all mainly in their Sensate form, whether refined to eudaemonism, or in the coarse forms of vulgar sensualism, utilitarianism, hedonism. These are the alternatives to be chosen : Man should seek pleasure and avoid pain ; utility is positive, disutility is negative. The maximum pleasure for the greatest number of beings, this is in essence the motto of Sensate moralists. Even the more refined systems, like eudaemonism or the "sensible and solid" utilitarianism of Jeremy Bentham or of John Stuart Mill, are no exception to this. They are but a more tempered and calculated expression of the same principles, where we are wisely told how to get maximum pleasure (or utility) for the cheapest prices (Bentham's "moral arithmetics").[26]

The second characteristic of the moral systems of a Sensate culture type is that they are never absolute, but are always relativistic, varying "according to circumstances and situations." They can be modified, have no sacred, unalterable, eternal imperatives. If under a given set of circumstances the maximum pleasure cannot be obtained in one way, it should be obtained in any other that is "efficient." No inflexible principles hinder such a shift.

[26] Just as I was giving this chapter a final reading, a copy of *Science* (New York), January 3, 1936, arrived, containing E. L. Thorndike's address, "Science and Values." As was to be expected, this is a good sample of a Sensate mentality in ethics paraded under the banner of "science."

The third quality of the Sensate code is that it has little to do with any transcendental or supersensory values, and either mocks at such values, ignores them, or mentions them only to repudiate them and to bolster up its own principles.

(d) Logically, *aesthetic value*, art, likewise cannot be identical in the Ideational and Sensate culture mentalities. They should be as profoundly different as are the other values. So far as the *style* of art is concerned — whether it be in painting, sculpture, music, literature, drama, architecture — in the Ideational mentality it is symbolic, its physical exemplars being merely the visible signs of the invisible world and inner values. But in the Sensate culture art must be sensate in form; "naturalistic," in the sense that its intention is to reproduce objects in a shape which imitates closely that in which they appear to our organs of sense. As to the *subjects* and the *aims* and *purposes* of art, they show analogous divergences in the two culture types. In general, Sensate art deals with those materials which serve and help to increase the sensate happiness of man; Ideational is the handmaid of religion, absolutistic ethics, eternal values.

(e) The same difference appears in regard to *social and practical values*. A regime professing Sensate ideals will approve anything that increases the sum total of Sensate enjoyment; and that leads to man's control over nature and over other men, as the means of satisfying ever-expanding needs. Of a special importance in such a state of society is the search for material objects which under the circumstances are particularly efficient in bringing satisfaction. As one of the most efficient means has always been *material wealth*, in a Sensate society it is the *alpha* and *omega* of comfort, of the satisfaction of all desires, of power, prestige, fame, happiness. With it everything can be bought, everything can be sold, and everything can be gratified. Therefore, it is quite comprehensible that the striving for wealth is inevitably one of the main activities of such a culture, that wealth is the standard by which almost all other values are judged, that it is, in fact, the supreme value of values. *Pecuniary value thus becomes the measuring stick* of scientific, artistic, moral, and other values. Those who are excellent moneymakers are the *leaders* of such a society. Those who are wealthy are its *aristocracy*. They are simultaneously public leaders, high priests, moral examples, kings who ennoble others, the Four Hundred which is envied, if not deeply esteemed. Under these conditions, writers, artists, scientists, ministers, public officials, and men of the professional classes hope and act mainly to write a "best seller," to obtain the best-paying position, to have the highest scale of remuneration, and so on. The exact conditions of individual Sensate societies may vary, but essentially the "practical" basis of all values, as this has just been described, is common in various degrees to all societies of this type. If arms and force, not money, are the main means to maximum happiness, then these instruments are the supreme arbiters of value, instead of money.

In this respect the Ideational mentality differs from the Sensate once again. Since the Ideationalist is but little interested in the external world and its sensate potentialities, he is not mad about either wealth or arms or material comfort or power or fame or luxury or any other external means of obtaining and increasing sensate comfort, pleasure, and happiness. On the contrary, an Ideationalist is either quite indifferent to all these illusory and transient values, or is even inimical to them as the sources of the disturbance of the peace of mind and of the perdition of the human soul. A perfect Ideationalist then will either flee from all this into a desert and become a hermit, or display in its presence all the profound indifference of a grown-up toward children's toys, or will attack it as being of negative value. In a thoroughgoing Ideational society wealth, or any Sensate value, not only cannot become dominant but at best will be tolerated only as turpitudinous. The most successful dealers in wealth do not have much chance to become the bearers of prestige, the leaders, the evaluators, the assessors of men, objects, and values, in such a society. The main values here are imperishable, absolute, everlasting, and consequently immaterial and transcendental, or near to it. Anything transient, including man's life itself, can have but a secondary and derivative significance.

Enough of contrast for the present. There are similar profound differences between the Ideational and Sensate mentalities in other fields of value. But a detailed analysis of all of them is unnecessary here, since this will be made in its proper place subsequently. For the present the summary examination which we have just completed is enough to indicate the essential nature of each of the chief types of culture mentality. Table 1, beginning on the next page, will make plain at a glance by its arrangement in tabular form the results of this examination of the seven types of culture mentalities.

TABLE 1.   SUMMARY OF THE MAIN TRAITS AND SATELLITES OF THE
DISCUSSED TYPES OF ADAPTATION

MAIN ELEMENTS	TYPES OF CULTURE MENTALITY						
	Ascetic Ideational	*Active Sensate*	*Active Ideational*	*Idealistic*	*Passive Sensate*	*Cynical Sensate*	*Pseudo-Ideational*
1. *Reality*	ultimate reality, eternal, nonsensate, transcendental	sensate, empirical, material	both, with emphasis on the eternal and nonsensate	both approximately equally represented	sensate, narrow, and shallow	sensate, but with spiritual mask	painfully sensate; spiritual, but undifferentiated; felt and sensed but not thought through (unintegrated)
2. *Main needs and ends*	spiritual	manifold and richly sensate	both, with predominance of spiritual	both approximately equally represented	narrow sensate	sensate, with a spiritual mask	mainly sensate, with elements of spiritual not differentiated
3. *Extent of satisfaction*	maximum	maximum	great, but moderated	great, but balanced	maximum for narrow sensate needs	according to circumstances	very limited
4. *Method of satisfaction*	mainly self-modification	mainly modification of external milieu	both ways, with the prevalence of self-modification	both ways	utilization of external milieu	milieu's utilization through superficial and purely external change of the psycho-social traits of the person, without change of itself	mere enforced endurance of the milieu
LOGICAL SATELLITES							
5. *Weltanschauung*	Being (*Sein*): lasting value; indifference to transient values; imperturbability; statism	Becoming (*Werden*): transient values; full-blooded sense of life, joy, and grief; dynamism and endless readjustment (progress, evolution)	both, with emphasis on Being	both equally represented	narrow and extreme Becoming, ("*Carpe diem*")	narrow Becoming, with a mask of *Being*	undifferentiated and not thought through, vague and fragmentary ideas (lack of integration)
6. *Power and object of control*	self-control, repression of the sensual man and of "self"	control of the sensate reality	both, with emphasis on self-control	both equally represented	no real control of either self or milieu	control of assuming and putting off masks	no control: mere endurance of the effects of other forces acted on by external power

TABLE 1.   SUMMARY OF THE MAIN TRAITS AND SATELLITES OF THE
DISCUSSED TYPES OF ADAPTATION — *continued*

LOGICAL SATELLITES	TYPES OF CULTURE MENTALITY						
	Ascetic Ideational	*Active Sensate*	*Active Ideational*	*Idealistic*	*Passive Sensate*	*Cynical Sensate*	*Pseudo-Ideational*
7. *Activity*	introvert	extrovert	both, with emphasis on intro-vert	both equally represented	parasitism of intro-vert-extro-vert type	specific introvert-extrovert	enforced extrovert-introvert; fatalistic
8. *Self*	highly inte-grated, spiritual, dissolved in the ulti-mate real-ity, aware of the sen-sual world as illusion or content of self; antimate-rialistic	highly inte-grated, sensate, dissolved in immediate physical reality; material-izes self and all the spiritual phenom-ena; mate-rialistic, caring for integrity of body and its sensual interest. Sensual lib-erty, sen-sual egotism	both, with emphasis on spirit-ual, etc.	both equally represented	no real in-tegration of self; mere flux of uninte-grated physical sensations; self almost identical with stom-ach, sex organs, etc.	no real in-tegration; similar to the passive sensate, but schem-ing and manipulat-ing	no inte-grated self, except as a vague cen-ter of sensa-tions; with some fanci-ful, animis-tic, or other, ideas and images; re-mains on a half-animal level (unin-tegrated)
9. *Knowledge*	develops insight into and cogni-tion of the spiritual, psychical, immaterial phenomena and experi-ences; con-centrates upon these exclu-sively; leads to arts of edu-cation and modifica-tion of man's inner life	develops science of natural phenomena and techni-cal inven-tions; con-centrates on these; leads to arts of technology, medicine, hygiene, sanitation, and modifi-cation of man's physical actions	both, but more mod-erately, with em-phasis on the spirit-ual	both, equally represented	develops only the "culinary" and "bed-room" techniques of sensual enjoyment	same as in passive sensate plus the technique of decep-tion and hypocrisy	does not give any real oppor-tunity to develop any form of in-tegrated knowledge and cogni-tion except some frag-ments acquired through im-posed "trial and error"
10. *Truth, its categories, criteria, and methods (of ar-riving at)*	based on inner ex-perience, "mystic way," con-centrated medita-tion; in-tuition and "reve-lation"; prophecy	based on observation of, meas-urement of, experimen-tation with, the exterior phenomena through exterior organs of senses, inductive logic	both, with the "inner way" em-phasized	both, equally emphasized (Scholasti-cism)	nothing coherent, no truth except sen-sations	nothing coherent	nothing dif-ferentiated and thought through clearly

TABLE 1. SUMMARY OF THE MAIN TRAITS AND SATELLITES OF THE DISCUSSED TYPES OF ADAPTATION — *continued*

LOGICAL SATELLITES	TYPES OF CULTURE MENTALITY						
	Ascetic Ideational	*Active Sensate*	*Active Ideational*	*Idealistic*	*Passive Sensate*	*Cynical Sensate*	*Pseudo-Ideational*
11. *Moral values and systems*	absolute, transcendental, categoric, imperative, everlasting, and unchangeable	relativistic and sensate: hedonistic, eudaemonistic, utilitarian; seeking maximum sensate happiness for largest number of human beings; "morals of rightly understood egotism"	both, with emphasis on the absolute and the external	both, equally emphasized	no real moral values, except sensual, "Wine, women, and song"; amoralism; nihilism	no real moral values, except sensate masked by spiritual; cynicism, nihilism	no differentiated moral system, except apathetic and dull submission to fate, and sensual disapproval of hard blows and approval of easier times followed by vague ideas about the other world's justice
12. *Aesthetic values*	"ideational" subservient to the main inner values, religious, nonsensate	sensate, secular, created to increase joys and beauties of a rich sensate life	both, with emphasis on the non-sensate	both, equally emphasized	narrow sensual; refinedly pathologic	sensate, masked with spiritual	undifferentiated and vague
13. *Social and practical values*	those which are lasting and lead to the ultimate reality: only such persons are leaders, only such things and events are positive, all others are valueless, or of negative value, particularly wealth, earthly comfort, etc.; principle of sacrifice	everything that gives joy of life to self and partly to others: particularly wealth, comfort, etc.; prestige is based on the above; wealth, money, physical might become "rights" and basis of all values; principle of sound egotism	both, with emphasis on spiritual	both, equally emphasized; live and let live	narrow and extremely sensual; "*après moi le déluge*"	narrow and extremely sensual with a mask of spiritual values; Tartufeism	no choice given; undifferentiated; as God or boss decides

The preceding pages outline the profound differences of various types of mentality, as they fall generally under the heading of Ideational or Sensate. Based on divergent major premises, they likewise differ throughout, if the implications of the premises are consistently carried through. A consistent adherence to these implications makes each type of mentality logical and integrated (according to the same canon of logic), in spite of their contrast. If the mentality of a given person or group or culture is indeed integrated according to one of these types, we shall find existing in it all the traits and satellites characteristic of the type as detailed above. In other words, logical integration will be coexistent with causal-functional integration. If such coexistence is not found, this means only that the mentalities in question are not integrated logically, but represent an "undigested" mixture of inconsistent elements.

The problems which next face us are these : first, to show that the above types of mentality have had actual historical existence ; second, to demonstrate that in these historical culture complexes the combination of the elements and satellites of each type was indeed exactly as outlined above.

If we succeed in solving these problems, three contentions will be established.

First, we shall have shown that the above types are not artificial inventions of the author, not a mere exercise in the field of logical classification, but represent classification which fits the empirical reality and serves as a fruitful instrument of dissecting, ordering, and understanding it.

Second, we shall have proved that the logico-meaningful method has indeed a heuristic value. If in the above types A and B and C and D elements of each type are put together as logically belonging to one another; and if in the factually given historical mentality A and B and C and D they are also found together whether in the A, B, C, D of the logically integrated mentalities or of logically unintegrated mentalities — various "Mixed" and "Pseudo-Ideational" persons, groups, and cultural conglomerations : this means that such formulas have the same cognitive value as any causal formula that contends that A, B, C, D are causally connected and are usually found together. In other words the above types become generalizing formulas indeed.

Third, we shall have shown that the historical culture mentalities have contained much logically consistent thought (within the major premises of each type) and in no way have been entirely or even overwhelmingly nonlogical or illogical, as Pareto and many others seem to believe.

When these tasks are done, there still remains another major problem : that of the relationship between the mentality and the external behavior, manifestation, events, processes, and other externalities of a culture. The point is that the *mentality* of a given person or group may be quite consistent and logical, but this does not entitle us, as yet, to conclude that it will be carried through in the activities, external patterns, and *behavior* of the person or group. A man may be a most brilliant commentator on Kant's *Critique of Practical Reason*, and yet in his behavior remain a scoundrel of the first degree. All the earmarks of the mentality of a given culture may appear to be Ascetic Ideational, and yet it is thinkable that the external aspect of such a culture may be a shocking contrast to that mentality: materialistic, comfortable, luxurious, ostentatious, mercenary.

In other words we must try to answer the question: What is the relationship between the mentality and the overt behavior or appearance of a given person, group, culture? Are they always also logically consistent with each other? or are they not? If not, when does the discrepancy occur and what are the reasons for it? Heuristically this means: Can we infer from the mentality type of a given person, group, culture, that the external behavior and patterns will be consistent with it? The question is too important to be overlooked. The present writer has not failed to understand that the study of a culture mentality has not as yet given us the authority to draw conclusions as to action, behavior, external patterns, processes. A study of this problem can be undertaken only after that of the first two is complete. Therefore, let us turn to the demonstration that the culture mentalities which we have been defining have existed in the actual world of culture; and that each Ideational, Sensate, Idealistic or Mixed culture which has had historical existence has consisted of such a combination of major premises and satellites as has been given in the above analysis and tables.

Chapter Three

CONCRETE ILLUSTRATIONS OF THE CHIEF TYPES OF CULTURE MENTALITY

It now becomes our main purpose to indicate by illustrations from the actual sociocultural world, both present and past, that the types of culture mentality distinguished in the last chapter are not artificially conceived abstractions without basis in empirical fact.

I. INDIVIDUALS AND SMALL GROUPS

We shall begin with a few generalized examples of the mentality and conduct of individuals and groups familiar to us in our daily experience. This should serve as an introduction to the more complex discussion of the vast systems of culture mentality which have existed since a time before the dawn of history, have been believed in, aspired to, and accepted by countless millions of individuals. These systems have each in their time affected to some extent the conduct of large masses of people, and have completely dominated the behavior of smaller or larger minorities who are their representatives par excellence.

With the characteristics of the chief culture types in our minds, even a superficial glance at our friends and acquaintances would show some of them to be conspicuously Active "Epicureans" to a larger or smaller degree; others to be Passive "Epicureans"; others Ideationalists with the traits of Active Ideationalism dominant (though in our culture this type is not common); and most of them to be of an intermediate type, providing examples of numerous varieties of the Mixed classification. Again, such traits as accompany the Cynical Sensate mentality may be perceptible among our acquaintances, quite conspicuous in some, very faint in others. In our age the pure Ascetic Ideational type is very rare, and we may not be able to find clear signs of it among those with whom we are in everyday contact; but such persons do exist even in our society,[1]

[1] A conspicuous example of this is offered by the mentality and culture of the Mount Athos monasteries. See M. Choukas, *Black Angels of Athos* (Brattleboro, Vt., 1934).

and especially in the Orient, and have existed in other ages in both the East and the West.

The same experience will be ours if we glance at the life and personality of many historical personages. It is enough to mention the names of Alexander the Great, Caesar, Augustus, Genghis Khan, Tamerlane, Peter the Great, Louis XIV, Frederick II of the Holy Roman Empire (or of Prussia), Danton, Napoleon, Cecil Rhodes, Carnegie, John D. Rockefeller, Sr., Lenin, or Henry Ford to put them without any difficulty in the class of Active "Epicureans." When we mention the names of Marcus Aurelius, St. Ambrose, Leo the Great, Gregory the Great, Gregory VII, Innocent III, Torquemada, St. Ignatius Loyola, Calvin, Wesley, Fox, there scarcely can be any doubt that they all exemplify various shades of the type of Active Ideationalism. Similarly, most hermits, mystics, ascetics, torturers of the body, some martyrs, such individuals as Diogenes and other Cynics and Stoics, all persons given to meditation and mysticism, have belonged to the Ascetic Ideationalist group.

Innumerable Tartufes, so well typified in Molière's comedy; all the hypocrites, the insincere, the dissimulators in speech, writing, and action; all the cynics, flatterers, and "good mixers," who are acting so in order to attract the good will of the rich and mighty or for some material profit, and always with an eye in the direction whence in their opinion the profit is most certain to come — all these Cynical "Epicureans" have always been, and are still, among us.

Again, who does not know of those who "burn the candle at both ends" in an incessant search for sensate pleasures. Usually concentrated in the class of the lazy posterity of rich fathers, this type, the Dorian Greys of the world, runs the gamut from those whose time is spent mainly in pursuit of ever new sex experience, and in refined or orgiastic eating and drinking, and in the constant improvement and refinement of other material comforts, to those who make their lives more refined eudaemonistic processes of the most "refined" enjoyment of all that the sensate art, science, comfort, technique, and riches can offer ("all that money can buy"), be it racing and polo, opera and symphony, poetry and theater, collecting art objects, hunting lions and cruising in yachts, or surrounding themselves with certain kinds of poets, intellectuals, philosophers. Each of us knows the type and would have no difficulty in pointing out several persons who exemplify this culture adaptation in its coarse and in its refined forms.

Moreover, all those in contact with the needy, the suppressed, the underprivileged, those bound hand and foot to follow what is ordered, who cannot do anything to change these conditions (slaves, serfs, prisoners, dependents, employees of inferior rank), would understand what is meant by Pseudo-Ideational adaptation. Large masses of individuals among the primitive tribes, as well as amidst a modern metropolis, have had a Pseudo-Ideational culture mentality. ·

Finally, most of our acquaintances, in all probability, belong to various of the Mixed culture types.   Some even exemplify the balanced Idealistic class, though most will be dominated by Sensate elements.   They like comfort, enjoy their meals and drinks, golf, bridge, and sex in a reasonable degree ; they are respectable, follow the rules of propriety and etiquette ("slips" are merely incidental) ; they discharge their business conscientiously, pay their taxes, make some philanthropic contributions, do their other duties, go to church on Sundays ; once in a while they ponder the great spiritual problems of humanity, and for such moments try to forget about business and money and comfort ; they sometimes make an effort to improve themselves and their inner life, sacrifice their narrow interests to family and sometimes to other people's welfare, and occasionally are even capable of doing something heroic.   In brief, these exemplary Rotarians, Kiwanians, Lions, Elks, Main Streeters (Babbitts), represent a wide variety of the Mixed type of mentality, but with a predominance of Sensate elements.

What has been said of our living acquaintances is also true of historical personages. Though any classification of such persons must be inferential, even when a complete record of their activities and state of mind exists ; and though, as with any conclusion based on inference, the classification may be in part erroneous and at best only approximately accurate, nevertheless there seems to be no particular difficulty in establishing with reasonable assurance the dominant types of culture mentality and conduct of a number of such individuals, especially when they belong to one of the extreme types.   In order generally to test this assumption and more specifically to see to what cultural type a series of kings and popes belongs (these being groups for which we have perhaps the fullest extant records), and in order also to ascertain whether these two social categories exhibit any marked differences as groups in respect to culture mentality, the present author, in co-operation with Mr. J. W. Boldyreff, undertook a detailed study of the popes together with the kings of four countries. As a means of minimizing the possibility of error, we divided all the kings and the popes first of all into three main classes : the Sensate, the Ideational, and the Mixed.[2]   In the Mixed group we placed all those

[2] The nature of the groups studied precludes the existence within them of the Pseudo-Ideational type.   Likewise, in view of the impossibility of our separating hypocrisy motivated

whose characteristics were not so clear as to permit our putting them with
certainty into one of the other classes. Then, later on, the class of the
Sensate was subdivided into two minor groups : Very Sensate and Sensate.
The same was done with the Ideational classification. Each of the
persons studied was put into one of these classes on the basis of all the
evidence available for his entire life : his activities, desires, aspirations,
sayings, as they are reported in authentic biographical and historical
works.[3]

The results are summarized in Table 2.

TABLE 2. DISTRIBUTION OF IDEATIONAL, MIXED, AND SENSATE TYPES
AMONG POPES AND KINGS

GROUP AND PERIOD	Total Number of Individuals Studied	Very Sensate		Sensate		Mixed		Ideational		Very Ideational	
		No.	Per cent of the total	No.	Per cent of the total	No.	Per cent of the total	No.	Per cent of the total	No.	Per cent of the total
Roman Catholic popes 42–1932	256	3	1.2	34	13.4	116	45.3	101	39.3	2	0.8
Russian czars 1290–1918	32	5	15.6	14	43.7	8	25.1	5	15.6	0	0
Austrian kings 1218–1922	30	1	3.3	13	43.3	9	30.0	7	23.4	0	0
English kings 1027–1910	35	3	8.6	18	51.4	8	22.9	6	17.1	0	0
French kings 938–1793	32	4	12.5	16	50.0	4	12.5	8	25.0	0	0

Table 2 shows that within each main group, that of the popes and
that of the kings (taking the four groups of kings as one), different types

by purely personal profit and that actuated by Church or State interests, we dropped also
the Cynical Sensate type. Finally, it must be noted that of the four major premises of each
type, dealing with the nature of reality, the needs to be satisfied, the method of the satisfaction, and the extent to which satisfaction is sought, the last three were heavily weighted.
This means that the significance of each type is somewhat simplified and slightly modified.
"Very Sensate" refers to persons who were very energetic and efficient in the transformation
of the social milieu and lavish in the satisfaction of their, mainly sensual, needs. "Sensate"
characterizes persons less energetic and more moderate in these respects. "Ideational"
describes those of the type of Active Idealism who for the sake of the transcendental or
semitranscendental value (salvation of the soul, God's commands, interests of Christianity,
and the Christian and Divine State, and so on), not overindulging their sensate needs, exerted
a notable influence in the modification of the social milieu. The category "Very Ideational"
applies to persons approaching somewhat to Ascetic Ideational type in its mild forms.

[3] A large body of literature was consulted. It is not detailed here in order to save over-
burdening the work with bibliographies which are secondary in importance and are otherwise
not unknown or difficult of access.

of "personality" — from the standpoint of culture mentality and conduct — have existed. As far as the popes are concerned, the predominant type has been the Mixed or Idealistic, followed by the Active Ideational. These two account for 85 per cent of the persons who occupied this position. Then about 13 per cent of the popes were persons of a moderate Sensate type, while the remaining 2 per cent were of the extreme Sensate and Ascetic Ideational types. We should not be surprised that the proportion of the Ascetic type is so small; the position of the pope, the supreme executive of the extensive Christian organization, does not permit, and consequently is not filled by, persons who are entirely other-worldly and unwilling to deal in any way with this sensate world.

Very different is the composition of the kings' group. Regardless of some differences among the four classes, we see that the " modal " type here is the Sensate; next comes the Mixed; then a moderate Active Ideational type (permeated considerably by sensate interests). The rest are of the extreme Sensate type, while there is practically none who can be put into the Ascetic Ideational group. Again, considering the nature of the position of secular rulers of a mainly material and sensate world, the divergence from the group of the popes is quite comprehensible. It would, in fact, have been surprising if the proportion of Sensatism to Ideationalism in this group had turned out to be about the same as that of the popes. It is to be expected that a conspicuous flight from the earthly world, and the position and functions of a king, should be incompatible.[4]

These results suggest that not only individuals but social groups and classes differ from one another in regard to the frequency of each type of culture mentality and conduct within its limits. The group of Roman Catholic popes as a whole is more Ideational than is the group of monarchs. If we had taken the group of slaves or serfs or other sub-merged classes, we probably should have found the Pseudo-Ideational type quite prevalent, while among popes and kings it is practically absent. In other words, *the types and the traits of culture mentality and conduct are unevenly distributed among various social groups, and, as we shall see, in the systems of integrated culture created and maintained by these groups.*

In Chapter Fifteen of Volume Three this principle will be worked out

---

[4] The detailed data which we have examined but which are not given here show, however, several interesting fluctuations of the frequency of each type in the course of time. In Chapter Fifteen of Volume Three, in connection with other topics, some of these data will be mentioned.

in greater detail. Here we shall merely point out briefly the distribution of types and traits which is perhaps typical, or at least most conspicuous, in each group.

A. Within any society the Active and Passive Sensate mentalities probably occupy more prominent positions in the adaptation of the rich and privileged classes than in that of the poor.

(1) In the period of vigor and ascendancy the Active Sensate form prevails among the rich.

(2) In the period of decay of this class the Passive Sensate form dominates.

B. Of all the types of mentality existent among the poor and disenfranchised classes, the Pseudo-Ideational type is perhaps the most prevalent; it is less frequent among the rich and privileged.

C. In a given society the Active Ideational mentality, and to some extent the Ascetic Ideational, occupy a relatively greater place in the life of the clergy or priesthood, or their equivalents (Shamans, Brahmans, moral leaders, etc.), than in the life of other groups. On the eve of the decay of, or a crisis in, a given religion, or moral and social ideology equivalent to it, both of these types of mentality tend to diminish among the clergy as a whole, and to be replaced either by the Idealistic or Mixed type or by Active and Passive "Epicureanism." The data on the popes offer corroboration of this statement.[5]

The reasons for the distribution indicated above are obvious. The rich and the privileged classes have more means (wealth) at their disposal for the satisfaction of their needs and therefore can indulge in more of such satisfaction than the poor. They have greater power to modify the external world and their social environment than the poor. Therefore, they do not practice giving up their fancies and needs, modifying themselves instead of their milieu to the extent to which the poor classes must. Hence the greater "Epicureanism" of the rich. This "Epicureanism" is Active at the vigorous stage, when any such class is struggling for ascendancy; and it tends to turn more and more into Passive "Epicu-

[5] It is to be noted in our detailed study of the popes that their mentality and conduct remain Active Ideational and intensely Ideational from 42 to 483. Then, still remaining Ideational, they become more permeated by the Sensate elements in the period 483–532; and for the first time become Mixed around 1032–1085. However, they again become mildly Ideational. But in the period from about 1350 to the end of the sixteenth century they definitely become Sensate, Active and Passive; and finally once more become slightly Sensate or Mixed in the second half of the eighteenth century and in the nineteenth century. As is known, almost all these periods of a decrease of Ideationalism were synchronous with, or slightly preceding, a crisis in the history of the Roman Catholic Church.

reanism" among the subsequent generations of those born in comfort and luxury and not obliged to fight for their existence.

For similar reasons the poor and the subjugated groups are more exposed to the Pseudo-Ideational mentality than the rich. Their circumstances do not permit them to be Active or Passive "Epicureans." As a whole they are not capable of lifting themselves to the high level of Ideationalism. Neither have they an opportunity or possibility of elevating themselves to the level of Active Ideationalism. Hence they have to be content with whatever the circumstances give them, and this is not enough to permit their developing a full Sensate mentality and behavior. Yet, in spite of all the limitations of their material standard of living, one would be greatly mistaken if he should interpret their poverty, lack of comfort, failure to satisfy many vital needs, as the signs of an Ideational type of mentality. True Ideationalism presupposes a free preference of such behavior where the possibility of satisfying physical needs also exists. The misery of the lower classes is not endured by choice, but imposed.[6] The oppressive power once removed and the means for satisfying their wishes being at hand, they would be no less, and possibly even more, "Epicurean" than the rich. The bridling of the bodily wants by the poor is Pseudo-Ideational, not truly Ideational, in the main.

As to the clergy and other religious and moral leaders, the nature of their profession requires of them a degree of Ideationalism, Ascetic or Active, greater than is required of other groups and classes. This, of course, does not mean that the clerical class always has it. Thus, during a period of the temporary or final decay of a religion, the clergy turn to "Epicureanism," and sometimes perhaps even more than the other classes. But such a situation leads to the complete disintegration of the clerical group. Normally, in spite of all the shortcomings of the clergy, at its vigorous stage of development it has been more Ideational than most of the other social classes. The statistics of crime show, for instance, that the participation of clergy in such activities is the lowest as compared with all other occupations. In addition, the clerical profession imposes upon its members certain duties that are "ascetic" in several

---

[6] This does not exclude the possibility that, once in a while when the chance comes, the submerged individual of Pseudo-Ideational personality may indulge in wild and coarse sensualism. Thus, the laborers in Liverpool, Chinese and Siamese coolies, etc., are said to indulge in occasional outbursts of most violent dissipation. Similar outbreaks of license are observed during, and on the eve of, great calamities and catastrophes among otherwise "balanced" groups. Such isolated cases should not destroy the validity of the general statement.

respects.[7] Violators of such duties have always existed, but not all members of the clergy are to be included among them, perhaps not even the majority.

Taking everything into consideration, the behavior of the clergy is well above the average in morality. Even in our predominantly Sensate age, as we shall see, the clergy, though it probably does not have much purely Ideational mentality, has a Mixed mentality which contains perhaps more Ideational elements than the Mixed mentalities of the other classes, and this despite the notable "worldliness" of some members of the clerical profession.[8]

It is also probable that the occupation of the clergy tends to bring into its behavior some of the Cynical Sensate type, and perhaps to an extent greater than for many other groups. Even those clergymen with the strongest leaning toward the Sensate must keep up appearances, otherwise they would lose their positions. Hence, hypocrisy, Elmer Gantryism, the putting on of the masks of decency, of Ideationalism, spiritualism, religiosity, and so on, which do not correspond to the inner *Gestalt* and to some of the outward actions of the persons involved.

The above general discussion serves to show that the distribution of culture types, with respect to the number of types included, their relative proportions, and the nature of their combinations, varies as between different social groups with one type generally predominant for each.

If we should examine simultaneously various societies and cultures, we would also easily see that all nations, cultures, or social aggregates do not have a like distribution of culture-mentality types. Even a superficial

---

[7] The sincere members of the clerical profession choose the ascetic duties of their church and religion rather than have them imposed by an external agency. Among clergy are found, however, individuals who enter the profession to escape material insecurity and danger. Such persons, when they perform their ascetic obligations, are exemplifying the Pseudo-Ideational or the Cynical Sensate mentality, or both.

[8] The whole history of monasticism testifies convincingly in favor of a much higher frequency of Ascetic and partly Active Ideationalists among the monks, nuns, and clergy. As we shall see, during the periods when the priestly class dominates a culture, it tends to be strongly Ideational. This will be found true, whether for sacerdotal Greece and Rome, the theocratic Europe of the Middle Ages, Taoist China, the Buddhist Tibet of the Lamas, Brahmanic India, or the theocratic primitive tribes like the Zuñi. Ample corroboration of this, as far as Christian monasticism is concerned, will be found in the following works on the subject: Montalembert, *The Monks of the West*, 2 vols. (Boston, 1860) ; N. B. Workman, *The Evolution of Monastic Ideal* (London, 1927) ; K. Lake, *The Early Days of Monasticism* (Oxford, 1909). See further all the works quoted in Chapters One, Two, Four, and Thirteen of Volume Two of the present work on the history of religion, monastic orders, and the related fields.

comparison of the present American or European societies with many Oriental, like the Chinese, the Indian,[9] and the Tibetan, shows at once the contrast between the conspicuously Sensate type of the former, and the Ideational or Pseudo-Ideational type of the latter. The first group has a much more luxurious standard of material well-being, satisfies more bountifully its material needs, displays great power in modifying the material environment, has more efficiency in its business and greater knowledge and control of external phenomena and processes, and is (as we shall see) conspicuously "worldly" in its culture patterns and aspirations. The second group is obliged to bridle many of its most urgent material needs; it displays much less external activity in transforming the material world; and in the heart of its integrated culture still remains predominantly Ideational, as is shown by its passivity and its religious, philosophical, mystical, moral, and aesthetic *Weltanschauung*. But it is backward in the knowledge of the material world, of material technique, of economics, and therefore far less able to control inorganic and organic material forces and processes than the first group. In spite of many gradations within each of these groups, the predominantly Ideational and Pseudo-Ideational character of most of the Oriental, especially the Hindu, and the conspicuously Sensate character of most of the contemporary Western societies, is indubitable and remains probably the fundamental difference between them.

II. LARGER CULTURAL SYSTEMS

Let us turn now to a more thorough examination of the types of culture mentality, selecting these not from among individuals and small groups, but largely from the vast and long-enduring psychosocial systems established by the great historical religions: Hinduism, Buddhism, Taoism, Jainism, Judaism, Christianity, Confucianism, and others. If it can be shown that these systems incorporate any one, or several, of the types of culture mentality differentiated in the preceding chapter, this would prove that those types, both as mental patterns and, in part, as systems of

[9] "It has been said that Greece and India were at opposite poles of the Aryan reaction to life. The Greek was devoted to life as reality and the Indian regarded life as illusion. With even greater truth such a distinction may be drawn between life as conceived by the American and the Indian respectively. The average American looks rather askance at the mental attitude of the average Indian. It savors to him too much of the impractical visionary. . . . In part it is due to the Indian disregard, through philosophic devotion to the Absolute, for what we call facts. Where so many are obsessed not with the phenomenal but with the ultimately real, we cannot expect much sense of chronology. Hence the Indian prefers to measure time by *Kalpas* of 4,320,000,000 mortal years rather than by decades and centuries." Herbert H. Gowen, *A History of Indian Literature* (New York, 1931), pp. 3–4.

conduct, are not artificial abstractions or products of imagination nor pathological exceptions, but abstractions based on living realities of immense magnitude and pertinent to the past as well as to the present.

I. SYSTEMS DOMINATED BY THE ASCETIC IDEATIONAL MENTALITY

A. *Hinduism (Brahmanism) and Buddhism.* Living in an age of a predominantly Sensate or Mixed type of culture mentality, we are prone to think that the Ascetic Ideational culture mentality is something rare, almost abnormal; and yet a brief survey of the mental patterns that have dominated and still dominate millions of human beings, that permeate the vastest systems of culture, shows that the Ascetic Ideational culture mentality comprises not an island but several of the largest continents in the world of culture. The systems of mentality of Hinduism, Buddhism, Jainism, Taoism, Sufism, early Christianity, and of many ascetic and mystical sects, groups, and movements (*i.e.*, the Cynics, Stoics, Gnostics, and the devotees of Orphism) have been predominantly Ideational, Ascetic Ideational at the highest level, Active Ideational on a lower, and Idealistic and Mixed on the lowest. All these systems set forth Ascetic Ideationalism as their sublime and supreme form; but, realizing that it is attainable only by the few, they admit for the mass of their adherents either the Active Ideational, or the Idealistic, or a Mixed mentality of a less Sensate sort.[10] In spite of this admission Ascetic Ideationalism remains

[10] Thus, for instance, in India thinkers often stress the principle of the *trivarga*, or "three-fold way of life." The first way is *dharma*, or "religious duty." It consists largely of the Ascetic and Active Ideational mentality and conduct. The second way is the *artha*, "the cult of the useful," which represents largely the Mixed type. And finally, there is the way of the *kāmā*, "the worship of the desirable," which results in the Active, and often Passive, Sensate mode of living. Often these different ways are prescribed for the same persons at different stages of their life: the stage of the student, of the householder (husband and father), of the forest dweller (when one retires to the jungles after the performance of the duties of husband and father).

For instance the manner of life prescribed for the householder is of a rather balanced Mixed type. Having finished his studentship, "let the regenerate man enter into the order of the householder, and, taking unto himself, with lawful ceremony, house, wife, and wealth, discharge, to the best of his ability, the duties of his station: satisfying the manes with funeral cakes; the gods with oblations; guests with hospitality; the sages with holy study; the progenitors of mankind with progeny . . . and all the world with words of truth."

Further on, his proper conduct is described in detail (how, whom, and when he is to marry, to eat, to work, and so on), and the whole character of this conduct is a balance between the Ideational and Sensate.

The same is true in regard to studentship. Beginning with the stage of hermit and ascetic, the Ideational form decidedly takes the upper hand and the Sensate form is reduced to almost nothing. (See a typical description of these stages and their duties in the *Vishnu Purānā*, III, ix–xii, trans. by H. H. Wilson (London, 1866), Vol. III, pp. 92–145. The same is given

the criterion of excellence for all the other mentalities. It decides their admissibility or nonadmissibility. It shapes and conditions them, controls them, permeates them, and thus the greater part of the culture mentality and, as we shall see, the actual culture dominated by these religious systems. If we consider that these systems of mentality have embraced, and still embrace, at least one-half of the human population of the world, we are forced to acknowledge the breadth and depth of their hold over human mind and human culture. We cannot, therefore, dismiss them as something "rare," "infrequent," "queer," "pathological," or as a mere survival of human ignorance, superstition, henceforth doomed to disappear forever.

The slightest acquaintance with these systems of mentality shows that their major premises and secondary, implied characteristics are exactly like those ascribed in the preceding chapter to the Ascetic Ideational type. It is not the task of this work to analyze in detail the history and the anatomy of each of these systems. I refer the reader who wishes further information in those directions to the works in the field. I confine myself to an outline of the essential characteristics and to a few quotations.

We shall begin with Hinduism (Brahmanism). Since Buddhism and Jainism are closely similar as far as their major premises are concerned, a somewhat more detailed exposition of the mentality of Hinduism-Brahmanism [11] will permit us to touch very briefly on the Buddhistic and Jainistic mentalities.

---

in the *Laws of Manu, Narada, Gautama*, and in other Brahmanic texts. The Ascetic "shall live without a fire, without a house, without pleasures, without protection. Remaining silent and uttering speech only on the occasion of the daily recitation of the Veda, begging so much food only in the villages as will sustain his life, he shall wander about, neither caring for this life nor for heaven." Progressing as the ascetic he subsequently "shall wander about, sustaining his life by roots, fruits, leaves, and grass. In the end he shall live on what has become detached spontaneously. Next he shall live on water, then on air, then on ether." (*Dharma-çastra* of Baudhāyana, quoted by Gowen, *op. cit.*, pp. 162–163.) Thus, not all are expected to have an ascetic mentality and conduct. In spite of this, however, in each of these stations the central idea — that the Ascetic Ideational mentality and conduct are the highest and the only forms having worth, goes through and through the whole culture, including its lower mentality forms. It characterizes the former and controls the latter.

[11] For the details of this system see the *Vedas*, the *Upanishads*, the *Vedantas*, the *Sacred Law Books*, of which the most important are translated in the volumes of *The Sacred Books of the East*, ed. by F. Max Müller (Oxford, 1884). See also F. Max Müller, *The Six Systems of Indian Philosophy* (New York, 1899); B. A. Keith, *A History of Sanskrit Literature* (Oxford, 1928); A. A. Macdonell, *A History of Sanskrit Literature* (New York, 1914); Z. J. Ragozin, *The Story of Vedic India* (New York, 1895); H. H. Gowen, *op. cit.;* E. J. Rapson (ed.), *The Cambridge History of India*, 3 vols. so far (Cambridge, 1922–28). These works contain bibliographies. Many other primary and secondary sources are quoted and mentioned elsewhere in the present work.

In all these systems ultimate reality is considered to be immaterial, hidden beyond the reach of the senses. It is Being, eternal and everlasting, having none of the properties of the sensate and material world. This note is struck in the *Rig-Veda* (x, 129) in the hymn of creation.

> Not being then existed not nor being . . .
> Death then existed not nor life immortal . . .
> Of neither night nor day was any token . . .
> By its inherent force the One breathed windless.
> No other thing than that beyond existed. . . .

It permeates practically all the texts of Hinduism and its philosophico-religious systems. All the six orthodox philosophies — the Mīmāmsa, the Vedānta, the Sāmkhya, the Yoga, the Vaiceshika, and the Nyāya — have this standpoint.[12] With variations it is reiterated in practically all the sources.

For example :

> This Universe is Brahma's self !
> He is Life-Intelligence pure !
> He is Truth and he is Light !
> His soul pervades the universe.
> He is the self within my heart . . .
> Smaller than the smallest seed,
> Greater than the earth and sky,
> Greater than all the worlds,
> Greater than the heaven on high.[13]

The following lines offer an even better formulation of the principle :

Beyond the senses there are the objects, beyond the objects there is the mind, beyond the mind there is the intellect, the Great Self is beyond the intellect. That Self is hidden in all beings and does not shine forth but it is seen by subtle seers. . . . It is not born, it dies not; it sprang from nothing; nothing sprang from it. The Ancient is unborn, eternal, everlasting. [It is] without sound, without touch, without form, without decay, without taste, eternal . . . without smell, beyond the great and unchangeable.[14]

---

[12] See F. M. Müller, *The Six Systems of Indian Philosophy.*

[13] From the *Chandogya Upanishad*, trans. by R. C. Dutt, in his *Lays of Ancient India* (London, 1894). See also the translation of G. F. Moore, in his *History of Religion* (New York, 1913), Vol. I, pp. 273–275.

[14] *The Upanishads*, pt. ii, third valli, 10–13 in *The Sacred Books of the East* (Oxford, 1884), Vol. XV. This philosophy of Being, with its sharp denial of reality of the sensate world, its insistence on the nonmaterial nature of the true reality (and the supreme value), its freedom from any association with physical phenomena, and so on, permeates all the classical works of Hinduism as well as of Buddhism. The Buddhist Nirvana is another name for the Great Self, or ultimate reality without beginning and end, without form, touch, smell, sound, or

Similarly, the true reality is described in all the Puránás under the different names of Brahma, Vishnu, and so on — all names having the same attributes, such as:[15] "the spirit"; "the support of all things"; "the smallest of the small; who is in all created things; the unchanged; imperishable; who is one with true wisdom; as truly known; eternal and incorrupt"; "who is the best of all things; the supreme soul, self-existent"; "who exist everywhere, and in whom all things here exist"; "of one essence, ever pure"; "durable"; "self-sustained, illimitable, un-decaying, and stable"; "devoid of sound or touch and possessing neither colour nor form; without beginning"; "imperceptible, inconceivable, indescribable"; "the cause of all things and without cause"; and so on.

The world of external sense perception is considered, therefore, to be unreal, unstable, transient, illusory — māyā. As A. A. Macdonell puts it :

The ultimate cause of all such false illusions [which take this illusory empirical world for reality] is *avidya*, or innate ignorance. It is this ignorance which prevents the soul from recognizing that the empirical world is mere māyā, or illusion. Thus to a Vedantist the universe is like a mirage, which the soul, under the influence of desire (*trishna*, or thirst) fancies it perceives. . . . The illusion vanishes as if by magic, when the scales fall from the eyes, on the acquisition of true knowledge. Then the semblance of any distinction between the soul and God disappears and salvation (*moksha*), the chief end of man, is attained.[16]

Such an illusion is not worth being cared for much. Only foolish men can prize it. "Wise men only, knowing the nature of what is immortal, do not look for anything here among things unstable." [17] Such wise men "care for nothing in this world." [18]

He whose conquest cannot be conquered again, into whose conquest no one in this world enters. He whom no desire with its snares and poisons can lead astray — is the Awakened, the Omniscient; even the gods envy him. . . . There is no satisfying lusts, even by a shower of gold pieces; he who knows that lusts have a short taste and cause pain, he is wise; he delights only in destruction of all desires.[19]

Only such men reach the Eternal, the Nirvana.

any other property of physical phenomena. See *Apastamba, The Vedanta Sutras*, the *Laws of Manu*, the *Institutes of Vishnu, Narada, Brihaspati*, in the same collection of *The Sacred Books of the East*, Vols. II, VII, XXXIII, XXXIV, and XXXVIII.

[15] *The Vishnu Puráná*, I, ii, and VI, v, trans. by H. H. Wilson, Vol. I (London, 1864), pp. 13 ff., and Vol. V (London, 1870), p. 211.

[16] A. A. Macdonell, *op. cit.*, p. 401. See also H. H. Gowen, *op. cit.*, chaps. viii–ix *et passim*.

[17] *The Upanishads*, pt. ii, fourth valli, 2.

[18] *The Dhammapada* (New York, n.d.), chap. i. This is one of the Buddhist classics.

[19] *Ibid.*, chap. xiv; see also chaps. xi, xv, *et passim*.

"Be not a friend of the [empirical] world!" [20]   In this world

All things hasten to decay and there is no permanency. . . . Everywhere I find old age, disease, and death. Therefore I search for the happiness of something that decays not, that never perishes, that never knows beginning, that looks with equal mind on enemy and friend, that needs not wealth, nor beauty, the happiness of one who finds repose alone in solitude . . . [with] all thoughts about the world destroyed.[21]

That holy man who stands immovable, as if erect upon a pinnacle, his appetites and organs all subdued, sated with knowledge, secular and sacred, to whom a lump of earth, a stone, or gold, to whom friends, relatives, or acquaintances, neutrals and enemies, the good and bad, are all alike, is called "one yoked with God,"

says the *Bhagavad-gītā*.[22]   Such a "way out" is found in giving up the whole empirical or sensate world, in separating oneself from it, from all its griefs, joys, and sensations; in "choking" their very source — sensations and perceptions — in looking at the world, even at oneself, as a mere dream to which one is not tied by anything, not by any bond, any empirical value, nor any desire. There is no other way out from griefs, sorrows, decay, death, and, likewise, no other way to eternal value and to immortality, because " body is fragile and before long, alas, it will lie in the earth, despised, without understanding, like a useless log." [23] Because any empirical joy is followed by sorrow, and the three greatest sorrows — old age, sickness, and death — are inescapable, "from pleasure comes grief; from pleasure comes fear; he who is free from pleasure knows neither grief, nor fear." [24]   Therefore, the way out, in one of the best formulations of Hindu and Buddhist principles, consists of giving up sensations themselves, even "self," because "they bring desire":

Contact [with the empirical world] is the cause of all sensations, producing the three kinds of pain or pleasure [of old age, sickness, and death].
Destroy contact, then will end sensation; destroy the six entrances [six organs of sense], then will contact cease; the six entrances all destroyed [not in physical sense, but in the sense of giving no value to what sense organs

[20] *Ibid.*, chap. xiii.
[21] Asvaghosha's *Bodhisattva*, trans. from the Sanskrit into Chinese in A.D. 420. Translated as the *Life of Buddha* into English by S. Beal (New York, n. d.), p. 319. This work, written by the most distinguished Buddhist Patriarch, is one of the best representatives of Buddhism and Hinduism.
[22] Trans. by M. Monier-Williams in his *Hinduism* (London, 1885), pp. 210–211.
[23] *The Dhammapada*, chap. iii; *Life of Buddha*, pp. 305 ff. *et passim*. See in the collection of *The Sacred Books of the East* all the volumes devoted to the Buddhist and Hindu texts.
[24] *The Dhammapada*, chap. xvi.

bring to "self" from the external world, and to sensual feelings that they give], from this, knowledge [empirical] ceases. Knowledge destroyed, names and things will cease; names and things destroyed, then knowledge perishes; ignorance [empirical knowledge is meant] destroyed, then the constituents of individual life will die.[25]

Such is the escape from individual self, from "I," and from the whole empirical world.

The restless busy nature of the [empirical] world, this I declare, says Buddha, is at the root of pain. Stop then the end by choking up the source. Desire not either life or its opposite. All is empty; neither "self" nor place for "self": but all the world like a phantasy.

Wealth, riches, self [empirical] all given up . . . I have no master; no honorable tribe, no point of excellence; self-taught in this profoundest doctrine I have arrived at superhuman wisdom.[26]

Such is the way that leads to Nirvana, and Nirvana itself is nothing but an absolute — superhuman, indeed — indifference to the whole empirical world of the senses, including not only our own body, but also our "self" with all its perceptions, sensations, memories, ideas, feelings, volitions, pains, and pleasures; our entire ego — anatomical, physiological, psychological, and social — in all its aspects. This means not only a mere minimization of all sensual needs and desires, but as close an approach to the extreme limit in the direction of their annihilation as one can imagine.

"A man who is free from desires and free from grief sees the majesty of nonempirical Self, by the Grace of the Creator." [27]   He is "freed from the jaws of death." [28]   "The man who knows the uncreated, who has cut all ties, removed all temptations, renounced all desires, he is the greatest of all men. . . .   There is no suffering for him who . . . abandoned grief, who has freed himself on all sides, and thrown off all [sensual] fetters." "The mind approaching the Eternal [Nirvana] has attained to the extinction of all desires." [29]   Such a man cannot be killed. Nothing can hurt him.

The Knowing Self is not born, it dies not. . . .   He is not killed [though the body is killed]. If the killer thinks he kills, if the killed thinks that he is killed, they do not understand: for this one does not kill, nor is that one killed.[30]

[25] *Life of Buddha*, pp. 375–378.
[26] *Ibid.*, pp. 397 and 380.
[27] *The Upanishads*, pt. ii, second valli, 20.
[28] *Ibid.*, pt. ii, third valli, 15.
[29] *The Dhammapada*, chaps. vi, vii, and xi.
[30] *The Upanishads*, pt. ii, second valli, 18–19.

As a solid rock is not shaken by the wind, wise people falter not amidst blame and praise.[31]

The reality of, and need for, adaptation to the empirical world (of any of the Sensate types) is definitely rejected as unreal and inferior and often ridiculed.

Long is a mile to him who is tired; long is a life to the foolish who do not know the true law. "This son belongs to me, and this wealth belongs to me" with such thoughts a fool is tormented. He himself does not belong himself: how much less sons and wealth?

He who lives looking for pleasures only, Mâra [the tempter] will certainly overthrow him.[32]

Look on this world as you would a bubble. Look upon it as you would upon a mirage; the king of death does not see him who thus looks down upon the world. . . . Come, look at this world, glittering like a royal chariot; the foolish are immersed in it, but the wise do not touch it.[33]

From the unreal lead me to the real; from darkness lead me to light; from death lead me to immortality.[34]

Sometimes this sarcasm and negative characterization of the Sensate world and of its values become in a sense poignantly realistic.

Foolishness has been the character of every king who has boasted: "All this earth is mine — everything is mine — it will be in my house forever": for he is dead. . . . They themselves are but foam upon the wave. Earth laughs at them. . . . Kings of great might, resistless valour and unbounded wealth . . . are now only a tale. All they have ceased, and all who are yet to come, will cease, to be.[35]

[31] *The Dhammapada*, chap. vi. All these principles are already given in the *Mahabharata* (about tenth century B.C.), especially in the *Bhagavad-gitā* or "*Divine Song*." See especially vi, 8 ff.; iii, 27; x, 19 ff.

[32] *The Dhammapada*, chaps. v and i. See, particularly, in Asvaghosha's *Life of Buddha*, his trials of various "ways out," or mentalities and forms of adaptation: physical tormenting of the body, and also the well-balanced adaptation of common sense taught to him by Bimbisara Raga. The latter said: Everything is to be taken sensibly, moderately, at the proper time and in the proper circumstances; when young, live and love and sow wild oats; "during middle life acquire wealth, and when old and all your abilities ripened, then is the time for the following the rules of religion"; and so on. This was the morality of most human beings. But Buddha rejects it without any hesitation, just as he rejects the method of tormenting the body as such, because it does not go beyond the sensate world, and so does not kill grief, sorrows, and self. Chaps. ii, iii, *et passim*.

[33] *The Dhammapada*, x, 27.

[34] *The Brihadaranyaka Upanishad*, I, iii, 28.

[35] *Vishnu Purâná*, Vol. IV, 237–242.

The empirical life believed by the foolish as reality turns out to be a cease-less chain of pains — bodily and mental. It begins with the embryo, which

exists surrounded by filth, floating in water, and distorted in its back, neck and bones . . . reposing amidst the slime of ordure and urine. . . .   Then comes the pain of birth. . . .   When the child is about to be born, its face is besmeared by excrement, urine, blood, mucus and semen. . . .   Thus born, the child is tortured in every limb. . . .   Unable to feel itself, unable to turn itself, it is dependent upon the will of others. . . .   [Later on] enveloped by the gloom of ignorance and internally bewildered, man knows not whence he is, who he is, whither he goes, nor what is his nature; what is cause, and what is not cause, what is right and what is wrong; what is virtue, what is vice. . . . When old age arrives, the body is infirm; the limbs are relaxed; the back is bowed; there is little appetite and little vigour; walking, rising, sleeping, sitting are all painful efforts, the ear is dull, eye is dim. . . .   [Then comes the agony of death.]   The body trembles; the man is exhausted.   The principle of selfishness afflicts him and he thinks: "What will become of my wealth, my lands, my children, my wife, my servants, my house?"   And when he "passes away" he has to undergo again the same sufferings in another body, being born again, if he does not reach Nirvana. . . .   Not in hell alone do the souls of the deceased undergo pain: there is no cessation, even in heaven. . . .   As long as he lives, he is immersed in manifold affliction. . . .   In acquiring, losing, and preserving wealth, there are many griefs; and so there are in the misfortunes of our friends. . . .   Whatever is most acceptable to man becomes a seed whence springs the tree of sorrow.[36]

Therefore, the way out is only in the engulfment by, and union with, the true ultimate reality.

All this is sufficient to show that the Hindu and Buddhist systems are dominated by what we have designated as the Ascetic Ideational culture type.[37]   The highest mentality of these systems contains these four elements.

(1) Ultimate reality is spiritual, toward which one must strive by throwing off the illusion of personality and by being absorbed in the Ultimate.

(2) Needs are purely spiritual.

[36] *Ibid.*, Vol. V, pp. 202 ff.; see also Vol. III, pp. 76 ff.

[37] This does not deny some variations in secondary matters, among various orthodox forms of Hindu thought and sects. For instance the Yoga system stresses much more physical self-mortification of the body with its detailed discipline for such a training ("restraints," "religious observances," "postures," "regulation of the breath," "restraint of the senses," "steadying of the mind," "contemplation," and "religious trance") than does the Vedanta system. Nevertheless these differences do not affect the essential similarity of these two systems.

(3) The extent of their satisfaction is maximal.

(4) The method of satisfaction consists in a complete mastery of all sensate needs, even to the point of the annihilation of their very source — that is, a complete modification (dissolution) of self, social, psychological, and biological.

More than that, we see also that the satellites with which this mentality is associated are exactly those which we have ascribed to the Ascetic Ideational type. From the above quotations (and the impression which they leave will only be strengthened by a more thorough knowledge of the systems of thought which they represent) it is evident that the main philosophy of Hinduism and Buddhism is that of Being, not of Becoming ; it develops in its followers a high ability to control the self ; its ideal of activity is entirely introvert, even to the point of advocating the relinquishing of sensations, contact with the external world, the disregard of the testimony of the "six entrances," and the assumption of a superhuman attitude of indifference to the whole external and material world. Of values it recognizes only the eternal, everlasting, and imperishable, rejecting all the transient and temporary as pseudo values. Likewise, its truth is not that of the senses, but is revealed in the mystic way, through intuition, meditation, and revelation. Its knowledge is, first and last, the sacred knowledge of the Vedas.[38] He who knows them is born a second time, such a spiritual birth being regarded as higher than the biological. Only such a man is exempted from the authority of the Yama (death) [39] — conquers it. The value of such a knowledge is unlimited even in the empirical sense.[40] Its truth is not relative ; it is

[38] "Science is declared to be a knowledge of the three Vedas, called Rig-Veda, Sama-Veda, and Yagur-Veda" : *Brihaspati*, xvi, 5. *The Sacred Books of the East* (Oxford, 1884), Vol. XXXIII. *Cf. Vishnu Puránâ*, VI, v (Vol. V, pp. 210 ff.).

[39] "Him [the teacher of the Vedas] he [the disciple] should never offend. For he causes him to be born [a second time] by imparting to him sacred learning. This second birth is the best. The father and the mother produce the body only." *Apastamba*, Pr. I, pat. i, kh. 1 : 13–18. See the same in the *Laws of Manu* and other laws. *The Sacred Books of the East* (Oxford, 1879), Vol. II.

[40] "A king and a Brahmana deeply versed in the Vedas, these two, uphold the moral order in the world. On them depends the existence of the fourfold human race [four main castes], of internally conscious beings, of those which move on foot and on wings, and those which creep." *Gautama*, viii, 1–2.

"The earth is upheld by the veracity of those who have subdued their passions and following righteous practices are never contaminated by desire, covetousness, and wrath." *Vishnu Puránâ*, III, xii (Vol. III, p. 144).

In complete harmony with this stands the division of Hindu literature into the *Çruti*, the "revealed literature," and *Smriti*, or "traditional literature." The first, embracing the *Vedas*, the *Upanishads*, the *Brahmanas*, and *Aranyakas*, is infinitely higher, more sacred, and more valuable than the *Smriti*, which in the form of various *Upa-vedas* and especially

absolute.   Absolute and eternal also are the moral and other values. They have nothing to do with relativistic and conditional utilitarianism, hedonism, positivism, eudaemonism, or any other empirical and transient values.   And all the events and phenomena of the empirical Sensate life and world are viewed and estimated from the standpoint of this transcendental Nirvana.

For the masses this highest form of mentality and conduct is impossible. Only those types which are closer to the Sensate can be achieved by them. Therefore, Hinduism and Buddhism provide another form of mentality and conduct which is identical in part with what I style Active Ideationalism, and in part with the Mixed.   These are the forms which are to be followed by ordinary human beings.   But even in them the relative values are judged by, and seriated in accordance with, the Ideational absolutes.   For the masses also is prescribed minimization of physical needs, avoidance to a considerable degree of sensate pleasures.   Thus, for instance, a student before he becomes "twice-born" through mastering the Sacred Learning, is admonished

not to look at the sun.   He shall avoid honey, meat, perfumes, garlands, sleep in the day-time, ointments, collyrium, a carriage, shoes, a parasol, love, anger, covetousness, perplexity, garrulity, playing musical instruments, bathing for pleasure, cleaning the teeth, elation, dancing, singing, calumny, and terror; to gaze at and to touch women; gambling, low service, to take things not offered, to injure animate beings, to make bitter speeches. . . .[41]

For the class of the "householder" the code is less severe, yet even he is required to abstain from many pleasures which would be regarded as proper in a normal Active Sensate society.   The positive scale of relative values shows the same tendency.   There follows one such scale.

---

the *Vedānyas*, deals with an empirical knowledge of the science of medicine and biology, of music, military science, architecture, the mechanical arts, grammar, poetry, law, etymology, astronomy, astrology, mathematics, physics, chemistry, etc.   While in our estimation these disciplines represent the only valuable knowledge, in the Hindu estimation they, though useful, in no way rival the *Çruti*.   Since the *Çruti* are revelation, it is comprehensible that they must not be changed in any part, line, word, syllable.   (The same is true of any revealed truth and literature in any system of beliefs.   This explains the wars and great social struggles because of a variation in one word or syllable, like *Filioque*, which led to the division of the Christian Church into the Eastern and Western; *Ucyc* and *Iucyc*, which led to a great schism in Russia in the seventeenth century; like the split of the Mohammedans into the faction of Sunnites and Shiites; like Monophysitic, Arian, and other schisms in the history of the first century of Christianity.)

[41] *Gautama*, ii, 12-19.   See also *Apastamba*, Pr. I, pat. i, kh. 2: 11-19; and the *Vishnu Purānā*, III, ix (Vol. III, pp. 92 ff.).

Wealth, relations, occupations, birth, learning, and age must be honoured; but each later named quality is more important than the preceding ones. But sacred learning is more important than all other qualities, because it is the root of the sacred law and because the Veda expressly declares it.[42]

This scale is diametrically opposed to that of the Sensate society!

The same inclination is seen in the ranking of various castes, in their prestige, and the prestige of spiritual and secular leaders. In the classical system of the four castes — Brahmans, Kshattriyas, Vaisýas, and Súdras — the Brahman caste is the highest of all.[43] Even the king is below them,[44] being only a Kshattriya; but the Brahman is the caste of priests and spiritual leaders. The rich man — his wealth — does not per se have any prestige; and the rich man is not even mentioned as a possible leader, nor wealth as value. "The king is the master of all, with the exception of Brâhmanas. He shall be holy in acts and speech. Fully instructed. Pure, of subdued senses. . . . All excepting Brâhmanas, shall worship him. . . ."[45] The Brahmanas do not yield the right of way to the king; on the contrary, the king should yield it to the Brahmanas.[46] Though the number of castes is now above three thousand, yet the superiority of the Brahmanas is still as indisputable as it has been for the last two thousand years: "In every scheme of grouping the Brahman heads the list," says one of the most competent investigators of the problem; and he is supported by all who have dealt with it.[47]

Thus, every characteristic of this system will find its counterpart among the traits of the Ascetic Ideational type or, in its milder mass form, among the traits of the Active Ideational and the Mixed types. This holds for the satellites as well as for the basic elements. More than this, later on

[42] *Gautama*, vi, 20–23. It is characteristic also that in the Vedas and the Brahmanas, except for Prajapati, the lord of creatures (eternal), the "gods appear to have become divine through acts of asceticism." (Gowen, *op. cit.* p. 99).

[43] See on this subject any of the "Sacred Laws": *Manu, Apastamba, Brihaspati, Narada, Institutes of Vishnu,* and any of the Sutras. Only in emergency is each of these three castes permitted to enter the occupations of the next lower caste. "In times of distress, the peculiar functions of the castes may be modified. A Brahman may follow the occupations of a Kshattriya or a Vaisýa; the Kshattriya may adopt those of the Vaisýa. But these two last should never descend to the functions of the Súdra." The *Vishnu Purâná,* III, viii (Vol. III, p. 90).

[44] *Gautama,* chap. xi.

[45] *Gautama,* chap. xi.

[46] *Apastamba,* Pr. II, pat. v, kh. 10 : 9–11.

[47] *The Imperial Gazetteer of India* (Oxford, 1907), Vol. I, p. 325. See also C. Bouglé, *Le régime des castes* (Paris, 1908), *passim; The Cambridge History of India,* ed. by E. J. Rapson, Vol. I, pp. 53 ff. *et passim;* M. Senart, *Les castes dans l'Inde* (Paris, 1896) — an English translation of this work has recently appeared; N. K. Dutt, *Origin and Growth of Caste in India* (London, 1931).

we shall see that many other minor traits associated with these abstract types of culture mentality (for instance, the nature of family relationships, personal liberty and restraint, forms of government, law, art) are to be found in the smaller groups and subsidiary systems of the Hindu-Buddhist culture, just as would logically be expected.

All this means that, at least as far as the culture mentalities involved in the Hindu-Buddhist systems are concerned, we have by an induction proved that the delineation of types in the preceding chapter is indeed no mere abstraction unrelated to, or distorting, empirical facts.

There is no time now for further details; yet, if the present writer presented here all the results of the analysis that he made, they would show clearly how even the smallest and most detailed traits of these systems (when Hinduism and Buddhism were purer, less "practical," and more enthusiastically believed in) fit their natures, and how the existence of these traits could be logically predicted if the nature of the dominant mentality were properly understood.

B. *Jainism.* What has been said of Hinduism and Buddhism also applies to Jainism. Founded by Parçva (about the sixth century B.C.), and remade by Vardhamaña Mahāvira (died *c.* 528 B.C.) about the time of the foundation of Buddhism, it was, like Buddhism, a reaction against Brahmanic Hinduism. Mahāvira, like Buddha, was the son of a noble warrior. He left home at the age of thirteen and became an ascetic, and after a period of thirteen years of ascetic training and practice reached "enlightenment and deliverance from the bonds of pleasures and pain." [48]

Jainism lays more stress than Hinduism and Buddhism on the torturing of the body and thus puts greater emphasis upon the physical aspect of the means to reach deliverance. The duties of a Jain are the same as those of a Brahman.

The duties of an ascetic consist in subduing his senses, withdrawal from worldly things and from communication with people . . . living in the forests,

---

[48] *The Cambridge History of India*, Vol. I, p. 159. The sixth century B.C. was exceedingly rich in religious and philosophical thought. It saw the emergence, or foundation, of Taoism, Confucianism, Buddhism, Jainism, of the Orphic-Pythagorean movement in Greece, of Zoroaster in Iran, of the Hebrew prophets, and of other religious, moral, and philosophical schools (at least sixty-three); and it probably has never been rivaled in fruitfulness and unique richness in this respect by any other century. In India it saw the revolt against Brahmanic Hinduism and the Vedas. Yet, as *The Cambridge History of India* rightly says (Vol. I, pp. 150–151), ". . . It is a strange characteristic of these sects that they adopted in their ascetic practices and in their whole mode of life the rules which had been already fixed by their Brahman antagonists." This is particularly true of Buddhism and Jainism.

cleanliness external and internal, abstinence from injury to living beings, and in sincerity, purity, freedom from envy, in kindness and patience.[49]

When these duties are fulfilled the Jain is entitled to part with the empirical world by self-starvation.

Jainism was originally merely a specialization and intensification of the old ascetic discipline. . . . So eager were the Jains to part with the world to the uttermost that many of their monks wore not a scrap of clothing. Twelve years of most severe asceticism were necessary for salvation. After that, if a monk did not wish to live, he was recommended to starve himself to death.[50]

The final goal is the same for the Jain as for the Brahman : Nirvana, kevala, or moksha; supreme and total enlightenment and absolute and everlasting deliverance from pain, sensate desires and values, and pleasure; "the complete and full, the unobstructed, unimpeded, infinite and supreme, best knowledge and intuition." [51]   In brief, Jainism in its pure form is a thoroughgoing example of our Ascetic Ideational type.

These principles, philosophies, and practices of Brahmanism, Buddhism, Jainism, extend throughout India, and not only in India of the ancient period, but in India of the Middle Ages and of the present; in India Brahmanic, Buddhistic, Jainistic, Mohammedan, Portuguese, and English.   They appear not only in its sacred literature, the *Çruti*, but also in the *Smriti, Vedantas, Puránás*, and the purely secular literature of India's greatest writers and thinkers.   They are found in the *Mahabharata* and *Ramayana* (whoever were their authors), in the works of Tiruvalluvara and Hemachandra (the greatest Jainist writer), in the dramas of the great writers like Bhāsa, Asvaghosha, Kālidāsa, and others, known and unknown; in other forms of supposedly secular literature of the Maurian, the Guptas, the slave king, the Mohammedan, the great Moghul periods.   Sometimes they appear directly, sometimes indirectly, now more, now less, but always the same in essentials.   Even the beast fables, like the *Panchatantra* and the *Hitopadeça*, besides presenting the more common morals of Mixed type, represent these principles as supreme. It is significant that, in the penetration of Mohammedanism into India, it is the Sufist, that is the ascetic, sect, which has had the best success.[52]

[49] *Ibid.*, Vol. I, p. 151.   See also H. Jacobi, "Jainism," in the *Encyclopedia of Religion and Ethics;*   H. H. Gowen, *op. cit.*, chap. xviii; M. S. Stevenson, *The Heart of Jainism* (Oxford, 1915); and especially *Achārāngā Sutra*, trans. by Jacobi, in *The Sacred Books of the East*, Vol. XXII; H. von Glasenapp, *Der Jainismus* (Berlin, 1925).

[50] J. N. Farquhar, *A Primer of Hinduism* (Oxford, 1912), p. 50.

[51] *The Cambridge History of India*, p. 159.

[52] See the works of Keith and Gowen; and Macdonell, *India's Past* (Oxford, 1927). In this sense in the history of Indian literature there is a "remarkable continuity, a continu-

C. *Taoism.* Another great system of culture mentality and conduct of the Ascetic Ideational type is represented by *Taoism* in its pure form. (It was supposedly founded by Lao-tse, born *c.* 604 B.C.) Like many other religious or moral systems, it has its highest forms which are within reach of only a few, and more "practical" forms accessible to the masses. In the latter forms the extremely pure are mixed with other, more earthly, and more sensate elements, and therefore the resulting mentality types on these levels are either Active Ideational [53] or Mixed. But even such forms, just as in the case of "practical" Hinduism and Buddhism, bear the marks of the purer Ascetic Ideational nature of the system as a whole. In this sense the Taoist is not only an Ideational system of thought and conduct, but also to some extent a formula of the actual culture and conduct of millions of men who have been affected by it.

The reader is referred to the Taoist system itself for details and characteristics not discussed here.[54] I confine myself to quoting a few lines from its teachings, which should be sufficient to show its connection with our Ascetic Ideational type.

The Taoist philosophy of Being (*Sein*), its stress on the eternal and permanent values, its control and minimization of sensate needs, and all its other traits are essentially similar to the Hindu-Buddhist, and to the characteristics of our Ascetic Ideational type.

There was something, undifferentiated and yet perfect, before heaven and earth came into being. So still, so incorporeal! It alone abides and changes not. It pervades all, but is not endangered. It may be regarded as the mother of all things. I know not its name: if I must designate it I call it Tao. Striving to give it a name, I call it great; great I call it transcending; transcending I call it far off; far off I call it returning. . . . Man takes its norm from earth; earth from heaven; heaven from Tao; the Tao from itself.[55]

---

ity unbroken, however much it has been modified, by an unexampled succession of native and foreign dynasties, from the days of the invading Aryans . . . to the present time." (Gowen, *op. cit.*, p. 9.) As we shall see, there were opposite currents of mentality — materialistic and Sensate — but they always were minor rivulets, even in the periods of their greatest success.

[53] Like the great Active Ideationalists of Christianity, the Taoist "furnished China with the most redoubtable chiefs of sects, with the most skillful politicians, with the most subtle dialecticians, the profoundest philosophers, and with the best writers." M. Granet, *La pensée chinoise* (Paris, 1934), p. 502.

[54] See M. Granet, *op. cit.*, pp. 501–551 (this brilliant interpretation suffers somewhat from an overemphasis on the positive and corporeal qualities of Taoism); H. A. Giles, *Religion of Ancient China* (London, 1905) and *Confucianism and Its Rivals* (London, 1915); P. L. Wieger, *Les pères du système taoïste* (Hien-hien, 1913); H. Maspero, *Le saint et la vie mystique chez Lao-Tseu et Tchouang-Tseu* (Paris, 1922).

[55] *Tao-Teh-King*, 6. The Texts of Taoism, in *The Sacred Books of the East*, Vol. XL; "The Classic of Purity," chap. 1, 3–5.

In this quotation are embraced, in brief, almost all the essential premises and satellites of the Ascetic Ideational form of adaptation. The nature of this adaptation will become clearer still from the following passages.

The mind of man loves stillness, but his desires draw it away. The reason why men are not able to attain to this is because their minds have not been cleansed and their desires have not been sent away. When no desire any longer arises, there is the true stillness and rest. In constant stillness there is the constant purity and rest.[56]

In order to achieve such a spiritual state, one should reject "the world of men" outside of the self, "the whole external reality," and finally the very idea of "existence" and "self." Then one enters the realm of "the diffuse light" where, "past and the present being annulled," "there is neither life nor death." "Banishing audition and vision, separating from every corporeal appearance, and eliminating every science, one enters a union with what permeates everything and all (ta t'ong) and what gives its continuity to the Universe (T'ien kiun)." [57]

As we see, "the way" is familiar: it consists of dismissing all desires and giving up the sensate world and its values. However, instead of "giving up" Taoism uses another term, namely "inaction," or nondoing, not making any effort to obtain any value of the empirical world, or performing any action to change it, to improve it, and so on. In essence the "inaction" of Taoism is similar to the "giving up" of Hinduism and Buddhism, and to the suppression of bodily desires of Jainism.

I consider doing nothing to obtain it [enjoyment] to be the great enjoyment. Heaven does nothing, and thence comes its serenity. Earth does nothing, and thence comes its rest. All things in all their variety grow from this inaction.[58]

Therefore, "the wise man will have no desires or ambitions, no aims, no purposeful and energetic activities: then everything will go right of itself." [59] Hence the maxim: "Doing nothing is better than to be busy doing nothing." Hence, also, the most radical laissez faire in governmental and social relationships which has ever been formulated, and such maxims as "the best government is that which governs the least," "a social reformer is the most impractical of men," or —

---

[56] The Texts of Taoism, in The Sacred Books of the East, Vol. XL, pp. 251–252.
[57] Giles, op. cit., Vol. I, pp. 245 and 257; Vol. II, p. 83. Granet, op. cit., pp. 530–531.
[58] "The Writings of Kwang-Zse," in The Sacred Books of the East, Vol. XL, pp. 3–4.
[59] G. F. Moore, History of Religions (New York, 1913), chap. iii, p. 52.

The more restrictions and prohibitions are in the empire, the poorer grow the people.   The more weapons the people have, the more troubled is the state.   The more there is cunning and skill, the more startling events will happen.   The more mandates and laws are enacted, the more there will be thieves and robbers.   Therefore the holy man says: I practice nonassertion, and the people of themselves reform.   I love quietude, and the peoples of themselves become righteous.   I use no diplomacy, and the people of themselves become rich.   I have no desire, and the people of themselves remain simple.[60]

In perfect logical conformity with the major premises of Taoism we find all the other characteristics of the Ideational mentality in it.   It holds as worthless all knowledge derived through the organs of sense. "Wise men are never scholars and scholars are never wise men," and "Vomit thy intelligence," says Kwang-tze, the other founder of Taoism.[61] Every sensation is corruptible; every dogma is misleading.   Only deep meditation and mystical ecstasy put one in contact with reality.   Hence its doctrines of silence, retreat into self, obscurity, and others of its teachings with reference to the theory of knowledge and wisdom.

Approach!   I am going to tell what is the Tao supreme [tche Tao].   Retreat! Retreat!   Obscurity!   Obscurity!   That is the apogee of the supreme Tao! Crepuscule, crepuscule, silence, silence: don't see anything, don't listen to anything. . . .   Conserve quietude, conserve thy essence: thou wilt enjoy long life!   Let thine eyes see nothing!   Let thine ears hear nothing!   Thy heart knows nothing!   Guard thine inner [self], close thyself to the external world: to know too many things is harmful.[62]

Don't talk!   Express yourself without talking!   He talks his whole life who says nothing!   He who talks does not say; he who says does not talk![63]

The real sage listens with his eyes and sees with his ears.

Do not cross thy door and thou shalt know the empire!   Do not look in the window; and the celestial Tao will appear to thee.

Hence Taoism's command: to empty one's mind of empirical knowledge, and its disapproval of popular education (the wise ruler "empties the people's mind").   "Forgetting in his immobility all that is but conventional knowledge, he purifies his heart of all false desires and all temptations invented by society."[64]   Hence its contempt of all the worldly

---

[60] Lao-tse's Canon of Reason and Virtue, 9, in the translation of W. S. A. Pott, *Chinese Political Philosophy* (New York, 1925), p. 106.

[61] See P. L. Wieger, *op. cit.*, p. 289.

[62] *Ibid.*, p. 287.

[63] H. A. Giles, *op. cit.*, Vol. II, pp. 143 and 100.

[64] *Ibid.*, p. 89.

values, including those related to kings and governments. "It is an axiom for the Taoists that a prince does not differ from a brigand." [65] Hence its antiutilitarian ethics. Sanctity or "Efficacy is exactly the opposite of the profane utility." [66] In conformity with the major premises is its stress upon the Total, Whole, Unity, in contradistinction to the Part, Detail, Congeries; its disapprobation of fighting, war, punishment; its sarcastic remarks about all earthly values (knowledge, justice, benevolence, prudence, righteousness, filial piety, morals, virtue, etc.); and its mottoes: "Recompense injury with kindness," and "To those who are good I am good, and to those who are not good, I am also good, and thus all gets to be good."

For a person who sees reality in what is designated as Tao, all the values in this reality are different from those in the reality of our sense-organs, and all the phenomena of this Sensate world become accordingly small and unimportant. From such a transcendental point of view,[67] all the agitation, all pains and pleasures, positive and negative values, and the rest of the phenomena of this world, become insignificant. One can assume toward them the attitude of inaction, the more so because this attitude is nearer to the nature of the ultimate reality and the supreme value.

The Taoism of the masses, naturally, is on a much lower level and presents combinations of specific forms of the Mixed mentality.

D. *Sufism.* In Mohammedanism the Sufist sect is a further example of the Ascetic Ideational mentality. This will appear from several quotations.

"Sufism is the renunciation of all selfish pleasures." This renunciation is of two kinds: formal and essential. For example, if one renounces a pleasure, and finds pleasure in the renunciation, this is formal renunciation; but if the pleasure renounces him, then the pleasure is annihilated, and this case falls

---

[65] Granet, *op. cit.*, p. 549.

[66] *Ibid.*, p. 545.

[67] M. Granet stresses the fact that "the wisdom of Taoism is of a mystical tendency" but has nothing to do either with spiritualism, or transcendentalism, or God, or soul. He prefers to style it as "a sort of naturalistic quietism." (*Ibid.*, pp. 519 and 586–591.) It is quite unimportant what terms we use in a shorthand characterization of the system. What is important for my purposes is that Taoism has all the earmarks of the Ideational mentality. Whether we style it "transcendental" or "naturalistic" is a secondary matter. Anyhow if it is naturalistic quietism, its naturalism has nothing common with the nature and naturalism of our organs of sense; its quietism has nothing to do with sensory "relaxation," "rest," and "being quiet." It is almost all supersensory, as fully supersensory as has been true of perhaps any real mystical current of mentality that has had historical existence. And this is excellently shown by M. Granet himself in his factual characterization of Taoism.

under the head of true contemplation (mushahabat).   Therefore renunciation of pleasure is the act of Man, but annihilation of pleasure is the act of God. The act of Man is formal and metaphorical, while the act of God is real.[68]

All the Shaykhs of this Path are agreed that when a man has escaped from the captivity of "stations" (maqamat), and gets rid of the impurity of "states" (ahwal), and is liberated from the abode of change and decay, and becomes endowed with all praiseworthy qualities, he is disjoined from all qualities. That is to say, he is not held in bondage by any praiseworthy quality of his own, nor does he regard it, nor is he made self-conceited thereby.   His state is hidden from the perception of intelligences, and his existence has no cause. And when he arrives at this degree, he becomes annihilated (fani) in this world and in the next, and is made divine (rabbani) in the disappearance of humanity; and gold and earth are the same in his eyes, and the ordinances which others find hard to keep become easy to him.

"Sufi is he that has nothing in his possession nor is himself possessed by anything."   This denotes the essence of annihilation (fana), since one whose qualities are annihilated neither possesses nor is possessed, in as much as the term "possession" can properly be applied only to existent things.   The meaning is that the Sufi does not make his own any good of this world or any glory of the next world, for he is not even in the possession and control of himself: he refrains from desiring authority over others that others may not desire submission from him.   This saying refers to a mystery of the Sufis which they call "complete annihilation" (fana-yi kulli).[69]

E. *Early and Ascetic Christianity and Other Ascetic Mystic Groups.* To the Ascetic Ideational type belong many branches of the Graeco-Roman currents of mentality: some Orphics, Cynics, Stoics, Gnostics, and Mystics; early and Monastic Christianity ("My Kingdom is not of this world"); and a great number of ascetic and mystical systems which in one way or another have existed, during all historical periods, among various peoples (many primitive tribes not excluded)[70] in various countries and under the most different names.

[68] Ali B. Utham Al-Jullabi Al-Hujwiri, *The Kashf Al-Mahjub, The Oldest Persian Treatise on Sufism*, E. J. W. Gibb Memorial Series (London, 1911), Vol. XVII, p. 327.

[69] *Ibid.*, pp. 24–25 and 33–37.

[70] Though the culture mentality of many preliterate peoples is little known, and is not always notably integrated logically, in a number of cases it is possible to discern the character of the dominant culture mentality among them.   For instance, the dominant type of the Zuñi culture mentality belongs clearly to the Ideational, partly Ascetic, partly Active, while that of either the Dobu, or the Trobriands, is much more Sensate and generally much less integrated logically.   In almost all "primitive cultures" there are present the elements of the Ideational mentality mostly in a poorly integrated form.   On this point see the subsequent parts of the present work.

As Graeco-Roman Ascetic and kindred systems,[71] and also Christianity, will be discussed in some detail in Volume Two, discussion of them is omitted here.   As to the numerous other groups whose mentalities belong to, or at least approach, the Ascetic Ideational type, it is possible to say, in general, that they are essentially the same, whether they are affiliated with Hindu, Buddhist, Jainist, Christian, Mohammedan, Puritan, Hebrew, or any other religion or group.   Taking all this into consideration and also the fact that this work is not a monograph about such groups, it is unnecessary for us to enter into detailed discussion of the traits and history of all these sects.   It will be enough to state emphatically their connection with the Ascetic Ideational type.   The truth of this can be tested by consulting any serious study of mysticism or asceticism by any competent investigator.   For example, we read in one of the best studies of mysticism :

The end which the mystic sets before him is conscious union with a living Absolute. . . .   He enjoys a certain contact of the soul with the Divinity; and it is God himself [or Eternity, or Nirvana, or the Absolute, or the Ultimate Reality, or the Godhead, etc.; the name may differ] who is then felt and tasted.

Such a person steps over the boundary line from the empirical or sensual world into the world of the Absolute Reality.

Its [mysticism's] aims are wholly transcendental and spiritual.   It is in no way concerned with adding to, exploring, rearranging, or improving anything in the visible universe.   The mystic brushes aside that universe even in its supernormal manifestations.   Though he does not neglect his duty to the many, his heart is always set upon the changeless One. . . .   This one is for the mystic, not merely reality of all that is, but also a living and personal Object of Love. . . .

Living union with this One is a definite state of form of enhanced life.   It is obtained neither from an intellectual realization of its delights, nor from the most acute emotional longing. . . .   It is arrived at by an arduous psychological and spiritual process — the so-called Mystic Way — entailing the complete remaking of character and the liberation of the new, or rather latent, form of consciousness [ecstasy, etc.]. . . .   Mysticism is not [only] an opinion; it is not [only] a philosophy.   It has nothing in common with the pursuit of occult

[71] On this subject see A. O. Lovejoy and G. Boas, *A Documentary History of Primitivism and Related Ideas* (Baltimore, 1935), Vol. I, where are given excerpts from the works of the Greek and the Roman "Primitivists."   Unfortunately under this name the authors include a large number of heterogeneous, and sometimes quite opposite, types of mentality.   Therefore, not all the "Primitivists" belong to the Ascetic Ideational type; however, a part are certainly of this type.   By a glance at the excerpts it is easy to see who of the Stoics, the Cynics, and other partisans of "self-sufficiency" are, and who are not, Ascetic Ideationalists.

knowledge. . . . It is the name of that organic process which involves the perfect consummation of the Love of God. . . . It is the art of establishing man's conscious relation with the Absolute.[72]

This, one can see, is practically identical with our definition of the Ascetic Ideational type. The study of the phenomena of mysticism will bring further conviction that, regardless of time or place, whether under the cloak of this or that religion or independently of any religion, or among the people of this or that race, or among the well educated or the uneducated, its essential forms, including the Mystic Way itself (with its stages of the Awakening of Self or Consciousness of Divine Reality, of Purification, of Illumination, of "Mystic Death," and of the Union with the Absolute Reality, or Nirvana)[73] are always and everywhere similar in their essential traits.

Whether it happened to Buddha, or Zoroaster, or Mahāvira, or Mohammed, or Christ, or St. Paul, or St. Augustine, or St. Francis of Assisi, or St. Ignatius, or Catherine of Genoa, or Pascal, or Master Eckhart, or St. John of the Cross, or George Fox, or other mystics of more recent time, the mystical experience has always followed the same path. The First Awakening is in essence the same for all and often comes abruptly.[74] After the First Awakening follows the stage of Purgation,

[72] Evelyn Underhill, *Mysticism, A Study in the Nature and Development of Man's Spiritual Consciousness* (London, 1931), pp. 73–81. See also W. James, *The Varieties of Religious Experience* (36th impression, New York, 1928), pp. 379–429; H. Silberer, *Problems of Mysticism and Its Symbolism* (New York, 1917); J. H. Leuba, *The Psychology of Religious Mysticism* (London, 1925); S. Dasgupta, *Hindu Mysticism* (Chicago, 1927); C. A. Bennett, *A Philosophical Study of Mysticism* (New Haven, 1923); E. A. Peers, *Spanish Mysticism* (New York, 1924); D. Knowles, *The English Mystics* (London, 1927); D. E. C. Butler, *Western Mysticism* (New York, 1933); and A. D. Nock, *Conversion* (Oxford, 1933); G. Quercy, *L'hallucination* (Paris, 1930), Vol. I, pp. 183 ff. and chaps. xxv–xxviii.

[73] For the details of the Mystic Way see Underhill, *op. cit.*, pp. 169 ff.

[74] Such an Awakening (or conversion) is well illustrated by the case of Pascal, one of the greatest scientists, who on receiving a sudden vision of a blazing cross and experiencing at the same time a new sensation, exclaims: "Not the God of philosophers and scholars! Joie, joie, pleurs de joie! Renunciation totale et douce!" F. von Hügel's *The Mystical Element of Religion as Studied in Saint Catherine of Genoa and Her Friends* (London, 1909), Vol. I, pp. 97–200, gives another good illustration in the conversion of St. Catherine. Having acquired a profound disgust for worldly things, she earnestly desired to become one with God; but to choose God meant a total renunciation of self. This, though she would, she could not accomplish. Then one day, during a confession, she experienced a sudden Awakening and kept crying within herself, "No more world; no more sins!" See other examples in Nock, *op. cit.* Starbuck, *The Psychology of Religion* (London, 1899), pp. 137–144, 262, 385, and 117 ff., distinguishes between two types of conversion: *the volitional type*, distinguished by the gradual building up, piece by piece, of a new set of moral and spiritual habits, and the *type by self-surrender*, sudden and instantaneous. (See also James, *op. cit.*, pp. 205–258.) But even in the volitional type, according to Starbuck, there are always critical points

in which "the self" attempts by discipline and mortification to eliminate its sensate nature completely — a very painful and difficult process.[75] It is the final self-stripping, the casting off of all material, immaterial, and finite things. Then comes Illumination, the stage of detachment from the whole empirical world and indifference toward all its temptations and values, and at the same time of contact with the Divine Reality. It is usually followed by a stage of final and complete purification and deliverance from the ties of the empirical world — the most terrible, most painful, and most trying of all the stages of the Mystic Way. Doubts, despair, the profound loneliness of one who has cut the ties of the world

---

at which the process seems much more rapid, and even in the most voluntarily built-up sort of regeneration (conversion or Awakening) there are passages where self-surrender becomes indispensable. Therefore, whatever the factors leading to it, the final phenomenon must be self-surrender. This self-surrender from the standpoint developed here is identical with the Mystical Awakening, and therefore may be said to occur always abruptly. The First Awakening may thus be considered as the climax in the conversion process. Thus we have no quarrel with those who see conversion as a gradual development, e.g., J. B. Pratt, *The Religious Consciousness* (New York, 1927), pp. 122–164. All we claim is that the turning point in conversion occurs unexpectedly and abruptly. The attitude taken here is supported, aside from the cases already mentioned and discussed and from the well-known conversions of Bunyan and Brainerd, by more than a hundred conversions mentioned by Mrs. Burr, *Religious Confessions and Confessants* (Boston, 1914), pp. 250–262, and particularly well exemplified by the unmistakable abruptness of Awakening in the conversions of Ramakrishna (Max Müller, *The Life and Sayings of Ramakrishna* (New York, 1899), p. 36), and of Chaitanya (see Professor J. Sarkar's trans. of the *Chaitanya-charit-amrita*, Calcutta, 1913). The following excerpts offer an example of such a surrender to the True Reality and renunciation of the world of the senses: "Man was created for this end, to praise and reverence the Lord, his God; so serving Him, as at length to be saved. The other things on the earth . . . are to be used, or to be abstained from, in reference to this end. All created things which are subject to us, should be indifferent to us. We ought not to seek health rather than sickness, not to prefer riches to poverty, nor honour to contempt, nor a long life to a short one. These things only must be chosen and desired, which lead to this end." "Receive, O Lord, my whole liberty; receive all my memory, intellect, and will. Thou hast given me whatever I have or possess; all I restore entirely to Thee, and I deliver it wholly to be governed by Thy will. Give me Thy love with Thy grace, and I am sufficiently rich; nor do I demand anything more." S. Ignatius Loyola, *Spiritual Exercises, The Foundation*, ed. by O. Shipley (London, 1870), pp. 15 and 39.

[75] It is to be noted that almost all the founders of great religions and the greatest educators of mankind underwent this experience, in the form of isolation from men and from the world, in the form of the mortification of their bodies, as well as through long and persistent self-discipline. Likewise in all ascetic and mystical movements and systems there is usually a special technique, sometimes highly developed, for this purpose. See, for example, the Brahmanic Yoga technique of conquering the lower self and freeing the transcendental self for fellowship with God, with its eight divisions of: *yama*, or "restraint"; *myama*, or "religious observances"; *asana*, or "postures"; *pranāyāma*, or "regulation of the breath"; *pratyāhāsa*, or "restraint of the senses"; *dhārana*, or "steadying of the mind"; *dhyāma*, or "contemplation"; *samādhi*, or "religious trance." There are similar techniques for other rationally (or irrationally) organized sects.

of the senses and does not yet feel the tie with the Ultimate Reality, accompany this spiritual torment where the "self now surrenders itself, its individuality, and its will completely. It desires nothing, asks nothing; is utterly passive." [76] Then, for those who pass successfully this stage of the "Mystic Death," comes the final stage of Union with the Divine Reality, Nirvana, where "the state of Absolute Life is not merely perceived and enjoyed by the self, as in illumination; but it is One with it.   It is the state of purely spiritual life characterized by peaceful joy, by enhanced powers, by intense certainty."   This is the state of Nirvana, of oneness with the Absolute, Everlasting, Divine, Final, and Infinite Value.   For those who have attained this stage, all the empirical world and its values are just illusion, no more.   Empirical knowledge and science are foolishness: witness St. Paul's "Wisdom of this world is foolishness with God"; all of St. Augustine's sarcasm over science; the *"Credo quia absurdum"* of Tertullian; Lao-tse's "Wise men are never scholars, and scholars are never wise men"; the belief among people of this sort in the superiority of Revelation over science in general.   On gaining this stage, the mystic reaches — or feels that he has reached — the world of Absolute Being, Absolute Certainty, and Absolute Value, and passes away from the world of Becoming and Relativity.

The discussion should by now have made clear all the essential traits, and also have shed some light on the profound, almost unfathomable, depths of the Ascetic Ideational mentality.   It should also have shown that this mentality is not a curious pathological or exceedingly rare case, but a form set forth and endorsed by, and incorporated in, the ideologies and practices of most of the world religions of the past and present and by innumerable smaller groups and sects, in comparison with which all the rationalistic, positivistic, scientific, intellectual, Sensate ideologies that have had historical existence are, in their diffusion and influence, as a flickering candlelight to the sun.   In other words, contrary to the opinion of most of the contemporary scholars and scientists, who are inclined to underestimate the role played by this mentality, it has been one of the most widespread, one of the most persistent, one of the most influential; it has played a major part in the vastest cultural systems that have shaped and conditioned the minds of hundreds of millions of human beings.   No scholar who studies the psychosocial reality, as it is, can ignore or pass by this form of mentality and culture.

Of course, the modern scholar who knows all the tittle-tattle and jargon

[76] Underhill, *op. cit.*, pp. 170 ff.

of the most "popular" texts — "stimulus-response," "environment-individual," "adjustment," "maladjustment," "lag," etc., is likely to say, "Well, perhaps the form does exist, and is well diffused; but it is a pathological form, and the place for its followers is the hospital for mental diseases." Very likely he would add, especially if he has taken one or two elementary courses in psychiatry for nurses and medical social workers, the name of the disease which he happens to remember from his "training." [77]

The answer to such a "scholar" is this: It is unimportant whether this form of mentality is pathological or not; it is also unimportant where the bearers of such a mentality should be placed. What is important is that such a form exists and this is all that is relevant to science. To this, perhaps, one can add that the place for Buddha, Lao-tse, Jesus Christ, St. Paul, Zoroaster, St. Augustine, Mohammed, St. Francis, St. Ignatius, Pascal, and many such individuals ought perhaps to have been a mental hospital; but since they were able to carry with them a large portion of mankind, our scholar would have found difficulty in putting them there. It is an old story that a Lilliputian finds all giants abnormally pathological!

The attitude of such a scholar is not the attitude of a real scientist. It is the pseudo science of one who judges by his own premises the logical nature of systems of mentality built on quite different premises. He shall not complain, therefore, when the partisans of these different systems style him also as a "fool."

II. THE ACTIVE IDEATIONAL CULTURE MENTALITY

This as well as the other remaining forms of mentality are generally better known than the Ascetic Ideational; therefore, I shall be briefer in giving concrete illustrations of each of them and in indicating the great

[77] This attitude was capitalized during the so-called "Next Friend's Suit," in which George Glover, son of Mary Baker Eddy, asked for the appointment of a receiver for her affairs. Representing Glover's interests in this trial at the Superior Court at Concord, Senator Chandler, in opening his plea, spoke thus of Mary Baker Eddy: "She was . . . suffering from systematized delusions and dementia. The first one is the delusion — fundamental, widespread, and deep rooted — of the nonexistence and nonreality of the physical universe, organic and inorganic. All her delusions are built upon this fundamental delusion, and they are systematized so that they are a part of her whole being. They are built upon and about a single insane delusion as to the nonexistence of the reality of the physical universe. . . . The world is known to astronomers, geologists, physicians, chemists, naturalists, and to the lawmakers of the country. Mrs. Eddy, controlled by her delusion, believes that the world is neither real nor existent!" Stefan Zweig, *Mental Healers: Franz Anton Mesmer, Mary Baker Eddy, Sigmund Freud*, English trans. by Eden and Cedar Paul (New York, 1932), p. 237.

organizations, systems, and agencies which incorporate, endorse, and practice these forms.

Beyond the behavior of individuals and small groups, the Active Ideational mentality is found in the great systems which spring to life from the Ascetic Ideational point of view. In a way it is the tragic and immanent destiny of the Ascetic Ideational culture system to turn into the Active Ideational. As soon as the Ascetic initiators attract the attention of other men, they begin to acquire followers. As the number of followers increases, an organization appears; and with it the pure Ascetic attitude — the attitude of complete indifference toward, and non-interference in, the affairs of the empirical world — becomes impossible. An "organization" or an "institution" is a phenomenon of this world. It requires management, direction, guidance, and the administration of many needs and relationships which are purely empirical. Thus, any Ascetic current, as soon as it grows in influence, becomes an organization; as soon as it becomes an organization, it necessarily becomes more and more Active Ideational; and the more Active, the more rapidly it grows. Such is the inevitable chain of transformation. Change comes also because it is impossible for large masses of the followers of an Ideational system to attain to, and remain upon, the high ground of Ascetic Ideationalism. Therefore, the transformation of the isolated Ascetic rivulets into a broad river is inevitably followed by the transformation of the Ascetic into the Active Ideational. But even at this stage there will remain within the organization a few who continue to follow the Ascetic point of view in contrast to the now Active Ideationalism of the majority. Such is the chain of destiny or "immanent causation."

One can see this in a great many cases. As soon as Brahmanism, or Buddhism, or Jainism, or Christianity, or Taoism, or, to take smaller groups, St. Francis of Assisi, or other hermits and ascetics, began to attract followers an organization appeared. Immediately the empirical world with its needs, affairs, relationships, pains and pleasures, sorrows and joys, poverty and property, sympathies and antipathies, became involved, and made pure Ascetic Ideationalism impossible for most members of the organization, and for the organization itself. The only form possible at this stage, when the moral powers of the current are still very strong and the demoralization of the stage of decay is as yet absent, is the Active Ideational. It stands for constitutions, rules, laws, and by-laws; often for empirical punishments and rewards, promotions and demotions, praise and blame; for the appearance of rulers and the ruled; in brief, for an organized network designed to enforce empirically the moral standard of life among the members of the organization as well as among outsiders. "The salvation of one's own soul turns into the salvation of the souls of others." The transcendental and the other worldly phenomena return to the empirical world and are more and more entangled by it.

Read from this standpoint the history of the growth of Brahmanism, Buddhism, Christianity, or Taoism, or of a religious order or center, or of a settlement which grew about some hermit or ascetic, or of many a minor current of mysticism. Everywhere you will find this transformation from Ascetic to Active Ideationalism. When we read about the activities of St. Paul, the great organizer of Christianity, we notice at once (from his Epistles) how he had to busy himself with worldly matters, and how the empirical world caught him more and more in its web. He had to give instructions to the brethren about this and that, censure them for some things, warn them of others, prohibit some activities, encourage others; and most of the matters in which his flock involved him, from riots and politics to property and wealth, were of this world. In the Acts of the Apostles we read that even in the earliest Christian community in Jerusalem its members were required to "pool" all their property, and when Ananias or other members did not do this, punishment, even capital punishment, at once made its entry into this supposedly Ascetic Ideational group. And the more Christianity grew, the more this transformation progressed. It is true that the Ascetic aspect remained very strong during the earliest centuries of its history; but its Active aspect grew rapidly, especially from the time of its legalization (after A.D. 313 and 321). More and more Christianity had to enter into world affairs, and into affairs for the salvation of mankind as a whole. Up to the time of its demoralization, when it temporarily weakened and its Active Ideational form began to be contaminated with various Sensate forms, the Christian organization remained (until the fourteenth century approximately) predominantly Active Ideational, the Sensate, Idealistic mentalities being minor currents.[78]

The following quotations from the letters of Pope Gregory VII show concretely the nature, and the inevitability, of this Active Ideational mentality into which the Church was driven from Ascetic Ideationalism.

[78] On a smaller scale the same is shown by history of many monasteries and orders. Most of them, in Egypt, Syria, or Europe, were "founded" by hermits and ascetics who did not want to found any organization. The Mount Athos monastic community may serve as an illustration. It grew around hermits and ascetics. The eremitical type of mentality conduct was there first, the organized "cenobitic" and "idiorhythmic" subsequently. See the cited works of Lake and Choukas.

Like all the great administrators of the Christian Church, and regardless of whether he wanted it or not, Gregory had to spend most of his energy in settling affairs of a worldly nature, trying to bring them nearer to the pure ideal of Christianity. "We urgently beg your Fraternity to crush out absolutely this absurd claim [upon a piece of property by one of the parties]," he commands in one of his letters of November 30, 1073. Similarly he had to fight adultery, the irregular sex life of the clergy, unlawful marriages of the low and the high, simony, avarice, bad political government, and so on. In order to enforce his Ideational commands he had to invoke, side by side with spiritual means, a full set of empirical rewards and punishments. The ideal remained purely Ideational; but reality made necessary the use of the empirical world in its most intensive and extensive forms. Thus, in a series of letters and commands to many kings and princes urging them to join the Crusades, the objective is spiritual; but the motives given as inducements are of a different nature. "And be assured," he writes to Count William of Burgundy, "that you, and all who join you in this undertaking, will receive a *double*, nay, as we believe, a *manifold*, reward from Peter and Paul, chiefs of the Apostles." This sounds quite commercial, like a good profit on an investment.

However, he rarely forgets to stress, and to strive for, the purely spiritual values for which the Church stands. In this sense his position remains purely Ideational. "We exhort . . . to love God and your neighbor as yourself; to keep peace among you; to live in chastity . . . to devote yourselves to charity and hospitality," he writes to the people of Bohemia. Or writing to Beatrice of Tuscany (June 24, 1073), he says:

It is fixed by the divine judge how much everyone is to suffer by adversity and how far he is to enjoy prosperity. Whoever, therefore, in times of temptations is led by fear of the one or hope of the other to stray from the right path shows that he neither hopes in God, nor respects the appeal of Holy Writ.

Or

If, then, they [the spiritual as well as the secular rulers] seek only their own glory and the lusts of this world, they cannot live without confusion to themselves and to their people.

In most of his letters written to kings, princes, and rulers he concludes with the wish, "May Almighty God enlighten your minds and lead you into eternal glory," or "that you may through his [St.Peter's] merit be delivered from your sins," and so on — wishes which from the Sensate

standard of our age would sound like an insult.   In a letter against
Philip I of France he writes:

Now everyone is committing every kind of abominable crimes.   They regard
neither divine nor human law.   They make nothing of perjury, sacrilege, incest
or mutual betrayal.   Of all these things your king — who is to be called a
tyrant rather than a king — is the cause and fountainhead under the inspiration of the Devil.   Every stage of his life is stained with vice and crime.   And
since he began his wretched and unhappy reign . . .

All this sounds spiritual and Ideational, though not as pure and unearthly
as "My kingdom is not of this world," and other mottoes of the Ascetic
Ideational sort.

But when we read of the measures taken to enforce these pieces of
advice, exhortations, or "commands," we discover that the empirical
world is very much present.   "By our apostolic authority we command
you" — this often repeated phrase has the very sound of worldliness.
And in giving warning, in applying anathema, in ejecting the disobedient
from the Church, and in using other purely physical pressure (punishment,
confiscation of property, and so on), Gregory VII almost invariably
quotes his favorite passages in the Bible as his divine authority, in justification of his interference in all these world affairs: "If thou dost not
speak to warn the wicked from his way, that wicked man shall die in his
iniquity, but his blood will I require at thine hands," he often quotes from
Ezekiel.   "Cursed be the man who holds back his sword from blood."
"Woe to him who keepeth back his sword from the incorrigible sinner." [79]

This shows that as soon as the Ascetic adaptation takes the form of an
organization, the main duty and the main function of the organization
becomes to "warn the wicked," because their sins would otherwise be the
responsibility of the organization.   It is driven to a policy of compulsory
saving of the wicked; and this policy forces it not to "hold back its
sword from the incorrigible sinner," and thus hopelessly involves it in the
affairs of the empirical world.

Thus, as soon as the Ascetic Ideational form becomes, however unwill-
ingly, the center of an organization, it is doomed to be transformed into
an efficient Active Ideational system (unless it degenerates to the Sensate
stage), and, for the masses striving to follow the Ascetic ideal, the level
of Active Ideationalism is the highest attainable.

[79] All these quotations are from *The Correspondence of Pope Gregory VII*, trans. by
E. Emerton (New York, 1932), pp. 8, 15, 20, 23, 39–40, 62, 65, 76, *et passim*.   Another
conspicuous incarnation of this mentality is found in the Buddhist Emperor Açoka.

What has been said of Christianity may be said of any other system which was Ascetic at its beginning. I have already pointed to a similar phenomenon with respect to Taoism. The history of Buddhism and Sufism offers further examples. This means that the Active Ideational type of mentality has always been widely spread in such systems when they entered the stage of attracting a large following and assumed an organized or institutionalized form. It is their destiny (until they become demoralized and lose their vigor and spirituality, and fall into the snares of the Sensate mentality).

The Active Ideational culture mentality can come to existence also directly, without passing through the Ascetic stage. Many groups have always been emerging in that direct way. As an example we may take the system of mentality of Mih-Teich in China — the system that was perhaps the most powerful in the fourth and third centuries B.C. It was rigidly organized as a sect. It attempted actively to transform the empirical world; it fought luxury, degeneration, egotism, anger, greed, by all means, including especially the compulsion, and autocratic enforcement, of its prescriptions. Logically moving along this line, the doctrine came to its culmination : to the *compulsory* introduction and maintenance of universal solidarity and love.[80] Here, then, we meet the same warning of the wicked, the same use of the sword for his salvation, that we found in the formulas of Gregory VII. Whether we take Calvinism or the Inquisition or any other movement or machinery of compulsion aimed to save the sinners from perdition and to bring this empirical world nearer to the "Kingdom of God," they are all the incarnations of this type of culture mentality.[81]

III. ACTIVE SENSATE CULTURE MENTALITY

This type of mentality is quite familiar to us. As we shall see, it pervades our contemporary culture. We find it in the behavior of most of the secular "executives" of history, be they great rulers, conquerors, organizers of political and business empires, efficient rebels against

---

[80] For Mih-Teich and his system see J. Legge, *The Life and Works of Mencius* (Philadelphia, 1875), pp. 99–121; H. A. Giles, *op. cit.*, Vol. II; M. Granet, *op. cit.*, pp. 490 ff.; A. Forke, "Mo Ti," *Mitteilungen des Seminars für orientalische Sprachen* (1923).

[81] Akin to it are all such movements of compulsion as Robespierre's terroristic salvation of the Republic, Lenin's and Stalin's Proletarian Dictatorship, and even the overenthusiasm of advocates of Prohibition who propose a pitiless punishment of all who partake of alcoholic beverages. However, the aims in such movements are of this world — utilitarian, hedonistic, eudaemonistic. Therefore they belong to a special brand of Active "Epicureanism" and not to Active Ideationalism.

various "spiritual" limitations and bonds. It is very widely spread, especially now, among businessmen, energetic professionals, scientists, scholars, laborers, "practical" ministers of the liberal "Social Gospel" — especially revolutionaries, and all those human groups which seek a "full, rich, beautiful, and active life"; who want their cups filled to the brim with sensate experience; who enjoy overcoming obstacles of an empirical nature, of transforming the environment in all its aspects; who enjoy and seek power over inorganic, organic, and psychosocial Nature; who delight in taming rivers, cutting canals, turning wilderness into civilization, hunting, breeding, changing, or exterminating animal and plant organisms, creating artistic, scientific, or other sensate values, fighting for political position, for superiority, fame, glory, wealth, comfort, and other values of this world. In brief, on a large and small scale, this type has always been incorporated by all the healthy, forceful, energetic, and active persons and groups who remain within this world in its widest, richest, and fullest meaning. These are the people who are "drunk with empirical life"; who are "power stations" from which an incessant stream of transforming activity flows upon the sensate world, bringing changes varying in importance from the small, gradual, imperceptible modification wrought by the "average man" to the startling, perhaps stupefying, revolution produced by the great Active "Epicureans" of history, the Caesars and the Lenins.

This type of mentality and examples of it in history are so well known, it is so common in this age, that no further commentary is necessary here.

IV. PASSIVE SENSATE CULTURE MENTALITY

This type is also very familiar to us in contemporary examples of both groups and individuals practicing it. It is found, in greater or lesser frequency, in practically all societies and virtually at all times. When and why it tends to increase, or to decrease, will be discussed further. The formulas of such a mentality have long existed and have been frequently repeated with a monotonous lack of variation in detail. Here are a few typical examples.

> Look upon this [the coffin with the mummy of the deceased], then drink and enjoy yourself; for when dead you will be like this.
> Be glad now, that thou mayest cause thine heart to forget that men will one day pay thee also thy funeral honours.
> Follow thy desire, so long as thou livest. Put myrrh on thy head, clothe thee in fine linen,
> And anoint thee with the genuine marvels of the things of the god.

And yet more to the delights which thou hast, and let not thine heart be
denied. Follow thy desire and do good to thyself.

Do what thou wishest on earth, and vex not thine heart — until that day
of lamentation cometh unto thee.

Yet He-with-the-Quiet-Heart [Osiris] heareth not their lamentations; and
cries deliver no man from the Under-world.

Celebrate the glad day,

Be not weary therein.

Lo, no man taketh his goods with him.

Yea, none returneth again that is gone thither.[82]

This is the old Egyptian expression of this type of mentality. It is difficult to find a more poignant example of the Passive "Epicureanism"!
The fact that such formulas are found in the little that has reached us
from Ancient Egypt, and that, according to Herodotus, such songs were
sung at the funeral banquets while the coffin was being carried about, are
good indications of a considerable spread of this mentality at some
periods of Egyptian history.

Similarly, in ancient China and India, as practically in every other
country, this type of culture adaptation not only was practiced but also
found its rationalizing philosophy and ideology, as, for example, in such a
hedonistic system as that of Yang-Choo who satirizes all values except
those of hedonism, and preaches an absolute "*Carpe diem*" attitude and
the complete disregard for any moral, social, religious, or other value
which may hinder or diminish the sensual pleasure of a given moment,
styling as fools all those who have sacrificed "wine, women, and song"
to any such values. Yang-Choo offers perhaps the most radical formulation of the most complete Sensate mentality of any time.[83] The great
Tu Fu was among those who sang the praises of this mentality conduct.

If carefully one reasons, one must own now is the time to grasp enjoyment's
hair. Why o'er a bubble moan, or lace us straight to meet the public stare?
Time is short, let us enjoy.[84]

In India the teaching and materialistic philosophy assigned to
Chārvākā (either contemporary with or earlier than the Mahabharata,

[82] The Song from the House [*i.e.*, the Tomb] of King Antef, written in front of the Harper,
in E. A. Wallis Budge, *The Teaching of Amen-em-apt* (London, 1924). See also several
similar fragments in the same work and in A. Erman, *The Literature of the Ancient Egyptians*
(London, 1927).

[83] See excerpts from his treatise in the translation of J. Legge, *The Life and Works of Mencius*, pp. 91–99.

[84] "The River Ch'ue," nos. 1 and 2, in W. J. B. Fletcher, *More Gems of Chinese Poetry,
Translated into English Verse* (Shanghai, 1923).

where he is represented as a demon, or rakshasa, slain by the virtuous
Brahmans) and to his followers, gives a closely similar formula.

> There is no heaven, no final liberation, nor any soul in another world. . . .
> While life remains, let man live happily, let him feed on glee, even though
> he runs in debt.
> When once the body becomes ashes, how can it ever return again?
> Hence it is only as means of livelihood the Brahmins have established here
> All these ceremonies for the dead — there is no other fruit anywhere.
> The three authors from the Vedas were buffoons, knaves and demons.[85]

As for Greece and Rome, the philosophical systems of vulgar Epicureanism (not that of Epicurus which is much nearer to a combination
of our Active Sensate mentality with partly Active and partly Ascetic
Ideationalism) are at some periods, as we shall see, widespread. The
works of many poets like Catullus, Horace, Ovid, epitaphs on tombstones,
give a rich variety of examples of the formulation and practice of this
mode of adaptation. The most famous brief formula is Juvenal's *"Carpe
diem."* Other formulas are represented by the following samples.

> Lesbia is beautiful, more beautiful than all women. . . .
> Let us live, let us love, my Lesbia, and together let us mock all severe old
> people.
> The sun dies to be born again, but as for us, once the ephemeral flame of our
> life is quenched we must sleep the eternal sleep.
> Therefore give me a thousand kisses, then a hundred, then a thousand, then
> a hundred more, then a thousand again and a hundred anew; after which
> we will confuse the account so as no longer to know it.[86]

And, "While I lived, I drank willingly; drink, ye who live." "Let us
eat and drink, for tomorrow we die," "What I have eaten and what I have
drunk; that is all that belongs to me." [87]

And so it goes with slight variations. Turning to later periods when
such mentality and conduct were again in flower, we find that the Renaissance offers many similar formulas. Boccaccio's *Decameron* is one example
of it. Here is another coming from Lorenzo the Magnificent.

---

[85] *Sarva-darçana-samgraha*, trans. by E. B. Cowell and A. E. Gough (London, 1882). For
the Sensate culture mentality in India, see the subsequent parts of this work, especially
Chapters One and Four of Volume Two.

[86] Catullus, *Carmina*, 86 and 5; Catullus himself exemplified this mentality conduct:
he squandered his fortune for his Lesbia (Clodia) and was dismissed by her, and then squandered his life and died from the grief of a repudiated lover.

[87] Epitaphs on Roman tombs, quoted in F. Cumont, *After Life in Roman Paganism* (New
Haven, 1922), pp. 11–12. See other examples in the same work.

Quanto e bella giovinezza,
Che si fugge tuttavia!
Chi vuol esse lieto, sia:
Di doman non c'e certezza.

Here is its replica in the French poet Ronsard's formulation.

Cueillez, cueillez votre jeunesse:
Comme à cette fleur la vieillesse
Fera ternir vostre beauté.[88]

This kind of formulation of the Passive Sensate mentality has never died and finds its expression in thousands of ideologies, moral systems, and so on, the mottoes of which are the same: "Enjoy life, for it is short!"; "Wine, women, and song"; or, as in the present-day advertising: "Unhappy? — Buy a Chevrolet!"; "Buy Swift's ham and be happy!"; "Are you happy? — If not hear Rudy Vallee, and you will be happy!"; "Do you inhale?"; "Reach for Luckies, instead . . ."; etc., etc., etc.

V. THE IDEALISTIC AND OTHER MIXED CULTURE MENTALITIES

The Idealistic, the only perfectly integrated and logically consistent form of the Mixed mentality, is not very frequently met with. Probably at all periods and in all societies there have been individuals and groups who have been its bearers, but they are the minority among the mass of those who represent the other varieties of the Mixed mentality. Moreover, as we shall see, though there have been periods in the history of several cultures when the Idealistic mentality became dominant, such periods were comparatively few and short in their duration. The reason for this is probably the exceedingly great difficulty of reaching a real synthesis of elements opposite in nature, the Ideational and the Sensate. A poorly integrated, a mechanical or eclectic, mixture of these elements is much easier to achieve than an organic synthesis. Synthesis requires not only a specific mood but a high intellect, an intellect far above the level of the average. In addition a special combination of cultural circumstances is necessary, namely, the beginning of the decline of an Ideational mentality, so that the Idealistic mentality may come to the front as a transition to a newly ascending Sensate mentality.

Despite the comparative infrequency of this type of Mixed mentality, its contribution to cultural value is qualitatively of a very high order.

[88] *Œuvres de P. de Ronsard*, ed. by Marty-Laveaux (Paris), Vol. II, p. 117. Or Ronsard's: " *Le temps s'en va ma Dame. Pour ce aymez-moi, cependant qu'estes belle.*" *Œuvres choisies de P. de Ronsard*, ed. by L. Moland (Paris, 1879), p. 315.

We shall meet it further in our consideration of the Greek and Western culture mentalities, where it will be properly analyzed.

As to the Mixed forms which represent a highly eclectic and low-grade integration of Ideational and Sensate elements, they have probably always been very widespread, except during periods of calamity and catastrophe. In fact, with all their variations in content, proportion, forms, mixtures of this sort probably represent the most common type of mentality to be found among individuals and groups. Since the major premises of such mentalities are eclectic, sometimes even irreconcilable, the mentalities as a whole are also eclectic and sometimes self-contra-dictory. Thus the logic of such a culture type is often nonlogical or illogical. In this sense the mentality is consistent with its mutually inconsistent major premises. This does not mean, however, that the whole mentality of those who represent this culture type is eclectic. Some compartments of their minds may be well integrated, to the extent that they are Idealistic in form.

All persons and groups who are "sensible," and "reasonable," who enjoy the life of this world but at the same time "give to God what belongs to God," perform their duties, do not go to extremes of sensualism or asceticism, are "good citizens," "honest men," who take good care of their bodies and at the same time do not entirely forget about their "souls" and the nonmaterial values, are the bearers of this form of mentality.

Among the great systems of human conduct Confucianism best embodies this culture type.[89] To this I may add that, so far as the surviving fragments show, this mentality seems also to have been typical for the Ancient Egyptians in the "normal" (noncatastrophic) times of their long history. In the whole range of ancient Egyptian literature, one finds almost no real note of Ascetic Ideationalism but plenty of teachings of the Mixed form of life. On one hand the individual is told, "Follow thy desires as long as thou livest"; on the other,

Be pious, diligent. Be discreet on visits. Beware of the harlot. Be reserved in thy conduct. . . . Be prudent in speech. Be reticent. Boast not of thy strength. Found the family. . . . Thou shouldest beget a son whilst thou art yet young, and shouldest live to see him become a man. Happy is the man who has much people and he is respected because of his children. . . . Be pious towards parents. Be not a drunkard. Lead an honest life.

[89] Here, as in all the preceding cases, the statement is not meant to deny the existence of ups and downs of this mentality in the history of all cultures where it has occurred. These fluctuations mark the main topic of this work, and will be studied further.

Be cautious in social intercourse. Be respectful. Learn : knowledge is useful. Be grateful to thy mother. Keep thyself far from tumults. Treat thy
wife well. Be careful of women.

and also,

Be mindful of death. Make for thyself a fair abode in the desert-valley,
the deep which will hide thy corpse. Have it before thine eyes in thine occupations. Say not : "I am too young for thee to carry off," for thou knowest
not thy death. . . . Possessions do not make for happiness. Wealth is
unstable. Eat not bread, if another is suffering want, and thou dost not stretch
out the hand to him with bread. One is rich and another is poor. He that
was rich in past years is in this year a groom. Be not greedy about filling
thy belly. The course of the water of last year, it is this year in another place.
Great seas have become dry places, and banks have become abysses.[90]

In all of the Egyptian literature that has reached us there is little, if anything, of transcendentalism and ideationalism in their pure form, and a
great deal of Sensate utilitarian egotism mitigated by utilitarian thoughts
on the advisability of moderation and consideration of the other fellow's
interests. The Ideational elements enter in the form of various observations on the afterlife but even there they are colored by the Sensate
utilitarian motivation. Almost all the important moral teachings of
Egypt, "the Teaching of Ptahhetep, the Teaching of King Khati, the
Teaching of Ani, the Teaching of Tuauf, etc., were all definitely written
. . . and were intended to teach how to achieve success in this world." [91]
"They exhorted a man to lead a moral life and to be good because
emoluments, promotion, and physical well-being were to be obtained
thereby." [92] Consequently, almost all of them were highly practical and
their main tone was this sound "Epicureanism" moderated by the
common sense necessary for the achievement of personal comfort and
happiness in this world.   Jules Baillet remarks that

The Egyptian benevolence does not aim, properly speaking, at the unfortunate whom it helps ; it aims at the benefactor himself, and only himself.
It ignores self-abnegation and devotion to self-sacrificing and self-forgetting.
In its heart the Egyptian benefaction has nothing in common with love for
neighbor and love for God like Christian charity.[93]

[90] A. Erman, *The Literature of the Ancient Egyptians*, trans. by A. M. Blackman (London,
1927), pp. 132–134 and 234–242.

[91] Wallis Budge, *op. cit.*, pp. 100–101.

[92] *Ibid.*, p. xiii.

[93] Jules Baillet, *Le régime pharaonique dans ses rapports avec l'évolution de la morale en
Egypt* (Paris, 1913), pp. 639–640.

It is an "investment" profitable to the benevolent investor who helps the poor, the widow, the unfortunate. Otherwise, "If thou wilt oppress the widow and usurp the orphans' possessions, and punish innocent men, and murder people, thou wilt be judged and punished after death." "Do right deeds, thou shalt remain on the earth." [94]

Here are a few other typical examples of this dominant tone.

Follow thy heart's desire as long as thou livest, and do no more than is ordered. Waste not the time in which thou canst follow thy heart's desire for it is hateful thing to the Ka [*i.e.*, the natural disposition] to limit its period. Weary not thyself concerning the affairs of the day, nor be anxious overmuch about thy house and estate; things happen [or come]; follow [thy] inclination.[95]

This sounds like the Passive Sensate "*Carpe diem.*" But these and similar maxims are preceded and followed by the moderating advice which changes its tone. Don't be too arrogant, too greedy, too sensual; obey thy superiors; protect the weak; mix even with the common people; satisfy thy servants because "no man knows what will happen as he meditates in the morning. . . . When the troublesome events come upon him it will be the trusted servants who will bid him 'Welcome'"; because "abuse brings a man to calamity"; because "the man who indulges in pleasure all the day long never acquires possessions"; because when a man pays too much and too close attention to the women, he is made a fool of.

A thousand men seeking what is beautiful are destroyed by them. A man is made a fool of their shining limbs, but they turn into things that are harder than quartzite sandstone. The pleasure is only for a little moment, and it (passes) like a dream, and a man at the end thereof finds death through knowing it.[96]

As we see, the reasons for the moderation in "the desires of one's heart" are purely practical, utilitarian, strictly sensate and materialistic. The entire motivation of all these restraints makes the whole behavior depicted Sensate.

With a slight variation, the same fundamental tone of moderate "Epicureanism" runs through almost all the literary sources of the Egyptians. The author of "The Teaching of Tuaf" instructs his son to school himself earnestly because without this he cannot choose the profession of the scribe. He should choose the scribe's profession because

---

[94] "The Teaching of Khati," § 13 in Wallis Budge, *op. cit.*
[95] "The Teaching of Pta-hetep," in *ibid.*, p. 56.
[96] "The Teaching of Pta-hetep," §§ 1–15 in *ibid.*

it is much better than that of a laborer, blacksmith, artisan, peasant, barber, waterman, weaver, spearmaker, sandalmaker, etc.; more comfortable, more enriching, less painful, from a purely material standpoint. "The goddess Meskhenit makes the scribe to flourish and to prosper." [97] The same can be said of almost all other Egyptian sources: their moral and religious teachings, their songs, their stories, their poems, their hymns, and what not.[98] Their predominant tone remains the same. Even the very reason why these teachings were written and why they ought to be studied and remembered by the people was based on the same common-sense utilitarian advantage to be gained.

The setting of them [these teachings] in thy heart will be advantageous to thee, and the rejection of them will be a calamity (for thee). I beseech thee to deposit them in the treasure-house of thy belly. Thou wilt find them beneficial in the season of adversity's trial . . . and a source of strength and safety as long as thou art upon the earth.[99]

So it is said even in this which is possibly the most "idealistic" teaching in the Egyptian literature. Still more conspicuously this utilitarianism is stressed in the other, less "idealistic," sources. "Do these things and your bodies shall be strong and healthy, and they shall prove of benefit to you for ever and ever." [100]

Such seems to have been the dominant mentality of this great nation throughout its history. The exact composition varied, now the Sensate, now the Ideational elements rising or falling. But in the periods of great calamity, this tone seems to have been sharply changed, a change marked by the rise of the Passive Sensate mentality of despair, with its "Carpe diem" attitude and the Ideationalism of despair, with its ascetic and otherworldly tendencies.[101]

With these reservations, one gets the impression on reading most of the documents of hearing a prominent Rotarian, or Kiwanian, or Elk,

[97] "The Teaching of Tuaf," *ibid.*, pp. 68–75.
[98] See the whole of Wallis Budge's book. See also A. Erman, *op. cit., passim.*
[99] "The Teaching of Amen-em-apt," in Wallis Budge, *op. cit.*, p. 145.
[100] "The Teaching of Sehetepabra," *ibid.*, p. 92.
[101] On this subject see the subsequent parts of the present work. For now it is enough merely to indicate documents like "The Admonitions of Ipuver," "The Prophecy of Neferrohu," "The Complaint of Khekheperre-Sonbu," "The Dispute with His Soul of a Man Who Is Tired of Life," which show this changed tone. And these documents seem to have come from the periods of the great catastrophes in the history of Egypt. See the texts in Wallis Budge, *op. cit.*, pp. 29 ff.; in A. Erman, pp. 86–134. "Even the most hopeful of them have a tang of bitterness and a sense of vanity of all human efforts and the lack of endurance of the best and greatest of human works," remarks J. Baikie in *A History of Egypt* (London, 1929), Vol. I, p. 363.

or a Lion — sensible, efficient, reasonable, and sound in body and mind — talking with his young son, who is also sensible and sound.

Yes, indeed, "the Egyptians loved life and hated death."[102] With such a mentality, well rounded, earthly, yet with a moderate element of spirituality and Ideationalism shown by their religiosity, their belief in the afterlife, their preparation for it,[103] their culture appears to be posited in both the Ideational and Sensate worlds, but with a decided predominance of the second. Therefore we shall not wonder at the efficiency of their external, sensate activity, as manifest in all fields of social life, from their harnessing of the Nile, their gigantic system of irrigation, to the creation of great empires, with marvelous architecture, sculpture, painting, and notable achievements in the field of the natural sciences and technology: astronomy, mathematics, geometry, medicine, and so on.[104] All this is in accordance with the nature of their mentality — Mixed, but integrated in a considerable degree.

A. *Confucianism.* As a theory of conduct, system of mentality, and philosophical-religious-moral code, Confucianism also represents a Mixed type considerably integrated but in a form different from that of the Ancient Egyptians: "To search for what is mysterious, and practice marvelous arts this is what I do not do." "When you do not know about life how can you know about death."[105] These quotations show the unwillingness of Confucius to go beyond the empirical world and its phenomena, and consequently the fact that the aspirations and interests of Confucianism have been mainly within the limits of the empirical world.[106] On the other hand it often mentioned heaven, thus indicating

[102] Sir E. Denison Ross, *The Art of Egypt* (New York, 1931), p. 16.

[103] Their strong religiosity was, however, also earthly in a sense. Their main deity is the pharaoh as the incarnation of the best deity and their afterlife a shadow of this life. "Le pharaon est la source, la règle, la sanction de toute vie morale. Cependent on croit aux dieux. Mais jamais il n'y a conflit entre le service du roi, et le service des dieux ou l'effort vers quelque idéal indépendent. On n'entrevoit les dieux, pharaons invisibles, qu'à travers le pharaon terrestre. . . . Il dirait non 'les dieux sont d'anciens rois qui ont existé réellement,' mais 'les dieux sont l'image et la synthèse des rois réels, des plus anciens et de leurs successeurs jusqu'au dernier survivant.' . . . Créateurs du monde, fondateurs d'empires, auteurs et protecteurs des lois morales, rois et dieux le sont tour à tour à l'instar les uns des autres." J. Baillet, *op. cit.*, pp. 624–625.

[104] See A. Rey, *La science orientale avant les Grecs* (Paris, 1931).

[105] "Confucian Analects" (chap. i), 15, in J. Legge's *The Life and Teachings of Confucius* (London, 1895); G. F. Moore, *History of Religions* (New York, 1913), Vol. I, pp. 33 ff.; M. Granet, *op. cit.*, p. 489. For Confucianism see the quoted works of H. A. Giles; H. Maspero; and A. Franke, *Das Confuzianische Dogma und die chinesische Staatsreligion* (1920).

[106] The Confucian system "is born out of experience, observations. . . . For such an art or knowledge the name of humanism is fitting. It has the inspiration of a positive mind (*d'un esprit positif*). It considers but the observable, living, concrete data. . . ." Thus

an introduction of Ideational premises, not in any profound way, perhaps, but hardly as a mere *façon de parler*.

Free from ascetic elements, this system at the same time represents a remarkable combination of the Ideational and Sensate; its main purpose being to indicate the empirical mean, to keep the balance, or, in its own language, to preserve "the state of equilibrium and harmony," meaning by this the state "when those feelings [of pleasure, anger, sorrow, or joy] have been stirred, and all in their due measure and degree." "This harmony is the universal path in which all human actings should proceed." When it exists "all things [are] nourished and flourish." [107]

Thus Confucianism defines itself, its main objective, and the conduct which it recommends, in such a way as to associate itself with our Mixed type. It recommends a proper gratification of all the important sensate needs but in due measure and degree, and with necessary limitations which are imposed by social duties, the general welfare of the people, and the commands of Heaven.[108]

All the other characteristics of Confucianism are summed up in the system of means which facilitate the realization of this goal. Such means are the doctrine of filial piety; the system of five fundamental social relationships; the preaching of reverence and benevolence; the exhortation to all, beginning with the ruler, to follow the path of harmony; the highest social ideal — the Society of the Great Similarity; the moral

---

writes M. Granet. "The dominant idea of Confucius and of his first disciples was to reject any speculation on the Universe and to make man the proper object of knowledge." M. Granet, *op. cit.*, pp. 489 and 486.

[107] "Confucian Analects" (chap. i), 5–6, in Legge, *op. cit.*

[108] The ideational elements in Confucianism, as in the ancient mentality of China, are included in the main categories of their systems, however positivistic these look at first glance. The concepts or symbols of the Yin and Yang, of the Tao, of Space, Time, Number, of Harmony, of Rites, of Order and Etiquette, of Ceremonies, of the Universe, of Reality, and so on, are all far from being free from purely supersensory and mystical ingredients. However positivistically M. Granet interprets these, he himself shows this clearly. In his work see pp. 301 ff., 325, 336, 339, 342, 389–390, 416, *et passim.* Confucianism and the ancient Chinese mentality may not use the words God, soul, transcendental, spiritual, and the like. Their logic (in accordance with its major premises) may be different in its concrete forms from ours; nevertheless, the classical categories of the Sensate (scientific) thought, beginning with "cause-effect," "time-space-identity," and ending with the theory of knowledge derived from and through organs of the senses, and the whole *Weltanschauung*, are fundamentally different from the categories of Confucianist thought and that of ancient China. The main difference is that the latter have, in a masked form, a great deal more of the ideational mentality than the strictly sensate-positivistic thought. As we shall see, this mixed character of the Confucianist and ancient Chinese mentality manifests itself clearly in all the most important compartments of their culture. Read from this standpoint M. Granet, *Chinese Civilization* (London, 1930); also his *Fêtes et chansons anciennes de la Chine* (Paris, 1919).

code; the technical use of poetry, music, ceremonies, habits, etc., as helpers in this task; and so on.[109]

The reward for following the behavior recommended is mainly earthly; the punishment or the consequences of its violations are chiefly earthly also. Therefore the main principle of social conduct is reasonable, practical, well balanced, but mainly earthly. It is expressed in the words, "What you do not want done to yourself, do not do to others," and "Requite injury with justice and kindness with kindness."

Such is this great system, which for more than twenty-five hundred years has been guiding the conduct of endless millions of human beings and groups. It was only systematized by Confucius, but as religion, as moral code, as political doctrine, as social philosophy, incorporating itself in the "spirit of China," it was the creation of many generations of the Chinese people.

Of other groups which have practiced the Mixed type of culture behavior, we have already spoken above.

VI. CYNICAL SENSATE AND PSEUDO-IDEATIONAL MENTALITY

As we shall see further, the Cynical Sensate form has not been endorsed *openly* by any great system or group. But, in fact, in a limited way, it enters the mentality and conduct of almost all human beings who do not always tell the whole truth, who follow the rules of courtesy and good education and often do not say what they think. In brief, those who are to some extent "liars," "hypocrites," "diplomats," "well-educated persons," "good mixers," "very pleasant and nice," "very courteous, polite, and polished men," and so on, all share, to some extent, in this type of mentality and conduct. Almost all adult human beings, in a slight or a great degree, are given to uttering falsehoods of the nature just indicated. Such lying, of course, leads to a modification of the psycho-social traits of individuals, particularly the speech reactions and expressive acting, which become false and insincere. When such a modification is made in order to secure or to keep, directly or indirectly, some means of satisfying the bodily needs, we have this type of mentality in action. Since "lying" for this purpose is indulged in by almost all human beings, this type of mentality enters as an element, though not necessarily the major element, into the cultural life of almost everyone.

[109] See, besides the Analects, the Texts of Confucianism (especially the Shih King, the Hsiâo King, the Lî Kî), in *The Sacred Books of the East*, Vol. III, particularly pp. 55 ff., 276–293, and 466–488; Vol. XXVII, pp. 1–10, 61 ff., 394 ff., and 401 ff.; Vol. XXVIII, pp. 87 ff., 93, 300 ff., and 367–393.

There are, of course, individuals and groups for whom this is the main form of culture mentality: "professional liars," so to speak, and those persons who are too ready to adapt themselves. "Flatterers" at courts, among the rich people, in business, in literature, in science, in the professions, exist everywhere. When a reviewer or critic praises a work which he thinks is bad but which he cannot afford not to praise in order to keep his job or to be praised in return; when the same is done by a scholar, a poet, an artist; when an employee is flattering to his employer; when these and other persons prefer not to say anything in spite of having a firm negative opinion, not desiring to "spoil the good relationship," and so on; all these are acting according to the Cynical Sensate mentality. And though such individuals have seldom composed a special class, they have nevertheless been present in every society.

Finally, the Pseudo-Ideational type has also existed at all times, in all societies, to a greater or lesser degree. All those who have been obliged to live in hard conditions, not because they chose them but because these conditions were imposed on them, either by other human agencies or by nature; all those who have had to bear their unfortunate lot, whether through their own fault like many imprisoned criminals or through the fault of the circumstances like slaves and serfs, the conquered, the subjugated; all those who have had, because of need and against their desire, to accept employment of a nature or under circumstances distasteful to them; all these are included under the Pseudo-Ideational type. Their number has always been legion.

The above discussion has made clear the nature of each type of mentality in its essentials. It demonstrates that each type has existed in the empirical cultural world and is composed of exactly the characteristics that are given to it in our abstract delineation. To this extent our first task is done. The classification of culture mentalities as proposed in the present work has thus shown itself a fruitful way of ordering the infinite chaos of cultural phenomena, at least in their inner aspect, into a few comprehensible systems. When the major premises of each of these systems are understood, all that is necessary is a logical unfolding of the rich content of each premise, uncovering all the detailed implications that are in it.

Thus the logico-meaningful reading of culture shows its "heuristic" value. It permits us to cast the logical net of relationship out over an enormous number of fragments of cultural phenomena often quite widely separated from one another; to establish a definite connection between them; and to find the proper place and the proper meaning for each fragment in the system. This means a transference of these fragments from the realm of incomprehensible chaos to that of comprehensible unity; from the realm of ignorance to that of cognition. Even for purely causal study the method of logical reading is exceedingly helpful; the logical connections indicate where we must look for causal relationships, which of the variables may be causally connected. They are like the indicators on a signpost; they point out in which direction the causalist must turn to find the causal relationships especially between variables which are widely separated in time and space. For, as we shall see, logical connection between fragments is often accompanied by causal association as well. The subsequent parts of this work will furnish ample corroboration of this statement.

We now have a grasp of one of the key principles for the study of the logical integration of cultural phenomena. The analysis of each type of mentality is far from having been exhaustive, but it has been sufficient to enable us to plunge into the main task of this work: a study of socio-cultural fluctuations. Let us, therefore, pass to a preliminary delineation of the principles involved in the study of fluctuation and change, or the dynamic aspects of cultural phenomena. In the next chapter these principles will be stated very concisely, only so far as is absolutely necessary for the understanding of the subsequent character of the study. In the process of the factual study of culture fluctuations throughout Volumes One, Two, and Three they will be, step by step, further unfolded and clarified. Then, in Volume Four of this work — that which deals with methodology — all such principles will be examined systematically to show what is the framework of the referential-methodological and logical principles of a study of sociocultural phenomena, and what should be the *règles de la méthode sociologique* as they appear to the writer.

Chapter Four

SOCIOCULTURAL FLUCTUATIONS: CONCEPT AND FORMS OF SOCIOCULTURAL PROCESS

Sociocultural fluctuations, *i.e.*, recurrent processes in social and cultural life and in human history — these are the main concern of the present study. The subject sounds fascinating but somewhat indefinite. The vagueness concerns not only the kind of processes the recurrence of which is to be studied, but also the very terms *process, recurrence,* and their derivatives. They have been used with such various senses and contain such a multitude of different connotations as to make necessary a special description of the meaning in which they are employed here. *By process is meant any kind of movement, or modification, or transformation, or alteration, or "evolution," in brief any change, of a given logical subject in the course of time, whether it be a change in its place in space or a modification of its quantitative or qualitative aspects.* Any process implies time and duration, is inseparable from, and unthinkable without, the time category. At least this is so understood here.[1] Hence any process can be divided into a series of sections related to one another according to the earlier-later, before-after patterns and associated with other processes and their sections according to the same categories, plus the additional one of simultaneity.

The definition sounds tautological, and in a way it is. However, there is sufficient excuse for such tautology, which, as we go further, will probably turn into something not quite so repetitious. The excuse consists in the fact that the concept of change or process in the above sense is an irreducible ultimate category of human thought and therefore indefinable in terms of another more ultimate category.[2] The usual

[1] Similar seems to be the situation in mechanics: with the exception of so-called translation, any motion of the material point is described with the variable of time. As far as the spatial change of the same logical subject is meant here, such change of the locus is subsumed under the same category of process and thus involves the time variable. For the details of this see the methodological part of this work to appear in Volume Four.

[2] So it is assumed from the Idealistic standpoint adopted here. From the extreme Ideational position, no change, no process, and no sensate time really exists; true reality is eternal and unchangeable. However, even from this standpoint the phenomena of change, though

method of definition through indication of the *genus* and *differentia specifica* is inapplicable in this case. An ultimate category can only be contrasted with, and supplemented by, another ultimate and corelated category of the opposite character, in the present instance by that of Unchangeable Being (German *Sein* in contradistinction to *Werden*). Like the concepts Father and Son, each of which becomes meaningful only when the other is given, the concept of Change or Process or Becoming is corelative with that of Unchangeable Being, and, being contrasted to it, gets its rich sense and profound meaning. To this extent the fullness of such a definition ceases to be tautology. When an analysis of the properties of process is added to the definition, the tautology fades, and, as we shall see, the concept of process becomes a fundamental point of reference, to which many a scientific construction can safely be tied for its orderly arrangement.[3]

I. Fundamental Specifications of the Concept Process

Any process, in order to be meaningful, implies specification (1) of its *unit*, the logical subject — that which is changing or is in process, (2) of its *time relationships*, (3) of its *space relationships*, (4) of its *direction*.

Without the *unit* or the logical subject, no process, no dynamic state generally, is observable, thinkable, or describable. Even physical mechanics in its description of the simplest motion has always to give, implicitly or explicitly, the unit in the form of a material point or a material body. The same is to be said of any other, more complex, process. The unit may be a thing; it may be a certain dynamic state, for instance, a process of integration, of disintegration, of growth, of degeneration, of expansion, etc. But some unit, as a logical subject, change, or modification of which we assert, must be given. Unitless or subjectless process is a word without meaning. More than that. This unit, though in a process or change, must be thought of as retaining its identity during the whole process in which it is involved. Any unit or subject exists as long as it retains its sameness or identity. When it

illusory, must be admitted in the illusory world of the senses. From the Idealistic standpoint the sensate reality is an aspect of true reality, therefore the process is also an aspect of true reality.

[3] Here I am giving an unbroken and concise delineation of the concepts of Being and Becoming as they are used in this work. One of the subsequent chapters gives a quantitative-qualitative analysis of the periods during which each of these categories rose and declined in their domination, from 580 B.C. to A.D. 1920, together with a consideration of some of the reasons for such recurrence. See Chapter Five of Volume Two, " Fluctuation of Eternalistic and Temporalistic Mentality."

loses this, it ceases to exist as a given unit, as the same logical subject. If it ceases to exist, it cannot be in any process or in any change, because the nonexistent cannot either change or remain unchangeable. At least, while concerned primarily with the change, we must think of this subject or unit as unchangeable, as a mode of *Being*. Whatever it is that changes, whether man, electron, plant, earth, the Universe, Boston, a Beethoven symphony, even a process which is in course of modification, we can talk of its change or of its being in process only when we assume that that which changes preserves its identity (its Being), that it remains the *same* throughout the process it goes through : that, in brief, it remains unchanged to the extent of preserving its identity. When we say, "Mr. J. B. Smith has changed during the last fifteen years," or "Boston has changed greatly during the three hundred years of its existence," or "The process of education has undergone great transformations in the last forty years," we assert that these subjects have been changed but at the same time we believe that, in spite of change, we are still dealing with Mr. J. B. Smith, and not Mr. A. B. Jones ; it is Boston and not New York ; it is the same process of education, not that of baking bread. In spite of change these units preserved their identity, remained in the domain of Being. Otherwise we cannot contend that there was any change in these units, because if they were not the same subject in each case then there would have been no change but just two or more subjects quite different from the very beginning.

This reconciliation of permanent sameness with change is not the illogical matter that it seems. It is based on the fact that if the unit of change A consists of the essential elements a, b, c, together with other elements which are not essential — now m, now n, now f, now k, now l, or some combination of these, A, as an integration of the elements a, b, c, can remain constant and at the same time be in a process of change with reference to m, n, f, k, l, or their combinations; and thus A may change without losing its identity. In other words, any proposition that describes a process or a change in any unit A always concerns these additional elements, whether they be qualities, quantities, or other "modalities" of A, the *differentia specifica* of its subclasses, sub-subclasses, varieties, or what not. But there must always remain some substratum as permanent and unchanging in the process. Otherwise, A ceases to exist. We can then state that the process of its change is ended by cessation of its existence, but we cannot say that A continues to change after it has ceased to exist. Such is the logic of the "paradox" of the unification of unchangeableness with change. It must be kept clearly in mind.

I — 12

Though briefly put here, it is of a cardinal importance for a proper understanding of any theory of process or change, as well as for uncovering
the vagueness and meaninglessness of many propositions that deal with
change and process.

Any Becoming, Change, Process, Motion, Movement, Dynamic State,
in contradistinction to Being, implies *time*. Without this second specification, process cannot be thought of nor described. Time is unavoidable to mark the beginning and end of process, its duration, its location
with regard to other processes (before, simultaneously, after), its velocity,
its time direction (from the past to the present, from the present to the
future, or vice versa), and a number of other important characteristics.
Even the simplest form of Becoming, the simplest motion of a material
point, cannot be described by the science of mechanics without the variable of time.[4] Still less possible is it to conceive or describe any more
complex process without the time co-ordinate.

Quite a different problem is the *kind of time* which must be used in
specifying various cultural processes. Without entering here into a discussion of this intricate matter, it is sufficient to say that the time suitable for the description of the motions of material bodies is often unfit
for the characterization of social and cultural processes. For these we
often must use another kind of time — *social time*. In spite of what
must to many readers be the incomprehensible nature of this statement,
I shall leave it without further explanation for the present. Otherwise
too great a deviation from our topic would be necessary to explain it.[5]

What has been said about time holds also, *mutatis mutandis*, for *space*.
Any process takes *place* somewhere and in spatial relationship with other
processes and phenomena chosen as points of reference. Otherwise, the
process cannot be located and remains indefinite. A different problem is

[4] Kinematics which deals with the fundamental forms of motion is, as Lagrange said,
geometry of four dimensions where the fourth dimension is time. "Kinematics is a study
of movement in its relation to time." P. Appel et S. Dautheville, *Précis de mécanique ration-
nelle* (Paris, 1924), p. 38. See also L. Lecornu, *La mécanique* (Paris, 1918), pp. 32 ff.; H.
Crew and K. Smith, *Mechanics* (New York, 1930), pp. 85 ff.; A. P. Y. Barcelo, *Essais de
mécanique sociale* (Paris, 1925), p. 22. Likewise, in kinetics also time is one of the unavoidable
variables. Geometry deals only with the geometrical forms of motion, but not with motion
properly; therefore it can deal with these forms without the variable of time. The same
is to be said of any analytical study of the static forms or relationships of a process.

[5] See Volume Two, Chapter Eleven, and the discussion of Social Time in the methodological part of this work to appear in Volume Four. If the reader reads attentively these
chapters he will not fail to see that the present statement about social time is quite clear and
that it involves a great problem, a problem which in a way affects the essential nature of the
social sciences and of their future. For a preliminary outline of the problem of social time see
P. Sorokin and R. Merton, " Social Time," in *American Journal of Sociology*, March, 1937.

raised in dealing with the *kind of space* and the *system of space co-ordinates* (vector) to be used for the "location" of cultural processes. *Physical or geometric space and its system of co-ordinates (vector of mechanics), which are suitable for the description of the spatial relationships of physical bodies, are often quite inadequate for that of psychosocial processes and of cultural phenomena generally.* Many social scientists are not quite aware, as yet, of this fact, and they still continue — with failure inevitably following their attempts — to use the system of physical space co-ordinates for the location of cultural processes. They should be excused for these attempts in this age of the domination of the physicochemical sciences and the mathematico-mechanical mentality. As a matter of fact, for their adequate description *many sociocultural phenomena require a special category of social space with its own system of co-ordinates.* This statement will be clarified in Volume Two, Chapter Eleven, and in the discussion of Social Space in the methodological part of the present work to appear in Volume Four.

Finally, the fourth essential specification with reference to process, namely, *direction*, is based on the fact that process proceeds *from* something *to* something, that change presupposes a passage *from* one status *to* another. Any dynamic state means some modification of the unit in the category of *From-To*. *This From-To movement is the direction of the process.*

The directions of a process may be various. *They can be reduced to four classes: time direction, space direction, quantitative direction, and qualitative direction.* *Time direction* is involved when we deal with such phrases as "from the past to the present," "from the Middle Ages to the Machine Age," "from 2500 B.C. to 1933," "from 6 P.M to 4 A.M." Often this time direction is expressed in other than From-To terms, like "before and after," "during," "within so many years, days, hours," and so on. It is evident, however, that these are virtually aspects of the same From-To category.

The time specification of a process most frequently comes out in the form of *duration*. For many processes it becomes necessary to know whether they have lasted a second, an hour, a day, a year, an age. This specification is often of utmost importance not only theoretically but practically. Likewise we often need to know the comparative duration of two or more processes : Are they equal, or are some longer than others? Moreover, if a process is recurrent, we must know something about the duration of the intervals between recurrence. Are they always of the same length? or do they increase or decrease in duration according to some rule which may be formulated? or are they strictly nonperiodical and without regularity as to duration? [6]

Another variety of time direction is *time sequence*. Given the objects, qualities, events a, b, c, which comes first, which second, which last? In other words, what is their *order* in time?

In these and many other forms the time specification of the direction of a process is often one of the most important traits to know, whether for theoretical or for practical purposes. All such specifications are varieties of time direction. Time direction, combined with either space direction or qualitative or quantitative direction, gives a series of "cumulative" or combined derivative directions styled by the terms velocity, tempo, rhythm of the process.

The second form of the direction of a process is *spatial direction:* either a purely geometrico-spatial direction, as in physical motion, in any movement of a material body in geometric space (such as driving from Dakota to New England) ; or a direction in social space—"climbing the social ladder," social promotion and demotion, social rapprochement, social separation.

Thirdly, a process may have a *quantitative* direction. When we say of a process that it increases, decreases, or remains constant; that it grows, multiplies, declines, becomes scarce — for instance that the birth rate falls from 10.2 to 9.6 per 1000 and that the suicide rate increases from 0.2 to 0.5 per 10,000, the direction of the process here is neither purely temporal nor purely spatial, it is *sui generis* and stresses the quantitative modification of the unit as such, and for this reason it is to be styled by a special name.

Propositions specifying the quantitative direction are of two varieties, *verbal* and *numerical*. A statement is verbal when it simply points out the direction in general terms: for instance, "War tends to decrease," "During the period studied social disorders greatly increased," and so on, without specification in exact numerical units. When such a specification is added, as in the above statements on the decrease and increase, respectively, of the birth and suicide rates, the quantitative direction assumes numerical form.[7]

The fourth form of direction is *qualitative* in the sense of a passage from one qualitative status to another, as from misery to happiness, childhood

[6] See E. B. Wilson, "The Periodogram of American Business Activity," in *Quarterly Journal of Economics*, May, 1934; also his "Are There Periods in American Business in Activity?" *Science*, August 31, 1934.

[7] As we shall see later on, many historians opposed to the quantitative method in the study of social phenomena use it, but only in its "verbal" form. They seem not to be aware that the verbal is merely a variety of the quantitative direction, not a negation of it.

to senility, health to sickness, hatred to love, the state of an amoeba to that of *homo sapiens*, the Gothic to the baroque, capitalism to communism, and so on. Such direction is exceedingly meaningful and perhaps the most important of all the kinds of direction so far as psychosocial and cultural phenomena are concerned. It is quite different from other directions and cannot be reduced to a mere aspect of any of them.

The belief, sanctioned by Hegel, still prevails that quality can be reduced to quantity, and, accordingly, the qualitative direction to the quantitative. This belief appears to be essentially baseless. Even in those few cases where quality can be described in the terms of quantity, the quality slips through, and evaporates from, the quantitative formulas. To a person who does not know red, green, blue, as perceptible to the sense of sight, the formulas of the number of the vibrations and the length of the waves of ether which correspond to red and green and blue can never give any idea of the quality of these colors.[8] In the case of most of the psychosocial qualitities this quantitative description has been and will probably remain useless, partly because these qualities do not have any unit of quantitative measurement, partly because the fundamental categories which compose the framework of reference in the social and cultural sciences are predominantly qualitative. Unlike the space and time of physics, social space, social time, and other categories are, as we shall see, not so much quantitative as qualitative. (See the methodological part of this work to appear in Volume Four.) For this reason alone the reduction of quality to quantity in the social sciences is impossible. If the fundamental frame of reference of these sciences is qualitative, most of the content of these sciences which is referred to the frame of reference is bound to be qualitative.[9] This does not mean that the category of quantity is to be excluded from such sciences. On the contrary, the category of quantitative direction takes care of this important aspect of social phenomena. But this is only one aspect and in no way should it be allowed to swallow the others, especially the qualitative aspect of psychosocial reality.[10]

[8] Compare H. Bergson, *Matter and Memory* (London, 1919), p. 259.

[9] This explains why most of the recent attempts in the social sciences to measure and to describe in quantitative terms many qualities of psychosocial phenomena have so utterly failed. They have led either to a pure quantitative verbosity, or to the painful elaboration of the obvious, or to rude blunders. On this subject see Sorokin, *Contemporary Sociological Theories*, chap. i and pp. 617 ff.; Sorokin, "Recent Social Trends," in *Journal of Political Economy*, Vol. XLI, April and June, 1933.

[10] This explains why an investigator of social processes cannot reduce them to a mere quantitative motion and define motion as a mere "change of position" (in geometrical space) as in the classical definition of mechanics by Kirchhoff. See his *Vorlesungen über mathe-*

Now there is an additional fact which must be observed with reference to direction. In mechanics each of its three *spatial* directions of vector

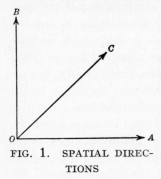

has two "senses"; as in Figure 1 for instance, from O to B and from B to O, from O to A, and from A to O, and so on.

Each of the four fundamental directions of sociocultural process may also have various senses. But just as the vector system of social phenomena is infinitely more complex than that of mechanics (this latter has only *spatial* vector, and even this is incomparably simpler than the vector of social space, which is a space not of three dimensions only but of

FIG. 1. SPATIAL DIREC-
TIONS

many more), each of our directions has not two but many more senses, especially qualitative direction. *This latter has potentially as great a number of senses as there are different irreducible qualities. Quantitative*

---

matische Physik: Mechanik (Leipzig, 1874), p. i. Compare H. Poincaré, *La science et l'hypothèse* (Paris, 1908), pp. 110 ff. Such an approach suitable for the material world is quite unfit for the world of the immaterial psychosocial phenomena and values. It can catch in its net only their quantitative aspect and no others. As shown, even spatial direction and change of position in the cultural world is in a degree qualitative.

Even in regard to the material world and material motion, the real situation is not exclusively quantitative at all. If mechanics can stick to Kirchhoff's definition and view the material world from the standpoint of quantity; on the contrary, chemistry and physics, not to mention biology, are already qualitative in a very considerable degree. But even mechanics cannot do without quality: its vector system is composed of at least three directions and six senses which are qualitative in their nature. When we take the motion of bodies, as a reality, it is notably different from abstract quantitative definition. This latter in a sense is a "bleached" and "mummified" skeleton of the real motion of material bodies. H. Bergson has shown this very well. His criticism of the concept of the motion of physical bodies as a mere change of position appears to contain a great deal of sense. "Movement is relative only for the mathematician [who measures it by the variation of the distance from the point of reference]. For the geometer all movement is relative: which signifies only that none of our mathematical symbols can express the fact that it is the moving body which is in motion rather than the axes or the points to which it is referred. And this is very natural, because these symbols, always meant for measurement, can express only distances. . . . But that there is real motion no one can seriously deny: if there were not, nothing in the universe would change. . . . The internal configuration of every real system varies." Differing from the mathematical motion which is infinitely divisible, "every movement, inasmuch as it is a passage from rest to rest, is absolutely indivisible." It is only the trajectory of a moving body — which is in fact the real object of study by the mathematician — that is divisible. "Motion studied in mechanics is but an abstraction or a symbol, a common measure, a common denominator, permitting the comparison of all real movements with each other, but these movements, regarded in themselves, are indivisible which occupy duration, link together the successive moments of time by a thread of variable quality similar to the continuity of our consciousness. . . ." "Real movement is rather the transference

direction has three main senses: increase, decrease, constancy. Furthermore, two or more senses of different directions can combine and give a
"cumulative sense." The number and variety of these mixed or cumulative senses is potentially infinite. Their main forms, however, may be
reduced to a manageable number, as we shall see further. This explains
why the sociocultural universe is incomparably more complex than the
physical universe of mechanics. And this complexity is not only quantitative but especially qualitative.

The four directions which we have just described [11] are sufficient for
the formation of a working concept of the nature of process and, together
with the other specifications (unit, time), for the classification of an
infinitely great variety of processes into a few kinds. Such descriptions
and classifications will be dealt with further on in the present work.

Let us now turn to a clarification of the second main concept of our
subject, the concept of *recurrence* and its derivatives.

II. Forms and Degrees of Uniqueness and Recurrence

If we have a phenomenon (or process) the characteristics of which
consist of the traits a, b, c; and if the most searching investigation does
not disclose anywhere and at any time any other phenomenon or process
which consists of the same characteristics, a, b, c, and is therefore identical with A, we may conclude that the phenomenon or process A is *unique.*

---

of a state than a thing," it is rather quality than quantity. Therefore, "real movements
cannot be merely changes of position." "I grasp the reality of movement when it appears
to me, within me, as a change of state or quality." See the further discussion of these points
in the works of Bergson, especially *Matter and Memory* (London, 1919), pp. 254 ff., 246 ff., 258,
267–271, *et passim.*

[11] One can but wonder at the clarity with which the problem was understood and analyzed
by some of the great thinkers of the past, particularly by Aristotle. After elaborating my
discussion of direction I was surprised to find that it coincided closely with what Aristotle
had said in this field (though my elaboration was done without knowing Aristotle's theory).
Here is the essence of his theory of change and its main specifications:

"In each change by which a phenomenon passes from one state to the opposite there exists
something that is the subject of this change. . . . If it is a change of locus [*secundum ubi,*
i.e., spatial direction] this something now is here and then is there. . . . If it is an augmentation [*secundum quantum, i.e.,* quantitative direction] this something now is of a certain
volume [or quantity or amount] while later on it will be either larger or smaller. If it is an
alteration [*secundum quale, i.e.,* qualitative direction] it is now healthy while later on it will
be sick. If it is a change in the very substance of this something [*secundum quid*], it is originated now and then will perish [the beginning and the end of the existence of the subject of
change]." *Metaphysics,* VII, i (*Aristotelis Opera,* ed. Didot, Vol. II, p. 558; Bohn's ed.,
London, 1857, pp. 212–213). See an excellent analysis of the Aristotelian theory of change in
P. Duhem's *Le système du monde, Histoire de doctrines cosmologiques de Platon à Copernicus*
(Paris, 1913), Vol. I, chap. iv.

If the investigation brings to light a phenomenon or process B which consists of the same characteristics, a, b, c, and is therefore identical with A, then A is not unique: it is reproduced in B and is therefore *repeated* or *recurring*. Phenomena (including the phenomena of process) are then either unique or recurring.

The uniqueness or recurrence of processes may, however, have different forms and degrees. Let us single out the main forms of unique and recurrent processes according to the process specifications which we have enumerated.

A. A process may be unique in *all its specifications*. This means that it happens only once in the eternity of time, only at one locus in the infinity of space, and also that the unit is unique in which the process occurs. Assuming that Socrates as a unit is unique and that all the important circumstances of his death do not have any duplicate in the eternity of time and infinity of space (no other man died anywhere at any time in exactly the same way as Socrates), we have an example of an *absolutely unique process: occurring to a unique individual and unrepeated in time and in space.*[12]

[12] If a unit is eternal and omnipresent, that is, unbounded in time and space, and the "process" goes on retaining its identity eternally and everywhere, such a phenomenon belongs not to the category of Changeable Becoming or Process but to that of Unchangeable Being. It is beyond such distinctions as uniqueness and recurrence. A *sine qua non* of any recurrence is that the phenomena recurring must be bounded in space or in time or in logical nature. In regard to the unbounded, eternal, and infinite, nothing can be said as to its recurrence.

Since any recurrence means the existence of two or more copies of a given phenomenon, including the phenomenon of process, it follows that each phenomenon process recurrent in time or repeated in space, in that part which is recurrent is finite or bounded or limited either in its time duration or in its extensity in space or in its logical nature. Of two or more infinities we cannot say whether or not they are representatives of the same phenomenon or process. Only because the columns of a classic building are bounded in space and separated from one another by something different from the columns, do we notice their similarity and their repetition in space. If each of the columns were spatially infinite (were the coexistence of several such infinities conceivable) we could not know whether there were one or many columns or whether they were repeated in space or not. The same is true of any phenomenon-process with regard to its duration. In order that we may distinguish recurrence in time, the process in question must be finite in duration and at each repetition preceded and followed by something different from it. *In other words, any recurrent phenomenon process must be bounded in time or space or both, and there must therefore be caesuras (spatial, temporal, or other) between each case of recurrence.* If there were not these pauses, for example, in duration, the process would be comparable to an infinite straight line. Without any "links" or "cuts" or "punctuations" in it, we cannot say that any part is recurrent in time. Like the Newtonian Absolute Time (see Newton, *Philosophiae Naturalis Principia Mathematica*, London, 1686, I, iii) it exists as Being (not Becoming) as far as time recurrence is concerned. If we conceive of several such eternally enduring lines stretched out in space, we can speak of their repetition in space, because in space each is bounded and separated from the others (in its cross section, as it were, but not in its length). Between the lines the space is occupied by something

B. A process related to a unique unit may be repeated *within this unit*. Socrates is a unique individual; however, such of his activities as sleeping and being awake, wandering in the streets of Athens, listening to the scoldings of Xantippe, and many others, were repeated many times during his life. Let us grant, for example, that the earth and Chinese culture are unique. The processes of the earth's revolution around its axis and around the sun; the processes, during the existence of Chinese culture, of business depression and prosperity, of peace and war, of decentralization and centralization, have occurred many times. Such processes, then, take place in a unique unit; and they are unique in space, in the sense that there is only one locus — one Socrates, one earth, one Chinese culture. But they are recurrent in this unique unit. For the sake of brevity we can call such processes *recurrent in time only*. By definition, then, the *processes recurrent in time* only are those *which occur in a unique unit and are repeated in it*.

C. There are two or more units essentially similar to one another, but a given process occurs only *once in the lifetime of each unit*. Let us assume that all human individuals are essentially alike. Since there are many human individuals, then by definition there are many similar units in which processes take place. But in the life span of each many processes occur only once: each is born once, passes the stage of childhood once, and dies once. *All such processes are unique in the time existence of each unit but repeated in social space, i.e., in other similar units*. Assuming that many cultures are similar and that each culture passes through the stages of childhood, maturity, and decay only once — or only once through the teological, metaphysical, and positive states — we have a further example of processes unique in time but recurrent in social space. All such recurrences may be called *recurrences in space only*.[13]

---

different from the line. Without this separation by things different from the lines all would merge and there would be, not a sense of eternally enduring lines, but continuous, unchangeable space, somewhat similar to Newtonian Absolute Space (*Principia*, II, iv). This would belong to the realm of Being, not Becoming.

[13] Of course, they can occur in various units at different times. Thus in one culture the termination of the stage of childhood may have taken place in 325 B.C., in another in A.D. 450, in a third in A.D. 1925. In this sense they may be styled as recurring in time also. However, the type in some respects is so fundamentally different from others (*i.e.*, those designated B and D in the present section), that it is advisable to distinguish it from them and to style it by a special name. The term *recurrence in space* stresses its specific nature, implying that the units in which the process occurs are not unique; and so far as the unit of the process is taken as the locus of the process, it recurs in space. Spengler's and numerous other similar theories of the life cycle of culture — that each culture passes through the stages of childhood, maturity, and old age — are, therefore, according to definition, theories of recurrence in space.

D. A process may not only occur in units which are not unique, but also be repeated several times in such units. Such a process is then *recurrent in time as well as in space.* The process of chemical association of many similar atoms of hydrogen and of oxygen in the combination H_2O (water) is recurrent in time as well as in space (providing the same atoms of oxygen and hydrogen are several times associated with and disassociated from one another). Under the assumption that human individuals are essentially similar, the alternating processes of sleep and wakefulness, of fatigue and rest, of cheer and gloom, and others which occur many times in all human beings, are processes repeated in both time and space. The same can be said, under the assumption of the essential similarity of various cultures, of the processes of prosperity and depression, war and peace, order and disorder, expansion and limitation of governmental control and so on.

Thus we have a range of processes from the absolutely unique to those recurrent in many units in time and space, as in Table 3.

TABLE 3. SUMMARY: MAIN FORMS OF UNIQUENESS AND RECURRENCE

1. Unique with respect to unit in which it occurs and in Time and Space.	1. No recurrence; the process is absolutely unique.
2. Occurring in a unique unit, but recurring in Time within this unit.	2. Recurrent in Time only.
3. Occurring in many similar units, but only once in Time within each.	3. Recurrent in Space only.
4. Occurring in many similar units and repeated in them.	4. Recurrent with respect to units and in Time and Space.

However pedantic this classification may appear to be, it will be of considerable service in our study. If the differences between these forms of recurrence and uniqueness had always been understood clearly, and if they had not often been lumped together in one class, many essential blunders would have been avoided and many a theory would have been more correctly appraised and interpreted.

Whether any process or phenomenon is recurrent or unique depends, by definition, on whether or not it is like some other phenomenon or process. If logically the concept of identity is absolute, empirically it is relative and has gradations. Any two phenomena or processes may be exactly alike in all their characteristics. Their identity in that case is complete. From this state of complete identity there may be gradations of decreasing identity until the phenomena become quite dissimilar. The passage from complete identity to dissimilarity may be depicted as in Table 4.

TABLE 4. THE PHENOMENA OF IDENTITY

	(Process) A	(Process) B
Complete identity	{ 1. a, b, c, d	a, b, c, d
	{ 2. a, b, c, d	a, b, c, e
Decreasing similarity	{ 3. a, b, c, d	a, b, e, f
	{ 4. a, b, c, d	a, e, f, j
Complete dissimilarity	5. a, b, c, d	e, f, j, m

From this it follows that whether two or more phenomena are identical, similar, or dissimilar depends first of all upon *the number of characteristics of the phenomena which are identical or dissimilar.* Other conditions being equal, the greater the number of identical and the less the number of dissimilar characteristics, the nearer the phenomena to identity, and vice versa.

But the number of identical and dissimilar traits is not all. Rather more important is the *essentiality* or *significance* of a trait for the characterization of the phenomenon involved. In empirical reality almost every phenomenon will have traits which are essential to it and traits which are inessential or accidental. To take the number of white spots on a cow as the essential traits for cows in general and on this basis to conclude that all cows which have the same number of white spots belong to the same species will evidently be wrong. White spots are a trait quite unimportant for the species of the cow. Though men generally wear shoes, to regard shoes as the essential characteristic of *homo sapiens* would be foolish. However great may be the number of such accidental traits occurring in phenomena under comparison, this would not justify our declaring these phenomena identical or similar. For identity or similarity it is necessary that the *traits essential to the nature of the phenomena be identical or similar.*

The essential traits are those which logically or causally, or — better still — logically and causally, are inseparable from the phenomenon, and without which the phenomenon ceases to be what it is. Take from water oxygen or hydrogen, and water ceases to exist. Take from any real social group (in contradistinction to the nominal) the elements of interaction and contact among all its members, and the group disappears. Unfortunately it is often impossible, among the numerous traits which cluster about a phenomenon, to decide by logic alone which are essential and which not. To make such distinctions often requires careful empirical observation in all its forms: experimental, statistical, "clinical," historical. When the number of occurrences of any traits is observed to be great in many examples of a particular kind of phenomenon, and when the number of exceptions to such occurrences is *nil* or very small, then we have strong empirical evidence that these traits are essential. On the contrary, the fewer the number of occurrences and the greater the number of exceptions, the less essential is the trait in question to the phenomenon in which it appears.

The greater, then, the number of identical traits which are essential (whether logically, causally, or by some other empirical necessity) *to the phenomena compared and the smaller the number of essential traits which are dissimilar, the more nearly identical are the phenomena.*

Our discussion should by now have made clearer the problems involved in testing phenomena for identity or dissimilarity. In its light it is reasonable to stress the relativity of these qualifications. We rarely deal in empirical reality with complete identity or complete dissimilarity. These "poles" are rather ideal limits. We usually deal in fact with phenomena showing greater and less similarity or dissimilarity. As long as the phenomena are similar in all or in the majority of their essential traits, they may be regarded as alike and as *repeated*. When they do not have any similar essential traits, they cannot be regarded as similar and therefore as recurrent. Between these limits there is considerable room for varying degrees of similarity and dissimilarity.

What has been said of phenomena applies generally to processes and their degrees of uniqueness or recurrence. The more complete the identity of the units of the processes and of their essential characteristics (their time-space-quantity-quality specifications), the greater is the degree of their likeness and the more complete their recurrence. When two or more processes are dissimilar in all their essential traits, they are not recurrent at all: they are different processes. Between these two ideal limits there are many gradations of recurrence.

(1) If a given process should recur in all its specifications this would be the most complete degree of recurrence. Many of the ancient thinkers (Hindu, Greek, Roman) contended that the cosmos as a whole and all the phenomena in it recur endlessly in absolutely identical cycles. This book and this chapter, the phenomenon of my writing these lines, have been repeated many times before in exactly the same form even with regard to the smallest detail, and will be repeated in the future in exactly the same situation. Such a recurrence is absolute and perfect.[14]

---

[14] This absolutely perfect recurrence may, however, take one of two different forms (Aristotle's numerical and generic recurrence). According to some of these thinkers, in such recurrences the *same* object or person recurs: the same Socrates, the same Xantippe, the

(2) The opposite pole is occupied by the processes which are quite dissimilar in their essential traits and which occur in units which are not alike. Such processes cannot be regarded as repeated or recurring.

(3) Between these ideal poles lies a large range of processes recurring more and less perfectly, according to the general criteria established above.

III. Are Sociocultural Processes Unique or Recurrent?

At this point it would be well to consider, at least briefly, the question : Are sociocultural processes recurrent? The problem arises from the fairly wide prevalence of the opinion that "history never repeats itself," that it is ever new, that there are no two sociocultural objects, values, groups, events, similar to each other either in time or in space. This is an abbreviated statement of the unicist conception of sociocultural and historical processes.[15] Since according to this conception there are no recurrences, no uniformities can be formulated ; consequently no discipline devoted to a study of recurrent sociocultural processes is possible, nor, indeed, any nomographic or generalizing social science whatsoever. Historians and social scientists must confine themselves merely to a straightforward description of a series of unique historical or sociocultural processes. Such are or should be the conclusions logically following from the premise of Uniqueness or Unrepeatedness.

same M. P. Smith, Jr., reappear. According to other thinkers, though the things, objects, relationships, persons, situations, which recur are alike, they are *only similar copies, not all the same original.* Though the person who recurs is like Socrates, has a wife like Xantippe, lives in a city like Athens, teaches in its streets the same subject and in the same manner as Socrates, is condemned to death under the same conditions, and by a court and on the charges of the leaders of the accusers who are like Anitus and Melitus, still this Socrates-like person in each recurrence is *not the same* person — he is another person in each recurrence, exactly like though he is to Socrates and to all the Socrates-like persons of all the past, present, and future recurrences. (For other examples see Chapter Ten of Volume Two on the history of recurrence theories.) Both types of recurrence involve perfect similarity between the objects and processes recurring, but one is the recurrence of the same — it contends for the continuity of everything; the other is the recurrence of the similar but not the same — it admits a discontinuity, finiteness in time of most empirical phenomena. For practical purposes the great difference between these conceptions is inessential. See the methodological part of this work to appear in Volume Four. Also see P. Duhem, *op. cit.*, Vol. I, pp. 261-296. Also A. Lovejoy and G. Boas, *Primitivism and Related Ideas in Antiquity* (Baltimore, 1935), Vol. I, chap. i *et passim.*

[15] See for instance A. D. Xénopol, *Principes fondamentaux de l'histoire*, pp. 214-215; in its second edition it is his *La théorie de l'histoire* (Paris, 1908). See especially the bibliographical references in *La théorie de l'histoire.* Explicitly and implicitly the assumption is shared by so many "classic historians" that it is needless to give references here. See, for instance, criticism of sociology by G. von Below, *Soziologie als Lehrfach* (München, 1920).

This conception has been stressed again and again, mainly by historians, though perhaps rarely in such a pointed form as in this work. Let us now ask to what extent it is valid. That it has some truth in it is beyond doubt : if one intentionally turns one's attention only to those characteristics of historical and sociocultural processes which are unique, one can find many traits which are unrepeated. Moreover, if one should consider all phenomena or processes down to their very last detail, it is true that in empirical reality every process or phenomenon must be unique, judged by an absolute standard. Certainly there was one Middle Kingdom in Egypt and no other, one Peloponnesian War and no other identical with it, one Caesar, one Plato, one Phidias, one King Charles V of Spain, one Beethoven's *Symphony No. 3*, one *Corpus Juris Civilis* of Justinian, one French Revolution of 1789.

Since the business of history, as a science, is to concentrate attention mainly (and in theory exclusively) on the unique aspect of historical processes,[16] we cannot wonder that such a business has habituated historians to see in all social life only the unique and not the recurrent aspect. If they claimed that their concentration is methodological only and that it does not deny the existence of Being in this Becoming, or of recurring phenomena and the possibility of investigating them by a special discipline which specializes in recurring aspects just as history specializes in the unique — if this were so, no criticism would be directed against the conception discussed, and its value would deserve full recognition. But as the theory does not confine itself to such methodological limits, but denies the existence of recurrence in social and historical processes generally, it exceeds its rights and falls into grave error. This error comprises several lesser missteps. Since no Becoming is possible without Being, as long as the unit in a process continues to exist (be it the Roman Empire, the Christian Church, Art, Science, etc.) there is unchangeable or recurrent (intermittent or continuous) process. Because sociocultural processes have an aspect of uniqueness it does not follow that they do not also have an aspect of repetition. As a matter of fact not only historical and social phenomena but all inorganic and organic phenomena are likewise unique in a way. There probably do not exist two identical drops of water, two cells, two organisms, even two atoms or electrons.

[16] See W. Dilthey, *Einleitung in die Geisteswissenschaften* (Leipzig, 1883), and *Der Aufbau der geschichtlichen Welt in der Geisteswissenschaften*, in *Abhandlungen der Berliner Akademie, philosophisch-historische Klasse* (1910) ; H. Rickert, *Die Grenzen der naturwissenschaftlichen Begriffsbildung* (Tübingen-Leipzig, 1902) ; Xénopol, *op. cit.* Also W. Windelbandt, *Die Praeludien* (Tübingen, 1911), Vol. II; A. Lappo-Danilevsky, *Methodology of History* (in Russian) (St. Petersburg, 1909), Vol. I.

And yet this does not prevent the organic and inorganic phenomena from having an aspect of similarity and repetition which may be studied by physics and chemistry; and it is this recurrence which physics and chemistry mainly study. As we shall see, the inorganic and organic worlds are full of the phenomena of recurrence in time and in space. The point is that all these phenomena have, side by side with the aspect of uniqueness, the aspect of similarity and identity which results in the repetition of the same chemical element, the same relationship of the elements, the same structure of cells or organisms, the same relationship between two or more inorganic or organic phenomena.

It is the same with the processes of social life and human history. If we set ourselves to ferret out only the unique traits in these processes we can do so. But if we wish to concentrate our attention on the repeated aspects of these phenomena we can find enough to suit us. Perhaps the uniformity of these repetitions is not so rigid here as in the inorganic world. Nevertheless it is still as important to recognize here as elsewhere the repetition of a given phenomenon, that is, the similarity of its essential traits in a given recurrence with those which occurred before or after, or here and there. That this is so the direct experience of all of us confirms without the slightest doubt.

What is the daily life of man but an alternation of activity and sleep, work and rest, breakfast, lunch, dinner; a repetition of the same grinding hours of work; an alternation of pain and pleasure, satisfaction and dissatisfaction; and a host of other daily repeated actions, movements, thoughts, desires, and psychical experiences? This "grinding routine" comprises the main fabric of our daily life: "day in, day out," each different from one another in some respects, but in larger aspects each much more like another than unlike. Of similar recurrences are woven the longer periods of existence. The Sunday rest and the six days of labor monotonously repeat themselves from week to week (for many with even such details as waffles for Sunday breakfast and Sunday movies). The monthly "paydays" flow untiringly one after another, here and there and in many societies, some quite different from one another. Seasonal variations of our mode of living come and go every new spring, summer, fall, and winter. The annual events of Christmas, birthday, nameday, maintain their endless rounds of recurrence each year, bringing minor differences in an overwhelming pattern of sameness. Finally, all of human life is composed of the same main phases of childhood, adolescence, maturity, and old age, which repeat themselves untiringly, if not in the life of the same individual, then in the life of numberless individuals through the earth and time. Verily

> One generation goeth and another generation cometh; but the earth abideth for ever. . . . The sun also ariseth, and the sun goeth down, and hasteth to its place where it ariseth. That which hath been is that which shall be; and that which hath been done is that which shall be done; and there is no new thing under the sun.

The old sage exaggerated the identity of recurring phenomena but put the fact of repetition unforgettably.

The great symphony of social life is "scored" for a countless number of separate processes, each proceeding in a wavelike manner and recurring in space, in time, in both space and time, periodically or nonperiodically, after short or long intervals. Briefly or for an extensive time, in the same or in several social systems, a process moves in a certain quantitative or qualitative or spatial direction, or in all these directions, reaches its "point of saturation," and then often reverses its movements. Economic processes fluctuate endlessly between prosperity and depression, enrichment and poverty; vital processes between births, deaths, marriages, divorces; all undergo their "ups and downs," which sometimes become monotonously uniform. Crime and licentiousness, religion and irreligion, social stability and revolt, recur endlessly. Social systems — associations, organizations, institutions — forever repeat the processes of recruiting, change, dismissal of their members, originate, grow, and dissolve. And so it goes with almost all social phenomena and process. Pulsations of war and peace, stable and critical periods, revolution and reaction, autocracy and democracy, individualism and collectivism, classicism and romanticism, idealism and materialism, convention and anarchy, growth and decay, integration and disintegration, have been going on without end.

These reminders are sufficient, for the present, to enable the reader to detect the one-sidedness of the partisans of the unicist conception of the processes of social life and human history. They have taken only one side of the coin and forgotten the other.

A much stronger argument, which virtually demolishes the theory of the unicists, is that their position is untenable logically. No unique historical process can be narrated without the admission, explicit or implicit, that many essential traits are repeated.[17] Suppose our historian wishes to describe Roman religion, or law, or the class composition

---

[17] "It is necessary to discern similarities even in the most different objects," says Aristotle. *Rhetoric* III, xi, 5.

of Roman society, or any other aspect of Roman history, as an absolutely unique event or process which has nothing in common with, or recurring in, other societies and other periods. Is such a task possible to accomplish? No, and for very obvious reasons. Let us take, for example, Roman religion. If any moment of any historical event or sociocultural process is unique, a difficulty arises at once: what moment of Roman religion is to be described? Is it to be the Roman religion of 8 P.M., July 1, 321 B.C., or of 7 A.M., May 10, 322 B.C.? If the historian wished to give such a description he could not because nobody knows what exactly were the religious beliefs, rites, and so on, at one of these moments, and how they changed from one moment to another. If he should say that so exact a concern with time is unnecessary, he would be denying his own claim that every process of history is unique. If he attempted to give a general picture of the religious situation in Rome during several decades or centuries, it would be not, as it were, a single photograph of a unique process but a composite photograph, a kind of average, a generalizing picture for a very long period. This would imply an admission that for decades or centuries a process had retained many traits unchanged or was recurring from generation to generation, was repeated in the actions and beliefs of numerous individuals and groups. In brief, it would mean a complete abandonment of the unicist contention. Such, then, is the difficulty with respect to time which this theory would meet with at once, and which would prevent the description of a process as really unique at every moment of its existence.

The next obstacle, which is no less difficult to surmount, is that connected with uniqueness or recurrence in space. The thesis of uniqueness demands that any phenomenon which shows some differences from every other in space or time is to be described as unique. There is no doubt that the religious beliefs and convictions of thousands of Roman individuals, families, and groups were not absolutely identical. To some degree they were different with every individual as they are among people of today. Since this is so, the problem arises whether our unicist means to describe the religious beliefs and rites of Roman X, or Roman Y, or Roman Z, or any other Roman individual, or whether he intends to describe Roman religion generally as it existed within such and such a group in Roman society. His concept of uniqueness would have been carried through only when he had described the religious beliefs of specific individuals, each taken separately. It is evident that such a task could not be performed for all the individuals in Roman society. If the unicist confined himself to one, or five, or ten Romans, his work could not be

styled a description of Roman religion generally, because it would be
the religion of only a few different Roman individuals out of hundreds of
thousands, each of whom, according to the thesis, would be unique.
Moreover, even with respect to these ten Romans — or, for that matter,
to one — adequate description would be impossible, because the religion
of any individual is changing throughout life, from childhood to senility.
Therefore, even in an individual every moment of religious belief is
unique.   Under such circumstances our unicist, to be consistent, may
not talk or write about the religion of such and such an individual generally, but must deal with the religion, for example, of X at the age of
7 years, 4 months, 23 days, 7 hours, 53 minutes, and 24 seconds.   But
this is only the beginning.   He must now proceed to record the religion
of this individual at intervals of a year, a month, a day, perhaps even an
hour — in any case at intervals of no more than several years.   Without the performance of this insuperable task — impossible with regard
to one Roman, and inconceivable for any large number of Romans —
the unicist can make no generalizations about Roman religion.   In effect,
history becomes merely the meaningless setting down of microscopically
minute facts.   Any deviation from this becomes an admission of the
fact of recurrence.

All these considerations show how the thesis of uniqueness, being consistently carried through, destroys itself.   As a matter of fact all the
historians who have written of Roman religion (if their writing is worth
anything scientifically, as I think much of it is) have generalized to a
greater or less degree.   They have always drawn a composite picture,
based on the explicit or implicit admission of recurrences — similarities
in the beliefs of Romans of different generations, of different times, of
different ages or sexes or groups — both in Rome proper and in the
provinces, and wherever else Romans lived.

But this is not all.   The greatest difficulty, seemingly unconquerable,
which the unicist meets with is that which springs from human language
and human logic, from the elementary but important rule that he may
style by the same term only phenomena which are identical, or at least
essentially similar, and that he must style by different terms phenomena
which are fundamentally different.   From this standpoint when our
unicist describes the *religion* of the Romans, the *art*, the *law*, the *class
composition*, the *wars*, the *imperialism*, the *decay*, the *vices* and *virtues*,
or the *sculpture* of the Romans — or when he talks of the Roman *rich* and
the Roman *poor classes*, the Roman *bourgeoisie*, or of Roman *expansion*,
and so on — he admits through his back door recurrences and repetitions

of social processes which he tried to bar from his front door. In styling a certain complex of social phenomena in Roman society as religion or a rich class or decay or law or art, the historian indicates that it is in some essential respects the same as religion, art, law, decay, and so on, among other peoples and at different periods. Otherwise, none of these terms, which imply classification and therefore recurrence, could be used. The point is that, for example, the Roman, Greek, Persian, Egyptian, medieval Christian, Protestant, Hindu, and other *religions*, whatever their differences and however each may be unique, must all have certain essential elements in common in order to belong to *the same class* of social phenomena styled religion. And since they belong to the same class and have common elements, then this means that in certain characteristics religion is a recurring phenomenon, repeated in different societies — at different periods, that is, in space and time. This is true of all categories of sociocultural and historical processes.

The crushing power of this argument is clear now. It has shown that the unicist cannot make any of his scientific descriptions without using the terms of human language which imply inevitably and unescapably the existence of recurrent elements and traits in any of the phenomena which are viewed as unique. If our unicist should wish to escape this inescapable logic, he might perhaps try to invent a type of terminology of his own which would be capable of giving expression to endless uniqueness; unfortunately, in that case his work would probably be put among the writings of the insane and he himself, very likely, in an asylum.

The weakness of the absolutely unicist position should now be plain. To it we grant what belongs to it rightfully : there is in any phenomenon a unique aspect. But we cannot concede what is based on an obvious, and even gross, violation of logic, which clearly leads to grave error. If any phenomena have their unique aspects, they also have their recurrent traits, characteristics which are common to other phenomena. In one sense sociocultural life and history never repeat themselves; and yet, in another, they always recur to some extent. Such seems to be the truth of the entire matter.

One may, therefore, as readily justify scientifically the study of the recurrent aspect of sociocultural processes as of their unique aspect. Hence, a discipline which specializes in the investigation of the first — be it called sociology, social philosophy, philosophy of history, or "abracadabra" — has as much right to exist as any unicist discipline that concentrates on the study of the second.

IV. Punctuation and Pulsation of Sociocultural Processes

If the unit and all the directions of a given process remain the same throughout its existence, it cannot have any "punctuation," "turn," "measure," "phase," "link," "beat," "rhythm." The unvarying nature of its directions in all their senses excludes, by definition, any pauses that separate one part of it from the others. Any accentuation that punctuates its "phases" and "turns," or marks the boundary line between its sections, or denotes its "measures" and "beats" and "rhythms" becomes impossible. Such a process may be compared to a musical note that, throughout its existence, goes on continuously and without any change whatsoever: or to a straight line, absolutely uniform and without divisions throughout its entire length. We might divide such a note or line artificially into sections, but our division would have no counterpart in the reality of the note or the line. This means that *a change in one or more directions, in any of their senses, of a process is necessary for its real punctuation.* More than this: *Any punctuation of a process is always the result of a change of one or more of its directions and their senses.* So far as a process is marked by caesuras, rhythm, "turns," change in tempo, or division into "phases," "links," "parts," and so on, all these marks are but a function of a change in any of the directions (in any of their senses) of a given process.

Thus, if the time direction in its various meanings remains the same, no time punctuation, no change of rhythm or tempo, no largo, prestissimo, accelerando, ritardando, is possible. On the other hand, as soon as the time direction changes (the tempo, let us say, passes from largo to presto), the process is divided at once into empirically existing links or phases, or, to speak in musical terms, measures and rhythms. Similarly, as soon as the quantitative direction shows any change (say the birth rate falls from 9.2 to 8.5 per 1000), this denotes a "turn" in the process, and breaks it into punctuated parts. When a process changes its qualitative direction (when something passes, for example, from health to sickness, red to blue, silence to noise, peace to war, prosperity to depression, childhood to puberty), the change of the qualitative direction divides the process into two or more different stages, phases, parts. In all such cases the punctuation is not imposed artificially, but exists within the process, and, when comprehended, provides an adequate indication of the real pulsation of the process.

From the principle thus explained there follows a series of conclusions which bear upon many important problems in the social sciences.

A. *The sharper the change in a given direction, the greater the modification of the process, so far as this direction is concerned.* In other words, the greater the change in direction, the sharper is the "turn" in the movement of the process, the clearer and more pronounced is the line that separates one phase from another, the more deeply punctuated the process becomes, and, last but not least, the easier it is to perceive and comprehend the pulsations.

B. Other conditions being equal, *simultaneous change in two directions punctuates a process more markedly than an* equal change in either of these directions alone. In such cases the caesura that separates one phase from the other becomes double or cumulative. When in a musical composition the tempo and the rhythm change together,[18] the modification becomes much more noticeable than when only one of these elements changes. If in such a field of sociocultural processes as, say, that of scientific discovery, there occurs at a certain moment not only a sharp change in the movement of the number of discoveries, from a preceding level to a sudden great increase (*i.e.*, a change in the quantitative direction) but also a shift in the field in which the discoveries are made, for example, from political economy to chemistry (*i.e.*, change in the qualitative direction), the turn becomes much more pronounced than if it were limited to only one of these directions.

C. From propositions A and B it follows that the greater the number of directions and their senses in which simultaneous change takes place, and the deeper or sharper the change in each of them, the greater will be the turn experienced by the process and the more easily this will be observed and understood.

[18] Even in writing about music, tempo and rhythm are confused often, in writing on social science almost always. They are very different things: the same musical score with the same measures and rhythm can be played at a slow tempo (largo) or at a very fast tempo (prestissimo). The same record can be played on a Victrola at 78 revolutions a minute, or at 156 or 39 revolutions. The tempo in all three cases will be quite different, the rhythm and measures the same. Generally, as we shall see in Volume Four, the terms, concepts, symbols, and other essentials of musical knowledge and theory are of invaluable help to any theorizer in the field of social processes. Hitherto social science has been using various curves and diagrams for the purpose of describing social processes. These, as compared with the technique and symbols of musical composition, are rude and inadequate. After all, the social scientist deals with the greatest and most complex symphony — the symphony of sociocultural life. In order to be able to read and to describe it, he needs at least as well developed a system of symbols and denotations as the composer of a symphony in music. If it were possible at the present moment to write treatises in social dynamics along the lines of a musical score, these treatises would probably gain a great deal in scientific value. I should not be surprised if in the social science of the future much of the musical system of concepts, terms, and symbols would be frequently used.

The essential meaning of all three preceding propositions may be formulated thus : *the depth, magnitude, and sharpness of each punctuation of a given process is directly proportional to the number of the directions in which the process synchronously changes, and to the sharpness of change in each of these directions.*

A change in one direction usually marks some "phase" in the life history of a process; a change in two or more directions marks a much larger "period" or "epoch" or "era." The change in one of the directions represents a comparatively slight turn; the change in two or more directions — of the same intensity in each, as in the first case — is a much more important turning point, signifying a much deeper and more pregnant transformation.

D. Finally, *when the unit in which the process takes place ceases to be identifiable, the process itself is to be regarded as ended.* Thus in accordance with the transformation of the unit itself in which movement takes place, the number of directions in which it changes, and the sharpness of change in each of these directions, a process contains a long series of punctuations from the most superficial "vibrations," "links," "phases," to "epochal" periods, "eras"; until a radical change in all its directions, accompanied by such a transformation of the unit as makes it unidentifiable, marks the end of the process altogether.

A few additional words in regard to the beginning and end of a process are not out of place here, since these extremes are the greatest, the ultimate, punctuations. *As long as the unit which is in process is identifiable, the process continues to exist in spite of all the changes in its directions. When the unit is changed to such an extent that it becomes unidentifiable, the process ends. The moment when the identification of the unit becomes impossible is the point at which the process ends. The moment when we observe the emergence of a new unit which, so far as our knowledge goes, did not exist before, a new process is started.*[19]

Identifying the unit of a process is a very complex and important problem. It will be considered in Volume Four. The above statement must now suffice together with that in the preceding section concerning the repetition of *essential* traits in recurrent processes.

[19] Some scholars prefer to say that a unit exists as long as it maintains its equilibrium. I prefer to use the criterion of "identification" because it is a clearer and more direct indication of whether or not the unit exists. If the unit is identifiable, it exists; if not, it does not. Moreover, without first having at our disposal any means of identifying the unit, we cannot say whether or not it possesses equilibrium. If we can identify it, then to add that it keeps its equilibrium is useless. See P. Sorokin, " *Le concept d'equilibre est-il necessaire aux sciences sociales,*" in *Revue international de sociologie*, September–October, 1936.

Only one additional point need be mentioned here, on the various classes of units and the various durations of processes. The point is understandingly observed by Aristotle. In the course of his discussion, he indicates that in some cyclical recurrences the same unit itself (*e.g.*, a heavenly body) is repeated, while in others only the species as represented by various and perishing individuals of the same kind.

It is evident that those things, whose "substance" — that which is undergoing the process — is imperishable, will be numerically as well as specifically, the same in their recurrence. . . . Those things, whose "substance" is perishable must return upon themselves in the sense that what recurs, though specifically the same [*i.e.*, of the same species], is not the same numerically [*i.e.*, not the same individually].[20]

In applying this principle to our case we must distinguish the finite recurring process in which the unit is genus, species, subspecies, from an individual of this genus, species, or subspecies. We can talk of the beginning and end of the process where the unit is individual, for instance, John Smith, a citizen of the United States. The end of this process (the life of John Smith) does not mean the end of the life process, the units of which are citizens of the United States generally. This second process existed before Smith and will continue to exist after his life process is ended. It will exist as long as the United States and, consequently, its citizens (comprising many individuals in successive generations) exist. The end of the process where the unit is the United States would not necessarily mean the end of the history of mankind. Mankind existed before the beginning of the United States and will probably continue to exist after its end. Many units of a process may be distributed thus among individuals, sub-subspecies, subspecies, species, and even genus. When we talk of the beginning or end of a process, we must remember that these extremes represent the points at which the process is merged with a narrower or broader process. The distribution may be represented by such classifications as these:

Class 1. The beginning and end of a recurrence series where the unit is the same individual.

Class 2. The beginning and end of a recurrence series where the unit is a subclass composed of various related individuals.

Class 3. The beginning and end of a recurrence series where the unit is a species composed of various subclasses.

Class 4. The beginning and end of a recurrence series where the unit is a genus composed of various species.

[20] Aristotle, *De generatione et corruptione*. *The Works of Aristotle*, trans. under the editorship of W. D. Ross (Oxford, 1930), Vol. II, pp. 337–338.

In accordance with the character of the classification, the number of classes may be fewer or greater than these four. Usually as we move from processes of Class 1 to those of Class 4, duration systematically increases. It is thus important that the investigator make clear each time what kind of duration he is talking of and, consequently, what kind of recurrences he is dealing with, whether those of a process in which the unit is an individual, or those in which a subclass is the unit, or those of a species or those of a genus. Usually recurrences involving an individual are contained in the recurrences of the subclass, species, and genus to which the individual belongs, but the recurrences of each class are not necessarily present in the processes of the succeeding subordinate classes nor of the individual of which the smallest unit is composed.

Thus, by developing logically the elements of process, the unit in which it works and the directions it takes — we have unfolded its fundamental nature, and have, on this basis, been able to discover, among other points, the system of the real punctuation of sociocultural processes, from the slightest and most superficial pauses to turns of epoch-making nature, as well as those ultimate points of punctuation which mark the beginning and end of processes. From the pragmatic point of view, the relatively superficial punctuations marked by a slight deviation in one of the directions of a process are the least important, not only because they are the least deep, but also because they often escape observation. The point is that in empirical reality none of the sociocultural processes exists in a state of isolation from the others but is inextricably interwoven with them, at least with respect to time and space. In addition, many have different rhythms and pulsations. Hence their combination results, not in a symphony with clearly defined tempos, measures, and rhythms but in a cacophony composed of different rhythms and tempos beaten simultaneously, so that they tend to obliterate and neutralize one another. The result is that we often fail to perceive the punctuation in a given process, if this is made only by a change in one of its directions. Under such circumstances, the cumulative punctuations or beats made by a synchronous change in two, three, or four of the directions of the process are noticeable more easily than the pulsations of the above "cacophony." They are like one marked rhythm and one clear tempo in which all the instruments of an orchestra play. Even an ear which is deaf musically can hear and understand these.

In the infinitely perplexing processes of sociocultural life, these cumulative pulsations are often comprehensible where the simpler beats fail us. They usually mark the especially important and long-time movement of an epoch or era.   Therefore we must open our ears to them in order that they do not get lost in the deadeningly noisy and amazingly complex cacophony of history.   This does not mean that the simpler signs are useless for orientation in the maze of social processes or that it is not worth while to try to study separately the beats representing time, space, quantity, and quality.   On the contrary all this is very important and often helpful.   But in addition the study of the cumulative punctuations is also exceedingly important and often more helpful.

What is quite useless for the investigation of the phases of processes and their recurrences in actuality is a purely artificial division into periods, based on a theory and not on empirical facts.   Such punctuation has been used often in the social sciences, whether in application to historical or economic or political or other processes.   It is used also to a considerable degree in several purely statistical studies where an artificial "mean," "median," or "average" is assumed in a mechanical way.   Such artificial beats, cycles, rhythms, punctuations, and what not, do not describe the real pulsations but something which either does not have any relationship at all to them or at most one which is very remote.   Their cognitive value is thus very limited, often nil.

For many scholars of a narrowly "empirical" outlook the problem of the punctuation and pulsation of sociocultural processes may appear too abstract and without urgent need for solution, in the sense that it does not confront a social scientist unless he himself seeks it.   It is needless to argue the fallacy of such an opinion.   The problem, in fact, faces the social scientist daily.   As soon as an economist engages in the study of business fluctuations, a demographer of vital processes, a criminologist of the movement of crime, or a social statistician of various social processes, he is confronted with it.   When he elucidates the "trends," the short- and long-time fluctuations of processes, he aims to describe their real punctuations, pulsations, and rhythms.   If he follows the path of least resistance in the form of giving artificial "means," "modes," and "medians," and restricts himself mostly to a study of the changes in the quantitative direction only, ignoring especially changes in the qualitative direction, such a drastic simplification of the problem does not mean that the question of real punctuation is not present and therefore not urgent.   The historians perhaps have to deal with it more closely than some others, first of all, in the work of dividing history into periods; second, in the attempt to mark properly the periods of the rise and decline of certain forms in the history of art, philosophy, religion, science, political organization.   This explains why they have dealt so much with the problem

itself of establishing periods. Some of them, like Kurt Breisig, say that
the end of one period and the beginning of another are marked by "a
change of the direction of the process" (*Richtungswechsel der Entwick-
lungsreihe*), and that such a change is always accentuated by some
important events.[21] Unfortunately, Breisig leaves his theory at that
point without developing it further. Other historians, especially in
connection with the problem of the division of history into the ancient,
medieval, and modern periods, have discussed the question more fully,
being concerned with the same problem which now confronts us. Thus
Spangenberg observes :

Historical process is a flowing continuity. It is like a stream which does
not have either standstill or separated parts. Though every periodization is
artificial, it is helpful and unavoidable. . . . Without a chronological sub-
division an historian cannot elucidate and master the richness of the historical
material and separate clearly the beginning, climax, and decline of the development studied.[22]

Thus the problem of the division of history into periods aiises. Most
historians, like C. J. Neumann, define a period as "a well-individualized
time span of historical life which by its content and configuration (*Inhalt*
and *Gehalt*) is bound into unity and through this separates itself from
what preceded and what followed it." "It is a part of the process
(*Entwicklung*) and at the same time it is a closed unity." [23]
This and similar theories are somewhat indefinite because they just
substitute for one unknown (period) another (unity different from what
preceded it and what followed). To be clear they must point to more
concrete signs of a unity as a separate "beat" in the process of history.
For such signs historians have been turning to some important event or
events, whether it be a catastrophe, like an invasion of the barbarians
or the Black Death ; or some political or social upheaval, like a change
in a political regime or a great revolution ; or a great new religious movement, like the Reformation ; or an important new invention, like printing ;

[21] K. Breisig, *Der Weg der Menschheit von geschichtlichen Werden* (Stuttgart, 1928), Vol. III,
pp. 1–20.
[22] H. Spangenberg, "*Die Perioden der Weltgeschichte*," in *Historische Zeitschrift*, Vol. CXVII
(1922), p. 3. Note the contradictory character of this statement: if a given process has
beginning, climax, and decline (and consequently an end) then "beats" or "phases" are really
present in it, and since they are present, to note them in a study is an artificiality no greater
than that of the statement that a tree usually has roots, trunk, branches, and leaves. Further
on, Spangenberg himself explicitly contradicts his statement as to the artificiality of period
divisions.
[23] C. J. Neumann, "*Perioden Römischer Kaisergeschichte*," in *Historische Zeitschrift*, Vol.
CXVII (1917), p. 378.

or an important scientific discovery, like those of Copernicus or Galileo; or a combination of such important events occurring synchronously.[24]

I have mentioned these problems and theories of the historians among other things in order to show that the problem confronting us is actual: it confronts all the social sciences, and even all the natural sciences. If among natural sciences the question is not discussed so much as among others the reason is that the punctuation — phases, beats, and recurrences — with which these sciences deal is relatively so simple, so clearly pronounced, so unquestionable, that there is very little reason to philosophize or to argue about it, but on the contrary every impetus to measure and to study it.

The preceding paragraphs have attempted to give a delineation of the concept of process, its elements, its main varieties, the nature of its uniqueness or its recurrence, and, finally, the bases and forms of its punctuation. The characterization has been intentionally concise and, in this sense, preliminary. Nevertheless, it is hoped that the description is sufficiently clear and logical to serve for what is to follow: a study of the great waves and recurrent fluctuations in the history of integrated cultures. In the last part of this work the concept of process will be unfolded in all its full details.

V. Linear and Nonlinear: Cyclical and Varyingly Recurrent Patterns of Process from the Standpoint of Their Direction

As we have mentioned, processes have directions with their senses. If the sense of a given direction and the direction itself remain the same throughout the existence of a process, its pattern may be said to be *linear* so far as the given direction and sense are concerned.

With reference to *spatial direction* linearity means a steady movement of the unit of process along the same line from one spatial center to another. Examples of such linearity are given in the following statements. "In the course of time the centers of civilization move northwardly from the tropical to the arctic regions." "The area of peace and solidarity progressively and concentrically expands in the course of time, while the area of antagonism and war progressively shrinks." "The stream of civilization shifts in the course of time from mountain to plain." [25] In

---

[24] See the discussion and the references in Spangenberg's article; also F. Stieve, *Die Perioden der Weltgeschichte* (Berlin, 1893), and J. Burckhardt, *Weltgeschichtliche Betrachtungen* (Stuttgart, 1905), W. Vogel, "*Über den Rhythmus im geschicht. Leben*," in *Historische Zeitschrift*, Vol. CXXIX (1923); and E. Troeltsch, "*Über die Maszstabe*," *ibid.*, Vol. CXVI. See in these papers a survey of various theories in the field.

[25] See my *Contemporary Sociological Theories*, pp. 106–109 *et passim*.

these and similar statements the social processes are represented as moving or radiating in the course of time from one spatial center to another, steadily, without any fundamental deviation from the spatial course assumed.

As applied to *quantitative direction* linearity means that the process either increases, or decreases, or remains constant during the time of its existence. Statements and theories that claim a progressive increase of human intelligence in the course of time, a progressive decrease of superstitions, an ever-increasing accumulation of knowledge, and so on, all assume quantitative linearity.

In application to the *time direction* linearity can mean only that the process maintains a steady and undeviating course from one time point to another, either from the past to the present and from the present to the future or vice versa. But linearity of time direction alone is not a particularly meaningful concept, since it is applicable to all patterns of process — both linear and nonlinear — from the standpoint of direction. As we shall see, however, *in combination with spatial and other directions, it can have a very distinct significance.* For instance, in such concepts as the acceleration or slowing of a process, time is a necessary element: acceleration means an ever-increasing tempo or, what is the same, an ever-decreasing consumption of time in the realization of a change which remains constant in magnitude and kind. In such a process we have time linearity in combination with linearity of the quantitative or qualitative direction. There is also some special meaning in time linearity when referred to those processes which occur only at a particular point in time and cannot be repeated or recovered, in contradistinction to processes which can be produced and reproduced at any time.

Finally, with regard to the *qualitative direction also, linearity is not quite applicable.* If a process passes from one quality A to another, B, quite different from A, or if it passes through a series of different qualities, A, B, C, D, such a passage is neither linear nor nonlinear. It is just beyond domain of these concepts. In moving through a series of qualitative states in which a certain quality becomes gradually more pronounced, clearer, purer (or fades and is contaminated), a process exhibits not so much a qualitative as a quantitative linearity. In the passage of a human being from childhood to maturity and old age, of a style from the Romanesque to the Gothic and to that of the Renaissance, or of a mentality from the theological to the metaphysical and the positive states, the series is neither linear nor nonlinear; it is a succession of qualitative states essentially different from one another and not associated in any way with the notions of linearity or nonlinearity. Linearity [26] means in all such cases a certain *uniform order of sequence of the qualitative states*. This is, in fact, the only meaning which qualitative linearity may have. For when, in the succession of these qualitative states a certain quality progressively increases or decreases, such a linearity becomes either quantitative or combined. Only in a combination with the quantitative or other directions, then, and for a few special shades of meaning, can linearity have significance when applied to the qualitative direction.

Such are the general meanings which the notion of linearity has as applied to the four forms of direction of a process. When these diverse linearities are combined, the result is synthetic or cumulative linearity, as, for example, in acceleration and retardation, expansion and contraction, increasing and decreasing purity, and many others.

Now linearity itself, when referred to the direction of a process, is of four main varieties: *unilinear, oscillating, spiral*, and *branching*. If the sense of a given direction remains the same throughout the existence of a process, and does not deviate for a moment from the linear trend, the process is unilinear. If the main linear trend remains, but the sense of a given direction deviates from it occasionally, we have either oscillating, or spiral, or branching varieties of linearity.

By the very logic of their being recurrent, processes cannot have a unilinear pattern of direction. If a process proceeds unilinearly throughout its existence — that is, continues without any change whatsoever — then it is like a straight line, without variation, punctuation, phases. It contains no sections (all divisions in it must be artificially made), no links, no stops. Hence there is no possibility of recurrence within it. Thus, a unit moving uniformly and rectilinearly in a spatial direction from A toward B, with an unvarying velocity and without any quantitative or qualitative change, contains no real punctuation, hence no recurrence. It is, as it were, a kind of spatially moving Being, instead of a Becoming. This means that as far as recurrent processes are concerned, there must be some deviation from the main linear trend, some modification of one of the senses of direction: *temporal, spatial, quantitative, or qualitative*.

---

[26] Most of the thinkers who regard such a series as linear really have in mind not the concept of linearity or nonlinearity, but the uniformity of the sequence of the qualitative states through which all the similar subjects of the process pass. According to them all people pass through the same sequence of the qualitative stages of evolution; the arts develop along the line of a uniform sequence of qualitative stages and the same is true of any other phenomena. The linearity of a process and *uniformity of the order of the qualities* through which the subject or subjects of the process pass are evidently quite different things. This point will be more fully discussed in Chapter Ten of Volume Two.

In recurrent processes, and in those aspects of each process which are repeated, linearity may be of the *oscillating, spiral,* or *branching* type, but not of the *unilinear.* (See Figure 2 for pictorial forms of these varieties of linear process.) In oscillating linearity, though the movement of the senses of direction (whether spatial, quantitative, qualitative, time, or composite) changes, these variations are purely secondary and temporary. After deviating for a short period from its main direction, an oscillating linear process resumes its course, and so continues to deviate and return throughout the whole of its existence. The line may signify the quantitative, qualitative, or spatial direction, or a combination of two or all of them.

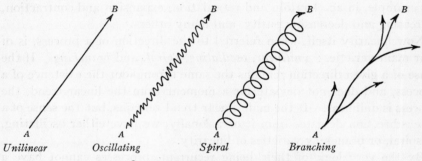

FIG. 2.   VARIETIES OF LINEAR PROCESS

Spiral is very much like oscillating linearity. The main difference between them (besides that in the spatial direction where the distinctive nature of the spiral line is self-evident) lies in the fact that *spiral linearity* involves a greater regularity in the occurrence and nature of the secondary deviations from the main direction; or to be more exact, a greater uniformity among all the deviations from the main route (including sometimes even uniformity of the sequence of phases through which each deviation passes).

Finally, *branching* linearity refers to a process which is separated into several branches, most of which, in spite of considerable deviations, still preserve the main direction and sense, like trees whose main vertical and upward growth is maintained despite many deviating and capriciously directed boughs. Such are the principal linear patterns of recurrence.

Let us now turn to a second type of recurrence: the *cyclical.* This type may be subdivided into the *completely cyclical* and the *relatively cyclical.* In the *completely cyclical* process the last phase of a given recurrence returns to its first phase, and the cycle begins again, traversing the same route through which it has passed before. In the *relatively cyclical* process, on the other hand, the direction of the recurring process does not coincide completely with that of the series of previous recurrences. There is some deviation from cycle to cycle. But in contradistinction to the linear pattern and especially to its oscillating and branching varieties, the relatively cyclical process does not have any main route *ex definitione* and returns partly to its previous direction, while the oscillating and branching linear processes do have such a route and in their recurrence never run twice over the same tracks.

As is true of linearity, the cyclic nature of a process may concern the *spatial* direction. If the space involved is geometric, then that a process is cyclic means that it moves circularly (including in circular motion the ellipsoid, etc.) and that the last spatial point of a given cycle coincides with its starting point. In the completely cyclical process the spatial trajectory of all recurrences is exactly the same. In the relatively cyclical it is not exactly the same in all parts, but the final point of the given cycle returns to its initial point.

A process may be cyclic with respect to its *quantitative* direction. In the completely cyclical process the "curve" of the quantitative senses of each cycle (increase, decrease, constancy — in whatever combination) is the same not only in the sequence of these senses but also in the amplitude of each. In brief, if laid one above the other, the quantitative curves of all the cycles of the process would coincide exactly. In the relatively cyclical process the curves of each recurrence are not quite alike, whether in respect to the amplitude or in some other respect; but the main sequence of the senses of the quantitative direction remains the same, and the last point of each recurrence coincides quantitatively with its starting point.

A process may be cyclic in its *qualitative* direction. The completely cyclical process would effect the passage of the unit of the process, in a uniform sequence through the same qualitative phases in each recurrence. The last qualitative status of a given recurrence would be identical with the first, and the cycle would begin again its undeviating course. Thus we may suppose a process going through the qualitative states a, b, c, d, e; a, b, c, d, e; a, b, c, d, e; and so on. One qualitative cycle is identical with the others. In the relatively cyclical qualitative process, however, the sequence of the qualities traversed in each cycle remains the same, and the last qualitative stage returns the cycle to the first; but in their intensity, purity, shading, and in other respects, the qualities do not correspond exactly from cycle to cycle throughout the process. This may be represented schematically in the following fashion: a, b, c, d, e; a, b, c^1, d^1, e^1; A, B, c, d, e; and so on.

Finally, cyclical recurrence may relate to *time direction*, but only, however, when the temporal is combined with other directions of the process. Such recurrence means a *periodical time rhythm*, of whatever kind of periodicity, in regard to the phases of the cycles or the entire cycles themselves (rhythms: 1–2; 1–2–3; 1–2–3–4; etc.). Periodicity here signifies that the time in which the cycle, or a phase of it, is realized remains the same from cycle to cycle, or from a phase in one cycle to the same phase in the other recurrent cycles.[27] In this sense the time punctuation then repeats itself from recurrence to recurrence in a given cyclical series. Hence, with regard to such regular periodicity, one may speak of processes which are cyclical in their time direction.

When a process is completely cyclical in all directions it becomes *absolutely cyclical*. Otherwise, a process may be completely cyclical in some of these directions and relatively cyclical or not cyclical at all in others.

The third fundamental pattern of recurrent processes may be styled *variably or creatively recurrent*. This applies to recurrences which are not absolutely identical, and the successive stages of which are not always linear or cyclical, or unchangeable or regular, but vary. In one link the movement may be unilinear, in another oscillating, in a third cyclical, in others curvilinear, and so on.

This variegated pattern runs counter to the theory of the linearists, since it indicates that not all process patterns need have a single, unchanging main trend. In similar fashion it denies the cyclicist contention. And its recognition of recurrences, despite variation and change of direction, is in disagreement with the conception of the unicists. It contains within itself all the varieties of the unicist, cyclical, and linear theories; but it admits each only as one element, only as applying to some processes, to some aspects of historical or sociocultural movements, never to all of them.

Thus the *variably recurrent pattern is the broadest and richest of these conceptions*. It does not ascribe to an entire historical process or to all sociocultural processes any perpetual tendency or direction which must be followed without change. It does not assume that social and historical processes must always proceed either along a straight line, or spirally, or in cycles, or in any other single manner or direction. Some social processes entire, and others in part, do indeed run along a straight line, but within definite limits, after which they continue, here in loops, there in irregular oscillations, elsewhere in waves and in other different forms. Since sociocultural processes are as manifold in pattern as life itself, as rich and creative as the activity of the highest human genius, it would be

[27] See the formula of periodicity in E. B. Wilson's articles cited in note 6.

strange if they should in fact be so poor in creative variations as to follow eternally one route, one direction, one pattern of trajectory which the limited sense or the nonsense of a theorizer would like them to follow.

Differing thus from the other two, the variably or creatively recurrent pattern stresses particularly the following three points. First, since there is no one permanent linear trend, and since the directions change, historical and social processes incessantly undergo ever new variations of the old themes. In this sense they are filled with surprise and are seldom predictable in their totality.[28] In this sense history as a whole never repeats itself, and the entire historical process has a unique aspect at any point of its existence, an aspect which is perhaps predictable only in its unpredictability.

So far this conception agrees with the unicist conception. However, as has been mentioned, processes with a unique aspect are not woven of entirely unique materials. They have recurrent and repeated elements. To the extent that they repeat themselves, either in units, or in space, or in time, or in two or more of these factors, this conception is congenial with the cyclical theory, which views all the processes as recurrent, absolutely or relatively. It fits with the linearists' point of view in admitting a linear trend for a portion of a process, and during a limited period, but sharply disagrees with them in their main contentions. This leads to the second point.

The variably recurrent conception stresses the *existence of limits* in the linear direction of most social processes.[29] This is the point at which the conception differs radically from those of the linearists and cyclicists. The latter either do not recognize the existence of limit in a given direction, or are obliged to claim that the direction changes all the time (since the process goes in a circle) but that the whole process runs in the same, or a similar, circle again and again. The variably recurrent conception, on the contrary, claims that many processes go on for some time without any appreciable change in their direction, but that sooner or later the trend reaches its limit, and then the process turns aside into a new path. This means the denial of the existence of a perpetual main linear trend in history and most of the social processes. As to history as a whole, since it is not finished as yet and since the future is unpredictable, we do not and cannot know whether there is any continuous and main trend

[28] See P. Sorokin, "Is Accurate Social Planning Possible?" in *American Sociological Review*, Vol. I (1936), pp. 12–25.

[29] See P. Sorokin, "The Principle of Limits," in *Publications of the Sociological Society of America*, Vol. XXVI (1932), no. 3.

and any terminal point to which mankind is being led. Moreover we do not detect such a trend in most of the important aspects of socio-cultural life; in economic, political, social organization, in arts and religion, in morals, in the forms of the political or economic bodies, in the family and other social organizations, in philosophy and ethics, in science and ideology. Instead we see in a way ever new creations, different from the preceding qualitatively and irreducible to any linear form; in a way we see that, instead of a linear trend, continued social processes exhibit turns and shifts in their directions, repetitions, ups and downs, approaches and retreats, recurrences of various kinds. If some processes have had linear direction from their beginning to the present time, they are in a decided minority. Besides, it is a question whether the trend will not change in the future (especially in connection with the cooling of the sun and the dying of life on the earth, that have been prophesied for us).

The third point involves the so-called principle of *immanent causation*, or self-regulation of sociocultural processes. According to this principle, when the unit is integrated the change in the direction of the process is caused not only and not so much by the interference of external forces but by the inner forces of the process itself and by the nature of its unit. Just as the living activity of an organism breeds its death, regardless of any external accident or external forces, so any sociocultural process occurring in an integrated unit and moving in a certain direction generates, by virtue of this activity, "forces" or "causes" which change the unit of the process and its direction. In other words any given direction of a process produces its own end and replacement by a different direction. This ancient conception (it is found in Aristotle) will be further developed in Volume Four.

The subsequent scheme recapitulates the discussed classification of processes.

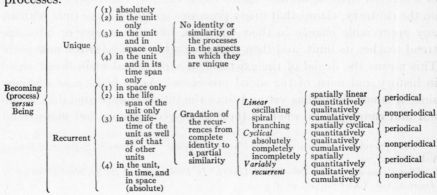

Into which of these patterns of process is the sociocultural life woven? Are all these patterns of process present in it, and, if so, in what proportion and in what fields? Which of these patterns has been particularly dominant in the mentality of this or that culture and period, and for what reasons? Are there oscillations in the emergence and prevalence of each of these patterns in the mentality of a given culture, and, if so, when and why has a given conception — whether linear or cyclical or varyingly recurrent — dominated? These and many related questions will be treated in the subsequent parts of this work and will be summed up analytically in Volume Four, the methodological section. There, likewise, will be considered many intricate problems connected with each of these conceptions, problems which are intentionally passed by here. For the present, the above brief definitions will serve as a sufficient "operational instrumentality" for the analytical and synthesizing constructions which are shortly to follow.

We are now about to turn to a study of sociocultural fluctuations mainly in the Graeco-Roman and the Western cultures, concentrating on the period from about 600 B.C. to the present time. These cultures are taken because they are better known to us than the others: they have left fuller and more accurate records than possibly any other culture. A period of, roughly, 2500 years is taken because long-time fluctuations cannot be studied properly in a shorter space of time, especially the profounder "waves" of history. Even this period is too short for the purposes of this study. But a lack of any even remotely satisfactory data for the time previous to 600 B.C. prevents our going beyond it into the past. But, though concentrating on these cultures and periods, we shall at the same time, in a study of the fluctuations of each class of phenomena, make additional, but much shorter, excursions into the sociocultural fluctuations of several other cultures, namely, the Hindu, the Chinese, and occasionally the Arabian. These special trips are undertaken for the purpose of verifying the validity of the results obtained through the study of the Graeco-Roman and Western fluctuations in "social space." I may be permitted to say that the brevity of these excursions should not suggest that the materials upon which they are based were studied hastily or incompletely. The specialists in the field of these cultures will perhaps admit that the necessary minimum of investigation has been done and that the important relevant sources and works have been consulted. So much for the limits of the treatment.

Now comes a more important question: What is studied in these cultures? What kind of fluctuations? What kind of problems? How are they investigated? For what purposes? A full and adequate answer to these questions is offered in the subsequent parts of the work. At the present we need only to indicate briefly a few of the main problems investigated. The questions dealt with are these: (1) Have the Graeco-Roman and the Western been logically integrated cultures? (2) If they have been, around what major premises have they been integrated? (3) Do the principles of the Ideational, the Sensate, and the Mixed types of culture offer a key for the solution of the problem of their integration? (4) If these principles do furnish a key, do they make it possible for the observer to comprehend the main forms of the science and philosophy, art and ethics, law and politics, economic and social organization, psychology and ideology, of the bearers of these cultures? (5) Has the logico-meaningful integration in these cultures been accompanied by the causal-functional? (6) Have these cultures and their main compartments remained unchanged in the course of time with respect to their predominant culture type, or have they undergone a substantial change in this respect? If they have experienced such alterations, then at what period were they predominantly Ideational, or Sensate, or Idealistic, or Mixed? (7) If there were these variations, what have been the main waves and alternations in these cultures? How long did each type last? Is any regular periodicity observable in the alternation of these types? (8) What have been the relationships in this process of various compartments of the cultures? Have they all been changing synchronously? Have some compartments been changing earlier than the others? Has the change in the direction of the cultural changes been always parallel or opposite or independent? (9) What have been the "causes" and factors of the change? And so many more questions might be specified without, however, exhausting the problems touched upon and discussed in the present work.

In a sense the work deals with one topic only: with the alternation of the domination of Ideational, Sensate, and Idealistic types of culture mentality and culture system. This one topic happens, however, to be of such a nature that its study demands and leads to the investigation of a legion of other topics involved in it, each of which is important enough to be the object of a special study.

The work represents a kind of grand fugue, the scoring of which involves the weaving into it of countless smaller fugues played by various sections of the orchestra. If the grand fugue is scored poorly, there is consolation for the composer : each little fugue may stand on its own feet and may have its own value, regardless of the value of the larger work which is intended to absorb all the smaller parts and to be the crowning climax of all of them. In a more prosaic way this means that if even the main synthesis of this work related to the Ideational and Sensate cultures proves unsatisfactory, each chapter or part that deals with a study of the fluctuation of the main sociocultural processes may not be valueless. These lines give a dim inkling of what the work as a whole deals with. To find out what is its real content, the reader must take his chance and look through its pages for himself.

If not for logical, then at least for pedagogical reasons, the study opens with a treatment of the fluctuation of the arts in the cultures studied. The pictorial and " concrete " nature of some of the art forms, particularly of painting and sculpture, and partly of music, architecture, and literature, seems to provide the best conditions for introducing the reader into the heart of the problem. Hence, we turn directly to a study of the arts.

PART TWO

Fluctuation of Ideational, Idealistic, and Sensate Forms of Art

Chapter Five

IS THERE ANY UNIFORM SEQUENCE IN THE FLOURISH-ING OF VARIOUS ARTS IN THE HISTORY OF A GIVEN CUL-TURE? PRELIMINARY CRITICAL SURVEY OF THEORIES ON THE SUBJECT

I. Introductory Remarks

We have already made a preliminary attempt, by an examination of various historical culture mentalities, to indicate that our conception of the Ideational, Sensate, and Mixed types entails no mere academic exercise in classification. It is now our intention to carry the attempt further. To establish conclusively the empirical value of our conceptions we must show that the various types are readily discernible in cultures which have had historical existence. They must be applicable to the main compartments of a given culture, whether the particular compartment be science, or philosophy, or art, or ethics, or *mores*, or forms of political, economic, or social organization. They must help us to understand the essential nature of any given form within the whole of a culture or in one or more of its compartments. They must throw light on the logico-meaningful and causal relationships (where these exist) between countless fragments, traits, details, events, processes; must order their chaotic multitude into comprehensible general formulas. Once grasped, they must serve as keys to open the doors to many sociocultural mysteries, or as arcs on which we can fasten a multitude of the perceptional fragments and characteristics of a given culture and its compartments. They must perform these functions in an "anatomic" or "taxonomic" diagnosis of culture as well as in a study of its "physiology": its change, its processes, its transformation, and its fluctuations. We shall begin this test in the field of art.

Our first step will consist in finding out whether the categories Ideational and Sensate are applicable to art phenomena. If they are so applicable, what does each category mean when referring specifically to painting, or sculpture, or music, or architecture, or literature, or the drama? Our next step in examining the cognitive value of the categories will consist in finding out to what extent and how successfully they serve, as detailed above, to generate understanding of the nature of a given art form, to order the fragmentary chaos of the art phenomena of a given culture or period into comprehensive systems, to answer a multitude of questions as to the causes and the manner of development in this field. Finally, the supreme test comes when we engage in investigating the dynamics of art phenomena in the course of time : their change, fluctuations, and transformations in terms, and from the standpoint, of these categories. Do they serve us satisfactorily in this particular problem? Do they help us greatly in this particular field where the perceptional data are so numerous, diverse, contrasting, fragmentary, and confused that we often do not see the wood for the trees? We have admirable and competent descriptive histories of art that detail for us all the changes the given art underwent. They often leave us hungry, however, if we wish to understand something of why these changes and forms have been what they have been ; what relationship, if any, exists between thousands of changing characteristics of a given art ; why now one form, now another, rises, becomes dominant, and then declines ; and especially, what relationship, if any, exists between the changes in a given branch of art, say painting, and those in other forms, say music or literature. Are the changes in each of the main fields of the arts connected in some way with those in other compartments of the same culture : its science, philosophy, ethics, law, religion, politics, economics, and other processes? Are there in these variations uniform relationships in the order or sequence of change? Do they change independently of one another? Is their change parallel? or contrapuntal? What regularity, if any, is there in these changes? Is there any continuous linear trend? or cyclical? or erratic fluctuation? Is there any periodicity? Finally, is the culture in question an integrated system that lives and changes organically, where a modification in the field of art means a corresponding and synchronous change in all the other compartments of the culture?

The purely descriptive and "factual" histories of art rarely answer, in a way that satisfies our curiosity, these and the hundreds of other similar questions which arise. They cannot be blamed for this. Such problems and tasks are not within their program. Sometimes they disdain them, often pass them by in order to avoid becoming entangled in "superficial philosophizing." Sometimes, they are simply not interested. Whatever the attitude of such histories, it is right from their standpoint. On the other hand, all who try to disentangle the confused mass of these problems are right also to make the effort. The problems exist ; they are there.   And they are at least as important as any of the problems of a descriptive history of art.   We may know well all the details of this or that picture of, say, Fra Angelico or Zeuxis; of this or that school of painting; and yet such a knowledge will remain "fragmentary," incapable of furnishing an answer to all the above questions.   Similar knowledge of many other paintings of other periods only increases our sense of chaos in this immense ocean of pictures, names, dates, traits, changes.

Whether we desire it or not, we somehow need an ordering of this chaos and the similar formlessness of other compartments of culture. Hence the necessity of some "ordering categories" like the proposed ones. If they are scientifically valuable categories, they will help in these difficulties.   If they are "dead categories," they will be of no assistance. Thus these last steps of the test play a decisive role.

Accordingly, the purpose of this part is to inquire into the meaning of the Ideational, Sensate, Idealistic, and the Mixed categories in the field of art phenomena.   The meaning once defined, we must then use these categories as the referential principles for diagnosing the given species of art.   The elucidation of these problems is but a preliminary step toward the fulfillment of the main purpose of the present part. This consists, with the help of these categories, first, in a study of the important aspects of the dynamics of art phenomena: the ways of their change, recurrences, trends, fluctuations, rhythms, periodicities, uniformities (or lack of them), and so on.   It consists, second, in an elucidation of the relationships, the causes and manners of association, of these aspects of the dynamics of art phenomena to similar aspects of the dynamics of other compartments of a given culture.   In this way we arrive at the very center of the study of the general problem of social change, social Becoming, social process, social trends and recurrences. And this is the task which the subsequent sections of this work will attempt to carry out, by taking into consideration, one after another, all the main compartments of culture.

Before passing to the realization of this plan and to the present writer's theories, it will be illuminating for us to glance, at least briefly, through the main body of theories in the field of these problems.   Such a glance will disclose generally the status of contemporary knowledge of the subject.   Thus, it will serve also as an introduction to the development of the special position taken in the present work.   The remainder of this and the subsequent chapter will be taken up entirely with some of the relevant theories, which, however, will be dealt with only as far as they concern the main problems, centered as they are about recurrent processes in culture generally and in art particularly. Let us turn to recurrences in the field of art phenomena.

As defined in the previous chapter recurrence may mean the repetition of a given unit in *time* only, or in *space* only, or in *both*. The culture which shows in its painting (*i.e.*, the unit in process) an alternation of periods of Expressionism and Impressionism offers an example of recurrence in *time*. If the art of a particular culture passes through the stages architectonic, sculptural, *malerisch*, and then disintegrates and decays; if such a sequence occurs only once in this culture; and if the same sequence takes place in the art of many other cultures, but only once in each, then, according to our definitions of recurrence, the case will be that of recurrence in *space* only. If, however, the same sequence not only occurs in many cultures, but is repeated in each, then we have recurrence in *both time and space*.

It is of especial importance that the differentiation here illustrated be kept clearly in mind, in view of the vitiation of numerous past theories of recurrence in social phenomena through the confusion of these three types. In the subsequent pages we shall try to keep them distinct.

II. Theories of the Recurrence of Art Phenomena in Space, in Time, and in Both Together

Like most of the cyclical theories of social process, the theories of recurrence in the field of art phenomena belong mostly to the class of those which hold for a repetition of certain uniformities in space. Strange to say, however, in most cases the authors of such theories seem to have a confused idea of the kind of recurrence the existence of which they are trying to prove: they mix recurrence in space with recurrence in time and therefore blunder at the very start. It goes without saying that many art phenomena, and especially the constituent or generic elements of art phenomena, recur in space as well as in time. Otherwise we should not be talking of the *art* of primitive and "civilized" peoples; of Greece, Babylon, Egypt, Russia, or France; of the Ancient period, the Middle Ages, or modern times. Since it is *art* and not something else (say law or science) that is thought of as appearing in all these societies, the constituent elements of this class of social phenomena must be the same everywhere and at any time that its phenomena are found and designated by the single term *art*. In spite of everchanging concrete forms in this mutable Becoming, there remains an unchangeable kernel of Being which generically, whether as a reality or a concept, always and everywhere remains the same. In other words it recurs in time as well as in space.

This is self-evident and therefore needs no further elucidation. Likewise, several other obvious, though often forgotten, statements need not detain us in this study. We are going to deal not with these obvious commonplaces, but with problems and with theories which are aimed not at these obvious matters but at things which are still subjects for controversy as far as the recurrence of art phenomena in social space is concerned. Of these theories and problems we shall take, one by one, only those which are concerned with the recurrence of the fundamental characteristics of art, and shall omit those which deal in detail with traits of very narrow scope and in a limited span of time and space. Probably for some purposes such a painstaking purely descriptive study is valuable. For our purposes, in this work which deals with the great variables of culture, which treats on a large scale of the widest sweeps of social history, such studies are irrelevant.

As the first problem of the recurrence of art phenomena in social space we ask ourselves: Is there any uniform sequence in the development and blossoming of various forms of art in cultures? For instance, in all cultures is it architecture (A) that develops and blossoms first, then sculpture (S), then painting (P), then music (M), and finally literature (L)? Does architecture lead, always and in all cultures, in the change of style, while all the other forms of art lag behind in the above sequential order? Does, therefore, this uniform sequence A, S, P, M, L recur universally in social space (in all cultures)? If not, then is there any other uniform sequence? If there is, what is it, with what stages in the life history of culture itself is it connected, and for what reasons? If such a uniform and universal sequence does not exist, do there exist any other main types of sequences which comprise the chief variations from it and which recur in various cultures and societies? Is a monistic (one universal sequence) or a pluralistic (several divers sequences) principle nearer to the known reality? Such, in brief, is the problem of the recurrence in social space which has been singled for treatment in this chapter. It is taken for its importance per se, and also because a considerable number of interesting theories have been set forth here, and need to be examined carefully from the point of view of their validity, and, finally, because it bears upon the general problem of existence of uniform sequences in cultural change.

Of several recent works which deal with this problem two of the most interesting, if not most important, are Sir Flinders Petrie's *The Revolutions of Civilization*,[1] whose contentions were recently reiterated in his article "History in Art," [2] and Paul Ligeti's *Der Weg aus dem Chaos*.[3]   According to Petrie not all forms of art in a given culture, or in its great period, blossom simultaneously.   Some branches of art always reach the stage of liberation from archaic, and advance into free and finer, forms earlier than others.   Generally, there is a uniform and regular sequence : such a turning point appears first in architecture and sculpture,

next comes Painting, then Literature, Music, Mechanics, Theoretic Science, and lastly Wealth.   When there is no survival of useful abilities, then the race is doomed, and only lives on its prestige and savings, until its wealth attracts a more vigorous people.   Mene, Tekel, Upharsin may be seen written on every full-blown civilization.[4]

Having studied from this standpoint the eight periods of Egyptian culture and several periods of the Graeco-Roman and European civilizations, he finds that this order has been uniformly recurrent.   For instance, for the European period corresponding to the eighth in his classification, he gives the following dates for the turning of the various branches of art and other kinds of creative activity from "archaic" form to "freedom" :

European sculpture	in	1240 A.D.
European painting	in	1400
European literature	in	1600
European music	in	1790
European mechanics	in	1890
European science	after	1910
European wealth	after	1910 [5]

Thus in that great cultural period the turning point from archaism to freedom, which is near the culmination point, lagged, if we take the advance in sculpture (and architecture) as the standard of comparison, in painting by about 160 years, in literature by about 360 years, in music by 550 years, and in science and wealth by almost 700 years.

A similar uniformity of sequence is shown, according to Petrie, in the development of all civilizations.   The sequence is always the same.   The lag may vary, however, tending to become longer as time advances.[6]

The theory of the eminent Egyptologist is undoubtedly very stimulating and suggestive.   Is it, however, valid?   I am afraid that he, like

[1] London and New York, 1912.   [2] In *Antiquity*, September, 1931.
[3] München, 1931.
[4] W. M. F. Petrie, *History in Art*, pp. 288–289.   See also O. G. S. Crawford, "Historical Cycles," in *Antiquity*, March, 1931, pp. 5–21.
[5] Petrie, *The Revolutions of Civilization*, p. 97.
[6] *Ibid.*   See also pp. 104–105, where he gives a summary table.

many others,[7] ascribes to social and historical processes a uniformity which they do not have.

In order to see this, let us examine his evidences. His sequence is based upon the "turning point from archaism to freedom" of each of the above cultural classes. Is the meaning of "turning point" clear enough and sufficiently definite so that such a point may be located and fixed? I am afraid not. And since the meaning is neither clear nor definite, it is not possible to locate the "turning point" objectively, whether in art, literature, music, or science; hence, any attempt to make such a location for each class of cultural phenomena is doomed to be questionable, and the entire sequence remains subjective.

A slight examination of Petrie's proof is sufficient to establish the validity of this criticism. Let us take two of his best cases, his Periods VIII and VII (European and Graeco-Roman). He writes:

In European sculpture the turning point has been here set at A.D. 1240, mainly on the strength of the well-dated Bamberg sculpture. . . . In architecture [which "goes closely together with sculpture in all ages"] Salisbury Cathedral stands for the perfect acquirement of freedom.[8]

This is practically the only basis upon which he makes A.D. 1240 the turning point in European sculpture and architecture from archaism to freedom. So far as architecture is concerned one wonders why only one cathedral is taken, and even this one not necessarily the best. No less remarkable cathedrals as "free" as the Salisbury were built: the marvelous Abbey Church at Jumièges c. 1048; cathedrals at Noyon c. 1140–1170, St. Denis c. 1144, Sens 1144–1168; Notre Dame at Senlis 1155–1185; Paris Cathedral 1162–1182, Chartres c. 1172, Reims 1211, Amiens 1215, Beauvais 1225, Canterbury 1174, Notre Dame at Paris completed about the middle of the thirteenth century.[9] It is clear, without extending this list, that the "turning point" can be fixed one or two centuries earlier than the

---

[7] For instance, the Marxian conception contends that in any culture and at any period the means and instruments of production change first, and social relationships and ideological facts change later. In a diluted and much more primitive form this theory is now circulated under the guise of a theory that the "immaterial" culture always lags behind the material culture in the process of social change. (See Ogburn, *Social Change* (New York, 1922) and most of the elementary texts in sociology.) On the other hand, writers like E. de Roberty contend that the material culture always lags behind the immaterial culture in the process of social change. At the first serious test these theories fall to pieces. Their general mistake is the assumption of a uniform sequence and a uniform and *invariable* order, where, in fact, it does not exist. (See the special chapter on that problem in Volume Four.)

[8] Petrie, *The Revolutions of Civilization*, pp. 94–95.

[9] W. R. Lethaby, "Mediaeval Architecture," in *The Legacy of the Middle Ages*, ed. by G. C. Crump and D. F. Jacob (Oxford, 1926), pp. 60–91.

year 1240, and for such a date there is as much reason as for that set by
Sir Flinders Petrie. The same can be said of sculpture. The turning
point had already appeared about the middle of the twelfth century (the
royal portal at Chartres *c.* 1145, and similar portals of other churches).[10]
It is true that at about the middle of the thirteenth century both Gothic
architecture and sculpture reached their climax, but the climax is not the
turning point. If it were, then again one would wonder why the climax
of European sculpture is put at 1240 and not at the period of the Renaissance and its great masters. One can admire the sculpture of the
thirteenth century, but cannot easily dispose of the sculpture of the Renaissance as inferior. Many specialists would rate it as superior to that of
the thirteenth century. Thus if we mean by the turning point in European sculpture and architecture the beginning of a new form, then it had
already appeared by the twelfth century. If we mean by the turning
point the climax in their achievement, then the date A.D. 1240 is no better
than several others which are earlier or later by several centuries.

However, Sir Flinders Petrie's claim with regard to sculpture and architecture is not nearly so open to question as that for other classes of cultural phenomena, for instance music, literature, mechanics, and science.
He puts the turning point of music *c.* 1790, for the following reasons :

Perhaps we may say that Haydn was still archaic in most of his life [?],
but steps freely for the first time in his great symphonies of 1790; while
Beethoven only shows some memories of archaism rarely in his earlier symphonies, from 1796 onwards. Hence, perhaps, 1790 may be accepted as the
turning point.[11]

That is the only argument for 1790 as the turning point from archaism
to freedom in music. Thus all the Flemish, French, Italian, English
Polyphonic schools of the fourteenth, fifteenth, sixteenth, and seventeenth
centuries; all the great, and very different, creators of music, like Dufay,
J. Okeghem, Josquin Deprès, Palestrina, C. Festa, da Victoria, Orlando
di Lasso, Gesualdo, W. Byrd, Alessandro Scarlatti, Rameau, Monteverde,
J. S. Bach, G. F. Handel, Gluck, and Mozart, not to mention many others,
are, according to Petrie, in one archaic stage of music ! And only since
Haydn (not Bach !) does music enter the stage of "freedom." I am afraid
such dating is quite subjective and will fail to be supported by the majority of musicians. If Sir Flinders means by "turning point" an innovation in music, then any of the men whose names I have mentioned have as

---

[10] P. Vitry, "Mediaeval Sculpture," *ibid.*, pp. 103 ff. See Chapter Eleven, on architecture, in this volume.

[11] Petrie, *The Revolutions of Civilization*, p. 96.

much right to be regarded as innovators as Haydn; and Bach, Palestrina, Mozart, Handel, Monteverde, and some others — much more. If he means a new spirit and mentality, then these had appeared already in the music of the minstrels and troubadours, or even earlier in such pieces as the celebrated Reading Rota or Rondel, "Sumer is icumen in," not to mention the diffusion of the *opera buffa*, or comic opera, especially in Italy of the seventeenth century.[12]   If he means the secular and Bohemian manner of life of musicians, this existed long before 1790.   If he means a change from religious to secular music, this had arisen by the sixteenth century, indeed much earlier.[13]   If, finally by "turning point" he perhaps means the climax of European music, even then opinions will be divided: some, for instance, view J. S. Bach as the pinnacle, some Beethoven; and there are some who would indicate other names and periods, from the Gregorian chant to Palestrina, to Wagner, to Stravinsky, and even to jazz.   Thus from any standpoint the date set by Petrie is exceedingly subjective.

Still more questionable are Petrie's turning points for mechanics and science, fixed, respectively, at 1890 and 1910.   Here is the essence of his argument.

In Mechanics . . . the full freedom of design was certainly not attained in the earlier railway work. [Why only the railway work?] . . . For the present we may put down 1890 as the close of archaism in Mechanics.[14]

It is obvious that in Natural Science discovery is still flowing rapidly, and that our conceptions have by no means outgrown the stage of casting off previous ideas, and not only developing what is in hand.[15]

That is all the argument for his dates of 1890 and 1910.   And these choices are, to be frank, very unfortunate.

Why is it impossible to accept Petrie's selection of 1910 as a turning point in science?   The reason is shown by the following figures in Table 5,[16] which give the number of important discoveries in all the natural sciences, technical inventions excluded.

A glance at these figures indicates that, if a turning point is to be established for science, it must be either the sixteenth or seventeenth or

[12] For these and other facts, see Chapter Twelve of this volume.

[13] See C. Gray, *The History of Music* (New York, 1928), the *Oxford History of Music*, and any other authoritative work on the history of music. See Chapter Twelve in this work.

[14] Petrie, *The Revolutions of Civilization*, pp. 96–97.

[15] *Ibid.*, p. 97.

[16] Computed from L. Darmstaedter, *Handbuch zur Geschichte der Naturwissenschaften und der Technik* (Berlin, 1908). See Chapter Three of Volume Two of this work, which deals with movement of discoveries and inventions.

TABLE 5.   DISCOVERIES IN THE NATURAL SCIENCES

Century Period	Number	Quarter-century Period	Number
1001–1100	2		
1101–1200	7		
1201–1300	39		
1301–1400	31		
1401–1500	45		
1501–1600	245		
1601–1700	492		
1701–1800	1034		
1801–1900	4937	1801–1825	686
		1826–1850	1191
		1851–1875	1443
		1876–1900	1617
		1900–1908	552

eighteenth or nineteenth centuries, or the period 1826–50, as far as the number of discoveries is concerned. If we take as a criterion the qualitative importance of scientific discoveries, then there is hardly any period which can take precedence over the period from the second half of the sixteenth to the beginning of the eighteenth century, when the main body of the fundamental principles and laws of the present natural sciences was established and formulated. If we take separately each of the natural sciences, we shall see that in the majority of them the peak of their achievement, quantitatively and perhaps qualitatively also, is quite over by 1910.[17] Moreover, since the beginning of the twentieth century there have been signs of a weakening, both quantitatively and qualitatively, in their progress. Perhaps in the future the situation will change, but thus far there is no reason whatever for us to join Sir Flinders Petrie in regarding 1910 as the turning point.

Similar is the situation with mechanics and technical inventions as shown by Table 6.[18]

So far as the number of inventions is concerned, we do not have any reason to place the entire period before 1910 in the "archaic" stage. As a matter of fact, the peak had been reached sometime previously; and since the beginning of the twentieth century, and particularly during the last fifteen years, there are signs of a quantitative and qualitative slowing

[17] For mathematics the greatest number of discoveries falls in the period 1701–50; for biology, 1851–75; for medicine, 1880–89 (see F. H. Garrison, *An Introduction to the History of Medicine*, 1929; and F. J. Cole and N. B. Eales, *A Statistical Analysis of the Literature of Comparative Anatomy*); and so on. Qualitatively, as mentioned, the period from the end of the sixteenth to the beginning of the eighteenth centuries is perhaps the most important and unrivaled. For the details, see Chapter Three of Volume Two, dealing with these subjects.

[18] Computed from L. Darmstaedter's *Handbuch*.

TABLE 6. MECHANICS AND TECHNICAL INVENTIONS

Century Period	Number of Technical Inventions	Quarter-century Period	Number of Technical Inventions
1001–1100	5		
1101–1200	5		
1201–1300	9		
1301–1400	25		
1401–1500	49		
1501–1600	121		
1601–1700	169		
1701–1800	519		
1801–1900	3477	1801–1825	378
		1826–1850	803
		1851–1875	1073
		1876–1900	1223
		1900–1908	309

of the rate of progress in inventions. Common opinion is to the contrary, but when one takes the statistics of the patent offices of the United States and Great Britain and analyzes their data, quantitatively and qualitatively, the above conclusion is the only one possible. For instance, the number of fundamental inventions in the United States was 25 for 1846–1855, 24 for 1856–1865, 20 for 1866–1875, 16 for 1876–1885, 13 for 1886–1895, 15 for 1896–1905, 10 for 1906–1915. The rate of increase of inventions declines especially between 1910–1930. The peak was 1866–1870. (At that time the average rate of annual increase of inventions was 1522; while the respective figure was 587 for the periods 1911–1915, 634 for 1916–1920, 616 for 1921–1925, and 625 for 1926–1930.)[19] So far as the railway industry (specially mentioned by Petrie) is concerned, the peaks of invention in this field were, according to the data of the Patent Office, in 1867 and 1889. Even in new industries, like automobile, radio, and airplane manufacture, the last few years show a quantitative decline in inventions.[20]

These data show that there is no foundation for regarding the periods before 1890 and 1910 as "archaic" in mechanics and natural science, respectively, and the periods since 1890 and 1910 as "free." The whole of Petrie's claim of the existence of the sequence of turning points established by him for various arts and other classes of cultural phenomena remains subjective, having no objective base in empirical facts.

If we should consider Sir Flinders's Period VII, it would be very easy to show how whimsical and subjective are his dates for the turning point

[19] These figures, a few out of many, are computed from the Report of the Commissioner of Patents, 1930. For inventions in Great Britain, see E. W. Hulme, *Statistical Bibliography in Relation to the Growth of Modern Civilization* (London, 1923).

[20] See the present work, Chapter Three of Volume Two.

in Graeco-Roman sculpture and architecture (450 B.C.); painting (350 B.C.); literature (200 B.C.); music, mechanics, science (A.D. 150); and wealth (A.D. 200).[21] Lack of space prevents the presentation of the evidences here. They will be given in subsequent parts of this work. I will mention only one case. Petrie fixes A.D. 150 as the turning point of science in the Graeco-Roman culture. As a matter of fact, in Greece the century from 400–300 B.C. was most fruitful in this respect, after which a decline rapidly set in; in Rome such a period was the first century A.D. For both countries taken together as a single whole the number of discoveries in the natural sciences and technical inventions is as in Table 7 [22] (as far as extant records show):

TABLE 7.   DISCOVERIES AND INVENTIONS IN GREECE AND ROME

Period	Number
600–501 B.C.	31
500–401	40
400–301	57
300–201	45
200–101	17
100–0	32
1–100 A.D.	60
101–200	18
201–300	6

These data do not at all warrant Petrie's conclusion. From the beginning of the second century A.D., a quite definite decline in science took place instead of a turning point from archaism to freedom.

These cases show that, since the dates of the turning point are incorrectly set forth, the entire theory of uniform sequence has little if any foundation. And still less warranted is the contention that the sequence is uniform for all cultures.

Let us now turn to a recent theory of Paul Ligeti, set forth in his interesting and impressive work *Der Weg aus dem Chaos*. In contradistinction to Petrie he does not think that "Sculpture and Architecture go closely together in all ages." [23] Ligeti thinks that the blossoming of architecture in all cultures always precedes that of sculpture. The essence of Ligeti's theory of the art sequence is as follows: in any great culture, at the be-

[21] F. Petrie, *The Revolutions of Civilization*, p. 101.

[22] Computed from L. Darmstaedter's *Handbuch*.

[23] Petrie, *The Revolutions of Civilization*, p. 94. A variation of Ligeti's theory is given still more recently in C. Gray's *Predicaments: Music and the Future* (New York, 1936), with a sequence: architecture, sculpture, painting, literature, music.

ginning of its development architecture is the first and earliest form of art to blossom; then comes the blossoming of sculpture, which happens at the period of maturity; and finally, the blossoming of painting takes place at the declining stage of the culture. This order is invariable and uniform in the development of all great cultures. In European culture the Middle Ages are marked by the greatest development of architecture, while sculpture and painting remain primitive and undeveloped. The Renaissance is the period of the triumph of sculpture, as the synthesis of architecture and painting. Finally, the modern time has created nothing remarkable in sculpture or architecture, but has achieved an incomparable level in painting. Similarly in Greek culture, the first centuries of Greek art are architectural; about 510 B.C. there was the sculptural or plastic age (statues of Harmodius and Aristogiton), culminating in the time of Pericles, and ending about 390 B.C. (Myron, Phidias, Polycleitus, and others). After 390 B.C. there was the age of painting, or the *malerisch* age. Likewise in Egypt the art of the Old Kingdom was architectonic, and its greatest achievement was in architecture; the end of the Middle Kingdom was plastic; the New Kingdom was marked predominantly by great achievement in the field of painting. The same sequence is observable in the history of China, Japan, and other countries. Thus:

Behind the rhythm of these arts there is a law, or the uniformity which operates everywhere that human culture is given. . . . Each culture begins with the architectonic period and ends with the period of painting.[24]

Side by side with these long waves, on which are based Ligeti's "law of the three states" in the development of art and culture, there are waves of a still longer duration, as well as other waves which are shorter. Thus, with regard to the longer waves, not only does every culture pass through these three states enumerated by Ligeti, but when all the cultures are taken together in their time succession, the same uniformity operates: the great ancient cultures, like the Egyptian, are predominantly architectural; later cultures, like those of Greece and Rome, are predominantly plastic; while modern cultures, like the European, are predominantly *malerisch*. Such is the long rhythm of the development of human art generally and human culture as a whole.[25]

As to the shorter waves, there are periods about one hundred and thirty years long, in which the same rhythm, architecture-sculpture-painting, takes place. In the history of Western culture there are seven waves of this kind.[26] These shorter waves are similar to surface rippling upon the

---

[24] Ligeti, *Der Weg aus dem Chaos*, p. 34; see also pp. 1–34 *et passim*.
[25] *Ibid.*, pp. 168 ff.   [26] *Ibid.*, pp. 51 ff.

longer waves of the ocean, while these longer movements are surface waves upon the tidal ebb and flow of the whole of human culture. Such is the main sequence of art development according to Ligeti.

For the moment we shall not enter into a discussion of the ingenious, sometimes profound, and always interesting interpretations of Ligeti of the meaning of this sequence, the reasons for its occurrence, and its social correlations with other forms of culture. All this will be discussed later. For the present we shall just inquire whether the existence of the sequence has been established conclusively from the standpoint of the facts. Ligeti's theory of the sequence of architecture, sculpture, and painting evidently refers to the sequence of the highest pinnacle reached by each of these arts, and therefore signifies that in each culture architecture reaches its highest development first, then sculpture, and after it painting.

It goes without saying that such a construction involves an estimation of what is the highest achievement in each of these arts, and as with all such evaluation, it contains an element of subjectivity. For one investigator the highest achievement in a given art may be of one kind, for another of a different kind. Correspondingly, the periods of the highest accomplishment would be different for such investigators. If, however, an investigator claims to have discovered a uniform law, the least that his theory must do is to run in general agreement with the estimates of the highest points as established by many competent investigators. When we take the statements of Ligeti and confront them with the estimates of other authorities, the result is that Ligeti's "uniform law" does not appear to be uniform at all, ceases to be a general law. Here are some facts which have been collected by Mr. Clarence Q. Berger, and elaborated upon by him in his term paper for my course in Social Dynamics.[27]

If we take the cultures of Egypt, India, China, Japan, France, Italy, Germany, England, Greece, and Rome, the time sequence in which the specified arts reached the zenith of their blossoming, and the periods in which this blossoming took place, appear to be as follows in Table 8 according to several historians of the respective art of each country.[28]

[27] For the sake of brevity I do not give here the numerous authorities upon whose work this table is based. It is enough to say that while Ligeti puts most of his estimates rather dogmatically, without either giving sufficient data or references to sources upon which his estimates of the highest points in the development of the arts are based, this table is based upon many data given by the standard works of a group of specialists in the history of each of the cultures given.

[28] These are not based on my estimates. As in other parts of this work, I attempt to eliminate my personal tastes and judgments in such evaluations. This means also that I do not necessarily subscribe to these estimates. I merely confront one set of estimates with another.

TABLE 8.   SEQUENCE OF BLOSSOMING OF THE MAIN ARTS IN
TEN GREAT CULTURES

Egypt		*Rome*	
1. Literature	2000–1225 B.C.	1. Literature	86–25 B.C.
2. Sculpture	1580–1350	2. Sculpture	30 B.C.–69 A.D.
3. Architecture	1580–1250	3. Painting	50–108
4. Music	1411–1284	4. Architecture	60–138
5. Painting	750–525	5. Music	466–495
India		*Germany*	
1. Literature	400 B.C.–100 A.D.	1. Architecture	1130–1260 A.D.
2. Sculpture	500 –725	2. Sculpture	1400–1500
3. Architecture	1489–1706	3. Painting	1491–1559
4. Music	1600–1771	4. Music	1720–1880
5. Painting	1615–1800	5. Literature	1756–1850
China		*England*	
1. Literature	479–300 B.C.	1. Architecture	1272–1377 A.D.
2. Sculpture	618–960 A.D.	2. Literature	1573–1618
3. Painting	960–1200	3. Music	1600–1675
4. Architecture	1400–1500	4. Painting	1717–1763
5. Music	1400–1500	5. Sculpture	1758–1787
Japan		*Italy*	
1. Literature	700–1142 A.D.	1. Literature	1290–1333 A.D.
2. Music	806–1146	2. Architecture	1444–1564
3. Sculpture	1000–1137	3. Painting	1472–1548
4. Painting	1350–1500	4. Sculpture	1500–1600
5. Architecture	1350–1583	5. Music	1560–1800
Greece		*France*	
1. Music	750–600 B.C.	1. Architecture	1150–1350 A.D.
2. Literature	524–450	2. Sculpture	1200–1250
3. Architecture	500–430	3. Music	1652–1700
4. Sculpture	450–350	4. Painting	1760–1853
5. Painting	430–350	5. Literature	1779–1895

It is granted that the periods of the climax for each art here indicated
are only approximate.   It is granted also that some elements of subjectivity are involved in this establishment of periods; for some countries
specialists have in some cases chosen for the blossoming of one of the arts
a period different from that which is given in the above list.   Nevertheless, it is not possible to regard these estimates as less valid than the claims
and estimates of Ligeti.   Under such circumstances it becomes clear at

once that Ligeti has elevated into a uniform law something which exists only in a limited number of cases: in only three cultures out of the ten considered — that is, in Greece, Germany, and France — does his sequence occur. In the other seven cultures the sequence is either the reverse of or quite different from his "law of lag" and his sequence. Thus we again have a case in which "an ugly fact kills a beautiful theory."

Postponing for a moment a characterization of the subsequent part of Ligeti's theory, let us review briefly some other theories of the uniform sequence of the development of various arts in various cultures or, what is the same, theories which claim that in all cultures certain arts always lead in the change of style while other arts always lag. Such a theory of a uniform lag is but the theory of uniform sequence of change in various arts. In either a systematic or an unsystematic way such contentions have been set forth many times before Ligeti and Petrie. For instance V. de Laprade developed a theory [29] that the art of the Orient (India, Egypt, Persia, China) was predominantly architectural; the art of Greece and Rome, predominantly sculptural; of Christian medieval Europe, mainly *malerisch;* and of the modern time, essentially musical. "Architecture responds to God; sculpture and painting, to an ideal or real man; music, to the external sensate world." [30]

The theories of Ligeti and Laprade, as well as several others of this type, are possibly influenced by the theory of G. W. F. Hegel's *Aesthetik.* In any case, there are several resemblances between Hegelian theories and the theories of these men. The essentials of that aspect of Hegel's theory which is relevant to this problem are as follows. In conformity with the chief principle of his philosophy, Hegel views the evolution of art as the process of self-realization, or of an unfolding of the Idea or Spirit, in the course of time.[31] In this process of unfolding there are three stages (*Hauptstufen*), each with its characteristic type of art: the *symbolic*, the *classical*, and the *romantic*.[32] In the symbolic stage and type of art

The Idea is still seeking for its true artistic expression, because it is here still essentially abstract and undetermined, and consequently has not mastered for itself the external appearance adequate to its own substance. . . .[33]

[29] Laprade's and Hegel's theories are those of recurrence in space as well as in time and partly in both.

[30] See V. de Laprade, *Le sentiment de la nature avant le Christianisme* (Paris, 1866), pp. i-civ *et passim;* also his *Le sentiment de la nature chez les modernes* (Paris, 1868), *passim.*

[31] See G. W. F. Hegel, *The Philosophy of Fine Art*, trans. by F. P. B. Osmaston, 4 vols. (London, 1920), Vol. I, pp. 125-147. This is the only complete translation of Hegel's *Aesthetik.*

[32] *Ibid.*, Vol. I, pp. 95-124; Vol. II, pp. 1-5; Vol. III, pp. 1-24; *et passim.*

[33] *Ibid.*, Vol. II, p. 3; Vol. I, pp. 103-104.

Therefore, only by symbolism can it express itself, in crude forms in which there is little real resemblance between the idea and the exterior forms in which it is clothed. Here matter dominates the Idea, and the Idea does not find an adequate expression in Sensate forms.

The second type of art, the classical, is based upon an absolutely homogeneous unity of content and form. . . .[34]

Here there is an adequate bridge between the Idea and its expression.

The symbolic configuration is imperfect because, first, Idea here only enters into consciousness in *abstract* determinacy or indeterminateness; and secondly, by reason of the fact that the coalescence of import with embodiment can only throughout remain defective, and in its turn wholly abstract. The classical art type solves both these difficulties. It is, in fact, the free and adequate embodiment of the Idea in the shape which is uniquely appropriate to the Idea itself. The Idea is consequently able to unite in free and completely assonant concord with it. For this reason the classical type of art is the first to present us with the creation and vision of the complete Ideal, and to establish the same as realized fact.[35]

Finally

The romantic type of art annuls the completed union of the Idea and its reality. . . . The classical type of art no doubt attained the highest excellence of which the sensuous embodiment of art is capable.

But as "Mind is the infinite subjectivity of Idea," it does not find a quite perfect expression in the finite nature of the sensate means of its objectization, even in the classical art.

To escape from such a condition the romantic type of art once more cancels that inseparable unity of the classical type, by securing a content which passes beyond the classical stage and its mode of expression.[36]

In the romantic type of art

We have the form in which the Idea of beauty grasps its own being as *absolute* Spirit, Spirit, that is to say, in the full consciousness of its untrammeled freedom. But for this very reason it is unable any more to obtain complete realization in forms which are external; its true determinate existence is now that which it possesses in itself as Spirit. That unity of the life of Spirit and its external appearance which we find in classical art is unbound, and it flees from the same once more into itself. It is this recoil which presents to us the fundamental type of the *romantic* type of art. Here we find, by the reason of the free spirituality which pervades the content, such content makes a more ideal demand upon expression than the mere representation through an external or

[34] *Ibid.*, Vol. II, p. 3.   [35] *Ibid.*, Vol. I, pp. 104–105.   [36] *Ibid.*, Vol. I, pp. 106–107.

physical medium is able to supply; the form on its external side sinks therefore to a relation of indifference; and in the romantic form of art we consequently meet with a separation between content and form as we previously found it in the symbolic form, with this difference that it is now due to the subordination of matter to spiritual expression rather than the predominance of externality over ideal significance.[37]

Thus in the symbolic stage and type of art the Idea is inadequately expressed and is dominated by external form; in the romantic stage the balance is again disrupted, because here the Idea, being infinite, strives to be free from the finite forms of external sensate expression, and therefore soars to itself in all its infiniteness and as a result demotes the external form to a place of secondary importance.

Such are the main types, and at the same time the stages, of art evolution.

Hegel develops these principles further, showing that the most adequate objectization of the symbolic stage and type is architecture; of the classical type and stage, sculpture; of the romantic, painting and then, especially, music and poetry.[38] This is not all. Each of the arts, in the process of its evolution, passes through these three stages; for instance, architecture evolves through symbolic, classical, and romantic periods. The same is true of other arts: sculpture, painting, music, poetry (though Hegel prefers to use somewhat different terms to designate the stages of poetic evolution).[39]

We have, then, a complex scale of progression from the smallest to the fullest unfolding of Spirit in the movement from architecture to poetry, and in the movement of each of the arts from the symbolic to the romantic stage. Viewed from the standpoint of the Hegelian classifications the art of the Orient has remained almost exclusively at the symbolic, the art of Greece and Rome at the classical, stage. The only art to reach the romantic stage has been the European, especially that of modern Europe.[40]

If we wish to describe Hegel's theory, with its assumption of a definite perpetual trend in all culture from symbolic to romantic and from architecture to poetry, in the terminology of the present work, it must be designated as *linear evolutionary* and, at the same time, *systematic*, because Hegel seems to assume the complete coincidence of the stages of cultural

[37] *Ibid.*, Vol. II, pp. 4–5.

[38] *Ibid.*, Vol. I, pp. 110–124; Vol. III, pp. 18 ff.; and all the last three volumes are mainly a development of this.

[39] See his explanations in *ibid.*, Vol. III, pp. 21 ff.

[40] See particularly *ibid.*, Vols. III and IV, which are devoted to a concrete analysis of the main forms of art: architecture, sculpture, painting, music, and poetry from these standpoints.

development with the types of art, according to his scheme. Finally, it contains as a secondary element some notions of recurrence, resulting from the dialectic triad and taking the form of a motion from the symbolic to the romantic form within each of the arts.

From this outline one can see the points of similarity between the Hegelian conception and that of Ligeti. Both consider architecture the earliest form of art, and point out its predominance in the Ancient Orient. Both place sculpture next and describe it as predominant in and typical of classical antiquity. Both regard it as a perfect balance between Hegel's Externality and Idea and Ligeti's Reality (*Sein*) and Appearance (*Schein*). Both consider painting as the third stage, in which the balance is again disrupted. Besides the similarities in these cardinal points there are many more likenesses in their interpretations of the details of each of the separate forms of art.

This does not mean that there are no differences; it means that, directly or indirectly, the stupendous work of Hegel has greatly influenced many philosophies and sociologies of art, as well as histories of art, theories, and ideologies. This influence has often been exerted without conscious knowledge on the part of many authors who have picked up their ideas from secondary works and from an "air" filled with ideological constructions evaporated from the work of this difficult, dull, but at the same time great, thinker. Like many such theorists, while latitudinarian in application, Hegel, in all his works, actually developed one, and only one, idea. His entire thought may be summed up in his conception of historical process as a dialectic unfolding of the *Geist*. (This is similar to the position of Herbert Spencer — all of Spencer's works are but an untiring development of his formula of evolution progress; or to that of August Comte, whose law of the three states is the main, in fact the only, topic of all his work, and so on.)

Since this whole work is a refutation of linear conceptions of sociocultural processes there is no need to make a special criticism of the Hegelian theory at this point. As far as its factual side is concerned the above data and the data of the subsequent chapters will be sufficient to show its inadequacies and blunders.

A further type which it is necessary to discuss is represented by the theory of J. Combarieu, according to which music, in the change of its style, uniformly lags behind the other arts.

Music almost always lags in social evolution. Schütz, Bach, Händel should be pushed back a century if one is to find a social mentality corresponding to their artistic mentality. In their sonatas Mozart and Beethoven express the charming conception of life which existed much earlier. The Germans had their musical romanticism about two generations later than their literary romanticism. Even Weber, in the songs of his *Freischütz* (1821), was lagging behind Herder and Bürger.

The same lagging of music in comparison with other arts occurred in the Middle Ages and in the time of the Renaissance.

Sculptors and painters of the Middle Ages were realists; those of the Renaissance painted only the "belles figures," like Raphael, and cultivated a "style." In music the evolution was rather the inverse. The musicians of the Middle Ages followed an abstract doctrine; those of the Renaissance began to approach life. Painters and sculptors reached long ago the ability to depict reality with remarkable accuracy; meanwhile music, a prisoner of the principles of the School, needed a long time to guess that its task was not only *construction* but also *expression*, and only lately began that conquest of the real [achieved long ago by other arts] which even now is not completed.[41]

At the dawn of the nineteenth century music was again lagging behind the other arts, though but slightly at this time. Literary romanticism had already appeared at the end of the eighteenth century. Goethe's *Werther* appeared in 1776, MacPherson's *Ossian* about the same time; Chateaubriand's *René* in 1802; Delacroix's *La Barque du Dante* in 1822; Victor Hugo's *Odes*, Byron's romantic poems, and Lamartine's *Meditations* and *Harmonies* all before, or not later than, 1830. Here again

Music was not the first voice of the romantic soul. It could not immediately assimilate the poetry which was diffused around it, and which seems to have solicited such an assimilation. Music was reluctant to abandon its carillons, official rhetoric, theatrical pomp, and . . . its aesthetics of the *petits riens*. It is true that musicians like Lesueur, Cherubini, Spontini show in some of their works that they are at the threshold of a new world; but it is necessary to go to the *Symphonie phantastique* (1830) and the *Robert le Diable* (1831) in order to get the first impressions of the clear change. The *Freischütz* of Weber (1821) was an isolated case, of a specific nature, and without any influence upon French art. Only somewhat later music took its full revenge with Berlioz, Chopin, Liszt, and R. Schumann.[42]

Such is the essence of this theory of lagging, formulated by one of the most competent historians of music.[43]

[41] J. Combarieu, *Histoire de la musique* (Paris, 1913), Vol. I, pp. 453–454.

[42] *Ibid.*, Vol. III, pp. 8–9.

[43] A similar theory has been set forth by V. d'Indy in his *Course de composition musical* (Paris, 1910), Vol. I, p. 216. "Music almost always lags behind the other arts because its domain is to be found in the depths of soul where, as in the depths of the ocean, the effects of the storms raging on the surface pass with retardation." See also Romain Roland, *Jean Christophe*, no. 4, *Le révolte* (1906), p. 141. According to L. R. Farnell, in Greece "poetry

The invalidity of this generalization follows from my previous remarks and from the data. In addition, the following criticism may be offered.

In another part of his excellent work Combarieu repudiates his own theory. We read there:

We had occasion to say that in the conquest of the Beautiful music sometimes lags behind the art of painting. . . . But here in J. S. Bach music achieved marvels . . . and by its science of construction and of expression it infinitely surpassed the contemporary art of architecture and painting. Who now knows the names of German architects and painters in 1729? [44]

What is this but the refutation of his own claim? It is easy to bring out many other exceptions to the theory. For instance, in Greece, the "classical" [45] period of music, if we accept the music of Terpander and his contemporaries as its representatives, preceded by about two centuries the classical age of literature and sculpture, or was at least not later than the classical age of literature and sculpture, if we consider as its representatives the choral lyric of Simonides, Pindar, and Bacchylides and the tragedies of Aeschylus, Sophocles, and Euripides. Likewise, in the medieval culture, its classical music, the Gregorian chant, was already in existence in the sixth century, while the classic age of medieval architecture (the Romanesque and the Gothic styles), or of medieval sculpture (the thirteenth century), or of medieval philosophy (Albertus Magnus and St. Thomas as the climax of Scholasticism in the thirteenth century), or of medieval literature, all came many centuries later. Furthermore, the music of Palestrina, Orlando di Lasso, and their contemporaries was in one sense far behind the other arts, but in another considerably in advance of them. The later classical age in music, the period of Bach, Handel, Mozart, Haydn, Beethoven, was either earlier than, or at least contemporaneous with, the classical age in German literature, with the period of Lessing, Schiller, Goethe, and Kant. Even the recent Romanticism in music could hardly be said to be behind that in literature or painting. We must not forget that Beethoven, in several of his later works, had a strong romantic vein; that Weber was contemporaneous with Delacroix, that Schumann, Mendelssohn, and Berlioz were contemporaneous with, or even earlier than, Heine, Hegel, and Schopenhauer. It is also a matter of doubt either that medieval painting and sculpture were "realistic" or that

---

attained a power of spiritual expression at a far earlier date than did painting or sculpture." *The Cults of the Greek States* (Oxford, 1896), Vol. I, pp. 9–10. *Cf.* Charles Lalo, *Esquisse d'une esthetique musicale scientifique* (Paris, 1908), pp. 310–311.

[44] Combarieu, *op. cit.*, Vol. II, pp. 270–271.

[45] For the time being I am obliged to use this and similar common terms in spite of their vagueness and subjectivity. In subsequent chapters my own terms are introduced.

medieval music "was lost in abstract doctrine." These statements on the arts of the Middle Ages are ambiguous. As we shall see, up to the fourteenth, even the fifteenth, century medieval painting and sculpture were still predominantly "conventional," Ideational, or Idealistic, and only since the Renaissance did they begin to become more and more "visual," "naturalistic," or "illusionistic." A stream of secular, "naturalistic" music may already be seen at the end of the twelfth century (the minstrels and the troubadours). Music broke its medieval, purely Ideational, forms (see Chapter Twelve) in the fourteenth, fifteenth, and sixteenth centuries. Palestrina, Orlando di Lasso, and others are contemporaries of Leonardo, Raphael, and other great masters of painting. Monteverde and the *opera buffa* were rather earlier than illusionistic baroque, and contemporaries of the Dutch naturalistic school in painting, and so on.[46]

In brief, there are so many exceptions to the rule of Combarieu, D'Indy, and others, that there remains no rule at all. Only by disregarding the extensive array of contradictory facts can one insist upon it.

Mutatis mutandis, the same may be said of many other theories of the existence of a universal and uniform lag of certain arts when compared with others. When writers like F. de Sanctis or F. Brunetière claim that literature usually leads in the change, and that the other arts, of which music is the latest because it is the most superficial,[47] usually lag, we have a variety of the theory which is even more inadequate than are the forms of it which we have just considered. These, as well as almost all similar theories of the uniformity sequence and lag, either are superficial or elevate the particular case or cases into a universal rule. As a matter of fact, general uniformity does not exist. In one country or period there is one sequence, not only in regard to the blossoming of, but also to the changes in, the various arts; in another country, as the above data of the sequences in various cultures have shown, the sequence may be different; in still other countries, like Germany in the eighteenth century, two or more arts and cultural "compartments" may blossom or undergo a similar change simultaneously (Haydn, Mozart, Beethoven and Lessing, Goethe, Schiller, Kant). To claim uniformity here means to disregard the facts.

Having given these samples of uniformist theories, and having indicated their shortcomings, we return now to a discussion of other parts of Ligeti's theories.

Since the sequential uniformity postulated by Ligeti and others is not a universal law at all, the bottom drops out of their sociological generaliza-

---

[46] See also the remarks in C. Lalo's *Esquisse*, pp. 310 ff.

[47] See F. Brunetière, *Évolution de la poésie lyrique* (Paris, 1894), ouverture lecture.

tions, and the validity of these now becomes highly questionable. Let us look closer at Ligeti's sociological correlations. If they are not all accurate, yet they are for the most part suggestive and ingenious. The chief of these generalizations may be summed up briefly as follows.

(1) Any culture (or a great period in a culture, or even the whole history of mankind) passes through three main stages as shown by its art: architectural, plastic, and *malerisch*.[48]

(2) At each of these stages the culture is characterized by several important traits, common to all cultures at the same stage of development.[49] In a concise form these traits may be described by Table 9.

TABLE 9. CULTURE CHARACTERISTICS

Architectural	Plastic	Malerisch
1. The beginning of an upswing of culture. It is virile and stern. It is marked by a collective state of mind and discipline.	Intermediate between the characteristics of the architectural and *malerisch* stages: their harmonious synthesis.	1. Decline of the culture or a great cultural period. It is stamped by feminity, Sensate mentality, and individualism.
2. It is a culture of volition and strong determination to achieve an ideal.		2. It is a culture of enjoyment of what has already been achieved before, culture of waste and sensual indulgence.
3. It is stamped by strong ethical idealism and morality (antisensate, antihedonistic, antiutilitarian).		3. Such terms as materialistic, skeptical, critical, "scientific," erotic, Epicurean, utilitarian, characterize such a culture.
4. It is dominated by religion, by belief, faith, and religious dogmatism. Its leaders are great religious and moral teachers.		4. There is a predominance of reason over belief. Intellectualism and the "scientific" attitude come to the fore.
5. Order and stability predominate over dynamic progress and change.		5. Freedom and progress predominate instead of order. There is variety, revolution, disorder, and mobility.
6. Its aristocracy is theocratic, noble because of its religious, moral, and social achievements, but not because of wealth.		6. Bureaucrats, moneymakers, imperialists, and "liberal" thinkers are the leaders.
7. There is a predominance of agriculture and handicraft.		7. There is a predominance of commerce, manufacture, "business," and machinery.
8. There is a mobilization and integration of mentality, and an awakening of the spiritual *Geist*.		8. There is a disintegration of mentality and decline of spiritual *Geist*.

[48] The term *malerisch* as it is used by Ligeti as well as by most of the German scholars in art (A. Riegl, H. Wölfflin, A. Schmarsow, O. Wulff, E. Panofsky, E. Utitz, H. Nohl, W. Worringer, M. Dvořák, E. Cohn-Wiener, L. Coellen, A. E. Brinckman, G. G. Weiszner, H. Schafer, K. Scheffler, and others) is almost untranslatable. It has a much more complex and deeper meaning than the term pictorial. Some of these meanings will be elucidated further. For this reason I prefer to use the German term, directly.

[49] Ligeti, *op. cit.*, pp. 65–111 *et passim*.

These represent the chief sociological correlations between the predominant art and other aspects of a culture. If we ask why these correlations occur, the answer of Ligeti is interesting. Like almost all investigators of art, he rightly says that art is one of the best barometers of culture.[50] What are the reasons for this association? They become comprehensible if we study the culture in which a given painting, piece of sculpture, or specimen of architecture was produced. We must consider to whom these objects were addressed and for whom they were created, and we must inquire into the very essence of architecture, sculpture, and painting. A painting is usually the work of *one* man and of one lifetime. A great building is always the work of many men, of a collectivity, and sometimes of several generations, as, for example, most of the cathedrals of the Middle Ages. He who is an individualist and wants to create alone is attracted by painting; those who want to create great things together, in a co-operative association, turn to architecture, because a great building can be but the work of many. "A picture is the message of one man, a building is that of many." [51] Hence, the connection of the *malerisch* stage with individualism and freedom, and the architectural stage with cordial, familistic collectivism and collective discipline.

Further, a painter addresses only a few people through his painting, and sometimes he paints for only one person. Pictures are always secluded in a building, and are only accessible to a few. Architecture addresses itself to the masses, because any great architectural creation, whether it be cathedral, pyramid, castle, palace, public hall, or government seat, is seen and can be seen by many, by unlimited, masses of people. "Painting can always be properly seen only from one point, by one eye. It is a message of a few, or even of one to the few, or even to one. Architecture is a message of many to many." Architecture is unwieldy, heavy, immobile, but always real. Its material is hard and rough: earth, stone, steel, and the like. It is little suited to express lightness, movement, change, anything merely showy. It is an expression of will, determination, and the demands of effort. There is nothing deceitful about it. It is the reality of the three dimensions, and it creates that reality itself. It is by nature somewhat ascetic and idealistic. It is the *Sein*, Existence, Being (in contradistinction to Becoming). Painting, on the contrary, is Show, Illusion, Deceit, mere Appearance. Its essence is to represent three-dimensional reality upon a two-dimensional surface, through light and shadow. Thus in its inner nature it is a show, deceit,

[50] *Ibid.*, pp. 60–61.   [51] *Ibid.*, pp. 60 ff.

appearance of the third dimension, which does not exist in fact. It is *Schein*, not *Sein*. In this sense it is not real. For the same reason it is inherently an imitation. Architecture does not imitate nature, it creates its own reality; painting imitates the things painted and gives us their illusory appearance. Therefore painting is especially suited to catching glimpses of the ever-changing shadows of things; it is apt to depict the dynamic, ever-changing, ever-moving, momentary play of light and shadow, color and contour. It is mobile, "progressive," and dynamic by its nature. Architecture must obey the laws and regularities of the realities on which it builds. It is and must be objective (because it is reality), while painting is and must be subjective and impressionistic, because it is and gives a mere show and appearance. Architecture must be orderly, disciplined, systematic, and free from mere fancifulness or whim, because otherwise it cannot produce anything lasting. It is Order, System, Effort, Law, and Discipline. Painting can be and is fanciful, individualistic, impressionistic, irregular, anarchistic, free, liberating, because it deals with the world of shadows, passing and momentary impressions. Here the artist is not forced by his material to obey the laws of the physical, objective world. He is free, and can give full freedom to his imagination and fancy. It does not require a disciplined order, and system, and effort. It is Fancifulness, Freedom, Life, and Accidental Impression of the moment.

When these properties of architecture and painting are considered, it becomes at once comprehensible why a culture at the architectural stage has the characteristics of order and stability, while at its *malerisch* stage it is stamped by individualism, freedom, intellectualism, impressionism, light-mindedness, momentary Epicureanism, a *Carpe diem* attitude, irreligiosity, revolution, disorder, and other traits. It is stamped by these traits not because of painting, but because painting is the form of art which is best suited for such a cultural *Gestalt*. It is structurally, logically, and causally a part, a symptom, and a quality of such a cultural status.

The more "architectural" is the inner life of a given culture the more architectural are its sculpture and painting. And vice versa, the more *malerisch*, showy, is the inner life of the culture, the more *malerisch* are its architecture and sculpture. The Middle Ages had painting and sculpture as well as architecture, but there was no perspective in the painting, no attempt to represent three-dimensional reality by two-dimensional surface: there was no Show, no Appearance. It depicted things as they were in the *mind* of the painter, in their eternal essence and idea, regardless of how they looked, not as they appeared to the artist's eye. Painting itself, then, was expressionistic, ideational, not visual, not impressionistic. In modern times, especially since the advent of baroque and rococo, at the *malerisch* stage of our culture architecture has become *malerisch*, full of movement and dynamic, purely impressionistic, illusionistic, and mere show for the sake of show. One is almost tempted to call it "Hollywoody." As to modern painting and sculpture, they have become purely impressionistic or visual. They depict, or try to depict, not the eternal essence of the phenomena or objects depicted, not their idea, but their purely visual appearance, even without reference to the other organs of sense. As the visual appearance of things incessantly changes, such artists grasp only the momentary show, give us purely visual snapshots of things, not their durable essence. Hence, impressionism in the arts of a culture in its *malerisch* period is in closest harmony with the organically impressionistic nature of all cultural life at this stage : it is constantly in turmoil and change; it becomes "progressive"; it is showy (providing, for example, in our own age motion pictures, advertising); it is momentary (*Carpe diem;* "Wine, Women, and Song"; jazz madness; crooning; and so on); it is individualistic, fanciful, disorderly.

Such is the explanation of the association of the predominant form of art with other important aspects of a culture.

Though many of these ideas are not new, and were set forth many times before Ligeti, nevertheless these pages of his work appear to be very suggestive and sometimes even profound. Even while rejecting his main theory of the existence of a uniform sequence in the development of art and, consequently, his main sociological conclusions about the future of our culture or other cultures, one must agree that his discussion contains a great deal that is perhaps valid — if not universally, then at least for some cultures and some periods. If he has done nothing else in these analyses Ligeti has shown beyond the possibility of doubt that there does in fact exist a close connection between the whole of a culture and the forms of its art. What is true and what is false in his theory will be shown in greater detail in subsequent chapters, where my own theory is developed.

The evidence presented in this chapter permits us to draw the following conclusions. Of the several theories under discussion which try to establish a definite and universal sequence in the development of various arts in all cultures and civilizations, we are obliged by the facts to adjudge their claim as, at best, only partially valid. No such uniform and universal sequence exists, and however valuable and interesting in other respects are the theories which have been tested, in this respect they must be regarded as a distortion of the truth.   They are like those theories which postulate a uniform and universal regularity of lag in the process of change from the material culture to the immaterial, from the economic phenomena (Marxianism and its diluted forms as represented by Ogburn and other American sociologists) to the ideological; or from science to religion and philosophy, from religion and philosophy to the arts, from the arts to economic and practical activity (see Roberty's sequence: science-religion-arts-practical activities).   They impose a complete uniformity where it either does not exist at all, or exists in a much more limited form than is claimed.   It is high time to liberate our minds from the popular delusion of the preceding two centuries that "nature" and, especially, the sociocultural processes are absolutely uniform and always proceed in the same monotonously invariable manner.   As a matter of fact, they are much more variable and creative than that.

Chapter Six

IS THE CURVE OF ART DEVELOPMENT UNIFORMLY SIMILAR
IN VARIOUS SOCIETIES AND CULTURES? PRELIMINARY CRITI-
CAL SURVEY OF THEORIES ON THE SUBJECT (*Continued*)

The preceding chapter shows that the sequence of the blossoming of
the various fine arts — painting, sculpture, architecture, music, and literature — is different in various cultures.　In this chapter I am going to
discuss a problem somewhat similar, namely : *Are the curves of art development in general, and of the specific arts in particular, essentially the same
in various cultures?　Do they pass through the same stages?*　Can we
maintain, for instance, from the standpoint of the style, or of the mentality, or of any other essential trait, that art in general, and its specific
forms in particular, undergo an "evolution" that is similar in various
societies and cultures?　If so, what is the correct general formula of
such an evolution?　If not, what is the scientific answer to the question
that should replace the theories and the formulas of the "uniformists"?

Since, as we shall see, the nineteenth and the beginning of the twentieth
centuries have been periods of belief in the existence of rigid uniformities
and, to a considerable extent, of a linear evolution in cosmology and
biology, as well as in sociology, it has been believed also that various
cultures and their art pass through the same stages of evolution.　A very
great number of social scientists and journalists, from Auguste Comte,
Herbert Spencer, and E. B. Tylor, to Letourneau and other *dii minores*,
have been busy with the formulation of "the laws of evolution," of "progress," of "stages of development," [1] of the historical trends and tendencies in all fields of culture, including art.　Dozens and dozens of such
"laws" have been manufactured with their curves of social evolutions
and art evolutions, and with three, four, five, and more stages through
which all peoples and cultures are supposed to pass.

During these years even many partisans of what may roughly be called
the creatively recurrent or cyclical interpretation of the direction of

[1] See the correct and humorous remarks of E. F. Gay in application to similar economic
theories in his "The Rhythm of History," in *Harvard Graduate Magazine*, September, 1923,
pp. 7 ff.

sociohistorical processes have also believed, despite the difference of their
conception from the linear, in the uniformity of the "curve" of cultural
development in general, and art development in particular, in various
cultures and societies.   They have also maintained that the stages or
phases of the development of various cultures are essentially the same.
In other words, they also subscribe to the thesis of the recurrence of art
phenomena in social space.   Their main variance lies in their conception
of the movement of culture in the finite and "parabolic" curve of cycles
instead of the unilinear, multilinear, or spiral line of a perpetual trend
projected into the infinity of the future, as advanced by the linearists
in their "bigger and better" evolution, which begins with the amoeba or
"primitive man" of the far-remote past.   Oswald Spengler may serve as an
example of a "cyclicist" who has succumbed to this obsession by "uniformity" in space.   In spite of his contempt of the social science of the
nineteenth century, like most of the "cyclicists" he did not succeed in
freeing himself from the tenets of the nineteenth-century dogmas of the
"universal uniformity" and "invariable rigidity" of the "laws of social
development" for all cultures and societies.   "Cultures are organisms,
and world-history is their collective biography."   "Every culture passes
through the age-phases of the individual man. . . .   Each has its childhood, youth, manhood and old age." [2]   This is not much different from
Auguste Comte's "law of the three states" through which, supposedly,
all cultures must pass, nor is it much different from most linearist conceptions.   It is characterized by the same belief in the uniformity of the
"curves" of the life history of cultures; the same belief in the similarity
of the stages through which they pass; and the same belief in the "invariability" of the laws for all peoples and times, styled "Destiny" by Spengler and "the iron law of determinism" by the linear evolutionists of
the nineteenth century.

Since the linearists as well as the cyclicists have believed in these
dogmas in regard to the evolution of whole cultures, it is natural that
the majority of theories of art evolution in various cultures have been
formulated with the same assumptions as to the uniformity of the curves
of evolution in various cultures, the similarity of the nature and sequence
of their stages of development, and the invariability of the "uniform"
laws determining their growth.   First, let us take the most general formulations of the uniformity of the growth of art in various cultures.

[2] Oswald Spengler, *The Decline of the West* (New York, 1929), Vol. I, pp. 104–108; see also
pp. 112–113 *et passim*.   See also F. Cornelius, *Die Weltgeschichte und ihre Rhythmus* (München, 1925) and H. Schneider, *Die Philosophie der Geschichte* (Breslau, 1923), Vol. II, pp. 68 ff.

The arts are subject to a beginning, progression, completion, and termination, a growth, a blooming, and a decay.[3]

Like all the human institutions, arts originate, grow, and prosper or decay according to certain laws. . . .   Among all peoples of a high culture they pass the periods of infancy, youth, maturity, and decadence. . . .   These periods of origin, splendor, and decline of arts exhibit certain common traits among the majority of peoples.   Take, for instance, the peoples who are original in art achievement and well known to us: the Greeks, the Italians, the French; you will be surprised to find everywhere the same traits.[4]

Each art which completely develops and runs its whole normal course without being interrupted by some external blow passes invariably through several phases, the order of sequence and constitutive character of which being constant are susceptible to a scientific study.[5]

To add similar quotations illustrating this type of theories is useless. Their first claim is that any art system is finite in its existence : it appears, blossoms, and declines.   I agree with this, because not only art but, as Plato says, "everything [on this earth] which has a beginning has also an end"; and therefore any empirical system, not only art, "will in time perish and come to dissolution."   There is no reason to insist further upon this platitude in special reference to art, nor painfully to try to prove its truth.   For this reason there is little in such formulas to inform us about the real nature of the curve of art development.   In brief, this claim is of very little cognitive value.

The second claim advanced by those holding such theories seems to be worthy of more serious consideration, namely, that the art systems of various cultures have the same or similar curves of development : origin, growth, zenith, and decline; or childhood, maturity, and senility. If they can show, with evidence, what the essential characteristics of art at each of these phases are, and that these phases, each with its special characteristics, are similar in the art systems of various cultures, then their contention becomes quite important, and is no longer platitudinous.

Do most of the theories discussed meet with these requirements? Unfortunately they do not.   Most of them give only figurative expressions without any serious attempt to substantiate them in the ways indicated above.   Without such a substantiation they hardly can be

---

[3] G. W. F. Hegel, *The Philosophy of Fine Art*, trans. by F. P. B. Osmaston (London, 1920), Vol. III, p. 5.

[4] C. Bayet, *Précis d'histoire de l'art* (Paris, 1905), pp. 11–13.

[5] Charles Lalo, *Esquisse d'une esthetique musicale scientifique* (Paris, 1908), pp. 259 ff. See similar contentions in A. Venturi, *La Madonna* (Milano, 1900), p. v; H. Rietsch, *Die deutsche Liedweise* (1904), and in many other works.

taken seriously and are of no scientific value.   Merely to say that each art system passes through the stages of childhood, maturity, senility, is but a meaningless expression, if it is not shown by means of concrete data what exactly are the characteristics of art childhood, art maturity, and art senility; when and where one stage ends and the next begins; how long is the duration of each stage; and so on.   Is the Gothic style the style of childhood, maturity, or senility, and why?   If it is one of these three "phases" that is in question, does it occur in all cultures, in all its essential traits?   It is enough to ask these questions to make clear the emptiness of such analogies, when they are not followed by the specification of exact details as suggested above.   Without such specifications they do not and cannot prove anything concerning either the uniformity or the nonuniformity of art evolution in various cultures, nor can they give us any real knowledge of the phases of development in art.

Mutatis mutandis, the same can be said of several other formulas when they are not substantiated and specified along the above lines.   Take, for instance, the formula stating that all art systems have the stages archaic, classical, and decadent.   Without factual substantiation it also is empty.   All such unsupported theories may be dismissed without further consideration.

The situation is different with all theories of uniform development in art which are supported by a solid factual substantiation and corroboration of their general contentions.   Such theories exist, and some of them are very discriminatingly elaborated.   Often they throw an interesting light on the dynamics of art phenomena.   They cannot be dismissed with a few remarks, as can the above; they deserve a more attentive analysis.   As our first example we shall take the theory of a distinguished historian of art, W. Deonna, which is brilliantly developed in his several works, and especially in the three large volumes of his *L'archéologie, sa valeur, ses méthodes*.[6]   The theories of W. Deonna, and of others whose contentions we shall consider later, do indeed go beyond a vague supposition and lay down a series of quite factual and concrete traits typical of the archaic, the classical, and the decadent stages of art. They try to show that those traits are found in various systems of art and follow a uniform sequence in the life course of divers art systems, and they also offer reasons why such a uniformity exists.

Deonna takes four great art systems in sculpture and, in part, painting — the paleolithic, the neolithic, the Graeco-Roman, and the Christian —

---

[6] Paris, 1912.

and tries to show that each of these systems has passed through similar fundamental periods of archaism, classicism, and finally decadence. In each of these phases the traits and style of all four systems of art are strikingly homogeneous and similar. The similarity is so great that the statues of early medieval Europe (before the twelfth century) can easily be mistaken for those of archaic Greece (before the sixth century B.C.), and vice versa. Likewise, comparing the Aurora of Michelangelo with the Niobide of Rome, the Nymphs of the Fountain by Jean Goujon (sixteenth century A.D.) with the Dancing Woman figure of Pergamum (third-second century B.C.); geometric statues of the archaic paleolithic with those of the archaic neolithic period, and with archaic Greek, archaic medieval, and so on, one cannot fail to see a striking similarity between them, even though they be separated from one another by centuries, even by thousands of years. Some of the statues of the Acropolis were pronounced by many specialists to be remarkably similar to the works of Mino da Fiesole, Francia, and Desiderio da Settignano; some of the sculptures of the Scopas school in Greece (fourth century B.C.) to the sculptures of Francia; some of the works of Praxiteles and Lysippus to those of Ghiberti and Donatello; some of the Greek and Pompeian vase paintings to the paintings of Mantegna, Roger van der Weyden, and Titian; some other works of ancient Greece and Rome, to those of Michelangelo, Velasquez, and Bernini;[7] and so on. Analyzing systematically the art objects of the four art systems, Deonna comes to the conclusion that, in essentials, each of them has passed through the same main stages, and when the art of the same phase in each of the four systems is taken separately it exhibits a remarkable similarity in all the systems. For instance, the art of Greece (mainly sculpture) before the sixth century is quite similar to that of Europe before the twelfth century; the art of Greece of the fifth century is a replica of the art of Europe of the thirteenth century; and so on. The Creto-Mycenaean art, viewed by Deonna as the last phase of neolithic art, is similar to that of the Graeco-Roman art of the Hellenistic period, and to the European art of the fifteenth and eighteenth centuries.[8] Volumes II and III of his work are devoted to the factual demonstration of this proposition. On the basis of an enormous amount of material, he proceeds to demonstrate the similarity of the phases in all four systems and the likeness

[7] W. Deonna, *L'archéologie*, Vol. III, pp. 6 ff. The many reproductions of these and other sculptures and paintings, though separated from one another by centuries and belonging to different art systems, indeed show a striking similarity in the whole as well as in technical details. See especially Vols. II and III, *passim*.

[8] *Ibid.*, Vol. III, p. 52 *et passim*. See the many reproductions printed in this work.

of the art of the four in corresponding phases. He deals not only with the general style of the art, but also with a series of details, such as the form of eye, ear, mouth; smile, frontality, nudity, composition of dress, posture; idealism or realism; emotionality or the lack of emotion; the presence or absence of landscape, portraiture, *genre* of a certain kind; and so on. His conclusions run as follows.

To sum up, we can consider art as developing according to a definite rhythm which leads to a recurrence of similar, if not identical, tendencies and forms separated by the intervals of centuries; using an image which is not quite exact but gives an idea of this regular course of art evolution, we can say that the evolution of the history of art can be compared to a spiral, where each curl superimposes over the lower one without touching it, as each period superimposes upon the anterior period. . . . That is what I plan to demonstrate.[9]

Further on Deonna shows that each of these four systems of art starts with the archaic form, the result mainly of inexperience and a lack of skill in the artists. Then each progresses, becomes perfected, and reaches its climax, or classical period, after which each begins to decline.

Each of these art systems, starting from a similar point of departure, develops with the same logical rhythm and in the course of its evolution produces analogical forms of art.[10]

The *archaic phase* of the art of the paleolithic, neolithic, Graeco-Roman (up to the sixth century B.C.), and the early medieval (up to the twelfth century A.D.) periods exhibits the same primitive technique, frontality, "horror of emptiness," lack of perspective or perspective by superposition of planes, lack of unity in the composition, triangular heads, "archaic smile," low foreheads, and a similar composition of ears, nose, hair, beard, and other parts of the human body.[11] Likewise, when the *classical phase* in these four art systems is considered, particularly the Greek art of the fifth century B.C. and the Christian art of the thirteenth century, one finds a complete similarity between them. The technique becomes perfect, the statues begin to live, frontality disappears, and simplicity of perfection takes place. Idealism becomes supreme, and art now

[9] *Ibid.*, Vol. III, pp. 36–37. He intentionally omits the art of other cultures partly because he does not feel quite competent in those fields, partly because he prefers to demonstrate more substantially in fewer art systems than less substantially in many; but in passing note that he indicates that the Egyptian, Chinese, Japanese, and other art systems display the same sequence of phases in their evolution.

[10] *Ibid.*, Vol. III, pp. 41–52.

[11] *Ibid.*, Vol. III, chap. v. See the many reproductions there and the detailed analysis by the author.

reproduces either the positively valuable and ideal object only, or idealizes natural objects : mortals are produced like young gods ; human beings, even though old, are shown as young and perfect ; nothing prosaic, ugly, defective, low, finds place in it. Not only the types of men, but even their postures, are idealized ; order, inner calm and peace, lack of passion and emotion characterize such an art ; perfect balance and harmony reign supreme. Idealization does not admit realistic portraiture. For this reason women (who are rare subjects of this art) are robust and athletic, old men are young, babies are depicted as grown up. Nothing pathetic, macabre, or passionate is shown. Eternally young and perfect human beings, with serenity on their faces — even in the funerary statues of the dead, calm and immortal, these are the types of the classical period. Neglect of landscape, of prosaic and realistic *genre*, and of profane historical scenes are further characteristics of the Greek as well as of the Christian art of this period. Idealistic symbolism, whether of the ideal of patriotism in Greece, or of that of Christianity and the Church in Europe, dominates the art. Both of these arts are profoundly religious. Both are essentially anonymous, and the artists retreat before the community ; both are local in detail but universal in topic ; both incorporate the unity of mind of their entire society and are the work of the entire society ; both are rationalistic, meditatively speculative, and free from any sensuality.[12]

If we then take the period of "overripeness" — the end of the classical period and the beginning of the period of decline, in the Mycenaean, the Hellenistic, and the modern European arts — we again find, in all of them, a series of striking resemblances. In spite of being separated by great intervals of time, they show the same style, the same spirit, and similar forms and content. We find skilled technique which can reproduce anything, but, having no strong "soul" of its own, it mixes all kinds of styles incongruously, and conscientiously imitates the "primitive" style. Not idealism but sensory (visual) naturalism is now supreme. Art is down to earth. While the idealistic art deified mortals, this naturalistic art mortalizes the immortals. It imitates sensate nature and empirical reality. It has a particular inclination to the reproduction of the negative, the macabre, the pathetic, the passionate, the prosaic, the picturesque, and the ugly phenomena of life. The old man is reproduced now with all the ugly and miserable traits of old age, and the prosaic scenes of life with all the reality of their everyday character. Calm serenity is gone, and instead we have distorted figures, suffering,

[12] *Ibid.*, Vol. III, chap. vi.

ugliness. Women, who figure little in the classical art, are one of the favorite subjects in this phase. They now are depicted "realistically," and the favorite modes of their reproduction are voluptuousness, sensuality, sexuality, seductiveness, and "prettiness." The spirit of a purely sensate Epicureanism is conspicuous. Men are also represented "naturalistically," often as effeminate, and usually smooth shaven. Masses and crowds, impressionistic portraiture, the *genre* of daily life, and especially of the lower classes and picturesque urchins, are also favorite subjects of the period. Lack of proportion and symmetry, fugitive and dynamic aspects of empirical reality, violent motion, incoherence and mixture of styles, "colossalism," urbanity, sophistication, and suavity are dominant. In brief, these "overripe" phases exhibit the same characteristics in all the three systems of art.[13]

The outline shows that Deonna was not content merely with vague generalizations, but presented a vast amount of factual material for its substantiation and verification. Whether or not the main claims of his theory are valid we shall see on further investigation. For the present let us take some other theories of the same type. A theory set forth by Frank Chambers will serve as a good example.

Frank Chambers also tries to prove that the curve of art evolution, and its essential stages, are very similar in Ancient Greece and in Europe. Making use of literature and literary criticism as the main body of his material, he comes to the following conclusions. Both arts have passed through two similar stages. The first stage is characterized by a nonaesthetic estimation of beauty and the fine arts. In this stage all the great art creations are produced, not for art's or beauty's sake but for the sake of religion, morals, patriotism, civic virtue, and other nonaesthetic ends. The fine arts as such, and beauty as beauty, are viewed negatively and resisted. However, this does not hinder the creation of the greatest art values. Such was the stage in Greece up to the fourth century B.C., and in Europe up to the Renaissance and the fall of classicism, *i.e.*, the Academies. In the second stage there appears an appreciation of the fine arts as such, and beauty for beauty's sake. At this stage the arts become free from their duties as the handmaid of religion or of other nonaesthetic values. "Aestheticism," art collecting, the connoisseur, art education, art criticism, and so on, now make their appearance. In spite of this, the art of the second stage hardly achieves the summits that were reached during the first stage, and it is soon destined to disintegration and decline.

[13] *Ibid.*, Vol. III, chaps. iv, viii, and ix, where the details and reproductions are given.

Both ancient and modern, both the Pagan and Christian eras, seem to have had a parallel aesthetic history. In both eras two aesthetic states of mind have existed successively. The first state of mind was that which, say, deified the sun and prayed to it; the second poetised self-consciously and said: "How beautiful!" It was the first state which caused the Parthenon to be built; it is the second state which now ponders its ruins, argues about its reconstruction, and sees passionate and romantic visions. The like of Homer, the Lyric poets, Herodotus, Thucydides, belong to the first state; the like of Strabo, Plutarch, Lucian, Athenaeus, Plotinus, to the second; Aristotle and, to a less extent, Plato are the links between the two.[14]

In his later work,[15] where he analyzes the development of European art, Chambers repeats the same conclusions in a somewhat modified form.

In both cycles, Graeco-Roman and European, the history of taste at bottom was the rise and fall of classicism. The emergence of the aesthetic consciousness, its crystallization and its dissolution recurred regularly and faithfully. The mediaeval gold-and-glitter is read in Homer and Herodotus, monastic aestheticism in the early law-givers and philosophers, signs of transition in Plato, a classic Renaissance in Aristotle and his Hellenistic successors, and finally a romantic decline in the authors of the late Graeco-Roman age. At this hour we live in a latter-day world, not unlike that of Lucian, Philostratus, Athenaeus, and Plotinus, and in a few generations our civilization and its art will have run its appointed course.[16]

While the theories of Deonna and Chambers deal mainly with the fields of *sculpture* and *painting*, other theories, making similar contentions concerning the uniformity of the main phases of art in various cultures, try to establish their claim with regard to *literature* and *music*. The theory of E. Bovet may be taken as an example for literature, and that of Charles Lalo for music. Both of these theories, however, go further than those of Deonna and Chambers and insist not only on the uniformity of the stages of the evolution of these arts in various cultures, but also on the recurrence of these stages (or cycles) in time in the same cultures: when one cycle ends, another, in a different concrete form but with similar stages, begins and, having run its course, is again succeeded by a new cycle with the same stages, and so on.

E. Bovet [17] develops a theory propounded by Victor Hugo in his *Cromwell*. In the preface to his work Hugo says that the literature of every people passes through three consecutive stages: lyric, epic, and dramatic.

[14] Frank Chambers, *Cycles of Taste* (Cambridge, 1928), pp. 119–120 *et passim*.

[15] Frank Chambers, *The History of Taste* (New York, 1932), pp. 302–303 *et passim*.

[16] See particularly the Appendix in Chambers's *The History of Taste*.

[17] E. Bovet, *Lyrisme, Épopée, Drame: Une loi de l'histoire littéraire expliquée par l'évolution général* (Paris, 1911).

Poetry has three stages each of which corresponds to an epoch of a society. The primitive times are lyrical, the antique times are epical, while the modern time is dramatic. The ode chants the eternity, epic solemnizes history, drama paints life. . . . In primitive times man chants: when he is young he is lyrical. Prayer is his whole religion; the ode is his whole poetry.

When larger groups and empires appear, battles and other heroic deeds occur, "man becomes epical" and tells of great deeds and events. Then, with the complication of social life, there appear drama, reflections, disappointment, and pity. Then poetry becomes dramatic. This universal law, according to Victor Hugo, is valid, whether we take the course of poetry in time, regardless of nations (the Bible is lyric, Homer epic, and Shakespeare dramatic) or within any great nation and great literature. The Book of Genesis in the Bible is lyrical; Kings, epic; Job, dramatic. In France Malherbe came before Chapelain, and Chapelain before Corneille; in Greece, Orpheus came before Homer, and Homer before Aeschylus.

Such is the essence of Hugo's generalization. With some reservations E. Bovet developed it further. In his interpretation, the sequence lyric-epic-dramatic is valid in regard to the development of the literature of all nations if it is not hindered by purely exterior circumstances, which in some cases may break its natural course. It is also valid in the sense that it recurs in this order several times in the history of a great literature. In other words, it recurs in social space as well as in social time.

For corroboration of this "law" Bovet makes especial use of the course of French literature. He divides its history into three eras and each era into three periods: lyric, epic, dramatic. The first era — "Feudal and Catholic" — covers the history of French literature from its beginning to 1520. Its first period, from the beginning to the twelfth century, was predominantly lyric, and this was also true of its whole mentality.[18] Its second period, from 1100 to 1328, in both its mentality and its litera-ture, was mainly epic (King Arthur's tales, epic of Roland, etc.). Its third period, from 1328 to 1520, was essentially dramatic and theatrical (Mystery Plays, Moralities, etc.). The second era, from 1520 to 1800, falls into three similar periods: the first, 1520–1610, was mainly lyrical and rationalistic (Rabelais, Ronsard, Du Bellay, Agrippa, etc.); the second, 1610–1715, was predominantly epic (classicism, the Academies, a great number of epics, the epic historical as the main and supreme *genre* of painting and sculpture); and the third, 1715–1800, was conspicuously dramatic. The same periodic sequence is set up in the third era, from

18 *Ibid.*, pp. 32 ff. and 40 ff.

1800 to the present time : the period from 1800 to 1840 was lyric (Romanticism) ; from 1840 to 1885 was epic (a flood of novels, and the development of the classic *roman*) ; and finally, the time from 1885 to the present time has been dramatic and theatrical in literature and in mentality. Thus :

In the course of one thousand years the French literature three times has passed the stages : lyric-epic-dramatic. This universal law has not, however, manifested itself so clearly and so regularly in any other literature. There is a reason for this.

It is the interference of external conditions which may cause — and has caused — deviation in the course of some of the literatures from the above natural sequence.[19]

Such is the essence of the Hugo-Bovet law. As we see, Bovet, contending for its universality, admits at the same time that external conditions may break the sequence. Therefore, he himself regards it as nonrigid and approximate. As a matter of fact, it is not universal at all. Even in regard to French literature, Bovet's periods and sequences are artificial to a considerable extent. In regard to other literatures his "law" has so many exceptions that it can hardly pretend to be even an approximate rule. We shall see this in Chapter Thirteen on literature. For the time being, with regard to the literatures of primitive peoples, we shall find illuminating the following statements of F. Boas, which have a bearing on Bovet's theory. First of all the epic is practically nonexistent in the native American literature. Likewise, the succession of various forms does not have any universal uniformity. "These forms are not necessary steps in the development of literary forms, but they occur only under certain conditions." And if some of the forms, for example epic, are not found in some of the cultures and their literature (for instance, among the American Indians) "it does not follow that they would have appeared at a later time." [20]

These remarks must suffice for the present to show the limited character of Bovet's generalization.

Turning to Charles Lalo's theory,[21] we find that, like Bovet, he claims the uniform sequence of the phases of development of music which he gives to be valid in social space as well as in time. Any fundamental musical system runs through the same stages during its life cycle. If in the history of a given culture several musical systems have followed

---

[19] *Ibid.*, pp. 139 ff.
[20] F. Boas, *Primitive Art* (Oslo, 1927), p. 339.
[21] *Op. cit.*

one another, each of them has run through the same stages. The number of stages, their character and sequence, may be observed in the following table, which gives all the essentials of the theory.[22]

SUCCESSION OF THE THREE PHASES IN THE HISTORY OF OCCIDENTAL MUSIC

A. Greek Music
    (1) *Preclassical Phase*
        (a) Primitives
            Greeks of Asia Minor: mythical personalities [?]
        (b) Predecessors
            Authors of the names taken by the classics: epical personalities [?]
    (2) *Classical Phase*
        (a) Great Classics
            Terpander of Sparta (end of eighth and beginning of seventh centuries B.C.)
        (b) Pseudo Classics
            Thaletas and the Doric musical instruments (middle of the seventh and beginning of sixth centuries B.C.)
    (3) *Postclassical Phase*
        (a) Romantics
            Phyrius, Timothy, the dithyramb, and tragedy in Athens (fifth century B.C.)
        (b) Decadents
            Alexandrian, Roman, and Hellenistic cosmopolitanism (since fourth century)
B. Christian Melody ·
    (1) *Preclassical Phase*
        (a) Primitives
            First Oriental and Roman hymns (second to third century A.D.)
        (b) Predecessors
            Ambrosian chant of Milan (fourth century A.D.)
    (2) *Classical Phase*
        (a) Gregorian chant of Rome (sixth or seventh [?] century A.D.)
    (3) *Postclassical Phase*
        (a) Romantics
            Tropes and sequences of Rhenish countries (ninth century)
        (b) Decadents
            Plain song (chant) in savant's language, then as dead, finally as liturgical (since eleventh century A.D.)
C. Polyphony of the Middle Ages
    (1) *Preclassical Phase*
        (a) Primitives
            Organum and counterpoint of Northern France (from tenth [?] to fourteenth century)

[22] *Ibid.*, p. 261.

       (*b*) Predecessors

           Gallo-Belgian and Flemish schools (fifteenth and beginning of sixteenth centuries)

   (2) *Classical Phase*

       (*a*) Grand Classics

           Palestrina's school in Rome (middle of sixteenth century)

       (*b*) Pseudo Classics

           Dramatic madrigal (end of sixteenth century)

   (3) *Postclassical Phase*

       (*a*) Romantics

           Dramatic and eclectic polyphony of Bach and Handel (the **beginning** of the eighteenth century)

       (*b*) Decadents

           Counterpoint and fugue of the school of the savant language, already almost liturgical (since eighteenth century)

 D. Modern Harmony

   (1) *Preclassical Phase*

       (*a*) Primitives

           Singers on lute; Florentine opera (beginning of seventeenth century)

       (*b*) Predecessors

           International dramatic music: France, Italy, Germany (end of seventeenth and beginning of eighteenth centuries)

   (2) *Classical Phase*

       (*a*) Grand Classics

           German symphony: Haydn, Mozart, Beethoven (end of eighteenth century)

       (*b*) Pseudo Classics

           Chopin, Mendelssohn, Schumann (beginning of nineteenth century)

   (3) *Postclassical Phase*

       (*a*) Romantics

           German and French symphonic drama and poem: Wagner and Berlioz (middle of nineteenth century)

       (*b*) Decadents

           Archaism, exoticism, symbolism, contemporary eclecticism

In all these systems the preclassical phase is characterized by an indeterminate confusion, incoherence, and complexity (contrary to Herbert Spencer's formulas of evolution), and poor technique and impure mixture. In the predecessor phase, the technique improves, and the confusion and mixture begin to decrease. The classical phase is marked by simplicity, pure internal harmony, and an organic unity of music with perfect technique. It puts an end to the incoherent complexity and unbalanced confusion of the preceding phase. These characteristics of the classical phase exist in the pseudo-classical phase of the period, but an admixture of romantic and other complexities begins to creep in. Finally, in the postclassical phase are found senility and sickness. It is marked by an increase of nonequilibrated complexities, by a lack of balance, by romanticism and patheticism, by eclecticism of styles, by "colossalism," by a growing attempt to find "new ways" and "new methods," which results in ever-increasing incoherence. Very notably there comes a desire to imitate the preclassical, particularly the primitive, music. Various extreme modernisms and radicalisms abound. Music loses its organic unity and becomes more and more difficult. Instead of a free creation of genius it tends to become increasingly the result of painful research, difficult calculation, scientifically computed excess. It turns into an impurity and becomes the product of the manipulation of savant prestidigitators and researchers.[23] In this way it gradually degenerates and finally dies, to give place to a new system which will run through similar phases during the course of its existence.

To complete the characterizations of the theories of Deonna, Chambers, Bovet, Lalo, and many others with similar views, it is necessary to add that almost all these authors view the likenesses in different art systems as the result not so much, if at all, of diffusion and imitation, as of spontaneity of origin, independent of imitation, copying, or diffusion. It is due partly to the similarity of human nature, partly to identical technical conditions (for instance, a lack of skill in archaic periods), partly to similar cultural configurations, and partly to the inner immanent logic of each art, the organization of which tends to create its own inner milieu in which, being isolated from the rest of the world, it lives its own life according to its own nature.[24]

These theories do not, of course, exhaust the list. There are numerous other theories of the uniform development of art among various peoples and cultures.[25] Such are, for instance, the theories which claim that

[23] *Ibid.*, pp. 262–320. My outline gives only a skeleton of the theory. Lalo fills the pages of his work with abundant factual material.

[24] *Ibid.*, p. 262. See also Deonna, *op. cit.*, Vol. II, chap. vii; Chambers, *The History of Taste*, pp. 269–270.

[25] For the moment I pass entirely by a large number of theories offering various generalizations in the field of art phenomena; such, for instance, as the theories of periodicity in the fluctuation of art forms, particularly the so-called generation periodicity set forth by a large number of ancient and modern writers; likewise many others of generalizing character. All such theories will be discussed in various other parts of this work, particularly in Volumes Three and Four. As samples of the writing on the subject the following few works may be mentioned: F. Mentré, *Les générations sociales* (Paris, 1920); F. Kummer, *Deutsche Literaturgeschichte des 19. und 20. Jahrhunderts nach Generationen dargestellt* (Dresden, 1922); E. Ermatingen (ed.), *Philosophie der Literaturwissenschaft* (Berlin, 1930); G. G. Wieszner, *Der Pulsschlag deutscher Stilgeschichte* (Stuttgart, 1933); J. L. Lowes, *Convention and Revolt in Literature* (Boston, 1926); Herbert L. Smith, *The Economic Laws of Art Production* (London, 1924); P. F. Baldensperger, *La littérature — création, succès, durée* (Paris, 1919); L. L.

among all peoples art passes from the "physioplastic" to the "ideoplastic" style (Max Verworn); from the expressionistic to the impressionistic (H. Schäfer and, in part, A. Rigle and A. Schmarsow); from the architectural, through the sculptural, to the *malerisch* style (Victor de Laprade, P. Ligeti, and others). Other theories claim that the art of all cultures passes, in the course of its development, through the stages decorative, plastic, architectural, and *malerisch* in conformity with a corresponding *Weltbegriff* (L. Coellen), and so on.[26] As many of these theories will have to be dealt with further on, and as their defects are somewhat similar to those of the theories of Deonna, Chambers, Bovet, Lalo, and others, it is not necessary to examine them here. Instead, we pass now to a brief examination of the validity of the theories outlined above and of their basic postulate as to the uniformity of art development in various cultures.

It can hardly be questioned that between the art systems of various cultures there exist many similarities in both small and great matters. Whether they are due to diffusion or to independent and spontaneous creation, or to both factors, such recurrences of similarities in space and time are readily observable. Whether we take the so-called geometric style or geometric ornamentation, or the physioplastic or ideoplastic style; or whether we consider the essentials of technique or subject matter, or the manner of their presentation, or other factors, the existence in the arts of divers peoples and cultures of an enormous number of similarities in these respects — similarities sometimes of a striking character — is beyond doubt. And *ceteris paribus* the nearer to each other the general characters of the whole culture of the peoples compared, the greater the probable similarity in their arts. The art forms of all nomadic hunters who have lived in quite different parts of the world seem to exhibit more similarities than can be found when the cultures of nomadic hunters are compared with those of industrialized and urbanized peoples. The

---

Schücking, *Die Soziologie der literarischen Geschmacksbieldung* (München, 1923); W. Hausenstein, *Die Kunst und die Gesellschaft*; F. I. Shmitt, *Iskusstvo: Osnovnyia Problemy teorii i istorii iskusstva* (Art: Fundamental Problems of History and Theory of Art) (Leningrad, 1925); P. Sakulin, *Sociological Method in Literature* (in Russian) (Moscow, 1925); N. I. Efimoff, *Sociology of Literature* (in Russian) (Leningrad, 1927).

These few titles, culled from an enormous literature in the field, give one an idea of the great variety of the problems touched on and generalizations made. But as most of the topics dealt with in these works do not concern directly the problem discussed in these two chapters, they are omitted here.

[26] See an outline of many of such theories in W. Passarge, *Die Philosophie der Kunstgeschichte in der Gegenwart* (Berlin, 1930). Most of these theories are but varieties of the Hegelian theory developed in his *Aesthetik*.

same is to be said of the art forms of all agricultural peoples, even though isolated from one another, and of the comparison between the arts of agricultural and nonagricultural peoples.[27] Similarities exist, are numerous and often essential. Otherwise we should expect the art of any people to differ completely from that of any other people, the arts of all people to have no common element whether in form, style, or pattern. Such a supposition is absurd. Thus far the theories concerned are valid and cannot be rejected.

Quite different, however, is the claim that the essential stages of the life history of all art systems are the same, that there exists a uniform sequence of these stages, and that therefore the life curve of all art systems has practically the same configuration, with its height in the classic period and a decline in the direction of the initial (archaic) and the final (postclassic) periods. These claims appear to me to be questionable. In subsequent chapters there will be offered a large body of material to support this doubt, and to show in detail what is true and what is fallacious in the above theories. Here, in the way of criticism, I shall limit my task to the formulation of brief statements which are sufficient to expose the weaker and unsupported aspects of the generalizations of the "uniformist" theories.

The life curve of the art systems of various cultures cannot be said to be the same in nature. Some art systems among so-called primitive peoples do not go beyond the archaic phase, in spite of the centuries of existence of their culture and art. The life curve of such systems remains, so to speak, on the same primitive level, without rising to the level of classicism.[28] On the other hand, as far as factual data are concerned, the art of the paleolithic peoples — this "miracle," as it is styled by many specialists — appears as already "mature" and far above the archaic phase. It shows skill in drawing, artistic perfection, ripeness.[29] It is true that Deonna foresees this objection and tries to obviate it by the assumption that the known perfected forms of the paleolithic art constitute the classical phase of its development, a phase which of necessity

[27] See the typical traits of the art of agricultural peoples in P. Sorokin, C. Zimmermann, and C. Galpin, *A Systematic Source Book in Rural Sociology* (Minneapolis, 1931), Vol. II, chaps. xv and xiv, where I tried to show this similarity.

[28] On this subject see E. von Sydow, *Die Kunst der Naturvölker und der Vorzeit*, 2d ed. (Berlin, 1927); F. Boas, *op. cit.* See the appropriate remarks in R. Thurnwald's "*Prinzipiengraden der ethnologischen Kunstforschung*," in the *Zeitschrift für Aesthetik*, Vol. XIX, pp. 349–355.

[29] See the reproductions and analysis of the paleolithic and neolithic art in the work of Von Sydow, pp. 66–67, 16–17, *et passim.* See also Max Verworn, *Zur Psychologie der Primitiven Kunst*, 2d ed. (Jena, 1917), and F. Boas, *op. cit.*

had been preceded by the archaic. This assumption sounds probable, but remains a mere guess, uncorroborated by data, and thus not convincing. Similarly, the known art of Crete and Mycenae belongs, in the main, to the "overripe" state of Deonna's curve. He again assumes that it was, of necessity, preceded by the archaic and classical stages of this art, but in its surviving examples there is little to support the assumption. For this reason, the life curve of such art systems lacks its first part, a line rising from the low level of the archaic to that of the classical stage. It thus differs from the uniform curve assumed in the theories discussed.

If we take such art systems as the Egyptian, the Chinese, or the Christian European, we are again confronted with a curve very different from that which is postulated. Indeed, the history of Egyptian art shows that it had not one parabolic "top," but several "tops" and several "bottoms." In other words, it follows a curve consisting of several waves rather than a single wave with one archaic, one classical, one declining phase. So far as sculpture is concerned, there was a classical period in the Old Kingdom, during the Second to Fourth dynasties, another in the Middle Kingdom, in the Eleventh and Twelfth dynasties, another in the New Kingdom, in the Eighteenth and Nineteenth dynasties; and later on, in sculpture as well as in architecture and painting, there were several more "ups and downs." [30] Any reasonable standard of judgment will disclose these ups and downs. To reduce this many-wave curve, with its several crests and troughs, to a single wave is impossible. Therefore, the form of the life curve of Egyptian art most sharply deviates from the uniform curve assumed in the theories under discussion. The same may be said of the Chinese art.[31] Its beginning is observed to have either a very short archaic stage, or none at all.

It may be said of Chinese painting, as well as of other forms of early Chinese art, that it appears from the beginning almost full-fledged. The earliest specimen known today reveals an art which has reached a high degree of independence and maturity.[32]

We reach the same conclusion if we take the history of European art. The impossibility of reducing its life curve to the postulated uniformity may be seen in the work of Deonna himself. His table runs as follows.[33]

[30] See Sir E. Denison Ross (ed.), *The Art of Egypt through the Ages* (New York and London, 1931); J. Capart, *Lectures on Egyptian Art* (Chapel Hill, 1928); J. Capart, *L'art egyptien* (Bruxelles, 1924), Vol. I; J. Baikie, *A History of Egypt* (New York, 1929), Vol. I, pp. 206 ff.

[31] See A. Waley, *An Introduction to the History of Chinese Painting* (London, 1923); O. Sirén, *A History of Early Chinese Painting*, 2 vols. (London, 1933); W. Cohn, *Chinese Art* (London, 1930); J. C. Ferguson, *Chinese Painting* (Chicago, 1927).

[32] O. Sirén, *op. cit.*, Vol. I, p. 1.   [33] Deonna, *op. cit.*, Vol. III, p. 52.

TABLE 10: PARALLELISM OF GREEK AND EUROPEAN ART

Art	Century					
Greek	Before VI B.C.	VI	V	IV	Hellenistic art	
European	Before XII A.D.	XII	XIII	XIV	XV	XVIII

This table shows that somehow he was not able to find the Greek counter-part to the European art of the seventeenth century; he had to place this art outside of his scheme. Moreover, he did not put the art of the nineteenth and twentieth centuries into his table.[34] Without bringing forward further points for discussion, one can see that the life curve of European art is not identical with that of Greek art and deviates greatly from the alleged uniform curve. In literature there are a great many cultures which it is impossible (like paleolithic painting) to plot with a parabolic curve, because the greatest literary creations in such cultures appear "miraculously" almost at the initial stages of their life history and are not excelled in the later stages. In Greek literature Homer's *Iliad* and *Odyssey*, in the Hindu literature *Mahabharata* and *Ramayana*, in the Finnish literature *Kalevala*, in the Assyro-Babylonian literature *Gilgamesh*, and in the Hebrew literature a part of the Bible, are cases in point. In such cultures the top, the most classical of all the classics, appears at an early — at almost the initial — stage but not at a later one. Something similar may be observed in the history of music in certain cultures. However limited our knowledge of Greek music may be, the existing evidences suggest that its great period, that of Terpander, was reached sometime in the eighth century B.C. during the archaic stage of Greek culture.

This conclusion is valid not only in regard to the general form of the curve of art development and its phases, but also in regard to many, if not all, of the most important changes in the style of an art. Their character and sequence are different in the art systems of various cultures. Here are a few instances.

(1) In some cultures the earliest art style is predominantly ideational or symbolic or ideoplastic (Max Verworn), or expressionistic (H. Schäfer); in other cultures it is predominantly visual, impressionistic, perspectivistic, illusionistic, or naturalistic; in still others both styles are found simultaneously.

[34] See the sound criticism of these points of Deonna's work by V. Chapot, "*Les méthodes archéologiques*," in *Revue de synthèse historique*, February, 1914, pp. 8-18. Compare J. Lagrange, *Mélanges d'histoire réligieuse* (Paris, 1915), pp. 227-279.

(2) The alternation of these styles from the standpoint of the length of domination, of the frequency of alternations, of the intensity of the shifts from one to another, and so on, are again considerably different in various cultures.

(3) The art of some cultures (*e.g.*, the Hindu) remains predominantly ideational throughout its history, while the art of other cultures (*e.g.*, the paleolithic, the Creto-Mycenaean, and, in part, the Greek) remains predominantly visual or naturalistic.

(4) The same propositions can be made with regard to the idealistic (not to be confused with ideational) and impressionistic (as the extreme form of the visual styles), their presence or absence, their alternations, and so on.

(5) The same propositions hold true for the linear and the *malerisch* styles — in the sense that these terms are used by H. Wölfflin, and for classicism and romanticism.

(6) Similar differences, implying a lack of universal uniformity, occur in the arts of various cultures among many other important characteristics, such as: (*a*) the proportion of the religious and secular subjects of the art, and its changes in the course of the existence of a given art in a given culture; (*b*) the proportion and intensity of the ascetic, of the Sensate (with the sexual as a form of this) mentality embodied in the art systems of various cultures at various stages of their existence; (*c*) the relative place occupied by such classes of painting and sculpture as portrait, *paysage, genre* of various types, historical, mythological, and others; by such musical works as oratorio, sonata, opera, symphony; by various forms of poetry and prose; (*d*) the relative predominance of the spirit of individualism and of collectivity; (*e*) the proportion of "pure" art or "art for art's sake" (which we shall see has never existed in the literal sense of the word) and of art not divorced from other cultural values, like religion, morals, patriotism, etc.

In all of these and in many other respects the art systems of various, and especially of very different, cultures offer a considerable diversity, and exhibit a clear lack of any uniformity. If we grant that this is really the situation, which it will be our attempt to prove in subsequent studies in the present work, then the laws of the uniform development of art in various cultures, of the uniform lagging of certain arts behind the others, of uniform curves of the quantitative and qualitative rhythms of the arts — all these and similar claims so dear to the linearists, cyclicists, evolutionists, and uniformists, in social sciences of the nineteenth and twentieth centuries — are not laws at all. They represent but the unwarranted elevation of a local and temporary relationship into a universal law. Such generalizations go far beyond the basis in fact upon which they are erected. No wonder that such unsafe buildings crumble at the first wind of factual examination. In the field of art, as well as in other fields of culture, the alleged uniformity of the curve of evolution, of the life history, of the phases and stages of development and progress, of historical destiny, happens to be no more than one of the pseudo-scientific beliefs of prosperous Europe in the second half of the nineteenth century. In the mental atmosphere of the cult of mechanico-materialistic but providential evolution, with its "Bigger and Better Progress," such a belief necessarily became popular, and was thought of as the last word in science. Since this Europe of the nineteenth century is gone, the above belief should lose some of its hypnotic fascination and an attitude of questioning inquiry should come increasingly to the fore. The results of such an inquiry show that this supposed last word of science is to a considerable degree marred by a fallacy arising from blind belief.

Chapter Seven

IDEATIONAL, SENSATE (Visual), AND MIXED (Idealistic, Cubistic, and Other) STYLES IN ART: PAINTING AND SCULPTURE

I. IDEATIONAL AND SENSATE (Visual) STYLES

In the two previous chapters I have shown the inadequacies of the theories of the "uniformists," of those who insist upon a rigid pattern of recurrence in the forms, styles, and content of art phenomena in various cultures and at various periods. Our rejection of these claims does not mean, however, that we must conclude that no recurrence at all takes place in the forms, styles, and content of the arts. Such repetition does surely occur; but the case should not be overstated as in these theories. Keeping constantly in mind that we mean by recurrence not the absolute reproduction in space or time of a given form or style or body of content (for such a thoroughgoing reproduction never takes place, involving as it must every unique characteristic), but the reappearance of a given form, style, or subject matter in its *essential* qualities, let us now turn to a study of some of the chief recurrences in the field of art phenomena. Both per se and for the purposes of this work, one of the most important forms of recurrence is the repetition (in space and time) and fluctuation of the Ideational, the Sensate (Visual), the Idealistic, and other Mixed styles in all their varieties and with all their secondary characteristics. It is important because, when it is understood, it makes comprehensible many essential traits of a given art in a given period, which otherwise would appear as meaningless *membra disjecta*. It is important also from the standpoint of the mentality incorporated in a given art: a proper understanding of the nature and dynamics of these styles permits us to grasp the nature of the mentality which lies behind the art, and behind the cultural constellation in which it appears, perhaps more adequately than would be possible if we approached it from the standpoint of some other key principle or, especially, if we studied separate paintings, sculptures, or buildings without any unifying principle.[1] Enough for the preliminary remarks. Now for the definitions.

[1] Compare A. N. Whitehead, *Adventures of Ideas* (New York, 1933), p. 14 and pt. i.

Among the objects most commonly depicted in the early Christian catacombs are a fish, a dove, an olive branch, an anchor, a good shepherd, scenes of the resurrection of Lazarus, Jonah in the whale's stomach, and Daniel in the lion's den.   If the reader thinks that for the early Christians the anchor in these frescoes is merely an anchor, the dove a dove, and that for some reason the early Christians were very fond of these objects as such, he is quite wrong.   As a matter of fact dove, fish, anchor, olive branch meant something radically different from what they appeared to be.   These objects were but symbols of nonempirical and supersensory values, like the human soul, God, salvation, and generally expressed "the hope of the Christian souls to reach the kingdom of God." [2]

Similarly the scenes of Lazarus and Daniel were there not for their own sake, but again as mere symbols of complex and superempirical values, which are well expressed in the prayer of the early Christians:

Father, deliver his [the deceased] soul as you delivered Jonas from the sea monster, the young Hebrews from the furnace, and Daniel from the lions' den. . . . I also pray to you, the Son of the God, to you who opened the eyes of the blind-born . . . who resurrected Lazarus . . .[3]

Here then we have a case where the objects depicted have no visual resemblance to their meaning, and where they are mere symbols of the superempirical values, mere "visible signs of the invisible world," or "a kind of diagram, expressing certain ideas, and not the likeness of anything on earth." [4]

The pictures of Plate I reproduce a few of the familiar geometric designs of the Indians.   The reader has probably seen such designs many times, has possibly even admired their beauty and ingenuity.   However, if the reader thinks that these lines and triangles and other "ornaments" meant for the Indians just the ornament as seen by the eye, he is again wrong.   Their meaning is quite different from and infinitely more complex than their visual form shows.   The real meanings of the pictures are as follows:

In No. 1, the upper zigzag line (a) represents a snake; the rectangular fields under it (b), the sea moved by the wind.   The dark corners of the rectangle (c) indicate calm on deep water, etc.[5]

[2] L. Bréhier, *L'art chrétien, son développement iconographique* (Paris, 1918), pp. 10–11.

[3] E. Mâle, *Art et artistes du Moyen Âge* (Paris, 1928), pp. 2–3.

[4] A. K. Coomaraswamy, *The Transformation of Nature in Art* (Harvard University Press, 1934), p. 5.

[5] F. Boas, *Primitive Art* (Oslo, 1927), p. 98.

PLATE I

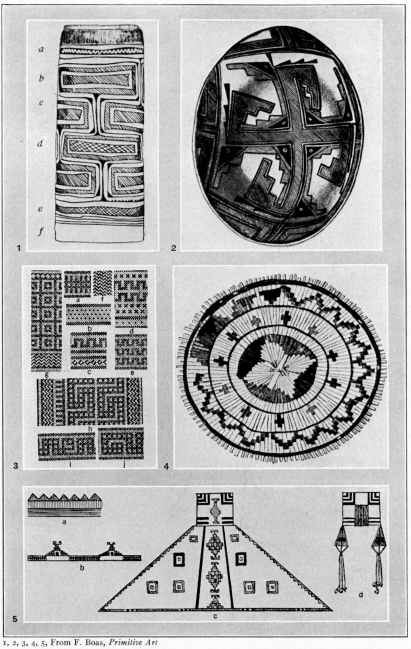

1, 2, 3, 4, 5, From F. Boas, *Primitive Art*

1, Bamboo case, from Melanesia.   **2,** Fragment of bowl, by the Zuñi Indians, New Mexico.
3, Patterns from baskets, from British Guiana.   **4,** Sacred shield, from the Huichol Indians,
Mexico.   **5,** Designs, from the Cheyenne Indians, northwestern United States.

The design of No. 2 is called "cloud all alone." Its meaning is still more complex. It is as follows, according to the Zuñi Indians.

When a person does not go to the dances when they dance for rain, after her death she goes to the Sacred Lake and when all the spirits of the other dead people come back to Zuni to make rain, she cannot go, but must wait there all alone, like a single little cloud left in the sky after the storm clouds have blown over. She just sits and waits all alone, always looking and looking in all directions, waiting for somebody to come. That is why we put eyes looking out in all directions.[6]

In No. 3 the main meanings of its various parts are as follows : (a) centipede; (b) savannah grass; (c-f) periwinkles; (g) butterflies; (h-j) snakes.[7] The meaning of No. 4 is :

The cross in the center represents four clouds on the horizon, the colored segments completing the inner circle represent red and blue birds soaring above the clouds. In the second circle are shown crosses representing red, yellow and blue corn. In the outer zone is a zig-zag line representing Mother Eastwater, a Deity. Nine triangles between head and tail of the serpent represent mescal which is . . . held as a prayer for rain and for health.[8]

In No. 5 figure (a) means mountains, a river, and a trail; figure (b), tents with fires in front. The meanings of the figures (d) and (c) are still more complex and abstract. There "the middle field represents the path of life of the child." The green dots in it symbolize "the child's good luck or the success that he will have in life. In this case green symbolizes growth and development; yellow, maturity and perfection; red means blood, life and good fortune." Other parts of the figures represent the age of the child, the heart, the unexpected events of life, and so on.[9]

These examples show the existence of a style in painting or drawing where the designs have no or an exceedingly remote visual (sensate) resemblance to the meanings symbolized by them. The artists do not paint the objects represented as they look to our eyes. Instead they create purely symbolic or ideational "signs" of the ideas or objects which they endeavor to depict.

Figures 1 to 4 of Plate II reproduce respectively Egyptian illustrations of a jug in a basin, a woman sleeping under a blanket, an Egyptian palace (in Amarna), and several prisoners. With these there are a picture (No. 5), entitled *Summer's Day*, by a distinguished modern

[6] *Ibid.*, p. 99.　　　　[7] *Ibid.*, p. 91.　　　　[8] *Ibid.*, p. 99.
[9] *Ibid.*, pp. 92–93. See also the many other pictures with their symbolic meanings, published in this same place.

artist (O. Nerlinger), and drawings by contemporary children (No. 6). A mere glance at the pictures is sufficient to see their visual (sensate) "unnaturalness." In fact the lower part of a jug in a basin cannot be seen from this position, yet our Egyptian artist without any hesitation draws the unseen line of the lower part of the jug. Likewise the body of the woman under the blanket cannot be seen, just as in the children's drawings the legs of a boy under his trousers and the body of a girl under her dress. They are here depicted contrary to the rule followed by any visual artist in attempting to imitate nature. As to the pictures of the Egyptian house and of the house on a summer's day by the modern artist, they are so different from the visual impression given by any house that without being informed of the meaning of these pictures the reader would have some difficulty to understand what they really mean or depict. Here again we have a set of pictures which seems to depict various objects not as they look to our eyes but as they exist in the mind of the artists, regardless of whether the picture has any visual resemblance to the objects when we look at them.

In Plate III, No. 1 is a reproduction of a famous work by Picasso. It depicts a cello or a violin, but again in a form quite different from that which it naturally impresses on the eye. The same is to be said of his *Lady with a Lute* (Plate IX), or of any "cubistic," "futuristic," or "modernistic" picture. They do not depict objects as they look to our eyes, but as they are in the mind of the artist, in their ideational essence, as it is thought of by the artist.

A few more examples. The next pictures we observe are a scene from a sarcophagus of approximately the fourth century A.D. (No. 2), and two scenes of the Crucifixion (Nos. 3 and 4) taken from the covers of a copy of the New Testament of about the ninth century. However the illustrations on Plates II and III differ from one another and from those on Plate I, these illustrations all have in common the trait that they do not reproduce the scenes and objects as they appear to our sight : such a conglomeration of figures and objects piled one upon another is impossible from the point of view of natural perspective. These pictures are ideational rather than visual or "natural."

If now we compare with these either the pictures created by paleolithic man, a sample of which (bison, No. 1) is given in Plate IV, or those of several contemporary primitive groups, a sample of which is also given (bushman rock paintings, No. 2), or the dying lion (No. 3) and the gazelle in the steppe (No. 4), from Assurbanipal's Palace in Nineveh, or virtually any other picture known to us as "natural," and the product of

PLATE II

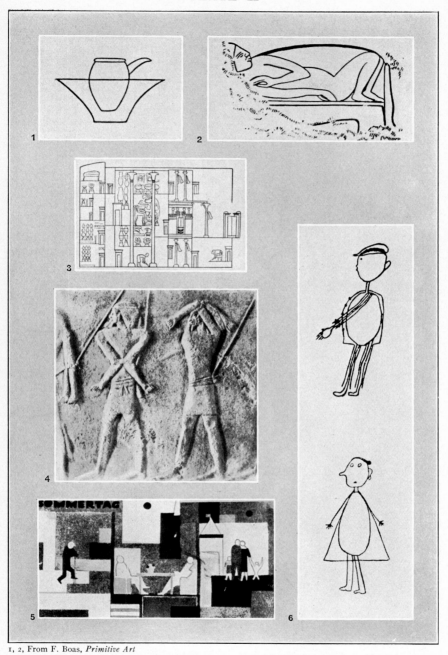

1, 2, From F. Boas, *Primitive Art*

1, Bowl and pitcher, from an Egyptian drawing. **2,** Sleeping person covered by blanket, from an Egyptian drawing. **3,** Palace in Amarna, from an Egyptian drawing. **4,** Egyptian sculpture of prisoners, from the Temple of King Sahure. **5,** Summer's Day, by O. Nerlinger. **6,** Drawings, by contemporary children.

"skill," the contrast is clear : while the preceding group does not strive to depict the objects as they appear to our eyes, these last all attempt to depict them in their exact visual impression — as we see them and only so. If a given trait, for instance a leg under trousers, is not seen in nature, being covered by the trousers, it is not depicted by the artist, though no doubt it is present under the trousers. In nature things have a perspective and appear foreshortened ; therefore the visual artist uses a convention to counterfeit foreshortening, though in reality it is misleading : foreshortened parts are in reality as long as some other parts which are made longer in the picture. In actual vision the play of light and shadow, perspective, changing colors often passing imperceptibly into one another, are all present, affecting the total visual impression made by any object seen. Hence their presence in a picture attempting to reproduce exactly visual impressions. In brief, in the pictures of this type an artist tries to render the visual (sensate), and only the visual, aspect of the objects. Anything else does not count and does not enter into the rendering.

After these remarks and examples the profound difference between what I here style the Ideational and the Visual (Sensate) styles must be clear in its essentials to the reader before we can proceed to a more detailed and more precise and more meaningful analysis of these styles and their intermediary or Mixed forms.

Each of these styles represents a characteristic mentality manifested in an appropriate external form.[10] As we have seen, the *Ideational* mentality seeks in the universe and in its parts *their unchangeable ultimate reality, their Being (Sein)*. This unchangeable Being is thought of as the essence of the reality of a given object or of the whole universe. It lies behind and beyond the appearances perceived by the eye and the other organs of sense. The sensory appearance of the objects is ever changing, ever in the process of Becoming (*Werden*), and is thus neither identical with the ultimate reality, with the permanent essence of it, nor similar to it. Hence, the Ideational mentality cannot and does not attempt to depict and to represent the phenomena as they look to our eyes, as they seem to our organs of sense, or as they are in their ever-changing empirical forms. The purely Ideational mentality is, by its very nature, immersed in the contemplation of the superempirical. So far as it is obliged to "depict" various objects, values, phenomena, in the language of art, it is

[10] For the relationship between mentality and art see, besides all the works quoted here, M. Dvořak, *Kunstgeschichte als Geistesgeschichte* (München, 1928), though this last work makes several points which represent an oversimplification of the truth and are thus not entirely valid.

not bound at all to depict them as they "look," as they appear to our eyes
(or to the other organs of sense), in those aspects, in short, which change
incessantly.   If need be, the Ideational mentality can strive to represent
the unchangeable Being (*Sein*) of these objects or values by symbols and
signs, and by other means having no resemblance to the visual appearance
of these objects, values, phenomena.   For such a mentality the sign of a
triangle may mean snake, buffalo, house, suffering, joy, glory, or anything
else.   This may be said of any purely Ideational sign, symbol, picture,
sculpture, music, and so on.

The Visual or (especially for arts other than the graphic) the Sensate
mentality is turned to the ever-changing aspect of the world and its parts
and objects.   It is the mentality of Becoming (*Werden*).   The sensory-
perceptual, or empirical, aspect of reality is its field.   Its reality is
incessantly changing, oscillating, vibrating, flowing.   The Visual mentality need not look — nor does it care to look — beyond this.   In art it
strives to render the picture, the image, the statue as nearly as possible
like the sensory appearance of the things depicted.   Bird, man, landscape,
nature morte, a scene of *genre*, a portrait, and what not — everything must
look in the picture or sculpture as it appears to our eyes (or, in the case of
music and literature, as it is presented to other organs of perception).
Foreshortening, perspective, *chiaroscuro*, the illusion of three-dimensionality on a two-dimensional surface, the play of colors identical with
that actually perceived by visual perception — these and thousands of
other illusions are the ideal, the necessity, the *condition sine qua non* of
the Visual or Sensate art.   It is bound by the *sensory appearance* (*Schein*)
of the world and its objects.   In its pure form it is Impressionism par
excellence trying to render the passing glimpse of the object or phenomenon, a living, momentary "snapshot" of it — or rather of the sensory impression of the empirical "stimulus" — as it is caught by eye (or other
organ of sense) in its vibration, its oscillation, its incessant change.   Such
a style cannot be either purely symbolic or abstract in which the symbol
or sign has no visual (or sensory) resemblance to the object depicted.
An art of this sort in its purest and extreme form does not need any mind,
intellect, thought, seeking the essence of the object or for its essential
lasting characteristics.   All it needs is a sharp eye (or other organ of
sense) and a good co-ordination of the "receptors" of the nervous system
with its "effectors," so that the visual impression may be fixed as accurately as possible.

To sum up : in their pure nature the Ideational and the Visual (Sensate)
styles, from the standpoint of the mentality which they represent and the

PLATE III

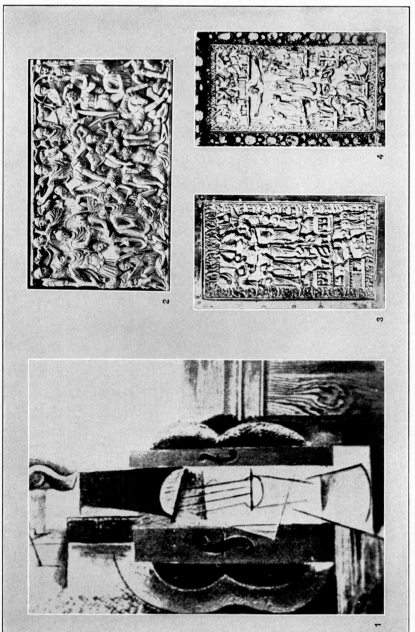

1, Cello, by Picasso. 2, Relief, from a Ludovisi sarcophagus of the fourth century. 3 and 4, Scenes of the Crucifixion, as represented on the covers of a New Testament of about the ninth century.

purposes and forms of depicting objects, are directly opposite and as different as can be. One is "transcendental," the other "empirical" or "naïve realistic." One lives in the supersensory world of Being, the other in the sensate world of Becoming. One is symbolic in its striving to depict by "visible signs the invisible world," the other is "impressionistic" and "illusionary." One is static, because the world of Being is unchangeable and remains always equal to itself, like Plato's Idea or the believer's God, or the philosopher's Ultimate Reality. The other is dynamic by its very nature, because its sensate world changes incessantly.

Which of these styles and mentalities is real or realistic? It is useless to ask. The answer depends upon what is meant by real, reality, realistic. If by these is meant the "unchangeable essence of an object," then the Ideational style is realistic. If the elusive appearance of the sensory-perceptual world is meant, then the Visual style is realistic. Both styles are equally entitled to use or not to use the term. On my part I shall not use it in application to either of these styles. Its use is unnecessary for my purposes.

II. Main Subclasses of Ideational, Visual, and Mixed Styles in Painting and Sculpture

Each of the two chief styles has different degrees of purity, beginning with the purest and ending with such a mixture of the elements of both styles that one cannot recognize in it either the Ideational or Visual and is obliged to put it into an intermediary Mixed, or Ideational Visual, style. The passage from the state of greatest purity to the Mixed state in either style is gradual and imperceptible, with the elements of either style varying both quantitatively and qualitatively. The chief steps in this gradual passage may be described thus:

I. IDEATIONAL STYLE

A. *Purest.* The subject matter is superempirical (supersensory) and immaterial (like God, the Virgin, the soul, the spirit, the Holy Ghost, and other religious and mystical topics) and its form (*i.e.*, the design, the picture, the sculpture) is purely symbolic, having no resemblance to the visual or sensory appearance of the object depicted. Since the topic is "invisible," its visible symbol naturally cannot have any visual resemblance to it. Examples of such an art are to be found in the Christian pictures in the Catacombs — an anchor, a dove, an olive branch, etc. — which signify ideational phenomena quite different from these objects.

B. *Impure Ideational Style.* (1) Though the subject is superempirical, the form in which it is rendered attempts to embody some visual resemblance to what is considered to be its empirical aspect, *e.g.*, pictures of Paradise, Inferno, the Last Judgment, *Pietà*, allegorical figures of Virtue, Vice, Patience, Temperance, the Muses, and similar topics, rendered in the conventional visual form in which they supposedly exist or will exist.

(2) The subject is empirical but the form is symbolic, having little or no visual resemblance to the physical appearance of the subject. The geometric designs of many primitive peoples, symbolizing buffalo, snake, hunting, fishing, etc., like the Indian pictures discussed above, belong to this type.

II. VISUAL (SENSATE) STYLE

A. *Purest.* The topic is purely empirical and material and the rendering is purely impressionistic, that is, illusionistic, in its visual similarity to a momentary appearance of the empirical and sensory reality depicted. A good camera snapshot and the most completely impressionistic pictures are the best samples of the purest Visual style. Such a style is dynamic, because the visual empirical reality, through incessant play of light and shade, incessantly changes. It must be impressionistic in the sense of catching visual appearance at a given moment. In this sense it is necessarily illusionistic, showy, presenting material objects in as illusionistic a form as they offer to our sense perceptions. The pictures of the leading French impressionists of the end of the nineteenth century are conspicuous samples of such a purely Visual style. Their rendering, as well as their theory, stresses the essentials of this purest Visual style.

For them in painting the only reality was the visual appearance of the objects. Behind and beyond it there was nothing. This visual reality was ever fugitive and changing. Therefore the task of artists like Manet, Degas, Renoir, and especially Claude Monet, was to catch the momentary glimpse of the empirical phenomena as illusionistically as possible. What phenomena? It does not matter at all what is depicted. There are no noble and ignoble, great and small phenomena. Everything is suitable for depiction, and the same landscape or object may be depicted as many times as one pleases because at each moment it will look different and thus will be new in this ever-changing world of Becoming. As a matter of fact, Monet and others painted the same landscape many times as a new object for a new picture. What mattered was not what was depicted but to what extent the illusionistic effect was caught. In conformity with

PLATE IV

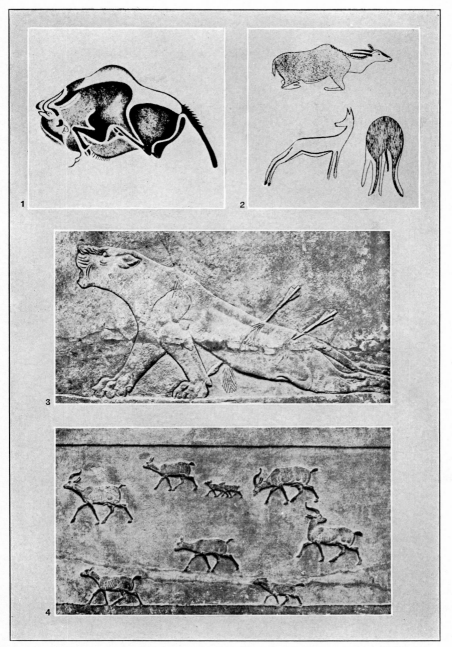

1, Cave painting of a bison dating from Paleolithic times, from southern France. 2, Bushman rock paintings, from South Africa. 3, Dying lion, and 4, Gazelle in the steppe, from Assurbanipal's Palace in Nineveh.

this the very necessity of thought or mind for painting was denied. All that was necessary was a good eye and a good connection or co-ordination of the eye with the painting muscles. The less the interference of mind or thought and the less its disfiguring influence, the better. In this sense impressionism was not only anti-intellectual but was radically sensate. In accordance with this it elaborated its own technique for painting and its own technical credo, which there is no need to go into here.[11] A careful study of the paintings of the impressionists discloses these traits quite clearly.[12]

A photographic snapshot is another example of the purely Visual style : it catches the momentary appearance of the material phenomena ; the next moment they would be different. It catches their purely Visual appearance, and catches with impartiality anything that is photographed. No thought, no idea, no brain, no ideationality is present or required for it. It just "snaps" and "shoots" the visual surface of the empirical objects.

The more completely Visual is the style, the more *dynamic* the picture. Since it strives to catch just a passing moment in the ever-fugitive appearance of the visual surface of the empirical world, the impression of change, of becoming, of dynamism, is unavoidable in such an art. Hence in conspicuously Visual pictures or sculptures or architectural creations (even in pictures of *nature morte*), the impression of dynamism, of restlessness, of fugitiveness, is, as we shall see, a usual satellite.

Moreover, the conspicuously Visual art in painting, sculpture, and, in part, even architecture, must be *malerisch*, and the more *malerisch* the more Visual it is. I use the term *malerisch* in H. Wölfflin's sense.[13] Visually almost no material objects are separated from the rest of the world by a clear and unbroken line. Similarly the parts of the object are not separated from one another clearly. The visual world is the world of patches of different colors, of light and shade, imperceptibly merging into one another. It is not a world where the boundaries of each object are clearly outlined by an unbroken line definitely separating one object and one color from the others. It is a world of somewhat indefinite forms and colors merging into one another. Hence the *malerisch* nature of the

[11] Not without a reason the postimpressionist critics styled it a "purely sensual art, an acephalic art, where only the sensations without any judgment of thought are noted, where eye devours brain," and so on. See L. Réau's chapter on Impressionism in A. Michel (ed.), *Histoire de l'art* (Paris, 1926), Vol. VIII, 2e partie, chap. xiii.

[12] A reproduction of their pictures in black and white does not do any particular justice to them. One must see them in original colors.

[13] See H. Wölfflin, *Principles of Art History* (New York, 1932).

pure Visual style. Its technique is not a linear delineation of the objects, but patches of color and light and shade which would give an illusionistic impression of the Visual world and in which all the corporeality of things has vanished.

As we shall see (and this has been excellently shown by H. Wölfflin), the painting of the second half of the sixteenth, and especially of the seventeenth and subsequent centuries, tended to be more and more *malerisch* in comparison with the linear character of the painting, sculpture, and architecture of the preceding centuries. In order to see the point a glance at Plate V is sufficient.

The first pair of pictures (Nos. 1 and 2) represent similar subjects — a woman, as treated by the linear Dürer and by the *malerisch* Rembrandt. Dürer's etching gives a clear linear representation of the body with all its details. It is sculptural, corporeal, tactile, architectonic. The artist separates the figure clearly from its surroundings not because it so clearly stands out from the rest of the world to our eyes but because he knows by his other organs of perception that it is a separate object with each part having clearly defined individuality. He supplements and "corrects" ideationally its visual appearance as this is given by our eyes only. Quite different is the sketch by Rembrandt. The figure imperceptibly merges into the rest of the world. No part is linearly defined; instead, the patches of light and shade (and in other pictures the patches of various colors) serve to give the visual and illusionistic impression of the subject. Nothing tactile or sculptural is in the picture. It is an illusionistic representation of a fugitive appearance.

The same difference is clear in the second pair of pictures, No. 3 by Dürer, No. 4 by Ostade, which treat a somewhat similar set of conditions. Ostade is *malerisch*, Dürer linear. One is purely visual, the other is only partly so.[14] Finally, Rubens's picture (No. 5) stresses the dynamism of the *malerisch* style.

Since the French Impressionistic school is, as we have mentioned, the extreme realization of the visual style, it should be expected to exhibit *malerisch* characteristics more conspicuously than do other schools, both in technique and results. And indeed this is the case. When one is looking at the masterly impressionistic paintings from a short distance one does see only incongruous, uneven, formless smearing of patches of color on the canvas. Its doctrine of painting *sub Jove crudo;* its mottoes that there are no black shades; that all shades are transparent and colored

---

[14] See in detail the discussion of the linear and *malerisch* in Wölfflin, *op. cit.*, chap. i *et passim.*

PLATE V

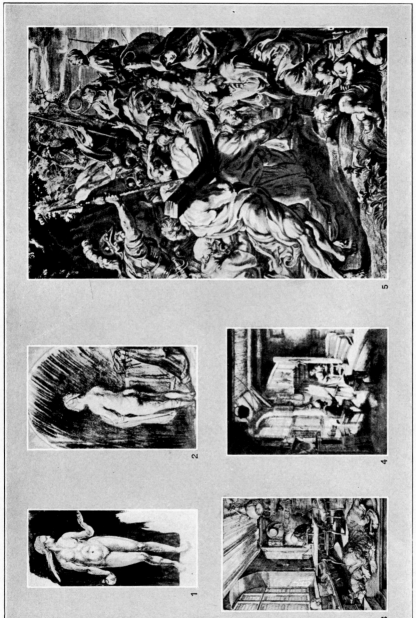

1, Study for Eve, by Dürer.   2, Woman dressing, by Rembrandt.   3, St. Jerome in His Cell, by Dürer.   4, The Artist in His Studio, by Ostade.
5, Christ Carrying the Cross, by Rubens.

and animated by thousands of reflections; that there are visually no fixed forms and no constant colors but that, instead, colors incessantly change from moment to moment through the play of light; that the subject per se is quite unimportant; and so on — these rules and *credos* led the impressionists to an extreme *malerisch* technique or to a sensory illusionism in pure form.[15]

These remarks are sufficient to indicate comprehensively to the reader the nature of the Visual style in its pure form. An increase of "dynamism" and of *malerisch* qualities in pictures or sculpture (or even architecture) in most cases *is* a certain sign of an increase of visualism.

B. *Impure Visual Style*. Like the Ideational style the Visual has different degrees of purity, running from the ideally pure — as outlined above — to less and less pure forms until the result becomes so mixed that the Visual strain in it ceases to be dominant. The main Impure varieties of the Visual style are as follows.

(1) The *topic* is empirical or visual, but the *rendering* is not based exclusively upon the visual impression. It gives something not presented by the momentary appearance of the object to the senses, or suppresses some "incidental" and "secondary" visual elements, or introduces some generally ideal and nonvisual elements either in the content or in the style of the picture, sculpture, or architecture. Such are, for instance, "character paintings" and "character portraits." In these the artist tends to render not merely the momentary appearance of the subject, but his essential, lasting, dominant nature. Moreover, many so-called expressionistic paintings conveying some central idea are of this sort; and this is true also of most of the "classical" paintings and sculptures with their careful selection of subject, of setting, of every detail of the picture or sculpture, and their elimination of everything incidental, unimportant, unclassical, debasing, and so on. Of this sort, likewise, are many stylizations and symbolizations and conventionalizations in the representation of empirical phenomena. Many Egyptian pictures and sculptural works; most of the linear or conventionalized art productions in the fields that we have studied; most of the "classical" works beginning with the Primitives of the fifteenth century and ending with the Academies of the seventeenth and eighteenth centuries, with the school of David, even with the expressionists of the end of the nineteenth century, some of

---

[15] See A. Michel, *op. cit.*, Vol. VIII, pp. 577 ff. See also W. Worringer, *Abstraction und Einfühlung* (München, 1909); Max Foth, "*Die Raumillusion und die unscharfe moderner Bilder*," in *Zeitschrift für Aesthetik und allgemeine Kunstwissenschaft* (1909), Vol. IV, pp. 456–463; E. Utitz, *Die Ueberwindung des Expressionismus* (Stuttgart, 1927); and the works of Wölfflin and Ligeti.

whom, like Cézanne, were near to the Impressionists in technique; many of the neoclassicists, "neorealists," and so on — all belong to the group working in the present subclass of the Impure Visual style.

The works of most of these periods, schools, and individuals fall so clearly into the present subclass that there is no need for illustrations. The case of the modern Expressionists like Cézanne is less clear. Therefore, illustrations of this school are not out of place here. It is enough to glance, on Plate VI, at the picture by Cézanne (No. 1), or E. Heckel's portrait of a woman (No. 2), or the Egyptian bust of the reformer-pharaoh Akhenaton (No. 3), to see clearly the point we have been discussing. Their technique is either impressionistic and *malerisch*, or linear (portraits). In content they represent "character painting" with much that is nonvisual worked into the rendering.

(2) Another main form of an Impure Visual style results when the topic is only partly empirical but the rendering is conspicuously visual. Such is, for instance, a purely "naturalistic" rendering of the Last Judgment, of the Christ Child sucking his finger, of the Madonna in the form of a lady of the world about us, of Virtues and Vices, of the migration of the Soul, of Justice, of Sin, and so on. Most of the visual representations of religious, transcendental, ethical, and other nonmaterial or nonsensory values belong to this type of the Impure Visual style. Such, for instance, are most of the religious pictures by the Italian masters of the Renaissance who gave to the religious personages like the Virgin, St. Mary, or St. Anne the likeness of their friends, wives, even mistresses. Such are most of the religious pictures of Rubens, some of Rembrandt, not to mention the work of lesser artists of these and later times. To the same class belong many allegorical pictures and statues — so fashionable in some periods — like the symbolization of Morning, Dawn, Virtue, Vice, Life, Death, Justice, Innocence, War, Peace, Discord, Abundance, Happiness, Conscience, and so on.

As we have mentioned, there are different degrees of impurity of the Ideational as well as of the Visual style. As long as one of these styles remains dominant in the work, the work is to be classed as a more or less pure sample of it.

III. MIXED STYLE

Though the Impure forms of the Ideational and of the Visual are in fact Mixed styles, the preponderance of the elements of one permits us to classify such renderings with the dominant style. By the *Mixed*, on the other hand, is meant a style containing such a mixture of the elements of

PLATE VI

1, Old Woman with a Rosary, by Cézanne. **2**, Etching, by Heckel. **3**, Egyptian bust of Akhenaton.

both main styles that one cannot without difficulty decide which elements are preponderant.

The varieties of the Mixed style, as this occurs empirically, are many. Of these I shall mention here especially three.

A. *Idealistic Style*. Exemplified most strikingly by the Greek art of the fifth century B.C. and the religious art of Europe in the thirteenth century, the Idealistic style is simultaneously Ideational and Visual. It is visual in the form in which it renders its subjects, but not entirely : as we shall see, it ignores on principle the profane, the incidental, the negative aspects of visual reality and adds the noblest, the sublimest, the most beautiful and typical values, which are not apparent in the objects perceived visually. It idealizes, modifies, typifies, and transforms visual reality in conformity with its ideals and ideas. To this extent it is not Visual, but Ideational. The same is true of the subjects represented. They are carefully selected and in most cases are either of the nonempirical kind, or of the half-empirical — typical, generalized in their nature. Nothing vulgar, debasing, ugly, unmoral, eccentric, can be the subject of such an art. If negative values are chosen for depiction, even these are beautified, are used mainly for stressing, by means of contrast, the positive values. If an individual is represented in portraiture, he is typified according to the idealized type. In all these respects the Idealistic art presents a marvelous balance and "organic" union of the elements of the Ideational and of the Visual style with some slight domination of the Ideational. Thus it is a specific form of the Mixed style. It has, of course, its own gradations and degrees with respect to the amount of dominance of, or the closeness of approach to, one or the other of the two opposed styles. But in its sublimest form the Idealistic maintains a steady balance between the two.

A glance at Plate VII, in which the Idealistic is confronted with a purely Visual or "naturalistic" rendering, will make clear the nature of the Idealistic art. Two sculptures of Pericles (Nos. 1 and 2), one of Christ (No. 4), two of the *Pietà* (thirteenth century — No. 3, and sixteenth century — No. 7), and two representing Church (No. 5) and Synagogue (No. 6, thirteenth century) offer examples of the Idealistic treatment of subjects. The five illustrations of Plate VIII give examples of an impure Visual or "naturalistic" rendering of, respectively, Caracalla (No. 1) and Christ (Nos. 2–5). The contrast is strikingly conspicuous. The Idealistic treatment does not show anything of decay, senility, death, imperfection, even of a purely human excess of emotion and passion. Even mortals are depicted as immortal, or noble, or sublime, or as an idealized type.

The "naturalistic" or impure Visual treatment depicts even the immortals (Christ) as mortal, the noble as vulgar, the great as debased. It is in a sense a "debunking" rendering which takes from its subjects most of their greatness, virtue, romance, charm, heroism, divinity, sublimity, and depicts them, naked, in their vulgar aspects. This is clearly shown by the pictures of Plate VIII. Christ in these pictures does not have anything divine or great. He is just a corpse, an imperfect corpse, an imperfect ordinary human being. The same contrast is easily seen in the busts of Pericles and of Caracalla. In the first we are given an ennobled and idealized type rather than an individual portrait with real — i.e., visual — traits. In the second, we see an individual as he "really" looks without idealized typification.

After these examples the nature of the Idealistic art and mentality is somewhat clarified. However, in view of its importance for our purposes, we must carry our analysis of it a few steps further.

The Idealistic art attempts to achieve results as far removed as possible from the photographic reproduction of reality; it substitutes a recreated, "beautified," typical reality in its most ideal manifestation. The purely Visual art attempts to be as faithful to "reality" as the camera, not necessarily in technique or rendering, but in achieving an "objective" likeness. The former closes its eye in the face of the ugly, incidental, secondary aspects of the world, though it knows of the existence of this ugliness and these secondary aspects. The latter delights to be "objective" and in a way enjoys the reproduction of the prosaic, ugly, distorted, singular, incidental, even more than the reproduction of the beautiful.

From these lines one can see that the Idealistic style of art is based on a specific *Weltanschauung* and philosophy of life, intermediary in nature between that of pure Ideationalism and pure Visualism (Sensatism).[16]

[16] W. Deonna describes these styles as follows (in application to the Idealistic art of Greece of the fifth century B.C. and the "naturalistic" Hellenistic art of the later centuries).

In the Idealistic art "the artist ignores the accidental [in his subjects] under all forms and wants to represent in man and in nature only what is eternal in them. He creates his divine types free from any defects of humanity and his mortal types participating in the divine essence. He ignores everything that can trouble the soul; his faces preserve calm and perfect serenity, and neither suffering nor joy can disturb them. Man, the supreme object of such an art, becomes an abstract and impersonal type depicted in the full power of his youthfulness equally far from the puerilities of infancy as from the miseries of old age. And such a man is placed in an ideal frame where all the details of the landscape are suppressed."

In the "realistic" art "the artist descends from heaven to the earth; he humanizes gods (instead of deifying the mortals); he is interested in all classes of society; he paints the purely individual traits and portraits (instead of an abstract idealized semidivine type); he depicts strong and tender passions; he views with curiosity a landscape; in brief, the

PLATE VII

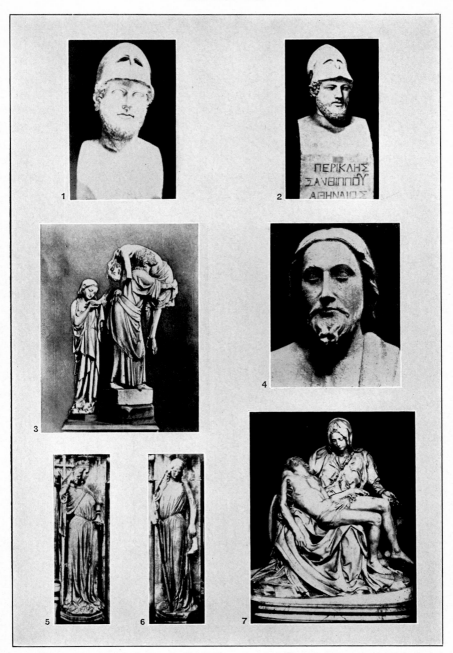

1 and 2, Greek busts of Pericles.   3, Pietà, eleventh or thirteenth century.   4, Head of Christ, thirteenth century.   5, Statue representing the Church, thirteenth century.   6, Statue representing the Synagogue, thirteenth century.   7, Pietà, by Michelangelo, sixteenth century.

From the very nature of the Idealistic and the Visual styles and the mentalities on which they are grounded, a series of associated traits follows. The most important of them may be mentioned here.

(1) To the extent that it does not try to reflect indiscriminately empirical reality as it is, but selects primarily those phenomena which conform to the supreme ideal, *the Idealistic art is almost always both a self-sufficient value created for its own sake, and a means to express, to manifest, to convey, to teach, to propagate the ideal and its values, which lie outside art.* Such an art is rarely art for art's sake, but almost always a partner or a companion, sometimes a handmaid, of religion, moral and civic virtue, or of other values of a nonaesthetic character. This does not, however, prevent such an art from reaching a position of supreme achievement in the realm of art alone. To this point what Chambers, Statham, and many others have stressed many times becomes relevant, namely, that any art in order to be great must have a great idea behind it ; otherwise it is liable to degenerate into a plaything suitable merely for the satisfaction of the sensate needs of man, and thus always temporary, short living, and shallow.[17] Thus, the idealistic art is always more closely correlated with the ideational than with the purely visual forms. In a degree it is always "ideational" so far as it always has the ideal or ideals behind it of which it becomes the mouthpiece.

The Visual (Sensate) art tends to be an art for art's sake so far as it does not tend to be a means to express anything except itself. It sees its main purpose and objectives in its reflection of the empirical reality as accurately as may be. It therefore is often associated with "aestheticism" in a particular sense, with that period in art history when art for art's sake appears, with its crowds of aesthetes, connoisseurs, collectors, professional critics, theorizers of beauty, professional artists who want to be artistic and nothing more. This is the period where art "liberates" itself, or rather believes that it liberates itself from any companionship with or subordination to anything outside of art itself : from religion, morality, civic duty, etc. This is the art which declares in its manifestoes

---

accidental which is never renewed or reborn, is what now is passionately studied and depicted." *L'archéologie*, Vol. III, pp. 503–504. See also the many other details given in the course of Deonna's admirable analysis of the art of various periods and countries from this standpoint.

[17] See Chambers's theory in his second essay. "If there is one thing that a survey of the history of architecture shows clearly, it is that all that is great in architecture has arisen from the desire to do something fine and noble for its own sake; and where there is not that desire [as in many modern commercial buildings] there will be no great architecture." Statham, *A Short Critical History of Architecture* (London, 1912), p. 545. See also A. Kingsley Porter, *Beyond Architecture* (Boston, 1918), *passim*, and particularly the essays entitled "Art of the Middle Ages," "Gothic Art," "The Gothic Way."

that it does not want to be subjected, or subordinated, or limited, or restrained by anything or anybody, that it wants to be absolutely free; and the artist views himself as a creature who *legibus solutus est.* Neither considerations of religion, public safety and decency, moral well-being, nor anything else should be permitted to bind his artistic fancies at all; he is above all these nonartistic values, just as art itself is beyond their reach.

In practice the situation of the "free" artist is quite different from that of his theory. Since the Visual (Sensate) art is to picture the actual empirical reality in its various aspects — objects, scenes, landscapes — as accurately as possible, without idealization or ideational stylization, the artist must reflect "reality" *as it is* — *i.e.*, as it looks to the eye. So far as some choice of a subject for depiction is necessary from among the endless details of this infinite empirical world — for no artist can paint or mold all its innumerable aspects — the choice is made not on the basis of the extra-aesthetic ideal, but on the basis of what *most frequently and most commonly* is met with (persons, scenes, *genre*, landscapes, objects of everyday experience), or of what is "fashionable" or of what is "picturesque," or of what is "pretty," or has sex appeal, or stimulates some pleasant sensuous experience, or, finally, has a high commercial value.

Whatever the choice is, it is always taken from this purely empirical world, always deals with it, and always tends to reflect it as accurately and "successfully" as may be. If the choice is the pretty face of Grisette or Lisette (look at the title pages of most of our weekly and monthly magazines), the face must be pretty or smart; if it is an everyday event or object, it must be depicted so "realistically" as to be taken for the object itself. If the choice is made for the sex reason, the figure must be voluptuous and seductive. If the choice is something empirically big, the art creation must be grand in its dimensions, "the greatest thing in the world" indeed.

This means, in a straight formulation, that such a "realistic" and supposedly absolutely "free" art is, in fact, the victim of its illusion. In fact it becomes also a servant, but a servant to different bosses from those of the Idealistic or Ideational art — to the Golden Calf; to the empirical visual reality; to the sensate — *i.e.*, eudaemonistic, hedonistic, and utilitarian — needs; to the sensual fancies of the Epicureans, the rich, the powerful.

(2) Since the Idealistic art has behind it, as its inspiration and soul, some great ideal, such an ideal or value is always the value of a genuine collectivity. It is not, and cannot be, mere individual fancy. It is

PLATE VIII

1, Head of Caracalla. 2, Head of Christ, Museum of Beauvais, fourteenth or fifteenth century.
3, Christ on the Cross, by G. Duvall. 4, The Crucifixion, by N. Gay. 5, The Dead Christ, by
Holbein the Younger.

logical, therefore, to expect that this value embraces within itself the collectivity as well as the individual artist creators. The creation then tends actively to involve the collectivity in which the individual artists are only the leaders. Everybody strives to contribute what he can to such a creation because the value is the common value of all. Hence the art of such periods tends to be stamped by the collective character of its creation, by the participation of masses in it, and by the anonymity of its individual artists. In this sense it is *nonindividualistic, collectivistic,* or *"familistic."* Often, as in the creation of many medieval Gothic and Romanesque or of early Byzantine cathedrals, or of some of the great Greek edifices, even the names of their builders and creators are either not preserved or were regarded as the names of the leaders only. Even when the real creator is an individual artist, his creation, if it is idealistic, reflects always a collective value and therefore remains collectivistic.

The Sensate (Visual) art, for the same reasons, tends to be, on the contrary, highly *individualistic.* It expresses the value of the artist, a value which may or may not be shared by the masses; here the artist is the creator; his name is attached to the creation and is inseparable from it. Since his creation is for him self-value, not a means to something else behind it, he is anxious to get a "copyright," to "immortalize" himself in it, to attach his name to it. Individualism in this sense and the Sensate (Visual) art are correlated to a high degree.

(3) Since the Idealistic art embodies some great values, any individual person of the common sort, any common landscape per se, any common event — unless they are symbols of the great value — can have no interest, or at best only a secondary interest. Only that object, person, or event which incarnates the value — has a direct relation to it — may properly be the subject of the Idealistic art. As to all other subjects, it either passes them by or strips them of any real individuality, turning them into rationalized and idealized types, a kind of algebraic formula without any concrete arithmetical value. Hence, the rationalistic, abstract, "typifying" nature of the Idealistic art. Under such circumstances, *the individual portrait, the empirical genre, the landscape, the historical scene, and anything concrete, not related to the ideal, are rare in such an art.* Its main content centers about its chief idealistic values. If these be religious, then it would represent deities, great religious events, religious history, doctrines, beliefs, and everything else of great significance as judged from the standpoint of these values.

In the Visual art the situation is the reverse. Only the empirical world, which always consists of individual objects, persons, events, is and can be

the concern of such an art.   It is the art of the portraiture of individuals;
the art of the depiction of the daily *genre;* the art of empirical events,
historical scenes, landscapes; in brief, the art of life and the world as
they appear to the organs of sense.

(4) The choice of the Idealistic art with regard to subject matter
and treatment is determined by the nature of the *ideal value*, not entirely
separated, however, from the empirical world, as it is in the Ideational art.
All that is foreign to this value is unimportant for such an art and is passed
over by it.   The nonidealistic phenomena, especially, or the phenomena
which are contrary to the ideal (unless they can be made to serve, by
contrast, for the augmentation of the glory of the ideal value) are out
of place in such an art.   *It passes by the prosaic, the debased, the defective,
the common, the earthly.*   It does not see the baby as a baby, the old man
as senile, the woman as womanish; what it sees is some general and
perfected type of man.   Therefore its babies are grown up; its old men
are youthful; its women are manly — there is no sex in them; its landscapes are just a background adapted each time to the requirement of the
main ideal topic; its scenes are only of the history of the ideal value,
as is the case, for example, with the scenes in the cathedrals of the thirteenth century, sculptures which have properly been styled the Bible
in stone.

The Visual art is *earthly* in its principle of selection.   It depicts what
may be interesting from the earthly standpoint, what may be "picturesque" ("Ah, how interesting!"), "stunning," "pretty," "effective,"
"romantic," "truthful," "sensational," "marketable."   By the law of
contrast, it tends to concentrate on common aspects of life and the world,
on the low, debased, perverse, evil, disgusting, sensual.   Hence its tendency to depict scenes of common or low life, historical events, the
drunkard, the prostitute, the street urchin, the criminal, the pretty face,
the seductive body, the nude erotic figure, the portrait, and so on; or to
render something that gives gratification to the eyes by its configuration
of forms and its play of colors.

(5) The world of the ideal is *thought to be eternal*.   It is the world
of Being.   *Eternal means static.   Static means quiet, calm, serene, immovable, and unagitated*, unshakably grounded and immersed in the ideal.
The world of the empirical, and especially of the visual empirical reality,
means *incessant change:* its forms, lights and shadows, colors and configurations, sounds, objects, and events, are in a ceaseless flux, moving
along the scale of time.   It is dynamic par excellence.   Its human subjects are eternally agitated, full of passions, emotions, activity, effort.

Their life is an endless succession of joys and sufferings, defeats and victories, comedies and tragedies, drama and boredom. Shall we wonder, then, that the Idealistic art tends to be relatively static? Its abstract figures are not agitated; they are calm and serene. Their whole world is also a kingdom of undisturbable, eternal, motionless unchangeableness. The Visual art, on the contrary, is charged with emotions, passions, agitation, and dynamics. It is dramatic, even comic and humorous, par excellence. It concentrates on dramatic scenes, on comic and picturesque moments. Its personages are in motion, often in violent motion; passions agitate their faces; emotions radiate from their attitudes; drama — whether tragic, as in the Laocoön group, or comical, as in the "funny picture" — is inseparable from it. In the Idealistic art of Greece of the fifth century or of the Middle Ages of the thirteenth century, even the expressions of the dead are divine, serene, and animated by never-failing faith and hope. In the Visual art of the seventeenth and subsequent centuries A.D. even Christ and the saints are hopelessly dead corpses with all the stamina of the corpse and of decay. No serenity, no divinity, but a dramatically dynamic and deadly passionate disintegration — that is what is seen. Similar is the dominant note of the Hellenistic art of the third and later centuries B.C.

(6) Since sensate gratification is not the object of the Idealistic art, one cannot expect from it gratification of sensate needs or desires. It is not and cannot be frivolous. Therefore the figures of women are relatively rare in it; figures, faces, and scenes which are frivolous, seductive, sexual, tempting, gratifying as "pretty," are out of place in it. In the Visual art the situation is the reverse.

(7) Since the Visual art depicts, not the lasting, but the passing visual aspect of things, an incessant novelty, change, and variety in its pictures and sculptures are its traits also; otherwise, the same thing becomes sensuously boring, too familiar, devoid of a sense of novelty. The Visual art must change incessantly; therefore it is and must be an *art* of *mode* and *fashion* and *fad:* the newer the better; the more variety the more enjoyment. Its fascination is in its looks; beyond and behind it there is no infinity of ideational content as in an Ideational art work. The Ideational art, on the contrary, is of necessity associated with slow change; it is an art of *lasting, ever-meaningful tradition:* ever old in its form and ever new in the content which it does and can absorb because it deals with infinity. Its values are the eternal values, well selected and well chosen: they do not require incessant change. Absolute value is the supreme value; and the supreme value need not be replaced by

other, inferior values, even if these are quite new, ever-changing, perfectly "modern." Therefore the period of the domination of the Ideational art is the age of tradition and convention. The period of the domination of the Visual art is the age of mode, fashion, seeking for the newest and the most modern. In such an age "*tout nouveau, tout beau.*"

Therefore there are no traditional and conventional forms in style; every artist tries to create his own style, different from the others. Hence, an incessant change of the forms and styles of art in such periods. In such an age men tend to enjoy everything only once: only once to read a new novel, once to see a play, once to glance at a picture, once to attend a show, once to hear a musical composition. To read the same novel over and over, to see the same show again and again, to hear the same song several times, means a decrease of enjoyment in direct proportion to the number of repetitions: a kind of "law of diminishing returns." For this reason the span of existence of most of the artistic creations of such periods is short. Today's best seller is forgotten tomorrow; today's musical, theatrical, or painting "sensation" falls quickly into oblivion. The very term "sensation" with its present-day meaning of "hit," "great success," "thriller," is characteristic. It does not exist in the period of the Ideational. In the Ideational periods men "enjoy" again and again the same thing, and the more conventional, traditional, familiar, are the external forms the more they tend to be appreciated. In such periods the "law of diminishing returns" with each repetition is to be reversed and becomes a "law of increasing returns" with each reading of the same work (say the Bible), each view of the same religious ceremony or Mystery play, each contemplation of the ikon with its familiar conventional traits, and so on. In such periods tradition, repetition, custom, convention, triumph. "*Je ne lis plus, je relis seulement*" is the motto of the period.[18]

---

[18] Compare R. Müller-Frienfels, "*Neucheit und Wiederholung im ästhetischen Geniessen,*" in *Zeitschrift für Aesthetik und allgemeine Kunstwissenschaft*, Vol. VII (1912), pp. 68–81. See also J. L. Lowes, *Convention and Revolt in Literature* (Boston, 1926). In connection with such an art in the Visual period stands the art of posters. They are intended to be even still shorter lived than the other pictures of the period: good advertising pictures have to change with the change of the mood of the public: in hot summer they must depict the half-nude swimming beauty (though this has no relationship to what is being advertised); in the baseball season the same brand has to use baseball pictures; or it must depict the fashionable movie star of the moment, or something else which is the moment's rage. These "hits" incessantly change; therefore the advertising art of painting and sculpture has also to be a kind of "perpetuum mobile." See P. Westheim, "*Plakatkunst,*" in *Zeitschrift für Aesthetik*, Vol. III (1908), pp. 119–132; and the vast literature about the *réclame, plakat*, poster, advertising.

Such are some of the typical traits of the Idealistic as contrasted with the Visual (Sensate) art. As to its difference from the Ideational art, it must be clear from the above characterization of the Ideational style. The main difference between them is that while the pure Ideational art is not attached in any way to the empirical (visual, sensate) reality either by its subject matter or by its form, the Idealistic does have such connections. Many of its ideals are not transcendental but empirical; its forms are visual; with one foot it stands in the ideational, with the other in the empirical, world. Its pictures are not mere symbols or signs, having no visual resemblance to the empirical forms of many of its empirical and half-empirical values. They have such a visual resemblance, though this is ennobled and typified. And the world of the ideal values of the Idealistic art and mentality is not entirely cut off from the empirical world: in some way it is inseparable from it, as soul is associated with body, thought with brain.

When this is properly understood, many differences existing between the Ideational and the Idealistic art, as profound as those between the Idealistic and the Visual but of a different nature, become comprehensible. Later they will be mentioned in more detail. Meanwhile the essentials of the Pure Visual, the Pure Ideational, and the Idealistic styles must be sufficiently clear to serve for the factual analysis soon to follow.

As we shall see, the *Idealistic* style usually occurs when the Ideational begins to decline, but without breaking entirely free from its "super-empirical" moorings; and when the Visual style begins to grow, without becoming, as yet, completely materialistic, mechanistic, hedonistic, and antireligious. When the descending line of Ideationalism and the ascending line of Visualism (Empirical Sensatism) cross each other at some theoretically "optimum" point, the result is Idealism and Idealistic art, in the sense of the words established above. The more these lines deviate from this marvelously balanced "optimum" point, the more the style becomes either Ideational or Visual, according to which of these styles becomes more and more dominant.

B. *Cubistic Mixed Style.* Another fundamental form of the Mixed style is represented by such styles as cubism, futurism, "imaginism," expressionism (as it is called often), and similar "modernistic" radical currents in art. These styles are neither predominantly Visual, nor Ideational. They are not Visual because they do not try to render the object as it looks to our eyes. No cubistic, futuristic, or other picture of a similar nature gives a purely visual impression of the object (see Plate IX). When painters of these schools try to depict the three-dimen-

sional corporeality of a material object in the forms of cubes, they aim
to represent not its visual form — because these three dimensions we
cannot see — but its ideational form : its three-dimensional solidity known
by other organs of sense and "stored" in our mind.　It is rightly
said of Picasso and can be said of most of the "modernists" that they
try "to substitute a conceptual reality for the visual one."　"They
confront the optic painting with the tactile evoking of the objects in all
their cubic or three-dimensional reality from several angles simultaneously."　"Not a reproduction of the visible surface of the objects,
not a painting of the objects as they appear to our eyes, but the rendering of them as they are in our mind," is the objective of their art.　"In
such a system painting is reduced to a geometric combination of colored
planes."　Most of these postimpressionistic schools — cubism, constructivism, expressionism, futurism, and other "isms" —

by reaction against the impressionistic sensualism attempt to restore in painting the long-time neglected rights of thought, while the care for *construction* [in
contrast to the impressionistic aim to reproduce the passing glimpse of the
visible reality as it is without any selection, choice, construction] affirms itself
in the provoking excesses of cubism.[19]

To this extent these currents in art are not Visual, but Ideational.

On the other hand, by these symbolic cubes or other nonvisual signs the
artists of these schools do not try to represent something superempirical,
nonmaterialistic.　On the contrary, these "modern" styles are in the
realm of empirical reality from top to bottom, and are perhaps more
empirical, sensate, materialistic, than even pure Visualism.　They aim to
depict all the solidity, spaciousness, weight, and other properties of the
material world.　They are strangers to any superempirical reality.　They
deny it, often despise it.　Therefore they are most radically different
from Ideationalism, which is always looking for a superempirical, supersensate reality.　In it the visible signs serve to symbolize the invisible
world.　Here the distorted or synthetic sensory signs serve to represent
the purely sensory, visible world.

Such is the peculiar combination or distortion of the elements of the
Visual and Ideational styles in the Cubistic Mixed style.

C. *Other Mixed Styles*.　Besides the Idealistic and the Cubistic
forms there are many other varieties of the Mixed style.　When one
studies, for instance, Egyptian sculpture, one notices, even in the
sculpture portraits from the Old Kingdom, the clearly and beautifully

[19] L. Réau's chapter in A. Michel (ed.), *op. cit.*, Vol. VIII, pp. 627 and 601.

PLATE IX

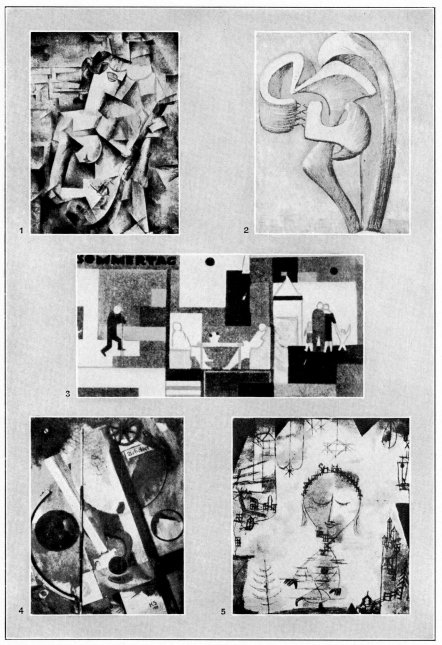

1, Lady with a Lute, by Picasso. 2, Abstract painting, by Picasso. 3, Summer's Day, by Nerlinger. 4, Das Arbeiterbild, by Kurt Schwitters. 5, Entfernung, by Paul Klee.

rendered Visual style of the face or of the head of the person, and the quite "unnatural" (from the Visual standpoint) rendering of the rest of the body: its posture, anatomy, configuration. The Visual style is thus closely combined with the nonvisual, sometimes conspicuously Ideational, form in the same sculpture or bas-relief or design. In this way we have an example of, so to speak, *the mechanical unification or the spatial adjacency of the elements of both styles in the same sculpture or design.*

Another variety of the Mixed style is exemplified in the predominant character of the early Chinese painting or pictorial art. It also often combines, in a peculiar way, elements of both styles. It is neither Ideational nor Visual; it is neither Idealistic nor Cubistic; nor is it even a mechanical mixture like that of the Egyptian. In one sense it is even extremely Visual, almost Impressionistic (especially in many a *paysage*); on the other hand, it is Ideational in several respects. If we take the predominant character of, say, the Chinese portrait, its essential traits are marked by Ideationalism, though the portraits are of actual, existing persons. "The Chinese artist considered its [art's] task to lie in preservation of the ideal forms of the visible world in order to hinder its [the world's] deformation." "The portrait should be a representation of the essence of man. . . ."

These ancient portraits must have been something very different from what we call now "portrait." This implies a drawing of trait after trait whose value lies in the resemblance with the face depicted. . . . This definition cannot be applied to the portrait of the Extreme Orient. . . . A Person's portrait was often executed after his death and the resemblance was not sought for, though the costume of the deceased that indicates its rank, his pose that manifests his dignity, all these social details had to be depicted in order that his image might serve as an example to his children and grand-children.

Accordingly the main objective of the portrait was to "transmit the spirit (*l'esprit*)" of the person.

On the other hand, these portraits, as well as many other Chinese pictures, are full of movement, of dynamism, and of several other Visual, almost Impressionistic, characteristics.[20]

A clear notion about a specific form of the Mixed style of the Chinese pictorial art is offered by the famous "Six Principles of Painting" formulated by Hsieh Ho (*c.* A.D. 495–501), which have been a canon for the Chinese painters. These Principles embody in themselves the Ideational as well as the Visual, demanding, on the one hand, "Resonance of Spirit

[20] S. Elisseev, "*Notes sur le portrait en extrême-orient*," in *Études d'orientalism à la mémoire de Raymonde Linossier* (Paris, 1933), pp. 170 ff.

and Movement of Life"; on the other, Visual likeness to the objects depicted. In comments of the no less famous Chang Yen-yüan of the T'ang period these principles mean:

Likeness to nature must be observed in the shapes, but these should have bone [i.e., structure] and spirit [i.e., life]. Structure, spirit, and shape originate in the directing idea and are expressed by the brush work.

This condition of "spirit" and "life" is regarded as paramount. Hence great painters are "highly cultured and noble-minded men. . . . Truly no worthless and mean loafers could do what they did." The paintings of Wu Tao-hsüan "are perfect in every respect. A god guided his hand; and the resonance of the spirit was so overwhelmingly strong [in his work] that it hardly could be confined on the silk. . . ." His contemporary painters "are fairly good in drawing the outer form and in obtaining some likeness, but they give no resonance of the spirit. . . . How can such things be called painting? Alas, for men of to-day, they do not reach the art." [21]

These lines are suggestive of the peculiar form of the Mixed style dealt with here. On looking through a good collection of Chinese pictures (or even a good reproduction of these, such as, for instance, those given in the volumes of O. Sirén), one can see the specific combination of the elements of both styles in Chinese art. [22]

Besides these forms there are many other varieties of the Mixed style.

Such, in outline, are the main styles into which fall all painting, sculpture, and (in a slightly modified form) architecture, music, literature, and drama. Each of these styles has many gradations; the main forms that we have discussed are only a few of the chief marks on the scale of these numerous gradations. But these signs are very useful for orientation in the tremendously vast and complex ocean of the art world, and especially in the study of the life of art: its courses, fluctuations, "cycles," turns, and changes, in the course of time.

The analysis which we have just made constitutes the first test through which our categories of culture mentality must pass. The fact that they happen to fit perfectly for the classification of the main styles in art —

[21] Quoted from O. Sirén, *A History of Early Chinese Painting* (London, 1933), Vol. I, pp. 32–36.

[22] See besides the works quoted also L. Binyon, *The Spirit of Man in Asian Art* (Harvard University Press, 1935), chaps. i–iii. It goes without saying that Chinese art has known also fluctuations; and the Taoist or Buddhist art of China differs from the Confucianist or even the more "Epicurean" art. The above characteristics are, so to speak, the "normal" and "predominant" traits of it.

that painting and sculpture fell quite naturally, so to speak, into these categories — indicates that they are not mere bloodless phantoms, a mere exercise in abstract logical classification. On the contrary, these preliminary concepts of Ideational, Sensate, and Mixed styles embrace principles which are conformable to and expressive of the actual, empirical reality, which bring clear meaning to the complexity and confusion in the field of art. We shall see further that this classification of the styles in art is one of the most "natural": it goes to the core of the predominant mentality shown in each style; it uncovers the essentials of the *Weltanschauung* of the artist and of his society; it stands in the closest relationship with the characteristics of other aspects of a given culture : its science and philosophy, religion and morals, forms of social and political organization, the nature of the social relationships — in brief, with all the essential traits of the given culture and its mentality. In this sense, an understanding of the *Gestalt* of a given culture at a given period helps us to understand the meaning, the origins, and methods of the predominant style of art; and an adequate knowledge of the art style and its proper interpretation in terms of these categories throws a peculiar light upon the culture in which it is born and prospers. These remarks are but "promissory notes" of what in the subsequent pages should be redeemed.

Since we have these categories at our disposal, we may venture now to use them for a study of several problems in the field of art phenomena as well as of the field of social phenomena generally.

(1) How have these styles, especially the Ideational and the Visual, been faring in the course of time in various cultures, particularly in the Graeco-Roman and the Western Christian as we pass from the earlier to the later periods of their life history? Has there been in the course of time a definite linear trend from one of these styles to the other, as many assure us: from Ideational to Visual, or from Visual to Ideational? If such a "line of progress" has existed, what has it been? If there has not been any steady and "eternal" trend of any kind from one style to the other, how have they been fluctuating: periodically? irregularly? Have they been replacing one another abruptly, moving from a "pure" variety of one directly to a "pure" variety of the other? or in their alternation have they been passing into one another gradually and imperceptibly, from the pure form of the one, through its less and less pure forms, to the Mixed forms, and then finally to the "pure" forms of the other style?

(2) Have these fluctuations been similar, uniform, and parallel in all the countries of the same "cultural continent," such as, for instance, all the European countries of the Western Christian cultural continent? Or

have these changes proceeded differently in different countries of the same "cultural continent"? If the configurations of these fluctuations have been similar in the different countries of the same cultural continent, have they been synchronous and simultaneous? If they have been nonsimultaneous, which countries have lagged behind which? And has the lagging of a certain country from the other been, so to speak, permanent, existing during the whole period studied? or has it been only temporary, a given country lagging in a certain period but leading in another period?

(3) Since most of us are particularly interested in our own time and in its art, what are its marks? Which of the styles dominates in it? Which tends to grow? Where exactly do we stand on the long historical road which has been traveled by art and its styles during the several centuries studied?

(4) Does a proper study of the trends, fluctuations, and pulsations of the styles show something in the field of the "spontaneous self-regulation of social processes" and the integrated or nonintegrated nature of art in these cultures? Does it exhibit, for instance, when one of the styles becomes extreme and excessive, that such a phenomenon is soon or immediately counteracted by the appearance and growth of the extreme forms of the opposite style? Does this phenomenon of "action and reaction" show itself in other ways?

(5) What, indeed, are the relationships of art dynamics to the changes and "curves" in the other fields of the *same* cultures? Is each of these styles associated positively or negatively with certain forms of the *Weltanschauung?* with certain forms of philosophy, whether materialism, idealism, or their varieties? with certain systems of epistemology and of truth: empiricism, rationalism, fideism, skepticism? with certain predominant systems of ethics: the ethics of Happiness, of Absolute Principles, or of any other? Is the growth of the power of one of the styles associated in some definite way with the movement of the natural sciences, with discoveries and technological inventions? How are they related to many other social phenomena, such as economic prosperity and depression, increase and decrease of wars, internal disturbances, political regimes, individualism, collectivism, contractualism, familism, etc.?

If the main concepts that we have elaborated above can throw some light on these problems, which are only in part concerned with art phenomena but are related to sociocultural phenomena generally, their introduction will be amply justified and my "promissory notes" will be promptly and fully repaid with liberal interest.

Chapter Eight

RECURRENCE IN SOCIAL SPACE AND FLUCTUATION IN TIME
OF THE IDEATIONAL, VISUAL, AND MIXED STYLES IN
PAINTING AND SCULPTURE (Qualitative Outline)

We shall begin our investigation with the problem of the existence or
nonexistence of any perpetual trend from one of the two opposed styles
to the other in the course of time generally and particularly in passing
from the earlier to the later stages of the history of the Graeco-Roman and
Western cultures.   These cultures will be at the center of our study of
the problem.   Other cultures and countries, especially the long-living
cultures of India and China, deserve special consideration.   But my
insufficient knowledge of them and the difficulties in the way of my
securing the necessary material about them for the present purpose, have
led me to pass them by, with the exception of a few remarks here and there.

I. IS THE STYLE OF PRIMITIVE ART VISUAL OR IDEATIONAL?

In the nineteenth century, with its evolutionary and linearly progressive
theories, it was pretty commonly accepted that in the development of art
style there was a perpetual linear tendency — unilinear, or spiral, or
oscillating — from primitive art, devoid of skill and technique, to the
present art, which supposedly is perfect and highly skillful.   Most writers
viewed almost all the forms of what is termed here the Ideational style as
the "primitive" style, which results from the inability of the artists to
draw or to paint or otherwise to reproduce the object properly.   Ideational and primitive were often taken to be identical, while any competent
rendering in the Visual style was regarded as a manifestation of artistic
skill, maturity of technique, progress in art and in aesthetic genius.   Even
now many people, looking at the paintings of Indians or Eskimos or
Egyptians or other ancient peoples, consider them certainly to be the
result of a lack of artistic skill and as a manifestation of the primitiveness
of the art of the ancients.   However natural such opinions seem to be, in
most cases they are wrong.   The fault of such theories consists in their
identification of Ideational with immature, of Visual with mature.   As a

matter of fact, the real situation in many cases is quite different. Often the Ideational and Visual styles are not so much a manifestation of the presence or absence of skill and highly developed technique, as the expression of quite different mentalities and different outlooks. One, as we have already observed in its definition, is the mentality of the Being; the other of the Becoming. One is posited not so much in the sensory world of the organs of perception, and particularly in that of the organ of seeing, as in the supersensory world of Mind — whether this be rational or irrational, superstitious or mystical, childish or visionary, does not matter here. What matters is that such a mentality does not look at the sensations and "telegrams" of the organs of the senses, particularly of the eyes where painting and sculpture are concerned, as furnishing the only or even the main data of reality. The other mentality — the Sensory Visual — is empirical through and through. Only that which is attested by the organs of sense is true, real, in actual existence. Therefore such a mentality can generate only the Visual style; whereas the Ideational mentality renders things in forms quite different from their visual appearance. It depicts things as they are in the mind but not as they appear to the eyes.[1] Some of the things depicted by it do not have any visual appearance. They are "immaterial," "incorporeal," "spiritual," no matter whether they are believed through superstition or wisdom. The ability or inability to depict things "visually" is the result of these mentalities: the sensory mentality strives and trains itself to depict objects visually. Therefore, it practices and learns how to do this. The Ideational mentality does not care to do this. Therefore it lacks practice. Instead, it trains itself to render things ideationally.

If this be true, then we must expect that the *primitive art of all cultures may have either of the two opposing styles at the same "stage" of development. This expectation is justified in fact. Some of the primitive peoples have predominantly Ideational, some predominantly Visual, and some both styles.* What is still more important and quite destructive of the theories of perpetual trends is that the Visual style, regarded by those who hold these theories as more perfect, mature, skillful, "progressive," etc., is found not only at the latest cultural stages but at the earliest as well. Such a situation evidently gives a decisive blow to most of the linear

---

[1] Maurice Denis, talking of the ideational paintings of the Italian Primitives and of their supposed clumsiness from the purely Visual standpoint, rightly says: "The Primitive . . . prefers reality to the appearance of reality. Rather than resign himself to the distortions of perspective which has no interest for his maiden eye, he makes the picture of things conform to the idea he has of them." It is then not a lack of skill but a manifestation of intellectualist realism. *Nouvelles théories* (Paris, 1922).

theories mentioned above.   Here are the corroborative data and the references.

The paintings, drawings, and sculptures of paleolithic man, as far as they are known to us, are predominantly Visual.   Some of them may be styled even Visual-Impressionistic, being excellent "snapshots" of an animal in motion — a reindeer, a buffalo, a mammoth.[2]   When we pass to the drawings, paintings, and sculptures of neolithic man, we observe that they are less Visual and much more Ideational.   In the art of the early stone age (to use the usual terminology)

there was more of realism and of naturalism than in the art of the late stone, bronze, and even iron ages.   The art of these later ages became schematized into abstract and ornamental designs. . . .   The living freshness of the art of the early stone age seems to have been entirely lost.[3]

This means that in transition from the earlier paleolithic to the later neolithic culture, art was moving not from ideationalism to visualism but, if anything, in quite the opposite direction.   The linear conception here, as in other cases, again shows itself wrong.[4]

[2] See the facts and the reproductions in the works of M. Verworn, E. von Sydow, F. Boas.

[3] Eckart von Sydow, *Die Kunst der Naturvölker und der Vorzeit*, 2d ed. (Berlin, 1927), pp. 16 ff.   See the reproductions, especially those numbered from 415 to 490.

[4] In passing it is to be noted that Max Verworn tried to find an explanation of this change in the difference of the nervous mechanism of the paleolithic and the neolithic man.   The drawings of the paleolithic man were the result of a direct transmission of the visual impression from the receptors to the effectors of the nervous system, without the disorganizing interference of the main centers of the nervous system.   The hand executed there what the eye saw, without the deranging influence of the beliefs, ideas, and other factors which tend to disfigure the freshness of impressions by their interference.   The neolithic man was already under the strong influence of various beliefs, superstitions, ideas, which did not permit the impression received by a receptor to pass directly to the effectors, but modified and disfigured them.   The neolithic art is not only an expression of what the eye sees but also of all the associations and biases which exist in the mind (brain).   Hence it is much more "ideoplastic" than the paleolithic art.   Here is the main generalization of Verworn.

"Die primitive Kunst hat um so mehr physioplastische [visual] Züge je mehr die sinnliche Beobachtung, sie hat um so mehr ideoplastische [ideational] Züge, je mehr das absrahierende, theoretisierende Vorstellungsleben der Völker im Vordergrund steht.   Den mächtigsten Impuls zur Entwicklung des theoretisierenden Vorstellungslebens in prähistorische Zeit gab die Konzeption der Seelenidee. . . .   Die aus dieser Idee entspringenden religiösen Vorstellungen lieferten die günstigsten Bedingungen für die Entstehuung einer ideoplastischen Kunst."

As secondary factors of such a shift from the Visual to the Ideational style, Verworn mentions the desire for ornamentation (why this must occur in a neolithic man only and not in the paleolithic also, is not explained) and the disfiguring role of copying by many people of the original, of its copy, of a copy of the copy, and so on.   See the details and pictures in Max Verworn, *Zur Psychologie der primitiven Kunst* (Jena, 1917), pp. 1–11, 20–29, *et passim*.

Such is the essence of this interesting theory.   Even while granting its ingenious character, one is forced to say that it is fallacious and unsatisfactory in many ways.   First, its assump-

If we turn to the styles of the *living primitive peoples*, we find both styles present among them.   Among some the Visual predominates, among the others the Ideational ; among many both are found.   But all in all there is no possibility of saying that one is dominant among the "more advanced," the other among the "less advanced," peoples.   The distribution of the styles does not show any such uniformity.   The Visual type "does not develop from the [ideational] as the result of evolution ; it is based on a distinct mental attitude, the early presence of which is manifested by the realistic, perspective paintings of a number of primitive tribes. . . ."   "The theory of a continuous development from symbolic [ideational] to realistic art" is wrong.   The Ideational drawings "are not by any means proof of inability to see and draw perspectively ; they

---

tion that the paleolithic man did not have any ideas, associations, beliefs, superstitions and the general ideological, "disorganizing" factors, is baseless. In all probability he had these in some forms.   If he had, then the factors which led the neolithic man to "ideoplastic art" were present also in the paleolithic man.   Therefore his theory does not explain the change discussed.   If the theory were right we should expect that as the mental life became more and more complex the art must have become more and more Ideational.   As a matter of fact, in Greece, from the fifth century to the end of the Hellenic culture, the Visual style became more and more dominant.   In the Western culture, from the fifteenth century to the very beginning of the twentieth century, it also has been growing at the cost of the Ideational style.   It is true that Verworn mentions that, though our mentality has been becoming more complex, at the same time it has been becoming more scientific, that is, realistic.   Granting this claim, we must not think that either now or, especially, in the sixteenth, seventeenth, eighteenth centuries, the whole mentality of society or of artists was scientific and did not have any "associations," "superstitions," "beliefs," "derivations," and other nonscientific ideologies.   If that is so — and it is certainly so — then it is incomprehensible how and why the Visual style has been dominant during all these centuries.

Furthermore, Verworn expected that according to his theory children whose minds are less deranged by "associations" and "ideas" than the minds of adult persons, would show more of the Visual style than grown-up persons.   His experimental verification of this hypothesis yielded quite the opposite result : children's drawings happened to be invariably Ideational.

As to the secondary factors, the theory does not explain why craving for decoration and ornamentation was present only in the neolithic and not also in the paleolithic man.   Why, furthermore, it reappeared and disappeared several times in the later periods of culture. Likewise, if copying facilitates a disfiguring of the Visual style in favor of the Ideational, why was the factor inoperative in the paleolithic society and in many later periods, before the invention of the mechanical means of reproducing a given object ?

These remarks are sufficient to indicate the purely speculative nature of the theory and its shortcomings.   Verworn seems to have been dominated by the popular notion that the Ideational is an artless, primitive, immature style, much the inferior of the Visual style. Accordingly he assumed that the evolution had to consist in a transition from the ideoplastic to the physioplastic style.   The assumptions led him to the above theory in spite of the fact that his own data sharply contradict it.   Here we have one additional case out of millions in which the preconceptions of a scientist lead him astray from scientific theory and incapacitate him for observing properly the data and giving them an adequate interpretation.

merely show that the interest of the people is centered in the full representation of the symbols." On the other hand, the Visual art "is not by any means absent in the drawing of primitive man as well as in those of children." "The two [styles] have distinct psychological sources which remain active in the early as well as in the late history of art." [5] In other words there is no serious basis for the claim that primitive art was uniformly Ideational or uniformly Visual; neither can we claim that in the course of time or "with the progress of civilization" it moved uniformly toward "bigger and better" visualism or ideationalism. The totality of the facts known seems to show that both currents were present from the earliest times; that in some groups the one and in others the other form was perhaps predominant; and that in some groups in the course of time a shift took place toward greater visualism, in others, toward greater ideationalism. No uniformity or linearity seems to have existed in this field in the process of change.[6]

[5] F. Boas, *Primitive Art* (Oslo, 1927), pp. 74–75 and 78–81. See the facts and evidences offered there. That the two styles are manifestations of two different mentalities mainly and have only a remote, if any, relationship to the presence or absence of skill and artistry, is accepted now by many authoritative historians and theorizers of art. They "correspond to radically different interests in the world." (H. Wölfflin, *Principles of Art History*, p. 14.) They are "manifestations of two different ways to see and to render things in accordance with two different mentalities. . . . To talk of one of them as superior to the other is an idle talk." (H. Schäfer, *"Agyptische und heutige Kunst,"* in *Die Antike*, Vol. III (1927), pp. 195 ff.) "The Egyptian [with his Mixed and partly Ideational style] is a realist who strives to render things just as they are; our artists are rather illusionists who try to show them as they appear. . . The Egyptian drawing aims at supplying us with the greatest number of elements possible, in order that we may be enabled to make a complete intellectual reconstruction of reality." J. Capart, *Lectures on Egyptian Art* (Chapel Hill, 1928), p. 91; see also his *L'art égyptien* (Bruxelles, 1924). See also A. Vierkandt, *"Das Zeichnen der Naturvölker,"* in *Zeitschrift für angewandte Psychologie*, Vol. VI, pp. 347 ff.; A. Coomaraswamy, *The Transformation of Nature in Art*, chap. i *et passim;* H. Nohl, *Stil und Weltanschauung* (Jena, 1920), p. 24; A. V. Scheltema, *Die altnordische Kunst* (Berlin, 1923); K. Lange, *"Zur Philosophie der Kunstgeschichte,"* in *Zeitschrift für Aesthetik und allgemeine Kunstgeschichte;* the works of O. Sirén, S. Elisseev, W. Worringer, Max Foth, E. Utitz, cited.

For a changing nature of resemblance between the picture or portrait and its object or person, see also A. H. Zadoks-Josephus Jitta, *Ancestral Portraiture in Rome* (Amsterdam, 1932), chap. ii; W. Waetzoldt, *Die Kunst des Porträts* (Leipzig, 1908); R. Delbrueck, *Antike Porträts* (Bonn, 1912); J. Capart, *Propos sur l'art égyptien* (Bruxelles, 1930).

[6] I am inclined to go still further in this direction and seriously to doubt the validity of other similar theories, like A. Riegl's and A. Schmarsow's theory that the tactile style (*Taktsinn*) predominated and developed earlier than the Visual style (*Gesichtsinn*) — see A. Riegl, *Stilfragen* (Berlin, 1893), A. Riegl, *Die spätromische Kunstindustrie* (Wien, 1901), A. Schmarsow, *Grundbegrieffe der Kunstwissenschaft* (Leipzig and Berlin, 1905); or the theory of H. Schäfer that the visual style was for the first time discovered in Greece in the fifth century B.C. and since that time became dominant; or the theory of Deonna that on account of lack of skill, the Ideational style had to predominate at the earlier stages — see Schäfer, *op. cit.*, and W. Deonna, *L'archéologie*, Vol. III, pp. 501 ff.

Side by side with this it may be noted that the *Ideational style tends to occur particularly in the fields of religion, magic, and other "sacred" and "hieratic" compartments of social life — no matter what they are concretely, while the Visual style more frequently occurs, even within the same culture, in the "profane," daily, routine, earthly fields of social life.* Even when the Visual art dominates the given society, the Ideational style often still continues to exist in such "hieratic" compartments, whether they be the fields of religion, of magic ceremonies and symbols, of the important state functions and festivities, or of what not. In common terminology such a phenomenon is often styled as survival of the "old forms" (old symbols, old forms of language,[7] relics, ancient ceremony). As a matter of fact it is Ideational rather than old, because the use of such ideational symbols as the national flag, heraldic signs, and so on, are often newly introduced; in spite of this they remain in most cases Ideational in their forms.

The reason for such a gravitation of each of these forms is evident: since the sacred and hieratic compartments of social life deal with "super-empirical," "transcendental," ideational abstract, noncorporeal and somewhat nonmaterial, complex values (whether religion, magic, or the dignity and honor of the nation, or family pride, or the glory of a group, or patriotism, justice, sacrifice, virtue), they cannot be expressed in any adequate Visual form because they do not have any. Hence the necessity of the Ideational signs or symbols — pure or impure — for denoting such phenomena and for making them "visible." On the other hand, purely empirical, daily, material phenomena have in the majority of the cases a visible form. Such a form can be rendered visually. Hence the existence of Visualism in such fields.

This "generalization" follows from the concept of Ideational and Visual and can easily be traced through, from the "primitive" cultures and tribes to the various "advanced" cultures and peoples. In a sharp or mild form it is discoverable in almost all the cases studied.

II. Brief Notes on Recurrence in Time and Space of the Main Styles in Egyptian, Assyrian, Chinese, and Hindu Pictorial Art

The conclusion we have just reached is corroborated by the history of painting and sculpture of various countries, especially of Egypt, China, Greece, Rome, and finally of the Western world. Their history shows an alternation of the ups and downs of each of the main styles without any

---

[7] See Karl Vossler, *The Spirit of Language in Civilisation* (London, 1932), pp. 24 ff. and 71 ff.

certain tendency toward the growth of one of the styles at the cost of the other.

A. *Egypt.*   In regard to Egypt we have seen in Chapter Three that the main tone of its mentality was Mixed, with deviation from it in either direction in some of the periods of catastrophe or excessive well-being. In conformity with this the dominant style of its art seems to have been also *Mixed,* especially in the form of the mechanical coexistence of both styles in the same sculpture.[8]   If the culture of Egypt was logically and causally integrated, such a harmony in the dominant type of its mentality and art should be expected.   This expectation seems to be justified by the actual character of Egyptian culture.   To this extent it is to be recognized as integrated logically as well as causally.

But the dominant character of the Egyptian mentality and art does not hinder the possibility of fluctuation in the nature of a relative increase or decrease of Ideational and Sensate elements during the long course of existence of Egyptian culture.   Such fluctuations seem to have occurred in fact.   Heinrich Schäfer indicated some of these alternations and rhythms.   According to him four distinct periods are noticeable from this standpoint: (1) The art of the Old Kingdom, characterized by a nonsentimental depicting of a sound material world; the style is only mildly Ideational and contains some elements of naturalism and visuality. (2) The art of the Middle Kingdom, where the Ideational style becomes somewhat more pronounced in the form of a particular inclination toward straight lines and geometric patterns.   (3) The style of the New Kingdom, where a return to the harmonious and curved lines of the first period is conspicuous, geometric style decreases, and some elements of "naturalism" are restored.   (4) The period of Akhenaton (a brief period), when a conspicuous Ideationalism and expressionism burst out, to be replaced again by much milder forms of it.[9]

This theory of the periods in its essentials seems to be not far from the reality.   In a little more detailed form the relative increase and decrease of the Ideational and the Visual elements within the main Mixed style appear to have occurred in the sculpture and drawing of Egypt at the following periods of its history.

(1) *The Old Kingdom.*   In its sculpture, at the very beginning of the Old Kingdom, and then from the fourth dynasty, there seems to have

---

[8] Egyptian portrait sculpture especially shows this in the perfection, even impressionism, of the face, as contrasted with the unnatural (visually) rendering of the rest of the body. Incidentally we have evidence here also that the artists had skill to render objects visually if they wished to.

[9] Schäfer, *op. cit.*, pp. 238 ff.   The terminology is, of course, mine.

been an increase of the Visual tendency as shown by the development of portrait sculpture dealing with private and ordinary persons, of the depiction of everyday life scenes, of "naturalism" even to the extent of representing figures with sex organs, of a tendency to voluptuousness, and by other symptoms of Visualism.[10]

(2) *The Middle Kingdom.* The art (mainly sculpture) of the beginning of this kingdom is much less Visual than that of the end of the Old Kingdom. It is Ideational-Idealistic in a greater degree.[11] However, in the later period of the Kingdom, roughly in the thirteenth dynasty, the visualism is much more pronounced than during the preceding dynasties. It is manifest in a great increase of the sculpture of ordinary persons and particularly in that of the *genre* which depicts the scenes of the everyday life of the common people : a house, a garden, a musical party; servants plying their tasks in kitchen, bakery, brewery; peasants in farmyard; fishermen; etc.[12]

(3) *The New Empire.* Again, the art of the very beginning of the Empire seems to have been less "realistic" than with its development later; in the time of Akhenaton it made a notable turn to Ideationalism and Idealism; during the period of Tutankhamen it sharply turned toward intimacy, picturesqueness, dynamism — in brief, to the Visual, the baroque; and then gradually shifted again toward Ideationalism and anti-Visualism.[13] Similar waves seem to have occurred during the *Saïte, the Ptolemaic, and the Roman periods,* because side by side with the purely Ideational and "primitivized" (ideationally normalized) sculptures, some of which exhibit a conspicuous Idealistic tendency, there are in those times sculptures which are brutally "realistic." Since it is impossible to place them accurately in the time sequence, it is probable that they belonged to different periods of this part of the history of Egypt. Toward the later part of this historical division, so far as this period witnessed a

---

[10] See J. Capart, *Lectures*, pp. 22 ff. and 74; E. D. Ross, *The Art of Egypt*, pp. 15–20 and the reproductions on pp. 100–112. See also G. Maspero, *Geschichte der Kunst in Aegypten* (Stuttgart, 1913). W. Wreszinski, *Atlas zur Altaegyptischen Kulturgeschichte* (Leipzig, 1914). W. Worringer, *Aegyptische Kunst (München, 1927).*

[11] This enormous change is usually described in terms of a decay. Here is an example of such a description. "Its [Egypt's] earliest remains (*c.* 4000 B.C.) display a marvelous capacity for rendering natural forms, and a technical skill almost impossible for us to comprehend. . . . But this early art was banished . . . and replaced in due course by a new phase where naturalism altogether gave place to conventionality." But later on, for instance in the seventh century, "Egyptian art was of a refined and delicate character, more like that of the earliest dynasties." H. B. Walters, *The Art of the Greeks* (New York, 1922), p. 27.

[12] Ross, *op. cit.*, pp. 21 ff.; see the reproductions on pp. 122–147.

[13] *Ibid.*, pp. 29–46; see the reproductions on pp. 177–203.

development of a quite realistic type of painting (the Fayum portraits, etc.), it is possible to conclude that the Visual tendency grew once again.[14]

However approximate are the above periods (even if we grant that some of them are indicated entirely tentatively), there can hardly be serious doubt that several waves of alternation really happened in the history of the Egyptian sculpture and painting.

It is to be mentioned that in Egypt as indicated, the Ideational style seems to have dominated particularly the art of the religious, of the magical, and generally of the sacred and hieratic compartments of social life; while the Visual art gravitated more to the secular art of the profane life.   This is shown by the fact that the purely religious art of Egypt bears upon itself the dominating marks of Ideationalism even in the periods of the ascendancy of the Visual art in other fields of social life.

B. *Assyria.*   Similar shifts seem to have occurred also in the history of Assyrian art.   It "was highly developed in its own line, manifested principally in the magnificent reliefs of Nimrud and Kouyunjik (Nineveh). . . . From a high degree of skill, however, it degenerated into mere conventionality, devoid of naturalism and feeling." [15]   Since the eminent author of this quotation assumes that the perfect style is the Visual style, the meaning of the quotation is that the Assyrian art shifted ("degenerated") toward an Ideational style "devoid of naturalism and feeling."   Hence, if he is correct as to the facts, this indicates the occurrence of a fluctuation from one style to the other in the history of Assyrian sculpture and pictorial art.[16]

C. *Early Chinese Pictorial Art.*   In Chapter Three it was indicated that the general mentality of the Chinese culture flowed in two streams: the Ideational, represented by Taoism and later on by Buddhism (especially by several mystic sects); and the Mixed, represented mainly by Confucianism (the purely Sensate mentality being always present, but representing a minor current).   If this diagnosis is correct, and if the Chinese culture was integrated logically and causally within each of these main streams, we should find two currents coexisting in the Chinese pictorial art also: the pure or impure Ideational pictorial art, and the Mixed pictorial art (with minor stream of the Visual art corresponding to the Epicurean mentality).   Are these expectations fulfilled?   It seems

[14] *Ibid.*, pp. 47–55 and the pictures on pp. 226 ff.

[15] Walters, *op. cit.*, p. 27.   See also E. Unger, *Babylon* (Berlin, 1931).

[16] That it had a perfect Visual form is seen even from the pictures, reproduced on Plate IV, of the magnificent Assyrian wounded lion and the gazelles rendered perfectly in all the dynamism and impressionism of their actions.   On the other hand, the hieratic art of Assyria remained much more Ideational, as far as the existing samples show it.

that they are. First, the historians of the Chinese pictorial art do not
fail to note many times that the regions or periods dominated by Taoism
or Buddhism or some Ideational mystic sects produced pictorial art of a
hieratic and Ideational type (in topics, in manner of rendering) essentially
different from the art produced in the courts or in periods dominated by
Confucianism or, sometimes, by Passive and Cynical "Epicureanism."
Second, they observe that the art dominated by Confucianism is indeed a
special variety of the Mixed style, where the Visual and Ideational elements coexist in a peculiar combination; and this is true no matter
whether we take a portrait, or a landscape, or *genre*, or animals, or what
not. A few quotations and references follow by way of a substantiation
of these statements. (Since I am not making this art the subject of a
more thorough study, I limit my notes to these remarks and quotations.
By carefully reading from this standpoint the works mentioned and other
works referred to in them, an investigator will find sufficient data by which
to test these statements.)

There is hardly any competent history of pictorial art in China which
fails to stress the specific character of the Taoist-Buddhist painting, in a
region, period, or sect where they were dominant. In their choice of
topics as well as in the manner of treatment, these streams stand out as
conspicuously different from the other streams.[17] What are the main
topics of this Ideational current in the Chinese thought and art? Dragons, devils, the Buddhist patriarchs or saints; the Archats, Lohans, the
Rishi (depicted often "with their minds in harmony"), the Kuanyin, the
Bodhisattvas, Buddha, the Taoist paradise, and similar topics. In other
words, the subjects are essentially supersensate and superempirical.
Even the landscape and portrait and animals depicted by this stream are
different in their spirit as well as in rendering. They are not a merely
visual reproduction of these seemingly sensory phenomena but something
very different: a kind of visible symbols of the invisible, that is, inner,
world and values. This statement is equally true of any period or region
or sect dominated by the Buddhist-Taoist mentalities, whether it be in
the period of the Han, the T'ang, the Sung, or other dynasties. Already
in the Han period the art of this stream was "a symbolic means for
the expression of ideas and the inner significance of things." For the
great artists of the period like Ku K'aichih, Lu T'an-wei, and others
"painting was not the representation of the outward shapes, but the
revealing of an inner character, the spirit or soul of things."[18] We find

[17] See L. Binyon, *The Spirit of Man in Asian Art* (Cambridge, 1935), pp. 31–32, 60 ff., 88 ff.,
and 96 ff.   [18] O. Sirén, *A History of Early Chinese Painting* (London, 1933), Vol. I, pp. 14–15.

similar traits in this stream in the period of the Six Dynasties (in the Korean Tomb Painting) : the figures of dragons, tigers, and others all rendered fantastically, like "proud chimaeras and winged lions." [19]

Likewise, during the time of the growth of Buddhism (always mixed in China with the elements of the Taoist mentality), in the Transition period and in the early T'ang period, especially during the Sui dynasty (A.D. 581–618) — when Buddhism was made the official religion and when "no fewer than 3792 new temples were built ; 106,580 statues of gold, silver, sandalwood, ivory, and stone were made for the sanctuaries ; thousands of old temples and statues were restored " — "the pictorial art . . . must have been of the religious type, and much of it was done by monks," and it "was of rather a hieratic type." [20]   Again, to jump to a later period — that of the Five Dynasties, the Buddhist painters (Kuan-hsiu and others) display the same characteristics : they paint the Archats, Shakyamuni's ten disciples, and try to depict again "the inner aspects" of things rather than their external visual appearance.[21]   Finally, when we come to the Sung period — the Northern Sung with painters like Li-Lung-mien and the Buddhist artists ; [22] the Southern Sung with the famous Buddhist school (having Taoist elements) of the Zen or Ch'an painters, who were mostly monks — or to the Neo-Confucian mentality developed by the great Chu-Hsi (1130–1200), we meet the same characteristics.

The Ch'an Buddhism was in this period "the spiritual undercurrent blended with the creative tendencies of the epoch." [23]   Art was to the Ch'an artists "delving down into the Buddha that each of us unknowingly carries within him." "Unless," says the Ch'an aesthete, "the artist's work is imbued with this vision of the subjective non-phenomenal aspect of life, his production will be mere toys." [24]   Even in their landscape and animal paintings

they gained the power of projecting their own consciousness into that of trees and birds or the figures they painted. All these things were not simply represented as phenomena of more or less individual character, but as parts or reflections of themselves, symbolic perhaps spiritually, because they reflected glimpses of reality, actual experiences from the painter's soul. This was more than romantic; it was vision, life, and truth.[25]

[19] *Ibid.*, Vol. I, pp. 25 ff.   [20] *Ibid.*, Vol. I, pp. 37 ff.   [21] *Ibid.*, Vol. I, pp. 107 ff.
[22] *Ibid.*, Vol. II, pp. 47 ff.   [23] *Ibid.*, Vol. II, p. 63.
[24] A. Waley, *Zen Buddhism in Its Relation to Art* (London, 1922), p. 22.
[25] Sirén, *op. cit.*, Vol. II, p. 95. Or, as Binyon puts it, "It is an escape not from life, but to life," stressing that it had nothing in common with European romanticism (*ibid.*, p. 96).

Their motives are often of the simplest kind: a few flowers or fruits, two birds . . . but they convey glimpses from the world that has no limits, embracing infinity of space and eternity of time, like the enlightened mind of the Ch'an student.[26]

Further, the bulk of the topics are supersensory: the Kuanyin, the dragons, the Archats, the Lohans, Bodhidharmas, etc. In painting, for instance, dragons, the "main idea is to press through the symbols of dragons the operation of Tao, the supreme principle of all manifested life." [27]

Thus this Ideational Taoist-Buddhist mentality gives rise to Ideational (either pure or impure) art, no matter at what period, in what region, in what sect.

And the opposite is also true. When we take periods marked by a decline and persecution of this Taoist-Buddhist stream and by a rise of either Orthodox Confucianism or of Passive Epicureanism (sometimes masked by the degenerated forms of Taoism), we notice a swing toward Visualism, both in the choice of subjects for depiction and in the manner of rendering pictures. One of such periods seems to have been the Middle T'ang period, especially the second part of the reign of Ming Huang, when an atmosphere of refined Passive Epicureanism prevailed: a period of the "Immortals of the Wine Cup," of dancers, singers, and girls, together with a decline of the religious systems and the rise of an Epicurean Humanism.[28]

In comformity with this the pictorial art of the period (Wu-Tao-tzu and others) was marked by an increase of the Visual elements. This is shown in the subjects of the period as well as in the manner of rendering them. The hieratic and religious topics seem to be in the minority. The representation of the beauty of the empirical world became the main topic of the art (animals, flowers, *genre*, landscapes, etc.). As to the manner of rendering, Wu-Tao-tzu and other "court painters"

mastered the technical means of representing space,[29] movement, and three-dimensional volumes in a hitherto unknown degree. His [Wu-Tao-tzu's] pic-

---

[26] *Ibid.*, Vol. II, pp. 95–96.

[27] *Ibid.*, Vol. II, p. 107. See the details as well as reproductions in the work of Sirén and in the other works mentioned. Further bibliography is given in these books.

[28] *Ibid.*, Vol. II, pp. 69–70.

[29] A fluctuation in the manner of representing space in the history of Chinese art is very instructive from our standpoint, when it is studied thus and is connected with the notion and apprehension of time in the Chinese mentality. See L. Bachhofer, "*Die Raumdarstellung in der Chinesischen Malerei des ersten Jahrtausends nach Christ*," in *Münchener Jahrbuch der Bild. Kunst* (1931); M. Granet, *La pensée chinoise*, pp. 83–114. See the chapter on Social Space in Volume Four of the present work.

tures must have possessed an extraordinary power of illusion. . . . The third dimension was rendered in a more convincing way than had been done by the earlier masters, and the figures were distinguished by an extraordinary degree of [visual] reality.[30]

Another period of the domination of Confucianism, mingled somewhat with the elements of the Sensate mentality, was the period of the Northern Sung (960–1126) and in it especially the reign of Hui Tsung (1101–1125).[31] Though the Ideational painters were not lacking there, they were out of favor; they were often opposed to the Imperial Academy of Painting. If we turn to the predominant type of the Academic painting, the painting of Hui Tsung himself being included, an extraordinary increase of visual naturalism — in the subjects as well as in the manner of rendering — is the outstanding trait of the period. The topics were "landscapes, often with the addition of animals, birds, and flowering plants." The Academicians "kept closer to objective [visual] reality." [32] As to the manner of rendering,

The formal criteria, which now were emphasized more than ever, were absolute fidelity to natural models. . . . This is illustrated by the emperor's own paintings as well as by various anecdotes about his way of criticizing the pictures of the academicians. . . . He used to gather the painters in the palace gardens and have them paint various kinds of flowers and birds, thus testing their power of observation and their faculty of reproducing exactly every feature of the charming models. Once some of them were called in to paint a pheasant walking in the garden. They made wonderful pictures . . . but the emperor said they all were wrong. Nobody could understand the reason for this condemnation.

The reason happened to be, as the emperor pointed out, that "when a pheasant is climbing a rockery, it does not lift the right foot first [as represented in their pictures] but the left." These and many other stories plus the character of the painting of the period — which becomes more

---

[30] Sirén, *op. cit.*, Vol. I, p. 77.

[31] Though short Taoist and Buddhist reactions took place in the period; though it is stamped by a sharp strife between Confucianism and Taoism; and though for political purposes the Emperor Hui Tsung adhered to a kind of Epicurean Taoism of "the romantic dreams of Taoist paradise and aesthetic speculations" and, of course, of "wine, women, and song"; the period shows, on the one hand, a definite decline of Buddhism, and Ideational Taoism, and a rise of Confucianism, and on the other, a development of humanistic and communistic agnosticism and even almost materialism: Wang-An-shih (1068–1085) and Ts'ai Ching — these "Soviet leaders" of the period at the head of the government were far from any Taoist or other Ideationalism. Their reforms were not far different from the State-Socialism or the State Capitalism of the Soviet system.

[32] Sirén, *op. cit.*, Vol. II, p. 40.

malerisch and less linear even in the technique (*e.g.*, Mi-Fei) — show the visual naturalism of the art of the period.[33]

We have by now, with these general remarks on Chinese painting, brought forward sufficient evidence in support of these statements: First, parallel to the two streams of culture mentality — the Ideational, represented by the real Taoism and Buddhism, and the Mixed, represented by Confucianism — we find two main streams in the style of Chinese painting: the Ideational and the Mixed. Second, the character of the general mentality of these two streams and the character of the style in painting which logically belongs to each type of mentality, happen to be notably integrated here in the causal-functional sense. This means that to this extent each stream in the Chinese culture was in fact integrated to a considerable degree. Third, Chinese art experienced also fluctuations in the comparative rise and decline of the Ideational and the Sensate styles, now the elements of the first rising at the cost of the elements of the second, now the opposite process taking place.

All this adds an additional case to our list of the recurrence of art styles in space as well as in time. It illustrates also the heuristic value of the logico-meaningful method for tracing even the causal connections between various compartments of a culture — in this case, between the dominant mentality and the style of pictorial art.

D. *Hindu Painting and Sculpture*. The dominant mentality of the Hindu culture — of Brahmanism-Hinduism as well as of Buddhism — has been Ideational, as was shown in Chapter Three. Logically we must expect its art to have been Ideational also. If the Hindu culture was in fact integrated, then this logical expectation should be corroborated by the reality. Such a corroboration would mean that the logico-meaningful relationships are followed by the causal-functional. What then has been the dominant style of the Hindu art? Has it been pre-eminently Ideational? The answer is given by the subsequent quotations from the works of eminent scholars in this field.

On the opening page of his work devoted to Oriental (mainly Indian and Chinese) aesthetic theory and art, A. K. Coomaraswamy says:

Whenever European art is referred to by way of contrast or elucidation, it should be remembered that "European art" is of two very different kinds, one Christian and scholastic, the other post-Renaissance and personal. . . . There was a time when Europe and Asia could and did actually understand each other very well. Asia remained herself.

[33] *Ibid.*, Vol. II, pp. 7 ff.

Europe after the Renaissance drifted to naturalism, quite different from the Asiatic as well as the Christian art of the Middle Ages. Further on, Coomaraswamy describes the characteristics of the Indian and, in considerable part, of the Chinese art, in the following terms. The Indian as well as the Christian icon is "a kind of diagram, expressing certain ideas, and not the likeness of anything on earth." "The formal element in art represents a purely mental activity." "The principle involved is that true knowledge of an object is not obtained by merely empirical observation or reflex registration, but only when the knower and known, seer and seen, meet in an act transcending distinction." "Here indeed European [medieval] and Asiatic art meet on absolutely common ground." "All the forms of Indian art and its derivatives in the Far East are ideally [virtually ideationally] determined." "Asiatic art is ideal in the mathematical sense : like Nature (*natura naturans*) not in appearance but in operation." "It is not the outward appearance as such, but rather the idea in the mind of the artist, or the immanent divine spirit, or the breath of life, that is to be revealed by a right use of natural forms. . . .   The painters painted the idea and not merely the shape." "Thus none of the terms cited by any means implies a view of art as finding its perfection in illusion ; for the East, as for St. Thomas, *ars imitatur naturam in sua operatione.*" "The Indian or Far Eastern icon, carved or painted, is neither a memory image nor an idealization, but a visual symbolism, ideal in mathematical sense." "The parts of icon are not organically [visually] related . . . but ideally related." "Asiatic and Christian art [in contradistinction to the later sensual or visual art] endeavour to represent things more nearly as they are in God, or nearer to their source" than as they look to our empirical senses. "The Eastern art sees them *sub specie aeternitatis*, but not as a passing appearance of the moment." [34]

The situation is summed up quite similarly in the following fragments taken from another authority in the field.

The Hindu view of art is the Hindu view of life, life as interpreted by religion and philosophy. There is in the Sanskrit language no exact equivalent for the word art [35] as it is used in modern European languages, for art in India has seldom been understood in the Modern Western sense of art for art's sake. In that country, mysteriously dominated by the urge to seek for and adore a reality more real than that offered by sensible or intellectual experience, art

[34] A. K. Coomaraswamy, *The Transformation of Nature in Art* (Cambridge, Mass., 1933), pp. 1–34, *passim*. See also the excellent bibliography of the works on Oriental art.

[35] As we shall see, the situation was similar in Greece, before the sixth century B.C. and in the early Middle Ages, with their Ideational art. No specific aesthetic existed and "the artist ranked simply as an artisan." J. Maritain, *Art and Scholasticism* (New York, 1930), p. 21·

has been consecrated to the service of the intuitively realised ideal of a religious philosophy and a philosophical religion.

For the most part it has been an hieratic art executed to meet the demands of the temple. . . . [The artist's] individual genius was not given the egotistical importance that is attached to it in the West. Rather it was merged into the anonymity of his caste. . . . Since all life is for the Hindus a sacrament, the same ideal of religion and philosophy which is the goal of priestly art dominates all other forms of art [industrial and narrative] too, and where it does not dominate the term Hindu, applied to the art of India, ceases to apply.

The religion and philosophy which dominates this art is embodied in the *Veda*, heard or revealed

media through which God, the Cosmic Soul, the Higher Self of Man, had revealed His inexhaustible source of truth. . . . As this view and others like it are in the mind of every artist in India, whether he be a great painter or a poor carpenter, there is in all Indian art a constancy of religious motives. Everything has a Divine meaning, and no element of life is treated for its own sake. . . . And since everything is thus seen through the God-intoxicated imagination, realism in the European [Visual] sense has no place in Indian art. . . .

The Hindu commonly regards the ordinary phenomenal world, not as reality which is an Absolute, infinite, unconditioned state of Being (God) knowledge of which is derived rather through intuition than through sense-perception, but as becoming the relative aspect of the infinite truth known to us under the limitation of our reason and ratiocination, the Unknowable as we know It. This conception of [the empirico-sensory] world as the Appearance (*Maya*) of God is familiar to the learned and the unlearned alike in India. . . . A symbolist technique was invented to express the various qualities of the Supreme Soul, and externalised form was given to Him in imaginary Superhuman types. . . . Anthropomorphic images thus came to be in India, as they did in Greece, representations of spiritual powers. Only, however, in India the artists did not embody their conception of God in the shapes of men and women as the Greeks did; but, insisting on the transcendence of God over men, the Hindus always portrayed Him as a Superhuman. . . . Hence, the many-headed gods, and many-armed goddesses of the Hindus, which, seeking to represent an eternal abstract ideal of beauty, have no exact counterpart in nature, and are purely mental creations, " works of pure design." [36]

And so on. We see that in the predominantly Ideational culture of India its art is indeed Ideational and has all the Ideational traits.

Thus, this brief glance through the pictorial art of these cultures has shown recurrence in them of the main styles, fluctuation in the ups and

[36] Mulk Raj Anand, *The Hindu View of Art* (London, 1933), pp. 37–48. See there, *passim*, the other characteristics of the Hindu art.

downs of each style, logico-meaningful as well as factual (causal-functional) association of the predominant type of mentality in each culture at a given period with the corresponding style in the pictorial art.   This means that in these two cultural variables, *i.e.*, the general mentality and the style of art, these cultures were observably integrated.

If we had examined the Tibetan or Arabian (Islamic) or several other cultures (for instance the Persian or the Japanese), all these phenomena and associations would in all probability have been found also.   But for various reasons such an additional survey has been omitted here.   Instead, we shall take the Graeco-Roman and the Western (European) cultures and study them more carefully and substantially for the phenomena we are considering.   Such a detailed analysis is likely to disclose many details and many evidences which cannot be given in a cursory survey like that given thus far in the present chapter.   So we turn now to the Graeco-Roman sculpture and painting.

III. Fluctuation of the Ideational, Visual, and Mixed Styles in the Course of the Greek Culture

The history of the Graeco-Roman culture and art offers somewhat better and fuller materials than do the other cultures for the study of the fluctuation of the art styles we have discussed and the mentality incorporated in them.   No doubt even here we are not quite safe, because the material preserved is scarce and insufficient.   For this reason the conjectural element is also unavoidable in any theory of the fluctuation of the styles in the history of the Graeco-Roman culture.   Nevertheless the existing material — the statues, the frescoes, the vase painting, and so on, together with the testimonies of the Graeco-Roman writers — furnishes a better basis for the construction of a theory of the fluctuations studied than was available in the cases just considered.

If we pay attention only to the greatest waves in the alternation of styles during the course of the Creto-Mycenaean and Graeco-Roman cultures up to the beginning of the Middle Ages, then the main periods of domination of each of the main styles may be delineated roughly as follows.

A.   The known phase of the Creto-Mycenaean culture, extending from the twelfth to the ninth century B.C., exhibits the domination of a Visual style of very refined form, amounting sometimes to an extreme Impressionistic Visualism.

B.   Whether the Greek culture properly was or was not a continuation of the Creto-Mycenaean culture, the period from about the ninth to the sixth century B.C. is marked by the domination of the Ideational art. If the Greek was a continuation of the Creto-Mycenaean culture, then such a fact means that a decay had taken place in the Visual style together with its passage into the Ideational. If the Greek culture was not a continuation of the Creto-Mycenaean, then all we can say is that the earliest known phase of the Greek art must be regarded as predominantly Ideational. In all probability there were connections between these cultures, and the Greek culture was, if not a direct descendant of the Creto-Mycenaean, then at least its relative. To this extent, at least, a partial transformation of the Visual into the Ideational seems to have taken place. The period of Homeric Art (the ninth and the eighth centuries, roughly) was something like a transition from the Mycenaean sensuousness to the Ideational art of the seventh and the sixth centuries.

C. From the second part of the sixth century B.C. on, the Ideational pattern of Greek art seems to have been relatively weakening while the Visual was rising. The descending course of the one and the ascending course of the other crossed in the fifth and fourth centuries B.C. and as a result gave the marvelous blend of both styles in the form of the great Idealistic art of Greece.

D. Toward the end of the fourth century B.C. the Ideational stream thinned so much and the Visual stream swelled to such an extent that the Visual style became already slightly dominant. Its swelling continued, at the cost of the Ideational, during the subsequent centuries of the Hellenistic culture. Therefore the period beginning with the end of the fourth century, and Hellenistic culture generally, were marked by a decisive domination of the Visual art with its centers at the Island of Rhodes, Alexandria, Pergamum, and other foci of the Hellenistic culture. In other words the purely Greek and Hellenistic phases of Greek culture ended with the domination of the Visual (Sensate) art and mentality.

E. The Etruscan art, the early "native" art of the Romans, was, before the influence of Hellenistic culture, a mixture of an Ideational with a Visual stream. Such a blend, not being perfect, yielded some Idealistic forms, but these were neither dominant nor perfectly balanced as in the case of Greece of the fifth century.

F. The free and autonomous development of the Roman art was sharply interfered with by the powerful influence of the Hellenistic and, in part, the Greek culture, especially from the end of the second century B.C. This interference led to a peculiar mixture of the native Etruscan and late — Hellenistic — Greek forms of art, which resulted in a kind of

rugged Idealistic mixed with overripe Visualism.   The main effect of this
was a series of imitative waves of Roman art : imitation of the Hellenistic
Visualism in the first century B.C. ; then imitation of the Idealistic art of
Greece in the time of Augustus; then again several waves — all of a short
duration — with quantitative-qualitative ups and downs of more or less
extreme Visualism, followed in some periods by a tiny stream of imitative
— primitive — Ideationalism.   Such is the essence of the Roman art
(omitting here the Christian) during the first century B.C. and the first
three centuries A.D.   In no period during these centuries was it conspicuously Ideational.   On the contrary it was predominantly Visual, but more
at one time and less at another.

G. However, into this world of Visualism, with the beginning of
Christianity, there entered a stream of pure Ideationalism in the form of
the early Christian art, the art of the catacombs.   At the beginning it was
just a tiny rivulet, almost unnoticeable and running far away from the
highway of Roman art.   Very rapidly, to the surprise of the intellectuals
of the Graeco-Roman world, Christianity grew into major power, and with
it the tiny rivulet of its Ideational art swelled into a broad river.   Partly
because of this fact, partly because the Roman (non-Christian) art itself,
especially after the third century, began to show more and more a swing
toward a bizarre Ideationalism which was somewhat like one of the
Mixed styles — because of these circumstances the non-Christian Roman
art underwent a comparatively rapid transformation from the dominant
Visual into an incongruous mixture of the extreme Visual with the Ideational elements (Roman "cubism" and "impressionism" of a cinematographic type) and finally, after being engulfed by the Christian art,
became, beginning with the end of the fifth century, predominantly
Ideational.   In this way it ushered art into the Ideational stream of the
Middle Ages.

Such schematically are the main waves of the alternation of the styles
and the main periods of the domination of each of them in the history of
the Creto-Mycenaean and Graeco-Roman cultures.

In order not to be accused of the usual sin of a sociologist, that of fitting
the facts to preconceived generalizations and of a superficial playing with
the facts of history, and for the sake of unfolding the sufficiently rich
content of the dry scheme presented above, I add a few typical details,
colors, and factual "shadings," which I am certain will be not superfluous.   They will be concisely given, and the reader who wants to check
their accuracy must consult the few references given, a selection from

among the many which were studied and which might have been listed if I wished merely to impress the reader by bibliographies.[37]

Whether the early stage of the Creto-Mycenaean art (*c.* 2500-900 B.C.) failed to survive, as some investigators think,[38] or whether it was from its beginning predominantly Visual, the fact is that most of what we have left from the Creto-Mycenaean art is of a highly Visual nature, and many of its objects, like the famous Vaphio cup (No. 1 on Plate X), are as perfect in their Visual artistry as anything produced later.[39]   It is true that there are some Ideational designs — geometric and others — on vases and painted pottery of Mycenae and on the ivory casket from Enkomi, Cyprus; but these are few in number.   The bulk of what we know of this art is clearly Visual, even impressionistic.   Of this nature are the excellent renderings of animals and human figures, with the mature knowledge of their anatomy which the art works show; such are the slender, pretty, voluptuous feminine figures, the Visual landscapes, the *genre* of daily life, the depiction of the common run of people; such are the picturesqueness, drama, dynamism, and sensuality.   These are the essential traits of this art.[40]   If a skillful Visual art is to be styled ripe or overripe, this art appears to us to be so.

This culture which existed between 2500 B.C. and 900 B.C. supposedly "disappears" as suddenly as it appears.   We can leave it to historians to unravel the mystery of this supposedly sudden change.   What is important for us is that the Greek art which comes after the Creto-Mycenaean, the art of the so-called Archaic period (*c.* 1000 or 900 to 500 or 460 B.C.), is fundamentally different.   The art of the ninth and possibly of the eighth century shows a growth of the geometric type (No. 2 on Plate X) — which in most cases is but a symbolic or Ideational art — together with another stream, exemplified by the shield of Achilles described in Homer which, with its visual delineation of daily life, bears the clear

[37] In this whole work so many sources have been studied and used, that if I wanted to mention them all, an additional volume of a purely bibliographical supplement would be necessary.   As this is inadvisable, I must limit my references and various appendixes (of sources, of detailed series of facts, of names of artists, philosophers, etc.) to the absolutely indispensable minimum.   Even with such limitation, as the reader can see, the appendixes occupy quite a large place in the work, and the sources quoted are long and substantial.

[38] See Deonna, *op. cit.*, Vol. III, pp. 61–123.

[39] "They form a work of art hardly surpassed by the product of any nation at any epoch." "The frescoes of Knossos and Tiryns are remarkable for their naturalism and power of rendering. . . ."   (H. B. Walters, *op. cit.*, p. 19.)

[40] See the description and analysis of it in Deonna, *op. cit.*, Vol. III, pp. 61 ff.; H. B. Walters, *op. cit.*, pp. 12 ff. and 142 ff.; and any good work in the history of Greek art.   See the literature referred to in these works.

PLATE X

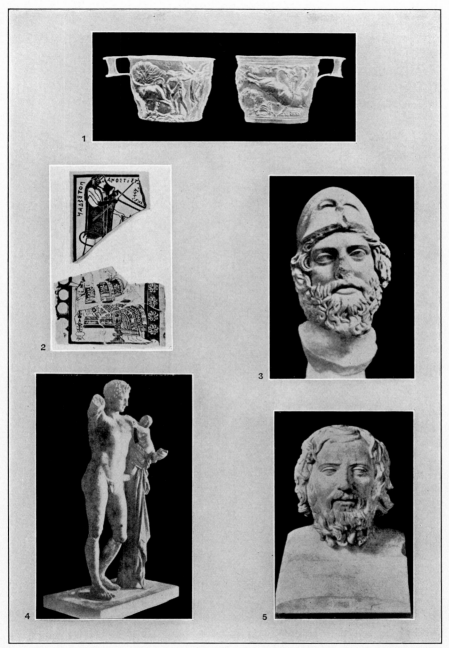

1, Vaphio gold cup.   2, Votive tablet and painted metope, from early Corinthian paintings.
3, Head of a strategos.   4, Hermes with the Child Dionysos, by Praxiteles.   5, Head of Anakreon.

stamp of the Visual type. These and other remains of the art of this period suggest its transitory nature, as it moves from the dominant Visual of the previous age to the Ideational type. Hence, the mixture of these two streams. From this standpoint the art of this period seems to have been similar to the art of the fourth and fifth centuries A.D. in Rome when, as we shall see, art and culture were also in a transition from the Visual to the Ideational. In the usual — though hardly adequate — terminology of a historian such a change is, of course, a "regression" and "degeneration." (How many times this has happened in various cultures !)

In no class of artistic products is this [regression, as compared with the Mycenaean period] more clearly seen than in the pottery of the age immediately succeeding the Mycenaean, in which the vigorous and lifelike portrayal of animals and plants is replaced by the simple geometric patterns characteristic of an uncultivated race.[41]

During the seventh and as late as the first half of the sixth century, the Ideational wave seems to have been rising higher. The geometrical and other forms of the Ideational style predominate ; the subjects, as they are exemplified by the Chest of Kypselos and the throne of Apollo at Amiklae, become almost exclusively religious and mythological. Of the previous refined Visualism there remains little, if anything, either in technique or in the content of art. Art becomes quite "conventional" and "formal" — terms which mean in most of the cases what I style Ideational.[42]

The same seems to be true in regard to the vase painting. In contradistinction to the mature Visual painting of the Cretan and Mycenaean pottery and of the frescoes of Knossos, the painting of the "Archaic" period is purely linear — it is drawing rather than painting — purely monochromic at the early period and then simple polychromic. As we have mentioned, the passage from linearism to *malerisch* painting is one of the definite signs of an increasing Visualism. The topics are again almost exclusively religious and "superempirical." The technique is not intended to create a visual illusion of the things rendered. Pliny's characterization of the painting of that period leaves no doubt as to its pre-

---

[41] H. Walters, *op. cit.*, p. 24. This "characteristic of an uncultivated race" is rather naïve : accustomed to the Visual standard, the author sees decay and lack of culture in anything that differs from it.

[42] Otherwise they have hardly any clear meaning. Any art is in a sense conventional and formal. The point therefore is : What kind of "convention" and "form"? When we add, Visual or Ideational, they acquire a real meaning.

dominantly Ideational ("conventional and formal") character.[43]   This
concerns equally the "draughtsmen" of the period, such as Philokles,
Kleanthes, Aridikes of Corinth, Telephanes of Sikyon, Deinias, Hy-
giainon, and others.

Beginning with the sixth century, especially the latter half, the first
signs of a shift from the Ideational toward the Visual style appear in
sculpture as well as in painting.   An effort to render subjects somewhat
more visually seems to have taken place in the Athenian school of sculpture and to a less degree in the school of Samos (Theodorus, Rhoikos,
Smilis, Telekles) and of Chios (Melas, Mikkiades, Archermos, Bupalos,
Athenis).   The same seems to be true of the vase painting of the schools
of Corinth, of Sikyon, and especially of Athens (Eumaros, c. 600–590
B.C.; Kimon of Kleonae, c. 520–500 B.C.).   However, the art still remains
predominantly Ideational, though the Ideationalism is progressively
declining before a growing Visualism.   But soon the descending curve
of Ideationalism and ascending curve of Visualism cross each other and
produce a marvelous blending in the form of the *sublime Idealistic art* of
the fifth century B.C.   It has all the perfections of the mature Visual
technique.   At the same time its "soul" is still in the Ideational —
religious, ethical, and nonsensate — world.   We are in the age of the
"predecessors" of Phidias : of Aegeladas of Argos (c. 520–516), of Myron,
of Onatas (c. 480), of Kalamis, of Pythagoras of Rhegion, and others.
The culmination point of the period — and of all time — in sculpture was
Phidias (500–432 B.C.),

the first sculptor to produce ideal embodiments of the highest moral qualities
of which a Greek could conceive, such as majesty, wisdom or beauty.   He was
the first sculptor who combined the idealism with the perfect mastery of his
material, thus producing a completer harmony than was attained by any before
or since.[44]

Then comes Polycletus (c. 440–410 B.C.), not to mention others like
Agorakritos, Alkamenes, Kolotes, Kallimachos.

The subjects of the sculpture of the fifth century are gods, heroes, or
ideational entities like Victory, Nemesis, and so on.   In this sense the
art is Ideational.   But the perfect technique is Visual.   Hence it unites
in itself both styles in an unrivaled form, and gives what I call the Idealistic art.

---

[43] See E. Jex-Blake and E. Sellers, *Pliny's Chapters on Art* (London, 1896) ; Deonna, *op.
cit.*, Vol. II, pp. 172 ff.; Vol. III, pp. 140 ff.   See also Herrmann-Brückman, *Denkmäler der
Malerei des Altertums* (München, 1931).

[44] Walters, *op. cit.*, p. 98 ;   G. Rodenwaldt, *Die Kunst der Antike* (Berlin, 1927), Vol. III.

The chief characteristics of the fifth century sculpture are breadth of style and ideality; these traits, though best exemplified in Pheidias, are by no means confined to the great master.[45]

The Greek painting of the fifth century is likewise Idealistic in nature. During the last part of the sixth and the fifth century it underwent a change similar to that experienced by sculpture. The shift of both these arts toward Visualism was almost simultaneous. If one lagged at all behind the other, it was a lag of short duration. The culmination of the fifth century painting was Polygnotus (*c.* 475–430 B.C.). He is rightly styled the Phidias of painting. Almost the same mastery of technique, the same idealistic and ennobling spirit, the same "soul," characterize his works as are found in Phidias. A similar idealism is present in the works of his school : in Mikon, Panaenos, and other painters of the period. Of all of them Aristotle rightly says that they were "the character painters" (in contradistinction to those who gave a purely Visual rendering of men) and "painted men greater than they are," while shortly after Polygnotus some painters painted men as they are or worse.

In view of the exceptional perfection of this Idealistic art of the fifth century, it is advisable to outline its characteristics a little more substantially. Such an analysis should help us to understand several typical traits of the Idealistic style. A few quotations from specialists will help us in this purpose.

This Idealism of the Greek painting and sculpture of the fifth century shows itself first in an excellent knowledge on the part of the artists of human anatomy and the means of rendering it in its ideal or perfect form, in the type of the persons represented, in their postures, in the abstractness of the human type; there are no concrete portraits, no ugliness, no defective traits or types; before us are immortals or idealized mortals; old age is rejuvenated; the baby is depicted as grown up; the women have little that is specifically womanish and appear like perfect athletes; there are no concrete landscapes. The postures and the expressions are free from any violent or debased or too human emotion and distorting passion. They are calm, serene, imperturbable like the gods. Even the dead shine with the same calmness and serene beauty. All the statues have a "Greek" profile; not because the Greeks were such, as Winkelmann thought, but because it was the profile thought to be perfect. The *chevelure* is simple but perfectly ordered; the drapery is perfectly adapted to the body, simple and marvelous in its orderly beauty. Eyes are

[45] *Ibid.*, p. 113.

natural and perfect, and shine with calmness and serenity; the lips and mouth are ideally cut; the postures are dignified and idealized.[46]

The artist of the fifth century does not try to reproduce nature in its integrity, but from his observation of it, — more precise than before — he abstracts an ideal. He knows how to render with precision the muscles of the human body, the folds and plaits of drapery, but he treats them soberly. . . . He does not ignore the realistic subjects, but he does not reproduce them for their own sake; they are but a means to a more sublime purpose. He wants especially to elevate himself above the common, to create abstractions and types not of a temporary but of eternal value. Eliminating the accidental and individual, he keeps only what is universal in man and nature, and this he does in sculpture as well as in literature.[47]

"The faces, do they express either joy or suffering? can one read in them the passions which agitate the human soul?" On the vase paintings the creatures of the lower and inferior orders, like slaves, centaurs, Silenes, fauns, and animals, show these passions, and this testifies that the artists knew how to express such aspects of life.

But the persons of a noble race, disdainful of manifesting their sentiments, consider unbecoming to them this mark of humanity. In the frontons of Olimpe, in the metopes of the Parthenon, while the Centaurs are convulsed by suffering, their adversaries, the gods and the mortals remain calm and impassive and permit their rage to be perceived only through minor details. . . . The conventional smile of the sixth century disappears now and, after the Persian wars, a grave expression is diffused over the faces. Neither joy nor sorrow but just a neutral expression. . . . Even when the body is engaged in a rude effort the face remains calm and the inward seething does not succeed in troubling this calm and serene surface. . . . Such is this ideal made up of muscular power and moral serenity, which by mistake many ascribed to the whole Greek art but which exists only in the art of the fifth century and reaches its supreme expression in the marbles of the Parthenon. . . . Pheidias, in the Parthenon, presents us with human creatures who do not permit us to see in the features of their faces any particular expression, any reflexion of a certain thought, or determined soul, and at the same time whose beauty appears to us divine and inspires us with religious admiration.[48]

In the fifth century there is no ugliness. Not because they did not know how to render it but because they avoided everything that can trouble the harmony of face or body. . . . [With few exceptions like the realistic statues of Demetrios of Alopéké or the sculpture of Olimpe] the general tendency is to

[46] See Deonna, *op. cit.*, Vol. III, pp. 200 ff., and the reproductions there.
[47] *Ibid.*, Vol. III, pp. 231–232.   [48] *Ibid.*, Vol. III, pp. 232–234.

embellish the types which at other times are depicted as horrible. Even the grimacing figure of the Gorgon is softened and appears now as a beautiful visage of the Medusa of Rondanini and the fauns, Silenes, and Centaurs lose their bestiality. . . .[49]

Further,

The Greeks of the fifth century neglected portraits not because they were unable to depict the distinctive traits of their models but on account of a principle. Pericles wears the helmet of a strategos but his face might have been that of another mortal or of a god. . . .[50]

"Greek art of the fifth century produced no portraits strictly speaking." According to Pliny the objective of an artist of the fifth century was "how to make noble men still nobler." Instead of a purely visual portrait this art gives "idealized abstractions" of men "in the prime of life with a luxuriant growth of hair," and so on. Even the head of Anakreon (No. 5 on Plate X) is attractive because in reality he "was an old man unable to give up love and wine"; as such he was senile and ruined; but in the portrait there is little of these characteristics.[51]

Women . . . appear in the art of the fifth century as robust athletes. . . . The baby does not have the disproportionate forms of real infancy . . . but by his proportions as well as by his musculature a baby is a small man who differs from the ephebes and athletes only in his dimensions.[52]

For an artist of the fifth century old age with its wrinkles, its parchment skin, its enfeebled attitude, is repellent. Priam wrote that the corpse of a youth is pleasant to see but that of an old man is a disgusting spectacle. . . .

In accordance with the idealism of the period it is comprehensible then that

if the masters of the fifth century made infants older and rendered them like the youth, inversely they rejuvenated the old men. In the vase paintings the traits of Priam and other old men . . . enframed by whiskers and grey hair remain, nevertheless, young, and their bodies look as robust as that of the ephebes.[53]

[49] *Ibid.*, Vol. III, pp. 236–237.
[50] *Ibid.*, Vol. III, p. 238. See No. 3 on Plate X.
[51] Anton Hekler, *Greek and Roman Portraits* (London, 1912), pp. vii–viii. One can look through the collection of the reproductions of the Greek and Roman portraits in this volume very profitably: in this particular field, going from the earliest to the latest times, one can easily detect the main waves of the styles discussed in the history of Graeco-Roman culture. Some of Hekler's statements, like "artistic activity always begins with abstractions," and so on, are rather questionable. See also R. Delbrück, *Antike Porträts* (Bonn, 1912).
[52] Deonna, *op. cit.*, Vol. III, pp. 238–239. See No. 4 on Plate X.
[53] *Ibid.*, Vol. III, pp. 239–243.

This particular trait of the rejuvenation of the old and of "aging the babies" to conform to the ideal type, is shown in other compartments of the Greek culture. A special study of this problem gives the following conclusions bearing upon our discussion.

As long as art was bound up with religion the artist was concerned with the representation of the young but mature figure, but as soon as the old faith began gradually to decompose . . . art made new conquest. The tendency corresponding to idealism is prior to that of realism. Polyclitus who was so directly concerned with the classical type was criticized by Quintilian for limiting his subjects to the representation of youthful figures and avoiding the stronger characterization of advanced age. (Quint. *Instr. Orat.* 12, 10, 8: *Quin aetatem quoque graviorem dicitur refugisse nihil ausus ultra leves genas.*) The fifth century was a transitional period preparatory to the full establishment of the old age type. At the end of the fifth century Greek art was changing from the typically beautiful to the individually characteristic. The glorious art of the fifth century . . . gave way to that of the fourth century which was concerned with pathos. Then in the last epoch of Greek art (from the death of Alexander the Great in 323 B.C. to the rise of the Roman dominion in Greece in 146 B.C.) sculpture lost its old ideals with the decline of the intellectual and artistic activity of Athens, and in spite of the persistence of the fondness for the human figure there was a weakening of the passion for beauty and the idealized tendency. The striving for the new effects, the giving up of much of the restraint so marked in the sculpture of the great period furthered by the continuation of the intensity and emotional qualities of Scopas produced figures which were the opposite of the calm and dignified types of the Periclean age.

In the Hellenistic age was created a stronger impulse toward portraiture. . . . The tendency toward greater realism and a more exact expression of individual traits became stronger after the Roman conquest, and in portrait statues and busts the Romans found a particularly promising field of endeavor. [This comes out in the architectural, decorative, sculptural, and literary arts, and vase painting. In the fourth and the third centuries] the old age portrayal burst into full bloom.[54]

All these traits of eternal youthfulness, ideal beauty, of absence of joy or sorrow, are united in the monuments of the funerary sculpture. . . . On the steles of the fifth century the dead is not at all such as he is in reality in his grave, but such as he was when alive. No sorrow upon his visage but a perfect serenity like that of the marbles of the Parthenon; no ugliness but an unalterable beauty; no portraits but the ideal traits of the gods; no senility but eternal youthfulness.[55]

[54] Bessie Ellen Richardson, *Old Age among the Ancient Greeks* (Baltimore, 1933), pp. 129–131. See also chaps. v–ix and reproductions.   [55] Deonna, *op. cit.*, Vol. III, p. 243.

Furthermore, "the art of the fifth century eliminates *paysage* from its compositions; it indicates the place where the action takes place, by but a few meagre and schematised shrubs." [56]   The Greek art ignores the sculpturing of historical scenes (before Alexander) because "history giving only some particular facts contradicts its general trend, and giving the real facts contradicts its idealistic tendency." [57]

Finally, this art was deeply religious, patriotic, instructive, moralizing, educating.   It was created not only for its own sake, but also as a means for such instruction and education.   It was not separated from, but was the partner of, religion, of civic and social morality.   What Chambers says about this stage of Greek art is essentially sound.   In their art the Greeks "saw a grandiose lesson of patriotism."   In the mythological plastic decorations of the temples, the fighting Greek deities and mythical ancestors "were their heroic ancestors who thus told them their exploits and repeated the ancient song of Tyrtaios: Let us fight courageously for this land, for our country, and let us die for our children without sparing our souls.   And you, young men, fight firmly one by the side of the others, let none of you show an example of shameful desertion or fear," etc. "To see his gods and heroes sculptured on the temples was for a Greek to receive a lesson of valiancy and faith."   In Greece sculpture, says Boutmy, was "a theological instruction, a veritable legendary bible, just as the façades of the Gothic cathedrals were an encyclopedia of the notions of that time." [58]   Such a thing was possible because "the fifth century was profoundly religious and the art was then but a form of a cult." [59]

From the same spirit comes its collective and in a way anonymous character.   "Temples and their art were the expression of the popular beliefs and were the collective work of all the citizens."   After the Persian wars, it was necessary to thank the gods for the victory, for peace, for prosperity; and "the whole Athenian people wanted to devote themselves to that national work which was to honour the gods and their own country."   There was a universal *élan*, ardent and enthusiastic desire to exalt the religion and the country.   Hence all tried to participate in the creation of the great national monument — the art of the fifth century. There was this idealism, there was unanimity, there was exaltation; hence the unity, harmony, and marvel of the art of that period.   "Each co-operated in this immense work; a feverish activity reigned everywhere

[56] *Ibid.*, Vol. III, p. 247.
[57] *Ibid.*, Vol. III, p. 247.
[58] *Ibid.*, Vol. III, pp. 250 ff.
[59] *Ibid.*, Vol. III, p. 252.   It should be remembered here that when Phidias and Anaxagoras offended the religious feelings they were punished and cast out, in spite of their fame.

in the Acropolis of Pericles." [60]　And the works were also for all : they were neither the palaces, nor the libraries for the savants, but the temples and civic common buildings.

Shall we wonder that in these conditions the

artist retreats before the community.　This does not mean that the fifth century did not know the great sculptors or painters — the names of Pheidias, Polycletus, Polygnotus, are present in everyone's memory — but means that they did not live as yet that particular mode of living which attracted attention to them ; they were not absorbed as yet wholly in their art as was true of their colleagues of the fourth century ; they took a part in the political life just as the other citizens.　They were aware of their value but this awareness did not grow yet to become exalted, and their genius was consecrated by them entirely to the well-being of the collectivity.[61]

In other words such great artists were but the leading members of a great collective enterprise but not the only creators of these great monuments.

It is needless to add that the age was simultaneously religious, rationalistic, speculative, ideological, and idealistic.[62]

I have paused for some length at the characterization of the Idealistic art of the fifth century because it shows clearly many typical traits of the Idealistic art generally.　When we approach the art of the thirteenth century in Christian Europe we shall meet most of these traits again. Let us now move on.

The period of pure Idealism in Greek art was short.　Though it remained Idealistic throughout the fifth and a part of the fourth century, nevertheless, after Phidias and Polygnotus the Ideational stream continued to become thinner, the Sensate ampler.　The marvelous balance of the Idealistic art was then more and more lost and this led to a gradual decline of the purity of the Idealistic style.

In sculpture, the first signs of a contamination of the pure Idealism of Phidias appear already in the works of Polycletus (active *c.* 440–410) with his idealization of the body (mainly athletes) rather than of the soul.　However, his works and that of the contemporary artists remain predominantly Idealistic still.　Idealism, though more and more contaminated, continues in the works of the first part of the fourth century,

---

[60] *Ibid.*, Vol. III, pp. 253 ff.

[61] *Ibid.*, Vol. III, pp. 255–257.

[62] Up to the fourth century "Greek art is the docile servant of official religion. . . .　It serves the gods and the dead."　The supreme product of Greek architecture, the temple, is "not a civil but a religious building."　(A. de Ridder and W. Deonna, *Art in Greece*, p. 54; see also pp. 63 ff.)

in those of Kephisodotus (active *c.* 395–370 B.C.), Praxiteles (*c.* 370–350 B.C.) (No. 4 on Plate X), Scopas (390–350 B.C.), and even partly of Lysippus (*c.* 330–315 B.C.), not to mention lesser sculptors. But the form becomes more and more Visual, the subjects more and more empirical; the spirit of ennoblement and idealization wanes more and more and all the other signs of Idealism mentioned above tend to either weaken or vanish. "From the ideal to the merely beautiful, and from the general to the individual . . . represents briefly, the transition from Pheidias to Praxiteles." [63]

Toward the end of the fourth century Idealism is over and the rising tide of Visualism definitely triumphs. Beginning with that period we have the Hellenistic sculpture, which is clearly and conspicuously Sensate or Visual, with all the traits of such an art.

A similar change took place also in painting during the fourth century. Already at the end of the fifth century a few painters, like Apollodorus, introduced a strong current of Visualism in painting: by using, for example, the effect of light and shade, by trying to paint men as "they seem to be" without any ennoblement, and by endeavoring to create a purely visual illusionism. Hence his contemporary nickname: "shadow painter." [64]

In the fourth century the tide of Visualism continues to rise while that of Ideationalism continues to dry out. In the first part of that century their balance was not yet destroyed entirely, and Idealism, though contaminated, still was dominant. But during the second half of the century the triumph of Visualism becomes unquestionable. Already in the works of Zeuxis (420–380 B.C.) there appears a search for striking and picturesque situations, for illusionistic Visual effects (remember the story of the grape painted by him and of a bird trying to pick it up); the subjects become more and more empirical and "realistic" (scenes of domestic life, children, women, *genre*); serenity and imperturbability of soul is gone, giving place to emotions and passions. In the works of Parrhasios these traits, especially emotionality, dynamism, and illusionism, seem to have been still more conspicuous. The same is even truer of the works of Timanthes and other painters of the end of the fourth century. Visualism definitely grows in the schools of Attica, Ionia, and Sikyon. "Classical Academism" of the period — with its efforts to paint with a Visual "academic accuracy and perfection" (Eupompos, Melanthios, Pamphilos, Pausias, Aristeides, Euphranor,

[63] Walters, *op. cit.*, p. 113.
[64] See the work of Walters and that of Blake and Sellers cited.

Nikomachos, Nikias, and others) ; with its use of the *malerisch* technique of chiaroscuro similar to that of Rembrandt, of foreshortening ; and with its other traits of Visualism — is a general trend.   In the works of Apelles, Protogenes, Antiphilos, Aëtion, and others, all the typical marks of Visualism are clear and conspicuous.   The Idealism of the fifth century is dead, and with it the Ideational stream is reduced to a thin rivulet as compared with the large river of Visualism.   The Hellenistic painting is quite Visual and is a further development of this trend of the fourth century.[65]

Again in order to give a more detailed idea of the characteristics of such an art, and at the same time to show its profound difference from the art of the preceding centuries in Greece, it is advisable to pause a little at this point and to give somewhat fuller treatment of the traits of the Hellenistic art (sculpture and painting), most of which are at the same time the traits of the Sensate or Visual style.

Here are most important characteristics : (1) The figures of women which before were rare now become quite common subjects of sculpture and painting.   (2) They are represented, not as robust and athletic — almost sexless — youths, but as slender, voluptuous, sexual, seductive figures, side by side with realistic figures of old women.   (3) A similar change takes place in regard to the figures of men.   (4) Portraits of individual persons, especially rulers and others on whom the artists depended, become more and more common.   (5) There appears more and more the representation of real landscapes and dramatic historical scenes.   (6) The everyday life, in form of the realistic *genre*, becomes a very common topic.   (7) Crowds, mobs, the common run of people, and especially pathological types: prostitutes, criminals, street urchins, etc., more and more replace the heroes and ideal men.   (8) The postures and expressions of the persons lose their idealized patterns and become realistic: serenity and calm are replaced by the pathetic, by passion and emotionality, including suffering, sorrow, pain, fear, agony, and distortion ; static immobility is driven out by dynamism and violent movement.   (9) Picturesqueness takes the upper hand over idealism : a

---

[65] Similar stages were passed through by vase painting.   The black-figured vases (*c.* 600–500 B.C.) are predominantly Ideational; the red-figured vases (*c.* 520–400 B.C.) predominantly Idealistic; the Vases of the Decadence (400–200 B.C.) are quite Visual and Sensuous, with all the earmarks of such an art: illusionism, showiness and splendor, large size, gaudy effects, lavish use of ornamentation, sensuality and eroticism, subjects from daily life, soft and effeminate effects of the Watteau type of figures.   See Walters, *op. cit.*, chap. ix, and *History of Ancient Pottery* (London, 1905) ; S. Reinach, *Répertoire des vases . . . grecs et étrusques*, 2 vols. (Paris, 1899–1900).

street urchin in his rags is preferred to the idealized demigod. An inclination to the macabre, nudity of a sexual nature, etc., is another aspect of it. (10) If before mortals were depicted like the immortals, now the gods tend to be depicted like mortals. (11) It is natural that now the baby is depicted as a baby and the old man as a semisenile person, the woman as very different from the man; and if before the women were masculinized now the men are frequently effeminized. (12) Behind the art object there is hardly noticeable any other ideal or value. "Art for art's sake" (just for a sensuous gratification!) becomes a norm; and the art's sake is considered purely sensuously, destined to give a sensate pleasure to the sensate man. (13) A tendency to gigantic quantitative proportions shows itself. What is lacking in quality is compensated for by hugeness, by large quantity (in size, in mass, in caliber). "The biggest" becomes one of the main means to be impressive. "The biggest," the "largest," tends to become the criterion of the best. Quantity tends to replace quality. In brief, we are on the earth, in a fleshy world, sensate, utilitarian, material, Epicurean.

On Plate XI, Nos. 1 and 2 show examples of everyday-life topics, with common type of people — females, "playing bridge" — which became the common topic of Hellenic art; Nos. 3 and 4 show the pathetic, dramatic, theatrical tendency, together with Visual dynamism. Nothing in the sculptures is at rest. Everything is in a violent motion. No. 5 is a sample of a Visual, matter-of-fact portrait, with all the peculiar traits of a given individual, without any idealization.

The subsequent quotations will elaborate these statements.[66]

The fourth century is an epoch of transition. . . . It was not the *subjects* that changed. In the fourth century they erected temples which told the same legends as before — so dear to the Greeks. But the spirit [*l'esprit*] which controlled the execution of these monuments now differed. The pure and noble idealism of the Parthenon began to become fleshy, art descended from the serene heights in order to approach nearer to humanity.[67]

In technical details this transition shows itself in a series of specific phenomena: (1) The postures of the figures become more indolent, subtle, and, in a way, graceful.[68] (2) Drapery tends to become more and picturesquely plaited: it ceases to be architectural and turns into the pictorial and movingly dynamic:[69] it is now adapted to the sex and the

---

[66] For the sake of brevity I am quoting only a few sources; the quoted statements can be duplicated in almost all the important works about this period of Graeco-Hellenistic art.

[67] Deonna, *op. cit.*, Vol. III, p. 261.

[68] *Ibid.*, Vol. III, pp. 262 ff.   [69] *Ibid.*, Vol. III, pp. 265 ff.

age of the figure, while before it was in a way sexless and ageless, being ideally arranged for an abstract ideal figure.[70]   (3) Now the visages show passions, melancholy, suffering, and other emotions.[71]   (4) What is still more important is that the fourth century secularized the religious creations of the fifth.[72]

The religious ideal of the fourth century is less elevated than that of the fifth, and from day to day the divine types approached the human ones more and more.   The weakening of the spirit of tradition, the progress of incredulity, the waning of religious beliefs, progressively detached man from the high idealistic conceptions and directed his attention to his immediate [needs]. While the religious and moral sentiments of the fifth century gave their unity to the literary and artistic creations of the age of Pericles, the unity of the art of the fourth century is found in human observation, in a study of man and of all that concerns him . . . Praxiteles and then Lysippus led sculpture step by step from the world of the immortals to that of the living. . . . Aphrodite is no more that chaste and austere goddess of the fifth century but became instead a beautiful and voluptuous woman, and her forms, so virile before, now became softened, more languishing and tender. . . . Apollo now became a young boy teasing a lizard; Artemis, a young lady busy with adjusting her *manteau* upon her shoulder; Hermes . . . rendered as an euphebe resting after the fatigues of palaestra amuses a midget-like Dionysus with a bunch of grapes.   These religious subjects become now a kind of a *genre* which begins to show its place.[73]

On the other hand, while the gods are descending from their heights and becoming more mortal, some mortals are rendered as immortals, but "humanly immortal."   Such, for instance, are the statues by Lysippus and others of Alexander the Great as well as the likenesses of some other persons, particularly of those upon whom an artist depended for patronage.

But whether the statues are those of gods or mortals, the visages of all are now marked by passions, emotions, and individual traits (portraiture).   "Gestures, draperies, visages, all concur now to express the sentiments which agitate the human heart.   The violent movement and frenzied attitude of the Menade of Dresden, as the symbols of the sacred delirium into which she is plunged," are typical.[74]   A little later, in works

[70] *Ibid.*, Vol. III, pp. 267 ff.

[71] *Ibid.*, Vol. III, pp. 268 ff.

[72] E. Pottier, *Diphilos* (Paris, 1909), p. 64.

[73] Deonna, *op. cit.*, Vol. III, pp. 272–273. See also F. Chambers, *The History of Taste*, Appendix; H. B. Walters, *The Art of the Greeks*, pp. 115 ff., 128 ff., *et passim*; E. Pfuhl, *Malerei und Zeichnung der Griechen* (München, 1923).

[74] Deonna, *op. cit.*, Vol. III, p. 276.

PLATE XI

1, Women conversing, from Myrina.   2, Women playing, from Capua.   3, Relief, from the altar
of Pergamum.   4, Laocoön.   5, Philetaerus of Pergamum.

like the Laocoön (No. 4, Plate XI), this pathetic emotionality reached its extreme expression, being joined also by a growing taste for the macabre, in part for the obscene, and for the cynical.

This search for the pathetic [says Collignon], this picturesque grouping, these violent attitudes imprinted upon the figures . . . such are the most positive evidences of the evolution which began to carry art in a new direction. There is no doubt that sculpture followed the movement already existing in literature [Euripides and others].[75]

While Praxiteles was the leader of sentimentalism, Scopas was the chief exponent of the pathetic, and these two human — excessively human — tendencies were one of the conspicuous signs of the rising tide of Visualism. Whether in the sculpture of other artists, or generally on the funerary steles, everywhere these tendencies began to appear.

Sorrowful passion, sweet melancholy, dolorous kindness, such are the sentiments stamped on the visages of the sculptures of the great artists-psychologists of the fourth century.

The melancholy is as yet light and rarely turns into physical pain, despair, suffering, as it did in the art of the Hellenistic period; but it is there, together with other signs of realism.[76] Praxiteles also was probably the first who tried to express the grace and seductiveness of the woman's body. "Portraits of the fourth century began to become more and more individualized and tended to reproduce exactly the characteristic traits of the model.[77]

It is true the Visualism did not here reach its climax, and that all this was only the forerunner of the utterly Visualistic portraiture of the Hellenistic period; but its beginning was made.[78] We are told that at that time they began to use the technique of making casts of the face of living persons and that Lysistratos of Sicyon, brother of Lysippus, was, according to Pliny, the first who introduced this technique. Its nature testifies as to its realistic objective.[79]

A careful study of the reproductions of the Greek portrait statues published in Hekler's work is sufficient to make the change clear. Demetrios of Alopéké (c. 420–390) supposedly was the first visualistic sculptor

[75] M. Collignon, *Histoire de la sculpture grecque* (Paris, 1897), Vol. II, pp. 103 ff. See also his *Scopas et Praxitèle* (Paris, 1907).

[76] Deonna, *op. cit.*, Vol. III, pp. 290–292; Chambers, *op. cit.*, pp. 292 ff.

[77] Deonna, *op. cit.*, Vol. III, p. 296.

[78] *Ibid.*, Vol. III, p. 297; Chambers, *op. cit.*, 295 ff. See also T. Graf, *Antike Porträts aus Hellenistischer Zeit.* (Wien, n. d.).

[79] Deonna, *op. cit.*, Vol. III, p. 298.

portraitist.   According to Pliny "likeness was more to him than beauty."
From the end of the fourth century this tendency triumphed, giving the
upper hand, now to a purely prosaic reproduction of portraits (schools
of Silanion and of Lysippus), now to theatrically dramatic, passionate,
mannered, *pseudo*-idealistic portraits, *e.g.*, lionlike bust of Alexander the
Great and others.   The same can be seen on the coin figures of these
periods.[80]

Finally, the position and the mentality of artists also changed greatly.
The artist became "emancipated" from the "fetters" of religion, community, *mores*, and what not.   From now on he became a servant of art
for art's sake.   Thus he began to depend upon various patrons, the rulers
and the rich.

He lost the noble and virile faith which animated his ancestors in the fifth
century. . . .   He ceased to look for the aspiration in the national, patriotic,
and religious life.   He was now interested more in man than in gods, and not
so much in the heroic man or a conqueror of the barbarians and monsters, or
a victorious athlete, but just in common man who did not accomplish any
heroism, who did not have any merit but that of mere living; and such a man
was looked for predominantly in the lowest classes of society. . . .   [Leochares
renders a slave merchant, Lysippus an intoxicated flute player (*une joueuse de
flute ivre*)].

Art, humanized in that way, tends to quit the exclusive service of gods in
order to devote itself to that of men; it secularizes itself.   Phydias immortalized Athena of the Parthenon or Zeus the Olympian; Lysippus multiplies the
portraits of Alexander whom he elevates to the rank of god; he keeps carefully his privilege to sign the royal statues, while Apelles has the exclusive
right to paint the conqueror and Pyrgoteles to engrave him upon fine stone.[81]

In this way there appeared a new type of artist in Greece, that of the
court; later on, that of the rich and influential men.   Thus, instead of
being free servants of the community and of the transcendental values,
they became "friends and valets" of the rich and of the powerful.

Take further, for instance, the treatment of gods, like Apollo, Dionysos,
or Eros:

What has the Eros of the fifth century, the serious young euphebus, in common with the boy-loves of the Alexandrian period?   Or the Aphrodite of the
fifth century, a vigorous woman chastely clad, with the soft voluptuousness of
the naked goddess of Hellenistic times!   What is there in common between

---

[80] Hekler, *op. cit.*, pp. ix-x, xvii, *et passim*.   See the plates preceding and following
No. 22, and No. 56 and following.
[81] *Ibid.*, Vol. III, pp. 301-302.

the bearded and garbed Dionysus of archaism and the youthful god, nude and effeminate, of the Graeco-Roman? And again between the virile Apollo of early days and the equivocal euphebus of Praxiteles, between the calm impassivity of these divine beings of the fifth century, and the dreamy, emotional or even suffering expressions which the Hellenists give them? [82]

Or take:

The Aegean Cretan avoided stripping completely, and the Egyptians, Chaldeans, Assyrians and Etruscans were averse to it except in the cases of the lower orders. . . . Woman . . . was draped from head to foot in the sixth century and the first half of the fifth. [The second half of the fifth introduced some beginning of nudity.] The fourth century went far along this road. . . . The draperies now slip off the shoulders altogether and only stop at the hips [Aphrodite of Milo, the Praxitelean Aphrodite of Arles, for instance]. Praxiteles is the first completely to undrape the goddess [e.g., Chidian Aphrodite]. No garment enwraps her. She is nude and completely displays all her beauties. [83]

Later on "Woman invaded art." [84] Eroticism and Sensate Epicureanism generally reign supreme in these Visual art creations.

And so it was with other human figures. The statue of a youth of the fifth century was, as we saw, religious and civic in character: he was a victor, strong, slim, perfect, a demigod; in the fourth century he becomes a robust fellow, with knit brows, strong muscles, somewhat negligent about his *chevelure* and other details; later on he appears as "a common little urchin," picturesque and quite real, free from any idealization, like hundreds of such beings in the streets of the Hellenistic cities. [85]

These tendencies became still more pronounced in the Hellenistic period. Here women became one of the main subjects of art. And, if the Aphrodites of the fourth century still retained something of the vigor and chastity of the fifth century,

the Hellenistic Aphrodites, the Nymphs, the Menades became charming and sensual women, of an easy virtue, somewhat similar to the influential courtesans, and from their bodies emanated the restless charm of voluptuousness. Gestures became gallant: Perseus delivering Andromede, and helping her gallantly to step down from a rock, is like a seigneur who helps a belle dame to descend from his carriage, with a somewhat coquettish gracefulness similar to the "mythologies" of the eighteenth century. [86]

[82] De Ridder and Deonna, *op. cit.*, p. 59.
[83] *Ibid.*, pp. 93–96.   [84] *Ibid.*, p. 115.
[85] *Ibid.*, p. 334.   [86] Deonna, *op. cit.*, Vol. III, p. 68.

Male visages are now rendered mainly as smooth shaven, in contrast with the preceding period.

The love of nature, of landscapes, grows, parallel to the preoccupation with the picturesque, assuming often the half-romantic tendency of the tired urbanist to find rest in the country among "pastoral" scenery. Likewise, an accurate rendering of animals and the frequent use of them as subjects became common in art. In brief, fashionably rendered plant and animal lore, so rare before, enters into the Hellenistic sculpture and painting.[87]

All this is followed by the disease of "colossalism" — by a tendency to substitute quantity for quality, the biggest and largest for the best. One can see this in virtually all forms of the Hellenistic art: in music and architecture, in literature ("the best sellers!"), in sculpture and painting. It is enough to remind the reader of the Colossus of Rhodes, about 105 feet high; of the Halicarnassus Mausoleum (or tomb of Mausolos), 140 feet high; of the large scale of the Pergamene Frieze (No. 3, Plate XI), and other sculptures; of the large buildings, and large paintings; in order to make clear this trait of the Visual art. Later on we shall see the same characteristic in the late Hellenistic and the Visual Graeco-Roman music and literature, theatrical performances, and other forms of art. Before us, in our own day, we have the "Hellenistic" Radio City, the biggest in the world! Where one cannot or does not want to provide quality, one attempts to achieve an impression by size, by the biggest quantity. And in such a culture such a means succeeds in its purpose!

Finally, it is enough to remind one of the Pergamene Frieze, the Dying Gaul, and other historical sculptures in order to bring agreement with the statement that "In these monuments we have for the first time [sic!] Historical Art, not symbolical but realistic records of contemporary events,"[88] with the specific traits of individuals, nationalities, races, and other social groups and persons. The world of symbols, abstract idealized types, is replaced by the Visual Sensate world of the empirical realities as they appear to our eyes. Mind is replaced by the organs of sense; thought by sensory images; abstract algebra by concrete arithmetic; generalization by perception; sociology and philosophy by biography and ethnography.

Such are main traits of this Visual art as they are manifest in the Hellenistic period. No doubt, during that period Idealism and even Ideationalism in art did not disappear entirely. But they became quite

---

[87] *Ibid.*, Vol. III, pp. 63–83.   [88] H. B. Walters, *The Art of the Greeks*, p. 130.

a thin stream just as Visualism had been a minor rivulet in the Greek art of the fifth and of the preceding centuries.

IV. FLUCTUATION OF THE STYLES IN ROMAN PAINTING AND SCULPTURE

The course of Roman painting and sculpture, considered from our present standpoint, can be briefly told. Its first source, the Italic art, was rather geometric cubistic (Ideational); its second source, the Etruscan art, so far as we know it, belonged to a mixed or moderate Visual ("naturalistic") style. The portrait busts, of which a sample is given (the so-called bust of a prominent orator, Arringatore, shown in No. 1 on Plate XII), show a clear inclination to the Visual style without any notable Ideational or Idealistic tendencies.

When the Greek art, unfortunately in its Hellenistic Visual style, began to influence Roman painting and sculpture, the result was, from about the end of the second century B.C., an interruption in the spontaneous development of the Roman arts, the development of eclecticism, and imitation, decay of Italic Ideational, and a softening and an extreme development of the Etruscan naturalism along the lines of the Hellenistic art. The somewhat "rugged" Etruscan Visual art was turned into a Visualism that was overripe, effeminate, exotic, idyllic, and impressionistic. This is partly exemplified by the paintings of Pompeii, and by other surviving pictures (see No. 2, Plate XII, an illustration of Hercules, from the paintings of a Pompeian house), partly by the rococo style of Arcesilaus and other painters of "boudoir mythology."[89] Since that

[89] H. B. Walters, *The Art of the Romans* (London, 1928), pp. 9–15 *et passim*. Again the main waves can be adequately grasped through a study of the evolution of Roman sculptural portraits. For this purpose the work of A. Hekler serves, with its more or less complete set of reproductions of the sculptural portraits. See also a much deeper analysis in A. H. Zadoks and J. Jitta, *Ancestral Portraiture in Rome* (Amsterdam, 1932), pp. 42 ff., 36–37 ff., 86, *et passim*.

"We may distinguish three periods in ancestral portraiture: in the first period till 200 B.C. ancestral portraiture has a *magic* significance; in the second period 200 B.C.–A.D. 20 it has an ethical one; about A.D. 20 the period of snobbery sets in."

In the first period no Visual likeness was demanded. Ancestral portraits were rather symbolic. Only from about 200 B.C. onwards "a more or less exact [Visual] likeness is demanded; about 150 B.C. the last consequence is drawn, and waxen death masks are made" [though the manner of making them, ascribed to Lysistratus, was discovered at least in the fourth century B.C.]. After that with pseudo-Idealistic and archaic imitations of the Augustan and subsequent periods, ancestral portraiture remained predominantly Visual up to the fourth century, when it became "cubistic." The authors rightly stress that the change was due to the change in mentality: to a replacement of religion by "the rationalization of religion [begun about 200 B.C.] which had grown into rationalism without religion." The

time the Roman arts became imitative, in a considerable degree, and remained so up to the end of the Visual (Sensate) culture of the Roman Empire, the change being mainly in the replacement of the models of the Greek art which were imitated. Of course, it was not a mere imitation : the Etruscan source remained and modified imitation. Nevertheless the main patterns were taken from Greece.

Throughout its history, from the first century B.C. to the fourth century A.D., Roman sculpture and painting were predominantly Visual. Their sculpture and painting remained "photographic" and large in size. But their Visualism had various shades and degrees. In the second part of the first century B.C. it imitated the sixth-century archaistic patterns (Pasiteles, Stephanus), and the Alexandrian effeminate rococo (Arcesilaus and his school). In the Augustan period it was pseudo-Idealistic Visualism, imitating the Idealistic art of Greece of the fifth century, but with a specific flavor of Visualism. It was not a real Idealism spontaneously springing from deep sources, it was rather a change of a fashion, of the pattern for imitation, as a reaction against the imitation of the Archaic Attic and of the overripe Hellenistic patterns of the preceding century. Hence, the Augustan imitative Idealistic art exemplified in the portrait statues, in the Augustan Parthenon, and in other sculptural and pictorial monuments of the time. Here are two examples of this art : an Idealized sculpture of Augustus (Nos. 3 and 4, Plate XII) and a part of the Augustan Parthenon — the *Ara pacis Augustae* (No. 5) — with its overabundance of decorations, and a lack of cohesion in the scheme.

This pseudo Idealism was short-lived, and soon after Augustus was replaced by a more extreme Visualism — impressionistic, photographic, singularistic, and illusionistic. In the Arch of Titus "each portrait is like a modern photograph, the reproduction of a passing impression." [90]

The chief post-Augustan fluctuations in the history of art may be summed up as follows.

Under the Flavian dynasty the chief aim of the artist was an imitative naturalism illusionism. Under Trajan (A.D. 98) a different tendency

---

authors state rightly that "Realism [Visualism] is mostly closely bound up with rationalism [Empiricism], never with belief in magical powers" [or mysticism, or even rationalism in the sense of medieval Scholastic rationalism].

[90] H. B. Walters, *The Art of the Romans*, p. 63. From this standpoint several of F. Wickhoff's claims, and in part of A. Riegl's contentions, about the "illusionistic" character of the Roman art of the second and the third centuries A.D. are valid. See F. Wickhoff, *Roman Art*, trans. by E. Strong (London, 1900); A. Riegl, *Die Spätromische Kunstindustrie* (Vienna, 1901). Also E. Strong, *La scultura romana da Augusto a Constantine*, 2 vols. (Firenze, 1923–1926).

PLATE XII

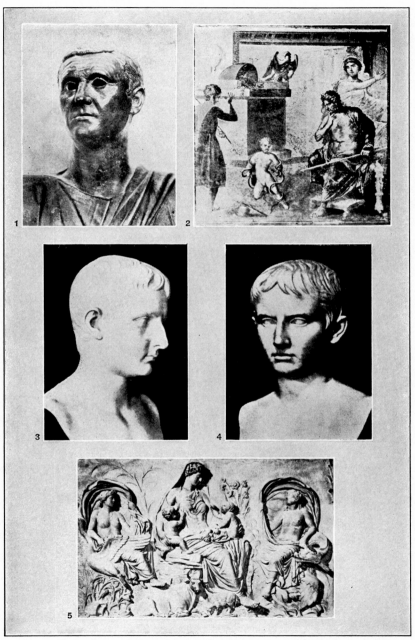

1, Portrait of Arringatore. 2, Pompeian wall painting. 3 and 4, Portrait of Augustus.
5, Ara Pacis, from the Augustan Parthenon.

is at work.   It is historicism, concentration on the rendering of the real historical scenes and personalities as they are.   Lastly, under Hadrian (A.D. 117) we have an archaistic reaction in the form of a cold academic imitation of the archaistic and idealistic art of Greece, but without its soul and mentality and with a sensuousness quite foreign to the Greek models.   Under Marcus Aurelius (A.D. 161) we are in a "rococo" age of an insipid refinement and effeminate elegance.   Under Caracalla (A.D. 212) came exaggerated passion, particularly rage, dynamism, and colossalism.   Then soon comes a "decay" of Roman art; more exactly, a decline of the Visual style and the reappearance of the Distorted Ideational style.   Their mixture, in the fourth and fifth centuries, gives a peculiar Mixed style — transitory, neither Ideational, nor Visual. With the continued decline of Visualism and the continued rise of the Christian Ideational style, we come to the Ideational art of the Middle Ages, as a new wave which replaced the preceding Visual wave of the Hellenistic and Roman Visual art.[91]   (See the illustrations of these waves in the sculpture portraits Nos. 1, 2, 3, 5, 6 on Plate XIII.)

Whatever the models imitated, the Sensate and Visual character of the Roman art during these centuries remains unquestionable.   It manifests itself in the photographic rendering of persons, even in the periods of Idealization; in everyday or historical topics; in an inclination toward huge size (e.g., Farnese Heracles, the Arch of Titus, the Column of Trajan, the Column of Marcus Aurelius, the Column of Constantine, huge palaces, etc.); in profuse overdecoration; in the spirit of sensuality, voluptuousness, eroticism, pervading even the idealized portraits (see the reproduction of portrait of Hadrian's favorite, Antinoüs, No. 4 on Plate XIII); in the cinematographic method of rendering figures; in the restless dynamism of their posture and setting; in the pathetic, emotional, and passionate rendering of feelings, in endless *amoretti* and sexuality; and in many other features which are the traits of the Visual style.

Similar, in essence, were the character and the changes in the styles of the Roman painting from the second century B.C. when the Hellenistic influence affected it.   As we pass from the "Incrustation Style" (second and first centuries to about 80 B.C.) to the "Architectural Style" (80 to 10 B.C.), then to the "Ornate Style" (10 B.C. to A.D. 50), and then to the "Intricate Style" (from A.D. 50 on), we observe an increase in the occurrence of the various signs of Visualism and Illusionism.

The Architectural Style introduced an element of Visual illusionism

[91] H. B. Walters, *The Art of the Romans*, pp. 69 ff.; Hekler, *op. cit.*, plates 137–164, 218 ff., 250 ff., 269 ff., 306–307, *et passim*.

in the form of design of the picture frame, which "produced a sort of illusory perspective," [92] in the sense that, though merely painted, it looked like a real architectural frame.   This element of illusionism and increasing complexity developed further in the Ornate Style with its overabundance of decoration and further growth of the illusionistic technique.   The Intricate style pushed all this still further, in technique as well as in content.   *Genre*, everyday events, ordinary persons — barbers, fishermen, hunters, cripples, courtesans, urchins, etc. — "historicism," and especially eroticism, sensuality, Cupid, Bacchus, dancing girls, Psyche, *amoretti*, were so much developed that the art of that painting was often styled "a school of immorality."   In addition all this was presented in a dramatic, emotional, impressionistic manner.   Caricature and satire also grew especially strong.

During the subsequent times, from the end of the first to the fourth century A.D., there were various imitative waves, somewhat similar to those in sculpture, but whatever was the pattern imitated — whether the Hellenistic refined and oversweet style, pastoralism and super-annuated idyllic themes, "classical examples," archaic, chilly academism, or what not — the dominant tone of all these varieties continued to be predominantly Visual, with all the traits of the Visual art, including complexity, colossalism, Epicureanism, and sensuality.   Vitruvius, Tacitus, Petronius Arbiter, Pliny, Dionysius of Halicarnassus, all stress the Visual character of the painting and unanimously complain of its complexity, overdeveloped technique, colossalism, voluptuousness, and contrast it unfavorably with the earlier painting, simpler but more original, more talented, more sound, and more beautiful.

Thus in sculpture as well as in painting — and further on we shall see also in music, literature, architecture, and drama — the Roman art (pagan) up to the second part of the fourth century remained predominantly Visual, with all the characteristics of such an art.

These, as schematized, were the main "pulsations" of the Ideational, Visual, Idealistic, and Mixed styles in the Graeco-Roman painting and sculpture.   The periods of rise, domination, and decline of each of these styles are only approximate, but that they did exist we can be sure.

[92] See particularly the quoted work of E. Jex-Blake and E. Sellers; Wickhoff's and Riegl's works, quoted; F. Chambers, *The History of Taste*, pp. 301 ff.; Pliny, *Natural History*, XXXV, 50; Dionysius of Halicarnassus, *De Isaeo;* H. B. Walters, *The Art of the Romans*, pp. 95 ff.; Deonna, *op. cit.*, Vol. III, pp. 506 ff.; E. Strong, *Roman Sculpture*, pp. 232 ff. (London, 1911).

PLATE XIII

1, Colossal bust of Titus.   2, Colossal bust of Domitian.   3, Head of the raging Caracalla.
4, Hadrian's favorite, Antinoüs.   5, Colossal bust of Constantine.   6, Colossal bust of Valentinian I.   7, Sarcophagus of the fourth century A.D.

Chapter Nine

FLUCTUATION OF THE MAIN STYLES IN THE PAINTING AND SCULPTURE OF WESTERN EUROPE
(Qualitative Outline, *Continued*)

I. Rise and Domination of Ideational Christian Art from the Sixth to the Twelfth Centuries

The "evolution" of the Graeco-Roman styles of painting and sculpture does not stop at the end of the fourth century. It continues its course in the subsequent centuries without any fundamental pause, without any disruption that is more absolute than many turns and caesuras experienced before. The art of the Middle Ages was not the end of the Graeco-Roman and the quite fresh beginning of a new art, but a continuation of the evolving Graeco-Roman art as subjected to additional new circumstances. In other forms such new conditions and elements had several times before been experienced by this art, from the twelfth century B.C. to the fifth century A.D.

Let us then resume the outline of this subsequent course of the Graeco-Roman art from the standpoint of its styles.

Even a layman, when he glances at the sculpture and painting of the time from the fifth century B.C. to the third A.D. and then at the colossal "cubistic" heads of Constantine and Valentinian, cannot help feeling that something "catastrophic" happened to the art in the fourth or the fifth century of our era. Indeed, all the artistic skill of the preceding centuries seems to have vanished; instead, we have very rough "blocks" cut apparently without any skill, very primitively, without showing any ability to render the individual traits of the persons rendered or even the anatomy of the head and other parts of the human body. It is as though we were suddenly plunged from the world of "skillful" and "mature" art with perfect technique into the world of the "primitive" art devoid of any artistry.

Such a change seems to mean nothing but a "decay," the "death" and the "end" of the Graeco-Roman art, whatever might have been the causes. And indeed, most of the historians of that art use these and similar terms for a characterization of the change we are considering. Consciously or unconsciously assuming that only the Visual art is the perfect art and only the Visual technique is the perfect artistic technique, they necessarily look at the change from the standpoint of this assumption and qualify it by the terms "decay," "degeneration," "decline," "fall," "end," and so on.

Such a description of the change is, however, utterly inadequate. Even if we omit mentioning the fact that "decay" and other similar terms imply a very subjective evaluation, based on the one-sided assumption of the superiority of only one real style — the Visual, we cannot neglect the fact that there is no ground to think that in the third or fourth century A.D. the course of the Graeco-Roman art was suddenly ended, or that the change took place there suddenly, without any previous preparation, or that it was really a decline of artistry in general, instead of being a decline of the Visual style only and its replacement by the entirely different Ideational style.[1]

As a matter of fact, the caesura in the course of the Graeco-Roman art in the fourth or the fifth century was hardly greater than several caesuras and turns in the preceding centuries. Moreover, the change did not spring out suddenly in the fourth or the fifth or the sixth century. It had appeared long before : at the very beginning of our era, in the form of the early Christian art, an art which was purely Ideational and quite different from the dominant pagan art of the first, the second, and the third centuries A.D. During these centuries it was the minor rivulet which, however, was steadily growing and which about the fourth or the fifth century began to become dominant. In other words, the change discussed was neither "decay" nor the "end" of the Graeco-Roman art, but merely one of its great transformations, that is, a decline of the Visual and a rise of the Ideational form of art — a process which seems also to have occurred in the passage from the overripe Mycenaean to the Archaic Greek art in the period from the ninth to the sixth centuries B.C. After the sixth century B.C. the Visual style began to ascend and dominated up to the third century A. D. ; now again it was sinking, and the Ideational style taking the upper hand. We are at the threshold of one of the great shifts in art from the dominant Visual form to the Ideational style which will be dominant throughout the Middle Ages. Such is the real nature of this change. Now let us glance at it a little more attentively.

---

[1] Concerning the Roman art of this period, besides the works of Wickhoff, Riegl, Walters, Zadock-Jitta, see G. Kaschnitz-Weinberg, "*Du réalism magique de la république romaine à l'art Constantin le Grand,*" in *Formes,* Vol. VIII, October, 1930.

The emergence of Christianity at the beginning of the first century meant, as we shall see, the beginning of a great transformation of the Sensate Graeco-Roman culture into the subsequent Ideational culture of the Middle Ages. Christianity was an Ideational cultural stream from its very emergence. Hence it necessarily gave rise to an extreme form of the Ideational art, as any such culture must if it is truly integrated. And, indeed, the earliest Christian art, that of the Catacombs,[2] was practically pure Ideational art : symbolic and transcendental in form as well as in content. Symbols of a dove, an olive branch, an anchor, a fish, the cross, a Good Shepherd, and a few others comprised its subjects. They meant not a fish nor an anchor, but a transcendental value quite different from these Visual signs. They were just the visible signs of the invisible world. Even the scenes from the Bible or from the lives of the saints were Ideational also — "imperfect" in their Visual technique and carrying much of symbolic meaning.[3] In brief, it was "otherworldly" art as Christianity itself was based on an "otherworldly" mentality.

In spite of that it was still Graeco-Roman (plus Oriental) art, being "a marriage of the antique Greek beauty with the Christian genius," "pure, innocent, and tender," "radiating peace and serenity." [4] Appearing as a small stream in the total Graeco-Roman — Visual — art, with the growth of Christianity it grew also more and more, until in the fourth and the fifth centuries it became practically a major stream. In this process of ascending to domination the Christian art, and with it the Ideational form, perhaps, lost something of their Ideational purity while admitting an element of Visualism.

This Ideationalism continues throughout the subsequent centuries of the Middle Ages, almost up to the thirteenth century. Beginning with about the sixth century the pagan art practically disappears, being engulfed by Christian art, which from that time became the only art of high achievement during the rest of the Middle Ages.

[2] See A. M. Mironoff, *History of Christian Art* (in Russian) (Kazan, 1914), pp. 23 ff.; T. Roller, *Les catacombes de Rome*, 2 vols. (Paris, 1881) ; Monsignor J. Wilpert, *Die Malereien der Katakomben*, 2 vols. (Freiburg, 1903–1904).

[3] These scenes were but symbols for what is expressed in the prayer of St. Cyprian of Antioch : "Father, deliver his soul as you delivered Jonas from the sea-monster; the young Hebrews from the furnace," etc.

[4] E. Mâle, *L'art religieux du XIIe siècle en France* (Paris, 1922), pp. 48–50 and 368. See also L. Bréhier, *L'art chrétien* (Paris, 1918), p. 55. "The foundation of Christian art was Hellenistic style up to the fifth century A.D. and only after that there began the Graeco-Oriental influence." N. P. Kondakov, *Ikonographia Bogomateri* (St. Petersburg, 1914), Vol. I, pp. 77 ff.; E. Mâle, *Art et artistes du Moyen Âge* (Paris, 1928), pp. 2 ff. and 8 ff.

Its topics are mainly superempirical and "transcendental." Its technique is Ideational, only in a minor part Visual, and even then Idealistic rather than purely Visual. Likewise:

Its objective was neither the aesthetic enjoyment nor the sensuous pleasure obtained from a contemplation of [visually] beautiful forms, but a reinforcement in the spirit of religion, and in its hopes, dogmas, beliefs, and rules of conduct.[5]

It was not until about A.D. 1000 that any striving after [sensuous] beauty entered into the art of the Christian nations of Europe.[6]

The Ideational otherworldliness of this art manifested itself in a kind of extreme asceticism and radical "puritanism," partly consciously, partly unconsciously, opposed to any sensuous objective as well as to sensuous enjoyment of art. The history of Christianity is marked by numerous explosions against any art and any representation of religious topics in painting or sculpture. This was one form of asceticism, the form of the rejection, prohibition, and persecution of any icons and iconography and painting. Its other form was manifested in innumerable demands and measures directed against any seductive, sensuously enjoyable forms of art. As to the first, already among the early Christian and Church Fathers there were not a few who opposed any painting, any sculpture, any icon or representation in Visual form. Later on several times in Byzantium, as well as in Western Christianity, there occurred small or large movements (like that of the eighth century in Byzantium, for instance) against images. Their reasons are expressed typically by the declaration of the Synod of the Bishops in 754 in Byzantium:

The sinful art of painting is an insult to the fundamental dogma of our salvation, Jesus Christ. . . . The Ignorant painter moved by the sacrilegious motive of profit, depicts what should be believed by the heart only. . . . Christ was simultaneously God and Man.[7]

For this reason he could not be depicted. The same should be applied to the images of all the saints, prophets, apostles, St. Mary, and so on.

There was always in the Church a strong vein of asceticism which objected to all religious representations, and considered them a concession to the spirit of the world and a danger to the spiritual life.[8]

As to the second form the Church authorities did not tire of protesting and prohibiting beautiful arts as such. To quote Mr. Baldwin Brown:

[5] Mironoff, *op. cit.*, p. 14.

[6] P. Gardner, *The Principles of Christian Art* (New York, 1928), p. 161.

[7] Mironoff, *op. cit.*, p. 12.   [8] Gardner, *op. cit.*, p. 185.

There was a puritan vein in monasticism that led to protest against what was regarded as over-exuberance in the use of the element of beauty in the furnishing forth of sacred structures.   The so-called Benedictine orders took as a rule this view, and a striking illustration of its working is to be found in the attitude of the Cistercians towards stained glass [in the churches].   The magnificent display of colour and imagery in the noble French storied windows of the twelfth and thirteenth centuries, such as those at Chartres, they considered too sumptuous for the House of God, and substituted geometrical patterns in grey and yellow.   Figures sculptured on the façades of their churches they also repudiated.[9]

Some authorities, like John Ruskin and G. G. Coulton, stress this "strong puritanism of the early Christianity"[10] so much that they formulate even a kind of law that "the religious passion is nearly always vividest when the art is weakest" (Ruskin)[11] and vice versa : arts blossom mainly in an age of relative unreligiousness.   Such a law probably goes too far and assumes that only the Visual form of art is real art; nevertheless it is true that the medieval art was guarded by the Church from an infiltration into it of the elements of sensuous beauty.   St. Jerome, St. Ambrose, St. Bernard, St. Anthony, St. Francis, St. Thomas Aquinas, the Cistercians, the Cluniacs, and many other leaders of Christianity as well as the Christian orders and institutions, did not weary of protesting, warning, prohibiting any art or any element in it that was for sensuous enjoyment.   They indefatigably cleansed it of such elements.   Bishop Bardock of London prohibits an artistic crucifix as heretical.   "The Cistercians vowed to remove from their lowly chapels everything which may flatter curious eyes and charm weak souls.   They banished painting and carving as vain things."[12]

Such an asceticism is a clear evidence of the Ideational character of that art.

Its Ideationalism is shown no less clearly by its *symbolic* character. Even more, it is shown by symbolism of a superempirical and transcendental nature.[13]   By very definition the Ideational art is that in which

---

[9] Hastings, *Encyclopedia of Religion and Ethics*, Vol. I, p. 850.

[10] See G. G. Coulton, *Art and the Reformation* (Oxford, 1928), p. 322.

[11] J. Ruskin, *The Queen of the Air* (New York, 1893) and Coulton, *op. cit.*, pp. 327–328.

[12] G. G. Coulton, *op. cit.*, pp. 329 ff. and 335.   See also P. Gardner, *op. cit.*, pp. 192–193; F. Chambers, *History of Taste* (New York, 1932), p. 111.   See the bibliography in the Appendix to Chapters Nine and Ten.

[13] As is shown elsewhere in this work there are symbolisms of different kinds and of different degrees of Ideationality.   Some symbolisms or "allegories" are not Ideational at all. On the other hand, the superempirical or transcendental symbolism almost always is highly Ideational.   See M. A. Ewer, *A Survey of Mystical Symbolism* (London, 1933); H. Silberer,

the visible signs are mere symbols of the invisible world. And this is exactly what we have in the Christian or in the central medieval art.

Medieval painting and sculpture are virtually iconography. An icon is not the same as a picture. After the thirteenth century the difference tended to decrease and the icon was in a sense swallowed by the picture. But before that time the picture was in a sense absorbed by the icon. The difference between them is, however, profound, and it is exactly the same as that between the Ideational and the Visual painting and sculpture. As one of the investigators of the Russian iconography puts it :

The objective of a picture is always in the picture itself ; it is simultaneously the means and the end of the artist. But the icon . . . is always a mere means, a mere way towards a purpose which lies beyond not only the art of painting, but beyond the whole visual [and sensory] world. The objective of an icon is always transcendental, otherworldly, beyond the earthly [sensory] reality. . . . It is a mere means for the soaring of the human soul and thought from the visible to the invisible world. . . .[14]

This means that the icon is a *symbol* of the transsensory world and values. Hence any real iconographic painting and sculpture are necessarily symbolic, that is, Ideational. Since this deduction is self-evident, the transcendentally symbolic character — so many times stressed — of the medieval art (and mentality) becomes comprehensible at once, and is seen to be inevitable if the contention that it was predominantly Ideational is true.

It is unnecessary for me to endeavor to prove that the medieval painting, sculpture, and other arts, as well as their whole mentality (as we shall see) were symbolic and therefore Ideational. Almost any competent investigator of the medieval art knows its symbolic character. As we have mentioned, the early Christian art was symbolic. Medieval architecture — Gothic and pre-Gothic — is symbolic, in the whole as well as in the details. In the thirteenth century Guillaume Durand, bishop of Mende in France, explained the symbolic meaning of every important detail of that architecture. And the same is still more true of the medieval sculpture and painting. As we shall see in the next chapter, they

---

Problems of Mysticism and Its Symbolism (New York, 1917) ; F. R. Webber, *Church Symbolism* (Cleveland, 1927).

[14] V. A. Nikolsky, *History of Russian Art* (in Russian) (Moscow, 1923), pp. 46–49. See also E. N. Troubetzkoy, *Two Worlds in the Ancient Russian Iconography* (in Russian) (Moscow, 1916), pp. 3–4 *et passim;* N. Pounin, *Russian Icon* (in Russian) (Leningrad, 1914) ; A. K. Coomaraswamy, *The Transformation of Nature in Art*, chap. i *et passim;* V. A. Riazanovsky, *About a Study of the Ancient Russian Iconography* (in Russian) (Harbin, 1934) ; A. N. Didron, *Christian Iconography*, 2 vols. (London, 1851–91).

are 95 to 100 per cent transcendentally symbolic in topic, as well as in form of rendering.[15] As is shown elsewhere, the other forms of art and the whole mentality of the Middle Ages were transcendentally symbolic or Ideational.[16] Finally, the art theories and the entire aesthetic mentality of the Middle Ages were again transcendentally symbolic. Thus, according to St. Thomas and the great Scholastics:

Beauty is essentially an object of *intelligence*, for what *knows* in the full meaning of the world is the mind, which alone is open to the infinity of being. The natural site of beauty is the intelligible world: thence it descends. . . . [It is] *splendor formae* . . . for *form*, that is to say the principle determining the peculiar perfection of everything which is, constituting and completing the things in their essence and their qualities, the *ontological secret, so to speak, of their innermost being, their spiritual essence*, their operative mystery, is above all the peculiar *principle of intelligibility*, the peculiar clarity of every thing.[17]

Hence it is perfectly Ideational, and thus inseparable from verity as well as from goodness. "The beautiful is the same thing as the good, differing only conceptually," says St. Thomas.[18] Finally its essence is the transcendental incarnated, emanating from God who is "beautiful by Himself, and in Himself, absolutely beautiful." Therefore *"quicumque appetit bonum, appetit ex hoc ipso pulchrum."* [19]

In brief, the art theories as well as the aesthetic mentality of the Middle Ages were Ideational par excellence.[20] When this central characteristic

---

[15] See the works of E. Mâle, Bréhier, Mironoff, Coulton (chaps. xiii and xiv), Kondakoff; André Michel, *Histoire de l'art* (Paris, 1904–1929), Vols. I and II; L. Gillet, in *Histoire du paysage en France* (Paris, 1908), pp. 35–41, and practically any serious investigation into the medieval art.

[16] See the chapters on literature, music, architecture, science, philosophy, and culture mentality in Volumes One and Two. See particularly H. O. Taylor, *The Mediaeval Mind* (London, 1927), Vol. II, chaps. xxviii and xxix; M. de Wulf, *Philosophy and Civilization in the Middle Ages* (Princeton, 1922); Lethaby, *Medieval Art* (London, 1904); J. Huizinga, *The Waning of the Middle Ages* (London, 1927), chaps. xii, xv, xxi, *et passim;* Maritain, *Art and Scholasticism* (New York, 1930).

[17] Maritain, *op. cit.*, pp. 23 ff.

[18] *Summa Theologica*, I–ii, q. 27, a. 1, ad. 3; and I, q. 5, a. 4, ad. 1. See the remarks on the Scholastic theory of the beautiful in Maritain's work, particularly chap. v, and notes 56 and 63b.

[19] Maritain, *op. cit.*, p. 31.

[20] W. J. Courthope, *A History of English Poetry* (New York, 1895), Vol. I, pp. 226 ff. and chap. ix; M. Denis, "*Le symbolisme et l'art religieux moderne*" in his *Nouvelles théories* (Paris, 1922). See also A. Coomaraswamy, *op. cit.*, and Chapter Thirteen, on criticism, in this volume. See also the works of F. Chambers.

"An appreciation of art [in the Middle Ages] was rather religious than artistic. . . . One of the fundamental traits of mind of the declining Middle Ages is the [increasing] predominance of the sense of sight [*i.e.*, Visualism] . . . connected with the atrophy of thought."

of the medieval art is grasped, virtually all its essential traits become comprehensible.

The characteristics of the Ideational art which we expect logically do in fact occur in it. No prosaic or profane topics are rendered in it. It is an art which instructs in, propagates, testifies to the victorious religion — a visible symbol for the invisible values. No sensatism is in it; nothing appears for a merely sensate enjoyment. It is limited to the religious symbols and the images of Christ, the Madonna, and the saints, and to Biblical scenes. In these scenes all the figures appear abstract and entirely idealized. Christ is depicted as the conqueror of evil, ruler of the world, Pantocrator glorious and majestic on his throne. Even when pictures depict some dolorous scene, like the Crucifixion, before you is shown not a suppressed criminal, not a humiliated man, suffering and miserable, but a king, in a royal crown, in royal robes, with a special plank on the cross under his feet, not suffering, free from mortal defects, with the letters signifying that this is the God. This art "saw in the Gospel its luminous, but not dolorous aspect." [21]

When on the sarcophagi they represent the Passions, they do not show either humiliation or suffering. The crown of thorns . . . over Jesus resembles a triumphal crown; before the judges Christ has an attitude of a hero or of a Stoic sage.

In other pictures he is depicted as a "young man, almost adolescent . . . with a charm of youth, an incarnation of beauty, eloquence, tenderness." In others (in the Syrian-Egyptian art) he becomes majestic, virile, with superhuman grandeur.[22]

Whatever is, however, the form given to Christ, one thing is clear, namely, the pictures deal with God, represent symbolically God, and in this sense are entirely Ideational, being mere symbols of the super-empirical values. The same is to be said of the Madonna, of the God-father, of the angels, and of other figures. The Madonna who even before the fifth century was depicted Ideationally Idealistically, in the form of a deaconess Oranta "with the usual traits of gentle simplicity and inner purity," now becomes Ideationalized and standardized in a different form: in the form of "a type somewhat austere and sublime

---

Huizinga, *op. cit.*, pp. 261–262 and 278. See also De Wulf, *Études historiques sur l'esthétique de St. Thomas d'Aquin* (Löwen, 1896). The medieval spirit of the art theories is well exemplified in the *Theophili, qui et Rugerus Libri III de diversio artibus*, trans. by R. Hendrie (London, 1847).

[21] Mâle, *L'art religieux du XIIe siècle en France*, pp. 50 ff.; L. Bréhier, *op. cit.*, pp. 76 ff. and chaps. iii–iv; A. Michel, *op. cit.*, Vol. I.

[22] Mâle, *L'art religieux*, pp. 50–51.

and at the same time simple and loving as a symbol of sympathy toward suffering human beings," with additional traits of a protectress of the true religion and, sometimes, of a Byzantine — abstract — woman figure who covers her face — the gesture of a woman who quits the world for the cloister.[23] It is "a purely spiritual concept," "the Virgin presaged by Isaiah," "divinity itself." [24]

A. *Byzantine Art.* This concerns not only Western art but that of Byzantium, which was a peculiar synthesis of the Graeco-Roman and Syrian-Egyptian styles. Here the Ideationalization of the abstract types of the triumphant Christ, the Madonna, the saints, became in a way still more pronounced and led to the marvelous creation of the image of God as a celestial emperor, the *Pantocrator;* to a similar standardized image of the Madonna — Odigitria — somewhat ascetic, free from any mortal traits, a symbolic image of the all-powerful and all-sublime Madonna, reminiscent now of the blonde Athena (*flava*), now of Pallas (*casta Pallas*), courageous and vigorous, the most wise (*doctissima domina*), stern and austere (*cruda virago*), pure and stainless (*innupta, intacta*), the protectress of mortals (*patrona*). All real mortal traits vanished from such a conceptual image.[25]

The same is to be said of the whole Byzantine art of this period.[26] Aside from its character, the very fact of a hieratic standardization of its Ideational images in the centuries after the sixth, and the prohibition of deviation from these standards, tells of its sacrosanct Ideational nature. "In that period the iconographic types were accepted as an unchangeable canon, and any deviation from them as well as a creation of any new types whatever almost entirely ceased." The types became hieratic, ideational symbols. They represented the invisible world in an Ideational Idealistic pattern. Its characteristics are:

iconographic idealisation of the attitudes; general kindness of the expressions of the visages; painting even the old faces rosy; exaggerated gracefulness of the body; forceful energy of movement and gesture, especially that of the foot stepping aside . . . poetically disheveled chevelure; "prophetic" or "Old Testament" lips; locks of small beards; an inspirationally directed look and a pupil turned profoundly to the corner of the eye.[27]

[23] Kondakov, *op. cit.*, Vol. I, pp. 369 ff.; Vol. II, p. 17.

[24] A. Venturi, *La Madonna* (Milano, 1900), pp. 2–6. See also J. Clément, *La représentation de la Madonna à travers les âges* (Paris, 1908).

[25] Kondakov, *op. cit.*, Vol. II, pp. 18, 152, *et passim.*

[26] See Bréhier, *op. cit.*, chaps. v–vi; Mâle, *Art et artistes du Moyen Âge*, pp. 9 ff.; C. Diehl, *Manuel d'art Byzantin* (Paris, 1926), *passim.*

[27] Kondakov, *op. cit.*, Vol. II, pp. 12–13. Also the plaits of the dress and the whole posture of Christ in even Crucifixion pictures is purely Ideational Idealistic. See many reproduc-

It was a great Ideational Idealization in accordance with the religious-aesthetic ideal of the period.

If we take the Byzantine art for the later period, it is enough to say for our purposes that the Ideational Idealistic style was dominant in it up to the twelfth and even thirteenth century, in spite of several important changes in that art in other respects. As the Visual elements were increasing, after the ninth century, the eleventh and, in part, twelfth in the history of the Byzantine art gave this rare and marvelous harmonious synthesis of the Ideational and Visual elements, the Byzantine *Idealistic* art, akin to the Greek idealistic art of the fifth century and the European of the thirteenth century.[28]

But after the end of the thirteenth century the Visual tide began to mount and the Byzantine art of the fourteenth and sixteenth centuries appears already Visual in its dominant aspect. Not without a reason was this change styled "the Byzantine Renaissance." Visualism, liveliness, emotionalism, dynamism, individualism; picturesqueness, daily *genre*, accurate Visual rendering draw art from the unearthly heights down to the earthly life. Secularization and other sensuous traits appeared in it. "A new art, lively and sincere, full of movement, expressiveness, picturesqueness, enamoured of exact and realistic observation" set in. "The artists now love to reproduce landscapes, to paint the individual persons, sometimes even rude and common." "This new art now looks for emotion, sentimentality, the pathetic, and for a soft and delicate sentiment of elegancy and gracefulness."[29]   /

Thus in the course of the Byzantine art (painting and sculpture) we have a domination of the Ideational style (with minor waves) up to about the twelfth century: in the thirteenth century Ideationalism begins to decline and Visualism to ascend, giving as a result the balanced Idealistic art of the thirteenth and partly of the fourteenth centuries. In the fourteenth century Visualism continues to grow and becomes even slightly dominant at its end and especially in the fifteenth and sixteenth centuries. As we shall see, these great fluctuations in the course of the Byzantine art were almost parallel with those of the Western art. The end of the Byzantine Empire and of its culture broke the process at that point without its continuation into a probable further growth of Visualism, as happened also in the life history of Western art.

---

tions in C. Diehl, *op. cit.*, Vol. II. Though Diehl stresses the realistic tendency of this art, his "realism" does not mean Visualism, Vol. II, pp. 502–504.

[28] C. Diehl, *op. cit.*, Vols. I and II, summary; Vol. II, pp. 904–905.

[29] *Ibid.*, Vol. II, pp. 739 ff., 857–859, 862–863.

Such is the bare sketch of the main fluctuations in the history of the Byzantine art, made mainly upon the basis of the qualitative studies of specialists. We can check the validity of this outline, and at the same time learn more accurately and substantially many details of these fluctuations, through the mass study of a sufficiently large sample of the ancient and the medieval Christian art (painting and sculpture), including both the Eastern (especially the Byzantine) and the Western taken together. This I shall do a little later. Meanwhile it will be proper, before such a quantitative study, to give a similar outline of the fluctuation of styles in the Western Christian art.

B. *Western Art.* For the period from about the sixth to the thirteenth century the Christian art was the only major, logically integrated art. The division of high art into the religious and the secular was practically nonexistent at that period. The course of this Western Christian art was in essentials similar to that of the Byzantine art. Throughout this period it remained essentially Ideational with an Idealistic treatment of the empirical-visual phenomena. It is true that from about the ninth century (the Carlovingian Renaissance) the elements of Visualism began to filter into that art. Nevertheless, up to the end of the twelfth century Ideationalism was the dominant characteristic of that art. It was somewhat different from the Ideationalism of the Byzantine art for that period: it was, so to speak, a more Greek than Oriental (Egyptian-Syrian) Ideationalism; less ascetic and less stern than the Ideationalism of the Byzantine art. Here Christ is more often depicted as a beautiful young Orpheus, or good youthful shepherd, than as a bearded Jewish prophet. Likewise, the figures and postures and expressions of the Madonna, of the saints, of the prophets and sages, were less stern and hieratic than in the Byzantine art. Possibly even the program and objectives of the Western Christian art were broader, embracing not only a theological and mystical education in how to reach the other world through a contemplation of the sensible figures and symbols, but also a catechistical and encyclopedic instruction in the affairs of this world within the limits of the medieval *trivium* and *quadrivium*.[30] This different shading does not, however, prevent its being essentially and dominantly Ideational and partly Ideational Idealistic.

As a detail this art —

---

[30] See the details in E. Mâle's *L'art religieux du XIIe siècle en France*, chaps. x and iii–iv. Other literature will be indicated later. See also the works indicated in the Appendix to this chapter, particularly those of O. Dalton, R. Garrucci, G. Dehio, and R. Muther.

bears upon itself the imprint of the monastic genius. . . .   The monk seems to have lived in a world of half-dreams.   For him there seems to have existed no boundary between the visible and invisible worlds.   He seems to have been no more surprised in being able to converse with the dead than with the living.[31]

The monks as a matter of normal occurrence saw the dead, conversed with angels, or demons and other phantoms.

Being almost entirely religious, it is concerned mainly with religious, transcendental, and conceptual symbols, and when it deals with "worldly" scenes, animals, and persons, it represents them in an Ideational Idealistic form.   Its method is the same whether it treats the figures of music, geometry, philosophy; or scenes of the Annunciation, of the Last Judgment, of the Visitation, of the Crucifixion; or plants and symbolic animals like Tritons, centaurs, griffons; not to mention the figures of Christ and the saints and the virtues.   If after the eleventh century the figures of the Vices and devils are not particularly attractive, the reason is that the negative values had of necessity to be negatively idealized, that is, exaggerated in their negative traits.[32]   But the tide of Sensate Visualism was rising.

Later on I shall present detailed data as to the manifestation of this rise of Visualism.   For the present it is enough to mention a few of its symptoms.   Representation of animal and plant lore becomes more pronounced in the art of the twelfth century, as compared with that of the preceding period.[33]   Half-moral historical scenes and figures of a secular character, like the images of Alexander the Great, of Roland, of the Arthurian cycle and the Knights of the Round Table, of the minstrels and troubadours, and so on, occur more and more often.[34]   The images of women more often appear now.[35]   And the technique begins to change, though slightly and almost imperceptibly, nevertheless definitely in the direction of Visualism.

II. The Thirteenth-century Idealistic Art

This rising tide of Visualism and ebb of Ideationalism resulted, in the thirteenth and partly in the fourteenth century, in one of those rare,

---

[31] *Ibid.*, pp. 365 ff.

[32] Even the images of Satan, up to the twelfth century (beginning with the sixth when such an image first appeared) "do not resemble at all the monster of the twelfth century.   Satan is depicted as a fallen angel, a son of God, who turned against Him, but who could not efface entirely his divine imprint. . . .   Images of demons, sufficiently rare in the Byzantine art, are never hideous."   Only at the end of the eleventh century and in the art of the twelfth the hideous and terrible image of Satan appears.   See *ibid.*, pp. 369–371.

[33] *Ibid.*, chap. ix.   [34] *Ibid.*, chap. vii.   [35] *Ibid.*, chaps. viii and ix.

but recurrent sublime blends of both styles in the form of the supreme Idealistic art of these centuries, an art in all its essential traits similar to the great Idealistic art of Greece of the fifth and, in part, of the fourth centuries B.C. It should be noted here that such an Idealistic art appeared again when the dominant Ideational style was declining and the moderate Visualism was rising. But not when Visualism was falling and Ideationalism rising. *The periods of a declining Visualism and of an ascending Ideationalism, like the transition from the Mycenaean art to the Archaic Greek art, or from the overripe Hellenistic Roman art to the Christian art of the fourth and the fifth centuries A.D., or perhaps like the change in the present period in which we live (as we shall see), seem to give not this marvelous Idealistic art but the incongruous results of a search for something different from overripe Visualism: cubism, futurism, and other Mixed "isms" which are neither the fish of Ideationalism nor the flesh of Visualism; nor are they a harmonious blend of both styles. They are just a revolt against, and a striving for, something different from the infatuated Visualism; but this search yields hardly any organic synthesis at all. Such periods seem to produce "modernistic incongruities," important as symptoms but far from representing the realization of the hopes of the Visual-Sensuous man who seeks to find the "bluebird" or a new and grand Art.*

Only the Ideational man and the Ideational culture which begin to pay more and more attention to the empirico-sensory world but which by one half, at least, are still in the supersensate world of Ideationalism, seem to be able to produce the great Idealistic art, as a blend of both styles.[36] Such exactly was the situation in the thirteenth century in Western culture generally, and especially in its art. As in Greece of the fifth century B.C., here again we are in an age of faith, all-embracing, understanding, and justifying all, including this world. It still does not see the central value in this world and in the earthly life. It sees this in the supersensory world; but the divine plan of this supersensory world somehow now includes also this earthly world and gives to it its meaning, blessing, and justification. Hence the art of the thirteenth century included (like the *Speculum majus* of Vincent of Beauvais): (1) the mirror of nature (humblest animals and plants), (2) the mirror of science (seven Muses of the *trivium* and the *quadrivium*, plus the eighth of philosophy), (3) the mirror of the virtues and of religion. This was

[36] "In the movement of religious human thought, but desirous to reconcile faith with reason . . . in this harmonious concurrence of all living forces . . . the art of the 13th century found such conditions which occur only in the greatest epochs of its history." André Michel, *op. cit.*, Vol. II, 2e partie, p. 991.

the chief division.   For the main place in art was given naturally (naturally in an Idealistic culture) to the representation of the providentially
controlled march of humanity, in which "it sees only Christ and looks
only for Christ in it." [37]

Never has art summed up the spirit of the time so magnificently. . . .   We
are in a century of certitude; therefore the art is but serenity.   All the violent
sentiments are discarded: what shines on the faces of the statues is not suffering, neither is it anxiety, nor worry about the infinite, but a profound peace,
unperturbable repose, silent love.   Death itself is conceived as a supreme
beauty, as a mere appearance.   Stretched out upon their tombs, the dead are
represented with a charm of youth, and, instead of closing their eyes, they
have them open to a light which the living do not see as yet.[38]

Since the dead and death itself were idealized in that art,[39] it goes
without saying that all the other phenomena were presented in the same
spirit of idealized serenity, calm, and charm, as the results of the unshakable faith and inner certitude of the believing soul.   If previously the
Virtues were represented as fighting the Vices, now "by a much more
profound comprehension of the essence of Virtue the Artists represent

[37] Mâle, *Art et artistes*, p. 16.   For this century see particularly the classical work of Mâle,
L'art religieux du XIIIe siècle en France; also L. Hourticq, *Art in France*, chap. iii.

[38] Mâle, *Art et artistes*, pp. 18–19.

[39] It is to be noted here again that if one should take the changes in style in such a limited
field as *ancestral portraiture*, in the specific form of tomb effigies, all the above waves would
clearly be noticed.   Zadoks and Jitta admirably outline the change in their excellent work.
They rightly stress the fact that a trend toward a sensory Visualism and the increasing use
of the death masks are "two coördinated consequences of one and the same mentality. . . .
This mentality will bring about as well portraits of extreme realism [Visualism in my sense;
so-called *verism*] as the practice of making moulds on the actual features" of the living or the
deceased person.   In Rome such molds came into practice (masks from the deceased person)
with the growth of Visualism as outlined before and as analyzed in detail in the work of
Zadoks and Jitta.   In Europe tomb effigies appeared about A.D. 1200.   "These statues first
represented the deceased not as he actually appeared after death but as he hoped and trusted
to be on the day of Judgment. . . .   This same sublime faith is apparent in the pure and
happy expression of all the equally youthful and equally beautiful faces which have lost
every trace of individuality.   [Ideationalism Idealism.]   Toward the end of the thirteenth
century . . . the period of transcendental and mystic faith has passed.   The eyes of the
faithful were lowered from Heaven to earth and saw now reality instead of vision.   Interest
turned from the heavenly Future to the worldly Present.   Not how the dead would perhaps
appear one day but how they had actually been in life was considered important.   More or
less [visual] likeness was now wanted. . . .   As the last consequence of this demand for
exact likeness the death mask, taken from the actual features, made its appearance," after
the thirteenth century, as a final step toward Visualism.   Hence all these skeletons, corpse-
like statues, "photographic mask-effigies" of the deceased, and so on.   We are in quite a
different atmosphere compared with that before and during the thirteenth century.   See
A. N. Zadoks and J. Jitta, *Ancestral Portraiture in Rome*, pp. 87 ff. and 92 ff.   See there
the factual details for Rome as well as for all of Europe.

them in a state of repose; they show us that their presence in the soul gives to it imperturbable stillness and peace." [40]

All the other earmarks of the Idealistic art are clearly shown by the art of the thirteenth century, this apex of the Christian European art.   Here are a few of its characteristics — already familiar to us.

(1) It was not an art for art's sake, but the "Bible in the stone."   Art was a means for the expression of the sublime religious conscience of the people.

The grand Gothic cathedrals of the thirteenth century were an effort to edify the House of God on a scale more gigantic than ever done before. . . . This was the period when the Christian art of the Occident became indeed religious and approached the theological and idealistic art of Byzantium of the twelfth century.[41]

The phenomenon of these cathedrals . . . is one of the miracles of history. We can hardly understand it now; so different we are from our ancestors! We create ports and channels, we construct engines, while our ancestors thought that their most urgent need was to erect the image of heaven upon the earth. . . . Peculiar economists who spent all the resources of the time on works which could not enrich anybody!   But, perhaps, these idealists distinguished the genuine wealth from the false?   And indeed he who enters our cathedrals and feels enveloped by power, purity, and religious silence, knows that these idealists did not err and that they bequeathed to France her most precious treasure.[42]

(2) We have already seen that its figures were idealized, even the dead.   Most of its statues are remarkable from this standpoint.   Their postures, gestures, expressions, appearance, all are lighted by the sublime serenity of the religious and moral ideal.

(3) The art of the thirteenth and of the preceding centuries, like that of the fifth B.C. and before, was an expression of a collective ideal, and thus it was a collective work.   All in some way participated in it, especially in the building of the cathedrals.   "Being such a collective work the Gothic cathedral is indeed an image of the Christian conscience of the thirteenth century." [43]   "The great monastic creations are striking for their impersonal and collective character." [44]

[40] Mâle, *Art et artistes*, p. 16.   [41] Bréhier, *op. cit.*, p. 279.
[42] Mâle, *Art et artistes*, pp. 19–20.   Notre Dame de Paris cost more than 100,000,000 francs.   In many of the cathedrals, like that of Chartres, there were more than 10,000 sculptures.   See also P. Vitry, "Medieval Sculpture," in G. Crump and E. Jacob's *The Legacy of the Middle Ages* (Oxford, 1926), pp. 104 and 94–95.
[43] Bréhier, *op. cit.*, p. 277.
[44] L. Gillet, *Histoire artistique des ordres mendiants* (Paris, 1912), p. 2.

(4) Again like the art of the fifth century B.C., the art of the thirteenth century "tends to convince but not to disturb emotionally." [45]

(5) Since it was a collective work and a realization of the ideal of the collectivity, the leading artists played only the role of the *primus inter pares*. They themselves neither regarded it as their own achievement only, nor were anxious to stamp their names and to take copyrights for it. Nor did they do it for the art's sake only. They did it as their service to God, *ad gloriam Dei*, for the realization of the ideal and not at all for the sake of a sensuous beauty or for a sensate enjoyment. Though the names of some of the leaders, like Villard de Honnecourt, are known, most of the artists remained anonymous, and their mood was very different from the Visual-individualistic artist who, at least, wants to immortalize himself through his creation. The spirit and mood of these artists are the same as those which were expressed somewhat earlier by the famous Theophilus, who as the only recompense for his work and instruction asks: "Pray for me for the pity of all powerful God."

Ores pro me apud misericordiam Dei omnipotentis, qui scit me nec humane laudis amore, nec temporalis premii cupiditate . . . sed in augmentum honoris et gloriae nominis ejus multorum necessitatibus succurrisse et profectibus consuluisse. . . .

And further:

Per spiritum sapientiae cognoscis a Deo cuncta creata procedere, et sino ipso nihil esse. . . . Per spiritum consilii talentum a Deo tibi concessum non abscondis. . . . Per spiritum timoris Domini te nihil ex te posse consideras, nihil inconcessum a Deo te habere seu velle cogitas, sed credendo, confitendo, gratias agendo, quicquid nosti, vel es, aut esse potes, divinae misericordiae reputas.[46]

Such was the spirit of the artists and of all the participants in the creation of these "miracles." Moved by such a spirit one does not care for "immortality" in this world, to take the credit for the achievement, to guard jealously one's interests, to strive for "originality," and so on.

In the powerfully social structure of mediaeval civilization the artist ranked simply as artisan, and every kind of anarchical development was prohibited to his individualism. He did not work for society people and the dealers, but for the faithful commons; it was his mission to house their prayers, to instruct their minds, to rejoice their souls and their eyes. Matchless epoch, in which

[45] Bréhier, *op. cit.*, p. 279.

[46] *Theophili, qui et Rugerus, presbyteri et monachi Libri III de diversio artibus* (London, 1847); parallel English trans. by R. Hendrie, pp. li and 200–206.

an ingenuous folk was educated in beauty without even noticing it, as perfect religious ought to pray without being aware of their prayers; when doctors and painters lovingly taught the poor, and the poor enjoyed their teaching, because they were all of the same royal race, born of water and the Spirit. More beautiful things were then created and there was less self-worship. The blessed humility in which the artist was situated exalted his strength and his freedom. The Renaissance was destined to drive the artist mad and make him the most miserable of men . . . by revealing to him his own grandeur and letting loose upon him the wild beast Beauty [visual Beauty] which Faith kept enchanted and led after it obedient, with a gossamer thread for leash.[47]

Similar was the situation in most of the similar periods of the domination of Idealism.

(6) The technique of art of the period was already so greatly developed that not without reason most of the investigators compare it and its creations with the technique of Phidias and of other great Greek masters of the fifth century. How such a miraculous development of the technique itself was possible does not concern us here. But the fact of such a miraculous ripening in a relatively short time is beyond doubt. This perfect Visual technique given into the hands of faithful and imperturbably idealistic souls permitted the miracle of the art of the thirteenth century, just as was the case previously with the Greek art of the fifth century.

This was the golden age of medieval sculpture, its classic period, because its development is serene and its mastery of its material complete, while it seems to shun all movement and over-expression. . . . [It shows] simplicity, rhythm, infinite amount of research, and an extraordinary precocity. . . . All the intricacies, all the awkwardness of the earlier art have gone; only a monumental grandeur remains. [In human scenes] a homeliness and justness of inspiration is combined with an austerity, terse and synthetic, which exclude all anecdote and mere picturesqueness.[48]

(7) As in the Greek classical art, there is calm and quiet and a lack of dynamism (the Platonic ideas do not change); there is no "show" and nothing *malerisch;* there is no patheticism, no sentimentality, no emotionalism; and there is no disorder. From the expressions of the visages to

[47] Maritain, *op. cit.*, pp. 21–22. See also the analysis of the evolution of the meanings of the word artist, artisan, and art, and the freedom of art and of the artist according to the theories and conditions of the Middle Ages, *passim*, and notes 42, 43, and 45.

[48] Paul Vitry, *op. cit.*, pp. 103–105. See besides the excellent (though not without minor exaggerations) parallel drawn between the Greek art of the fifth century B.C. and the art of the thirteenth century A.D. in Deonna's *L'archéologie*, Vol. III, chap. vi (note also the many reproductions). See also, Hourticq, *op. cit.*, chap. iii; A. Michel, *op. cit.*, Vols. I and II.

the chevelure or to the plaits of the drapery, everything is harmonious and perfect, but free from the sweet and sentimental orderliness or "perfection" of a perfumed doll.[49]   Likewise the art of the preceding centuries, as well as of the thirteenth century, had a "contemptuous attitude towards [Sensate] virtuosity, was free from dilettantism, and disdainful of art for the sake of art." [50]

Such was this golden age of the idealistic art of Christian Europe.

III. Rise of Visualism from the Fourteenth to the Sixteenth Centuries

The tide of Visualism continued, however, to rise and the "optimum" point of the marvelous blending of the two opposite styles was soon passed.   Its duration was short (as was the case with the Greek Idealistic art).   Already at the end of the thirteenth century the "optimum" point was left behind, and the art of the fourteenth and fifteenth centuries already represents the period of transition from a waning Idealism toward a full-blooded Visualism.   "The 'fact' is that after the climax of what is styled 'idealism' there followed a birth of 'realism.'" [51]

A new ideal appeared, more graceful, finer, more sharply cut; the skill of the carver increased, but his interest in style, in dignity, in adaptation of his work to buildings diminished.   A single statue, or statuette, an altar reredos, took the place of the great work of yore, just as painted panels replaced huge decorative frescoes. . . .   Striving after violent feeling, passion, suffering [was the mark of the time]. . . .   Instead of Christ, lofty and serene, the Man of Sorrows is represented: cheeks were hollowed . . . eyes . . . were distorted with feeling. . . .   It was the beginning of "naturalism!"

[Portraiture] the art hitherto unknown [began to develop].   A sense of the picturesque develops.

By the end of the fourteenth century the saints lose their simple attributes and begin to be surrounded with a multitude of picturesque accessories borrowed from everyday life.

The Virgin Mother is now less lofty but more tender than of old. . . . [Often now she is] charming . . . a little stereotyped, sometimes slipping into the insipid elegance of merely pious imagery. . . .   Taste deteriorated and the noble lady of the thirteenth century became a simple housewife in everyday clothes by the end of the fourteenth, or a peasant woman dandling or suckling her quite ordinary babe. . . .   [She is now] lightly veiled, the outline of the hip strongly marked.[52]

[49] See particularly E. Mâle's and W. Deonna's works.
[50] L. Gillet, *Histoire artistique des ordres mendiants*, pp. 2 ff.
[51] Michel, *op. cit.*, Vol. II, p. 992.
[52] Vitry, *op. cit.*, pp. 110–114.

The Virgin partook more of the nature of common humanity. . . . She was shown now smiling at the gambols of her infant. . . . Nudity began to appear more often than before. The folds and plaits became more realistic and complicated. . . . Statuary gradually turned into portraiture. . . . Expressive violence marks the close of the Medieval sculpture.[53]

The visual tendency grew in the fourteenth and the fifteenth centuries, but "this attractive art lacked vigour." [54]

Its topics began to become more and more secular and, of the secular, more and more everyday and common. They become increasingly "fleshly." The drapery of the thirteenth century was architectural; now it becomes complicated, plaited, picturesque, even burlesque, imitating real drapery in its numerous details and losing more and more in unity and sobriety of texture. Agitation, dynamism, passionateness, emotionalism, particularly pathetic and macabre moods, combined with voluptuousness, all this begins to permeate the figures, the scenes, the expressions, the postures, the clothing as reproduced in painting and sculpture.

If previously mortals were idealized like gods, now the gods are depicted as mortals,[55] with the exception of the few powerful mortals who are rendered godlike out of flattery. Individualism of artists, Epicureanism, voluptuousness, sensuality, all are rising. Virtually all the traits of the transitional period from Idealism to Visualism, which we saw in the Greek art of the fourth century B.C., are repeated, in a new setting and under different conditions.[56]

In order that the picture may be still clearer, a few additional quotations will not be out of place.

"About 1380 the old iconography is profoundly transformed" and "the end of the Middle Ages is an epoch of dissolution."

[53] Hourticq, *op. cit.*, pp. 104–109.

[54] *Ibid.*, pp. 117 ff. and 124. See also many of the details in the work of E. Mâle, and of A. Michel, Vol. II.

[55] Especially is this conspicuous in the types of the Madonna, Christ, and many of the saints. If the Madonnas of Nicola Pisano and Giotto are still half-Gothic, the Madonnas of almost all the subsequent masters become more and more human, mortal, until they are in effect pretty girls, or seductive ladies, or half-coarse women, or sexually suggestive feminine figures of the Renaissance where little, if any, piety, blessedness, sublimity, purity, or divinity is present. They were, as Savonarola said, "Florentine belles under the traits of the Virgin and the saints in the clothes of courtesans." The same is to be said of other religious figures not to mention those of the mortals which began to become more and more common. See A. Venturi's and J. Clement's monographs on the Madonna; Hourticq, *op. cit.*, p. 124; Michel, *op. cit.*, Vol. II, pp. 990 ff. and Vol. III, pp. 515 ff. and 590 ff.

[56] For this parallelism see W. Deonna, *op. cit.*, Vol. III, chap. vii, and the many reproductions there.

The spirit as well as the style is changed.   The spirit of medieval art was "the faith which does not argue but chants."   "Such an art could not be inspired by doubt."   When doubt and intellectualism and reason came, such an art could not survive.   Moreover:

> The principle of the Medieval art was in complete opposition to that of the Renaissance.   The former is of profound humility: the veritable spirit of Christianity itself.   The principle of the second is pride: from now on man is self-sufficient and aspires to be God.   The highest expression of that art is the naked human body [carefully studied and correctly rendered].[57]

Or as the same author says:

> The thirteenth century art was addressed to intelligence; the art of the fourteenth and the fifteenth speaks of sensitiveness. . . . Dolour is the great inspirer of this age. . . . The Passion became its ordinary theme.
> The Idealism of the thirteenth century was succeeded by researches in detailed exactness and individual resemblance which assured the triumph of realism.[58]

In sculpture, the poses, expressions, traits, etc., became more individual, free, and picturesque.   The positive as well as the negative phenomena — e.g., ugliness, senility, suffering, and so on (Plate XIV) — began to be reproduced, with an increasing preference for the negative.

> The result of this innovation was a loss of beautiful unity by the religious art. . . .   The collective work of the Christian people was replaced by that of individual persons and foundations, which was often a work of vanity. . . . At the same time the execution of pious imagery assumed commercial and industrial character.[59]

Unflinching faith having been lost and man being thrown upon himself, emotionality, passionateness, dolor, pessimism, suffering, side by side with the attempt to see salvation in pleasure, seized the Christian world. With the previous world (which once seemed unshakable) falling to pieces, and a new world not yet assured, such dolor and despair are rather comprehensible.   Shall we wonder that exactly at that time such themes as Death, in its ugliness, the dance macabre, corpses (including Christ) in all their reality, became, as it were, epidemic?

[57] E. Mâle, *L'art religieux de la fin du Moyen Âge en France* (Paris, 1908), pp. vii–ix, 525–528, and 541.

[58] E. Mâle, *Art et artistes*, pp. 20–21 and 23 ff.

[59] *Ibid.*

PLATE XIV

1, 2, and **4,** from the Dance of Death, by Hans Holbein the Younger. **3,** Melancholia, by Dürer.

Beginning with the opening of the fifteenth century and continuing in the sixteenth, the images of corpses, and death's heads, and skulls, multiplied in the churches, on the church glass, in pictures.[60]

Finally, art itself was greatly influenced by the religious theater, by its mysteries, and as a result became more and more *theatrical*, that is Visual, with representation of all the passions, emotionality, and sensibility described above.[61]

Religious art thus ceased to be not only all of art exclusively, but even the main form of art; it tended more and more to become a small stream, and even this small stream ceased to be a united stream but was broken into a series of small individual rivulets. Since that time "there have been Christian artists; but there is no more a Christian art." [62]

In the religious as well as the secular art, the Virgin now becomes a mere tender mother or a coquettish woman; Christ becomes just a babe sucking his finger, or playing with St. John like any other child in the street; the saints and apostles do not differ in anything from the people in general. Even the nimbus, as a sign of divinity, is often lacking.

Instead of being represented as an abstract type the saints, not to mention mortals, are individualized and turned into a kind hardly distinguished from the common run of people. St. Joseph is a common carpenter; St. Elizabeth, a young bourgeois; St. Anne, a grave matron; and so on.[63] It was this sensuous Visualism which provoked Savonarola's indignation and characterization:

The figures which you cause to be painted in your churches are the images of your gods. . . . Meanwhile young men, seeing this or that woman, are saying, "Here comes Magdalen . . . here is St. Joan," because you had painted in the churches figures which exactly resemble this or that person: which is too bad and constitutes a grave insult to the things of God. . . .

[60] Bréhier, *op. cit.*, pp. 335 ff. and 371 ff.; see also Hourticq, *op. cit.*, pp. 127–128; J. Huizinga, *op. cit.*, chaps. xi and xix–xxi; H. O. Taylor, *The Mediaeval Mind* (London, 1914), Vol. II, Bk. VII.

[61] See E. Mâle, *L'art religieux de la fin du Moyen Âge en France*, chap. i *et passim*. Mâle, though right in stressing the influence of the religious theater upon art, at the same time is in error in his explanation that the change of art came about merely through this factor. The rise of the religious theater and theatricality was but one of the symptoms of a deeper change of the whole mentality of the culture.

[62] *Ibid.*, p. 541. Though in his later work, *L'art religieux après le concile de Trente* (Paris, 1932), Mâle somewhat modified this statement, nevertheless in essence it remains true.

[63] Mâle, *L'art religieux de la fin du Moyen Âge en France*, pp. 159 ff. See the reproductions of the Virgin and religious scenes in Venturi's book. A glance is sufficient to see what an enormous change took place in comparison with the thirteenth century!

You have given the Virgin the dresses of courtesans. . . . That is how the divine cult is profaned.[64]

A little later even the cynical and malicious Aretino reproached Michelangelo that "your angels do not have any earthly decency while your saints are deprived of any celestial ornament."[65]

Now the verdict "like life itself" becomes the highest praise of a work of art. And *visual illusionism* becomes more and more the fundamental criterion of the perfection of the artistic technique. An exactly similar thing occurred in the Greek art of the fourth and following centuries and in Roman art, where to find in a work such an illusionism was also the greatest compliment to the artist. Just as stories once began to circulate about a painted picture of grapes or of something else so similar to the reality that animals were deceived and took the painting for the real thing (*e.g.*, the grape painted by Zeuxis), so it was now; and Vasari tells us with pride that he painted a strawberry bush with such success that the peacock was deceived and tried to pick the berries from the picture! Already at the end of the fourteenth century Gennino Gennini instructs artists: "Remember that the most perfect guide and the best pilot you can have is a mere copying of nature [in her Visual appearance]."[66] To render things as they look becomes from now on the main objective of art. Hence it is not accidental that Leonardo da Vinci was indignant at the Scholastics of the twelfth and the thirteenth centuries for their underestimation of the importance of painting and of the sense of sight. "Painting rightly complains of not being reckoned among the liberal arts, for she is a true daughter of Nature and works through the eye, the noblest of our senses." For him painting — and he means Visual painting — is superior to sculpture, music, and poetry, because poetry represents with words and for the ear, while painting represents for the eye and "by true likeness." "Take a poet who describes the beauty of a lady to her lover and a painter who represents her, and you will see to which nature guides the enamored critic."[67] Generally, the shift from the Ideational to the Visual art (and culture) is marked by a great stress on the value of the *eye* among the organs of sense, and of *sight* among all the senses.

In conformity with this the *technical style of sculpture and painting* begins to move also toward an ever-increasing *malerisch* quality, illusionism, and their satellites: dynamism, emotionality, sensuality, and

[64] Deonna, *op. cit.*, Vol. III, p. 344.   [65] *Ibid.*

[66] See P. Monnier, *Le Quattrocento* (Paris, 1901), Vol. I; Deonna, *op. cit.*, Vol. III, p. 450; F. Chamber, *The History of Taste*, pp. 56 ff.

[67] See Leonardo da Vinci, *Textes choisis* (Paris, 1907), pp. 355 and 368.

so forth. When we study the change of technique, moving from the thirteenth century to the "Primitives" of the fourteenth and the fifteenth centuries, and from them to the "Classics" of the Renaissance, and then to the baroque of the seventeenth century, we are immediately aware of the movement from less illusionism to greater, from the linear style to the *malerisch* (in Wölfflin's sense). Since Wölfflin has described this movement fully, there is no need for me to go into the matter in detail, and for my purpose it is enough briefly to outline the essence of his conclusions.

Wölfflin rightly remarks that "Vision itself has its history, and the revelation of these visual strata must be regarded as the primary task of art history." [68] Following this principle he indicates the five fundamental pairs of the representational forms of Art: (1) Linear versus Malerisch, (2) Plane versus Recession, (3) Closeness versus Openness, (4) Multiplicity versus Unity, (5) Clearness versus Unclearness. The first elements of all of these pairs are mutually interconnected, and this is true also of the second elements. Now what Wölfflin styles the linear form (correlated with the plane, the closed, the multiple, the clear) approaches the Ideational; while his *malerisch* form (with its related kinds) is nearer to the Visual style.

[In the linear style] the stress is laid on the limits of things; in the painterly the work tends to look limitless. . . . In the one case interest lies more in the perception of the individual material objects, as solid, tangible bodies; in the other, in the apprehension of the world as a shifting semblance. . . . Linear represents the things as they are, the painterly as they seem to be.

The linear appeals to touch; the painterly to the eye only; "The painterly eye perceives everything as vibrating, and suffers nothing to settle into definite lines and surfaces." It is dynamic; it catches the passing appearances of the things, which change from moment to moment. The linear, on the contrary, has a distinctness of plasticity; it is tactile; in it "representation and things are, so to speak, identical." In the painterly style "only the visual appearance of reality is seized." "It has its roots only in the eye and appeals only to the eye." Therefore, a transition from the linear to the painterly style means "a triumph of seeming over being. . . ." It reaches its climax in illusionism, as the extreme degree of Visualism.[69]

From these characterizations one can see why the linear style with its satellites is much nearer to the Ideational, while the *malerisch* ("painterly") comes closest to the Visual style; and why a transition

[68] H. Wölfflin, *Principles of Art History*, p. 11. [69] *Ibid.*, pp. 11–28.

I — 23

from the linear to the *malerisch*, or vice versa, is a quite definite transition from one grade of Ideationalism or Visualism to another, different grade.

It now becomes easy to understand how the European painting and sculpture in the period from the fifteenth to the seventeenth century passed from the clear-cut linearism of the Primitives of the fifteenth century, through the Classics of the sixteenth century, to the baroque of the seventeenth, which is a clear-cut *malerisch* art (*i.e.*, from the linear classics, like Leonardo da Vinci, Botticelli, Dürer, Raphael, Massys, Wolf Huber, Holbein, Sansovino, H. Aldegrever, Benedetto da Mariano, Michelangelo (partly), Altdorfer, Ter Borch, etc.; to the *malerisch* Frans Hals, Van Dyck, Rembrandt, Velasquez, Grünewald, Ostade, Jan Lievens, Metsu, A. van de Velde, Bernini, Puget, Rubens, Van Goyen, Vermeer, Ruysdael, and so on).[70]

This trend toward an ever-increasing *malerisch* quality continues with slight fluctuations, up to about the end of the eighteenth century.[71] Then comes a temporary lull in the form of neo-classicism, an imitation of the imitation of the antique by the Renaissance. Though in technique it is somewhat less *malerisch* than the baroque (and the rococo), it still remains conspicuously Visual in form and especially in content; in fact the neo-classicism of the end of the eighteenth and of the beginning of the nineteenth century is rather more sensate and "worldly" than the baroque. Just as in the Roman art, especially after the neo-classicism of Augustus, the subsequent course of art was mainly a change in waves of imitation, whether of the classic, the archaic, the Hellenistic, and other patterns, each wave remaining conspicuously Visual and Sensate; so the history of art after the neo-classicism of the Western world was, up to the end of the nineteenth century, a replacement of one imitative wave by another: neo-classicism by "romanticism," then this by a short turn again toward something nearer to neo-classicism and the Academy; then impressionism as the extremest form of the Visual art, followed by "expressionism" and "cubism" and other "isms." Whatever was the name of the predominant wave, and however they differed from one another (for instance, the romantic school from the neo-classic), nevertheless all these waves remained, up to the end of the nineteenth century — up to the appearance of the "cubists," "futurists," and other extreme modernists — Visual and Sensate. None of the important and powerful streams was nearer to Ideationalism than to Visualism. Only the very

[70] See the analysis and the reproductions in Wölfflin's work, *passim*. See also P. Ligeti's analysis and many reproductions.
[71] See Wölfflin, *op. cit.*, p. 31.

end of the nineteenth and the beginning of the twentieth century have given something that may be styled a revolt against Visualism, though it is in no way Ideationalism. It is that "cubistic" incongruous Mixed style which usually comes at the periods of the ebbing Visualism and before the dawn of Ideationalism.

Such in brief is the outline of the main fluctuations of the technique of the arts of painting and sculpture from the standpoint of Ideationalism and Visualism.

As to *the other traits* of the art of the fifteenth and in part of the sixteenth century, the sculpture as well as the painting shows the same trend toward Visualism, being in this respect an art of a transition.

However different are the various painters and sculptors of the fifteenth century (Ghiberti, Brunelleschi, Donatello, Jacopo della Quercia, Luca della Robbia, Giotto, Masaccio, Ghirlandajo, Perugini, Masovino, Lippi, Botticelli, Fra Angelico, Verocchio, Andrea Mantegna, Leonardo da Vinci, and others in Italy; Michel Colombe, Peter of Milan, Laurana, Jean Foucquet, Bourdichon, and others in France; Schongauer, Martin Schaffner, Bernard Strigel, Holbein Senior, Pacher, Dürer, and, in part, Lucas Cranach, and Martin Grünewald in Germany; the Van Eycks, Dirk Bouts, Thierry Bouts and his sons, A. van Ouwater, Gerard de Saint-Jean, Quentin Massys, H. Memling, Gerard David, H. van der Goes, J. van Wassenhove in Holland; known and unknown artists of Spain), and however great are the differences in the sculpture and painting of various countries, the trend toward Visualism is common to almost all of them and to all countries. "In spite of appreciable differences in style the tendencies [in all these countries] remain essentially the same." The main motto of all of them is Giotto's (Visual): "Verity taken from Nature." Of all of them it can be said that they have a "Charm, in which gracefulness and discreet emotion, observation and invention . . . take turns . . . and dramatic sentiment is strong but still reserved." "Realism, an audacious sense of [visual] truth, of life, of passion," are growing.[72] In some they are expressed very strongly, in others moderately.

The Middle Ages and Ideationalism are still alive, still noticeable, but they are waning. Individualism grows. Portraiture also. *Genre* also. Dynamism and emotionalism also. A secular spirit rises both in subjects and in manner. Similarly to the Greek art of the fourth century sensualism, voluptuousness, eroticism make further headway. The pretty woman begins to become more and more a common subject of art.

[72] A. Michel, *op. cit.*, Vol. III, pp. 526, 553-555, *et passim;* also Vol. IV, *passim*.

The purity of the thirteenth century has disappeared. Then, in the Cathedral of Lyons, the artist who carved the history of the world left unfilled the medallion which was to tell the story of Lot. Now, even the saints are depicted nude. It is not enough to render the voluptuous bodies; sensuality looks for something exotic in this field; and various artists like the creator of the Florence statue of the Hermaphrodite (a replica of the indecent but famous *Hermaphroditus* of Beccadelli) soon will supply the proper commodity, praising, depicting, stimulating sodomy, and other exotic forms of sexual voluptuousness. Here again Savonarola (1452–1498) was probably not far from the truth when he said to his contemporaries: "Your life is that of a swine; you pass it in bed, in idle gossiping, in the streets, in orgies and in debauchery." [73]

We see . . . in the cynical or refined pleasures of the Dukes of Ferrara and Milan, in the dainty epicureanism or in the open license of the Medicis, how far the quest for any description of pleasure was carried. . . . [In such an atmosphere the poets, sculptors, and scholars who depended upon them, filled their palaces with] hunting and amorous scenes. In the direction of painting they praised the nudities of Dello and Pollaiolo; they sharpened the . . . sentiment of paganism with a point of voluptuous sensuality. And many artists, like Fra Philippo Lippi who carried off a nun, were no better in regard to license and voluptuousness.[74] (See No. 2, Plate XV.)

In other countries this trend was not so sharply expressed, but it was the same.

All the other traits of Visualism were not lacking: emotionality, the pathetic, individualized portraits, *genre*, historical scenes, picturesqueness, physical dolor, dolorous sentimentality, pessimism, even theatricality, bust portraiture, naturalism, historical scenes, the common nature of the topics, everyday-life subjects, landscapes, and so on.[75]

This is its dominant tone. Of course, the Idealistic stream did not disappear entirely (*e.g.*, Fra Angelico), but it was secondary, and even then it lost most of its purity and sublimity.

In the sixteenth century — the century of the Renaissance — all these tendencies became quite clear and pronounced. Ideationalism in its pure form is practically dead; Visualism triumphs. Only a somewhat diluted Idealism still lingers and temporarily flares up; but even it is moored to the earth rather than to heaven. It is in most cases an Idealism of the empirical and of the sensory human body, of landscape, of

[73] On this subject see particularly Monnier, *op. cit.*, Vol. I, pp. 47 ff., and Vol. II, p. 412; H. Taine, *Philosophie de l'art* (Paris, 1881), p. 179.

[74] H. Taine, *Lectures on Art*, trans. by J. Durand (New York, 1889), p. 70.

[75] See Deonna, *op. cit.*, Vol. III, chap. viii.

PLATE XV

1, St. Anne and the Child Jesus, by Leonardo da Vinci.   2, Sleeping Venus, by Giorgione.

visual form generally; but not the idealization of the transcendental and supersensory. The Flemish school develops as entirely Visual, undilutedly "naturalistic." The Italian classics idealize and select and beautify the objects rendered, but do this in a purely empirical sense, from an empirical standpoint, and with empirical objects mainly. They do not attempt to paint the singular, the incidental, the occasional; to render portraits; to paint landscapes; the passionate. They select man mainly as their subject and they want to "perfect nature." But their nature is almost exclusively Sensate and they perfect it in a purely empirical sense. Even when they paint the religious subject it is "visualized," "materialized," dragged from its transcendental heaven to an earthly Sensate form, and treated from the standpoint of a purely Sensate psychology. (See No. 1, Plate XV, and No. 5, Plate VIII.)

The reason is that their idealism was purely humanistic, earthly, scientific, wingless, to soar to the heights of transcendental idealism, an idealism which does not fear anything, does not question itself, in a way is blind and unreservedly believing. Here in the earthly idealism, vested entirely in mortal man, such a power was impossible. In the second place, being an earthly idealism it was bound hand and foot to the empirical appearance of man and his milieu. It could not divorce itself decisively from this empirical reality, as does the Ideational and purely Idealistic art. Since it rejected the transcendental world, it had only the empirical world; [76] it had to study it and to render it as it appeared to the eyes, at the best beautifying it but again on the basis merely of this Visual reality. "The main thing in the art of design," says Cellini, "is to cleverly fashion a naked man or woman." [77]

Such is its motto. These masters studied, studied most patiently; and, as Leonardo da Vinci said, this seems sometimes to have led to a mere pedantic and scientific exercise instead of an art creation.[78] Being so closely bound to that reality — the only reality they really believed in — they could not get free from it entirely.

But the main thing was the whole mentality of the age, reflected by and in the art.

[76] This was the tragedy of these wingless realists. And Michelangelo himself seems to have felt it in his later years, because in his old age he often wondered if he had loved his art too much and his Heavenly Father too little.

[77] Taine, *Lectures on Art*, p. 17.

[78] "Peintre anatomiste, veille bien que ton excessive connaissance des os, des tendons et des muscles ne fasse pas de toi un pédant à force de faire montre de ton savoire sur ce point." A. Michel, *Nouvelles études sur l'histoire de l'art* (Paris, 1908), p. 334. See also Deonna, *op. cit.*, Vol. III, p. 419. Michelangelo himself was not free from that entirely.

This art is neither mystic, nor dramatic, nor spiritual. . . . Its aim is not to present to the eye the incorporeal and sublime world, the innocent and ecstatic spirits, the theological or ecclesiastical dogmas . . . it abandons the Christian and monastic period to enter on the laic and pagan period. . . . It is not preoccupied with the moral order of things at the expense of the physical. . . .[79]

They are preoccupied with form. After their painstaking study of human and animal anatomy their objective is

to present to the eye, first, the natural human body, that is to say, healthy, active, and energetic, endowed with all animal and athletic aptitudes; and, besides this, the ideal human body, akin to the Greek type, so well proportioned and balanced . . . posed in such a happy attitude, draped and surrounded by other bodies so well grouped that the whole forms a harmony, and the entire work conveys the idea of a corporeal world . . . heroic or divine, in any case, superior and complete. Such is the peculiar genius of these artists.[80]

The whole process of transition from the fourteenth to the sixteenth century in Italy is depicted as follows.

The order of painting remained symbolic and mystic up to the end of the fourteenth century, under the control of Christian theological ideas. It perpetuated the symbolic and mystic school down to the middle of the fifteenth century (Paro Spinello and the Bicci), during the long contest between the Christian spirit and the pagan spirit. In the middle of the fifteenth century its most angelic interpreter (Fra Angelico) is found in a holy spirit preserved from paganism by the seclusion of the cloister. It began to be interested in the real and substantial body during the early years of the fifteenth century . . . and substituted for the hope of celestial felicity the search for terrestrial happiness. It passed over from exact imitation to creative beauty (at the time of Leonardo da Vinci, Michael Angelo). . . . It maintained itself at Venice half a century later than elsewhere. . . . It became enfeebled in the time of Correggio, and chilled under the successors of Michael Angelo . . . when habits assumed a decorous air and minds took a sentimental turn; when the painter . . . became a polished cavalier; when the shop with its apprentices gave way to an "Academy"; when the bold and free artist . . . became a diplomatic courtier convinced of his own importance, a respecter of etiquette, a defender of rules, and the vain flatterer of prelates and the great.[81]

In brief, we are entering the age of the *malerisch* and in many respects still more Visual baroque, and of the Academies which arose as the natural successor of this Italian classicism.[82]

[79] H. Taine, *Lectures on Art*, p. 15.   [80] *Ibid.*, p. 17.   [81] *Ibid.*, pp. 153–156.
[82] Deonna rightly says that "the refinement of the beaux ésprits in the Hellenic age, as well as in the fifteenth and sixteenth centuries, witnessed a development by reaction of the

In other countries which occupied a leading place in the art of the fifteenth and sixteenth centuries, even this reaction of a feeble Idealism scarcely took place. I mean first of all the Netherlands. Its art, beginning with Hubert van Eyck, grew in Visualism and became Visual par excellence during the first half of the sixteenth century. Later on, under the influence of the Italian art perhaps, there occurred a brief weakening of this naturalism, but all in all even then art stayed on the earth. What objects did it represent? Artists were

copying actual life — the contemporary in his ordinary dress, in the midst of his daily duties, amongst veritable pieces of furniture, taking his walks, at market, at the table, at the town hall, in the tavern, just as the eye sees him, a gentleman, a bourgeois, a peasant, with the innumerable and striking particulars which belong to his character, profession, and condition.[83]

The early Flemings (contrary to the classical Greeks) not only did not depict an abstract and idealized type of man, but, producing only exact individualized portraits, they

translated into portraiture the ideal personification of the Virgin, the apostles, the prophets and the martyrs, ever striving to represent in an exact manner the petty details of nature [whether landscape or person or animal or plant]. . . . The Flemings strove to render them precisely as they saw them. . . . They created a realistic school, a school of landscape. . . . If your imagination is filled with noble Italian or with elegant French forms, your eyes will be offended: you will often fancy the [Flemish] artist purposely studied the ugly. The truth is that he is not repelled by the trivialities and deformities of life. . . . They were incapable of simplifying nature; they aimed to reproduce her entire. They did not concentrate her in the nude body: they assigned equal importance to all her appearances — landscapes, edifices, animals, costumes and accessories. They are not qualified to comprehend and prize the ideal body; they are constituted to paint and enforce the actual body. . . . They almost always paint man in a well-to-do condition and content with his lot. . . . When they exalt him it is without raising him above his terrestrial conditions. . . . Generally they leave him as he is. The Dutch school confines itself to reproducing the repose of the bourgeois interior, the comforts of shop and farm, out-door sports and tavern enjoyments, all the petty satisfactions of an orderly and tranquil existence. . . . They are Flemings, and they stick to the earth.[84]

---

taste for the burlesque, for parody, for rudeness itself, and for the grotesque forms treated not in a summary manner as in the monsters of the cathedrals but with all the realism of science." *Op. cit.*, Vol. III, p. 420.

[83] H. Taine, *Lectures on Art*, p. 14.

[84] *Ibid.*, pp. 221–224 and 263.

Here is an excellent summary of the Flemish school. After the art of the thirteenth century almost entirely devoted to God, to Moral Order, and to Physical Order as a Work of God, the Flemish art now devotes itself to rendering such empirical objects as :

the armour, the polished glass of a window, the scrolls of a carpet, the hairs of fur, the undraped body, a canon's massive, wrinkled and obese features, a bourgomaster's or soldier's massive shoulders, projecting chin and prominent nose, the spindling shanks of a hangman, the overlarge head and diminutive limbs of a child, the costumes and furniture of the age ; their entire work being a glorification of this present life. . . . Art falls from heaven to earth, and is no longer to treat divine but human incidents.[85]

If to this list we add the tavern, the kitchen, the bedroom, the mill ; the prosaic figures of merchants, of beggars, of housewives, some comely, some ugly ; of fish, game, ham ; club and council meetings ; scenes of brawling, love making ; street boys ; farms, landscapes ; if further we recall the great specialization of artists — like Paul Potter in the painting of cows, like Philips Wouwerman in that of gray horses, like Houdecoeter in that of poultry, like William van de Velde in the painting of ships, like Abraham van Beijeren in the painting of oysters and lobsters, like Jan van Huysum in flowers, like Peter Claesz in fine silverware ; if we consider further that art now becomes greatly commercialized — when we consider all this, we can hardly imagine a greater contrast in the style, in the content, in the mentality of an art than that between the Flemish school and the art of the Middle Ages — of the thirteenth and, in part, of the fourteenth century. We are magically transferred from the Kingdom of Ideationalism and Idealism into the earthly realm of Sensate and Visual "naturalism" !

Other countries of Europe, France, Spain, Germany, England, occupy an intermediary position between the earthly Idealism of Italy and the purely Visual naturalism of Holland.

In France, as we move from the time of Michel Colombe (c. 1430) to the time of Primatice, Jean Goujon (d. c. 1568), Germain Pilon (d. 1590), Les Clouets, and Jean Cousin, to mention but a few names, the growth of the Sensate mentality, as well as of the Visual manner in sculpture and painting, is strikingly evident.[86] The Visualism of the French art of the

[85] *Ibid.*, pp. 263–264 and 274. See the details in A. Michel, *Histoire de l'art*, Vol. V, pp. 195 ff. Even when they paint religious topics, the rendering is entirely profane. Charming saints, beautiful Herodias, and the lithe Salome of Quentin Massys, Christs and Magdalens of Lucas van Leyden, are typical examples.

[86] One can see it easily also in a homogeneous series of the tomb monuments. Before the thirteenth century there is usually a mere symbol, a figure or scene from the Bible or the

period did not go so far as that of the Flemish, partly because French art was represented by a considerable number of Italian artists (Cellini, Primatice, and others), who exerted the classic Italian influence.[87]

In Germany, under the domination of the bourgeoisie and Protestantism, art assumed many further Visual traits but even at the apex of the period, about 1500 to 1540, it preserved more of the Ideational elements than the Flemish art, though in the works of Cranach, Grünewald, the Holbeins (Senior and, especially, Junior), H. Crien, and others, it was definitely marked by all the most important traits of Visualism : "Naturalism," interest in portraits, *malerisch* qualities, patheticism, emotionality, the macabre, sensuality, theatricality, picturesqueness, and so on, are displayed in it conspicuously and powerfully. After that period, with the greater permeation of the Italian and Dutch influences (from 1540) the elements of Visualism, in a modified form, increased still more.[88]

We have a similar mixture during that period in Spain and Portugal, a mixture of the Oriental, Italian, Flemish, and French influences. The works of the great artists of these countries, and especially of Antonio Goncalves in Portugal, show the same tide of rising Visualism.[89]

The same can be said of the art of England.[90]

To sum up the general trend in all the European countries at the end of the fifteenth and in the first half of the sixteenth century we can say : During that period the art of "humility, of suffering, of sorrow," or resignation, of acceptance of divine guidance, was replaced by another art which Pascal defined as "concupiscence of eyes, concupiscence of flesh and lust (*orgueil*) of life." [91]

At that time there began a clear separation and even an opposition of the secular and of the religious art, which up to the end of the fifteenth century had been one, that is, religious.[92] The fact of the separation and the fact that the religious art from now on becomes a minor stream are in

Gospel; in the thirteenth century an Idealistic figure, serene and peaceful; in the fourteenth and the fifteenth centuries pathetic and macabre figures and scenes, especially skeletons, death, etc.; in the sixteenth century the macabre plus sensuality and paganism.

[87] See the history and characterization in A. Michel, *Histoire de l'art*, Vol. IV, pp. 498 to the end of the volume.

[88] See the details in *ibid.*, Vol. V, 1e partie.

[89] *Ibid.*, Vol. IV, 2e partie.

[90] *Ibid.*, Vol. V, pp. 336 ff.

[91] *Ibid.*, Vol. IV, p. 490.

[92] *Ibid.*, Vol. IV, p. 490. "Religious art during the preceding centuries had been the total art; from now on there appeared religious and profane arts." E. Mâle, *L'art religieux après le concile de Trente* (Paris, 1932), p. 5.

themselves most important symptoms of the great shift from Ideation-alism toward a secular and sensuous Visualism.

IV. THE END OF THE SIXTEENTH AND THE SEVENTEENTH CENTURY. THE BAROQUE AS A FURTHER GROWTH OF SENSATE VISUALISM

A superficial glance at the art of the end of the sixteenth and of the seventeenth century may suggest that during that period painting and sculpture make a shift from Visualism toward Ideationalism. The main reason for such a contention would be the fact of a tightening moral and religious control over paintings and sculpture, and their "cleansing" and "purification," carried on by the Church after the twenty-fifth session of the Council of Trent in 1563, as well as by other, secular agencies of the Western society of that time, including Protestantism and its "icono-clastic" and "puritanic" tendencies. Many previous liberalities in painting were declared indecent; nudity and seductive love scenes were proscribed, and many other "sinful" topics. One moral limitation after another was imposed upon art. Censorship of the art creations and pressure upon the artists were greatly reinforced.

Side by side with this, in the field of the purely secular art the estab-lishment of the Academies of Art, especially in France around the middle of the seventeenth century, with their Academic classicism, modeled supposedly on the Greek "classic" art and the art of the classics of the Italian Renaissance; with Academic rules — at the beginning stressing line at the cost of color, proscribing the incidental, the ugly, the individual, and, in part, landscape and *genre* and portraiture; demanding an ideal-ization of the typical and beautiful: all this seems to suggest also a shift from a comparatively strong to less strong Visualism, from a compara-tively weak to a stronger Idealism.

However, such a conclusion would be wrong. It would have been based upon a few artificially selected data favorable to it, and would have overlooked an infinitely greater body of quite contradictory facts. In brief, the period in reality undergoes not a shift from Visualism but a further promotion of its success at the cost not only of the weak remnants of Ideationalism but even of Idealism. A very concise survey of the main features of both the religious and the secular painting and sculpture of the period is sufficient to make this clear. And we can conveniently begin with the *religious* art, which is now fairly definitely separated from the secular art and all in all is the minor rather than the major stream.

A. *Religious Art.* Protestantism assumed an iconoclastic attitude; therefore it would not and did not have a religious art, though several

Protestant painters treated religious topics. As to the Catholic religious art, the austere censorship applied, after the Council of Trent of 1563, to religious pictures and sculpture succeeded somewhat in achieving a mechanical suppression of "indecency," "nudity," and "light-mindedness." However, even in this the success was not complete: for in mythological, historical, and heroic pictures, especially outside of churches, nudity and other "indecencies" were still permitted. The measures taken attempted to impose — again mechanically — a standardized idealization of the figures, postures, scenes depicted (for instance in the scenes of the Crucifixion it was prohibited to depict St. Mary in a faint, etc.); but this instilled not so much the spirit of real Idealism in art as an artificial "powder" and "rouge" ennobling things superficially only [93] — a kind of convulsive, ecstatic, desperate religiosity, where spontaneous feeling was lacking.

Aside from this all the other traits of the religious art of the period, in the content as well as in the technique, were more Visual than the art of even the preceding period.

(1) It became controversially propagandist and political in the fight with Protestantism and other sects. Therefore the spirit of calmness, untroubled faith, serenity was gone from it: it was now on the earth and heavily engaged in a political conflict.

All that Protestantism attacked: the cult of the Virgin, the supremacy of St. Peter, the belief in the sacraments, in the efficacy of prayers for the dead, in that of good deeds; the belief in an intervention of the saints; veneration of the images and relics; all these dogmas were defended now by the art allied with the Catholic Church.[94]

Such "political" art can hardly be genuinely Ideational.

(2) Idealistic art is serene and calm. The religious art of the seventeenth century was supercharged with an almost pathological, in a sense sadistic, terrible and terrifying emotionalism and patheticism, particularly in the pictures of the martyrs, in tortures and sufferings, which are depicted in all their Visual horror. The scenes of the cutting of tongues, of the putting of people into a grave alive, of cutting the stomach and pulling out the intestines and kidneys, and so on — these scenes, depicted in all their last horrible details, evidently are even farther from Ideationalism or Idealism than the Laocoön group or emotionally Visual creations of the Hellenistic and Roman Sensate art.

[93] For these and subsequent characteristics, see the details and the reproductions in E. Mâle, *L'art religieux après le concile de Trente*, chap. i; L. Bréhier, *op. cit.*, chap. xiv.
[94] E. Mâle, *L'art religieux après le concile de Trente*, p. 107 and the whole of chap. ii.

The genius of the Renaissance sympathized little with suffering and death and therefore rarely depicted the tortures of the martyrs. Only beginning with the end of the sixteenth century these terrible and violent images began to multiply.[95]

This is true also of the secular art.

It is extremely curious to see that the artists of the seventeenth century ordinarily depicted only the most violent scenes of ancient history: Lucretia knifing herself, the dying Dido and Cleopatra, Sophonias drinking poison, Seneca opening his veins. . . . These dolorous figures now multiplied the number of pictures of violent death.[96]

The period glittered, so to speak, in the lurid light of violence and blood and dolorous emotion. And the treatment of such topics was so Visual and "realistic" that E. Mâle says, not without reason, that even for us "the spectacle of these terrible paintings is almost unbearable." [97]   It is an art of the theater of cruelties and horrors.

(3) The same absolutely un-Ideational and un-Idealistic — almost pathological — emotionalism is shown by the appearance of a great multitude of pictures of ecstasy, visions, ecstatic and convulsed expressions on the faces, in the postures and attitudes of saints and other persons depicted. In the religious as well as in the secular art these scenes and expressions are everywhere. Nothing remains of the inner calmness, serenity, imperturbability of the Ideational and Idealistic art. Unshakable and unquestioning faith is gone, in its place a society which desperately, artificially, painfully — and hopelessly — tries to cling to a lost paradise. Of the medieval, of the thirteenth-century, deep inner harmony there survives very little. "Now all is *élan*, aspiration, dolorous effort to escape human nature and to get to be engulfed by God." [98] Therefore all is in a desperate and violent motion and movement; all is convulsive Becoming, filled to the brim with sensibility, emotionality, exaltation, the pathetic, with dolor, despair, pain, suffering — in brief, with the extremest forms of dynamic emotionality of a particularly terrible and ecstatic kind.

(4) The period is marked by a great multiplication of the scenes of death and of death itself, rendered in all their Visual reality and morbid appearance (Plate XVI and No. 5, Plate VIII). Skulls, corpses, disintegration, skeletons, rotten bones, graves, coffins, and similar topics are to be found everywhere.

[95] *Ibid.*, p. 127; see also chap. iii and the reproductions there.
[96] *Ibid.*, p. 148.   [97] *Ibid.*, p. 112.   [98] *Ibid.*, p. 152.

PLATE XVI

1, Saint Teresa, by Bernini.   2, Christ Carrying the Cross, by Rubens.

Suddenly, several years after the Council of Trent, beginning with 1570 . . . there appears now on tombs with the bust of the deceased the skull of death. This skull is of a terrifying naturalness: it has the colour of an aged ivory. It looks like a real skull.[99]

The same is true of the skeletons and other signs and scenes of death. In the most Visual form possible, art depicts these topics and reminds the beholder of *Finis, Cinis, Vermis, Lapis, Oblivio*, or of *Hic jacet pulvis et nihil*. And the dead, in a contrast to the living dead with open eyes of the Idealistic or Ideational period, are now corpses, rendered in all the Visual "naturalness" of a corpse, sometimes disintegrated, sometimes wormy. While the tombs of the Ideational and of the Idealistic age calm and elevate us, "the tombs of the seventeenth century terrify." [100] And this is true not only of the tombs, but of the whole religious art of the period; and not only of the religious art, but of the secular art as well. So much for the content.

(5) As to the form, it became, so we have already observed, much more Visual — more *malerisch* — and less linear; more dynamic and less static; more showy than before; more allegorical and less symbolic. Artificial perspectives to give illusion, *malerisch* technique, dynamism of postures and expressions, invention and application of several new devices to give "realistic" effects and to increase the Visual deceit — the growth of all this is unquestionable, has been stressed by many historians and critics, and need not be discussed here at length.[101] (See Plate XVI.)

Only one point remains to be mentioned, namely, a further decay of transcendental symbolism and its replacement, in part, by hypostatized abstractions and allegories of a purely intellectual type — a phenomenon common to virtually all the compartments of art of the seventeenth century: literature, drama, theater, and, to some extent, to the whole mentality of the age. As explained elsewhere there is a profound difference between the transcendental symbolism of the Middle Ages, or any Ideational symbolism, and an allegory composed of hypostatized intellectual abstractions. The first consists in visible signs of the invisible world of God; the second, in visible signs of either visible things of the Sensate world or of the hypostatized abstractions of the same sensuous world, usually some desirable — Sensate — qualities of a man or a group. The transcendental symbolism does not endeavor to make the visible signs visually similar to the symbolized values, neither does it aim to

---

[99] *Ibid.*, p. 206.   [100] *Ibid.*, p. 206.
[101] For the religious art see *ibid.*, pp. 191 and 201; for the art of the seventeenth century, see the works on the baroque mentioned in the Appendix to this chapter.

make these visible signs pleasant visually. Allegory attempts to render the figure used Visually like the allegorized object, and almost always tends to make the allegorical figure pleasant and enjoyable sensuously and to make its meaning rationalistically and intellectually justifiable. W. J. Courthope well understood certain profound differences between allegory and the transcendental, or medieval, symbolism, comparing Dante's symbolism with the allegory of the later centuries.

Both adopt the machinery of allegory, but put it to completely opposite uses. With Dante allegory is an integral part of his system of thought. Following the lead of St. Thomas Aquinas, he held that the visible universe and human society were images of the mind of God, and hence in his system, every phenomenal object was a symbol of some form of existence in the real world of spiritual being. The entire scene and action of the Divine Comedy is placed in the universe invisible to mortal eyes. [The purpose of the symbol here is] to convey a spiritual idea to the mind by means of a sensible image.

> "Così parlar conviensi al vostro ingegno,
> Perocche solo da sensato apprende
> Cio che fa poscia d'intelletto degno.
> Per questo la Scrittura condiscende
> A vostra facultate, e piedi e mano
> Attribuisce a Deo, ed altro entende."
>
> (*Paradiso*, iv, 40–45)

Each feature in the topography of the poem and all its *dramatis personae* are symbolical of some hidden truth.[102]

The allegorical method of the later centuries "is the exact reverse of all this. Allegory has there nothing to do with philosophy, but is merely a poetical vehicle of moral thought." In Dante the persons are actual, but they symbolize some invisible form of existence; in the later allegory "all the actors are for the most part abstract qualities, though their deeds and words resemble those of persons in real life."

The difference is that between philosophical realism, where "*universalia sunt realia*" — more real than the concrete sensations and individual images, and nominalism, for which abstract concepts do not have any reality — neither in the objective world nor in the mind, being mere fictions while the concrete sensory objects and sensations and images are the only reality.[103]

---

[102] W. J. Courthope, *A History of English Poetry* (New York, 1895), Vol. I, pp. 237 ff. and chap. ix.

[103] See H. O. Taylor, *The Mediaeval Mind*, Vol. II, Bk. V, "Symbolism"; it is somewhat regrettable that the author of this work failed somewhat to stress the profound difference

If, then, the seventeenth-century art shows an increase of Visualism, we must expect logically a further decline in the transcendental symbolism of the Ideational Art of the Middle Ages and its replacement by Visual allegories. This deduction is corroborated by the facts.

The Middle Ages were the age of symbols. . . . Art was profoundly symbolic. . . . Already weakened in the fifteenth century the symbolic genius declined entirely in the seventeenth century.[104]

Instead there came the abstract and "worldly" allegories, a flood of allegories in the art of the period : innumerable pictures and statues of *Simplex, Humilis, Fidelis, Verecunda, Secreta, Lacrimabilis; Verity, Justice, Benignity, Poverty, Vigilance, Force, Possession, Prudence, Memory, Volition, Intellect, Liberty, Friendship, Sleep*, and all the other abstractions of Cesar Ripa's *Iconologia* compiled soon into a whole encyclopedia of abstractions. "The allegories of Ripa were everywhere" : in books, in churches, on medals.[105] Mâle says further that this allegory was quite different either from the Greek symbolism of the classical age or from that of the Middle Ages.

Greece was always [an exaggeration !] Platonic and believed in the reality of Ideas ; its allegories were never [*sic!* but what about the Hellenistic and sensate period ?] poor abstractions. . . . The allegories of the grand centuries of the Middle Ages were also more beautiful and profound than those of Ripa. The Battle of Vices and Virtues had a high significance : it was the image of an inner struggle. In the thirteenth century the noble images of Virtues . . . expressed a doctrine, and were in a perfect harmony with the teaching of the Church. . . . [It was only with the beginning of the fifteenth century that] allegories surcharged with strange attributes made their appearance. They were the real enigmas whose meaning it was difficult to divine. It was then that the phantasy of individuals replaced the previous teaching.[106]

Ripa and the seventeenth century continued that process. The allegories of the seventeenth century "gave to its art something artificial and cold." Yes, we are in an age of a premeditated theatricality, the planned and "scientific" Visualism of Despair; in an age of "illusion," of exalted "show."

So much for the religious art of the period.

---

between various forms of symbolism and allegory. But in his analysis of the Scriptural Allegories and the works of Hugo of St. Victor and of others, he makes the above meaning clear.

[104] E. Mâle, *L'art religieux après le concile de Trente,* p. 335.
[105] *Ibid.,* pp. 405 ff.
[106] *Ibid.,* pp. 427 ff.

B. *Secular Art*. It should be noted, first, that the religious art (as we have previously pointed out) is now already a minor stream, as compared with the secular, which became from now on the major current; second, that in the total of both the streams the proportion of religious topics continues rapidly to decline. These two facts are eloquent enough testimony that art was moving farther and farther away from its Ideational form toward the Visual.

In other respects the essential characteristics of the secular sculpture and painting of the period are similar to those of the religious art. This happens because both are manifestations of the predominant mentality and of the cultural configurations of the period.

If we wish to characterize the specific traits of the art of the end of the sixteenth, of the seventeenth, and, with modifications, of the first part of the eighteenth century, we must use several terms which, as a matter of fact, are employed by nearly all the historians of the art of that period and which by themselves point to its particularly conspicuous Visualism. These words are: theatricality, illusionism, illusionistic artificiality, showiness manifest in the ostentation of art, sumptuousness, pomp, luxury, overabundance of decoration, impurity, latent or open sensuality and sexuality, paganism, dynamism, patheticism, twisted and convulsive exaltation of ecstasy and other strong emotions, imitative, purely cerebral and chilly Academism with its pseudo idealism paralleled by the pure Visual naturalism of the Flemish school. Such are the characteristics of the baroque.

Baroque first of all is a theatrical pomp, an exaggerated "show," and therefore Visualism. It is enough to glance at a typical baroque architectural creation in order to see this. The façade is profusely decorated with arcades and colonnades which, with the chiaroscuro they provide, give illusionistic and dynamic effects; with loggias and galleries; with broken lines, curved in the most artificial way; with sculpture and even color used for ornamental purposes; and all in overabundance. And all this is done ostentatiously, sumptuously, in the most luxurious way, like the first official reception of a *nouveau riche*. When, however, one happens to glance at the sides of the building, one is surprised to find that the other parts are left as though unfinished, forgotten to the extent even of being left without an elementary decent order. Each time that I see such a building, I am reminded of a person who goes into a beauty parlor and orders her face to be "beautified" in the most luxurious manner "without any consideration of expense," and at the same time forgets to wash the other side of her head, and comes out of the parlor with dirt behind her ears, unwashed and unclean everywhere except for her face. The baroque and the person care mainly to give a visual illusion of their being clean and beautified, a mere show of surface, of façade. In this sense the baroque is "show," "surface," Visual illusion.

When its other traits are observed, its restlessness, dynamism, fluidity, this theatrical Visualism comes out still stronger. When, besides the exterior, the interior decoration of the baroque is considered, with its gluttony for mirrors, damask flowers, gilt, stucco, garlands (even petty angels, which are hybrids between the angels of religion and vulgar cupids), the baroque is at once recognized as the world of theatrical and ostentatious Visualism, as a purely illusionistic world created only for the eyes, as a mere show — but with the intention to pass this show for a genuine world.

When this ostentatious and sumptuous display became tiresome after some fifty or sixty years, the same visual and theatrical mentality changed the decorations of the baroque into its direct descendant, the rococo. The rococo of the eighteenth century is the direct outcome of the baroque and belongs to the same family of theatricality and show, but the decorations are changed for the sake of variety. The rococo world is the same illusionistic artificial world, the world of seen surfaces and appearances, but they now are made in an effeminate, enfeebled, idyllic, pastoral, coquettish fashion. It is the "boudoir" world with its "bosoms," with artificial and illusionistic rocks, waterfalls, gorges, fountains, idyllic shepherds and pastorals, cupids and nymphs, with artificial disorderliness of shrubbery and trees (trimmed and clipped to give this effect), with theatrical "simplicity," in most cases fashioned supposedly à la Chinese, with other exotic freaks and illusionistic devices of an enfeebled, weary, bored, overripe, and half-senile society. This play with "freaks" was styled and believed to be a "return to nature," to "simplicity," to "innocence." [107]

These indications are sufficient to substantiate my claim. Since a detailed survey of the sculpture and painting of the period in various

---

[107] About baroque and rococo see H. Wölfflin, *op. cit., passim;* also his *Renaissance und Barock* (München, 1888); C. Ricci, *Vita barocca* (Milan, 1904); A. Schmarsow, *Barock und Rokoko* (Leipzig, 1897); A. Riegl, *Die Entstehung der Barockkunst in Rom* (Wien, 1908); J. Strygowski, *Das Werden des Barock* (Strassburg, 1898); A. Michel, *Histoire de l'art*, Vols. V, VI, VII, and VIII; works cited in the Appendix. For the rococo mentality see particularly A. Lovejoy, "The First Gothic Revival and the Return to Nature," in *Modern Language Notes*, XLVII (November, 1932); A. Lovejoy, "The Chinese Origin of Romanticism," in *The Journal of English and Germanic Philology*, Vol. XXXII (1933), pp. 1-20.

countries is beyond the scope of this work, a few additional remarks will suffice to bring to view other symptomatic details.

However different is the sculpture and painting of the period in various countries, especially in the Netherlands on the one hand and in Italy, France, and Spain, on the other; however profound are the contrasts between the artists of the same country (*e.g.*, Rubens and Rembrandt; Caravaggio and Carracci and Bernini in Italy; Poussin, Le Brun, and Claude Lorrain in France; El Greco, Velásquez, Murillo, Zurbarán, and Montañés in Spain); almost all of them are similar in having in common the properties of the Visual art of the baroque described above.

First of all, in all countries the architecture, sculpture, and painting, from a purely technical standpoint, became less linear and more *malerisch* (in Wölfflin's sense). This "Visualization" of art, in technique as well as subject, is one of its most important characteristics, as Wölfflin has so excellently shown in his work.

The *malerisch* method now triumphs over linearism, eye over mind and other organs of perception; vibrating and restless dynamism over static immobility; the momentary impression over the eternal aspect; violence of emotions, movements, expressions, and actions over serenity and calmness; recession over painting on a plane; openness over closeness; obscurity over clarity; visual theatricality over Ideational reality.[108] These changes concerned the art of the whole of Western Europe and by themselves are sufficient again to prove the fact of a further shift to visualism.

In the Netherlands the previous naturalism developed further, in technique as well as in content. Color and the *malerisch* treatment made enormous progress through the works of Rembrandt, Rubens, Van Dyke, Janssens, Jordaens, Franz Hals, Ruysdael, and other great masters of the period. Linearism practically disappeared in the works of all these men. *Dynamism* and *motion* stamp all their works, whether their topics be religious (see, for instance, the religious pictures of Rubens and Rembrandt; all are permeated by violent dynamism, as though they caught the depicted events at the moment of their most violent and dramatic movement) or secular (portrait or *paysage*, *genre* of everyday life or of historical events). Even the *paysage* becomes full of motion and vibration. In other terms this means increasing *emotionality* and *patheticism*. This emotionality begins to become more and more *fleshly* and *sensuous*. Even the religious personalities, especially the women, and

---

[108] See the discussion and the pictures in H. Wölfflin, *op. cit.* See also Ligeti's book, which stresses particularly this point ("*Schein* versus *Sein*," "Appearance versus Reality," "Becoming versus Being").

particularly the women of Rubens become rosy, fleshly, full of biological vigor and appetite, where there is little if anything of otherworldliness, asceticism, Ideationalism. We are amidst a very "real" world of sensory perceptions, "disfigured" little, if at all, by any idealism or ideationalism. As a natural consequence the topics themselves become more and more of that sensory daily world : portraiture develops further, especially that of quite ordinary men ; the everyday *genre* progresses ; no selection is made between noble and ignoble subjects ; everything, and particularly ordinary routine events — eating, sleeping, fighting, quarreling, doing this or that job — these are now the main materials dealt with. In addition, caricature and satire for the first time make their entrance into the world of art on a relatively large scale. In brief, before us is Visualism in its *fully developed* form. It has not very much further to go in order to reach its *extreme* form of impressionism, a result which was achieved at the end of the nineteenth century.[109]

As far as the Flemish influence upon the art of other countries was growing at that period, fully developed Visualism in its "naturalistic" form was making headway in other countries.

In the other line of the development of art in the seventeenth century stand Italy, France, and Spain, where the progress of Visualism assumed a pseudo-Idealistic and pseudo-classical form different from that of the Netherlands. In Italy we have the epigoni of Michelangelo, the genius of the baroque, Bernini and his followers, and the growth of the school of Caravaggio. Here the progress of Visualism assumed not the form of a further development of Flemish naturalism, but that of an artificial, pompous, sumptuous, luxurious *theatricality*, with its voluptuousness of ecstasy and sensuality. Some part of the halo of the Renaissance idealization of the empirical world still hovers above the works of Carracci, Guido, Albani, Guercino, and a few others ; but it is more and more dispelled by the theatricality and by the "sensuous naturalism" of the followers of Caravaggio. However different this theatricality is from the Flemish naturalism, nevertheless it is but another form of triumphant Visualism. The above characterization of the baroque is particularly applicable to the art of Italy of that period. The usual satellites of Visualism are naturally not lacking here : patheticism, dynamism, picturesqueness, latent and open sensualism and sexualism, growth of *genre*, of individual portraiture, and so on.[110]   (See Plates XV and XVI.)

---

[109] See the details in A. Michel, *Histoire de l'art*, Vol. VI, chap. iv, and the references there.

[110] See A. Michel, *Histoire de l'art*, Vol. V, chap. xi; Vol. VI, chap. i; *et passim*, and H. Voss, Weese, Weisbach, Pauli, Glück in the Appendix to this chapter.

In France the growth of Visualism assumed the form of *Academic art* [111] with Le Brun as its lawgiver, after the French baroque of the first half of the seventeenth century. As Hourticq rightly remarks, this was the second wave of imitation of what was supposed to be classical art in France, the first imitative "submission" to classical discipline being in the time of Francis I (the Renaissance properly in its Italian fashion), and the third being later on, at the end of the eighteenth century, in the form of the neo-classical school of David.[112] Here we have something very similar to the waves of imitative classicism in ancient Rome, under Augustus and later, each subsequent imitation being more and more dissimilar from the pattern of the original Greek classicism, and each successive imitation being more and more Visual than the preceding one.[113] The same is true in regard to the waves of imitative classicism here. In spite of the rules of the Academy, which at least in part have some relationship to the rules of the classic art, the Academic "classicism" was no less removed from the real classic art of Greece of the fifth century B.C. than the "classic" dramas and tragedies of Racine and Corneille were from the classic drama of Greece of the fifth century. In fact it was a pseudo classicism and pseudo idealism, or more exactly, a chill theatrical, "rationalized" sensate Visualism. Even the supreme *genre* of the Academy, the historic *genre*, shows this clearly.

With its artificial themes taken either from the Bible or from classical antiquity (Poussin), it began in the former to select more and more of such topics as the bathing Suzanne and the elderly onlookers, and Lot and his daughters, where the voluptuous feminine bodies and erotic associations were evident; in the themes of antiquity (Apollo and Daphne, the Shepherds of Arcadia, Orpheus and Eurydice, and so on) again it painted mainly nude bodies, and again not so much those of the antiquity as of the France of the seventeenth century, with its own dreams and aspirations garbed in what was believed to be the patterns of antiquity. Whether in the works of Poussin (1594–1665), or Simon Vouet (1590–1649), or somewhat later in those of Claude Lorrain, Bourdon, Le Sueur, and others, theatrical Visualism with its artificiality remains present. After the foundation of the Academies, in the works of Le Brun and other academicians, it is still stronger. Subdued artificiality and theatrical Visualism permeate it from top to bottom: in its preference for topics of imaginary antiquity, in its cold, rational rules, in its hierarchy of the

---

[111] The Academy of Painting and Sculpture was founded in 1648, of Architecture in 1671, of Music in 1672, and the French Academy of Rome in 1666.

[112] Hourticq, *op. cit.*, p. 303.   [113] See pages 306–308.

various *genres*, and so on. What is still more important, these rules were far from being followed by all the artists. Portraiture grows, *paysage* grows, nonhistorical *genre* shows the same tendency. The method of rendering remains Visual. Allegories (Charity, Intelligence, Memory, etc.) are used but — and this again is a typical trait — for some reason all these abstractions are given the form of nude — and seductive — females. The topics of antiquity seem to be a mere pretext for the representation of naked and sensuous bodies, and especially feminine bodies. Even when, as in the tomb monuments, they try to imitate the idealistic figures, the result is very different: the figures of the dead for some reason or other are given often the dress and forms of the Greeks and of the Romans; their posture and attitude are again full of movement and dramatic action; their facial expressions have little if anything of Idealistic calm and serenity. The Academism was cerebral, elegant, of the beauty parlor, with subdued tones of an aristocratic "idealization" of purely sensuous objects, phenomena, events. There was no Ideationalism in it and little, if anything, of a transcendental Idealism. If, in comparison with the pure Visual naturalism of the Flemish type, it was not so naturally Visualistic, it was, on the other hand, more theatrically Visualistic than the former. Anyhow this wave of pseudo-classical Idealism was weak, shallow, and comparatively short lived. Toward the beginning of the eighteenth century there remained little if anything of this intellectual pseudo Idealism of the Academy. The Visual trend was continued.[114]

In Spain the same tendency toward Visualism existed, though perhaps not so blatantly as in the Netherlands or Italy. The Spanish painting was in its golden age, in the age of Velásquez, Murillo, Ribera, Zurbarán, Montañés, V. Leal, and other great masters of the age. It was neither so naturalistic as the Flemish art nor so theatrical as the Bernini school in Italy, nor even so cerebral and cold as the Academic art of France. It represented a real synthesis of the remnants of the earthly Idealism of the Renaissance plus remnants even of the real medieval Idealism, with exquisite Visual tendencies. In this sense it was an art nearest to the art of the Italian Renaissance though less "pagan," but in technique more Visual and *malerisch*.[115]

The other countries, England and Germany, like Spain occupied an intermediate position between the Italo-French and the Flemish forms of Visualism.[116]

---

[114] See the details in Michel, *Histoire de l'art*, Vol. VI, and the literature referred to there.
[115] See the details, *ibid.*, Vol. VI, chap. viii.   [116] See *ibid.*, Vol. VI, chap. xii.

Thus Visualism took two main forms in that period: the Flemish naturalistic, and the Italo-French theatrical. In conformity with this main trend, its satellites, like the growth of individualism; the transformation of the artist into the professional who is paid for his art by fame, by popularity, by wealth, by nearness to the powerful of the period; the growth of so-called aestheticism in society; the development of a literature devoted to the problem of art; the reasoning and chattering about it; the rise of connoisseurism in art; the appearance of professional critics; the increase of art education; and so on — all the satellites already familiar from the Visual phase of the Graeco-Roman art did not fail to appear. In many respects the period was indeed similar to the phase of the Hellenistic and of the Roman art after the second century B.C. Generally its "increasing sensualism ushered into painting [and also sculpture] what Pascal styled 'vanity' and what Mother Angelica accused as satisfying 'two senses at once'!" [117] The age and culture of Ideationalism was over; over was the age of Idealism of the thirteenth century. The European world passed definitely into the Sensate Visual stage of its culture.

V. Eighteenth Century

I have remarked, in regard to the Hellenistic and the Roman post-Augustan art, that their subsequent course was a series of waves of imitation of previous forms of art, changing more and more quickly as we pass to the later centuries of these cultures — imitation of the early "archaic," the "classic," then the previous Idealistic and purely Visual forms, and so on. *In this sequence of the various fashions and imitations the previous Ideational form as well as a real Idealistic form was never successfully achieved, all the imitative waves remaining generally in the Visual stream and the change consisting in a variation of different Visual forms in spite of the efforts to give a real Idealistic or even Ideational art.* And this varying Visualism dominated up to the end of the Sensate phase of the Graeco-Roman culture and its replacement by the beginning of the Ideational culture.

This fact comes spontaneously to one's mind when one is following the destinies of the European art after the Idealistic art of the thirteenth and in part of the fourteenth century. There have been many waves of changed styles, several attempts to revive the "idealistic classicism," and to achieve an Idealistic art; quite recently there has been attempted even something near to the Ideational style. But in spite of all this, all these

[117] *Ibid.*, Vol. VI, p. 935.

changes have moved in a Visual stream, never giving real Idealistic or Ideational art. And Visualism, since the fifteenth century, has steadily progressed up to the end of the nineteenth century. The waves of various styles have been mainly a change of one variety of Visual style to the other varieties of the same style. And the change of these fashions seems to have tended to go on more quickly as we move from the preceding centuries to our own times.

The Renaissance was the first imitative wave of the supposedly Idealistic art of Greece, for which it mistook the overripe stage of the Hellenistic and the Roman art. The Renaissance failed, as we have mentioned, to produce real Idealistic art, giving instead a brilliant but pseudo-classic and pseudo-Idealistic Visual art. Then came as a reaction the purely naturalistic Visualism of the Flemish school, the baroque of the Italian, with Academism as its offshoot and as the second imitative wave of a pseudo classicism. In spite of their differences they all happen to be no less but more Visual than the Renaissance. Toward the end of the seventeenth and the beginning of the eighteenth century, the baroque as well as Academism was worn out and gave place to the rococo style on the one hand, and to the Flemish "sweetened" naturalism on the other. Both by their very nature are fully Visual and sensuous, each in its own manner. In neither one is there even the pretense of being classical, or Ideational, or Idealistic. The Flemish naturalism aims to render the real (empirical) world as it looks, in its everyday aspects, in all its visual appearance. The rococo does the same but in a particularly effeminate, perfumed, boudoirish, "sweet" way, with superannuated and theatrical innocence, with all the artificiality of the hedonists satiated with the usual sensuous impressions and dreaming of a delicate coquettish innocence, of fresh shepherdesses, of romantic ruins, of romantic nature, of pastorals, and similar Rousseauistic delicacies; all of them tempting to the boudoirish, artificial, gallant, polished, and worn-out Epicureans. If the baroque was a magnificent theatrical pageant staged on a large scale, and in splendid sumptuousness, the rococo is a diminutive theatrical freak, intimate, jolly, boudoirish, sentimental, and theoretically "simple," but in fact containing endless freaks and complexities.

About the beginning of the second part of the eighteenth century the rococo was practically worn out and the first signs of a return, for the third time, to "classicism" appeared. This return was an accomplished fact at the end of the eighteenth century. Thus within one century art made a whole circle: beginning with classical Academism, it went to the romantic rococo, and at the end of the century returned to classicism.

The domination of the third imitation of classicism was short, however: around 1825 it was almost over and soon was replaced by the romanticism of the second quarter of the nineteenth century. Romanticism did not last longer, and within one quarter of a century was outmoded. It was replaced by something like "naturalism," and several other currents, one of which developed into the impressionistic school of the last quarter of the nineteenth century. In it Visualism reached its extremest and purest form: there was and there is no possibility of going further along the line of Visualism. Its triumph was again short, and toward the end of the nineteenth century its fashionableness was already on the decline: "expressionists," and especially "cubists," "futurists," "symbolists," appeared as the opponents of not only the impressionistic school but almost the Visual style itself.

At the present moment we have a most diversified conglomeration of many schools and currents, among them even the challengers of the Visual style generally and the first symptoms of the search for something akin to the Ideational style. But these symptoms as yet are weak; the searchers look but have not yet found what they desire.

Thus within the nineteenth century we have several waves, each of a duration hardly longer than a quarter of a century. In the eighteenth century the duration of the rococo and of classicism was about half of a century; in the seventeenth century the baroque and Academism lasted almost a century; the Flemish naturalism lasted even longer; and the Renaissance "classicism" also continued for more than a century.

Such, roughly speaking, was the main course of European art, with its trend to an acceleration of the change of the fashionable varieties of the Visual style. This acceleration seems to mean that Visualism is perhaps beginning to wear itself out, since one variety of it after another is tried and quickly discarded, and this trial and discarding, becoming quicker and more short lived, is perhaps an indication of the decline of the Visual style. The subject must, however, be discussed further.

Let us now turn to a brief substantiation of the above statements about the main styles of the eighteenth century.

In France, "from 1690 — the date of the death of Le Brun — to 1785, which marks the arrival of David, French painting described a complete cycle which brought it back to the point of its departure." In the first part of the century Academism and classicism were dethroned in favor of the free and romantic rococo; from about 1750 the rococo and romanticism were dethroned in favor of neo-classicism.[118]

[118] *Ibid.*, Vol. VII, pp. 483 and 1.

The general traits of the rococo were given above. It is a style "where purely decorative research and passion for ornamentation pushed to excess predominate." [119] In architecture it is marked by "light and gayety stressed by grand recesses, made ornate by leaves, fantastic masks, and especially by jolly and smiling feminine figures." Horror of straight lines and straight angles; curvatures, and curved lines; "flexibility and dyssymmetry"; and all this loaded by the garlands of Hymen, by rustic attributes, by amours, by Chinese dragons, and by voluptuous — light, smiling, and promising — feminine figures: this is the rococo. These traits, conspicuous in the French rococo, were still more pronounced in the German, Italian, and the Dutch.[120]

In sculpture it imitated "living, animated, passionate nature" in its dynamic aspect, even "to the slightest and most fugitive palpitations of life." Hence, the passion, sentimentality, sensuality, Visualism, hedonism, of that sculpture.[121]

In painting

by reaction against the disciplined, intellectualist, and Italianizing art of the Academy [after 1690, the date of Le Brun's death] there arose a more free and more sensual art which preferred Rubens to Carracci, and which, trying first of all to please, deliberately sacrificed some of the boring correctnesses of the Academic art to the charm of colour.[122]

It was a petty art by its nature: intimate, domestic, gallant, coquettish, boudoirish, theatrical par excellence. "The art of the fifteenth century reflected mysteries; the art of the eighteenth, the Opera." Even in the religious painting

the grave and serene faith which inspired Le Sueur and Phil. of Champaigne does not now find any interpreters. The Bible for the painters of the Regency is no more than a repertory of gallant subjects, among which they chose preferably two: Lot and his daughters, and Suzanne and the Elders.[123]

These quotations are sufficient to indicate that this petty art was Visual from head to foot, with all the usual satellites of Visualism. Watteau (b. 1684), idyllic, *malerisch*, picturesque, "everyday" (with his endless Venuses, sleeping, walking, talking, bathing); Boucher (1703–1770), boudoirish; Greuze (1725–1805), sentimental and erotic in his sugar-sweet, lachrymose, apparent innocence; Fragonard (1732–1806), a mixture of all of these; La Tour and others, skillful in their Visual portraiture; and H. Robert, Jos, and Vernet, romantic in their predilection for "romantic"

[119] *Ibid.*, Vol. VII, p. 178.   [120] *Ibid.*, Vol. VII, pp. 14 ff.   [121] *Ibid.*, Vol. VII, p. 37.   [122] *Ibid.*, Vol. VII, p. 87.   [123] *Ibid.*, Vol. VII, p. 91.

ruins — these artists illustrate typically the style of the period. Other satellites of Visualism were not lacking: the growth of individualism and freedom among the artists; the growth of portrait painting, of the everyday *genre* (a boy, a love scene, a snatched kiss, etc.); of picturesque, theatrical *paysage* especially. (Ruins and dramatic nature everywhere.) In regard to this last we find the following generalization:

Each time a revival of the classical doctrine approaches, you can see that man is becoming more important as a subject of the classic art, while landscape tends to fade and be effaced around him; and *vice versa:* whenever you notice [in art] that the sky spreads over the head and the soil extends under the feet and becomes land instead of being merely a pedestal for a human figure this is a sign of the time when art descends from the heights of the absolute to the relative world, to the world of the accidental, of the [visually] real. Such is the profound significance of the history of the landscape.[124]

Whether the rule is universally true or not will be discussed further; in application to the rococo art, it is certainly true: *paysage*, mainly of the artificial, theatrical kind, grew proportionately very much in that period.[125]

Moreover, "aestheticism" and the discussion of the problems of art, connoisseurism, art education, and so on, were among the most fashionable topics and hobbies.

Aesthetic questions and questions of good taste in the eighteenth century occupied an ever increasing place in the daily conversations of society, in the philosophical and critical discussions. . . . The number of art amateurs and of the "curieux" multiplied enormously.[126]

This seems to happen often when art is becoming shallow in its Visual character. So it was in Greece after the fourth century; so it was in the Hellenistic world; so it was in Rome after Augustus; so it happened several times in the history of the Western culture.[127]

As the French art was gradually imitated throughout Europe, the rococo style penetrated and became dominant in Germany, the Netherlands, and Italy, in Spain and Portugal (in the first part of the eighteenth

[124] L. Gillet, *Histoire du paysage en France* (Paris, 1908), p. 36.

[125] For the details, see Michel's and Hourticq's works.

[126] Michel, *Histoire de l'art*, Vol. VII, p. 2. Dominant aesthetic theories were also illusionistic. See K. Lange, "*Die asthetische Illusion in 18 Jahrhundert*," in *Zeitschrift für Aesthetik und allgemeine Kunstwissenschaft* (1906), pp. 30–43.

[127] See this point stressed strongly in F. Chambers's works. Generally, when a social value begins to become shallow or a social institution to become disorganized, the society begins vividly to discuss it and to offer various — mostly useless — remedies. In our days this is conspicuously shown by the problem of the family and the literature about it: there is a flood of such writings at the present time.

century); only England escaped its influence in any great degree. For this reason it is unnecessary to survey each of these countries. Even in England, where art in the eighteenth century was great (Hogarth, Reynolds, Gainsborough, Wilson, Crome, Ward, Lawrence), even there it was Visual, almost impressionistically Visual, though in a way different from the rococo.[128]

VI. THE END OF THE EIGHTEENTH CENTURY AND THE NINETEENTH CENTURY

As we have mentioned, beginning with about the second part of the eighteenth century a reaction against the rococo and romanticism began to appear. Around 1780 it triumphed and ushered in again a "neo-classic" style in the work of David and his school in France, and similar painting and sculpture in other countries. In one respect it seems to have moved somewhat away from Visualism — it was more linear and less *malerisch* than the rococo or the baroque. Born as an intellectualist movement in a considerable degree, under the influence of Winckelmann's rediscovery of the antique art in his *Geschichte der Kunst des Alterthums* (which happened to represent it quite wrongly and considered as the antique art the latest Hellenistic and Roman Visual art) it claimed to be in a sense an Ideational movement (the *Gedankenkunst* of Winckelmann!) and therefore stressed line as against color, scarcity of ornamentation as against its profusion, the architectural type of painting as against the visual, antique topics in opposition to the romantic, nudity in opposition to drapery, the heroic as against the daily and common, the static and reposeful as against dynamism and movement; man as against nature. In brief, it sought to be Ideational, or Idealistic, in a "classic" manner.

In reality it was a simulacrum of all this, an even poorer simulacrum perhaps than the Academism of the second half of the seventeenth century had provided. Even more artificial, cold, and boring than the earlier imitation, it followed the purely external traits of the classic art, without its inner spirit. The results were about the same as in several of the ancient Roman waves of pseudo classicism: cold theatricality, *ennui*, incongruity (especially when some contemporary persons were represented either naked or in Roman togas), and other traits of a purely imitative movement:

First, colossalism: it was thought that antiquity was necessarily colossal and, as Quatremère de Quincy insisted, "Physical grandeur is one of the main reasons for the value and the effects in architecture,"

---

[128] See the history in A. Michel, *op. cit.*, Vol. VII, *passim*.

and "grandeur must be not only real but also apparent." [129]   We have seen the same colossalism developing in the Hellenistic and Roman cultures in the Visual stage of their art.

Second, the lack of any real Idealistic spirit in the art : it deals only with purely empirical topics, and even with those quite artificially.

Third, in spite of its proscription of dynamism, it was, beginning with the first famous picture of David, *Le serment des Horaces*, dynamic, dramatic, passionate.   The real calm and serenity of the Idealistic art was never achieved by it.   Shall we add that it was Sensate, often even erotic, with all the voluptuousness of Canova's *Amour et Psyche, Danseuses*, to mention but the best examples; that it was quite earthly in its subservience to the powerful of this world, of which David himself gives an excellent example with his too flexible subservience to the revolutionaries, to Napoleon, to the Bourbons after their restoration.[130]   In brief, if in some respects the neo-classicism of the end of the eighteenth and the beginning of the nineteenth century was a reaction against the Visualism of the rococo, this was indeed slight, and art remained in the Visual current, never being able to soar either to the real Idealism or, especially, to Ideationalism.   It was just a slight rippling upon the wave of Visual art, no more.

Again this neo-classicism was not only French but practically European ; therefore what has just been said is applicable, with slight variation, to the art of virtually all the main countries of Europe.   In spite of all its attempts, Western art was not able to get out of the stream of Visualism, which it had entered after the decline of the Idealistic art of the thirteenth century.

In the anarchical and many-colored conglomeration of numerous and various schools of art of the nineteenth century — all of which, to the end, remained in the Visual stream — there were some alternations in the slight domination of the neo-neo-neo-classic and of the neo-neo-neo-anti-classic, the neo-romantic, the neo-Primitivist, the pre-Raphaelite, the rationalist, and other currents.   The neo-classicism of the David-Winckelmann school continued to about 1820–1830.   Its place was taken by the anticlassical Romantic school, which dominated up to about 1848–1850.   Then its place was taken in turn by the realism (practically the Visual naturalism [131] so excellently developed before by the Flemish

---

[129] See L. Hautecoeur's study in A. Michel's work, Vol. VIII, pp. 6 ff.

[130] See A. Michel, *Histoire de l'art*, Vol. VIII (Paris, 1925), 1e partie.

[131] "Aesthetically realism is opposite to idealism.   It consists in the reproduction of objects just as they [Visually] are without any attempt to purify, to ennoble, or to beautify them by

artists of the seventeenth century) of Gericault, of the *paysagists* of the Barbizon school (Courbet, Daumier, Millet, and others). It flourished from about 1848 to 1870. Its further development, and purest form of the Visual art, was *impressionism*, which succeeded realism and dominated from about 1870 to the end of the nineteenth century. All these currents were Visual. Impressionism is Visual par excellence.

Then only, as a reaction to it and to Visualism generally, appeared symbolism, constructivism, expressionism, neo-Primitivism, cubism, futurism, and similar movements which at least in their negative program and aspirations broke sharply and decisively with Visualism for the first time since the entrance of Visualism into the Western art. As I have pointed out, they did not succeed in becoming real Ideationalism or even Idealism; they are just transitory, incoherent movements, whose aversion to Visualism is clear and determined. In this sense they are a real landmark in the course of the Western art. But in their positive search for a new form of art they remain, so far, unsuccessful. The result is incoherence, inner contradiction, "queerness," and, in a sense, sterility. They are the children of divorce from Visuality; they have lost the old family shelter, but they have not found, as yet, a new family. Therefore they are "in the street," a kind of homeless, formless wild urchins running here and there and failing in their attempt to find a safe and pleasant place to live and really creative work to do.[132] This is a tendency common, as we shall see, to practically all the main forms of contemporary art: painting and sculpture, architecture, music, drama, and literature.

That romanticism, realism (or rather Visual naturalism), and impressionism are quite Visual currents is evident. They do not even pretend to be Idealistic or Ideational. For this reason it is needless to discuss them. What is worth doing here is to point out some of the traits of impressionism which make it the last and the extremest development of Visualism to the limit beyond which there is *non plus ultra*. It replaced composition (choice, selection, arrangement — omitting the incidental, stressing the essential) by the impression of a moment. It painted things as they

---

the work of mind. The artist must represent what he sees." L. Réau in Michel, *Histoire de l'art*, Vol. VIII, p. 548.

However, some principle of choice of subjects, often a certain propaganda, for instance, in favor of laboring classes by Millet and others, plus an effort to give the Visually typical in the object rendered — not just the purely incidental — has always been present in "realism." Only Impressionism, as its logical development, expelled all these "Ideational" elements and became the triumph of a pure Visualism.

[132] For the history of art in the nineteenth and twentieth centuries, see A. Michel, *Histoire de l'art*, Vol. VIII, 1e, 2e, and 3e partie.

looked at a given point in an incessant fugitive change of Visual appearance due to the vibration of light and shade. It did not aim to stress
anything essential, lasting, eternal in the objects. It was *malerisch* par
excellence. There were no fixed linear forms, no constant color, because
"forms and colours incessantly change from moment to moment," and
because "all shades are transparent and coloured, animated by thousands
of reflexions." [133]   Accordingly they painted out of doors, in full sun-
light, *sub Jove crudo*, with a specially elaborated technique of extreme
malerisch characters (patches of various colors put side by side) made
possible through the photographic and optical discoveries of Chevreul.

The theorizers of impressionism and the artists claimed quite consistently that such an art did not need either mind or thought or any
idea ; all that it needed was a sharp eye and a trained hand to render
the impression of the eye either in painting or in sculpture. Also, they
contended quite consistently that it was a matter of indifference what
was painted ; the subject was a secondary matter and anything would do.
"*Sujet* is quite unimportant : a pile of earth or the most vulgar and common object may become, in certain moments, quite fascinating." The
same object could be rendered many times, each time giving a new
picture or new sculpture because at different moments this object would
look different. And many of the artists indeed painted the same landscape or other object several times. *Paysage* and portrait — these two
forms of art profited essentially from impressionism. No particular
selection in the topics, no idealization, no ideationalization, have a place
in impressionism. It aimed to be "empty minded," like a photographic
camera that would "shoot" anything. Like the camera, impressionism
desired to take "snapshots" of the passing Visual surface of objects. It
was not an accident that impressionism developed simultaneously and in
connection with the development of photography : both were the offshoots
of the same deep forces which concentrated the attention mainly on the
Visual appearance of the world, on its "surface," on its "visible illusion"
— moreover, on the surface of a given passing moment, proscribing and
refusing to go "deeper" into what is behind the visual aspect, behind the
world of the senses. In all these respects the principle of Becoming and
of the Visualist outlook on the world (*Weltanschauung*) reached its climax
in impressionism. There is no possibility of going further along that path.
Even photography ; even "movies," which also began to develop almost
simultaneously with all this and the appearance of which at the end
of the nineteenth century is again not purely accidental ; even these can

[133] *Ibid.*, Vol. VIII, pp. 577 ff.

hardly go further along the line of Visualism than impressionism has already gone.

Here then is a conception of the external world entirely new, if not in philosophy, at least in painting [an exaggeration !]. Figures and objects, which the painters of the Occident tried to paint since the fifteenth century with the maximum of relief and materiality, now lost all their fixity, and all their consistency. Nature appeared now as a mere succession of appearances, as an unstable phantasmagoria, as a deceiving mirage.[134]

Plates XVII, XVIII, and XIX give an idea of the moderately impressionistic, impressionistic, and imitative sculptural and expressionistic pictures, with the sex motive, of the second part of the nineteenth century and the beginning of the twentieth. In Plate XVII, No. 1, *Naked Woman* by Gustave Courbet (1819–1877), is sculptural; No. 2, *Street in Bern* by Edouard Manet (1832–1883), is mildly impressionistic. Nos. 1 and 2 on Plate XVIII, *Boulevard* and *The Breakfast of the Boaters* by Auguste Renoir (1841–1920), and No. 3, *Ugolino and His Sons* by J. B. Carpeaux (1827–1875), and No. 4, a bust of H. von —— by Auguste Rodin (1840–1917), represent the impressionistic in painting and sculpture. Plate XIX shows *Scene from Tahiti* by Paul Gaugin (1848–1903) with " primitivistic" tendency, and *Field in Spring* by Claude Monet (1840–1928) impressionistic especially. For an example of the *pathétique* similar to the Laocoön group (Plate XI), Carpeaux's group may be taken. Cubistic and other expressionistic works may be found on Plate IX.

Impressionism, photography, movies — all three are excellent testimony that at the end of the nineteenth and at the beginning of the twentieth century the mentality of the Western society, so far as it was expressed in art (and, as we shall see, in philosophy, science, and all the compartments of culture), became extremely Visual and illusionistic. Reality was reduced in that mentality to the mere surface of the sensory phenomena; even in that surface the reality was thought of as a purely momentary, fugitive, and passing glimpse. "The real is only what your eye sees at a given moment." Such is this "visually solipsistic" philosophy of illusionism and radical illusionistic Visual "shallowness." "All the world is but a momentary Visual appearance," a "momentary Visual impression," such is another formula. And all this results from the development of Visualism to its logical limits. When this limit, in the form of impressionism (and other illusion philosophies), has been reached, Visualism, and its foundation Sensatism (*Nihil esse in intellectu quod non*

---

[134] L. Reau's study in Michel, *Histoire de l'art*, Vol. VIII, p. 548.

fuerit prius in sensu), suddenly find themselves at "the end of their rope," in a blind alley, in imminent danger of self-annihilation. Since the whole of reality has been reduced by Visualism to the mere passing impression, to the momentary appearance, the reality amounts to mere illusion and mirage, to self-deceit and dreaming; even these being purely fugitive and momentary.

Such a "reality" became so "thin" (thinner even than the outermost surface of the things), and so "immaterial," that it reduced itself to something less substantial than even the proverbial ashes. Ashes have at least some material being; in the Impressionistic Visualism there is left nothing but the passing mirage. Paradoxically Visualism and Sensatism, pushed to their limits, came to self-destruction. Both rejected any "Ideational" reality, any mind, any thought, any planned construction in their purposes and creations. Their ultimate foundation, at the beginning, was the materiality of the external world. Now this materiality has evaporated in "illusionism." Therefore this basis has disappeared. The Ideational foundation had been rejected from the very beginning. Therefore it could not become the new foundation. In this way reality was reduced to almost nothingness, and the mentality of Visualism found itself in emptiness: without reality, without any foundation to rest upon.

For a time it could live in the illusionistic world of fugitive phantasmagorias, amidst the restless mirages of incessant Becoming; but nobody and no movement can live for a long time in such a world of illusionistic appearances. Impressionism could not do it; and at the beginning of the twentieth century its triumph was over; it destroyed itself; it called forth a vigorous reaction and criticism. And since it was the most extreme form of Visualism; and since other, more moderate, forms had been tried before, there seems to have been no possibility of advancing along this path. The only "new" way or way further was the *non-Visual* way. Hence, "the blind alley" of Visualism suddenly began to be abandoned and there appeared an ever-increasing number of artists who decisively refused to enter into any part of the Visual highway. They believed that all Visual routes had been tried and that all led, after a time, to a blind alley. The only possibility was to try to find a new, non-Visual road. Expressionism, constructivism, cubism, futurism, "pointilism," "dadaism," "surrealism," "tactilism," and many other modern "isms" were exactly this "getting-off" the Visual highway and searching for a new non-Visual pass leading to new horizons and to new summits of artistic creation. "The dominant trait of the contemporary paint-

PLATE XVII

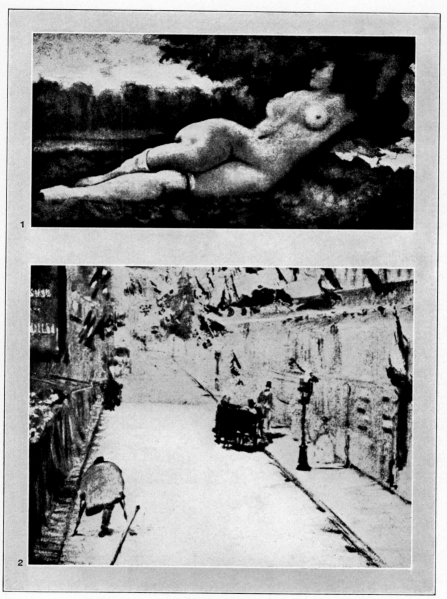

1, Naked Woman, by Courbet.   2, Street in Bern, by Manet.

ing is a vigorous reaction against Impressionism. Almost all the post-Impressionists are anti-Impressionists." [135]

The main criticisms raised against impressionism are :

(1) Absence of thought, style, and construction.

(2) Its purely Sensate nature — "an acephalic art." It notes only sensations, without any judgment of thought; "eye eats the brain in it."

(3) Its nihilism. For impressionism there is nothing noble or ignoble. There is no gradation of values, no hierarchy of *genres;* no qualitative scale of topics. Everything is potentially equal to everything else as mere impression.

It led to the disappearance or to the neglect of many noble *genres* which involved an effort of thought: religious painting, grand decorative painting, and to some extent even portraiture. . . . Only *paysage* gained from it.[136]

However great are the differences between the various post- and anti-impressionistic schools, the trait common to all of them — in various forms and degrees — is that :

By reaction against the Impressionistic sensatism the new art attempts to restore in painting the long-neglected rights of thought, while the care for construction affirms itself [not only in its recognition by these schools, but especially] by the provocative excesses of cubism.[137]

In this sense all these schools — the neo-classicists, the constructionists, the expressionists, the neo-impressionists, the cubists, and others — show a retreat from extreme Visualism and therefore approach to some Ideationalism (as far as the role of thought and construction is concerned).

However, this trait is manifest in different degrees in these schools. The most radical rupture with Visualism is made by what are often called cubism and futurism. As indicated at the beginning of this chapter, they reject the very idea of representing things as they look. They want "to substitute the conceptual reality for the visual one." Their purpose is "not a reproduction of the surface of the objects, not rendering them as they appear to the eyes, but painting them as they are in the mind." [138] If one looks at the pictures of Picasso on Plate XI, one sees this point immediately. It is not a visual cello or girl with lute but a conceptional one.

This formulation sounds perfectly Ideational. However, it is not, so far as the positive program of cubists and similar schools is concerned.

---

[135] Michel, *Histoire de l'art*, Vol. VIII, p. 600.　　　　[136] *Ibid.*, pp. 600 ff.
[137] *Ibid.*, p. 601.　　　　[138] *Ibid.*, pp. 627 ff.

They are Ideationalists as far as their negative attitude toward Visualism is concerned: they make a resolute rupture with the very principle of Visualism. However, when we inquire what kind of conceptual reality they want to paint and how they conceive it in their minds, the answer is: Sensate — almost rude — materialistic reality. The main difference between their Sensatism and that of Visualism is that while Visualism renders things as they look to our eyes only — only to one organ of our senses — the cubists want to render them as they are presented by two or more organs of sense: by the eye and by the tactile sense. Through these we know that the material-sensory things have usually three dimensions; these three dimensions are not made apparent by our eyes alone but they are presented, in all their materiality, by touch, and perhaps by other organs of sense. Hence cubism. It aims to render — to show — all the three dimensions of material objects. These three dimensions are there, in these objects. Accordingly it tends to render three-dimensionality and corporeality of material things by a geometrical combination of colored planes. Hence all these peculiar cubes, planes, and cuts, which are so strange to the public for centuries educated in Visualism, and typical for many modernistic schools.

To this extent these schools are free of Visualism. But are they Ideational? Not at all. The reality which they believe and try to render remains purely material, corporeal reality. They do not go beyond it, do not strive to render by visible signs the invisible and immaterial world. Even their "mind" is not supreme thought and master of sensations, independent of them, and having its own existence, but is a mere "box" with not only one entrance — the eye, as is the "mind" of the pure impressionists, but with two or more entrances in the form of the other organs of sense. In this way they remain in "purgatory": out of the realm of Visualism, but also out of the kingdom of Ideationalism. Just between. They quitted the former and did not reach the latter. Hence their transitory nature, their incoherence, their queerness, and their fruitlessness. So far as their rupture with Visualism is concerned, they are a very important symptom: a sign of the time, maybe the real, first indication of the end of one great epoch in art and culture and of the coming of a new era. But they are not themselves the bearers of the new spring: they look in a wrong direction; they are too deeply sunk in the Sensate material world, have no wings to soar over it into the stratosphere of the real mind, real Ideationality. Therefore they creep hopelessly, biting strongly at Visualism but unable to build the palace of Ideationalism. Like the Roman transitory art of the second

PLATE XVIII

1, Boulevard, by Renoir.   2, The Breakfast of the Boaters, by Renoir.   3, Ugolino and His Sons, by Carpeaux.   4, Bust of H. von ——, by Rodin.

to the fourth centuries of our era they are just the shining derelicts of a great crisis or great cultural turn. For the real Ideationalists we have still to look into the future.

Such is the deep significance of impressionism and cubism from the standpoint of the present work.

Since the most anti-Visual currents are neither Ideational nor Idealistic, and besides are still the minor currents in the river of contemporary art, this means that the art of the end of the nineteenth and of the twentieth centuries is still conspicuously and extremely Visual. Therefore we should expect the usual satellites of the Visual art also to be displayed in it conspicuously. The expectation is sustained by the facts. Is this contemporary art *individualistic?* Of course. From this follows the contemporary "anarchy" of art. "The word school has no longer its old significance. Individualism which has shattered this uniformity, has destroyed both state and school in the early sense. There is no longer either victor or vanquished [but as many schools as there are artists]." [139] To call any artist unoriginal and without individuality is an insult. Right or wrong, the artists want to be individualists, original, peculiar, especially free from any restraint, even extravagant and queer. Likewise the contemporary artist is a highly professional artist. He wants to be free from any tutelage of religion, moral decency, of anything except his fancy.[140] He wants to mark his creation with his name and is willing in no way to be just an anonymous creator, the *primus inter pares* of a collectivity, as the Ideational artists were. On the other hand, he is a member of the professional union of artists, a kind of caste separate from the rest of the collectivity and ready to protect its interests at the cost of this collectivity.

What is the basis of the selection of the topics by artists of our time? There are several, among them in a few cases some which are purely Ideational. But in the bulk the basis is neither the glory of God nor the glory of the country nor a service to some ideal as such, but the *market demand, profit,* either through commercial sale of pictures and sculptures or through getting an order from a rich magnate, from politicians, or from the state. In all such cases, with publicity as an instrument toward such a commercial goal, Mammon is what dictates the patterns as well as the topics of the art of today. The professional artist has to make

---

[139] Hourticq, *op. cit.*, p. 433.

[140] "The modern artist (in contradistinction to the medieval) seems to regard any limiting conditions imposed as a sacrilegious attempt on his *freedom* as a maker of beauty." J. Maritain, *op. cit.*, p. 158.

his living.   To make it he must be able to sell his services or creations. To sell them he must adapt them to the existing demand of the market. Hence the highly commercialized character of his work and the vulgarism which controls it.   The artist, instead of lifting the vulgar tastes to sublime heights, must debase himself to the low level of vulgarism.[141]

Connected with this is the phenomenon of the development of aestheticism, art dilettantism, art connoisseurism, mass art education, art promotion, art journals, art critics, art dealers, and other phenomena of that kind.   We have seen, and shall see further, that in the Graeco-Roman Visual phase all this grew to huge proportions.   It is needless to point out that we too have all this with us on an enormous scale : hundreds of art journals, thousands of art reviewers, art critics, art managers, art promoters ; thousands of art connoisseurs, art amateurs, art collectors ; hundreds of thousands of art dealers.   Art education is everywhere — on the radio, in the newspapers, in the schools, in the churches, in private houses ; it has become one of the main topics of education.   Even men's and women's clubs and the rural and Four-H clubs have it as a major interest.   Oceans of art !   Another question is how good all this is.   But it is not my task to discuss this problem here.

Further, we have seen that colossalism is one of the satellites of the Visual art.   Do we have it with us?   More than enough.   Sheer quantity springs to the eye everywhere and tends more and more to replace quality.   We build one art museum bigger than the others.   A strenuous competition exists in that respect.   And if a building is the "biggest in the world," this is advertised *urbi et orbi;* and the building is proudly thought of as the best in the world.   The same is true of the pictures, of the mural frescoes, of the statues and sculptural decorations.   "Biggest in the world," or "the greatest number of art galleries, art schools, art courses, art trades" — as with the best sellers, this is thought of as equivalent to being the leader in art, the highest and the best !   We are in the grip of this mania of colossalism, and it manifests itself everywhere and in all fields of art, as will be shown further.

Moreover, as has happened before, the main topics of our art are the persons, the events, the sights of common, daily life, with an inclination for the picaresque, picturesque, for the doubtful aspects and types of life : to crime, to criminals, to prostitutes, to ragamuffins, to urchins,

---

[141] "Unable to enjoy the substance and the peace of wisdom [as the ideational artists did] he is . . . condemned to every servile misery of temporal practice and production. . . . Now the modern world, which had promised the artists all things, will soon scarcely leave him even the bare means of subsistence."   *Ibid.,* pp. 35 and 37.

PLATE XIX

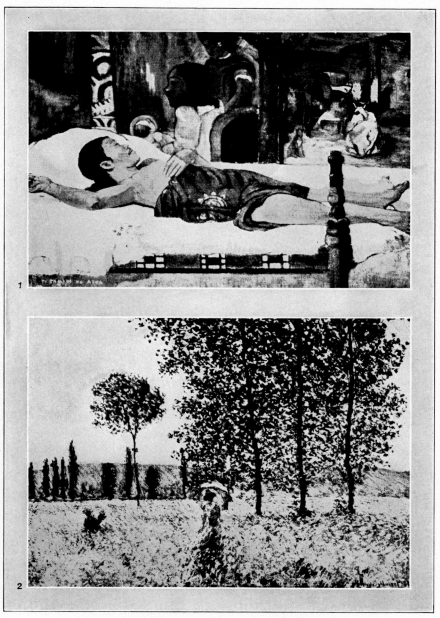

1, Scene from Tahiti, by Gaugin.   **2,** Field in Spring, by Monet.

to the "poorer classes," to abnormal types, and so on. The "proletariat," labor, the "misadapted," Cinderellas, tramps, criminals, and so on, play a very large part in the paintings and sculpture of our time. Here again we are simply repeating what has happened several times before.

Sex, eroticism, voluptuous nudity, the invasion of the pretty — and not too chaste — woman, have been the usual satellites of such a Visual art.[142] It is enough to pick up almost any copy of one of our contemporary magazines, in order to find such a pretty face, be it a movie star, a prostitute, a pretty stenographer, society lady, or just the anonymous mistress of the artist or of the editor. It is enough to go to any annual salon of the new pictures in order to see everywhere old and young female bodies, sitting, lying, standing, quite nude, almost completely nude, three-quarters naked, half-naked but coquettishly dressed so that the figure looks more sexual, having a stronger voluptuous appeal than many naked contemporary Venuses. The same is true of the males: they also are depicted either as "brutes" and "cave men-like" or "fine and dandy," effeminate, and with "sex appeal." One can go at random a dozen times to the movies and see all this in this modern and most Visual form of art.

Other satellites are not lacking. Patheticism, emotionality, dynamism — we have all that in an even supermelodramatic portion. *Satirical, cynical, skeptical* topics abound. In the Ideational and Idealistic there is no place for such an art, because there is no such mentality. The Sensate Visualist cannot help having them. Hence widespread development of caricature, satirical cartoons, pictures, sculptures, portraits, and the satirization of all kinds of events, persons, values. Each newspaper copy has a section containing such satire and caricature; and there are dozens and dozens of special magazines (*The New Yorker, Ballyhoo*) devoted exclusively to satirizing and caricaturing and ridiculing everything and everybody. This is our "stimulant" and refreshment.

We have also seen that the development of *paysage* is connected with Visualism. We, too, have a great development of landscape painting, landscape architecture, and decorative art.

Finally, as the crowning jewel of the four-hundred-year development of Sensate Visualism we have — and not by accident — photography and movies. That they were invented when Visualism in form of Visual realism and impressionism was reaching its extreme development is not

---

[142] The chief topics of the films in 1930 were: sex, 15 per cent of the total; crime, 27.4 per cent; and love, 29.6 per cent. See E. Dale, *The Content of Motion Pictures* (New York, 1935). Thus more than 70 per cent of the films is taken up with these three topics.

to be overlooked. It is in an excellent harmony with the style of time. It is the "finishing touch." And the success of, for example, the movies, amounting for many to their having a "good time" in movies and their regarding the rest of real life as waste — this phenomenal success is really symptomatic and symbolic. Our life is becoming more and more "Hollywoody," more and more "appearance," "illusion," "mirage," which is felt as reality, whereas the reality is felt to be less real than this theatrical deceit.

This is a real finishing touch to the Visualization of our whole life and mentality, of our growing rupture with, and movement away from, the deeper reality. We begin to live in a more and more theatrical, "decorative," "illusionary" world of Visual shadows. As we shall see, our science is becoming more and more illusionistic; our culture tends to be more and more a "show," our criteria of right and wrong, great and small, good and bad, beneficial and harmful, respectable and shameful, all tend to become Visual, a mere "decorum of appearance," of publicity, of advertising, of exhibition, of "objective Visual behaviorism," Visual tests, Visual evidence, the triumph of Visuality in all compartments of culture. We shall see that we are indeed living in the most scientific, most Visual, most illusionary, and therefore most unreal world.

This outline shows the main long-time waves of alternation of the Ideational and the Visual forms of painting and sculpture, together with the main periods of the domination of the intermediary styles, particularly of the Idealistic and cubistic, and with the shorter and shallower ripplings in these alternations. All this probably is sufficient not only for the clarification of my main concepts and for showing that these concepts are not something artificially built up by me, but are indeed at the very base of each form of art and condition hundreds of other detailed traits of a given art of a given period; but also for the inductive corroboration of the "cycles" or "fluctuations" that we have postulated. To this extent the logico-meaningful method is vindicated further: knowing the type of the art, we know and "can deduce" hundreds of its details, and these details are found indeed to exist in the empirical reality.

My task, however, is not finished with this chapter. We have yet to study the history of art further and more accurately, at least in its quantitative aspects. Hence, an invitation to the reader to proceed to the next chapter, which may give something newer and more basic — even for specialists in the history of art — than the qualitative sketch of the course of art from my standpoint, which we have just completed.

Chapter Ten

QUANTITATIVE DESCRIPTION OF THE FLUCTUATION OF THE
MAIN STYLES AND THEIR SATELLITES IN THE PAINTING
AND SCULPTURE OF WESTERN EUROPE [1]

I. Preliminary Methodological Remarks

The verbal and qualitative outline of the fluctuation studied in the preceding chapter is supposedly correct in the essentials, since it agrees with the conclusions of most historians of art.   Nevertheless the accuracy of the historians' conclusions may be questioned.   The point is that these conclusions are based not so much upon the total output of the paintings and sculptures of each period as upon a limited and relatively small collection chosen from the works of the most prominent artists.   This sample is neither so large as to embrace the greater part of the artistic works of the period, nor is it necessarily a random and therefore a representative sample.   Often only a few pictures or sculptures which suit the thesis of the author have been used as "illustrations," leaving the bulk unconsidered and unanalyzed.   The danger of such a method is apparent.   Out of hundreds of thousands of pictures and sculptures, one can always pick up a few dozens which fit any preconceived theory. In that way, one can prove practically any contention in the field, because, as a matter of fact, there are always major and minor streams of art and one always can back up his theory by ascribing the traits of the minor stream to the whole or to the majority of the art creations of the period. There is another point of danger in such a method : in so far as it takes only a few of the works of the greatest artists of the time and assumes that they are representative of the bulk of the works by more numerous and less prominent artists, one is making an arbitrary assumption : it may or may not be true.   For instance, it is very probable that the changes in the forms of art (styles as well as the contents) in the work of the "top artists" occur more rapidly, and perhaps even fluctuate more violently, than those in the bulk of art produced by the mass of the less prominent and mediocre artists.   A great artist is always original to

[1] In co-operation with N. L. Okuneff, Harold Cross, and others.

369

some degree. When we "jump" from the few great artists of a given period to the few of the next period, there always will be found a notable change, due to the factor that these artists, being great, are original. The situation is different with the great bulk of art creations by the mediocre or merely talented majority of artists. Inertia, tradition, imitation, continuity, are likely to predominate here; therefore more time is necessary to produce a notable change in the bulk of the art creations. Hence these fluctuations may be slower and less violent than in the "thin rivulet" of the creations of the greatest artists.

These reasons explain why the conclusions reached in the previous chapter, as well as those of any historian of art, need a further test and corroboration. This should consist in taking practically *all* the known pictures and sculptures of any period studied — or at least, the greater bulk of them — and in studying them all from the standpoint of the problems investigated. When such a "mass study" is made for all the periods investigated, and the data are summed up in a quantitative way, and the diagrams are constructed, and when these support the conclusions, then and then only can we feel relatively sure that these conclusions are roughly valid.

This explains why I had to undertake such a study, in spite of the enormous labor it required, the enormous knowledge it demands, and the "Egyptian load" of monotonous work which is necessary to carry through such a study. I had other reasons also for undertaking such a task. We shall see that it permits us to check and to test many other theories in the field of art which are, in a sense, "a side issue" to my main thesis but which, nevertheless, have a direct bearing on the problems of the dynamics of culture generally. Besides, in later parts of this work, where I attempt to study the existence or nonexistence of "the correlations" or "associations" in the change and fluctuation of various sociocultural processes in different compartments of culture — science, philosophy, art, law, political phenomena, economic phenomena, etc. — I naturally need some real "statistical curves and data" in the field of art fluctuation in order that such data and curves can be compared with those in other fields of culture.

This is enough to show why the subsequent laborious, almost appalling, quantitative study of the paintings and sculptures of Western culture was undertaken. Before giving its results, a few methodological remarks and reservations will explain how these data were obtained and what they mean. Putting the matter as briefly as possible, the following has to be stated.

A. For each of the countries and for each of the periods we tried to include for our analysis all the pictures and all the sculptural works known in the history of art, regardless of whether they belong to great or small or anonymous artists; though all that is known represents, especially for the early centuries, only a small part of what must have existed then. We are sure that our samples embrace — for most of the countries — the bulk of the works of each period, as the reader himself can judge from the tables herein; but it is more than probable that for various reasons we succeeded in getting only a part — though possibly the major part — of the known paintings and sculptures. This part, however, is so large that it is fairly representative, and is certainly larger and more representative than any "samples" used in any study hitherto made.

B. The location of the exact date and place of production of many pictures and sculptural works meets with difficulties, especially in regard to the works of the earlier centuries. The exact dates of their creation, not only the year, but the decade or even the century, are not known. For this reason alone, the periodization for the earlier works had to be made in large time units, such as a century or even two centuries. Within such large units of time, their location in all probability is accurate, at least in regard to the enormous majority of "the dateless art creations."

C. As we shall see, this large section of the world's artistic works is studied from several standpoints, and studied quantitatively. Some of these points, as to whether the topic of the picture or sculpture is religious or secular; whether the portrait is of a woman or a man; whether the work belongs to the landscape, to the everyday *genre*, or to the portraiture class; whether the subject is royalty, the aristocracy, the clergy, the artist, *bourgeoisie*, or the labor class — such points involve practically no subjectivity of the investigators and are computed and classified easily. Other points are more complex and involve some amount of subjectivity. Such, for instance, as whether the nudity of the figure is ascetic, or sensuous (erotic), or neutral; whether (in some of the pictures of not purely Ideational or obviously Visual or Idealistic type) the predominant style is Ideational or Visual or Mixed or what. And there are a few other points of similar character, where the qualification depends, to a degree, upon the "personal equation" of the classifier. This danger was foreseen at the beginning of the study; therefore the workers tried to compare the qualifications in many cases and give the verdict which won either the unanimous or the majority opinion. Besides, for the sake of testing how great may be the element of subjectivity in such cases, the art of Italy [2] was studied independently in two places by the investigators, who did not even know that a parallel study was being made in Prague under the direction of Professor N. L. Okuneff and his associates (whom I asked to do the greater part of this enormous work), and in Cambridge, Massachusetts, by Harold Cross, to whom I gave the task here. The samples in both studies happened to be not exactly the same: the sample studied in Prague included 32,299 pictures and sculptures; the Cambridge sample had 13,427 pictures and 3252 sculptures, altogether 16,679. On account of this difference, some discrepancy in the results was to be expected, regardless of the subjective element involved in the study of some of the points mentioned. This supposition is corroborated by the fact that some discrepancy appears even in the points which, like the "religious and secular" subjects of the pictures, or percentage of male and female portraits, involve practically no subjective element and can be counted easily. The following data give an idea of the discrepancies in the "objective" and the "subjective" points. Let us take first such points in both studies which *do not involve any appreciable subjectivity* — as, for instance, the point of what percentage in the total sample studied is religious and what is secular, according to the topic of the picture or sculpture. In the Prague sample and the Cambridge sample respectively, the percentages are: for the thirteenth century 99.7 religious and .3 secular, 97.5 religious and 2.5 secular; for the period 1301–1350 the religious percentages are respectively (the secular is 100 per cent, minus the per cent of the religious): 98.5 and 94.7; for 1351–1400, 82.4 and 94.0; for 1401–1450, 84.9 and 89.8; for 1451–1500, 80.4 and 76.5; for 1501–1550, 68.8 and 74.6; for 1551–1600, 54.8 and 56.1; for 1601–1650, 50.3 and 59.5; for 1651–1700, 56.1 and 53.5; for 1701–1750, 36.4 and 27.3; for 1751–1800, 42.2 and 20.1; for 1801–1850, 34.1 and 7.56; for 1851–1900, 12.0 and 8.66. The figures show a discrepancy even in this relatively objective point. It is undoubtedly due mainly to the difference in the size of the samples, one being practically twice as large as the other. The difference for most of the periods — even for half-century periods — is, however, comparatively insignificant: only in four periods out of fourteen is the movement of the two curves opposite, and even there, with two exceptions,

[2] Regretfully I had to give up similar parallel studies for the other countries. Besides the Italian art, the French and the Byzantine art were studied, but upon quite an insufficient collection. The reader can easily realize what an amount of work is involved and the expense of the labor of the investigators, though they, for the sake of the study, agreed to do this spadework for a very modest remuneration, taking it as a labor of love and scientific interest, rather than a job with proper remuneration.

the curves of the percentages run practically parallel, so far as the main
trends and fluctuations are concerned. As the Prague sample is larger
and the study was made under the close supervision of a prominent professor of the history of art, it gives probably more accurate data than
the Cambridge study.

An idea of the discrepancy in the two studies, in the points which
involve an element of subjectivity, is given by comparing the percentages
of both studies concerning the measure of spirituality or sensuality in
the pictures and sculptures in which the human body figures (all the
pictures practically, minus *paysage* and few others, where the human
body does not figure. These latter are put into the neutral class).
All such pictures were divided into three classes: spiritual (ascetic or
near to it), sensual (fleshy and partly erotic), and neutral. The results
in both studies in the terms of the percentages are as follows in Table 11 :

TABLE 11. PRAGUE AND CAMBRIDGE STUDIES COMPARED

PERIOD	Prague Study Percentages			Cambridge Study Percentages		
	Spiritual	Sensual	Neutral	Spiritual	Sensual	Neutral
1201–1300	72.9 (5.7) [1]	0.0 (0.0) [2]	27.1	6.8	0.0	93.2
1301–1350	9.2 (2.2)	0.0 (0.0)	90.8	4.8	3.0	92.2
1351–1400	69.9 (11.6)	0.0 (0.0)	30.1	7.6	7.6	85.0
1401–1450	45.2 (4.2)	5.4 (0.9)	50.4	6.4	14.3	79.3
1451–1500	39.4 (5.9)	5.5 (1.2)	55.1	6.8	21.8	71.4
1501–1550	27.8 (5.5)	16.7 (6.9)	55.4	3.9	29.0	67.1
1551–1600	35.1 (15.1)	12.8 (6.1)	51.1	3.4	29.4	67.2
1601–1650	34.1 (15.8)	16.9 (7.6)	50.1	3.7	36.2	60.1
1651–1700	42.1 (16.9)	22.4 (8.3)	35.5	2.1	39.0	58.9
1701–1750	30.1 (8.7)	32.6 (13.0)	37.3	9.1	32.4	58.8
1751–1800	15.4 (3.6)	20.4 (7.7)	64.2	1.0	27.0	72.0
1801–1850	28.9 (5.1)	36.0 (11.7)	35.3	0.0	2.0	98.0
1851–1900	22.7 (3.3)	29.6 (11.3)	47.7	1.4	6.6	92.0
1901–1933	6.2 (1.4)	18.3 (7.9)	75.5	0.0	5.4	94.6

[1] Among the spiritual a part which is extremely spiritual.
[2] Among the sensual the part which is extremely sensual (erotic, sexual).

I took this point which, by its nature, involves possibly the greatest
subjectivity of any point in my study. At the first glance the results
of the two studies seem to be absolutely different. However, a closer
study of the data and a few words of explanation suffice in order to change
such a conclusion and cause one to wonder rather that the discrepancy
is so small relatively and the results of both studies so similar. In the
Prague study, my instruction was to classify all pictures into five categories: spiritual, extremely spiritual (ascetic), sensual, extremely
sensual (erotic), and neutral. In the Cambridge study, only three cate-

gories were given : spiritual, sensual, neutral. The natural result was that in the Cambridge study only the conspicuously spiritual and the conspicuously sensual (almost corresponding to the Prague study's extremely spiritual and extremely sensual) were put into these classes, while all the others were put into the neutral class. In the Prague study, into the general classes of spiritual and sensual were put many pictures where some domination — though inconspicuous — of one of these "intangible traits" was noticeable; therefore, the neutral class there happened naturally to be smaller than in the Cambridge study. Under these circumstances, the real points of comparison of the results of both studies are the percentages of the extremely spiritual, and the extremely sensual in the Prague study (in parentheses) with the percentages of the Cambridge study. When such a comparison is made for all the periods studied, one can see that, all in all, the curves of the two percentages are going in the same direction, if the century periods are taken; and even in the half-century periods they either run parallel or partly parallel for all the periods, with the exception of four (out of fourteen): 1551–1600, 1701–1750, 1801–1850, and 1851–1900. In other periods the curves have parallel direction in their ups and downs. In other words, the number of periods where the two curves go in different ways in both the "objective" and the "subjective" points happens to be the same (four out of the fourteen); and the general character of the discrepancy is altogether very similar in both cases. This suggests that it is due mainly to the difference in the number as well as in the somewhat different composition of the samples (because many pictures studied in one place were not studied in the other); and only secondarily to "the subjective element" which enters into the study and computation of some of the points. In other words, as this — the worst — case shows, the subjective element happened in fact to be very similar in both studies.

When two or more competent persons say that the color of a given picture is, say, red, though color is in a sense a subjective impression, such a unanimous statement is objectively accurate. With less force, the same is to be said of our subject. The similarity of the results obtained by both studies, where one investigator did not even know that the other study was being made, is good evidence that "the correlation" between both studies even in the most "subjective" points is quite tangible. If, in both cases, the pictures studied had been identical, there is hardly any doubt that the discrepancy would have been still lower. All this means that, even in regard to such points, the possible criticism that they involve too much of the subjective element to be studied quantitatively, and to give reliable results, is possible but would probably be premature and hasty if it tried to deny the rough and approximate accuracy of the figures as indicators.   Anyhow, they cannot be brushed aside until several independent studies are made along the same line, with possibly still larger samples, by a large group of investigators, because outside of such a study there is no better or even as good a basis on which to contend that in the painting and sculpture of a given period such and such traits or characteristics increased or decreased in comparison with the preceding period.   Such statements will be based either on the few quite unsafe illustrative cases selected to suit the theory, or upon mere guesswork, or upon a small and neither random nor representative sample.   For the sake of brevity, I shall not mention other reservations, well realized and comprehensible to any real investigator.

So much about the reservations, and the test of the validity, and the reliability of the results.   To sum up, *they may be unreliable but they are more reliable than any data presented up to the present time, so far as the general course of art fluctuation in the countries studied is concerned.*

In subsequent tables, I am presenting the figures and the diagrams based upon the Prague study as more complete and covering all the countries, while the Cambridge study was made only for Italy and in a small way for Byzantium and France, with too few samples to be of any real significance or to serve as a check for the results of the Prague study. This study deals with the paintings and sculptures of the following countries or cultures: (1) Italy, (2) France, (3) England, (4) Central Europe (Germany, Austria, Czechoslovakia), (5) the Netherlands, (6) Spain, (7) Russia, (8) Islam, (9) ancient and medieval Christian art (including the religious art of Byzantium), without differentiation by countries.   The periods with which the study begins for each country, as well as the periodization itself, are indicated in the tables and diagrams. In order to give an idea upon what sources the table for each country is based and the works of what artists are studied, in the Appendix for this chapter.   I am giving for a few of these countries the bibliography of the sources consulted and the list of the artists whose works were studied.   Perusal of these data will show that we tried to include all that is known and to consult the vast body of sources and literature about each country studied.   It will also show that some of the countries (Italy, Central Europe, France, Russia) were studied more extensively than the others, like Spain or England.

The investigation is made and the data are presented separately for all the above countries and cultures.   This is done in order to elucidate several additional problems, such as whether the changes have been going on synchronously and parallel in all the countries; whether some of the countries lagged regularly; whether the movement has been similar in the countries which, like the European countries, belong to the same Christian, "cultural continent," and in the countries which, like the Islamic world, belong to a different cultural continent; and several other problems. Accordingly, the diagrams are made in such a way that the reader can see at once what has been the situation in these and in several other respects, in all these countries.

II. Fluctuation of Ideational and Visual Forms of Art

A. *Religious and Secular Subjects*. As defined above, these forms of art differ from one another in their content as well as in their style. Therefore, the first step in the study of the fluctuation is to find out how things have been moving from the standpoint of the *content* of art. The first step to ascertain whether a picture is Visual or Ideational in *content* is to determine the religious or secular character of its subject. The religious subject generally, and in Christian culture particularly, belongs, as a rule, to the supersensory and superempirical world; it is then Ideational in its nature. The secular picture is almost always empirical in its subject; therefore, by definition, it belongs to the Visual world. This is sufficient to explain why, in the study of the problem of the Ideational and Visual fluctuation in art by its *content*, the changes in the proportion of the religious and secular pictures and sculptures in the total for each period are symptomatic and serve as the best available barometer for the purpose. Besides, a study of the change in the proportion of the religious and secular art in the total art of the country for a certain period is important in itself and throws a light upon many cultural changes. If, for instance, in the course of the art evolution of a country, one notices that the proportion of the religious pictures decreases systematically — that the art becomes more and more secular — this may be one of the most important symptoms of what is happening with the religion of the country and with the country itself: the religion which does not exert any influence upon art (even Ideational art), which does not influence the philosophical and scientific mentality of the people and does not exert any influence upon it, which likewise does not affect and mold the law and mores of the country, its "rights" and "wrongs," its political, social, and economic organization — such a religion in all probability is dead and does not live and function any more. Like a dead constitution of the State, which exists upon paper and may be mentioned and referred to once in a while, it is probably just a "mummy" removed from the world of living realities into that of the museum of history. This is just one of the illustrations why and how the problem of the change in the proportion of the religious and secular subjects (in pictures and sculptures) may have significance per se, besides the problem of their fluctuations.

Having taken, then, the total sample of paintings and sculptures for each period as 100 per cent and divided it into religious and secular, we have the following results, given in the absolute and percentage figures in Table 12 and summed up on the percentage basis in Figure 3. Table 12 and Figure 3 suggest the following conclusions.

(1) So far as the art data by countries are concerned, for most of the European countries they begin only about the fifteenth century, when the differentiation into national art, as well as into the secular and religious, began to crystallize. Before that, especially before the thirteenth century, the art of Europe is taken as a whole, as a Christian art. Therefore, to see the situation in medieval Europe and Byzantium, one has to turn to the figure and to those tables which are styled "Ancient and Medieval Christian" art. Here, unfortunately, before the tenth century, the date of the art object in most cases is unknown. For this reason all the pictures and sculptural works studied, some 5032 units, had to be "lumped together" into one period, "before the tenth century." [3]

[3] A more specific study of the Byzantine art made in Cambridge, limited to the objects whose dates are approximately known, gives the following results.

Century	Total Number of Units Studied	Percentage of the Religious
4	20	80.0
5	21	80.9
6	109	89.0
7	23	69.6
8	22	90.9
9	38	79.0
10	54	79.6
11	179	92.7
12	182	89.0
13	136	98.6
14	109	92.7

As the samples are small, no certain conclusion can be obtained. It is to be noted, however, that the data agree almost perfectly with those given in the text, concerning the ancient and medieval Christian art generally. There the percentage of religious pictures before the tenth century is 81.9; here it is about the same, fluctuating from century to century (from the fourth to the tenth) between 69.6 and 90.9, standing for most of the centuries around 80 per cent. Quite similar are the data in both cases for the centuries from the tenth to the fifteenth. This additional test speaks well for the approximate validity of the results obtained, because, as mentioned, the two studies were carried on — one in Cambridge (the Byzantine), the other in Prague — independently, by different persons.

TABLE 12. FLUCTUATION OF THE RELIGIOUS AND SECULAR IN ART

R = Religious   S = Secular

Ancient and Medieval Christian

(Numbers)

	-X	X-XI	XII-XIII	XIV-XV	XVI-XVII	XVIII	Total
R	4119	2365	3764	3080	1133	437	14,898
S	913	134	142	603	247	—	2,039
Total	5032	2499	3906	3683	1380	437	16,937

(Percentages)

	-X	X-XI	XII-XIII	XIV-XV	XVI-XVII	XVIII	Total
R	81.9	94.6	96.4	83.6	82.1	100.0	88.0
S	18.1	5.4	3.6	16.4	17.9	—	12.0
Total	100.0	100.0	100.0	100.0	100.0	100.0	100.0

Islamic

(Numbers)

	-X	X-XI	XII-XIII	XIV-XV	XVI	XVII	XVIII	Total
R	15	20	10	30	120	10	30	235
S	60	575	490	530	780	1200	920	4555
Total	75	595	500	560	900	1210	950	4790

(Percentages)

	-X	X-XI	XII-XIII	XIV-XV	XVI	XVII	XVIII	Total
R	20.0	3.4	2.0	5.4	13.3	.8	3.2	4.1
S	80.0	96.6	98.0	94.6	86.7	99.2	96.8	95.9
Total	100.0	100.0	100.0	100.0	100.0	100.0	100.0	100.0

Dutch

(Numbers)

	-1500	1500-1600	1600-1620	1620-1640	1640-1660	1660-1680	1680-1780	1780-1880	1880-1933	Total
R	1116	630	276	242	490	90	56	42	34	2976
S	182	466	466	726	894	728	414	532	348	4756
Total	1298	1096	742	968	1384	818	470	574	382	7732

(Percentages)

	-1500	1500-1600	1600-1620	1620-1640	1640-1660	1660-1680	1680-1780	1780-1880	1880-1933	Total
R	86.0	57.5	37.2	25.0	35.4	11.0	11.9	7.3	8.1	38.4
S	14.0	42.5	62.8	75.0	64.6	89.0	88.1	92.7	91.9	61.6
Total	100.0	100.0	100.0	100.0	100.0	100.0	100.0	100.0	100.0	100.0

English

(Numbers)

	XV	XVI	XVII	1700-1750	1750-1800	1800-1850	1850-1900	1900-1933	Total
R	395	68	31	4	3	12	10	8	531
S	8	18	32	104	128	175	193	136	794
Total	403	86	63	108	131	187	203	144	1325

(Percentages)

	XV	XVI	XVII	1700-1750	1750-1800	1800-1850	1850-1900	1900-1933	Total
R	98.0	79.1	49.2	3.7	2.3	6.4	4.9	5.6	40.1
S	2.0	20.9	50.8	96.3	97.7	93.6	95.1	94.4	59.9
Total	100.0	100.0	100.0	100.0	100.0	100.0	100.0	100.0	100.0

R = Religious   S = Secular

TABLE 12.   FLUCTUATION OF THE RELIGIOUS AND SECULAR IN ART—*continued*

Spanish

(Numbers)

	XV	XVI	XVII	1700–1750	1750–1800	1800–1850	1850–1900	1900–1933	Total
R	282	311	285	18	6	6	9	—	917
S	10	72	234	273	309	111	102	171	1282
Total	292	383	519	291	315	117	111	171	2199

(Percentages)

	XV	XVI	XVII	1700–1750	1750–1800	1800–1850	1850–1900	1900–1933	Total
R	96.6	81.2	54.2	6.2	1.9	5.2	8.3	—	41.7
S	3.4	18.8	45.8	93.8	98.1	94.8	91.7	100.0	58.3
Total	100.0	100.0	100.0	100.0	100.0	100.0	100.0	100.0	100.0

Italian

(Numbers)

	1200–1300	1300–1350	1350–1400	1400–1450	1450–1500	1500–1550	1550–1600	1600–1650	1650–1700	1700–1750	1750–1800	1800–1850	1850–1900	1900–1933	Total
R	871	702	534	1166	2812	2105	2388	1923	2565	1331	1212	416	118	78	18,221
S	3	11	114	207	686	957	1972	1898	2011	2320	1672	802	861	564	14,078
Total	874	713	648	1373	3498	3062	4360	3821	4576	3651	2884	1218	979	642	32,299

(Percentages)

	1200–1300	1300–1350	1350–1400	1400–1450	1450–1500	1500–1550	1550–1600	1600–1650	1650–1700	1700–1750	1750–1800	1800–1850	1850–1900	1900–1933	Total
R	99.7	98.5	82.4	84.9	80.4	68.8	54.8	50.3	56.1	36.4	42.0	34.1	12.0	12.1	56.4
S	.3	1.5	17.6	15.1	19.6	31.2	45.2	49.7	43.9	63.6	58.0	65.9	88.0	87.9	43.6
Total	100.0	100.0	100.0	100.0	100.0	100.0	100.0	100.0	100.0	100.0	100.0	100.0	100.0	100.0	100.0

French

(Numbers)

	1500–1600	1600–1650	1650–1700	1700–1750	1750–1800	1800–1850	1850–1880	1880–1900	1900–1933	Total
R	1044	555	603	126	177	36	63	21	9	2,634
S	372	390	363	2541	2454	3033	1803	1029	1272	13,257
Total	1416	945	966	2667	2631	3069	1866	1050	1281	15,891

(Percentages)

	1500–1600	1600–1650	1650–1700	1700–1750	1750–1800	1800–1850	1850–1880	1880–1900	1900–1933	Total
R	72.3	58.7	62.4	4.7	6.7	1.2	3.4	1.1	.7	16.6
S	27.7	41.3	37.6	95.3	93.3	98.8	96.6	98.9	99.3	83.4
Total	100.0	100.0	100.0	100.0	100.0	100.0	100.0	100.0	100.0	100.0

Central Europe

(Numbers)

	1500–1600	1600–1650	1650–1700	1700–1750	1750–1800	1800–1830	1830–1860	1860–1880	1880–1900	1900–1933	Total
R	999	78	97	45	51	153	48	45	33	222	1,771
S	618	102	95	285	331	918	768	1326	930	4089	9,462
Total	1617	180	192	330	383	1071	816	1371	963	4311	11,233

(Percentages)

	1500–1600	1600–1650	1650–1700	1700–1750	1750–1800	1800–1830	1830–1860	1860–1880	1880–1900	1900–1933	Total
R	61.8	43.3	53.6	13.6	13.4	14.3	5.9	3.2	3.4	5.1	15.8
S	38.2	56.7	46.4	86.4	86.6	85.8	94.1	96.8	96.6	94.9	84.2
Total	100.0	100.0	100.0	100.0	100.0	100.0	100.0	100.0	100.0	100.0	100.0

R = Religious TABLE 12. FLUCTUATION OF THE RELIGIOUS AND SECULAR IN ART — *continued* S = Secular

Russian

	-XII	XII-XIII	XIV-XV	XVI	XVII	XVIII	1801-1825	1826-1850	1851-1875	1876-1900	1900-1933	Total
						(Numbers)						
R	22	82	240	311	378	117	121	249	96	351	157	2,124
S	—	—	—	—	18	470	546	480	520	2287	5849	10,170
Total	22	82	240	311	396	587	667	729	616	2638	6006	12,294
						(Percentages)						
R	100.0	100.0	100.0	100.0	95.5	19.9	18.1	34.2	15.6	13.2	2.6	17.3
S	—	—	—	—	4.5	80.1	81.9	65.8	84.4	86.8	97.4	82.7
Total	100.0	100.0	100.0	100.0	100.0	100.0	100.0	100.0	100.0	100.0	100.0	100.0

Europe as a Whole [1]

	-X	X-XI	XII-XIII	XIV-XV	XVI	XVII	XVIII	XIX	XX
					(Numbers)				
R	4119	2387	4717	12,148	8,418	8,176[2]	3,583[3]	1,829[3]	508[3]
S	913	134	145	1,821	4,598	8,080	11,301	16,416	12,429
Total	5032	2521	4862	13,969	13,016	16,256	14,884	18,245	12,937
					(Percentages)				
R	81.9	94.7	97.0	85.0	64.7	50.2	24.1	10.0	3.0
S	18.1	5.3	3.0	15.0	35.3	49.8	75.9	90.0	96.1
Total	100.0	100.0	100.0	100.0	100.0	100.0	100.0	100.0	100.0

[1] All the seven European countries, plus the ancient and medieval Christian.
[2] Obtained by taking one-half of the entire "Christian art" for the sixteenth and seventeenth centuries.
[3] For Holland, the eighteenth century means the data for the period 1680-1780, the nineteenth century, 1780-1880, the twentieth century, and 1880-1933.

The data of both studies show that before the tenth century the grand total of all art (religious and secular), according to its content, was overwhelmingly religious; more than 81 per cent of its subjects were religious. As such, especially for that period of Christianity, it was Ideational in type. The art mentality of the period was concentrated mainly on "otherworldly" ideas; it depicted, principally in symbolic form (as we shall see), the invisible Kingdom of God and of His Gospel. Only a small stream of secular subjects was reflected in it; and even those were used mainly because of their indirect connection with the religious Ideational world. The situation remains similar in the centuries from the tenth to the thirteenth inclusive. The total art continued to be overwhelmingly religious and depicted mainly — about 90 per cent — religious subjects and problems. After the fourteenth century in religious art itself, not to mention the secular art, which began to be a separate stream, we notice a notable decrease of the percentage of the religious element. The decrease continues up to the eighteenth century, when the religious art was

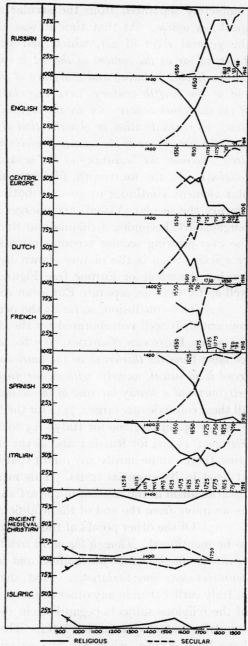

FIG. 3.   RELIGIOUS AND SECULAR ART BY
COUNTRIES

completely separated from the secular and had to be religious, so to speak, *ex officio*. At that time it was already a very minor stream in the general river of art, which had become overwhelmingly secular. *Thus, so far as the content of the art is concerned, the data entirely justify the thesis that painting and sculpture of the Middle Ages, up to about the end of the twelfth century, were overwhelmingly Ideational. At the end of the thirteenth century, we see the beginning of the process of "secularization," or sensualization or visualization of the content of art in two forms: first, the percentage of the secular subjects begins to grow in the religious art itself; second, the beginning of the separation of the secular art from the religious.* In the fourteenth, fifteenth, and sixteenth centuries, the secular element continues to grow in both forms and in the seventeenth century the secular (Visual) art emerges as already dominant, while the religious art, becoming a thinner and thinner rivulet in comparison with the ever-growing secular stream, retreats to a purely religious position *ex officio*. Such is the picture shown by the section of Table 12 concerning the whole of Europe (see Figure 9 for Europe on page 418) as well as by that for separate European countries.

(2) This conclusion, so far as the period after the twelfth century is concerned, is well corroborated by the data and the curves concerning the seven European countries. *In the total art of all these countries, as we move from the thirteenth or the fourteenth century to our time, the main trend is identical, namely, with minor fluctuations, a steady decrease of the religious and a steady increase of the secular elements.* As the samples for all these countries are large : 7732 for the Netherlands ; 1325 for England ; 2199 for Spain ; 32,299 for Italy ; 15,891 for France ; 11,233 for Central Europe ; 12,294 for Russia ; and as the trend is similar in all these countries, there can be hardly any doubt that it reflects the reality accurately, at least in its essential traits. This means, then, a steady decrease of Ideationalism in the content of the art and a steady increase of Visualism as we move from the end of the Middle Ages to our time.

(3) Of the other points of the data and the curves, the following are to be mentioned : *Though the main trend is the same in all the European countries, in the minor fluctuations and in the time of its appearance, the countries show some variations.* First, the trend of secularization emerged in Italy earlier than in any other country. The decrease of the proportion of the religious subjects began here in the thirteenth century. In other countries it started somewhat later. The latest in this respect appears to have been Russia, when the process emerged only in the seventeenth century, but after emergence progressed very abruptly.

(4) Of the minor fluctuations in Europe, it is to be noted that in Italy, France, Central Europe, and the Netherlands, either the end of the sixteenth or the seventeenth century is marked by a temporary rise of the proportion of the religious subjects and a respective fall of the percentage of the secular pictures and sculptures. This is probably a reflection of the Counter-Reformation, of the Ascetic Protestantism,[4] and, in central Europe, of the Thirty Years' War and the sufferings and despair which were its aftermath. When the total historical configuration of that period is considered, the results appear to be entirely consistent with the situation known. For most of these countries — Spain, England, partly the Netherlands, and France — the most "pagan" centuries were the eighteenth, the nineteenth, and the twentieth. The beginning of the nineteenth century in several countries is marked by a temporary slight increase of the religious class compared with the eighteenth century, probably as a consequence of the Revolutions and the Napoleonic Wars, but the rise seems to have been temporary and soon was replaced by the continuation of the main trend. Finally, if we inquire what has been the situation in our time — at the end of the nineteenth and in the twentieth century — the answer is: In Holland, England, Spain, Italy, and Central Europe there has been a slight increase of the percentage of religious art, while in Russia and France there has been a continuation of its decrease. Due to these two countries exclusively, the total for Europe shows a fall of the religious pictures from 10 per cent in the nineteenth to 3.9 per cent in the twentieth century. If these countries were excluded, then the twentieth century would show a slight increase of the percentage of the religious subjects in comparison with that of the nineteenth century. If the postwar art up to the present year were analyzed more fully, possibly even in France (in Russia, on account of the severe policy of extermination of religion, the trend could not manifest itself openly) the trend of increase of the religious pictures and sculpture would appear also. Anyhow, the fact that such a tendency is shown by the data for most of the countries studied is interesting. It becomes particularly symptomatic in the light of the subsequent data concerning the style of art: these data, as we shall see, show for this latest period a

[4] Though several branches of Protestantism were iconoclastic so far as the placement of art creation in the churches is concerned, outside of that Protestantism did not inhibit either a rendering of the religious theme in secular art, or the emergence of a number of great artists in the Protestant countries who created many paintings, pictures, sculptural works, on a series of religious subjects. Germany and Holland are the countries conspicuous in that respect. The asceticism of several branches of Protestantism in that period seems to have led to an increase of the concentration of the artists' interests on the religious subjects.

decisive turn away from Visualism. We shall see a similar movement in music and in literature and in other compartments of the Western culture. The consistency of all these data warrants the conclusion that the discussed increase of the percentage of the religious element, however slight it is for some countries, is not a mere play of incomplete data, but something that possibly reflects the real process. Whether this slight increase of the religious subjects or Ideational content of art is just one of the temporary short-lived fluctuations or the "first swallow" of the coming long-time trend toward increase of Ideationalism in art remains to be seen. In Volume Four some consideration of this problem will be given in the light of all the data.

(5) Finally, if one glances at the curves of Islamic art, one can see at once that its course was very different and little related to that of either the Christian art or the art of the European countries. This suggests that the Islamic art belongs to a quite different "cultural continent" than European Christian culture; it demonstrates also that all the European countries seem to belong to the same cultural continent because their main trends are practically the same. We shall see a similar situation in regard to many other items of art and other compartments of culture. Historical knowledge corroborates such a conclusion. In spite of all the differences of one European country from another, Europe is one cultural continent, and the main sociocultural processes in all the fundamental compartments of culture have been going on there along essentially similar lines.

So much about the fluctuation of Ideational and Visual content in painting and sculpture of Europe. The data given so far corroborate the conclusions given in the preceding chapter. We turn now to a study of the same problem from the standpoint of style.

III. Fluctuation of Ideational and Visual Styles

Besides the content, the second criterion of Visuality or Ideationality and their intermediary forms in painting and sculpture is the style or the manner of presenting the objects. The essential traits of each of the fundamental as well as of the main intermediary styles were indicated and discussed in Chapters Seven to Nine. Now the question is: What is shown in the field of the styles by our quantitative data?

Classification of paintings and sculptures from this standpoint is both easy and difficult. It is very easy in regard to clear-cut Ideational or impressionistic Visual works; it involves a certain degree of subjectivity in regard to intermediary types of work — partly Visual, partly "formal" and "conventional," partly "expressionistic." However, in regard to most of these, the degree of subjectivity at the worst concerns not so much the nature of the two principal styles in which painting has to be classed as the various shadings of the intermediary styles. If a special class is set forth, into which all such "mixed" works of art from the standpoint of their style are put, the results seem to give at least a somewhat simplified but roughly adequate picture of the complex reality. This is especially true if one does not attempt to give in these classes too delicate shadings. However much such a shading is desirable, I preferred to sacrifice it in order to make a more adequate study of the fluctuations of the main classes.[5] Table 13 and Figure 4 attempt to give an answer to the question posited ; in these all paintings and sculptures are classified first into five classes.

(1) Impressionistic, as extremely Visual.

(2) "Formal" or "purely conventional" rendering, which means the Ideational style in either its pure or in its moderate form, but as the dominant style.

(3) "Naturalistic," which means a moderately visual, and visually naturalistic rendering, without the impressionistic extreme of visualism.

(4) Expressionistic, as partly Visual in its technique, but with its Visualism "corrected" by omission of the Visual traits present in the object but incidental to the central idea of the artist, and stressing the traits which are regarded as essential. It embraces also such streams as "cubism," "constructivism," "primitivism," and other antivisual styles discussed before. This class generally differs from the impressionistic and Visual class in that it strives to express not a momentary glimpse of the object, but its essential, central character, deprived of incidental, passing, Visual traits. From the purely formal or Ideational class, it differs in that partly it uses Visual, sometimes even impressionistic technique. From the naturalistic class it differs in its effort to express the central idea of the visual object, by the choice of the details ; some- times by its much more extreme Visual technique, sometimes (like cubism)

[5] Here again the results of the two independent studies made in Prague and in Cambridge in regard to the Italian and partly the Byzantine and French paintings and sculpture give sufficiently close similarity. Thus, the Byzantine art (from the fourth to the fourteenth century) does not give any percentage of the purely impressionistic style in the Cambridge study, as the Christian — ancient and medieval — art does not give it in the Prague study. Likewise, the Italian art gives, in both studies, the maximum of the impressionistic works in the second half of the nineteenth and in the twentieth century. Similarly, the French art shows a recession of impressionism in the twentieth century compared with the nineteenth. Not essentially different are the results in regard to other main styles in both studies.

by its sharp anti-Visualism. In brief, the expressionistic class is a peculiar Mixed class, in some respects quite antagonistic to pure Visualism and impressionism, in some others to Ideationalism.

(5) Mixed class, where are put all the works which do not belong to one of the above classes and which represent a mixture of the Ideational and Visual styles in various forms, without any definite preponderance of either.

Table 13 and Figure 4 show the fluctuation of the main styles for the various cultures.

The data give, then, the following picture.

A. To begin with the *impressionistic* style as the extreme and purest visual style, it is totally absent in the Christian — ancient and medieval — art, from its beginning to its end (to the nineteenth century). It is also totally absent in the art of all the European countries studied up to the second half of the nineteenth century. Finally, it is entirely absent in the Islamic art. So far as it is the most illusionistic style, its emergence and growth in the second part of the nineteenth century means an inclination of our modern culture and of its mentality to substitute appearances for reality — symptomatic detachment from the world of reality in the age which has been supposedly most scientific, most realistic, and the most matter-of-fact. However strange may appear these results and their interpretation, we shall see that a careful study of other compartments of culture of that period corroborates the loss of the sense of reality by the society of the period and its replacement by mere "looks," appearance, "show," theatrical decorations, by *als ob* — by "as if." The second half of the nineteenth century seems to have been the period when society began to live in the most unreal, most deceptive, most illusionistic *milieu* ever created by it and accepted by it as a genuine reality. The data show that with the exception of France, impressionism has continued to grow up to the present time. This means, then, that this society and culture of ours is particularly showy, "Hollywoody," illusionary. Such is one of the paradoxical inferences given by the data. However strange they seem, the reader must have patience to examine the evidences given by art as well as by other main classes of cultural phenomena. It is to be noted, however, that in France, where impressionism developed and reached its purest and best form, we notice a sign of its recession with the beginning of the twentieth century. In other countries, as we shall see, it has been developing not at the cost of the non-Visual or Ideational style, but at that of the Visual — naturalistic. This signifies not a further recession of the Ideational stream but a growth of extremism in a part

TABLE 13. FLUCTUATION OF THE MAIN STYLES IN ART

N = Naturalistic   F = Formal (Ideational)   I = Impressionistic   E = Expressionistic   M = Mixed

Ancient and Medieval Christian

(Numbers)

	-X	X-XI	XII-XIII	XIV-XV	XVI-XVII	XVIII	Total
N	673	57	22	76	64	—	892
F	3857	2301	1880	2514	1210	341	12,103
I	—	—	—	—	—	—	—
E	—	—	—	—	—	—	—
M	502	141	2004	1093	106	96	3,942
Total	5032	2499	3906	2683	1380	437	16,937

(Percentages)

	-X	X-XI	XII-XIII	XIV-XV	XVI-XVII	XVIII	Total
N	13.4	2.3	.6	2.1	4.6	—	5.3
F	77.0	92.1	47.6	68.2	87.7	78.5	71.4
I	—	—	—	—	—	—	—
E	—	—	—	—	—	—	—
M	9.6	5.6	51.8	29.7	7.7	21.5	23.3
Total	100.0	100.0	100.0	100.0	100.0	100.0	100.0

English

(Numbers)

	XV	XVI	XVII	1700-1750	1750-1800	1800-1850	1850-1900	1900-1933	Total
N	311	56	51	108	131	187	149	39	1032
F	60	12	—	—	—	—	—	—	72
I	—	—	—	—	—	—	39	46	85
E	—	—	12	—	—	—	—	38	38
M	32	18	—	—	—	—	15	21	98
Total	403	86	63	108	131	187	203	144	1325

(Percentages)

	XV	XVI	XVII	1700-1750	1750-1800	1800-1850	1850-1900	1900-1933	Total
N	77.2	65.1	81.0	100.0	100.0	100.0	73.4	27.0	77.9
F	14.9	14.0	—	—	—	—	—	—	5.4
I	—	—	—	—	—	—	19.2	32.0	6.4
E	—	—	19.0	—	—	—	—	26.4	2.9
M	7.9	20.9	—	—	—	—	7.4	14.6	7.4
Total	100.0	100.0	100.0	100.0	100.0	100.0	100.0	100.0	100.0

N = Naturalistic   F = Formal (Ideational)   I = Impressionistic   E = Expressionistic   M = Mixed

TABLE 13. FLUCTUATION OF THE MAIN STYLES IN ART—*continued*

Central Europe

(Numbers)

	XVI	1600–1650	1650–1700	1700–1750	1750–1800	1800–1830	1830–1860	1860–1880	1880–1900	1900–1933	Total
N	396	129	192	330	382	1071	816	1239	813	804	6,172
F	1218	51									1,269
I								132	99	663	894
E									27	2418	2,445
M									24	105	129
Total	1617	180	192	330	382	1071	816	1371	963	3990	10,909

(Percentages)

	XVI	1600–1650	1650–1700	1700–1750	1750–1800	1800–1830	1830–1860	1860–1880	1880–1900	1900–1933	Total
N	24.5	71.7	100.0	100.0	100.0	100.0	100.0	90.4	84.4	18.7	57.8
F	75.5	28.3									11.3
I								9.6	10.3	15.4	8.0
E									2.8	63.5	21.7
M									2.5	2.4	1.2
Total	100.0	100.0	100.0	100.0	100.0	100.0	100.0	100.0	100.0	100.0	100.0

Dutch

(Numbers)

	–1500	1500–1600	1600–1620	1620–1640	1640–1660	1660–1680	1680–1780	1780–1880	1880–1933	Total
N	1298	1096	742	968	1384	818	470	524	79	7379
F								50	82	132
I									120	120
E									101	101
M										
Total	1298	1096	742	968	1384	818	470	574	382	7732

(Percentages)

	–1500	1500–1600	1600–1620	1620–1640	1640–1660	1660–1680	1680–1780	1780–1880	1880–1933	Total
N	100.0	100.0	100.0	100.0	100.0	100.0	100.0	91.3	20.7	95.4
F								8.7	21.5	1.7
I									31.4	1.6
E									26.4	1.3
M										
Total	100.0	100.0	100.0	100.0	100.0	100.0	100.0	100.0	100.0	100.0

French

(Numbers)

	XVI	1600–1650	1650–1700	1700–1750	1750–1800	1800–1850	1850–1880	1880–1900	1900–1933	Total
N	354	600	890	2667	2631	3069	822	471	305	11,809
F	441	—	—	—	—	—	759	310	217	441
I	—	—	—	—	—	—	210	269	759	1,286
E	—	—	—	—	—	—	75	—	—	1,238
M	621	345	76	—	—	—	—	—	—	1,117
Total	1416	945	966	2667	2631	3069	1866	1050	1281	15,891

(Percentages)

	XVI	1600–1650	1650–1700	1700–1750	1750–1800	1800–1850	1850–1880	1880–1900	1900–1933	Total
N	25.0	63.5	92.1	100.0	100.0	100.0	44.1	45.1	23.8	74.3
F	31.1	—	—	—	—	—	40.7	29.5	16.9	2.8
I	—	—	—	—	—	—	11.3	25.4	59.3	8.1
E	—	—	—	—	—	—	4.0	—	—	7.8
M	43.9	36.5	7.9	—	—	—	—	—	—	7.0
Total	100.0	100.0	100.0	100.0	100.0	100.0	100.0	100.0	100.0	100.0

Spanish

(Numbers)

	XV	XVI	XVII	1700–1750	1750–1800	1800–1850	1850–1900	1900–1933	Total
N	112	183	519	291	315	117	75	42	1654
F	72	69	—	—	—	—	—	63	141
I	—	—	—	—	—	—	36	54	99
E	108	131	—	—	—	—	—	—	54
M	—	—	—	—	—	—	—	12	251
Total	292	383	519	291	315	117	111	171	2199

(Percentages)

	XV	XVI	XVII	1700–1750	1750–1800	1800–1850	1850–1900	1900–1933	Total
N	38.3	47.8	100.0	100.0	100.0	100.0	67.6	24.6	75.1
F	24.7	18.0	—	—	—	—	—	36.8	6.5
I	—	—	—	—	—	—	32.4	31.6	4.5
E	37.0	34.2	—	—	—	—	—	—	2.5
M	—	—	—	—	—	—	—	7.0	11.4
Total	100.0	100.0	100.0	100.0	100.0	100.0	100.0	100.0	100.0

TABLE 13. FLUCTUATION OF THE MAIN STYLES IN ART — *continued*

N = Naturalistic　　F = Formal (Ideational)　　I = Impressionistic　　E = Expressionistic　　M = Mixed

Italian

(Numbers)

	1200–1300	1300–1350	1350–1400	1400–1450	1450–1500	1500–1550	1550–1600	1600–1650	1650–1700	1700–1750	1750–1800	1800–1850	1850–1900	1900–1933	Total
N	185	152	390	922	3297	2958	4360	3821	4576	3651	2884	1218	512	110	29,036
F	588	500	—	15	116	—	—	—	—	—	—	—	325	281	1,219
I	—	—	—	—	—	—	—	—	—	—	—	—	—	204	606
E	—	—	—	—	—	—	—	—	—	—	—	—	—	—	204
M	101	61	258	436	85	104	—	—	—	—	—	—	142	47	1,234
Total	874	713	648	1373	3498	3062	4360	3821	4576	3651	2884	1218	979	642	32,299

(Percentages)

	1200–1300	1300–1350	1350–1400	1400–1450	1450–1500	1500–1550	1550–1600	1600–1650	1650–1700	1700–1750	1750–1800	1800–1850	1850–1900	1900–1933	Total
N	21.2	21.0	60.2	66.4	94.3	96.6	100.0	100.0	100.0	100.0	100.0	100.0	52.3	17.1	89.9
F	67.3	70.4	—	1.1	3.3	—	—	—	—	—	—	—	33.2	43.8	3.8
I	—	—	—	—	—	—	—	—	—	—	—	—	—	31.8	1.9
E	—	—	—	—	—	—	—	—	—	—	—	—	—	—	.6
M	11.5	8.6	39.8	32.5	2.4	3.4	—	—	—	—	—	—	14.5	7.3	3.8
Total	100.0	100.0	100.0	100.0	100.0	100.0	100.0	100.0	100.0	100.0	100.0	100.0	100.0	100.0	100.0

Russian

(Numbers)

	–XII	XII–XIII	XIV–XV	XVI	XVII	XVIII	1801–1825	1826–1850	1851–1875	1876–1900	XX	Total
N	—	—	—	—	—	492	667	729	616	1784	106	4,394
F	22	82	240	311	313	24	—	—	—	27	87	1,106
I	—	—	—	—	—	—	—	—	—	827	4926	5,753
E	—	—	—	—	—	—	—	—	—	—	887	887
M	—	—	—	—	83	71	—	—	—	—	—	154
Total	22	82	240	311	396	587	667	729	616	2638	6006	12,249

(Percentages)

	–XII	XII–XIII	XIV–XV	XVI	XVII	XVIII	1801–1825	1826–1850	1851–1875	1876–1900	XX	Total
N	—	—	—	—	—	84.1	100.0	100.0	100.0	67.9	1.8	35.7
F	100.0	100.0	100.0	100.0	78.9	4.0	—	—	—	1.0	1.4	8.1
I	—	—	—	—	—	—	—	—	—	31.1	82.0	46.8
E	—	—	—	—	—	—	—	—	—	—	14.8	8.2
M	—	—	—	—	21.1	11.9	—	—	—	—	—	1.2
Total	100.0	100.0	100.0	100.0	100.0	100.0	100.0	100.0	100.0	100.0	100.0	100.0

Islamic

	-X	X-XI	XII-XIII	XIV-XV	XVI	XVII	XVIII	Total
				(Numbers)				
N				60		350	21	431
F								
I	75	595	500	500	900	860	929	4359
E								
M								
Total	75	595	500	560	900	1210	950	4790
				(Percentages)				
N				10.7		29.0	2.2	10.0
F								
I	100.0	100.0	100.0	89.3	100.0	71.0	97.8	90.0
E								
M								
Total	100.0	100.0	100.0	100.0	100.0	100.0	100.0	100.0

Europe as a Whole

(Seven Countries plus the Christian Art United)

	-X	X-XI	XII-XIII	XIV-XV	XVI	XVII	XVIII	XIX	XX
					(Numbers)				
Visual[1]	673	57	307	6458	9435	14,722	14,352	16,856	7763
Ideational	3857	2323	2550	3517	2656	969	365	27	87
Expressionistic								506	4480
Mixed	502	141	2065	2073	1010	569	167	256	285
					(Percentages)				
Visual	13.4	2.3	6.0	53.6	72.0	90.6	96.4	95.5	61.5
Ideational	77.0	92.2	51.1	29.2	20.3	5.9	2.5	0.3	0.7
Expressionistic								2.8	35.5
Mixed	9.6	5.5	42.9	17.2	7.7	3.5	1.1	1.4	2.3

[1] Visual is Naturalistic plus Impressionistic.

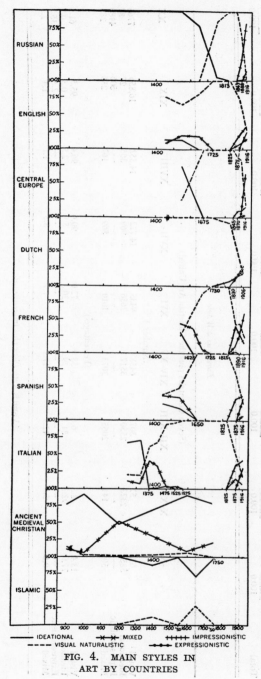

FIG. 4.   MAIN STYLES IN
ART BY COUNTRIES

of the moderate forms of Visualism which, together with all
the currents of Visual and pro-
Visual styles, shows a sign of
decrease in the twentieth century as compared with the
nineteenth. There is hardly
any doubt that the recession
of impressionism in other
countries is a mere question
of time. If it were possible
to "measure" adequately the
present-day situation, perhaps
the results would already show
such a recession. Since in
France, which led here (as in
several other waves of art), the
tide already has passed its
apex and has been receding,
in all probability the other
countries will follow the same
course. If the supposition is
to be realized, this would mean
also a recession from the illusionistic mentality to something nearer the Ideational
one.

B. Take now the opposite
style, the *formal* or *Ideational*.
Glancing at the figures and
the curve in the Christian —
ancient and medieval — art,
which up to the fourteenth
century was the *one* grand art
of Europe, we see that up to
the twelfth and the thirteenth
centuries it was overwhelmingly Ideational (in various
degrees). Up to the tenth
century it included 77 per cent

of all paintings and sculptures; in the tenth and the eleventh centuries, the percentage rises to 92.1; and then in the twelfth and — especially — in the thirteenth centuries, when practically all the art was Christian, we see a sudden drop of the percentage to 47.6 in the Christian art and to 51.1 per cent for the whole of Europe (that is, in the total art of all the countries studied). After that century the percentage in the Christian art again rises, but we know already that beginning with the fourteenth century the secular art began to separate from the Christian art, and for this reason, even if the Christian art did become somewhat more Ideational in the quantity of the artistic works, this means only that it had to become such *ex officio* and does *not* mean at all that the total — the Christian as well as the secular — art became (percentably) more Ideational after the thirteenth century. This is shown, for the whole of Europe, by Table 13 and by Figure 9. The data show that the percentage of the Ideational art in the fourteenth to fifteenth centuries fell to 29.2 per cent instead of 51.1 per cent, as in the twelfth and the thirteenth centuries.

These data are interesting in several respects. First, in the above discussion of the movement of the religious and secular subjects in paintings and sculpture, we saw that the tenth and the eleventh centuries also showed a rise of the religious subjects, compared with the period before the tenth century (from 81.9 to 94.6 per cent). Here we see quite a parallel movement in the styles: Ideational style gives for the tenth to eleventh centuries 92.1 per cent instead of 77.0 per cent before the tenth century. Its percentages rise parallel with those of the religious subjects. For the twelfth and the thirteenth centuries the parallelism disappears: the percentage of the religious subjects rises to 96.4, the percentage of the Ideational renderings falls from 92.1 to 51.1 (for the whole of Europe). What is the meaning of such a divergence? Mainly a replacement of unquestioning faith by rationalistic Scholasticism, which tried to harmonize faith and reason, faith and logic, faith and testimony, of the senses. That is the essence of Scholasticism and of Scholastic rationalism, as we shall see. They are a marvelous endeavor to give *suum quique:* to faith and to logic, to revelation and sensory experience. In this sense Scholasticism and its *Summae* are a remarkable organic synthesis of the Ideational with the Sensate mentality. The mere Ideationalism of an intuitive and unquestioning faith disappeared by the thirteenth century and was replaced by religious rationalism — where God and intelligence went together, and intelligence, logic, and syllogism, together with the organs of senses, were called on for justification of the faith which before

I — 27

did not need any justification. It was the Idealistic century of a marvelous balance between the Ideational and the Sensate mentalities. (See Chapters One and Two of Volume Two, on philosophical mentality and its changes.)

This is exactly what is shown by the above figure of 51.1 per cent — practically half of the art creations were Ideational in the thirteenth century; the other half were Mixed, and there was 6.0 per cent of the Visual art. The subjects of art remained religious but, just as in Scholasticism, they were treated now not exclusively Ideationally; about half of them were treated with a great deal of Visual element (42.9 per cent of the Mixed and 6.0 per cent of the Visual). Here, then, we have a direct and rather remarkable corroboration of the fact that the thirteenth century was indeed (like the fifth century B.C.) the age of a marvelous balance — even quantitative — of the Ideational and Visual styles and mentalities, which resulted in the sublime Idealistic art of the thirteenth century. In this way the statement made in Chapter Nine is justified in its essentials. In the sixteenth century, the Ideational art falls still more — to 20.3 per cent, and after the sixteenth century it practically disappears in all European countries with the exception of Russia, which lags by about two centuries and there disappears after the eighteenth century — a lag quite similar to what we saw in the curve of the religious and secular art. It does not reappear at all, with the exception of Russia again, where it returns, but only to about one per cent at the end of the nineteenth century. When the figures for the Ideational art are taken for European art as a whole (including Christian art), they give 5.9 per cent for the seventeenth, 2.5 for the eighteenth, 0.2 for the nineteenth, and 0.7 for the twentieth centuries.

This is a direct corroboration of the contention that the art as well as the mentality and culture of the Western world, after the fifteenth century, has been becoming overwhelmingly Sensate and almost non-Ideational. The emergence of impressionism in the second half of the nineteenth century was a further sign of the progress of Visualism, even from a qualitative standpoint. It was one of the best barometers that the Sensate (Visual) mentality and culture had reached their logical and factual limit: the world of Becoming was triumphant over that of Being; change over stationary existence; progress over lasting order; sensoriness over mind; "objective science" over logic and especially over concentrated meditation; the empirical system of truth over all the others. Whether there are signs that in the twentieth century the reaction to this triumphant Visualism is emerging, we shall discuss a little later.

Notice, further, that the curves of impressionism, as well as of Ideation-alism, have been moving practically in quite similar ways in all the European countries. In the Islamic art, on the contrary, impressionism is entirely lacking, while Ideationalism has been the predominant style throughout the whole existence of Islamic art. This shows again that the European countries all belong to the same "cultural continent" and that deep and important changes occur in a similar way in all of them, while the Islamic countries seem to belong to a very different cultural continent. Its currents move in a very different way from the European currents.

C. As to the *naturalistic* or *Moderate Visual* style, it played a modest part in the Christian art up to the tenth century and after that became a very tiny stream, to be replaced mainly by the Mixed style. In the painting and sculpture of the European countries it became the principal element after the fifteenth century (with the familiar lag of about two centuries for Russia); it was about the only style in the second half of the seventeenth, in the eighteenth, and in the first part of the nineteenth centuries (there are slight differences in the periods from country to country). Beginning with the second part of the nineteenth century, it shows very definite signs of recession. That is again a rather interesting fact. It corroborates again the theory that the art and the mentality and the culture of these periods were almost entirely Visual and Sensate, though in a moderate or tempered form. Now what is the meaning of the recession of this naturalism, beginning with the second half of the nine-teenth century? Table 13 and Figure 4 give some indication of the answer. The recession has been due first to an extremization of moderate Visualism into impressionism, which has grown at the cost of the natural-istic style discussed; second, to a reaction against Visualism generally, which manifested itself in various expressionistic movements: symbolism, constructivism, cubism, and other similar "isms," whose anti-Visual nature has already been discussed. Toward the end of the first part of the nineteenth century it split itself into impressionism, and a little later into expressionism. These two currents took a great deal of "water" from the main stream and left it more and more shallow and dry. As both of these currents — impressionism and expressionism — are more extreme and "less balanced" than the good, *bourgeois*, well-rounded naturalism, the split speaks of the differentiation of such a balanced Visual style into two extreme factions. A kind of splitting of a *bourgeois* "liberal party" or "middle class" into the "laborites" and "fascists." In this case, the victim of the split is art and mentality and the Western culture itself.

To those who can read the "letters on the wall" all the time being written by art, this fact of the splitting of the well-rounded, almost Victorian naturalistic style into the two opposite and more extreme factions would have given a good warning of the coming splitting of the Western *bourgeois* Visual and Sensate mentality, society, and culture into the extreme factions of "cubists" and "impressionists" in politics, science, philosophy, behavior; into communists and fascists, revolutionaries and Tories. But, helas! There have been few, if any, wise men who could really read the signs of the coming changes in art or in any other compartments of culture. Most of the "readers" *ex officio*, politicians, professors, journalists, writers and lecturers and critics and theorizers have been themselves men of purely Visual culture and as such have been able rarely, if ever, to understand anything but the "show," the "looks," the appearance, the decorations, or the surface of cultural and social processes, never going deeper to that reality which lies behind them. Therefore, most of the writers on art have not been able to read its real meaning and often its prophetic and diagnostic symptoms.

As to the Islamic art, it has only intermittently and in a modest proportion the naturalistic style. It has always been predominantly "formal." Here again we see that its whole pattern, as well as the course of its changes, is very different, unrelated to those in the art of the European countries.

D. Finally, turn to *expressionism*. As mentioned, under this name are united several — and very different — styles, from symbolism and cubism to expressionistic impressionism or even neo-impressionism. The general trait common to all of these different currents is that they are more or less opposed to the Visual principle in art generally — some radically, others modestly; and particularly are they opposed to impressionistic Visualism. All of these currents stand for "construction," for using subjects with some central idea, and in conformity with it correcting and modifying its Visual aspect as much as the idea requires, even up to a complete disregard of it.

As explained in the preceding chapter, they are anti-Visual in their negative program; but almost all of them are not, at the same time, Ideational, for the reason indicated. They have cut their moorings from the Visual shore, but have not arrived, as yet, at the real Ideational shore. The data show that in the Christian art the expressionistic style, in that sense, did not exist at all, being quite unnecessary in view of the wide use of the Ideational style (anyhow, expressionism in most of its varieties is at the best Ideationalism in embryo form). As for the European countries, it emerged at the end of the nineteenth century and has rapidly grown since that time, having become now one of the major streams. Having a zero percentage for all centuries up to the nineteenth, in the nineteenth it receives 2.8 per cent; in the twentieth, 35.5 per cent! The fact is interesting in many respects. First, it undoubtedly means a sharp reaction against Visualism and especially its extreme form — impressionism. In this sense it testifies in favor of a possible exhaustion (for the given period) of Visual art, Visual mentality, Visual culture, and Visualism and sensualism generally. That this is so is shown by the total percentage of the Visual art (naturalistic and impressionistic). Its percentage declined in the twentieth century to 61.5, compared with 96.4 in the eighteenth and 95.4 in the nineteenth! Quite a fall! Whether the rise of expressionism in recent times is the beginning of a decline of the Visual style (and mentality) and indicates its future "rest" for a long time (just as the Ideational style and mentality declined after the thirteenth century and rested up to the present time) remains to be seen. It may be so; it may also mean only a short time recession of Visualism and sensualism. Anyhow, it signifies a strong reaction (but does not signify as yet an advent of Ideationalism, because, as explained, expressionism is a kind of "communistic perversion of capitalism": it violently denies it, but at the same time is even more materialistic, mercenary, greedy for Sensate value than capitalism, and is more anti-Idealistic and anti-Ideational. Similar, exactly, is the position of most expressionistic currents in contemporary art).

A second interesting thing is that it appeared very soon after the emergence and growth of impressionism. This has been the extreme form of Visualism. It was followed by a similarly extreme reaction of expressionism.

Here again (as well as in the long domination of the Ideational style in the Middle Ages, replaced by a long domination of the Visual art after the fifteenth century) we have a case as outlined in my "principle of limit," in my "varyingly recurrent concept of the direction of the socio-cultural processes," and in what I call the self-regulation of the socio-cultural processes: a certain movement calls for its opposite, and the more extreme the former the more extreme the latter, which replaces the former eventually. The facts of this kind are met and analyzed in practically all the compartments of culture and are discussed more in detail elsewhere. Any school or style in art is but a passing triumph: today it is conqueror, tomorrow it is victim.

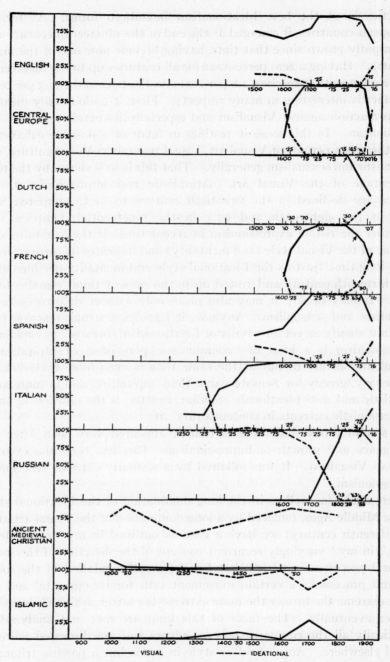

FIG. 5.   THE VISUAL AND IDEATIONAL IN ART BY COUNTRIES

E. As to the *Mixed* class, it needs no special attention after the main streams have been discussed.   I shall only remark that the thirteenth century appears here again as a perfectly balanced period, from even the quantitative standpoint : the Mixed style includes 42.9 per cent of all the art creations of that century for the whole of Europe.

Such are the main conclusions given by Table 13.   These conclusions, however, do not give a direct answer to the question as to whether the Visual stream, in all its pure and impure varieties, or the Ideational — again in all its varieties — has been dominant and is now growing.   In order to answer that question and a few others connected with it, let us simplify the situation somewhat.   Since impressionism is just the extreme variety of the Visual style, let us unite these two into one class of Visual style.   Since expressionism is anti-Visual (though not Ideational in the proper sense of this term) let us unite this with the formal or Ideational class, under the name of the anti-Visual current (or conditionally Ideational).   And after that, let us look at the results.   They are given in Figure 5, based upon the table where naturalistic and impressionistic numbers are united into one class ; the same is done for the formal and the expressionistic ; all the pictures and sculptures of each period are taken as 100 per cent and divided into three classes : Visual, anti-Visual (Ideational and quasi-Ideational), and Mixed.[6]   On the figure are given the percentages of the Visual and of the anti-Visual (the Mixed is not shown) in the total of all the pictures and sculptures of each period.   Now turn to Figure 5.   It shows again that the Visual rendering played an insignificant part in the ancient and medieval Christian art ; that the non-Visual or Ideational rendering had its maximum in the tenth and the eleventh centuries ; in the thirteenth century it went down and became, as mentioned, marvelously balanced and produced the great Idealistic art of that century ; then it rose again quantitatively (not qualitatively) and reached its climax about the middle of the seventeenth century (*ex officio*, Ideational style in religious art), after which it has been tending gradually to decline.   In other words, here in Christian art we have had two long-time waves, one with its top in the tenth and the eleventh centuries, the other in the seventeenth.

As to the total European art, religious and secular (see Table 13 and Figure 9), it shows that the Ideational art has been decreasing steadily after the eleventh century, giving 51.1 per cent for the twelfth to the thirteenth centuries ; 29.2 for the fourteenth to fifteenth ; 20.3 for the

---

[6] For the sake of economy of space I do not give tables : they can be easily computed from the preceding tables.

sixteenth ; 5.9 for the seventeenth ; 2.5 for the eighteenth ; 0.3 for the nineteenth ; and — a sign of revival — 0.7 for the twentieth.   If we include in it — under the category of the non-Visual style — expressionism, then the percentage for the non-Visual style will be the same for all these centuries, with the exception of the nineteenth, where the percentage will be 3.1, and the twentieth, where it will be 36.2 !   A very sharp reaction against Visualism has taken place at the end of the nineteenth and in the twentieth century !

As to the art of the specified European countries, as a whole they show essentially similar curves of the movement of the Visual as well as of the non-Visual styles, the main difference being only in the minor fluctuations and in the period when decrease of the non-Visual and growth of the Visual took place.   For all these countries we have a steady and rapid sliding down of the proportion of the non-Visual style — in Italy since the middle of the thirteenth century, in other countries somewhat later, the latest being Russia, when the process began only in the seventeenth and the eighteenth centuries.   Generally, the centuries from the sixteenth up to the last part of the nineteenth century were dominated almost monopolistically by the Visual style in all the European countries. In all of them the non-Visual style is at the zero line, especially for the eighteenth and the first half of the nineteenth century.   Beginning with the second part or the last quarter of the nineteenth century, however, in all these countries, without any exception, we see the opposite process : a decline of the percentage of the Visual pictures and sculptures and a rise of the percentage of the non-Visual ones.   This fact, noticed before, comes out here with especial clearness since we united into one class all the Visual and all the non-Visual streams.   Even in the particularly naturalistic and Visual country of Holland, the trend of rise of non-Visualism is as pronounced as in other countries.   I mentioned above that though impressionism does not show as yet any definite decrease in the twentieth century, with the exception of France, nevertheless, the whole Visual stream, of which impressionism is but a part, has been on a rapid decline in the twentieth century from 95.4 in the nineteenth to 61.5 per cent in the twentieth.   The non-Visual tide has been rising. This can hardly be questioned in the light of the data given.   Is it just a temporary rise or the first symptom of a coming long-time wave of domination of the non-Visual style, which in that case will probably turn into the Ideational?   This remains to be seen.   Personally I am inclined to regard it as the first wave of the coming growth of Ideationalism.   But whichever of these possibilities is realized, the demonstrated rise of the non-Visual styles is a fairly sure symptom that Visual, Sensate mentality and culture are shaken in their solidity, in their integrity, and in their fascination. In art they are more and more rejected, though the revolters against it do not know, as yet, what they really want and what are the values which they wish to substitute for the Visual values. The situation is very similar to that in the Hellenic-Roman world, especially after the third century A.D., when Visualism, after many imitative waves of classic, archaic, Hellenic, and other patterns, and after transformation into a kind of Roman impressionism, also wore itself out and began to be rejected more and more. As a result, art began to assume the style of incoherent non-Visualism in the third and the fourth and, partly, even in the fifth century. This stage of incoherent non-Visualism was present but as a passage toward the emergence and rapid rise of the Ideational art, which dominated about nine centuries of the culture of Europe. At the present time we have a somewhat similar situation. After the Renaissance there were several imitative waves of various "classic" forms, "Gothic" forms, "primitive" forms, each wave being shorter and shorter. At the end of the nineteenth century Visualism turned into impressionism as its last "card" and ultimate form. It rapidly rose, produced some wonderful creations, and seems to be fading already. There hardly is any progress on the highway of Visualism. For the time being, it seems to have exhausted itself. Hence the necessity of pioneering in a new, non-Visual way. This is shown by the rise of the incoherent non-Visualism of the end of the nineteenth and twentieth centuries. The pioneers are still on their way to the "promised land" where they can settle. This promised land seems to be but Ideationalism in some form.

This concerns not only the style of painting and sculpture, but the mentality and the culture which are behind it and of which it is a manifestation. To be brief, art viewed in that perspective points to the exhaustion of the Visual, Sensate mentality and culture; to a rise of its opponents; and to the transitory position of our present mentality and culture, between the wave of the ending Sensate culture and the dawn of the Ideational culture.

I have indicated that the data show a slight increase of the religious subjects in the twentieth century in all European countries, with the exception of Russia and France. This fact well fits with the rising tide of the non-Visual style in the same period. Though not in the minor fluctuations, certainly in all the big movements the religious or transcendental subjects have been positively associated with the Ideational form (which form is in a sense a logical necessity, because the transcendental phenomena do not have, as such, any Visual form), while the secular-empirical subjects have been positively associated with the Visual style. The Middle Ages were predominantly religious in their art; and their style in art was overwhelmingly Ideational. The decline of the religious subjects in art was followed by decline of Ideationalism after the thirteenth century. The last four centuries were predominantly secular and they were also visual in the style of their art. The end of the nineteenth century and the twentieth have shown a slight rise of religious subjects, and the same period is marked by rise of the non-Visual style. Thus the data here agree with one another and mutually reinforce their validity. Yes, we seem to be in a very interesting transitional period, at the end of one long wave of Sensate culture and before the beginning of another wave of the coming Ideational culture. Hence the incoherency of contemporary art, and its search for something new and different from the worn-out Visualism.

Figure 6 sums up very roughly long-time waves of the domination of each of the main styles and their alternation in the course of time.

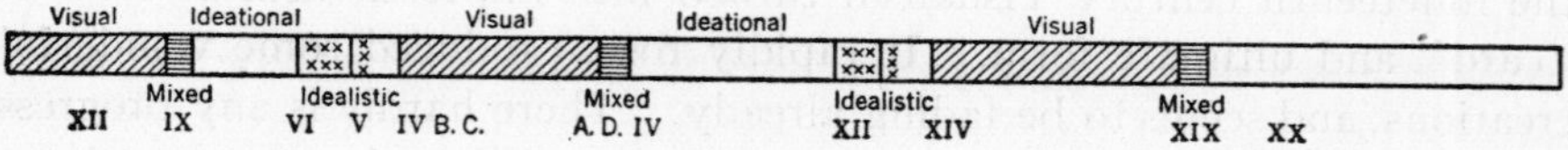

FIG. 6. LONG-TIME WAVES OF THE MAIN STYLES IN ART

In a rough form the figure sums up the course of the alternation of the main styles for a period of some thirty-one centuries, from the Creto-Mycenaean through the Greek, through the Roman, through the medieval, up to the present time. As mentioned, there are plenty of reasons to regard these links as a continuation of each other, because — regardless of whether the Greek culture was a transformation of the Creto-Mycenaean or its direct descendent, and whether we shall consider the medieval culture as a modification of the Graeco-Roman or its continuation — the fact of a connection and continuation of the Mycenaean culture by the Greek, and of the Graeco-Roman by the medieval, is rather certain. From such a perspective we see, first, that *there are indeed long-time waves in domination of each of the main styles, and an alternation of that domination in the course of time.* Second, *there is a certain order in that alternation: Visual, through the period of incoherent Mixed transition, is followed by Ideational; the Ideational, when it begins to wane and the Visual begins to grow, is followed by a short period of the Idealistic art, which is supplanted again by the Visual phase, after which, through the period of another incoherent Mixed transition, comes again the Ideational phase,*

which through the Idealistic phase is followed by the Visual, and so on.
Such a sequence is logically comprehensible, as explained above, and
factually has taken place at least three times in the period of thirty-one
centuries studied.   Third, *at the present time our art and culture seem to
have entered the transitional period of the Mixed "incoherency" which
usually comes at the end of the Visual wave and before the rise of the Ideational wave.*   Fourth, however strange it appears, and however unnecessary to expect a mere mechanical equality of the duration of each of the
waves of both styles, from my standpoint, nevertheless, the scheme shows
that the periods of the domination of each style are approximately equal in
their duration.   We have the duration of about three centuries of domination of the Visual and Ideational styles in the chain of the Creto-
Mycenaean-Greek phases; then comes a period of about eight or nine
centuries of domination of the Visual, followed by about as long a period
of domination of the Ideational form (from the fifth or the sixth century
to the thirteenth).   The last waves of the dominant Visual form have
lasted, so far, about five and a half centuries.   Two Idealistic periods
lasted each about one hundred and fifty years.   Here then, quite unexpectedly, we meet again the phenomenon of "self-regulation" of sociocultural processes, of the "limit" in the direction of social processes, and
of a lack of any perpetual trend and the presence of the "erratically
recurrent waves" in the course of sociocultural processes.   These principles, as explained in Volume Two, do not require an arithmetical equality
of action and reaction — they remain valid without it; and yet, here as
in several other processes shown further, the length of the domination of
each of these styles, in two periods of recurrence, happens to be almost
arithmetically equal: about three hundred years in the first recurrence
and about eight hundred years in the second.   Thus not looking intentionally for a corroboration of these principles, the data supply such
corroboration by, so to speak, their own initiative.

F. *Other Theories in the Field.*   In the light of the above, I can
touch now two theories which concern closely the same problem of waves
in the style of art.   First of those is H. Schäfer's theory, the second is
that of H. Krauss.   H. Schäfer accepts the wavelike fluctuation of styles,
but contrary to his own thesis he claims that the Visual style was discovered for the first time in Greece in the fifth century and only since
that time has it spread and existed.[7]   Such a supposition is factually
untenable: we have seen that even the art of the primitive peoples, not

[7] H. Schäfer, "*Agyptische und heutige Kunst,*" in *Die Antike* (1927), Vol. III, pp. 209, 213,
et passim.

to mention that of the Mycenaean period, has been Visual, and sometimes perfect in its Visuality. Otherwise, his very general sketch of the periods of domination of the impressionistic and expressionistic styles marks properly the main boundaries of the main periods. He also finds that contemporary art seems to show more and more an expressionistic trend somewhat similar to the art of ancient Egypt and to what I call non-Visual style.

More substantially the problem was treated by H. Krauss in a special monographic work. He attempted systematically to show long and short waves of the recurring swings from a form near to what I call Ideational to the form near to my Visual, and back; correlated with the waves from the plastic or tactile to the *malerisch;* from the plane to the recess — all three movements mutually correlated with one another — in the history of the Graeco-Roman and the Christian-European art.[8] His study led him to the following conclusions.

These tendencies coexist side by side at any moment; but one of them at a given period grows and pushes the other underneath; subsequently, however, the other gathers power and takes the upper hand until it too is replaced by the opposite tendency. From this standpoint there are definite epochs in the life history of any art system; each epoch consists of four major waves, the fourth of which is transitional to the new epoch, beginning with the wave opposite to the last wave of the preceding epoch. Analyzing from this standpoint the painting, sculpture, and architecture of Greece, Rome, Byzantium, and Europe, Krauss attempts to give the approximate chronological points of each of the epochs and of the tops and bottoms of the four waves which comprise the art history of each epoch. Here are his data.

---

[8] Unfortunately he does not give any large sample or quantitative data for substantiation of his propositions. The same must be said of several other theories in this field. Here is Krauss's formulation of the problem.

"Sind rhythmisch sich wiederholende stets zu ihrem Ausgangspunkt zurückkehrende Bewegungen festzustellen, die etwa

(1) von einer *naturwahren* Formgestaltung zu einer *naturfernen* ubergehen?

(2) von einer *extrem-plastischen* Tendenz ausgehend in einer *extrem-malerischen* endigen?

(3) von *Flächeneigung* resp. *gedrängten Raumgefühl* zur *Tiefeneigung* resp. *erweitertem Raumgefühl* führen? ferner

(4) Lassen sich aus dem *Wechsel*·etwa *sich ablösender Stile* Schlüsse ziehen, die auf eine Periodizität hinzielen?"

H. Krauss, *Das Wellengesetz in der Geschichte* (Bern and Leipzig, 1929), p. 13. See other and more general theories in W. Ziegenfuss, "*Kunst,*" in *Handwörterbuch der Soziologie* (Stuttgart, 1931), pp. 308–338; F. Adama van Scheltema, "*Rhythmus,*" in *Zeitschrift für Aesthetik* (1927), Vol. XXI.

TABLE 14.   APPROXIMATE ESTIMATES OF THE CURVES DATA [9]

Epochs	Wave A		Wave B		Wave C		Wave D	
1. *Graeco-Roman art* B.C.	530	430	380	320	290	200	135	60	10
2. *Early Byzantine* A.D.	330	440	480	550	585	685	750	825	875
3. *Late Byzantine*	875	970	1010	1090	1120	1220	1270	1340	1390
4. *European, medieval*	875	970	1010	1090	1120	1220	1270	1340	1390
5. *European, later*	1390	1470	1500	1540	1560	1630	1670	1740	1780
6. *European, latest*	1780	1820	1832	1850	1858	1885	1898	1925	—

Festgestellt wurde :

I. Ein rhythmisch sich wiederholendes Zurückdrängen eines periodisch auftauchenden, intensiv-plastischen Empfindens:

II. Ein mit dem progressiv steigenden malerischen Empfinden parallel sich entwickelndes Raumgefühl, das, ursprunglich gedrängt, sich in ein unbegrenztes, ein "kosmischs" umwandelt.

Durch das periodische Sich-Ausleben der beiden Triebe ist die Epoche räumlich und zeitlich bestimmt. Die Höchststeigerung des malerischen und räumlichen Empfindens und die unmittelbar darauf folgende Einengung des Raumgefühls zeigt den Abschluss der alten, den Anfang einer neuen Epoche an.

Der gesetzmässig sich vollziehende Ablauf jeder Epoche lässt sich durch eine mehrfach gegliederte Kurve ausdrücken, deren drei Partialkurven durch eine vierte mit der Kurve einer neuen Epoche verbunden ist. Diese letzte Partialkurve, die sogenannte Uebergangskurve, gehort nur zum Teil der alten Epoche an. . . . Aus der Uebergangszeit erhebt sich die Frühzeitwelle A (die romantische Welle). Sie wird von der rasch emporsteigen Stosswelle B gefolgt (die realistische). Diese geht nun in die Reife und Spätzeitwelle C (die Barockwelle) über, die schliesslich in der letzten Welle D (der Uebergangswelle) formal and inhaltlich nachklingt. Die Kurve ist zunächst durch die Bewegung, durch die Wandlung der Form bedingt. Innerhalb der Kurve vollzieht sich die Auseinanderzetzung zwischen malerischem und plastischem Empfinden, zwischen Differenzierung und Integrierung, zwischen idealistischer und realistischer Gestaltung der Form. In der Kurve jedoch gelangt auch das malerische Empfinden begleitende Raumgefühl zum Ausdruck. Die Kurve spiegelt den Kampf und den Sieg des räumlich-malerischen Empfindens ab.[10]

Not denying the existence of the rhythms and the essential accuracy of some of the author's data, I must say that his concrete conclusions are not entirely convincing. He is victimized somewhat by his desire to find quite a rhythmic and clearly cut regularity in all the systems of art

[9] *Ibid.*, p. 115.   [10] *Ibid.*, p. 100.

he considers. In this point he makes the same mistake which is made by the contenders of the existence of a uniform regularity in the development of all the art systems, discussed before.

And the text of his work is not sufficient to warrant Table 14 where all the six "epochs" of art fluctuate so uniformly. More than that: even the table itself, especially the "epochs" 5 and 6, with their periods of twelve, eighteen, and even eight, years, testify that the dates are fitted to the assumed curve, rather than that the curve follows from the real data. The author is vague in his factual analysis of the "evolution curve" of these art systems. He indiscriminately talks now of the Ideational and Visual; now replaces them with the "Frühzeit," now with the Romantic, now with the Idealistic, and so on, as though all these terms are identical, and as though to be "romantic" necessarily means to be Ideational or Visual. This vagueness goes through his work, vitiates its clearness and factualness, and the author's final conclusion. Even with all that, the factual basis of the work does not warrant the final table given above. It springs up as a *deus ex machina* at the end of the book.

For these reasons, I cannot accept these conclusions, though the idea of the existence of rhythm or waves in the changes of the Ideational and Visual styles and their satellites appears to me to be sound. H. Wölfflin also states the recurrence of the main forms of art, saying that "There is classic and baroque, not only in more modern times and not only in antique building, but on so different ground as Gothic," and farther on he says that the rhythm of the "linear versus *malerisch*" studied by him in the history of the European art of the fifteenth to the eighteenth centuries is also recurrent in the history of art of other countries and of other periods. Unfortunately, however, he does not go into the matter beyond these statements and the period studied.[11]

Karl Scheffler affirms also that there is an eternal rhythm of the "Gothic" and the "Greek" styles, meaning by the first a spontaneous, creative, symbolic, vertical, wild, emotional, pathetic, changeable, masculine style and by the Greek a mathematical [though in fact the Parthenon was asymmetrical in a purely mathematical sense], planned, clear, unemotional, static, feminine art.[12] The division and the definitions of each of these styles is so indefinite, dark, and fantastic, that the theory can hardly be taken seriously. It is much better formulated by those who claim the rhythm of the "classic" and the "romantic" forms; of the Apollonian and Dionysian arts, and so on.

[11] H. Wölfflin, *Principles*, p. 231.
[12] See K. Scheffler, *Der Geist der Gothik* (Leipzig, 1919).

Generally, almost every investigator of the phenomena of art dynamics hardly fails to notice the phenomena of rhythm of various styles in the course of art existence. And there are many theories of this kind, of which the most important have been discussed in the previous chapters. In regard to many of them, however, it is to be noticed that they either do not try to substantiate their contentions by a factual, and especially by quantitative analysis of the data, or, like Krauss, do so rather fragmentarily and superficially; that the theories which attempt it seriously are not numerous; and that even among these, the ones which have to be recognized as quite adequate scientifically are so few that they can easily be counted on the fingers of one hand. More numerous are those which give an important part of truth and something indeed new; but the truthful part in them is usually followed by a great deal of exaggeration, one-sidedness, or similar defects.

Now we can return to a continuation of our study.

IV. Fluctuation of the Spiritual and Sensual Character of Painting and Sculpture

The Sensate culture and its art are expected to be more "Epicurean" than the Ideational culture and art. To give sensual pleasure is one of the main objects of the first, while upholding the world of the eternal and spiritual values is one of the main objectives of the second. This follows from the definition of these cultures and from the concept of the Visual (Sensate) and Ideational forms of art. Therefore, we shall expect deductively that the Ideational art and the periods of its domination will be positively associated with the "spiritual character" of the pictures and sculptures, while the art of the periods of the domination of the Sensate (Visual) form will show a positive "correlation" with the sensuous character of its pictures and sculptures.

To discover to what extent this expectation is corroborated by the facts, a special study was made of the art of the same countries and periods with which we deal in this chapter. As mentioned, classification of pictures and sculptures according to their spirituality or sensuality involves some element of subjectivity. But granting this to some extent, nevertheless the main results seem to give a fairly adequate picture of the changes in the art reality and in the art mentality. Here again the essential results of the two independent studies, in Cambridge and Prague, come close together. Furthermore, in order to reduce the element of subjectivity, the paintings and sculptures were divided into three main classes: Spiritual (with subclasses: moderately and extremely), Sensual (with the same subclasses), and Neutral. Only the works which indeed embodied, conspicuously and almost unquestionably, spirituality or sensuality were put into the extreme classes. All the pictures and sculptures which did not show clearly either one of these characteristics were put into the Neutral class. And the reader, going through the tables, can see for himself that the enormous majority of the art works were placed in this class. Those which were put into the other two classes show to any specialist or normal man their spirituality or sensuality almost as clearly as pictures with bright blue or red tones would show to a normal man their predominant colors.

By spirituality is meant the ascetic, otherworldly, stoic, or idealistic atmosphere of the picture or sculpture; by sensuality, the "Epicurean," materialistic, sensualistic, hedonistic, carnal, or sensuous — sometimes even sexual — atmosphere prevailing in the work. If one takes the pictures of Fra Angelico, or El Greco, or most of the pictures of the "Primitives" or of the thirteenth and of the preceding centuries, on the one hand; and those of Giorgione, partly Rubens, or Boucher, or many of the "nude women bodies" of the modern artists, one can see at once the difference in these "atmospheres" almost as clearly as the difference between the black and white, red and blue, pink and green.

Now let us turn to Table 15, which gives in detailed form the data of the five main subdivisions, and to Figures 7 and 8, Figure 7 gives them in the form of the three curves: Spiritual (in which both subclasses are united), Sensual (covering also both subclasses), and Neutral; Figure 8 depicts the movement of the percentages of the "extremely spiritual" and the "extremely sensual" pictures and sculptures.

Table 15 and Figures 7 and 8 warrant the following conclusions. If we take the whole of Europe (Figures 9 and 10), we see that its art up to the fourteenth and fifteenth centuries was Spiritual and Neutral, sensualism being practically lacking; only 0.8 per cent of the pictures and sculptures before the tenth century (mainly in the period of the Carlovingian Renaissance) show even moderate sensuality. For the centuries from the tenth to the thirteenth inclusive, the sensuality is again entirely lacking. Here the centuries tenth to eleventh, quite consistent with the previous data concerning the percentage of the religious and ideational works, give a somewhat higher percentage of spiritual art works than the period before the tenth. The twelfth and partly the thirteenth centuries remain even more spiritual and pious than the previous ones — a result quite consistent with the data already given. For the fourteenth to fifteenth centuries we have an even still higher proportion of spiritual works (38.7 instead

TABLE 15. FLUCTUATION OF THE SPIRITUAL AND SENSUAL CHARACTER IN ART

Sp = Spiritual   Se = Sensual   N = Neutral   e = extremely   m = moderately

Ancient and Medieval Christian

	-X	X-XI	XII-XIII	XIV-XV	XVI-XVII	XVIII	Total
			(Numbers)				
Sp—m	557	229	83	673	156	—	1,698
e	51	160	137	277	110	—	735
Se—m	43	—	—	—	—	—	43
e	—	—	—	—	—	—	—
N	4381	2110	3686	2733	1114	437	14,461
Total	5032	2499	3906	3683	1380	437	16,937
			(Percentages)				
Sp—m	11.1	9.2	2.2	18.3	11.0	—	10.0
e	1.0	6.4	3.4	7.5	8.0	—	4.3
Se—m	.8	—	—	—	—	—	.3
e	—	—	—	—	—	—	—
N	87.1	84.4	94.4	74.2	81.0	100.0	85.4
Total	100.0	100.0	100.0	100.0	100.0	100.0	100.0

Islamic

	-X	X-XI	XII-XIII	XIV-XV	XVI	XVII	XVIII	Total
				(Numbers)				
Sp—m	5	5	28	22	6	28	34	128
e	—	—	—	4	—	10	—	14
Se—m	5	65	20	44	12	76	36	258
e	20	5	4	10	8	76	34	157
N	45	520	448	480	874	1020	846	4233
Total	75	595	500	560	900	1210	950	4790
				(Percentages)				
Sp—m	6.7	.8	5.6	3.9	.7	2.3	3.5	2.6
e	—	—	—	.7	—	.8	—	.3
Se—m	6.7	11.0	4.0	7.9	1.3	6.3	3.8	5.0
e	26.6	.8	.8	1.8	.9	6.3	3.6	3.3
N	60.0	87.4	89.6	85.7	97.1	84.3	89.1	88.8
Total	100.0	100.0	100.0	100.0	100.0	100.0	100.0	100.0

TABLE 15. FLUCTUATION OF THE SPIRITUAL AND SENSUAL CHARACTER IN ART — continued

Sp = Spiritual   Se = Sensual   N = Neutral   e = extremely   m = moderately

Russian

	-XII	XII–XIII	XIV–XV	XVI	XVII	XVIII	1801–1825	1826–1850	1851–1875	1876–1900	XX	Total
						(Numbers)						
Sp—m	—	20	57	62	84	27	52	31	27	219	587	1,166
e	—	6	12	21	10	3	8	4	6	73	153	296
Se—m	—	—	—	—	—	107	176	169	341	201	578	1,572
e	—	—	—	—	—	12	34	38	72	67	149	372
N	22	56	171	228	302	438	397	487	170	2078	4539	8,888
Total	22	82	240	311	396	587	667	729	616	2638	6006	12,294
						(Percentages)						
Sp—m		24.4	23.8	19.9	21.2	4.6	7.8	4.3	4.4	8.3	9.8	9.5
e		7.3	5.0	6.8	2.5	.6	1.2	.5	1.0	2.8	2.5	2.4
Se—m		—	—	—	—	18.2	26.4	23.2	55.4	7.6	9.6	12.8
e		—	—	—	—	2.0	5.1	5.2	11.6	2.5	2.5	3.0
N	100.0	68.3	71.2	73.3	76.3	74.6	59.5	66.8	27.6	78.8	75.6	72.3
Total	100.0	100.0	100.0	100.0	100.0	100.0	100.0	100.0	100.0	100.0	100.0	100.0

Italian

	1200–1300	1300–1350	1350–1400	1400–1450	1450–1500	1500–1550	1550–1600	1600–1650	1650–1700	1700–1750	1750–1800	1800–1850	1850–1900	1900–1933	Total
							(Numbers)								
Sp—m	586	50	378	563	1171	684	872	702	1161	782	340	287	160	31	7,767
e	51	16	75	57	208	169	659	612	773	318	105	62	32	9	3,146
Se—m	—	—	—	62	150	301	291	317	647	715	367	296	179	67	3,392
e	—	—	—	13	41	212	267	289	379	476	222	143	112	51	2,205
N	237	647	195	678	1928	1696	2271	1901	1616	1360	1850	430	496	484	15,789
Total	874	713	648	1373	3498	3062	4360	3821	4576	3651	2884	1218	979	642	32,299
							(Percentages)								
Sp—m	67.2	7.0	58.3	40.0	33.5	22.4	21.0	17.3	25.2	21.4	11.8	23.6	19.4	4.8	24.0
e	5.7	2.2	11.6	4.2	5.9	5.5	15.1	15.8	16.9	8.7	3.6	5.1	3.3	1.4	9.7
Se—m	—	—	—	4.5	4.3	9.8	6.7	9.3	14.1	19.6	12.7	24.3	18.3	10.4	10.6
e	—	—	—	.9	1.2	6.9	6.1	7.5	8.3	13.0	7.7	11.7	11.3	7.9	6.8
N	27.1	90.8	30.1	50.4	55.1	55.4	51.1	50.1	35.5	37.3	64.2	35.3	47.7	75.5	48.9
Total	100.0	100.0	100.0	100.0	100.0	100.0	100.0	100.0	100.0	100.0	100.0	100.0	100.0	100.0	100.0

Spanish

(Numbers)

	XV	XVI	XVII	1700–1750	1750–1800	1800–1850	1850–1900	1900–1933	Total
Sp—m	195	225	66	11	6	27	15	—	545
e	97	63	55	—	—	—	—	—	215
Se—m	—	—	—	80	67	19	16	33	215
e	—	—	—	—	—	—	—	—	—
N	—	95	398	200	242	71	80	138	1224
Total	292	383	519	291	315	117	111	171	2199

(Percentages)

	XV	XVI	XVII	1700–1750	1750–1800	1800–1850	1850–1900	1900–1933	Total
Sp—m	66.8	58.7	12.7	3.8	1.9	23.1	13.5	—	24.7
e	33.2	16.5	10.6	—	—	—	—	—	9.8
Se—m	—	—	—	27.5	23.0	16.2	14.4	19.3	9.8
e	—	—	—	—	—	—	—	—	—
N	—	24.8	76.7	68.7	75.1	60.7	72.1	80.7	55.7
Total	100.0	100.0	100.0	100.0	100.0	100.0	100.0	100.0	100.0

French

(Numbers)

	XVI	1600–1650	1650–1700	1700–1750	1750–1800	1800–1850	1850–1880	1880–1900	1900–1933	Total
Sp—m	201	108	123	21	11	87	60	121	272	1,004
e	36	15	24	3	—	18	21	47	69	233
Se—m	126	69	144	108	123	147	204	182	197	1,300
e	21	36	90	390	534	228	303	127	93	1,822
N	1032	717	585	2145	1963	2589	1278	573	650	11,532
Total	1416	945	966	2667	2631	3069	1866	1050	1281	15,891

(Percentages)

	XVI	1600–1650	1650–1700	1700–1750	1750–1800	1800–1850	1850–1880	1880–1900	1900–1933	Total
Sp—m	14.2	11.4	12.7	.8	.4	2.8	3.2	11.5	21.2	6.3
e	2.5	1.6	2.5	.1	—	.6	1.1	4.5	5.4	1.5
Se—m	9.7	7.3	14.9	4.0	4.7	4.8	11.0	17.3	15.4	8.1
e	1.5	3.8	9.3	14.6	20.3	7.4	16.2	12.1	7.3	11.5
N	72.1	75.9	60.6	80.5	74.6	84.4	68.5	54.6	50.7	72.6
Total	100.0	100.0	100.0	100.0	100.0	100.0	100.0	100.0	100.0	100.0

TABLE 15. FLUCTUATION OF THE SPIRITUAL AND SENSUAL CHARACTER IN ART — continued

Sp = Spiritual   Se = Sensual   N = Neutral   e = extremely   m = moderately

Dutch

(Numbers)

	-1500	1500-1600	1600-1620	1620-1640	1640-1660	1660-1680	1680-1780	1780-1880	1880-1933	Total
Sp — m	504	292	—	—	—	—	—	—	6	802
e	—	—	—	—	—	—	—	—	—	—
Se — m	—	—	84	164	—	—	—	—	89	337
e	—	—	456	218	150	168	—	—	16	1008
N	794	804	202	586	1234	650	470	574	271	5585
Total	1298	1096	742	968	1384	818	470	574	382	7732

(Percentages)

	-1500	1500-1600	1600-1620	1620-1640	1640-1660	1660-1680	1680-1780	1780-1880	1880-1933	Total
Sp — m	38.9	26.6	—	—	—	—	—	—	1.6	10.5
e	—	—	—	—	—	—	—	—	—	—
Se — m	—	—	11.3	16.9	—	—	—	—	23.3	4.5
e	—	—	61.5	22.5	10.8	20.5	—	—	4.2	12.7
N	61.1	73.4	27.2	60.6	89.2	79.5	100.0	100.0	70.9	72.3
Total	100.0	100.0	100.0	100.0	100.0	100.0	100.0	100.0	100.0	100.0

Central Europe

(Numbers)

	XVI	1600-1650	1650-1700	1700-1750	1750-1800	1800-1830	1830-1860	1860-1880	1880-1900	1900-1933	Total
Sp — m	705	36	38	72	21	216	75	141	84	348	1,736
e	57	—	6	3	—	9	—	—	6	33	114
Se — m	147	9	23	24	119	57	69	51	96	213	808
e	21	—	7	—	18	9	12	—	6	36	109
N	687	135	118	231	224	780	660	1179	771	3681	8,466
Total	1617	180	192	330	382	1071	816	1371	963	4311	11,233

(Percentages)

	XVI	1600-1650	1650-1700	1700-1750	1750-1800	1800-1830	1830-1860	1860-1880	1880-1900	1900-1933	Total
Sp — m	43.6	20.0	17.8	21.8	5.5	20.2	9.2	10.3	8.7	8.1	15.4
e	3.5	—	3.1	.9	—	.8	—	—	.6	.8	1.0
Se — m	9.1	5.0	12.0	7.6	31.2	5.4	8.5	3.7	10.0	4.9	7.2
e	1.3	—	3.6	—	4.7	.8	1.5	—	.6	.8	.9
N	42.5	75.0	61.5	69.7	58.6	72.8	80.8	86.0	80.1	85.4	75.5
Total	100.0	100.0	100.0	100.0	100.0	100.0	100.0	100.0	100.0	100.0	100.0

English

(Numbers)

	XV	XVI	XVII	1700-1750	1750-1800	1800-1850	1850-1900	1900-1933	Total
Sp—m	341	16	7	—	—	—	—	—	364
e	62	2	—	—	—	45	78	9	196
Se—m	—	—	12	57	82	—	—	15	166
e	—	—	—	3	11	—	—	—	14
N	—	68	44	48	38	142	125	120	585
Total	403	86	63	108	131	187	203	144	1325

(Percentages)

	XV	XVI	XVII	1700-1750	1750-1800	1800-1850	1850-1900	1900-1933	Total
Sp—m	84.6	18.6	11.1	—	—	—	—	—	26.7
e	15.4	2.3	—	—	—	24.1	38.4	6.3	14.8
Se—m	—	—	19.0	56.4	62.6	—	—	10.4	12.5
e	—	—	—	2.9	8.4	—	—	—	1.0
N	—	79.1	69.9	40.7	29.0	75.9	61.6	83.3	45.0
Total	100.0	100.0	100.0	100.0	100.0	100.0	100.0	100.0	100.0

Europe as a Whole

(Numbers)

	-X	X-XI	XII-XIII	XIV-XV	XVI	XVII	XVIII	XIX	XX
Spiritual	608	389	883	4716	4197	3953	1723	2,007	1508
Sensual	43	—	—	266	1386	3262	3525	3,354	1537
Neutral	4781	2132	3978	7203	7438	8945	9646	12,880	9893

(Percentages)

	-X	X-XI	XII-XIII	XIV-XV	XVI	XVII	XVIII	XIX	XX
Spiritual	12.1	15.5	18.2	38.7	32.2	24.5	11.5	11.0	11.7
Sensual	0.8	—	—	2.2	10.6	20.2	23.6	18.4	11.9
Neutral	87.1	84.5	81.8	59.1	57.2	55.3	64.9	60.6	76.4
Total	100.0	100.0	100.0	100.0	100.0	100.0	100.0	100.0	100.0

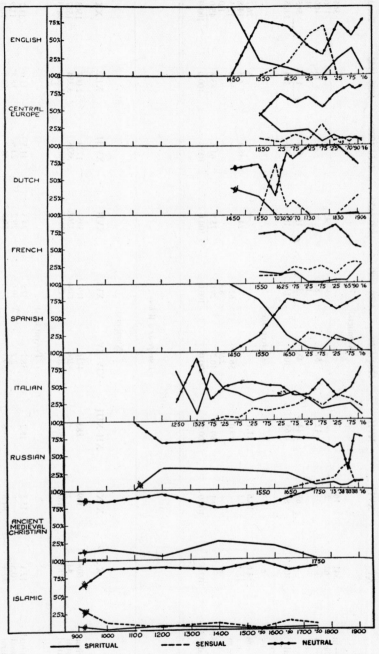

FIG. 7. THE SPIRITUAL AND SENSUAL IN ART BY COUNTRIES

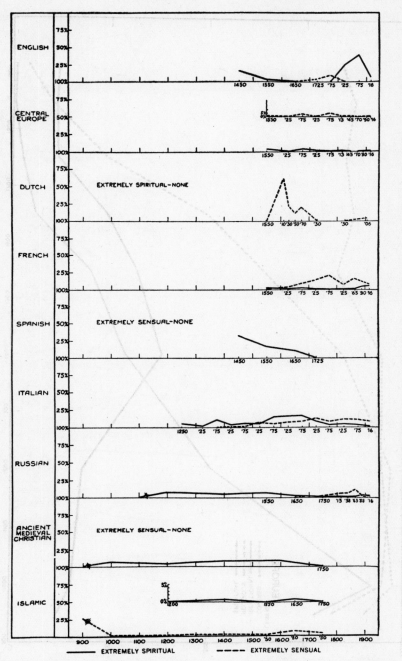

FIG. 8.   THE EXTREMELY SPIRITUAL AND SENSUAL BY COUNTRIES

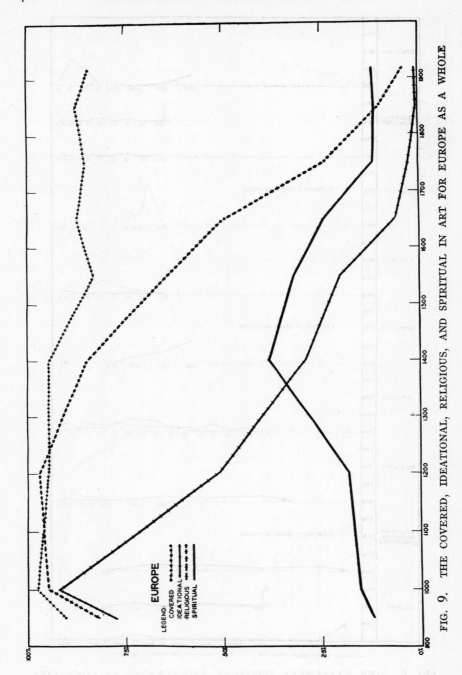

FIG. 9. THE COVERED, IDEATIONAL, RELIGIOUS, AND SPIRITUAL IN ART FOR EUROPE AS A WHOLE

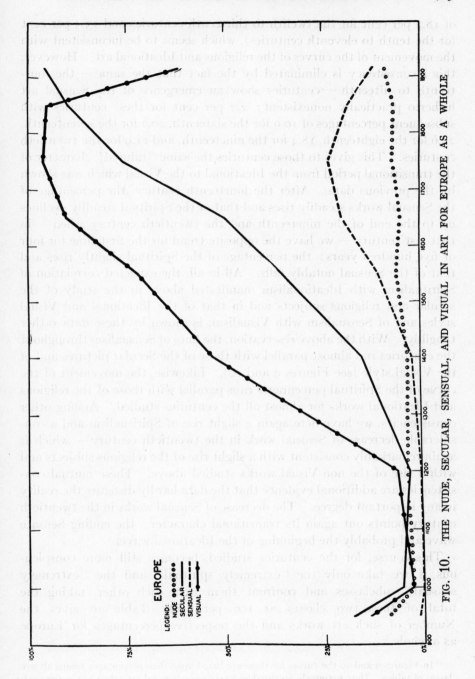

FIG. 10. THE NUDE, SECULAR, SENSUAL, AND VISUAL IN ART FOR EUROPE AS A WHOLE

LEGEND:
EUROPE
NUDE
SECULAR
SENSUAL
VISUAL

of 18.2 per cent for the twelfth to thirteenth centuries and 15.5 per cent for the tenth to eleventh centuries), which seems to be inconsistent with the movement of the curves of the religious and Ideational art. However, this inconsistency is eliminated by the fact that the same — the fourteenth to fifteenth — centuries show an emergence of the Sensual art hitherto practically nonexistent : 2.2 per cent for these centuries with subsequent percentages of 10.6 for the sixteenth, 20.2 for the seventeenth, 23.6 for the eighteenth, 18.4 for the nineteenth, and 11.9 for the twentieth centuries. This gives to those centuries the same "tainted" character of the transitional period from the Ideational to the Visual which was shown by the previous data. After the fourteenth century, the percentage of the Sensual works steadily rises and that of the Spiritual steadily declines up to the end of the nineteenth and the twentieth century when — in that last century — we have the opposite trend for the first time for four or five hundred years : the percentage of the Spiritual slightly rises and that of the Sensual notably falls. All in all, the expected correlation of Spiritualism with Ideationalism manifested above in the study of the secular and religious subjects and in that of the Ideational and Visual styles and of Sensualism with Visualism, is shown by these data rather tangibly. With the above reservation, the lines of Sensualism throughout the centuries run almost parallel with those of the Secular pictures and of the Visual style (see Figures 9 and 10). Likewise, the movement of the curve of the Spiritual percentages runs parallel with those of the religious and Ideational works for almost all the centuries studied. Among other consistencies, we have here again a slight rise of Spiritualism and a considerable decrease of Sensual work in the twentieth century — which is again remarkably consistent with a slight rise of the religious subjects and with a rise of the non-Visual works studied above. These mutual consistencies are additional evidence that the data hardly disfigure the reality in any important degree. The decrease of Sensual works in the twentieth century points out again its transitional character; the ending Sensate wave and probably the beginning of the Ideational wave.

This course, for the centuries studied, becomes still more conspicuous if we take only the "extremely spiritual" and the "extremely sensual" subclasses and confront them with each other, taking the total of these two classes as 100 per cent. Table 16 gives the Number of such art works and the respective percentages for Europe as a whole.[13]

---

[13] In Figures 9 and 10 the curves for these are based upon their percentages among all five classes of tables. Here extremely Spiritual and extremely Sensual are taken as 100 per cent.

TABLE 16.   FLUCTUATION OF EXTREMELY SPIRITUAL AND SENSUAL ART

Europe by Centuries

	-X	X–XI	XII–XIII	XIV–XV	XVI	XVII	XVIII	XIX	XX
Extremely Spiritual									
Number	51	160	194	804	1072	1550	432	409	273
Per cent	100	100	100	95.2	67.3	46.4	20.6	26.2	44.2
Extremely Sensual									
Number	—	—	—	41	521	1793	1666	1151	345
Per cent	—	—	—	4.8	32.7	53.6	79.4	73.8	55.8

As the reader can see, the proportion of these classes follows in essentials the same course as that of Table 15.   But here the changes in the "sensualization" and "spiritualization" in their extreme and, therefore, most unquestionable form come out still more clearly.   After the thirteenth century there began a steady and rapid trend toward the sensualization of art — even its eroticism — which from 4.8 per cent of the extremely sensual works in the fourteenth and fifteenth centuries reached 79.4 per cent in the eighteenth and 73.8 per cent in the nineteenth century.   Its recession began at the end of the nineteenth century and has moved rapidly in the twentieth century, falling back to 55.8 per cent.

Thus all the above data give rather consistent results as to the fluctuation of the Ideational and of the Visual (Sensate) forms of art and art mentality.   Among other things they quite consistently point out that the twentieth century was the century of at least temporary reversal of the trend which had been going on during the last four centuries.

If now we take the data for the separate European countries, the essential configuration of the Sensual, Spiritual, and Neutral curves in these countries follows the same course, namely, a decrease of spirituality after the thirteenth century.   But in secondary traits, there are differences in time, when this decrease or increase of the Sensual wave took place, Italy, as usual, leading in time and Russia, as usual, lagging; in the minor fluctuations of each of the curves (for instance, the seventeenth century showed a temporary rise of the spiritual curve in several — mainly Catholic — countries) and in the relative proportion of the Spiritual, Sensual, and Neutral works.   But these are details; therefore, it is unnecessary to go into their laborious discussion.   One point is to be mentioned, however: the Islamic art here again follows its own course, unrelated to and quite dissimilar to the countries of the European Christian culture.

V. FLUCTUATION OF QUANTITATIVE AND QUALITATIVE NUDITY

As a further test of the sensual or spiritual character of the art works in the centuries studied, I have taken nudity as it is given in the pictures and sculptures which depict the human body. In the sample used, all the pictures — for instance, landscape — where the human figure is not depicted are naturally excluded. Only those with human figures are taken. Per se, nudity is not necessarily a mark either of sensuality or spirituality. But in the cultural configuration of the Western Christian world, a complete nudity has mostly been regarded as something indecent, or with a flavoring of indecency. Under a few special circumstances it has been regarded as appropriate — as, for instance, baptism, or other special event; likewise some ascetic, spiritual forms of nudity have always been treated as "holy," "innocent," "sacred," and decent. But aside from such special conditions and forms, complete nudity has been under a taboo in that culture, and the pictures or sculptures which present it have had, with the exception of mythological and religious, magic and moral, subjects, a flavoring, at least in most cases, of something sensual. Anyhow, the "quantity" of nudity — meaning by this whether the body is completely covered or completely uncovered, with sex organs depicted — is not quite a neutral phenomenon in regard to sensuality and spirituality. If passing from century to century, we notice that (other conditions being equal) the percentage of pictures with human figures which are completely nude increases, as compared with those having the figures completely covered (except faces, hands, and possibly feet); this is a fairly good symptom (in the conditions of Christian European culture) that art is becoming more sensual, perhaps even sexual. Hence, the advisability of the study of nudity from this quantitative standpoint, in connection with the Ideationality or Visuality (Sensateness) of art and culture.

It is granted, however, that the mere quantity of nudity is not an entirely sufficient symptom for that purpose: theoretically, we can imagine a situation in a given century when the percentage of the pictures and sculptures with completely nude bodies (except perhaps the sex organs) increases, but the nude bodies are all ascetic, like some of El Greco's pictures. Such a situation, however factually improbable it is, evidently does not warrant the conclusion that on this basis alone the art of such a century is more sensual than that of some other century, where the percentage of the nude bodies is smaller. Frankly, in the conditions of the Christian European culture, such a theoretical possibility factually has rarely been possible; but in order to be sure, I made a further study

TABLE 17. FLUCTUATION OF NUDITY IN ART — QUALITATIVE

1 = Ascetic   2 = Neutral   3 = Erotic

Ancient and Medieval Christian

	-X	X-XI	XII-XIII	XIV-XV	XVI-XVII	XVIII
			(Numbers)			
1	29	75	192	6	37	12
2	671	206	480	979	221	102
3	—	—	—	11	—	—
Total	700	281	672	996	258	114
			(Percentages)			
1	4.1	26.6	28.6	.6	14.3	10.5
2	95.9	73.4	71.4	98.3	85.7	89.5
3	—	—	—	1.1	—	—
Total	100.0	100.0	100.0	100.0	100.0	100.0

Russian

	-XII	XII-XIII	XIV-XV	XVI	XVII	XVIII	1801–1825	1826–1850	1851–1875	1876–1900	XX	Total
						(Numbers)						
1	2	2	27	21	89	10	5	—	—	32	67	255
2	—	—	3	—	16	167	334	307	197	437	1090	2551
3	—	—	—	—	—	33	62	92	73	189	574	1023
Total	2	2	30	21	105	210	401	399	270	658	1731	3829
						(Percentages)						
1	100.0	100.0	90.0	100.0	84.8	4.8	1.2	—	—	4.9	1.8	
2	—	—	10.0	—	15.2	79.5	83.4	76.9	73.0	66.4	63.0	
3	—	—	—	—	—	15.7	15.4	23.1	27.0	28.7	33.2	
Total	100.0	100.0	100.0	100.0	100.0	100.0	100.0	100.0	100.0	100.0	100.0	

1 = Ascetic   2 = Neutral   3 = Erotic

TABLE 17. FLUCTUATION OF NUDITY IN ART — QUALITATIVE — continued

Islamic

(Numbers)

	-X	X-XI	XII-XIII	XIV-XV	XVI	XVII	XVIII	Total
1	—	—	—	—	—	—	—	—
2	20	10	42	13	40	98	21	244
3	—	—	—	—	—	65	11	76
Total	20	10	42	13	40	163	32	320

(Percentages)

	-X	X-XI	XII-XIII	XIV-XV	XVI	XVII	XVIII
1	—	—	—	—	—	—	—
2	100.0	100.0	100.0	100.0	100.0	60.2	65.7
3	—	—	—	—	—	39.8	34.3
Total	100.0	100.0	100.0	100.0	100.0	100.0	100.0

Dutch

(Numbers)

	-1500	1500-1600	1600-1620	1620-1640	1640-1660	1660-1680	1680-1780	1780-1880	1880-1933	Total
1	22	4	4	—	—	—	—	—	—	30
2	36	66	82	24	—	10	10	18	41	287
3	—	—	70	182	46	12	—	2	8	320
Total	58	70	156	206	46	22	10	20	49	637

(Percentages)

	-1500	1500-1600	1600-1620	1620-1640	1640-1660	1660-1680	1680-1780	1780-1880	1880-1933
1	38.0	5.7	2.6	—	—	—	—	—	—
2	62.0	94.3	52.4	11.6	—	45.5	100.0	90.0	83.7
3	—	—	45.0	88.4	100.0	54.5	—	10.0	16.3
Total	100.0	100.0	100.0	100.0	100.0	100.0	100.0	100.0	100.0

English

(Numbers)

	XV	XVI	XVII	1700–1750	1750–1800	1800–1850	1850–1900	1900–1933	Total
1	6	7	2	—	—	—	1	3	19
2	6	7	32	41	37	19	24	58	224
3	—	—	4	17	14	6	8	7	56
Total	12	14	38	58	51	25	33	68	299

(Percentages)

	XV	XVI	XVII	1700–1750	1750–1800	1800–1850	1850–1900	1900–1933
1	50.0	50.0	5.3	—	—	—	3.1	4.4
2	50.0	50.0	84.2	70.7	72.5	76.0	72.7	85.3
3	—	—	10.5	29.3	27.5	24.0	24.2	10.3
Total	100.0	100.0	100.0	100.0	100.0	100.0	100.0	100.0

Spanish

(Numbers)

	XV	XVI	XVII	1700–1750	1750–1800	1800–1850	1850–1900	1900–1933	Total
1	7	5	—	—	—	—	—	—	12
2	1	16	11	—	—	—	—	—	55
3	—	—	—	3	3	9	3	12	
Total	8	21	11	3	3	9	3	12	67

(Percentages)

	XV	XVI	XVII	1700–1750	1750–1800	1800–1850	1850–1900	1900–1933
1	87.5	23.8	—	—	—	—	—	—
2	12.5	76.2	100.0	—	—	—	—	—
3	—	—	—	100.0	100.0	100.0	100.0	100.0
Total	100.0	100.0	100.0	100.0	100.0	100.0	100.0	100.0

TABLE 17. FLUCTUATION OF NUDITY IN ART — QUALITATIVE — *continued*

1 = Ascetic　　2 = Neutral　　3 = Erotic

Italian

(Numbers)

	1200–1300	1300–1350	1350–1400	1400–1450	1450–1500	1500–1550	1550–1600	1600–1650	1650–1700	1700–1750	1750–1800	1800–1850	1850–1900	1900–1933	Total
1	13	15	21	27	—	15	37	31	41	3	—	—	—	—	203
2	113	50	96	261	962	1140	784	952	801	819	612	505	239	205	7539
3			20	35	99	101	127	290	389	206	117	102	57	1543
Total	126	65	117	308	997	1254	922	1110	1132	1211	818	622	341	262	9285

(Percentages)

	1200–1300	1300–1350	1350–1400	1400–1450	1450–1500	1500–1550	1550–1600	1600–1650	1650–1700	1700–1750	1750–1800	1800–1850	1850–1900	1900–1933
1	10.3	23.0	18.0	8.8	—	1.2	4.0	2.8	3.6	.2	—	—	—	—
2	89.7	77.0	82.0	84.7	96.5	90.9	85.0	85.8	70.8	67.6	74.8	81.2	70.0	78.2
3	—	—	6.5	3.5	7.9	11.0	11.4	25.6	32.2	25.2	18.8	30.0	21.8
Total	100.0	100.0	100.0	100.0	100.0	100.0	100.0	100.0	100.0	100.0	100.0	100.0	100.0	100.0

French

(Numbers)

	XVI	1600–1650	1650–1700	1700–1750	1750–1800	1800–1850	1850–1880	1880–1900	1900–1933	Total
1	183	61	72	—	—	—	28	17	21	382
2	99	274	214	237	90	90	96	119	237	1456
3	9	12	21	276	324	138	63	152	222	1217
Total	291	347	307	513	414	228	187	288	480	3055

(Percentages)

	XVI	1600–1650	1650–1700	1700–1750	1750–1800	1800–1850	1850–1880	1880–1900	1900–1933
1	62.9	17.6	23.5	—	—	—	15.0	5.9	4.4
2	34.0	78.9	69.7	46.2	21.7	39.5	51.3	41.3	49.4
3	3.1	3.5	6.8	53.8	78.3	60.5	33.7	52.8	46.2
Total	100.0	100.0	100.0	100.0	100.0	100.0	100.0	100.0	100.0

Central Europe

(Numbers)

	XVI	1600–1650	1650–1700	1700–1750	1750–1800	1800–1830	1830–1860	1860–1880	1880–1900	1900–1933	Total
1	162	9	4	6	3	12	6	6	3	93	304
2	123	27	40	60	127	153	15	81	117	132	875
3	99	9	20	15	62	15	9	27	54	339	649
Total	384	45	64	81	192	180	30	114	174	564	1828

(Percentages)

	XVI	1600–1650	1650–1700	1700–1750	1750–1800	1800–1830	1830–1860	1860–1880	1880–1900	1900–1933	Total
1	42.2	20.0	6.3	7.4	1.6	6.7	20.0	5.3	1.8	16.5	5.8
2	32.0	60.0	62.5	74.0	66.1	85.0	50.0	71.0	67.2	23.4	56.1
3	25.8	20.0	31.2	18.6	32.3	8.3	30.0	23.7	31.0	60.1	38.1
Total	100.0	100.0	100.0	100.0	100.0	100.0	100.0	100.0	100.0	100.0	100.0

Europe as a Whole

(Numbers)

	X	X–XI	XII–XIII	XIV–XV	XVI	XVII	XVIII	XIX	XX
1	29	77	207	131	453	331	34	110	184
2	671	206	593	2394	2346	2593	2335	2763	1765
3	—	—	—	11	341	793	1336	965	1207

(Percentages)

	X	X–XI	XII–XIII	XIV–XV	XVI	XVII	XVIII	XIX	XX
1	4.1	27.0	34.5	5.2	14.4	9.0	0.9	2.9	5.8
2	95.9	73.0	65.5	94.4	74.8	69.7	62.7	72.0	56.1
3	—	—	—	0.4	10.8	21.3	36.4	25.1	38.1
Total	100.0	100.0	100.0	100.0	100.0	100.0	100.0	100.0	100.0

of nudity from its qualitative standpoint : whether it is ascetic or erotic (with "sex appeal") or neutral; putting into the classes "ascetic" and "erotic" only the quite conspicuous works of art in this respect, all the works with human bodies which clearly do not show either of these traits were put into the neutral class. Thus, side by side with the quantitative study of the quantity of nudity, I studied the quality of it. Such a double study can serve as a barometer of sensuality or spirituality, Visuality or Ideationality.

Let us see now what is the situation first of all with the qualitative character of nudity and the percentage of the specified classes of nudity, in the pictures and sculptures of centuries studied. From the qualitative standpoint, we divided all art works with the human body uncovered into three classes : Ascetic, Erotic, and Neutral.

Then each picture or sculpture with such nude body (or bodies) was taken as a unit,[14] and according to the prevalent type of its nudity either as a whole, or according to its central figure (or figures), was put into one of these classes. The total number of such works of each class for each specified century was computed, and the results are given in Table 17, in numbers as well as in percentages.

Table 18 shows the changes in the quality of the nudity for the whole of Europe (that is, the total of the seven countries, plus Christian art).

TABLE 18. FLUCTUATION OF ASCETIC, NEUTRAL, AND EROTIC IN ART

				Europe by Centuries					
	-X	X–XI	XII–XIII	XIV–XV	XVI	XVII	XVIII	XIX	XX
Ascetic									
Number	29	77	207	131	453	331	34	110	184
Per cent	4.1	27.0	34.5	5.2	14.4	9.0	0.9	2.9	5.8
Neutral									
Number	671	206	593	2394	2346	2593	2335	2763	1765
Per cent	95.9	73.0	65.5	94.4	74.8	69.7	62.7	72.0	56.1
Erotic (Sexual)									
Number	—	—	—	11	341	793	1336	965	1207
Per cent	—	—	—	0.4	10.8	21.3	36.4	25.1	38.1

[14] In the computation of the quantity of the nudity, the unit was not always just a picture or sculpture but, when the work contained more than one central nude body (not just a silhouette in the background), such figures were taken as a unit. As a result, one picture sometimes is counted as two or more units; and if one of the central figures is covered while the other is nude, one unit was given to each of these different classes (or one picture was counted more than once). This explains why the absolute numbers in the tables on Quantitative and Qualitative nudity differ widely from one another as well as from the numbers

Here the sample is quite different from the previous ones; and yet the results are essentially similar to the results given by the study of the religious and secular subjects, Ideational and Visual styles, sensual and spiritual character of the art works. As there, up to the fourteenth and fifteenth centuries we do not find any case of erotic nudity; the tenth and eleventh centuries show a rise of ascetic nudity in comparison with the centuries before the tenth, the same as has been shown by all the previous tables; the twelfth and the thirteenth centuries give a further rise of ascetic pictures that is quite consistent with the increase of the religious subjects and of spirituality in these centuries, also shown by previous tables. After the thirteenth century the erotic nudity in art appears for the first time in the fourteenth and fifteenth centuries and then rapidly grows in the subsequent centuries, while the ascetic nudity, with

given in other tables. In the study of the quality of the nudity, only those pictures were included which depict the human body naked. In the study of the quantity of nudity, all the pictures and sculptures where the human body is the central subject were included; all others, like landscapes or purely symbolic and ornamental works, were excluded.

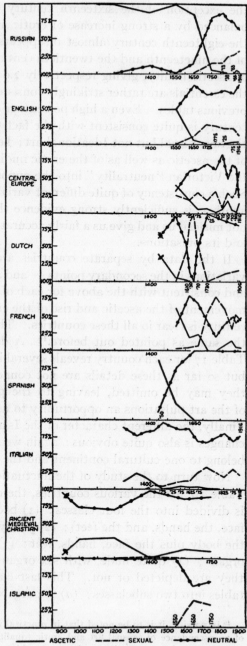

FIG. 11.   ASCETIC, SEXUAL, AND NEUTRAL IN ART BY COUNTRIES

the exception of the sixteenth century, where its increase is counter-balanced by a strong increase of erotic nudity, tends to decrease and in the eighteenth century almost disappears (0.9 per cent only). The end of the nineteenth and the twentieth century show a rise of the percentage of ascetic nudity, giving respectively 2.9 and 5.8 per cent. In brief, all the essentials are rather strikingly consistent with the results given by the previous tables. Even a high percentage of erotic nudity in the twentieth century is quite consistent with the fact that this century gives a rise of the non-Visual but not Ideational art; hence a simultaneous growth here of the ascetic as well as of the erotic nudity, the phenomenon of splitting the Victorian "neutrality" into the opposite factions pointed out earlier. Such a consistency of quite different variables, but inwardly related to one another, is sufficiently strong evidence that the data and the results do not mislead us and give us a fairly accurate reflection of the reality studied and its pulsations.

If the data by separate countries are taken, they show, as before, variations in the secondary points — and again these variations are similar and consistent with the above for each of the countries; but a downward movement of the ascetic and rise of the erotic nudity after the fourteenth century is clear in all these countries. Their mutual differences are about the same as pointed out before.[15] A detailed study of Figure 11 and Table 17 for each country reveals several interesting and important traits; but so far as these details are not connected with my main topic here, they may be omitted, leaving to the persons interested in the study of the art pulsations an opportunity to use the data for such an analysis. Finally, the different character of the Islamic nudity and the course of its changes is also quite obvious: again we see that the European countries belong to one cultural continent and the Islamic world to another.

Now turn to the study of the fluctuation of the *quantity of nudity*. In Table 19, for the various countries, the quantity of nudity in the figures is divided into the four classes: (1) body entirely covered (except the face, the hands, and the feet); (2) partly covered, leaving nude a part of the body plus the face, hands, feet; (3) uncovered entirely, except sex organs; (4) quite nude, with sex organs not draped or veiled, whether they are depicted or not. This last class is further subdivided in the tables into two subclasses: (*a*) sex organs depicted and (*b*) not depicted.

---

[15] In passing, it is to be noted that in practically all the European countries, the periods of an ascendance of sensual art and erotic (qualitatively) nudity are the periods of great power, expansion, prosperity, and sensuous blossoming. Later on, we shall discuss this matter more fully.

The results are given in the tables.   In the section of Table 19 for the whole of Europe, classes 1 and 2 are united into one class; classes 4 *a* and 4 *b* are grouped also into one class.

As to Figure 12, it summarizes two curves: one "body covered or partly covered," which is a unification into one class of the classes 1 and 2 of the tables; second, body uncovered (nude), which is a unification into one class of the classes 3 and 4 (*a* and *b*) into one class.   Now let us see the results.

Turning to the table for Europe, we find that, in spite of several secondary deviations, the changes in the quantity of nudity are in essential agreement with the previous curves.   The centuries before the tenth and then from the tenth to the fifteenth give an exceptionally high percentage of the "covered bodies" (from 90.2 to 94.6) and an exceptionally low percentage of the nude bodies (with the exception of the period before the tenth).   Here again the tenth and eleventh centuries appear as the most "holy" and the least nude.   After the fifteenth century the percentage of the "covered bodies" falls while that of the nude goes up.   So far the data agree with the outlined expectation.   The main disagreement consists in the fact that the trend toward nudity does not steadily increase and the trend away from the "covered" bodies does not steadily decrease, as we go from the fifteenth to the later centuries; the second deviation is that the twentieth century does not come out here as less nude or more "covered" than the nineteenth and the eighteenth centuries, as was the case in all the other variables studied.

Considering, however, that the quantity of nudity per se is not necessarily a sign of either sensuality or spirituality, we can hardly be surprised at these deviations.   I am rather surprised to find that the movement of the quantity of nudity shows a tangible association in the essentials with all the previous "barometers" of sensuality (Visuality) and Ideationality of art, art mentality, and the respective cultures.   It gives for the medieval centuries a notably higher percentage of the figures depicted which are covered, and a notably lower percentage of the figures which are nude, than for the centuries after the fourteenth and fifteenth.   This contrast is still more conspicuous if one takes the percentage of the nude bodies with sex organs depicted for the centuries before the fifteenth and after it.   So far the quantity of nudity is associated with Ideational and Visual art and their mentality.   But in view of the decisive role of the quality of nudity, the association cannot be expected to be close, and indeed it is not.   The quality of nudity studied above shows a much closer association with Ideationality and Visuality (sensuality) in art.

TABLE 19. FLUCTUATION OF NUDITY IN ART — QUANTITATIVE

1 = body covered   2 = partly covered   3 = uncovered, except sex organs   4 a = nude: sex organs depicted   4 b = nude: sex organs not depicted

Ancient and Medieval Christian

(Numbers)

	-X	X-XI	XII-XIII	XIV-XV	XVI-XVII	XVIII	Total
1	4285	2103	3817	3620	1367	421	15,613
2	208	218	392	702	169	41	1,730
3	52	6	89	73	21	17	258
4 a	102	—	—	27	—	—	132
4 b	338	54	191	194	68	56	901
Total	4985	2384	4489	4616	1625	535	18,634

(Percentages)

	-X	X-XI	XII-XIII	XIV-XV	XVI-XVII	XVIII
1	86.0	88.1	85.0	78.4	84.1	78.6
2	4.2	9.2	8.7	15.2	10.4	7.7
3	1.0	.3	2.0	1.6	1.3	3.2
4 a	2.0	.1		.6		
4 b	6.8	2.3	4.3	4.2	4.2	10.5
Total	100.0	100.0	100.0	100.0	100.0	100.0

English

(Numbers)

	XV	XVI	XVII	1700–1750	1750–1800	1800–1850	1850–1900	1900–1933	Total
1	396	82	57	96	120	158	192	121	1222
2	5	8	21	33	41	7	13	27	155
3	7	3	8	10	4	6	5	18	61
4 a	—	—	7	15	6	12	15	23	78
4 b	—	3	2	—	—	—	—	—	5
Total	408	96	95	154	171	183	225	189	1521

(Percentages)

	XV	XVI	XVII	1700–1750	1750–1800	1800–1850	1850–1900	1900–1933
1	97.1	85.5	60.0	62.4	70.2	86.3	85.3	64.0
2	1.2	8.3	22.1	21.4	24.0	3.8	5.8	14.3
3	1.7	3.1	8.4	6.5	2.3	3.3	2.2	9.5
4 a			7.4	9.7	3.5	6.6	6.7	12.2
4 b		3.1	2.1					
Total	100.0	100.0	100.0	100.0	100.0	100.0	100.0	100.0

Islamic

(Numbers)

	-X	X-XI	XII-XIII	XIV-XV	XVI	XVII	XVIII	Total
1	55	585	467	560	874	1203	934	4678
2	10	10	30	13	40	140	32	275
3	10	—	—	—	—	12	—	22
4 b	—	—	12	—	—	11	—	23
Total	75	595	509	573	914	1366	966	4998

(Percentages)

	-X	X-XI	XII-XIII	XIV-XV	XVI	XVII	XVIII
1	73.4	98.3	91.7	97.7	95.6	88.1	96.7
2	13.3	1.7	5.9	2.3	4.4	10.2	3.3
3	13.3	—	—	—	—	.9	—
4 b	—	—	2.4	—	—	.8	—
Total	100.0	100.0	100.0	100.0	100.0	100.0	100.0

Russian

(Numbers)

	-XII	XII-XIII	XIV-XV	XVI	XVII	XVIII	1801-1825	1826-1850	1851-1875	1876-1900	XX	Total
1	20	78	210	308	382	527	521	665	547	2508	5279	11,045
2	2	—	10	—	25	3	117	182	83	428	788	1,638
3	—	2	10	11	40	49	106	76	85	113	554	1,046
4 a	—	—	3	4	—	116	172	115	102	117	379	1,008
4 b	—	2	7	6	40	10	6	26	—	—	—	97
Total	22	82	240	329	487	705	922	1064	817	3166	7000	14,834

(Percentages)

	-XII	XII-XIII	XIV-XV	XVI	XVII	XVIII	1801-1825	1826-1850	1851-1875	1876-1900	XX
1	90.9	95.2	87.4	93.7	78.5	74.8	56.4	62.6	67.0	79.2	75.4
2	9.1	—	4.2	—	5.1	.4	12.7	17.1	10.1	13.5	11.3
3	—	2.4	4.2	3.3	8.2	6.9	11.5	7.1	10.4	3.6	7.9
4 a	—	—	1.3	1.2	—	16.5	18.7	10.8	12.5	3.7	5.4
4 b	—	2.4	2.9	1.8	8.2	1.4	.7	2.4	—	—	—
Total	100.0	100.0	100.0	100.0	100.0	100.0	100.0	100.0	100.0	100.0	100.0

TABLE 19. FLUCTUATION OF NUDITY IN ART — QUANTITATIVE — continued

1 = body covered   2 = partly covered   3 = uncovered, except sex organs   4 a = nude: sex organs depicted   4 b = nude: sex organs not depicted

Italian

(Numbers)

	1200–1300	1300–1350	1350–1400	1400–1450	1450–1500	1500–1550	1550–1600	1600–1650	1650–1700	1700–1750	1750–1800	1800–1850	1850–1900	1900–1933	Total
1	763	642	627	1201	3110	2872	3991	3219	3463	2912	2124	871	707	416	26,918
2	114	48	54	93	191	147	113	287	417	627	431	319	198	102	3,141
3	—	7	30	99	496	644	574	512	426	371	280	216	131	97	3,883
4 a	—	—	12	90	292	463	235	311	289	213	107	87	62	63	2,227
4 b	12	7	21	26	18	—	—	—	—	—	—	—	—	—	84
Total	889	707	744	1509	4107	4126	4913	4329	4595	4123	2942	1493	1098	678	36,253

(Percentages)

	1200–1300	1300–1350	1350–1400	1400–1450	1450–1500	1500–1550	1550–1600	1600–1650	1650–1700	1700–1750	1750–1800	1800–1850	1850–1900	1900–1933
1	85.8	90.8	84.3	79.5	75.7	69.6	81.2	74.4	75.3	70.6	72.3	58.3	64.5	61.4
2	12.8	6.8	7.3	6.2	4.7	3.6	2.3	6.6	9.1	15.2	14.6	21.4	18.0	15.0
3	—	1.0	4.0	6.6	12.1	15.6	11.7	11.8	9.3	9.0	9.5	14.5	11.9	14.3
4 a	—	.4	1.6	6.0	7.1	11.2	4.8	7.2	6.3	5.2	3.6	5.8	5.6	9.3
4 b	1.4	1.0	2.8	1.7	.4	—	—	—	—	—	—	—	—	—
Total	100.0	100.0	100.0	100.0	100.0	100.0	100.0	100.0	100.0	100.0	100.0	100.0	100.0	100.0

Spanish

(Numbers)

	XV	XVI	XVII	1700–1750	1750–1800	1800–1850	1850–1900	1900–1933	Total
1	284	354	491	285	291	108	108	159	2080
2	8	3	7	—	—	—	—	3	21
3	—	18	2	—	—	3	3	3	26
4 a	—	—	1	—	3	3	—	—	10
4 b	—	—	—	—	—	3	—	6	9
Total	292	375	501	285	294	117	111	171	2146

(Percentages)

	XV	XVI	XVII	1700–1750	1750–1800	1800–1850	1850–1900	1900–1933
1	97.3	94.4	98.0	100.0	99.0	92.2	97.3	92.9
2	2.7	.8	1.4	—	—	—	—	1.8
3	—	4.8	.4	—	—	2.6	2.7	1.8
4 a	—	—	.2	—	1.0	2.6	—	—
4 b	—	—	—	—	—	2.6	—	3.5
Total	100.0	100.0	100.0	100.0	100.0	100.0	100.0	100.0

French

(Numbers)

	XVI	1600–1650	1650–1700	1700–1750	1750–1800	1800–1850	1850–1880	1880–1900	1900–1933	Total
1	1236	810	783	2010	1953	2358	1010	772	801	11,733
2	111	118	127	51	99	48	104	127	217	1,002
3	120	137	108	168	156	—	20	60	63	832
4 a	24	92	72	225	186	45	81	86	149	960
4 b	36	—	—	69	63	126	45	15	51	405
Total	1527	1157	1090	2523	2457	2577	1260	1060	1281	14,932

(Percentages)

	XVI	1600–1650	1650–1700	1700–1750	1750–1800	1800–1850	1850–1880	1880–1900	1900–1933
1	80.9	70.0	71.8	79.8	79.5	91.5	80.1	72.8	62.6
2	7.3	10.2	11.7	2.0	4.0	1.9	8.3	12.0	16.9
3	7.9	11.9	9.9	6.7	6.3	—	1.6	5.7	4.9
4 a	1.6	7.9	6.6	8.9	7.6	1.7	6.4	8.1	11.6
4 b	2.3	—	—	2.6	2.6	4.9	3.6	1.4	4.0
Total	100.0	100.0	100.0	100.0	100.0	100.0	100.0	100.0	100.0

Dutch

(Numbers)

	–1500	1500–1600	1600–1620	1620–1640	1640–1660	1660–1680	1680–1780	1780–1880	1880–1933	Total
1	1234	936	436	734	1270	762	460	452	346	6630
2	8	36	82	36	—	—	10	16	21	209
3	50	8	42	16	18	18	—	—	—	152
4 a	—	—	—	60	38	4	—	4	28	134
4 b	—	—	4	18	10	—	—	—	—	32
Total	1292	980	564	864	1336	784	470	472	395	7157

(Percentages)

	–1500	1500–1600	1600–1620	1620–1640	1640–1660	1660–1680	1680–1780	1780–1880	1880–1933
1	95.5	95.5	77.4	84.9	95.2	97.2	97.9	95.8	87.6
2	.6	3.7	14.5	4.2	—	—	2.1	3.4	5.3
3	3.9	.8	7.4	1.9	1.3	2.3	—	—	—
4 a	—	—	—	6.9	2.8	.5	—	.8	7.1
4 b	—	—	.7	2.1	.7	—	—	—	—
Total	100.0	100.0	100.0	100.0	100.0	100.0	100.0	100.0	100.0

TABLE 19. FLUCTUATION OF NUDITY IN ART — QUANTITATIVE — *continued*

1 = body covered   2 = partly covered   3 = uncovered, except sex organs   4 a = nude: sex organs depicted   4 b = nude: sex organs not depicted

Central Europe

(Numbers)

	XVI	1600–1650	1650–1700	1700–1750	1750–1800	1800–1830	1830–1860	1860–1880	1880–1900	1900–1933	Total
1	1221	105	180	221	367	717	639	867	413	1887	6617
2	147	33	42	63	78	132	42	81	33	267	918
3	210	9	12	69	92	84	21	48	54	156	755
4 a	84	3	7	9	21	39	9	39	99	384	694
4 b	42	—	3	3	—	—	—	27	21	24	120
Total	1704	150	244	365	558	972	711	1062	620	2718	9104

(Percentages)

	XVI	1600–1650	1650–1700	1700–1750	1750–1800	1800–1830	1830–1860	1860–1880	1880–1900	1900–1933
1	71.7	70.0	73.8	60.5	65.8	73.8	90.0	81.7	66.6	69.3
2	8.6	22.0	17.2	17.3	13.9	13.6	5.9	7.6	5.3	9.8
3	12.3	6.0	4.9	18.9	16.5	8.6	2.9	4.5	8.7	5.8
4 a	4.9	2.0	2.9	2.5	3.8	4.0	1.2	3.7	16.0	14.2
4 b	2.5	—	1.2	.8	—	—	—	2.5	3.4	.9
Total	100.0	100.0	100.0	100.0	100.0	100.0	100.0	100.0	100.0	100.0

Europe as a Whole

1 = covered and partly covered   2 = uncovered except sex organs   3 = nude

(Numbers)

	-X	X–XI	XII–XIII	XIV–XV	XVI	XVII	XVIII	XIX	XX
1	4493	2343	5164	7848	12,334	15,854	13,264	15,545	10,434
2	52	6	91	177	1,599	1,369	1,216	1,028	891
3	440	57	205	274	931	927	1,102	1,188	1,107
Total	4985	2406	5460	8299	14,864	18,150	15,582	17,761	12,432

(Percentages)

	-X	X–XI	XII–XIII	XIV–XV	XVI	XVII	XVIII	XIX	XX
1	90.2	97.4	94.6	94.6	83.2	87.4	85.2	87.5	83.9
2	1.0	0.3	1.7	2.1	10.7	7.5	7.7	5.8	7.2
3	8.8	2.3	3.7	3.3	6.1	5.1	7.1	6.7	8.9
Total	100.0	100.0	100.0	100.0	100.0	100.0	100.0	100.0	100.0

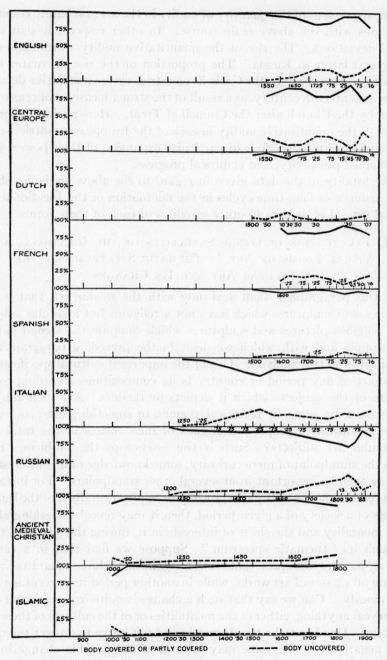

FIG. 12.   FLUCTUATION OF NUDITY IN ART BY COUNTRIES

The movement of the quantity of nudity in the art of separate countries coincides with the above main course. In other respects it shows the usual deviations. The rise of the quantitative nudity starts earliest in Italy and latest in Russia. The proportion of the rise fluctuates from country to country. In the Catholic countries we see its relative decrease in the seventeenth century, as a result of the strong measures of censorship taken by the Church after the Council of Trent. Here again the periods of rise of the quantitative nudity in each of the European countries seems to coincide with the periods of particular expansion of their power, their commercial prosperity, and empirical progress.

The totality of the data given in regard to the above variables shows the existence of long-time cycles in the fluctuation of the Ideational and Visual art. Let us turn to other satellites of each of these forms.

VI. Fluctuation of Other Satellites of the Ideational and Visual Forms of Art. "Thematic Spectrum" of the Secular Art and Its Changes

In this paragraph I shall deal only with the *secular* art, that is, the pictures and sculptures which have not a religious but a secular subject. The religious pictures and sculptures which compose the second part of our sample and with which we dealt in the preceding paragraphs are excluded from this analysis. One of the important cultural specifications of an art of any period or country is its composition, according to the nature of the subjects which it depicts or renders. Are such subjects landscapes, or *genre,* or historical themes, or something else; and what is the quantitative proportion of each of such classes in the total sum of secular art subjects? Such is the essence of the problem. Even from the standpoint of mere curiosity, some knowledge of it is interesting. It may even be important from several other standpoints. For instance, if art reflects the mentality of its society or, more accurately, of the leading classes of a society of a given period, then it may reveal something about that mentality and the shifts of interests in it, during the course of time, through its "thematic spectrum." Suppose we find that in a certain period *paysage* occupies quite an insignificant place (quantitatively) among all classes of art works, while in another period its percentage rises enormously. Can we say that such a change is quite irrelevant and does not reveal anything, either of the mentalities or of the cultures of these two periods? One has to be too dogmatic and too brave to answer the question negatively. The same may be said of the notable change in the percentages of any main class of subjects.

By the specialists in the theory and history of art, the problem has been raised, though, so far as I know, it has hardly had any real detailed treatment based upon sufficiently large samples for each period. The subsequent pages try to fill, to some extent, this hiatus. In the process of the subsequent analysis, its importance to my theory of the Ideational and Visual art as well as for several other problems will become clear.

All the secular pictures and subjects are divided in this study into seven main classes, according to their *Visual* nature, namely: (1) Subjects of antiquity (mainly historical and pseudo-historical events), (2) Portrait, (3) *Genre*, (4) *Paysage*, (5) Fantastic subjects, (6) Animals, (7) *Nature morte*. Table 20 and Figures 13, 14, 15, and 16 give the respective data in their absolute number and in the percentages which each class composes in the total of the seven classes, which is taken as 100 per cent. It is to be noted that the total number of the secular pictures for each country here is not exactly the same as in Table 12 of the total number of religious and secular pictures. The slight discrepancy is due to several circumstances. First, some of the secular pictures which are simultaneously, say, *paysage* and *animal* pictures are counted twice and are placed in both categories. The same concerns all pictures that are not exclusively either portrait or *genre* or any of the seven categories mentioned but are " intermediary " and belong to two or more of these classes. Second, the copies of some of the pictures or sculptures could not be obtained for a detailed investigation: from their general description in the sources it was possible to say whether they were secular or religious and therefore they could be counted as a unit in these tables dealing with the number of religious and secular pictures. But what kind of secular picture such a picture was exactly, it was impossible to say definitely from the description, without an investigation of the picture or its copy. All such secular pictures were therefore excluded from the present sample. These two circumstances explain the slight discrepancy between the number of the secular pictures in existence and in the above tables mentioned. Let us now point out a few outstanding results revealed or confirmed by the data. To begin with, we start with *paysage*.

I. PAYSAGE AND THE FLUCTUATION OF ITS PROPORTIONS IN THE TOTAL OF SECULAR ART

Several investigators have already pointed out the fact that *paysage* as *paysage*, depicted for its own sake and not just as a background for human figures or for other subjects, appeared in the history of art

TABLE 20. FLUCTUATION OF THE CONTENT OF SECULAR ART

0 = Subjects of antiquity   1 = Portrait   2 = Genre   3 = Paysage   4 = Fantastic subjects   5 = Animals   6 = Nature morte

Ancient and Medieval Christian

(Numbers)

	-X	X-XI	XII-XIII	XIV-XV	XVI-XVII	XVIII	Total
0	121	11	40	101	97	—	370
1	73	41	23	406	32	—	575
2	271	—	—	—	—	—	271
3	—	4	2	—	—	—	6
4	26	36	54	70	78	—	264
5	376	12	23	26	40	—	477
6	46	—	—	—	—	—	46
Total	913	104	142	603	247	—	2009

(Percentages)

	-X	X-XI	XII-XIII	XIV-XV	XVI-XVII	XVIII
0	13.2	10.6	28.4	16.7	39.2	—
1	8.0	39.4	16.2	67.4	13.0	—
2	29.7	—	—	—	—	—
3	—	3.8	1.4	—	—	—
4	2.9	34.6	38.0	11.6	31.5	—
5	41.2	11.6	16.0	4.3	16.3	—
6	5.0	—	—	—	—	—
Total	100.0	100.0	100.0	100.0	100.0	—

Islamic

(Numbers)

	-X	X-XI	XII-XIII	XIV-XV	XVI	XVII	XVIII	Total
0	9	38	176	50	140	630	105	1148
1	30	185	150	230	500	350	513	1958
2	—	—	—	—	—	—	—	—
3	6	27	32	21	20	56	84	246
4	15	325	132	229	35	112	32	880
5	—	—	—	—	85	24	212	321
6	—	—	—	—	—	—	—	—
Total	60	575	490	530	780	1172	946	4553

(Percentages)

	-X	X-XI	XII-XIII	XIV-XV	XVI	XVII	XVIII
0	15.0	6.6	35.9	9.4	17.9	53.8	11.1
1	50.0	32.2	30.6	43.4	64.1	29.8	54.2
2	—	—	—	—	—	—	—
3	10.0	4.7	6.5	4.0	2.6	4.8	8.9
4	25.0	56.5	27.0	43.2	4.5	9.6	3.4
5	—	—	—	—	10.9	2.0	22.4
6	—	—	—	—	—	—	—
Total	100.0	100.0	100.0	100.0	100.0	100.0	100.0

Russian

(Numbers)

	-XII	XII-XIII	XIV-XV	XVI	XVII	XVIII	1801-1825	1821-1850	1851-1875	1876-1900	XX	Total
0	—	—	—	—	—	48	53	30	21	27	48	227
1	—	—	—	—	—	292	220	129	78	354	755	1832
2	—	—	—	—	—	60	92	187	183	524	2376	3422
3	—	—	—	—	4	19	57	66	64	608	1215	2029
4	—	—	—	—	—	18	8	9	15	153	536	751
5	—	—	—	—	12	5	17	11	13	57	62	165
6	—	—	—	—	—	6	—	—	7	25	167	205
Total	—	—	—	—	16	448	447	432	381	1748	5159	8631

(Percentages)

	-XII	XII-XIII	XIV-XV	XVI	XVII	XVIII	1801-1825	1821-1850	1851-1875	1876-1900	XX	Total
0	—	—	—	—	—	10.8	11.9	6.9	5.5	1.5	.9	
1	—	—	—	—	25.0	65.1	49.2	29.9	20.5	20.2	14.6	
2	—	—	—	—	—	13.4	20.6	43.3	48.1	30.0	46.3	
3	—	—	—	—	—	4.3	12.7	15.3	16.8	34.8	23.4	
4	—	—	—	—	—	4.0	1.8	2.1	3.9	8.8	10.4	
5	—	—	—	—	75.0	1.1	3.8	2.5	3.4	3.3	1.2	
6	—	—	—	—	—	1.3	—	—	1.8	1.4	3.2	
Total	—	—	—	—	100.0	100.0	100.0	100.0	100.0	100.0	100.0	

Italian

(Numbers)

	1200-1300	1300-1350	1350-1400	1400-1450	1450-1500	1500-1550	1550-1600	1600-1650	1650-1700	1700-1750	1750-1800	1800-1850	1850-1900	1900-1933	Total
0	—	10	59	227	445	560	617	893	688	552	273	42	7		4,375
1	3	43	103	317	368	593	524	826	1015	641	377	362	250		5,429
2	—	35	45	79	98	243	373	573	826	613	706	660	240		4,493
3	—	—	2	7	16	34	56	105	215	260	176	265	148		1,284
4	—	—	—	11	7	3	8	—	12	3	7	14	12		77
5	—	16	15	9	12	8	18	5	17	3	5	12	5		125
6	—	—	1	3	5	4	12	49	148	71	12	21	59		385
Total	3	11	104	225	653	951	1445	1608	2451	2921	2143	1556	1376	721	16,168

(Percentages)

	1200-1300	1300-1350	1350-1400	1400-1450	1450-1500	1500-1550	1550-1600	1600-1650	1650-1700	1700-1750	1750-1800	1800-1850	1850-1900	1900-1933	Total
0	—	9.6	26.2	34.8	46.7	38.7	38.3	36.4	23.6	25.8	17.6	3.1	1.0		
1	100.0	41.3	45.8	48.5	38.8	40.9	32.6	33.7	34.6	29.9	24.2	26.3	34.6		
2	—	33.7	20.0	12.0	10.3	16.9	23.3	23.4	28.3	28.7	45.3	48.0	33.2		
3	—	—	.9	1.1	1.7	2.4	3.5	4.3	7.4	12.1	11.3	19.2	20.6		
4	—	—	—	1.7	.7	.2	.5	—	.4	.1	.5	1.0	1.7		
5	—	15.4	6.7	1.4	1.3	.6	1.1	.2	.6	.1	.3	.9	.7		
6	—	—	.4	.5	.5	.3	.7	2.0	5.1	3.3	.8	1.5	8.2		
Total	100.0	100.0	100.0	100.0	100.0	100.0	100.0	100.0	100.0	100.0	100.0	100.0	100.0	100.0	

TABLE 20. FLUCTUATION OF THE CONTENT OF SECULAR ART — continued

0 = Subjects of antiquity   1 = Portrait   2 = Genre   3 = Paysage   4 = Fantastic subjects   5 = Animals   6 = Nature morte

Spanish

(Numbers)

	XV	XVI	XVII	1700-1750	1750-1800	1800-1850	1850-1900	1900-1933	Total
0	—	—	9	9	15	12	6	—	51
1	10	40	107	90	141	30	21	69	508
2	—	10	45	120	84	71	60	69	459
3	—	4	13	13	28	33	31	44	166
4	—	8	11	3	—	—	—	—	22
5	—	—	15	8	4	2	—	—	29
6	—	—	—	—	—	—	10	24	34
Total	10	62	200	243	272	148	128	206	1269

(Percentages)

	XV	XVI	XVII	1700-1750	1750-1800	1800-1850	1850-1900	1900-1933	
0	—	—	4.5	3.7	5.5	8.1	4.7	—	
1	100.0	64.5	53.5	37.0	51.9	20.3	16.4	33.5	
2	—	16.1	22.5	49.4	30.8	48.0	46.9	33.5	
3	—	6.5	6.5	5.4	10.3	22.3	24.2	21.3	
4	—	12.9	5.5	1.2	—	—	—	—	
5	—	—	7.5	3.3	1.5	1.3	—	—	
6	—	—	—	—	—	—	7.8	11.7	
Total	100.0	100.0	100.0	100.0	100.0	100.0	100.0	100.0	

French

(Numbers)

	XVI	1600-1650	1650-1700	1700-1750	1750-1800	1800-1850	1850-1880	1880-1900	1900-1933	Total
0	12	30	63	540	294	138	10	—	—	1087
1	96	60	93	384	434	414	138	124	146	1889
2	129	96	156	717	808	668	759	443	497	4273
3	—	9	18	144	177	351	351	240	282	1572
4	39	33	30	135	117	57	71	24	21	527
5	24	18	21	3	15	75	12	12	6	186
6	—	—	—	—	—	—	69	90	114	273
Total	300	246	381	1923	1845	1703	1410	933	1066	9807

(Percentages)

	XVI	1600-1650	1650-1700	1700-1750	1750-1800	1800-1850	1850-1880	1880-1900	1900-1933	
0	4.0	12.2	16.5	28.1	16.0	8.1	.7	—	—	
1	32.0	24.4	24.4	20.0	23.5	24.3	9.8	13.3	13.7	
2	43.0	39.0	41.0	37.3	43.8	39.2	53.9	47.4	46.6	
3	—	3.7	4.7	7.5	9.6	20.6	24.8	25.7	26.4	
4	13.0	13.4	7.9	7.0	6.3	3.4	5.0	2.6	2.0	
5	8.0	7.3	5.5	.1	.8	4.4	.9	1.3	.6	
6	—	—	—	—	—	—	4.9	9.7	10.7	
Total	100.0	100.0	100.0	100.0	100.0	100.0	100.0	100.0	100.0	

Dutch

(Numbers)

	−1500	1500–1600	1600–1620	1620–1640	1640–1660	1660–1680	1680–1780	1780–1880	1880–1933	Total
0	16	14	44	70	46	—	—	—	—	190
1	34	78	184	200	204	124	26	40	118	1008
2	—	72	110	212	324	402	250	136	171	1677
3	6	116	122	68	48	28	10	90	92	580
4	30	34	8	44	32	—	—	—	13	161
5	—	12	14	12	6	—	—	10	8	62
6	—	—	—	32	42	90	6	20	56	246
Total	86	326	482	638	702	644	292	296	458	3924

(Percentages)

	−1500	1500–1600	1600–1620	1620–1640	1640–1660	1660–1680	1680–1780	1780–1880	1880–1933
0	18.6	4.3	9.1	11.0	6.5	—	—	—	—
1	39.6	23.9	38.2	31.3	29.0	19.3	8.9	13.5	25.8
2	—	22.1	22.8	33.2	46.2	62.3	85.6	46.0	37.4
3	7.0	35.6	25.3	10.7	6.8	4.4	3.4	30.4	20.1
4	34.8	10.4	1.7	6.9	4.6	—	—	—	2.8
5	—	3.7	2.9	1.9	.9	—	—	3.4	1.7
6	—	—	—	5.0	6.0	14.0	2.1	6.7	12.2
Total	100.0	100.0	100.0	100.0	100.0	100.0	100.0	100.0	100.0

Central Europe

(Numbers)

	XVI	1600–1650	1650–1700	1700–1750	1750–1800	1800–1830	1830–1860	1860–1880	1880–1900	1900–1933	Total
0	78	15	21	45	67	93	24	69	33	51	496
1	264	39	56	66	66	180	120	222	156	597	1766
2	126	30	84	90	138	252	429	859	486	1548	4042
3	45	6	10	15	27	135	102	74	117	981	1512
4	72	6	8	39	17	57	45	39	15	183	481
5	15	3	4	3	18	18	15	21	39	57	193
6	6	—	2	6	9	12	9	33	36	122	235
Total	606	99	185	264	342	747	744	1317	882	3539	8725

(Percentages)

	XVI	1600–1650	1650–1700	1700–1750	1750–1800	1800–1830	1830–1860	1860–1880	1880–1900	1900–1933
0	12.9	15.1	11.3	17.0	19.6	12.4	3.2	5.2	3.3	1.4
1	43.5	39.4	30.3	25.0	19.3	24.2	16.1	16.9	17.7	16.9
2	20.8	30.3	45.4	34.1	40.3	33.7	57.7	65.2	55.4	43.8
3	7.4	6.1	5.4	5.7	7.9	18.1	13.7	5.6	13.4	27.7
4	11.9	6.1	4.3	14.8	5.0	7.6	6.1	3.0	1.7	5.2
5	2.5	3.0	2.2	1.1	5.3	2.4	2.0	1.6	4.4	1.6
6	1.0	—	1.1	2.3	2.6	1.6	1.2	2.5	4.1	3.4
Total	100.0	100.0	100.0	100.0	100.0	100.0	100.0	100.0	100.0	100.0

TABLE 20. FLUCTUATION OF THE CONTENT OF SECULAR ART — continued

0 = Subjects of antiquity   1 = Portrait   2 = Genre   3 = Paysage   4 = Fantastic subjects   5 = Animals   6 = Nature morte

English

(Numbers)

	XV	XVI	XVII	1700–1750	1750–1800	1800–1850	1850–1900	1900–1933	Total
0	—	—	—	20	23	11	21	—	75
1	8	21	28	37	51	38	31	27	241
2	—	—	—	31	35	26	13	22	127
3	—	—	—	40	47	25	25	36	173
4	—	—	—	11	12	35	85	12	155
5	7	10	23	8	10	6	5	2	66
6	—	—	—	—	—	—	—	9	14
Total	15	31	51	147	178	141	180	108	851

(Percentages)

	XV	XVI	XVII	1700–1750	1750–1800	1800–1850	1850–1900	1900–1933
0	—	—	—	13.6	12.9	7.8	11.7	—
1	53.3	67.8	55.0	25.2	28.7	27.0	17.2	25.0
2	—	—	—	21.1	19.7	18.4	7.2	20.4
3	—	—	—	27.2	26.4	17.8	13.9	33.3
4	—	—	—	7.5	6.7	24.8	47.2	11.1
5	46.7	32.2	45.0	5.4	5.6	4.2	2.8	1.9
6	—	—	—	—	—	—	—	8.3
Total	100.0	100.0	100.0	100.0	100.0	100.0	100.0	100.0

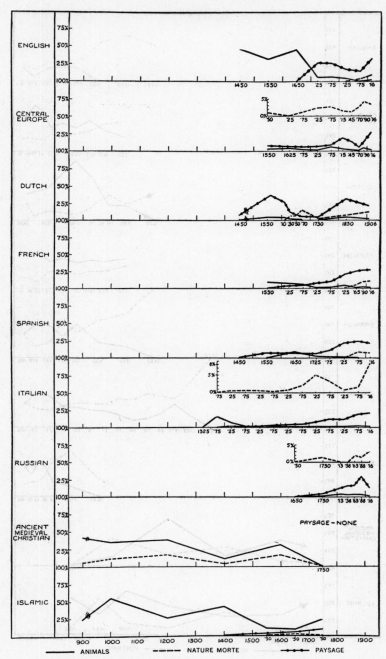

FIG. 13. ANIMALS, NATURE MORTE, PAYSAGE IN ART BY COUNTRIES

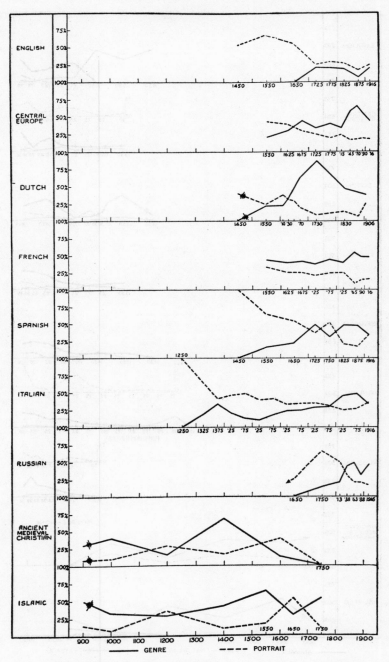

FIG. 14.   GENRE AND PORTRAIT IN ART BY COUNTRIES

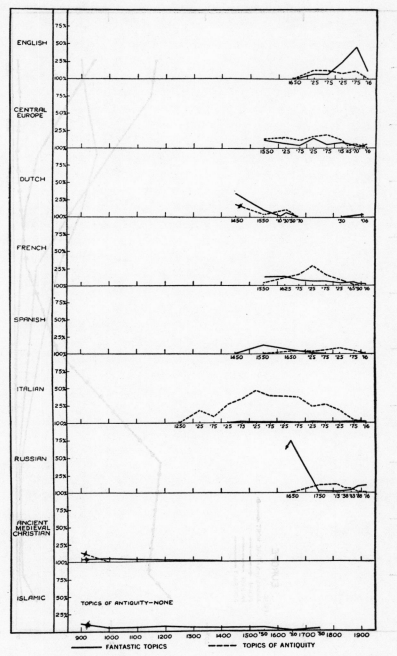

FIG. 15.   THE FANTASTIC AND ANTIQUE IN ART BY COUNTRIES

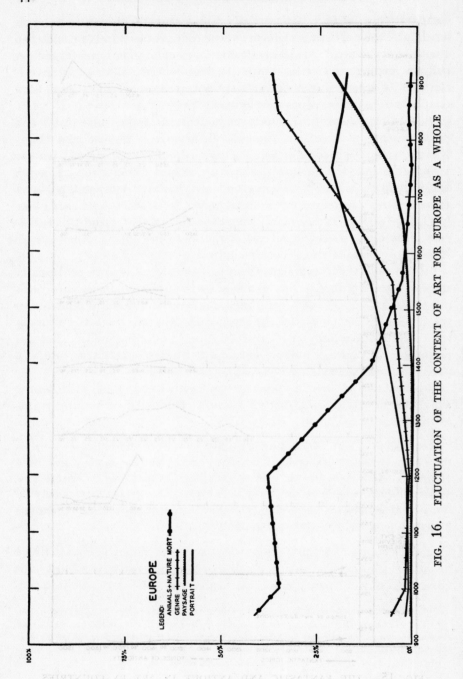

FIG. 16. FLUCTUATION OF THE CONTENT OF ART FOR EUROPE AS A WHOLE

comparatively lately. "Historically the sentiment of nature emerges much later than artistic sentiment, whose rudimentary forms we find even among the cavemen." It was little developed among the Oriental ancient cultures, among the Greeks, and in the Middle Ages, so far as art is concerned. It emerges only in a relatively urbanized society and at a relatively late period of its development.[16]

In this statement A. Dauzat reproduces the more substantial and deeper theory of Victor de Laprade, developed in his essential three-volume work, *Le sentiment de la nature*. De Laprade starts with the assumption that the mentality of culture is best reflected in art, much better than in science. "Poetry and arts have that advantage (over science, historical, economic, political and other sources) that they alone furnish us with the inner man throughout the ages." From this standpoint they give us a direct picture of the soul while all the other sources supply only indirect and unreliable data.[17]

Viewed from this standpoint, the art of the early cultures, or the early stages of the cultures — for instance, of the Oriental cultures — deals mainly with God ; the art of the later stages or later cultures, like that of the Greeks, deals mainly with the heroic man ; the late stages of culture or late cultures deal mainly with nature considered purely visually. For this reason *paysage* appears and grows mainly at much later stages, and as a particular case among ourselves, among the "moderns." [18]

Now man is a slave to the material world more than ever before. Therefore he depicts this material world, especially its nature, in his art abundantly.

Domination of man over nature is assured by science and industry ; so runs the common belief. In fact, at no other epoch has the human soul been oppressed so strongly by the external world as in our times. Nature now dominates man more unconditionally than ever. The tyranny of the material things over the soul — innerly and externally — of matter over spirit, increases with each progress of science and industry.[19]

From this standpoint the discovery of nature in the eighteenth century is not incidental. The nature discovered is purely external nature, as it appears to our organs of sense. As such, now, "it colors our literature

[16] A. Dauzat, *Le sentiment de la nature et son expression artistique* (Paris, 1914), pp. 138 ff.

[17] V. de Laprade, *Le sentiment de la nature chez les modernes* (Paris, 1868), pp. 6 ff. Also, *Le sentiment de la nature avant le christianisme* (Paris, 1866), Introduction. Also his *Prolégomènes* (Paris, 1882).

[18] Laprade, *Le sentiment de la nature avant le christianisme*, pp. 1–104.

[19] *Ibid.*, p. 82.

and plastic arts, destroys our moral sentiment, and weakens society. In the right characterization of a sect, it is but a rehabilitation of flesh." [20]

In his three volumes, Laprade attempts to demonstrate this proposition. I have stopped at his work because, as the reader can see from the few quotations, he gives some inklings of the deeper connection of this seemingly technical question — how large is the percentage of *paysage* in art — with much deeper configurations of the mentality and of the nature of a culture.

More technically and factually, the question has been considered by several prominent specialists of the *L'École d'Art* in the collective work : *Histoire du paysage en France*. There H. Marcel, H. Bouchot, L. Gillet, and C. Diehl state that *paysage* is a modern invention. In the Oriental and antique paintings it played a purely decorative role; in the Middle Ages this role was still less because even the mere elements of nature had there an "ideogrammatic (Ideational) meaning only." Before the fifteenth century there was practically no *paysage*. *Paysage* begins with an appearance of the sky in the pictures — not just a blue or gold background over the heads of the figures, as in the medieval pictures — but of the sky with clouds and other of its characteristics.

It was a fundamental fact in the history of painting . . . an invention comparable to that of a language. . . . In the Middle Ages there was no *paysage*. . . . For the Classic and the Gothic art there was only one hero-man. . . . [Everything else was neglected.] A single tree depicted symbolized country; two trees, the forest; a rock, a whole mountain; a tower, a city. Such a rendering is not so much a comprehensible language as a mere alphabet or even a cipher.[21]

With the appearance of the sky in the paintings, everything changes. We are ushered into the period of the existence of *paysage* in art. This happened in the fifteenth century. "A new and modern mentality (*l'esprit*) was born on a day when a mountain was taken, not for a symbol of flesh or of a woman, but simply for what it is — a mountain." [22]

In the fifteenth century *paysage* appears suddenly in France "with all its resources" in the form of the famous *Très riches heures* of Chantilly made for the Duke of Berry in 1416, and the *Heures* of Tourin, made in 1418 by

---

[20] Laprade, *Le sentiment de la nature chez les modernes*, p. 83.

[21] L. Gillet, "Le paysage dans la miniature," in *Histoire du paysage en France*, by Benoit and others, pp. 34–35 (Paris, 1908). See there H. Marcel, Introduction; H. Bouchot, "*Le paysage chez les primitifes*," pp. 1–26; C. Diehl, "*Le paysage en Italie au XVe et au XVIe siècle*," pp. 55–70; L. Gillet, "*Le paysage français au XVIe siècle*," pp. 71–99; and all the other studies by R. Bouger, P. Marcel, L. Deshairs, F. Benoit, L. Rosenthal, and others. See also L. Hautecouer, M. Aubert, and others, *Le romantisme et l'art* (Paris, 1928).

[22] *Ibid.*, p. 41.

the three Limbourg brothers and the two Van Eycks.   Then Jean Fouquet and, partly, J. Colombe, Bourdichon, and others contributed to its development.   In Italy, it appears also in the fifteenth century, but slightly and as a means rather than for its own sake (Pollaiuolo, Pinturicchio, G. da Fabriano, E. Pisanello, and a few others).

The Renaissance, with its imitation of antiquity, neglected *paysage* again.   Man was the center of its interest and therefore Botticelli and Leonardo, Michelangelo and other masters regarded *paysage* rather contemptuously.   So, with the exception of the Flemish school, landscape painting tended to disappear again in the sixteenth century, at least in France and Italy.   "Circa 1520, painters renounce suddenly their previous admirable achievement in *paysage*," and it almost disappears. From that time on "Nature does not play any role; eclipses and disappears" in paintings and tapestry.[23]

Respectively the theorizers on art of that period, like Rossi, Primatice, and others, recommended a suppression of *paysage*, viewed it as the most inferior *genre* of painting, and glorified the human figure, antiquity, and "denaturing of nature."

In the seventeenth century, *paysage* in France undergoes a short-time rise in the works of N. Poussin and Claude Lorrain, mainly; but with the triumph of the Academic art in the work of the best artists, it experiences a new setback in the second part of the seventeenth and becomes again rather a background for figures, in the form of the heroic and pastoral *paysage* admitted by the Academy and by the most prominent theorizer on art of the time, Roger de Piles, in his all-influential *Cours de peinture par principles*.   However, under the pressure of public taste, and with the decline of the Academy, a visual-naturalistic *paysage* rises again, toward the end of the seventeenth and in the eighteenth century (the Flemish school, F. Desportes, Watteau, Oudry, and others).   In the second part, in general agreement with the rococo style and "discovery of nature," a pastoral, idyllic, wild, romantic *paysage* becomes particularly dominant.   Then, at the very end of the eighteenth century, due to the triumph of the neo-classic school and the Revolution, *paysage* again sinks and is even proscribed.   Its new "boom" comes with romanticism and results in a blossoming of the romantic *paysage* particularly; again a temporary — but slight — setback is caused by a new short wave of the neo-classicism, under the July Monarchy, but this is rapidly superseded

[23] *Ibid.*, pp. 71 ff.   The contemptuous attitude of Michelangelo and most of the Italian masters of the Renaissance toward *paysage* and the Flemish paintings which cultivated it is too well known to need illustration by quotations from the statements of these masters.

by a blossoming of the naturalistic *paysage*, superseded in its turn by the great flaring-up of the impressionistic *paysage* of the last quarter of the nineteenth century. Such is the essence of the qualitative-quantitative ups and downs of *paysage* in the course of French painting, according to these specialists. Their main conclusions or generalizations sum up the essential results as follows:

First, *paysage is a relatively modern invention which appeared in our culture only in the fifteenth and reached its climax in the nineteenth century.*

Second, *there is the eternal law of alternation of the ups and downs of paysage*, "*due to that obscure law of alternation which seems to rule this world.*" [24]

Third, *the recurrent negative association of paysage with classical style.* "Each time, when art swings toward a classical doctrine, one can expect an aggrandizement of man in art and a fading and disappearing of *paysage* around him," and vice versa.[25]

Without including several other — and somewhat similar — theories in the field,[26] the above shows that the seemingly technical problem of *paysage* in art has a much deeper meaning and involves several problems on the nature of mentality and of culture; it also gives an idea of the character of the quantitative fluctuation of *paysage* in the history of Western painting and sculpture, according to the authors quoted.

Their curve of the fluctuation of *paysage* can be roughly summed up as follows:

(1) Up to the fifteenth century there was no *paysage* as such. No real *paysage* existed also in the antique or the Oriental art.

(2) In the fifteenth century a real (Visual) *paysage* emerges suddenly, with all its resources, mature and perfect.

(3) In the sixteenth century *paysage* decreases and fades quantitatively.

(4) In the middle of the seventeenth century it flares up, but it is short lived and sinks under the influence of the Academic art.

[24] *Ibid.*, p. 8.

[25] *Ibid.*, p. 36. By the way, in a sense the first generalization that *paysage* appeared for the first time only in the fifteenth century somewhat contradicts the second and the third generalizations which indicate "an eternal law of alternations in ups and downs of *paysage*" and in its positive or negative associations with classicism and anticlassicism.

[26] See, for instance, Michel Epuy, *Le sentiment de la nature* (Paris, 1907); Fred. W. Moormon, *The Interpretation of Nature in English Poetry from Beowulf to Shakespeare* (London, 1905); F. Paulhan, *L'esthétique du paysage* (Paris, 1913); P. Gaultier, "Les sentiments de la nature" in his *Reflet d'histoire*" (Paris, 1909); A. Lovejoy and others, *Primitivism and Related Ideas.* See other literature in Sorokin and Zimmerman, *Principles of Rural-Urban Sociology* (New York, 1929), chap. xxi.

(5) In the eighteenth century, especially after about 1730–1740, the pastoral, the idyllic, the romantic, the "Rousseauan" *paysage*, partly also "boudoirish" *paysage*, greatly increases and becomes a passion.

(6) At the end of the eighteenth, in the time of the Revolution and the Empire, *paysage* again suffers an enormous setback.

(7) In the Restored Monarchy, simultaneously with an explosion of Romanticism, it again shines and blossoms.

(8) Under the July Monarchy it slightly suffers but soon recovers its forces and in form of the "naturalistic" and then especially impressionistic *paysage*, it triumphantly reaches its greatest qualitative and quantitative development in the nineteenth and twentieth centuries.

Such is its course in France and, with slight variations, in the other European countries, with the exception of the Flemish school, which had to all appearances a different course of fluctuation.

To what extent are these conclusions valid? The subsequent data presented in Tables 21 and 22 and Figure 17 answer this question; in addition, they tell us what the quantitative course of *paysage* has been in other European countries — a course practically little touched upon by the studies quoted. They reveal also similarities and dissimilarities in the art of various European countries. Perhaps they give something else. Before turning to the tables, a few preliminary remarks seem to be necessary.

First, we must agree whether we mean by *paysage* only its visual rendering or also the symbolic and Ideational presentation of the scenery of nature (sea, river, forest, mountain, etc.) and of its elements (branch, plant, tree, etc.). Since everything can be depicted in these two widely different styles, *paysage* can also be Visual and Ideational or symbolic. When this is understood, then it becomes quite clear that *paysage*, either Ideational or Visual, appeared as early as, perhaps even earlier than, several other types of painting. In the art of almost any primitive people, especially of the agricultural peoples, as well as at the earliest stages of art of the so-called historical nations, the Egyptian, the Greek, the Babylonian, the Chinese, etc., we find more than enough of such renderings either in the Ideational or in the symbolic forms.[27] For this evident reason it is fallacious to claim that *paysage* did not exist up to

[27] For primitive art, see the data and the facts and the pictures in the quoted works of F. Boas and von Sydow. For the agricultural peoples, see Sorokin and Zimmerman, *op. cit.*, chap. xxi, and Sorokin, Zimmerman and Galpin, *A Systematic Source Book in Rural Sociology*, Vol. II, chap. xv. See in these works the literature and the data. For the early stages of the art of practically any of the so-called "historical cultures," almost any serious work on the history of art will verify the validity of my statement.

the fifteenth century. It certainly did exist and was one of the main forms of art, at least in the Ideational style. I am more than doubtful also as to the validity of the statement that even the Visual *paysage* appeared late, and was nonexistent either among the primitive peoples or in the Oriental (think of the multitude of excellent Chinese[28] and Japanese landscapes!) or in the Greek or other cultures. It is true that in the art of Egypt, of Greece, and of Rome, Visual *paysage* occupied a very small space; but it existed at least in the Ideational form, whether there or in the early Christian and medieval art. Such, then, is the answer which we have to give in regard to the contentions of the above investigators. *Paysage* existed as early as any other type, but often it was presented in its Ideational form. It existed also early in Visual form, at least among several primitive and early cultures, though in many of them it seems to have been little developed.[29] With these limitations and qualifications the statement about the slow development of the Visual *paysage* in the art of Greece, of Rome, and of the Middle Ages seems to be true. At least, the preceding and subsequent tables corroborate that. In these tables, the term *paysage* means *Visual paysage* only (not the Ideational). For the countries and for the centuries where and when the table gives zero, this zero means not a lack of *paysage* in any of its forms, but merely lack of the visual type. This being understood, we return now to the study of Table 20 and Figures 13 and 16.

The main conclusions suggested by Table 20 can be summed up as follows.

(1) It is true that in the secular pictures of the Christian art, and the ancient and the medieval Christian art, indeed in the whole of the grand art of the Middle Ages, we do not find *Visual paysage* at all. As that art was predominantly Ideational, the statement that the Ideational art and the Visual *paysage* are negatively associated finds its direct corroboration. Since the Ideational mind is turned "inwardly" toward the nonempirical realities, and since the Visual, empirical reality is a mere mirage for it, such a negative association is logically comprehensible. So far, in application to the Visual *paysage*, the above statements of the scholars quoted are to be accepted (though their explanations hardly go deep enough).

(2) This conclusion, furthermore, is clearly supported by the figures for most of the European countries. In Russian art the Visual *paysage*

[28] A *Landscape with a Hunter* has survived from Ku-K'ai-chih, that is, from the earliest known Chinese pictures. See its reproduction, Plate 9, in Sirén, *op. cit.*, Vol. I.

[29] In China also, Visual *paysage* developed fully "three or four centuries later" in comparison with other forms of painting. Sirén, *op. cit.*, Vol. I, p. 18.

appears only in the eighteenth century; in Italy only in the fifteenth and remains up to almost the eighteenth century but slightly developed quantitatively; in Spain, only in the sixteenth; in France, after the fifteenth century, it practically disappeared in the sixteenth and re-emerged only in the seventeenth century; in England it appeared on a considerable scale only in the eighteenth century; and in Central Europe only in the sixteenth. The Flemish school represented an exception in the sense that there the Visual *paysage* emerged even before the fifteenth century. Even the Idealistic art of the thirteenth century did not have it in any tangible degree. I can now put in a modified and much more general, and I hope more accurate, form the above proposition of Gillet, saying: For the logical reason indicated and on the basis of the factual test, one can claim: *Where and when the Ideational form of art is dominant, there and then one can expect to have an absence of Visual paysage in that art; when and where the Visual form of art is dominant, the Visual paysage is to be expected and the larger the scale, the more visual is the art.*

(3) If we take Europe as a whole, then the movement of the percentages of the Visual *paysage*, in the centuries studied, of the total of the Secular painting and sculpture appears as in Table 21 and in Figure 16.

TABLE 21.   FLUCTUATION OF PAYSAGE IN ART

			Europe by Centuries						
	-X	X–XI	XII–XIII	XIV–XV	XVI	XVII	XVIII	XIX	XX
Number	—	—	—	15	215	483	993	2810	2798
Percentage in total secular art	—	—	—	0.8	5.6	6.2	9.0	19.3	23.0
Percentage in total secular and religious art	—	—	—	0.1	1.6	2.9	6.6	15.4	21.6

Table 21 and Figure 16 show clearly a total lack of the Visual *paysage* in the Middle Ages, its emergence in the fifteenth century, and its progressive increase from that century on until it reaches its high proportion in the nineteenth and in the twentieth centuries. These figures give a corroboration of an increasing visualization (sensualization) of the Western culture (and mentality) in the last five centuries. In distinction from several above symptoms, this "barometer" does not show as yet a reaction against Visual art in the twentieth century: *paysage* is still growing and going strong. But in the transitory century, one can hardly expect that all the "barometers" would show definitely the same "weather." The figures show also what is the relative proportion of *paysage* among all the seven classes into which the total secular art is divided.

(4) A glance at the Islamic art shows that, in accordance with the statement of the quoted investigators, the Islamic art throughout the whole period of its existence contained little of *paysage:* in that culture it has been much less developed and appeared only in the sixteenth century, but after that it also grew.

(5) Changes in the proportion of *paysage* in separate countries are depicted in Table 20 and Figure 13. The main trend in all the European countries has been the same. But in minor fluctuations there are of course differences, though most of them are of the type already met. Thus, for instance, Russia again lags by about two centuries from most of the European countries in emergence of *paysage*. In the fourteenth, the fifteenth, the sixteenth, and the seventeenth centuries the Netherlands leads all the other countries in the quantitative development of landscape painting, but after that time the leadership passes to other countries. Other differences can be seen from the data. In most of the countries the movement of the percentages of *paysage* fluctuates more erratically than in the curve for the whole of Europe.

A. *Content of Paysage.* If we inquire what scenery or topics of nature, and in what proportion, have been rendered in *paysage* in various countries and in various centuries, the answer is given by Table 22, which tries to subdivide *paysage* according to its main topics into five main classes : *urban, rural, mountains, sea, seasons;* to these classes, for different purposes, are added three other classes, "joyful (sunny)," "sad (gloomy)," and "with human beings," which, however, have to be considered separately from the above five.

As one picture may be a "rural landscape" and at the same time may depict, for instance, autumn with rural scenery, and be either joyful (sunny) or sad (gloomy) in tone, it may enter two or more of the above classes. For this reason, the number of the picture units for any given century cannot be expected to equal absolutely the number of the *paysage* pictures for that century given in the tables about *paysage* generally.

On the basis of absolute numbers, one can compute various percentages of each category in various combinations. Let us take a few of the "spotlights" revealed by the data. First, let us see how the comparative proportion of the "rural" and "urban" *paysage* changes in the course

TABLE 22. FLUCTUATION OF PAYSAGE TYPES IN ART

a = urban b = rural c = mountains d = sea e = seasons f = sunny g = gloomy h = with human beings

Ancient and Medieval Christian

(No items in this category)

Islamic

(Numbers)

	-X	X-XI	XII-XIII	XIV-XV	XVI	XVII	XVIII	Total
a	—	—	—	—	—	14	32	46
b	—	—	—	—	20	21	14	55
c	—	—	—	—	—	21	12	33
d	—	—	—	—	—	—	26	26
e	—	—	—	—	—	—	—	—
f	—	—	—	—	—	—	—	—
g	—	—	—	—	—	—	—	—
h	—	—	—	—	—	—	—	—
Total	—	—	—	—	20	56	84	160

Russian

(Numbers)

	-XII	XII-XIII	XIV-XV	XVI	XVII	XVIII	1801-1825	1826-1850	1851-1875	1876-1900	XX	Total
a	—	—	—	—	—	15	29	29	21	78	695	867
b	—	—	—	—	—	4	19	21	15	387	359	805
c	—	—	—	—	—	—	—	8	7	54	83	152
d	—	—	—	—	—	—	9	8	21	89	78	205
Total	—	—	—	—	—	19	57	66	64	608	1215	2029
e	—	—	—	—	—	10	12	22	100	460	575	1179
f	—	—	—	—	—	7	4	27	32	121	217	408
g	—	—	—	—	—	5	6	36	57	147	189	440
Total	—	—	—	—	—	12	10	63	89	268	406	848
h	—	—	—	—	—	12	8	7	21	67	47	162

TABLE 22. FLUCTUATION OF PAYSAGE TYPES IN ART — continued

a = urban   b = rural   c = mountains   d = sea   e = seasons   f = sunny   g = gloomy   h = with human beings

Italian

(Numbers)

	1200–1300	1300–1350	1350–1400	1400–1450	1450–1500	1500–1550	1550–1600	1600–1650	1650–1700	1700–1750	1750–1800	1800–1850	1850–1900	1900–1933	Total
a	—	—	—	—	3	4	6	12	31	89	118	57	89	46	455
b	—	—	—	1	2	8	21	33	50	61	72	61	92	53	454
c	—	—	—	1	2	4	7	9	18	47	51	31	46	17	233
d	—	—	—	—	—	—	—	2	6	18	19	27	38	32	142
Total	—	—	—	2	7	16	34	56	105	215	260	176	265	148	1284
e	—	—	—	—	—	—	—	—	—	—	—	—	173	173	346
f	—	—	—	—	—	—	—	—	—	298	170	189	147	156	960
g	—	—	—	—	—	—	—	—	—	32	12	27	18	31	120
Total	—	—	—	—	—	—	—	—	—	330	182	216	165	187	1080
h	—	—	—	—	4	17	31	141	87	112	89	62	13	11	567

Spanish

(Numbers)

	XV	XVI	XVII	1700–1750	1750–1800	1800–1850	1850–1900	1900–1933	Total
a	—	4	8	3	6	6	15	26	68
b	—	—	2	—	12	7	10	12	43
c	—	—	3	—	3	3	6	—	15
d	—	—	—	10	7	17	—	6	40
Total	—	4	13	13	28	33	31	44	166
e	—	4	13	13	28	33	31	44	166
f	—	—	—	—	—	—	—	—	—
g	—	—	—	—	—	—	—	—	—
h	—	4	13	8	9	12	3	—	49

French

(Numbers)

	XVI	1600–1650	1650–1700	1700–1750	1750–1800	1800–1850	1850–1880	1880–1900	1900–1933	Total
a	—	9	18	105	87	189	186	60	66	720
b	—	—	—	39	54	84	96	99	126	498
c	—	—	—	—	21	54	6	12	15	108
d	—	—	—	15	15	24	63	69	75	246
Total	—	9	18	144	177	351	351	240	282	1572
e	—	—	—	—	12	18	54	60	69	213
f	—	—	—	—	—	33	12	21	24	90
g	—	—	—	—	—	15	9	9	18	51
Total	—	—	—	—	—	48	21	30	42	141
h	21	27	31	66	54	—	51	30	39	319

Dutch

(Numbers)

	–1500	1500–1600	1600–1620	1620–1640	1640–1660	1660–1680	1680–1780	1780–1880	1880–1933	Total
a	6	16	30	18	6	10	10	34	32	162
b	—	64	64	42	24	18	—	26	30	268
c	—	—	6	—	—	—	—	—	—	6
d	—	36	22	8	18	—	—	30	30	144
Total	6	116	122	68	48	28	10	90	92	580
e	—	8	14	22	2	—	—	2	16	64
f	—	—	—	4	—	—	—	—	14	18
g	—	24	28	18	12	6	—	—	18	106
Total	—	24	28	22	12	6	—	—	32	124
h	10	16	42	16	—	—	—	—	8	92

I—31

TABLE 22.   FLUCTUATION OF PAYSAGE TYPES IN ART — *continued*

a = urban   b = rural   c = mountains   d = sea   e = seasons   f = sunny   g = gloomy   h = with human beings

Central Europe

(Numbers)

	XVI	1600–1650	1650–1700	1700–1750	1750–1800	1800–1830	1830–1860	1860–1880	1880–1900	1900–1933	Total
a	6	—	2	—	5	30	63	6	69	450	631
b	24	6	8	6	7	69	24	41	24	438	647
c	15	—	—	3	8	24	12	6	9	57	134
d	—	—	—	6	7	12	3	21	15	36	100
Total	45	6	10	15	27	135	102	74	117	981	1512
e	9	—	12	—	13	39	15	63	15	111	277
f	—	—	—	—	—	3	—	9	6	6	24
g	—	—	—	3	—	9	—	—	3	3	15
Total	—	—	—	3	—	12	—	9	9	9	39
h	3	3	12	21	41	108	9	27	15	54	293

English

(Numbers)

	XV	XVI	XVII	1700–1750	1750–1800	1800–1850	1850–1900	1900–1933	Total
a	—	—	—	18	19	9	12	16	74
b	—	—	—	22	27	12	1	10	72
c	—	—	—	—	—	2	4	3	9
d	—	—	—	—	1	2	8	7	18
Total	—	—	—	40	47	25	25	36	173
e	—	—	—	19	17	8	13	18	75
f	—	—	—	—	—	—	—	9	9
g	—	—	—	—	—	3	4	2	9
Total	—	—	—	—	—	3	4	11	18
h	—	—	—	40	42	7	2	4	95

of time. If we take the total of the pictures for both of these classes for each specified period as 100 per cent, then we can get an idea of their changes.

(1) *Urban and Rural Paysage*. Generally it seems reasonable to expect that with the growth of urbanization, the percentage of urban *paysage* will grow also, while that of rural scenery will decrease. The figures in the tables do not support such an expectation. For instance, in Russia, the percentages of the urban and rural *paysage* respectively were : in the eighteenth century, 79 and 21 ; in the nineteenth, especially in its last quarter, when the urbanization had progressed a great deal, they were 26 and 74 ; in the twentieth century, 66 and 34. In other words, the proportion of the urban and rural *paysage* is not determined directly by urbanization but by some other factors. Similar are the results given by other countries : none of them shows an increase of urban landscape painting with an increase of urbanization. Table 23 shows the percentages of urban and rural *paysage* in Italy, beginning with 1400–1450, for each subsequent half-century period, up to 1900–1933, and in France and England for the specified periods.

TABLE 23.   URBAN AND RURAL PAYSAGE IN ART

	1400–1450	–1500	–1550	–1600	–1650	–1700	–1750	–1800	–1850	–1900	1900–1933
Italy											
Urban	—	60	34	22	34	32	59	62	48	44	47
Rural	100	40	66	78	66	68	41	38	52	56	53
France											
Urban	—	—	—	—	100	100	73	62	69	56	34
Rural	—	—	—	—	—	—	27	38	31	44	66
England											
Urban	—	—	—	—	—	—	40	41	43	92	52
Rural	—	—	—	—	—	—	60	59	57	8	38

In the Netherlands, for the period before 1500, 100 per cent of the *paysage* is urban ; for the sixteenth century it falls to 20, while the rural has 80 per cent ; for the eighteenth century, the urban is again 100 per cent ; for the nineteenth, the percentages are 40 and 60 respectively ; for the twentieth, 52 and 48.

It is granted that the samples, especially for the previous centuries, are possibly few (though not too few, considering the small number of *paysage* pictures registered in the annals of history of art).   Nevertheless, there can hardly be any doubt that roughly the figures reflect the reality : the progress of urbanization is not followed by a corresponding increase of the urban *paysage* at the cost of the rural.   Its movement in all countries is erratic.   Such a situation is due probably to many and various factors, among them the law of contrast : many inhabitants of highly urbanized centers are fond of and like to own pictures of rural scenery, hence the demand for the rural landscapes.   Again the social origin of the painters may have something to do with the matter : if the artists are of urban origin, they may concentrate upon the urban *paysage;* if of rural, upon rural scenes, as more familiar to them.   But this is just a series of guesses. The whole thing seems to depend on the prevailing fashions within the upper and the well-to-do classes who are the buyers of such pictures. There seem to have been alternating waves of fashion of "urbanity" (for instance, in France in the seventeenth century; in Italy, in the fifteenth; in Russia, in the eighteenth; in England, in the second part of the nineteenth; in Holland, in the fifteenth and the eighteenth) and the wave of "rusticity" and "pastoral," "idyllic" scenery, for instance, in Italy, in the sixteenth; in France, in the twentieth; in Russia, in the nineteenth; in Holland, in the nineteenth.

The twentieth century gives different results for various countries: growing "urbanism" in Russia; "rusticity" in France; "equilibrium" in Italy and Holland.   In the Islamic art, from the sixteenth to the eighteenth century, there was a steadily growing trend of "urbanity" in such paintings.

(2) *"Pure Paysage and Paysage with Human Figures."* It is enough to glance through the tables for practically all the European countries to see that the absolute and the relative proportion of *paysage* with human figures (or of the human figure with a landscape background) [30] has tended systematically to decrease, as we move from the earlier centuries to the present time.   *Paysage* has been growing more and more "pure," not "contaminated" with any human figure.   This is evidently another corroboration of the above trend of the growth of the Visual *paysage* during the last four or five centuries.   It has grown, then, not only quantitatively, in the sense of an increase of its percentage

[30] This explains why in several cases the number of the pictures of "*paysage* with human figures" exceeds the total number of the *paysage* pictures: the pictures which represent "human figure with some landscape background" were often not counted as *paysage* at all and therefore were not entered in that class; but for this specific class, "*paysage* with human figure," many such pictures have to be entered in that class.   Hence, the above "puzzling" fact that in some cases the number of such pictures exceeds the total number of the *paysage* pictures.

in the total of the secular pictures, but qualitatively also. God and man, as the theme or the hero of the Ideational and Idealistic art, have more and more been replaced by "nature" — its empirical and visual appearance — free from man and his Ideational values. An enormous change in the whole mentality of art when it is understood properly!

(3) *Joyful (Sunny) and Sad (Gloomy) Paysage.* Putting aside the idea as to whether a sunny *paysage* expresses cheerfulness and a gloomy one a sadness of mood — which may or may not be true — it is interesting to see which of these two types (excluding pictures which are neutral and indefinite in this respect) is prevalent in various countries, and how their relative percentage fluctuates from century to century. The answer is given in Table 24 and Figure 17. Taking both classes as 100 per cent, we have for the whole of Europe the following percentages.

TABLE 24.   JOYFUL AND SAD PAYSAGE IN ART

	Europe by Centuries				
	XVI	XVII	XVIII	XIX	XX
Joyful	—	6	83	74	77
Sad	100	94	17	36	33

The landscapes of the sixteenth and the seventeenth centuries are almost wholly gloomy; those of the eighteenth are mainly sunny (and cheerful); somewhat less — but still predominantly — "sunny" remains the *paysage* of the nineteenth and twentieth centuries. Such is the result when the data for all the seven European countries are taken together. When each country is studied separately, there is a considerable divergence from one another. Russian *paysage* has been more sunny in the eighteenth and in the twentieth centuries; in the nineteenth it was comparatively more gloomy. The Italian likewise was more sunny in the eighteenth than in the nineteenth and the twentieth centuries. The Spanish has been predominantly neutral. The French was more sunny in the nineteenth than in the twentieth century. The Dutch is most sunny in the twentieth century and for the previous centuries was predominantly gloomy. The Central European landscape was most sunny in the period 1860–1880 (growth and triumph of German Empire); most gloomy in 1800–1830, and in the last part of the nineteenth and in the twentieth century less cheerful than in 1860–1880. The English *paysage* of the nineteenth century was exceedingly gloomy but has become more sunny in the twentieth century.

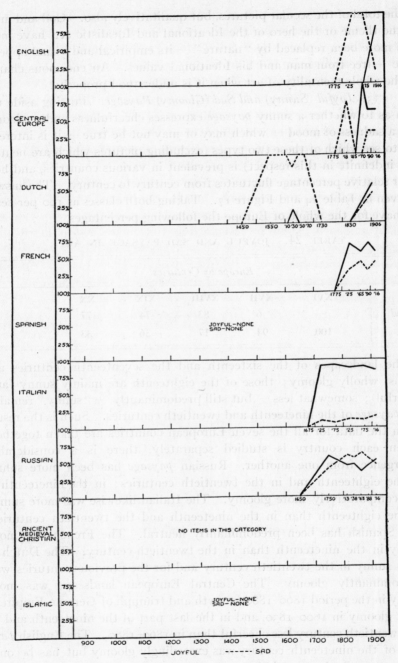

FIG. 17.   JOYFUL AND SAD PAYSAGE IN ART BY COUNTRIES

The abnormally high percentage of gloomy *paysage* in Holland and England and the exceedingly high percentage of sunny *paysage* in Italy, then in France, then in Central Europe, and the middle position occupied by Russia, are in all probability a reflection of climate: gloomy and foggy in England and Holland; sunny in Italy, France, and in Central Europe; and intermediate in Russia. In this way we have, unexpectedly, an interesting illustration of the influence of climatic conditions upon painting, and since the Visual *paysage* reflects — illusionistically — the appearance of the prevalent aspect of nature, such a hypothesis appears to be fairly probable.[31]

If this predominant tone of the *paysage* of the various countries can be explained by their prevalent climatic conditions, the fluctuation of the "sunny" and "gloomy" percentages in various periods for the same country evidently cannot be explained by that factor. Whether it is due to the fluctuation of the cheerful and gloomy moods in the country remains an open question. Possibly it is, to some extent. At least, in Central Europe and in Holland and partly in other countries, some of the periods of increase of the "cheerful" *paysage* are the periods of the uplift of the countries. However, no definite conclusion is possible.

II. ANIMALS AND STILL LIFE

Each of these two classes of pictures and sculptures is composed of those whose main subject is an animal (or animals) or the *nature morte*. Here again we must clearly distinguish between the Ideational and Visual forms of each class. Many pictures of animals, especially in ancient and medieval art, were purely symbolic and Ideational (hieratic); a familiar example is given by the pictures of the four evangelists with their traditional animals — lion, griffon, ox; the dove and fish of the early Christian art, Apocalyptic figures, and the animals in other works of Ideational art.[32] The same is to be said of the still-life pictures.

[31] The same thing is shown partly by the number and proportion of the "sea" and "mountain" pictures in various countries. In Holland, England, and partly in Russia and France, "mountain" *paysage* is much more modest quantitatively than in Italy or Spain, while in Holland and England the "sea" paintings are more numerous.

[32] About the long life and continuity of many animal images, and about the change of their meanings in various periods and countries, especially such animal images as the signs of the zodiac, which functioned in ancient Babylon, Egypt, Greece, Rome, in the Middle Ages, changing the meaning of each animal image from period to period, from culture to culture, see L. Hourticq, *La vie des images* (Paris, 1927), pp. 15 ff. and chap. iii. "These images travel through the ages, carrying different meanings, thoughts and associations," he rightly says. Such a change of meaning of the image of the same animal, or of a still-life object, is a direct evidence of the Ideational character of many of such images. Another familiar example of

The olive branch, or grape, or palm leaf, or many other forms of still life in the ancient Christian and medieval art were ideational in their meaning and character. Thus visually similar pictures of animals and of still life may mean, and often do mean, radically different things.

Keeping this in mind, one has to say that in a quantitative study of such pictures and sculptures it is impossible, unfortunately, to keep this profound distinction. We had to classify in the class of "animal" pictures and sculptures all such works where visually the central figure was animal, no matter whether in Ideational or Visual meaning. The same is true of the *nature morte*. In other words, the tables give the number and percentages of these pictures classified from the *Visual standpoint*, without an attempt to divide them into Ideational and Visual classes.

A careful glance at Tables 20 and 25 and Figures 13 and 16 shows that *the percentage of the "animal pictures" has tended to decrease, with some fluctuations, in most of the European countries and in Europe taken as a whole, as we pass from the medieval art to the present time.*

TABLE 25. NUMBER AND PER CENT OF ANIMAL PICTURES AND SCULPTURES IN THE TOTAL SECULAR ART

	Europe by Centuries								
	–X	X–XI	XII–XIII	XIV–XV	XVI	XVII	XVIII	XIX	XX
Total number	913	104	142	1707	3845	7826	11,018	14,569	11,257
Number (animal)	376	36	54	117	120	177	85	329	140
Percentage	41.2	34.6	38.0	6.8	3.2	2.3	0.8	2.2	1.2

From Table 25 and Figures 13 and 16 we see a rapid and systematic decline of the percentage of animal pictures from the early Middle Ages to the eighteenth century, when it reaches its lowest point, and then rises in the nineteenth century and falls again in the twentieth century. This means that *in the period of the domination of the Ideational art, the animal images are more used — and doubtless in the Ideational sense — than in the period of domination of the Visual art.* In this sense, animal lore (in symbolic form) is more developed in the Ideational cultures than in the Visual.

the Ideationality of such images is given by the images of animals or of the still-life objects on coats of arms and in heraldic literature. Even contemporary "insignias" of many states, like a one- or two-headed eagle, a wolf, a lion, a leopard, a bear, and so on are mainly Ideational. About the medieval symbolism of such images see the quoted works of Mâle, Bréhier, Huizinga, and others.

Whether such a result, so far as the quantity is concerned, is a consequence of the *inner connection* of Ideational mentality with the animal images, used as one of the most convenient ways to express transcendental, religious, and nonempirical values and ideas — and one can see that animal images are indeed a convenient tool for that — or is the result of an *incidental* connection, due to the fact that the centuries of the Ideational culture were the centuries, little mechanized and little industrialized, which used animals and animal power more than the recent eras of steam and electricity — which of these explanations is accurate is uncertain. It seems that the inner connection must play some role in the results. Otherwise, we would expect a decrease of *paysage*, and especially of the rural *paysage*, in the modern art of the Visual culture (because urbanization made it also "more rare" and less common). And yet, we saw that it increased instead of decreasing. The incidental connection also seems to have played some part, but hardly a decisive one : if it were the main factor we should have obtained a further decrease of animal pictures in the nineteenth and in the twentieth centuries in comparison with the eighteenth. Instead, we have an increase that again suggests the inner connection. It is possible the Visual art finds that animals, as animals, are neither so picturesque nor such satisfactory subjects as a *paysage* or other type of art.

If the art of separate countries is taken, the main trends in all the European countries are similar to the above; in secondary fluctuations as well as in the total comparative proportion of the animal pictures, there are several differences. For instance, Italian art has a much lower percentage of such pictures and sculptures generally, compared with the English or the Central European. But it is outside the scope of this work to go into a discussion of these secondary traits. As to the Islamic art, it is marked by a very high percentage of such art works, compared with almost all the European countries after the fifteenth century. Here appears again its heterogeneity from the art of the countries belonging to the Western Christian cultural continent.

III. NATURE MORTE

A glance at Table 20 and Figures 13 and 16 is sufficient to show that the still-life pictures and sculptures have had a main trend rather opposite to that of the animal pictures and sculptures: in practically all the European countries their part in the total secular art has tended to increase as we pass from the early centuries to the thirteenth; then it fell in the fourteenth, but after the fifteenth century it has steadily grown. Especially great is the increase in the twentieth century. Their number is now much greater than that of the animal pictures in practically all the European countries. This increase seems to represent a compensation for the decrease of the animal pictures. Their proportion was sufficiently high in the Middle Ages, but there the images of still life were used mainly symbolically or ideationally. The twelfth and thirteenth centuries give the highest (for Europe) percentage of this class. Considering Vincent de Beauvais's *Mirror of Nature*, the thirteenth century seems to have been interested in them ideationally as well as visually. When the Visual trend was started in the fourteenth and the fifteenth centuries, they lost their ideational interest; from the purely visual standpoint, they possibly were less interesting than other types of painting and sculpture. But step by step, perhaps with the growth of the materialistic-mechanistic mentality, they began to attract greater and greater attention, until in the twentieth century they have risen to quite a large class among the other divisions of secular art. These facts suggest the following hypothesis as to their association with the main forms of art studied; per se, they are neither positively nor negatively associated with Ideationalism or Visualism. They occupy a place in Ideational art, but of a purely symbolic nature. This place, however, is much more modest than that held by the animal pictures and sculptures. This means that they are not so convenient a tool for the "incarnation" of transcendental ideas and values as the images of animals. The Idealistic art uses the images of the *nature morte* still more extensively but in a mixed way: partly as symbols, partly for their own purposes. In the Visual art they function only as visual images. In this capacity they may or may not occupy a large place. In our culture, their percentage has been growing, whether due to an increase of the materialistic-mechanistic mentality (an increase shown in other ways), which may be inclined to prefer the *nature morte* to the living nature, or to some other reasons, remains uncertain. One guess is that most of the *nature morte* pictures are made for, and are interesting mainly from, the standpoint of technique. *Technique* is what more and more replaces the living spirit, the mind, the thought, and real creativeness in the later stages of the Visual wave. This is shown in other parts of this work. Therefore, the increase discussed is perhaps a reflection of this general phenomenon in the field of art.

If we pay attention to the similarities and differences of the art of each country, we discover some secondary variations in the configuration of the curve, in the general proportion of this class to the total of the

secular art, in its periods of secondary ups and downs.   But the main
trend of increase in the present century is common to all the European
countries.   The Islamic art is marked by an almost total absence of this
type.   (Its substitute is probably the ornamental and decorative designs
where, as elements, the objects of the *nature morte* enter.) [33]

IV. PORTRAITURE AND THE FLUCTUATION OF ITS PROPORTION
IN SECULAR ART

I have already indicated the reasons why portraiture as a visual likeness of man developed (quantitatively and also qualitatively) in the
periods of domination of Visual art and was undeveloped in those of
domination of the Ideational art.   The general outline of the movement
of portrait painting in the Graeco-Roman and the European art has been
given.   Now we shall test the validity of this outline and of the above
"correlation" upon our quantitative material.   In addition, it may
yield some other results.   Let us turn first to Table 20 and Figures 14 and
16, which give the percentages of portraits in the total secular art (of all
seven classes into which it is divided) by countries and cultures for the
centuries studied.

For the whole of Europe, so far as the secular art is concerned, the
situation is depicted as follows.

TABLE 26.   FLUCTUATION OF PORTRAITURE

	Europe by Centuries								
	–X	X–XI	XII–XIII	XIV–XV	XVI	XVII	XVIII	XIX	XX
Portrait number	73	11	43	928	1508	2498	3243	3453	2313
Total secular number	913	104	142	1707	3845	7826	11,018	14,569	11,257
Percentage of total secular	8.0	10.6	29.0	54.4	39.2	31.9	29.4	23.7	20.6
Percentage of total secular and religious	1.4	0.4	0.9	6.6	11.5	17.8	21.8	18.9	18.0

[33] Of 790 pictures and sculptures of Ancient Egypt in my sample, there is none of still
life and 105 or 13.3 per cent of the animal class.   In this respect the Egyptian art resembles
the Islamic.   Of 3540 drawings and sculptures of Graeco-Roman art in my sample, there
is none of the *nature morte* and 65 or about 2 per cent of the animal class.   The Graeco-
Roman art, then, had in general both of these classes developed (quantitatively) less than
either the medieval or modern art.

At first glance, the figures seem to contradict the suggested association, at least in part : after the fifteenth century the percentage of portrait pictures and sculpture does not increase but decreases. However, one has to keep in mind that for the centuries before the fourteenth the total of the secular pictures makes only a small fraction of the total pictures — secular and religious — 18.1 per cent for the centuries before the tenth, 5.3 for the tenth and eleventh, and only 3 per cent for the twelfth and thirteenth centuries; while in the centuries after the thirteenth the percentage of the secular systematically rises : 15.0, 35.3, 49.8, 75.9, 90.0, and 96.1 for the twentieth century. When this fact is considered, it becomes evident at once that in the total art of the Middle Ages, portrait painting occupied a quite insignificant place (73 pictures out of 5032 for the centuries before the tenth; 11 out of 2521 for the tenth and eleventh centuries; 43 out of 4863 for the twelfth and the thirteenth centuries). It was almost absent in that Ideational art. Even in the total secular art of that period the percentage of portraiture is notably lower than that for the subsequent centuries. Even for the fourteenth and the fifteenth centuries, which give the highest percentage of portraits in the total of the secular art, the percentage of portraits in the total — secular and religious — art of these centuries is only about 6 : 928 portraits out of the total 13,969. For the sixteenth century this percentage becomes (in regard to the total — religious and secular) more than 11 ; for the seventeenth century, more than 17 ; for the eighteenth century, more than 21 ; for the nineteenth, around 19 ; and for the twentieth century, around 18. So far the contention that *portraiture and the Ideational art are negatively associated while portraiture and Visual art are associated positively* is corroborated by the data. Even a slight decrease of the percentage for the nineteenth and the twentieth centuries is in agreement with similar deviations from "Visualism" which we have met before. The percentages (in regard to the total art) show that, beginning with the fourteenth century, portraiture has systematically and rapidly grown, up to the end of the nineteenth century, when it shows a slight decrease.

In the total of the secular art only, portraiture has been fairly steadily decreasing in its percentage among the seven main classes of painting and sculpture. The absolute number of portraits increases, but the percentage to the secular art decreases. The reason for that is probably technical mainly. It is certainly not a decreasing tendency in the modern man to have his own portrait ; as everybody knows, nowadays thousands of individuals order their portraits, not to mention millions of photographs and movies, through which this craving is satisfied. The reasons for a decrease in the nineteenth and the twentieth centuries is because of the invention of photography. It permits everyone to obtain most accurate visual snapshots of oneself and makes a painted portrait not so necessary. Another reason is that, as we shall see, with the decay of the aristocracy and clergy, the demand for a portrait made by a great artist — and only such portraits enter the history of art or the grand art — which costs a great deal, has possibly decreased also; the bulk of *bourgeoisie* and rich philistines are well satisfied with photographs or with inexpensive "home-made" portraits painted by home-made artists, which portraiture does not reach the treasury of grand art. On the other hand, the great artists, under these conditions of a decreased portrait demand, are forced to create some other type which will have a wider market; except the man whose portrait is painted and his immediate circle and devotees, the portrait of the average man does not have a public market: the public would prefer to buy some other type than a picture of this or that manufacturer, or grocery king, or politician, or *literati*, or scientist, or professor, or any other person, with the exception of perhaps a few really famous or great or notable figures.

These reasons seem to me fairly sufficient to explain the decreasing proportion of portraiture in the total secular art of the last two centuries.

The data for the separate countries show several variations in the secondary characteristics: In the majority of the countries, the golden age of portrait painting quantitatively was the eighteenth century, when sensuous Visualism was at one of its highest levels. If there had been no invention of photography and movies, the nineteenth century would possibly give a still higher percentage.

The figures do not show anything as to the quality of the portrait painting. But from the preceding chapter we know that it has been growing, to the end of the nineteenth century, more and more visual, impressionistic, illusionary. Only at the very end of the nineteenth century did the expressionistic portraiture raise its head, as a manifestation of the general trend away from extreme — impressionistic — Visualism.

So much for the porportion of portraits in the total paintings and sculptures of each of the centuries studied.[34] We can now turn to Table 27 and the social sciences in portraiture.

[34] In the Graeco-Roman art, out of 3540 works studied, 316 or 9 per cent were portraits. In the Egyptian art, out of 790 works studied, 123 or 16 per cent were portraits. Thus the average of the Graeco-Roman art was near to the situation in Europe in the fifteenth and sixteenth centuries. The Egyptian art gives a percentage near to that of the seventeenth century in Europe. The Egyptian portraiture, with the exception of the late Saite and Roman period, has been mainly of the "mixed" type — somewhat idealistic — rather than quite Visual.

TABLE 27. FLUCTUATION OF SOCIAL CLASSES AND SEXES IN PORTRAITURE

a = aristocracy　b = clergy　c = bourgeoisie　d = intellectuals, artists　e = military　f = lower classes　g = male　h = female　i = caricature

	-X	X-XI	XII-XIII	XIV-XV	XVI-XVII	XVIII	Total
			Ancient and Medieval Christian				
			(Numbers)				
a	54	11	31	80	18	—	194
b	10	—	9	21	42	—	82
c	9	—	—	—	37	—	46
d	—	—	—	—	—	—	—
e	—	—	—	—	—	—	—
f	—	—	—	—	—	—	—
Total	73	11	40	101	97	—	322
g	67	34	32	74	79	—	286
h	8	7	8	27	18	—	68
Total	75	41	40	101	97	—	354
i	—	—	—	—	—	—	—
			(Percentages)				
a	74.0	100.0	77.5	79.2	18.6	—	—
b	13.7	—	22.5	20.8	43.3	—	—
c	12.3	—	—	—	38.1	—	—
d	—	—	—	—	—	—	—
e	—	—	—	—	—	—	—
f	—	—	—	—	—	—	—
Total	100.0	100.0	100.0	100.0	100.0	—	—
g	89.3	83.0	80.0	73.3	81.4	—	—
h	10.7	17.0	20.0	26.7	18.6	—	—
Total	100.0	100.0	100.0	100.0	100.0	—	—
i	—	—	—	—	—	—	—

Islamic

(Numbers)

	-X	X-XI	XII-XIII	XIV-XV	XVI	XVII	XVIII	Total
a	6	29	128	37	85	511	105	895
b	—	—	8	—	20	21	—	49
c	—	—	—	—	—	42	—	42
d	—	—	—	13	35	—	—	48
e	—	9	40	—	—	28	—	77
f	3	—	—	—	—	28	—	37
Total	9	38	176	50	140	630	105	1148
g	6	16	128	37	105	581	92	965
h	3	13	9	—	35	77	13	150
Total	9	29	137	37	140	658	105	1115
i	—	—	—	—	—	14	—	14

(Percentages)

	-X	X-XI	XII-XIII	XIV-XV	XVI	XVII	XVIII	Total
a	66.7	76.3	72.8	74.0	60.7	81.2	100.0	
b	—	—	4.5	—	14.3	3.3	—	
c	—	—	—	—	—	6.7	—	
d	—	—	—	26.0	25.0	—	—	
e	—	23.7	22.7	—	—	4.4	—	
f	33.3	—	—	—	—	4.4	—	
Total	100.0	100.0	100.0	100.0	100.0	100.0	100.0	
g	66.7	55.2	93.4	100.0	75.0	88.3	87.6	
h	33.3	44.8	6.6	—	25.0	11.7	12.4	
Total	100.0	100.0	100.0	100.0	100.0	100.0	100.0	
i	—	—	—	—	—	2.2	—	

TABLE 27. FLUCTUATION OF SOCIAL CLASSES AND SEXES IN PORTRAITURE — *continued*

a = aristocracy b = clergy c = bourgeoisie d = intellectuals, artists e = military f = lower classes g = male h = female i = caricature

Russian

(Numbers)

	-XII	XII–XIII	XIV–XV	XVI	XVII	XVIII	1801–1825	1826–1850	1851–1875	1876–1900	XX	Total
a	—	—	—	—	4	164	76	28	20	48	52	392
b	—	—	—	—	—	20	10	6	3	9	2	50
c	—	—	—	—	—	61	58	45	15	117	387	683
d	—	—	—	—	—	19	35	30	20	138	239	481
e	—	—	—	—	—	20	22	14	5	15	28	104
f	—	—	—	—	—	8	19	6	15	27	47	122
Total	—	—	—	—	4	292	220	129	78	354	755	1832
g	—	—	—	—	4	217	148	97	64	280	506	1316
h	—	—	—	—	—	75	72	32	14	74	249	516
Total	—	—	—	—	4	292	220	129	78	354	755	1832
i	—	—	—	—	—	—	8	15	18	4	68	113

(Percentages)

	-XII	XII–XIII	XIV–XV	XVI	XVII	XVIII	1801–1825	1826–1850	1851–1875	1876–1900	XX
a	—	—	—	—	100.0	56.2	34.6	21.7	25.7	13.7	6.9
b	—	—	—	—	—	6.9	4.5	4.6	3.8	2.5	.3
c	—	—	—	—	—	20.8	26.4	35.0	19.2	33.0	51.2
d	—	—	—	—	—	6.5	15.9	23.3	25.7	39.0	31.7
e	—	—	—	—	—	6.9	10.0	10.8	6.4	4.2	3.7
f	—	—	—	—	—	2.7	8.6	4.6	19.2	7.6	6.2
Total	—	—	—	—	100.0	100.0	100.0	100.0	100.0	100.0	100.0
g	—	—	—	—	100.0	74.3	67.3	75.2	82.0	79.1	67.0
h	—	—	—	—	—	25.7	32.7	24.8	18.0	20.9	33.0
Total	—	—	—	—	100.0	100.0	100.0	100.0	100.0	100.0	100.0
i	—	—	—	—	—	—	3.6	11.6	23.1	1.1	9.0

Italian

(Numbers)

	1200-1300	1300-1350	1350-1400	1400-1450	1450-1500	1500-1550	1550-1600	1600-1650	1650-1700	1700-1750	1750-1800	1800-1850	1850-1900	1900-1933	Total
a	2	4	21	55	113	137	294	312	561	666	401	172	112	58	2908
b	1	3	14	27	52	27	32	26	41	30	18	5	6	2	284
c	—	—	—	5	88	152	167	115	121	218	127	133	178	112	1416
d	—	—	8	7	43	38	58	42	67	41	32	21	26	15	408
e	—	—	—	9	21	8	29	17	21	39	41	18	9	6	208
f	—	—	—	—	—	6	13	12	15	21	22	28	31	57	205
Total	3	7	43	103	317	368	593	524	826	1015	641	377	362	250	5429
g	3	5	30	47	257	252	321	276	511	637	360	235	211	127	3272
h	—	2	13	29	61	117	272	248	315	378	281	142	101	123	2082
Total	3	7	43	76	318	369	593	524	826	1015	641	377	312	250	5354
i	—	—	—	—	—	—	—	—	6	27	31	57	62	46	229

(Percentages)

	1200-1300	1300-1350	1350-1400	1400-1450	1450-1500	1500-1550	1550-1600	1600-1650	1650-1700	1700-1750	1750-1800	1800-1850	1850-1900	1900-1933	Total
a	66.7	57.2	48.8	53.4	35.7	37.3	49.5	59.7	67.9	65.6	62.6	45.6	30.9	23.2	
b	33.3	42.8	32.6	26.2	16.4	7.3	5.4	5.0	5.0	3.0	2.8	1.3	1.7	.8	
c	—	—	—	4.9	27.7	41.3	28.2	21.8	14.7	21.5	19.8	35.3	49.1	44.8	
d	—	—	18.6	6.8	13.6	10.3	9.8	8.0	8.1	4.0	5.0	5.6	7.2	6.0	
e	—	—	—	8.7	6.6	2.2	4.9	3.2	2.5	3.8	6.4	4.8	2.5	2.4	
f	—	—	—	—	—	1.6	2.2	2.3	1.8	2.1	3.4	7.4	8.6	22.8	
Total	100.0	100.0	100.0	100.0	100.0	100.0	100.0	100.0	100.0	100.0	100.0	100.0	100.0	100.0	
g	100.0	71.4	69.8	61.8	80.8	68.3	54.2	52.6	61.8	62.7	56.2	62.4	67.6	50.8	
h	—	28.6	30.2	38.2	19.2	31.7	45.8	47.4	38.2	37.3	43.8	37.6	32.4	49.2	
Total	100.0	100.0	100.0	100.0	100.0	100.0	100.0	100.0	100.0	100.0	100.0	100.0	100.0	100.0	
i	—	—	—	—	—	—	—	—	.7	2.7	4.8	15.1	17.1	18.4	

TABLE 27. FLUCTUATION OF SOCIAL CLASSES AND SEXES IN PORTRAITURE — *continued*

a = aristocracy b = clergy c = bourgeoisie d = intellectuals, artists e = military f = lower classes g = male h = female i = caricature

Spanish

(Numbers)

	XV	XVI	XVII	1700–1750	1750–1800	1800–1850	1850–1900	1900–1933	Total
a	6	22	45	36	27	30	21	15	202
b	4	3	14	21	15	—	—	—	57
c	—	9	13	9	18	—	—	18	67
d	—	6	12	6	18	—	—	—	42
e	—	—	9	3	21	—	—	—	33
f	—	—	14	15	42	—	—	36	107
Total	10	40	107	90	141	30	21	69	508
g	6	21	62	53	89	13	10	31	285
h	4	19	45	37	52	17	11	38	223
Total	10	40	107	90	141	30	21	69	508
i	—	—	3	15	12	6	4	7	64

(Percentages)

	XV	XVI	XVII	1700–1750	1750–1800	1800–1850	1850–1900	1900–1933
a	60.0	55.0	42.1	40.0	19.1	100.0	100.0	21.7
b	40.0	7.5	13.1	23.3	10.6	—	—	—
c		22.5	12.1	10.0	12.8	—	—	26.1
d		15.0	11.2	6.7	12.8	—	—	—
e			8.4	3.3	14.9	—	—	—
f			13.1	16.7	29.8	—	—	52.2
Total	100.0	100.0	100.0	100.0	100.0	100.0	100.0	100.0
g	60.0	52.5	58.0	59.0	63.2	43.3	47.6	45.0
h	40.0	47.5	42.0	41.0	36.8	56.7	52.4	55.0
Total	100.0	100.0	100.0	100.0	100.0	100.0	100.0	100.0
i	—	—	2.8	16.7	8.5	20.0	20.0	10.2

French

	XVI	1600–1650	1650–1700	1700–1750	1750–1800	1800–1850	1850–1880	1880–1900	1900–1933	Total
					(Numbers)					
a	36	21	42	228	201	78	36	—	3	645
b	30	24	30	69	101	3	—	—	2	259
c	—	3	6	54	60	21	6	67	49	266
d	21	6	9	6	21	96	48	52	71	330
e	9	6	6	18	36	126	15	—	4	220
f	—	—	—	9	15	90	33	5	17	169
Total	96	60	93	384	434	414	138	124	146	1889
g	72	27	53	288	303	210	40	67	85	1145
h	24	23	46	96	131	204	98	57	61	740
Total	96	50	99	384	434	414	138	124	146	1885
i	—	—	—	—	27	216	46	89	71	449
					(Percentages)					
a	37.5	35.0	45.2	59.3	46.3	18.8	26.1	—	2.1	
b	31.2	40.0	32.3	18.0	23.3	.7	—	—	1.4	
c	—	5.0	6.4	14.1	13.8	5.1	4.4	54.0	33.5	
d	21.9	10.0	9.7	1.6	4.8	23.2	34.8	42.0	48.6	
e	9.4	10.0	6.4	4.7	8.3	30.4	10.9	—	2.7	
f	—	—	—	2.3	3.5	21.8	23.8	4.0	11.7	
Total	100.0	100.0	100.0	100.0	100.0	100.0	100.0	100.0	100.0	
g	75.0	54.0	53.6	75.0	69.8	50.7	29.0	54.0	58.2	
h	25.0	46.0	46.4	25.0	30.2	49.3	71.0	46.0	41.8	
Total	100.0	100.0	100.0	100.0	100.0	100.0	100.0	100.0	100.0	
i	—	—	—	—	6.2	52.2	33.3	71.8	48.6	

TABLE 27. FLUCTUATION OF SOCIAL CLASSES AND SEXES IN PORTRAITURE — *continued*

a = aristocracy   b = clergy   c = bourgeoisie   d = intellectuals, artists   e = military   f = lower classes   g = male   h = female   i = caricature

Dutch

(Numbers)

	-1500	1500–1600	1600–1620	1620–1640	1640–1660	1660–1680	1680–1780	1780–1880	1880–1933	Total
a	10	20	82	124	118	24	—	—	8	386
b	16	24	18	4	—	—	—	—	3	65
c	8	28	24	—	—	22	26	—	64	172
d	—	6	20	16	18	28	—	18	21	127
e	—	—	24	38	44	42	—	—	4	152
f	—	—	16	18	24	8	—	22	18	106
Total	34	78	184	200	204	124	26	40	118	1008
g	62	76	78	56	74	60	92	110	67	675
h	24	16	82	66	90	18	30	112	51	489
Total	86	92	160	122	164	78	122	222	118	1164
i	—	—	—	10	14	—	—	—	23	47

(Percentages)

	-1500	1500–1600	1600–1620	1620–1640	1640–1660	1660–1680	1680–1780	1780–1880	1880–1933	Total
a	29.4	25.7	44.6	62.0	57.8	19.4	—	—	6.8	
b	47.0	30.8	9.8	2.0	—	—	—	—	2.5	
c	23.6	35.8	13.0	—	—	17.8	100.0	—	54.3	
d	—	7.7	10.9	8.0	8.8	22.6	—	45.0	17.8	
e	—	—	13.0	19.0	21.6	33.8	—	—	3.4	
f	—	—	8.7	9.0	11.8	6.4	—	55.0	15.2	
Total	100.0	100.0	100.0	100.0	100.0	100.0	100.0	100.0	100.0	
g	72.1	82.6	48.7	45.8	45.2	77.0	75.4	49.5	56.8	
h	27.9	17.4	51.3	54.2	54.8	23.0	24.6	50.5	43.2	
Total	100.0	100.0	100.0	100.0	100.0	100.0	100.0	100.0	100.0	
i	—	—	—	5.0	6.9	—	—	—	19.5	

Central Europe

(Numbers)

	XVI	1600–1650	1650–1700	1700–1750	1750–1800	1800–1830	1830–1860	1860–1880	1880–1900	1900–1993	Total
a	129	15	30	45	23	72	51	138	33	24	560
b	48	15	12	3	3	12	12	6	6	6	123
c	24	—	8	6	15	12	12	24	36	381	518
d	21	3	—	12	10	30	24	36	57	159	352
e	18	6	4	—	3	39	9	12	9	12	112
f	24	—	2	—	12	15	12	6	15	15	101
Total	264	39	56	66	66	180	120	222	156	597	1766
g	237	36	34	60	35	138	81	120	111	396	1248
h	27	3	20	6	31	42	39	102	45	221	536
Total	264	39	54	66	66	180	120	222	156	617	1784
i	—	3	2	—	8	12	9	—	9	9	52

(Percentages)

	XVI	1600–1650	1650–1700	1700–1750	1750–1800	1800–1830	1830–1860	1860–1880	1880–1900	1900–1993
a	48.9	38.5	53.6	68.2	34.9	40.0	42.5	62.2	21.2	4.0
b	18.2	38.5	21.4	4.5	4.5	6.6	10.0	2.7	3.8	1.0
c	9.1	—	14.3	9.1	22.7	6.6	10.0	10.8	23.1	63.8
d	7.9	7.6	—	18.2	15.2	16.6	20.0	16.2	36.5	26.7
e	6.8	15.4	7.1	—	4.5	21.6	7.5	5.4	5.8	2.0
f	9.1	—	3.6	—	18.2	8.6	10.0	2.7	9.6	2.5
Total	100.0	100.0	100.0	100.0	100.0	100.0	100.0	100.0	100.0	100.0
g	89.8	92.4	63.0	90.9	53.0	76.6	67.5	54.0	71.2	64.2
h	10.2	7.6	37.0	9.1	47.0	23.4	32.5	46.0	28.8	35.8
Total	100.0	100.0	100.0	100.0	100.0	100.0	100.0	100.0	100.0	100.0
i	—	7.6	3.6	—	12.1	6.6	7.5	—	5.8	1.5

TABLE 27. FLUCTUATION OF SOCIAL CLASSES AND SEXES IN PORTRAITURE — continued

a = aristocracy b = clergy c = bourgeoisie d = intellectuals, artists e = military f = lower classes g = male h = female i = caricature

English

(Numbers)

	XV	XVI	XVII	1700–1750	1750–1800	1800–1850	1850–1900	1900–1933	Total
a	8	12	17	12	21	6	5	5	86
b	—	9	11	4	4	—	2	—	30
c	—	—	—	3	4	4	2	15	28
d	—	—	—	10	11	13	16	7	57
e	—	—	—	5	7	—	—	—	12
f	—	—	—	3	4	15	6	—	28
Total	8	21	28	37	51	38	31	27	241
g	6	15	21	25	27	18	16	10	138
h	2	6	7	22	24	30	25	7	123
Total	8	21	28	47	51	48	41	17	261
i	—	—	—	3	4	2	—	—	9

(Percentages)

	XV	XVI	XVII	1700–1750	1750–1800	1800–1850	1850–1900	1900–1933	Total
a	100.0	57.2	60.7	32.4	41.3	15.8	16.1	18.5	
b	—	42.8	39.3	10.8	7.8	—	6.5	—	
c	—	—	—	8.1	7.8	10.5	6.5	55.6	
d	—	—	—	27.1	21.6	34.2	51.6	25.9	
e	—	—	—	13.5	13.7	—	—	—	
f	—	—	—	8.1	7.8	39.5	19.3	—	
Total	100.0	100.0	100.0	100.0	100.0	100.0	100.0	100.0	
g	75.0	71.4	75.0	53.2	53.0	37.5	39.0	58.9	
h	25.0	28.6	25.0	46.8	47.0	62.5	61.0	41.1	
Total	100.0	100.0	100.0	100.0	100.0	100.0	100.0	100.0	
i	—	—	—	8.1	7.8	5.3	—	—	

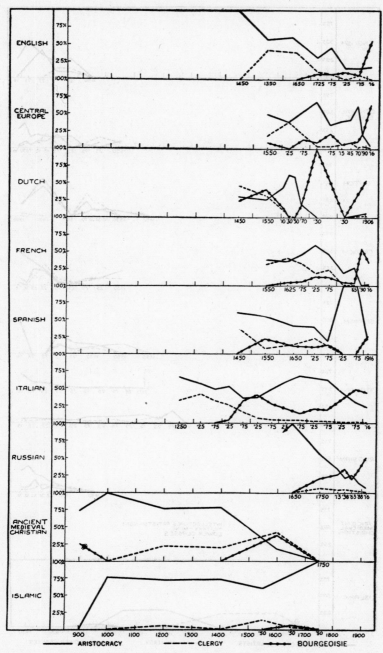

FIG. 18. ARISTOCRACY, CLERGY, AND BOURGEOISIE BY COUNTRIES

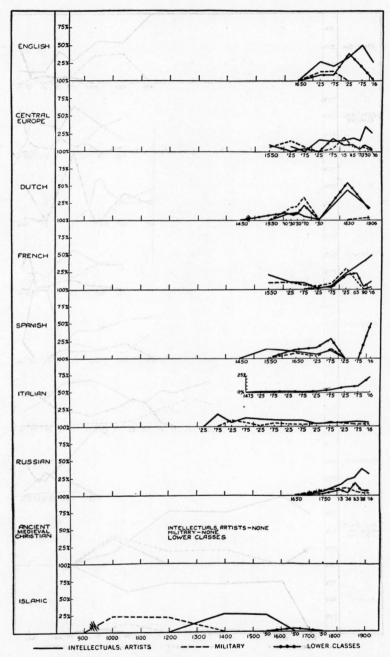

FIG. 19.   INTELLECTUALS, MILITARY, AND LOWER CLASSES BY COUNTRIES

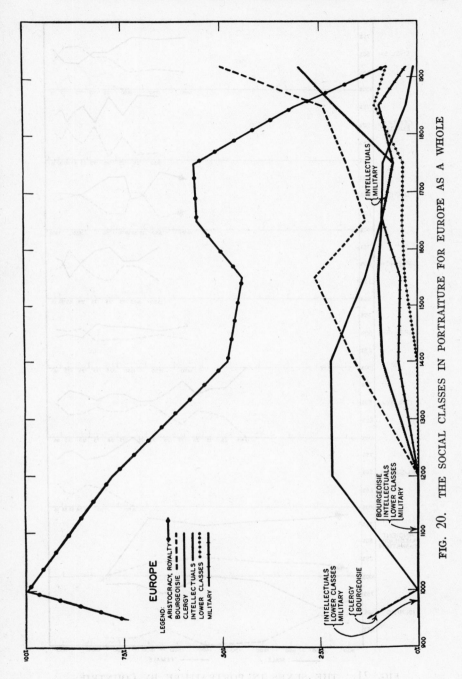

FIG. 20.   THE SOCIAL CLASSES IN PORTRAITURE FOR EUROPE AS A WHOLE

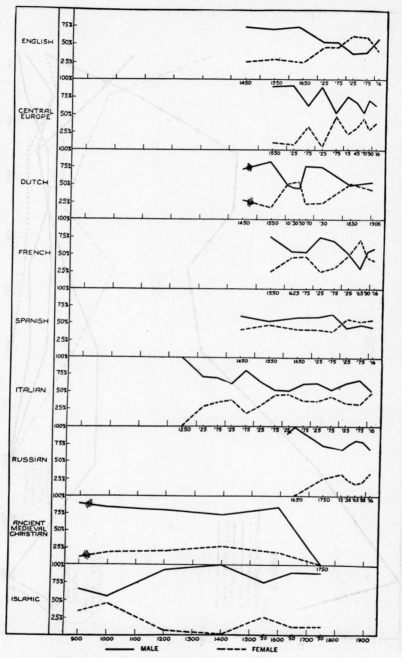

FIG. 21.   THE SEXES IN PORTRAITURE BY COUNTRIES

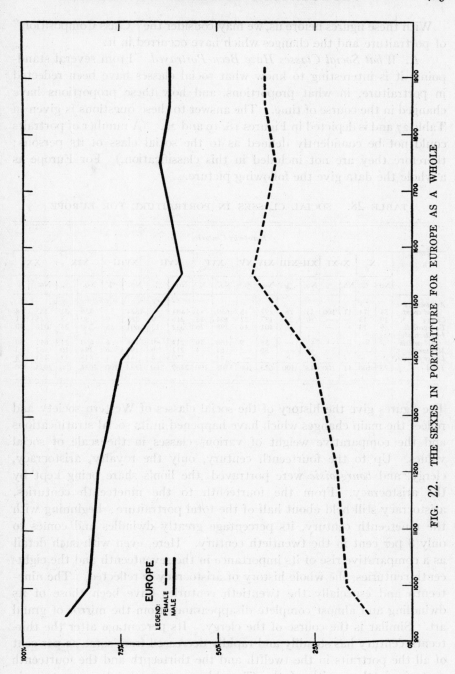

FIG. 22. THE SEXES IN PORTRAITURE FOR EUROPE AS A WHOLE

With these figures before us, we may consider the "Class Composition" of portraiture and the changes which have occurred in it.

A. *What Social Classes Have Been Portrayed.* From several standpoints it is interesting to know what social classes have been reflected in portraiture, in what proportions, and how these proportions have changed in the course of time. The answer to these questions is given in Table 27 and is depicted in Figures 18, 19 and 20. (A number of portraits could not be confidently defined as to the social class of its persons; therefore they are not included in this classification.) For Europe as a whole the data give the following picture.

TABLE 28. SOCIAL CLASSES IN PORTRAITURE FOR EUROPE

	Europe by Centuries																	
	-X		X-XI		XII-XIII		XIV-XV		XVI		XVII		XVIII		XIX		XX	
	No.	%	No.	%	No.	%	No.	%	No.	%	No.	%	No.	%	No.	%	No.	%
Aristocracy and court	54	74	11	100	33	78	297	48	659	44	1404	56	1824	57	926	31	165	8
Clergy	10	13	—	—	10	22	137	22	194	13	216	9	288	9	80	3	15	1
Bourgeoisie	9	13	—	—	—	—	101	16	398	26	332	13	601	18	730	24	1026	50
Intellectuals and artists	—	—	—	—	—	—	58	9	150	10	211	9	186	6	660	21	612	30
Military	—	—	—	—	—	—	30	5	64	4	217	9	193	6	293	10	52	3
Lower classes	—	—	—	—	—	—	—	—	43	3	109	4	141	4	345	11	154	8
Total	73	100	11	100	43	100	623	100	1508	100	2489	100	3233	100	3034	100	2024	100

The figures give the history of the social classes of Western society and reflect the main changes which have happened in its social stratifications and the comparative weight of various classes in the scale of social values. Up to the fourteenth century, only the royalty, aristocracy, clergy, and *bourgeoisie* were portrayed, the lion's share being kept by the aristocracy. From the fourteenth to the nineteenth centuries, aristocracy still held about half of the total portraiture; beginning with the nineteenth century, its percentage greatly dwindles and comes to only 8 per cent in the twentieth century. Here, even with such detail as a comparative rise of its importance in the seventeenth and the eighteenth centuries, the whole history of aristocracy is reflected. The nineteenth and especially the twentieth centuries have been those of its dwindling and almost complete disappearance from the mirror of grand art. Similar is the course of the clergy. Its percentage after the thirteenth century has steadily and rapidly decreased from some 22 per cent of all the portraits in the twelfth and the thirteenth and the fourteenth centuries — the zenith of the Church's power and role — up to only

0.8 per cent. *Sic transit gloria mundi!* Again a very instructive and hardly misleading reflection of the comparative prestige and glory and influence of the clergy among other social classes.

Different is the "carrier curve" of the *bourgeoisie*. Up to the four-teenth century, it is almost unreflected in art. (The few portraits before the tenth century are those of secular Christian pious men, some saints and donors rather than the portraits of *bourgeoisie* as such.) In the fourteenth century this class steps out and, with a temporary moderate setback in the seventeenth century — which is again in conformity with many setbacks of the Sensate variables in that century of a desperate effort to reinforce the dwindling Ideationalism — steadily grows, reach-ing in the nineteenth century 24 per cent of all the portraits and 50 per cent in the twentieth century. These figures are sufficiently eloquent to demonstrate the growing power of this class — the wealthy and the rich class — during these centuries after the thirteenth, its increasing leadership and comparative weight among the other classes. The nature of the class — the distinction of being wealthy — tells also of the moneyed, the sensual, the materialistic character of the Sensate culture of these centuries. It also tells that the leaders in such a culture are the rich and the wealthy and corroborates thus this "logical satellite" of Sensate culture. What will be its share in the remainder of the twentieth cen-tury remains to be seen; so far, we have been living in an age of the aristocracy of the moneymakers and business leaders. As reflected in the mirror of art this class is much more important than the aristocracy and clergy taken together. It is probable that here again the mirror of art reflects accurately the social realities.

Somewhat similar has been the progress of the professional classes in portraiture: intellectuals, *literati*, and artists. This class first appeared mirrored in the art of the fourteenth century; then, with minor fluctua-tions, it reaches 21 and 30 per cent of the portraits of all the classes in the nineteenth and twentieth centuries. The "brain-trust" class thus became in these centuries next in power to the *bourgeois* class, showing its objective "congeniality" to that class, which many of the "brain-trusters" themselves do not realize.

The military class has had a fluctuating career: it emerges in the mirror of art in the fourteenth century, gives the highest percentage in the seventeenth and nineteenth, but it has occupied a relatively modest place throughout all the centuries in the number of its portraits. Finally, the portraiture of the lower classes began only with the sixteenth century — the latest of all the classes. But their share more than doubled in the nineteenth century and occupies the place in the twentieth century equal to that of the aristocracy.

Such is the story told by these data. They give an additional illustration that art is a fairly sensitive barometer of social changes and reflects fairly accurately even such "gross movements" in social life as the changes in the class composition and stratification of society, which do not concern art directly. In regard to more delicate and more intimate changes in the mentality, art possibly is one of the very best mirrors and barometers.

The data have another bearing, tied up somewhat with our main topic : the Ideational and Sensate art. In the analysis of the satellites of each of these styles, I indicated that as we pass from Ideational to Visual art, the topics depicted tend to become less transcendental, less sublime, less idealistic, more picturesque, materialistic, and "earthly." The Ideational art depicts mainly God, and transcendental values. Only by the way does it render earthly things. The Idealistic art — partly of these values, partly of idealized man (the hero, as incarnation of the positive values, so far as the portraiture is concerned) — is bound to render mainly those classes and groups, like the aristocracy, clergy, and so on, which occupy the top of the social pyramid and, in the scale of the values of these periods, are considered as "superior," "nobler," "better," more valuable than the lower classes. Visual art, on the contrary, even in the field of portraiture, is bound to depict in a much greater proportion the lower classes and the common man, and even the negative types, like the criminal, prostitute, ragamuffin, street urchin, and so on. And the more Visualism grows, the more pronounced is such a trend expected to be. Such are the deductions which follow from the very concept of the Ideational and Visual styles (and mentalities and cultures). Are these deductions justified by an inductive study of art works? Yes, such a validization has been given above, in the study of the percentages of the religious and secular subjects. It will be touched when I pass to the study of *genre*. But in a small degree some indications are given also by the data on portraiture.

Whatever are the reasons, they show that in the Ideational and Idealistic phases of even the *secular* art (which for these centuries was, as we saw, just a small rivulet), not to mention the main stream of religious art, the *bourgeoisie* and the lower classes were absent. As the art has become more and more Visual, they emerged, and have been steadily growing, while the aristocracy and the clergy have been as steadily declining. The man hero of the Middle Ages is replaced by a more and more common type of man, having little of heroism or any real halo around his head.   The gods, deities, saints of the Ideational period, are replaced by heroes, kings, princes, dukes, and popes of the Idealistic period; and these are more and more crowded out by the Babbitts from Main Street, and by honest plain peasants or laborers or by the criminal and hobo and urchin of the lower classes.   So far the deduction is in agreement with the results received.   In the next section we shall see this more clearly.[35]

As to the changes in the class composition of portraiture of separate countries, they are given in Table 27 and Figures 18 and 19, and need not be discussed here.   It is enough to say that main trends are similar in all the European countries studied; but in the secondary fluctuations there are differences, some of them of considerable interest for a sociologist, historian, theorizer on art, and economist.   But these aspects of the data are outside the immediate objectives of this work and therefore may be passed by without discussion.[36]

B. *Male and Female in Portraiture*.   What is the representation of the sexes in the portraits?   What is the proportion of each sex and how does the proportion vary?   The answer to these inquiries is given by Tables 27 and 29 and Figures 21 and 22.   When computed for all European countries taken together, the results give the following picture.

TABLE 29.   MALE AND FEMALE IN PORTRAITURE

				Europe by Centuries						
	-X	X–XI	XII–XIII	XIV–XV	XVI	XVII	XVIII	XIX	XX
Percentage of male	89	83	81	75	59	62	65	62	62
Percentage of female	11	17	19	25	41	38	35	38	38

[35] In the Graeco-Roman art the class composition of the portraits is as follows: aristocracy, 67 per cent; clergy, 7; *bourgeoisie*, 2; intellectuals, 13; military, 7; lower classes, 4 per cent. In the Egyptian art aristocratic portraiture gives 79 per cent; clergy, 10 per cent; *bourgeoisie* and other classes, 11 per cent (among the aristocracy enter several portraits of intellectuals; but as these occupied a high position at the court, they belong to and are computed among the class of aristocracy). Thus both Graeco-Roman as well as Egyptian portraiture is much more aristocratic in its class composition than the European for the centuries of the Visual culture. They approach the class composition of the medieval portrait in Europe. They both are also near to the composition of portraiture of the Islamic art.

[36] In subsequent tables the totals for the social classes and sexes very often are different for obvious reasons, *e.g.*, in many cases the social class of the person(s) portrayed is unknown,

The figures reflect in a way the process of "emancipation" of women. As we pass from the medieval centuries, the percentage of the female portraits increases, reaching its maximum in the sixteenth century, after which it falls slightly and stabilizes around 38 per cent. All the centuries after the thirteenth show a notably increased percentage of female portraits. This increase undoubtedly reflects the process of increased participation of women in sociocultural functions — among them the artistic, scientific, and political activities — which has taken place in comparison with women's activities in the Middle Ages. On the other hand, it corroborates the theory of the satellites of the Ideational and Visual art mentioned above — that the predominance of Visual art seems to manifest itself in a greater proportion of the pictures and sculptures which depict woman, and especially pretty and voluptuous woman. A partial manifestation of that is shown by the above figures.[37]

The data for separate European countries show a similar main trend but with several variations in the secondary points. They show a series of waves of increase and decrease of the percentage of portraits of each sex. They show further that some of the nations are more "female inclined" than the others. The process of the rise of the female percentage is again found lagging in Russian art, as before in other items.

C. *Caricature.* It has been mentioned that picturesqueness and caricature and satire are more congenial to the Sensate mentality than to the Ideational, with its serenity and faith. For this reason it is possible to expect that the Ideational art would show much less of caricature and satire than the Visual art. In order to check that, special attention was paid to this point, in portraiture, as well as in the field of *genre*. This expectation seems to be well corroborated by the data. A glance at Table 27 shows that the religious — ancient and medieval — art does not have it at all; that in secular art up to the seventeenth, and for most of the European countries even up to the eighteenth century, the caricature portrait is practically lacking in the temple of the grand art. It is a satellite of the Sensate mentality. As such it functions as friendly humor, as a weapon in the social and political struggle with

while its sex is known; in a number of pictures there are portraits of not one person, but two or more persons; and so on. Percentages of the caricature are those of the totals for the social classes.

[37] In the Islamic art the percentage of female portraiture is generally lower than in the "Visual centuries" of the European art. In the Egyptian art it comes to 9 per cent only; in the Graeco-Roman art it is about 21 per cent higher than in Egypt, but lower than in our culture for the Visual period.

opponents and enemies, as "fun" and so on. Emerging in the seventeenth century, it stays in the field of art with some fluctuations.[38]

So much for portraiture as a class in the field of secular art. The results given here well corroborate the deductions made from the very nature of the Ideational and Visual art (and mentality) and throw a definite light upon the nature of our culture.

Let us now discuss the next big section of secular art, *genre*, as a class of painting and sculpture which depicts the daily and usual occurrences in the life of mortals.

V. GENRE

In an outline of the satellites of each of the two types of art and their mentality, I indicated that the very nature of the Ideational art is little conducive toward the *genre* pictures and sculpture which depict the empirical daily events of ordinary people, their work, their festivities, their games, their fights, their lovemaking, marriages, funerals, and so on and so forth. The Visual art and mentality, on the contrary, would be interested in such subjects greatly, and therefore it is to be expected that with a passage from the Ideational to the Visual art, the quantitative proportion of such subjects and such a class of painting and sculpture would increase.

Qualitatively, the *genre* has to become more and more "common," depicting not the sublimest and noblest and most elevating events and figures, but the common people and, at the overripe stage of the Visual art, the picturesque, and especially the negative types of men (criminal, prostitute, hobo, urchin, glutton, drunkard, etc.). How well is this deduction corroborated by the material at hand? Very well, indeed. The tables again tell their instructive tale in their own way. Here is the summary result for Europe as a whole, while Table 20 and Figure 14 can give the data for the separate countries (see also Figure 16).

TABLE 30.   GENRE IN SECULAR AND RELIGIOUS ART

Europe by Centuries									
	-X	X–XI	XII–XIII	XIV–XV	XVI	XVII	XVIII	XIX	XX
Secular	29.7	39.4	16.2	35.3	18.0	31.0	34.2	45.0	43.1
Secular and religious	5.4	1.6	0.5	4.1	5.3	14.9	25.3	35.9	37.4

[38] In the Islamic art, caricature portrait is practically unknown. It is practically absent also in the sample of the Graeco-Roman art studied here.

I — 33

Even in regard to the secular art, the last three centuries exceeded the centuries of the Middle Ages (up to the fourteenth). But, as already explained, the more adequate picture demands that the proportion be taken not in regard to the secular art only, which composed an insignificant part in the Ideational and Idealistic centuries of the Middle Ages, but in regard to the total secular and religious art. In that case, as the figures of the lower row show, they support excellently the deduction mentioned. With the growth of the Sensate culture and the Visual art after the thirteenth century, the proportion of the *genre* grows steadily until in the last two centuries it reaches about 35 to 38 per cent of all the pictures and sculptures. There can hardly be expected a better corroboration of the deduction.

In the Islamic art, the *genre* is somewhat more developed (quantitatively) than in European art. The sample at hand of the Graeco-Roman art gives about 32 per cent of the *genre* of all the works studied (1135 out of 3540). Thus it is near to the percentage in the nineteenth century. The Egyptian art gives about 58 per cent of the total (458 out of 790), thus approaching the Islamic art and even surpassing it. As mentioned, these are the samples without any periodization. There is no doubt that they belong mainly to the later periods (Visual) of art in these cultures.

As to the movement of the data in separate countries, they show variations in several points, but again the essentials are alike in the European countries. The comparatively greatest development (quantitatively, in proportion to the total of the secular art) we find in Holland, as is to be expected; and one of the lowest, in England, Italy, and France. (Here the influence of the Academy and of classicism is evident.) Furthermore, it is interesting to notice that the curves of *genre* and portraiture go (within the secular art) in almost opposite ways: when one rises, the other falls (in the total art both have been growing at the cost of the religious and ideational art). The rise of the portrait coincides in most cases with a revival of the "classical pattern" while the *genre* rises with a wave of romanticism. As the *genre* has repeatedly been considered by the Academies and the classicists an inferior form of painting and sculpture, such a coincidence is comprehensible.

So much for the quantitative aspect of the problem and its connection with Ideational and Visual art. Turn now to a more detailed study of the main topics or classes of *genre*. The results are summarized in Table 31. It may tell something about the changes in its inner content in the course of time and thus throw some light upon its qualitative

TABLE 31. FLUCTUATION OF TYPES OF GENRE IN ART

a = everyday life   b = festivals, etc.   c = satire, humor   d = dramatic events   e = military scenes   f = love scenes

Ancient and Medieval Christian

(Numbers)

	-X	X-XI	XII-XIII	XIV-XV	XVI-XVII	XVIII	Total
a	188	23	15	146	—	—	372
b	49	6	—	40	—	—	95
c	—	—	8	29	—	—	37
d	—	—	—	19	—	—	19
e	34	12	—	47	32	—	125
f	—	—	—	125	—	—	125
Total	271	41	23	406	32	—	773

(Percentages)

	-X	X-XI	XII-XIII	XIV-XV	XVI-XVII	XVIII	Total
a	69.4	56.1	65.2	36.0	—	—	
b	18.1	14.6	—	9.9	—	—	
c	—	—	34.8	7.1	—	—	
d	—	—	—	4.7	—	—	
e	12.5	29.3	—	11.6	100.0	—	
f	—	—	—	30.7	—	—	
Total	100.0	100.0	100.0	100.0	100.0	—	

Islamic

(Numbers)

	-X	X-XI	XII-XIII	XIV-XV	XVI	XVII	XVIII	Total
a	15	91	42	76	170	98	62	554
b	12	69	96	101	245	133	113	769
c	—	—	—	—	—	21	242	263
d	—	—	—	—	50	42	12	104
e	3	25	12	53	—	14	63	170
f	—	—	—	—	35	42	21	98
Total	30	185	150	230	500	350	513	1958

(Percentages)

	-X	X-XI	XII-XIII	XIV-XV	XVI	XVII	XVIII	Total
a	50.0	49.2	28.0	33.0	34.0	28.0	12.1	
b	40.0	37.3	64.0	43.9	49.0	38.0	22.0	
c	—	—	—	—	—	6.0	47.2	
d	—	—	—	—	10.0	12.0	2.3	
e	10.0	13.5	8.0	23.1	—	4.0	12.3	
f	—	—	—	—	7.0	12.0	4.1	
Total	100.0	100.0	100.0	100.0	100.0	100.0	100.0	

a = everyday life   b = festivals, etc.   c = satire, humor   d = dramatic events   e = military scenes   f = love scenes

TABLE 31. FLUCTUATION OF TYPES OF GENRE IN ART — *continued*

Dutch

(Numbers)

	-1500	1500–1600	1600–1620	1620–1640	1640–1660	1660–1680	1680–1780	1780–1880	1880–1933	Total
a	—	16	44	130	270	398	250	110	121	1339
b	—	36	42	30	28	—	—	—	12	148
c	—	—	4	18	4	—	—	—	—	26
d	—	14	12	28	16	4	—	12	8	46
e	—	—	—	—	—	—	—	4	6	58
f	—	6	8	6	6	—	—	10	24	60
Total	—	72	110	212	324	402	250	136	171	1677

(Percentages)

	1500–1600	1600–1620	1620–1640	1640–1660	1660–1680	1680–1780	1780–1880	1880–1933
a	22.2	40.0	61.3	83.4	99.0	100.0	80.9	70.7
b	50.0	38.2	14.2	8.6	—	—	—	7.0
c	—	3.6	8.5	1.2	—	—	8.8	4.7
d	19.4	10.9	13.2	4.9	1.0	—	2.9	3.5
e	—	—	—	—	—	—	—	—
f	8.4	7.3	2.8	1.9	—	—	7.4	14.1
Total	100.0	100.0	100.0	100.0	100.0	100.0	100.0	100.0

English

(Numbers)

	XV	XVI	XVII	1700–1750	1750–1800	1800–1850	1850–1900	1900–1933	Total
a	—	—	—	20	21	8	3	—	52
b	—	—	—	2	4	8	—	5	19
c	—	—	—	6	7	—	—	8	21
d	—	—	—	3	3	8	4	3	21
e	—	—	—	—	—	—	—	—	—
f	—	—	—	—	—	2	6	6	14
Total	—	—	—	31	35	26	13	22	127

(Percentages)

	1700–1750	1750–1800	1800–1850	1850–1900	1900–1933
a	64.5	60.0	30.8	23.1	—
b	6.4	11.4	30.8	—	22.7
c	19.4	20.0	—	—	36.4
d	9.7	8.6	30.8	30.8	13.6
e	—	—	—	—	—
f	—	—	7.6	46.1	27.3
Total	100.0	100.0	100.0	100.0	100.0

Spanish

(Numbers)

	XV	XVI	XVII	1700–1750	1750–1800	1800–1850	1850–1900	1900–1933	Total
a	—	—	12	30	30	30	27	36	165
b	—	2	4	54	15	3	12	15	105
c	—	3	12	3	12	—	6	—	36
d	—	1	6	24	12	17	9	3	72
e	—	4	9	6	6	14	2	—	41
f	—	—	2	3	9	7	4	15	40
Total	—	10	45	120	84	71	60	69	459

(Percentages)

	XV	XVI	XVII	1700–1750	1750–1800	1800–1850	1850–1900	1900–1933
a	—	—	26.7	25.0	35.7	42.3	45.0	52.2
b	—	20.0	8.9	45.0	17.8	4.2	20.0	21.8
c	—	30.0	26.7	2.5	14.3	—	10.0	—
d	—	10.0	13.3	20.0	14.3	24.0	15.0	4.2
e	—	40.0	20.0	5.0	7.2	19.7	3.3	—
f	—	—	4.4	2.5	10.7	9.8	6.7	21.8
Total	—	100.0	100.0	100.0	100.0	100.0	100.0	100.0

Italian

(Numbers)

	1200–1300	1300–1350	1350–1400	1400–1450	1450–1500	1500–1550	1550–1600	1600–1650	1650–1700	1700–1750	1750–1800	1800–1850	1850–1900	1900–1933	Total
a	2	—	15	22	34	38	63	87	89	61	220	231	382	147	1391
b	—	—	13	16	19	18	96	115	311	489	111	80	93	21	1382
c	—	—	—	—	—	—	—	—	—	8	12	17	9	5	51
d	—	—	—	2	10	8	3	47	51	93	102	210	108	27	661
e	—	—	7	5	12	26	72	88	60	57	46	31	17	8	429
f	—	—	—	—	4	8	9	36	62	118	122	137	51	32	579
Total	2	—	35	45	79	98	243	373	573	826	613	706	660	240	4493

(Percentages)

	1200–1300	1300–1350	1350–1400	1400–1450	1450–1500	1500–1550	1550–1600	1600–1650	1650–1700	1700–1750	1750–1800	1800–1850	1850–1900	1900–1933
a	100.0	—	42.8	48.9	43.0	38.8	25.9	23.3	15.5	7.4	35.8	32.7	57.9	61.4
b	—	—	37.2	35.6	24.1	18.4	39.5	30.9	54.3	59.1	18.1	11.4	14.1	8.7
c	—	—	—	—	—	—	—	—	—	1.0	2.0	2.4	1.4	2.1
d	—	—	—	4.4	12.6	8.1	1.2	12.6	8.9	11.3	16.7	29.7	16.3	11.2
e	—	—	20.0	11.1	15.2	26.6	29.7	23.6	10.5	6.9	7.5	4.4	2.6	3.3
f	—	—	—	—	5.1	8.1	3.7	9.6	10.8	14.3	19.9	19.4	7.7	13.3
Total	100.0	—	100.0	100.0	100.0	100.0	100.0	100.0	100.0	100.0	100.0	100.0	100.0	100.0

TABLE 31.   FLUCTUATION OF TYPES OF GENRE IN ART — continued

a = everyday life   b = festivals, etc.   c = satire, humor   d = dramatic events   e = military scenes   f = love scenes

French

	XVI	1600–1650	1650–1700	1700–1750	1750–1800	1800–1850	1850–1880	1880–1900	1900–1933	Total
					(Numbers)					
a	36	30	54	189	231	219	396	225	249	1629
b	54	36	60	147	201	66	102	132	161	959
c	—	—	—	108	69	191	135	15	24	542
d	12	6	9	54	46	165	63	48	30	433
e	18	12	18	63	102	15	27	15	9	279
f	9	12	15	156	159	12	36	18	24	441
Total	129	96	156	717	808	668	759	453	497	4283
					(Percentages)					
a	27.9	31.3	34.6	26.3	28.6	32.8	52.2	49.7	50.1	
b	41.9	37.5	38.5	20.5	24.9	9.9	13.4	29.1	32.4	
c	—	—	—	15.1	8.5	28.6	17.8	3.3	4.8	
d	9.3	6.2	5.8	7.5	5.7	24.7	8.3	10.6	6.1	
e	14.0	12.5	11.5	8.8	12.6	2.2	3.6	3.3	1.8	
f	6.9	12.5	9.6	21.8	19.7	1.8	4.7	4.0	4.8	
Total	100.0	100.0	100.0	100.0	100.0	100.0	100.0	100.0	100.0	

Central Europe

	XVI	1600–1650	1650–1700	1700–1750	1750–1800	1800–1830	1830–1860	1860–1880	1880–1900	1900–1933	Total
						(Numbers)					
a	42	9	17	60	41	78	168	547	246	1257	2465
b	21	9	25	12	37	36	39	48	54	117	398
c	—	—	—	—	8	3	57	6	3	69	146
d	15	6	19	—	10	39	27	75	39	66	296
e	39	3	7	6	15	60	123	171	105	24	553
f	9	3	16	12	27	36	15	12	39	15	184
Total	126	30	84	90	138	252	429	859	486	1548	4042
						(Percentages)					
a	33.4	30.0	20.2	66.7	29.7	31.0	39.1	63.7	50.6	81.4	
b	16.7	30.0	29.7	13.3	26.8	14.3	9.1	5.6	11.1	7.6	
c	—	—	—	—	5.8	1.2	13.3	.7	.6	4.5	
d	11.9	20.0	22.7	—	7.2	15.5	6.3	8.7	8.0	3.9	
e	30.9	10.0	8.3	6.7	10.9	23.7	28.7	19.9	21.7	1.6	
f	7.1	10.0	19.1	13.3	19.6	14.3	3.5	1.4	8.0	1.0	
Total	100.0	100.0	100.0	100.0	100.0	100.0	100.0	100.0	100.0	100.0	

Russian

(Numbers)

	-XII	XII-XIII	XIV-XV	XVI	XVII	XVIII	1801–1825	1826–1850	1851–1875	1876–1900	XX	Total
a						21	52	99	89	326	1810	2397
b						14	14	15	27	82	377	529
c						5	8	45	9	10	23	100
d						8	12	15	30	63	75	203
e						8	4	7	21	25	23	88
f						4	2	6	7	18	68	105
Total						60	92	187	183	524	2376	3422

(Percentages)

	-XII	XII-XIII	XIV-XV	XVI	XVII	XVIII	1801–1825	1826–1850	1851–1875	1876–1900	XX
a						35.0	56.6	53.0	48.6	62.3	76.1
b						23.4	15.2	8.0	14.8	15.6	15.8
c						8.3	8.7	24.0	4.9	1.9	1.0
d						13.3	13.0	8.0	16.4	12.0	3.2
e						13.3	4.3	3.8	11.5	4.8	1.0
f						6.7	2.2	3.2	3.8	3.4	2.9
Total						100.0	100.0	100.0	100.0	100.0	100.0

changes and their connection with our main topic. First, what it tells
is that in most of the European countries *"the love scenes" have been,
with some fluctuations, tending to increase as we move from the Middle
Ages to our times*. The centuries before the fourteenth do not have
love scenes at all. They appear only in the fourteenth and the fifteenth centuries. This is a direct corroboration of the results reached
concerning the nonsensual, nonerotic character of the Ideational art and
its small quantitative nudity and lack of sensual nudity. Emerging in the fourteenth and fifteenth centuries, the love scenes tend
to increase, with some fluctuations, during the subsequent centuries,
reaching their maximum percentage in most countries in the eighteenth
(partly), the nineteenth, and the twentieth centuries. This is to be
expected from the very nature of our main concepts of the two forms of
art, and the expectation is amply corroborated. In the light of these
data, it is comprehensible why in our day the grand painting and sculpture
have an abundance of the love subject in various forms; and why, in the
field of inferior art especially, love and eroticism permeate them from
top to bottom: erotic movies; erotic pictures; pretty and voluptuous
women's faces or bodies in advertising (look at the automobile advertising,
for instance — he embraces her, while steering with one hand; or adver-
tisements of "swimming beauties" sponsoring cigarettes or hundreds of
other commodities — always the inevitable pretty and seductive girl,
with her unmasked "sex appeal"); the quantity of nude and recumbent
females in the annual exhibitions of paintings and sculpture, the same on
the front pages of almost every monthly and weekly; the movie stars,
posing everywhere; and so on. Yes, the tables tell interesting and
instructive things in this respect.

The second thing which they reveal is that *satire and humor* were
practically lacking in the medieval Ideational period. (There are only
eight pictures in all the centuries before the fourteenth.) They appear
upon the canvas of the grand art of the European countries only in the
eighteenth, in the seventeenth, and in the sixteenth centuries. After
that, they reach their greatest percentage in most countries in some period
of the nineteenth century (see Table 31). Above, discussing caricature,
I indicated that caricature and satire are little compatible with the
Ideational mentality and art; while they fit well with the Visual art and
Sensate mentality. They are good stimulants for digestion (after-dinner
talks); for fighting enemies — private and public; for refreshment of
mood; and for hundreds of other — empirical — purposes. The complete lack of satire in the Ideational art and its considerable proportion

in the art of the Visual centuries is again a good corroboration of the expectation and of the theory. This fact throws also a peculiar light upon the mentality of our times and that of the Middle Ages.

Third, I mentioned that Ideational and Idealistic art are little interested in the empirical common events and daily run of common life which is neither virtue nor sin, and they are especially hostile to the negative type of men, negative empirical events and values. The visual eye and mind cannot help paying attention to the daily, habitual aspects of life because they are common occurrences with almost all the people. The expectation is again fairly well corroborated by the data. Though at the first glance the percentages of "everyday life" depicted in the centuries before the fourteenth appear to be high, one must remember that the secular art occupied quite an insignificant proportion in the total — religious and secular — art of these centuries. Therefore 188 pictures of such a *genre* with scenes from daily life out of the 5032 before the tenth century, 23 out of the total 2499 for the tenth and eleventh centuries, and 15 out of the total 3906 for the twelfth and the thirteenth centuries make quite an insignificant proportion of the whole. On the other hand, when in the nineteenth or the twentieth century the "everyday life" gives 70, 80, or more per cent of the total *genre*, and becomes the main form of painting, it means a really high percentage in regard to the total art of the period, because the art of that period is 90 to 96 per cent secular. In the light of these considerations, the data show that the subjects of "everyday life," with their common run of people, occupied little place in Ideational and Idealistic art. They emerge and grow after the thirteenth, even after the fourteenth and the fifteenth centuries, in most European countries, and in most of them they attain their maximum in the twentieth, and the nineteenth, and then in the eighteenth centuries. (In Italy the period 1300–1350 gives 100 per cent, but this is made up of only two pictures — which are in our sample all there are in that century from the *genre* in Italian art.)

If it were possible — and it is possible if one takes such a subject as a special study — for me to investigate in similar manner the fluctuations of the positive and the negative or picturesque, the exotic and queer types of human persons reflected in the *genre* school, I am almost certain that such an investigation would show an increasing proportion of the "human derelicts" and "pathological types" with the growth of the Visual art (and mentality), especially in the overripe stage of the Visual art and culture. Criminals, prostitutes, courtesans, ladies of easy virtue, beggars, street urchins, ragamuffins, exotic Oriental personalities and scenes, "the

poor," "the oppressed," "the poverty-crushed persons," the social derelicts of all kinds, the socially and mentally maladjusted, the bloody, the
greedy, the gluttons, the sick, the pathological — these and similar types
of human beings become more and more favored topics of such an art and
mentality. And the art of our days (just as we shall see, in its literature,
its science, its politics, its ethics, its philosophy) is filled with such types
and events. The "physio-dirty" stream of interpretation of man in the
so-called science and philosophy of our days ("psychoanalytic," which
reduces man to a bag filled with sex — and dirty sex — only; "the
economic," which reduces him and his culture to a stomach only; the
"behavioristic," which tells us that man is a mere combination of reflexes
— conditional and unconditional; the biological and evolutionary, which
makes of him a mere animal; the mechanistic, which assures us that
man is merely a mechanism and so on) is the same phenomenon that we
meet in our art. The "physio-dirty" and pathological literature and
theater of our days reflect the same quality. Finally, the contemporary
political and social thought, with its social reform, devote to the criminal
and prostitute, the insane, the sick, the unbalanced, much greater attention and care and even devotion than to the normal noncriminal and not
destitute and honest people. And all the contemporary fuss about
making the prisons better than the first-class hotels; safeguarding the
comfort, life, and interest of criminals, at the cost of the life and interest
of the noncriminals; sacrificing the creative and successful elements of the
population for the less talented and unsuccessful and so on — all this is
the same phenomenon which is reflected in our modest percentages of the
"everyday life" in contemporary painting and sculpture. Other subdivisions of the *genre* are neither very important nor do they show any trend
significant enough to be discussed here. They fluctuate irregularly. Only
one thing is to be indicated in passing. In several of the European
countries the percentage of the "military scenes" is tending somewhere
to decrease, especially in the twentieth century. Here perhaps we have
a reflection in art of the "pacifistic" tendencies of these centuries —
pacifistic in the field of the wishes but not in that of social realities (as is
shown in the parts of this work which deal with the movement of war).

VI. SUBJECTS OF ANTIQUITY AND FANTASTIC TOPICS

Of the remaining main classes of the secular art, a few words will suffice
to point out some of the significant traits given by Figure 15 and Table 20.

A. It has been mentioned that the *subjects of antiquity* become a
fashion and therefore their percentage rises with each wave of imitation

of antiquity and of "classical" Graeco-Roman art or, more exactly, of what has been thought to be "classical" (and what has not been in most cases).   In Italy, earlier than anywhere else, the subjects of antiquity begin to rise in favor after the thirteenth century, reach their climax in the period 1500–1550, and then steadily decline, with very slight fluctuations up to the present time.   The curve tells concisely the whole course of the Italian Renaissance from its emergence to our days.   In France the curve is similar, but it starts to rise later and reaches its climax also later, 1650–1750, and then steadily declines.   There have been minor fluctuations, but they are not reflected in the figures and the curve, because of the large periods of half a century and a century taken.   The curves of Central Europe have two slight elevations — one in 1600–1650, the other, and the highest, in 1700–1800 — after which the subjects of antiquity decline also.   In England the rise starts only in the eighteenth century, at once reaches its top (1700–1750), and then declines.   In Spain also the Renaissance was lagging and not very strong: starting in the seventeenth century, the subjects of antiquity reach their climax in 1800–1850 and then decline.   In Russia they start in the eighteenth century and as in England at once reach their climax and after 1825 decline.   Different is the curve for Holland, where they played some part in the fifteenth and the sixteenth centuries; but after 1640–1660 they declined there.   Comparing the height of the curves, we can see also that the "Renaissance" and "antiquity" and "classicism" had their greatest vogue in Italy and France.   In other European countries the wave has been much lower and shallower.   The medieval art after the ninth century (before that there remained a heritage of the Graeco-Roman culture) had nothing to do with such subjects.

B. As to the *fantastic art*, the class itself is very indefinite.   From the monsters, devils, and fantastic and mythological creatures which at the time of their creation were believed to be real and existing, up to the purely intentional display of imagination in delineating such "creatures" not believed to be real by the artist, all such subjects — quite heterogeneous in their nature and meaning — had to be entered in that class.   Therefore the data and the curve disclose only that after the sixteenth century such subjects began to grow less in most countries (with the exception of England, where the top is the nineteenth century) and are still dying out or have entirely disappeared.   In the twentieth century in Russia and Holland only do they show a slight revival, but it is a revival of the "imaginative fantastic subjects," not those believed to be real.   Decline of this form of art after the sixteenth century may mean a decline of the Ideational mentality and growth of the Visual and Sensate mentality, for which such creatures, be they angels or devils or monsters or what not, do not exist.   The slight revival of the class means probably the search for something exotic or theatrical, rather than a search for "superempirical" realities.

VII. SUMMARY

The main results given by the quantitative study are summed up as follows.

A. The data show that art before the thirteenth century, and especially from the tenth to the thirteenth, was almost exclusively Ideational.   The art of the thirteenth century was predominantly Idealistic.   After the thirteenth century the Visual tide began to rise, the Ideational to ebb rapidly, and the nineteenth century was the climax, so far, of this Visualism.

B. Side by side with these big waves, there have been minor ripples, but they are not caught in our net of big periods of half a century, a century, and even of two centuries.

C. This main course has manifested itself in several changes in the content as well as in the form or style of painting and sculpture, during the period studied, which content and style are the essential traits of the Ideational and the Visual styles.

(1) Art subjects have been, after the thirteenth century, more and more secular and less and less religious, transcendental, superempirical.   At the present time more than 96 per cent of all art is secular, while in the period before the fourteenth century the situation was reversed. A slight reaction, however, is noticeable in the twentieth century.

(2) The style of depicting the objects of painting and sculpture was predominantly Ideational before the thirteenth century; Idealistic in the thirteenth and part of the fourteenth; then it became more and more Visual, until at the end of the nineteenth century it reached the limit of Visualism, becoming impressionistic.   The twentieth century is marked by a strong anti-Visual reaction, showing itself in a notable increase of such anti-Visual forms as cubistic, expressionistic, constructistic, and other Mixed styles.   They are not as yet, however, Ideational.

(3) Parallel is the course of the spiritual and sensual character of art in these centuries; likewise, Visual centuries are marked by a quantitative increase of nudity, and by a growth of the sensuous, voluptuous, erotic, fleshy nudity at the cost of ascetic, martyrlike, or nonhuman nudity of the Middle Ages.

(4) Parallel is the course of the Visual portraiture, *paysage*, *genre*, and partly of the *nature morte*. They all increase in the centuries after the thirteenth, while in the Ideational period before that they occupy little space in art, and even so not in the visual sense but as mere symbols of the superempirical realities.

(5) Many subclasses of each of these main classes of painting and sculpture move in agreement with the expectations given by the very concepts of Ideational, Idealistic, and Visual art, and in this way support the whole hypothesis as well as many of its details.

D. As an additional conclusion given by the data and directly sustaining the theory of the whole pattern of the Ideational and Sensate cultures and mentality, we can say that the following "variables" are usually associated with one another, and in their quantitative ups and downs move parallel, or almost so, in their essential fluctuations.

Ideational Art	*Visual Art*
Prevalence of religious topics	Prevalence of secular topics
Spiritual character of the objects rendered	Sensual character of the objects rendered
Ideational style	Visual, especially impressionistic style
Lack of or little nudity	A considerable nudity (quantitatively)
Ascetic and nonsensual and nonerotic nudity qualitatively	Sensual and erotic and fleshy character of it, qualitatively
Lack of, or little place occupied by, portraiture, *genre*, *paysage*, and fantastic subjects (in a merely imaginative sense)	Ever-increasing proportion of *paysage*, portraiture, *genre*. Portraiture tends to become more and more "democratic," replacing the hero, the aristocracy, by the man of the lower classes, *bourgeoisie*, and in part intellectuals. *Genre* becomes also more and more erotic; more and more of "everyday life," more and more devoted to
Lack of the daily events, exotic, picturesque, and negative types, values, and events	the exotic, negative, and pathological types and events

E. All the European countries studied show, in these changes, that they belong to the same "cultural continent," and the main changes are essentially similar in all of them, though not in all simultaneous and synchronous.

F. The data and the curves support the theory of limit, the variationally recurring character of social processes, the theory of autonomous self-regulation of sociocultural processes, and a lack of any permanent and perpetual tendency.

G. When the whole period studied is taken, beginning with the Creto-Mycenaean and Graeco-Roman cultures and ending with the present time, the curves of Ideational and Visual art give several alternating big waves of domination of either one of these main styles. Roughly the main periods are :

(1) From the twelfth to the ninth centuries B.C., domination of Visual art.

(2) From about the eighth to the sixth centuries (inclusive), domination of Ideational style, with a possible transitory non-Visual but not Ideational reaction in the ninth century.

(3) The end of the sixth and the fifth centuries and partly the beginning of the fourth century B.C., domination of marvelously mixed Idealistic art.

(4) Centuries from the end of the fourth B.C. to the fourth A.D. were dominated again by the Hellenistic and Roman Visual art, though there were several smaller, shorter, and shallower ripplings of Ideational, Idealistic, and Visual fluctuations upon the surface of the main long-time tides of the main styles.

(5) Centuries from the fourth to the sixth were transitory (so far as the whole of the Graeco-Roman art is concerned) in the sense of the noncoherent anti-Visual reaction, looking for something new and different from Visualism but not having found it as yet.

(6) The art of the centuries from about the sixth to the twelfth was predominantly Ideational with several slighter fluctuations : in the Carolingian Renaissance, according to all our data, there was a slight reversal to Visualism or rather to Idealism; the tenth and eleventh centuries and partly the beginning of the twelfth were particularly rigorous in their Ideationalism.

(7) The art of the end of the twelfth and of the thirteenth and partly of the fourteenth centuries was predominantly Idealistic.

(8) After the fourteenth century the rising tide of Visualism continued, with secondary fluctuations, especially in the seventeenth century, up to the twentieth century.

(9) The twentieth century shows a conspicuous reaction against Visualism but as yet has not found the Ideational style. Its art, in its non-Visual part, is marked by the usual incoherency of such a transitory period of declining Visual wave and coming Ideational wave. Whether this reaction of the twentieth century is the sign of the end of the Visual period and of the coming long-time domination of the Ideational style remains to be seen. In the totality of the evidences given in this work, I

am inclined to interpret it in that sense.   Such are the main landmarks of
the long-time alternations of the main styles for the period covering some
three thousand years.

H.   When art enters a transition from the dominant Ideational form
to the coming-to-dominate Visual form, the descending line of Ideationalism and the ascending line of Visualism usually give an "optimum point"
of perfect balance of both styles, which results in the marvelous Idealistic
art similar to that of the fifth century B.C. and the thirteenth century
A.D.   When art passes from the domination of the Visual art to the
domination of the Ideational, the art of that transitory period is marked
by an incoherent, impure, queer form of anti-Visualism which is not
Ideational.

I.   The art of various countries, and especially of quite different
cultures, shows different proportions of general domination of Visualism
and Ideationalism.

J.   Finally, in the last two chapters I have paid, to some extent,
"the promissory note" concerning the heuristic value of the logico-
meaningful method in the study of the sociocultural phenomena, as well
as the fruitfulness of the integrating principles of the Ideational and
Sensate mentality.   These chapters show that these principles not
only fit the art phenomena as the integrating principles, but that they are
important heuristic instrumentalities : when their nature is properly
understood and the logical elements involved clearly realized, one can
deduce most of the important traits of a given art of a given period, in
its content as well as in its form or style, as soon as one learns to which
of the main types the art of the period belongs.   Like an algebraic formula,
the categories contain all the important arithmetic figures.   Heuristically,
the categories help not only to discern between what variables in art we
should expect the existence of the functional-causal relationships, but help
to establish them in fact and to decide the integrated or unintegrated nature
of a given compartment of culture — in this case, the compartment of art
in painting and sculpture.   The above quantitative and qualitative study
has warranted the logical expectations and deductions resulting from the
nature of the dominant styles and their main waves.   The contentions
set forth in the first two chapters of this work about the logico-meaningful
method and logical reading of culture, their nature, their heuristic and
other value, now are demonstrated factually ; therefore, what might
appear unclear is now clarified to a considerable extent.   However, this
part payment of the "promissory note" in no way finishes its "redemption."   It will be paid fully and with liberal interest ; and this promise

will be fulfilled. The above is only a first "installment." All the subsequent chapters will continue the redemption. But the reader, and especially the not too thoughtful reader, perhaps, has to be reminded that the payment of the promises has begun.[39]

[39] See Appendix to this chapter at the end of this volume for the lists of the known artists whose works, together with the works of unknown artists, entered the above samples. See there also the sources consulted.

Chapter Eleven

FLUCTUATION OF IDEATIONAL AND VISUAL FORMS OF ARCHITECTURE

Having treated in considerable detail the fluctuation and recurrence of the Ideational and Visual and main intermediary styles in painting and sculpture, in this and the subsequent chapters I want to show briefly, first, that the same categories can be applied to other classes of art phenomena — namely, architecture, music, literature, and criticism; second, that somewhat similar recurrences and fluctuations of these styles go on also in these fields of art; third, what the relationship is to one another of the waves of Ideationalism and Visualism in each of them. Do they occur synchronously, or do they fluctuate independently, not being "timed"? If so, is there a uniform order to the fields in which the changes occur? Which field leads in time and which lags? And several other related problems.

The fluctuations discussed here will not be treated with the same detail as those in the arts of painting and sculpture. Rather, I shall give outlines. However, in spite of their brevity, the outlines will, I hope, be sufficiently accurate and factually correct to escape being considered as "too general" or "superficial." The treatment may be concise, but behind that conciseness is a study of the facts much greater than appears on the surface.

The first question which confronts us is whether the concepts of the Ideational and Visual (Sensate) styles, with their intermediaries, are applicable to architecture as a whole. With a slight modification of their shading, and with a proper "adjustment" of these categories to the nature of architecture, the question seems to be answered positively. Regardless of the variety of the architectural types from other standpoints, it is possible to distinguish the elements of both the Ideational and Visual styles (with the linear and pictorial, static and dynamic, open and closed forms, unity and multiplicity, and other satellites of these fundamental categories) in architectural creations. As to the "content" or *inner characteristic* of Ideational architecture, it is the same as in other Ideational forms: the symbolism (and allegory of impure Ideational style) permeates the building in its entirety as well as in its details.   The meaning and value of Ideational architectural form lie not in its visual aspect but in what is beyond and behind it, and of which it is only a visible symbol.   If, for instance, the foundations of many churches are in the pattern of a cross, the pattern is chosen and valued not so much because it visually is a cross but because the cross is a symbol of Christianity, of Christ, of His Cross, and so on.   The same is to be said of many details.   If, for instance, the buildings of many churches in the Oriental Christianity have one central cupola with four smaller cupolas around it, its "beauty" or "value" lies not merely in the visible pleasant effect but in the fact that the central cupola represents Christ, and the other four, the four evangelists.   In the Visual style of architecture such a symbolism is absent: its value lies in its visual effects and in its success in meeting the utilitarian needs which it has to serve, and that is all.   Behind or beyond that, no symbolic meaning is to be looked for.   The quality of the building depends entirely upon its visual form and utility as such.   Therefore, most of the Ideational architecture is to be sought for mainly in the religious, magical, or other fields, where buildings are constructed to serve these — at least in part — superempirical and transcendental purposes. In a word, the characteristics of Ideationality, from the standpoint of the "inner content," are the same in architecture as in painting and sculpture. This is also true of the "*external*" forms of architecture: here the *criteria* also remain the same as in painting and sculpture.   The Ideational architecture (in any concrete pattern) is marked by a relative simplicity and external unpretentiousness of form; by freedom from anything merely "illusionary" and "showy"; by the static nature of the building; by the perfect fulfillment of the structural functions of all its important parts; by a strong atmosphere of independence of its empirical surroundings; by its inner richness and harmony and beauty, compared and contrasted with its exterior simplicity; it is "solid, definite, enduring," built for eternity, tactile, clear, complete in itself, and "architectural."

In the Visual architecture, the principles of dynamism (catching in stone or steel or wood the passing glimpses of phenomena), movement, "show," change, mere exterior appearance, illusion, and artificiality (for instance, various devices of the baroque to prolong the perspective and size and other "light and shade" effects in their purely visual illusion), intricacy of forms, superabundance of embellishments and decorations to catch the eye but having no structural functions; unclearness; inner plainness in comparison with the external ornateness, etc. — such are its traits. What is meant will be much clearer after a glance at the plates.

Numbers 1, 2, and 3 of Plate XX show three main orders of Greek columns, the Doric, the Ionic, and the Corinthian, and No. 4 is a Roman Composite order, made, in a way, out of all the other three. As we pass from the Doric order to the Ionic, then to the Corinthian, and finally to the Roman Composite order, we see a progressive growth of complication, ornamentation, and "showiness." The Ionic column begins to portray this element of show and illusion and deceit: its façade is all right but its side view is already less satisfactory than the Doric and impresses us as though, after taking great care to wash its face (façade), the builders neglected to wash (to take care of) its sides. The showy nature of the Corinthian order, with its abundance of purely decorative and purely Visual elements, is obvious. Finally, the Roman Composite order is the most overdecorated, most complicated, and most Visual, in the sense that these decorations have almost no architectural function; they are placed entirely for visual effects.

Numbers 5 and 6 on Plate XX depict two Egyptian architectural monuments very similar in their form, but one much simpler and Ideational in character, while the other is decorated externally with rows of columns which have hardly any real architectural function and are placed mainly for visual effect. (No. 5 is the pyramid of Ne-woser-re, reconstructed by Borchardt; No. 6 is the grave and the temple of Mentuhotep III.)

Pictures 1 and 2 of Plate XXI show the exterior and the interior appearance of the Hagia Sophia, sixth century A.D. (the exterior appearance was complicated by the minarets, added by the Turks) and 3 and 4 of the San Giovanni in Fonte, Ravenna, ninth century A.D. Externally both buildings are extremely simple, having almost no purely decorative elements and nothing for effect. They are just cutting a part of real space from the rest of the world in a real way by real walls. Internally, they represent a creation of their own world, perfect and harmonious. They remind one of a man dressed very plainly and modestly but with a beautiful, pure, and harmonious soul.

The Visual architecture, on the contrary, tends to make a show of externalities, to load and to overload them with decorations, and to use devices which through visual illusion, shade and light, foreshortening and other means, give, for instance, an impression of a long row of rooms, where in fact such a row does not exist (increasing the length and the height of the building through purely visual devices, without increasing them factually).

Finally, if one looks at the two baroque churches on Plate XXII, their dynamic, showy, overdecorated character hits the eye. Their Visualism is shown also by the fact that being overdecorated on the façade, their sides impress us as forgotten. The face is "powdered and rouged," the ears and other features are neglected.

These illustrations possibly make clearer the idea of the Ideational and Visual externality in architecture, at least for the nonspecialists in the field.

Viewed from this standpoint, the life history of the architecture of various cultures, as well as that of a certain and definite architectural style, like the Gothic or the classic, shows long-time and short-time oscillations between Ideationalism and Visualism with their intermediaries.

If one does not pretend, as Ligeti, Krauss, and some others do, that these swings are periodical (happen after more or less equal spans of time), or that they are uniform in all cultures, or that they invariably tend to follow the trend from non-*malerisch* to ever-increasing *malerisch*, then one can hardly deny the existence of the swings from the Ideational to the Visual and vice versa. These various cultures and their architectural systems may exhibit a considerable difference, in being more Ideational (for instance, the Egyptian architecture) or more Visual (partly like Persian, partly Saracenic, or European, since about the thirteenth century) throughout their whole history. Such differences do exist, just as the painting of one culture may be more Visual than that of some other. And yet, whatever is the dominant constant "tone" of the architecture, in almost every system the swings discussed seem to have taken place, although we lack the complete data of their development. Egyptian architecture throughout its history was predominantly Ideational. It was mainly religious architecture — pyramid and temple. Internally, therefore, it served Ideational purposes. Externally on many of its buildings, "there is not the slightest ornament."

The architecture . . . is almost entirely for interior effect. Externally the Egyptian temple is a box; except the pyloned entrance, there is nothing externally but a blind wall, of great thickness, surrounding the whole. There might be obelisks set up in front of it, and an avenue of sphinxes giving dignity to the approach; there was one two miles long, connecting the temples of Luxor and Karnak; but these are outlying sentinels. The building itself is a vast windowless mass externally; all the architectural grandeur is in the interior.[1] In its essence, it is a conspicuously "symbolic architecture," symbolizing religious ideas.

[1] H. H. Statham, *A Short Critical History of Architecture* (London, 1912), pp. 21 and 31. See also F. Kimball and G. H. Edgell, *A History of Architecture* (New York, 1918), pp. 10 ff.; L. Curtius, *Die antike Kunst*, Vol. I (*Ägypten und Vorderasien*), in Burger's *Handbuch der Kunstwissenshaft* (Berlin, 1913).

PLATE XX

1, Doric column and capital, from the Parthenon. 2, Ionic column and capital, from Erech-
theion. 3, Corinthian column and capital, from the monument of Lysistrates. 4, Roman
Composite column and capital, from the Arch of Titus. 5, Pyramid of Ne-woser-re, reconstructed by Borchardt. 6, Grave temple of Mentuhotep III, restored.

This means, in my terminology, that it was predominantly Ideational architecture, innerly being religious, externally simple and symbolic. There was little added for mere "show"— little attempt to build for a mere visual appearance, little illusionary device. What there is, is all real, tactile, corporeal. Inside it was "a magnificence . . . the gloomy and awful grandeur." [2]

In spite of that predominantly Ideational order, and in spite of the scarcity of the material which survived, there seem to have occurred several times the alternating rise and ebb of each of the two main styles, somewhat similar to such waves in the field of painting and sculpture. Whether we take one important element of an architectural building of Egypt, or the types of grand buildings as a whole, such waves can be traced. For instance, under the Fourth Dynasty "we find square monolithic pillars without division or ornament of any kind." [3] Under the Fifth Dynasty, and toward the end of the Old Kingdom, there appears a circular column, with palm leaves already notably complicated and ornamental. We have seen that at the later stage of the Old Kingdom, the sculpture and painting seem to have also become more Visual.

The beginning of the Middle Kingdom starts with a very simple column — simpler than the palm or papyrus pillar of the later Old Kingdom — "abstractly geometrical." [4] Toward the end of the Middle Kingdom, the column is again more Visual and complicated. Then, under the Empire — sometime — appears the inverted "bellshaped column." Toward its end, and especially in the Saite and the Roman periods, we have generally "a tendency to overloading of decoration and mingling of various architectural forms." [5]

In the same period there appears a new type of capital, with a human head beneath each face of the abacus. Under the Ptolemies and the Romans, columns become generally more ornamented and more and more fanciful, like the columns in the temple at Denderah (c. the end of the first century B.C.).[6]

Above, we have seen that these periods of growth of Visualism in architecture were also those of an increase of Visualism in Egyptian painting and sculpture.

[2] Statham, op. cit., p. 32.
[3] Kimball and Edgell, op. cit., p. 22. See also Statham, op. cit., p. 33.
[4] Kimball and Edgell, op. cit., p. 22.
[5] E. A. Gardner, "The Saite, Ptolemaic, and Roman Periods," in E. D. Ross, The Art of Egypt through the Ages (New York and London, 1931), p. 48. See also Statham, op. cit., p. 33.
[6] Statham, op. cit., pp. 176–177.

What is said of the column can possibly be said of the character of the grand architecture generally. On the basis of the few remnants left, the grand Egyptian architecture seems to have been more Ideational (externally and internally) at the earlier stages of each of the great epochs of the Egyptian culture — the old Kingdom, the Middle Kingdom, the New Empire — than at the later stages of each epoch. In the Saite and the Roman periods it generally became more Visual than in the preceding periods.

In the Old Kingdom "the architectural forms, though simple, were of the greatest refinement." The period "set a standard of size and workmanship never afterward equaled."

In the Middle Kingdom the forms are already more complicated and reach the summit of splendor. But at its end "the buildings of Rameses III, last of the great imperial Pharaohs, already show heaviness of design and carelessness of execution."

At the beginning of the Saite period there seems to have been a period of simplification or an imitative return to Ideationalism, but soon it was superseded by the opposite trend of Visual ornamentation in an undue proportion.[7]

If this be true, it would mean that the great risings and ebbings of Ideationalism and Visualism in architecture were almost parallel with similar waves in painting and sculpture in Egypt.[8] The "swings" between the Ideational and Visual styles are more noticeable in the life history of the Graeco-Roman architecture.

Let us take the main forms of the columns — the Doric, the Ionic, and the Corinthian — and the respective place which each of them occupies in the Graeco-Roman architecture at different periods, and consider the swings. The Doric column is the most Ideational. It is structural and organic in its pure simplicity; in its pure form it has nothing for decorative purposes. The Corinthian, the most Visual in its

_____

[7] Kimball and Edgell, op. cit., pp. 12–16.

[8] With these limitations, the hypothesis of Ligeti seems to be suggestive. According to him, in every culture and in the Egyptian also, as we move from its earlier to the later stages, Visualism steadily progresses. More accurate seems to be the statement that Visualism tends to grow from the earlier to the later stages of a *great cultural epoch* (long-time waves) or from the earlier to the later stages of a *given architectural form*, which is often shorter than the span of the epoch, and such waves therefore are often shorter than the preceding waves; but it does not necessarily steadily progress from the beginning to the end of a *given culture*. In the Egyptian culture there were several ups and downs of Ideationalism and Visualism in each of its great epochs, as mentioned. But even this cannot be expected to be a uniform rule for the cultures. Sometimes we have the impure complicated and Visual form at the beginning of the epoch or at the emergence of an architectural form, not at its end.

PLATE XXI

1, The Hagia Sophia, Constantinople. 2, Interior of the Hagia Sophia. 3, Exterior of San Giovanni, in Ravenna. 4, Interior of San Giovanni.

relatively rich ornamentation, existed in great part for the sake of ornamentation, from the visual standpoint. The Ionic occupies an intermediate place between these two forms.[9]

At the earlier stages of the continental Greek architecture, the Doric order was used almost exclusively. Then the Ionic order, somewhat Doricized, began to spread more and more. Finally, about the beginning of the fourth century B.C., while "the Doric style was almost abandoned by the middle of the fourth"[10] the Corinthian style appeared. The Ionic and the Corinthian both grew at the cost of the Doric. The Hellenistic and the Roman architects used more and more the Corinthian, and ever more complicated forms of it, until they produced a still more complicated "Composite order" where all the styles were mixed and decoration and Visualism reached a kind of climax.

The Corinthian Order was the favorite with the Roman architects and their treatment of it is typical of the whole spirit of Roman art, in its richness, costliness, exuberance of ornament, and its want of reticence.[11]

Thus a study of the history of these orders gives a convincing evidence of the existence of the waves discussed. The same conclusion is suggested if, instead of the history of columns, we take another element: for instance, the *number of the external columns* in the Greek temples. Comparing the earlier and the later stages in temple architecture, we see that their number tended, with fluctuations, to increase, and the increase was dictated not so much by architectural as by purely visual reasons. The earlier Doric temples were *in antis* (two external columns); then came the *prostyle* (four columns); then the *amphiprostyle* (eight), the *peripetal* and *dipteral*, each step loading the building more and more with the ornamental elements.[12] In still later stages —

[9] "Critics have been unanimous in recognizing in the mature Doric system an organic whole of the most expressive character. . . ." Kimball and Edgell, *op. cit.*, pp. 58–60. "It is the most essentially Greek." Statham, *op. cit.*, p. 82. On the other hand, "We may accept the idea of Choisy that . . . the Corinthian capital was a kind of decorative phantasy." Statham, *op. cit.*, p. 120. The show-side of the Ionic capital is seen, among other things, in "that it is only a satisfactory design in its face view, the side view giving us . . . a heavy and awkward appearance." Statham, *op. cit.*, p. 111. Such a stress on a façade view is typical of the baroque and other "visual" styles. "The Ionic order is richer and less severe than the Doric." H. Walters, *The Art of the Greeks* (New York, 1922), p. 45.

[10] Kimball and Edgell, *op. cit.*, p. 64, and see pp. 83 ff. See also H. Walters, *op. cit.*, p. 50.

[11] Statham, *op. cit.*, p. 142. See also Walters, *op. cit.*, p. 50. See the factual details in the quoted histories of architecture or in any other standard work in this field.

[12] Walters, *op. cit.*, pp. 35 ff.

there is in the later temples a tendency to mix the styles, as at Phigaleia and Tegea; even in the Parthenon the Ionic columns were used to support the roof of the opisthodomus. . . . [Likewise] little molding was employed about Doric buildings as compared with the Ionic and Corinthian styles; they consist indeed mainly of plain surfaces with painted ornaments, whereas two orders consist of molded surfaces with carved ornaments.[13]

The Hellenistic and the Roman architecture complicated all this still more, in a Visual direction.

If now we turn to architecture as a whole, its early stage *before the fifth century* B.C. was simple Doric, externally; and internally the grand buildings were temples, devoted to the worship of deities and other super-empirical purposes. In other words, it was predominantly *Ideational*, according to the *internal as well as external criteria of Ideationality*. Internally it was a temple, "*not a civil but a religious building.*" "*It served the gods and the dead.*" "Luxury and beauty were entirely reserved for the gods." [14]

Externally this Doric architecture was simple even in details. It was free from any colossalism. The Greek artist of that period "saw beauty not in material grandeur or riches but in proportion and simplicity"; likewise he "did not care for rare and glittering materials, such as gold, silver, and precious stones." [15]

The buildings were modest in size. Up to the fifth century "decoration by figure sculpture had scarcely been employed in Doric temples, except in the triangular fields of the two pediments, and in the series of metopes on the ends." [16]

In brief, just as painting and sculpture before the fifth century were pre-eminently Ideational, the Greek architecture was also Ideational in that period.

The fifth century was the Idealistic period in Greek painting and sculpture. And it seems to have been *Idealistic also in architecture*. The Parthenon is its evidence and incarnation. Internally it was still devoted to God but also to the civic virtues, and, to a degree, to the noble empirical values. Externally, this manifests itself in a marvelous harmony and proportion between the Ideational otherworldliness and visual beauty. Hence, its greater decorativeness and visual appeal as compared with the preceding period. It is larger in size. It is more ornamented.

[13] *Ibid.*, pp. 42–43.
[14] A. de Ridder and W. Deonna, *Art in Greece* (New York, 1927), pp. 54 and 55.
[15] *Ibid.*, p. 68.
[16] Kimball and Edgell, *op. cit.*, p. 84.

PLATE XXII

1, Baroque façade of the San Andrea della Valle in Rome.
2, Baroque façade of the Santa Crocé in Lecce.

Instead of an almost complete lack of decorative elements "now, in the design of the Parthenon, all the metopes of the external Doric order were filled with sculpture, and a continuous Ionic frieze was added around the cella."

The Doric order was complicated by the infusion of an element of the Ionic order. In brief, here again we see all the typical earmarks of Idealistic art in an unexcelled beauty, proportion, and balance in the whole as well as in detail.

Since about the middle of the fourth century, the balance line in the rising tide of Visualism and falling tide of Ideationalism seems to have been passed. From that time on, the architecture becomes, with minor fluctuations and reactions, more and more Visual, like the Greek, the Hellenistic, and then the Roman painting and sculpture.[17] Again a change takes place in the inner character of the buildings as well as in their externality: both become more and more Visual. From the inner standpoint, side by side with temples, the princes' palaces, the theaters, public civic buildings, triumphal arches, aqueducts, mansions of the potentates and other secular buildings, "for every variety of purpose which public and private life on a scale of magnificence demanded," [18] became more and more the incarnation of the grand architecture. It begins to serve less and less the gods and the dead and more and more the empirical needs of the powerful, the rich, and the privileged. It ceases to be symbolic and becomes Visual in its beauty or ugliness. All forms of art now —

placed themselves at the disposal of kings and princes. Pheidias had immortalized Athena and the Olympian Zeus and Polycleitos had celebrated the athletic champions. Lysippus (at the end of the fourth century) for his part made innumerable images of Alexander, whom he elevated to the divine rank." [19]

Then came the potentate, the rich, and the privileged. With this change of the inner character of the Graeco-Roman art, including architecture, the external earmarks of Visualism did not fail to appear: great size, profusion of ornamentation, luxury, costliness, visual magnificence, increase of illusionary devices, mixture of all styles, and all the other external symptoms of Visual art.

Sobriety [of the early Greek temples] begins to disappear in it beginning with the fourth century B.C. and during the Hellenistic epoch the Doric order is sweetened in the temple of Dionysos in Pergamon, the Ionic is surcharged

---

[17] *Ibid.*, pp. 84–85.   [18] Statham, *op. cit.*, p. 139.
[19] Ridder and Deonna, *op. cit.*, p. 111.

by ornaments and the Corinthian is preferred because it is more rich and exuberant; the temples of Asia Minor, like the temples of Didymes and of Aphrodisias cover the capitals with a profusion of motives.[20]

"Luxury, love of the colossal and grandiose, pompousness and theatrical display, the very things Greek art had once avoided, now appeared." [21]

All this is manifest throughout the whole of the buildings as well as in their details: in the Roman architecture which "is entirely founded on Greek and forms indeed a kind of continuation of the latter in the spirit of lavishness and display and inferior refinement" [22] — all this reached a kind of climax of Visualism. On the whole

it was more profuse and exuberant than Greek. [In it] the original [Greek] structural significance tended to be lost, as in the later and more sophisticated days of Greece itself. Columns and entablatures were used as decorative adjuncts to a wall or to an arch, where they had no structural functions but where they served . . . to give visible expression to the classical cultivation of their builders. . . . The Romans proceeded to enrich [the Greek orders] still further in ornamentation and in scale.[23]

Add to this an ever-increasing taste for magnificence and size. The result was enormous buildings, like the Pompeian theater (of which Cicero said that since he could not make it beautiful he made it rich), the Maison Carrée, the Temple of the Sun, the Baths of Diana, and many others.

With the Flavian Emperors, 69–96 A.D., the tendencies toward regal luxury of accommodations and toward elaboration of detail reached their height. Their palace on the Palatine hill, their temples and fora, in the entablatures of which there was scarcely a member left undecorated, the "Composite" capital, in which elements of the Ionic and Corinthian were combined, attest their striving for enrichment of form.[24]

Then came again a reaction, under Trajan and Hadrian, toward simplicity and austerity; then again complication, with a mixture of the new Oriental elements. Some of the preserved Roman buildings of this period, like the Temple of Venus, Baalbek (c. A.D. 200), show a use of light and shade to effect visual illusion, and are similar in that respect to what, in

[20] Deonna, L'archéologie, Vol. III, p. 455. See also E. Muntz, Histoire de l'art pendant la Renaissance (Paris, 1895), Vol. III, p. 312; A. Michel, Histoire de l'art, Vol. III, p. 5; Kimball and Edgell, op. cit., pp. 84 ff.

[21] Ridder and Deonna, op. cit., p. 111.

[22] Statham, op. cit., pp. 136 and 173.

[23] Kimball and Edgell, op. cit., pp. 103–104. See also H. Walters, The Art of the Romans, pp. 21 ff.

[24] Kimball and Edgell, op. cit., p. 114.

European architecture, is styled baroque.[25]   And so it went, with minor fluctuations until the whole Graeco-Roman architecture, as well as the Visual form of its painting and sculpture, was replaced more and more by the early Christian and Byzantine types which introduced the Ideational style and made it more and more triumphant until it became dominant in the Middle Ages.

To sum up, then, *the Graeco-Roman architecture in its Ideational Visual aspects seems to have had main waves fairly synchronous with those in the Graeco-Roman painting and sculpture: it was predominantly Ideational up to the fifth century* B.C.; *in the fifth century it became Idealistic; beginning with the end of the fourth century* B.C. *it began to be dominated more and more by Visualism. Temporary and shallow short-lived reactions and minor fluctuations occurred, but they were only ripples upon the above main tides. Beginning with about the end of the fourth century* A.D., *the Visual phase of that architecture began to decline more and more and a new rising tide of Ideational-Christian architecture began to replace it until that became triumphant during the next century. In this way, the wave of Visualism which dominated for some seven or even eight centuries was ended and succeeded by a new wave of Ideational Christian architecture.*

This Christian architecture — the basilica type, the Byzantine dome style, and then the Romanesque and the Gothic — was but a continuation of the Graeco-Roman architecture, not its absolute end and an absolutely new form.   There was nowhere a complete break between the Roman basilica, already established at the end of the Graeco-Roman visual wave, and the subsequent main styles of the Middle Ages.   Contrary to popular opinion, the medieval architecture is not separated by an absolute caesura from the Graeco-Roman; on the contrary, it is a continuation of it, but in a form of a new Ideational wave which replaced the Visual wave, just as the Visual wave succeeded the Ideational and Idealistic, after the fifth century B.C.   Thus far one can view the whole architectural process from the centuries before the fifth up to the present time as a continuity punctuated by the alternation of the great and the small waves of Ideationalism and Visualism.

As to the early Christian (the basilica type) and the early Byzantine architecture (dome style) their Ideational character is shown by both their internal and external traits.   Internally again the *grand buildings*

[25] In this respect L. Réau rightly says: "Strictly speaking, the Baroque is less a distinct style than a phase which appears in the evolution of all styles.   The Antique art and the Gothic art, as well as the architecture of the Renaissance, passed through the Baroque phase." "*L'architecture de la Renaissance en Allemagne*" in A. Michel's *Histoire de l'art* (Paris, 1912), Vol. V, p. 155.

of architecture are churches and cathedrals, serving religious purposes and devoted to God and to the superempirical values. Even the external trait of the comparative size of the religious and secular buildings shows that "however tall and threatening the houses of noblemen and merchants might be in the aspect of the town, the lofty mass of the churches always remained dominant." [26]

When we are approaching a contemporary city or village, especially in the countries which have been built recently, and do not have buildings left from the Middle Ages, like the United States of America, we do not see on the horizon church domes or Gothic church towers looming above and dominating all the other buildings. They are lost among the contemporary skyscrapers built for business and other secular purposes. Among these the cathedrals and churches are overshadowed as insignificant midgets. The landscape and the skyline of the Middle Ages were quite different.

Every powerful religious movement has a tendency to create a civilization embodying its ideas and ideals. But hardly ever has this ideal been so perfectly attained by any religion as by Medieval Christianity.[27] Not only custom and law, but also social economic conditions, the organization of teaching, of learning, of artistic activity, — and even the outward appearance of the civilized landscape, all, down to the beginning of the sixteenth century, betrayed throughout the Occident the overwhelming influence of the Church. The city announced itself from a distance by the high uprising roofs and towers of its numerous churches and monasteries, and in a flat country the extremely stately buildings of the rich old abbeys and convents struck the eye far more than the fortresses and castles.[28]

Cologne's landscape in 1562 was determined by 19 parish churches; 22 great monasteries; 11 religious foundations; more than 100 chapels; 76 religious convents; 106 houses of Beguines; 12 religious hospitals.

Mainz (in 1450) with 7050 inhabitants had 19 religious foundations; 8 monasteries; 7 nunneries; 3 establishments of the Spiritual Orders of Knights.

Worms, in 1500 with 7000 inhabitants, had 5 foundations; 9 monasteries; 5 nunneries; 8 parish churches; 2 establishments of spiritual orders; in total about 1500 ecclesiastics or more than 20 per cent of the total population.[29]

In England there was more than one parish church to every hundred families, without counting chapels or wayside shrines. The proportion was even greater

---

[26] J. Huizinga, *The Waning of the Middle Ages* (London, 1927), p. 2.

[27] That is an exaggeration: Hinduism and Buddhism reached it perhaps even more than Christianity.

[28] Heinrich Boehmer, *Luther* (New York, 1930), pp. 314–315.

[29] *Ibid.*, pp. 315–316.

in towns than in the villages. Norwich had about 50 churches when its total population was more probably 8000 than 12,000 souls, Lincoln had 49, York 41.[30]

At least there was one clergyman to every thirty adult persons. "The church bells were tolled" on every important occasion. "Villagers felt at home within the four walls of the church." "The church and its graveyard were certainly the most decorous corners of the parish"; they afforded guidance to the living and comfort to the dying.[31]

Such was the landscape and the situation up to the fifteenth century. Beginning with that century the grand architecture becomes more and more secular: the palace, the *Rathaus*, the mansion, the commercial edifice, the parliament buildings, and so on become more and more dominant.

Being religious, the buildings and their important details are *symbolic*: in the basilica, or in the Romanesque, or in the Gothic cathedral, almost every part has its definite symbol: a visible sign of the invisible values. And the "beauty" of the whole or of the part of the building is, so to speak, not in its visible form, but in the value of the invisible which it symbolizes.[32] This inner mark of the Ideationalism of this architecture is well seconded by its external characteristics, quite typical of the Ideational architecture. Outwardly the buildings were, like the Egyptian architecture or the early Greek, of the simplest form, free from any ornamentation, intended only to "cut off" space and making no display and no visual show. No pretension to visual effect stamps them. Externally they are pure symbols; judged by themselves, regardless of their symbolic (Ideational) meaning, they will be found "dull." But, and here is the other side of the problem, in these architectures, "Ample compensation for the dull exterior of the basilica was made by the gorgeous polychromatic decoration of the interior . . . for the greater glory of God." [33]

And this can be said generally of all the early Christian churches, beginning with the fourth century of our era. Like the churches of Ravenna, "their exterior is plain. . . . The interior shows (under the Oriental influence) a complete incrustation of precious glass mosaic in the Alexandrian manner." [34]

Judged as a whole the Early Christian architecture "is a self-sufficient style, amply providing the early Church with buildings beautiful in themselves and even finer in their complete fulfillment of the needs for which they were designed." [35]

[30] G. G. Coulton, *Art and the Reformation* (Oxford, 1928), pp. 323–324.
[31] G. G. Coulton, *The Medieval Scene* (Cambridge, 1930), pp. 44–45.
[32] See F. R. Webber, *Church Symbolism* (Cleveland, 1927).
[33] Kimball and Edgell, *op. cit.*, p. 166.   [34] *Ibid.*, p. 179.   [35] *Ibid.*, p. 180.

The same is to be said of the Byzantine early architecture up to its climax, represented by the Hagia Sophia (A.D. 537–563). Even this marvel "externally seems a mass of huge and not very shapely buttressing, and it must be admitted that its architectural glory is rather internal than external." [36]   Its "decoration is drab on the exterior but brilliant in the interior." [37]

It is known that internally it amounted to a marvel, and was "rich and splendid in the extreme." [38]   There it is a world — and a most beautiful world — by itself self-sufficient and supreme — like the internal world of the self-sufficient and beautiful soul, marvelous in its infinite richness and independent from the external *milieu*. "From the coldness and the superficial and pompous spirit of display which characterizes Roman architecture it is as alien as possible." [39]

This Ideational character — innerly as well as externally — architecture retained throughout the few subsequent centuries, in Byzantium as well as in Western Europe, having smaller and shorter swings between the main types discussed. One of these swings toward Visualism seems to have taken place, in the West, in the period of the Carolingian Renaissance in the ninth century — the period which was marked, as we saw above, also by a swing toward Visualism in painting and sculpture — and at about the same time in Byzantium, in "the Second Golden Age" of Byzantine art, soon after the ascendance of the Macedonian dynasty. But in both cases this swing was minor and was soon superseded by a reaction (what we saw in painting and sculpture also, because in almost all the important *criteria* of Ideationalism the tenth and the eleventh centuries give a more Ideational picture in the above tables than the centuries before the tenth). Nevertheless, beginning with the eleventh century, the visual tide in the architecture of Byzantium as well as of the West begins to rise. In Byzantium the churches of the twelfth century were already much richer in exterior decoration and in the use of polychromy and other visual ornamentations. "The exterior of a twelfth-century Byzantine church bears but slight resemblance to that of one of the sixth." [40]

In the Western churches of the Byzantine type, like that of Saint Mark at Venice (*c.* 1063), the Visual and decorative tendencies came out quite clearly, beginning with false domes and ending with lavishness in external decoration, profusion of marble columns, precious mosaic, polychrome, marble veneer, etc. In spite of the great merit of the architecture of the

---

[36] Statham, *op. cit.*, p. 199.   [37] Kimball and Edgell, *op. cit.*, p. 193.
[38] *Ibid.*, pp. 199 ff.   [39] Statham, *op. cit.*, p. 219.   [40] Kimball and Edgell, *op. cit.*, p. 198.

Byzantine Renaissance from the thirteenth to the fifteenth centuries, its architecture was not Ideational but Idealistic, with a preponderance of Visual elements.[41]

Somewhat similar was the course of architecture in the West. That the early Christian basilica was Ideational has already been stated.

When, after the experimentation and transitional period from the basilica to the Romanesque — a style not quite definite, up to the emergence of the Gothic in the twelfth century — the style crystallized, it revealed itself as conspicuously Ideational. It was a notable simplification, in its reduction and reticence in regard to exterior decorations, theatricality, and Visualism, when compared with the later stages of the Visual Graeco-Roman architecture. Its Ideationalism, as in the Hagia Sophia and other churches in Byzantium, is manifest in the attention paid to the interior decoration. This change meant a great deal more than the mere statement it conveys. First of all it means "a change from the external to the internal ranging of columns, or supports which do duty as columns." In the Romanesque, like the Egyptian and unlike the classic architecture, "the column became again an internal feature," and what is still more important, not for ornamental but for structural purposes.[42]   Second, "The exterior . . . was of the greatest simplicity; the architectural effect was reserved for the interior."[43]   Third, it was pre-eminently church architecture. All this is, according to the definition, a mark of the Ideational type.

In the course of existence from about the sixth to the twelfth century, there seem to have occurred minor swings to more or less Ideationalism versus Visualism. Nevertheless, the Ideational style was dominant up to the eleventh century. Beginning with that time, the Visual tide began to rise and manifested itself in the late Romanesque of the eleventh and the twelfth centuries, typified by the Cathedral of Pisa and by several French, German, and Italian buildings, with their much greater complication, picturesqueness, and theatrical decorativeness, and with the reduced massiveness, simplicity, and other traits of Ideationalism. As a detail, one can see in some of these buildings, like the group at Pisa, a tendency to transference — for decorative purposes mainly — of many undeveloped columns to the outside.[44]

---

[41] *Ibid.*, pp. 205–206.   [42] Statham, *op. cit.*, pp. 222–223.

[43] *Ibid.*, pp. 229 and 244.   Color decorations were eschewed in the exterior.   Some sculptured decoration appeared but it was confined to portals, lintels, and capitals.   See also Kimball and Edgell, *op. cit.*, p. 230.

[44] See the details in L. Hourticq, *Art in France* (New York, 1924), p. 29.   See also Statham, *op. cit.*, pp. 321 ff.;   Kimball and Edgell, *op. cit.*, pp. 230 ff.

This increasing tide of Visualism finally manifested itself in the emergence of the Gothic of the twelfth and of the thirteenth centuries — the style which is a marvelous balance of the Ideational and the Visual elements and is neither one nor the other but a straight Idealistic style, like the Idealistic sculpture and painting of the same centuries. Its course of development from the early to the late "flamboyant" Gothic of the fifteenth and sixteenth centuries, which evolved into the baroque and the late baroque, or the rococo, is a steady rise of Visualism, which with the late "flamboyant" Gothic became dominant and in the baroque reached its great heights.

It is enough to compare the Gothic of the transitional period (c. 1140 to 1220) with the Gothic of the second half of the thirteenth century — the climax of Idealism — and finally with the late Gothic of the fourteenth, fifteenth, and the beginning of the sixteenth century, in order to see the growth of the picturesquely Visual. The early Gothic, beginning with the abbey church of St. Denis (c. 1144), was still predominantly Ideational, with a strong vein of Visualism, in the form of an admixture of the elements heterogeneous to the style. The Gothic of the thirteenth century is the climax where the Visual and Ideational elements are marvelously balanced. The late Gothic is already picturesque, overdecorated, "oversweetened." It is properly styled "flamboyant."

Beginning with the treatment of the window and window tracery (with its stages of the "transitional" — possibly the least *malerisch* and illusory treatment — then geometrically decorated, then curvilinear and flamboyant; [45] passing through the interior and exterior decorations, considered in their decorative and structural functions, in their abundance, forms, and inner content; and ending with the whole configuration of architecture, the swing seems to be supported by the details as well as by the whole architecture of these periods.

The later flamboyant style "is accompanied by a greatly increased general richness of ornamentation, especially externally." [46]

"Decorations and carved ornaments of the late Gothic are overelaborated and used without reticence." [47]

It shows "a certain abuse in research," "tormented and nervous forms."[48]

---

[45] See Statham, *op. cit.*, pp. 385 ff.; Kimball and Edgell, *op. cit.*, pp. 282–283; also W. R. Lethaby, "Medieval Architecture," in G. C. Crump and E. F. Jacob (editors), *The Legacy of the Middle Ages* (Oxford, 1926).

[46] Statham, *op. cit.*, pp. 389 ff. See also Kimball and Edgell, *op. cit.*, p. 337 and the whole chapter on Gothic architecture.   [47] *Ibid.*, pp. 404 ff.

[48] André Michel, *Histoire de l'art* (Paris, 1906), Vol. II, p. 523. See there chap. vi; also Vol. III, chap. i; Vol. IV, pp. 493 ff.

In addition, its whole character, especially of its sculpture, changed greatly, shifting definitely from Ideationalism to a sentimentalized Visualism. [49]

"It is an architecture subtle rather than vigorous." [50]

Many of these late Gothic buildings and their details are like sweet confectionery toys, in their overloaded decoration.

Like many another great style, "Gothic architecture, continually on the strain for improvement, arrived in the sixteenth century at the point where it seemed nothing further could be done." It had "exhausted its resources." [51] "From the end of the fourteenth century up to the Renaissance, the flamboyant Gothic did not produce any new principle . . . but brought only a taste for complexity." [52]

Its course was run; in the rising tide of Visualism it could not continue; either a new architectural style had to be created, or there had to be a return to one previously abandoned. This latter happened to be the Renaissance form of architecture.

Beginning with the Renaissance, "architecture, for the first time in her great history, took to looking not forward but backward, to the precedents of what was considered to be, and was in some senses, a greater age." [53]

After that time it became aware of itself, in the sense that it became "a conscious artistic effort, the outcome not of habit but of choice and culture." Since that time it has been, not a collective achievement, but "the work of an individual architect; and is connected with his name." [54]

In spite of its seeming simplicity in its initial stages, represented by Brunelleschi (1377–1446), Michelozzo (1391–1472), L. B. Alberti (1404–1472), the Renaissance architecture represented a further step toward Visualism. *Innerly*, since that time, the grand architecture has ceased to be exclusively religious, but has tended to be more and more secular: the palace of a prince, king, monarch, magnate, the rich, the powerful; the public building, and so on, began to be the form more and more often used to incarnate the grand architecture. So far, it ceases to be symbolic and loses any "invisible meaning" of its visible sign. The visible, visual

---

[49] On this, see especially E. Mâle, *L'art religieux de la fin du moyen âge en France* (Paris, 1908), *passim*, and L. Bréhier, *L'art chrétien* (Paris, 1918), chaps. xi, xii, and xiii.

[50] L. Hourticq, *op. cit.*, pp. 103–104.

[51] Statham, *op. cit.*, pp. 442–443.

[52] Deonna, *L'archéologie*, Vol. III, p. 455.   See also A. Michel, *op. cit.*, Vol. III, p. 5.

[53] Statham, *op. cit.*, p. 444.

[54] Statham, *op. cit.*, p. 444.

form becomes more and more self-sufficient. This means a waning of the inner criterion of Ideationalism.[55]

Externally, all the earmarks of Visual architecture emerged and grew with the beginning of the Renaissance and continued with the subsequent forms of the baroque and the rococo.

Here are a few details: "Architecture of the Renaissance began to borrow from the antiquity patterns of two kinds." First it revived column, pilaster, and entablature in a Roman way, not for structural but for decorative purposes. Second, it imitated the decorative patterns of antiquity — also in the later, visual forms rather than in an earlier one.[56]

"Structure becomes of less importance in its control of design, and is less certainly expressed; the question became, for a long time at least, not how a building was constructed but how it looked." [57]

These statements bring out clearly the essence of the visual nature of the architecture discussed.

After Bramante the Visualism came out quite clearly and resulted, in spite of inner reactions like Palladianism and others, in the architecture of Michelangelo and Bernini and of the Academy, with their "luxury in decoration and ornamental richness," [58] with their intentional Visualism, illusion, magnificence, pompousness, and other satellites of that style.

In countries like Germany, which did not have to any notable degree this supposedly "classical-style" intermezzo, the growing Visualism expressed itself in a passage from more and more complicated Gothic directly to the baroque, whose excessive Visualism needs no discussion.[59] Already "at the end of the fifteenth century architecture (in Germany and the Northern Countries) is not any more a major art: incapable of imposing its laws upon painting and sculpture, it limits itself merely to furnishing a frame for the fantasies of the decorators." [60]

"The façades [are] seduced by their search for picturesqueness and intimacy." [61] A small detail, typical of the Visual world of the *Becoming*.

In the Middle Ages it required the life span of several generations to build a cathedral. Now such "constructions, which demanded the work

[55] About the growth of the secular architecture (beginning with the fifteenth century) at the cost of the religious, with all the satellites of such a change, see A. Michel, *op. cit.*, Vol. IV, pp. 562 ff.; Vol. V, pp. 1 ff. and 156 ff.

[56] *Ibid.*, Vol. III, pp. 467–468.

[57] Statham, *op. cit.*, p. 445.

[58] Michel, *op. cit.*, Vol. IV, pp. 56 ff.

[59] *Ibid.*, Vol. V, pp. 3–4.

[60] *Ibid.*, Vol. V, p. 153.   [61] *Ibid.*, Vol. V, p. 157.

of several generations, were repellent to the practical and timorous *l'esprit* of *bourgeoisie*." [62] Therefore such constructions tend to disappear in this Visual and changeable world of Becoming.

Whether through an intermezzo of the Renaissance classicism, or continuing directly from the flamboyant Gothic, at the end of the sixteenth and in the seventeenth century, Western architecture assumed the so-called baroque style. The mere word "baroque" is quite sufficient to suggest its excessive visualism. "The Baroque style . . . is characterized by a taste for contrast and movement, by an appetite for the colossal, by search for theatrical effects, and by arbitrariness in the treatment of the combination of forms." [63] This definition sounds as though it were intended to stress specifically the Visual theory discussed here. "Art became more brilliant and sumptuous; churches by their luxury testified to the glories of the papacy." . . . "They resembled theaters." [64]

The secular as well as the religious architecture was marked further by illusionism. "Antique orders became mere decorations." . . . The main reason was that "as soon as they please the eyes, by this reason they have a right to exist." [65]

Richness of decoration was pushed to the limit: sculpture, painting, color, gold, polychrome marble, all were used in this age of the *goût de luxe*. All the other satellites of an extreme Visualism in architecture were not lacking. Ligeti rightly stresses the visual mania of the period as well as the growing victory of the *Schein* over the *Sein*, beginning with the Renaissance and ending with the nineteenth century. [66]

In the baroque architecture, on the contrary, this so to speak real tactile creation is greatly sacrificed in favor of the illusory, visual show. The baroque buildings, with their light and shadow play, with their artificial devices to change the perspective, with their sumptuous façades and the exterior appearances, with their dynamics, "sich mit dem *Build* begnügend, das sie dem Auge darbieten, sich mit der Licht-Schatten-Symphonie begnügend, die auf unserer Netzhaut ensteht, mit einem Wort: sich begnügend mit dem, was man den *Schein* nennt." [67]

---

[62] *Ibid.*, Vol. V, p. 156.

[63] *Ibid.*, Vol. VII, p. 253. See also the quoted works on the baroque, by Wölfflin, Schmarsow, and Riegl.

[64] *Ibid.*, Vol. VI, p. 8.

[65] P. Ligeti, *Der Weg aus dem Chaos* (München, 1931), pp. 18–20.

[66] *Ibid.*, pp. 40–41 and 51 ff., and diagram 137.

[67] *Ibid.*, diagram 146. See also G. G. Wieszner, *Der Pulsschlag deutscher Stilgeschichte* (Stuttgart, 1930); and Wölfflin's *Principles of Art History* (New York, 1932).

In its very essence the baroque is the architecture of the Becoming, of change, of dynamism, of the fugitive aspect of the empirical reality embodied in stone.

All this concerns equally the architecture of practically all the main Western countries, including even the artificially, cerebrally severe style of some of the constructions of the Counter-Reformation, like the Spanish Escurial; or Palladianism, or the Monarchical architecture of France, or the heavy and massive baroque of Germany and the Netherlands; or the eclectic mixture of all styles, present in many countries. In all these variations, the elements of Visualism, of show (among them "a severe and stern show," purely cerebral) are conspicuously present.

After the baroque came the rococo, still more Visual, erotic, futile, reduced almost entirely to puerile decorations: it was a confectioner's sweet and toyland architecture.[68]

Then came the neo-classic reaction, but it was, exactly as in painting and sculpture, a change of one form of Visualism for another, but not an abandonment of Visualism, or even hardly its moderation.

After that, during the nineteenth century we had several waves of romanticism and classicism, a revival of the Gothic, of the Renaissance, and several other hopeless revivals, but none succeeded in creating an Ideational style, or any original style at all. And all were visual with a passion for size, external appearance, decorativeness; purely sensual; devoid of any symbolism; aimed entirely at a pleasant impression upon the eye and utilitarian convenience for the satisfaction of economic and physiological needs.[69]

And these "revivals" and "eclectic mixtures" have been going on up to this day, up to the "new architecture" of the skyscrapers and other modern designs. Whether the skyscraper architecture represents a departure of a new — and a real — style in architecture, as some are claiming, remains to be seen. But compared with most of the imitative styles of the second half of the nineteenth and of the beginning of the twentieth centuries, this modern architecture shows undoubtedly a trend toward structural simplicity, but hardly Ideationality.

Its simplicity and structural form suggest that it is perhaps the *anti-Visual* (cubistic) *reaction* in architecture, similar to that in painting and sculpture at the end of the nineteenth and of the twentieth century. Its many traits support such an interpretation. On the other hand, it is,

[68] See the factual data and the details in A. Michel's work quoted, Vol. VII, and quoted works of Statham, Kimball and Edgell, and others.

[69] See the factual history, Michel, *op. cit.*, Vol. VIII.

so far, not an Ideational architecture. Practically all these buildings are secular. They do not pretend to symbolize any transcendental reality. On the contrary, they are mainly railroad stations, commercial buildings, theaters (especially the movie theaters), Radio City, the Woolworth, the Empire State, the Chrysler buildings, and others, serving the most material, the most commercial, the most empirical, and the most visual needs. There is nothing of the characteristic of the Ideational style. Outwardly, in spite of their greater simplicity, they have all the earmarks of Visualism : first of all, their main passion for quantitative size : The biggest building in the world! — this is regarded as the highest praise, its glory and pride. In this respect we witness a real race for the biggest and largest. A real mania of quantitative colossalism, typical of an over-ripe era of Visualism. Next to it comes the "scientism," and "the rationalistic cerebrality" of this simplicity. It is not an outflow of a spontaneous creation, but mathematically calculated, from the real-estate standpoint of profit. It is perfectly, geometrically accurate, measured, thought through, especially from the standpoint of dividends and profit. But "the Parthenon was not geometrically regular. It obeys a very much higher logic and regularity." And irregular also were the great cathedrals of the thirteenth century. To quote :

The architects of the Middle Ages did not restore "in the style" like Viollet-le-Duc. If the choir of a Romanesque church was destroyed by fire, they would rebuild it in Gothic, without another thought. But consider in the Cathedral at le Mans the accord of the two, and the transition, the sudden leap, with such self-assurance, into splendor : there is living logic, like the logic of the Alps or the anatomy of man." [70]

This too cerebral, mathematical, commercial, "scientific" planning — quite regular, almost deadly correct — so far has not resulted in the creation of any new style, except hugeness and a new type of decoration of the buildings. They are the fruit of the "interior decorators" : eclectic, luxurious, representing a mixture of everything, from Greek frescoes to the baroque and the rococo, from the Gothic to the "Primitives," and almost all imitative even when the subjects of the decorative ornaments are supposed to be perfectly modern, like the industrial world, the machine, and, of course, a proletarian blessed by Lenin. So far, there is nothing from Ideationalism. It is, from a purely empirical standpoint, quite a justifiable "cubism" and "constructivism" in architecture, similar in its nature to the anti-Visual reaction in painting

[70] J. Maritain, *Art and Scholasticism* (New York, 1931), p. 53.

and sculpture. Whether, as such, it is the forerunner of a coming Ideationalism, or just a temporary reaction of the twentieth century, remains to be seen.

Summing up this sketch, we can make these conclusions.

(1) Our main categories fit, without any difficulty, the field of architecture also. They help to order into graspable systems the perceptional chaos of architectural phenomena and show that in its main traits architecture is not something incidental, but a logical manifestation of the respective Ideational, Idealistic, Sensate, and Mixed mentality of a given culture. Thus the second installment is paid on the "promissory note."

(2) In architecture, as in painting and sculpture, there are long-time and short-time waves of ascendance and domination of the Ideational and Visual styles, with their intermediary ones.

(3) So far as the short and long waves of this alternation are concerned in the course of the Graeco-Roman and the Western Christian cultures, these waves in essentials have been running parallel to those in painting and sculpture. The architecture of Greece, up to the fifth century B.C., was predominantly Ideational, as were Greek painting and sculpture. The architecture of the fifth century was mainly Idealistic, as were painting and sculpture. The architecture after the first part of the fourth century became more and more Visual and remained such up to the fifth century A.D. So with painting and sculpture. After the fifth century, the architecture began to grow more and more Ideational and remained so, small fluctuations disregarded, up to the twelfth century. So it was with painting and sculpture. The architecture of the thirteenth century was pre-eminently Idealistic. So were painting and sculpture. Since the fourteenth century, the Visual tide has been rising and dominant up to the present time. So it is in painting and sculpture. At the present time, we have an anti-Visual reaction in architecture, painting, and sculpture. But this reaction is not as yet Ideationalism. It is the symptom of a possible end of the Visual wave and of the coming domination of the Ideational wave; but that is a guess.

(4) Thus the main waves in all these fields are more or less synchronous, when only the main waves are considered and in such relatively long units of time as century periods. In their minor fluctuations there seem to be present some "lags" and "leads" in time, when the time units are shorter. But as shown before, these "non-synchronisms" concerned only the smaller waves; and in these lags and leads there hardly is present any universal uniformity as to which of these three

fields uniformly lags and which uniformly leads.   More accurate seems to be the picture of a diversity in these "lags and leads."   At one period architecture may be in the lead; at another, painting or sculpture. In this respect history does not stick to any universal uniformity and prefers a theme with many variations.   So much for the rhythm of Ideationality and Sensuality in architecture.

(5) If to the foregoing data one adds that similar swings from Ideationality to Visuality and vice versa took place in the history of the Persian and the Saracenic architecture, where the later stages of a given style exhibit a similar trend toward visuality, decorativeness, complication, etc.,[71] then the above sketch is sufficient to claim that the contended swings and the rhythm of Ideationality and Visuality indeed exist and indeed are shown by the dynamics of the architectural styles of almost any culture.

(6) This sketch shows also that the swings are not periodical; that the duration of the domination of each of the fundamental forms studied varies from country to country, from period to period, becoming perhaps somewhat shorter as we approach our own time.   But we will discuss that, as well as the causes and meaning of these swings, in Volume Four. For the time being, we turn to music.

[71] This is shown by the earlier and later Arabian architectural creations; by the earlier and later Mohammedan mosques; by the Persian buildings of the earlier and later periods. See Statham, *op. cit.*, pp. 58 ff. and chap. v.

FLUCTUATION OF IDEATIONAL, SENSATE, AND MIXED FORMS OF MUSIC[1]

I. IDEATIONAL, SENSATE, AND MIXED FORMS OF MUSIC

The generic categories — Ideational and Sensate — are as fundamental in and applicable to music as they are to painting, sculpture, and architecture.

The famous definition of music given by Boethius (*c.* A.D. 500) can serve as an excellent introduction to the nature and the difference of these forms of music. Commenting on the views of Pythagoras, Plato, Aristotle, and other Greek philosophers, he says that these ancients distinguished three forms of music: (1) Celestial, or the music of the world (made by the revolutions of the heavenly bodies and by the world's motion); (2) Human music; and (3) Instrumental music. As to the Human music, the famous author of the *Consolations*, and one of the most influential philosophers of his time and of subsequent centuries, defines it in the following very strange way:

"*Humanam vero musicam quisquis in sese ipsum descendit, intellegit*" — "Human music is that which is understood by anyone who descends into himself or enters into himself."

A strange definition indeed! Boethius's further commentaries sound no less strange. He most highly commends Pythagoras (and others) for their rejection of the testimony of the ear ("*relicto aurium judicio*") in their investigation of music. Certainly a very peculiar commendation. Furthermore:

Quanto praeclarior est scientia musicae in cognitione rationis quam in opere efficiendi atque actu! Tantum scilicet quantum corpus mente superatur. . . . Is vero est musicus qui, ratione perpensa, canendi scientiam non servitio operis sed imperio speculationis assumpsit. . . . Quod totum in ratione ac speculatione positum est." [2] (How much superior is the science of music, in

[1] In co-operation with I. Lapshin and N. Evreinoff, who collected some of the statistical data used in this chapter.

[2] Boethius, *De Institutione Musica*, I, 33. See also J. Combarieu, *Histoire de la musique* (Paris, 1913), Vol. I, pp. 221 ff.

the knowledge of its rationality, compared with its practice. As much superior as intelligence, compared with body. The real musician is he who acquires the science of chant by reason, with the help of the sovereign speculation, but not through the servitude of practice. . . . The whole music is posited in the reason and speculation.)

What is still stranger is that this theory was supported by most of the Greek philosophers and was practically unanimously accepted by the thinkers of the Middle Ages and reigned supreme for almost one thousand years.[3]

All this sounds strange to us. And yet a little study and analysis are sufficient to make clear its important meaning. It is no more strange than the concept of Ideational painting. Boethius and his famous predecessors and followers by this meant what I style the Ideational or symbolic form of music, in contradistinction to the Sensately audible. Just as in Ideational painting the visual impression (through the eye) plays a secondary role, and the aim of the picture is to give the idea of the object as it exists in the mind, likewise in Ideational music the main thing is not how it sounds — pleasant or unpleasant — but what is hidden behind the sounds for which they are mere signs or symbols. The music is not in the sounds as they are heard by the ear but in this "behind the sounds," which can be grasped only by the mind and not by an organ of perception like the ear.

In order to grasp "what is hidden behind the sounds" one does not need a purely sensual ear, but, so to speak, an immaterial, supersensual organ of perception, a special intuition, reason, and mind, or, as Boethius says, one has to "descend into oneself." A given combination of sounds, as perceived by the ear, may be most ugly — most inharmonious, unpleasant, unenjoyable — and yet, if it means to the mind something great, for which it is a mere symbol, a mere "symbolic" stimulus, it is great, "heavenly" Ideational music.[4]

In the Sensate music, on the contrary, the aim is to please the ear. The criterion is its "audible beauty," at its face value, regardless of any hidden meaning. If there is such a meaning, as in so-called program music, it is the meaning of this perceptional, empirical world (descriptive music, program music, etc.). The ear is here the supreme judge and it

---

[3] See Combarieu, *op. cit.*, Vol. I, pp. 221 ff. Especially see H. Abert, *Die Musikanschauung des Mittelalters und ihre Grundlagen* (Halle, 1905).

[4] It goes without saying that in order for such music to be beautiful music for many, these many have to have a highly identical mentality, and a similar education in the interpretation of sound symbols (conditioned stimuli). Such a music can be social only in highly homogeneous sociocultural conditions.

decides whether the sounds are pleasant, enjoyable, charming, ravishing; whether they describe well "clouds," "love," "summer night," "dreams," "terror," etc. The music stands or falls by its "audible beauty" just as in the Visual painting the picture stands or falls by the purely visual impression made on the eye by the object perceived. Such music or painting does not strive to suggest anything hidden behind its audible or visible form; it is not a mere symbol for something else; it is an end in itself. If, incidentally, it happens to mean something else, this "else" is secondary and unessential. This explanation should make the meaning of Ideational and Sensate music somewhat clearer.

These two forms of music represent two different mentalities, two different mental attitudes toward the world of sound and the world of reality. One takes sounds at their face value and does not go farther than their empirical, sensate quality. The other takes them as merely imperfect symbols of a hidden nonsensate reality and estimates them in the light of these hidden values.

Like painting, both Ideational and Sensate music are found in the most primitive as well as in the most civilized cultures. As to the primitive societies, it is sufficient to outline a series of the theories on primitive music, and on its forms and sources, to prove that. In spite of all the factual inadequacy, we may grant that there is an element of truth (but not the whole truth) in Herbert Spencer's theory that the singing or chanting of the primitive societies is the result of a physiological law, according to which every intense emotion influences the organs of speech and respiration in a way which results in the production of sounds, or singing. In other words, music is a mere reflex of physiological factors. We may also hypothetically agree in part with Charles Darwin's hypothesis that chanting originated from an appeal of a male to its mate, and was thus closely connected with love and sex. We may accept as partly true the claim that "chanting is a play, a pleasant discharge of the surplus energy of the body," as E. Grosse tried to show. We may not totally decline either the theories of Hermann Smidt, Otto Bockel, Wallascheck, Bücher, and others, that chanting exists just because it gives pleasure, or has a biological utility, or results from the necessity of the co-ordination of the labor activities of the members of a group.

It is quite probable that primitive peoples sing when they are excited, when they have an abundance of energy, or merely because they enjoy it, because music and singing are pleasant and biologically useful. And all such chanting and singing are merely forms of Sensate music, in our terminology, which means that this form really exists among the most primitive groups.[5]

But this does not exhaust the fundamental forms of music among the primitives. Side by side with it, there is an Ideational form. It has two main varieties, the music of magic and that of religion.[6] Both of these forms are in their essentials Ideational music, not Sensate. The use of music in performing magical acts and in religious ceremonies is universal and is found even among the most primitive societies.

Musical magic [and the same is to be said of musical religion] whose existence is shown by innumerable evidences, reposes upon a profound idea: it identifies the laws of music with those of the social and moral life of man, projected into the world of inanimate objects and with laws of the whole universe." To music is ascribed a hidden meaning, hidden efficacy, hidden charm. For this reason it assumes specific forms; for each specific action is established a specific form of music or sound combination. For the same reasons, music is usually given a divine origin. "With the magic chant everything is possible, believe the primitive peoples." [7]

There are the magic incantations for communication with spirits, for curing animals, for obtaining rain or fair weather, for facilitation of love, for help in childbearing, for vengeance, for appeasing evil spirits, for changing or shaping man's character in a desirable direction, and so on and so forth. Since every detail is supposed to have great effect, the incantations are specific for each purpose. The sense, the importance, and the influence of such a music is not then in the sounds as such but in this magico-mystical or religious value which lies behind them. If these values are great and are longed for, the music which corresponds to them will also be great (though from the standpoint of the ear perception of one unfamiliar with its hidden meaning it may sound most ugly and intolerable). It is evident, then, that Ideational music was known as early as the purely Sensate and coexisted with it.

[5] See H. Spencer's *Principles of Sociology*, Vol. III, chapters devoted to art; V. R. Wallascheck, *Anfänge der Tonkunst* (Leipzig, 1903); K. Bücher, *Arbeit und Rhythmus* (Leipzig, 1902); H. Smidt, *The World's Earliest Music Traced to Its Beginning in Ancient Lands* (London, 1908); F. Boas, *Primitive Art* (Oslo, 1927); C. Lalo, *L'art et la vie sociale* (Paris, 1921) and *Esquisse d'une esthétique musicale scientifique* (Paris, 1908); J. Combarieu, *La musique et la magie* (Paris, 1909). See other literature, especially numerous anthropological studies of music among the Indians and other "primitive tribes" in these works.

[6] Just now it is unimportant for our purposes whether one of these forms genetically preceded the other, as Combarieu and some others contend. Without giving here the reasons, I think that the purely religious music existed as early as that of magic, because religion itself is evident as early as magic.

[7] J. Combarieu, *op. cit.*, Vol. I, p. 40; see there the details. And see especially his *La musique et la magie*.

Let us not think that Ideational music is limited to these magico-religious forms. In many varieties it has existed among the most different cultures and has been praised by a host of thinkers of various cultures at various stages of history.

Those who are acquainted with the history of music will realize at once that in the Oriental countries as well as in Greece and Rome, not to mention the Middle Ages, such a music existed in many forms. We are prone to associate with the term "Oriental" music something effeminate, sweet, highly hedonistic, suggestive of the harem, and created specifically for the increase of sensual joys of life. No doubt such highly sensual music did exist there, but it was not the only music, and even not always its main form.

Ideational music existed side by side with it. The music which in Egypt, in China, in India, and in several other Oriental countries was the business of the State and of the public authorities — which was selected, cultivated, purified, and controlled by them — was possibly in its greater part predominantly Ideational or symbolic.

For the ancient inhabitants of the Nile region music was symbolic, that is, it was the system of signs indicating mystic *liens*, rather than an art whose purpose was to influence the sensibility. . . . For the Chinese, music was the same, a mystical science at the beginning.[8]

The same is to be said of many other peoples. Just because this mystical or Ideational or symbolic meaning was given to it explains why it was considered one of the important businesses of the government; why it was hieratically controlled; why the sages, the thinkers, the statesmen — Confucius, Pythagoras, Plato, and Aristotle — were busy with it and gave to it great thought. "To set forth correctly the successes and failures (of government), to affect Heaven and Earth, and to move spiritual beings, there is no readier instrument than poetry (and music)."[9]

This is a Chinese motto. It shows the Ideational meaning given to music, and explains why Confucius himself composed and selected the odes and music which were to be used and practiced.[10]

[8] L. Bourguès and A. Denéréaz, *La musique et la vie interieure* (Paris and Lausanne, 1921), pp. 73 ff.; M. Granet, *La pensée Chinoise* (Paris, 1934), pp. 124 ff., 289 ff., and 408 ff. For the sake of brevity I do not give here either the literature or the body of the facts bearing these statements; see them in the works of Combarieu, *Histoire*, Vol. I, chap. vi ff. and chap. xi; Lalo, and others, quoted.

[9] The Shih King, p. 276, in the *Sacred Books of the East*, Vol. III; see also the Lî-Kî, *ibid.*, Vol. XXVII, p. 1.

[10] In the classical texts of Confucianism, as well as in the historical works of other Chinese scholars of the past, this symbolic or Ideational nature of music was stressed *expressis verbis*.

In a similar way Plato in his *Republic* (mainly Bk. CXI) and *Laws* (Bk. XI) devotes pages and pages to music, and his interpretation — typical of the Greek thinkers, at least since Pythagoras — is essentially the same as that of Confucius. He ascribes the same Ideational meaning to it; analyzes its main forms and their effects; requires that the State choose the best and only the best — the best for moralizing, educating, reinforcing, penetrating, but not the best from the standpoint of the pleasure of the ear — since only such a music should be heard by youth. Similar is the standpoint of Aristotle.[11]

In all these ideas they were expressing what in essentials existed in Greece before their time, and what in a modified form continued to exist through almost all the brilliant period of Greek history. That the early public music of the Greeks was predominantly magico-religious or Ideational can hardly be questioned. Even later on, this Ideationality continued to exist, as the doctrine of the *ethos* in Greek music plainly shows. By this doctrine is meant a theory or belief in the specific expression and influence of various modes of music, as they were classified by the Greeks. The hypo-Dorian mode (*la-la* in our diatonic minor) was believed to express ardor and joyfulness, etc., at the same time moving the soul to feel these emotions. The Doric mode (diatonic *mi-mi*) is an incarnation and effectuation of courage, patriotism, fortitude, justice, valor, grandness, and virility. The Phrygian mode (diatonic *re-re*) is the instrument, symbol, expression, and agency of intoxication, passion, etc. This doctrine of the *ethos* shows that each of these four modes was

For instance, one of the great Chinese thinkers and statesmen of the past, Sou-ma-Ch'ien, writes: "When the ancient kings made their ordinances, concerning rites and music, they did not try to look for a *satisfaction of ears or eyes*, but they wanted to teach the people to be just," and so on. See Combarieu, *Histoire*, Vol. I, pp. 153 ff. See *Mémoires historiques de Se-ma-Ts'ien*, trans. by E. Chavannes, 5 vols. (Paris, 1895–1905). In view of this prevalent mentality and Ideational nature of music it is quite comprehensible why it was the business of the government. "The ancients had a state music. . . . Nothing could be more easily explained. If music was supposed to have an influence upon the spirits and minds (*les esprits*) it follows that it should similarly affect all; it should become a quite certain means for creation of certain states of soul and sentiment; it should become the main instrument of education; and in these capacities it should be regulated by the State as an important means of control. Such was the Greek conception and such also the Chinese conception." Combarieu, *Histoire*, Vol. I, p. 153.

[11] Like Plato and many others, Aristotle clearly distinguishes the difference between the Sensate music, with its pleasure as an end in itself, its place in the class of "sleep, wine, and dancing," and the Ideational music, which affects men's souls, serves as a means of education, influences man's character and mind. Its value is not in its audible pleasure, but in the things which lie behind the sounds, like the Lydian music and grief and "contraction of the soul"; or courage and firmness, and the Doric music; or enthusiasm, and the Phrygian music, and so on. *Politics*, 1339a–1340b.

perceived, interpreted, and estimated not for and by their audible sounds, but for and by the values of which these sounds were the mere symbols.[12]

All this is but another way of expressing Boethius's definition of music as that which is understood by anyone who descends into himself, and for which the testimony of the ear is unessential or secondary. As a matter of fact, Boethius did not invent this interpretation, but merely formulated what was the general conception of his great inspirer, Pythagoras, and subsequent great Greek thinkers.

Though the concepts of Ideational and Sensate music are now sufficiently clear, let us take the predominant form of medieval music, the plain chant and more specifically the Gregorian chant, in order to clarify the difference still more adequately. Many readers probably know that the plain chant was not only the main music in the Middle Ages, but almost the only great music that existed. All the other forms were absorbed or eliminated by it. "During centuries it was the only music known, practiced, and taught." [13]

Anyone can make an interesting experiment. Take nonspecialists in music and non-Catholic clergymen; take contemporaries, whether farmers, laborers, college students, college professors, journalists, scientists, etc. Play the records of the Gregorian chant on a phonograph without telling what it is, and then ask the listeners whether they like it or not. I venture to say that at least 95, if not 100, per cent would answer negatively. And in a sense they could not be blamed. Because, from the standpoint of a sensually audible criterion, the chant is no music at all; it is something queer; unenjoyable, primitive, dry; in brief, it has none of the earmarks of what we are accustomed to style music — neither measure, nor harmony, nor polyphony.

From the standpoint of melody, the plain chant seems to contradict every common sense. . . . It has a very mediocre respect for words and their rhythmic disposition. . . . (It divides the words and phrases without any regard for their sense and unity.) Another queerness — there are vocalisms in it (which again go contrary to every rule of music).[14]

These defects are already sufficiently enormous. But they are not all and not the most apparent. . . . This music is disconcerting. It is devoid of everything that constitutes our musical art. It ignores measure. It does

---

[12] For that, see the excellent work of H. Abert, *Die Lehre vom Ethos in der Griechische Musik* (Leipzig, 1899).

[13] Combarieu, *Histoire*, Vol. I, p. 254.

[14] In its predecessor, the Ambrosian chant, there were sometimes as many as 332 notes to one syllable. See C. Lalo, *Esquisse*, quoted p. 282, and "Ambrosien" in *Dictionnaire d'archéologie chrétienne*, col. 1368.

not care at all, or very rarely, for what is styled "expression." . . . It does not have any indicated tempo. It does not have the advantages of the nuances of intensity (*forte, piano*); the tones it employs are practically unrealizable; also it does not make any transposition; it permits the basso to sing all that is written in the seventh tone! Finally, does this music give at least enjoyment to the ear? That is very doubtful. . . . We can add that it is unfit for any audience (concert hall). It was not made to be listened to. In the church there were not meant to be present any listeners, but only the performers. All this means that the plain chant is . . . in opposition to all our ideas and all our habits. In brief: it is anti-musical." [15]

Such is this music. It has nothing musical in the sense of Sensate music. But is it indeed of purely negative value? If one tried to say that, he would have an unconquerable difficulty in explaining why and how it was able to be not only the supreme, but the only grand music in the whole Western Christian world for almost a thousand years. It is absolutely incomprehensible that a purely negative value could exist, dominate, and be performed unquestioned for such a length of time and on such a vast "cultural continent." And many other — no less important — difficulties will beset the partisans of such an answer. All these unconquerable contradictions indicate that the answer is wrong. And it is wrong, indeed. Its main mistake is that it applies to Ideational music the criterion of perfection of Sensate music, a perfectly wrong procedure which leads to an absurd solution. The point is that the plain chant is one of the most conspicuous, perhaps even the *most* conspicuous, pure, and the most characteristic example of Ideational music. When this is understood, then, it will appear as a marvel. Let me continue to quote Combarieu, who does not have in view the proposed theory of two types of music, but who, like almost all the competent historians of music, does not fail to put in his own terminology quite clearly what I mean by Ideational music. After the seemingly negative estimate of the plain chant, Combarieu asks:

Does all this mean that its "originality" is purely negative? On the contrary, it is admirable. Enumerating all the embellishments of which the plain chant is voluntarily and conscientiously devoid, we . . . were doing that in order to stress the following proposition: the plain chant is above all forms of expression of profane art because it is connected with such a disposition of

---

[15] Combarieu, *Histoire*, Vol. I, pp. 261–262. One can add to this that, in spite of slightly different "modes," its lack of expression goes so far as such different and opposite feelings and words, as *Kyrie Eleison, Gloria, Agnus Dei* are sung almost without any difference in tempo, intensity, mood, and melody. This is to have the same music for funeral processions and merry dancing.

soul which itself is above all the [empirical] sentiments in which the musical expression takes habitually its place.   Perhaps it would be too much to say that the plain chant is mystic and that it has a kind of spiritual richness, where the followers of the profane, viewing the matter from a purely exterior stand-point, see in it but an apparent poverty.   To say this would be to ignore its fineness and variety (because in fact it is not dry, not abstract, and not inca-pable of touching and of impressing). . . .   It is an admirable expression of Christian idealism. . . .   It is serene.   It is a triumph of pure form. . . . It is an epoch.[16]

These statements are sufficient to show the Ideational nature of the dominant medieval music and to clarify still more the concept of the Ideational and Sensate forms of music.   As a final stroke to this clari-fication, let me remind you of the fact that practically any one of us has, knows, and appreciates some forms — though perhaps neither pure nor sublime — of Ideational music, in spite of the fact that, as we shall see later, we are brought up and live in an epoch of the predominance of Sensate music.   Indeed most of us like, love, and adore the music of our national anthem, not because it is particularly musical from the stand-point of the ear, but because it is a symbol of a great value — our coun-try, its glory, welfare, honor, virtue — which is hidden and enveloped in the more than mediocre (from the sensual standpoint) music of the anthem.   The same is to be said of many religious hymns of our church, if we are earnest believers, or of the songs of our college, our fraternity, our "gang," which sound quite flat to the ear of an outsider who does not comprehend the precious values associated with them.   And yet, to the "insider" they are "heavenly"; they touch and move him to the depths of his soul, just on account of their hidden values.   More than that. Almost all of us have a pet tune of two or three notes, or sometimes just a silly and nonsensical combination of sounds, with or without words, which we love and appreciate very highly.   Why?   Not because it is sensually beautiful, but because it is associated with some very im-portant moment of our life, perhaps, for instance, with the first kiss, or love, or achievement of some importance, etc.   Therefore the nonsen-

---

[16] *Ibid.*, Vol. I, pp. 262 ff. and 254.   It is "the art in which the early Christian values are best expressed and embodied," says another historian of music.   C. Gray, *The History of Music* (London and New York, 1928), p. 23.   All this is clearly expressed by St. Augustine and other Church Fathers.   St. Augustine, who before his conversion was an outstanding representative of the pagan culture, shows the inner struggle for and against Ideational music and ends with its acceptance.   "I am moved, not with the singing, but with the things sung," is an excellent formula for Ideational music.   See *Confessions*, Bk. X, chap. xxxiii, pp. 234 ff. in Everyman's Library ed.   See also H. Abert, *Die Musikanschauung des Mittelalters;* C. Lalo, *Esquisse*, quoted, pp. 282-283.

sical sound or tune, comprehensible only to us, and possibly to a few others who were also participants in the event, is an incarnation of this value and therefore it is beautiful, so far as we are concerned. To an outsider it is just nonsense and a silly nuisance, or causes wonder that So-and-so should enjoy such nonsense or ugliness. Of course such music is not necessarily Ideational; in most cases it is just antisensual, something similar to antivisual painting. Nevertheless, it gives an idea of Ideational music.

Sensate music is hedonistic in its nature. It has its *raison d'être* only as much and as long as it has its sensual beauty (like a woman physically beautiful, but mentally flat, who is appreciated so long as she keeps her beauty — physical loveliness gone, she becomes uninteresting, lifeless, boring). If the sounds are pleasing, it is good music. If they are not, it is poor music.

Ideational music, in its pure form, is quite opposite to that. It is not tied to sounds. These can be sensually beautiful or ugly; queer or flat; they are unessential to the beauty of this music. What is important is the beauty of the inner values, for which such music or sounds stand. If this inner beauty is great, its vehicle may be any sound, even to the ugliest one. Despite that, though only "ugly" to the outsider, such music is the greatest of all to the "insider."

Innerly its purest form is when it is "an audible sign for inaudible, superempirical, and transcendental values," like the values of religion. Its less pure form is when the values are not entirely transcendental but half-empirical and half-transcendental. Such, for instance, are Beethoven's Destiny, "the Gladness that such be of music," the *Weltgeist*, the tragedy, in the Greek sense, the great moral, social, and scientific values far above the philistine and empirical system of values; or something like Richard Wagner's "supreme ecstasy of the consciousness of Infinity," or what is stated in the motto: *universalia ante rem;* and so on.

As in the field of painting, sculpture, and architecture, there are *Mixed forms of music:* one of the most important variety is the *Idealistic* and the *cubistic* music, corresponding to the nonvisual style of painting.

In the *Idealistic* music the Ideational values are perfectly blended with sensual beauty. Such, for instance, are many compositions of Palestrina, of Bach, of Beethoven. They are neither quite Sensate, like many sensually beautiful musical pieces, nor quite Ideational, like the Gregorian chants.

Similar gradations are given in the Sensate music, from the purest to the impure, passing into Mixed. In practical reality, the Ideational and Sensate forms of music not always, and perhaps rarely, are heard in their pure forms. More often they are mixed together in some proportion in the same piece of music. And the whole music of any people at any time represents also a mixture and coexistence of these two forms. Of the general characteristics associated with each of the two types of music, the following can be mentioned.

A. Ideational music tends to be "inner," while the Sensate is inclined to be theatrical and external. Being "inner," the Ideational music does not need either impressive technical means or any external impressiveness aimed to "hit," to "stun," to impress sensationally. No "smartness" is necessary to it. It is like the silent communion of a soul with God. It can achieve its purpose with the simplest means. Therefore it is not intended for popularity, for success, for public approval; nor to be considered the biggest, the loudest, the best selling. Neither does it demand enormous choruses, concert halls, advertising, applause, etc. Take the Gregorian or the Ambrosian chants as the purest form of Ideational music. How small and simple, then, was its technical apparatus. The Roman *Schola* had, in the time of St. Gregory, only seven singers. Later on, with all the luxury of the Papal Sistine Chapel, there were hardly more than thirty-seven singers, which number was reduced to twenty-four in 1565 (the year of Palestrina's *Mass of the Pope Marcel*).[17] No orchestra; no instrumental means. In an ordinary monastery or church, the singers and means to perform the chants were still more meager and simple. Even if we take, as we shall later on, the mixed Ideational Sensate music in its sublime and noble forms, where the Ideationalism is still considerable and Sensateness is of a sublime type, like the orchestras of Bach, Beethoven, Haydn, Handel, Mozart, and compare them with the noblest forms of the predominantly Sensate music, be it Wagner, Berlioz, or Mahler, we cannot fail to see that these latter employed means enormously larger, more varied, more theatrical, more complex, than the former. The Sensate music in its growth, and the Ideational in its retreat, have been parallel during the last few centuries with the growth of the theatricalness, the bigger and

---

[17] Berlioz summed this up well after his visit to St. Peter's in Rome. "Immense, sublime . . . crushing . . . terrifying (*écrasant*)! I am terrified. These pictures, these statues, these columns, this architecture of the giants; all this is but the body of the monument . . . music is the soul. . . . But where is the organ?" He expected to find an enormous organ. Instead he found a mere harmonium "sur des roulettes." He expected to find an enormous chorus, whose members "have to be counted by thousands." Instead the chorus contained only eighteen members on ordinary days, and thirty-two for solemn festivals! J. Combarieu, *Histoire*, Vol. I, p. 121.

bigger choruses, orchestras, music halls, until they created such a "marvelous" *chef d'œuvre* as Radio City — the largest amusement center in the world, with the largest orchestras, presenting the music of crooners, of jazz, contaminated sometimes by the insertion of the "light forms" of "classical music" profaned and badly played. We shall see that such things have happened many times in the past. Verily "history repeats itself."

Sensate music cannot, however, be blamed for its theatricalness, its bent to stun, to be "smart," to be a sensation, and for these purposes to utilize anything that may be useful — the deadening quantity and the tricks. It cannot be blamed for all that because it is its very nature. It has to be interesting, enjoyable, entertaining, successful, popular. Otherwise it will not exist at all: it cannot rely upon the quality of Ideational music, since it does not have it. It has, so to speak, to stand upon its own feet for its sensual impression. If it cannot, its existence is ended.

This difference shows itself not only in the quantity of the technical means employed by each type of music, but in many other traits. The Gregorian chants use no instrumental accompaniment; only human voices. And these voices sing in unison: there is no polyphony. And the melody is almost all within one octave. What a poverty of means, indeed! No beautification! And such asceticism was due not to chance or "primitiveness" but was conscientiously and intentionally introduced through deliberate elimination of any sensual beauty.

The noblest forms of the Mixed music, like that of Palestrina, Monteverde, Mozart, Beethoven, Bach, and some other classics, use naturally richer and more varied technical means. And yet, when compared with the Wagnerian, or Berliozian, or Mahlerian, or Richard Straussian musical creations, the scale of the voices, the chromatics, and dozens of other devices used in these are incomparably greater and richer. They use and abuse any means which can increase the sensual effects, and in this quest they naturally turn to those which also are sensate: be it massing of voices; their enormous range; their modulations; all kinds of consonances, and especially dissonances; chromatics; contrasts of rhythms, intensity, etc.

In the low-grade Sensate music, all this is evident to anybody who attends movies, vaudeville, and other musical entertainments. There are massed on the largest scale the most diversified methods to produce the "richest, loudest, and biggest in the world."

B. Ideational music tends to be and is comparatively *pure* in its style, meaning by purity its inner self-consistency and the elimination of everything that does not belong to it. The Sensate music has to be the opposite to that; it is not and cannot afford to be pure. Since Ideational music is for an "inner" use only or mainly, it does not need any lipsticks and powder and other "beautifications." It does not strive to captivate the public; it does not seek popularity and success; therefore it need not embellish itself with all the bric-a-brac which helps to impress, to captivate the public, and to make itself "popular" (not to mention, profitable). Sensate music has to do all this. It is like a movie "star": as long as it captivates it lives; as soon as the charms are lacking, nobody employs it. It is in its nature to seek popularity; to adapt itself to all the fancies and tastes of the large masses — or those who pay — and to make the front page and "fame" and "glory"! Therefore it has to contaminate itself with all the tricks necessary for a "success." It has to be entertaining. In its lowest forms, in the vaudevilles, musical comedy, the heterogeneity of the styles, means, forms, colors interwoven into the music is self-evident and unlimited, from classical music to jazz, dancing, athletics, comedy actors, magicians, and what not. All this is further complicated by light effects, scenery effects, sound effects, and even by the sale of ice cream and candies and nuts for the unoccupied mouths of the listeners. The same is true of the musical-sound movies where all this is perhaps still more exaggerated. In brief, the great Ideational music is almost ascetic purity. The great Sensate music is impurity, a Mixture, a bazaar, where anything "popular" can be found. The intermediary forms occupy intermediary positions. Palestrina, Vittoria, and Orlando di Lasso, Bach, Handel, Mozart, and Beethoven, all have a considerable purity of style (because their music is Idealistic in greater part); but it is not so "pure" as that of the Gregorian chants. It has already an admixture of the noblest music with elements heterogeneous to the main theme. When you come to the greatest stage manager of the nineteenth century, Richard Wagner, we find anything but purity: the very idea of the Wagnerian musical drama is mixture: of music, of poetry, of dancing, of stage, with all the imaginable tricks and effects and stunts; of popular topics and legends. In brief, it is the most magnificent incarnation of impurity, in the noblest forms of Sensate art.

C. Ideational music, being "inner," does not force its author or creator to protect his rights, insure his name and authorship. Since it is not music for the listeners but a communion of a soul with itself or its god, there is no motive for all that. In the Sensate music all this is inevitable. It has to be "individualistic."

D. Since Ideational music is an audible sign for inaudible great values, these values are and have to be, ordinarily, the values of a collectivity. Purely individual values are too weak, too fragile and uncertain to be great. Only the values that are approved, generated, and sanctified by collectivity — and by that of several generations — are usually the great values and appear such. This explains why Ideational music is produced mainly in a society where the values are not atomized, and are unanimously recognized as such, without any particularism, singularism, party division, and individualism. In other words, the grand Ideational music has to have a fairly homogeneous society mentally; otherwise its "audible signs" would be incomprehensible and as such unrecognized. For Sensate music all this is unnecessary. It is music for a heterogeneous market, just for a buyer. Besides, it appeals to the ear, and to be pleasant for the ear is much easier than to be great ideationally. This is another reason why Ideational music is associated — appears and lives — in more homogeneous society and collective culture, while the Sensate music is more individualistic and functions mainly in the heterogeneous society.

E. Purely Ideational music does not need any special aesthetic theorizing and aesthetic critics and professional art appraisers. Instead it needs and usually has religious and moral *censors*, whose business is to find whether it conveys properly the superempirical and other values which lie behind the sound symbols. As the symbols chosen to convey these values are usually pre-existing in the social *milieu* and precede the individual creators of such music, these creators usually accept them and only purify and modify them, without a radical alteration. This we shall see in the history of the Greek, the Roman, and the Western music, where the Ideational and Idealistic classics did not introduce a radical departure from the existing forms of music and drama. For these reasons, even the religious and moral censorship in the creative period of pure Ideational music is little developed. The necessary forms come spontaneously from the collective soul. Only when the Ideational stage begins to decline does it become more pronounced and step by step merges with the sensually aesthetic theorizing and criticism.

Different is the situation in the periods of the domination of the Sensate music. Its very nature calls for a criterion of its beauty and perfection, therefore for a development of theorizing and professional criticism. Why? Because in the Ideational music the criterion is simple and definite : the conformity of the sound symbols to the value as it is established in the practice of the group, if the music is social, or in the practice of an individual, if the music is just individual. By its very nature it pertains to the habitual collective associations as they have grown in the collective religious practices and habits. No other criterion or theorizing is necessary. The Sensate music does not have this. Its aim is to please sensually. Therefore it has to have some criteria which would show that this is better music than that because it pleases more or is nearer to the aesthetic criterion set forth by this or that author. As the field of the sensual tastes is exceedingly variable and changes from man to man, from group to group, from period to period, this diversity calls forth an ever-increasing number of theories of beauty, aesthetic perfection, and of aesthetic theorizing, each of which tends to justify the specific taste of their authors and the groups or factions of which they are representatives. Hence, the necessity of the development of aesthetic criticism, theorizing, professional critics, "reviewers," "estimators," in the period of the Sensate music. Such is the inner connection between these two.

When we have the stage of marvelous mixture of the Ideational and Sensate music — the great "classical" period in the history of any art — the theorizing and criticism, though already present, are not fully developed as yet. The art itself is so beautiful and perfect that it needs no theoretical justification and reasoned proofs that it is great and beautiful. Art itself is the best and the most convincing incarnation of its perfection and beauty — far more convincing than any literary or critical essay on what is beautiful and what is not. Besides, the artists themselves are so filled with their creative power and create so spontaneously that they do not have time or inclination for dry and analytical theorizing. They create spontaneously, as spontaneously sings a nightingale. They have an inner — often half-intuitional — feeling of beauty, which is a "law unto itself." No cold, rationalized, and cerebrally dissected anatomy of beauty is needed by them.[18] They themselves set forth the law of what is beautiful by their spontaneous creations instead of following the dissected theorizing of the great and small professional art critics. And the grandeur of their creations is so convincing that the critics themselves have to bow and accept the criteria given in the creations. For such a period Tolstoi's caustic statements about professional art critics is quite applicable. In comparison with the real great master,

[18] See here interesting thoughts given by J. Maritain in his *Art and Scholasticism*, quoted; also by W. Deonna and F. Chambers in their quoted works. See Chapter Thirteen in this volume, on literary criticism.

the professional art critics are the fools who dispute the sages. They say that their function is to explain the art objects. Explain and interpret! What is it in art that they have to explain? An artist, if he is a real artist, through his work transmits most successfully to other men the sentiments which he experienced. In such conditions what remains or needs to be explained? [19]

These considerations explain why in such periods art criticism and art theorizing, with all its crowd of professional art critics, art guides, art managers, are little developed, though not absent.

It is only when the Idealistic stage is passed and even when the Sensate art has passed its peak and begins to decline that a great development of all these phenomena becomes necessary. Why? Because there is no grand work equally convincing to all; and there are a great many works, very different from one another, each of which is admired by some and detested by others. In these circumstances, as in a court case with incomplete and contradictory evidences, each party needs many "lawyers" and a crowd of witnesses and helpers, to show that their party is right and the other parties are wrong. Hence an enormous development of "the professional art lawyers," that is, critics and theorizers. Hence a blossoming of heated disputes in the incessant controversies; hence, in brief, a development of art criticism, in the period when the grand works of art are absent. Instead of the beautiful flowers of art, there spread the "weeds" of art theorizers and critics; "aestheticism and aestheticians," professional art critics, reviewers, and "amateurs in art," each of whom, even the greatest ones, are at best third-rate creators. Such is the connection between such epochs in art — in this case in music — and the presence or absence of art criticism and theorizing. There are other satellites of either of the two forms, but they will be mentioned later.

II. FLUCTUATION OF THE MAIN STYLES IN TIME AND SPACE

Like painting, sculpture, architecture, and literature, music, so far as these forms are concerned, has different dominant styles in various cultures at the same moment, and at various stages of the same culture in the course of time. As mentioned, both forms are found in practically all cultures at all stages. But the proportion of each form as well as its purity is not constant. In one culture or in one period the Ideational form may be dominant; in another culture or period the Sensate music may be the main form. Side by side with these conspicuous differences,

[19] L. Tolstoi, *Qu'est-ce que l'art?* (Paris, 1903), pp. 142 ff.

the purity or intensity of each style may also fluctuate. In this way we have short-time and long-time, strong and weak, waves of domination, now of one, now of the other form. Besides the periods of domination of one of these forms, there are their periods of either mechanical or organic mixture, where neither form is dominant. When the periods of organic, harmonious, and well-balanced mixture occur, these periods, as we shall see, give possibly the highest peaks of musical creativeness and the greatest music.

Why and how these fluctuations occur; what are their factors; in which cultural constellations they happen; in what relationship they stand toward other cultural processes and their waves, all this is to be discussed in the later parts of this work. For the present we merely outline some of the fluctuations.

Since music is only one of the numerous topics of this work, the factual corroboration can be reduced to an indication of the main periods of domination of each of these styles, mainly in the life history of the Graeco-Roman and the Western culture studied by us. We have to limit our task by the great waves of each type, because in music it is impossible to "measure" and to indicate exactly the smallest fluctuations. The details and the actual facts are to be found in the works referred to.

A. *Preliterate Cultures.* So far as the primitive peoples are concerned, they all seem to have had in some form and in some proportion both forms of music: Sensate and non-Sensate, or rude Ideational. Any primitive people, so far as known, has some form of magical and religious music chants and incantations, and some instrumental music used in these performances and ceremonies; in so far, any people has a non-Sensate form approaching Ideational music. And any people has, side by side with such a music, a form of music performed just for the sensual joy of it, without any magical, religious, or ideational implication. Be it shouting or singing or just "sound producing" from surplus of energy, love, intoxication, joy, sadness, longing, and what not, such psychophysiological sound reactions, consciously or unconsciously made for their own sake, in some form seem to have existed among all the primitive peoples. Such music is in greater part Sensate. Finally, it is hardly necessary to mention that Mixed music is certainly found also.

How great is the proportion of each form among a given tribe and which form is dominant — if any — cannot be stated because of lack of data. Of course, if we agree with the theory that at the initial stage there was only the magic music, or with the theory that at that stage there was only the labor music, or love music, or any other, then respectively we must recognize that at that stage the Ideational or the Sensate dominated, according to which of these theories we accept. But neither of these exclusive theories appears to be adequate; each overstresses its own pet point; therefore we must leave the problem unsolved.

In a purely conjectural way it appears to me that if the problem were studied carefully, such a field study would probably disclose that the proportions are not constant among all the primitives; that in some tribes with Ideational mentality dominant (e.g., the Zuñi) the Ideational form dominates, while in some other tribes with Sensate mentality dominant this form holds the upper hand. But this is mere conjecture. What one can be certain about is that both forms in some proportion are seemingly found in all the primitive organizations.

So far as the highest purity of the Ideational music is concerned, it requires the tensest and finest spirituality, free from physiological, sensual, and instinctive admixtures. Such a spirituality can be achieved only after an intensive and long and deep mental development; after long meditation, contemplation, and self-education, control, and training. Without these, no pure and fine Ideationalism or spirituality are possible. Without these, no sublime and pure Ideational music is possible either. So far as the data of anthropology, history, archeology, ethnology, and sociology show, the primitive peoples do not possess these mental qualifications. For this reason we can hardly expect to find among them the sublime and pure forms of Ideational music. It has to be of a considerable crudeness or of a "low grade," only akin to the real Ideationality. A study of the magico-religious chants and incantations seems to support that expectation. Their music is Ideational but of a crude type. It is not the Ideationality of the human soul after it had known all the empirical joys and sorrows of the sensual world, its tragedies and comedies and happiness; after it had overcome griefs and temptations, rejected them as mere appearance and nonessentials, and turned toward an inaudible, transcendental world and an inaudible (to the ear) "heavenly music." [20] In other words, the sublimest form of Ideational music presupposes a mind and soul which, like Christ in the desert, conquered all the temptations of the empirical world and soared over it to the nonempirical Infinity. Meanwhile the magico-religious beliefs and music of the primitives are not superempirical, but rather subempirical. They are

[20] An excellent example of that is given by St. Augustine. Before the conversion to Christianity, "The delights of the ear had more entangled and subdued me," he writes, "but Thou didst loosen, and free me." *Confessions*, Bk. X, chap. xxxiii, p. 234, in Everyman's Library ed.

not the result of the overcoming and giving up of the empirical reality with its values, but of a dependence, fear, and weakness toward it; and their object in most cases is not giving up the empirical values but, on the contrary, acquiring them through magico-religious operations — trying to get what otherwise could not be obtained. This explains why the Ideationality of their music is of a low and crude grade.

Somewhat similar considerations suggest that their Sensate music had to be also of a low grade. First of all because for the finest forms of its creation a highly developed technical skill and technical means are necessary. A man who does not know the A B C of musical composition cannot create Bach's or Beethoven's music. This technical skill as yet is lacking among them. Then an impressive array of technical means and instruments is necessary to enchant the ear sensually. These are also lacking. Furthermore, an intense sensualism is necessary, an artificially reinforced emotionalism, unconditionally Epicurean mentality — to squeeze from the empirical world of sounds all their sensual beauty and to enjoy them to the full — which is also lacking in most cases among them. Neither their love, nor erotism, nor sensualism reaches the high pitch found in ripe cultural stages. Finally, even for the sublime sensual music, a highly developed intellectuality and mental ripeness, including the very mentality of eudaemonism, hedonism, and epicureanism, are necessary. They are again lacking here. Therefore, we may find a "rough diamond" of the sensual music in the tunes and songs and melodies of the primitive peoples; but they are rough and not polished, and not set in a dazzling frame of harmony, measure, rhythm, counterpoint, or polyphony. They remain crude and primitive.

These considerations, plus the body of the existing facts which seem to support them, are sufficient to make these conclusions probable.[21]

B. *Oriental Cultures.* For lack of data, and especially data as to the nature of the music predominant at various periods of the history of the Oriental cultures, there is no possibility of indicating directly the cycles of the domination of each of the types studied. What can be said with a reasonable certainty is that both types existed in the music of Ancient Egypt, Assyria, China, India, and of the Hebrew culture. That the Ideational music existed is witnessed by the beliefs in the divine and mysterious origin of music; by its use in magico-religious activities;

---

[21] See the facts partly in the works of Combarieu, Lalo, Smith, Boas, quoted, and especially in the enormous number of the field studies of the music of various primitive groups which are given in the bibliographical references of these works. For the reasons indicated above, I am not giving these references and the literature.

by a belief in its magic power; in its connection with the laws of nature; by the social control of music by the State and by religious authorities; and by direct testimony of the writers and thinkers of these cultures, who clearly distinguish between music for pleasure and the other kind of music which has mysterious social, moral, educational, magical meaning and value. On the other hand, music for pleasure, purely Sensate, in a class with "wine, women, and song," is also certain from the evidences which have survived. Whether we take the Chinese, or Hindu, or Sumerian, or Assyrian, or Egyptian, or the Hebrew music, in all these cultures the origin of music is ascribed to a divine or mysterious power, be it the legendary bird, Foung-Hoang of the Chinese; the Egyptian Hermes, who invented the lyre; Jehovah's revelation to Moses (Numbers x. 1–10); the Assyrian god of music, Nébo, and Ishtar, characterized as "a harmonious flute with the tenderest music"; the Sumerian goddess Nina; or the Hindu god Nareda, the inventor of the *Vina*, and the goddess of music Saraswati, not to mention Krishna, Ganesa, and other gods, depicted usually with a musical instrument.

Likewise in all these cultures the music was credited with a magical and mysterious power which has led to careful formal discrimination of various forms of hieratic music suitable for various occasions.

Similarly the oldest forms are met in religious and magical ceremonies.

In all of these cultures, music was carefully controlled either by the religious or State authorities, and the earliest musicians were the religious priests, the prophets, the seers, or other persons and groups in whose hands were the social, mental, and moral control of the people. Among the Chinese, the Egyptians, the Hebrews, the Assyrians, the Hindus, we find evidences of an existence of a special corporation (the Chinese Board of Control of Music; the School of Samuel and the Levitic corporation among the Hebrews; a similar board of music among the Egyptians; and so on) which created, chose, and controlled music as the magical and sacred power for religious, social, and moral purposes, which had little, if any, relationship to sensual enjoyment. Therefore, as such a sacred power, it was formal, in the sense of being Ideational and serving as a symbol of the superempirical values. As such it was forbidden to be changed and tampered with. What H. Woollett says of the Chinese music, *mutatis mutandis*, can be said of all of them.

Subjected to too rigid religious and hierarchical laws it remained at its primitive form . . . and represents an immovable block which resists the assault of the centuries, the influences of the neighborly peoples, and the variations of the mode.

Though nothing has survived from the early music of these cultures, the testimonies show that in most cases such a music was relatively simple, serene, and, in a sense, "otherworldly." The place of its performance was the temple, the altar, or other place of religious services.

What the Chinese thinker Ssu-Ma-Chien says of the Chinese music and the principles of its regulation, estimation, and specification can be said of all the Oriental cultures and their music.

Those who are generous and calm, tender and correct, should sing the *Song;* those who are magnanimous and calm, penetrating and sincere, should sing the *Ta-ya;* those who are respectable, moderate, and like the rites, should sing the *Siea-ya*. . . . The airs of the *Tcheng*-country are enjoyed by the excessive and debauched minds; the airs of the *Song*-country annihilate the will power and effeminate; the airs of the *Wei*-country are vivid and mobile and trouble the mind; the airs of the *Ts'i*-country are violent and excessive and make one arrogant. . . .

As we shall see, the same is said by Greek philosophers and the Christian Church Fathers.

Like a doctor's prescription for various diseases, for each ceremony, for each occasion, there was its own appropriate music, and sometimes the deviation from the rule was regarded as a great sin or blunder.

In accordance with that, each musical phrase, often each tone, was a special symbol of some value.

Usually the main topic of the Sensate music — love — played little, if any, part in such a music.

All this means that the Ideational values ruled the character and estimate of the music, and the existence — possibly even the predominance — of the Ideational music in these cultures seems certain.

Side by side with it there existed also Sensate music. The contemporary thinkers and the sources make the distinction between these two forms rather clear and fundamental. It is the music used in secular feasts, orgies, during repasts, in places of sensual pleasure — the court, the harem, the palace of the noble, the house of the rich man, the house of love sold and bought; in brief, the place and activity of sensual enjoyment. And curiously enough, for such music the musicians were often women with a not particularly enviable reputation. They themselves and their music were equally the means of purely sensual pleasure. The first kind of music is treated as service to God, to the country, or to some other superempirical or great value; the second is regarded as a mere instrument of pleasure.[22]

Finally, between these two types there were several intermediate forms of music, partly Ideational, partly Sensate. Such, for instance, was the music used in military activities, festivities, and so on. In brief we have more evidences than we need of the existence of these two types of music in the Oriental cultures.[23]

Which of these forms predominated at various stages of history of these cultures we cannot say. In a purely hypothetical way, on the basis of the association between certain forms of culture and certain kinds of art, it is probable that the Sensate music was predominant at the stages of the ripeness of these cultures, when the large urban centers, luxury, comfort, upper comfortable classes, and, in brief, an Epicurean mentality and culture blossomed. So it seems to have been in the time of Solomon among the Hebrews, compared with the time of Samuel or David. In India the periods of use and revival of Brahmanism seem to have been marked by depression of Sensate music; the periods of its weakening, by the revival of the art. In Assyria the music of the time of Assurbanipal or Nebuchadnezzar seems to have been more sensual than before. That the conjecture is not entirely void is witnessed by the fact that the music of these countries was highly developed; that at these stages there appeared numerous and varied musical instruments; that it assumed the forms not only of religious but also secular "symphonies," chamber music, and other forms of works which served mainly for the purposes of enjoyment. All this is very probable. Unfortunately, we cannot fix exactly the dates and the periods; therefore it is better to drop the matter here and pass to Greek music.

[22] Not giving here all the sources, I refer just to the better known source, the Bible, where the difference between the Ideational and Sensate music is clear in many places; and the Bible's distinction is typical for other Oriental countries. See Ecclesiastes xxii. 6, xxxii. 7, and xlix. 2; Job xxi. 9 and 32; Amos vi; II Kings xix. 14 and 15; Apocalypse xvii; many Psalms. Even the terminology clearly shows the distinction between the two types.

[23] See the facts and the details in Combarieu, *Histoire*, Vol. I; W. Jones, *The Musical Modes of the Hindus* in E. Rosenthal, *The Story of Indian Music* (London, 1929); F. A. Gevaërt, *Les origines du chant liturgique* (Paris, 1890); H. Woollett, *Histoire de la musique* (Paris, 1920), Vol. I; A. Machabey, *Les époques de la musique* (Paris, 1920), Vol. I; *Encyclopédie de la musique*, 5 vols. (Paris, 1913–1922) — see in Volume I particularly: V. Loret, *"Egypte"*; Violleaut and F. Pélagand, *"Assyrie-Chaldée"*; A. Cahen, *"Hebreux"*; M. Courant, *"Chine-Corée"*; J. Grosset, *"Inde"*; M. Emmanuel, *"Grèce."* See also H. E. Wooldridge, *The Oxford History of Music* (Oxford, 1901), Vol. I; H. Riemann, *Handbuch der Musikgeschichte* (Leipzig, 1904); M. Emmanuel, *Histoire de la langue musicale* (Paris, 1911), Vol. I.

C. *Graeco-Roman Culture.* (1) So far as the existing evidences show, the earliest stages of the Greek music (not of the Creto-Mycenaean, of which little is known, nor even of the later stage of the Ionic music) seem to have been predominantly Ideational. And this domination of Ideational music seems to have continued up to the middle of the fifth century B.C. and, with an admixture of the growing Sensate as a subordinate factor, throughout the fifth century B.C.

(2) The fifth century gives a marvelous balance of both kinds, with a still notable domination of the Ideational music. It is the period of Idealistic music.

(3) After the fifth century, or even at its end, the Sensate music continues to rise, and becomes particularly dominant in the Hellenistic culture, especially in Alexandria, Pergamum, and other centers.

(4) As to Roman music, its earliest stages, not yet touched by the pronounced Greek influence, were also mainly non-Sensate, crudely Ideational, though the Ideationality seems to have been of a lower grade and more primitive than that of the Greeks, particularly in the classic period of the times of Terpander, when were produced the great classics of Greek choral religious music. The Roman music seems not to have had either the marvelous balance of the Ideational and Sensate music, reached by the Greek music in the sixth and fifth centuries, the period of Aeschylus (525–456 B.C.), Pindar (522–448 B.C.), Sophocles (496–406 B.C.), Euripides (480–406 B.C.), and others. The Roman music, from its primitive predominant Ideationality, passed, under the influence of the decadent Sensate music of the Greeks, directly to the stage of predominating Sensate music of possibly a coarser and more decadent type than the Greek Sensate music at its best period.

(5) This predomination of Sensate music in the Hellenic as well as in the Roman world continued during the first three or four centuries of the Christian era, when it was gradually replaced by the conspicuous forms of the Christian music, which, after the fourth century, became Ideational par excellence, since the Ambrosian and then Gregorian chants had swept away the Sensate music from the "highway" of grand music.

Such, in a schematic way, were the grand waves of Ideational and Sensate music in the history of the Graeco-Roman culture.

Now a few data to explain and corroborate this "curve of the waves."

(*a*) The predominant Ideational character of the early Greek music follows from the fact that it was principally for magic and religious use, and as such was Ideational in its essence, though perhaps of not a very high quality.

(*b*) The high degree of Ideationality of the "classic" period of Greek music — the period of Terpander, his contemporaries, and immediate successors, like Archilochos (b. *c.* 720 B.C.), Clonas of Argos, Aristonicos of Argos, Simonides of Samos, Thaletas, Olympus, Polymnastes of Colophon, Tyrtaeus, Stesichoros, Alkman, Sakadas, and many others who lived at the end of the eighth, in the seventh, and during the first part of the sixth century — can hardly be questioned. Though practically no single note of their music has survived, the evidences are not lacking that it was only in a minor part Sensate, and mainly religious and religiously civic.

The Greeks made music to interfere in all their relationships with the Spirits who became gods; they made it a necessary part of their cult; that is, they regarded it as a bond between man and the Invisible, as a charm.[24]

Later on the cult was socialized; charm music was purified of its "instinctive" elements and became a form of socially religious art. This was done by the school of Terpander and the other classicists of the eighth, seventh, and sixth centuries.

The essential traits of their music can be summed up as follows. It was religious and religiously civic, as indicated by the very terms of the musical forms: *nome* meant a religious chant in honor of this or that god of a given province; *dithyramb*, a lyric hymn to Dionysos; *paean*, a chant to Apollo; other terms — like the *prosody* — the chants of the march of the religious cortege to the temple; the *threnody* and other terms are equally of religious (or magic) nature. At that stage, these forms of the grand music were all religious. If there were some profane forms of music, like lullabies, work songs, love songs, etc., they seem to have also borne the print of Ideationality, or were a mere minority in the stream of grand musical art. Their "golden day" was to come later.

This grand music functioned invariably in connection with religious ceremonies and religiously civic performances — like the religious festivities of Dionysos and Apollo (not to mention the other deities). The altar, temple, or religious theater were the places of their performance. They were one of the most important functions of the state and religious authorities. All performances were in charge of the first *archon* and of special authorities. How seriously the task was regarded can be judged from Demosthenes' speech (*Contra Midias*), where for a supposedly unlawful interference in the functions of the person given charge of the

[24] Combarieu, *Histoire*, Vol. I, p. 61.

chorus in these festivals, capital punishment was demanded. And this in the fourth century when the previous severity and religious character of music were already considerably weakened. The State and religious authorities controlled and censored the music produced quite as severely as the early Christian Church did. Any transgression of the rules was a sacrilege.

The creation of music was not intended to present something new or quite different from the existing traditional forms and rules. Like any sacred value, the traditional forms were regarded as obligatory, inviolable. All the creators could do was to devise a variation of the forms sanctified by tradition and by religious practices and beliefs. Thus there was no spirit of novelty, modernism, difference, or revolutionary initiative; and no pleasant sensual impression was demanded, but the genius which could leave all the essentials untouched and nevertheless produce an improved variation of the old theme.

It goes without saying that the theme of the music and the mimetic ceremonies (dances and religious mysteries) was not of a profane nature, but concerned the world of the Invisible in its relationship to man. At that period, and not even in the fifth century B.C., the main and almost the only theme of our music, operas, dramas, oratorios, and so on — love, romantic, and sexual — did not enter at all into the music and ceremonies. Still less were the common man and his daily life the theme. The music was highly symbolic. It was merely a sign for the invisible and superempirical realities.

As religiously Ideational, it was a collective task and performance. Creators were regarded as one of the many agencies, and as such did not have the spirit of professional individuals nor other qualities of modern composers in regard to personal ambitions, professional vanity, and high commercial returns. They created *ad gloriam Dei* and regarded their work as a performance of their religious and patriotic duties. All they aspired to was to be the victor at the national contest, usual during these religious festivities. Hence the central role was that of the chorus, and not of the individual performer. For the same reasons, only the fully pledged citizens were admitted to the audience. Noninitiates and strangers were not permitted to participate in this sacred activity, either as listeners or performers.

Shall we wonder that this music contained hardly any tendency to new effects, to smartness, to a mixture of various elements, to a desire to impress by sensation, or by mere quantity and mass? As any real Ideational music, it was pure, simple, serene, and "inner."

I — 37

Here are a few quotations which characterize the music from this standpoint.

This music was exceedingly closely connected with religion. . . . The Greeks ignored singing by many parties . . . what practically amounts to unison. [Accompanied by instrumental music in vocal-instrumental forms.] . . . They did not have a taste for noisy music. Their instruments were too poor to emit the power and variety of timbres. . . . No doubt the music was very simple, of great serenity, probably analogous to the Gregorian plain chant. [Dances which accompanied the music were in fact not dances, but more properly mimetic ceremonies of religious character.]
If one considers the conditions [attendance of the ceremonies by thousands and thousands] and especially the enormous proportions of the [religious] theater, one will be surprised at the small number of the choristers in the lyrical dramas of Greece: only sixteen or twenty-four maximum! In order to understand that, one should forget our modern theaters and consider that at its origin the Greek drama was an entirely religious ceremony. In our greatest religious basilicas music also played an important part, but also without any deadening noise. . . . This observation is also applicable to the instrument which accompanied the chorus and which alone was what we call "orchestra": flute, or more accurately the *auloi*. It is very probable that only a double flute was employed in the theater. . . . According to Varro, one of the two flutes played the chant; the other accompanied it. . . .[25]

All this shows clearly the purity and simplicity of the Ideational music of the Greeks and supports my statement about its usual characteristics. Farther on Combarieu says:

Modern opera, since Monteverde and Lulli, seems to have for its principle, or subject matter, an expression of love. On our lyrical stage, love occupies as much of a place as it does in our novels. It reigns there as sovereign and everything comes to it. . . . Nothing similar in the Greek theater. There is practically no love. . . . Not only the Greeks ignored love, as it is understood by the modern poets, but — what is still more remarkable — every place where, according to our notion, they had an excellent opportunity to write a scene of love, they forgot, neglected, disdained to do it.

And not only in the period under discussion, when no love as such existed in the music and drama of the Greeks, but even later on, in the " golden age " of the Greek drama, of Aeschylus, Sophocles, Euripides, in the fifth century B.C., when, as we shall see, the Sensate music and art generally progressed to a considerable degree.

[25] From J. Combarieu, *Histoire*, Vol. I, pp. 65, 92, 94, 117, 118, 120–121, and 127–130.

The topics were the gods and their actions and their relations to man. Later on, came man's struggle against the Invisible, the gigantic duel against the superhuman and superempirical forces, as in the tragedies of the fifth century B.C. Nothing vulgar, of everyday occurrence, of the "Main Street" life, was to be found in this nonnaturalistic Ideational art.

Such a theater was mythical; expressing humanity — universal and local simultaneously — it used only the legends where the marvelous, miraculous, still believed to be real, occupied an exclusive place. . . . And the poet-musicians of Greece treated only the subjects which were consecrated and fixed by the national beliefs.

These extracts are sufficient to make my statements clearer and warranted.[26]

(c) This magico-religious ideationality of music of the eighth to the sixth century did not continue in the subsequent period. Parallel to the change in other arts — from Ideationality to Sensateness — music underwent a similar change. In the sixth century the Sensate form began to gain. Toward its end and in the fifth century B.C. — roughly speaking — the descending line of Ideational music and the ascending line of Sensate music crossed each other, and this crossing resulted in the marvel of the Idealistic music of the fifth century.[27] It reached its point of maturity or a perfect equilibrium between religion and pure art in the music and, associated with it, poetry and drama (tragedy and comedy) of Pindar, Aeschylus, Sophocles; partly Euripides, Aristophanes, Simonides of Klos (likened often to P. E. Bach), Agathocles, Melanippides the Older (master of counterpoint), Bacchylides (likened often to Mozart), Lamprocles, Diagoras, Likymnos, Damon, and others.

In its essential parts it still remains Ideational and keeps the forms of the hieratic music (and drama) demanded and sanctified by traditional beliefs. But the elements of Sensate music began to creep in. If the tragedies of Aeschylus exhibit these but slightly, in the works of Euripides they are already in considerable evidence, and this is the reason why most of the thinkers who immediately succeeded him, like Plato, take him as the boundary line of what they styled decadence.

The main changes in comparison with the preceding stage were schematically as follows:[28]

[26] See for details and further corroboration, ibid., Vol. I, chaps. vii–xiii. See also the works of H. Riemann, F. A. Gevaërt, C. Lalo, L. Bourguès and A. Denéréaz, quoted. M. Emmanuel, "Grèce" in the Encyclopédie de la musique (Paris, 1913), Vol. I.

[27] Combarieu, Histoire, Vol. I, p. 145.

[28] Ibid., Vol. I, pp. 145–146.

(i) Progressive abandonment of the purely sacerdotal art in favor of music to please.

(ii) Increasing substitution of Destiny for the gods and other "metaphysical abstractions" (as August Comte would say).

(iii) Complication of the technicality of music, intended to make a greater impression and to please more.

(iv) Increase of the purely "human" theme of music and drama associated with it.

(v) Increase of the comical, satirical, and sarcastic veins, in ridiculing and satirizing, in a roughly human way, human affairs and events and relationships. (Aristophanes and the increasing number of comedies.)

(vi) Decreasing role of the chorus and increasing role of individual performers. Likewise the increasing individualism at the cost of collectivity is seen in the authors also. They begin to be more and more individualistic and less and less to erase themselves before anonymous collectivity.

(vii) Progressive permeation of the profane spirit in art.

(viii) Progressive loss of calm serenity in music in favor of its increasing passionate, pathetic, individual emotionality.

(ix) Even such details as the introduction of the feminine element upon the stage are not lacking. "Such an introduction (by Euripides) opened to the melodic imagination unexplored domains. The heroines of Euripides chant beautifully. Wherever a violent emotion is to be expressed, or a cry of the heart to be issued, three-metrical iamb gives place to the melic rhythms. Hence these monodies and duets — the predecessors of our operas — as characteristics of the new tragedy," rightly says Gevaërt. "The music of Venus could be but ardent, nervous, and dissolving. Euripides was already on the border of decay." [29]

Comparing Aeschylus (525–456 B.C.) with Euripides (480–406 B.C.), one can find these tendencies which in the works of the minor poets and after Euripides grew still stronger.

(d) After the fourth century B.C. the Sensate music, already strong, continues to grow and to dominate over the Ideational music of the preceding period. The marvelous balance of the fifth century is disrupted in favor of Sensate music. The contemporary and subsequent thinkers used to mention the names of Euripides, Melanippides the Younger, Phrynis, and his disciple Timothy (446–357) as the "corrupters of taste." From now on, to please sensually becomes the ever-increasing

---

[29] Bourguès and Denéréaz, *op. cit.*, p. 85.

aim of music (and of other arts also). Subsequent masters, like Philoxenes of Cytherea (b. 436), Telestes (b. 420), Agathon (b. 415), Cleomenes of Rhegium, and a crowd of parodists continued this tendency, and introduced important innovations most favorably accepted by the public but denounced by Plato, Aristophanes, Aristoxenes, who accused these composers of "corruption" of "real music." [30]

The essential traits of this Sensate music were as follows. It became

(i) More and more profane.

(ii) More and more sensual.

(iii) More and more "human," free, individualistic.

(iv) More and more intended to produce "effects," sensation.

(v) More and more impure, complicated, with ever-increasing tendency to be "bigger" in mass and quantity.

(vi) More and more "professional."

(vii) Not the gods, nor even the metaphysical abstractions and entities, nor even the half-mythical heroes, but just the "common man" and his affairs tended to be the theme of that music. Respectively the spirit of profanity, love, sex, "wine, women and song," the hunt for popularity and applause, with commercial returns, and all the earmarks of modernism permeated it.

A few quotations will make these statements clearer to the non-specialist.

The Greek music underwent an evolution parallel with that of the religious beliefs and of the constitutions of various Greek States, moving from the most austere liturgy to the sharpest profane modernism.[31] . . . They chanted, first addressing themselves to the spirits and gods, then, step by step, gods were replaced by the legendary heroes, who had served their country, then by the powerful and rich aristocracy, and finally by ordinary man. . . . This evolution took place in all *genres* of music. . . .

The dithyramb lost its previous character of simplicity. They introduced into it monodies, "tortured melodies"; there appeared new and additional chords on the cythara; they began to seek for effects, overstressing what we call modernism! "I do not chant the superannuated," said Timothy; "the modern and new is much more preferable. Now young Zeus is reigning while in the past the old Kronos [Krony] was the maître. To the devil with the old Muse." [As though one were hearing a crowd of modernists in our own day; here also history seems to repeat itself.] . . .

[30] Combarieu, *Histoire*, Vol. I, p. 101.
[31] For the sake of brevity, I quote only from Combarieu, but what he says is sustained by the other competent historians of Greek music. Quotations are from his *Histoire*, Vol. I, pp. 144–145, 149, 101, and 151–152.

"The school of Terpander guarded its simplicity up to the time of Phrynis," says Plutarch in his *De Musica;* "because it was not permitted in the past to make pieces of music in the modern manner, nor to change the mode nor the rhythm in the course of the composition." Now Phrynis and his pupils "seek for unforeseen effects, stunning contrasts, and intentional difficulties"; while Timothy transformed the dithyramb into "a piece of bravura aimed to exhibit the talent of the virtuoso." . . .

[On the other hand, Aristoxenes (b. 329) tells that the main aim of the musician now was] "to get the applause of the multitude; its corollary was a series of technical transformations of music leading to an ever-increasing conspicuity of the virtuoso. . . . Technique developed from simplicity into complexity." The *auloi* became more complicated and capable of rivaling the trumpet. The cithara received additional strings (the eighth and the ninth) and eventually was still more complicated, reaching in the second century A.D. as many as fifteen strings. Before Phrynis only the Dorian and Aeolian modes were used; after him, according to contemporary comedy poets, there appeared the "torturers of melody," who "mixed in one piece the Dorian, the Phrygian, the Lydian, the diatonic, the chromatic, the enharmonic, and took hitherto unpermitted liberties with the rhythms" (Dionysus Halicarnaensis, *De compositione verborum*, xix). Add to this vocalisms, mixture of *genres*, etc. The complications of this type were numerous.[32]

It is obvious that purity of style was lost. The new music was a mixture of all types and *genres*, of tragic and comic elements, and all sorts of tricks which might be successful. It was transformed into theatricalness, with all the impurity of styles typical of the ripe Sensate music.[33] In a way it became on the one hand the Wagnerian theater, on the other the hodgepodge of Radio City theaters.

If the forms of Melanippides' music are not yet quite gone, Kinesias of Athens is already lost in these bizarre researches. Timothy plunges into the depths of impressionism and embarrasses his contemporaries with the audacity of his realistic innovations. . . . Philemon of Cythera — a remote predecessor of R. Strauss — pushed naturalism to an imitation of a goat's bleating in his tragedy *Cyclopes*. Agathon imagined grand operas, where the accompaniment supported easy and sweet melodies, which prolonged themselves into the interminable solos and duets — vain efforts to achieve the sublime by virtuosity and "effects." Naturally the parodists took their part. . . . Already Aristophanes in his comedies caricatured, with an infinite *esprit*, the musical

---

[32] C. Lalo, *Esquisse*, pp. 298 ff. See also Aristophanes, *Thermophories*, v. 100; Plutarch, *De Musica*, chaps. xvii and xxx; Aristoxenes, *Elemente der Harmonie*, ed. by Marguard (Berlin, 1869), 23, and also testimonies of Plato and Aristotle.

[33] C. Lalo, *Esquisse*, pp. 301 ff.

and literary style of the grand masters. His successors are but just insipid clowns. Before us is a plain dilettantism, and this dilettantism had a long existence because it amused the masses during the whole Alexandrian period and up to the Renaissance of music in the medieval plain chant. . . . Aristoxenes tried in the fourth century to preach a return to the classic traditions, but the people, *blasé*, did not listen any more. Their taste was for pirouettes. It was the singer Moschos who triumphed, and only because he could sustain a note longer than his competitors. The aberration even went so far as to erect a temple to the joyful flute of Lamia — a courtesan who made her entrance into Athens in the cortege of Demetrios Poliorcetes. On that day music was dead.[34]

Side by side with this transformation, music and its instruments tended to become more complicated and more numerous. What could not be achieved by creative quality was attempted by mere quantity, by huge masses and ever-increasing scales. We saw that at the Ideational stage the variety and number of the instruments, the size of the chorus, the scale of tones, the volume of sound, and so on, were almost blushingly modest. Now the picture changes. Huge private buildings were erected for musical and other performances. Monster concerts, with hundreds and even thousands of artists were given. At the funeral games organized by Alexander the Great in honor of Ephestion, more than three thousand artists gathered from all parts of Greece. Other similar monster performances were not lacking in Greece, as well as later on in Rome. Yes, they stole the novelty of our contemporaries' efforts to make the art (or antiart rather) the "biggest in the world" and regarded this "bigness and largeness" as the very criterion of its perfection. The biggest building, the biggest orchestra and chorus of singers, the biggest noise, the biggest of everything, since quality is lost. The amplitude of tones, the power of the instruments, the contrasts of consonances and dissonances, the technical difficulties and puzzles, the pronounced role of technique as such, these and many other things increased and became ever more noisy, like some modern compositions.

Add to this a fundamental transformation of the status and the functions of the music maker. At the early stages he was a priest, a prophet, a magician. Then he was a moral and social leader. Now he became a professional and an individualist. His creation was his own monopoly. Through it he sought to make his living — and a most luxurious one — to be famous, to be popular, to be the idol of a crowd

---

[34] L. Bourguès and A. Denéréaz, *op. cit.*, pp. 84–85. See also Combarieu, *Histoire*, Vol. I, chap. ix.

of emotional and half-hysterical followers. His creation was intended
to "make a hit" and through that to procure for him all these things.
To make a hit it had to please the public; to please, it had to adapt itself
to the predominant mass tastes, which at such a period are invariably
vulgar, in whatever concrete forms they appear. All this aroused in
the creator an insatiable vanity and appetite. In order to protect
better their individual interests, a crowd of such professionals would
unite themselves into unions, those numerous *Dionysiae Synodes* (*c.* 300
B.C. and later), *Dionysiac Associations of Artists of Ionia and Hellespont*
(*c.* 279 B.C.), *Union of the Itinerant Musicians*, and so on. Out of a sacred
and sacrosanct activity, the disinterested service to God and to mankind,
art activity turned now into a mere business which, since "business is
business," became a commercial activity with all its paraphernalia and
quest for a market and a marketable commodity. In this way the art
was debased, though the secular position of the artist improved materially
to an enormous degree. Music became the fashion. Beginning with
the upper classes, and ending with any dull boy or girl of the rich, all
began to aspire to it, to be trained in it, to become the aestheticians and
musicians, from an emperor in Rome to the Graeco-Roman Babbitt.
It became as necessary to a good education as the ability to play golf
and bridge, to enjoy crossword and jigsaw puzzles in our time. Hence,
the enormous incomes and profits of the popular musicians and artists;
the elevated social position they occupied (no lower than the heavyweight
world champion, or Babe Ruth, or the golf and the tennis and football
czars of our day). Fame, popularity, prestige, friendship of the greatest
rulers and leaders, love of the ladies of all classes — these and scores of
other world values were showered upon the popular musicians. The
cult of many of them was hardly less than that of Richard Wagner, with
the enormous crowd of half-crazy Wagnerian devotees throughout the
world, from Peking and Moscow to Berlin and Paris. Cities vied for the
honor of having a famous musician among their citizens; some of them
were named for artists; statues were erected to composers; enormous
sums were paid for their concerts. In brief, the popular musician was
a manufacturer of an important sensual pleasure, and as such he was
paid well by sensual values, from applause and fame to wealth and
sensual and sexual love. In this way the situation continued (with
slighter ups and downs) until the victorious Ideational music of Christianity put an end to this sensual music, great in a way in its initial stages,
but completely degenerated during the Alexandrian, Pergamene, and
the Roman period.

(e) As for Roman music, its story can be told briefly. The Etruscan and early Roman music seems to have been predominantly Ideational, at least in its religious, social, and public forms. As mentioned, the Ideationality must have been of a low grade. Before it was fully developed and before the "homemade" Sensate form had time to grow, the Greek music infiltrated and was superimposed upon the Roman music, still native and primitive. The result was that the intermediate stage, the "classic miracle" of the Idealistic music, was hardly known to Rome, as it was unknown in painting, sculpture, and architecture, except by imitation. It skipped this greatest stage and from the predominance of the primitive Ideational jumped directly to the superannuated and overripe Sensate music which was imported from Greece. "Generally the Romans imitated and continued merrily and in a poorer form the music of Greece. They developed it in an inartistic way, bringing it to the terminal point of decadence." [35]

Therefore in that stage of imitative music, the Roman musical art had all the above traits of the Greek Sensate music still more conspicuous and overemphasized. Here the principle of quantitative hugeness reached an enormous development. The theaters they built, like that erected by Pompey in 55 B.C., were enormous, being intended for forty thousand persons, as Pliny the Elder tells. "Not being able to make it beautiful, they made it rich." Such is the moral of this "quantitative bigness," formulated by Pliny.[36]

This colossalism comes out everywhere. Their musical festivals often were on a gigantic scale. Concerts where simultaneously a hundred trumpets blared, a hundred players accompanied thousands of actors and acrobats, were not rare.[37] Purity of style disappeared. "The contemporaries of Terentius and Plautus, Livius Andronicus and Attius, were incapable of enjoying a melody as such without words, gesticulation, and pantomime." [38]

Cicero's letter to Marius in 55 B.C. gives a fairly accurate idea of this Roman art. Describing the theatrical performances he attended, Cicero complains:

I must tell you that though our entertainments were extremely magnificent, yet they were by no means such as you would have relished. . . . The enormous parade with which they were attended . . . destroyed all the grace of

---

[35] Combarieu, *Histoire*, Vol. I, p. 175.
[36] See Pliny, *Natural Histories*, XXXVI, 15.
[37] Bourguès and Denéréaz, *op. cit.*, pp. 98–100. Combarieu, *Histoire*, Vol. I, pp. 176 ff.
[38] Combarieu, *Histoire*, Vol. I, pp. 177–178.

the performance. What pleasure could it afford to a judicious spectator to see a thousand mules prancing about the stage, in the tragedy of *Clytemnestra;* or whole regiments accoutered in foreign armor in that of the *Trojan Horse?* In a word, what man of sense could be entertained with viewing a mock army drawn up on the stage in battle array? These, I confess, are spectacles extremely well adapted to captivate vulgar eyes; but undoubtedly would have had no charm in yours. In plain truth, my friend, you would have received more amusement from the dullest piece that Protogenes (Marius' slave) could possibly have read to you, than we met at these ridiculous shows.[39]

The Oriental and Greek Sensate art invaded Rome about 187 B.C. There were several attempts on the part of the conservative groups either to prohibit this *luxuriae peregrinae* (*e.g.*, in 115 B.C.) or to replace the Greek Sensate and decadent art by forms of the Greek classic music (*e.g.*, Vespasian and others); but all these efforts were ineffective; the result was a further lowering of the standard of the Greek Sensate music.

The Romans [of the Empire] hardly enjoyed the music as such. They were particularly sensitive to the quantity of the instruments, to the sonorous volume, or to the queerness of certain performances. Monster concerts are not rare. Seneca (*Epistolae* LXXXIV, 10) tells that there are more singers in the theater of his time than listeners in the theaters of the past. . . . And indeed the Roman theater contained from 7000 to 12,000 spectators.[40]

Then comes an increase in the size of the instruments; complication of their character; and an enormous increase of their number.[41]

It is needless to describe in detail the popularity of music, from the emperors to the *bourgeoisie;* the musical training of children; musical aestheticism and aestheticians; the lucrativeness of the musical profession; the vanity of the artists; the crowd of admirers (especially female) of the popular musicians; the sex scandals about them. Artists were accepted and eagerly invited into the best houses; they were the close friends of emperors and potentates; they were given, by Nero and other powerful and rich people, palaces, fortunes, and what not. "Snobbism produced in the virtuosos unlimited vanity. . . . They became capricious."[42]

In brief, all the traits of the Greek Sensate music were present in the Roman Sensate music in an exaggerated and cruder form.

[39] Cicero, *The Offices. Essays and Selected Letters*, pp. 274–275, Everyman's Library ed.
[40] Combarieu, *Histoire*, Vol. I, p. 183.
[41] For these and other traits see Cicero, *Pro Roscio Amerino*, 45, 134; *Pro Milone*, 21; *Pro Coelio*, 15; Seneca, *Epistolae*, 151; Plutarch, *De Musica*, 15, 1; *Questiones Convivalium*, IX, 15 and 17.
[42] Combarieu, *Histoire*, Vol. I, pp. 186–188.

Such a music continued during the first few centuries of our era, degenerating more and more, parallel with the decay of the Sensate Graeco-Roman civilization. Christianity early enough rejected it and soon intentionally began to purify music of all its sensual embellishments, at the same time elaborating from the Graeco-Hebrew sources of its own music. In the form of the plain chant, Christianity put an end to the eight-hundred-year (from about 400 B.C. to A.D. 400) domination of Sensate music and ushered in the domination of Ideational music on the level of the grand art. And this domination also continued during some eight hundred to nine hundred years (from about A.D. 400 to 1300–1400). Then we come to the medieval period, with its unquestionable and almost monopolistic domination of the plain chant — one of the sublimest and purest forms of Ideational music.

(f) In the above, I have indicated the abundance of art critics and professional aestheticians during the period of the domination of Sensate music and their absence — with the presence of socioreligious and moral censorships — in the period of Ideational music, especially in the initial stages of its decline. The association claimed is well corroborated in the history of the Graeco-Roman music and musical theorizing and criticism.

(i) We hear hardly anything of the existence of art criticism and art theorizing in the early Ideational stage of Greek music, the period of Terpander, and the subsequent period up to the sixth century.[43]

[43] "The great Greek poets of the classic epoch, though practicing a very complex art of poetry, never created any theory of versification; it was the grammarians who came after the creators of the *chefs d'œuvres* who invented the metrical theory and theory of prosody. . . . The same is true of music. Rhetoric was not, as Renan said, 'the only error of the Greeks.' From the sixth century B.C., the discovery, though admirable, made by the great founder of the theory of numbers (Pythagoras) engaged the theorizers of music along the lines on which the musical theorizing continued for centuries," rightly says Combarieu, conveying the same idea. *Histoire*, Vol. I, p. 83. Lalo still more clearly stresses it.

"Classics create their works spontaneously and naturally, without either rational calculation or preponderant passionate affectivity. Mozart was a spontaneous composer, just as La Fontaine could not help becoming naturally a 'fableist.' . . . In such an age there is little of theorizing and little of ethology in contradistinction to 'the age of the predecessors and of the subsequent romantics.' The classical 'rules' diffuse and impose themselves without any effort. Classics provide the examples and the works but not theories and reasoned principles. It was not Mozart but Monteverde; not Beethoven but Wagner . . . not Racine and Molière, but the Pleiade and the Romantic coterie who reasoned out their technique before their creations and for the sake of their creations." C. Lalo, *Esquisse*, p. 295.

See further many theories and my criticism and my data about the relationship between the creative and the "critical" periods in art in the preceding and subsequent chapters where the problem is discussed more substantially.

(ii) Only in the sixth century rises the first and the greatest theorizer of Greek music, Pythagoras. But his theorizing is mathematico-mystical, or Ideational, and in it there is little of Sensate theory, evaluation, and criticism of music.

(iii) The subsequent Pythagorean school (Philolaos, Lasos of Hermione, Hippasos of Metaponte, Archytas of Tarent) continued in the footpath of its teacher, during the sixth and partly the fifth century, and theorizing and Sensate criticism tended to increase more and more.

(iv) Plato, Aristotle, and Aristoxenes of Tarent, the disciple of Aristotle (the fourth century B.C.), Euclid (third century B.C.), not to mention the *dii minores*, already occupy an intermediate position. Their theories, here as in other fields of art, are still somewhat Ideational and, in their specific principle of *imitation*, they hold as one of the main criteria of beauty what we would style the religious and moral fitness of the art creation. In this sense their theories are still predominantly Ideational, though already mixed with the Sensate criteria of beauty. In the works of the lesser critics and philosophers, the same characteristic prevails. Just as music in the fourth century B.C. was passing from the Ideational to the Sensate form, so the criticism and theorizing were increasing and becoming more and more Sensate.

(v) As we pass to the subsequent centuries, we find also a growth of professional "aestheticism," art criticism, art evaluation, where the criteria of perfection and grandeur become more and more sensual, more and more divergent, more and more complicated in technicality and divergent principles. A crowd of grammarians, rhetoricians, philosophers, and art amateurs, something very similar to our own crowd of art critics, art reviewers, evaluators, and educators, appears. Among them there were few relatively prominent names — like Eratosthenes (third to second centuries, B.C.), Heron of Alexandria, Ktesibios (first century), Aristides Quintilian (first century B.C.), then T. Varro (first century B.C.), Philodemus of Gadara, Didymus, Cleonides, Theon of Smyrna, Nicomachus of Gerase, Claudius Ptolemy, Gaudencius, Alypius, Censorinus — but most of them are of the same caliber as the main ranks of contemporary art reviewers and critics, most of whom are neither artists nor know anything about art except the beggarly superficialities. But they occupy the front stage, become noisy, influential, authoritative, and write innumerable texts and compendiums, not to mention articles in which and through which they crush many talents and create "best sellers out of nullities." Innumerable aesthetic theories spring into existence; heated discussion develops; everybody begins to discuss art, to give his evaluations, his theories. In brief, creation of the great masterpieces ceases, but a sterile, sophisticated, and sensate art theory and art criticism blossoms.[44]

Even when a moralizing voice like Plutarch's is heard in this noisy crowd, it is a voice crying in the wilderness; besides, even his moralizing preaching is not spontaneous, not otherworldly or mystic or Ideational, but entirely reasoned, rationally calculated, and based not so much upon Ideational principle as upon very earthly, very utilitarian, noble, but Sensate considerations. Therefore even such exceptions are in fact not exceptions really, but only a variety of the same predominant trend. Briefly, the history of the Graeco-Roman music supports definitely the expectation outlined.

D. *Medieval Music.* The movement of medieval and modern music can be characterized from the standpoint of the forms discussed, as follows.

(1) On the highway of the great music, the medieval music, during almost nine hundred years (from about the fifth century A.D. to the fourteenth century) was either exclusively Ideational, or (from the twelfth to the fourteenth centuries) predominantly so.

(2) The Ideationality of this music was of the purest and most sublime.

(3) Up to the end of the eleventh century, Ideational music was almost the only grand music existing; after the end of that century, there appeared the first signs of its mixture with the Sensate, in the music of troubadours, trouvères, minnesingers, and other forms of secular music, which had acquired many traits of the Sensate. After that time, this stream of Sensate music — not without fluctuations — tended to increase, in the form of secular motets, madrigals, and later on, in the form of the *ars nova*, and then in that of symphonies, operas, musical comedies, and so on. The growing sensatization of music manifested itself in the Sensate musical mentality, in the rapid increase of Sensate music, in its technical forms, in its themes, in the occasions for which it was written, in the social events which it immortalized. In brief, in the inner nature as well as in the external traits.

(4) In contradistinction to some other forms of art, especially of painting and sculpture, which attained, as we saw, the marvelous Idealistic phase in the thirteenth and fourteenth centuries, *music seems to have reached the Idealistic point somewhat later:* around the sixteenth and

---

[44] See some details in Combarieu, *Histoire*, Vol. I, chaps. viii, ix, xii, and xiii; especially see H. Abert, *Lehre vom Ethos in der griechische Musik*, and the works of Gevaërt, quoted. See the literature and data in the other chapters of this work.

seventeenth and partly the eighteenth century (Palestrina, Vittoria, Bach, Handel, Mozart, and Beethoven) when these forms were wonderfully blended and resulted in the miracle of the Idealistic music of the sixteenth to the eighteenth centuries, inclusive.

This marvelous balance, though with a slightly and slowly increasing predominance of the Sensate music, was not broken during the eighteenth century. Great masters of the period, like the Bachs, Gluck, Handel, Rameau, Mozart, Haydn, Beethoven are still mainly within the borderline of this balance; therefore the Idealistic period may be extended up to the very beginning of the nineteenth century, including such great masterpieces as Beethoven's last five quartets and the *Ninth Symphony*, with the transcendental heights of some parts of these works. Though in some of the works of these great masters there is little Ideationality, nevertheless all the while in the bulk of these creations, the balance — more and more sensualized — still persisted.

(5) After the beginning of the nineteenth century, the Sensate form begins to predominate definitely and more and more radically. In the music of Wagner and other Romantics, it possibly reached its highest peak. After that, and especially after the end of the nineteenth century, it began to show all the symptoms of disorganization, demoralization, and degeneration, which — again not without exceptions and oscillations — has been continuing up to the present time. It witnesses on the one hand an utter degradation, vulgarization, "jazzing," and modernistic-impressionistic musical anarchy and impotency (in spite of the gigantic technical skill and complexities of many a modern composition); on the other hand, it exhibits the first signs of the efforts to seek new, anti-Sensate forms of music. Thus schematically:

(a) The period from the fifth to the twelfth centuries is that of the monopolistic domination of the pure and sublime Ideational music (on the highway of grand music, because on the lower levels in all times and in all places and societies there always were both types of music).

(b) The period from the twelfth to the fifteenth is the time of entrance of the Sensate music, but still definitely in a secondary place.

(c) The period from the end of the fifteenth to the beginning of the nineteenth century was that of balance of the Ideational and Sensate forms — a long period of Idealistic music. In the centuries from the end of the fifteenth to the second part of the seventeenth the Ideational music seems still to have predominated; beginning with the second part of the seventeenth and especially in the eighteenth century the Sensate, but in its noblest forms, began to gain the ascendancy.

(d) The nineteenth century is the period of decisive domination of Sensate music, and the closer we come to the twentieth century, the stronger it becomes.

(e) The present century is the age showing the first symptoms of recession of Sensate music and at the same time the age of seeking for new, non-Sensate forms; in this sense it is a period of transition. This reaction against Sensate music is very similar to that against Visualism in painting, sculpture, and architecture. Let us now somewhat corroborate the above statements.

That the grand music of the fifth to the twelfth centuries was almost monopolistically Ideational is testified to by the fact that the main and almost its only form was the plain chant, first the Ambrosian version, then the Gregorian classical improvement, and then the religious hymns and psalmodies. (The same is still more true of the religious grand music of the Eastern Church.) I have already given a characterization of this chant and the reasons why it is sublimely Ideational. In the words of one historian of music, the Gregorian chant, consisting roughly of about three hundred Introits and Communions, one hundred Graduals, one hundred Alleluias, twenty Tracts, and one hundred Offertories, has

a curiously ethereal, static, arrested, timeless quality . . . the spirit of gentleness, humility and resignation is its dominant character . . . [and in it] the disembodied soul, released from the tyranny of flesh, soars ecstatically upwards to Heaven, like the Holy Dove of the Scriptures.[45]

Since it was the result of the work of generations in the Orient and then in the Occident, it assumed its Ideational form not entirely spontaneously, but was to a degree the result of intentional efforts to purify the Christian music of all the worldly embellishments and thus create a music quite harmonious with the Christian spirit of "otherworldliness." We know how hard many of the Church Fathers (St. Augustine, St. Benedict, St. Jerome, pseudo Justin, Clement of Alexandria, and others) worked in that direction, dropping both instruments and instrumental music and after the fourth century prohibiting their use in the churches; excluding chromatics and disharmony as unbecoming to the Christian spirit. Only "*moralitas artis musicae* was admitted and even this only when it is sung with all the heart and all the determination to

[45] C. Gray, *op. cit.*, pp. 14, 18, 19, and 32. As mentioned, records of a part of it are now readily available so the reader can verify for himself the accuracy of this characterization by listening to the most important parts of it as well as to the works of the composers discussed, since a considerable part of these is now recorded.

practice the Christian faith and morality. . . . *Cantate oribus cantate moribus,*" as St. Augustine said.[46]

"It is possible to admit only modest and decent harmonies; and it is necessary to exclude all the effeminate and sensual accords," said Clement of Alexandria. Their allurement leads to an enervating and mollifying manner of living, while the grave modulations inspire temperance and inhibit licence and debauchery. Therefore it is quite necessary to avoid chromatic and light harmonies because they are used in the impudent orgies of the courtesans.[47]

In a similar way one after another of the charms of the Sensate music were excluded,[48] and as a result we have the simple, unisonous, otherworldly, unmusical — from the Sensate standpoint — grand music of early Christianity and of the Middle Ages.

This shift from the Sensate to the Ideational form did not happen at once; it required about two or three centuries; but when it had been completed, the contrast between the degraded music of the Graeco-Roman and Alexandrian period and the Christian music of the fifth and sixth centuries was as great as it could be. They are two opposite poles, having little in common. Similarly, all the ideas on the nature of music, its goodness or badness and so on, changed also. A sample of the new Ideational conception has been given from Boethius, and it is typical of the Christian critics and those of the Middle Ages.

During the centuries of the domination of this music, in the circles of the common people there was undoubtedly circulating another — more Sensate — type of music, of folk songs; but these do not belong to the grand music; they do not stamp the integrated culture of the period; and besides, even these were considerably influenced by the plain chant and its forms and spirit. For this reason they are out of the field of our study.

[46] See H. Abert, "*Die musikaestetischen Auschannungen der frühesten Christlichen Kirche,*" in *Zeitschrift für Aesthetik und allgemeine Kunstwissenschaft* (1906), Vol. I, pp. 526–541; St. Augustine, *Confessions*, Bk. X, chap. xxxiii in Everyman's Library ed; T. Gérold, *Les pères de l'église et la musique* (Strassburg, 1931). Also T. Gérold, *La musique au moyen âge,* (Paris, 1932).

[47] Combarieu, *Histoire*, Vol. I, p. 200. See many important facts and details there, as well as in other histories of music quoted, especially the *Die Musikanschauung des Mittelalters* (Halle, 1905) by H. Abert; P. Wagner, *Einführung in die gregorianischen Melodien* (1910), Vol. I; A. Gastoué, "*La musique byzantine et le chant des églises d'Orient,*" in the *Encyclopédie de la musique.* Also A. Gastoué, *L'art grégorien* (Paris, 1913).

[48] This anti-Sensate spirit of the early Christian Church went so far as to cause, at the earliest stages of its development, a controversy between the Christians as to whether any music is admissible. Many hermits, ascetics, and monks argued against even the plainest chants in religious services and in Christian life generally.

Plain chant dominated monopolistically up to the end of the eleventh century.[49]

Then on the highway of grand music for the first time appears secular music, more worldly, more embellished and less Ideational than the chants. I mean the debut of the music of the troubadours, trouvères and their German replicas, the minnesingers. The curve of their rise and decay stretches from 1090 to 1290.[50] Their *chansons* were numerous (more than 260 *chansons* of trouvères and about 2000 *chansons* of troubadours are preserved). In its spirit and character this music and its themes are very different from the chants. Its subjects — mainly love and sentiment — are of this world; its nature is much more Sensate. These songs and their words signify the first break in the domination of the purely Ideational music. This is shown also by the technical traits of this music. It introduces some of the embellishments expelled from the chants. Their monodies were sentimental and gallant. Instrumental accompaniment was used. Some other novelties of a nobly Sensate nature were introduced. Nevertheless in spite of profane love being the main subject of these *chansons*, they do not differ in their music and technique radically from the Ideational music; and even in their spirit the *chansons d'histoire, dramatique, de danse*, the *reverie*, the *pastorelle*, the *aube*, the *chansons courtoises*, the *débats*, and the *chansons religieuses*, the main forms, are far from being entirely Sensate and are rather midway between the pious-religious and the nobly Sensate Ideal-

[49] As we have seen, other forms of art of the Middle Ages had the same predominant Ideational character, not excepting even the religious theater. It was not only religious exclusively, but highly symbolic, that is, Ideational. See about that in Combarieu, *Histoire*, Vol. I, chap. xx. See there also the bibliography.

So far as the Byzantine music is concerned, there the classic expression of Ideational music falls in the fifth, sixth, and seventh centuries A.D. (Timocles, Anthimos in the fifth; Sophronios, Sergios, Anastasios and the greatest of all these, Romanos — *princeps melodorum* — in the sixth and at the beginning of the seventh). The high level is continued in the seventh (Andreos of Crete, and St. John the Damascene in the eighth century). So Ideational music there was about synchronous with the crystallization and classic expression of Ideationalism in the form of the Gregorian chants in the West. In the centuries from the tenth to the twelfth, there seems to have begun a penetration of the Sensate elements into the grand music — which was almost exclusively religious. It manifested itself by complication, increase of affectation and artificiality, mannerisms and frivolity. This penetration continues and in the thirteenth, fourteenth, and fifteenth centuries results in the great Idealistic music of Byzantium. Thus the process of its establishment happened somewhat earlier than in the West. But the difference is neither great nor radical. See details in E. Wellesz, *Byzantinische Musik* (Breslau, 1927); Metallov, *Religious Songs of the Russian Church, Bogoslujebnoie penie rousskoi tzerkvi* (Moscow, 1912); and Gastoué's work, quoted.

[50] Possibly the famous "Sumer is icumen in" appeared somewhat earlier; but it remains, so far, a unique phenomenon of its kind.

I — 38

istic standpoints. The reason for this, just as for the almost contemporary "Courts of Love," is that profane love and otherworldly subjects are still shot through by the modified, idealistic, Platonic spirit. They are but a transposition of the Divine love. Their subtleties of "fine amour" maintain the cult of an ideal lady, like the Madonna, the mother of the Savior, the object of devotion, adoration, pure and ideal. It is the idealization of love and the elevation of this tender emotion of mortals to the heights of immortal forms — a phenomenon typical of any period when the Ideational forms begin to be mixed with a moderate injection of the nobler Sensate elements.

The appearance and rise of these *chansons* do not signify the end of the domination of Ideationalism, but only the end of its monopoly and the beginning of a further growth of Sensateness and, for several centuries, the organic mixture of both forms.[51]

After the thirteenth century, then,[52] with some ups and downs, the Sensate music rises, in the secular as well as in the religious fields, and its rise leads to the wonderful balance of both forms, which gives, as it often does, the peak of musical art.

As for the technical side, it acquires one audible embellishment after another, and becomes steadily richer and more beautiful. After the thirteenth century it becomes "measured" (quite a symbolic phenomenon in its significance); it develops polyphony; it produces and develops counterpoint (the fifteenth century being its "golden age"); introduces and cultivates the richest variety of rhythms; then develops harmony and "vertical" writing, instead of the horizontal; begins artistically to use intensity — *piano, forte*, etc.; achieves wonderful perfection in its use of chromatics, consonances, and dissonances; tends to become more and more expressive; introduces and expands and perfects the use of instrumental music and blends it with vocal; enlarges the scale of the choruses as well as that of the orchestras; combines the sound impression with the visual in form, color, motion, and so on.

Parallel to that development the theory of music and its interpretation

[51] For trouvères and minnesingers see Combarieu, *Histoire*, Vol. I, chap. xxi; P. Aubry, *Trouvères et troubadours* (Paris, 1909); C. Gray, *op. cit.*, chap. iii.

[52] Toward its end the changes must have been considerable, since in 1322 Pope John XXII issued a special bull directed against this revolution. This bull describes the change in the spirit as well as in the technical aspects of music. "The multitude of its (new music's) notes obscures the modest and tempered deductions through which the tones distinguished themselves from one another in the plain chant. They run and never make a rest, enervate the ear and do not cure the souls. . . . Hence the devotion which they search for is forgotten and the effeminacy which should be avoided has a great day." Combarieu, *Histoire*, Vol. I, p. 384.

undergoes a similar change. The attention of the theorizers of music is more turned toward making it richer, pleasanter, and more beautiful in its sensate appeal. This is the objective which is increasingly evident as we pass from the medieval writers on music who followed in the footsteps of Boethius — Leander and Isidor of Seville, St. John the Damascene, Romanos, Alcuin, the school of the St. Gall Monastery, Hucbald and others — to Guido d'Arezzo (c. 1050), who shows quite clearly this new objective, Walter Odington of Oxford, Adam de la Halle (1240–1287), and subsequent theorizers on this subject.

As to the technical changes which appeared and began to develop, especially after the thirteenth century, in the musical creations of the fourteenth (the *ars nova*), the fifteenth, and the sixteenth centuries, they become quite conspicuous. These tendencies are equally clear in the *ars nova* in its Italian and French branches (Philippe de Vitry, 1290–1361; Francesco Landino, 1225–1377; Francesco da Cesaro; Guillaume Machant, d. 1367; and others); in the Flemish Polyphonic school (John Dunstable, d. 1453; Guillaume Dufay, 1400–1474; Pierre de la Rue, d. 1518; Okeghem, 1430–1495; and Josquin Deprès, 1450–1521, to mention only the main names); in the French school (Clément Jannequin; Goudimel, 1510–1564; Claudin Le Jeune, 1530–1564); in the Italian schools (Costanzo Festa, b. 1505; Wallaërt, 1510–1562; Cyprian van Rore, 1516–1565; A. Gabrieli, 1510–1586; G. Gabrieli, 1557–1612; Gesualdo, d. 1614; Palestrina, 1524–1594; Orlando di Lasso, 1530–1594); and even in the Spanish school (Christobal Morales, b. 1512; Vittoria, 1540–1608, and others); in the English school (R. Fairfax, John Taverner, William Bird, and others); among the German Meistersingers and other currents there (Hans Sach, 1496–1576). The trend was general for Western European culture.

So far as the inner character of the change is concerned, the trend of Sensualization shows itself unquestionably in many forms.

(i) *First of all the proportion of religious music tends to decrease while that of the secular music tends to increase.* Though the categories of the religious and secular are not identical with the Ideational and Sensate, nevertheless as a rule religious music is more closely associated with the Ideational and secular with the Sensate. There are no exact statistics on the proportion of each of these forms of music or of the composers or their musical creations for these centuries. Nevertheless, it is safe to say that in the realm of grand music, the medieval music from the fourth to the twelfth century was almost 100 per cent religious. With the arrival of the trouvère-troubadour music this percentage decreases and the secular music comes into the field of grand music. After that, with the *ars nova*, with the ever-increasing number of madrigals, sonnets, and so on; with the continually growing number of composers of secular music and those who, besides religious compositions, began to compose secular music also — and almost all the religious composers of these three centuries and subsequent ones began to do that — it is safe to deduce that the proportion of the secular music was growing.

In co-operation with I. Lapshin, I computed the changes in the proportion of religious and secular music, according to the number of composers of each type as well as to the compositions belonging to the grand music (see Tables 32 and 33). Taking as a basis the fundamental histories of music, those of J. Combarieu, H. Woollett, *The Oxford History of Music*, and that by A. Schering, and registering any name characterized as a predominantly religious or predominantly secular composer on the one hand, and all the works mentioned as religious or secular, the percentage of either form of music was computed according to both methods. When the sixteenth-century music was studied, the ratios of the secular-religious music computed according to the character of the composition as well as according to the number of the composers (both religious and secular) happened to be not far apart: 44 per cent religious and 56 per cent secular, according to the number of works; and 54 per cent and 47 per cent respectively, according to the number of composers. Nevertheless, it soon became evident that no valid statistical study of the proportions was possible. Such a study makes indefinite the unit of work to be taken. If every opus is taken as an equal unit — for instance, a short madrigal and a whole Mass — such an equalization is absurd. Then it is impossible to secure even relatively complete data about most works; even in regard to many that are known, it is impossible to decide whether they are religious or secular. For these reasons, this basis for computation of the proportions was dropped and we turned to the number of composers predominantly religious or secular. This basis has also its deficiencies. For instance, Palestrina and Orlando di Lasso in such a procedure would be given one unit each, equal to other not only less influential but to much less productive composers. Compared with more than a thousand compositions produced by Palestrina and at least twenty-three hundred by di Lasso, such an equalization of these creators with those who produced only a few works is quite unpermissible. In addition, for the period before the fifteenth century, either method is misleading, since at that time, as in the early Middle Ages, the Christian Church used and permitted only the approved chants and rather discouraged any novelty in religious music. In a statistical study, such a situation results in the obviously misleading conclusion that Gregorian chants, for instance, used *urbi et orbi* in the Christian Church, would count only one unit, equal to a madrigal known only to a small circle and used a short time. For the same reason the number of secular composers would supply a greater number of names, though all their output was used much less than the chants alone.[53]

TABLE 32. PROPORTION OF RELIGIOUS AND SECULAR COMPOSERS BY CENTURIES

Century	Period	Number of Religious Composers	Number of Secular Composers	Per Cent Religious	Per Cent Secular
XVI	1500–1520	26	19	—	—
	1520–1540	19	30	—	—
	1540–1560	22	16	53	47
	1560–1580	18	16	—	—
	1580–1600	31	21	—	—
XVII	1600–1620	28	47	—	—
	1620–1640	22	25	—	—
	1640–1660	31	37	46	54
	1660–1680	47	48	—	—
	1680–1700	64	64	—	—
XVIII	1700–1720	68	57	—	—
	1720–1740	69	72	44	56
	1740–1760	41	55	—	—
	1760–1780	27	55	—	—
	1780–1800	28	52	—	—
XIX	1800–1820	27	73	—	—
	1820–1840	31	67	—	—
	1840–1860	47	87	24	76
	1860–1880	22	126	—	—
	1880–1900	35	163	—	—

For these reasons either method is inadequate and in application to the centuries before the sixteenth entirely unreliable. They are also very deficient when applied to the musical works and composers after the fifteenth century; but the deficiency here is somewhat mitigated because at that time the composers were given more freedom in the

[53] As a matter of fact, in our computation by the number of composers whose names are mentioned in the above histories of music, plus the value of one assigned to anonymous single or collective pieces of secular music, we arrived at approximately the following percentages; of the composers for the thirteenth century, 69 secular and 31 religious; for the fourteenth, 61 and 39 respectively; for the fifteenth, 54 and 46. Thus these figures show a preponderance of secular composers in these centuries and a decreasing proportion of them as we pass from the thirteenth to the fifteenth century. These results are entirely misleading, in my opinion. The evidence existing leaves hardly any doubt that the situation was rather reversed.

field of religious music and the creation of appropriate religious music began to be welcomed by the Church. Likewise their works could be performed in various religious ceremonies, and in this way they were stimulated to creativeness. Even under these circumstances, the quantitative data are likely to be misleading, but the figures in Table 32 were secured as to the number of the religious and secular composers for the specified period.[54]

Taking into consideration all the circumstances known and the trends in other fields of art, these figures seem to show the situation correctly. The results are supported by other data — the data of the religious and secular compositions of the prominent composers (Table 33).

For the religious compositions were taken oratorios, Passion music, cantatas, Masses, and other compositions, such as the Magnificat, Stabat Mater, Requiem, chorales, etc. For secular music, sonatas, chamber music (quartets, quintets, etc.), operas, concertos, symphonies, overtures, symphonic poems, suites, and a few songs.

TABLE 33.   PROPORTION OF RELIGIOUS AND SECULAR COMPOSITIONS
BY CENTURIES

Century	Period	Number of Great Religious Works	Number of Great Secular Works	Per Cent Religious	Per Cent Secular
XVII	1600–1620	19	47	—	—
	1620–1640	19	25	—	—
	1640–1660	25	37	42	58
	1660–1680	42	48	—	—
	1680–1700	54	64	—	—
XVIII	1700–1720	60	57	—	—
	1720–1740	60	72	—	—
	1740–1760	40	55	42	58
	1760–1680	27	55	—	—
	1780–1800	27	52	—	—
XIX	1800–1820	25	73	—	—
	1820–1840	29	67	—	—
	1840–1860	42	87	21	79
	1860–1880	19	126	—	—
	1880–1900	25	163	—	—
	1900–1920	7	138	5	95

The results of Tables 32 and 33 are rather close. The trends are the same — toward ever-increasing secularization which in the nineteenth and (especially) in the twentieth centuries has become not only dominant but crushingly so (especially if one takes into consideration that many

[54] If a composer created in both fields without any definite preponderance in either, he was put into both classes.

religious compositions like Verdi's *Requiem* or Berlioz's *Tuba mirum* — even, in parts, Beethoven's *Missa solemnis* — are half pagan in their spirit and character). Not only the trends but even the proportions in both tables come remarkably close to each other. They are almost identical in spite of the quite different basis of their computation.

The above considerations and the data warrant the assumption that the trend started at least as far back as the thirteenth century, perhaps even in the second part of the twelfth, when the music of the trouvères and troubadours came into existence.

This secularization has been proceeding not only quantitatively but qualitatively. As mentioned, even the religious music after the four-teenth and fifteenth centuries has been showing an increasingly profane and worldly character.[55] Specialists in music know that even such great religious compositions as J. S. Bach's *Mass* and *Magnificat*, the *St. John* and *St. Matthew Passions*, some of Palestrina's, Vittoria's, and especially Orlando di Lasso's religious works, Beethoven's *Missa solemnis*, Mozart's *Requiem*, Berlioz's *Tuba mirum*, not to mention works like Verdi's *Requiem* or Brahms's *German Requiem*, or Stravinsky's *Symphony of Psalms*, were at best religious only in part; in other parts they were magnificent failures as religious music.[56] If some parts were religious in spirit, the other parts were Sensate, the music of opera or symphony. Further-more, in their technique the religious compositions of these centuries have almost invariably been Sensate.[57]

[55] Since the seventeenth century, "almost all the religious music is penetrated by the profane spirit, which abandons, or what is still worse, alters the traditions. There are many Christian artists, but there is little of pure Christian art." Combarieu, *Histoire*, Vol. XI, p. 208.

[56] "The Masses and other sacred compositions of Haydn and Mozart contain a great deal of beautiful music, but they are utterly unsuited to the purpose of the ritual. They strike one as being distinctly pagan, both in style and sentiment. Those of Haydn, one feels, would be a more appropriate accompaniment to the bucolic rites of Ceres and Demeter than to those of the Catholic Church, while those of Mozart, not even excepting the famous Requiem, with their subtle sensuous charm, suggest pagan divinities in disguise, like the Saint John and Sainte Anne of Leonardo da Vinci. . . . As to the great *Missa Solemnis* of Beethoven, it is pantheistic rather than Christian, mystical rather than religious," and has "frequently a dramatic, secular style." Even it, from this standpoint, "is a magnificent failure." Even Bach's Mass is not quite perfect in this respect. C. Gray, *op. cit.*, pp. 194 and 183.

[57] One can listen to the religious music of different periods through the records issued. Take, for instance, a series: a Gregorian chant (or some part of it, *e.g.*, Agnus Dei), Pales-trina's Agnus Dei from his Mass, Orlando di Lasso's Agnus Dei, Bach's *Mass in B minor*, Beethoven's Agnus Dei, from his *Missa solemnis*, the requiems of Mozart, Berlioz, Brahms, Verdi, and so on. If one listens attentively to this series, one hears quite clearly the trends discussed. Such evidence is of the first class, more valid than any statistical table or even any indirect corroboration.

Since religious music has been dwindling, becoming less and less Ideational and more Sensate, it follows that the Sensate music for the last eight centuries has been correspondingly increasing.[58]

It is to be said, on the other hand, that in the period from the end of the fifteenth century to the beginning of the nineteenth, all in all the grand music represented (special currents exempted) a mixture of both forms, without an extreme or monopolistic preponderance of either. In the fifteenth and sixteenth centuries, and in the first part of the seventeenth, the Ideational form was still slightly preponderant; in the second part of the seventeenth and in the eighteenth century the Sensate form was increasingly preponderant, but without decisively breaking the balance. The Idealistic music of these centuries incorporated in itself all the purest, noblest, and richest there is in Sensate beauty — was free from its rude, vulgar, cheap, too sensational and smart aspects; at the same time it still soared in the realm of the superempirical values, still was attached to them, guided and inspired by them and by their inner beauty. In that music the supreme inspiration still comes from the sublime ideals and idealistic values, which were a substitution for the entirely otherworldly values of the pure Ideational music. As such it uplifted the common man to the heights of the immortal values, showing him the kingdom of infinity; telling him in the Sensate language about *universalia ante rem;* ennobling, purifying, and giving him wings on which to soar far above the plains of the empirical world.

It is not incidental that the religious and the secular music of this period differ from each other very little. Bach, Mozart, Handel, Beethoven often use similar airs and music in their secular and religious compositions. This means that both kinds are Idealistic, neither otherworldly religious, nor sensually hedonistic.

With different shadings all this is true of the great works of the great masters of these centuries. In Palestrina's works, vocal music reaches its heights in purity, nobility, idealism, and sensuous perfection. After J. S. Bach, Handel, Haydn, Mozart, and Beethoven, the greatest of the

---

[58] Here are a few quotations from Combarieu, *Histoire*, Vol. I, which corroborate the above. Since the fourteenth century, "The profane *chanson* develops more and more and tends to acquire a supremacy equal to that of the religious chants; but it is treated as a motet, while *en revanche*, they compose many Masses with melodies taken from the popular tunes" (p. 447). "Then music makes another decisive conquest, namely that of the qualities thanks to which music is an art of charm and seduction, not in the primitive and magic sense, but in the modern sense of these terms" (p. 447). Music begins "to express these human sentiments which are not entirely spiritual and sometimes are of the lowest part of our inner life" (p. 451). "In the Renaissance, music sometimes humanizes itself and becomes realistic" (p. 452).

great, in whose works music reached its highest Idealistic peaks, the descent to the cheaper and more extreme sensatism is indicated clearly.

Though there is no doubt that in the music of these centuries there were several "muddy" streams of an exaggerated and too earthly sensualism, and though there is also no doubt that even in the works of these great masters there were several places where they fell from the heights and produced something very sensual, nevertheless, when the bulk of the great works of the period is considered, the characteristics of the Idealistic music are unquestionably true of them, from Palestrina to Beethoven's *Ninth Symphony* and his last quartets (especially opera 127, 131, 132, and 135). In the Palestrina-Vittoria-Lasso-Bach period, the inspiration and the main value of the music is still religious, and even Christian religious,[59] superempirical, serene and absolute, dressed in the noblest and sublimest robes of empirical beauty. There is still the cathedral and *Adoremus*, Christ and the Kingdom of God in it, and either unquestioning faith or a rationalistic will to believe. This faith transforms into Idealistic colors even the folk songs. In the Lulli-Rameau and Gluck-Mozart-Haydn streams, the purely religious value is less noticeable, but the music is like a pure dream on a spring morning, of a beautiful and innocent youth, not yet touched by the prose of everyday life; still living in a world of dreams, free from hatred, even from tragedy. It is a fresh, pure, spontaneous song of youth, idealistic, imaginative, with silver laughter; without any burden of sin or tragedy, or worry or "dirt of daily vulgarity." In Beethoven, finally, we have the music of a sage, to whom all the ecstasy of wisdom and all the tragedy of reality are known; who has scaled the heights of empirical pain and pleasure, with its noble and vulgar aspects; who has fathomed all this and has not been seduced by it. He knows its inexorability as Destiny, but he knows also that beside and beyond it there is another world, the world of the Godhead, the supersensual values, something difficult to define and put into words, but expressible in the mysterious language of music. This comes out with special intensity, in spite of many relapses, in the works of Beethoven of the third and last period, that achieve the unachievable and definitely cross the boundary line between the Sensate and noumenal worlds. Other streams were nearer to the earth, especially the theatrical

---

[59] Some of them, like Vittoria (the El Greco of music), remained intensely religious and wanted to be purely ideational. "Many evil and depraved men abuse music as an excitant in order to plunge into earthly delight, instead of raising themselves by means of it to the contemplation of God and divine things. The art of song should be entirely devoted to the aim and end for which it was originally intended, namely, praise and glory of God," writes Vittoria. C. Gray, *op. cit.*, p. 83.

streams of musical drama and musical comedy (*opera buffa*) — which, headed by Monteverde, emerged in the sixteenth and seventeenth centuries — and the gallant streams of Rameau, but even they were free from the vulgarities of naturalism and exaggerated theatricality which invaded music in the nineteenth and twentieth centuries.

The trend toward ever-increasing sensatism in music is shown by various data. One of these concerns the *theatricalism of music*. It has been indicated that this quality is one of the important characteristics of Sensate art in any field. There is no doubt that quantitatively and qualitatively the theatricalism of music has grown steadily in the last two or three centuries. This is manifest in the fact that opera, especially comic opera, not to mention vaudeville and entertainments of a similar low order, emerged only at the end of the sixteenth and in the seventeenth century. "By the middle of the seventeenth century opera . . . had become a popular form of entertainment. In Venice alone there were no fewer than seventeen opera houses." [60] Somewhat similar was the situation in other urban centers.

In the field of religious music, oratorio, as a theatrical form of music, emerged in the seventeenth century.[61] This is a direct evidence of my contention, but it is not all the evidence.[62] What is important also is that these theatrical forms of music have been rapidly growing during the last three centuries. We divided the important musical works mentioned in the above histories into the "theatrical" (oratorio, opera, and comic opera) and the nontheatrical (cantata, organ and chamber music, symphony, concerto, suite, etc.) and roughly computed their number in these centuries. The results are shown in Table 34.

TABLE 34.   FLUCTUATION OF THEATRICAL AND NONTHEATRICAL
COMPOSITIONS BY CENTURIES

Century	Number of Important Theatrical Combinations (opera, musical drama, musical comedy, oratorio)	Number of Important Nontheatrical Compositions
XVII	96	317
XVIII	163	353
XIX	207	395

[60] *Ibid.*, pp. 13 and 136.   [61] See Combarieu, *Histoire*, Vol. XI, chap. xli.

[62] Do not confuse this theatricalism with the religious medieval mysteries. These were symbolic and dealt with superempirical values. As such, they did not try to "sell" a fictitious empirical reality to an audience, instead of the real one. They did not function for the sake of amusement and sensual pleasure. In these and many other traits the mysteries and religious dramas of the Middle Ages are radically different from the theatrical productions in the modern sense of the word.

Thus while the number of nontheatrical works increased but slightly, that of important theatrical works increased more than twice, an additional evidence of the "theatrical" nature of modern culture, shown by other compartments of art.

C. Lalo indicates, in his own way, the sensate and superficial nature of theatrical music, as opposed to "classic" music.

The great classics are not dramaturgies and the great dramaturgies are not and cannot be classics. The reason for that is that by its nature the technique of drama is a hash, an inevitable impurity. . . . The great works of the classics do not intend to put a drama into a symphony, as it is often said; but, on the contrary, to relegate the theater and drama to the class of an inferior *genre* of music. It is romanticism which made a grand art out of the theater. The theater is in the same relationship to music that journalism is to literature. It is not to be wondered at that the classics did not try to be journalists.[63]

The theatricalism of the music of the nineteenth and twentieth centuries is manifested in many other forms, both quantitative and qualitative. They give additional support to the above data and acquire a peculiar meaning in its light. Take one or two examples.

According to the majority of the critics, the greatest and certainly the most influential composer of the nineteenth century is Richard Wagner. He is its mightiest musical dramatist. His music is theatrical, not only in the sense of being opera, but music drama, produced with the co-operation of all the arts — poetry, painting, mimic, music, by all the means which can impress, and with music used as a component of the drama, rather than as an end in itself. This sounds like Ideational music. But when one considers that his is human drama, centered, as usual, around profane love, which is beautified by legendary and romantic figures, one can understand that Wagner is the radically opposite pole to any Ideational music. "Wagner was neither a musician who made poems, nor a poet who made music, but a 'theatricalist,' who made both whenever he wanted them,"[64] is one of the best definitions of Wagner I have come across, in spite of the superficiality of its author.

Other postclassics and Romantics, be they Schubert or Schumann, Bruckner or Smetana, Berlioz or Verdi, Bizet, Brahms, Tschaikovsky, Moussorgsky, or Debussy, show the same tendency, but perhaps in a less degree.[65]

[63] Lalo, *Esquisse*, p. 292.

[64] Egon Friedel, *A Cultural History of the Modern Age* (New York, 1932), Vol. III, p. 309.

[65] On the level of the vulgar art of the present time, this unholy theatricalism and its tasteless mixture of everything without the slightest reason is shown by the popular "shows,"

The next satellite of the sensual art generally, and of sensual music particularly, is *quantitative colossalism*. We saw how successfully it invaded the Graeco-Roman music in its Sensate stage. The same is evident in the music of the last three centuries, and especially of the nineteenth and twentieth. Yes, the music of this period has certainly grown to be the "biggest" and the most colossal in a quantitative respect. I have indicated how small was the number of the performers, whether in Greece in the period of its Ideational and Idealistic music, or in the Middle Ages, or even in the centuries of the European Idealistic music. As we pass from the Middle Ages to the twentieth century, the colossalism grows in many ways. Take, for instance, the *size of the orchestra* for which musical compositions are scored. Here are typical data. Monteverde's *Orpheus* (1607) is scored, all in all, for about thirty instruments: two gravicembalos, two contrabassi de viola, ten viola da braccio, one double harp, one small flute, two morgani di ligno, etc. The orchestras of Lulli, Bach, or Stamitz were ordinarily not larger.[66]

From the seventeenth to the eighteenth centuries new instruments are introduced, one after another, enlarging the orchestra, and the number of players on the same instruments is increased. In 1720 the flute is introduced. Handel introduced the trombone and valtorna; Mozart the clarinet; Gosseck several percussion instruments; then came the tuba corva (Lesueur), the organ (Rust), celesta, piano, bell, piccolo, various horns, and so on.

In spite of this, excepting the "parade music" of the time of the French Revolution, with its monster orchestras and choruses, the orchestra of the eighteenth century was still moderate in its size. Even the orchestra for which Beethoven scored his first to the fifth symphonies was still moderate and well balanced.

When we come to the nineteenth and twentieth centuries the size notably increases. Berlioz's *Fantastic Symphony* (1830) is scored for

---

musical comedies, and our "talkies." They mix everything — music, conversation, songs, pantomimes, and heaven knows what else. And what is still more typical is that in many "comedies" and "talkies" the hero suddenly plunges without any reason, in the most important moments (when he is about to kiss the heroine), into a long and mostly raucous singing of some current "crooning hit." In these vulgar *chef d'œuvres* of our time in this unmusical "Music Goes Round and Round" interpolation, the discussed trait assumes great conspicuousness and exhibits the lowest grade of taste one can imagine, even from the standpoint of a keen sensualism.

[66] See the details in H. Kretzschmar's *Geschichte der Oper* (Leipzig, 1919). Also E. Wellesz, *Der Beginn des musikalischen barock und die Anfänge der Oper in Wien* (Leipzig, 1922); R. Haas, *Die musik des barocks* (Potsdam, 1928); R. Rolland, "L'opera," in the *Encyclopédie de la musique*, quoted.

more than a hundred instruments. His *Tuba mirum* (1838) for a still larger orchestra (not to mention the chorus). About the size of the *Fantastic Symphony* orchestra was that for the *Rienzi* of Wagner (1840). As we come to Wagner's *Gotterdämmerung* (1877), Bruckner's *Eighth Symphony* (1884), Mahler's *First Symphony* (1888), Richard Strauss's *Heldenleben* (1899), the size and complexity of the orchestra still further increase. In Strauss's *Electra* (1908), Mahler's *Fifth Symphony* (1904) and then his *Eighth* (1910), Schönberg's *Gurrelieder* (1901), and Stravinsky's *Sacré du printemps* (1913), the necessary instruments number one hundred and twenty and more.

From seven singers in the Gregorian *Schola*, from four to twenty for Palestrina's music, from some thirty to sixty instruments in the regular orchestras of Bach and Mozart, the orchestra of the nineteenth and twentieth centuries has certainly grown to be colossal.

The same is true of the choruses and other instrumentalities of music, beginning with the buildings and ending with the stage. We live in the age of the highest and largest halls, in an age of monster choruses, even in provincial music festivals, in an age of large-scale technical means of providing music in every form. The totality of the modern technical musical equipment of a regular good-sized stage used in vaudeville and ordinary shows is probably larger than that used in the greatest musical festival of the Middle Ages or even of the centuries from the fifteenth to the eighteenth inclusive.

One sees the same trait in many more intimate forms of music : the scale of tonality has grown wider in range; the polytonality greater; the contrasts sharper, more used and more abused, especially in the *fortissimo;* the scale of dissonances has been growing; the proportion and character of noises, which tend more and more to replace melody; also the variety of chromatics, of timbres, of rhythms, of tempos, as well.

In passing, it is worth while to mention another trend very symbolic in its character. It is an aftermath of this quantitative growth and also a mark of sensuality. It consists of a steady increase of the brass, wood wind, and percussion instruments in orchestration. While in the compositions of the seventeenth and eighteenth centuries they played a very modest role — and the brass and percussion instruments often played hardly any — the compositions of the nineteenth and twentieth centuries have been giving them a more and more important part. In the field of vulgar music, it has led to the modern domination of the brass band and the saxophone. The fact is hardly incidental, it is symbolic, the brass music driving out the more delicate music of the strings. Causally it is one of the satellites of the Sensate music and its passion for size. We have in our days a replica of what happened in Greece and Rome in the period of domination of such music.

The evidences of the trend discussed and of the powerful domination of Sensate music in the nineteenth and twentieth centuries are not limited by the above. There are many others. Such is the *ever-increasing complication of the texture of music and the deliberate creation of technical difficulties.* While ordinary orchestras can play the works of the classics, many a modern work, like some by Stravinsky, Smidt, Schönberg, Honegger, Mahler, taxes to the limit the resources of even the very best and most virtuosic orchestras. Another aspect is the *ever-increasing role of technique,* not of genius or talent, but technique which is the result of long training in order to be capable of the most difficult "tricks," whatever they may be. The great masterpieces in art and literature and science have mostly been spontaneous in the sense that they were the result of a free flow of the creative forces of a genius not dominated by technique, to whom technique is a minor matter and who creates his own. *The decadent periods, whether in art or science or religion, have often been marked by this substitution of technique for genius;* of specific training in technical skill rather than real creativeness or inspiration. *In such periods, technique usually dominates the field;* scientists talk mainly of scientific technique, with which they usually do not produce anything but mediocrity; critics and artists talk of the technique of scoring, of playing, of writing, of painting. Technique becomes the alpha and omega of art. And artist creators strive to show first of all their mastery of it, and especially some of their own inventions in it. Hence the cerebral character of music or art created according to the prescription of the approved technique. Hence their striving for difficulties and a technical *tour de force* as supposedly the highest mark of mastery. Thus the technical virtuosity of such periods becomes indeed amazing. All these things are various aspects of the same phenomenon: the Sensate character of art. And of all that we have more than enough, in the music of the last part of the nineteenth and the twentieth century.[67]

I shall mention just a few additional satellites of Sensate music which

---

[67] So far as the domination of Sensate music is concerned, it was naturally described and formulated long ago. One of the prominent theorizers in the call to "naturalism" and "imitation" of empirical life was J. J. Rousseau. Somewhat later one of the voices clamoring for Sensate music was A. Reicha, who in his *Art du compositeur dramatique* (Paris, 1833), p. 107, says: "We think that the ancient music of the Church in the famous style of Palestrina is unfitted to our age. This style is devoid of musical ideas, of air, of symmetry, of grace, of variety; it can interest us but little. It should be replaced by a new style."

have appeared during the nineteenth and twentieth centuries. Such are the *professionalism and individualism* of the music composers. Anonymity and collectivity of creative activities do not exist. Everybody wants to attach his name to his work. Everybody wants to be "original," "singular," "individual." To say of somebody's achievement, whether composition or performance, that it is "regular," "common," or devoid of individuality, is to offend the artist deeply. Professionalism and decay of collective activities have gone so far that nowadays every distant farm woman and every village lad needs a professional instructor to tell them how they shall sing, how to play musical instruments, or how to musically educate themselves. Collective creation, be it folk song or just a tune, has practically disappeared. Instead, the last "hit" of the crooner or of a successful song writer is broadcast over the country. In the Four H clubs and county singing clubs, the people, like puppets, are drilled by professionals in what is called the singing of masterpieces, from Aïda to the last popular song. The results are — well, many of the readers have probably heard these famous concerts, pretentious but as a rule mechanical and poor musically.

On the other hand there are professional unions of composers, singers, musicians, quite similar to the Dionysiac unions of musicians in Greece and similar unions in Rome. But the collective creation in music by the body of the people, as it was practiced in the Ideational and Idealistic periods, has practically disappeared.

Another satellite and symptom of the trend discussed is the *enormous development of musical education, musical criticism, musical discussion, and musical aestheticism.* Nowadays almost every boy and girl of good family is obliged to be "musically educated." Innumerable public and private agencies strive to give a musical education to every child through singing clubs, governmental organizations, public schools, etc. Musical criticism blossoms in every copy of practically every newspaper. Musical journals, musical schools, musical discussions, departments of music in every college and high school — all these are present in abundance. If the production of masterpieces depended upon the number of people involved in musical activities, then certainly we should expect a generous crop. The reality, however, does not agree with that expectation.

Sensate art is created for a market. Nowadays, when the artist is a professional and makes his living by his activity, he has to create a marketable commodity. Therefore he has to create, not perhaps what he would like to, but what can make money. In order to do this, he has to adapt his work to the prevailing taste of the largest class of consumers. Such an adaptation means *vulgarization and commercialization*. Hence their presence in our musical culture. It can hardly be helped.

Its other aspect is a *cheap sensationalism*. If an artist is to make money, he has to make a "hit." To make a "hit," his work has to have something sensational which will get wide publicity, arouse interest, attract a full house, and so on. All this we have to a degree hardly equaled before.

Sensate music and culture are of the world of Becoming, of incessant and rapid change. Since the value of Sensate music is in its *sounds* as such; and since many repetitions of the same combination of sounds soon become familiar and boring, *musical art, under such conditions, demands an incessant change, unceasing variety, contrasting fashions.* Of all this we have also more than enough. The best sellers in music, like those in literature, are acclaimed, and then forgotten the next season; something new has to come incessantly, and not merely new, but contrastingly new. Hence the rapid change in fads and fashions in the music of these centuries. Within the nineteenth century alone, there were at least three waves of classicism-romanticism. As for smaller changes, they are almost seasonal. Even the leading musical critics, in their reviews of the performances of the great orchestras or conductors, make it almost a rule to complain that "only last season such and such a composition was played, and now it is again on the program." One of the commonest criticisms is that the programs have little variety; and so on. We are so accustomed to this psychology that we do not notice the extraordinary character of such everyday statements. Imagine a medieval "highbrow" saying that only last season the Chants, or the Kyrie, or the Gloria was performed, and now it is again on the program! Such a statement would have been impossible in the period of Ideational music, and in such periods every Kyrie, Gloria, Agnus Dei, Sanctus, and so on was performed several times a day, and yet one can hardly discover any inscription or statement of the medieval intellectuals that they were given too often and that they should be replaced by something new and different. When this is understood, all the significance of the daily statements of our critics and of our public will become clear. Yes, we cannot help striving for something ever new and varied and contrasting. If we even want to stick to something, we cannot, because such is the nature of Sensate art generally and of Sensate music particularly. We have to chase after novelty and variety of subject, of technique, of "trick," whether we want to or not.

The result of this unceasing change is an ever-increasing trend of Sensate music toward something not just beautiful, but *striking, extreme, exotic, picturesque, and monstrous.* Sensual beauty of normal form soon becomes familiar and tiresome. In a mediocre form it is bound to be quickly exhausted. The artist who is striving to give something quite new and the public who is possessed by the passion for novelty both sooner or later are driven to look for that new and original in the realms little exploited by the classics: in the field of the unusual and especially the extreme; in the vast region of the perverse and negative phenomena of life unexploited and avoided by Ideational as well as by Idealistic music. In the fields of positive values, the sensual music cannot compete with the Ideational or Idealistic. If their topics were God and the absolute values, or the hero and the ideal types of man and sociocultural values, the sensual music is bound to take something either perverse, exotic or negative, or empirically dramatic or just mediocre — types such as *The Emperor Jones, Heldenleben, Sinfonia Domestica,* or the urbanized cavemen (in the *Sacré*), with human sacrifice, of course, interwoven around sex (also of course), or comedians (*Petrushka*) or clowns (*Pagliacci*), or a pregnant woman with her lover (Schönberg), or gypsies and smugglers (*Carmen*), or railroad business (*Pacific*), or romantic brigands (*Robert le Diable*), or the Voceks, and so on. As we shall see, in literature and dramatic art, this trend is still more conspicuous (remember the success of the series of perverse types given in O'Neill's plays), but it is quite tangible in music also.

One of the most important evidences of that is the *growth of musical comedy.* Like almost any comedy, it is woven mainly around the negative types and events and values. The grand art of the Middle Ages did not know it. In the form of the *opera buffa,* it appeared in the sixteenth century and has been growing ever since. In our sample we got twenty-four for the seventeenth century, ninety-seven for the eighteenth, and one hundred and six for the nineteenth. Quite a growth! Like caricature and satire in painting, comedy in literature and drama, the musical comedy, by its very nature, deals with the ridiculous, stupid, perverse, criminal aspects of life.[68] Its growth, therefore, is a direct corroboration of the statements previously made.

Besides the directly negative and perverse subjects, another refuge and source of supply for new and unusual subjects is the *types, phenomena, and*

---

[68] See in Combarieu, *Histoire,* Vol. III, pp. 444–452, a list of comic operas and musical comedies with the number of the performances of each in the *Opéra,* since 1805 to 1914, and in the *Opéra Comique,* since 1807 to 1910.

*values on the level of commonness and mediocrity, devoid of any heroism or
halo.* Since these fields were also intentionally avoided by the Ideational-
Idealistic art, the sensational art naturally appropriates them, depicts
them with all the empirical circumstances of real life, and proudly parades
them as "naturalism," "realism," and truth. This naturalism, in all its
flatness, is another variety of the phenomenon typical of a sensual mentality and sensual music and is present abundantly in contemporary
music.[69] The railroad-airplane (Honegger), factory (Molotov), toccata
(Prokoffieff), *May First Symphony* (Shostakovitch), *Noises of London*
(Elgar), football (Martinou), are just a few recent examples of that.

The third source for the novelty to which the musician of sensualism
turns is something exotic, sensually exotic particularly, which, like a
cocktail or mystery or detective story, can provide a diversion from the
habitual routine of life (office hours, day-in and day-out drudgery).
Hence the *exotic, the picturesque, the sexually charged "romanticism"*
of the Hollywood type — "Isn't It Romantic?" Egyptians, Chinese,
Persians, Africans, Turks, Mongols, ancient peoples, cavemen, Romans,
Jews, are presented in the most naïvely fantastic but picturesque manner,
quite different from our own society. These and many other exoticisms
(woven around sex chiefly, of course) have been one of the most popular
sources of supply of the ever new and different to which sensual music is
doomed. *Samson and Delilah, Islamey, Salammbo, Île de Calypso,
Oberon, Salomé, Aïda, Thaïs, Astarté, Thamara, L'Africaine, Coppelia,
Sappho, Faire, Othello, Le Prise de Trois, Ariadne, Bacchus*, the whole
Wagnerian series of the Ring, *Tristan and Isolde*, each more exotic than its
predecessor! The majority of the operas and a considerable part of
other musical compositions of the end of the eighteenth and of the nineteenth and twentieth centuries have subjects of this kind.[70]

Finally, *pathos, dramatism, emotion* — especially woven around love:
love tragic and comic, light and heavy, of the caveman type and of the
chorus-girl type, Don Juanish, Othelloish, of the Romeo type; love
ancient, medieval, of modern Broadway; love of gods, of devils; love
angelic; love in every imaginable form, with veiled and unveiled sex —
all this naturally pervades our music and our art generally, as it always
does in the period of dominant sensual art and mentality. The more
dramatic, pathetic, emotional the work, the better, the greater, the more
successful it is.

[69] Compare Combarieu, *Histoire*, Vol. III, p. 452.

[70] An analysis of the list of operas and of the comic operas given by Combarieu is exceedingly suggestive, from this standpoint.

One of the manifestations of this emotionality and pathos is an increasing sentimental sadness of grand as well as of the vulgar contemporary music. This has been noticed by several historians of music. Speaking of that Combarieu says that this *triste sentimentality* has been growing, even in comic opera. "Music of the comic theater, which by definition has to be gay, has become sad and dolorous. Already in the melodies of Massenet, in *Werther* and *Manon*, the intensity of the expression of love is a voice of suffering. In the *Louise* of Charpentier, it is a poignant sadness." [71]

In agreement with this is the moronic and sentimentally sad crooning in the field of contemporary vulgar music. Our study of the major and minor keys in which great compositions are written indicates that the proportion of those written in the minor key has been increasing. The minor as such was regarded rather negatively up to the eighteenth century (in the sixteenth century it was considered something painful and abnormal: *si lontano un poco della perfezione del harmonia; flebile nescio quid*, as it was characterized by Zarlino in 1558). And Rameau in 1750 in his *Demonstration du principe de l'harmonie* had to plead especially for its right in music. Through Bach the minor became equal to the major and then, parallel with an increase of the harmonic complexity of music and its tonality, the minor tended to be used more and more. Professor I. Lapshin's study of the dominant tonality of the works shows the following coefficient of tonality — the coefficient being the sum of major and minor keys of the six tonalities of the major and of the six tonalities of the minor, which are dominant in the work of the composer studied.

Mozart, 20; Haydn, 21; Beethoven, 26; Glinka, 20; Weber, 24; Meyerbeer, 23; Chopin, 42; Rimsky-Korsakoff, 28; Grieg, 24; Moussorgsky, 27; Scriabin, 45; Tschaikovsky, 25. In the percentages of the works written in the major and minor keys the results are somewhat similar. For the eighteenth century the percentage (computed upon the basis of the works of the main composers) is 22; from 1800 to 1850 it rises to 25; from 1850 to 1900 to 38.5.

The figures can be only roughly representative, but they show the trend. Though the sad or gay impression of music depends upon the total means used, and among them the minor may sound gay and the major dolorous, nevertheless, normally the statements expressed many times from Aristotle up to Pierre Maillard [72] that the minor usually

[71] Combarieu, *Histoire*, Vol. III, p. 452.
[72] See *Traité de sons* (Paris, 1910).

sounds sad, dolorous, lamentable, are hardly wrong.   Under such an assumption — and I subscribe to it — an increase of the minor is also a
symptom of growing sentimental sadness, emotionality, and lamentability
of music.   We have seen that these qualities and the pathetic are the
usual satellites of Sensate art in all its compartments, and this is an
additional corroboration of the growth of Sensate music in the last
two centuries.

The growth of all these tendencies to ultrasensatism, sexualism, exoticism, and naturalism in the effort, on the one hand, to reflect in music the
empirical Sensate reality — and especially its common, everyday, or
pathological aspects — and, on the other — as a counterpoison — some
exotic and fantastic aspects of it as a remedy for the boredom of prosaism
is shown also in the approximate statistics of the main subjects or themes
of the prominent operas for the last three centuries.   Table 35 gives the
figures from our sample taken from the same sources.

In the classification, by mythological and pseudo-historical operas are
meant the operas and music where the subject is taken from ancient
mythology and pseudo history, like most of the operas of Lulli, the aristocratic operas of the Venetian school, and the *galant* operas of Rameau.
Similar subjects have been used in symphonic poems, like the *Prometheus*
of Beethoven, the *Orpheus* of Monteverde, Glück, and Liszt, the *Ariadne*
of Richard Strauss, the *Oedipus* of Stravinsky, *Psychée* of César Franck,
etc.

By comic and *genre* music are meant most of the classical comic operas
and similar works, like Rossini's *Barber of Seville*, Pergolesi's *Serva-
Padrona* (1733), Moussorgsky's *Fair of Sorochnitzy*, Smetana's *Bartered
Bride*, and the works of Weber, Cherubini, Cambini, and others.

By revolutionary and war types are meant works like Tschaikovsky's
1812, Gossek's, Catel's, Lesueur's, Cherubini's, Cambini's revolutionary
music; Cretri's *Dionys le tyran*, Beethoven's *Leonora* and *Fidelio*, Rossini's *William Tell*, Meyerbeer's *Huguenots* and *Prophet*, Moussorgsky's
Khovantzchina, étc.

By animalism and *paysage*, clouds, sea, morning, night, seasons, forest,
thunderstorm; songs about a flea or a rat or a lion; the waterfall, desert;
birds and other creatures and the *paysage* subjects expressed in musical
terms, like Debussy's *Clouds* and *Sea;* Rimsky-Korsakoff's *Scheherazade*,
Wagner's *Siegfried's Idyll*, Berlioz's *Damnation of Faust*, Haydn's and
Glazunoff's *Seasons*, and so on.

By historical works, those like Moussorgsky's *Boris Godunoff*, Wagner's
Meistersinger, the *Kitege* of Rimsky-Korsakoff, etc.

By exoticism, works like Lesueur's *Île de Calypso*, Beethoven's *Ruins of Athens*, Weber's *Oberon* (Turkish theme), *Tourandott* (Chinese), Glinka's *Ruslan*, Balakireff's *Islamey*, Strauss's *Salomé*, etc.

By urbanism and *nature morte*, the naturalistic reflection of the industrial, urban, and mechanized or still-life phenomena, like the factory, railway, airplane, subway, machine, engine, skyscraper, noises of the city, football, city crowds, etc.

TABLE 35. FLUCTUATION OF COMPOSITIONS BY CONTENT

Period	Mythology Pseudo history	Genre Comedy	Revolution War	Folk Legend Paysage Animalism	Historism	Exoticism	Urbanism Nature morte
1600–1620 ⎫	30	5	—	—	—	—	—
1620–1640 ⎭	—	—	—	—	—	—	—
1640–1660	18	2	—	—	—	—	—
1660–1680	25	7	—	—	—	—	—
1680–1700	50	10	—	—	—	—	—
1600–1700	*123*	*24*	—	—	—	—	—
1700–1720	23	10	—	—	—	—	—
1720–1740	34	6	—	—	—	—	—
1740–1760	17	13	—	—	—	—	—
1760–1780	26	47	—	—	—	—	—
1780–1800	12	21	11	—	—	—	—
1700–1800	*112*	*97*	*11*	—	—	—	—
1800–1820	14	26	3	—	—	—	—
1820–1840	14	14	5	2	4	—	—
1840–1860	14	12	4	16	5	8	
1860–1880	9	40	15	20	10	13	12
1880–1900	12	14	3	25	8	20	8
1800–1900	*63*	*106*	*30*	*63*	*27*	*41*	*20*
1900–1920	15	15	6	19	6	11	20

The sample is of course incomplete and only approximate, but roughly it reflects the reality. It shows that animalism and *paysage, nature morte*, exoticism, and urbanism emerged only in the nineteenth century; here the trend is identical with what we have seen in the fields of painting and sculpture. Urbanism reflects in the most naturalistic way the routine of daily life of the common average type of man. The same is shown by the increase of the *genre* and comedy music. Historism, which grows usually only in the period of the domination of sensatism in art, appears also here only in the nineteenth century. Revolution and war is an incarnation of the pathetic, dramatic, and emotional. It emerged in the eighteenth century.

As a contrast to these growing classes, "mythology" and "pseudo history," which deal mainly with the hero, with the deeply tragic and heroic aspects of life, the class which is the favorite subject of Idealistic art, shows a rapid decrease; the little halo of the heroic, not to mention the divine, fades in the realm of growing Sensate music. The music of the nineteenth and the twentieth centuries has turned away more and more from such a "superstition" as God and the superempirical values, and from such a "prejudice" of the aristocratic old regime as a hero; instead, like all the fields of art, it has been captivated by the Voceks, by the Carmens, by the seduced Marguerites, by the criminals, by the proletarians, and others like them. This is the essence of what modern art calls proudly "realism," "naturalism," "free art," and often the "art as a great educator."

It is really an interpretation of man and of all the sociocultural values on a decidedly low level, and is a general characteristic of the overripe phase of any Sensate culture and mentality. From the heavens and heroic heights it always descends to social gutters and cellars. That is its destiny!

Under these conditions, one can hardly expect from contemporary music either great — eternal — creations or any consistent style or any inner harmony and peace. Inner emptiness and brilliant technique — that is its present situation. It is probably doomed to go more and more to pieces; to break into smaller and smaller fragments, each of which tends to be more and more peculiar, but all innerly incoherent, fragmentary, and impressing us more by their freakiness than by their beauty. Inner emptiness and the most complicated and brilliant technique are the destiny to which it is doomed until it is replaced by the Ideational music, which has still to appear, but will probably grow eventually. The first clumsy signs of it, in some of the modern "isms," seem already to have come to the surface. The works of many of the most modern composers, like Stravinsky and Honegger, show already a rupture with the purely Sensate music, quite similar to the reaction of the anti-Visualists in painting. These modernists, or "Cubists in Music," are in real revolt against the prevalent forms of Sensate music. Some of them quite openly brush aside the sensually pleasing functions of music and profess something quite different from them, as the objectives of their compositions.[73] So far, like the anti-Visualists, they are reactionists. Like the cubists, they have cut their moorings from the shore of sensualism, but they have not arrived at any new and real port where they and their music can settle permanently. They are still searching, but they do not know what they are looking for, or, if they think they

---

[73] See, for instance, I. Stravinsky's *Chronicle of My Life* (London, 1936).

know, they still remain children of the Sensate age, with all its Sensate mentality.

Whether they constitute one of the "twists" of the sensual stream, or are the forerunners of a coming Ideational wave remains to be seen. What is significant is that here in music we find exactly the same situation as in other fields of art studied. The Sensate wave has reached its height; in its traits it shows all the signs of overripeness. How long will it stay there? Is its tide going to rise still higher, or is it going to ebb? Let us abstain from prophecy. What is important is a comprehension of the position where our culture stands at the present moment. The above gives some information in this respect. And it is significant that this anti-Sensate twist at the end of the nineteenth and in the twentieth century is met in other fields of the fine arts, and we shall meet it again in almost all the other compartments of our culture. Such a unanimity guarantees the validity of the result. The "twist" is but a reflection of what has happened in the sociocultural reality.

The above sums up the main waves of the Ideational and Sensate music, during some twenty-five hundred to twenty-seven hundred years studied. Besides these tidal fluctuations, there have been many minor ones, but they are outside the scope of this work, though the most important are reflected in the data given. So far as the tidal waves are concerned, they have proceeded in their essentials parallel with similar waves in other fields of art. The main discrepancies in time are as follows.

First, music became classically Ideational in the fifth and sixth centuries A.D., while other arts — painting, sculpture, architecture — achieved their classic Ideationality somewhat later, by two or three centuries.

Second, the Idealistic phase of music lagged, compared with that phase in the other arts; while these reached the Idealistic stage in the thirteenth century, music entered it in the fifteenth and stayed in that phase longer, up to the beginning of the nineteenth century.

Such are the main differences. They answer the problem to what extent various generalizations of the theories considered in Chapters Five and Six are valid. The answer is rather negative in regard to the existence of a universally uniform sequence of leading and lagging claimed by such theories. In one period music was leading painting, sculpture, and architecture; in another, it was lagging. We shall meet these phenomena many times.

Finally, the results show that, all in all, the four forms of art studied moved together in their changes, but the simultaneousness of the change was neither very close nor perfectly integrated. We shall discuss the meaning of this later; for the time being, let us just note it. The last remark is recurrent: by this chapter, an additional installment is paid toward the redemption of the promissory note.[74]

[74] The list of musicians and compositions studied in the above samples of this chapter will be given in the fourth volume of this work, in a chapter on the fluctuation of the curve of creativeness in music.

Chapter Thirteen

FLUCTUATION OF IDEATIONAL AND SENSATE FORMS OF LITERATURE AND CRITICISM

I. PRELITERARY GROUPS

Literature, like the other forms of art, may be of two fundamental types: Ideational and Sensate. And between these extremes lie the many Mixed varieties. The literary work which deals with the "invisible" world, superempirical and transcendental, and in which words and images are but symbols of this world, is, according to definition, Ideational literature. The work which depicts and describes empirical phenomena in their sensory aspect, where words and images have nothing but their empirical meaning, is Sensate literature. A considerable number of purely religious and magical literary works (hymns, dithyrambs, prayers, odes, narratives, proverbs, riddles, incantations, etc.), on the one hand, and such works as Dante's *Divine Comedy*, on the other, are examples of the first type; purely "realistic" and "naturalistic" novels, dramas, plays, lyrics (for example, the works of Zola and Sinclair Lewis) are examples of the second. The pure Ideational literature is not concerned with the empirical world of the senses; it does not strive at all to reflect this world accurately. Moreover, its objective is not to give a purely sensate enjoyment. Its "soul" and its objectives are beyond these purposes. The Sensate work aims always to give pleasure, to entertain, to amuse, to help pass the time, with or without any moral, didactic, or utilitarian purposes. It strives to reflect empirical reality and, in its pure examples, to describe this reality with all the accuracy of "scientific" observation. In other respects, each of these types of literature has practically the same characteristics, respectively, as Ideational and Sensate painting, sculpture, music, and architecture. Without further elaboration here (since the subject will be discussed later), I shall merely state that the division into Ideational and Sensate cuts across, and in no way coincides with, such categories as "realistic," "symbolistic," "classic," "romantic," and many other classifications at present current in the theories and histories of literature and art in general.

In a rough or highly developed form both of these types of literature seem to have coexisted in virtually all cultures, at all periods. Even among "primitive" peoples we find crude Ideational literature (religious and magical prayers, songs, incantations, proverbs, formulas, dithyrambs, etc.) as well as the Sensate, whether in the form of some empirical narrative, labor song, love song, or coarse sexual or drinking song. Both are found in some form and in some degree. In the religious and magical literature, especially, the symbolic interpretation is quite common. Just as in primitive decorative art "a geometric form often receives a secondary meaning that is read into it, so the narrative," or song, or formula, or even seemingly senseless group of syllables, "is given an interpretative significance that is quite foreign to the original tale." For instance, the image of a girl who married a dog signifies in one Alaskan myth the origin of the Milky Way, in British Columbia the origin of the culture hero, in other places the tribal ancestor and his emergence, or a constellation or some other cosmological fact or myth.[1] Similar symbolism has existed in many forms among almost all primitive tribes, as well as in the early stages of so-called historical cultures. Many of what are named the metaphors and metaphoric expressions in these literatures are but symbols, not metaphors at all in our sense of the word. We may expect to find that, as long as music (song) was inseparably associated with words, and as long as both the magico-religious and Sensate music existed among primitive peoples, both forms of literature also occurred. And the expectation is well met by the facts.

Though present in almost every sociocultural constellation, both styles naturally occur, however, in different states of purity and in different proportions. Among primitive tribes both forms, and especially the Ideational, are to a large extent impure. Most of the literature of such peoples is of a Mixed form, where the Ideational and Sensate elements are interwoven — in some cases exceedingly well, in others rather poorly. For instance, most of the early epics, anonymous or connected with some individual name, whether the *Mahabharata* and *Ramayana*, the *Gilgamesh* epic, or parts of the Bible, the *Iliad*, the *Odyssey*, the *Edda*, the *Scop's Song*, the *Song of Beowulf*, or the Russian folk epics about the great heroes Iliya Murometz, Dobrynia Nikititch, Sviatopolk, Mikula Selianinovitch, and others — these and many other early epics represent in principle the Mixed — that is, the Ideational-Sensate — literature in

---

[1] Franz Boas, *Primitive Art* (Oslo, 1927), pp. 336–337. See also the other examples given in this work for the religious and secular forms of literature, especially on pp. 326–327 and 324, and in the chapter on literature.

their character. They deal in part with the empirical heroic types, in part with superempirical forces (gods, the Fates, and so on). They stand in part in this world, and the description is empirical, devoid of any particular and, especially, transcendental symbolism; and in part in a superempirical world of religious, moral, and other values described by symbolic imagery. To their contemporaries these epics must have been much more symbolic than they now appear, because many of the images, metaphors, descriptions, and even syllables, which sound empirical to us, were probably symbols with meanings very different from their empirical content.[2] Some of them were to all purposes Idealistic in the sense given to that term in this work.

It is probable that the literatures of different peoples contain different proportions of the two extreme forms at a given moment, some having more, some less of each of these types. It is also probable that these proportions do not remain constant in the course of the literature, but vary, giving domination now to one, now to the other. At least such has been the case (on a high, logically integrated plane) during the history of several cultures, particularly those studied here: the Graeco-Roman and Western Christian. More than ever, when one examines the main waves of the transformation of literature from the Ideational to the Sensate types with their Mixed forms, or vice versa, one is led to the conclusion that in their main movements *these fluctuations follow in a close parallel those in the fields of painting and sculpture, and also, to a less degree, in other fields of art.* At least such is the conclusion obtained after a study of the literature of the Western Christian and, to some extent, of the Graeco-Roman cultures. Whether such a parallelism is universal for all cultures and times, I am not prepared to say. We must not be too hasty with generalizations. We may, perhaps, expect its existence, but this must be corroborated by an actual study of the problem based on the empirical facts of these cultures. Such an extensive study need not be attempted here.[3]

[2] For several examples of what appear to us meaningless syllables (like *hei-hei, aya, iya, ham-ham,* and so on), reiterated in songs of some primitive peoples, which in fact have a symbolic meaning (the cannibal spirit, grizzly bear, several supernatural beings, and other meanings), see F. Boas, *op. cit.,* p. 301.

[3] The immense vastness of the field of all literatures, and the great difficulties to be met in such a study, force me to limit myself to the Christian European literature only, and even there to that of the main countries. The Graeco-Roman literature has been included also, but somewhat more superficially. Subsequently German and French literature are treated in some detail. See the Appendix to this chapter for the works upon which the conclusions are based.

II. Graeco-Roman Literature and Criticism

As to the Graeco-Roman literature [4] (omitting the Creto-Mycenaean), it seems that in the centuries from about the eighth to the fifth B.C. this was predominantly Ideational. The precise century to which Homer and Hesiod belong is unknown, but it is possibly the eighth. The same is true of the legendary Orpheus and the Orphic literature. If the great works of these writers and groups cannot be styled purely Ideational, they are mainly so, for the rest being at least Idealistic. The poets of the Homeric, the Orphic, and the Hesiodic schools are all mainly the "spokesmen of deity" and "prophets." [5] To their contemporaries and to the Greeks up to about the time of Plato and Aristotle they were, in all probability, much more Ideational than they now appear to us.[6] To the Greeks before the fourth century the *Iliad* and *Odyssey* were religious, moral, and educational, rather than art creations. The Bible and the Gospels to the early Christians were not aesthetic works of art but divine revelation, and the attitude of the Greeks to Homer and Hesiod was similar. At least when one takes the discussions and commentaries of Homer by the early Greek thinkers and "critics" one finds in them no trace of what we term interpretation and criticism from the standpoint of art as an aesthetic criterion of beauty.

Their criticism was criticism of matter only; they treated Homer as a historical, a religious, a philosophical document, not as a work of art. . . . [It was an] allegorical interpretation of Homer and perhaps of other poets [Anaximander, Stesimbrotus, Glaucus, and others]. . . . For criticism there was no room.[7]

Since the writings of Homer and other poets of that time were not looked upon as sheer poetry, but were viewed religiously and morally, in part perhaps symbolically, this is a sufficiently good indication that they were perceived and interpreted much more Ideationally than we

---

[4] See any standard history of the Greek literature and mythology, but especially W. von Christ, W. Schmid, and O. Stählin, *Geschichte der griechischen Literatur* (München, 1924), 2 vols.; A. F. Pauly and G. Wissowa, *Realenzyklopädie der Klassischen Altertumswissenschaft* (Stuttgart, 1894–1936), 16 vols.

[5] Wilamowitz-Moellendorff, *Der Glaube der Hellenen* (Berlin, 1931), Vol. I, pp. 39 ff. See also A. Lang, *The World of Homer* (London, 1920); M. P. Nilsson, *Homer and Mycenae* (London, 1933).

[6] Up to the fourth century B.C. the poets were regarded as divinely inspired. See, for instance, Plato, *Republic I*, 331e; *Ion*, 539d and e; Aristophanes, *Frogs*, 686, where he styles his chorus "holy"; *Wasps*, 1043; and Herakleitos, *Quaestiones Homericae*.

[7] G. Saintsbury, *A History of Criticism and Literary Taste of Europe* (London, 1900), Vol. I, pp. 11–13. See also F. Chambers, *Cycles of Taste* (Cambridge, 1928), *passim*.

understand and interpret them today.[8] These works thus show to some extent the strength of the Ideational current of that period. But more indicative by far is the fact that the bulk of the literature, which was practically inseparable from music and hardly existed apart from it, was definitely religious, magical, and symbolic. This literature was represented by the Doric choral lyric of religious *nomes, dithyrambs, paeans, prosodies, threnodies,* and other magico-religious songs, hymns, and literary-musical creations (Terpander, Alkman, Lasos, Simonides of Samos, Arion, Stesichoros, Simonides of Keos, and others). In so far as these were predominantly Ideational the literature of the period may be said to be predominantly Ideational.[9] There is no doubt that the Sensate literature, especially the Ionic stream of literature somewhat later (Theognis, Sappho, Anakreon, the Sicilian comic but moralizing and philosophizing poets such as Epicharmos, Sophron, and others of the sixth century), existed side by side with the Ideational stream; but it was, to all appearances, a subordinate and minor current, and even this current was greatly permeated by Ideationalism and Idealism. This impression is supported by Aristotle, who says that after poetry originated it

naturally divided itself into two different kinds. They who were of a grave and lofty spirit chose for their imitation the actions and the adventures of elevated characters; while poets of a lighter turn represented those of the vicious and contemptible. And these composed originally satires, as the former did hymns and encomia. Of the lighter kind, we have no poem anterior to the time of Homer, though many such in all probability there were [possibly on the lower planes of literature]. . . . [The first of these forms, developed later into tragedy,] originated from the dithyrambic hymn, the other [comedy] from those phallic songs. . . . [And further,] the successive improvements of tragedy, and the respective authors of them, have not escaped our knowledge; but those of comedy, from the little attention that was paid to it in its origin, remain in obscurity. For it is not till late that comedy was authorized by the magistrate and carried on at the public expense; it was at first a private and voluntary exhibition. . . .[10]

Here we have testimony that the religious and moral and Ideational forms of literature appeared earlier than the "lighter" (more Sensate) forms; that the first current, until late, was on the high plane of socially

---

[8] See the quoted works of F. de Coulanges, Saintsbury, Christ-Schmid-Stählin, and others referred to in this chapter.

[9] See A. W. Pickard-Cambridge, *Dithyramb, Tragedy, Comedy* (Oxford, 1927).

[10] Aristotle, *Poetics*, I, 6-8 (pp. 10-12 in Everyman's Library ed.).

recognized literature, "authorized by the magistrate," predominant, almost monopolistic; that the Sensate forms emerged only later and from the lower sources (phallic songs) and only quite late received social sanction, although on the lower level of literature they had previously existed for some time.

The end of the sixth and the fifth century B.C. — the period of the great Ideational-Idealistic lyricist Pindar and of the great tragedies and comedies (Aeschylus, Sophocles, and to some extent Euripides and Aristophanes) — was, as was indicated in Chapter Twelve, the *Idealistic period of Greek literature* (and of other arts). Both Sensate and Ideational elements were so marvelously balanced in the inner content, as well as in the external form, that the tragedies of the fifth century reach the peak of the literary art of Greece.[11]

After the first half of the fifth century, and especially beginning with the end of the fourth century B.C., Greek literature as well as Greek literary criticism, like the other forms of art already studied, definitely move toward ever-increasing Sensatism. *The manifestations of this rising tide of Sensate literature are exactly the same as those which we have pointed out in Greek painting, sculpture, music, and to some extent, architecture.*

A. The subject matter becomes more secular and less religious.

B. Gradually not only gods but even heroes are depicted as mortal.[12] The common, vulgar type of personages, the negative, the picturesque, the subsocial types begin to become more and more popular as themes for works.

C. Description itself, especially in the Alexandrian school, becomes more "realistic" and empirically "scientific." Symbolism, especially transcendental symbolism, practically disappears. Its place is taken by a "naturalistic realism," by a correct, detailed, scientific characterization of personages, events, places.

D. The portrayal of *genre* of a banal character ("here, certainly we are in the very heart of a banal and everyday reality"),[13] on the one hand, and the paysage, the pastoral, the idyll (whether in the style of Theocritus or others still more sentimental), on the other hand, develop increasingly — a fact analogous to what we have observed in painting and sculpture.

[11] Compare Pickard-Cambridge, *op. cit.;* G. Norwood, *Greek Tragedy* (London, 1920); A. David-Sauvageot, *Le réalisme et le naturalisme dans la littérature et dans l'art* (Paris, 1889), p. 20; P. Lenoir, *Histoire du réalisme et du naturalisme dans la poésie et dans l'art* (Paris, 1889), pp. 69–151.

[12] David-Sauvageot, *op. cit.*, p. 25. See also S. Ranulf, *The Jealousy of the Gods* (Copenhagen, 1933–1934), *passim.*   [13] *Ibid.*, p. 27.

E. Tragedy slowly begins to give way to comedy, to satire, to burlesque, to picaresque — again a trait indicated in the preceding chapters as one of the usual satellites of the Sensate art.

F. Just as the Western literature of the Renaissance and the period of the Academies, in attempting to revive antiquity, of necessity hid under the forms of antiquity the sensational subject matter and interests of the sixteenth and seventeenth centuries, so did the Greek, especially from the third century B.C. in its "renaissances" of the archaic forms, including many of ancient legendary and mythological content. For "these false archaisms were but mere mannerisms," because the poets and literati "did not take care at all to give any accurate restitution of the legendary past, and their mythological disguise was for them but a pretext to dress up in picturesque disguise the real life of their time." [14] This is a phenomenon many times repeated, and typical of the many revivals of the primitive and of the archaic forms of art.

G. Sensualism and eroticism, sometimes crude, sometimes refined, occasionally in the form of "innocence" of the type of Greuze's "innocent doves," permeates the literary work.

H. Sensual pleasure becomes, more and more, the main and often the only objective.

I. In conformity with this we find "art for art's sake," aestheticism, art criticism, art education, art fashion, "art appreciation," and so on, developing rapidly, and the art criticism becomes what we mean by that term today : pure aesthetic analysis and interpretation of literary works from the purely artistic standpoint ; it deals with beauty as consciously Sensate, aestheticism as "pure aesthetism" (which in fact is a Sensate aestheticism), criticism as purely "literary criticism" (which in fact is a form of Sensate art).

J. We find the growth of individualism, among the literati, and of their "professionalization," mannerisms, vanity, influence, and the improvement of their position in social and material respects.[15] In brief we have all the familiar satellites of the art dominated by the Sensate form.

Instead of my offering a detailed historical corroboration of these statements — which is beyond the scope of this work — it will be enough to remind the reader of a few of the "milestones," a few of the chief

---

[14] *Ibid.*, p. 24. See J. Girard, *Études sur la poésie grecque* (Paris, 1884).

[15] See W. S. Ferguson, *Hellenistic Athens* (London, 1911), pp. 165 ff., 212 ff., *et passim;* U. von Wilamowitz-Moellendorff, *Hellenistische Dichtung in der Zeit des Kallimachos* (Berlin, 1924).

names which mark the long course of Greek literature. After Euripides and a few epigoni, Greek tragedy died and was replaced by the *Old Greek Comedy*, with Aristophanes as its greatest creator. Though the Greek Comedy in its origin and early stages was also religious and therefore Ideational to a considerable degree, nevertheless even the Old Comedy, when compared with the Tragedy, represented a step farther from the Ideationalism Idealism toward Sensatism. The replacement of the Old Comedy by the so-called *Middle Comedy*, and this by the *New Comedy*, were further milestones in the movement of Greek literature toward an ever-increasing Sensatism. The movement from Aristophanes to Menander and Philemon and other representatives of the New Comedy was a great shift from the world of gods and heroes to that of ordinary men, and even to that of negative subsocial personalities and affairs. In the New Comedy there is nothing mythological, religious, heroic. Practically all the comedies deal with very ordinary people, often with the sexual, with low morality and with all the ordinary and pathological paraphernalia of such a social world. We are virtually in the same world as that of today's Broadway "shows" and musical and other comedy.

When we pass onward to the Hellenistic literature, we are practically at the extreme point of the Sensate. What this literature consists of is imitative epics with old gods and heroes in whom nobody now believes and in whose trappings are dressed the potentates of the time, those patrons on whom depend the well-being and position and income of the writer (Ptolemy in the guise of Zeus or some other deity or mythological hero) ; or the pedantically learned and superscholarly poetry of the rococo type, thoroughly "technical" and "scientific" and therefore perfectly mediocre even in the works of its greatest representatives, like Kallimachos, Apollonius of Rhodes, Aratos (with his versification of a textbook in astronomy), Nikandros (who does the same with medicine) ; or the bucolic and pastoral poetry of Theokritus with his sugary shepherds and shepherdesses ; or the still more typical riddle and the figure poetry of Lykophoron and others, where the supreme end was to write a poem with the length of the lines so shaped as to give the figure of an ax or an altar or wings or some other shape — and all this permeated with the notorious Alexandrian eroticism and indecency, as represented not only by such specialists in this line as Sotades and others, but also in almost all the other works, the pedantically learned not excluded. Add to this the development of epigrammatic, satirical literature, the "detective and mystery stories" — and the general character of the Hellenistic literature (about its criticism much more will be said further) will be comprehensible. We are in a world of overripe Sensatism, pushed to the extremes of sensuality and matter-of-fact empiricism and "positivism" even in poetry and literature. Little, if anything, is left of the Ideationalism and not much of the Idealism of the previous centuries. We breathe there the peculiar atmosphere of the Greek rococo, mixed with naturalism, pedantry, normal and abnormal eroticism, and Hollywood-like "romanticism." [16]

This picture will appear still clearer if we glance briefly at the evolution of literary criticism before and after the end of the fourth century B.C. As has previously been mentioned, before Plato and Aristotle literary criticism as such virtually did not exist. Saintsbury finds the first weak glimmerings of it in only one of the six writers named Democritus. Its place was taken by estimation and censorship of the literary works from the standpoint of religion, moral and philosophical values. "For [pure art and literary] criticism there could be no room." This is true of the criticism of Anaximander, Stesimbrotus, Glaucus, Xenophanes, Parmenides, Empedocles, of even the sophists like Georgias, Protagoras, and others.[17] In other words we are dealing mainly with Ideational or Idealistic literature, and of this nature also was its criticism, censorship, and evaluation. The same idea is well expressed by F. Chambers, who shows that among the early Greek writers, critics, and appraisers of art phenomena, there is no trace of a sensate aesthetic approach. The lack is so remarkable that it has led the author to contend that at that stage the very appreciation and feeling for beauty, the aesthetic consciousness itself, was lacking among the Greeks.

In literature and the arts the aesthetic consciousness did not exist [up to approximately the Peloponnesian War].[18]

When a race of men had that ancestral faith that can see gods and demons in every avenue of life, in the sky, the sea, the countryside, aesthetic notions must be as foreign to the soul as a philosophy of rationalism. . . . It is only when gods and demons are outgrown and when men begin to think, as modern men think, that a beauty is discovered.

If literary records are to be trusted, it is evident that the archaic and the fifth-century Greek possessed no consciousness of Fine Art in the modern

---

[16] See the works of Wilamowitz-Moellendorff and Girard; and Christ and Schmid, *Die ncchklassische Periode der griechischen Literatur von 320 vor Christus bis 100 nach Christus* (Berlin, 1920).

[17] Saintsbury, *op. cit.*, Vol. I, pp. 13–16.

[18] Chambers, *History of Taste* (New York, 1932), p. 273.

sense. . . . The truth is that Greek art in its earliest and in its finest epoch was completely bound up with the life and religion of the people. . . . Greek statues and pictures represented Gods, heroes, and men [mainly for religious, moralizing, and political reasons]. Buildings supplied practical needs and perhaps embodied chosen traditional symbols. To these things the Greek dedicated his most precious possessions, his riches and his gold-and-glitter. But beyond the simplicity of such immediate ends, early Greek art had no self-conscious exalted ideals per se.[19]

As Pausanias put it, "All the statues and everything else equally on the Acropolis at Athens are votive offerings." [20]

I would rather say "the Sensate aesthetic consciousness" and "Sensate beauty" were then discovered, because before that time a feeling for beauty certainly existed, but it was a feeling of an Ideational and Idealistic beauty. With this reservation Chambers's statement is well substantiated.

The period from Plato to Aristotle was transitory in art, literature, and criticism, from the Idealistic to the Sensate. Hence the intermediary character of their positions in the field of art criticism. Plato, with the exception of some "aesthetic" liberalism of a very modest type in *Phedrus*, remains "nonaesthetic" like his predecessors. We all know how in his *Republic* and *Laws* he admonishes poets and artists, calling them "drones," when they were not endeavoring to inculcate appropriate moral, religious, political, and social values; considering them dangerous; prohibiting unexpurgated in his Commonwealth Homer, Hesiod, and Euripides; prescribing the kind and the style of art creations, and banishing all the artists who would not comply with these prescriptions, and so on.[21] "We shall request Homer and the other poets not to be indignant if we erase these things; . . . the more poetical they are the less ought they to be heard by children, and by men who ought to be free, and more afraid of slavery than of death." [22] In brief, for him "pure" art does not exist; only when interwoven organically with religious, philosophical, and moral and other values, and in so far as it does not contradict or become isolated from these values, is it recognized.

The same is to be said of other of Plato's contemporaries and immediate successors, such as Aristophanes with his satire on the men of letters,

[19] Chambers, *Cycles of Taste*, pp. 14–16 and 106; especially the careful analysis of all the passages concerning art phenomena among the ancient Greek writers.

[20] Pausanias, V, 21.

[21] See Plato, *Republic*, II, 377; III, 386 ff., 390–397, *et passim*, and *The Dialogues of Plato*, trans. by B. Jowett (New York, 1874), Vol. II, pp. 200 ff.

[22] *Republic*, III, 387 *et passim*.

on "highbrows" like Socrates and Euripides, and on other "underminers" of social values, such as Isocrates with his moral and religious, but little aesthetic, criticism of art objects.[23]

Even Aristotle stands essentially in a somewhat similar position. His principle of *mimesis*, or imitation, as the object and criterion of art, does not mean a mere naturalistic reproduction of everything as it exists in empirical sensory reality. It is rather the principle of an idealized and typified reproduction of such phenomena, an imitation of such a nature as to accomplish the purgation of emotions and to lead to ennoblement, to the moral and social uplifting of man. Saintsbury is right in saying that "Aristotle . . . is doubly and triply ethical" in his attitude and appraisal of art phenomena. For Aristotle and his predecessors, Sensate art as "art for art's sake" does not exist, although here and there they lean more nearly to such a position than Plato and his predecessors.[24]

After Aristotle the literature as well as art criticism rapidly changes and shows all the characteristics of the Sensate literature, and these changes become increasingly conspicuous. Up to that time "criticism had not yet assumed the position of a recognized art. . . . Rhetoric, from this time onward, more and more tends to become the Art of Literary Criticism in general." [25] A considerable and ever-increasing literature of art criticism from a purely aesthetic standpoint develops. (Writings of Menander, Theophrastus, Pausanias, Athenaeus, Polemo, and others.) Dozens and dozens of texts, guides, manuals, in the field of such criticism began to appear. In contradistinction to the previous period the criticism deals with such problems as: "Is this writer or this work good or bad as writer or work? What variety of the poetical or prosaic pleasure does he or it give? What is the special idiosyncrasy of the author or the book?" and so on.[26] The standpoint is Sensate, with its own aesthetic criteria of perfection. Professional art criticism and critics make their entrance and multiply, especially in the Pergamene and Alexandrian schools, during the third and second centuries B.C. Zenodotus, Crates of Mallos, Aristarchus, and the grammarians Aristophanes and Zoilus, are typical. Criticism also becomes erudite and scholastic. Scholia are piled upon

---

[23] Saintsbury, *op. cit.*, Vol. I, pp. 29–59.

[24] See Aristotle, *Poetics*, I, vi, trans. by Jowett, pp. xv *et passim*. "It is not the poet's province to relate such things as have actually happened, but such as might happen." "Poetry is chiefly concerned about general truth." Further, the things related "should be good and told with propriety."

[25] Saintsbury, *op. cit.*, Vol. I, pp. 61–71. See also Chambers, *Cycles of Taste*, pp. 1–117.

[26] *Ibid.*, Vol. I, p. 71.

scholia, commentaries, notes, references, grow.   For instance in scholia on Homer

we have the thrice, nay, thirty-times decocted essence of the critical study of generations, centuries, millennia, of study of the writer who entered Greek life, Greek thought, Greek education, as no book save the English Bible has ever entered into the life, the thought, the education, of any other country. We have it in ample bulk, of all ages, preserved . . . of comment on comment, of annotated annotation. . . .   We find [there] laborious comment on etymology, on grammar, on mythology, etc., etc.   We get the most painstaking discussions on the poet's meaning, handled simply, handled allegorically, handled "this way, that way, which way you please."   Two volumes of comment on the Odyssey contain endless discussion of the aesthetic technique of it concerning accentuation and punctuation, athetesis, anakephalaiosis; endless classifications of narratives into classes: homiletic, apangeltic, hypostatic, mixed, etc., etc.[27]

Many a contemporary critic, commentator, annotator can but envy this scholarly erudition and professional art criticism, until the polishing of words, expressions, technical details, the mutual "backpatting" of the critics, writers, and artists turns into a purely technical and aesthetic sport or display of learning, and becomes more and more dead "pigeonholing," more and more empty; as is true after Hermogenes (c. A.D. 170), when we find such critics as Dion Chrysostom (between the first and second centuries A.D.), Aristides of Smyrna, Maximus Tyrius, Philostratus, and later Libanius, Themistius, and Julian in the fourth century.   A specimen of this sort of later " criticism " is given by Julian in his literary epistle to Libanius.

Thou art blessed to write thus, and still more to be able to think thus! O speech! O brains! O composition! O division! O epicheiremes! O ordonnance! O departures of style! O harmony! O symphony!

"To which we may add," as Saintsbury so correctly remarks, "O clichés! O tickets! O fudge!"[28]   In brief:

For three centuries between Aristotle and Dionysius [of Halicarnassus] . . . attention was entirely devoted . . . to verbal or material criticism of the Alexandrian and Pergamene schools, and to technical rhetoric.   [Progressing in that way art as well as criticism] was in itself becoming more and more a futile technique.[29]

In this way the Sensate "art for art's sake" and the no less Sensate criticism began to defeat their purpose.   They became more and more

[27] *Ibid.*, Vol. I, pp. 76–88.   [28] *Ibid.*, Vol. I, p. 126.   [29] *Ibid.*, Vol. I, p. 194.

futile, sterile, and uncreative. Thus, the movement which began for the sake of a supposedly "pure art," in its name and for its freedom, brought decay instead of blossoming. Art became separated from other values — religion, morals, idealism, philosophy, etc. — and, freed from their tutelage, turned into a mere source of sensual pleasure, ceasing to produce anything comparable to Homer or Hesiod, Theognis, Pindar, Aeschylus, Sophocles, Euripides, Aristophanes, or even the lesser creators in literature.[30] These minor writers, minor art critics in this period of Sensate art, never reach the sublime height of creation as did those in the Ideational and Idealistic period.

This second stage of Greek art merges into the Hellenistic, and then into the Roman literature and criticism. Being archaic but sincere, the art and literature of the Romans before the Greek influence, though it never reached the height of the Greek at its peak of glory, were also predominantly Ideational or Idealistic, and mainly religious, magical, and moral. Even here, however, we sense a strong undercurrent of "rugged" naturalism and rough but subdued Sensatism. Greek influence, mainly in the Sensate Hellenistic form, shortened the life of this primitive Ideational and Idealistic literature and quickened the growth of its Sensate form. At the intersection of this decline of the Ideational stream and the forced rise of the Sensate stream we have the period of the Mixed type, the Roman Idealistic literature of about the first century B.C. and the beginning of the first century A.D. Similar to Roman painting, sculpture, music, and architecture of the same period, it never reached the sublimity of the Idealistic originals of the Greeks; nevertheless it gave a "golden age" to Roman literature, and its main stream was essentially Idealistic. I refer to the creations of Virgil and, to some extent, of Horace, Lucretius (whose materialistic poem was permeated by a specific kind of "materialistic idealism" or "idealistic materialism" presented as gospel), Livy, Sallust, Cicero, Seneca, Varro, Cato, and others. Although simultaneously with this stream there existed an almost purely Sensate stream — represented by Horace, and especially Catullus, Ovid, and a few others — it was secondary to the other. In brief, the literature of the period is a counterpart of the "neo-classic" forms of painting, sculpture, music, and architecture of that time. All, for a short time, undergo a transition, and we find the traits of a waning Ideationalism mixing with a ripe Sensatism, a reflection of the Graeco-Hellenistic Sensate influence. The period was short, however, corresponding to the pseudo-Idealistic, neo-classic period in other forms of art,

---

[30] See also F. Chambers, *Cycles of Taste*, pp. 119 *et passim*, and *History of Taste*, pp. 292 ff.

which we have already dealt with. The rising tide of Sensatism in art and literature generally was progressing rapidly.[31]

Already in the second part of the first century A.D. Sensatism became dominant in literature, and this tendency developed more and more during the next two or three centuries, in spite of the moralizing influence of Plutarch and a few others. Beginning with the first century, all the traits of the Sensate literature become quite noticeable. Roman society now became highly literary and aesthetically minded, as the works of Persius, Petronius, Seneca the Younger, Juvenal, and Martial show. "The literary discussion was as indispensable at a Roman supper of the better class as broiled bones at an English one . . . while supper lasted. . . ."[32] Persius tells us: "Ecce inter pocula quaerunt Romulidae satieri, quid dia poemata narrent. . . . Ventosa et enormis loquacitas" was going on. There appeared literary salons; women took most intense interest in art and literature. There appeared groups of hysterical and enthusiastic admirers of this or that artist. Literary and artistic novelties stirred and excited cities — as the bigger football games in our day. Tacitus, in a work ascribed to him, *Dialogus de claris Oratoribus*, tells us, for instance, that C. Maternus's tragedy on Cato was such a sensation. Everybody seems to have aspired to become a professional artist, writer, orator, etc., and for this purpose subjected himself, or herself, to a long training under professionals. There was an enormous production of texts in every field, which multiplied as time went on. These characteristics of the times are pictured in a few lines of the *Arbiter elegantiarum* of Petronius. At the opening of the work he denounces the dominance of the bombastic and polished language of the writers and critics of his day.

If you will excuse my saying so, you rhetoricians were the first to ruin litera-ture [with your polished, bombastic, and empty phraseology]. . . . Youth had not been enslaved yet to declamations when Sophocles and Euripides devised the words in which they were to speak. [Likewise Plato and Pindar were not subject to the rules of these] schoolmasters. . . . Of late this windy and extravagant loquacity has shifted from Asia to Athens. And forthwith true eloquence, its rule corrupted, has been . . . put to silence. Tell me, who has since equaled the fame of Thucydides, of Hyperides? Not so much as a lyric of wholesome complexion has appeared, and everything, as if poisoned with the same food, has been unable to last to a natural grey old age. Even painting has made no better end. . . .[33]

---

[31] This applies chiefly to the pagan literature of the time. The emerging and purely Ideational literature of Christianity, quite inimical toward Sensate art, was then only in its infancy, and therefore was a very small stream. Only after some three or four centuries did it become the main river. [32] Saintsbury, *op. cit.*, Vol. I, p. 243. [33] *Ibid.*, Vol. I, pp. 234-244.

Similarly, Seneca decries all this literary and artistic bustle; Persius satirizes the common figure of "a literary dandy" in hyacinthine garment, mincing and twanging through his nose some rancid stuff (*rancidulum quiddam*), "these effeminate drivels" who are scribbling in their study, arraying themselves in their best clothes before sitting down to read — and he adds in a hopeless *desiderium*, "Whatever you write, write it in a manly fashion, with no aesthetic trifling!" [34] Still more sharply Juvenal (in his tenth *Satire*) denounces all this Sensate aestheticism, beginning with "the learned lady who talks for hours on the comparative merits of Homer and Virgil," and ending with the rhetoricians, book and art collectors, writers of artificial Greek epics, sham-heroic poems, and the like. A similar picture, with the same negative estimate, is given by Martial and even by such writers as the talkative Statius, Pliny, and Tacitus, to mention only a few names.

To be a bookish aesthete became popular. Pliny the Younger tells us [35] that he himself, even during boar-hunting "sat at the nets with a pencil and notebook." And quite naturally he coins the formula so familiar to us: "The bigger the better." ("Ut aliae bonae res, ita bonus liber melior est quisque, quo major.") A picture essentially no different is given by Tacitus. Just as in Hellenistic Greece, erudition goes hand in hand with aestheticism. The age was polyhistoric, and a disproportionate place was given to rhetoric, oratory, criticism, literary occupations; and withal there was little if any originality or creativeness. Pure aestheticism found its best expression and theoretical formulation in the works of Quintilian and other leading critics. Quintilian, the best of these, laid down the canons of style for various types of writing: how to write jokes; what is the difference between *venustum, salsum, facetum;* what makes for perspicuity, elegance, beauty of style; what are the forms of tapeinoisis, meiosis, homology, macrology, pleonasm, cacozelon, tropes, figures, and so on. And all this is for the glory of pure Sensate beauty, because "True beauty, in merely being beautiful, is the highest utility," because "Grace of style will captivate," in other words, for the sake of Sensate pleasure. Other critics and writers, as Aulus Gellius, Macrobius, Servius Honoratus, Curius Fortunatianus, and so on, are still more "learned" and more sterile. They busy themselves almost entirely about "technique," classifications, standardizations, textbooks; laying down law after law, standard after standard, annotation and commentary after annotation and commentary; indulging, of course, in mutual backslapping; being perhaps "logical" and "technical," but quite without power either as

[34] *Ibid.*, Vol. I, pp. 249 ff.   [35] *Epistles*, 20th letter of the first book to Tacitus.

creators or as critics. And all is permeated with an Epicurean Sensate spirit. Statius's remark that in case of failure his wife's caresses would console him is just a typical symbol of this spirit. Even later, among some "versatile" Christians, as for example Sidonius Apollinarius (a fifth-sixth century bishop, count, poet, critic), this empty erudition and sterile aestheticism still lingers, as one can see from the following specimen of his style, as given by Saintsbury.

O book, multifariously pollent, he addresses Claudiano suo in his letter à propos of a new work of Claudian. O language, not of a thin but a subtle mind! He feels like Pythagoras! He divides like Aristotle. . . . He "suades" like Cato, dissuades like Appius, per-suades like Tully. . . . He is instructive like Augustine. He soars like Hilary, and abuses himself like John, reproves like Basil, consoles like Gregory, etc.[36]

At the beginning of this rising tide of Sensatism, the demands for the absolute freedom of a poet, a writer, an artist, were naturally not lacking. Already Cicero pleads for it.[37] In the second century A.D. Lucian gives its formula: "Poetry enjoys unrestricted freedom; the poet's fancy is her only law."[38] Thus a literary man declares that he *"legibus solutus est."* Shall we wonder that St. Augustine, himself previously one of these literary men, professor of rhetoric, critic, and orator, denounces all this, after his conversion, in the strongest terms, styling it all as foolishness, the "art of deceiving," "seduction of men," buying and selling of grammar rules and talks, and so on?[39] Now there were no great names in literature; no great achievements in other fields of art. Sensate art carried to an extreme, as if it had dried up the springs of creativeness, could offer only imitations and second-rate productions. And the contemporaries themselves well understood this: "What are we to say if an old picture of a few colors delights some men more than a highly finished one?" wrote Cicero.[40]

In the past when artists used only few colours painting was greater; but now when India herself contributes the ooze of her rivers and the blood of dragons and elephants, no famous picture is ever painted.[41]

The earliest paintings were executed in simple colours and without contrasts; they were, however, correct in drawing and very pleasing. Paintings of a later

[36] *Ibid.*, Vol. I, pp. 385–386.   [37] *De Oratore*, II, 57; *cf.* I, 32.
[38] *De historia conscribenda*, § 8.
[39] See Augustine, *The City of God*, Bks. III, VI, *et passim; Confessions*, trans. by Sir Tobie Matthew (London, 1923), pp. 25 ff., 48–50, *et passim.*
[40] *Orator at Brutum*, § 80.
[41] Pliny, *Natural History*, XXXV, 50.

date were less correct in drawing, but more elaborated, more varied in their light and shades, and depending in their effects on the multitude of their colours.[42]

Longinus speaks of "the world-wide bareness that pervades our life."

Such were the voices of this period. To these can be added the voices and testimonies of Seneca, Petronius, Persius, Statius, Juvenal, Martial, Tacitus, the elder Pliny, Augustine and other Church Fathers, Quintilian, and almost all the other notable writers. Some of these were mentioned above.[43]

The artist was free indeed and his art exalted to all but a divine office. Yet there seemed to be a regrettable longing for the rigid past. The artist would fain go back and attempt to express his melancholy memories in revivals of bygone styles. Hence came the "archaistic" schools of the Graeco-Roman sculptures [and literature] and the deliberate imitation of the conventionalities, which the archaic sculptor carved [or poet sang], in all ignorance and innocence of heart. But a spirit of disillusionment was abroad.[44]

The creative spirit was gone. Not the imitative idylls or sentimental pastorals, nor sham-heroic poems, nor mystery-adventure-detective stories, nor realistic and naturalistic novels, nor mannered and sensual poetry, nor still cruder erotic literature, nor different kinds of propaganda literature (from the antireligious and materialistic and erotic works of Lucian to the moral propaganda pieces), nor divers imitations of the archaic, classic, Oriental patterns of literature — none of these varieties, quite common in the literature of the period, produced anything great or durable. The *genre* which possibly strove the most was satire, ridiculing, scourging, and gibing at the contemporary life and culture, as represented by Lucian, Petronius, Juvenal, Martial, Persius, and others. But this *genre*, as we already know, is a satellite of the late stages of Sensate art. So the fact that satirical literature developed more than the other forms of literary creation is additional evidence of the Sensate character of the literature of the period discussed. Sensate literature, reduced to a mere instrument of pleasure, freed from a union and co-operation with other sociocultural values (or as some like to say, from being "handmaiden" to religion, moral, and other values), and not kindled from within by these values, became more and more empty, sterile, bored with itself, as a man who becomes saturated with "wine, women, and song." Sooner or later such a man and such a literature have to pay the price, and the inevitable

---

[42] Dionysius Halicarnassus, *De Isaeo.*
[43] See Chambers, *History of Taste*, pp. 300 ff., and Saintsbury, *op. cit.*, Vol. I, *passim.*
[44] Chambers, *History of Taste*, p. 300.

"day of reckoning" must be faced, their *dies irae*. Both become worn
out, more and more debilitated, shallow, and impotent. Both are bound
to "dig their own grave," the more Sensate they are and the longer they
persist in that course. Toward the end of the fourth and beginning of
the fifth centuries the Sensate wave of Graeco-Hellenic-Roman literature
had worn itself out. It had run its span of life and now was dead. In its
place there came the rising tide of Christian Ideational literature, a tiny
stream at the beginning of our era but the dominant stream in the fifth
century and after. Thus, in all essentials, the main fluctuations in the
alternation of Ideational and Sensate forms of literature in the course of a
Graeco-Roman culture went parallel with similar waves in painting,
sculpture, music, and architecture. There is no doubt that in the minor
ripplings there were deviations from this parallelism and synchronization,
but in the main fluctuations all these forms of art moved parallel, in a
similar direction, and at about the same periods of time.

III. MEDIEVAL IDEATIONAL LITERATURE AND CRITICISM

Originating as an insignificant current at the beginning of our era, the
Ideational literature of the Christians grew and, as we have already
observed, about the end of the fifth century became the main current,
pushing underground the dried-up Sensate stream which had dominated
from the end of the fourth century B.C. In turn the Ideational stream
remained dominant for about seven or eight hundred years. And in the
thirteenth and, in part, the fourteenth centuries, when its decline began
to be paralleled by the growth of the Sensate stream, it gave rise to an
Idealistic literature, which was a balanced mixture of the two currents.
Subsequently, from the fifteenth to the twentieth centuries, the Sensate
literature was once again dominant. Such in brief is the great pulsation
of the Ideational and the Sensate in the course of the Western Christian
literature. Let us now glance a little more closely at this pulsation.

That the chief literature of the centuries from the fifth to the end of
the twelfth was mainly Ideational is beyond question. Its characteristics
and the quantitative-qualitative changes in its nature were exactly the
same as those which we have studied in some detail in the field of painting, sculpture, and other forms of art.

A. *Inner Traits.* From the point of view of its inner character
the literature [45] *of the centuries from the fifth to the tenth was almost entirely*

---

[45] There is no doubt that on the lower levels of literature there existed a great many pagan
and partly heroic, partly Sensate, and even indecent songs, poems, stories, tales. But, as
mentioned, these levels are beyond the scope of this work.

religious. In that period there is almost nothing which can be styled secular.
From the beginning Christianity assumed a purely negative attitude
toward secular and Sensate literature, well exemplified by the famous
case of St. Jerome's vision, in which he was warned of celestial condemnation for his "Ciceronianus," that is, for his being fond of great secular
literature. Tertullian called the whole *doctrina secularis literaturae*
stupid in the eyes of God. Hence the purely religious character of the
literature of the period indicated. Indeed, in the history of French
literature there is virtually nothing of the secular up to the twelfth
century. The literature consists of such works as saints' lives (Ste.
Eulalie, St. Leger, St. Alexis), translations and commentaries on sacred
books and prayers, and the like. In German literature the situation
is exactly the same. Only in the ninth century does there appear the
heroic poem *Hildebrandslied* and other works like the *Heliand, Otfried,*
and the *Ludwigslied,* all religious in their essence. In the tenth and eleventh centuries we have another semisecular literary work, the *Ruodlied,*
and the first few sprinklings of secular literature (*Waltharius,* and the
Schwänke: Modus Florum, modus Liebung, the *Meregarte,* the *Physiologus*),
but they are few and incidental. We must wait until the second half of
the twelfth century before secular literature really emerges.[46] Not much
different is the situation with English literature. Except for a few poems
dealing with subjects surviving from the pre-Christian stage of the
Teutonic poetry, like the *Scop's Song, Song of Beowulf,* and the *Death
of Byrhtnoth,* after the advent of Christianity literature becomes almost
entirely religious and clerical, like Cynewulf's works, the *Legend of St.
Guthlac,* the metrical paraphrase of Caedmon, the saints' lives, the
translations of the works of Bede, Orosius, Boethius, St. Gregory, and
so on.[47]

[46] These as well as many subsequent data are the result of a special study of the French
and German literatures made in co-operation with Dr. H. R. Phelps and Dr. P. Parker. Of a
large amount of detailed data, and sources and literature consulted, I am giving here only
a quite insignificant part. This has to be done for the sake of economy of space. At my
disposal remain, however, detailed lists with analysis of almost all the important literary works
of each century studied and of the detailed results given by such a study. For practical
reasons, I am giving only a few references to the relatively authoritative courses in the
history of the French and the German literatures where a corroboration of my statements can
be found. See for the main works and sources used the Appendix to this chapter at the end
of this volume.

[47] See for France W. Foerster und E. Koschwitz, *Altfranzösisches Übungsbuch* (Leipzig,
1915); Collection of the *Société d'ancient Textes,* ed. by Langlois and others; V. Langlois, *La
vie en France au Moyen Âge* (Paris, 1926), Vol. I. For German literature see J. G. Robertson,
History of German Literature (New York, 1931), pp. 15–41; F. Vogt und M. Koch, *Geschichte
der Deutschen Literatur* (Leipzig and Wien 1919), Vol. I, pp. 1–62; the *Deutsche National-*

Similar was the situation in other European Christian countries. In
some the emergence of literary work came a little later, in some a little
earlier, but in all on the level of high literature the religious dominated,
to the exclusion of other types, until the twelfth century. Only in that
century, and mainly in its second half, the hitherto subterranean stream
of the secular literature emerges and begins more and more to expand at
the expense of the religious writing.

In brief, the situation is quite similar to that in painting, sculpture,
architecture, and music. And this virtually exclusively religious literature was Ideational not only quantitatively but qualitatively. It is
"otherworldly" and *expressis verbis* does not tire of repeating its negative,
contemptuous, even inimical attitude toward the empirical life, sensate
joys and sufferings, as a short-living mirage, at the best as a brief preparation for the "other life" beyond.

B. *External Traits.* Being Ideational inwardly, in its external form
the literature is also Ideational, that is, mainly *symbolical.* The symbolic, or as it is sometimes called, "allegorical," language appeared in the
Western writings almost as early as the Christian literature itself. The
Church Fathers used it widely, whether in the interpretation of the Bible
or any other religious source, or in the interpretation of the pagan writers :
of Cicero, or Ovid, or Virgil, or others. Origen, Gregory the Great
(especially in his commentary on the Book of Job), Dionysius the Areopa-
gite, Cassiodorus, Martianus, Boethius, Scotus Erigena, and practically
every other Christian writer (and simultaneously many of the neo-Plato-
nists and mystics among the pagan writers of the first centuries of our era,
like Porphyry, Plotinus, Ammonius, and others who were in the Ideational stream of the period also) made *symbolism and allegory a fundamental category of thought, which from that time on dominates all the thinking
and writing of the Middle Ages.* With the emergence of Christianity we
have symbolism and "the thick-coming allegoric fancies of the early
Christian homilists and commentators which were to thicken ever and
spread till the full blossoming of allegory in the *Romance of the Rose,* and
its busy decadence thence forward." Even the pagan works and notions
were interpreted symbolically. An example is given in Fulgentius's
Expositio Virgiliana. Here "every word [of Virgil], every syllable
almost . . . is tortured to yield an allegory." The same is true of the

Literatur, ed. by J. Kurschner (Berlin, 1885). For the English literature see W. J. Courthope,
A History of English Literature (New York, 1895), Vol. I, pp. i–iv. For a general survey see C.
Jenkins, "Some Aspects of Mediaeval Literature," in *The Legacy of the Middle Ages,* ed. by
Crump and Jacobs (Oxford, 1926). There also C. Foligno's "Vernacular Literature," P. C. de
Labriolle, *History and Literature of Christianity from Tertullian to Boethius* (New York, 1925).

works of Venantus Fortunatus, Isidore of Seville, Bede, and others.[48] In everything and everywhere the hidden meaning was looked for, found, and interpreted. The empirical world, and the words themselves which denote various objects of the empirical reality, were regarded as just a symbol, a sign, a mere imperfect indication of the superempirical reality, and of its parts and elements. Huizinga well sums up the situation: "In the Middle Ages the symbolist attitude was much more in evidence than the causal or the genetic attitude." The symbolic — and especially the transcendentally symbolic principle became there the main category of thought. Hence

Symbolism's image of the world is distinguished by impeccable order, architectonic structure, hierarchic subordination. . . . It permits of an infinity of relations between things. . . . The [empirical] world, objectionable in itself, became acceptable by its symbolic purport.[49]

"The symbol has become a reality." [50] "Allegory became an obsession." [51]

This concerns equally the theological, the philosophical, and the poetical writings. They all become symbolic, and in the earlier part of the Middle Ages *transcendentally symbolic*, that is, they contain not allegory as a convention or mere metaphor, but a real belief that every empirical phenomenon and every empirical word are but signs of the corresponding part in the world of the superempirical reality — the only reality which is true.[52] Just as the empirical world is mere appearance, a mere congeries of "accidents" which come into being and pass away whereas the real essence of things is superempirical and eternal, so language itself is but an imperfect sign using empirical terms and images for pointing out the superempirical realities in the world of God. In conformity with this even the most difficult and the most obscene passages from the Bible or from Ovid or Virgil or any other source, were symbolized, reinterpreted, and Ideationalized.

This symbolic language of writing and thinking was dominant up to the thirteenth century. Thus, here again, not accidentally but quite

---

[48] Saintsbury, *op. cit.*, Vol. I, pp. 393 ff.

[49] J. Huizinga, *The Waning of the Middle Ages* (London, 1927), pp. 184 and 188.

[50] W. W. Lawrence, "The Middle Ages," in *Columbia University Lectures* (Lectures on Literature, New York, 1911), p. 141.

[51] C. Foligno, "Vernacular Literature," in *The Legacy of the Middle Ages*, ed. by G. Crump and E. Jacob, pp. 190 ff. See also the chapter on Symbolism in H. O. Taylor, *Mediaeval Mind* (London, 1927), and Courthope, *op. cit.*, Vol. I, pp. 101 ff. and chap. ix.

[52] For other examples of transcendental symbolism see M. A. Ewer, *A Survey of Mystical Symbolism* (New York, 1933); H. Silberer, *Problems of Mysticism and Its Symbolism* (New York, 1927); F. R. Webber, *Church Symbolism* (Cleveland, 1927).

logically, we find the Ideational content of literature associated with symbolic external form; and both taken together testify definitely to the fact of the Ideational character of the literature of the period.

There is no need to point out that this Ideational literature was free from all the characteristics of the Sensate art and literature: it did not deal with everyday phenomena, did not have such a *genre* at all. It did not give any realistic portraiture of any individual (the lives of saints were in no way such portraiture). It was not sensual or sexual in any way. It did not attempt any novels of either historical character in the sense of an accurate reproduction of empirical historical events and personages; or of entertaining character — mystery and detective and adventure stories; or of satirical and picaresque nature; or just "romantic" in the modern sense of romanticism. Not only the negative type of personages, and the negative and low aspects of empirical life, were neglected by it; but even empirical heroic types and events occupy little space in it, and those are not so much empirical and "real" as abstract and formalized types, half otherworldly, half legendary. In brief, the reader may consider all the specific characteristics of the Ideational and Sensate art discussed at some length in Chapter Seven on painting and sculpture, and he will discover that practically all of those which belonged to the Ideational painting are to be found in the Ideational literature of the period also.

When studied in much greater detail than here, the literature exhibits several peculiar details perfectly suited to the Ideational type and hardly comprehensible from another standpoint. Here is an example. Several investigators of the medieval literature have noticed a lack of historical time and space perspective in it.

Never was there less sense of historical perspective [than in the medieval literature]: Mediaeval, classical, and Biblical heroes and heroines ran joyously along side by side. Time and space were forgotten. Mediaeval literature is, like Mediaeval painting, out of perspective and proportion.[53]

The statement is quite accurate; medieval literature indeed has little of this time-space perspective; but this is true also of the Hindu literature, and the literature of any Ideational period and type. The reason is evident: Ideational literature deals with and is moored to the world of Being, not to that of Becoming. The empirical time-space perspective has place, importance, and role in the world of fleeting and changing Becoming, while the world of Being is eternal, unchangeable. There-

[53] W. W. Lawrence, *op. cit.*, p. 152.

fore the world of Being does not need these co-ordinates of the empirical Space and Time (see Chapter Eleven of Volume Two, on Ideational and Sensate time-space conceptions). Hence the lack of Sensate space-time perspective in the medieval as well as any conspicuously Ideational literature; and the purer and sublimer its Ideationality the greater is the lack of this perspective. It is not an accident that the highly Ideational Brahmanic writings of India did not develop history virtually at all, and that the smallest unit of time in that literature is about 320,000 mortal years! This appears strange and paradoxical. But when the Ideational nature of the literature is recognized, this appears perfectly logical and in complete harmony with the very essence of Ideationalism.

Other similar traits, strange at first glance, but in perfect agreement with the nature of Ideationalism, are also present in the literature we are discussing.

C. *Literary Criticism.* Finally, in conformity with all this, stands also the character of the *literary and art criticism* of the period from the fifth to the thirteenth century. This character, in contrast to that of the preceding Sensate criticism, is purely Ideational. Sensate art, pure aestheticism, "art for art's sake," beauty for the sake of beauty with all the satellites of these traits discussed above, have vanished from literary criticism. They are rejected, decried, and stamped sinful, impure, unpermissible. In brief, these categories disappeared almost entirely from the highway of the art mentality of the Middle Ages and at the best remained as a secondary stream underground, somewhere in the depths of paganism, and even there were in part remodeled in accordance with the new spirit and the new art.

The criterion of beauty and art became again religious and moral. Whatever contradicted this criterion became nonart, nonbeauty. Such a situation continued almost unbroken up to the twelfth century. In the works of the Church Fathers — Augustine, Cassiodorus, Boethius, Martianus, Venantus Fortunatus, Fulgentius, Isidore of Seville, Bede, Scotus Erigena, St. Bernard, St. Benedictine, St. Francis — one does not find anything of this aestheticism and pure aesthetic criticism. Even the great theorizers of the twelfth and thirteenth centuries, like St. Thomas Aquinas, do not exhibit much of it. Whatever criticism there was — and there was certainly a great deal — it was not Sensately aesthetic, but religious and moral. In other words it was an Ideational judgment. "The Middle Ages was innocent as hardly indulging in criticism [Sensate] at all. . . ." Purely "literary criticism is impossible" in the medieval frame of mind.   Its "very essence was opposed to criticism [of that kind]." [54]

Thus, the purely religious content and Ideational (mainly symbolic) form of the chief medieval literature, the absence of the Sensate literary and art criticism, and the presence, instead, of a purely Ideational censorship and estimation of literary works — all these make obvious the Ideational character of that literature up to the twelfth century.   This is still more obvious when one remembers that until the twelfth century the other forms of art, and especially painting, music, and sculpture, were in exactly the same situation, that is, both inwardly and externally were quite Ideational.

IV. IDEALISTIC LITERATURE AND CRITICISM OF THE THIRTEENTH AND FOURTEENTH CENTURIES

Just as in the various fields of art the first observable emergence of a mildly Sensate form took place in the twelfth and the thirteenth centuries, and led to the Idealistic style in painting, sculpture, architecture, and — somewhat later — music, so also is it with literary work during this same period. *In literature also these are transitional centuries of an Idealistic mixture of the declining Ideationalism and the reawakening Sensatism.   The Idealistic character is manifest in all the main aspects of what is styled here Idealistic art, namely, in the inner content of the literature, in its external forms, and finally in the character of the art and literary criticism of the period.*

A. *Inner Traits.*   As to the *inner content* of the literature of these centuries, it now represents, first of all, a *mixture of religious with secular topics*, though the secular is still predominantly *heroic*, and still does not deal with the banal, everyday events and personages and still less with the vulgar, negative, low, debased, pathological aspects of empirical life. This mixture is one of the inner characteristics of the Idealistic art.

On the level of the major literature, according to our rough computation, the proportion of the religious writings, which was about 95 per cent previously, now falls for these centuries to about 30 to 55, in the French, the German, and the English literatures; the remaining 70 to 45 per cent being secular or semisecular.   Somewhat similar is the situation in the literature of the other Western countries of Europe (with the exception of Russia, which lags here also).   This decrease is due not to an absolute decrease in the quantity of religious literature, but to an enormous increase of secular and semisecular writing.   In Germany this is the period of the

[54] Saintsbury, *op. cit.*, Vol. I, pp. 484, 373, and 381.

Ruodlieb (a chivalric romance written by a monk, begun in the eleventh century), of the *Kaiserchronik, Rolandslied* (a secular heroic poem, but still permeated by the religious point of view), *Alexanderlied, Tristrant, Lanzelet, Nibelungenlied, Salman und Morolf, Gregorius, Barlaam, Parzival, Iwein, Lied von Troye*, the works of Hartmann von Aue, of Wolfram von Eschenbach, of Ulrich von Lichtenstein, of Gottfried von Strassburg, of Walter von der Vogelweide, and of a number of other "historico-legendary romances" and epics, with a little sprinkling of somewhat less heroic and more Sensate works. The character of these writings shows that even in the secular world they deal mainly with heroes, with outstanding persons, and with the positive values of empirical reality as they were understood then. Even these secular works are permeated considerably by the Ideational — religious and moral — atmosphere. The remaining portion of the literature, some 40 per cent, was still religious.[55]

Not much different is the situation in the French or English or general Western European literature of the period.

In France the secular literature is represented by similar epics and heroic romances: *La Chanson de Roland, Le Couronnement de Louis, Raoul de Cambrai, Tristan et Iseult*, and so on; by a number of shorter narratives like Marie de France's *Seven Lais, La mule sans frein, Richeut*, by the *De amore* of André Chapelain; by a few secular dramas, like Adam de la Halle's *Jeu de Robin et Marion;* by fables, like the *Roman de Renard;* by lyrics and by fabliaux (thought they were on the lower level of literature); and at the end of the fourteenth century by historical works (Joinville and Froissart); and finally, by probably the greatest of all these writings, the *Roman de la Rose*.

As we shall see, the character of these is very like that of the German works of the same period. It is mainly heroic, positive, ennobling, moralizing, permeated still by the religious spirit. A few more "earthly" and, among the *fabliaux*, even indecent works emerged; but they again were a much smaller stream and even part of that stream circulated not as literature but as a kind of stories told ("not for the children and the ladies") while drinking and under similar circumstances.[56]

In England, side by side with still predominant religious literature, the secular literature is represented by similar Arthurian romances and epics, by fables, by modified *chansons de geste*, by political songs, and at the close of the fourteenth century by Langland's *The Vision Concerning Piers*

---

[55] See the details in the works of J. G. Robertson and Vogt und Koch, cited.

[56] See the works of Langlois, Foerster and Koschwitz, and the other volumes referred to above.

Plowman; and it culminates in the appearance of Chaucer, who by all rights not so much closes the period as opens the next one.[57]

Similar was the situation in other Western European literatures, the peak and the summit of which, as well as for all Europe, was Dante's *Divine Comedy.*

Thus the quantitative proportions of the religious and secular literatures and their general qualitative character, so far as their inner content is concerned, testify to the Idealistic nature of the literature of those centuries.

The empirical world, the Sensate *Weltanschauung*, with its joys and griefs, its passions and emotions, had already entered into, and left its stamp upon, literature. But still, in the main, the noblest, the most elevating, the heroic, the best side of this empirical reality is reflected. The other side — the prosaic, the daily, the vulgar, the debased, the pathological — is still reflected little.

If one should go into a deeper study of the inner character of this literature — the religious and especially the secular — one would find this Idealistic nature more fully confirmed. Here are some of the symptomatic items and the manner in which they are treated in the literature of the preceding period, and that of the period under discussion.[58]

If we glance at the literature of the preceding period (before the twelfth century) and of the period under discussion from the standpoint of *asceticism versus sensuality*, the result is that the literature of the preceding period is seen to be ascetic and even extremely ascetic in a considerable part; and at the same time, when it is not, it is almost entirely free from any conspicuous Sensatism and especially from that of coarse and erotic sensuality. This naturally holds for the saints' lives, not to mention the purely theological literature. To attain holiness one must give up all sensate comfort, home, friends, family, and any physical joy of this world. St. Alexis abandoning his bride on the night of his marriage in order to avoid temptation to the detriment of the holy life he wants to enter, or chastity as glorified by Hroswitha, is in a sense typical. Love as the relationship of the sexes, whether in a noble or coarse form, plays generally little role in that literature, and in no way is one of its chief objects. If a few references to sexual immorality are found, as for instance in the eighth-century *Altdeutsche Gespräche*, or in *Modus Liebung*,

[57] See Courthope, *op. cit.*, Vol. I, *passim.*

[58] The subsequent conclusions are a short summary of a rather detailed investigation made with the help of Dr. Phelps and Dr. Parker. Lack of space and the voluminousness of the details force me to extract from the study only its main results.

they are condemnatory mostly and serve as a contrast to what is held to be good and proper.

When we pass to the period of the twelfth to the fourteenth century, inclusive, the atmosphere notably changes. The ascetic strain decreases, quantitatively and in part qualitatively, and the Sensate strain increases. First of all, love now begins to occupy a much larger place. It becomes one of the main topics of the epics and of the romances, not to mention the *fabliaux* and the lyric poetry. And not only love but other pleasure-giving objects and processes: feasts, eating, luxury of dwelling, fine clothing, fine weapons and arms, fighting, hunting, vengeance, etc. — to all these now a greater attention is devoted, and all are described with a sense of enjoyment. On the other hand — and this is important for the Idealistic nature of this literature — these sensate joys and strains and motives are still on a level of a high nobility, idealization, refinement, and free from the debased, low, coarse, and vulgar forms. These low forms crop up once in a while in the *Schwänke*, in the *fabliaux*, and in a few other works of the period; but these were regarded as the literature of the bourgeoisie and of the lower classes and as such either did not compose the "high-grade" literature of the period or got into it rather rarely. Only at the very end of the fourteenth century and afterwards did they have their heyday.

From this standpoint the famous *Roman de la Rose*, perhaps the greatest and the most popular work of its kind in the period, composed by two different authors in the thirteenth century, is in many respects typical. Its topic is love. In the first part composed by Guillaume de Lorris, we have an allegorical treatment of sensate love in its sublimest (but not ascetic), noblest, most decent, most delicate, and most romantic form. Nothing coarse or cynical is in it. It is the finest conception of what often is styled Platonic love. In this part this conception is quite representative of the conception of love in many epics and romances of the period, and of what was formulated in, and to a degree practiced according to, the *Regulations of the Court of Love* of the twelfth and the thirteenth centuries. André Chapelain in his *De amore* gives an adequate presentation of this Code, with its thirty-one articles of the Laws of Love.

Such rules as article 2: *Nemo duplici potest amore ligari* (love of only one and forever) or article 20: *Amorosus semper est timorosus*, and the general principle of the worship of women and the like, indicate the nature of the chivalric Code of Love. Of the same kind is the love of most of the epics and the romances of the period. Even when it breaks the rules of morality, as for instance in the *Tristan*, it breaks them not by the erotic fancy of the heroes or heroines, but by the inescapable dictum of Destiny, as was true also of the *Oedipus* and other tragedies of the Idealistic Greek literature of the fifth century B.C., and turns the event into tragedy instead of an adulterous sex adventure.

Side by side with this type of the Idealized and ennobled love, there is a still purer and still more delicate type represented by such literary works as the *Livre des cent ballades* and the writings of Marie of France, with their unstained glorification of the pure, sublime, and faithful love of knights. On the other hand, in the second part of the *Roman de la Rose*, composed somewhat later by another author, Jean de Meung, we face a different symphony of love — more fleshy, more sensate, partly cynical, erotic, and scoffing. Its motto, *Fais ce que tu voudras*, repeated later on by Rabelais, gives an idea of the change. After the first part where there is nothing of the "physiology of sex," we are thrown into a love romance where procreation and physiology and "sex appeal," in the modern sense, play a considerable part. In addition to this Jean de Meung attacks satirically chastity, the clergy, kings, the nobility, the monastic orders, and other qualities and institutions. His advice with regard to success in love is: Have "a great heavy purse."

Again, in this part also the *Roman de la Rose* is very typical of a section of the literature of the period. The motives of this part are paralleled in several other contemporary works, like the *Pélerinage de Charlemagne* in which Oliver boasts of his sexual strength and is put to the test; like the fabliau *Richeut* in which Martin Hopart says:

> *Il n'est paradis fors deniers*
> *Et mengier et boire bon vin*
> *Et gesir sus draps desliez.*

(There is no paradise except hard cash, eating, and drinking good wine, and lying on a nice smooth bed.)

In varying forms these motives recur in several German and other works of the period.

Thus the *Roman de la Rose* in both its parts is typical for the period in regard to asceticism versus Sensatism, and represents the situation accurately.[59] When along with these two streams of Sensate love —

---

[59] This mixed or double character of the period from the twelfth to the fourteenth century is shown also in such details as the appearance of women in art and literature. First, parallel to what we have seen in the field of painting and sculpture, woman figures more often and occupies a more conspicuous place in the literature of this period than in that of the preceding. Second, in the preceding period woman as woman in the sense of the sex essentially different from the male sex is not stressed, and consequently no specific attitude in regard to her is developed. Saints, of either sex, are described just as saints, without specific exhibition of

Platonic and physiological — the ascetic stream is also considered — the ascetic stream which runs still strong in a considerable part of the literature of these centuries and becomes even somewhat more sharp and extreme as a reaction against the rising tide of eroticism and sensualism [60] — then one can hardly question the validity of my statement that the literature was Mixed in its character, and that as a result of this mixture it was indeed Idealistic.[61]

---

the female characteristics as something quite apart and radically different from the male. Now the attitude changes. Woman is now treated as something quite different from man. In this treatment again two opposite attitudes — and these attitudes are meant to be applied only to woman — appear: one, the chivalrous attitude of the *lumen caeli, sancta rosa*, a worship of the lady, adoration, almost deification of her; another the "bourgeois" attitude which rails and rants at women as untrustworthy, sensual creatures, a necessary evil and pest. The same attitude is taken now by the clerical writers and art as probably a reaction against the sensuous adoration of woman and of its consequences. In the preceding period such an attitude in the art and the literature of the clergy and church was absent. The first is typical for most of the aristocratic epics and romances; the second, for the fabliaux and the coarser class of literature. Here the *Roman de la Rose* reflects again this situation faithfully: in the first part we see the first attitude; in the second, mild forms of the second. E. Mâle very discriminatingly notices the same phenomenon in painting and sculpture. Before the twelfth century we do not see in the religious art representations of a woman with serpents coming from her breasts and similar images. Beginning with the twelfth century such figures appear more and more often. "It is strange to note the appearance of this sombre figure of culpable woman in the art of the twelfth century in the Southern France where poets began to deify her and to eulogize her weaknesses with much greater pleasure than her virtues. While monks carved upon the portals of their churches woman as an image of degradation, Guillaume d'Aquitaine told his pleasant fortunes in ironic verses and with pleasure untroubled by any remorse. Bernard de Ventadour saw in love the unique objective of life and expressed this in words of voluptuous tenderness. The moral of the world began to oppose that of the cloister." E. Mâle, *L'art religieux du XIIe siècle en France*, p. 376.

Thus in this detailed trait again the Ideational and the Idealistic character of the literatures of the two periods comes out clearly and in conformity with what has been observed in the two parts of the *Roman de la Rose* (where, however, the sternly ascetic reaction is not represented).

[60] As is known, the *Roman de la Rose* aroused sharp criticism on the part of the partisans of asceticism and they criticized it, though without crushing its popularity, most severely. Among its critics the most prominent is perhaps Jean Gerson, the famous chancellor of the University of Paris, who in 1402 published his treatise against it, where he says: "The fool rails at marriage and monastic life. He teaches how all young girls should sell their persons early and dear without shame . . ." and that "Nature does not wish that a woman should be content with one single man. . . . He carried his blasphemy so far as to show from the Gospel of St. Luke that formerly a woman's genitals, the rose of the romance, were sacred," and so on.

[61] For those who delight in statistics and demand a strictly quantitative corroboration of any contention, I point out that we carried on several more specific and more definitely quantitative studies of the problem. One of them, for instance, concerns how often cases of adultery or illicit sex relations are described and the nature of the remarks about it — whether condemned, praised, or left without ethical comment. The essential results of such study are again in agreement with the characteristics indicated above. In the preceding

The ascetic and, more generally, Ideational stream, strongly present in that literature, found its greatest expression in Dante's *Divine Comedy*. When all the works of the Italian poet are considered, including his sonnets and lyric poetry in which the Sensate motives are conspicuous, he alone is found to incorporate in his works the perfect balance of the Ideational and Sensate currents and to be in this sense a manifestation of the Idealistic art of the period. In his *Divine Comedy*, however, he is much nearer to Ideationalism than to Idealism. Of course, many sensate elements are present in it, in the very description of the types of the persons whom he meets, especially in the *Inferno* and in part in the *Purgatorio*, and in the account of the deeds for which they are placed there. Nevertheless, these elements are relegated to a secondary position; the main content and the soul of the work, as well as its principal form — a real transcendental symbolism — are undoubtedly and strongly Ideational.

Thus when what are probably the two main works of the period are taken into consideration — the two differing parts of the *Roman de la Rose*

---

period such cases are very rarely mentioned and when mentioned practically always condemned. They serve in these few cases as a pretext to show what is or is not right conduct. In this Idealistic period the situation changes step by step: the number of the cases of adultery and illicit sex relations increases and the proportion of those which either are not condemned at all but praised or just left uncommented on increases also. For instance, in the German literature, before the twelfth century adultery is mentioned only twice and in both cases is strongly condemned. In the first half of the twelfth century it is mentioned as a historical event (the case of Lucretia) in the *Kaiserchronik* and condemned; similarly are mentioned and condemned the efforts to seduce two different queens. Only the illicit relations of Alexander and the queen in the *Alexanderlied* are left without comment. In the second half of the twelfth century illicit sex relations are mentioned in eight works and only in two of these (*Salman und Morolf* and *Lanzelet*) are they condemned. In two, in the beast fable of *Reinhart* and in the *Tristrant*, they are rather approved or, at least, excused. More specifically we have eleven cases of adultery in *Tristrant*, *Salman* (twice), *Reinhart*. The cases of illicit sex relations in the *Floire und Blanchefleur*, *Eneide*, *Böchlein*, *Lanzelet;* incests in the *Gregorius* (between brother and sister, knowing; and son and mother, unknowing), are condemned and repented for. In the lyric there are numerous cases. In the thirteenth century adultery and illicit sex relations are mentioned in more than twelve important works, and half of them, at least, are either not condemned at all or are condemned but not strongly (see two *Tristan* poems, *Parzival*, *Eraclius*, *Herzemaere*, two *Alexander* poems, *Engelhardt*, *Partenopier*, three *Troyanische Krieg* poems, and a few others). In the fourteenth century, in the much smaller volume of literature extant, we find several cases mentioned at least in five important works — a larger proportion than before — and of these in two they are condemned and in three works they are not condemned. Thus, however rough and in a sense inaccurate are such statistics, nevertheless they also reflect the trend discussed and show the "divided" mind, or rather the Mixed — the Ideational Sensate — mentality of the period, notably different from the preceding one. In a similar manner several other items symptomatic of the change in the attitude, asceticism versus sensuality, have been studied, and yielded a similar result. Their presentation here, however, would make the work still more cumbersome than it already is. Therefore, they are omitted.

and the *Divine Comedy* — these two works are found to incorporate in themselves all the three main streams of the literature of the period : predominantly Ideational, nobly and idealistically Sensate, and openly erotic. The presence and the mixture of these three streams in the literature are themselves excellent evidence of its Idealistic character. The fact that the period created these great masterpieces, not to mention many smaller ones, is additional evidence of such a character because, as has been indicated several times in this work, the greatest blossoming of art usually occurs in the Idealistic periods when the Ideational stream begins to decline and the Sensate to rise, and these streams cross each other and blend together and produce, as the result of such a blending, the great Idealistic art, not yet loosened from its Ideational moorings and at the same time dressed in the dazzling and noblest and purest forms of Sensate beauty.

From this standpoint the very fact of the creation of these two works — so different and at the same time so congenial — is not an accident but the manifestation of the deep and subtle logic of an integrated culture and art.

The Mixed or Idealistic manner of treatment of love in the period is shown also by the Mixed religious-Sensate terminology of many works in which religious language is sprinkled with the erotic and eroticism is given religious forms. In the thirteenth and fourteenth centuries love associations were dominated by the religious. After the fifteenth century religious terms were made subservient to the erotic ones. The *Roman de la Rose* offers examples of the former; Charles d'Orleans (fifteenth century) gives an illustration of the latter, with his "These are the ten commandments, True God of Love," or when, lamenting his dead love, he says : "I have celebrated the obsequies of my Lady in the Church of Love ; and the service of her soul was sung by dolorous Thought. . . . I had the tomb made of Regrets," and so on. Comparisons of amorous longings and sadness with the sufferings of ascetics and the martyrs and other expressions of *les amoureux de l'observance* are quite common in the period. Of these two elements the Ideational religious used more often to take the upper hand in the earlier part of the period and resulted usually in the *Memento mori* and *vanitas vanitatum* of Sensate love and its beauty and pleasures. At the end of the fourteenth century and after, while this manner of mixing religious and erotic terminology lingered, the erotic element began to dominate and resulted in the *Carpe diem* — Life is short ; after death there is nothing but dust and worms ; therefore, snatch every pleasure you can. Wine, women, and song ! Examples are found in Olivier de la Marche's *Parement et triumphe de dames*, in Villon, in Boccaccio, in F. de la Salle, in Lorenzo the Magnificent, in Lorenzo de Valla, in Rabelais, in Ronsard, to mention but a few names.

If now we take another item relevant to the problem under discussion it gives similar indications : for instance, *divorce* as the outlet for a sensately unhappy marriage. In the literature before the twelfth century it is practically absent. In the period considered, a few mentions of divorce already occur (Marie de France's *Eliduc*, and *Le Friesne*, and the *Oesterreichische Reichschronik*, and a few others). Another item which appears concerns *economic problems* in whatever form. Nowadays, in our Sensate culture there is hardly any problem and any work, whether in literature, art, philosophy, social science, which does not start with, or at least consider as one of the important factors, the economic problems. In the Ideational culture this "economic mentality" is practically absent. Therefore we expect that in the literature of the Ideational period up to the twelfth century economic problems must either be absent or play a very modest role. The expectation is borne out by the facts. The economic problem virtually does not occur at all, remains almost completely unmentioned. The mind turned to eternity is little interested in such matters and follows the Gospel's prescription not to worry from this standpoint about tomorrow. In the literature of the Idealistic period we may expect the problem to appear, in modest degree. And it does, several times, *e.g.*, in *Der Welsche Gast* of the thirteenth century Thomasin inveighs against a moneylender, but from the purely religious point of view. Similarly it is mentioned in the *Edelstein* of the fourteenth century from the same standpoint. It is discussed also in the form of a complaint at the poverty of the author in the *Miracle de Théophile* by Rutebeuf of the thirteenth century. It comes out in the form of the laments over the sad condition of the peasantry in the *Miserere, Lamentations de Mahieu, Contrefait de Renard*. In the literature of the fourteenth century in France, Gilles li Muisis decries the evils of speculation, the shortage of labor, the overtaxation of the laboring classes, avarice, and so on. Similar motives are found in the *Divine Comedy* of Dante, as well as in the *Piers Plowman* and other works of the period. In the Idealistic literature this motive is to be expected. But it cannot be the main problem, or a problem considered purely from the standpoint of the sensate well-being. Such an attitude is that of the predominantly Sensate literature. The Idealistic literature is expected to consider it as one among many other — and no less important — problems and to consider it from the Idealistic — religious, moral, social, or other — standpoint. The literature of the period considers it exactly in that fashion, and therefore this symptom shows once more that my qualification and diagnosis of the literature as Idealistic are supported by the facts.

As a further test of the Ideationality, Idealism, or Sensatism of the literature before the twelfth century and from the twelfth to the fourteenth, I considered the attitudes which may be expressed in the terms *duty versus revolt*, that is, willingness or unwillingness to carry on acts or ways of life recognized as obligatory in painful and uncomfortable empirical conditions — and I consider as revolt any fact of criticism, complaint, any violation of what was regarded as duty, whether religious, moral, or juridico-social. Again the results corroborate what we should expect. In the Ideational literature and mentality, duty, especially the religious and moral duty, is absolute and the only category which counts. (See Part Two of Volume Two on Fluctuations of Ethical Systems.) The cases in which this attitude is violated are exceedingly few in the literature before the twelfth century and are followed almost always by a statement of disapproval and by retribution. The inflexible attitude is shown by the manner in which the violations of duty are dealt with and by the general treatment of crime in various fields. It is shown also by the conduct of the persons involved, who do not neglect their duty through any comfort or discomfort of a Sensate nature, but perform it, even paying for its fulfillment with their life. This is the general view of the literature of the period, and in this it again exhibits its Ideational character clearly. In the literature of the Idealistic period, it is to be expected that such a rigidity will be somewhat mitigated; some violations of duty and in a moderate degree will be somewhat excused. And this is exactly what we find in fact. The fulfillment of duty under all circumstances is still the main ideal. But in several cases, as in the instance of the fatalistic passion in the *Tristan*, or in the instances of *Parzival*, *Meier Helmbrecht*, *Pfaffe Ameis*, and Ganelon of the *Chanson de Roland*, where in certain circumstances the Sensate point of view finds an excuse, or much more often in the case of the literature of the bourgeoisie — the *fabliaux* — duty begins to yield fairly often to material convenience and personal advantage. In the fourteenth century even in some epics, for instance in the *Hue Capet*, self-interest becomes more and more dominant at the cost of duty. This concerns equally the religious, the feudal, the chivalrous, the moral, or the patriotic duty.

An additional difference in the literatures of the two periods is that, in what I style Idealistic, the religious duty becomes less conspicuous than, for instance, the patriotic or the chivalrous duty and wanes faster than those which are nearer to the Sensate world.   Besides, even when duty is emphasized in the literature of the twelfth to the fourteenth century, one feels it is emphasized as a matter of routine and as something more superficial than it was in the mentality and the literature of the preceding period.

Thus this barometer once more confirms our diagnosis of the literature of the period as Idealistic.   In the preceding, the Ideational, literature, duty is the categorical imperative which does not yield to any exigencies and Sensate considerations.   There it is *dura lex sed lex* and is in a sense in harmony with the *fiat justitia et pereat mundus* [Sensate].   In the period from the twelfth to the fourteenth century the *lex* is still *lex* and *duty is still duty*, but they begin to be broken here and there by the material exigencies, by the utilitarian, hedonistic, and eudaemonistic balancing of advantages and disadvantages.   In the later period, with the rise of the Sensate culture, the *lex* and the *duty* will be further undermined and sacrificed more and more in favor of utilitarian and Sensate considerations, until finally the *lex* and the *duty* will be destroyed as the categoric and absolute values, and replaced by what may be styled a bookkeeper's balance of Sensate advantages and disadvantages in this or that line of conduct, computed allegedly in a purely scientific and mathematical manner, but in fact representing one of the most foolish, shortsighted, and stupid systems of recommended conduct in spite of all the scientific (in fact pseudo-scientific) halo attributed to it by almost everybody.

Of the other inner "symptoms" studied I shall mention only five more : (1) *What proportion in the literatures of both periods is occupied by description of nature (paysage*, landscape)?   (2) *What proportion is occupied by the genre of everyday life?*   (3) *How often are real historical personages in their real empirical settings of time, place, and social conditions found in that literature?*   (4) *How often do persons of low grade, of the lower classes, of mediocre nature, especially of picturesque, picaresque, negative, debased, and similar character, figure in the literature of both periods, and what place do they occupy?*   (5) *What is the "emotional tone" of these literatures: Is it calm and serene, or is it dramatic, emotional, pathetic, and if the second, in what specific form: joy, pessimism, sadness?*

The brief answer to all these questions is that in the literatures of the two periods compared, we find the situation similar to what we found in the study of painting and sculpture for the same times.   Landscape as landscape and appreciation of nature ; the realistic *genre* of everyday life ; historical romances, novels, or biographies, as well as descriptions of characters in their realistic types ; persons and events of the debased and low order, or of picaresque and picturesque character, occupy little, if any, place in the literature before the twelfth century.   And this shows again its Ideational character.   Likewise, in emotional tone the literature is simple, serene, calm, unperturbed by anything empirical in its unfaltering faith in God and His providence.   The literature of the second period shows already an increasing tendency to give place to *paysage*, to the daily *genre*, to mediocre types of men (especially in the *fabliaux* and in the "bourgeois" literature).   In that period emerges *historical narrative* (*e.g.*, the work of Froissart, Joinville, and several other chroniclers); there appears a kind of biography as person portraiture.   The emotional tone of the literature becomes less serene and calm, more alive; and in the fourteenth century, especially, it becomes *very* melancholy, sad, pessimistic, particularly in the lyric poetry — for instance, of E. Deschamps, Jean Meschinot, Georges Chastellain, Jean Gerson, and many others.[62]   So it happens almost always, when one fundamental form of culture comes to an end and the next form has not yet arrived.   When the new does come, the sadness will be replaced by the most optimistic assurances of progress and by joy of life.

If, further, we consider that most of the literature of the first period is *anonymous* and in a sense *collective*, while in the second period a considerable part of it becomes *individualistic*, in the sense that its single maker begins more and more to stamp his name upon the creation and to regard it as his and his only; in this trait again we see a complete parallelism with what we have observed of painting and sculpture.   This trait shows

[62] See J. Huizinga's work, where he particularly emphasizes this pessimism.   "At the close of the Middle Ages a sombre melancholy weighs on the people's soul."   There was an "immense sadness."   "The note of despair and profound dejection is predominantly sounded not by ascetic monks, but by the court poets and the chroniclers — the laymen, living in aristocratic circles and amidst aristocratic ideas."   Deschamps cries:

"Temps de doleur et de temptacion,
Aages de plour, d'envie et de tourment,
Temps de langour et de dampnaccion,"

and so on.   And adds: "The age of decline nigh to the end; Time full of horrors which does all things falsely; Lying age, full of pride and of envy.   Time without honor and without a true judgment.   Age of sadness which shortens life."

Similarly Jean Meschinot complains: "O miserable and very sad life! Have mercy, O Lord, upon our wicked persons whose life is short."

And so on.   The attitude is quite typical not only for the literature of the period but, as we have seen, for its painting and sculpture, too.   See Huizinga, *op. cit.*, chap. ii; for painting and sculpture see E. Mâle, *L'art religieux de la fin du Moyen Âge en France* (Paris, 1908), *passim*.   "A strange thing this century [the fifteenth], which is also that of the Renaissance, is sad.   Fear grows with the coming of the modern age.   Never was the restlessness of souls greater and more profound."   L. Gillet, *Histoire artistique des ordres mendiants*, (Paris, 1912), p. 208.

once more the Ideational nature of the literature of the first period and the Idealistic character of that of the second.

Thus the totality of the inner symptomatic traits leaves no doubt about the predominantly Ideational character of the literature from the sixth to the twelfth century, and its Idealistic character from the twelfth century.[63] The main fluctuations in literature accompany those in painting and sculpture.

B. *External Traits*. The Idealistic character of the literature of the period comes out no less clearly from a consideration of its *external* form or style. The external form of the Ideational art is transcendental symbolism, in which the sensory signs and images are but "visible symbols of the invisible world." The external form of the Sensate art is sensory realism or naturalism, or visualism. The characteristic external form of the mixed Idealistic art is a union of these different styles, resulting either in their simple intermingling, or in *allegory*, which is the organic or "chemical" synthesis of the two and not mere mechanical and spatial existence. In the preceding chapter I pointed out *the deep difference between transcendental symbolism and allegory*. The second is a metaphorical personification and hypostatization of abstractions taken mostly from this sensory world. The first is the representation by signs from the empirical world of the superempirical realities, which are beyond the empirical world and which can be but imperfectly indicated by the code of sensory signs. From this standpoint the literature of the preceding period, that is to the twelfth century, is mainly symbolic but not allegorical. The literature of the period under consideration displays the coexistence of all three styles: symbolism, for instance, in the *Divine Comedy;* "visual naturalism" in the *fabliaux*, in many short novels, and to some extent in the epics, romances, and lyrical poetry; and "allegory" in the *Roman de la Rose*. Such coexistence, with each style represented in a strong proportion, is by itself evidence of the Mixed Idealistic character of the literature. What, however, is more important, is that *allegory* is a new and particularly powerful trait. It is in this period that allegory in the present sense first enters literature (and the other arts, also). It lingers there for several centuries, especially in the *Moralities* and *Mystery* plays, gradually degenerating into "marinism," "Gongorism," "euphuism," and other highly artificial mannerisms in the literature of the fifteenth, the sixteenth, the seventeenth, and in part of the eighteenth century, when allegory in all its forms declines and almost disappears. A similar situation existed, as we should remember,

---

[63] Compare A. David-Sauvageot, *op. cit.*, pp. 40 ff., 68, and 91 ff.

in painting and sculpture. It is in the period following the twelfth century, whether in the *Roman de la Rose* or in other literary works, that all the innumerable allegorical personifications emerge: Love, Beauty, Wealth, Youth, Gaiety, Leisure, Frankness, Liberty, Hope, Fear, Sweet Thought, Sweet Speech, Sweet Looks, Courtesy, Danger, Shame, Reason, Virginity, Seduction, Purity, Innocence, and so on. I have taken these allegorical figures from the *Roman de la Rose* only, and they are but a small part of those which occur in that work. Each personified abstraction is depicted as a concrete personality, acting, and talking, having the various other characteristics of a real person, often possessing even sex traits. Some of the figures are female (*e.g.*, Dame Leisure); others are male. In the *Roman de la Rose* the Lover approaches the walls of the Mysterious Garden of Love; Dame Leisure opens the gates (so here we have a female gatekeeper); Gaiety conducts the Lover; and there follows an introduction to Amor who holds Beauty by the hand in the presence of her court, which consists of Sir and Madame Wealth, Liberality, Frankness, Courtesy, Youth, and other people of high society. Such is the form and the language of the *Roman de la Rose* and, in a less subtle form, of hundreds of other allegorical works of the period. Moreover, the literature of the subsequent period is flooded with allegories, including such figures as Everyman, Virtue, Gluttony, Stomach, and Foot.

It is evident that this allegorical language is something radically different from both the transcendental symbolism and naturalistic description. It is a style *sui generis*, in which the abstract aspects of the empirical world are forged into the visual similitude of concrete empirical persons, actions, objects, traits. Such language is, as it were, a chemical compound of the Sensate and the Ideational aspects of reality. And in this respect it is an Idealistic mixture and therefore specifically typical of the Idealistic art. Its emergence in the literature of the period is a striking proof of the Mixed, and Idealistic, nature of that literature.

Thus, the external forms of the literature show its Idealistic nature no less clearly than its inner character. We have the coexistence of the symbolic, the allegorical, and the naturalistic forms; and we witness the emergence and rapid rise of Allegory as a particular style.

C. *Art Criticism.* If, finally, we turn to the *art and literary criticism* of the period, we find it consistent in character with the inner and external nature of the literature proper. In the preceding period, as has been indicated, there was but an Ideational appreciation or judgment of art and literature. Sensate beauty, Sensate art appreciation, and Sensate criticism did not exist at all. Now the situation begins to change. The

Ideational standpoint is still strong and dominant, but its monopoly is broken: art and literary criticism, as we understand it now, begins to emerge. The first signs of this are seen in St. Thomas Aquinas's conceptions and in Dante's *De vulgari eloquentia* and even in such a mystic as Meister Eckhart (b. *c.* 1260). Others soon follow in their footsteps, and in the fifteenth century the literary (Sensate) criticism is already quite widespread, especially in Italy.[64]

It is true that in the thirteenth and the fourteenth century there are no more than the first symptoms of such a criticism. For criticism necessarily lags somewhat behind literature proper and behind art: only when the phenomena of a Sensate art have emerged and become crystallized and conspicuous do the critics become cognizant of its existence and begin to dissect it and to ponder over what has already taken place. In a similar manner, the critics at the end of the Graeco-Roman Sensate culture, in the fourth, the fifth, and even the sixth century, continued still to examine, to estimate, to criticize art and literature from the Sensate standpoint, while in reality the Sensate art was already dead and the Ideational art and literature were already emerging and becoming dominant. In our case the Sensate literary and art criticism emerges clearly only in the fifteenth and sixteenth centuries, but in the period under discussion we have only its first signs.

Thus, the inner nature of the writings, their external forms — especially the allegorical style—and, finally, the character of the art appreciation and what we call art and literary criticism all demonstrate unequivocally the Mixed, and Idealistically Mixed, quality of the literature of the twelfth to the fourteenth century, inclusive. And this is the result of the waning of the previous Ideational stream and the swelling of the Sensate stream, which had previously been dry. Then, as in practically any such Idealistic period, literature, like the other arts, gave rise to some of its finest blossoms, whether in the form of Dante's *Divine Comedy*, or in that of the *Roman de la Rose* or of numerous other wonderful epics and romances, or in the shape of the great Scholastic works of philosophy and theology, which also contained much of the special theory of art.[65]

[64] See G. Saintsbury, *op. cit.*, Vol. I, pp. 416 ff.; J. Schlosser, *Die Kunstliteratur* (Vienna, 1924), pp. 66–77; M. de Wulf, *Études historiques sur l'Esthétique de St. Thomas d'Aquin;* A. K. Coomaraswamy, *The Transformation of Nature in Art* (Cambridge, 1933), chap. ii *et passim.*

[65] Anybody who knows something of medieval art and literature can but agree with Saintsbury (and the competent investigators are now virtually unanimous in this point) that the medieval literature created several fresh and beautiful forms — the story, the romance, the pathos of love, etc. — and that they gave " the immense provision of new kinds of literature side by side with almost total abstinence from [Sensate] criticism." (Saintsbury, *op. cit.*, Vol. I, p. 486.)

The period thus once more confirms the statement that the peaks of art are usually reached in the Idealistic phase, just as the marvelous balance of the literature and art of the twelfth, the thirteenth, and the fourteenth centuries is in turn a testimony of its Idealistic nature. Now we can move to the next period.

V. The Period of the Domination of Sensate Literature and Criticism

After the fourteenth century the decline of the Ideational stream and the rising tide of Sensatism progressed and led to the domination of the Sensate form of literature from about the fifteenth century to the present. There were of course minor fluctuations, short-time and shallow ups and downs of Sensatism and Ideationalism. However, they were merely ripplings upon a fairly continuous rising tide of Sensatism, until, at the end of the nineteenth century, the first large reaction against Sensatism (though not a setting up of Ideationalism) appeared. This conclusion is substantiated once again by the inner character of the literature of the period, by its external forms, and by the character of the art and literary criticism. Let us survey concisely but accurately the literature of the "modern" period from all these standpoints.

A. *Inner Traits. First of all, the literature becomes more and more secular and less and less religious in its topics.* In our rough quantitative estimation of the masterpieces in France, the percentage of the literature dealing with religious subjects, which had been about 100 up to the twelfth century and had fallen to some 55 to 30 during the period from the twelfth to the fourteenth centuries, decreases to some 25 to 20 per cent in the fifteenth century, rises to 25 to 35 in the sixteenth, seventeenth, and eighteenth centuries, and then falls again to some 10 per cent in the nineteenth and twentieth centuries. The figures are very approximate, but indicative of the trend. It is similar to what we have seen in painting and sculpture and music and architecture.

What is much more important, however, is not so much the quantitative proportions as the qualitative aspects of this literature of religious interest. If its proportions increased somewhat from the sixteenth to the eighteenth century,[66] as compared with the fifteenth, the increase is due mainly to

---

[66] This increase of the quantitative proportion of the religious literature is accompanied by an increase in the number of prominent ecclesiastical writers in these centuries, as compared with the previous ones. Taking the twenty-seven volumes of M. N. S. Guillon's *Bibliothèque choisie des pères de l'église grecque et latine* (Paris, 1828–1834), we computed the number of the names listed for each century, with the following result: the twelfth century,

the purely controversial and, especially in the eighteenth century, anti-religious character of this body of writing. It deals with the religious topics, but deals with them either by way of dispute (the quarrel of Protestantism with Catholicism, of various sects with one another, in which the authors are busy mainly with denouncing and slandering their opponents), or in a purely aesthetic or negative way, like the work of Rabelais, Jodelle's *Eugène* (1552), Régnier's (seventeenth century) work, Diderot's *La religieuse*, most of the writings of the Encyclopedists, of the men of the Enlightenment, of the materialists, of the Communists Mably, Morelli, and the like. Even in the writings of somewhat more positively religious type, for instance that of the Deists, the religious question is reduced to the almost purely empirical problem of finding what line of conduct and mentality is most conducive to the happiness of the empirical nature.[67]

Somewhat similar is the situation in German, English, Italian, Dutch, and other European literatures, except for Russia and the Slavic countries generally, which lagged here also and where the same trend appeared later but, once it had appeared, proceeded much faster in its tempo. The fact of this quantitative and qualitative decline of the religious content of the literature is so evident and so indisputable, and is in such an agreement with the same trend in other fields of art, that there is no need to argue it extensively. So far as the transcendental religious traits are associated with Ideationality, their quantitative and qualitative decrease is equivalent to the decrease of Ideationality and the increase of Sensatism in this literature.

Other *inner* characteristics of the literature of the period clearly show the same symptoms of the rise of the Sensate and a progressive drying up

---

38; the thirteenth, 27; the fourteenth, 24; the fifteenth, 47; the sixteenth, 40; the seventeenth, 138; for the years 1701–1728 (the dictionary does not go later), 39. Thus the enormous increase of the ecclesiastical writers in the seventeenth and the eighteenth century is clear. And this in spite of the fact that Guillon is somewhat biased against Protestants and does not list a number of the prominent writers among them. If he had done that, the increase for these centuries would have been notably greater. The figures show also a decrease of the number from the twelfth to the fourteenth centuries. Only the number for the fifteenth century differs somewhat from the estimate of the proportion of the religious and secular literature in that century. The computation was made by J. W. Boldyreff.

[67] In a strict sense their religious writings were rather antireligious so far as Christianity and its *credo* and Scriptures are concerned, not to mention the clergy, the monastic life, and so on. Such are Locke's, Toland's, Shaftesbury's, Swift's, or Mandeville's works in England and, on the Continent, Voltaire's and other writings of the Enlightenment. On this point see L. Reynaud, *Le Romanticisme: Les origines anglo-germanique* (Paris, 1926), chap. i *et passim;* L. Whitney, *Primitivism and the Idea of Progress in English Popular Literature of the 18th Century* (Baltimore, 1934).

of the Ideational. Take *asceticism and Ideational otherworldliness versus Sensualism* (erotic, nutritional, *i.e.*, gluttony and drinking, immoderacy in various kinds of refined and coarse sensual pleasures). Our study particularly of the German and the French literature shows, first, that *the ascetico-religious ideals and aspirations sound less and less often, and less and less strongly, as we pass from the fourteenth to the twentieth century.* To be sure, until the beginning of the nineteenth they are still occasionally heard and met with ; in some periods, particularly at the time of ascetic puritanism and the Counter-Reformation of the end of the sixteenth and in the seventeenth century, they assume even a sharp and desperate form (corresponding to El Greco's painting and Vittoria's music) or become sublimely mystical. But all this is "a voice crying in the wilderness," becoming weaker and weaker. The main trend of any ascetic or anti-Sensate mentality was a progressive *piano* and *pianissimo*, and then *sub voce*. After the French Revolution there also was a brief resuscitation of a romantic "otherworldliness" combined with eroticism (Chateaubriand, *Les martyrs*, *Atala*, and a few others), but all this was a passing and incidental "reactionary" fashion. The main course continued in the Sensate direction. In the nineteenth and the twentieth century (to the postwar years) the ascetic, otherworldly motives, as presented in positive form, disappear almost entirely from literature. On the other hand, as we move from the fourteenth to the twentieth century, the satirical, the condemnatory, the ironical, and generally the adverse attitude toward asceticism, religious piety, monasteries, monks, the clergy, the Church, Scripture, chastity, celibacy — in brief, almost all the religious-Ideational values of Christianity — systematically increases. These topics become more and more the favorites for every kind of denunciation, for ridicule, for satire. To them are ascribed all imaginable evils, especially erotic and sexual depravity and immorality. Various types of this adverse criticism are exemplified in Boccaccio's *Decameron*, with its sex-conscious nuns, monks, and priests ; in Jodelle's comedy *Eugène* (1552), in which an abbé hires a chaplain to serve as a pimp and to find a husband for his mistress ; in Antoine de la Salle's *Cent nouvelles nouvelles;* in Cyrano de Bergerac ; in Rabelais's *Gargantua;* in Molière's comedies ; in Diderot's *La religieuse;* in the satires of Régnier (especially the eighth) ; in Swift's *Tale of a Tub;* in Le Sage's *Gil Blas;* in several works of the Enlightenment, like Voltaire's *Pucelle;* and in hundreds of others, like the writings of Anatole France, Flaubert, Zola, like Sinclair Lewis's *Elmer Gantry*, and other iconoclastic and muckraking works of recent years in all the Western countries, including America.

I — 42

This decline of religious and ascetic Ideationalism was followed by the *progress of straightforward Sensatism from the fourteenth to the twentieth century.* In some of the countries, like Italy, the shift was violent and already manifested itself in full in the period from the fourteenth to the sixteenth century, after which it underwent a temporary though superficial recession and then proceeded on its course. In other countries, like Germany and Scandinavia, which did not have the Renaissance but instead, primarily, the Reformation, the shift was slower and more gradual during these centuries, but still steadily increasing.

This long-time trend toward an ever greater, more conspicuous, and more varied Sensatism in the literature of the last five centuries manifests itself in hundreds of forms, among which we find all those met with in the study of painting, sculpture, and other forms of art.

First, let us take the main changes in the description of *love.* In Italy, in place of the Idealistic love of Dante for Beatrice, a love almost free from any signs of Sensatism, comes Petrarch's love for Laura, still delicate and not devoid of Idealization, but certainly more permeated by the Sensate motives than Dante's. Then comes Boccaccio's *Decameron*, where love is already sensual, though served lightly and with gallantry. It is already a love almost purely of the bedroom. And this strain continues and more openly develops into a mere sex physiology, an even perverted sex physiology. It is enough to mention Aretino's obscenities in his *Ragionamenti* and other works, Beccadelli's *Hermaphroditus*, Giraldi's *Hecatommithi*, Lorenzo Valla's *Voluptas*,[68] Lorenzo the Magnificent's [69] *Carpe diem* and the *Facetiae*, Berni's burlesque lyric, Politian's buffoonisms, and other works of high literary attainment, to see the enormous change in the modes of the treatment of love. From the heavenly love of the first medieval period, and the sublime and delicate knightly love of the second period, we are now reduced to mere sex affairs and bedroom entertainment.

Even somewhat less sensual works, perfectly decent and good, according to the time, in their advice and standards (like the popular and widely

[68] L. Valla preached "free love" openly. "Si mulier mihi et ego mulieri placeo, quid tu tamquam medius nos dirimere conaberis? . . . Omnino nihil interest, utrum cum marito coeat mulier an cum amatore." (*De voluptate ac de vero bono*, I, c. 38.) Similar teachings were given by several others, like Cosma Raimondi, and those who resurrected the ideas of Epicurus.

[69] It is well expressed in his famous verses:

> "Quanto é bella giovinezza,
> Che si fugge tuttavia !
> Chi vuol esse lieto, sia ;
> Di doman non c'e certezza. "

circulated work of Castiglione, *Il Cortigiano*, Francesco Barbaro's *De re uxoria*, and the similar treatises of Poggio, C. Urceo, Dardano, B. da Cesena, and others) are permeated by the same spirit, but here it is somewhat moderated by various considerations of utility and expediency, and more carefully veiled by the rules of etiquette.   Even in these works there is little either of sublime inner Ideationality or even of Idealism. The whole matter is considered only from the aspect of external appearances.   If appearance is kept, everything is all right.   In brief, within some two hundred years love as it is treated in the high literature "progressed" from a purely platonic, almost Ideational, form, devoid of sensuality, to a mere bedroom affair, and this, in addition, in a perverse form here and there.   Logically there was no possibility of going farther along this road.   Therefore the later period, after the sixteenth century, did not "improve" qualitatively (because the limit of physiological sensuality was already reached), but it could advance quantitatively, spreading these "whims" of the humanists, of the tyrants, of the *condottieri*, of the intelligentsia of the period, to other classes of the population through the popularization and multiplication of such writings and their wider dissemination.   And this, in spite of temporary reactions like that of the end of the sixteenth and the first part of the seventeenth century, has indeed been going on during all the subsequent years.[70]

The second part of the *Roman de la Rose* had already exhibited the trend.   In the fifteenth and the subsequent centuries it was sharpened. Instead of the Idealistic love found in the works of Marie de France, in the first part of the *Roman* and in the *Livre des cent ballades*, and instead of the gallant and still Idealistic (though less than before) pattern of love of the romances and epics, there come now in the fifteenth and sixteenth centuries the open sensuality of Antoine de la Salle's *Cent nouvelles nouvelles*, *Les quinze joies de mariage*, and *Petit Jehan de Saintré*, the riotousness and sensuality of François Villon, the sophistication and eroticism (with a religious flavor) of Charles d'Orleans, the sensuality and realism of Jodelle, the unruliness and satiric sensuality of Rabelais, the more delicate sensuality of Marguerite of Navarre (imitator of Boccaccio's *Decameron*), the romanticism even of the Pléiade (Du Bellay, Ronsard, and others in

[70] Of course literature reflected to a considerable degree the real social life, which in the period of the Renaissance was perhaps even more sensual with respect to love and sex than the literature.   See J. Burckhardt, *The Civilization of the Renaissance in Italy* (London, 1909), pt. v *et passim;* R. Davidson, *Geschichte von Florenz* (Berlin, 1922), Vol. IV, pt. i, chap. i; A. von Martin, *Soziologie der Renaissance* (Stuttgart, 1922); P. Villari, *The Life and Times of N. Machiavelli*, Vol. I, *passim;* also his monograph on Savonarola.   The writings of Machiavelli, Guiciardini, and other contemporaries show this also.

whose works the *Carpe diem* motive is observable [71]), and the salty coarseness of large numbers of the comedies and *sottises* and *farces*. In the seventeenth century there are Cyrano de Bergerac, Régnier, Scarron, C. Sorel, Furetière, and others with their satirical, picaresque, "naturalistic," and cynical novels and lyrics.

After a slight reaction in the second part of the seventeenth century, with its "classical revival," the trend is resumed in the eighteenth century and proceeds *crescendo* in the disreputable works of Voltaire, like *La Pucelle* and the less obscene *Jeannot et Colin*, and others; in Le Sage's novels of the interminable sexual adventures of a traveler, *Gil Blas*, from one bedroom to another; in the works of Marivaux; in the half-obscene *La religieuse* and *Les bijoux indiscrète* of Diderot; in Rousseaux's *Confessions;* and in other works. In the nineteenth and twentieth centuries the main topic of French literature is sensual and sexual love, both normal and pathological: the love of the old and of the young; of the poor and of the rich; love bought, love granted; love in this way, love in that — but love always hovering near the bedroom and rarely if ever idealized and never ideationalized. This concerns equally Chateaubriand, Mme. de Staël, George Sand, Musset, Stendhal, Balzac, Hugo, Mérimée, Baudelaire, Zola, Maupassant, Verlaine, Daudet, France, Flaubert, Goncourt, and others. The main difference between them is that some, like Maupassant, made the sex affair their main and almost only topic; some enjoyed particularly poetizing and depicting either sadistic forms of sex (Mirbeau and others), or pathological forms (for instance, with a corpse, Baudelaire, Verlaine); while others described mainly the predominant sexual-sensual life of married or unmarried heroes who did not show any sadism or abnormality.

It is true that the Idealistic representation of love did not disappear at once from literature after the fourteenth century. A few writers, like Christine de Pisan and others, continued the earlier tradition.[72] But their voices were drowned out by the large Sensate chorus of the majority of the writers and literati. Even such Idealistic voices as these grow fewer and weaker in the high literature as we move from the fifteenth toward the twentieth century.

The trend unfolded itself more slowly in Germany and the Scandinavian

[71] For instance, Ronsard's
> " Cueillez, cueillez votre jeunesse :
> Comme à cette fleur la vieillesse
> Fera ternir votre beauté."

[72] See for the centuries of the French Renaissance, A. Tilley, *Literature of the French Renaissance* (Cambridge, 1904).

countries. But in essentials it proceeded there in the same direction. During the centuries from the fifteenth to the eighteenth, it manifested itself not so much in the production, on the level of the higher literature, of indecent or obscene masterpieces, as in a gradual slackening of the Idealistic and Idealized patterns of love; in the progressive rarity of the motive of the vanity of the world, and in a progressive permeation of the conception of love by "physiology" and sex in the writings recounting the affairs of heroes and in the lyrical poetry. But this was done in "decent forms," almost imperceptibly, without "exhibitionism" and cynicism and parading sexuality, such as occurred in the Italian and to some extent in the French literature of these centuries. From the fifteenth to the seventeenth century, inclusive, the progress of the trend is made mainly through the rise and diffusion of satirical works, then of the *Schwänke*, the realistic novels, and the *Fastnachtsspiele*. The seventeenth century gives rise to a typical baroque dualism of mysticism and religious ecstasy with eroticism and sexuality. In the eighteenth century the family and moral standards are openly attacked; and to the end of the eighteenth century the prevailing romanticism and sentimentalism are full of the most intense passion, whether in the preclassical works of Goethe, or in Schiller, or in other of the literary men of the time. After that century the motives of the vanity of the world practically disappear from literature. Love, adultery, illicit sex relations, become more and more common topics. And even disapproval of them is stressed less and less, and the attitude of liberation from the tyranny of the bonds imposed by moral and legal laws is more and more approved.

In the nineteenth century, especially after the *Junges Deutschland*, Germany catches up with other European countries and the realistic portraiture of love becomes the main topic of the literary works, to such an extent that, at the end of the century, it begins to be played up erotically with all the traits of such a literature (Sudermann, Fontane, Wassermann, and many others).

In other countries, such as Spain and England, the trend was the same, though in each of them there have been local variations in accordance with local conditions. In England, Chaucer (1340?–1400) is already a landmark denoting a decided turn toward Sensatism in the presentation of love. In his *Canterbury Tales* we are in an atmosphere very different from either Ideational, of which there are no traces, or Idealistic, of which there also is almost nothing. With a naturalistic genius, he realistically and in part satirically depicts love on a bourgeois level. It is true that he appeared somewhat prematurely and that after him in the works of Gower, Sir

Thomas Wyatt, and several others, the medieval Idealism, mingled with a powerful religious strain, continued to linger for some time. But these later works were the sunset glow, while the new light was in the direction indicated by Chaucer. The Elizabethan *Paradise of Dainty Devices*, *The Phoenix Nest*, *The Princely Pleasures of Kenilworth*, and so on, have little of the Idealistic representation of love. Then John Lyly and the schools of euphuism and Gongorism, the pastorals (Spenser), Sir Philip Sidney, and others; still later the more Sensate streams represented by Thomas Carew (1598–1638), Sir John Suckling, and others; and then the scandalous and debauched court literature of the Restoration (Duke of Buckingham and others) — all this brought the Sensatism almost to its furthest limits. Even in greater works, including Shakespeare, Idealistic love is practically absent. Before us are great passions, but they are of this world, sometimes even openly of the bedroom character.

There were of course several temporary pauses in that trend, like the Puritan reaction, the *moderato* of the end of the seventeenth century and the first part of the eighteenth. But even these were permeated by the atmosphere of a moderate Epicureanism or of a sensible utilitarianism. The end of the eighteenth and the nineteenth century (the Lake School, Byron, romanticism) continued the trend, pushing it sometimes to extremes (pathology of sex: Oscar Wilde and others).

It is true that in most cases the movement proceeded gradually and with some "propriety," at least up to the seventeenth century. But nevertheless it remained the trend to the Sensate representation of love, whether in poetry, or drama, or epic, or novel, or in other forms of literature. Everywhere

we see the same principle at work, namely, a movement away from the original didactic purpose of poetry, either toward the direct imitation of nature, or toward the mere technical development of art. Thus the moral [or, still better, Ideational or Idealistic, because many moralities were utilitarian and hedonistic] character of the tale . . . changes gradually into the epical representation of human actions and passions. The elaborate "moralization" with which the ecclesiastic storyteller of the *Gesta Romanorum* sanctifies profane fables is dropped in the Canterbury Tales.[73]

Since Chaucer, this trend, after several fluctuations, has driven out practically all Ideational, even almost all Idealistic, representations of love. At the present moment, not uninfluenced by the physical-sensual interpretation of man by so-called psychoanalysis and similar currents

[73] Courthope, *op. cit.*, Vol. I, p. 471.

of pseudo-scientific fashion (literature being generally negativistic and pathological, as we shall see further), it treats also with great gusto predominantly the pathology of love and sex affairs.   In English as well as in other literatures of the European countries the atmosphere is thick with such pathology.

So much for the trend toward Sensatism as it is reflected in the treatment of love.   All in all, it is the same as that which we found in the field of painting and sculpture and music.

But there are also other inner traits which make the trend still clearer. Take such a matter as the reflection of *economic problems* in literature. We saw that in the first medieval period such problems were virtually absent from the literary work.   In the Idealistic period they emerge but still occupy a small place and in very few writings.   As we pass from the fifteenth to the twentieth century, they begin to occupy more and more space and become increasingly important, until, finally, in the nineteenth and twentieth centuries, they rank among the most important topics of literature, almost as important as love.   The economic aspects of life, of love itself, began to be depicted, dissected, chewed over by almost all the literary men, who now depicted poverty, exploitation, the wickedness or generosity of the rich, the perpetration of crimes through poverty ; who now made apologies for scoundrels, "unfortunate" criminals, prostitutes, idiots, paranoiacs, and all those whose failure is conceived as the result of poverty.   Side by side with these the laboring and poorer classes enter literature ; and this has given many an opportunity to depict the avarice, greed, unfaithfulness, hypocrisy, and so on, of many types of personality and social groups.   In brief, in the nineteenth- and the twentieth-century economic problems, economic motives, economic behavior, economic ideology, the economic interpretation of almost all the actions of the heroes of literary works, became a mania, an obsession, a fashion, the sign of a supposedly deep insight into human nature, and the prophetic and scientific sense, mind, and intuition of the author.   In this respect literature reflects the same physiological-sensual interpretation of man — so inescapable in a ripe Sensate culture — which by so-called science is reflected in the economic interpretation of history and of all social life and of almost all human behavior.   Since the beginning of the nineteenth century this economic interpretation has invaded the social and the other sciences dealing with man [74] and flooded our psychology with that faithful satellite of the ripe Sensate culture.   The point is so unquestionable for literature and so clear even from this outline that I

[74] See P. Sorokin, *Contemporary Sociological Theories* (New York, 1928), chap. x.

shall not bother myself or the reader with a more detailed presentation of the facts, though I have collected a quite convincing body of data for that purpose.

We have previously explained why fixing an increasingly greater attention on the economic aspects of life is necessarily a satellite of the Sensate culture mentality. The economic is the most empirical aspect of the empirical Sensate reality. It is perceived and felt by all the organs of sense, from the interio- and proprio-receptors of the nervous system (located over the alimentary tract and in the muscles and glands) to the exterio-receptors. It is "objective." It is felt most intensely. It is "quantitative." In brief, it is the most conspicuous side of sensory reality, comprehensible to almost any moron. As reality is reduced more and more to the purely sensory, the economic aspect of everything necessarily comes to the front. And it usually comes only under such conditions and imposes itself upon the human mind. As a result it is reflected in literature among the chief traits of the Sensate culture. Hence the exceptional part which the economic problem has played in the writings of the period considered, and especially in the nineteenth and to some extent in the twentieth century. As we have mentioned, literature here is in harmony with so-called science and with the philosophy and the religion and the morals of the same period. All these compartments of the modern culture have been influenced more and more by materialism and economic considerations.

Another symptom of the nature of a culture mentality is found in the *kind of heroes* depicted by its literary works. In the first period — the Ideational — of painting, sculpture, music, and literature, the heroes were God Himself, other superhuman beings (the Madonna, the Holy Ghost, the apostles and saints), and a number of absolute values. In the Idealistic period, the personages were semideified heroes: great knights and other incarnations of the positive values of empirical and semiempirical reality. After the fourteenth century their place is taken by the common run of people, by merchants, servants, peasants, polished courtiers, artisans, and what not; by rogues, criminals, prostitutes, failures, derelicts, and the wretched; by pathological types; by murderers, swindlers, exploiters, hypocrites, scoundrels, profligates, idiots, morons; by various picturesque and picaresque personalities. What Courthope says of English literature since the time of Chaucer is applicable, with a slight variation, to the whole of European literature during the fifteenth, sixteenth, and seventeenth centuries. The *personae* of the literary works from that time on become "butchers and fishmongers, soldiers and monks, abbots and learned ladies, midwives, pilgrims, beggars, scholars, travellers." [75]

From the seventeenth to the twentieth century this gallery has been enriched *crescendo* by a more common, negative, and disgusting collection of still lower, still less noble types of human derelicts, and of the sweepings of social sewers; until finally we are faced with the overwhelming crowd of pathological and negative personages which monopolize contemporary literature.

Any careful reader of present-day writing can but agree with the following statements: from the seventeenth century on, most of the heroes of literature

are either pathological or are on their way to becoming such. Shakespeare attentively follows their insanity and makes them exhibit scientifically all the stages which lead from soundness to insanity. The folly of Lear is complete; also that of Ophelia; Hamlet is rather sane than insane at the beginning, but the events give him such a great shock that his mind is disturbed. The pretended folly becomes real without the possibility of our marking the moment of this transformation. . . .

Thus this naturalism has learned every form of the inferior nature; it has observed the human body — the machine at rest, the machine in movement, the temperament, the instincts, the appetites, the passions; it has explored the mysteries of sensations; but its every essence has made impossible its climbing higher. It knows neither reason nor volition; in most cases it remains at the mere threshold of the moral world. . . . Its heroes remain what their temperament forces them to be, incapable either of improving or of controlling themselves.[76]

This is said of Shakespeare and early "naturalism." Of our contemporary realistic-naturalistic literature, the same author says:

The persons of the realistic novel and the theater of our times do not fare better than the Shakespearean heroes. These are also maladies, vice, passion, virtue itself being, according to the materialist doctrine, a mere consequence of a certain nervous situation. . . . Psychology is reduced to pathology, and physiological anatomy replaces the ancient moral anatomy. Try to pay attention to the moral aspect of every book, every play, every picture that appears: you will not find in any either beautiful sanity or genuine virtue. Everything that is not quite negative is of an honest mediocrity and quite hopeless. Virtue is more and more despised and outfashioned; it ends by being put into the group of manners and usages which our scepticism ridicules pitilessly. . . . On the other hand, the bad subjects of every kind, the im-

[75] Courthope, *op. cit.*, Vol. II, p. 29.   [76] David-Sauvageot, *op. cit.*, pp. 112–113.

moral, the debauched, the criminal, abound. Each personage has his own "neurosis," his own ulcer; and each limps somewhat. These persons wear, now the blouse of a laborer, now the full evening dress of society; but they rarely differ from one another under these disguises. One can see at once where they came from: they escaped one fine night from the insane asylum (la cour des Miracles).[77]

Another investigator notes as the most important characteristic of the literature after the sixteenth century "its penetration by everyday reality and especially the disdained one. Such a reality furnishes a new basis for theatrical plays as well as novels." [78]

Thus knights and aristocracy, kings and saints, were replaced (as in portraiture in the field of painting) more and more by merchants, the rich, the bourgeois, and the powerful upstarts; then these began to be replaced more and more by serfs, servants, valets, artisans, peasants, farmers, laborers, proletarians; then side by side with these classes there began a big parade of the poor, of the oppressed, of the unfortunate of all kinds in company with rogues, gamins, ragamuffins, hypocrites, mistresses, profligates of both sexes, married and unmarried, prostitutes; the victims of gigantic passions, unbalanced and abnormal. Then came the romantic criminal and adventurer, the pirate and buccaneer; the savage, either of the Rousseau type, or the "caveman," or enchanting sheik, the exotic Oriental; then just criminals — terrible and plain, with the detective, of course, either clever or stupid. Then, to put the final touches on the trend, the most varied collection of pathological types is let out upon the front page of literature: idiots and morons, often romantically introduced; paranoiacs of different kinds; the pathological in sex, in crime, in virtue (rarely), in body, in mind, in general behavior, in everything imaginable. Side by side with them there parade the common — quite common — and almost always dishonest and hypocritical, and often sexual, Babbitts, or Elmer Gantrys, or Arrowsmiths, or Forsytes, or the Wang-Lungs, or the Trader Horns, or this or that farmer, merchant, duke, proletarian, secretary, stenographer, doctor, newspaperman, teacher, housewife, miner, carpenter, minister, or other ordinary, mediocre, insignificant, unheroic, flat kind of human beings. When this or that pathology for some reason cannot be conveniently incarnated in the form of a contemporary figure, many authors take some Greek or Roman or Egyptian or Hindu or Chinese or Bushman or other savage figure, or a beast,[79]

---

[77] *Ibid.*, pp. 319–320.   [78] L. Reynaud, *Le romantisme*, p. 65.

[79] See, for instance, G. Boas, *The Happy Beast in French Thought of the Seventeenth Century* (Baltimore, 1933), L. Whitney's *Primitivism*, quoted, and A. Lovejoy's *Primitivism and Related Ideas in Antiquity*, quoted.

stuff it with all the abnormalities and passions and unbalanced mind and body and conduct, and place within the stuffing a kind of mechanical motor and force him to walk to and fro upon the pages of the best sellers and the "serious" literature.

Such has been the trend — a trend identical with what we have seen in painting and other fields of art.

I have somewhat overstressed the case, for the sake of brevity and clarity, but even if we introduce all the necessary shadings and all the more complex variations of the general tendency, the essence of the characterization which we have just discussed remains perfectly valid.   This can be demonstrated in detail, step by step, century by century, in the major literature of practically all the European countries.   If we take *epics* and *novels*, for example, and examine the nature of their heroes, we get the following sequence as we move from the fifteenth to the twentieth century.   *In the fourteenth, fifteenth, sixteenth, and the first part of the seventeenth centuries the heroes of epics are still drawn on a grand scale, and the epics deal with persons and events far above the level of the mediocre, the vulgar, the everyday, the banal.*   This is true of almost all the writings of this class, whether the heroic, mythological, or Christian.   Take, for example, in Italy, Boccaccio's *Teseide* and the *Nymphs of Fiesole*, Pulci's *Morgante*, Boiardo's *Orlando Amoroso*, Ariosto's *Orlando Furioso*, Tasso's *Jerusalem Delivered;* in Spain and Portugal, Marini's *Adonis*, Camoëns's *Lusiada*, Ercilla's *Arancana;* and generally in Europe, Ronsard's *La Franciade*, Zrinyi's *The Zriniade*, Spenser's *Faerie Queene*, D'Aubigné's *Tragiques*, Guillaume du Bartas's *Judith*, Arrebo's *Hexaemeron*, Sternhjelm's *Hercules* and, stretching into the middle of the seventeenth century, Milton's great epic, *Paradise Lost*.   These are but the outstanding representatives of a much larger group of such epics, which were produced in these centuries.

"Beginning with the end of the seventeenth century, the classical, the romanesque, or the religious epics lose their ground." [80]   And with their disappearance the heroic and grand personages and events disappear also from the literature of that kind, to give place to the less and less heroic persons and happenings.

Similarly heroic are the leading characters of the *roman*, the *novel*, and the *story* of the same centuries.   This is true, for example, of the heroes of the chivalric romances so widely produced and read at this time : the cycle of the Arthurian romances (Malory) and especially the innumerable

---

[80] P. van Tieghem, *Précis d'histoire littéraire de l'Europe depuis la Renaissance* (Paris, 1925), p. 36.

Amadis epics beginning with the *Amadis de Gaule* by Montalvo (1492) —
still idealistic, clean, and romantic — and ending with countless imitations
of it : *Esplandian, Florisand, Primaleon, Palmerin of Olive, Palmerin of
England, Lisuart, Florisel, Clarisel, Belianis, Amadis of Greece*, and so on,
by F. de Silva, F. de Moraes, and many others, who flourished mainly
between 1510 and 1580.   Their heroes are still wonderful knights, marvelous in their achievements, brave, unconquerable, audacious, just, noble,
loyal, enchanted by love and, for its own and chivalry's sake, performing
great and heroic deeds.   With the end of the sixteenth century the chivalric romances, like the heroic epics, disappear, and the place of their heroes
begins to be taken by much less heroic persons and types.   The note of
mockery at these heroes and heroic epics and romances had of course
already appeared in the sixteenth century (Rabelais's *Pantagruel and
Gargantua*, 1535–1552; Cervantes's *Don Quixote*, 1605–1615), but in the
fourteenth, the fifteenth, and even in the sixteenth century they still
blossomed, and their decline began only in the seventeenth, in which
only a few of such works still continued, by way of imitation, to
appear (for instance, Georges's and Madelaine's romances imitating the
Amadis type).

Then as we move on toward the twentieth century, in the novels and
romances and tales and in the more prosaic literature, the heroic element
tends to be replaced by nonheroic heroes, by "average" mortals, as well
as by the picturesque and picaresque characters and then later by the
negative and pathological types.

Here are the main steps by which was accomplished this gradual process
of making heroes unheroic.   In the sixteenth century already side by side
with the declining heroic epics and romances there appeared the *pastoral
romances*, some parts of which still deal with heroic, though less heroic,
personages — especially women — and in this sense are a remoter replica
of the Amadis type; other parts of which deal with much less heroic
mortals — tired, melancholy, turning to the simple life of the shepherd,
but still rarely negative, still rather romantic and effervescent.   In this
sense the *pastoral* romances were a step down from the heroic, but still
remain with their heroes above the level of the mediocre.   They are represented in the sixteenth and seventeenth centuries by innumerable Arcadias
(of Sannazaro, Lope de Vega, Philip Sidney, and others), by numerous
Diana Amorosas (of J. de Montemayor, Gil Polo, and others), by the
Galatea of Cervantes, by the *Young Girl and the Woman* of Ribeiro, by
L'Astrée of Honoré d'Urfé, by the *Euphues* of John Lyly, and so on.   Even
in this brand of romances the heroic element tends to decrease as we pass

from the pastorals of the end of the fifteenth to those of the end of the seventeenth centuries.

The next step in this trend among the novels and romances leads to the *picaresque*, *satirical*, and *realistic* tales, novels, and romances.

The *picaresque* novel as a notable current emerges a little later than the pastoral, somewhere in the second part of the sixteenth century (before the fifteenth we have hardly any of it in artistic literature, and of course it is entirely absent in the Ideational period), and reaches its climax only in the seventeenth and eighteenth centuries, when the pastoral romances had somewhat declined.

The very term picaresque denotes that the heroes of such romances and novels are *rogues*, *adventurers* (beggars, hobos, valets, soldiers, students), who live by their wits. Some of them are rather pleasant and sympathetic, others less so, but the type is generally opposite to that of the noble *Amadis*, though all in all not yet criminal or pathological. It is a shrewd, witty, knockabout but amiable kind.

It is evident that this type is a further downward step from the idealistic and noble personages of the heroic and pastoral epics and romances. Examples of this kind of picaresque novels are the anonymous *Life of Lazarillo of Tormes* (1544), Mateo Aleman's *Life of the Picaro Guzman*, the *Picara Justina* (with its woman hero), Quevedo's *El Buscon* (1626), Espinel's *Marcos of Obregon*, *Till Eulenspiegel*, Grimmelshausen's *Simplicissimus* (1669), Cervantes's *Don Quixote*, the imitative works of Thomas Nashe, and others.

Here again as we move from the earlier to the later types of the *picaro*, especially to some of the eighteenth century, like *Gil Blas*, he becomes, as it were, more and more picaresque, more sexual, of a lower order, less heroic, and even less romantic. The earlier rogues are often depicted as the defenders of freedom, of poor and innocent people, and in this way in a diluted form perform the functions of the earlier heroic knight errant. The rogues of the later picaresque novels, however, perform few if any such deeds: they become, like *Gil Blas*, mainly roguish pilgrims from one bedroom to another.[81]

Then, simultaneously with the picaresque novel or a little later (mainly in the seventeenth century), there emerges and grows the *realistic novel* (in its diverse varieties: classic, romantic, sentimental, etc.) and *satirical works*. The very name *realistic* or *naturalistic* implies that such a literature reflects mainly what is seen and met with most frequently and most commonly in the empirical reality. This means the average, mediocre,

[81] See H. Norman, *Swindlers and Rogues in French Drama* (Chicago, 1928).

most common type of human beings (because the hero and the genius are rare flowers), the most common and routine events and affairs and conduct, repeated daily and seen everywhere and all the time. Hence the heroes of the realistic novels and tales and other naturalistic literature are themselves of necessity common, everyday, mediocre men.

In this way the emergence and expansion of realistic-naturalistic literature implies a shift from heroes, heroism, idealization; from the sublime, the elevated, the romantic, the noble, and the above-the-average to the very average level of men and the motivations and events associated with them. From the heavenly heights of the Ideational literature before the twelfth century, through the Idealistic and heroic plateaus of the literature of the twelfth to the fifteenth century, we descend now, at the end of the sixteenth and subsequent centuries, to the earthly Main Street, to the village and the city (mansion, apartment, slum tenement), to the poverty-stricken, disease-stricken, demoralized, and mentally stricken persons and their affairs. In the earlier stages of the realistic novel people and events were rather normal and sound, though neither heroic nor sublime; in the later stages the pathological, the diseased, the unsound aspects of empirical reality, the social dregs and sweepings, began to be depicted more and more, thus dragging even the realistic literature down from its common and normal level to the very gutters of social life and to the debased and perverse types of human personality.

Simultaneously with the realistic novel there arose to the level of conscious literature, the *satirical*, *ironical*, and *comical* tale and novel. Again the very terms indicate that such a literature is the opposite to the Idealistic. The latter chooses the positive and the noblest aspects of empirical reality, beautifies and glorifies them; the former selects the negative aspects and paints them still more negatively through an exaggeration of the vices and shortcomings, whatever they may be. From this standpoint the growth of satirical literature is a further step down from the Idealistic heights.

Now even within the satirical literature itself, as it developed, there was manifest the same downward movement in its debasing, tearing to pieces, ridiculing, smashing, slandering progressively greater and more fundamental values. If the satirical works of the earlier phase ridiculed the stupid or comic or silly aspects of an old husband married to a young wife or vice versa, the gluttony of an abbot, the difficulty of an adventurous lover, the shortsightedness of an elderly chaperon, they rarely if ever attacked the fundamental sociocultural values and institutions — religious, scientific, moral, artistic: God and the saints and the credo of religion, the family, the government, the Church, chastity, heroism, genius, duty, sacrifice, and so on. As time went on and as we move into the eighteenth, the nineteenth, and the twentieth centuries, the black and poisonous brush of satire reaches higher, and more boldly stains and vilifies the fundamental values, until at the present moment there is nothing left which has not been slandered, ridiculed, and debased by it. Religion, God, the saints, the Virgin, angels, devils, sacraments, Paradise, Inferno, the Credo, the State, the Government, aristocracy, nobility, talent, genius, sacrifice, altruism, marriage, the family, asceticism, idealism, chastity, faithfulness, loyalty, science, philosophy, moral duty, property, order, truth, beauty, righteousness, man himself — everything and everybody is slandered and satirized and defiled. I cannot find any single value whatever which has escaped. Everything has been covered with the worst kind of dirt, and dragged into the mental and sociocultural sewer : Religion is called opium, God a heartless deceiver and murderer, the Virgin a mistress, angels and devils erotic loafers, and so on and so forth. Idealism immortalized the mortals ; now the contemporary "debunking" satirical literature paints the immortals as low-grade animals. In man it sees nothing and leaves nothing divine or human in the real and noble sense of the terms, it sees nothing except "reflexes" and "complexes" and "drives" of the lowest animal order. In this the physical-sensual mentality of the ripe Sensate culture is reflected once more.

Such, schematically, has been the course of the realistic-satirical literature during the last four centuries.

Finally, since the emergence of the *realistic novel* and *romance*, their heroes, no matter to what class they belong, have rarely been heroic in any true sense. They are just ordinary mortals, either light-minded and easy-going (like many sexual adventurers of the type of the famous Don Juan), or boring, unhappy, and suffering — but they are always "common," rarely, if ever, above the level of mediocrity. This is true of almost all the realistic novels, beginning with the earliest and ending with the contemporary ones. Such are the heroes of the realistic-satirical novels of the fifteenth, the sixteenth, and the seventeenth centuries : in Italy the *Novelino* (one hundred anonymous stories) of the end of the thirteenth century ; the novels and the romances of the type of Boccaccio (1313–1375), F. Sacchetti (1335–1400), and Masuccio (*c.* 1465) ; of Bandello, Giraldi Cinthio, Grazzini, Straparola, Machiavelli, and Luigi da Porto in the sixteenth century ; in France the realistic novels of A. de la Salle (1398–1462), Marguerite de Valois, Bonaventure des Périers, Noël du

Fail (1520–1586), of D'Aubigné, Scarron, Furetière, Charles Sorel; in Spain the novels of A. Martinez (*Corbacho*, in 1438), Fernando de Rojas (*c.* 1475–1540), Gomez de Quevedo (1570–1644); in England the tales of Chaucer — to mention but the outstanding names.

In these centuries, however, the realistic novels were much more cheerful, light-hearted, adventurous; much more free from pessimism, lachrymose sentimentality, and somber, sinister, and painful scenes, characters, and tragedies, than were the later realistic romances and novels. But in the latter, in spite of this difference, the tragic or suffering or wretched persons are again almost all the mediocrities or failures or negative types. This is the case with almost all the heroes and heroines of the sentimental, psychological, moralizing, satirical realistic novels of the eighteenth century — the novels and romances of Le Sage, of Rousseau, of Goethe (*Werther*), of Foscolo, of Mörk, and of the most prominent writers of English novels and romances, such as Richardson, Fielding, Smollett, Sterne, Mackenzie, and others. As to the nineteenth and the twentieth centuries, not only are the chief characters of the realistic literature a common type of people, and not only do they tend to be of a more and more negative, "subnormal" level (prostitutes, mistresses, unfaithful wives and husbands, thieves, murderers, oppressors, exploiters, swindlers, hypocrites, idiots, morons, the poverty-stricken, the mentally and morally dumb, dull, stupid, cowardly, etc.), but, what is very curious, all the attempts to create in a realistic novel a positive social type have led to invariable failure. The realistic writers were obliged to look for such a positive type either in queer and abnormal kinds of personality (for instance, Tolstoi's Pierre Bezoukhy or Dostoevsky's Raskolnikoff and Prince Myshkin, most of Ibsen's and Hauptmann's characters; or some of Zola's, Maupassant's, and Balzac's heroes, or even the best types of Charles Dickens), or to create quite unreal, purely "paper-made" synthetic *resonneurs* like Romain Roland's Jean Christophe, or to offer vaguely and schematically delineated figures like the Zossima of Dostoevsky, or to give a positive type something very cheap, very ordinary, and of doubtful quality, like some of the "proletarian" characters of socialist-communist literature, or, to be specific, like Sinclair Lewis's Ann Vickers. The realistic mentality, turned entirely to the sensory perception and conception of men, necessarily sees human beings only as they are empirically with all their "physiology," "reflexes," "instincts," shortcomings, defects, biases, "residues," and ordinary daily traits. When it attempts to soar and to reach a great vision of a real hero, it finds its wings to be clipped too short to permit much soaring; therefore, it is forced to crawl and to creep over the surface of the earth, and can comprehend only various varieties of the very ordinary and very mortal beings, remote from any "immortality" and real heroism.

Furthermore, the closer we come to the end of the nineteenth and to the beginning of the twentieth century, the more it seems that even the normal low types of human beings are replaced by the pathological and negative, that we are led from the living room of ordinary mortals to their cellars and toilet rooms, from the room of the common and honest citizen to the den of the criminal, to the prison, to the lodging of the prostitute, that we are shown the empirical reality stripped of any decorum and holiday costumes and color. The Babbitts, the Forsytes, Gorki's hobos, the pathological types of O'Neill, the paranoiacs or impotent loafers of Chekhov, the Arrowsmiths and Elmer Gantrys, the people of Hotel Imperial, the empty-souled dandies of D'Annunzio, the psychoanalytical — and almost invariably sexual — heroes and heroines of almost all the best sellers, even the supposedly realistic farmers, laborers, clerks, stenographers, gangsters, bookkeepers, merchants, notaries, mayors, housewives, teachers, professors, ministers, engineers, mechanics, secretaries, actors, artists, show girls, businessmen, and so on, of most of our contemporary novels — all tend to be touched by this or that sign of abnormality. Very rarely are they "idealized." When they are, the idealization is as obvious as cheap rouge on the face of a superannuated streetwalker. More than that: even the real and, up to recent times somewhat glorified, historical personages are more and more depicted in a debunking way in our novels, delineated in the same physical-sensual style.[82]

---

[82] For the last two decades this trait has been pronounced not only in realistic fiction but in biographical works. Take, for instance, the recent biographies of Washington, of Lincoln, of Queen Victoria, of Edward VII, of Goethe, of Napoleon — they are all permeated by this debunking spirit and rival one another in the sensual interpretation of the hero in whom they leave nothing of heroism. The same is true of the recent historical works. In my seminar Miss Helen Sorenson made a special study of biographies in the United States from 1865 to 1932. Her study shows that the main differences of biographies written in the period 1865–1880 and in 1910–1932 are that in the first period "the tendency was to regard the great men as moulding the events of the time" (Carlyle's *Heroes and Hero Worship*). Now, "the tendency has been to stress the influence of environment" — typified in *The Education of Henry Adams* (Cambridge, Mass., 1918) and others. The biographers of the first period idealized their subjects. Now (already in 1884 Froude showed this in his *Life of Thomas Carlyle*) the fashion is to debase and to degrade them, showing all their shady sides, mainly (typified in Strachey's biographies, Rupert Hughes's *Washington*, W. Ellis's *John Ruskin*, R. Millar's *Wellington*, and hundreds of "psychoanalytical" biographies of all the Ludwigs and other "dirt painters"). In addition, they now are fragmentary and patchy, as almost everything nowadays, when we have "Music cut up into notes, pictures cut up into cubes,

To sum up: *from God and His Kingdom and His saints, the heroes of literature became the semideified knights of the Idealistic period; from these they turned into more and more human beings, until everything heroic disappeared almost entirely in the realistic literature and the scene was entirely occupied by ordinary mortals with their ordinary life events, which in their turn began to be replaced more and more by the subnormal and negative types and events of human society. The sequence — purely religious literature, heroic epic, chivalric romance, pastoral romance, picaresque story, realistic and satirical fiction — is the track along which these landmarks denote the main stages of the long-distance descent of literature from the Ideational heaven to the Sensual sewer.*

Thus far we have been concerned mainly with narrative prose (epics, stories, romances, novels, etc.). The *drama* and *poetry* have been intentionally excluded. But now let us briefly consider the "evolution" of these forms as well. All in all, the trend toward the progressive lowering of the type of heroes occurs in the drama no less than in narrative literature. The chief figures of the *medieval mysteries* were God, the saints, the angels, and other divine beings. The heroes of the subsequent semi-religious plays and *moralities* were already of a lower order, but side by side with the mortals or with even the sinful types there always were present the religious or allegorical figures of the positive virtues and the semidivine and divine beings. Moreover, the characters of the even more secular plays of the fifteenth, the sixteenth, the seventeenth, and the first part of the eighteenth centuries, that is, of the Renaissance and then of the Classical Age, were (except for comedies) still mainly either biblical or otherwise prominent historically, great in their passions and deeds; in brief, they were far above the level of mediocrity. For the fifteenth and sixteenth centuries (except the comedies and the farces, of which further) this concerns the plays in Spain and Portugal of Juan del Engina (1465–1539; *Resurrection, Christmas*, etc.), of Gil Vicente (b. 1460), in part of Ines Pereira (*c.* 1523), of Juan de la Cueva (1550–1610), all with their religious or moralizing or national dramas; or even many of the dramatic pastorals of the sixteenth and of the first part of the seventeenth century. In England during these years the theater (except the comedies) was represented not only by Moralities but also mainly by the biblical, heroic, moralizing, and historical plays of Lyly, of Robert Greene, of Peele, of Thomas Kyd, of Lodge, of Christopher Marlowe; or by the dramatic

---

prose cut up into impressions and episodes, and poetry often cut up into isolated images." In addition the proportion of biographies now among all books published has increased to 8 per cent, while in 1886 it was only about 3 per cent.

pastorals of Fletcher, Ben Jonson, and others.   The heroes of these plays are still mainly either divine or heroic.   Somewhat similar was the situation in other European countries; with the difference that in Italy and France the imitation of the antique tragedies was particularly strong; but their heroes were, however, heroic.

The heroic characters still remain the main figures of the drama and tragedy of the seventeenth and of the beginning of the eighteenth century. This is true of the greatest plays of the period in England, from Shakespeare to Dryden, in France from Corneille and Racine to most of the tragedies of Voltaire, in Italy from the atrocious tragedies of Cinthio or Speroni to the less violent pastorals and operas.   Similar was the situation in Spain, and also in Germany, though in a somewhat different way (Schiller, Goethe, the earlier Gottsched, Lessing, C. F. Weisse, and others).

In all these dramas and tragedies of Europe the heroes are often abnormal, often pathological, sometimes insane, but they are "heroic" in their passions, deeds, vices, and virtues.

From about the second half of the eighteenth century (with the short interlude of the Revolutionary theater at the end of the eighteenth and the beginning of the nineteenth) the classical tragedy declines, and with its decline the heroes of the drama become decidedly more "human," less heroic, and more the common type of persons, and the topics and events around which the plot of the play is woven become also of an ordinary, everyday type, much nearer to one's common experience in empirical reality.   There were a few romantic attempts to revive the heroic drama, but they were rare exceptions which in no way weaken the trend.

The predominant type of leading persons in the theater from the end of the nineteenth century to the present day has been the common man, regardless of his occupation and social status.   Even in this respect there has been a trend toward a more frequent choice of a hero from the lower and laboring classes, from the poor, the disenfranchised, and the unfortunate.   Even more: there has also been a steadily increasing fashion to choose the hero or the heroine from somewhat abnormal, pathological, and defective types or criminal groups.[83]   Here, as in other fields of literature and art, the same gravitation toward the "social sewer" is also quite noticeable.

This trend in the theater is still more conspicuous *in comedy*, considered separately.   Comedy did not exist — on the level of the great literature

---

[83] The trend is quite evident also in the moving-picture plays, where it is vulgarized to a *non plus ultra*.

— in the Ideational period. It appeared but was still rare and mild in the period of Idealism. Its real emergence as a strong current in the main stream of literature was about the fifteenth and the sixteenth centuries. And it reached great heights in Spain in the sixteenth and seventeenth centuries with the plays of Lope de Rueda, Torres Naharro, Juan de la Cueva, Lope de Vega, de Castro, Tirso de Molina, Alarcón, and Calderon. In other countries comedy emerged somewhat later still. Thus from its beginning it is a specific brand of the Sensate literature. It has been developing progressively in Sensate quality during the subsequent centuries, not only quantitatively but also qualitatively, ridiculing, satirizing, and stressing the comical and the negative aspects of greater and greater values. The early comedy was rather mild, poking fun mainly at the delicate situations of a passionate love, with its *bouffon* (*gracioso*), its dame, its old husband and young wife, its chaperon. It not only did not attack either religion, or the king, or the family, or any important social value and institution, but on the contrary was didactic and moralizing and perfectly loyal. But soon it began to touch more sharply ever higher institutions and values, until in the nineteenth and twentieth centuries practically nothing has remained sacred, nothing has escaped being ridiculed, satirized, sometimes defiled by comedy and theatrical satire.

Now the particularly strong development of the dramatic and the theatrical literature after the fourteenth century has a further significance. Though the Ideational period of the Western literature knew *Mystery Plays*, they were neither so common nor played so often as the dramas, tragedies, comedies, and farces of the later times. Besides, the Ideational Mysteries, by their very nature as well as by the reasons for which they were staged, were never a mere entertainment for amusement or pleasure. They were practically a variety of the religious comedy, little different from the liturgy or other formal services. By this nature and by their infrequent staging, they differ radically from what we understand now by a theatrical performance. They had nothing of "show," of "appearance," of "illusion." The play as we understand it is an illusion, a temporary substitute for some reality, not even real in an empirical sense, but it has within limits the effect of reality for some short time. From this standpoint, *the very development of theatrical literature is itself a highly important symptom of the growth of the Sensate culture.* As we have mentioned before, the essence of the Sensate is appearance, looks, show, illusion. Accordingly such a culture, mentality, and art necessarily develop theatricality as their *alter ego*. The successful growth of the

Western theatrical literature in all its numerous forms is but the normal realization of a tendency inherent in the nature of the culture. Vice versa, the large body of existing drama for the period from the fourteenth century on is itself powerful evidence of the predominance of the Sensate culture stream.

So much for this point.

Of other *inner* evidences of the predominantly Sensate nature of the Western literature after the fourteenth century I shall mention briefly only a few. If we take such symptoms as *duty versus sensate comfort* (and this symptom is certainly a good indicator of the Ideational or Sensate mentality, because, as we shall see in Part Two of Volume Two on ethical systems, the Ideational mentality tends to have the ethics of absolute principles, regardless of their physical comfort or discomfort, while the Sensate mentality tends to be utilitarian, eudaemonistic, and hedonistic), the study of the conduct of the persons in literature shows that, as we pass from the fourteenth century to the present time, duty begins to be sacrificed more and more in favor of comfort, and the consequent growing neglect of obligations — whether religious, moral, civic, familistic, political, or what not — is more and more approved by writers. In the literature before the twelfth century, duty is uppermost and as a rule is never subjected to scrutiny from the utilitarian, hedonistic, or eudaemonistic standpoints. Correspondingly, as we have seen, there is nothing of the *spirit of revolt* against duty in any form. Duty is absolute and remains so. In the Idealistic period of literature the transgression of duty appears but remains relatively rare, and in most cases is condemned or disapproved. But as we pass to the subsequent centuries the number of actions in violation of duty tends to increase, with some minor fluctuations. The heroes begin more and more often to neglect their religious, moral, familistic, and other obligations. An accurate statistical study of this problem is impossible for obvious reasons. But roughly, the change in this respect may, on the basis of our study of the French and partly of the German literature from this standpoint, be represented by the following figures.

The percentage of cases in which duty is placed above comfort and material convenience is, in the literature before the twelfth century, about 100; in the twelfth about 75; in the thirteenth and fourteenth, about 60; in the fifteenth, about 50; in the sixteenth and the first part of the seventeenth, about 60; in the later seventeenth, about 50; in the eighteenth, 35; in the nineteenth and twentieth, about 30 to 25. The figures for other countries would probably be somewhat different; but there is hardly any doubt that their main trend would be roughly the same. This quantitative increase of the frequency of the violation of duty in favor of Sensate comfort, convenience, and expediency is in perfect agreement with a similar trend in the ethical mentality for these centuries as will be shown in subsequent parts of this work.

Now we may add to this increasing frequency of the violation of duty, the evidence of the changing tone with which these transgressions are treated in literary works. Let us take as an example the cases of the violation of marital loyalty and family duty. In the writings of even so late a date as the middle of the nineteenth century (*e.g.*, Flaubert's *Madame Bovary*, or Leo Tolstoi's *Anna Karenina*, or Dumas fils's *La Dame aux camélias*, or Constant's *Adolphe*, or others), the breach of duty is almost invariably depicted as a tragedy, and in most cases the violators pay for it very dearly, often with their life. At the end of the nineteenth and the beginning of the twentieth century, such violations become rather common, the heroes marry and remarry, change their bed partners easily and cheerfully and, as it were, with the blessing of the author. The sense of tragedy has evaporated; the breach is reduced to a mere change from an uncomfortable "convention" to another, more suitable to the hero. And the hero does it as easily as he would discard an ill-fitting suit of clothes for one more comfortable. The feeling for marital and family duty seems to be entirely atrophied in these "free" individuals and in the liberal authors who created them. With some small variations, the same may be said of the breach of any other duty in any socioreligious and moral field of conduct. We are in an atmosphere radically different from that which existed not only in the Ideational and Idealistic periods, but even in the centuries from the fifteenth to the seventeenth.

The other side of this situation is the *increasing frequency with which heroes in literature revolt against any duty, any inconvenient bond, obligation, or, as they liberally style it, "social convention."* They become more and more "revolters," whether conscious or unconscious, reasoning or unreasoning, in their actions. And many of the popular works of the period have been popular just because their heroes and heroines possessed this trait, of which authors approved. Revolters against God and religion, against "political tyranny," against economic oppression, against domestic slavery, against everything and everybody, have arisen in swarms. When, for some reason or other, an author could not find his rebel in the upper or the middle classes, or in the honest and respectable groups, he turned to robbers (Schiller and others), criminals (Hugo and others), prostitutes (Dostoevsky and others), or to plain housewives (Flaubert,

Sudermann, and others), and skillfully dressed up these types and presented them in such a sympathetic and dazzling form that the public heartily approved him and his heroes — always in the name of "freedom," "the maximum happiness for the maximum number of people," and of similar slogans, often helped out by a sprinkling of references to God and the Bible, though such references have been becoming less and less fashionable.

This increasing frequency of the breach of duty and of the revolt against all inconvenient conventions and values is certain evidence of a rising *individualism*, as opposed to the social or collective aspects of literature. This individualism has manifested itself also in the "proprietary" appropriation of a literary creation by its author, whether from the economic or any other standpoint. The writers of these centuries can do without, and can forget, everything but to put their name — their own individual name — upon the work. This is their child, their pet, their care, and they cannot and will not share "the honor of authorship" with anybody. They want to have it all, and view this possession as the road to fame, money, comfort, popularity, and — immortality.

We have seen that individualism is something belonging organically to the Sensate art, culture, and mentality. We shall meet it in practically all compartments of the Sensate culture. Hence, the individualism, egotism, and eccentricity of the literature of the period is additional evidence of its predominantly Sensate character.

In painting, sculpture, and music the Ideational and Idealistic creations are calm, serene, and imperturbable, while the Sensate are *dynamic, passionate, pathetic, sensational, emotional*. The same is to be observed in literature. Even the lives of the saints, when they tell the most horrible or pathetic events, like tortures, recount them in a calm way, just as the Bible narrates the creation of the world or the passion of Christ in the same imperturbable manner. When we turn to literature after the fourteenth century, we find that calmness and serenity and imperturbability have vanished. It becomes more and more passionate; it begins to strive intentionally to be pathetic, emotional, to impress, to make a sensation, to "move," to "strike." Not only poetry, but also the novel and the tale; not only tragedy, but also comedy and vaudeville; not only drama but also the epic and the poetic — all show this drift.

Every means is used to achieve that purpose. Hence, incidentally, the inevitable development of the mystery, detective, adventure, spook, horror stories, and novels, whether in the form of the Gothic tales of Walpole, Clara Reeve, Anna Radcliffe, "Monk" Lewis, and others of the eighteenth century, or in the form of the contemporary Sherlock Holmes crime stories and the innumerable detective-mystery-adventure stories, which provide a kind of "relaxation" for most of us. Hence also the "sentimental" literary works, whether in the form of the lachrymose *Pamela* of Richardson and novels of the type written by Sterne and Rousseau, or in the form of the "pastoral stories" of the seventeenth and eighteenth centuries, or in the form of the contemporary "weeping" novels which depict the sufferings of the poor, of noble but persecuted criminals, of the pure virgins who become prostitutes, of the great geniuses who become failures, of the saviors of mankind who turn into mere parlor socialists or first-class murderers or loafers of the type of Jean Christophe, and so on. All this is to be expected from the very nature of the Sensate literature, and all this the literature of the period under consideration presents abundantly.

The literature of a Sensate culture and mentality is the literature of the world of *Becoming*. It must be dynamic and ever-changing. It must exhibit all possible variety and incessant novelty in its form and content. Hence, if my diagnosis of the literature of these centuries is accurate, we should expect a continued and ever-increasing rapidity of change of vogue and fashion in it. It must strive without pause to be "new," "different," "original," "fresh," "unusual." The expectation is well borne out by the event. Perhaps investigators like Drommel and others, who claim that about every fifteen or thirty years there has been a change in the fundamental form of literature, stress unduly the periodicity and the regularity of the change (see Volume Four of this work, devoted to the problem of the periodicity of social recurrences). But they seem to be right in the contention that the literature of the last three centuries did indeed undergo rapid changes in fundamental forms. Today romanticism is in vogue, tomorrow realism and naturalism; at one period the heroic epic is the fashion, at another it is discarded in favor of something quite different. Even in the fifteenth, sixteenth, and seventeenth centuries the main forms of literary works were changing in periods of some sixty to eighty years. This was the case with the blossoming of the heroic epic, of the chivalric romance, of the pastoral *roman*, of the picaresque story, of the heroic or classical drama and tragedy. Still shorter were the periods for the rise of the sentimental novel, the mystery story, and what not. At the present moment the tempo of change as well as the passion for variety is well shown by the kind of best sellers and books promoted by various "literary guilds," "Book of the Month Clubs," and similar organizations for the spread of the standardized pabulum. They change in character with magic rapidity. Today *Trader Horn*, tomorrow Ludwig's intolerable concoction on Napoleon, the day after a psychoanalytical sex story, after that something romantic on China or India or Soviet Russia, and then . . . well, one cannot enumerate all the surprising "variety" and astounding contrasts presented by the ever-changing best sellers and "hits" of contemporary literature, which have their day and are forgotten within a few weeks.

Such dynamism and variety and contrast in present-day literary vogues are but a reflection of the Sensate nature of our literature.

Finally, the trait of *quantity and colossalism*, as against *quality*, is a typical sign of the Sensate culture and its art. This also is highly conspicuous in contemporary literature. One of its manifestations is the judgment of what work is good and what is poor. The most unquestionable contemporary criterion of this is the *number of copies sold*. If a work is a best seller, it is great. Its author is a genius; he becomes "famous." This is our main and almost only standard. Its very nature indicates the "colossalism" pervading our literature.

I shall not continue the enumeration of the traits associated with Sensate literature, and conspicuously evident in the writings of the period under consideration. The totality of the traits already discussed is sufficiently imposing to warrant the truth of our contention that, since the fourteenth century, literature has indeed been predominantly, and progressively, more Sensate in its nature.

This conclusion is corroborated by other considerations, namely, by the external form of the literature and by the character of the criticism of the period. Let us make the test.

B. *External Traits.* It has been shown that the literature of the Ideational period is characteristically symbolic and that this was the case with European writing up to the twelfth century; that the literature of the Idealistic period is by nature in part *allegorical*, in part Ideational, in part realistic, and that this was so for the period after the twelfth century. The *Sensate literature is predominantly naturalistic and realistic*, like the Visual painting, which describes the empirical reality as it appears to our eyes and other organs of sense. Zola, as one of the most prominent exponents of this "realistic" or "naturalistic" style in literature, expressed well the essence of the style: "Our quarrel with the idealists consists exclusively in the fact that we start with observation and experience while they start with the absolute." [84] The "realistic" or "naturalistic" style is well outlined in a more developed form by

[84] E. Zola, *Le roman expérimental*, p. 87.

A. David-Sauvageot : [85] "Realism is a system which forces art to reproduce the sensible reality such as our experience makes known. . . ." In contradistinction to Ideationalism or Idealism it does not select exclusively either the positive or the negative values but "without any preference accepts all the elements [positive and negative] with which nature [empirical reality] furnishes it." It does not "correct" the sensory reality through the omission of some traits and the addition of some others, as the nonrealistic writers and artists do, but "it copies, without retouching, that which it sees." Since any sensory reality is always fragmentary and never represents a complete and unified system, "realism, instead of trying to give an account of the *ensembles*, limits itself to fragmentary studies."

If realism had been consistent with itself and if it could have embraced the whole of [the empirical] reality, it would have depicted order as well as disorder, the general as well as the particular, the sublime as well as the debased, sentiments as well as sensations, the beautiful as well as the ugly; but even so it is always constrained to satisfy itself with the mere surface of the phenomena, with the purely external aspects, never being able to reach the mind [*l'esprit*].

Judged by the modern realistic and naturalistic literature "realism can then be defined as a system which reproduces from reality only that which impresses the senses most directly, that is, the external and the material aspect of human beings and objects."

This realistic style emerged, on the level of the major literature, only after the fourteenth century, in the form of the realistic novel, of the so-called *tableaux de moeurs*, and in part of the comedies. Afterwards it developed so greatly [86] that in the nineteenth and twentieth centuries it has had a virtual monopoly.

An exception to this appears, at the very end of the nineteenth century and in the twentieth, in the work of such literary schools as the *symbolist*,

[85] David-Sauvageot, *op. cit.*, pp. 7–11.

[86] From the standpoint of the meaning given here to realism-naturalism such literary currents as the romanticism of the second quarter of the nineteenth century, often opposed to realism-naturalism, are but a variety of it. The Romantics do not use the symbolic or allegorical or purely imaginary and conceptual technique in their works; they also copy the empirical reality and try to render it in all its specific characteristics. But in the choice of the objects and events and types which they make the topic of their works they are more eccentric, fanciful, and whimsical than the so-called realists and naturalists. That is all the difference between them from the standpoint of our definitions. The same idea is expressed in different form by L. Reynaud: "Realism and Parnassan aestheticism are but a variety of Romanticism." *Op. cit.*, p. 264. Cf. A. Machen, *Hieroglyphics: A Note upon Ecstasy in Literature* (New York, 1923), pp. 63–66.

futurist, surrealist, and others similar.   But these have been, so far, minor rivulets.   Moreover, like the anti-Visual painting and the anti-Sensate music, none of these currents is either Ideational or Idealistic; they are but a manifestation of reaction against realism and naturalism.   In this respect they are important, but they have nothing in common with Ideational symbolism or Idealistic allegory, whether in their external form or in their inward nature.   Like cubism, they are in several respects even more Sensate than the standard realistic literature of these centuries.[87]   They are simultaneously an extreme form of the Sensate and a revolt against it, and in this they are similar to corresponding currents in other contemporaneous fields of art.   But they are not, as yet, the patterns of the coming Ideational or Idealistic literature.

C. *Criticism.*   Finally, the art and literary criticism of that period also has all the earmarks of the Sensate type, already familiar to the reader from the discussion of the Graeco-Roman culture.   With a mere change of names and places, all that was said about the character of the Graeco-Roman criticism of the Sensate period can be applied literally to the critical writing in the West of the period following the fifteenth and sixteenth centuries.

First of all, the purely aesthetic criticism of art and literary works which was nonexistent in the Ideational period and had in a very inconspicuous and still uncertain form barely begun to emerge in the Idealistic period now became definitely established.   Its nature is to analyze, to criticize, and to estimate from the so-called purely artistic and aesthetic standpoint, from the standpoint of "art for art's sake" or of "pure beauty."   The real meaning of all this, however, is that art and literature are evaluated entirely from the standpoint of their power of providing sensate enjoyment, whether that enjoyment be utilitarian, eudaemonistic, or hedonistic.   This is the essence of the Sensate criticism of art.   Beginning with the fifteenth and becoming stronger in the sixteenth century, such criticism grows very rapidly and soon begins to be dominant.

In the period from about 1530 to 1600

the extant critical writing, excluding mere rhetorical schoolbooks, probably exceeds, and very largely exceeds, the total of classical and mediaeval work

[87] Reynaud from this standpoint notes rightly: "Symbolism [of our times] is in fact but a return to a personal poetry of the romantic epoch par excellence, and is even a still more personal poetry than the romantic poetry [of the nineteenth century]. . . . All the characteristics of romanticism are found in it.   Like romanticism it loves the restless, disordered, legendary periods of history but it observes and describes them with a still stronger Alexandrian voluptuousness and seeks in them for still rarer and subtler sensations." *Op. cit.*, p. 265.

on the subject which we possess, even inclusive of school books. . . . For
the first time criticism . . . received a really large share of the intellectual
attention of the period.[88]

A great number of treatises on poetry (*Arte poetica, De poeta, Poetics,
Versie regole*) appear. They deal from the purely aesthetic standpoint
with technical analysis, and with the problems of what are art and
poetry; what their matter and instruments, their modes, manners,
traits; what their classes — prose, and poetry; what tragedy, comedy,
heroic. They consider whether Tasso or Ariosto is better and more
beautiful, and so on. This criticism springs up and blossoms, first in
Italy, a little later in France, England, and other European countries.
"In 1600 criticism is a classed and recognized department of literature." [89]

Just as in Greece the period from about the fourth century B.C. to the
beginning of the third century — the period of Plato and Aristotle —
was transitory in this respect and the critical works still viewed the works
of art not from the purely aesthetic standpoint but also from the religious,
moral, and civic; and just as such "pure" criticism emerges only in the
third century so it does here in the West during the fifteenth and sixteenth
centuries: the criticism is still Mixed, being only partly aesthetic and
still having strong nonaesthetic religious, moral, and other motives in it.
In some of the works of the period the aesthetic motive plays a quite
insignificant role. Savonarola's *De scientiis* (1452–1498), for example,
still stands upon an Ideational basis with the claim:

The end [of literature] is to induce men to live virtuously by decent representation; that one should not style poetry or art "divine" because divine
may be applied only to the science the object of which is God and not to the
discipline the object of which is a mere example (*Scientia autem divina est
cuius objectum Deus, non illa cuius objectum exemplum*).

Several other writers, however, adopt a Mixed standpoint and consider
the purely aesthetic as only one aspect among many — the scientific,
moral, philosophical, religious, etc. — in respect to which an artistic
work is to be judged great and positive, or, on the contrary, poor and
negative. Such in Italy were Erasmus (the *Ciceronianus* and the *Collo-
quies*, in which he sarcastically criticizes the pure aestheticians), Vida,
Pazzi, Berni, Danielo, Fracastoro, Minturno, L. Giraldus, Scaliger,
Castelvetro, and even Politian himself, with whom the Sensate art criticism properly begins.[90]

[88] Saintsbury, *op. cit.*, Vol. II, p. 211; see also pp. 37 ff.
[89] *Ibid.*, Vol. II, p. 229.　　[90] See the details in *ibid.*, Vol. II, chaps. ii and iii.

However, as we move from the fifteenth to the sixteenth, and from the sixteenth to the subsequent centuries, these nonaesthetic (Ideational) motives become rarer and weaker, and the purely Sensate criticism, except for temporary and secondary fluctuations, grows progressively — in both the quantitative and the qualitative aspects.

With a slight lag the same movement of criticism took place in France, England, and the rest of Europe, with the exception of Russia and some other Slavic countries, where the lag was much greater (corresponding to what we discovered in the field of painting).

In fifteenth- and sixteenth-century France most of the critics occupied the Mixed position, some being nearer to the Ideational, others to the Sensate, standpoint. This is the position of Deschamps, of Sibilet, of Du Bellay with his epoch-making *Défense et illustration de la langue française*, of Pelletier, Ronsard, Vauquelin de la Fresnaye, Montaigne, and others. Among these, the critics like Montaigne are the most nearly completely Sensate, viewing literature and art chiefly as a means of amusement, of enjoyment, and to some extent of knowledge. But from the seventeenth century on, the nonaesthetic — Ideational — elements in criticism decline and the Sensate grows in number and importance.[91]

England shows essentially a similar picture at the end of the fifteenth and in the sixteenth century. Sir Thomas Wilson, Sir John Cheke, Roger Ascham, Edmund Spenser, Gabriel Harvey, Sir Philip Sidney, Stephen Gosson, even Bacon and Ben Jonson, are still in the Mixed position: some, like Ascham, Sidney, and Gosson, are nearer to the Ideational; others, like Harvey, Bacon, and Ben Jonson, approach the Sensate standpoint.

And this in general is the situation in Spain and Germany.[92]

With the advance of the seventeenth century the purely aesthetic standpoint crystallizes in the form of the codes and canons formulated by the Academies. As Saintsbury rightly says, "in the Middle Ages there was no such creed at all," because there was no Sensate criticism, but only the Ideational — religious and moral — censorship and estimation. The first weak inklings of it emerged in the centuries from the thirteenth to the fifteenth; the fifteenth and sixteenth centuries prepared it; the seventeenth formulated it, made it uniform and monopolistic. The subsequent centuries revolted occasionally against the given credo of the Academy, but not against the Sensate principle upon which the credo was built. In fact in many ways the subsequent centuries developed the

<hr />

[91] See *ibid.*, Vol. II, chap. iv.   [92] *Ibid.*, Vol. II, chap. v *et passim*.

Sensate point of view much further and threw away many "neo-classic" and "academic" moderating rules to give a quite free play to the principle of Sensatism.

The essential traits of the creed of the Academy in regard to art criticism are well known to the specialists. It is enough to say that it took the place of the religious creed in many ways; that in it "it is generally admitted that a poem [or other literary or art work] must please"; that it was almost unanimously accepted and that "the absence of dissidence, except on minor points, is most remarkable"; that the so-called Romantic Revolt was but a variety of the same creed; that, finally, "this accepted faith of Criticism . . . is a very peculiar Catholicity." [93] It is best formulated in the classical treatises of Roger de Piles (b. 1635) and Boileau's *Art poétique*. Other critics like Malherbe, Régnier, and Jean Balzac expressed the same attitudes.

All in all it was sensible, rationalistic, moderated, scientific, even mathematical Sensate criticism, free from vagaries, from any extreme and unbalanced radicalism and eccentricity, still slightly touched by the fading light of Idealism, and well protected from the vulgar, grossly hedonistic sensualism. And it reigned through the seventeenth century and in part in the eighteenth century.

The eighteenth century continued it by sheer inertia, but soon began to move in the Sensate direction. It discarded many moderating principles, turned to romantic and passionate and in many respects uncontrolled Sensate criticism. From this time forward the Idealistic is doomed, for, moving further in this direction with the changing of concrete forms, it finally gives way almost completely to the Sensate criticism, which has reigned supreme and virtually alone up to the present time. The literary and artistic criticism of the last two centuries has been stupid and wise, ignorant and learned, boring and witty, but withal virtually always Sensate. The categories "beauty as beauty" and "art as art" have been accepted by all the critics, who have judged literary or art works primarily on the basis of their sensate effect, on the pleasure, the enjoyment, the delight which they afford. No standard divergent from this — for instance, the religious, the scientific, the moral, the civic, or any other — has played an important part on the level of the high literary and art criticism. Values of this sort have guided the activities of the police, of the various "Watch and Ward" societies, of political parties, of religious groups; but such groups are outside the field of art and literary criticism proper and do not per se concern it.

[93] *Ibid.*, Vol. II, pp. 408–409.

Centrally, criticism has been what is called purely aesthetic and artistic. Hence, about it are to be found all the satellites of the Sensate type. In the first place the very growth of the discussion, criticism, analysis, and conscious awareness of literature and art, which, as we saw, had already begun in the fifteenth and sixteenth centuries, and which continued to increase quantitatively in the subsequent ages, is of high significance. Just as the Graeco-Roman literature of a similar period was very critical and "scholarly," just as aesthetic problems became the favorite topic for everybody's discussion, and on every occasion, so has it been in the Western culture. "English and French, the two leading literatures of Europe [of the seventeenth and eighteenth centuries] became copiously and intensely critical. Addison, Johnson, Pope, Voltaire, are all dictators of literature . . . and they are all critics. . . ." The names of Goethe, Shaftesbury, Lessing, Buffon, Diderot, and of many others can be added to these. "Moreover, criticism has enormously multiplied its appearances and opportunities: it has become popular. The *Critical Review* — the periodical — becomes common. The critic as such is no longer regarded as a mere pedant." [94]

Now the *professional critic* makes his big appearance, now the professional aesthetician, the professional theorizer on art and literature. More than that : he becomes a powerful figure not only in literature but in social life and politics. The critic becomes a kind of lawgiver and intellectual and social leader, often a figure with whom kings and prelates and magnates and powerful nobles have to reckon. He gets a big following among all sorts of people from clever politicians to hysterical females. Literary problems become one of the main topics of conversation in any gathering, from the tavern to the salon. Art and literary education begin to be one of the prerequisites of any "educated" man or woman. One can apply literally what Persius says of his Roman contemporaries: "*Ecce inter pocula quaerunt Romulidae satieri, quid dia poemata narrent.*" And the same, probably even greater, *ventosa et enormis loquacitas* on art and literary topics began among the upper and the middle classes. Such problems were discussed everywhere and by everyone. Concomitantly, critical journals, reviews, articles, pamphlets, essays, treatises, not to mention the number of critics and reviewers and "Book of the Month Clubs," increased and expanded greatly. In brief, the situation is an accurate example, on a large scale, of what usually takes place in such a phase of culture and of what took place in the history of the Graeco-Roman during an analogous period.

[94] *Ibid.*, Vol. II, pp. 560–561. For the nineteenth century see Volume III of his work.

This Sensatism in the criticism of art and literature has continued to the present day. It has subsided in part occasionally during the period of the last two and a half centuries; but its sensate nature has remained dominant, has tended to become sharper, more extreme, less "bridled," and often more indecent, sterile, empty, dishonest, and so on, as we move nearer to our own times. The present situation is well known to any "educated" man who is interested in art and literature. And who is not interested now? and if not, who would dare to say so openly? Is there any man's or woman's club which does not have a section of its programs and meetings reserved for literary and critical activities? No newspaper, magazine, journal, weekly appears without its book review or article about literature or art. Art appreciation and literary education are practically obligatory for every boy and girl. Reading (or at least buying) the newest best seller recommended by this or that coterie of critics is the habitual practice of most of the husbands and wives who pretend to be "cultured." The number of professional aestheticians and critics — from the Menckens to the Wall Street collectors, to the connoisseurs, to the specialists in "home decorating," and to the newspaper book-review reporters — makes up a very large occupational group, and some of its members are to be reckoned with by rulers and bosses either in business, or in statesmanship, or in any other field.

On the other hand, as in Rome, most of this criticism is empty, ignorant, thoughtless, negligible, so far as its inner content is concerned. It is, however, powerful in other respects: it determines the "best sellers" and thus the success or failure, the fame or tragedy, the victory or defeat, the poverty or fortune of the artists and writers. It also shapes the taste of the public itself toward good or bad. In these and other respects its influence is often in inverse proportion to its inner worth.

As in Rome, it became commercialized through and through. Hence, in most cases it lacks even a consistent principle of estimation, and has been more and more inclined to take for a criterion of success the mere *quantitative success* which can be achieved for a given work: if copies are sold in great quantity or if there is a long "run" in the theater, criticism either is forced to praise the work or, more often, is enthusiastically willing to praise it, and for this very reason.

In conformity with this the efforts of the authors as well as of the critics are primarily directed toward such quantitative success. Not only is the character of the work itself shaped to achieve success, but all possible external means are used, from advertising to the formation of a kind of mutual "backslapping" coterie (again paralleling Hellenistic

Roman coteries), to make the work a "huge success," "a hit," a "best seller." As the level of the taste of the large masses is, in most cases, far from being very high, such production for a large market tends to lower the standard of both creative works and criticism. Hence the inner emptiness of both at the present day. We produce great quantities of literary and critical writings; and yet, most of the best sellers are forgotten within a few months or, at the best, a few years; and, in spite of the great number of the literary and art critics, there is hardly a single figure among them who is great. We have a few very "influential" critics, go-betweens for the literary producers and consumers, but that is all that one can say. They are as far from greatness as possible.

Finally, a kind of anarchy in the field of criticism must be expected in such a phase; and we find this to be so indeed. Since most of the theories and principles are fragmentary, poorly thought out, every critic follows his own fancy or the fancy of the financial bosses of the papers and magazines for which he writes. The result is confusion, superficiality, bickering between factions and cliques, each trying to promulgate its own Lilliputian standard.

Under such conditions criticism is beginning to lose its prestige and influence. Even now best sellers are determined not so much by critics as by various business agencies and commercial techniques, like the group of persons upon whom depends the distribution of a given book throughout all the public libraries, like the amount of advertising done for the book, or like the success of the publisher in getting the book included among the monthly book selections of various "book clubs," and so on. Most of these agencies are practically anonymous and purely profit making, administered by men who make no claim to be connoisseurs of art or literature, or critics. This situation is a kind of Nemesis for the progressively declining criticism itself.

The emptiness of modern criticism explains also the emergence at the very end of the nineteenth and in the twentieth century of the *criticism of the critics*. It is a kind of revolt against Sensate judgments of whatever kind — a revolt similar to that against the Visual painting, and the Sensate music, architecture, and literature, such as has been marked above. It has manifested itself in various forms, from Leo Tolstoi's sarcastic castigation in his *What Is Art?* and in his attack on Shakespeare and contemporary literature and art and criticism, to the *manifestos* of mainly young and wild hotheads — futurists, symbolists, surrealists, and other "arch-modernists," who violently and quite disrespectfully assail the predominant Sensate critical currents, declare them

I—44

to be outmoded, and reject them practically entire. In their negative reaction these revolutionaries are quite definite and are therefore a symptom of the crisis in the Sensate criticism. But in their positive program they have not yet found a new path leading to a new and great kingdom of art and literature and criticism. Like similar rebels in other fields of art, they are in great confusion, they are lost in the sea between the old forsaken land and the new country earnestly sought for. Hence the chaotic and incoherent character of their positive ideals and aspirations and aims. But as a sign of reaction against the superannuated Sensatism of modern criticism, they are of high significance.

Thus from the fifteenth century to the present time literature does indeed show all the characteristics of a predominantly Sensate mentality, whether it is considered from the standpoint of its inner properties, or its external forms, or of the nature of the art and literary criticism of the period. These characteristics have been manifesting themselves more and more conspicuously and sharply until toward the end of the nineteenth and in the twentieth century the Sensate development seems to have reached its logical and empirical limits. The first signs of revolt against it have appeared during the last few decades. But these revolutionary currents are still minor rivulets, and the bulk of the literature is still very Sensate, showing all the marks of an overripe Sensatism. It can hardly continue for a very long time to stay in this overripe form. In all probability it will shift more and more to a kind of Ideationalism. But this is a guess and, even if correct, would not warrant our expecting the shift to begin to be fairly under way in less than several generations.

VI. Related Problems Considered in the Light of the Present Theory

"PURPOSEFUL" AND "PURE" ART

The theory developed above permits the concise elucidation of several problems which have been heatedly discussed for a long time. Moreover, it enables us to indicate, in a different wording and context, some other sociocultural fluctuations. Finally, it provides an answer concerning the validity of certain general theories which have been set forth in the field of art.

The first problem which we may consider is the controversy between the theories of *art for art's sake or "pure" art, and art as the servant or handmaid of religion, public welfare, moral, and other nonaesthetic values.*

It is not my purpose, of course, to take sides in this controversy.   I intend, rather, first, to point out that it is not a controversy which has appeared recently but has been going on for ages and recurring again and again ; second, to show the real meaning of each of the opposite conceptions of art ; third, to make clear that the controversy means a great deal more than its partisans usually imply.

The formula "art for art's sake," or "beauty for beauty's sake," seemingly means that art and beauty are great values per se, independently of any other value, and that the artist has to heed only the purely aesthetic consideration and nothing else.   It means also that art does not need the support of nor is itself merely the means of expressing religious, moral, civic, and other nonaesthetic values.   This places beauty on a level with any other primary quality or purpose.   All this sounds well. But a further analysis of such assumptions shows their indefiniteness. Indeed, what works are works of pure art and what are not?   Are the Bible, the *Iliad*, the *Divine Comedy*, *Hamlet*, the Gregorian chants, the sculptures of the thirteenth century, the Cathedral of Chartres, Bach's Mass, Wagner's *Tristan and Isolde*, Stravinsky's *Sacré*, Baudelaire's poetry, and Rodin's works — are they all works of pure art? or are some pure, and some not?   If the first answer is considered correct, then everything seems to be pure art, and there is no other art whatever.   If the second answer is correct, then what is the criterion by which pure art may be separated from the other kind?   It is enough to proceed along this line of analysis in order to see that the formulas either do not have any meaning or that their meaning is exceedingly vague.   It is not my purpose to go into a full examination and criticism of what has been written in controversy on this subject.   It is enough to point out that the entire terminology — "pure" and "impure" art, "art for art's sake," "art for the sake of something else" — is very unsatisfactory.

We get much nearer to the reality and a much clearer insight into the essence of the problem when we replace these poor shibboleths with the conception of the Sensate, the Ideational, and the Idealistic.   The point is that the real issue in the controversy has been the opposition between the partisans of the Ideational and of the Sensate art.   *Those who champion "art for art's sake" have really been fighting for the Sensate form of art, the direct and main function of which is to give sensate gratification, delight, pleasure, joy.*   If such a purpose is achieved by the artistic work, it is, from this point of view, of no importance whether or not the work serves, in either a positive or negative sense, religion, morality, civics, science, or any other value.   The partisans of the "purposeful" art —

that is, the art which makes manifest or promulgates religious, moral, political, scientific, and other values — have been fighting for some form of Ideational or Idealistic art because by definition the Ideational or the Idealistic incorporates in itself these values. It is inseparable from them by its very nature. Such is the real meaning of the controversy and the forms of art which the opposing parties defend.

When this is understood, all the sonorous phrases especially of the champions of "pure" art — the claims that they are those who adore, esteem, and admire art as art, release it from servility or subordination to religion and other values; that they are for "free" beauty; and so on — take on a greatly changed meaning. Yes, these artists and critics "free" art, or rather separate it, from other great sociocultural values; but they simultaneously enslave it to sensations. They make art a mere servant, a mere instrumentality of sensate gratification. If the art does not serve this purpose, it ceases to be art; it is thrown away and disqualified. *In other words, the true difference between the "pure" (Sensate) and the "impure" (Ideational) art consists not in the fact that the one is free and the other is not ("handmaid of religion" is the most common formula), but that they are "subordinated" to quite different masters: one to hedonism, to emotions and sensations; the other to the Ideational and Idealistic values of religion, morals, civics, science, philosophy, etc.* One is divorced from the duty of fostering Ideational values but is inevitably bound to the gratification of the senses; the other is inseparably united with the Ideational, but escapes becoming a "plaything" of sensations and emotions. Both are free and unfree, pure and impure, but each in a different way and in regard to different values. When these divergent values are translated into concrete sociocultural terms, then naturally the Ideational art will be found co-operating with, or, if the term is preferable, serving religious, moral, civic, philosophical, and other similar values; while the Sensate art will be discovered serving the pleasure seekers, be they individuals or groups. The Ideational and to some extent the Idealistic, artist will be working on the cathedrals, Parthenons, chapels, sacred public buildings. The subjects which he selects will be Ideational: Athena, Zeus, Apollo, Christ, God, or, as in the Idealistic period, the superempirical and the noblest and sublimest topics of the empirical world. And the urge and inspiration to creation in such an artist will be the desire to do great service to God and to these values. And the greater the artist, the greater will be the Ideational value of the topic which he selects. The Sensate artist, on the other hand, will be working for whoever will hire him and give him the highest material or money value for his work. As the highest bidders are usually the rich and the powerful, such an artist becomes the servant of the rich, the powerful, or of those who can indirectly enable him to acquire the maximum money value (or its substitute), like publicity agencies, commercial managers, bosses of the commercial art market, or their favorites, mistresses, wives, and so on. Believing the Ideational artist to be a serf of this or that Ideational institution or of its managers, the Sensate artist boasts of his "freedom," being all the time in fact the servant of the rich and the powerful, while the Ideational artist has been serving God or the superempirical. If anything, the position of the second is rather more elevated and freer from servility than the position of the first, who is obliged to fulfill the whims, now of Alexander the Great, now of Madame Pompadour, now of a financial magnate or his wife or his mistress, now of the editor of a magazine, now of his commercial manager, and now of the prevalent vogues of the "market."

Such in brief is the real character of the "pure" and "impure" forms of art, about which so much controversy has raged.

In the course of the history of art there are periods of domination of the "pure" and of the "purposeful," which alternate. It is when the Sensate art dominates that the formulas of "art for art's sake," of "pure beauty," of absolute freedom of art from any control by, or even co-operation with, other sociocultural values of an Ideational nature, arise, come into vogue, and are accepted and defended by artists and critics. This was the situation in the Sensate periods of the Graeco-Roman and the Western European culture. The art dominated by the Ideational mentality does not support such conceptions and claims ; therefore in the predominantly Ideational periods of the Graeco-Roman and the medieval European art, such opinions, theories, contentions, do not play an important role. We have seen this in the chapters of the present work devoted to art and to art criticism and theorizing. We have observed that there was nothing of the theory of "pure" art in Greece before the fourth century, that it appeared and spread only later, beginning with the end of the fourth century. Plato and Aristotle still occupied an intermediate position. Likewise, from about the fifth century A.D. to the thirteenth and fourteenth centuries there was nothing of it. Only after the fourteenth century do the literary criticism of the Sensate type and the theory of "pure" art emerge and develop.

All the previous analysis of the fluctuation of the main forms of art and of art criticism provides evidence of the alternation of the domination of the "pure" and the "purposeful" art. The existence of "cycles," in the rise of "art for art's sake" and of art with a nonaesthetic purpose, is merely one aspect of the cycles of domination of the Ideational and the Sensate.

Viewed in a different light; this alternation of "pure" (Sensate) art and art with a "purpose" (Ideational Idealistic) means the existence of an *alternation of the periods of the "organic unification" of art with other sociocultural values of an Ideational character, and the periods of the isolation or separation of art from these values. In the Ideational and to some extent in the Idealistic periods art is inseparably, organically united with other sociocultural values of an Ideational nature.* It is inaccurate to say (as is usually said) that it is subservient to them. It would be more correct to state that it is organically united with them : all these values are one and are "unconscious" of their separate existence, each being organically blended with the others, being neither master nor servant, but a part of a culture where all values exist together in harmonious unity. And as we shall see later on, this concerns not only the union of art with Ideational values but also the union of these values themselves with one another. In the Greek culture up to the end of the fourth century B.C., religion, philosophy, science, art, morals, civic patriotism— all were one. There was not and could not be any antagonism between them, as there is no antagonism between the vital parts of one organism. The same is true of the Ideational medieval period in the West. It was also a period of the united existence of all these values. They were one ; none existed separately from any other ; still less was there any antagonism between them. The Ideational culture is integrated into organic unity with the principle of the interdependence of subordinate values.

In the Sensate cultures and periods, art, as we have seen, separates itself from the other values. It is "independent" and "free" of them, just as all other values are "independent" and "free" of one another. Each strives to live its separate life. Hence, "art for art's sake." Thus art pays little attention to the other values and is often openly antagonistic to them. As we shall see, the same is true of the other values with respect to one another. In such periods religion is divorced from science, and they often oppose each other. The same is true of religion and philosophy, philosophy and science, science and morals, morals and religion, and so on. Here the oneness of the Ideational period is split up and broken ; and each of these values divorces itself from the others and becomes "free." *The Sensate culture is also an integrated culture but integrated around the principle of diversity, and the mutual independence of its main values and compartments.* It is not an absolute "patriarchal monarchy" with one "we" of its values, but a federal republic based upon the principle of the separation and division of its main states.

In application to art all this means that the art of Ideational periods is "purposeful," filled inevitably with other values. The art of the Sensate periods is "pure"; it may be and usually is empty of the other values. It aspires to "beauty." The aesthetic category seeks to be autonomous and separate from the other categories of truth, wisdom, righteousness, religion, moral principles.

Since the periods of the domination of the Ideational and Sensate art alternate, the "pure" art and the art with a purpose alternate also. In other words, *we have a rhythm of the periods of union and separation of art from sociocultural values of an Ideational character*. This rhythm is, in turn, but a part of a more general alternation of periods of the united, organic existence of the main sociocultural values of Ideational nature in one undivided whole and the periods of their separate and divorced and often mutually antagonistic existence.

This rhythm is sufficiently important by itself to be mentioned here and to be discussed more substantially later on. Saint-Simon grasped one aspect of it and made it one of his main laws.[95] We see that it is a mere result of the more fundamental rhythm of alternation of the Ideational and Sensate culture mentalities.

In the light of the immediately preceding chapters we can now easily see the merits and defects in various theories of art phenomena which were outlined in the very first chapters of this part. Ligeti's theory, which endeavors to see what I style Ideational art only in architecture, what I style Idealistic only in sculpture, and what I call Sensate only in painting, and which tries also to establish a uniform law for their sequence in the history of culture — this theory is wrong in its very premises. It is fallacious because not only architecture, but sculpture, painting, literature, and music also, may be and have been Ideational. All of them have also been Idealistic and Sensate. And all of these arts have existed side by side at all periods. Therefore it is impossible to talk of art periods as being architectural or sculptural or pictorial. Still less is it correct to talk of the uniform sequence of their blossoming in all cultures, with all the sociocultural generalizations which Ligeti attaches to such a sequence. What we have, instead, is an alternation of the Ideational and Sensate art; and it concerns all the arts equally, not only one or two, and proceeds more or less synchronously in all of them. This is evidently

[95] See *Œuvres de Saint-Simon et d'Enfantin* (Paris, 1877), Vol. XLI, pp. 170–171.

quite different from what Ligeti claims.   Therefore, his theory in most of its essential parts must be rejected.

The same, with slight variation, should be said of all the other theories discussed above.

A few words concerning Chambers's theory will not be out of place. He is right in his claim that in the Greek, as well as in the Western, culture there were periods when art for art's sake, "pure" beauty and the appreciation of it, and all the accompaniment of this — art education, aestheticians, art critics, professional artists, and so on — did not exist. But he is inaccurate in his terminology and mistaken in his fundamental notion when he characterizes these periods as times in which the "aesthetic consciousness" and the appreciation and sense of the "fine arts" and "beauty" did not exist at all.   He is wrong because, in the first place, even among primitive peoples many of these phenomena, being "economically useless" and requiring much time and energy for their creation, can be accounted for only if we admit the existence of this "sense of beauty."   And, as a matter of fact,

no people known to us, however hard their lives may be, spend all their time, all their energies, in the acquisition of food and shelter.   Even the poorest tribes have produced work that gives to them aesthetic pleasure. . . .   In one way or another aesthetic pleasure is felt by all members of mankind.[96]

Moreover, if in such periods there had been no sense of beauty, no art consciousness, no appreciation of fine arts, one might well wonder how it was possible for these periods to create the greatest art values, creations which Chambers himself calls special attention to.   Why did Homer compose his *Iliad* at such a time?   Why did the Greeks go to such "uneconomical expense" to build the Parthenon?   Why did Phidias labor over his great statues?   For what reason did Christians build great cathedrals, and the crowd of anonymous artists toil to put up ten thousand sculptural pieces on only one cathedral like that of Chartres?   If there had been no sense of beauty, all this would have been quite unnecessary, in fact strange, because worshipers could have prayed to their gods anywhere, on an altar made of rough stones or in a hut or in a quite ordinary building.   More than this, the artists themselves (for instance Homer in several places), and others in such periods, definitely use the very word beauty and its derivatives and related terms.   Therefore it is quite wrong to assume that such periods did not have aesthetic consciousness, appreciation of the fine arts, and so on.

[96] F. Boas, *op. cit.*, p. 9.

The source of this error of Chambers is not difficult to discover.   Consciously or unconsciously he assumed that "fine arts" and "a sense of beauty" and "aesthetic consciousness" exist only in what I call the Sensate form.   (And his language in the description of the attitude of the Church Fathers toward art, and in other places, shows clearly such an assumption.)   From this point of view it would naturally appear that all the periods in which art was Ideational were periods of the nonexistence of art consciousness and art appreciation.   The fallacy of such a conclusion is now evident.   Chambers's theory notwithstanding, aesthetic consciousness and the appreciation of the fine arts existed in Greece before the fourth century, in Europe throughout the Middle Ages — and there is not the slightest doubt of it.   But all this occurred in Ideational form, not in the Sensate, and thus was merged organically with religion, philosophy, morals, and civics.   Hence it was not separately observable during these periods.

Another error in Chambers's theory concerns a more detailed point. As a result of his assumption, he concludes that creativeness in art is in an inverse proportion to the development of art consciousness, art appreciation, aesthetic criticism, and so on.   The greatest art creations were made in the periods when, according to Chambers, this art appreciation, art criticism, art education, did not exist.   But when aestheticism grew in great quantity, whether it was in Hellenistic Greece or in the Europe of the last two centuries, the creative impulse in art diminished.   This conclusion needs serious modification.   First, it is inaccurate to say that art criticism did not exist in the periods which I style Ideational and which coincide with Chambers's periods of the nonexistence of the sense of beauty and art criticism.   We know well that Church Fathers and medieval thinkers and early Greeks, before Phidias and in his time, had art criticism and criticism of a very severe sort, which took the form of finding out to what extent a given work is in agreement with, and expresses well, the main nonaesthetic Ideational values.   It was thorough, but it was radically different from the Sensate criticism. For this reason, it is inaccurate to say that no art criticism and analysis existed in the Ideational periods, when the greatest art creations were made; and since they existed, it is wrong to claim that creativeness in art is in inverse proportion to the development of art criticism and aesthetic consciousness.   At best one may say only that it is in inverse proportion to the development of the Sensate aesthetic consciousness and art criticism.   Such a statement would seem not to violate the empirical facts, at least not obviously.   But even this can hardly be sustained seriously. The point is that it assumes a certain and narrow and subjective basis for what is great and not great in art. It postulates that only the creations of the Ideational and Idealistic art are great while all the others are less great. To this the admirer of the Sensate art can oppose a quite contrary statement; and there is no judge who can say with assurance which of the opponents is right or wrong.

Much more accurate seems to be the position which states that there are different forms of art, each great and each beautiful in its own way: Ideational and Sensate. Each has its masterpieces. Each has enriched the treasure house of beauty with wonderful jewels. An objective investigator does not have any impartial reason for rejecting the jewels of either type of art. All that he can say is that usually in the latest stages of a given period of Ideational or Sensate art there is a tendency toward the increase of the dominant type of art analysis and criticism; and that usually these stages happen ordinarily [97] to be more sterile in their creativity, and this is one of the reasons that these are stages of decay and that another form of art must come to give an outlet to the creative instinct. With several reservations it may also be said that one of the greatest peaks of creativity in art occurs usually in the Idealistic

---

[97] This more modest statement itself needs several qualifications. One of them is that within even the period of domination of one of the types of art, the development of criticism and art theorizing and art appreciation is not always in inverse proportion to creation. Here is an example concerning the relationship between literary criticism and literature, in the words of G. Saintsbury: "No constant ratio exists between periods of creation and periods of criticism — they may go hand in hand or one may follow the other or both may fail to put in any important appearance as Fate and metaphysical aid may determine." *Op. cit.*, Vol. II, p. 411.

In Italy of the seventeenth century both declined; in England and France of the second part of the seventeenth and in the eighteenth century both seem to have been flourishing. In Rome after the first century A.D. literature was declining while criticism was swelling quantitatively. In the thirteenth century the Ideational censorship was possibly the least severe and the Scholastic theorizing did not pay particular attention to art criticism; and yet, art generally and literature particularly were blossoming. In the period of "Protestant asceticism" and the Counter-Reformation, the religious censorship of both religious and secular art was most strenuous; and yet, in the Protestant countries it did not create any great religious art; in the Catholic countries it created — baroque! Thus the relationship is rather checkered. However, the latest stages of the given Ideational or Sensate wave in art are ordinarily marked by increasing sterility of the dominant form and by a notable quantitative increase of, respectively, qualitatively hollow Ideational criticism (censorship) or Sensate criticism and art theorizing, whether of the "libertine" type or of "Parnassian aestheticism," or just an empty and thoughtless and mannered verbosity, examples of which are found in the Roman art criticism of the centuries from the first to the fifth A.D., and may be seen every day in the present-day literary criticism: libertine, hollow in its Parnassian pretensions, empty in its mannerism, and quite devoid of any thought in 99 per cent of the ordinary "book reviews," musical-concerts reviews, or exhibition reviews, in practically all the periodicals, from daily to monthly, including the reviews of special art journals.

periods, when art is not yet divorced from the Ideational world and at the same time dresses itself in the noblest forms of the Sensate reality. So it was in the fifth century B.C. in Greece, and in the thirteenth to the fifteenth for architecture and sculpture, to the seventeenth for painting, and to the nineteenth for music in the Western culture.

In this formulation the real situation is described more accurately than in Chambers's sweeping generalization, even than in the corrected version of Chambers given above.

One more remark. Since the nature of the Ideational mentality is absolutistic, centered about a fixed value, this value is and can be only one. Being one, *it is opposed to the principle of diversity and variety.* Hence, the lack of variety in the art and other compartments of the Ideational culture (as we shall see). The mind that has found the absolute does not seek anything else and does not need any diversity. It is like a lover who has discovered his ideal and therefore does not seek nor see other women. Such a lack of variety may appear, from the Sensate standpoint, to be a kind of poverty, monotonous and boring; just as from the standpoint of a polygamist the lover may appear a poor creature, unfortunate in his monogamic attachment. And as a matter of fact, the art as well as the other compartments of the Ideational culture have indeed been found poor by the assessors of the Sensate culture. Many historians, social philosophers, and social scientists have stressed the poverty, uncreativeness, sterility of the culture of the "Dark Ages," for instance. Their verdict is but natural. The Sensate culture is "diverse," "variegated," and "polygamic" by definition. It is relativistic by its nature; therefore it is necessarily creative of diversity and desirous of variety. Measured by its stick the Ideational culture must seem "poor," "uncreative," "unfortunate."

However, at the beginning of the present work it was pointed out that if we want to understand any culture we must measure and appraise it by its own stick, not by that taken from a culture with quite different major premises. This means that we are not entitled to pass unfavorable judgment on the Ideational art because it is not diverse and varied, nor upon the art of the Sensate culture because it is extremely varied. The partisans of each culture may shower upon one another such compliments as they like, without convincing one another (because their major premises are quite different — incommensurable). Instead, we can only indicate the principle of diversity and that of absolutistic "monotony" in art as logically belonging to each of these cultures, respectively, and as having in the course of history actually been prevalent in each. Those who like cultural diversity may not care for the Ideational culture and its art; those who prefer cultural absolutism and singleness may feel repelled by the Sensate culture and its art. But these likes and dislikes are the personal concern of the respective individuals and groups. The task of an investigator is to indicate the essential characteristics of each culture, leaving the evaluations to the sense or the nonsense of others.

This point must be brought out because, in the subsequent parts of this work, we shall meet it frequently. For instance, in a study of the movement of scientific discoveries and various philosophical currents, we shall find a very small number of discoveries and almost no diversity of philosophical, religious, and ethical thought in the periods of Ideationalism. If one should make a curve indicating the movement of discoveries and of creativity in philosophico-religious thought based upon the number of discoveries, scientists, scholars, and thinkers, or the number of divergent currents of thought, it may be expected that in the Ideational culture the "indices" of progress in all these respects would be low. Shall we conclude from this that such a culture is stagnant, ignorant, regressive, and in mental, moral, and religious decay? Evidently such an evaluation would be as little warranted as the assumed superiority of the champions of cultural diversity over the cultural absolutist. All that such data permit us to conclude is that the Ideational culture typically gives a low result in all these respects and the Sensate culture a high result. They may in addition perhaps indicate the exact nature and the reasons for such a difference. No more and no less. Evaluation is a private matter in which neither of the opposite parties can convince the other. It is beyond the realm of an objective investigator. In indicating accurately the traits A and B as belonging logically and causally to the cultures N and M, respectively, he fulfills his task. The rest is a matter of personal taste, his as well as that of any other assessor.

These remarks must be borne in mind if we wish to avoid blunders.

VII. GENERAL SUMMARY ON ART FLUCTUATION

Our study of the fluctuation of the Ideational and Sensate forms of art in its main fields warrants the following conclusions.

A. The history of the Graeco-Roman and Western European art shows that the long-time fluctuation or alternation of the Sensate and Ideational forms really occurs in all fields of art: painting, sculpture, music, architecture, literature, and drama.

B. When one of these forms becomes dominant, various traits logically belonging to it begin in fact to infiltrate into the art and manifest themselves in all fields.   These characteristics are at once logical elements of each of these forms and symptomatic of its presence. In other words, they are logically and in fact associated with each of these forms and with one another and should be expected, and can be foreseen, if we learn that the predominant art of such and such a period is either Sensate or Ideational or Idealistic, and if the art in question is indeed integrated. Most of these specific traits have been discussed above in some detail.   Here, for the sake of clarity and conciseness, the most important of them are briefly repeated in the form of an inventory of the elements of each of the main styles.

ELEMENTS AND SPECIFIC CHARACTERISTICS OF THE MAIN STYLES OF ART

Ideational	*Idealistic*	*Sensate*
	A. Inner Traits	
1. Predominantly religious topics.	1. Religious-secular, heroic.	1. Secular predominantly.
2. Persons are God, deities, superhuman beings, saints. Mainly "otherworldly."	2. Semidivine and human heroic and positive types, noble, beautiful, virtuous. Abstract idealized types rather than individual persons.	2. Mortals, common type of people; at the later stages picturesque, picaresque, negative, pathological: rogues, urchins, insane, criminal, etc. Mainly individual persons with their purely individual traits and environment.
3. Events dealt with: transcendental events in the kingdom of the invisible, mainly; or the visible signs of such events.	3. Noble, heroic, positive, virtuous deeds and events, partly in the super-Sensate world, partly in the Sensate world.	3. Everyday events, deeds, actions, of a common character, or picturesque, amusing adventures of the same Sensate world.
4. Emotional tone: otherworldly, ascetic, anti-sensual: negative to the joys and pleasures of this world. Unquestioning faith.	4. Idealistic; partly otherworldly, partly earthly, but noble, sublime, pure, free from hedonistic emotionalism, from pathetic, macabre passions. Serene and calm. Faith in harmony with reason and the senses.	4. Emotional, sentimental, passionate, pathetic, often macabre, still more often sensual and sexual. Skepticism and cerebral intellectualism.
5. Little of nudity, and even then ascetic and non-fleshly.	5. Some nudity, but it is neither ascetic nor sensual. It is abstract in its idealized forms	5. A great deal of nudity. It is erotic, sensual, voluptuous, and fleshly.

Ideational	*Idealistic*	*Sensate*

6. Turned mainly to the super-Sensate world, it pays little attention to *paysage*, to concrete and real historical events, to earthly *genre*, to individual portraiture of real persons. It deals with the eternal world of Being, of God, wherein there is no change.

6. Concentrates upon the relatively durable and positive *types*, and not upon individual persons, events, nature, and other concrete traits of empirical reality. The types are invariably positive, ennobled, idealized. When negative types are given, they serve only as a foil for the positive types.

6. Singularistic individualism: of persons — hence portraiture: of nature — hence *paysage;* of events — hence the daily *genre.*

7. No satire and caricature; in the Ideational mentality there is no place for that. No comedy, no operetta, no farce, no vaudeville.

7. Some satire but free from vulgarity, coarseness, and bitterness, and from serving daily purposes. First signs of a noble and moralizing and didactic comedy.

7. Development of satire, the debunking skeptical attitude. Great development of comic opera, of comedy, of farce, of vaudeville, and so on.

8. Transcendental anonymity and union in God.

9. Art is religion and inseparable from it. Therefore it is in a sense sacred and is service to God and to His kingdom.

8. Familistic and harmonious free collectivism.

9. Art is a great moral and civic and religious agent, serving man and the empirical world, and representing one of its semi-Ideational and semi-Sensate values.

8. Individualism and "professionalism."

9. Art is an instrument of a refined Sensate enjoyment: its function to give pleasure, joy, amusement, entertainment; to increase the sensate happiness of sensate human beings. It is in the class of such other instrumentalities, but somewhat more refined than "wine, women, and song."

B. *External Traits*

1. Symbolic; "formal," "conventional."

1. Allegorical, typological.

1. Visual, sensual, realistic, naturalistic, impressionistic, singularistic.

2. Static: in its character as well as in its resistance to change.

2. Static-dynamic: in character and in the slow tempo of its change.

2. Dynamic: in character and in a progressively accelerating tempo of change.

Ideational	*Idealistic*	*Sensate*
3. Simplest means, instrumentalities, and technique. Simple and "archaic"; often intentionally stripped of all the beautifying trimmings and accessories.	3. Moderate but marvelously effective in its means, technique, and instrumentalities. Harmonious in its inner and external synthesis of Ideational and Sensate beauty.	3. Most complex. Colossal. Quantitative "biggerness and betterness." Most complicated technique, artificially designed to sensually impress, to stun, to "hit." Enormous apparatus of instruments, means, accessories.
4. Art of performers concentrated on inner significance, rather than art for an audience.	4. Inner-external. Art of performers and audience, collectively participating, but in various degrees, in creation or performance.	4. All external; behavioristic, carried by professional performers or artists for passive audience (so far as participation in creativeness is concerned). "Showy" and designed to be "Hollywoody."
5. No professionals, as artists; division of functions mainly upon the basis of the religious and magical roles played by various individuals.	5. Professionals as *primus inter pares*.	5. Artist is professional.
6. No Sensate criticism, connoisseurism, aestheticism. Instead censorship of the work according to whether it is compatible or incompatible with the religious or other leading values.	6. Emergence of criticism, but still in Mixed form: it is religio-ethico-aesthetical.	6. Sensate criticism and universal art education, discussion, estimation, from the standpoint of the Sensate delight.

Are the association of these traits in characteristic groups and the association of these groups each with its proper form of art something peculiar only to the Graeco-Roman and the Western arts, or can they pretend to the status of a uniformity of a general type, not only in time — that is, in the course of the Graeco-Roman and the Western culture — but also in space, in the sense that these specific traits can be expected to occur in any Ideational art no matter where and when the culture, the group, the personality, whether it concern the Hindu, the Tibetan, the Chinese Taoist, or any other? In other words, do the associations which we have found occur in many cultures at various times? or are they to be considered a particular association applicable only to the cultures studied and to none outside of these?

In spite of my dislike for the sweeping generalizations for all times and societies, so foolishly favored by sociologists and so severely criticized by me in the first chapters — indeed the whole — of this work and elsewhere,[98] I am inclined to say that these associations are valid far beyond the periods of the Graeco-Roman and Western cultures which we have examined.   This is not the place to enter into a detailed discussion of this problem, which in itself would provide the subject of a monograph.   But on the basis of my study of the problem, I have come to the conclusion that practically all the associations and correlations established in the course of the preceding chapters are valid for at least several great cultures, and to many social groups and personalities.   Here are some of the crucial cases.

We have seen that the Brahmanic-Hindu culture, the Buddhist, the Taoist, the Lamaist-Tibetan, the Jainist, are and have been throughout their long existence, predominantly Ideational (not, however, without some, though slight, fluctuations).   That this is their character will be agreed upon by everybody who has studied them.   This being so, then if the characteristic associations of traits which we found in Graeco-Roman and Western art are valid for these Eastern cultures also, we should find in their art specific elements which we have listed as belonging with the Ideational.

Is such an expectation sustained by the facts?   It seems that it is. In the preceding chapters we have shown, especially in regard to painting, that the pictorial art of the Taoist, Hindu, Buddhist Ideational cultures has been Ideational; that the pictorial art of the Mixed cultures, like the Egyptian or the Confucianist, was also Mixed; that finally, so far as we note the fluctuations of the Ideational and Sensate phases in these cultures, the forms of art fluctuate also with a corresponding rise and decline of the satellites of each form.[99]

To repeat, this means that the associations and correlations established above go far beyond the Graeco-Roman and the Western Christian cultures.   In other words, they recur in social space as well as in social time.

---

[98] See my *Contemporary Sociological Theories, passim.*

[99] A. K. Coomaraswamy (*The Transformation of Nature in Art*, pp. 1-34 *et passim*) admirably demonstrates the similarity, in a sense even identity, of the art mentality and the art theories of the Hindus with those of St. Thomas Aquinas, Meister Eckhart, and other medieval thinkers.   He rightly says also that the Asiatic art and the Christian European art before the Renaissance belong to the same type: and that only with the Renaissance and later the European art became illusionistic, naturalistic, or Sensate (in my terms), while the Asiatic art remained mainly upon the Ideational or the Mixed ground.

We get further and striking corroboration from a study of the nature of social groups and their peculiar forms of art. What social group is the creator and bearer par excellence of the Ideational art? Obviously that composed of the priesthood[100] and clergy whose main vocation is the service of God and His kingdom. Its mentality is posited in the Ideational world, not in the empirical. Therefore, the art which it creates, whether the group be the Christian clergy, the Taoist priests, the Hindu Brahmans, the Tibetan[101] and Buddhist lamas, or the Mt. Athos monks,[102] is necessarily Ideational. If on the other hand we take the bourgeoisie, the intellectual proletariat, and other empiricists of any kind, their business is posited entirely or mainly in the empirical world, and even here in its most materialistic and Sensate compartments. For this reason their art cannot be Ideational; on the contrary it is Sensate. And the Western art since the fifteenth century has been more and more bourgeois, the art of the merchants and financiers and businessmen, and, in addition, the art of the half-atheistic and in a considerable degree parasitic descendants of the previous nobility and aristocracy. As for the Idealistic art, it has been in considerable degree the work of the aristocracy and nobility, great, chivalrous, noble, and idealistic, whether hereditary or not, whether in the form of the great Greeks who readily sacrificed themselves for the glory of gods and country at Marathon or elsewhere, or in the form of the feudal aristocracy at its apex.

The present contention is easily verified by a detailed examination of any number of specific groups, beginning with some seemingly Ideational preliterate tribes, like the Zuñi Indians. The little that I know of the Zuñis shows a crudely Ideational art and mentality.[103] However,

[100] There has always been — and there exists in a great abundance especially now — a priesthood which is quite Sensate. Such a clergy can never create or be a bearer of ideational art. The Elmer Gantrys are but hypocritical sensualists of the worst type. The early Greek or early medieval Christian clergy was in its bulk Ideationally religious, as was the bulk of the people of that period.

[101] See, for instance, A. MacDonald, *Twenty Years in Tibet* (London, 1932); G. Tucci and E. Ghersi, *Secrets of Tibet* (London, 1935); L. A. Waddell, *Lhasa and Its Mysteries* (London, 1905).

[102] A. Chukas, *Black Angels* (Brattleboro, Vt., 1934).

[103] See R. Benedict's *Patterns of Culture* (Boston, 1934). A somewhat cursory and insufficient analysis of the cultures and mentality of a few preliterate tribes from this standpoint led me to think that among these tribes there are clearly Ideational and Sensate types of cultures and that the art forms are correspondingly also crudely Ideational or Sensate or Mixed. In others, the culture and mentality are nonintegrated logically, of the Pseudo-Ideational type. In such logically unintegrated cultures one finds naturally unintegrated forms of art — which confirms the rule still more. This, however, is a tentative statement. A further serious study of these tribes from this standpoint is necessary.

I — 45

there are many other, better-known groups for our examination. Suppose we take the *Mendicant Orders*. They have been numerous. Their mentality (before their decay and demoralization) was Ideational par excellence. What was the art which they created, and stood for? What was the art championed by St. Francis, St. Dominic, and their immediate successors, before these orders began too actively and less spiritually to interfere in earthly politics and affairs? It was Ideational.[104] The same is true of any similar order, in any culture, be it the monks of Mt. Athos, or the Sufist monks, or any others. And in this they are at the opposite pole from any group of libertines, the partisans of "wine, women, and song" in whatever form and from whatever classes, who have always stood for the most voluptuous forms of the Sensate art.

Finally, to take, on the one hand, individuals with Ideational (religious, mystical, ascetic) personality, like Meister Eckhart or St. Thomas or St. John of the Cross or Savonarola or some nameless hermit or other; on the other hand, persons of the Gargantuan type, fleshly sensual, with the psychology of the *Carpe diem* — it is the rule that those of the Ideational type have been inclined toward Ideational forms of art, while those of the Sensate type have favored the Sensate art.

All these considerations suggest that the theory of the Ideational and Sensate types of art, with their characteristics and satellites and association correlations as developed in the present work, has a bearing far beyond the two chief cultures studied. It is in fact applicable, if not to all times and places, then at least to many of the great cultures, and to countless groups and persons. To this extent it is a generalization of relatively broad validity.

C. The tempo of change varies characteristically for each style of art. It has been stressed that the Ideational art tends to be static in its absolute, sacred, hieratic nature. However, in the course of time it is subject to some change, but the tempo of change is very slow and mostly gradual. The Idealistic art occupies a middle position in this respect. As to the Sensate art, by definition it is dynamic in its nature and therefore obliged to change incessantly as the art of never-ceasing Becoming. Therefore, the tempo of change of the Sensate art is somewhat faster than the tempo of the Ideational and the Idealistic. Moreover, as the Sensate art grows the tempo tends more and more to accelerate, until in the overripe stage it becomes so fast that various currents are superimposed one upon another in the same period and result in the variety and heterogeneity of various styles and schools.

[104] See L. Gillet, *Histoire artistique des Ordres Mendiants*, chaps. i, ii, *et passim.*

This follows logically from the nature of the art, and the empirical reality seems to support the deduction. We have seen that in the late Hellenistic and in the Roman phase of the Sensate art, various fashions and waves of imitative archaism, classicism, and other "isms" came and departed within the space of a few decades until they began, so to speak, to tread on the tails of the preceding phase — so that finally several different "fashions" began to coexist simultaneously and gave the familiar picture of an archaic chaos of schools and of fads and fancies. We noticed that in Western culture as we approach the seventeenth, the eighteenth, the nineteenth, and then the twentieth century, this acceleration becomes obvious also. The Renaissance style existed for about two centuries, but the baroque existed hardly more than one century, the rococo still less; and the various neo-classic, romantic, impressionistic, expressionistic, cubistic, and other waves have existed for still shorter and shorter times the nearer we get to our own day. If the contention of Dromel, that the style of art changes every fifteen years, is questionable;[105] if the contention of many others that the style changes fundamentally every twenty-five to thirty-three years is also open to question as a broad generalization; there can hardly be any doubt that at the present moment fashions in art come and go very rapidly, some being even shorter than fifteen years in duration.

This tendency to acceleration in the Sensate art is worth special notice, because we are likely to meet it in other compartments of culture. But it must not be confused with the many "laws" of the acceleration of social change and progress formulated by numerous social scientists of the past as well as of the present. I do not claim that there is a progressively universal acceleration of anything as time goes on. I contend only that the tempo of change of the Sensate culture and art may be logically expected to be faster than that of the Ideational and the Idealistic; and that, with the rise of the Sensate, the tempo of change accelerates as we move from the initial to the overripe stages of the culture. This has little in common with the universal "laws" of acceleration from the beginning of human history to the present. In fact my theory to some extent contradicts such "laws," indicating that, if after a phase of the Sensate culture there comes again domination of an Ideational culture and art, the tempo of the change will be slower than that of the preceding Sensate

[105] J. Dromel, *La loi des révolutions, les générations, les nationalités, les dynasties, les religions* (Paris, 1862). See also the works of F. Mentré, F. Kummer, and many others, quoted in Chapter Ten of Volume Two of this work.

culture, even though this Ideational phase (like the medieval after the Graeco-Roman) comes relatively late.

D. Generally speaking, the fluctuations from one main type to another go hand in hand in all fields of art. If we take fairly long periods, say not shorter than a century, then with very few exceptions all the arts — painting and sculpture, architecture and music, literature and drama — pass simultaneously from one, say Ideational, to another, say Idealistic or Sensate form. Only in the field of the European music was there a noticeable lag in its passing from the Ideational to the Idealistic and from that to the Sensate phase. But even so, the lag was neither exceedingly great nor contradictory to the kind of transformation in the other forms of art. It consisted mainly in the fact that the specific traits of music in each of these phases did not manifest themselves so clearly and conspicuously at once as in some other fields. This is due mainly to the nature of music.

If shorter periods are taken and the smaller fluctuations are studied, a lack of simultaneity seems to occur somewhat more often, as was shown in part in Chapter Twelve and all the preceding chapters. But these short-time fluctuations are similar to ripplings upon great waves; they are neither deep nor fundamental. In these short-time and nonsynchronous fluctuations there is hardly any uniformity, in the sense that the change invariably takes place first in a certain field of art with a lag in some other. The reality is that at one time one art may be leading, another lagging; at another period, the situation may be reversed. This means that all the theories of the existence of a uniform sequence in the change of various arts, with a certain art always leading and others lagging in a uniform order — that all such theories (many of which were discussed in Chapters Five and Six) are fallacious.

E. To the extent that the long-time changes in all the arts are parallel and more or less synchronous it is suggested that all the arts of the cultures studied have been integrated logically and causally to a high degree; that all the fine arts of these cultures are part of one living unity, the manifestation of one system; and that therefore when this culture begins to undergo the process of transformation, they all naturally follow the same path and change in the same direction.

Later on we shall see that not only the arts but practically all the main compartments of a culture: science and philosophy, law and ethics; forms of social, political, and economic organization — all change synchronously and in the same direction. This shows that in their mentality such cultures are living unities, real systems, though not quite rigid and closely knit; and not a mere agglomeration of various compartments accidentally placed side by side in time or in space — capable of change in quite divergent ways in its different parts.

F. Since, within the period of some twenty-five hundred years which we have studied, there have been several rising tides of each of the cultural forms, there is no foundation for claiming the existence of any perpetual linear tendency in this respect: in the course of time art has been moving neither steadily toward bigger and better Ideationalism nor in the opposite direction. It moves merely from one side to another in alternating fashion. When one of the forms has completed its immanent course and has lived the span of time destined to it, it decays and is replaced, after the proper intermediary stages, by the other form. So it has been in the past, and so probably it will continue to be. Since the dominant form of art for the last five centuries has been Sensate, when this has run its life course its place will be taken, in all probability after a Mixed phase of transition, by Ideational art. When that has lived its appointed span, the Sensate culture will recur again, and so it will go until integrated culture or mankind disappears.

In other words, here again we see the validity of the erratically or creatively recurrent conception of sociocultural processes.[106]

G. I have pointed to many indications that at the end of the nineteenth and in the twentieth century there has appeared in all the fields of art a strong reaction against the dominant Sensate-Visual-naturalistic form. The revolt is clear, but its positive program is as yet confused, chaotic, incoherent, similar to that of the transitional period of the third and the fourth centuries A.D., when art began to pass from the overripe Sensate to the developing Ideational form. Whether this reaction is the first swallow of the coming Ideational spring or just a temporary reaction nobody can tell certainly. But considering the overripeness of our Sensate art and its other characteristics, which point to the possible

---

[106] As a matter of fact among serious scholars in the field of art there are very few now who fail to notice the "cyclical" or the erratically recurrent direction of the change of art phenomena. Here are two quotations out of hundreds: "Nothing in literature dies: things only wane and wax, retire and come forward." Saintsbury, *op. cit.*, Vol. II, p. 566.

Fluctuations and alternations of styles and currents in art go on all the time. "Et ce sera indéfiniment ainsi, en vertu de cette obscure loi d'alternance qui semble l'assise de ce monde, pour la perpétuelle déception des ésprits de pure logique, épris de synthèse totale, qui oublient, dans leur pourchas de l'absolu, que la vie n'est que l'équilibre instable de forces contraires, un passage incessant d'éléments substitutifs dans un cadre, mobile lui-même, et qu'a en vouloir arreter le cours, on ne fait que des cadavres, ou, tout au plus, des momies." Henry Marcel, in *Histoire du paysage en France* (Paris, 1908), p. viii.

Other theories were quoted and discussed in Chapters Five and Six.

exhaustion of a wave which has lasted from the fifteenth to the twentieth century, it is not improbable that this change is indeed the beginning of something new. At least such an interpretation is no less warranted than the opposite. As we shall see in Volumes Two and Three, such an interpretation is well supported by a similar revolt against Sensate mentality in science, philosophy, religion, law, ethics, and in practically all the compartments of our culture. Such a " totalitarian " revolt can hardly be a mere short-time ripple. More probably it is the symptom of a coming great turn in the course of our culture and society.

APPENDIXES

Appendix to Chapters Nine and Ten

The following Appendix gives two lists for the countries of Europe that are studied quantitatively: one of sources and the other of artists whose works are included in the tables of these chapters. The lists give an idea of the sources consulted and of the works of the known artists, which, together with the works of the unknown artists, make up the basis of the tables. When the exact dates of birth and death of the artists are known, they are given. When only the century in which the artist flourished is known, that century is given. Finally, for the artists who are active in the twentieth century, this century or only the date of their birth, without that of their death (if they are already dead), is given.

In so far as possible names and dates of the artists are given as they are listed in Thieme and Becker's *Allgemeines Lexikon der Bildenden Künstler*,[1] which is the standard reference in the field. In the cases of French and Dutch artists E. Bénézit's *Dictionnaire des peintres*[2] and A. Wurzbach's *Niederländisches Künstler-Lexikon*[3] are used because of their special application to the artists of the countries concerned. Otherwise reference is made to the sources noted.

A small number of the artists are listed not in the country of their birth but in the country where they lived and worked. A few of the artists are put in two countries because of their creative activity in both of such countries.

The samples examined consist not only of the works of the artists given in the lists, but also of a very considerable part of the works of unknown artists. For Europe before the thirteenth century almost all the samples are anonymous. An overwhelming majority of the works of Islamic countries are anonymous.

From the tables, as well as from these lists, one can see that all the countries were not studied with the same care. Some, such as England and Spain, were studied less comprehensively, and their samples are comparatively few. Other countries, such as Italy, France, Russia, and those of Central Europe, were studied more thoroughly, so the samples are more numerous and undoubtedly more complete. Inasmuch as this work is not a detailed history of art, the total number of paintings and sculptures of known and unknown artists examined and compressed in the tables of Chapters Nine and Ten is thought to be quite sufficient for the purposes of the present investigation.

Finally, though every possible effort was made to avoid errors, it is quite possible that a few of them are present, because the author could not personally check every picture and every date of the more than 100,000 pictures and sculptures examined and classified by N. Okunev and his associates. It is reasonably certain that the number of such errors is small. If any have slipped into the tabulations they hardly could affect the results in any appreciable way.

CHRISTIAN ART: ANCIENT AND MEDIEVAL

SOURCES

Bossert, H. and W. Storek. *Das mittelalterliche Hausbuch.* Leipzig, 1912.
Codices e Vaticanis selecti, Vol. VIII, *Il Menologio di Basilio II* (Cod. Vatic. gr. 1613). Torino, 1907.
———— Vol. X, C. Stornajolo, *Le miniature della topografia cristiana di Cosma Indicopleuste* (Cod. Vatic. gr. 699). Milano, 1908.
Dalton, O. M. *Byzantine Art and Archaeology.* Oxford, 1911.
Diehl, C. *Manuel d'art byzantin,* 2 vols. Paris, 1927.
Ebersolt, J. *La miniature byzantine.* Paris, 1926.
Garrucci, R. *Storia della arte christiana,* 6 vols. Prato, 1872.

Goldschmidt, A. *Die Elfenbeinskulpturen,* 3 vols. Berlin, 1914.
Haseloff, A. *Codex purpureus Rossanensis.* Berlin, 1898.
Hevesy, A. de. *Le bréviaire de Sigismont de Luxemburg.* Paris, 1911.
Jerphanion, G. de. *Les églises rupestres de Cappadoce,* 2 vols. Paris, 1925–1928.
Koechlin, R. *Les ivoires gothiques Français,* 2 vols. et album. Paris, 1924.
Königliche Museen zu Berlin. *Beschreibung der Bildwerke der christlichen Epochen. Die Elfenbeinbildwerke.* Berlin, 1902.
"*L'art byzantin chez les Slaves. Les Balkans,*" in *Récueils d'études.* Paris, 1930.
Marucchi, O. *I Monumenti del Museo Cristiano Pio-Lateranense.* Milano, 1910.
Matzulewitsch, L. *Byzantinische Antike.* Berlin, 1929.

---

[1] U. Thieme and F. Becker, *Allgemeines Lexikon der Bildenden Künstler*, 30 vols. (Leipzig, 1907–1936).
[2] E. Bénézit, *Dictionnaire des peintres, sculpteurs, dessinateurs et graveurs*, 3 vols. (Paris, 1911–1923).
[3] A. von Wurzbach, *Niederländisches Künstler-Lexikon*, 3 vols. (Leipzig, 1911–1923).

Millet, G. *Monuments de l'Athos*, Vol. I, *Les peintures*. Paris, 1927.
—— *Monastere de Daphni*. Paris, 1899.
—— *Recherches sur l'iconographie de l'Évangile*. Paris, 1916.
—— *Monuments byzantins de Mistra*. Paris, 1910.
Omont, H. *Miniatures des plus anciens manuscrits grecs de la Bibliothèque Nationale du VIe au XIVe siècle*. Paris, 1929.
Sauerland, H. and A. Haseloff. *Der Psalter Erzbischof Egberts von Trier. Codex Gertrudianus in Cividale*. Trier, 1901.
Strzygowski, J. *Byzantinische Denkmäler*, 3 vols. Wien, 1891, 1893, and 1903.
Swarzenski, G. *Die Salzburger Malerei*. Leipzig, 1908.

—— *Die Regensburger Buchmalerei des X und XI Jahrhunderts*. Leipzig, 1901.
Wilpert, J. *Die Malereien der Katakomben Roms*. Freiburg, 1903.
Wölfflin, H. *Die Bamberger Apokalypse*. München, 1918.
Zimmermann, H. *Vorkarolingische Miniaturen*, 4 vols. Berlin, 1916.

Other works cited in the text.

ARTISTS

A list of the artists is not given, since their names, with few exceptions, are unknown.

ITALY

SOURCES

Ancona, Paolo. *La miniature italienne du Xe au XVIe*. Paris, 1925.
Babelon, J. *Pisanello*. Paris, 1931.
Badt, K. *Andrea Solario*. Leipzig, 1914.
Basch, V. *Titien*. Paris, 1920.
Bercken, E. von der. *Malerei der Renaissance in Italien*. Potsdam, 1927.
Bercken, E. von der and A. L. Mayer. *Jacopo Tintoretto*, 2 vols. München, 1923.
Berenson, B. *Die Mäler der Renaissance*, 4 vols. München, 1925.
—— *The Study and Criticism of Italian Art*, 3 vols. London, 1920–1927.
Biehl, W. *Toskanische Plastik des frühen und hohen Mittelalters*. Leipzig, 1926.
Bindi, V. *Artisti abbruzzesi*. Napoli, 1883.
Bode, W. *Die Kunst der Frührenaissance in Italien*. Berlin, 1923.
—— *Florentiner Bildhauer der Renaissance*. Berlin, 1921.
—— *Die Italienischen Bronzestatuetten der Renaissance*. Berlin, 1912.
Callari, L. *Storia dell' arte contemporanea italiana*. Roma, 1909.
Colasanti, A. *La galleria nazionale di arte moderna in Roma*. Milano, 1923.
Dvořák, M. *Geschichte der Italienischen Kunst im Zeitalter der Renaissance*, 2 vols. München, 1928.
Escher, K. *Malerei der Renaissance in Italien*, 2 vols. Berlin, 1922.
Federici, N. G. = Althan, Nino d'. *Gli artisti italiani*. Torino, 1902.
Fiocco, G. *Francesco Guardi*. Firenze, 1923.
—— *L'arte di Andrea Mantegna*. Bologna, 1927.
—— *Die Venezianische Malerei des XVII und XVIII Jahrhunderts*. Berlin, 1929.
Flat, P. *Les premiers Vénitiens*. Paris, 1899.
Focillon, H. *Benvenuto Cellini*. Paris, 1910.
Fraschetti, S. *Il Bernini*. Milano, 1900.

Fröhlich-Bum, L. *Parmigianino und der Manierismus*. Wien, 1921.
Gabelentz, H. von der. *Fra Bartolommeo und die florentiner Renaissance*, 2 vols. Leipzig, 1922.
Gauthiez, P. *Luini*. Paris, 1907.
Geiger, B. *Alessandro Magnasco*. Wien, 1923.
Gnoli, U. *L'arte umbra alla mostra di Perugia*. Bergamo, 1908.
—— *Pittori e miniatori nell' Umbria*. Spoleto, 1923.
Goloubew, V. *Les dessins de Jacopo Bellini*, 2 vols. Bruxelles, 1912.
Grunwald, A. *Florentiner Studien*. Prague, 1914.
Habich, G. *Die Medaillen der italienischen Renaissance*. Berlin, 1923.
Hadeln, Detlev F. von. *Zeichnungen des Giacomo Tintoretto*. Berlin, 1922.
—— *Zeichnungen des Tizian*. Berlin, 1924.
Hamann, R. *Die Frührenaissance der Italienischen Malerei*. Jena, 1909.
Hausenstein, W. *Das Werk des Vittore Carpaccio*. Stuttgart, 1925.
Kristeller, P. *Andrea Mantegna*. Berlin, 1902.
—— *Jacopo de Barbari*. Paris, 1896.
—— *Tizian. Il trionfo della fede*. Berlin, 1906.
Malaguzzi-Valeri, F. *Leonardo da Vinci e la scultura*. Bologna, 1922.
Melani, A. *Manuale di scultura italiana*. Milano, 1899.
Mendelssohn, H. *Fra Filippo Lippi*. Berlin, 1909.
Michelangelo. *Mappe des Kunstwarts*. München, 1911–1914.
Missirini, M. *Storia della romana Accademia di San Lucca*. Roma, 1823.
Molmenti, P. *Acque-forti dei Tiepolo*. Venezia, 1896.
Nicodemi, G. *La pittura milanese dell' età neoclassica*. Milano, 1915.
—— *L'arte italiana*. Padova, 1923.
Ojetti, U., L. Dami, and N. Tarchiani. *La pittura italiana del seicento e del settecento alla mostra di Palazzo Pitti*. Roma, 1924.
Pevsner, N. *Die Italienische Malerei von Ende*

der Renaissance bis zum Ausgehenden Rokoko. Potsdam, 1927.

Planiscig, L. *Venezianische Bildhauer der Renaissance.* Wien, 1921.

Posse, H. *Der römische Maler Andrea Sacchi.* Leipzig, 1925.

Rava, A. *G. B. Piazzetta.* Firenze, 1921.

Ricci, C. *Pier della Francesca.* Roma, 1910.

—— *Melozzo da Forlì.* Roma, 1911.

—— *Luca Signorelli.* Roma, 1912.

Roger-Miles, L. *Leonard de Vinci et les Jocondes.* Paris, 1923.

Rolfs, W. *Geschichte der Malerei Neapels.* Leipzig, 1910.

Rusconi, A. J. *Sandro Botticelli.* Bergamo, 1907.

Saltini. *Le arti belle in Toscana da mezzo il secolo XVIII al di nostri.* Firenze, 1862.

Schlosser, J. *Tommaso da Modena.* Wien, 1898.

Schmarsow, A. *Italienische Kunst im Zeitalter Dantes.* Augsburg, 1928.

—— *Masaccio Studien,* 4 vols. Kassel, 1895-1898.

Schottmüller, F. *Donatello.* München, 1904.

Schubring, P. *Die Kunst der Hochrenaissance in Italien.* Berlin, 1926.

Sirén, O. *Toskanische Maler im XIII Jahrhundert.* Berlin, 1922.

—— *Dessins et tableaux de la renaissance italienne dans les collections de Suède.* Stockholm, 1902.

—— *Don Lorenzo Monaco.* Strassburg, 1905.

Somaré, E. *Masaccio.* Milano, 1924.

Springer, A. and C. Ricci. *Manuale di storia dell' arte.* Bergamo, 1924.

Steinmann, E. *Die Sixtinische Kapelle,* 2 vols. München, 1901-1905.

Toesca, P. *Masolino da Panicale.* Bergamo, 1908.

Venturi, A. *Storia dell' arte italiana,* 10 vols. Milano, 1901-1936.

—— *Studi dal vero.* Milano, 1927.

—— *Botticelli.* Roma, 1926.

Venturi, L. *Le Origini della pittura veneziana, 1300-1500.* Venezia, 1907.

Voss, H. *Die Malerei der Spätrenaissance in Rom und Florenz,* 2 vols. Berlin, 1920.

Weigelt, C. *Duccio di Buoninsegna.* Leipzig, 1911.

Willard, A. R. *History of Modern Italian Art.* London, 1899.

Zahn, L. and G. Kirsta. *Caravaggio.* Berlin, 1928.

Catalogues of art museums. Art journals. Other works cited in the text.

ARTISTS

Abate, Pier Antonio dell' = Pietro Antonio da Modena. ?-1473.
Abbate, Nicolo. 1512-1571.
Abbiati, Filippo. 1640-1715.
Ademollo, Carlo. 1825-1911.
Agabiti, Pietro Paolo. *c.* 1470-*c.* 1540.

Agnolo da Siena = Agostino di Giovanni. XIII-XIV centuries.
Agnolo di Ventura. XIV century.
Agostino d'Antonio di Duccio. 1418-1481.
Agostino di Federigo. XV (?) century.
Agresti, Livio. XVI century.
Agricola, Filippo. 1776-1857.
Alamagna, Giovanni d'. ?-1450.
Alari Bonacolsi, Pietro Giacomo = L'Antico. *c.* 1460-1528.
Albacini, Carlo. 1777-1858.
Albani, Francesco. 1578-1660.
Alberti, Cherubino. 1553-1615.
Alberti, Leon Battista degli. 1404-1472.
Albertinelli, Mariotto. 1474-1515.
Albertis, Sebastiano d'. 1828-1897.
Alenis, Tommaso de. XV-XVI centuries.
Alexii, Andreas. XV century.
Alfani, Domenico. *c.* 1480-1553.
Alfani, Orazio. *c.* 1510-1583.
Algardi, Alessandro. 1602-1654.
Aliprandi, Giacomo. XVI century.
Allamagna, Giusto d'. XV century.
Allegretto, Nuzi. XIV century.
Allegri, Pomponio. 1521-1593.
Allori, Cristofano. 1577-1621.
Altichiero da Zevio. *c.* 1320-*c.* 1385.
Alvergna, Fra Antonio dell'. XIV (?) century.
Amadeo, Giovanni Antonio. 1447-1522.
Amato, Giovanni Antonio d'. *c.* 1475-*c.* 1555.
Ambrogio da Milano. XV-XVI centuries.
Amici, Luigi. 1813-1897.
Amidano, Giulio Cesare. 1566-1630.
Amigoni, Jacopo. 1675-1752.
Ammanati, Bartolomeo. 1511-1592.
Anderlini, Giovanni Paolo. XVIII century.
Andrea di Ardito. XIV century.
Andrea di Mino da Siena. XIV century.
Andrea da Murano. XV-XVI centuries.
Anesi, Paolo. XVIII century.
Angeli, Giuseppe. *c.* 1709-1798.
Angelico, Fra Beato = Guidolino di Pietro da Mugello. 1387-1455.
Angelini, Giuseppe. 1735-1811.
Angelini, Tito. 1806-1878.
Ansaldo, Andrea. 1584-1638.
Anselmi, Michelangelo. 1491-1554.
Ansuino da Forlì. XV century.
Antonello da Messina. *c.* 1430-1479.
Antonello de Saliba. ?-1535.
Antoniazzo, Romano = Antoniazzo di Benedetto Aquilio. XV-XVI centuries.
Antonio di Chellino da Pisa. XV century.
Antonio di Cristiforo. XV century.
Antonio da Viterbo. XV-XVI centuries.
Antonio di Orlando. XIII century.
Antonio da Padova. XIV century.
Apollonio da Firenze. XIII-XIV centuries.
Appiani, Andrea. 1754-1817.
Aquila, Andrea dall'. XV century.
Aquilio, Bernardino. XV-XVI centuries.
Aquilio, Marcantonio. XV-XVI centuries.
Aretusi, Pellegrino de = il Munari = Pellegrino da Modena. 1460/65-1523.
Argenti, Giosué. 1819-1892.

Argomento di Ugolino. XIV century.
Arienti, Carlo. 1801–1873.
Aspetti, Tiziano. 1565–1607.
Asta, Andrea dell'. 1673–1721.
Aulista, Angelo d'. XV century.
Avanzo, Jacopo. XIV–XV centuries.
Azeglio, Taparelli d'. 1798–1866.
Baboccio, Antonio. 1351–1435.
Badalocchio, Sisto Tosa. 1581–1647.
Badile, Antonio. c. 1516–1560.
Baglione, Giovanni. 1571–1644.
Baglioni, Cesare. c. 1560–c. 1610.
Balbi, Filippo. 1806–1890.
Baldini, Baccio. XV century.
Baldovinetti, Alesso. 1425–1499.
Balducci, Matteo. XV–XVI centuries.
Balestra, Antonio. 1666–1740.
Bambini, Nicolo. 1651–1736.
Banco, Nanni di. c. 1373–c. 1420.
Bandinelli, Baccio. 1493–1560.
Bandini, Tommaso. 1807–1849.
Barabino, Nicolo. 1832–1891.
Baratta, Francesco. ?–1666.
Baratta, Pietro. XVIII century.
Barbari, Jacopo de'. c. 1450–c. 1515.
Barbella, Costatino. 1852–
Barile, Antonio. 1453–1516.
Barnaba da Modena. XIV century.
Barocci, Frederigo Jacopo = Vignola. 1526/28–1612.
Baroncelli, Nicolo di Giovanni = Nicolo dal Cavallo. XV century.
Bartoli, Taddeo di. 1363–1422.
Bartolini, Lorenzo. 1777–1850.
Bartolo di Fredi. ?–c. 1410.
Bartolomeo da Pian Castagnajo. XV century.
Bartolommeo, Fra = Baccio della Porta. 1472–1517.
Bartolommeo di Vanni. XIV century.
Bartolommeo Veneto. XV–XVI centuries.
Baruzzi, Cincinnato. 1790–1878.
Barzaghi, Francesco. 1839–1892.
Basaiti, Marco. 1470–c. 1521.
Basoli, Antonio. 1848–
Bassano, Francesco il Giovane = Francesco da Ponte. 1549–1592.
Bassano, Francesco il Vecchio. c. 1475–1530.
Bassano, Giacomo da Ponte. 1510–1592.
Bassano, Giambattista. 1553–1613.
Bastiani, Lazzaro. 1425–1512.
Bastianini, Giovanni. 1830–1868.
Batoni, Pompeo Girolamo. 1708–1787.
Battagio, Giovanni di Domenico da Lodi. XV century.
Battista, Martino di = Pellegrino da San Daniele. 1460/70–1547.
Beaumont, Claudio Francesco. 1694–1766.
Beccafumi, Domenico. 1486–1551.
Beccaria, Angelo. 1820–1897.
Begarelli, Antonio. c. 1500–1565.
Bella, Stefano della. 1610–1664.
Bellano, Bartolommeo. c. 1434–1496/97.
Bellini, Gentile. 1429–1507.
Bellini, Giovanni = Giambellino. c. 1430–1516.
Bellini, Jacopo. 1400–c. 1470.

Belliniano, Vittore. XV–XVI centuries.
Bellosio, Carlo. 1801–1849.
Bellotto, Bernardo. 1720–1780.
Bellucci, Antonio. 1654–1726.
Bembo, Benedetto. XV century.
Bembo, Bonifazio. XV century.
Bencovich, Federico = il Dalmatino. c. 1670–c. 1740.
Benedetto di Baldassare. XVI century.
Benedetto Ranuci di Spoleto. XII–XIII centuries.
Benedetto da Rovezzano. 1474–c. 1552.
Benfatto, Alvise = Dal Friso. 1559–1611.
Benvenuti, Pietro. 1769–1844.
Berlinghieri, Berlinghiero. XIII century.
Berlinghieri, Bonaventura. XIII century.
Bernardino di Mariotto dello Stagno. XVI century.
Bernini, Giovanni Lorenzo. 1598–1680.
Berretoni, Niccoló. 1637–1682.
Bertini, Francesco di Fausto. XVII century.
Bertini, Giuseppe. 1825–1898.
Berto di Giovanni. XV–XVI centuries.
Bertoldo di Giovanni. c. 1420–1491.
Bertucci, Giovanni Battista = Bertucci da Faenza. c. 1540–1614.
Bettini, Domenico. 1644–1705.
Bevilacqua, Giovanni Ambrogio. XV–XVI centuries.
Bezzi, Bartolomeo. 1851–
Bezzuoli, Giuseppe. 1784–1855.
Bianco, Bartolommeo. c. 1590–1657.
Bibiena, Ferdinando Galli = Galli da Bibiena. 1657–1743.
Bicci Family. XIV–XV centuries.
Biscaino, Bartolommeo. c. 1632–1657.
Biscarra. Cesare. XX century.
Bison, Giuseppe Bernardino. 1762–1844.
Bissolo, Francesco. c. 1470–1554.
Bistolfi, Leandro. 1859–
Boccaccino, Boccaccio. 1467–1525.
Boccati, Giovanni. c. 1420–?
Boccioni, Umberto. 1882–1916.
Bocco, Fabriano da. XIII–XIV centuries.
Boigi, Andrea. XVII century.
Boldini, Jean Giovanni. 1845–1931.
Bolgarini, Bartolommeo. ?–1378.
Bologna, Andrea da. XIV century.
Bologna, Giovanni = Giambologna. c. 1524–1608.
Boltraffio, Giovanni Antonio. 1467–1516.
Bombelli, Sebastiano. 1635–1716.
Bonajuto, Andrea di = Andrea Bonaiti. ?–1377.
Bonascia, Bartholommeo. c. 1450–1527.
Bonesi, Gian Girolamo. 1653–1725.
Bonfigli, Benedetto. c. 1420–1496.
Bongi, Domenico. XVI century.
Bonifo, Giuseppe. 1707–1789.
Bon o Buno, Bartolommeo. ?–1529.
Bono, Giovanni di Bertuccio. ?–1442.
Bono da Ferrara. XV century.
Bonofacio, di Pitati = Bonifazio Veronese. 1487–1553.
Bonozza, Giovanni. XVII–XVIII centuries.
Bonsignori, Francesco. c. 1455–1519.

Bordone, Paris. 1500–1570.
Borghese, Ippolito. XVII century.
Borghesi da Parma, Giambattista. 1790–1846.
Borgino dal Pozzo. XIV century.
Borgognone, Ambrogio di Stefano. c. 1455–1523.
Borromini, Francesco. 1599–1667.
Bosa, Antonio. 1780–1845.
Boselli, Felice. 1650–1732.
Bossi, Giuseppe. 1777–1815.
Botticelli, Sandro = Alessandro di Mariano da Vanni Filipepi. 1444–1510.
Bracci, Pietro. 1700–1773.
Braccini, Andrea. XIV century.
Bramante, Donato. c. 1444–1514.
Bramantino = Bartolommeo Suardi. c. 1470–1536.
Brandi, Giacinto. 1623–1691.
Brea, Lucovico. c. 1443–c. 1520.
Bregno, Andrea = Andrea da Milano. 1421–1506.
Breschia, Bartolommeo da. 1506–c. 1578.
Brescianino, Andrea del = Piccinelli. c. 1485–?
Brina, Francesco. c. 1540–c. 1586.
Brini, Giovanni. ?–1599.
Brizio, Francesco. c. 1575–1623.
Bronzino, Angelo = Agnolo di Cosimo di Mariano. 1503–1572.
Brunelleschi, Filippo di ser. 1377–1446.
Bruni, Bruno di. XVII century.
Brusasorci, Domenico. c. 1516–1567.
Brusasorci, Felice. 1542–1605.
Brusco, Paolo Girolamo. 1742–1820.
Brustolon, Andrea. 1662–1732.
Buffalmacco = Cristofani Buonamico. XIII–XIV centuries.
Bugatti, Zanetto di. XV century.
Bugiardini, Giuliano. 1475–1554.
Buonamato, Luigi. 1795–1878.
Buonconsiglio, Giovanni = il Marescalco. ?–1537.
Buntalenti, Bernardo. 1536–1608.
Busciolano, Antonio. 1823–1871.
Busi, Giovanni = il Cariani. 1485/90–1547.
Busti, Agostino = il Bambaja. 1483–1548.
Butinone, Bernardino Jacobi. XV–XVI centuries.
Cabianca, Vincenzo. 1827–1902.
Caccavello, Annibale. c. 1515–?
Cacciatori, Benedetto. 1794–1871.
Cafaro, Giuseppe. XVI century.
Caffa, Melchiorre. 1635(?)–1667.
Caggiano, Fidele. 1804–1880.
Cagnacci = Guido Canlassi. 1601–1681.
Calandra, David. 1856–
Calegari, Antonio. 1698–1777.
Caliari, Benedetto. 1538–1598.
Caliari, Carlo. 1570–1596.
Caliari, Gabriele. 1568–1631.
Callani, Gaetano. 1736–1809.
Calvi, Lazzaro. 1502–1607.
Calvi, Pantaleone. 1502–1595.
Cambiaso, Luca. 1527–1585.
Cambio, Arnolfo di. ?–1302.
Cametti, Bernadino. 1682–1736.
Cammarano, Michele. 1849–1920.
Camogli, Bartolommeo da. XIV–XV centuries.

Campagna, Girolamo. 1549/50–1626.
Campagnola, Domenico. ?–1582.
Campagnola, Giulio. 1482–?
Campi, Bernardino. 1522–1590/95.
Campi, Giulio. 1502–1572.
Camuccini, Vincenzo. 1771–1844.
Canal, Antonio = il Canaletto. 1697–1768.
Canavesi di Pinerolo, Giovanni. XV century.
Canerio, Anselmo. XVI century.
Canesi, Ulisse. 1807–1895.
Canonica, Pietro. 1869–
Canova, Antonio. 1757–1822.
Cantagallina, Remigio. 1582–1635.
Cantarini, Simone = il Pesarese. 1612–1648.
Canzio, Michele. 1787–1868.
Capalti, Alessandro. c. 1810–1868.
Capanna da Siena. XV–XVI centuries.
Caporali, Bartolommeo. XV century.
Cappella, Francesco. 1714–1784.
Cappella, Scipione. XVIII century.
Capponi, Luigi di Giampietro. XV century.
Capriolo, Domenico. 1494–1528.
Caracciolo, Giovanni Battista = Battistello. c. 1570–1637.
Caratti, Franz. ?–1679.
Caravaggio Michelangelo da Caravaggio. c. 1565–1609.
Carbone, Giovanni Bernardo. 1614–1683.
Carcano, Filippo. 1840–
Cardelli, Domenico. XVIII century.
Carducci, Bartolommeo. 1560–1608.
Carducci, Michelangelo. XVI century.
Carducci, Vicenzo. 1578–1638.
Carena, Felice. 1880–
Carlevaris, Luca. 1665–1731.
Carloni, Taddeo. 1543–1613.
Carloni, Giovanni Andrea. 1590–1630.
Carloni, Giovanni Battista. 1592–1677.
Carnevali, Giovanni. 1806–1873.
Carnevalle, Bartolommeo della Corradini fra. ?–1484.
Carona, Pietro Lombardo da. XVI century.
Caroto, Giovanni. 1488/95–1563/66.
Caroto, Giovanni. 1491–1563.
Caroto, Giovanni Francesco. c. 1480–1555.
Carpaccio, Vittore. 1455–1526.
Carpi, Girolamo da. 1501–1556.
Carpioni, Giulio. 1611–1674.
Carrá, Carlo Dalmazzo. 1881–
Carracci, Annibale. 1560–1609.
Carracci, Lodovico. 1555–1619.
Carradori, Francesco. 1747–1825.
Carrea, Bartolommeo. c. 1750–1839.
Carriera, Rosalba. 1675–1757.
Carta, Natale. 1790–1884.
Cartei, Luigi. 1822–1891.
Casareggio, Andrea. 1741–1799.
Caselli, Cristoforo = il Temperello. ?–1521.
Casnedi, Raffaello. 1822–1892.
Cassioli, Amos. 1832–1891.
Castagno, Andrea dal. 1410–1457.
Castello, Giovan Battista = Bergamasco. 1509–1579.
Castello, Francesco da = il Tifernate. XV–XVI centuries.

Castiglione, Giovanni Benedetto = il Grechetto. 1616–1670.
Catena, Giovanni Gherardo dalle. XVI century.
Catena, Vicenzo di Biagio. c. 1470–1531.
Cattaneo, Danese. c. 1509–1573.
Cavalcanti, Andrea di Lazzaro = il Buggiano. 1412–1462.
Cavalleri, Ferdinando. 1794–1865.
Cavallini, Francesco. XVII century.
Cavallini, Pietro. XIII–XIV centuries.
Cavallino, Bernardo. 1622–1654.
Cavalori, Mirabello. 1510/20–1572.
Cavazzola, Paolo Morando. 1486–1522.
Cavazzoni Zanotti, Giovanni Pietro. 1674–1765.
Cavedoni, Giacomo. 1577–1660.
Ceccarini, Giovanni. XVIII–XIX centuries.
Celentano, Bernardo. 1835–1863.
Celesti, Andrea. 1637–1706.
Celio, Gaspero. 1571–1640.
Cellini, Benvenuto. 1500–1571.
Cenni di Francesco di ser Cenni. XIV–XV centuries.
Cennini, Cennino di Drea. 1370–?
Cerquozzi, Michelangelo = delle Battaglie = delle Bambociate. 1602–1660.
Cerrachi, Giuseppe. 1751–1802.
Ceruti, Giacomo. XVIII century.
Cesari, Giuseppe = il cavaliere d'Arpino. 1568–1640.
Cesariano, Cesare di Lorenzo. 1483–1543.
Cesi, Bartolommeo. 1556–1629.
Chiaradia, Enrico. 1851–1901.
Chirico, Giacomo di. 1844/45–1884.
Ciardi, Guglielmo. 1843–1907.
Cignani, Carlo. 1628–1719.
Cignani, Felice. 1660–1724.
Cignaroli, Gianbettino. 1706–1770.
Cima da Coneglino, Gianbattista. 1459–1518.
Cimabue = Cenni di Pepi. c. 1240–1302.
Cini, Branco. XIV century.
Ciseri, Antonio. 1821–1891.
Cittadini, Pietro Francesco. 1616–1681.
Ciuffagni, Bernardo di Piero di Bartolommeo. 1381–1457.
Civerchio, Vincenzo = Fanone. 1468/70–1544.
Civitali, Matteo di Giovanni. 1436–1501.
Cocari, Niccolo di Giovanni = Niccolo Fiorentino. 1430–1514.
Coducci, Moro di Martino = il Moretto. c. 1440–1504.
Coghetti, Francesco. 1804–1875.
Colle, Raffaello dal. c. 1500–1566.
Colli, Giovanni. 1636–1681.
Colonna, Angelo Michele. 1600–1687.
Commodi, Andrea. 1560–1638.
Comolli, Giovanni Battista. 1775–1830.
Conca, Sebastiano. 1680–1764.
Consani, Vincenco. 1818–1887.
Consoni, Niccolo. 1814–1884.
Conti, Bernardino dei. ?–1522.
Conti, Primo. 1900–
Conventi, Giulio Cesare. 1577–1640.
Coppi, Giacomo = del Meglio. 1523–1591.
Coppo di Marcovaldo. 1225/30–?
Corenzio, Belisario. 1558–1643.

Cornacchini, Agostino. 1685–1740.
Cornevalle, Bartolommeo della Corradini fra. ?–1484.
Cornienti, Cherubino. 1816–1860.
Corona, Anselmo. XVI century.
Corona, Claudio. XVI century.
Corradini, Antonio. ?–1752.
Correggio = Antonio Allegri. 1494–1534.
Cortona, Pietro da = Berrettini. 1596–1669.
Cossa, Francesco del. 1435–1477.
Costa, Lorenzo. c. 1460–1535.
Costoli, Aristodemo. 1803–1871.
Cozzarelli, Giacomo di Bartolomeo di Marco. 1453–1515.
Credi, Lorenzo di. 1459–1537.
Cremona, Tranquillo. 1837–1878.
Cremonini, Giovanni Battista. c. 1550–1610.
Crescenzio, Antonello de = il Palermitano. c. 1467–1542.
Crespi, Daniele. 1590–1630.
Crespi, Giovanni Battista = il Cerano. 1557–1633.
Crespi, Giuseppe Maria = lo Spagnuolo. 1665–1747.
Creti, Giuseppe. 1634–1714.
Criscuolo, Giovan Filippo. c. 1500–1584.
Cristoforo, Romano Giovanni. c. 1470–1512.
Crivelli, Angelo Maria. ?–1730.
Crivelli, Carlo. 1430/35–1495.
Curia, Francesco. 1538–1610.
Curti, Girolamo = Dentone. c. 1576–1632.
Daddi, Barnardo. ?–1350.
Dalbono, Edoardo. 1843–1915.
Danti, Vincenzo. 1530–1576.
Demi, Paolo Emilio. 1797–1863.
Demin, Giovanni. 1786–1859.
De Pisis, Filippo. 1896–
Desiderio, Settignano da. 1428–1464.
Diamantini, Giuseppe. 1621–1705.
Diotti, Giuseppe. 1779–1846.
Diziani, Gasparo. 1689–1767.
Dolci, Carlo. 1616–1686.
Domenichino = Domenico Zampieri. 1581–1641.
Domenico di Paris padovano, del Cavallo. XV century.
Donatello = Donato di Niccolo di Betto Bardi. 1386–1466.
Doni, Dono dei. c. 1500–1575.
Dossi, Battista. ?–1548.
Dossi Dosso = Giovanni de Luteri. 1479–1542.
Duccio di Buoninsegna. c. 1255–1319.
Duknowich da Trau, Giovanni = Giovanni Dalmata. c. 1440–1509.
Dupré, Giovanni. 1817–1882.
Duquesnoy, Francesco = il Flamingo. 1594–1643.
Durandi, Giacomo. 1410–1469.
Durante, Fortunato. 1787–1863.
Eismann, Carlo. 1679–1718.
Emanueli, Giovanni. 1816–1894.
Enrico di Tedice. XIII century.
Errante, Giuseppe. 1760–1821.
Este, Antonio d'. 1754–1837.
Evangelista di Pian di Meleto. c. 1458–1549.
Fabriano, Gentile da. ?–1427.

Fabris, Giuseppe de. 1790–1860.
Fadiga, Domenico. c. XVIII–XIX centuries.
Falcone, Aniello. 1600–1656.
Falconetto, Maria. c. 1468–1534.
Fanachiotti, Cesare. 1809–1877.
Fancelli, Bartolo di Bernardo. XVI century.
Farinati, Giovanni Battista. 1532–1592.
Farinati, Paolo. 1524–1606.
Faruffini, Federico. 1831–1869.
Fasolo, Giovanni Antonio. 1530–1572.
Fasolo, Lorenzo. XV–XVI centuries.
Fattori, Giovanni. 1824–1908.
Favretto, Giacomo. 1849–1887.
Federighi, Antonio. c. 1420–1490.
Fedi, Pio. 1816–1892.
Ferramola, Floriano. 1480–1528.
Ferrari, Bartolommeo. 1780–1844.
Ferrari, Ettore. 1849–
Ferrari, Eusebio. XV–XVI centuries.
Ferrari, Gaudenzio. c. 1471–1546.
Ferrari, Giovanni Andrea dei. 1598–1669.
Ferrari, Giovanni = Torretti. 1744–1826.
Ferrari, Luigi. 1810–1894.
Ferrata, Ercole. 1610–1686.
Ferri, Ciro. 1634–1689.
Ferrucci, Andrea di Piero = Andrea da Fiesole. 1465–1526.
Ferrucci da Fiesole, Francesco di Simone. 1437–1493.
Feti, Domenico. c. 1589–1624.
Filarete, Antonio di Pietro Averlino. 1400–c. 1469.
Finelli, Carlo. 1785–1853.
Fiorenzo di Lorenzo. c. 1445–1522/25.
Fiori, Ernesto de. 1884–
Florigerio, Sebastiano. c. 1500–c. 1543.
Fogolino, Marcello. XV–XVI centuries.
Fonduti, Agostino dei. XV century.
Fontana, Prospero. 1512–1597.
Fontanesi di Reggio Emilia, Antonio. 1818–1882.
Fontebasso, Francesco. 1709–1768/69.
Foppa, Vincenzo. c. 1427–c. 1515.
Forabosco, Girolamo. XVII century.
Fraccaroli, Innocenzo. 1805–1882.
Fracassini, Cesare. 1838–1868.
Fragiacomo, Pietro. 1856–1922.
Francesca, Piero della. c. 1420–1492.
Franceschi, Alessandro. 1789–1834.
Franceschini, Marcantonio. 1648–1729.
Francesco da Siena. XVI century.
Franchi, Alessandro. 1838–1914.
Franchi, Giuseppe. 1731–1806.
Francia, Giacomo. c. 1486–1557.
Franciabigio = Francesco Bigi di Cristofano. 1482–1525.
Fumiani, Giovanni Antonio. 1643–1710.
Fungai, Bernardino. c. 1460–1516.
Furini, Francesco. 1604–1646.
Gabbiani, Anton Domenico. 1652–1726.
Gaddi, Taddeo. c. 1300–1366.
Gaggini, Giuseppe. 1791–1867.
Gaggini, Pace. XV–XVI centuries.
Gagini, Domenico. ?–1492.
Gagliardi, Pietro. 1809–1890.
Galli, Antonio. ?–1862.

Galli, Pietro. 1804–1877.
Gamba, Enrico. 1831–1883.
Gamba, Francesco. 1818–1887.
Gambarini, Giuseppe. 1680–1725.
Gambello, Antonio. XV century.
Gandini del Grano, Giorgio. 1489–1538.
Gandolfino d'Asti. XV–XVI centuries.
Garaventa, Giambattista. 1777–1840.
Garguilo, Domenico = Micco Spadaro. 1612–1679.
Garofalo, il Benvenuto Tisi. 1481–1559.
Gastaldi, Andrea. 1826–1889.
Gatta, Bartolommeo della Dei, Pier d' Antonio. 1448–1502.
Gatti, Barnardino = Sojaro. 1495–1575.
Gatti, Fortunato. 1597–1651.
Gatti, Saturnino de'. 1463–c. 1521.
Gaulli, Giambattista = il Baciccia. 1639–1709.
Gemito, Vincenzo. 1852–
Genga, Bartolommeo. 1516–1558.
Genga, Girolamo. c. 1476–1551.
Gennari, Benedetto. c. 1575–1610.
Gerini, Lorenzo di Niccolo. XIV–XV centuries.
Gerino da Pistoia. XV–XVI centuries.
Gessi, Giovanni Francesco. 1588–1649.
Gherardi, Cristofaro = Doceno. 1508–1556.
Gherardi, Filippo. 1643–1704.
Ghiberti, Lorenzo. 1378–1455.
Ghiberti, Vittorio. 1416–1496.
Ghirlandaio, Davide = Davide Bigordi. 1452–1525.
Ghirlandaio, Domenico = Domenico Bigordi. 1449–1494.
Ghirlandaio, Ridolfo. 1483–1561.
Ghislandi, Fra Vittore. 1655–1743.
Ghisolfi, Giovanni. 1623–1683.
Giacomo di Zambonino da Campione. ?–1398.
Giambologna = Giovanni Bologna. c. 1524–1608.
Gianelli, Bartolommeo. 1824–1894.
Giaquinti, Corrado. 1699–1765.
Gigante, Giacinto. 1806–1876.
Giolfino, Niccoló di Niccoló. 1476–1555.
Giordano, Luca. 1632–1705.
Giorgio di Matteo = Orsini da Zara. ?–1475.
Giorgione = Giorgio da Castelfranco. c. 1477–1510.
Giotto di Bondone. 1266–1337.
Giovanni di Bartolommeo. XIV century.
Giovanni di Jacopo di Guido Kaverzaio. XIV century.
Giovanni di Martino da Fiesole. XV century.
Giovanni di Niccola di Pisa. XIV century.
Giovanni di Paolo. c. 1400–1482.
Giovanni di Stefano. c. 1446–c. 1506.
Girolamo di Bernardino. ?–1512.
Giudici, Carlo Maria. 1723–1804.
Giungi, Innocenzo. 1800–1840.
Giunta Pisano. XIII century.
Gnoccarini, Francesco. XIX century.
Gola, Emilio. 1851–1923.
Gonin, Francesco. 1808–1889.
Gozzoli, Benozzo = Benozzo di Lese. 1420–1498.
Granacci, Francesco. 1477–1543.

Grande, Antonio del. XVII century.
Grandi, Ercole. *c.* 1468–1531.
Grandi, Francesco. 1831–1891.
Grassi, Giovannino di. ?–1398.
Graziani, Ercole. 1688–1765.
Grigoletti, Michelangelo. 1801–1870.
Grimaldi, Giovanni Francesco. 1606–1680.
Gros, Pierre le (the Younger). 1656–1719.
Gualtieri, Gualterio. XVI century.
Guardi, Francesco de. 1712–1793.
Guariento padovano. XIV century.
Guarini, Guarino. 1624–1683.
Guarino, Francesco. 1611–1654.
Gubbio, Oderisio. XIII century.
Guercino = Giovanni Francesco Barbieri. 1591–1666.
Guerrazi, Temistocle. 1806–1884.
Guidi, Domenico. 1625–1701.
Guidi, Jacopo di Pietro. XIV–XV centuries.
Guido Reni, 1575–1642.
Guido da Siena. XIII century.
Hayez, Francesco. 1791–1881.
Ibi, Sinibaldo. *c.* 1475–*c.* 1550.
Imola, Innocenzo Francucci da. 1490–1547.
Indaco, Jacopo = Jacopo Torni. 1476–*c.* 1544.
Induno, Domenico. 1815–1878.
Induno, Gerolamo. 1828–1890.
Ingegno, l' = Andrea di Luigi. XV–XVI centuries.
Isola, Giuseppe. 1806–1893.
Jacobello, Jacopo d'Antonello. *c.* 1455–?
Jacometti, Ignazio. 1819–1883.
Jacopo di Guglielmo. ?–1525.
Jacovetti, Rinaldo. XVI century.
Jerace, Francesco. 1854–
Jufre, Antonio = Guffre da Messina. XV century.
Juvara, Filippo. 1676–1736.
Lama, Giovanni Bernardo. XVI century.
Lamberti, Nicoló di Piero. 1393–1451.
Landi, Gaspare. 1756–1830.
Landi, Neroccio di Bartolomeo di Benedetto de'. 1447–1500.
Lanfranco, Giovanni. 1582–1647.
Langetti, Giovanni Battista. 1625–1676.
Lanino, Bernardino. 1510/15–1583.
Lappoli, Matteo. *c.* 1450–1504.
Lattanzio da Rimini. XV–XVI centuries.
Laurana, Francesco. 1420/25–1502.
Laurana, Luciano. 1420/25–1479.
Laureti, Tommaso. 1530–1602.
Lauri, Filippo. 1623–1694.
Lazzarini, Gregorio. 1655–1730.
Lega, Silvestro. 1826–1895.
Lendinara, Bartolommeo. ?–1520.
Lendinara, Cristoforo. XV century.
Leonardo da Pavia. XV century.
Leonardo Grazia. XVI century.
Leoni, Leone = Leone Aretino. 1509–1590.
Leoni, Ottavio Mario. 1578–1630.
Liberale da Verona. 1445–1536.
Liberi, Pietro. 1614–1687.
Libri, Girolamo dai. 1474–1555.
Licinio, Bernardino. *c.* 1489–*c.* 1550.
Ligorio, Pirro. *c.* 1500–1583.

Lipparini, Lodovico. 1800–1856.
Lippi, Filippino. *c.* 1457–1504.
Lippi, Fra Filippo. *c.* 1406–1469.
Lironi, Giuseppe. 1689–1749.
Lista, Stanislao. 1824–1908.
Locatelli, Andrea. 1695–1741.
Lomazzo, Giovanni Paolo. 1538–1600.
Lombardi, Alfonso = Citadella. 1497–1537.
Lombardo, Antonio. *c.* 1458–1516(?).
Lombardo, Martino. XV century.
Lombardo, Tullio. *c.* 1455–1532.
Lomi, Oraxio = Gentileschi. 1562–1647.
Londonio, Francesco. 1723–1783.
Longhi, Alessandro. 1733–1813.
Longhi, Luca. 1507–1580.
Longhi, Pietro. 1702–1785.
Lorentino d'Andrea. *c.* 1430–1506.
Lorenzetti, Ambrogio. ?–1348.
Lorenzetti, Pietro. XIV century.
Lorenzo di Pietro = Vecchietta. *c.* 1412–1480.
Lorenzo Veneziano. XIV century.
Lorenzo di Viterbo. 1437–*c.* 1476.
Lotto, Lorenzo. 1480–1556.
Lucchetti, Giuseppe. 1823–1867.
Luini, Bernardino. *c.* 1480/85–1532.
Lunghi, Martino. 1602–1657.
Luti, Benedetto. 1666–1724.
Luzzi, Lorenzo. ?–1526/27.
Macchietti, Girolamo. 1535–1592.
Macrino, d'Alba. *c.* 1465–?
Maderna, Carlo. 1556–1629.
Maderno, Stefano. *c.* 1576–1636.
Magagni, Girolamo = Giomo del Sodoma. 1507–1562.
Maggiotto, Domenico. 1713–1794.
Magnasco, Alessandro = Lissandrino. 1677–1749.
Magni, Pietro. 1817–1877.
Magno, Cesare. XVI century.
Maiano, Benedetto da = Benedetto di Leonardo. 1442–1497.
Maiano, Giuliano di Leonardo d'Antonio da. 1432–1490.
Maini, Giovanni Battista. 1690–1752.
Mainoni, Luigi. 1804–1850.
Malatesta, Adeodato. 1806–1891.
Malatini, Girolamo. XIV (?) century.
Malvito, Tommaso. XV century.
Manaigo, Silvestro. *c.* 1670–*c.* 1734.
Mancini, Antonio. 1852–1931.
Mancini, Domenico. XVI century.
Manerbio, Andrea da. XVI century.
Manetti, Antonio. XVIII century.
Manfredi, Bartolommeo. 1580–*c.* 1620.
Manni, Giannicola di Paolo. *c.* 1460–1544.
Manno, Francesco. 1752–1831.
Manozzi, Giovanni = Giovanni da San Giovanni. 1592–1636.
Mansueti, Giovanni di Niccolò. XV–XVI centuries.
Mantegazza, Cristoforo. ?–1482.
Mantegna, Andrea. 1431–1506.
Manzuoli, Tommaso d'Antonio = **Maso da San** Friano. 1536–1571.
Maratta, Carlo. 1625–1713.

Marchesi, Girolamo = Girolamo da Cotignola. *c.* 1481–*c.* 1550.
Marchesi, Pompeo. 1789–1858.
Marchiori, Giovanni. 1696–1778.
Marconi, Rocco. ?–1529.
Marescalco, Pietro da = lo Spada. 1503–1583.
Margaritone d'Arezzo. ?–1293.
Maria, Giacomo de. 1762–1838.
Mariano di Eusterio = Mariano da Perugia. *c.* 1470–?
Marieschi, Michele. 1696–1743.
Mariotto, Bernardino di. XVI century.
Marochetti, Carlo. 1805–1867.
Martinelli, Domenico. 1650–1718.
Martini, Arturo. ?–1889.
Martini, Bernardino = Zenale. 1436–1526.
Martini, Giovanni = Giovanni da Udine. ?–1535.
Marziale, Marco. ?–*c.* 1507.
Masaccio = Tommaso di Giovanni di Simone Guidi. 1401–1428.
Masolino = Tommaso di Cristoforo Fini. 1383–1447.
Massarani, Tullo. 1826–1905.
Matteis, Paolo de. 1662–1728.
Mattielli, Lorenzo. 1682–1748.
Maturino Fiorentino. XVI century.
Mazone, Giovanni. *c.* 1433–1512.
Mazza, Camillo. 1602–1672.
Mazza, Damiano. XVI century.
Mazzola-Bedoli, Girolamo. *c.* 1500–1569.
Mazzola, Filippo. *c.* 1460–1505.
Mazzoli, Pamfili. XVII century.
Mazzolino, Lodovico. *c.* 1480–1528.
Mazzoni, Guido = il Paganino. *c.* 1450–1518.
Mazzuoli, Giuseppe. 1644–1725.
Meloni, Marco. XVI century.
Melozzo da Forli. 1438–1494.
Memmi, Lippo. XIV century.
Menabuoi, Giusto di Giovanni de'. ?–1393.
Meo da Siena. XIII century.
Melanzio, Francesco. XV–XVI centuries.
Melone, Altobello. XV–XVI centuries.
Melzi, Francesco. 1493–*c.* 1570.
Menzocchi, Francesco. 1513–1574.
Metalli, Agostino. 1609–1660.
Michelangelo, Buonarroti, 1475–1564.
Michele da Verona. 1470–1536/44.
Micheli, Parrasio. *c.* 1516–1578.
Michelozzo di Bartolommeo. 1396–1472.
Michetti, Francesco Paolo. 1851–1929.
Michieli, Andrea = Vicentino Michieli. 1539–1614.
Migliori, Francesco. 1684–1734.
Minardi, Tommaso. 1787–1871.
Mino da Fiesole = Mino da Poppio. 1430/31–1484.
Minozzi, Bernadino. 1699–1769.
Miralietti, Giovanni. XV century.
Mocetto, Girolamo = Mozetto. *c.* 1458–*c.* 1531.
Mochi, Francesco. 1580–1654.
Moderati, Francesco. *c.* 1680–?
Modigliani, Amadeo. 1884–1920.
Mola, Francesco. 1612–1666.
Molinari, Antonio. 1665–1727.

Molinari, Giovanni Battista. 1636–1682
Molmenti, Pompeo. 1819–1894.
Monaco, Lorenzo. *c.* 1370–1425.
Montagna, Bartolomeo. *c.* 1450–1523.
Montagna, Benedetto. XV–XVI centuries.
Montalto = Giovanni Stefano Danedi. 1608–1689.
Montani, Tommaso. XVI–XVII centuries.
Montauti, Antonio. ?–*c.* 1740.
Montelupo, Baccio da. 1469–1535.
Montemezzano, Francesco. *c.* 1540–*c.* 1602.
Montemezzo, Antonio. 1841–1898.
Montersoli, Fra Giovanni. 1507–1563.
Montevarchi, Francesco da. XVI century.
Monteverde, Giulio. 1837–1917.
Monti, Cesare. XX century.
Monti, Gaetano Matteo. 1776–1847.
Morandi, Giorgio. XX century.
Morazzone, Pietro Francesco = Mazzuchelli. 1571–1626.
Morelli, Domenico. 1826–1901.
Morelli, Lazzaro. 1608–1690.
Moretti-Larese, Eugenio. 1822–1874.
Moretto, Alessandro = Alessandre Bonvicino. 1498–1554.
Morgari, Paolo Emilio. 1815–1882.
Moricci, Giuseppe. 1806–1879.
Morone, Domenico. 1442–1517.
Morone, Francesco. 1471–1529.
Moroni, Giovanni Battista. *c.* 1525–1578.
Mosca, Giovanni Maria = Zuan Maria Padovna. XVI century.
Motelli, Gaetano. 1805–1858.
Mura, Francesco de = Franceschiello. 1696–1782.
Mussini, Luigi. 1813–1888.
Nacherino, Michelangelo. 1550–1622.
Naldini, Battista. 1537–1591.
Nani, Giovanni. XV century.
Nanni, Giovanni. 1487–1564.
Nardo di Cione. XIV century.
Nardo, Evangelista di Maestro. XVI century.
Nazari, Bartolommeo. 1699–1758.
Nebbia, Cesare. 1536–1614.
Negri, Pietro. XVII century.
Nelli, Ottaviano di Martino. 1370/75–*c.* 1444.
Netti, Francesco. 1832–1894.
Niccolo l'Allunno = Niccolo di Liberatore. *c.* 1430–1502.
Niccolo di Bari = dall Arco. *c.* 1440–1494.
Niccoló da Bologna. XIV century.
Niccoló di Piero Lamberti = il Pela. ?–1451.
Niccolo di Segna. XIV century.
Nittis, Giuseppe de. 1846–1884.
Nogari, Giuseppe. 1699–1763.
Nola, Giovanni da. XVI century.
Nuvoloni, Carlo Francesco. 1608–*c.* 1665.
Obici, Giuseppe. XIX century.
Ognabene, Andrea di Jacopo d'. XIII–XIV centuries.
Onofri, Vincenzo. 1503–1524.
Oppi, Ubaldo. 1889–
Orcagna, Andrea di Cione. 1308–1368.
Orlandi, Deodato. XIII–XIV centuries.
Orsi, Achille d'. 1845–1929.

Ortolano, l' = Giovanni Battista Benvenuti. ?-c. 1525.
Pacchia, Girolamo. 1477-1533(?).
Pacchiarotti, Giacomo. 1474-1540.
Pacetti, Camillo. 1758-1826.
Pagani, Gaspare. 1518-1543.
Pagani, Lattanzio = Lattanzio della Marco. XVI century.
Pagani, Paolo. 1661-1716.
Pagano, Francesco = Francesco Napoletano. XV century.
Pagliano, Eleuterio. 1826-1903.
Paladino, Filippo di Benedetto. 1544-1614.
Palagi, Pelagio. 1775-1860.
Palizzi, Filippo. 1818-1899.
Palladio, Andrea. 1508-1580.
Palma, Antonio = Antonio Nigreti. c. 1510/15-1575.
Palma, Jacopo = Palma Vecchio. 1480-1528.
Palmezzano, Marco. ?-1539.
Palmieri, Giuseppe. 1674-1740.
Paltronieri, Pietro. 1673-1741.
Pampaloni, Luigi. 1791-1847.
Pandolfi da Pesaro, Giovanni Giacomo. XVI-XVII centuries.
Pannini, Giovanni Paolo. 1691/92-1765.
Paoletti, Pietro. 1801-1847.
Paolino da Pistoia, Fra. 1490-1547.
Paolo di Giovanni. XIV-XV centuries.
Paolo da Ragusa. XV century.
Papacello, Maso = Tommaso Barnabei. c. 1500-1559.
Parigi, Giulio. ?-1635.
Parmigianino, il = Francesco Mazzola. 1503-1540.
Parodi, Domenico. 1668-1740.
Parodi, Philippo. 1630-1702.
Pasinelli, Lorenzo. 1629-1700.
Pasini, Alberto. 1826-1899.
Passeri, Giambattista. 1610/16-1679.
Pasti, Matteo di Andrea de'. XV century.
Pastura, il = Antonio Massari da Viterbo. XV-XVI centuries.
Pecori, Domenico. c. 1480-1527.
Pedrini, Giovanni = Giampetrino = Gian Pietro Rizzi. XVI century.
Pellegrini, Giovanni Antonio. 1675-1741.
Pennachi = Gerolamo da Traviso. 1497-1544.
Pennacchi, Pier Maria. 1464-1528(?).
Penni, Giovanni Francesco = il Fattore. 1488(?)-c. 1528.
Penso, Francesco = Cabianca. 1665-1737.
Persico, Luigi. 1791-1860.
Perugino = Pietro de Cristoforo Vannucci. c. 1450-1523.
Peruzzi, Baldassare Tommaso. 1481-1536.
Pesello, Francesco di Stefano = il Pesellino. 1422-1457.
Piacenza, Carlo. 1814-1887.
Piaggio, Teramo. XV-XVI centuries.
Piazza, Calisto. ?-1561.
Piazzetta, Giovanni Battista. 1682-1754.
Piccinelli, Andrea del Breschianino. c. 1485-?
Piero di Cosimo. 1462-1521.
Pietro di Francia. XIV century.

Pietro di Martino da Milano. ?-1473.
Pietro de Rondo = da Rondo. XV century.
Pino da Siena = Marco dal Pino. c. 1525-c. 1587/88.
Pintaricchio = Bernadino di Betto-Benedetto di Biagio. c. 1454-1513.
Piola, Paolo Girolamo. 1666-1724.
Piombo, Sebastiano del = Sebastiano Luciani. 1485-1547.
Pisa, Giovanni da. XV century.
Pisanello, il = Antonio di Puccio Pisano. c. 1395-1455.
Pisani, Giovanni Paolo. 1574-1637.
Pisano, Andrea. ?-1348/49.
Pisano Giovanni. XIII century.
Pittoni, Giovanni Battista. 1687-1767.
Pittoni, Battista = Vincentino. c. 1520-1584.
Pizzi, Angelo. 1775-1819.
Pizzolo, Nicoló. 1421-1453.
Po, Giacomo del. 1652-1726.
Podesti, Francesco. 1800-1895.
Polidoro da Caravaggio = Polidoro Caldara. 1490/1500-1543.
Polidoro da Lanciano = Polidoro Lanzani. 1515-1565.
Politi, Odorico. 1785-1846.
Pollaiuolo, Jacopo d'Antonio del. 1433-1498.
Pollaiuolo, Pier di Jacopo d'Antonio Benci del. 1443-1496.
Pomarancio, il = Cristoforo Roncalli. 1552-1626.
Ponchino, Giovanni Batista = Bozzato. 1500-1570.
Ponsonelli, Giacomo Antonio. c. 1654-1735.
Pontormo, il = Jacopo Carrucci. 1494-1557.
Pordenone, Giovanni Antonio. 1484-1539.
Porissimi, Claudio. XVII century.
Porta, Giacomo della. c. 1537-1602.
Porta, Guglielmo della. ?-1577.
Portelli, Carlo. ?-1574.
Portigiani, Pagno di Lapo. 1408-1470.
Pozzi, Giovanni Battista. 1561-1589.
Pozzo, Andrea. 1642-1709.
Predis, Ambrogio de. c. 1455-?
Preti, Mattia. 1613-1699.
Previati, Gaetano. 1852-1920.
Previtali, Andrea = Cordeliaghi. c. 1470-1528.
Primaticcio, Francesco = Bologna. 1504-1570.
Procaccini, Camillo. ?-1629.
Procaccini, Giulio Cesare. c. 1570-1625.
Puccinelli, Angelo. XIV century.
Puligo, Domenico. 1492-1527.
Pupini, Biagio dalle = Biagio dalle Lame. XVI century.
Putti, Giovanni. 1771-1847.
Quaini, Luigi. 1643-1717.
Quartararo palermitano, Riccardo. XV-XVI centuries.
Queirolo, Francesco. 1704-1762.
Querena, Lattanzio. 1768-1853.
Quercia, Jacopo della = Jacopo della Fonte. 1367-1438.
Raffaelli Santi. 1483-1520.
Raggi, Antonio = il Lombardo. 1624-1686.
Raggi, Pietro Paolo. c. 1646-1724.

Raibolini, Francesco = Francia Francesco. c. 1450–1517.
Raimondi, Marcantonio. c. 1480–c. 1534.
Rainaldi, Carlo. 1611–1691.
Ramenghi, Bartolommeo = Bagnacavallo. 1484–1542.
Rasconi, Giacomo. XV century.
Raverti, Matteo de. XIV–XV centuries.
Recco, Giuseppe. 1634–1695.
Revelli, Salvator. 1816–1859.
Ricci, Giovanni Battista. 1537–1627.
Ricci, Marco. 1676–1729.
Ricci, Sebastiano. 1659–1734.
Ricci, Stefano. 1765–1837.
Ricciarelli, Daniele = Daniele da Volterra. 1509–1566.
Riccio, Andrea = Andrea Briosco. 1470–1532.
Riccio, Antonello. XVI century.
Riccio, il = Bartolommeo Neroni. 1500(?)–1571/73.
Riccomanni, Leonardo di. XV century.
Richter, Giovanni. 1665–1745.
Ridolfi da Verona, Claudio. 1560–1644.
Rignardi, Andrea. XIV (?) century.
Rinaldi, Rinaldo. 1793–1873.
Ristori, Fra. ?–1283.
Rizzo, Antonio. XV century.
Robbia, Andrea della. 1435–1525.
Robbia, Luca di Simone di Marco della. 1400–1482.
Roberti, Domenico. c. 1642–1707.
Roberti, Ercole de. 1456–1496.
Robusti, Domenico. 1562–1637.
Robusti, Marietta. 1560–1590.
Roccatagliata, Nicoló. XVI–XVII centuries.
Rodriguez, Luigi = il Siciliano. XVI–XVII centuries.
Romanelli, Giovanni Francesco. 1610(?)–1662.
Romanelli, Pasquale. 1812–1887.
Romanelli, Romano. 1882–
Romanino, Girolamo. 1484/87–1562.
Romano, Giulio = Giulio Peppi. 1499–1546.
Romazzani, Ercole. XV (?) century.
Rondani, Francesco Maria. 1490–1548.
Rondinello, Nicoló. XV–XVI centuries.
Rosa, Ercole. 1846–1893.
Rosa, Salvator. 1615–1673.
Rosselli, Cosimo. 1439–1507.
Rossellino, Antonio = Antonio di Matteo di Domenico Gamberelli. 1427–1479.
Rossellino, Bernardo = Bernardo di Matteo di Domenico Gamberelli. 1409–1464.
Rossello, Domenico di Giovanni di Bartolomeo. c. 1439–1497/98.
Rossetti, Giovanni Battista. XV–XVI centuries.
Rossetti, Giovanni Paolo. ?–1586.
Rossi, Francesco de'. 1510–1563.
Rossi-Scotti, Lemno Conte. 1848–
Rosso, Fiorentino il = Giovan Battista di Jacopo di Gasparre. 1494–1540.
Rosso, Giovanni di Bartolo. XV century.
Rosso, Menardo. XX century.
Rotari, Conte Pietro Antonio. 1707–1762.
Rotta, Antonio. 1828–1903.
Rozzolone, Pietro. XV–XVI centuries.

Rubio, Luigi. 1808–1882.
Ruggeri, Quirino. 1883–
Ruoppolo, Giovanni Battista. 1620–1685.
Rusconi, Benedetto = Benedetto-Diana. c. 1460–1525.
Rusconi, Camillo. 1658–1728.
Russolo, Luigi. 1885–
Rustici, Giovanni Francesco. 1474–1554.
Rustici, Lorenzo = il Rustico. 1521–1572.
Rusuti, Filippo. XIII–XIV centuries.
Sabatelli, Francesco. 1803–1829.
Sabatelli, Giuseppe. 1813–1843.
Sabatelli, Luigi. 1772–1850.
Sabatini, Andrea = Andrea da Salerno. 1484–1530.
Sacchi, Andrea. c. 1599–1661.
Saccocia, Cola. XV century.
Sachi, Pier Francesco. 1485–1528.
Salai, Andrea = Gian Giacomo di Caprotti. c. 1480–1524.
Saliba, Pietro de. XV–XVI centuries.
Salietti, Alberto. 1892–
Salimbeni, Arcangelo. XVI century.
Salvi, Nicola. 1697–1751.
Salvini, Salvino. 1824–1899.
Salvo d'Antonio = Gian Salvo. 1493–1525.
San Gallo = Aristotile Bastiano. 1481–1551.
Sangallo, Francesco da = il Margotta. 1494–1576.
Sangallo, Giuliano da. 1445–1516.
Sangiorgio, Abbondio. 1798–1879.
San Giorgio, Eusebio da. 1465/70–?
Sanmartino, Giuseppe. 1720–1793.
Sanseverino, Lorenzo d'Alessandro da. c. 1445–1503(?).
Sansovino, Andrea = Andrea Contucci. c. 1460–1529.
Santafede, Fabrizio. XVI–XVII centuries.
Sant' Agata, Francesco da. XVI century.
Santarelli, Emilio. 1801–1886.
Santi, Andriolo di. XIV century.
Santi, Giovanni. c. 1435–1494.
Santo, Girolamo dal. XVI century.
Sarrocchi, Tito. 1824–1900.
Sarti, Ignazio. 1791–1854.
Sarto, Andrea del = Andrea di Agnolo. 1486–1530.
Sartorio, Giulio Aristide. 1860–1932.
Sassetta, Stefano di Giovanni = il Sassetta. 1392–1450.
Sassoferrato = Giovanni Battista Salvi. 1609–1685.
Savoldo, Giovanni Girolamo. c. 1480–c. 1550.
Savonanzi, Emilio. 1580–1660.
Scarsallino = Ippolito-Scarsella. 1551–1620.
Schedoni, Bartolomeo. c. 1570–1615.
Schiaffino, Bernardo. 1680–1725.
Schiaffino, Francesco Maria. 1691–1765.
Schiavone, lo = Andrea Meldolla. ?–1563.
Schiavone, Giorgio di Tommaso = Giorgio Chiulinovich. 1436/37–1504.
Scotti, Gottardo. ?–1485.
Scuri, Enrico. 1805–1884.
Sega, Giovanni del. ?–1527.
Segna di Bonaventura. XIII–XIV centuries.

Semeghini, Pio. 1878–
Sementi, Giacomo. 1580–1636.
Semino, Andrea. 1525(?)–1595(?).
Semino, Antonio. c. 1485–1554/55.
Semino, Ottavio. 1520–1604.
Sergantini, Giovanni. 1858–1899.
Sesto, Cesare da. c. 1477–1523.
Severini, Gino. 1883–
Siciliano, Francesco. XVIII century.
Siciolante, Girolamo = il Sermoneta. 1521–c. 1580.
Signorelli, Francesco. XVI century.
Signorelli, Luca. c. 1441–1523.
Silvagni, Giovanni. c. 1790–1854.
Silvestro da Sulmona = l'Ariscola = Silvestro dall'Aquila.
Simone, Martini. 1283–1344.
Sirani, Elisabetta d'Andrea. 1638–1665.
Sirani, Giovanni Andrea. 1610–1670.
Sironi, Mario. 1893–
Slodtz, René Michel = Michel-ange. 1705–1764.
Sodoma, il = Giovanni Antonio de'Bazzi. 1477–1549.
Soffici, Ardengo. 1879–
Soggi, Niccoló. 1480–1551.
Sogliani, Giovanni Antonio. 1492–1544.
Solari, Angelo. 1755–1846.
Solari, Pietro. XV century.
Solario, Andrea. c. 1460–c. 1530.
Solario, Antonio da. 1382–1455.
Solario, Cristoforo. XV–XVI centuries.
Solimena, Francesco. 1657–1747.
Somaini, Francesco. 1815–1855.
Sorbili, Giuseppe Antonio. 1824–
Sorri, Pietro. 1556–1622.
Sotio, Alberto. XII century.
Spada, Lionello. 1576–1622.
Spadini, Armando. 1883–
Spagna, lo = Giovanni di Pietro = Giovanni Spagniolo. ?–1528/30.
Spani, Bartolommeo. XV (?) century.
Spanzotti, Martino. ?–1524/28.
Sperandio, Niccoló. c. 1425–1500.
Speranza, Giovanni. XVI century.
Spezza, Andrea. ?–1628.
Spinazzi, Innocenzio. XVIII century.
Spinello, Aretino = Luca Spinelli. c. 1333–1410.
Spolverini, Ilario. 1657–1734.
Squarcione, Francesco. 1394–1474.
Stanzioni, Massimo. 1585–1656.
Stella Guglielmo. XIX century.
Strazza, Giovanni. 1817/18–1875.
Strozzi, Bernardo = il Capuccino. 1581–1644.
Tacca, Ferdinando. 1619–1685.
Tacca, Pietro. 1577–1640.
Tacconi, Francesco. 1464–1490.
Taddeo di Giovanni. XIV (?) century.
Tadolini, Adamo. 1789–1868.
Tafi, Andrea. XIII–XIV centuries.
Tamagni, Vincenzo. 1492–c. 1530.
Tantardini, Antonio. 1829–1879.
Tartari, Giulio. XVII century.
Tatti, Jacopo = Jacopo Sansovino. 1486–1570.
Tempesta, Antonio. 1555–1630.

Tenerani, Pietro. 1789–1869.
Testa, Pietro = il Lucchesino. 1617–1650.
Tiarini, Alessandro. 1577–1668.
Tiberio d'Assisi. XV–XVI centuries.
Tiepolo, Giovanni Battista. 1696–1770.
Tiepolo, Giovanni Domenico. 1726–1804.
Tintoretto, il = Jacopo Robusti. 1518–1594.
Tiziano Vecelli. 1476/77–1576.
Tommaso da Modena. 1325–1379.
Torbido, Francesco = il Moro. c. 1486–c. 1546.
Torre, Flaminio. 1621–1661.
Torretti, Giuseppe II. ?–1772.
Torrigiani, Bastiano. 1573–1586.
Torriti, Jacopo. XIII century.
Toschi, Orazio. XX century.
Tosi, Arturo. 1871–
Traballesi, Giuliano. 1726–1796.
Tradate, Jacopino da. ?–1440.
Traini, Francesco. XIV century.
Traverso, Niccoló. 1745–1823.
Trevisano, Angelo. 1669–1753.
Trevisano, Francesco. 1656–1746.
Tribolo, il = Niccoló Pericoli. 1485–1550.
Trometto, Niccola. c. 1550–c. 1620.
Trotti, Giovanni Battista = il Malosso. 1555–1619.
Tucci, Giovanni Maria. XVI century.
Tura Cosimo. c. 1432–1495.
Turchi, Alessandro = l'Orbetto. 1582–1648.
Turino, Barna di. XIV century.
Turola, Bartolommeo. XIV century.
Ubertini, Antonio. XVI century.
Ubertini, Baccio. XV–XVI centuries.
Ubertini, Francesco d' = Bacchiacca. 1494–1557.
Ubriachi, Baldassare. XIV century.
Ucello, Paolo = Paolo di Doni. 1396/97–1475.
Ugolino da Siena. ?–1339.
Ugolino di Tedice. XIII century.
Ussi, Stefano. 1822–1901.
Vaccaro, Andrea. 1598–1670.
Vaga, Perino del = Piero Buonaccorsi. 1499–1547.
Valle. 1696–1778.
Vanni, Andrea. 1332–c. 1414.
Vannutelli, Scipione. 1839–1894.
Varni, Santo. 1807–1885.
Varotari, Alessandro = il Padovanino. 1590–1650.
Vasari, Giorgio. 1511–1574.
Vasilacchi = Antonio l'Aliense. 1556–1629.
Vela, Vincenzo. 1822–1891.
Veneziano, Antonio. XIV century.
Veneziano, Domenico di Bartolommeo. c. 1410–1461.
Venusti, Marcello. 1515–1579.
Verla, Francesco. XV–XVI centuries.
Veronese, Paolo = Paolo Caliari. 1528–1588.
Verrocchio, Andre del = Andrea di Michele di Francesco de' Gioni. 1435–1488.
Viani, Domenico Maria. 1668–1711.
Vidolenghi, Leonardo. XV century.
Vigilia, Tommaso de. 1435–c. 1495.
Vignola Giacomo Barozzi. 1507–1573.
Vincenzo da Pavia. ?–1540.

Vinci, Leonardo da. 1452–1519.
Visentino, Antonio. 1688–1782.
Vite, Antonio. XIV–XV centuries.
Vite, Timoteo della. 1469–1523.
Vittoria, Alessandro. 1525–1608.
Vivarini, Alvise. 1446/47–1502/3.
Vivarini, Bartolommeo. XV century.
Vivo, Tommaso da. 1790–1884.
Wildt, Adolfo. 1868–1931.
Zaccagna, Turpino = Turpino Zaccagna. XVI century.
Zaganelli, Francesco dei = il Cotignola. XV–XVI centuries.
Zagari, Saro. 1825–?

Zais, Giuseppe. *c.* 1750–1784.
Zanchi, Antonio d'. 1639–1722.
Zandomenighi, Luigi. 1779–1850.
Zanelli, Angelo. XX century.
Zevio, Stefano da. 1393–1450.
Zocchi, Giuseppe. *c.* 1711–1767.
Zona, Antonio. *c.* 1810–1892.
Zoppo, Marco. XV century.
Zotto, Antonio del. 1841–?
Zuccarelli, Francesco. 1702–1788.
Zuccaro, Federigo. 1543–1609.
Zuccari, Taddeo. 1529–1566.
Zucconi, Adolfo. XX century.
Zurretti, Emilio. XX century.

FRANCE

SOURCES

Bruwaert, E. *Jacques Callot.* Paris, 1913.
Clément, C. *Decamps.* Paris, 1886.
Courboin, F. *La gravure en France des origines à 1900.* Paris, 1923.
Dimier, L. *Histoire de la peinture française du retour de Vouet à la mort de Lebrun (1627 à 1690),* 2 vols. Paris, 1926.
——— *Histoire de la peinture française des origines au retour de Vouet (1300 à 1627).* Paris, 1925.
Dorbec, P. *Théodore Rousseau.* Paris, 1910.
Fointainas, A. and L. Vauxcelles. *Histoire générale de l'art français de la révolution à nos jours,* 3 vols. Paris, 1922.
Fosca, F. *Renoir.* Paris, 1923.
Fuchs, E. *Der Maler Doumier.* München, 1927.
Gasquet, J. *Cézanne.* Paris, 1911.
Hourtied, L. *Ingres. L'œuvre du maître.* Paris, 1928.
Kahn, G. *Boucher.* Paris, 1904.
Labande, L. H. *Les primitifs français.* Marseille, 1932.
Leclère, T. *Hubert Robert et les paysagistes français du XVIIIᵉ siècle.* Paris, 1913.
Léger, C. *Courbet.* Paris, 1929.
Magne, E. *Nicolas Poussin.* Bruxelles and Paris, 1914.
Mâle, E. *L'art religieux de la fin du moyen âge en France.* Paris, 1922.
Marcel, H. *J. F. Millet.* Paris, 1904.
Mauclair, C. *Claude Monet.* Paris, 1924.
Meier-Graefe, J. *Eugène Delacroix. Beitrage zu einer Analyse.* München, 1922.
——— *Cézanne.* München, 1920.
——— *Courbet.* München, 1921.
——— *Degas.* München, 1920.
Pilon, E. *Watteau et son école.* Paris, 1912.
Réau, L. *Histoire de la peinture française au XVIIIᵉ siècle,* 2 vols. Paris, 1925.
Rey, R. *Gauguin.* Paris, 1923.
Robaut, A. *Camille Corot.* Paris, 1884.
Rümann, A. *Honoré Daumier. Sein Holzschnittwerk.* München, 1914.
Véron, E. *Eugène Delacroix.* Paris, 1887.
Vogelstein, J. *Von französischer Buchmalerei.* München, 1914.

Vollard, A. *Paul Cézanne.* München, 1921.
Weese, D. A. *Sculptur und Malerei in Frankreich vom XV bis zum XVII Jahrhundert.* Berlin, 1917.
Yriarte, C. *J. F. Millet.* Paris, 1885.

Catalogues of art museums. Art journals. Other works cited in the text.

ARTISTS

Abbate, Nicolo. 1512–1571.
Achard, Jean Alexis. 1807–1884.
Androuet, Jacques Ducerceau. 1510–1584.
Angers, Pierre Jean David d'. 1788–1856.
Audran, Claude. 1639–1684.
Audran, Gerard. 1640–1703.
Bailly, Louis L. 1761–1845.
Baléchou, Jean Joseph. 1719–1764.
Baquoy, Jean Charles. 1721–1777.
Bar, Bonaventure de. 1700–1729.
Bartelié, L. 1842–1913.
Barye, Antoine-Louis. 1796–1875.
Beauvarlet, Jacques Firmin. 1731–1797.
Bellechose, Henri. ?–1440/44.
Bellegambe, Jean. 1470/80–1535.
Bérain, Jean-Louis. 1637–1711.
Berthault, Pierre Gabriel. 1748–1819.
Bertin, Edouard. 1797–1871.
Bertin, Jean Victor. 1775–1842.
Besbard, Paul Albert. 1849–
Biard, Pierre. 1559–1609.
Bonington, Richard Parkes. 1801–1828.
Bontemps, Pierre. XVI century.
Bosse, Abraham. 1602–1676.
Bouchardon, Edme. 1698–1762.
Boucher, François. 1703–1770.
Boudin, Eugène Louis. 1825–1908.
Bourdichon, Jean. 1457–1521.
Bracquemond, Félix Henry. 1833–1914.
Braque, Georges. 1882–
Brébiette, Pierre. 1598–1650.
Broederlam, Melchior. 1388–
Bruges, Jean de. XIV century.
Buhot, Felix Hilaire. 1847–1898.
Callot, Jacques. 1592–1635.
Carpeaux, Jean Baptiste. 1827–1875.

Carrand, Louis Hilaire. 1821–1899.
Carrière, Eugène. 1849–1906.
Cars, Laurent. 1702–1771.
Cézanne, Paul. 1839–1906.
Champaigne, Philippe de. 1602–1674.
Chapuy, Jean Baptiste. 1760–1802.
Chardin, Jean Baptiste Siméon. 1699–1779.
Chasseriar, Theodore. 1819–1856.
Chastillon, Claude. 1560–1616.
Chauveau, François. 1613–1676.
Chavannes, Puvis de. 1824–1898.
Chenu, Pierre. 1730–1800.
Clerc, Sebastian le. 1637–1714.
Clouet, François. 1510–1572.
Clouet, Jean. 1485–1541.
Cochin, Charles Nicolas (the Elder). 1688–1754.
Colombe, Michel. 1430–1512.
Colson, Jean François. 1733–1803.
Constant, Benjamin. 1845–1902.
Corneille, Claude. ?–1574.
Corot, Jean Baptiste Camille. 1796–1875.
Courbet, Gustave. 1819–1877.
Cousin, Jean (the Elder). 1490–1560.
Cousin, Jean (the Younger). 1522–1594.
Coypel, Antoine. 1661–1722.
Coypel, Charles Antoine. 1694–1752.
Coypel, Noel. 1628–1707.
Darcis, Louis. ?–1801.
Daubigny, Charles François. 1817–1878.
Daullé, Jean. 1707–1763.
Daumier, Honoré. 1808–1879.
David, Jacques Louis. 1748–1825.
Debucourt, Philibert Louis. 1755–1832.
Decamps, Gabriel Alexander. 1803–1860.
Decourt, Jean. XVI century.
Degas, Hilaire Germain Edgar. 1834–1917.
Delacroix, Ferdinand Victor Eugène. 1798–1863.
Delaune, Etienne. 1518–1595.
Demarteau, Gilles. 1729–1776.
Denis, Maurice. 1870–?
Derain, André. ?–1880.
Descourtis, Charles Melchior. 1753–1826.
Desportes, François. 1661–1743.
Diaz de la Pena, Narcisse Virgil. 1807–1876.
Didier, Adrien. 1838–?
Doré, Paul Gustave Louis Christophe. 1833–1883.
Dorigny, Michel. 1617–1685.
Doyen, Gabriel François. 1726–1806.
Drevet, Pierre Imbert. 1697–1739.
Drouais, Jean Germain. 1763–1788.
Dubois, Ambroise. 1543–1614.
Dubreuil, Toussaint. 1561–1602.
Duclos, Antoine Jean. 1742–1795.
Dumonstier, Etienne. ?–1603.
Dumonstier, Pierre. 1585–1656.
Duplessi-Bertaux, Jean. 1747–1818.
Duplessis, Joseph Silfrede. 1725–1802.
Dupré, Jules. 1811–1889.
Duvet, Jean. 1485–1561.
Edelinck, Gérard. 1640–1707.
Enguerrand, Charanton. 1410–?
Fautin-Latour, Ignace Henri Jean Théodore. 1836–1902.
Febvre, Claude le. 1632–1675.

Flandrien, Hypolite Jean. 1809–1864.
Flandrin, Jules. 1871–?
Fosse, Charles de la. 1636–1716.
Fouquet, Jean. 1415/20–1480.
Fragonard, Jean Honoré. 1732–1806.
François, Alphonse. 1811–1883.
François, Jules Charles Remy. 1809–1861.
Froment, Nicolas. XV century.
Gaillard, Claude Ferdinand. 1834–1887.
Gaultier, Leonard. 1560–1641.
Gellée, Claude = le Lorrain. 1600–1682.
Gérard, François. 1770–1837.
Géricault, Jean Louis André Théodore. 1791–1824.
Gillot, Claude. 1673–1722.
Girardet, Abraham Louis. 1772–1820.
Godefroy, François. 1743–1819.
Goujon, Jean. ?–1567.
Gourmont, Jean de. 1483–1560.
Granet, François Marius. 1775–1849.
Greuze, Jean Baptiste. 1725–1805.
Gros, Antoine Jean. 1771–1835.
Guérin, Pierre Narcisse. 1774–1833.
Hayon, Leon Albert. 1840–1882.
Helman, Isodore Stanislaus. 1743–1809.
Henriquel-Dupont, Louis Pierre. 1797–1892.
Hesdin, Jacquemart de. XIV century.
Hilaire, Jean Baptiste. XVIII–XIX centuries.
Hoey, Nicolas. XVI–XVII centuries.
Hoin, Claude Jean Baptiste. 1750–1817.
Honnecourt, Villard de. XIII century.
Huet, Paul. 1803–1869.
Ingres, Jean Auguste Dominique. 1780–1867.
Jacquet, Jules. 1841–1913.
Janinet, Jean François. 1752–1814.
Jazet, Jean Pierre Marie. 1788–1871.
Jongkind, J. Barthelemy. 1822–1891.
Jouvenet, Jean Baptiste. 1644–1717.
Juste, Jean. 1505–1559.
Labille-Guiard, Adelaide. 1749–1803.
Lancret, Nicolas. 1690–1743.
Largillière, Nicolas de. 1656–1746.
Larmessin, Nicolas de. 1684–1755.
Launay, Nicolas de. 1647–1727.
Le Bas, Jacques Phillipe. 1707–1783.
Lebrun, Charles. 1619–1690.
Lemoine, François. 1688–1737.
Lepère, August. 1849–1918.
Lépicie, Bernard. 1700–1755.
Lépine, Louis. 1825–1892.
Leprince, Jean Baptiste. 1733–1781.
Leu, Thomas de. 1560–1612.
Loo, Charles Andre van. 1705–1765.
Loo, Louis Michel van. 1707–1771.
Loubon, Emile. 1809–1863.
Lyon, Corneille de. XVI century.
Malouel, Jean. 1370–1415.
Manet, Edouard. 1832–1883.
Marmion, Simon. 1425–1489.
Marot, Daniel. 1653/55–1718.
Marquet, Albert. 1875–
Masson, Antoine. 1636–1700.
Matisse, Henri. ?–1869.
Mellan, Claude. 1598–1688.
Mercier, Philippe. 1689–1760.

Meryon, Charles. 1821–1868.
Mignard, Pierre. 1610/12–1695.
Millet, Jean François. 1814–1874.
Miralhet, Jean. 1394–1457.
Monet, Claude. 1840–1926.
Monticelli, Adolphe Joseph Thomas. 1824–1886.
Moreau, Gustave. 1826–1897.
Moreau, Jean Michel. 1741–1814.
Moreau, Louis Gabriel. 1740–1806.
Morin, Jean. 1609–1650.
Morse, Auguste Achille. ?–1885.
Nain, Antoine le. 1593–1648.
Nain, Louis le. 1588–1648.
Nanteuil, Robert. 1623/25–1678.
Natoire, Charles Joséph. 1700–1777.
Nattier, Jean Marc. 1685–1766.
Olivier, Michel Barthelemy. 1712–1784.
Oudry, Jean Baptiste. 1686–1755.
Patas, Charles Emmanuel. 1744–1802.
Pater, Jean Baptiste. 1695–1736.
le Paultre. 1618–1682.
Perronneau, Jean Baptiste. 1731–1783.
Pesne, Antoine. 1683–1757.
Pesne, Jean. ?–1700.
Pierre, Jean Baptiste Marie. 1714–1789.
Pigalle, Jean Baptiste. 1714–1785.
Pilon, Germain. 1535–1590.
Pissarro, Camille. 1830–1903.
Poilly, François de. 1622/23–1693.
Pourbus, François (the Elder). 1545–1581.
Pourbus, François (the Younger). 1569/70–1622.
Poussin, Nicolas. 1594–1665.
Prevost, Benoit Louis. 1735–1809.
Prieur, Barthelemy. 1545–1601.
Primatiecio. 1504–1570.
Prud'hon, Pierre. 1758–1823.
Pucelle, Jehan. XIII–XIV centuries.
Quénedey, Edme. 1756–1860.
Rabel, Daniel. 1578–1637.
Raoux, Jean. 1677–1734.
Redon, Odilon. 1840–1916.
Renoir, Pierre Auguste. 1841–1920.

Restout, Jean. 1692–1768.
Ricard, Louis Gaston. 1823–1872.
Richier, Ligier. 1500–1567.
Rigaud, Hyacinthe. 1659–1743.
Rigaud, Jacques. 1681–1753.
Rodin, René François Auguste. 1840–1917.
Roger, Barthelemy Joseph Fulevau. 1767–1841.
Rossi, Rosso. 1494–1541.
Rousseau, Emile Alfred. 1831–1874.
Rousseau, Henri. 1875–1933.
Rousseau, Théodore. 1812–1867.
Rude, François. 1784–1855.
Saint-Aubin, Augustin de. 1737–1807.
Saint-Aubin, Gabriel Jacques de. 1724–1780.
Saint-Jean, Jean de. XVII century.
Santerre, Jean Baptiste. 1651–1717.
Seurat, Georges. 1859–1891.
Signac, Paul. 1863–
Silvestre, Israel. 1621–1691.
Sisley, Alfred. 1840–1899.
Sluyter, Claus. ?–1405.
Sueur, Eustache. 1616/17–1655.
Tissot, James Jacques Joseph. 1837–1902.
Tocqué, Louis. 1696–1772.
Tory, Godefroid. 1485–1533.
Toulouse-Lautrec, Henri de. 1864–1901.
Tour, Maurice Quentin de la. 1704–1788.
Tournier, Jean Jacques. XVII century.
Trouvain, Antoine. 1656–1708.
Troy, Jean François de. 1679–1752.
Utrillo, Maurice. 1883–
Vallatton, Félix Edouard. 1865–1925.
Vernet, Claude Joseph. 1714–1789.
Vestier, Antoine. 1740–1824.
Vien, Joseph Marie. 1716–1809.
Vigée-Lebrun, Elizabeth Louise. 1755–1842.
Vivien, Joseph. 1657–1734/35.
Voltigeant, Josse de. XVII century.
Vouet, Simon. 1590–1649.
Vuillard, Jean Edouard. 1868–
Watelet, Claude Henri. 1718–1786.
Watteau, Jean Antoine. 1684–1721.

CENTRAL EUROPE

CENTRAL EUROPE: SOURCES

Aldenhoven, C. *Geschichte der Kölner Maler-schule.* Lübek, 1902.
Antoniewicz, J. B. *Grottger.* Lwów, n.d.
Baum, I. *Deutsche Bildwerke des Mittelalters.* Stuttgart, 1924.
Biermann, G. *Deutsche Barock und Rokoko.* Leipzig, 1914.
Bock, E. *Die deutsche Graphik.* München, 1922.
Burger, F. *Die deutsche Malerei vom Ausgeheuten Mittelalter bis zum Ende der Renaissance.* Berlin, 1913.
Dehio, G. *Geschichte der deutschen Kunst,* 4 vols. Berlin, 1921–1934.
Deri, M. *Die Malerei im XIX Jahrhundert,* Vols. I and II. Berlin, 1920.

Dostál, E. *Venceslas Hollar.* Praha, 1924.
Drost, W. *Barockmalerei in den germanischen Ländern.* (*Handbuch der Kunstwissenschaft,* ed. by A. E. Brinckmann.) Potsdam, 1926.
Einstein, C. *Die Kunst des XX Jahrhunderts.* Berlin, 1928.
Esswein, H. and W. Hausenstein. *Das Deutsche Bild des XVI Jahrhunderts.* München, 1923.
Feuchtmayer, K. *Oberdeutsche Kunst der Spät-gotik und Reformationzeit.* Augsburg, 1924.
Feulner, A. *Die deutsche Plastik des XVI Jahrhunderts.* München, 1926.
—— *Die deutsche Plastik des XVII Jahrhunderts.* München, 1926.
Giedion-Welcker, C. *Bayrische Rokokoplastik.* München, 1922.
Glaser, C. *Zwei Jahrhunderte deutschen Malerei.* München, 1916.
—— *Lukas Cranach.* Leipzig, 1923.

Glück, G. *Die Kunst der Renaissance in Deutschland.* Berlin, 1928.
Grisebach, A. *Carl Friedrich Schinkel.* Leipzig, 1924.
Gurlitt, C. *Die Deutsche Kunst.* Berlin, 1924.
Heidrich, E. *Die Altdeutsche Malerei.* Jena, 1909.
Heise, C. G. *Norddeutsche Malerei.* Leipzig, 1918.
Jiránek, M. *Nanuš Schwaiger.* Praha, 1908.
Jiřík, X. *František Genišek.* Praha, 1906.
—— *Karel Pukyně.* Praha, 1919.
Kállai, E. *Neue Malerei in Ungarn.* Leipzig, 1925.
"Klassiker der Kunst" in *Gesamtausgaben*, Vol. XXXVI.
Knackfuss, H. *Künstler-Monographien*, Nos. 1–115.
Kopera, F. *Dzieje malarstwa w Polsce*, 4 vols. Krákow, 1929.
Kuhn, A. *Die polnische Kunst von 1800 bis zur Gegenwart.* Berlin, 1930.
Mádl, K. B. *Antonin Machek.* Praha, 1929.
—— *Bohumil Kafka.* Praha, 1919.
Matějček, A. *Samtida konsti Tjekoslovakien.* Molmö, 1931.
—— *Max Švabinský.* Praha, 1923.
Meder, I. *Die Handzeichnung.* Wien, 1923.
Muther, R. *Geschichte der Malerei*, Vols. II and III. Leipzig, 1909.
Oldenburg, A. *Die Münchner Malerei im XIX Jahrhundert.* München, 1922.
Palkovský, B. *Max Švabinský.* Praha, 1923.
Pauli, G. *Die Kunst des Klassizismus und der Romantik.* Berlin, 1925.
Pinder, W. *Die deutsche Plastik des fünfzehnten Jahrhunderts.* München, 1924.
Pretter, M. *Samtida Kost i Polen.* Molmö,1930.
Sauerland, M. *Die deutsche Plastik des XVIII Jahrhunderts.* München, 1926.
Scheffler, K. and C. Glaser. *Deutsche Meister. M. Friedlander. Albrecht Dürer.* Leipzig, 1921.
Štech, V. and F. X. Jiřík. *Mikoláš Aleš.* Praha, n.d.
Wagner, V. *Dejiny výtvarného umenia na Slovensku.* Trnava, 1930.
Waldmann, E. *Die Kunst des Realizmus und des Impressionizmus im XIX Jahrhundert.* Berlin, 1927.
Weisbach, W. *Die Kunst des Barock.* Berlin, 1924.
Worringer, W. *Die Anfänge der Tafelmalerei.* Leipzig, 1924.

Catalogues of art museums. Other works cited in the text.

HUNGARY: ARTISTS

Aba-Novák, Vilmos. 1894–
Benczúr, Gyula. 1844–1920.
Benedek, Peter. XX century.
Berény, Robert. XIX–XX centuries.
Bernáth, Aurel. XX century.
Bornemisza, Géza. XX century.
Bortnyik, Alexander. XX century.
Csóka, Istvan. 1865–
Csontváry, Theodor. XX century.
Czigány, Desideř. XX century.
Czillich, Anna. XX century.
Czóbel, Béla. XIX century.
Deli, Anton. XX century.
Dénes, Valerie. XX century.
Derkovits, Julius. XX century.
Dunajský, László. 1822–1904.
Egry, József. 1883–
Fadrusz, Janos. 1858–1903.
Fényes, Adolf. 1867–
Ferenczy, Károly. 1862–1915.
Forbat, Alfred. XX century.
Galimberti, Sándor. 1883–1915.
Grünwald, Béla Iványi. XX century.
Gulacsi, Lajos Kálmán. 1882–
Hatvany, Ferencz. 1881–
Hollósy, Simon. 1857–1918.
Huszár, Adolf Wilhelm. 1843–1885.
Jándi. XX century.
Kádár, Béla. 1877–
Kassák, Lajos. 1887–
Kernstok, Károly. 1873–
Kmetty, János. XX century.
Korda, Vince. 1897–
Körösföi-Kriesch, Aladár. 1863–1920.
Koszta, József. 1864–
Lampérth, Josef. 1891–1923.
Madarász, Viktor von. 1830–1917.
Márffy, Ödön. 1878–
Mattis-Teutsch, János. 1884–
Medgyes, László. 1892–
Mednyánszky, László. 1852–1919.
Mészoly, Geza. 1844–1887.
Moholy-Nagy, László. 1895–
Molnár, Farkas (Wolfgang). 1897–
Munkácsy, Mihály. 1844–1909.
Nagy, Sándor. 1869–
Nagy-Balogh, János. 1874–1919.
Paál, László. 1846–1879.
Péri, László. 1889–
Perlrott-Csaba, Vilmos. 1880–
Pór, Bertalan. 1880–
Rippl-Ronai, Jozsef. 1861–1927.
Scheiber, Hugo. 1873–
Schönberger, Armand. 1885–
Simon, F. Georg. XX century.
Székeley, Bartholomäus. XX century.
Szinyei-Merse, Paul. XX century.
Szobotka, Emerich. XX century.
Szönyi, Stefan. XX century.
Tihanyi, Ludwig. XX century.
Uitz, Béla. XX century.
Vaszary, Johann. XX century.

POLAND: ARTISTS

Augustynowicz, Aleksander. 1865–
Axentowicz, Teodor. 1859–
Bartlomiejczyk, Edmund. 1885–
Borowski, Waclaw. 1886–

Boruciński, Michal. 1885–
Boznańska, Olga. 1865–
Brandt, Josef von. 1841–1915.
Chełmonski, Josef. 1850–1914.
Chodowiecki, Daniel. 1726–1801.
Cieślewski, Tadensz. 1895–
Czajkowski, Stanisław. 1878–
Czyzewski, Tytus. 1883–
Debicki, Stanisław. 1866–1924.
Dotzycki, Leon. 1888–
Dunikowsi, Ksawery. 1876–
Duninówna, Marja. XX century.
Falat, Juljan. 1853–1919.
Fedkowicz, Jerzy. 1891–
Fendi, Peter. 1796–1842.
Filipkiewicz, Stefan. 1879–
Führich, Josef von. 1800–1876.
Gerson, Wojciech. 1831–1901.
Gierymski, Aleksander. 1849–1901.
Gierymiski, Maks. 1846–1874.
Godebski, Cyprian. 1835–1909.
Goryńska, Wiktoria. 1902–
Grottger, Artur. 1837–1867.
Hofmann, Włastimił. 1881–
Hrynkowski, Jan Piotr. 1891–
Jarocki, Władysław. 1879–
Kaminski, Sigismund. 1888–
Kamocki, Stanisław. 1875–
Kedzierski, Apoloniusz. 1851–
Komicz, Tadensz. 1700–1780.
Konarska, Janina. XVIII century.
Kossak, Juliusz. 1824–1899.
Kotarbinski, Mieczysław. 1890–
Kowalewskij, Bromisław. 1870–
Kowalski-Wiernsz, Alfred, 1849–1915.
Kowarski, Szczesny F. 1890–
Krafft, Johann Peter. 1780–1856.
Kramsztyk, Roman. 1885–
Krzyżanowski, Konrad. 1872–1922.
Kucharski, Aleksander. 1741–1819.
Kulisiewicz, Tadeusz. XX century.
Lam, Władysław. 1893–
Laszczka, Konstant. 1865–
Lednicka, Maryla. 1895–
Lentz, Stanisław. 1863–1920.
Madeyski, Anton. 1862–
Małczewski, Jacek von. 1854–1929.
Małczewski, Rafel. 1892–
Masłowski, Stanisław. 1853–1926.
Matejko, Jan. 1838–1893.
Mehoffer, Josef. 1869–
Michalowski, Piotr. 1801–1855.
Mierzejewski, Jacek. 1884–1925.
Niesiołowski, Tymon. 1879–
Orlowski, Aleksandr Ossipowitsch. 1777–1832.
Ostrowski, Stanisław. 1879–
Pankiewicz, Jósef. 1866–
Pautsch, Fryderyk. 1877–
Pienkowski, Ignacy. 1877–
Płonski, Michal. 1778–1812.
Pochwalski, Kazimierz. 1855–
Podkowinski, Wladysław. 1866–1895.
Pronaszko, Andrzej. 1889–
Pronaszko, Zbigniew. 1885–
Pruszkowski, Tadeusz. 1888–

Pruszkowski, Witold. 1846–1896.
Rembowski, Jan. 1879–1923.
Rodakowski, Henry Hipolit. 1823–1894.
Roguski, Wladysław. 1890–
Rożek, Marcin. 1885–
Rubczak, Jan. 1884–
Russ, Karl. 1779–1843.
Rustem, Jan. 1762–1835.
Rygier, Teodor. 1841–1913.
Rzecki, Stanisław. 1888–
Samlicki, Marcin. 1878–
Sichulski, Kazimierz. 1879–
Siemiradzki, Hendryk. 1843–1902.
Simmler, Josef. 1823–1868.
Skoczylas, Władysław. 1883–1934.
Sléndzinski, Ludomir. 1889–
Slewinski, Władysław. 1855–1918.
Stachowicz, Michal. 1768–1835.
Stanislawski, Jan. 1860–1906.
Stobrowski, Kazimierz. 1867–1929.
Strassgschwandtner, Antonin. 1826–1881.
Stryjenska, Zofia. 1897–
Szczepkowski, Jan. 1878–
Szymanowski, Waclaw. 1859–
Tetmajer, Wlodimierz. 1862–1923.
Wasowicz, Waclaw. 1891–
Weiss, Wojciech. 1875–
Welonski, Pio. 1879–1931.
Winkler, Konrad. XX century.
Witkiewicz, Stanisław. 1851–1915.
Wittig, Edward. 1881–
Wojniakowski, Kazimierz. 1772–1812.
Wojtkiewicz, Witold. 1880–1909.
Wyczolkowski, Léon. 1852–
Wyspianski, Stanisław. 1869–1907.
Zak, Eugenijusz. 1884–1926.
Zamoyski, August de. 1893–
Zmurkos, Franciszck. 1859–1910.

CZECHOSLOVAKIA: ARTISTS

Aleš, Nikolaus. 1852–1913.
Alexius, Daniel. XVI–XVII (?) centuries.
Balas, Zdenek. 1904–
Bauch, Jan. XX century.
Benda, Jarolsav. 1882–
Beneš, Ladislav. 1883–
Beneš, Vincens. 1883–
Bílek, František. 1872–
Blažiček, Oldřich. 1887–
Boettinger, Hugo. 1880–
Boháček, Karel. XX century.
Bohun, Petr. 1822–1879.
Brandel, Peter. 1668–1739.
Březa, Rudolf. XX century.
Brömse, August. 1873–1925.
Brozik, Václav. 1851–1901.
Brunner, V. H. 1886–1928.
Čapek, Josef. 1888–
Čermák, Jaroslav. 1831–1878.
Chittussi, Antonin. 1847–1891.
Duša, Ferdyš. XX century.
Dvořáček, Ludvik. XX century.
Dvořák, Karel. 1873–

Feigl, Friedrich. 1884–
Filla, Emil. 1882–
Fritsch, Josef Anton. 1714–1770.
Führich, Josef von. 1800–1876.
Grund, Norbert. 1717–1767.
Gutfreund, Otto. 1889–1927.
Hartmann, Johann Jacob. 1680–1728/45.
Hartmann, Vaclav. XVIII century.
Heintz, Josef. 1564–1609.
Hellich, Josef. 1807/10–1880.
Heyer, Miroslav. 1891–
Holan, Karel. 1893–
Holy, Miraslav. 1897–
Huber, Wolfgang. c. 1490–1553.
Hudeček, Antonin. 1872–
Jareš, Jaroslav. XX century.
Jičinska, Veřa. XX century.
Jiránek, Milos. 1875–1911.
Kafka, Bohumil. 1878–
Kars, Georg. 1882–
Kausek, Fritz. 1890–
Kerhart, Oldřich. 1895–
Kloncek, Celda. 1885–
Knüpfer, Beneš. 1848–1910.
Kofránek, Ladislav. 1880–
Kohl, Ludvik. 1746–1821.
Korf, Maxim. 1892–
Kosarek, Adolf. 1830–1859.
Kotrba, Karel. XX century.
Kramolin, Josef. 1730–1802.
Kratochvil, Zdeněk. 1883–
Krattner, Karel. 1862–1926.
Kremlička, Rudolf. 1886–
Kubiček, Jóža. XX century.
Kubiček, Leo. XX century.
Kubin, Otakar. 1883–
Kubišta, Bohumil. 1884–1918.
Kupezky, Jan. 1667–1740.
Kupka, Frantisek. 1871–
Kutski, Mathias. 1546–?
Kysela, František. 1881–
Lada, Josef. 1887–
Lauda, Jan. 1898–
Liška, Jan Kristof. ?–1712.
Lolek, Stanislav. 1873–
Machek, Antonin. 1775–1844.
Majer, Antonin. 1882–
Mánes, Antonin. 1784–1843.
Mánes, Josef. 1820–1871.
Mařák, Julius. 1832–1899.
Mařatka, Josef. 1874–
Marold, Luděk. 1865–1898.
Melnik, Paul von. XVI century.
Mokrý, František. 1892–
Moravec, Alois. 1899–
Mrkvička, O. XX century.
Mucha, Alfons. 1860–
Mudroch, Bedřich. XX century.
Myslbek, Josef. 1848–1922.
Nechleba, Vratislav. 1885–
Nejedlý, Otakar. 1883–
Nekolová, Gusta. XX century.
Norák, V. V. 1901–
Nosecky, Siard. 1693–1753.
Novák, Josef. XX century.

Nowak, Willy. 1886–
Nutsky, Simon (Mathias). 1546–?
Obrovský, Jakub. 1882–
Ondrušora-Melkorá, Ludmila. XX century.
Ornys, Matouš. XVI century.
Palko, Franz Karl. 1724–1767.
Pappe, Gustav. 1828–1859.
Pinkas, Sobeslav. 1827–1901.
Pokorný, Karel. 1891–
Polivka, Václav. XX century.
Prachně, Václav Kollar Z. XVII century.
Prachner, Václav. 1812–
Preisler, Jan. 1872–1918.
Purkyne, Karel. 1834–1868.
Raab, Ignaz. 1715–1787.
Rabas, Václav. 1885–
Rada, Vlastimil. 1895–
Radous, Matouš. XVII century.
Rambousek, Jan. 1895–
Rambouská, Ludmila. XX century.
Ratiboie, Jilji Z. XVI century.
Redelmayer, Josef. 1727–1788.
Reiner, Wenzel. 1689–1743.
Režek, Tro. XX century.
Riedl, Jaroslav. 1893–
Salcman, Martin. 1896–
Šalieun, Ladislav. 1870–
Schnirch, Bohuslav. 1845–1901.
Schwaiger, Hans. 1854–1912.
Šedivý, Jan. XX century.
Sedláček, Vojtech. 1892–
Silorsky, Vladimir. 1891–
Šima, Josef. 1891–
Šimak, L. 1898–
Šimon, František. 1877–
Slaviček, Antonin. 1870–1910.
Sochor, Václav. 1895–
Sotnorsky, Karll Skreta. XVII century.
Špála, Vaclav. 1885–
Španiel, Otakar. 1881–
Špilar, Jaroslav. 1869–1917.
Špilar, Karel. 1871–
Spranger, Bartholomeus. 1546–1627.
Stary, Jan Kantor. XVI century.
Steiner, Hugo. 1880–
Stretti, Victor. 1872–
Štursa, Jan. 1880–1925.
Sucharda, Stanislav. 1866–1916.
Sutnar, Ladislav. XX century.
Švabinsky, Max. 1873–
Svoboda, Karel. 1824–1870.
Taborsky, Jan. XVI century.
Terency, Stepan. 1792–1856.
Thiele, Franz. 1868–
Tilgner, Viktor. 1844–1896.
Tulka, Josef. 1846–1882.
Ullrych, Bohumil. 1893–
Úprka, František. 1868–1929.
Úprka, Jóža. 1861–
Vagner, Bohumil. 1921–
Vik, Karel. 1883–
Voiechora, Marie. XX century.
Wagner, Antonin. 1834–1895.
Wagner, Karl. 1887–

Willmann, Michael Lucas. 1630–1706.
Ženišek, František. 1849–1916.
Živec, Václav. XX century.
Zrzarý, Jan. 1890–

GERMANY AND AUSTRIA: ARTISTS

Abel, Josef. 1764–1818.
Abt, Ulrich. 1486–1532.
Achen, Hans von. 1552–1615.
Achenbach, Andrea. 1815–1910.
Achenbach, Oswald. 1827–1901.
Adam, Albrecht. 1786–1862.
Albiker, Karl. 1878–
Aldegrever, Heinrich. 1502–c. 1555.
Alt, Rudolf von. 1812–1905.
Alt, Theodor. 1846–
Altdorfer, Albrecht. c. 1480–1538.
Amberger, Christoph. 1500/10–1561/62.
Amerling, Friedrich von. 1803–1887.
Amiet, Kuno. 1868–
Amman, Jobst. 1539–1591.
Andri, Ferdinand. 1871–
Asam, Cosmas Damian. 1686–1739.
Asam, Egid Guirin. 1692–1750.
Bach, Johann Samuel. 1749–1778.
Backoffen, Hans. ?–1519.
Baldung, Hans. c. 1480–1545.
Baluschek, Hans. 1870–
Bandel, Ernst von. 1800–1876.
Bantzer, Karl. 1857–
Barlach, Ernst. 1870–
Bartels, Hans von. 1856–1913.
Baum, Paul. 1859–1932.
Baumeister, Willy. 1889–
Becker, Jacob. 1810–1872.
Beckman, Max. 1884–
Begas, Karl. 1794–1854.
Begas, Reinhold. 1831–1911.
Beham, Bartel. 1502–1540.
Beham, Hans Sebald. 1500–1550.
Belling, Rudolf. 1886–
Bendemen, Eduard. 1811–1889.
Berg, Claus. XVI century.
Blau-Lang, Tina. 1845–1916.
Blechen, Karl. 1798–1840.
Bochmann, Gregor von. 1850–
Böcklin, Arnold. 1827–1901.
Boehle, Fritz. 1873–1916.
Breu, Jörg. 1480–1537.
Bruyn, Bartholomäus. 1493–1555.
Bucher, Franz. 1836–1890.
Buckholz, Karl. 1849–1889.
Burger, Anton. 1824–1905.
Burgkmair, Hans. 1473–1531.
Buri, Max Alfred. 1868–1925.
Bürkel, Heinrich. 1802–1869.
Burnitz, Karl Peter. 1824–1886.
Campendonk, Heinrich. 1889–
Candid, Peter. c. 1548–1628.
Canon, Hans. 1829–1885.
Carstens, Asmus. 1754–1798.
Carus, Carl Gustav. 1789–1869.

Caspar-Filser, Maria. 1878–
Chodowiecki, Daniel Nikolaus. 1726–1801.
Corinth, Joseph Louis. 1858–1925.
Cornelius, Peter von. 1783–1867.
Cranach, Hans. ?–1537.
Cranach, Lucas (the Elder). 1472–1553.
Dahl, Johann Christian. 1788–1857.
Danhauser, Josef. 1805–1845.
Dannecker, Johann Heinrich von. 1758–1841.
Daucher, Adolf. 1460/65–1523.
Daucher, Hans. 1485–1538.
Defregger, Franz von. 1835–1921.
Denner, Balthasar. 1685–1749.
Dettmann, Ludwig. 1865–
Deutsch, Nikolaus Manuel. 1484–1530.
Dietrich, Christian Wilhelm Ernst. 1712–1774.
Diez, Robert. 1844–1922.
Diez, Wilhelm von. 1839–1907.
Dill, Ludwig. 1848–
Dillis, Georg Johann. 1759–1841.
Dix, Otto. 1891–
Donner, Georg Raphael. 1693–1741.
Douvermann, Heinrich. ?–c. 1544.
Dreber, Heinrich. 1822–1875.
Dreyer, Benedikt. ?–1555.
Dufresnes, Rudolf. 1846–1916.
Dürer, Albrecht. 1471–1528.
Eberz, Josef. 1880–
Edlinger, Joseph Georg von. 1741–1819.
Egell, Paul. 1691–1752.
Egger-Lienz, Albin. 1868–1926.
Eichhorst, Franz. 1885–
Elkan, Benno. 1877–
Elsheimer, Adam. 1578–1610.
Ende, Hans am. 1864–
Engert, Erasmus. 1796–1871.
Erbslöh, Adolf. 1881–
Erhart, Gregor. ?–c. 1540.
Erler, Fritz. 1868–
Ermels, Johann Franciscus. 1641–1693.
Ernst, Max. 1891–
Eysen, Louis. 1843–1899.
Feichtmayer, Johann Michael. 1709–1772.
Feininger, Lyonel. 1871–
Felixmüller, Konrad. 1898–
Feselen, Melchior. ?–1538.
Feuerbach, Anselm. 1829–1880.
Fischer, Martin. 1741–1820.
Flötner, Peter. c. 1485–1546.
Fohr, Carl Philipp. 1795–1818.
Friedrich, Kaspar David. 1774–1840.
Fries, Ernst. 1801–1833.
Fries, Hans. c. 1465–c. 1520.
Fritsch, Ernst. XX century.
Frölich, Lorens. 1820–1908.
Füger, Friedrich H. 1751–1818.
Führich, Joseph Ritter von. 1800–1876.
Furtmeyer, Berthold. ?–c. 1501.
Füssli, Johann. 1741–1825.
Gabriel, Max. 1840–1915.
Gaertner, Eduard. 1801–1877.
Gaul, August. 1869–1921.
Gawell, Oskar. XX century.
Gebhart, Eduard von. 1838–1925.
Geiger, Willi. XX century.

Genelli, Bonaventura. 1798–1868.
Gensler, Gunther. 1808–1845.
Gensler, Jakob. 1803–1884.
Gerhard, Hubert. 1540/50–1620.
Gessner, Salomon. 1730–1788.
Gille, Christian Friedrich. 1805–1899.
Graff, Anton. 1736–1813.
Grassi, Josef. c. 1758–1838.
Gröninger, Gerhard. 1582–c. 1652.
Gröninger, Johann Mauritz. ?–1707.
Gröninger, Johann W. 1675/77–1732.
Grossman, Rudolf. 1882–
Grosz, Georg. 1893–
Grund, Norbert. 1717–1767.
Grünewald, Matthias. 1470/82–c. 1530.
Guggenbichler, Johann Meinrad. 1649–1723.
Gültlinger, Johannes Gumpolt. c. 1460–1522.
Günther, Ignatz. 1725–1775.
Günther, Joachim Johann. 1717–1789.
Gurlitt, Louis. 1812–1897.
Habermann, Hugo von. 1849–1929.
Hackert, Philipp. 1737–1807.
Haider, Karl. 1846–1912.
Haller, Hermann. 1880–
Hanak, Anton. 1875–
Hasenclever, Johann Peter. 1810–1853.
Heckel, Erich. 1883–
Hees, Peter von. 1709–1782.
Heinz, Josef. 1564–1609.
Herbig, Otto. 1889–
Hering, Loy. c. 1485–c. 1554.
Hermann, Curt. 1854–1929.
Herrlein, Johann Andreas. 1720–1796.
Herterich, Ludwig von. 1856–
Hess, Heinrich Maria von. 1798–1863.
Hetsch, Philipp Friedrich von. 1758–1838.
Hildebrandt, Theodor. 1804–1874.
Hirschvogel, Augustin. 1503–1553.
Hodler, Ferdinand. 1853–1918.
Hofer, Karl. 1878–
Hoffmann, Ludwig von. 1861–
Holbein, Hans (the Elder). 1460–1524.
Holbein, Hans (the Younger). 1497/98–1543.
Hölzel, Adolf. 1853–
Hosemann, Theodor. 1807–1875.
Huber, Ernst. 1895–
Huber, Wolfgang. 1490–1553.
Hübner, Ulrich. 1872–
Hummel, Johann Erdmann. 1769–1852.
Issel, Georg Wilhelm. 1785–1870.
Jamnitzer, Wenzel. 1568–1585.
Jank, Angelo. 1868–
Janssen, Viktor Emil. 1807–1845.
Jensen, F. M. XX century.
Jettel, Eugen. 1845–1901.
Jordan, Rudolf. 1810–1887.
Juncker, Johann. 1582–c. 1625.
Juncker, Justus. 1703–1767.
Juppe, Ludwig. c. 1465–?
Kalckreuth, Leopold von. 1855–1928.
Kallmorgen, Friedrich. 1856–1924.
Kanoldt, Alexander. 1881–
Kapup, Christoph. XVI–XVII centuries.
Kauffmann, Angelica. 1741–1807.
Kaulbach, Wilhelm von. 1805–1874.

Keller, Albert von. 1844–1920.
Kern, Leonhard. 1585/88–1662.
Kern, Michael. 1580–1649.
Kersting, Georg Friedrich. 1785–1847.
Kirchner, Ernst Ludwig. 1880–
Klee, Paul. 1879–
Klein, Johann Adam. 1792–1875.
Klimt, Gustav. 1862–1918.
Klinger, Max. 1857–1920.
Knaus, Ludwig. 1829–1910.
Kobell, Wilhelm von. 1766–1855.
Koch, Joseph Anton. 1768–1839.
Koetger, Bernard. 1874–
Kokoschka, Oskar. 1886–
Kolbe, Georg. 1877–
Kollwitz, Kathe. 1867–
König, Leo von. 1871–
Krafft, Adam. 1455/60–1508/9.
Krafft, Johann August. 1798–1829.
Kraus, Georg Melchior. 1737–1806.
Kriehuber, Josef. 1800–1876.
Krüger, Franz. 1797–1857.
Krumper, Hans. c. 1570–1634.
Kubin, Alfred. 1877–
Kuehl, Gotthardt. 1850–1915.
Kügelgen, Gerhard von. 1772–1820.
Kulmbach, Hans Suess von. c. 1480–1522.
Kunstmann, Ludwig. XX century.
Labenwolf, Pankias. 1492–1563.
Lang, Albert. 1847–
Lang, Georg. XX century.
Lederer, Jugo. 1871–
Lehmbruck, Wilhelm. 1881–1919.
Leinberger, Hans. ?–1530.
Leistikow, Walter. 1865–1908.
Lenbach, Franz von. 1836–1904.
Lessing, Karl Friedrich. 1808–1880.
Leutze, Emmanuel. 1816–1868.
Levy, Rudolf. 1875–
Liebl, Wilhelm Maria Hubertus. 1844–1900.
Lier, Adolf Heinrich. 1826–1882.
Lys, Johann. 1590/1600–1629.
Macke, August. 1887–1914.
Mackensen, Fritz. 1866–
Magnus, Eduard. 1799–1872.
Makart, Hans. 1840–1884.
Marc, Franz. 1880–1916.
Marées, Hans von. 1837–1887.
Martin, Oskar. XX century.
Maulbertsch, Franz Anton. 1724–1796.
Meit, Conrad. XVI century.
Mengs, Anton Raphael. 1728–1779.
Mense, Karl. 1886–
Menzel, Adolf. 1815–1905.
Merian, Matthäus. 1593–1650.
Messerschmidt, Franz Xaver. 1736–1783.
Messkirch, Meister von.
Metzner, Franz. 1870–1919.
Meyerheim, Eduard. 1808–1879.
Meyerheim, Paul Friedrich. 1842–1915.
Meyer-Marton, George. 1897–
Modersohn, Otto. 1865–
Modersohn-Becker, Paul. 1876–1907.
Moll, Carl. 1861–
Moll, Oskar. 1875–

Morgenstern, Andreas. XVI century.
Morgenstern, Christian Ernst Bernard. 1805–1867.
Müller, Otto. 1874–1930.
Müller, Victor. 1829–1871.
Munkassy, Mihaly von. 1844–1909.
Münstermann, Ludwig. 1570/80–1637/38.
Nahl, Johann August. 1752–1825.
Nauen, Heinrich. 1880–
Neureuther, Eugen Napoleon. 1806–1882.
Nolde, Emil. 1867–
Oeser, Adam Friedrich. 1717–1799.
Ohmacht, Landolin. 1760–1834.
Oldach, Julius. 1804–1830.
Olde, Hans. 1855–1917.
Olivier, Ferdinand. 1785–1841.
Oppenheimer, Max. XX century.
Orlik, Emil. 1870–1932.
Ostendorfer, Michael. c. 1490–1559.
Ovens, Jürgen. 1623–1678.
Overbeck, Friedrich. 1789–1869.
Pascin, Jules. 1885–1930.
Pechstein, Max. 1881–
Peerdt, Ernst Carl Friedrich. 1852–1932.
Pencz, Georg. c. 1500–1550.
Permoser, Balthasar. 1651–1732.
Pesne, Antoine. 1683–1757.
Pettenkofen, August Xaver Karl von. 1822–1889.
Pforr, Franz. 1788–1812.
Piglhein, Bruno. 1848–1894.
Piloty, Karl Theodor von. 1826–1886.
Pippel, Otto Eduard. XX century.
Pock, Tobias. XVII century.
Preller, Friedrich. 1804–1878.
Purrmann, Hans. 1880–
Quaglio, Domenico. 1786–1837.
Radziwill, Franz. 1895–
Raemisch, Waldemar. 1888–
Ramberg, Johann Heinrich. 1763–1840.
Rauch, Christian Daniel. 1777–1857.
Rauchmüller, Matthias. 1645–1686.
Reichel, Hans. 1570–1642.
Reinhart, Johann Christian. 1761–1847.
Rethel, Alfred. 1816–1859.
Richter, Adrian Ludwig. 1803–1884.
Riedinger, Johann Elias. 1698–1767.
Rietschel, Ernst Friedrich. 1804–1861.
Rohden, Johann Martin von. 1778–1868.
Rohlfs, Christian. 1849–
Roos, Johann Heinrich. 1631–1685.
Rottenhammer, Hans. 1564–1625.
Rottman, Carl. 1797–1850.
Rottmayr, Johann. 1654–1730.
Runge, Philipp Otto. 1777–1810.
Russ, Karl. 1779–1843.
Ruthart, Carl Andreas. 1630(?)–1703(?).
Ruths, Valentin Georg. 1825–1905.
Sandrart, Joachim von. 1606–1688.
Schachinger, Gabriel. 1850–1912.
Schadow, Friedrich Wilhelm von. 1788–1862.
Schadow, Johann Gottfried. 1764–1850.
Schaffner, Martin. 1480–1541.
Schaper, Fritz. 1841–1919.
Schäuffelein, Hans Leonhard. c. 1480–1539/40.

Scheits, Matthias. c. 1640–c. 1700.
Schick, Gottlieb. 1779–1812.
Schider, Fritz. 1846–1907.
Schindler, Emil Jakob. 1842–1892.
Schirmer, Johann Wilhelm. 1807–1863.
Schleich, Eduard. 1812–1874.
Schlemmer, Oskar. 1888–
Schlichter, Rudolf. 1890–
Schlüter, Andreas. 1664–1714.
Schmidt-Rotluff, Karl. 1881–
Schmitson, Tentwart. 1830–1863.
Schmitt, Georg Philipp. 1808–1873.
Schmitt-Reutte, Ludwig. 1863–1909.
Schnorr von Karolsfeld, Julius. 1794–1872.
Scholderer, Otto. 1834–1902.
Schön, Otto. 1893–
Schönfeldt, Johann. 1609–c. 1675.
Schrimpf, Georg. 1889–
Schröder, Heinrich. XX century.
Schroedter, Adolf. 1805–1875.
Schück, Karl. 1846–1903.
Schültz, Daniel. c. 1620–1686.
Schütz, Georg. 1718–1791.
Schwanthaler, Ludwig. 1802–1848.
Schwarz, Christoph. 1550–1597.
Schwind, Moritz von. 1804–1871.
Schwitters, Kurt. 1887–
Seekatz, Konrad. 1719–1768.
Seewad, Richard. 1889–
Seibels, Karl. 1844–1877.
Skarbina, Franz. 1849–1910.
Slevogt, Max. 1868–1932.
Solis, Virgil. 1514–1562.
Sonnenschein, Johann Valentin. 1749–1816.
Speckter, Erwin. 1808–1835.
Speckter, Hans. 1848–1888.
Sperl, Johann. 1840–
Spilnberger, Johann. 1628–1679.
Spitzweg, Karl. 1808–1885.
Spranger, Bartholomäus. 1546–1611(?).
Stammel, Joseph Thaddäus. c. 1700–1765.
Stauffer-Bern, Karl. 1857–1891.
Steffeck, Karl. 1818–1890.
Steinle, Eduard von. 1810–1886.
Steppes, Edmund. 1873–
Stimmer, Tobias. 1539–1584/87.
Strack, Ludwig Philipp. 1761–1836.
Strassgschwandtner, Antonin. 1826–1881.
Straub, Johann Baptist. 1704–c. 1785.
Strigel, Bernhard. 1461–1528.
Stuck, Franz. 1863–1928.
Stügel, Bernhard. 1461–1528.
Szinyei-Merse, Pal. 1845–
Tassaert, Jan Pieter Anthoon. 1729–1788.
Ternite, Wilhelm. 1786–1871.
Thoma, Hans. 1839–1924.
Tilgner, Victor. 1844–1896.
Tischbein, Johann Friedrich August. 1750–1812.
Tischbein, Johann H. 1722–1789.
Tischbein, Johann Heinrich Wilhelm. 1751–1829.
Tischler, Victor. 1890–
Trant, Wolf. ?–1520.
Trauttman, Johann Georg. 1713–1769.
Trippel, Alexander. 1744–1793.
Trübner, Wilhelm. 1851–1917.

Trumm, Peter.   XX century.
Ubbelohde, Otto.   1867–1922.
Uhde, Fritz von.   1848–1911.
Unold, Max.   XX century.
Urlaub, Georg Karl.   1749–1809.
Ury, Lesser.   1862–1931.
Vautier, Benjamin.   1829–1898.
Veit, Philipp.   1793–1877.
Vischer, Hans.   1488–1550.
Vischer, Hermann.   ?–1516.
Vischer, Paul.   XVI century.
Vischer, Peter (the Elder).   c. 1460–1529.
Vischer, Peter (the Younger).   1487–1528.
Vogel, Christian Leberecht.   1759–1816.
Vogel, Hugo.   1855–
Vogeler, Heinrich.   1872–
Vries, Adrian de.   1560–1627(?).
Wächter, Eberhard.   1762–1852.
Wagenbauer, Max.   1774–1829.
Wagmüller, Michael.   1839–1881.
Wagner, Johann.   1730–1809.
Wagner, Johann Martin.   1777–1858.

Waldmann, Kaspar.   ?–1720.
Waldmüller, Ferdinand Georg.   1793–1865.
Wassmann, Rudolf Friedrich.   1805–1865.
Weba, Georg.   1872–
Weissgerber, Albert.   1878–1915.
Weisz, Josef.   XX century.
Werner, Joseph.   1637–1710.
Weyer, Johann Mathias.   c. 1620–c. 1690.
Wild, Hans.   XV century.
Winterhalter, Franz X.   1806–1873.
Wolff, Elbert.   ?–1609.
Wurzelbauer, Benedikt.   1548–1620.
Zauner, Franz.   1746–1822.
Zerbe, Karl.   XX century.
Zick, Januarius.   1732–1797.
Ziesenis, Johann Georg.   1716–1777.
Zimmerman, Johann B.   c. 1680–1758.
Zingg, Adrian.   1734–1816.
Zügel, Heinrich von.   1850–
Zumbusch, Kaspar von.   1830–1915.
Zürn, Jörg.   XVII century.
Zustris, Frederick.   1524–1591.

THE NETHERLANDS

SOURCES

Baldass, L.   *Joos van Cleve.*   Wien, 1925.
Bode, Wilhelm van.   *Die Meister der holländischen und vlämischen Malerschulen.*   Leipzig, 1921.
——— *Adriaen Brouwer.*   Berlin, 1924.
Buchwald, C.   *Adriaen de Vries.*   Leipzig, 1899.
Destrée, Jos.   *Hugo van der Goes.*   Bruxelles and Paris, 1914.
Durrieu, Paul.   *La miniature Flamande.*   Bruxelles and Paris, 1921.
Friedländer, Max J.   *Die altniederländische Malerei*, 12 vols.   Berlin, 1924–1935.
——— *Von Eyck bis Bruegel.*   Berlin, 1916.
Hejmans, O.   *Die belgische Malerei im XIX Jahrhundert.*   Leipzig, 1906.
Kaemmerer, L.   *Memling.*   Leipzig, 1899.
Knackfuss, H.   *Franz Hals.*   Leipzig, 1903.
Lafond, P.   *Roger van der Weyden.*   Bruxelles and Paris, 1912.
Lamborte, Paul and H. Grimsditch.   *Flemish Painting.*   London, 1927.
Legard, A.   *Jean Gossart dit Mabuse.*   Bruxelles and Paris, 1914.
Lemonnier, C.   *L'école belge de peinture.*   Bruxelles, 1906.
Marius, G.   *Die holländische Malerei im XIX Jahrhundert.*   Berlin, 1906.
Moes, E. W.   *Frans Hals. Sa vie et son œuvre.*   Bruxelles, 1909.
Muther, R.   *Die belgische Malerei.*   Berlin, 1903.
Oldenbourg, Rudolf.   *P. P. Rubens.*   München and Berlin, 1922.
Posse, H.   *Die Gemäldegalerie des Kaiser Friedrich Museum.*   Berlin, 1911.
Reiffenberg, B. and W. Hansenstein.   *Vermeer van Delft.*   München, 1924.
Roh, Franz.   *Holländische Malerei (Die Kunst in Bildern).*   Jena, 1921.

Rosenberg, A.   *P. P. Rubens. Des Meisters Gemälde.*   Stuttgart and Leipzig, 1911.
——— *Teniers der Jüngere.*   Leipzig, 1903.
——— *Terborch und Jan Steen.*   Leipzig, 1897.
Rosenberg, H.   *Adriaen und Isack van Ostade.*   Leipzig, 1900.
Schäffer. E.   *Van Dyck. Des Meisters Gemälde.*   Stuttgart and Leipzig, 1909.
Valentiner, W. K.   *Pieter de Hooch. Des Meisters Gemälde.*   Berlin and Leipzig, 1929.
Willigen, A. van der.   *Les artistes de Harlem.*   Harlem, 1870.
Winkler, Friedrich.   *Die altniederländische Malerei (von 1400–1600).*   Berlin, 1924.
——— *Der Meister von Flémalle und Rogier van der Weyden.*   Strassburg, 1913.

Catalogues of art museums.   Other works cited in the text.

ARTISTS

Aertsen, Pieter.   1508–1575.
Amstel, Jan van.   c. 1500–c. 1540.
Apol, Louis.   1850–
Artan de Saint Marten, Louis.   1837–1890.
Artz, David Adolf Constant.   1837–1890.
Asselijn, Jan.   c. 1610–1652.
Avercamp, Hendrick.   1585–c. 1663.
Backer, Jakob Adriaenz.   1608/9–1651.
Baron, Théodore.   1840–1899.
Bastert, Nicolas.   1854–
Bauer, Marius Alexander Jacques.   1862–
Berchen, Claes Pietersz.   1620–1683.
Berckheyde, Gerrit Adriaensz.   1638–1698.
Berckheyde, Job Adriaensz.   1630–1693.
Beyeren, Abraham Hendricksz van.   1620–1675.
Bisschop, Christoffel.   1828–1904.
Bloemart, Abraham.   1564–1651.

Blommers, Bernard Johannes. 1845–1914.
Bock, Achille de. 1854–1904.
Bol, Ferdinand. 1616–1680.
Bosboom, Johannes. 1817–1891.
Bosch, Hieronymus. c. 1460–1516.
Both, Jan Dirchaz. 1610–1652.
Boulenger, Hippolyte. 1838–1874.
Boursse, Esaias. 1631–1672.
Bouts, Alfred. c. 1455–1548.
Bouts, Dierick. ?–1475.
Braekeller, Henri. 1830–1888.
Bray, Jan de. ?–1697.
Breitner, Georges. 1857–
Breughel, Jan 1568–1625.
Breughel, Pieter. 1525–1569.
Bril, Paul. 1554–1626.
Brouwer, Adriaan. c. 1606–1638.
Buékelaer, Joachim. 1533–1573.
Caisne, Henri de. 1799–1852.
Campin, Robert. c. 1375–1444.
Capelle, Jan van de. c. 1624–1679.
Caristus, Petrus. XV century.
Claesz, Pieter. c. 1600–1661.
Claus, Emil. 1849–1924.
Cleve, Joos van. XVI century.
Codde, Pieter Jacobs. c. 1600–1678.
Coques, Gonzales. c. 1618–1684.
Cornelissen von Harlem, Cornelis. 1562–1638.
Cornelisz,ꞌJacob = Jacob van Amsterdam. XV–
  XVI centuries.
Coter, Colijn de. XV century.
Craesbeeck, Joos van. 1606–c. 1654.
Crayer, Jasper de. 1584–1669.
Cuyp, Aelbert. 1620–1691.
Cuyp, Jacob Gerritsz. 1594–c. 1651.
David, Gerard. c. 1450–1523.
Dillens, Adolf Alexander. 1821–1877.
Dou, Gerard. 1613–1675.
Dubois, Louis. 1830–1880.
Duchatel, François. 1625–1694.
Dujardin, Karel. c. 1622–1678.
Dusart, Cornelis. 1660–1704.
Duyster, Willem Cornelisz. 1600–1635.
Dyck, Antoon van. 1599–1641.
Eeckhout, Gebrand van den. 1621–1674.
Elias, Nicolaes = Nicolaes Eliasz Pickenoy.
  1590–1658.
Engelbertz, Cornelis = Engelbrechten. 1468–
  1533.
Evenepoel, Henri Jacques Edouard. 1872–1899.
Everdingen, Allart van. 1621–1675.
Eyck, Hubert van. c. 1366–1426.
Eyck, Jan van. 1386–1441.
Fabritius, Bernard. XVII century.
Fabritius, Carel. c. 1620–1654.
Flinck, Govaert. 1615–1660.
Floris, Frans de Vriendt. c. 1516–1570.
Fourmois, Theodore. 1814–1871.
Francken, Frans. 1581–1643.
Fréderic, Léon. 1856–
Fyt, Jan. 1611–1661.
Gallait, Louis. 1810–1887.
Geertgen van Sint Jans = Gerard van Haarlem.
  c. 1465–1493.
Gelder, Aart de. 1645–1727.

Gent, Joos van = Joos van Wassenhoven. XV
  century.
Goes, Hugo van der. 1435–1482.
Gogh, Vincent van. 1853–1890.
Gossart, Jan. c. 1472–c. 1533.
Goyen, Jan Josefsz van. 1596–1656.
Graat, Barent. 1628–1709.
Groux, Charles de. 1825–1870.
Haas, Johannes Hubertus de. 1832–1880.
Hackaert, Jan. 1629–c. 1699.
Hals, Dirk. 1591–1656.
Hals, Frans. c. 1580–c. 1666.
Haverman, Hendrick Johann. 1859–
Heem, Jan Davidz de. 1606–1683/84.
Heemskerk, Marten Jacobsz van. 1498–1574.
Helst, Bartholomeus van der. c. 1612–1670.
Hemessen, Jan. 1506–1566
Henkes, Gerke. 1844–
Hermans, Charles. 1839–
Heyden, Jan van der. 1637–1712.
Heymans, Adrien Joseph. 1839–1921.
Hobbema, Meindert. 1638–1709.
Hondecoeter, Melchior d'. 1636–1695.
Honthorst, Gerrit van. 1590–1656.
Hoogh, Pieter de. 1629–c. 1677.
Houckgeest, Gerard. c. 1600–?
Jacobz, Dirck. c. 1500–1567.
Joost, Jan. ?–c. 1519.
Jordaens, Jacob. 1593–1678.
Kalf, Willem. 1622–1693.
Ketel, Cornelis. 1548–1616.
Key, Willem. c. 1515–1568.
Keyser, Nicaise de. 1813–1887.
Keyser, Thomas de. 1596/97–1667.
Khnopff, Fernand. 1858–1921.
Klinkenberg, Johannes Karel. 1852–1924.
Koninck, Philips de. 1619–1688.
Kraels, Josef. 1824–
Laermans, Eugene. 1864–
Lastman, Pieter Pietersz. 1583–1633.
Leyden, Lukas van. 1494–1533.
Leys, Jan August Henri. 1815–1869.
Madou, Jean Baptiste. 1796–1877.
Maes, Nicolas. 1632–1693.
Maris, Jakobus Hendricus. 1837–1899.
Maris, Willem. 1844–1910.
Massys, Quentin. c. 1466–1530.
Mathieu, Paul. 1872–1932.
Mauve, Anton. 1838–1888.
Memlinc, Hans. 1433/35–1494.
Mennier, Constantin. 1831–1905.
Mennuijs, Albert. 1844–
Mesdag, Hendrik Willem. 1831–1915.
Metsu, Gabriel. c. 1630–1667.
Meyer, Hendrik de (the Elder). c. 1620–c. 1690.
Mieris, Franz van (the Elder). 1635–1681.
Millet, Jean Francis. 1642–1679.
Mirevelt, Michiel Janszoon van. 1567–1641.
Moeyaert, Claesz Cornelisz. c. 1600–c. 1669.
Molenaer, Jan Mienze. c. 1605–1668.
Moreelse, Paulus. 1571–1638.
Moro, Antonis. c. 1512–1575.
Mosscher, Jacob van. c. 1590–1650.
Moyaert, Nicolaes. 1592–1655.
Mytens, Daniel Martensz. c. 1590–c. 1660.

Navez, François Joseph. 1787–1869.
Neer, Aart van der. 1603–1677.
Netscher, Caspar. 1639–1684.
Nitenbroeck, Moses van. 1590–1648.
Oleffe, Gustav. 1867–1932.
Orley, Bernard d'. 1493–1542.
Ostade, Adriaen van. 1610–1685.
Ostade, Isaack van. 1621–1649.
Patinir, Joachim. c. 1485–1524.
Poelenburgh, Cornelis. c. 1586–1667.
Porcellis, Jan. 1585–1632.
Post, Frans Jansz. 1612–1680.
Pot, Hendrick Gerritsz. 1585–1657.
Potter, Paulus. 1625–1654.
Pourbus, Frans. 1545–1581.
Provost, Jean. 1462–1529.
Pynacker, Adam. 1622–1673.
Ravestijn, Antonisz van. 1572–1657.
Rembrandt van Ryn. 1606–1669.
Roemerswaelen, Marinus van. c. 1497–c. 1567.
Rops, Felicien. 1833–1898.
Rubens, Peter Paul. 1577–1640.
Ruisdael, Jacob Izaakszoon. c. 1625–1682.
Ruysdael, Saloman van. 1600–1670.
Saenredam, Pieter Jansz. 1597–1665.
Saft-leven, Herman. c. 1608–1685.
Sande-Backhuyzen, Julius van den. 1835–
Santvoort, Dirck van. 1610–1680.
Schalcken, Godfried. 1643–1706.
Schut, Cornelis. 1597–1655.
Scoreel, Jan. 1495–1562.
Seghers, Hercules Pietersz. c. 1590–c. 1640.
Siberechts, Jan. 1627–1703.
Slingeland, Pieter Cornelisz van. 1640–1691.
Slingeneyer, Ernest. c. 1820–1894.
Smits, Jakob. 1855–1928.
Snyders, Frans. 1579–1657.
Steen, Jan Havicksz. 1626–1679.

Stevens, Alfred. 1828–1906.
Stevens, Joseph. 1822–1892.
Stobbaerts, Jean Baptiste. 1838–1914.
Teniers, David (the Elder). 1582–1649.
Teniers, David (the Younger). 1610–1690.
Ter Borch, Gerard. 1617–1681.
Ter Brugghen, Henrick. 1588–1629.
Termeulen, François Pieter. 1843–
Tholen, William Bastian. 1860–1931.
Toorop, Jan Theodoor. 1859–1928.
Uytewael, Joachim Antonisz. 1566–1638.
Valckert, Werner van den. c. 1580–1630.
Valkenborch, Lukas van. c. 1540–1625(?).
Veen, Otto van. 1556–1629.
Velde, Adriaen van der. c. 1635–1672.
Velde, Esaias van de. c. 1590–1630.
Velde, Willem van de (the Elder). c. 1611–1693.
Velde, Willem van de (the Younger). 1633–1707.
Venne, Adriaen Pietersz van de. 1589–1662.
Vermeer van Delft, Jan. 1632–1675.
Verspronck, Johannes Cornelisz. 1597–1662.
Verwee, Alfred. 1838–1895.
Veth, Jan Pieter. 1864–1925.
Victors, Johannes. 1620–1676.
Vlieger, Simon Jacobsz de. 1600–1653.
Vos, Cornelis de. c. 1585–1651.
Vos, Marten de. 1532–1603.
Vries, Paul Vredeman de. 1567–1604.
Wappers, Gustav. 1838–1874.
Wauters, Emil Charles. 1846–1933.
Wauters, R. 1882–1916.
Weenix, Jan Baptist. 1621–1660.
Wiertz, Antoine Joseph. 1806–1865.
Wildens, Jan. 1586–1653.
Witte, Emanuel de. 1618–1692.
Wouwerman, Philips. 1619–1668.
Wynants, Jan. c. 1620–1682.

ENGLAND

SOURCES

Borenius, T. and E. W. Tristram, *Englische Malerei des Mittelalters.* Firenze and München, 1927.
Millar, E. *La miniature anglaise du Xe au XIIIe siècle.* Paris and Bruxelles, 1926.
Muther, R. *Geschichte der Malerei*, Vol. III. Leipzig, 1909.
—— *Geschichte der englischen Malerei.* Berlin, 1902.
Pauli, G. *Die Kunst des Klassizismus und der Romantik.* Berlin, 1925.
Rilke, R. M. *Worpswede.* Leipzig, 1905.
Saunders, O. Elfrida. *Englische Buchmalerei*, 2 vols. Firenze and München, 1928.
Schleinitz, O. von. *Walter Crane.* Leipzig, 1902.
—— *Burne Jones.* Leipzig, 1901.
—— *William Holman Hunt.* Leipzig, 1907.
Sizeranne, Robert de la. *La Peinture contemporaine.* Paris, 1895.

Catalogues of art museums. Art journals. Other works cited in the text.

ARTISTS

Alma-Tadema, Sir Lawrence. 1836–1912.
Beechey, Sir William. 1753–1839.
Blake, William. 1757–1827.
Brangwyn, Frank W. 1867–
Brown, Ford Madox. 1821–1893.
Burne-Jones, Sir Edward C. B. 1833–1898.
Collins, William. 1787–1847.
Constable, John. 1776–1837.
Crane, Walter. 1845–1915.
Crome, John. 1769–1821.
Devon, William de. XIII century.
Dicksee, Frank. 1853–
Dyce, William. 1806–1864.
Faed, Thomas. 1826–1900.
Flaxman, John. 1755–1826.
Frith, William. 1819–1909.
Füssli, Johann Heinrich. 1741–1825.

Gainsborough, Thomas. 1727–1788.
Greiffenhagen, Maurice William. 1862–1932.
Herkomer, Hubert. 1849–1914.
Hogarth, William. 1697–1764.
Holman-Hunt, William. 1827–1910.
Hoppner, John. 1758–1810.
Horsley, John. 1817–1903.
Johnson, Thomas. 1708–1767.
Landseer, Sir Edwin. 1802–1873.
Lawrence, Sir Thomas. 1769–1830.
Leighton, Lord Frederick. 1830–1896.
Leslie, Charles R. 1794–1859.
Maclise, Daniel. 1811–1870.
Millais, Sir John Everett. 1829–1896.
Moore, Albert. 1841–1893.
Morland, George. 1763–1804.
Mulready, William. 1786–1863.
Opie, John. 1761–1807.
Ouless, Walter W. 1848–

Paris, Matthew. XIII century.
Raeburn, Henry. 1756–1823.
Reynolds, Sir Joshua. 1723–1792.
Richmond, George. 1809–1896.
Romney, George. 1734–1802.
Rossetti, Dante Gabriel. 1828–1882.
Sandys, Anthony Frederick. 1829–1904.
Shannon, James Jegusha. 1862–1923.
Shaw, Byam. 1872–1919.
Solomon, Soloman Joseph. 1860–1927.
Stanhope, J. R. Spencer. 1829–1908.
Strudwick, John. 1848–
Turner, Joseph William. 1775–1851.
Walker, Frederick. 1840–1875.
Ward, James. 1769–1859.
Watts, George Frederick. 1817–1904.
Webster, Thomas. 1800–1886.
Wilkie, David. 1785–1841.
Wilson, Richard. 1714–1782.

SPAIN

SOURCES

Gensel, W. *Velasquez. Des Meisters Gemälde.*
Leipzig, 1908.
Justi, C. *Diego Velasquez*, 2 vols. Bonn, 1922.
Kehrer, H. *Francisco de Zurbarán.* München,
1918.
Knackfuss, H. *Velasquez.* Leipzig, 1905.
—— *Murillo.* Leipzig, 1904.
Loga, Valerian von. *Francisco de Goya.* Berlin,
1903.
Mayer, August L. *Murillo. Des Meisters Ge-
mälde.* Leipzig, 1913.
—— *Die Sevillaner Malerschule.* Leipzig, 1911.
Muther, R. *Geschichte der Malerei*, Vols. II and
III. Leipzig, 1909.
Weisbach, W. *Die Kunst des Barock.* Berlin,
1924.

Catalogues of art museums. Other works cited
in the text.

ARTISTS

Alejo, Vera. XX century.
Anglad-Camarasa, Hermangildo. 1873–
Antolinez, José. 1639–1676.
Becerra, Gaspar. 1520–1570.
Cano, Alonzo. 1601–1667.
Carbonero, José Moreno. 1860–
Carducho, Vicente. 1578–1638.
Casado del Alisal, Don José. 1832–1886.
Castillo, Juan del. 1584–1640.
Cerezo, Matteo. 1635–1685.
Cespedes, Pablo de. 1538–1608.
Churriguerra, José. 1650–1723.
Coella, Alonzo Sanchez. 1531/32–1588.
Coello, Claudio. 1630/35–1692.
Cruz, Juan Pantoja de la. 1551–1608.

Fernandez, Alxo. 1470–1543.
Fernandez, Gregorio. 1576–1635.
Fernandez de Navarrete, Juan. *c.* 1526–1579.
Fortuny y Carbo, Mariano. 1838–1874.
Goya y Lucientes, Francisco José de. 1746–1828.
Guadalupe, Pedro de. *c.* 1470–*c.* 1531.
Herrera, Francisco (the Elder). 1588–1652.
Herrera, Francisco (the Younger). 1622–1685.
Hispalense, Juan. 1440–?
Juni, Juan de. ?–1577.
Legote, Pablo. *c.* 1590–*c.* 1670/72.
Llanos y Valdez, Sebastiano. ?–1668.
Maçip, Vicente Juanes. 1523–1579.
Mayorga, Cristobal de. ?–1533.
Mazo, Juan Battista del. 1612–1667.
Montañez, Juan Martinez. 1568–1649.
Mor, Antonis. 1519–1575.
Morales, Luis de. 1509–1586.
Nunez, Juan. 1480–1530.
Pacecho, Francesco. 1564/71–1654.
Pereira, Vasco. *c.* 1535–1609.
Pareja, Juan de. 1606–1670.
Perez de Alesio, Matteo. 1547–*c.* 1600.
Pradilla y Ortiz, Francisco. 1848–1921.
Ribalta, Francisco. 1555(?)–1625.
Ribera, Jusèpe de. 1590–1652.
Rizi, Fray Juan. 1595–1675.
Ruela, Juan de. 1558/60–1625.
Sanchez de Castro, Juan. XV century.
Sanchez, Coello Alonzo. 1531/32–1588.
Sanchez, Pedro. XV century.
Theotocopuli, Domenico. 1545/48–1614.
Tomé, Narciso. XVIII century.
Tristan, Luis. 1586–1640.
Valdes-Leal, Don Juan. *c.* 1630–1691.
Vargas, Luis de. 1502–1568.
Villegas Marmole, Pedro. 1520–1597.
Zamora, Andrés de. ?–1554.
Zamora, Juan. XVII century.
Zuloaga y Zabaleta, Ignacio. 1870–
Zurbarąn, Francisco de. 1598–1662.

RUSSIA

SOURCES [1]

Ainalov, D. *Geschichte der russischen Monumentalkunst vormoskovitischen Zeit*, 2 vols. Berlin, 1932–1933.

Alpatov, M. and N. Brunov. *Geschichte der altrussischen Kunst.* Baden bei Wien, 1932.

Babenchikoff, M., E. Zamiatin, M. Kuzmin, and J. Annenkov. *Portraits.* 1922.

Bakushinski, A. *Paintings and Drawings of the XVIII and XIX Centuries in Tzvetkov's Gallery.* 1930.

Benois, A. N. *Russian Museum of Emperor Alexander III.* 1906.

——— *Russian School of Painting.* 1904.

Diagileff, S. P. *D. G. Levitski* (1735–1822). n. d.

Efros, A. *Portrait of Natan Altman.* 1922.

Efros, A. and N. Punin. *S. Tschekhonin.* 1924.

Ernst, S. *K. A. Somov.* 1918.

——— *I. E. Repin.* 1927.

Evdokimoff, I. *Province. Etchings of I. Pavlov.* 1925.

Fritsche, V. (ed.). *Russian Painting in the XIX Century.* 1929.

Ge, P. N. *The Main Currents of Russian Painting in the XIX Century.* 1898.

Georgievski, V. T. *Frescoes of Ferapont Monastery.* 1911.

Glagol, S. *M. V. Nesterov, Life and Work.* n. d.

——— *Konenkov.* 1920.

Glagol, S. and I. Grabar. *I. I. Levitan, Life and Work.* n. d.

Gollerbach, E. *Paintings of M. Dobujinski.* 1923.

——— *A History of Etching.* 1924.

——— *Portrait Painting in Russia in the XVIII Century.* 1923.

——— *A. Golovin, Life and Work.* 1928.

Grabar, I. *V. A. Seroff, Life and Work.* 1913.

——— *A History of Russian Art*, 6 vols. 1909.

——— *"Andrei Rubleff,"* in *Voprosy Restavratzii,* Vol. I. 1926.

Grabar, I. and F. Rokotov. *Exhibition of Portraits.* 1923.

Iaremitch, S. *M. A. Vrubel, Life and Work.* 1924.

Iavorskaia, N. V. *Silvester Tschedrin* (1791–1830). 1931.

Ivanov, A. P. *M. A. Vrubel.* 1928.

Jidkov, G. V. *Moscow Painting of the Middle of the XIV Century.* 1929.

Kondakov, N. P. *Russian Ikon*, 4 vols. 1928–1933.

Kovalenskaia, N. *V. A. Tropinin.* 1930.

Kusmin, M. and V. Voinov. *D. Mitrokhin.* 1928.

Kusmitski, N. *A. Ageev.* 1923.

Kusnetzoff, P. *Turkestan.* 1923.

Likhatcheff, N. P. *Materials for History of Russian Ikon Painting.* 1905.

Muratov, P. *Painting of Konchalovski.* 1924.

Muratov, P. and B. Griftzoff. *N. P. Ulianov.* 1925.

Nevedomski, M. and I. Repin. *A. I. Kuindji.* 1913.

Nikolski, V. A. *A History of Russian Art.* 1923.

Pervukhin, N. *The Church of Bogoiavlenia in Iaroslavl.* 1916.

——— *The Church of Elias in Iaroslavl,* 1915.

Pokrovski, N. P. *Church Archeology in Its Relationship to the History of Christian Art.* 1916.

Polovtzeff, A. *F. A. Bruni.* 1907.

Punin, N. *V. V. Lebedeff.* 1928.

Radlov, N. *From Repin to Grigorieff.* 1923.

Réau, L. *L'art russe*, 2 vols. Paris, 1922.

Riazanovski, V. A. *A Study of Ancient Russian Painting.* 1934.

Rovinski, D. *A Survey of Ikon Painting in Russia.* 1903.

Schweinfurt, T. *Geschichte der Russischen Malerei im Mittelalters.* Haag, 1930.

Sobko, N. P. *Dictionary of Russian Painters.* 1893.

Tschepkin, V. N. *"Novgorod School of Painting,"* in *Trudy XI Archeologicheskago, Siezda,* Vol. II. 1902.

Uspenski, A. I. *Studies in History of Russian Art.* 1910.

——— *V. M. Vasnetzoff.* 1906.

Voinoff, V. *B. Kustodieff.* 1926.

——— *V. D. Polenoff.* 1930.

Wrangel, N. N. *O. Kiprenski.* n. d.

——— *A. G. Venezianoff.* n. d.

Wulff, O. *Die neurussische Kunst.* Augsburg, 1932.

Zamiatin, E. *Russia. Russian Types of B. Kustodieff.* 1923.

Art journals: *Apollon, Jar-Ptitza, Mir Iskusstva, Russkoie Iskustvo, Sofia, Zlatozvet, Zolotoie Runo.* A series of special publications like: *U Istokov Russkoi Jivopisi,* 1925; and others. Catalogues and publications of Russian museums.

[1] With the exception of the works given in French and German, all other works are in Russian. The bibliography gives English translation of the Russian titles of the works. Place of publication is either Moscow or St. Petersburg (Leningrad).

ARTISTS

Agin, A. A.   1816–1875.
Aivasovski, I. K.   1817–1900.
Akimoff, I.   XVIII century.
Alexandroff, I. P.   1781–1822.
Alexandroff, P. A.   XIX–XX centuries.
Alexandrova, E. V.   XX century.
Alexeeff, A.   XX century.
Alexeeff, F.   1753–1824.
Altman, N.   XX century.
Ammon, V. F.   XX century.
Amosoff, S. N.   XX century.
Anisfeld, B.   XX century.
Annenkov, G.   XX century.

Antokolski, M. M.   1843–1902.
Antropoff, A. P.   1716–1795.
Arapoff, A. A.   XX century.
Argunoff, I. P.   1727–1797.
Argunoff, N. I.   1771–1829.
Arkhipenko, A.   XX century.
Arkhipoff, A. E.   1862–?
Aronson, N.   XX century.
Averkieff, P.   XVII century.
Bakalovitch, S. V.   1857–?
Bakanoff, I. M.   XIX–XX centuries.
Baksheef, V. N.   XX century.
Bakst, L.   XX Century.
Basin, P. V.   1793–1877.
Beklemisheff, V. A.   1861–?
Belski, A. I.   1730–1796.
Benois, A. A.   XX century.
Benois, A. N.   XX century.
Benois, N. A.   XX century.
Benois, N. L.   XX century.
Bernadski, E.   XX century.
Bilibin, I.   XX century.
Bogaievski, K.   XX century.
Bogdanoff, I. P.   XIX–XX centuries.
Bogdanoff-Belski, N. P.   1868–?
Bogoliuboff, A. P.   1824–1896.
Bok, A. P.   1829–1895.
Borisoff-Musatoff, V. E.   XX century.
Borovikovski, V. L.   1758–1825.
Botkin, F.   XX century.
Braz, O.   1872–
Brodski, I.   XX century.
Brulloff, A. P.   1789–1877.
Brulloff, K. P.   1799–1852.
Bruni, F. A.   1800–1875.
Bruni, L. A.   XIX century.
Bugaievski-Blagodarny, I. V.   1783–1859.
Bunin, L.   XVII century.
Dionisius.   XVI century.
Dobujinski, M.   XX century.
Drojjin, P. S.   1745–1805.
Dubovskoi, N. N.   1859–?
Egoroff, A. E.   1776–1851.
Endokuroff, I. I.   1861–1898.
Ermeneeff, I.   XVIII century.
Ernsfeld.   XX century.
Esakoff, A. E.   1787–1815.
Falileeff, V.   XX century.
Falk, R.   XX century.
Fedotoff, P.   1816–1852.
Feshin, N. I.   1881–?
Flavitzki, K.   1830–1866.
Floroff, A.   XX century.
Gagarin, N. N.   1810–1893.
Galaktionoff, S. F.   1779–1854.
Galberg, S. I.   1787–1839.
Gattenberg, F. I.   ?–1820.
Ge, N. N.   1831–1894.
Gilferding, F.   XVIII century.
Ginzburg, I.   1859–?
Golovin, A.   XX century.
Goncharova, N.   XX century.
Grabar, I. E.   XX century.
Grigorieff, B.   XX century.
Groot, G. X.   1716–1749.

Grube, G.   XVIII century.
Gutenbroon, L.   XVIII century.
Iakoby, V. I.   1834–1902.
Iakovleff, A. E.   XX century.
Iakovleff, I. E.   1787–1843.
Iaroshenko, N. A.   1846–1898.
Iensen, D.   1816–?
Iordan, F.   1800–1883.
Istomin, V.   XVIII century.
Iuon, K.   XX century.
Ivanov, A.   1821–?
Ivanov, A. A.   1806–1858.
Ivanov, A. I.   1775–1848.
Ivanov, D. I.   1782–1818.
Ivanov, M.   XVIII century.
Ivanov, M. M.   1748–1823.
Ivanov, S. V.   1864–1910.
Jille, N.   1709–1793.
Joukovski, P. V.   XX century.
Joukovski, S.   1873–?
Joukovski, V. A.   XIX century.
Jouravleff, F. S.   1836–1901.
Kankov, I. S.   1816–1854.
Karavak, L.   ?–1754.
Kardovski, D. N.   1866–?
Kasakov, I. S.   1873–?
Kasatkin, N. A.   1859–?
Khristinek.   1762–1813.
Kiprenski, O. A.   1783–1836.
Kisseleff, A. A.   1838–?
Kivshenko, A. D.   1851–1895.
Klever, J.   XIX–XX centuries.
Klodt, M. K.   1832–1902.
Klodt, P. K.   1805–1867.
Koslov.   1738–1791.
Koslovski, M. I.   1753–1820.
Konchalovski, P.   XX century.
Konenkoff, S. T.   XX century.
Korovin, K. A.   1861–
Korsukhin, A. I.   1835–?
Kostenko, S. P.   1861–1898.
Kostromitin, P.   XVIII century.
Kotzebu, A.   1815–1889.
Kovalevski, P. O.   1843–1903.
Kovalski, L.   1870–?
Krachkovski, I.   1854–?
Kramskoi, I. N.   1837–1887.
Krichevski, F.   1879–?
Kryjitski, K.   1858–1911.
Kuindji, A. I.   1842–1910.
Kukharevski, A.   1804–1841.
Kurennoi, A.   1869–?
Kustodieff, B.   XX century.
Kuznetzoff, N.   1850–?
Kuznetzoff, P.   XX century.
Lagorio.   XX century.
Lagrene, L.   1724–1805.
Lampi, A.   1775–1837.
Lampi, N. B.   1751–1830.
Lanceré, E. A.   XX century.
Lanceré, E. E.   XX century.
Larionoff, M.   XX century.
Lebedeff, M. I.   1812–1837.
Lebedeff, V. V.   XX century.
Leman, J.   1834–1902.

Lemox, K. V.   1841-?
Lentuloff, A.   XX century.
Levitan, I.   1861-1900.
Levitski, D. G.   1735-1822.
Levitski, G. K.   XVIII century.
Liders, D.   1710-1759.
Lipshitz, I.   XX century.
Lisheff, V.   1877-?
Litovtschenko, A. D.   1835-1890.
Loganovski, P.   XX century.
Losenko, A. P.   1737-1773.
Lukomski, G. K.   XX century.
Makaroff, I. K.   1822-1897.
Makhaieff, M.   XVIII century.
Makovski, V. E.   1846-?
Maliavin, F.   1869-?
Markoff, M. T.   1802-1878.
Martos, I.   1754-1835.
Martynoff, A.   1768-1826.
Maté, V.   1856-1917.
Matveeff, A.   1701-1739.
Matveeff, F.   1758-1826.
Maximoff, V. M.   1844-?
Miagkoff, M.   1799-1852.
Miassoiedoff, G.   1835-1911.
Mikhailov, G.   1814-1867.
Miropolski, L.   XX century.
Mitrokhin, D.   XX century.
Narbut, G.   XX century.
Nasarieff, M.   XVII century.
Nesteroff, M.   1862-?
Nevreff, N.   1830-1904.
Nikitin, G.   XVII century.
Nikitin, I. M.   1690-1741.
Novoskoltzeff, A. H.   1853-?
Ober, A.   1843-?
Orlova, X.   XX century.
Orlovski, A.   1777-1832.
Orlovski, V.   1793-1837.
Ossipoff, A.   XX century.
Ostroumova-Lebedeva, A.   XX century.
Paissi.   XV century.
Pasternack, L.   1862-
Pavlov, C.   XVII century.
Pavlov, I.   XX century.
Pavlovetz, N.   XVII century.
Pelevin, G.   XX century.
Perepletchikoff, V.   XX century.
Peroff, V.   1833-1882.
Perro, I.   XX century.
Petrov, N.   XX century.
Petrov, V.   1770-1811.
Petrov-Vodkin.   XX century.
Pimenoff, N.   1812-1864.
Pimenoff, S.   1784-1833.
Pimonenko.   XX century.
Pnin, P.   XX century.
Polenoff, V.   1844-1927.
Poplavski, A.   XX century.
Prenner, G. K.   1720-1766.
Prianishnikoff, I.   1840-1894.
Prokoffieff, I.   1758-1828.
Purvit, V.   1872-?
Pushkareff, P.   XX century.
Pushnov, M.   1716-1797.

Radlov, N.   XX century.
Rashett, G.   1744-1809.
Rastrelli, K. B.   XVIII century.
Reder, K.   XX century.
Reimers, I.   1818-1868.
Reitern, E. P.   1794-1865.
Remisoff, N.   XX century.
Repin, I.   1844-1930.
Rerikh, N. K.   1874-
Riabushkin, A.   1861-1904.
Riabushinski, A. P.   XX century.
Rokotoff, F.   1735-1808.
Roslin, A.   1718-1793.
Rubleff, A.   XIV-XV centuries.
Ryloff, A.   XX century.
Sakharova, O.   XX century.
Samokish-Sudkovski.   XX century.
Sapunoff, N.   XX century.
Sarian, M.   XX century.
Sasonoff, V.   XX century.
Savin, Istoma.   XVII century.
Savin, Nikifor.   XVII century.
Savin, Sila.   XVII century.
Savitski, K.   1845-?
Savrassoff, A.   1830-1897.
Semiradski, G.   1843-1902.
Serebriakova, E.   XX century.
Serebriakova, S.   XX century.
Seriakoff, L.   XX century.
Serov, V.   1865-?
Shagal, M.   XX century.
Shanks, E.   XX century.
Shebuieff, V.   1777-1851.
Shevtchenko, T.   1814-1861.
Shibanoff, M.   XVIII century.
Shishkin, I.   1831-1898.
Shmidt, G.   XVIII century.
Shubin, F.   1740-1805.
Shukhaieff, V.   XX century.
Shwartz, V.   1838-1869.
Skorodumoff, G.   1755-1792.
Skotnikoff, E.   1780-1843.
Sokolov, P. F.   1791-1848.
Sokolov, P. I.   1753-1791.
Sokolov, P. P.   1821-1899.
Solomatkin, L.   XX century.
Somov, K.   1869-
Sorokin, E.   1821-1892.
Stelletzki, D.   XX century.
Sudeikin, S.   XX century.
Sudkovski, P.   1850-1885.
Surikoff, V.   1848-1916.
Tatlin, V.   XX century.
Terebeneff, I.   XX century.
Tikhobrasoff, N.   1818-1874.
Tolstoi, F.   1783-1873.
Torelli, S.   1712-1784.
Tropinin, V.   1776-1857.
Trubetzkoi, P.   XX century.
Trukhmenski, A.   XVII century.
Tschedrin, F.   1751-1825.
Tschedrin, S.   1798-1830.
Tschedrovski, I.   XX century.
Tschekhonin, S.   XX century.
Tschernysheff, A.   XX century.

Tschesski, I. 1762–1848.
Tschirin, P. XVII century.
Tschistiakoff, P. 1832–?
Tschukin, S. XX century.
Tschurlianis, N. XX century.
Tupyleff, I. 1758–1821.
Turjanski, L. XX century.
Tyrsa, N. XX century.
Varnek, A. 1782–1831.
Vasnetzoff, A. 1856–1933.
Vasnetzoff, V. 1848–?
Vassilieff, F. 1850–1873.
Velli, J. de. 1730–1804.
Venezianoff, A. 1779–1847.

Venig, K. 1830–?
Veretschagin, V. 1842–1904.
Vinogradoff, S. XX century.
Vishniakoff, I. 1699–1763.
Vitali, I. 1794–1855.
Volkoff, A. XX century.
Vorobieff, M. 1787–1855.
Vrubel, M. 1856–1910.
Zack, E. XX century.
Zagorski, N. XX century
Zakharoff, P. 1816–1852.
Zaleman, G. 1859–?
Zelentzoff, K. XX century.
Zuboff, A. XVIII century.

ISLAM

SOURCES

Diez, E. *Die Kunst der Islamischen Volker*, in *Handbuch der Kunstwissenschaft*. Berlin, 1915.
Gluck, H. and E. Diez, *Die Kunst der Islam*. Berlin, 1925.
Herzfeld, E. *Die Malereien von Samarra*, in *Forschungen zur Islamischen Kunst*, Vol. II. Berlin, 1927.
Kühnel, E. *Maurische Kunst*. Berlin, 1924.
Migeon, G. *Manuel d'art musulman. Arts plastiques*, 2 vols. Paris, 1927.
Stchoukine, L. *La peinture Indiene à l'époque des Grands Moghols*. Paris, 1929.

Art journals: *Der Islam. Zeitschrift für Geschichte und Kultur des Islamischen Orients.* Berlin, 1912
——— *Orientalisches Archiv*, ed. by Hugo Grothe. Berlin, 1910 ff.
——— *Syria. Revue d'art oriental et d'archéologie.* Paris, 1920 ff.

ARTISTS

Abd Allah Hussein. XVII century. Persia.
Abdalla. XV century. Persia.

Abul Fadl Ibn Abi Ishak. XIV century. Mesopotamia.
Aga Mirek. XV century. Persia.
Aga Risa Abbassy. XVI–XVII centuries. Persia.
Geneid es Sultani. XIV century. Bagdad.
Iakhia ibn Mahmut. XIII century. Mesopotamia.
Kassim Ali. XV century. Afghanistan.
Kemal Ed-Din Behsad. XV century. Afghanistan.
Khiar Ed-Din Khalil. XV century. Afghanistan.
Mehmad. XV century. Persia.
Mehmed Kassim. XVII century. Persia.
Mir Mohammed Ali. XVII century. Persia.
Mohammed Jussuff. XVII century. Persia.
Mohammed Sultan. XV–XVI century. Persia.
Nipatch. XVII century. India.
Sadik Beg. XVII century. Persia.
Shafi Abbassi. XVII century. Persia.
Shah Kassim. XVII century. Persia.
Sheikh Mohammed of Shiraz. XVI–XVII centuries. Persia.
Sheikhzade Mahmud. XV century. Persia.
Ustad Abd Allah. XV century. Persia.
Ustad Mohammadi. XVI century. Persia.

Appendix to Chapter Thirteen

This Appendix gives, first, a list of the works in German literature — all in all more than 600 — which have been studied and upon which the conclusions of Chapter Thirteen are based, so far as they concern German literature; second, an abbreviated list of the representative works in French literature, which do not exhaust the works studied but which have been given a representative importance in this study. These lists give an idea of the character and the size of the material upon which the conclusions concerning these two literatures are based. The main literary works of other countries are mentioned in the text of Chapter Thirteen. For both countries the works are given by century or half-century periods.

BIBLIOGRAPHY — GERMAN LITERATURE

IV–XI CENTURIES

Reference books:

Robertson, J. G. *History of German Literature*, rev. ed. New York, 1931.

Vogt, F. and M. Koch. *Geschichte der Deutschen Litteratur*, 3 vols. Leipzig, 1919.

Sources:

Abh. d. Berl. Akad. d. W. (*Abhandlungen der Berliner Akademie der Wissenschaften*). 1851.

Annolied, ed. by Roediger, in *Monumenta Germanica*, Vol. I, pp. 115–132.

D N L (*Deutsche National Literatur*), ed. by J. Kürschner. Berlin, 1885 ff.

Ecbasis Captivi, ed. by J. Grimm and A. Schmeller, in *Lateinische Gedichte des X und XI Jahrhunderts*, pp. 243–285. Göttingen, 1838.

Freisinger Dreikönigsspiel, in H. Anz, *Lateinische Magierspiele*, pp. 154–158. 1905.

Heliand, ed. by O. Behaghel, 1922. Trans. by E. Behringer. 1898.

Hroswith. *Opera Omnia*, ed. by K. Barack. Nürnberg, 1858.

——— *Plays*, trans. by C. St. John. London, 1923.

M and S (Müllenhoff and Scherer). *Denkmäler deutscher Poesie und Prosa aus dem VIII–XII Jahrhunderts*. Berlin, 1864.

Old Saxon Genesis, in Behaghel's ed. of *Heliand* (see above).

Otfrids Evangelienbuch, trans. by J. Kelle. Prague, 1870.

Ruodlieb, trans. by M. Heyne. Leipzig, 1897.

Tatian, ed. by E. Sievers. Paderborn, 1872.

Waltharius, ed. by J. W. Beck. Groningen, 1908. Trans. by Althof. Berlin, 1920.

Williram, ed. by Seemüller, in *Quellen und Forschungen*, Vol. XXVIII. 1878.

XII CENTURY

1110. Exodus and Genesis, ed. by J. Diemer. 1862.

1120. Lamprecht. *Alexanderlied*, ed. by H. Weismann. 1850.

Short religious poems in *Kleinere deutsche Gedichte des XI und XII Jahrhunderts*, ed. by A. Waag, 2d ed. 1916.

1132. Konrad. *Rolandslied*, ed. by K. Bartsch, in *Dichtungen des deutschen Mittelalters*, Vol. III. Leipzig, 1874.

1140. Melker. *Marienlied*, in *Kleinere deutsche Gedichte*, cited, pp. 173–176.

1147. *Kaiserchronik*, ed. by J. Diemer. 1849.

1150. Hartmann. *Vom Glauben*, ed. by F. von der Leyen, in *Germanische Abhandlungen*. Berlin, 1907.

Shorter religious poems, in *Kleinere deutsche Gedichte*, cited.

1160. *König Rother*, ed. by H. Rückert, in *Deutsche Dichtungen des Mittelalters*, cited, Vol. I. Leipzig, 1872.

Himmel und Hölle. Müllendorf and Scherer, Denkmäler. Berlin, 1864.

Tegernseer Antichristspiel (*Ludus de Antichristo*), ed. by F. Wilhelm, 2d ed. München, 1912.

1170. Wernher. *Drei Lieder von der Jungfrau*, ed. by C. Wesle. Halle, 1927.

Floire und Blanschefleur, in *Zeitschrift für deutsches Altertum*, Vol. XXI, pp. 320–331. 1877.

Heinrich von Veldeke. *Servatius*, in *D N L*, Vol. IV., pt. i, pp. 81–241.

Graf Rudolf (synopsis), in *D N L*, Vol. II, pt. ii, pp. 292–295.

1180. *Herzog Ernst*, ed. by K. Bartsch. Wien, 1869.

Heinrich von Veldeke. *Eneide*, ed. by L. Eltmüller. 1852.

Eilhart von Oberge. *Tristrant*, ed. by K. Wagner, in *Rheinische Beiträge*, Vol. V. Bonn, 1924.

Salman und Morolf, ed. by F. Vogt. Halle, 1880.

Orendel, ed. by A. Berger. Bonn, 1888.

Oswald, ed. by G. Baesecke. Breslau, 1917.

Heinrich der Glichezaere. *Reinhart*, ed. by G. Baesecke. Halle, 1925.

1190. Hartmann von Aue. *Büchlein*, with *Armer Heinrich*, below.

———— *Erec*, ed. by F. Bech (Hartmann, Vol. I). 1870.

1195. Ulrich V. Zatzikoven. *Lanzelet*, ed. by K. Hahn. 1845.

Hartmann. *Gregorius*, ed. by H. Paul, 1929.

———— *Der arme Heinrich* (and *Büchlein*), ed. by M. Haupt, 2d ed. 1881.

End of Century. *Carmina Burana*, ed. by J. Schmeller, 3d ed. 1894.

1200. *Das Nibelungenlied*, ed. by K. Bartsch, Leipzig, 1923.

Lyrics:

Des Minnesangs Frühling, ed. by F. Vogt. 1930.

XIII CENTURY (FIRST HALF)

1205. Wirnt von Gravenberg. *Wigalois*, ed. by J. Kapsteyn, in *Rheinische Beiträge*, Vol. IX. Bonn, 1926.

Hartmann. *Iwein*, ed. by G. Benecke and K. Lachmann, 5th ed. Berlin, 1926.

1210. Wolfram von Eschenbach. *Parzival*, ed. by A. Leitzmann, 3 vols. Halle, 1903, 1926, and 1928.

Otte. *Eraclius*, ed. by H. Gräf, in *Quellen und Forschungen*, Vol. L. Strasburg, 1883.

Konrad von Fussesbrunnen. *Kindheit Jesu*, ed. by K. Köchendorffer, in *Quellen und Forschungen*, Vol. XLIII. Strasburg, 1881.

1212. Stricker. *Daniel vom Blühenden Tal*, ed. by G. Rosenhagen, in *Germanische Abhandlungen*, Vol. IX. Breslau, 1894.

1215. Gottfried von Strasburg. *Tristan*, ed. by F. Ranke. Berlin, 1930.

1220. Herbort von Fritslar. *Lied von Troye*, ed. by K. Frommann. Quedlinburg, 1837.

———— *Der Winsbeke*, ed. by M. Haupt. Leipzig, 1845.

Wolfram. *Willehalm* and *Titurel*, ed. by K. Lachmann. Berlin, 1926.

Thomasin von Zirclaere. *Der Welsche Gast*, ed. by H. Rückert. Quedlinburg, 1852.

Konrad Fleck. *Flore und Blanschefleur*, ed. by W. Golther, in *D N L*, Vol. II, pp. 249–470.

1225. Ortnit. *Wolfdietrich*, ed. by J. Lunze. Tübingen, 1906.

1230. Rudolf von Ems. *Guter Gerhard*, ed. by M. Haupt. Leipzig, 1840.

———— *Barlaam und Josaphat*, ed. by F. Pfeiffer, in *Dichtungen des deutschen Mittelalters*, Vol. III. Leipzig, 1843.

Stricker. *Pfaffe Ameis*, ed. by H. Lambel, in *Deutsche Klassiker des Mittelalters*, Vol. XII. Leipzig, 1883.

Freidank. *Bescheidenheit*, ed. by F. Sandvoss. Berlin, 1877.

1235. Stricker. *Karl der Grosse*, ed. by K. Bartsch. Quedlinburg, 1857.

1240. *Gudrun*, ed. by E. Martin. Halle, 1872.

Ulrich von Türheim. *Tristan*, ed. by H. Massmann, in *Dichtungen des deutschen Mittelalters*, Vol. II, pp. 488–590. Leipzig, 1843.

Rudolf von Ems. *Weltchronik*, ed. by G. Ehrismann. Berlin, 1915.

Reinbot von Durne. *Heiliger Georg*, ed. by C. von Kraus. Heidelberg, 1907.

Mai und Beaflor, ed. by F. Pfeiffer, in *Dichtungen des deutschen Mittelalters*, Vol. VII. Leipzig, 1848.

1250. Rudolf von Ems. *Wilhelm von Orlens*, ed. by V. Junk. Berlin, 1905.

Biterolf und Dietlieb and *Laurin*, ed. by O. Jänicke, in *Deutsches Heldenbuch*, Vol. I. Berlin, 1866.

Rosengarten, ed. by G. Holz. Halle, 1893.

Eckenlied, Sigenot, and *Virginal*, ed. by J. Zupitza, in *Deutsches Heldenbuch*, Vol. V. Berlin, 1870.

Wernher der Gaertenaere. *Meier Helmbrecht*, ed. by H. Lambel, in *Deutsche Klassiker des Mittelalters*, Vol. XII. Leipzig, 1883.

Lyrics:

Deutsche National Literatur, ed. by F. Pfaff, Vol. VIII, pts. i and ii. Stuttgart, 1894.

XIII CENTURY (SECOND HALF)

1255. Ulrich von Lichtenstein. *Frauendienst*, ed. by K. Lachmann. Berlin, 1841.

Berthold von Holle. *Die Krane*, ed. by K. Bartsch. Nürnberg, 1858.

1257. Ulrich von Lichtenstein. *Frauenbuch*. See *Frauendienst*, above.

1260. Konrad von Würzburg. *Silvester* and *Alexius*, ed. by P. Gereke, in *Konrad von Würzburgs Legenden*. Halle, 1925.

———— *Der Welt Lohn*, ed. by E. Schröder, in *Konrad von Würzburgs kleinere Dichtungen*, Vol. I. Berlin, 1924.

———— *Goldene Schmiede*, ed. by W. Grimm. Berlin, 1840.

1260–1280. Der Pleier. *Garel vom Blühenden Tal*, ed. by M. Walz. Freiburg, i. B. 1892.

———— *Tandareis*, ed. by F. Khull. Graz, 1885.

———— *Meleranz*, ed. by K. Bartsch. Stuttgart, 1861.

Konrad von Stoffeln. *Gauriel von Muntabel*, ed. by F. Khull. Graz, 1885.

1265–1275. Konrad von Würzburg. *Kaiser Otto*, ed. by K. Hahan. Quedlinburg, 1838.

———— *Herzemaere*, ed by E. Schröder, in *Kleinere Dichtungen*, Vol. I. Berlin, 1924.

1270. Albrecht von Scharfenberg. *Der jüngere Titurel*, ed. by K. Hahn. Quedlinburg, 1842.

1280. Konrad von Würzburg. *Partenopier und Meliur*, ed. by K. Bartsch. Wien, 1872.
1285. *Lohengrin*, ed. by H. Rückert. Quedlinburg, 1838.
Konrad von Würzburg. *Der trojanischer Krieg*, ed. by A. von Keller. Stuttgart, 1858.
Ulrich von Eschenbach. *Alexander*, ed. by W. Toischer. Tübingen, 1888.
1290–1300. *Alpharts Tod, Dietrichs Flucht, Rabenschlacht*, in *Das deutsches Heldenbuch*, ed. by E. Martin, Vol. II. Berlin, 1866.
Passional, ed. by K. Köpke. Quedlinburg, 1852.
Buch der Väter, ed. by K. Reissenberger. Berlin, 1914.
Die heilige Elisabeth, ed. by M. Rieger, in *Bibliothek des Stuttgarter Literar Vereins*, Vol. XC. Stuttgart, 1868.

Lyrics:

Tannhäuser, ed. by S. Singer. Tübingen, 1922.
Der Marner, ed. by P. Strauch, in *Quellen und Forschungen*, Vol. XIV. Strasburg, 1876.
Seifried Helbling, ed. by J. Seemüller. Halle, 1876.

Preaching:

Berthold von Regensburg, ed. by F. Pfeiffer. Wien, 1862.

XIV CENTURY

1300. Hugo von Trimberg. *Der Renner*, ed. by G. Ehrismann. Tübingen, 1908–1909.
Heinrich von Hesler. *Die Apokalypse*, ed. by K. Helm. Berlin, 1907.
Heinrich von Neustadt. *Apollonius von Tyrus*, ed. by S. Singer. Berlin, 1906.
Heinrich von Freiberg. *Werke*, ed. by A. Bernt. Halle, 1906.
1310. Ottokar von Steier. *Österreichische Reimchronik*, ed. by J. Seemüller. Hannover, 1890.
1335. Wisse und Colin. *Parzival*, ed. by K. Schorbach. Strasburg, 1888.
Tilo von Kulm. *Buch von den Siben Ingesigeln*, ed. by Köchendorffer. Berlin, 1907.
1340. Hadamar von Laber. *Die Jagd*, ed. by K. Stejskal. Vienna, 1880.
Ulrich Boner. *Der Edelstein*, ed. by F. Pfeiffer. Leipzig, 1844.
1350. *Theophilus*, ed. by R. Petsch. Heidelberg, 1908.
1386–1388. *Semperschlacht* and *Schlacht zu Nävels*, in R. von Lilliencron, *Historische Volkslieder der Deutschen*, Vol. I, pp. 109–151. Leipzig, 1865.
1400. Johannes von Saaz. *Der Ackermann aus Böhmen*, ed. by A. Bernt. Reichenberg, 1925.

Lyrics:

Hadlaub, in F. von der Hagen, *Minnesinger*, Vol. II, pp. 278–308. Leipzig, 1838.
Frauenlob (Heinrich von Meissen), ed. by L. Ettmüller. Leipzig, 1843.

XV CENTURY

1400. Hans von Bühel. *Die Königstochter von Frankreich*, ed. by J. Merzdorf. Oldenburg, 1867.
1413. Heinrich von Wittenweiler. *Der Ring*, ed. by E. Wiessner. Leipzig, 1931.
1437. Elisabeth von Nassau-Saarbrücken. (*Loher und Maller*); *Hug Schapeler*, in *Volksbücher vom sterbender Rittertum*, ed. by H. Kindermann. Leipzig, 1928.
1453. Hermann von Sachsenheim. *Die Mörin*, ed. by E. Martin. Tübingen, 1878.
1462. M. Beheim. *Buch von der Wienern*, ed. by T. Karajan. Vienna, 1853.
1470. J. Wimpfeling. *Stylpho*, ed. by H. Holstein. Berlin, 1892.
1472. Casper von der Röen. *Dresdener Heldenbuch*, in F. von der Hagen, *Deutsche Gedichte des Mittelalters*, Vol. II. Berlin, 1820.
Albrecht von Eyb. *Ehebüchlein*, ed. by M. Herrmann. Berlin, 1890.
1473. Frankfürter. *Der Pfarrer von Kalenberg*, ed. by F. Ebeling. Berlin, 1890.
1483. *Till Eulenspiegel*, ed. by F. von Zobeltitz. Hamburg, 1924.
1485. H. Steinhöwel. *Esopus*, ed. by H. Österley. Tübingen, 1873.
1490. V. Füetrer. *Buch der Abenteuer* (*Auswahl*), ed. by F. Panzer. Tübingen, 1902.
1494. S. Brant. *Narrenschiff*, ed. by F. Schultz. Strasburg, 1913.
J. Geiler. *Christlicher Pilger*, ed. by P. de Lorenzi, Vol. III. Trier, 1883.
1497. Reuchlin. *Henno*, ed. by H. Holstein. Halle, 1888.
1498. *Reynke de Vos*, ed. by A. Leitzmann. Halle, 1925.

Lyrics and folk songs:

Hugo von Montfort, ed. by J. Wackernell. Innsbruck, 1881.
Oswald von Wolkenstein, ed. by J. Schatz. Göttingen, 1904.
Püterich von Reichertshausen. *Ehrenbrief*, ed. by F. Behrend and R. Wolkan. Weimar, 1920.
Historische Volkslieder der Deutschen, ed. by R. von Liliencron. Leipzig, 1865.
Volkslieder, ed. by L. Uhland, 3d ed. Stuttgart, 1893.

Drama:

In *DNL*, Vol. XIV, pts. i, ii, and iii, ed. by R. Froning. Stuttgart, 1892.
Deutsche Volksspiele des Mittelalters. Leipzig, 1917–1918.

XVI CENTURY

Alberus, E. *Buch von der Tugend und der Weisheit*, ed. by W. Braune. Halle, 1892.

Alsfelder Passionspiel, in *D N L*, Vol. XIV, ed. by R. Froning. Stuttgart, 1892.

Ayrer, J. *Dramen*, in *Schauspiele aus dem XVI Jahrhundert*, ed. by J. Tittmann. Leipzig, 1868.

Birck, S. *Dramen*, in *Schweizerische Schauspiele des sechszehnten Jahrhunderts*, ed. by J. Baechtold. Zürich, 1890–1893.

Dedekind, F. *Grobianus*, ed. by A. Bömer. Berlin, 1903.

Die 4 Haimonskinder, ed. by A. Bachmann. Tübingen, 1895.

Epistolae Obscurorum Virorum, ed. by F. Stokes. New Haven, 1925.

Fischart, J. *Werke*, ed. by H. Kurz. Leipzig, 1866.

——— *Eulenspiegel Reimenweis* and *Ritter vom Stauffenberg* in *Werke*, in *D N L*, Vol. XVIII, ed. by A. Hauffen. Stuttgart, 1890.

Frey, J. *Gartengesellschaft*, ed. by J. Bolte. Tübingen, 1896.

Frischlin, N. Latin dramas in *Opera Poetica*. Strasburg, 1587.

——— *Deutsche Dichtungen*, ed. by D. F. Strauss. Stuttgart, 1857.

——— *Phasma*. 1592.

Geiler, J. *Narrenschiff*, in *Werke*, ed. by P. de Lorenzi. Trier, 1881.

Gengenbach, P. *Werke*, ed. by K. Goedeke. Hannover, 1856.

Heinrich Julius von Braunschweig. *Dramen*, in *Deutsche Dichter des XVI Jahrhunderts*, Vol. XIV, ed. by J. Tittmann. Leipzig, 1880.

Historia Dr. Johann Fausti, ed. by W. Braune. Halle, 1878.

Hutten, U. von. *Gesprächbüchlein*, ed. by R. Zoozmann. Dresden, 1905.

——— *Clag und Vermanung*, in *D N L*, Vol. XVII, ed. by Dr. Balke. Stuttgart, 1891.

Kirchhoff, H. *Wendunmuth*, ed. by H. Österley. Tübingen, 1869.

Kolross, J. *Spiel von Funferley Betrachtnissen*, in *Bächtold, Schweizer Schauspiele des XVI Jahrhunderts*. Zürich, 1890 ff.

Krüger, B. *Anfang und Ende der Welt*, in Tittmann, *Schauspiele aus dem XVI Jahrhundert*.

Lalenbuch, ed. by K. von Bahder. Halle, 1914.

Lindener, M. *Katzipori* and *Rastbüchlein*, ed. by F. Lichtenstein. Tübingen, 1869.

Luther, M. *Geistliche Lieder*, ed. by F. Klippgen. Halle, 1912.

——— *Fabeln*, ed. by E. Thiele. Halle, 1888.

Macropedius. *Hecatus*, in *Drei Schauspiele*, ed. by J. Bolte. Leipzig, 1927.

Magelone, ed. by J. Bolte. Weimar, 1894.

Manuel, N. *Werke*, ed. by J. Baechtold. Frauenfeld, 1878.

Maximilian I. *Teuerdank*, ed. by K. Goedeke. Leipzig, 1878.

——— *Der Weisskunig*. Vienna.

Montanus, M. *Wegkürzer*, ed. by J. Bolte. Tübingen, 1899.

Murner, T. *Werke*, ed. by F. Schultz and others. Berlin and Strasburg, 1918 ff.

Naogeorgus, T. *Pammachius*, in *D N L*, Vol. XXII, ed. by R. Froning.

——— *Mercator*, in *Drei Schauspiele*, ed. by J. Bolte.

Pauli, J. *Schimpf und Ernst*, ed. by J. Bolte. Berlin, 1924.

Rebhun, P. *Susanna*, in *D N L*, Vol. XXII, ed. by R. Froning and others.

——— *Hochzeit zu Cana*, in *Dramen*, ed. by H. Palm. Stuttgart, 1859.

Ringwalt, B. *Werke*, in *D N L*, Vol. XIX, ed. by E. Wolff. Stuttgart, 1893.

Rollenhagen, G. *Froschmeuseler*, ed. by K. Goedeke. Leipzig, 1876.

Ruof, J. *Wilhelm Tell*, in J. Bächtold, *Schweizer Schauspiele des XVI Jahrhunderts*.

Sachs, H. *Fastnachtsspiele* and *Opferung Isaacs*, in *Werke*, ed. by A. von Keller and E. Goetze. Tübingen, 1882.

——— *Tristrand und Isalde* and *Hörnen Sewfriedt*, in *Werke*, ed. by J. Büsching, Vol. II. Nürnberg, 1819.

——— Other works, in *Werke*, ed. by P. Merker and R. Buchwald. Leipzig, 1925.

Schumann, V. *Nachtbüchlein*, in *Deutsche Schwänke des XVI Jahrhunderts*, ed. by E. Blümml, Vol. III.

Waldis, B. *Parabell vom verloren Sohn*, in *D N L*, Vol. XXII, ed. by R. Froning and others.

——— *Esopus*, ed. by J. Tittmann. Leipzig, 1882.

Wickram, J. *Werke*, ed. by J. Bolte. Tübingen, 1901 ff.

Widmann, G. *Histori Peter Lewen*, ed. by F. Eberling. Berlin, 1890.

——— *Faustbuch*, ed. by A. von Keller. Stuttgart, 1880.

Wimpfeling, J. *Germania*, trans. by E. Martin. Strasburg, 1885.

XVII CENTURY

Reference books:

Robertson, *op. cit.*, pp. 206–236.

Vogt and Koch, *op. cit.*, Vol. II, pp. 1–60 and 69.

For the Silesian poets (Hofmannswaldau, Gryphius, Lohenstein, Angelus Silesius, Neukirch, especially), Heckel, H., *Geschichte der deutschen Literatur in Schlesien*, Vol. I. Breslau, 1929.

Abraham a Santa Clara. *Judas der Erzschelm*, ed. by F. Bogertag, in *D N L*, Vol. XI. Stuttgart, 1884.

Angelus Silesius. *Werke*, ed. by H. Held. München, 1924.

Balde, J. *Carmina Lyrica*, ed. by P. Müller. München, 1884.

Böhme, J. *Aurora*, in *Schriften*, ed. by H. Kayser. Leipzig, 1923.

Bucholtz, A. *Herkules und Valiska.* Brunswick, 1659.
Canitz, R. von. *Nebenstunden,* in *Gedichte.* Berlin, 1765.
Dach, S. *Werke,* ed. by H. Österley. Tübingen, 1876.
Englische Comödien, ed. by J. Tittmann, in *Deutsche Dichtungen des XVII Jahrhunderts,* Vol. XIII. Leipzig, 1880.
Fleming, P. *Deutsche Poemata,* ed. by J. Lappenberg. Stuttgart, 1865.
Gerhardt, P. *Gedichte,* ed. by K. Goedeke, in *Deutsche Dichtungen des XVII Jahrhunderts,* Vol. XII. Leipzig, 1877.
Grimmelshausen, J. J. C. von. *Werke,* ed. by A. Keller. Stuttgart, 1854–1862.
Gryphius, A. *Cardenio und Celinde,* in *Werke,* in *D N L,* Vol. XXIX. Stuttgart, 1883.
―――― *Geliebte Dornrose, Peter Squentz,* and *Horribilicribrifax,* in *Lustspiele,* ed. by H. Palm. Tübingen, 1878.
Hock, T. *Schönes Blumenfeld,* ed. by M. Koch. Halle, 1899.
Hollonius, L. *Somnium Vitae Humanae,* ed. by F. Spengler. Halle, 1891.
Israel, S. *Pyramus und Thisbe,* ed. by A. Schaer. Tübingen, 1921.
Lauremberg, J. *Scherzgedichte,* ed. by W. Braune. Halle, 1879.
Logau, F. von. *Sämtliche Sinngedichte,* ed. by G. Eitner. Tübingen, 1872.
Lohenstein, D. von. *Arminius.* Leipzig, 1689.
―――― *Cleopatra* and *Sophonisbe,* in *Poetische Werke.* Leipzig, 1748.
Moscherosch, H. *Philander,* ed. by F. Bobertag, in *D N L,* Vol. XXXII.
―――― *Insomnis Cura Parentum,* ed. by L. Pariser. Halle, 1893.
Neukirch, B. *Hofmannswaldaus und andere deutsche Gedichte.* Leipzig, 1697.
Opitz, M. *Works (Dichtung),* ed. by H. Oesterley, in *D N L,* Vol. XXVII. Stuttgart, 1890.
Rachel, J. *Satirische Gedichte,* ed. by K. Drescher. Halle, 1903.
Reuter, C. *Schelmuffsky,* ed. by G. Witkowski. Leipzig, 1916.
Rist, J. *Dichtungen,* ed. by K. Goedeke, in *Deutsche Dichtungen des XVII Jahrhunderts,* Vol. XVI. Leipzig, 1885.
Sandrub, L. *Werke,* ed. by G. Milchsack. Halle, 1878.
Spee, F. von. *Trutznachtigal,* ed. by G. Balke, in *Deutsche Dichtungen des XVII Jahrhunderts,* Vol. XIII. Leipzig, 1879.
Weckherlin, G. *Gedichte,* ed. by H. Fischer. Tübingen, 1894 ff.
Weise, C. *Bäurischer Machiavell,* ed. by L. Fulda, in *D N L,* Vol. XXXIX. Stuttgart, 1884.
―――― *Drei ärgste Erznarren,* ed. by W. Braune. Halle, 1878.
―――― *Überflüssige Gedanken,* ed. by M. von Waldberg. Halle, 1914.
Wernigke, C. *Epigrammata,* ed. by R. Pechel. Berlin, 1909.

Zesen, P. von. *Adriatische Rosamund,* ed. by M. Jellinek. Halle, 1899.
Ziegler, A. von. *Asiatische Banise,* ed. by F. Bobertag, in *D N L,* Vol. XXXVII.
Zincgref, J. W. *Auserlesene Gedichte,* ed. by W. Braune. Halle, 1879.

―――――――――――――――――――

XVIII CENTURY

Reference books:
Robertson, *op. cit.,* pp. 237–411.
Schneider, F. J. *Die deutsche Dichtung zwischen Barock und Klassizismus* (1700–1785). Stuttgart, 1924. (Especially good for its period.)
Vogt and Koch, *op. cit.,* Vol. II, pp. 55 ff. and 61–310; Vol. III, pp. 1–23, 31–34, and 38–42.

Besser, J. V. *Schriften.* Leipzig, 1720.
Bodmer, J. *Noachide.* Berlin, 1765.
Brawe, J. von. *Brutus,* ed. by J. Minor, in *D N L,* Vol. LXXII.
Brockes, B. H. *Bethlehemitischer Kindermord.* Cologne, 1715.
―――― *Irdisches Vergnügen an Gott.* Hamburg, 1730 ff.
Christlich Meynende. *Faust,* ed. by S. Szamatolski. Stuttgart, 1891.
Cronegk, J. von. *Codrus,* in *Schriften,* below. Reutlingen, 1777.
Gellert, C. *Schriften.* Leipzig, 1839.
Gemmingen, O. von. *Der deutsche Hausvater,* ed. by A. Hauffen, in *D N L,* Vol. CXXXIX, pt. i.
Gerstenberg, H. W. von. *Ugolino,* ed. by R. Hamel, in *D N L,* Vol. XLVIII.
―――― *Gedicht eines Skalden,* in *Schriften,* Vol. II. Altona, 1815.
Gessner, S. *Idyllen,* in *Schriften,* Vol. III. Zürich, 1818.
Gleim, J. *Werke.* Halberstadt, 1811.
Goethe, J. W. von. *Werke,* Propyläen ed. München, 1909.
Gottsched, J. C. *Der sterbende Cato,* ed. by J. Crüger, in *D N L,* Vol. XLII.
―――― *Deutsche Schaubühne.* Leipzig, 1740–1745.
Günther, J. *Gedichte,* ed. by W. Krämer. Leipzig, 1930 f.
Hagedorn, F. von. *Poetische Werke.* Hamburg, 1825.
Haller, A. von. *Versuch schweizerische Gedichte,* 11th ed. Bern, 1777.
Heinse, J. J. *Ardinghello,* ed. by C. Schüddekopf, in *Werke,* Vol. IV. Leipzig, 1902.
Hermes, J. *Sophiens Reise,* 3d ed. Leipzig, 1778.
Hölderlin, F. *Hyperion,* in *Werke,* Vol. II. Berlin, 1923.
Iffland, A. *Die Jaeger,* in *Werke,* Vol. I. Leipzig, 1858.
Kleist, C. E. von. *Der Frühling,* ed. by W. Körte, in *Werke,* Vol. I. Berlin, 1903.
Klinger, F. M. *Werke.* Leipzig, 1832.
Klopstock, F. *Werke.* Karlsruhe, 1821 f.
Kotzebue, A. von. *Menschenhass und Reue,* in *Werke,* Vol. III. Leipzig, 1867.

Leisewitz, J. *Julius von Tarent*, ed. by A. Sauer, in *DNL*, Vol. LXXIX.

Lenz, J. M. R. *Der Hofmeister* and *Die Soldaten*, ed. by A. Sauer, in *DNL*, Vol. LXXX.

Lessing, G. E. *Werke*, ed. by K. Lachmann and F. Muncker, 3d ed. Stuttgart, 1886.

Miller, J. M. *Siegwart*, 2d ed. Leipzig, 1777.

Moritz, K. P. *Anton Reiser*, ed. by L. Geiger. Heilbronn, 1886.

Müller, J. F. *Werke*. Heidelberg, 1811.

Nicolai, C. F. *Sebaldus Nothanker*. Berlin, 1773.

Pestalozzi, J. *Lienhart und Gertrud*, ed. by K. Richter. Leipzig, 1882.

Rabener, G. *Satirische Schriften*, 4th ed. Leipzig, 1759.

Richter, J. P. F. (Jean Paul). *Werke*. Weimar, 1929.

Schikaneder, E. *Die Zauberflöte*, in *Deutsche Schaubuehne*, Vol. II. Augsburg, 1793.

Schiller, J. F. *Werke*, Horen ed. München, 1910.

Schlegel, F. *Lucinde*. Leipzig, 1929.

Schlegel, J. E. *Werke*. Leipzig, 1771.

Schnabel, J. G. *Insel Felsenburg*, ed. by L. Tieck. Breslau, 1828.

Tersteegen, J. *Geistliche Lieder*, ed. by W. Nelle. Guetersloh, 1897.

Tieck, L. *William Lovell*. Berlin, 1795–1797.

―――― *Franz Sternbald*. Berlin, 1798.

Uz, J. *Werke*. Karlsruhe, 1818.

Voss, J. *Idyllen*, in *Gedichte*, ed. by K. Goedeke. Leipzig, 1869.

Wagner, H. L. *Die Kindermörderin*, ed. by A. Sauer, in *DNL*, Vol. LXXX.

Weise, C. *Die böse Catharine*, ed. by L. Fulda, in *DNL*, Vol. XXXIX.

Wieland, C. M. *Werke*. Leipzig, 1794 ff.

―――――――――――――――――――――――

XIX CENTURY (FIRST HALF)

―――――――――――――――――――――――

Reference books:

H. Bieber. *Der Kampf um die Tradition*, in *Deutsche Dichtung*, 1830–1880. Stuttgart, 1928.

Robertson, J. G., *op. cit.*, pp. 411–617.

Vogt and Koch, *op. cit.*, Vol. III, pp. 1–234.

Wiegler, P. *Geschichte der deutschen Literatur*, Vol. II, pp. 1–682. Berlin, 1930.

Alexis, W. *Cabanis*, Berlin, 1871.

―――― *Roland von Berlin*, 3d ed. Berlin, 1872.

Arndt, E. M. *Lieder für Deutsche*, ed. by H. Meisner, in *Werke*, Vols. III and IV. Leipzig, 1895.

Arnim, A. von. *Werke*. Berlin, 1840.

Brentano, C. von. *Godwi* and *Braver Kasperl und schönes Annerl*, ed. by H. Amerling and K. Vietor, in *Werke*, Vols. I and II. Frankfurt-am-Main, 1923.

―――― *Gründung Prags*, ed. by C. Schüdderkopf, in *Werke*, Vol. X. München, 1910.

Büchner, G. *Dantons Tod*. Maastricht, 1930.

Chamisso, A. von. *Peter Schlemihl*, ed. by H. Jardel, in *Werke*, Vol. II. Leipzig, 1922.

Collin, H. von. *Regulus*, in *Werke*, Vol. I. Wien, 1812.

Droste-Hülshoff, A. *Werke*. München, 1925.

Eichendorff, J. von. *Werke*. Leipzig, 1864.

Fouque, F. *Sigurd*. Berlin, 1808.

―――― *Zauberring*. Nürnberg, 1816.

Freiligrath, F. *Glaubensbekenntnis*, in *Dichtungen*, Vol. III. Stuttgart, 1877.

Freytag, G. *Werke*. Leipzig, 1887.

Geibel, E. *Zeitstimmen*, ed. by W. Stammler, in *Werke*, Vol. I. Leipzig.

Goethe, J. W. von. *Werke*, Propyläen ed. München, 1912.

Gotthelf, J. *Werke*, ed. by R. Hunziker and H. Bloesch. Zürich, 1921.

Grabbe, C. *Werke*, ed. by P. Friedrich. Weimar, 1923.

Grillparzer, F. *Werke*. Stuttgart, 1874.

Grün, A. *Letzter Ritter*, in *Werke*, Vol. III. Berlin, 1877.

Gutzkow, K. *Werke*, ed. by P. Müller. Leipzig.

Hauff, W. *Lichtenstein*, ed. by M. Drescher, in *Werke*, Vol. IV. Berlin, 1930.

Hebbel, C. F. *Werke*, ed. by W. von Scholz. Stuttgart, 1923.

Heine, H. *Werke*, ed. by E. Elster, 2d ed. Leipzig.

Herwegh, G. *Gedichte eines Lebendigen*, ed. by H. Tardel, in *Werke*, Vol. I. Berlin.

Hoffmann, E. T. A. *Dichtungen*, ed. by W. Harich. Weimar, 1924.

Hoffmann, V. Fallersleben. *Lieder und Romanzen*, in *Werke*, Vols. I–III. Berlin, 1891.

Immermann, K. *Münchhausen* and *Trauerspiel in Tirol*, ed. by M. Koch, in *DNL*, Vols. CLIX and CLX. Stuttgart.

―――― *Epiconen*, Berlin, 1854.

Kleist, H. von. *Werke*, ed. by E. Schmidt. Leipzig, 1904.

Körner, J. *Zriny*, ed. by M. Fuchs, in *Werke*. Berlin, 1911.

Laube, H. *Werke*, ed. by H. Houben. Leipzig, 1909.

Lenau, N. *Werke*, ed. by E. Castle. Leipzig, 1911.

Ludwig, O. *Erbförster*, ed. by P. Merker, in *Werke*, Vol. VI. München, 1914.

Mörike, E. *Werke*. Stuttgart, 1878.

Müller, W. *Schöne Müllerin*, in *Gedichte*. Leipzig, 1868.

Müllner, A. *Die Schuld*, in *Theater*, Vol. II. Stuttgart, 1820.

Münch-Bellinghausen, E. *Griseldis*, in *Werke*, Vol. II. Wien, 1856.

Novalis (F. von Hardenberg). *Heinrich von Ofterdingen*, ed. by J. Minor, in *Schriften*, Vol. IV. Jena, 1923.

Platen, A. von. *Romantischer Ödipus*, ed. by M. Koch, in *Werke*. Leipzig.

Raimund, F. *Werke*, ed. by C. Glossy and A. Sauer. Wien, 1881.

Richter, J. P. F. *Titan*, in *Werke*, Vols. X–XII. Berlin, 1848.

Rückert, F. *Werke*. Frankfurt-am-Main, 1882.

Schiller, J. F. *Werke*, Horen ed. Berlin.

Schlegel, F. *Alarkos*, in *Werke*, Vol. I. Berlin, 1809.
Tieck, L. *Aufruhr in den Cevennen*, in *Schriften*, Vol. XXVI. Berlin, 1854.
—— *Phantasus*, 2d ed. Berlin, 1845.
—— *Vittoria Accorombona*, 2d ed. Breslau. 1841.
Tiedge, C. *Urania*. Reutlingen, 1802.
Uhland, L. *Gedichte und Dramen*. Stuttgart, 1885.
Wagner, R. *Schriften*. Leipzig, 1871 ff.
Wernep, Z. *Werke*. Grimma.

XIX CENTURY (SECOND HALF)

Alexis, W. *Ruhe ist die erste Bürgerpflicht*, 3d ed. Berlin, 1872.
Anzengruber, L. *Werke*, ed. by R. Latzke and O. Rommel. Wien, 1922.
Bodenstedt, F. *Mirza Schaffy*. Berlin, 1917.
Dehmel, R. *Weib und Welt*, in *Werke*, Vol. III. Berlin, 1907 ff.
Droste-Hülshoff, A. *Werke*. München, 1925.
Ebers, G. *Ägyptische Königstochter*, 7th ed. Stuttgart, 1879.
Ebner-Eschenbach, M. *Werke*. Berlin.
Fontane, T. *Werke*. Berlin, 1920.
Freytag, G. *Werke*. Leipzig, 1887.
Fulda, L. *Talisman*, 13th ed. Stuttgart, 1895.
Geibel, E. *Werke*, ed. by W. Stammler. Leipzig.
George, S. *Werke*. Berlin, 1928.
Gutzkow, K. *Ritter vom Geiste*, 2d ed. Leipzig, 1852.
Halbe, M. *Jugend*. Dresden, 1895.
Hartleben, O. *Werke*. Berlin, 1909.
Hauptmann, G. *Biberpelz*. Berlin, 1899.
—— *Einsame Menschen*. Berlin, 1899.
—— *Fuhrmann Henschel*. Berlin, 1899.
—— *Hanneles Himmelfahrt*. Berlin, 1902.
—— *Versunkene Glocke*. Berlin, 1897.
—— *Vor Sonnenaufgang*. Berlin, 1892.
—— *Weber*. Berlin, 1899.
Hebbel, C. F. *Werke*, ed. by W. von Scholz. Stuttgart, 1923.
Heine, H. *Werke*, ed. by E. Elster, 2d ed. Leipzig.
Heyse, P. *Werke*. Berlin.
Hirschfeld, L. *Mütter*. Berlin, 1896.
Hofmannsthal, H. von. *Tor und Tod*, in *Kleinere Dramen*, Vol. I. Leipzig, 1919.
Holz, A. und Schlaf. *Familie Selicke*. Berlin, 1890.
Jensen, W. *Braune Erica*, ed. by E. Joynes. Boston, 1894.
Keller, G. *Leute von Seldwyla*, Vol. I, ed. by J. Fränkel, in *Werke*, Vol. VII. Zürich and München, 1927.
—— Other works in *Werke*, new ed. Stuttgart.
Kretzer, M. *Gesicht Christi*. Leipzig, 1919.
Laube, H. *Der deutsche Krieg*, ed. by H. Houben, in *Werke*. Leipzig, 1909.
Liliencron, D. von. *Poggfred*, ed. by R. Dehmel, in *Werke*, Vol. I. Berlin, 1913.
Ludwig, O. *Werke*, ed. by G. Freytag. Berlin.

Meyer, C. F. *Sämtliche Werke*, Taschen ed. Leipzig.
Nissel, F. *Agnes von Meran*, in *Dramatische Werke*. Stuttgart, 1912.
Raabe, W. *Hungerpastor*, in *Sämtliche Werke*, Vol. I. Berlin-Gruenewald.
Ruederer, J. *Fahnenweihe*. München, 1913.
Scheffel, J. V. *Trompeter von Säkkingen*, ed. by F. Payer, in *Werke*, Vol. II. Leipzig and Wien.
Schnitzler, A. *Theaterstücke*. Berlin.
Spielhagen, F. *Werke*. Leipzig, 1890.
Spitteler, C. *Prometheus und Epimetheus*. Aarau, 1881.
Stifter, A. *Nachsommer*, ed. by K. Eben and F. Hüller, in *Werke*, Vols. VI–VIII. Prague.
Storm, T. *Schimmelreiter*, ed. by A. Koester, in *Werke*, Vol. VII. Leipzig, 1920.
Sudermann, H. *Ehre*. Stuttgart, 1901.
—— *Es war*. Stuttgart, 1895.
—— *Frau Sorge*. Stuttgart, 1897.
—— *Glück im Winkel*. Stuttgart, 1902.
—— *Heimat*. Stuttgart, 1893.
—— *Johannes*. Stuttgart, 1899.
—— *Sodoms Ende*. Stuttgart, 1893.
Vischer, F. T. *Auch Einer*. Stuttgart, 1908.
Wagner, R. *Schriften*. Leipzig, 1871 ff.
Weber, F. W. *Dreizehnlinden*, ed. by E. Weber and F. Weber, in *Dichtungen*, Vol. III. Paderborn, 1922.
Wildenbruch, E. von. *Werke*, ed. by B. Litzmann. Berlin, 1912.

XX CENTURY

Reference books:

Robertson, *op. cit.*, pp. 621–640.
Vogt and Koch, *op. cit.*, Vol. III, pp. 234–365.
Wiegler, P., *op. cit.*, Vol. II, pp. 682–858.

Alverdes, P. *Pfeiferstube*, trans. New York, 1930.
Bahr, H. *Konze*. Berlin, 1910.
Barlach, E. *Suendflut*. Berlin, 1925.
Brecht, B. *Trommeln in der Nacht*. Berlin, 1923.
Brod, M. *Tycho Brahe*. Leipzig, 1915.
Bronnen, A. *Vatermord*. Berlin, 1925.
Dehmel, R. *Zwei Menschen*, in *Werke*, Vol. V. Berlin, 1908.
Döblin, A. *Berge Meere und Giganten*. Berlin, 1924.
—— *Berlin Alexanderplatz*. Berlin, 1930.
Frank, L. *Karl und Anna*. Leipzig, 1929.
Frenssen, G. *Jörn Uhl*. Berlin, 1909.
George, S. *Werke*. Berlin, 1928.
Goering, R. *Scapa Flow*. Berlin, 1919.
—— *Seeschlacht*. Berlin, 1919.
Hardt, E. *Tantris der Narr*. Leipzig, 1911.
Hasenclever, W. *Der Sohn*. München, 1917.
Hauptmann, G. *Dorothea Angermann*. Berlin, 1926.
—— *Emanuel Quint*. Berlin, 1910.
—— *Indipohdi*. Berlin, 1921.
—— *Rose Bernd*. Berlin, 1904.

Hesse, H. *Demian.* Berlin, 1922.
Johst, H. *Der König.* München, 1924.
Kaiser, G. *Bürger von Calais.* Berlin, 1920.
——— *Gas,* Vols. I and II. Potsdam, 1924–1925.
——— *Von Morgens bis Mitternachts.* Potsdam, 1920.
Mann, H. *Die Armen.* Leipzig, 1917.
——— *Der Kopf.* Berlin, 1925.
Mann, T. *Buddenbrooks.* Berlin, 1929.
——— *Königliche Hoheit,* in *Werke,* Vol. V. Berlin, 1925.
——— *Tonio Kröger.* Berlin.
——— *Zauberberg.* Berlin, 1930.
Mombert, A. *Aon.* Berlin, 1907–1911.
Remarque, E. *Im Westen nichts Neues.* Berlin, 1929.
Renn, L. *Krieg,* trans. London, 1930.
Rilke, R. M. *Werke.* Leipzig, 1927.
Scholz, W. von. *Jude von Konstanz,* in *Werke,* Vol. II. Stuttgart, 1924.
Schönherr, K. *Glaube und Heimat.* Leipzig, 1911.
Sorge, R. *Bettler,* 4th ed. Berlin, 1919.
Spitteler, C. *Olympischer Frühling.* Jena, 1911.
Sternheim, C. *Bürger Schippel.* München, 1920.
——— *Hose.* Leipzig, 1919.

——— *Snob.* München, 1920.
Sudermann, H. *Hohes Lied.* Stuttgart, 1909.
Thoma, L. *Moral.* München, 1908.
Toller, E. *Deutscher Hinkemann.* Potsdam, 1923.
——— *Maschinenstürmer.* Leipzig, 1922.
——— *Masse-Mensch.* Potsdam, 1925.
——— *Wandlung.* Potsdam, 1922.
Unruh, F. von. *Ein Geschlecht.* Leipzig, 1918.
——— *Offiziere.* Frankfurt-am-Main, 1925.
——— *Platz.* München, 1920.
Viebig, C. *Wacht am Rhein.* Berlin, 1906.
Wassermann, J. *Christian Wahnschaffe.* Berlin, 1919.
Wedekind, F. *Werke.* München, 1919.
Werfel, F. *Gedichte.* Berlin, 1927.
——— *Spiegelmensch.* Leipzig, 1920.
——— *Verdi,* trans. New York, 1925.
——— *Tod des Kleinbürgers.* Berlin, 1927.
Wildgans, A. *Dies Irae.* Leipzig, 1918.
Zuckmayer, C. *Fröhlicher Weinberg.* Berlin, 1925.
——— *Hauptmann von Köpenick.*
Zweig, A. *Streit um den Sergeanten Grischa.* Potsdam, 1928.

BIBLIOGRAPHY — FRENCH LITERATURE

This is an abbreviated list of the works which have been studied and compose the material upon which the conclusions of Chapter Thirteen are based, so far as French literature is concerned. In this list are enumerated only those works that are regarded representative in the study of the problems of this chapter.[1] For the nineteenth century the list is composed almost exclusively of novels and plays in which social ideas and attitudes are seen at work. Social ideas expressed in political, social, and philosophical treatises are studied in Volumes Two and Three of this work; for this reason they are not included here.

BEFORE 1100

Saints' lives (3)
Sainte Eulalie, Saint Léger, and *Saint Alexis.* All from W. Foerster and E. Koschwitz, *Altfranzösisches Übungsbuch,* 5th ed. Leipzig, 1915.

XII CENTURY

Epics:
La Chanson de Roland, var. eds.
Le Pèlerinage Charlemagne, ed. by Koschwitz, 5th ed. Leipzig, 1907.
Le Couronnement Louis, ed. by Langlois. Paris, 1888; same ed., Paris, 1925.
Le Roman de Thèbes, Anc. Textes ed. Paris, 1890.
Raoul de Cambrai, ed. by Tuffrau. Paris, 1924.

Moralists:
Livre des manières and *Le Proverbe au vilain.*

Both in chap. v, Langlois, *La Vie en France au moyen âge,* Vol. II. Paris, 1926–1928.

Romances:
Tristan et Iseult, ed. by J. Bédier. Paris, 1926. Modernized.
Chrétien de Troyes. *Yvain* and *Erec et Enide,* var. eds. Both ed. by W. Foerster. Halle.

Shorter narratives:
Marie de France. *Seven Lais,* ed. by E. Ruckert. New York, 1901.
La Mule sans frein, ed. by Orlowski. Paris, 1911.
Richeut, in Méon, *Nouveau recueil de fabliaux,* Vol. I. 1823.

XIII CENTURY

Romances:
Aucassin et Nicolette, var. eds.
Galeran, Joufrois, La Chastelaine de Vergi, and

[1] Editions published in Paris unless otherwise indicated.

Le Chastelain de Couci. These in chap. v, Langlois, *op. cit.*, Vol. I.

Religious literature:

Rutebeuf. *Le Miracle de Théophile,* var. eds.
Bodel, Jean. *Le Jeu de Saint Nicolas,* var. eds.
Gautier de Coinci. [50] *Miracles de la Sainte Vierge.*
Poems, ed. by Poquet. Paris, 1857.

Secular drama:

Adam de la Halle. *Jeu de Robin et Marion,* ed. by Champion.
——— *Jeu de la feuillée,* ed. by Champion.

Lyric poetry:

Rutebeuf, ed. by Kressner and Wolfenbüttel. 1885.
Also various anonymous lyrics.

Allegory:

Roman de la Rose, Soc. Anc. Textes ed.

Moralists:

La Bible Guiot, La Bible au Seigneur de Berzé, Le Besant de Dieu, La Riote du monde, Le Roman de Carité, Miserere, Les Quatre âges de l'homme, Les Lamentations de Mahieu, and *Le Contrefait de Renard.* All in Langlois, *op. cit.*, Vol. II.

Fables and short stories:

Roman de Renard, 4 vols. 1882.
Montaiglon, A. Selections from *Recueil géneral des fabliaux.* Paris, 1872–1890.

XIV CENTURY

Epics:

Hue Capet and *Floovent,* var. eds.

Romances:

La Patience de la Comtesse d'Anjou and *Sone de Nansai.* Both in Langlois, *op. cit.*, Vol. I.

Moralists:

Le Livre de la Chevalier de la Tour Landry, in English. London, 1930.
Contes moralisés de Nicole Bozon. Paris, 1889.
Le Registre de Gilles li Muisis, in Langlois, *op. cit.*, Vol. II.
Colonna, Egidio (Gilles de Rome). *Du Gouvernement des rois,* ed. by Molenaer. New York and London, 1899.

Religious drama:

Miracles de Notre Dame, Soc. Anc. Textes ed., Vol. I.

Fabliaux:

Montaiglon, *op. cit.*

Lyric poetry:

Deschamps, E., various eds., including "*Miroir du mariage,*" Soc. Anc. Textes ed.

History:

Joinville, ed. by Wailly. Paris, 1874.
Froissart, ed. by K. de Lettenhove. Paris, 1870–1877.

XV CENTURY TO 1515

Moralists:

Christine de Pisan. *See* M. J. Pinet, *Christine de Pisan.* Paris, 1927.
Chartier, Alain. *Le Quadrilogue invectif.* Paris, 1923; series *Classiques françaises du moyen âge.*

Drama:

Picot, E. and C. Nyrop [6]. *Nouveau recueil de farces françaises.* Paris, 1880.
Recueil géneral des sotties [9], Soc. Anc. Textes ed. Paris, 1902.
Maistre Pierre Pathelin. Paris, 1924.

Short stories:

Antoine de la Salle. *Cent nouvelles nouvelles* and *Les Quinze joies du mariage,* 2 vols. Paris, 1928 and 1888.

Novel:

A. de la Salle. *Petit Jehan de Saintré.* Paris, 1926.

Lyric poets:

Machault, G. Paris, 1909.
Villon, Fr., var. eds.
Charles d'Orléans, 2 vols. Paris, 1896.

XVI CENTURY

Historian:

Commines, Ph. de, in résumé, 2 vols. Paris, 1924–1925.

Lyric poets:

Marot, C. Paris, 1911.
Du Bellay, Joachim, 5 vols. 1908–1923.
Du Bartas, G. 1611.
Scève, M. 1927.
Marguerite de Navarre (d'Angoulême). 1873.
Houx, J. le. *Vaux de Vire.* 1875.
Ronsard, P. de. *Œuvres,* var. eds.
In general for sixteenth century see A. Tilley, *Literature of the French Renaissance,* 2 vols. Cambridge, 1904.

Drama:

Jodelle. *Eugène,* in *Œuvres,* 2 vols. 1868–1870.
Odet de Turnèbe. *Les Contents.* 1584.
Jean de la Taille. *Les Corrivaux,* in *Œuvres,* Vol. IV. 1879.

Translations :

Amyot. *Les Vies de Plutarque.* 1574.

Philosophy, religion, moralizations, etc. (4 authors):

Rabelais. *Gargantua* and *Pantagruel,* var. eds.

Calvin. *Institution chrétienne*. Geneva, 1888,
Périers, B. des. *Cymbalum mundi*, in *Œuvres*.
2 vols. 1856.
Montaigne. *Essais*, var. eds.

Romance:
Amadis de Gaule, 12 vols. Antwerp, 1561.

Short stories:
Marguerite de Navarre (d'Angoulême). *Hepta-méron*. New York, 1925.
Périers, B. des. *Joyeux devis*, in *Œuvres*, 2 vols. 1856.

History, politics, and memoirs:
Anon. *Histoire de Bayart*.
Pasquier, E. *Recherches de la France*, in *Œuvres*, 2 vols. 1849.
Noue, F. de la. *Discours*. Basle, 1587.
Bodin, Jean. *Six Livres de la République*. 1586.
Thou, J. A. de. *Historiarum sui temporis*, 12 vols. 1734.
Hotman, F. *Franco-Gallia*, in English. London, 1721.
—— *Satire Ménippée*. 1878.
Brantôme. *Œuvres*, 13 vols. 1858–1895.

Science:
Paré, Ambroise. *Œuvres*, 3 vols. 1840.
Palissy, Bernard. *Œuvres*. 1890.

XVII CENTURY

Satires:
Régnier, M. 1930.
Boileau, var. eds.
Pascal. *Lettres Provinciales*, var. eds.
Cyrano de Bergerac. *Lettres satiriques*, in *Œuvres*. 1921.

Drama:
Corneille. *Le Cid, Horace*, and *Le Menteur*, var. eds.
Molière. *Les Précieuses ridicules, Le Bourgeois gentilhomme, Tartuffe, Femmes savantes*, and *École des femmes*, var. eds.
Racine. *Andromaque, Phèdre*, and *Athalie*, var. eds.
Cyrano de Bergerac. *Le Pédant joué*, in *Œuvres*. 1921.

Novels:
Scudéry, Mlle de. *Artamène*, 10 vols. 1654.
Sorel, Ch. *Histoire comique de Francion*. 1858.
La Fayette, Mme de. *La Princesse de Clèves*, var. eds.
Fénelon, *Télémaque*, var. eds.

Philosophy, history, moralizations, etc. (5 authors):
Descartes. *Discours de la méthode*, var. eds.
Pascal. *Pensées*, var. eds.
Bossuet. *Histoire universelle*, var. eds.
Fontenelle. *Entretiens sur la pluralité des mondes* and *Digression sur les anciens et modernes*, var. eds.
La Bruyère. *Caractères*, var. eds.

Religion:
St. François de Sales. *Introduction à la vie dévote*, var. eds.

Fables:
La Fontaine, var. eds.

XVIII CENTURY

Drama:
Régnard. *Le Légataire universel*, var. eds.
Lesage. *Turcaret*, var. eds.
Voltaire. *Mahomet*, var eds.
Marivaux. *Le Jeu de l'amour et du hasard*, var. eds.
Beaumarchais. *Le Barbier de Séville* and *Le Mariage de Figaro*, var. eds.
Sedaine. *Le Philosophe sans le savoir*. 1914.

Novels and stories:
Lesage. *Gil Blas*, var. eds.
Marivaux. *Le Paysan parvenu*. 1825.
Prévost. *Manon Lescaut*, var. eds.
Voltaire. *Zadig, Candide, La Pucelle*, and *Jeannot et Colin*, var. eds.
Rousseau. *Julie* and *Emile*, var. eds.
Diderot. *La Religieuse*. 1822.
Les Bijoux indiscrets. 1748.
B. de Saint Pierre. *Paul et Virginie*, var. eds.

Philosophers and reformers:
Bayle, P. *Pensées sur la comète*, 2 vols. 1911–1912.
Dictionnaire historique et critique. 1820–1824.
Rousseau. *Contrat social*, var. eds.
Mably, as analyzed in E. A. Whitfield. *Gabriel Bonnot de Mably*. London, 1930.
Montesquieu. *Lettres persanes*, var. eds.
Holbach, Baron d'. *Système de la nature*. 1821.
Condillac. *Traité des sensations*. 1788.

XIX AND XX CENTURIES

Reference books:

General bibliography:
Thième, Hugo. *Guide bibliographique de la littérature française de 1800 à 1906*. Paris, 1907. See particularly pt. ii, B, pp. 483 ff.

French civilization:
Rambaud, A. *Histoire de la civilisation française*, 2 vols. Paris, 1885.
—— *Histoire de la civilisation contemporaine de la France*. 1888.
Ducoudray, G. *Histoire et civilisation de la France*, 3 vols. 1904.

Special topics:
Wood, Mary M. *The Spirit of Protest in Old French Literature*. New York, 1917.
Norman, H. *Swindlers and Rogues in French Drama*. Chicago, 1928.

Abensour, L. *La Femme et le féminisme avant la Révolution* (diss.). Paris, 1923.

Epic:

Chateaubriand. *Les Martyrs.*

Novels:

Chateaubriand. *Atala* and *René*, var. eds.
Mme. de Staël. *Corinne*, var. eds.
Constant, B. *Adolphe*, var. eds.
Hugo. *Notre Dame de Paris* and *Les Misérables*, var. eds.
Dumas père. *Les Trois mousquetaires*, var. eds.
Sand, George. *Indiana, La Petite Fadette*, and *Le Meunier d'Angibault*, var. eds.
Musset. *Confessions d'un enfant du siècle*, var. eds.
Balzac. *Eugénie Grandet* and *Le Père Goriot*, var. eds.
Stendhal. *La Chartreuse de Parme*, var. eds.
Mérimée. *Colomba, Carmen*, and *Matteo Falcone*, var. eds.
Flaubert. *Madame Bovary* and *Un cœur simple*, var. eds.
Goncourt. *Sœur Philomène*, var. eds.
Zola. *L'Assommoir* and *La Terre*, var. eds.

France, A. *Le Crime de Sylvestre Bonnard, Thaïs. L'Ile des Pingouins*, and *Les Dieux ont soif*, var. eds.
Maupassant. *Une vie*, var. eds.
Barrès, M. *L'Appel au soldat*, var. eds.
Bourget, P. *L'Etape* and *Un divorce*, var. eds.

Dramas:

Hugo. *Hernani, Ruy Blas*, and *Le Roi s'amuse*, var. eds.
Musset. *On ne badine pas avec l'amour*, var eds.
Dumas père. *Antony*, var. eds.
Vigny. *Chatterton*, var. eds.
Dumas fils. *La Dame aux camélias, Le Demi-Monde, Le Fils naturel, La Femme de Claude, Les Idées de Mme Aubray*, and *La Question d'argent*, var. eds.
Augier. *Le Gendre de M. Poirier* and *Le Fils de Giboyer*, var. eds.
Becque, H. *Les Corbeaux*, var. eds.
Hervieu, P. *Les Tenailles*, var. eds.
Rostand. *Cyrano de Bergerac*, var. eds.
Sardou. *Divorçons*, var. eds.
Brieux. *La Robe rouge* and *Blanchette*, var. eds.
Curel, F. de. *Le Repas du lion*, var. eds.

INDEXES

INDEXES

Index of Authors

All names given in the Appendixes, including those of the authors of reference and other works cited, are not included in the Index. For these names see the Appendixes.

Abbott, W. C., vii
Abert, H., 532, 537, 539, 567, 570
Abert, H., 570
Allport, G. W., 84
Anand, M. R., 284
Anderson, C. A., vii
Appel, P., 156
Aristophanes, 560, 598
Aristotle, 55, 56, 170, 177, 599, 605
Aristoxenes, 560
Aubert, M., 450
Aubry, P., 572
Augustine, St. See St. Augustine

Bachofer, L., 280
Baikie, J., 147, 239
Baillet, J., 145, 148
Baldensperger, M. F., 236
Baldwin, J. M., 84
Barcelo, A. P. Y., 156
Bayet, C., 225
Beal, S., 116
Beauvais, V. de. See De Beauvais, V.
Becker, H., 5
Beethoven, 59
Below, G. von. See Von Below, G.
Benedict, R., 6, 39, 41–43, 45, 683
Bennett, C. A., 131
Benoit, F., 450
Berger, C. Q., vii, 208
Bergson, H., 159, 161
Bernard, C., 86
Binyon, L., 266, 278
Boas, F., 233–36, 238, 244–45, 271, 273, 453, 534, 596–97, 674
Boas, G., 130, 167, 644
Boccaccio, 142
Boehme, J., 84
Boehmer, H., 518
Boethius, 531
Boldyreff, J. W., vii, 105, 634
Borel, E., 11
Bouchot, H., 450
Bouger, R., 450
Bouglé, C., 122
Bourguès, L., 535, 557, 558, 561, 563
Bovet, E., 231–33
Bréhier, L., 244, 311, 317, 323, 324, 329, 341, 466, 523
Breisig, K., 180
Bridgman, P. W., 19
Brown, J., 86
Brunetière, F., 216
Bücher, K., 534

Budge, E. A. W., 141, 145, 146
Bullock, C. J., vii
Burckhardt, J., 181, 637
Burr, C. S., 132
Butler, D. E. C., 131

Cahen, A., 552
Capart, J., 239, 273, 276
Carlyle, T., 651
Catullus, 142
Chambers, F., 231, 236, 257, 300, 301, 308, 313, 330, 356, 545, 598, 603–4, 605, 606–7, 611, 674–75, 677
Chapot, V., 240
Chaucer, 639–40
Choukas, M., 103, 683
Christ, W. von. See Von Christ, W.
Cicero, 89, 564
Clément, J., 317, 327
Cohn, W., 239
Cole, F. J., 204
Collignon, M., 301
Combarieu, J., 214, 215, 531–32, 534, 535, 536, 537, 552, 554–57, 558–59, 561, 563, 564, 565, 567, 570, 571, 572, 574, 577, 578, 587–89
Comte, A., x, 9, 29, 38
Coomaraswamy, A. K., 244, 282–83, 314, 315, 632, 682
Cornelius, F., 224
Coulton, G. G., 313, 315, 519
Cournot, A., 11
Courthope, W. J., 315, 344, 614, 615, 620, 641, 643
Crawford, O. G. S., 200
Crew, H., 156
Cross, H., vii, 372
Crump, G., 323
Cumont, F., 142
Curtius, L., 510

Dale, E., 367
Dante, 57, 624, 626
Darmstaedter, L., 203–4, 206
Darwin, C., 59
Dasgupta, S., 131
Dautheville, S., 156
Dauzat, A., 449
David-Sauvageot, A., 600, 630, 643–44, 660
Davidson, R., 637
Da Vinci, Leonardo, 330
De Beauvais, V., 468
De Flore, Joachim, 91
De Labriolle, P. C., 614
De Laprade, V., 210, 449–50
Delbrueck, R., 273, 293

De Lorris, G., 621
De Meung, J., 622
Denéréaz, A., 535, 557, 558, 561, 563
Denis, M., 270, 315
De Nood, N. B., vii
Déonna, W., 226–30, 236, 239, 256–57, 273, 288, 290, 292–96, 299–300, 301, 303–4, 308, 325–26, 327, 330, 334, 335, 336–37, 514, 515–16, 523, 545
De Ridder, A., 296, 303, 514, 515, 516
De Roberty, E., 4
Descartes, 26
Deshairs, L., 450
De Wulf, M., 315–16, 632
Didron, A. N., 314
Diehl, C., 317–18, 450
Dilthey, W., 26, 168
D'Indy, V., 214
Diogenes Laertius, 81, 90, 104
Dionysius Halicarnassus, 611
Dixon, R. B., 6, 14
Dromel, J., 684
Duhem, P., 161, 167
Duprat, G. L., 30
Durkheim, E., 4, 38
Dutt, N. K., 122
Dutt, R. C., 114
Dvořák, M., 247

Eales, N. B., 204
Eddy, M. B., 134
Edgell, G. H., 510, 511, 512, 513, 514, 515, 516, 519, 520–21, 522
Efimoff, N. I., 237
Elisséev, S., vii, 265, 273
Ellis, W., 651
Ellwood, C. A., vii
Emmanuel, M., 552, 557
Ennemoser, J., 84
Epuy, M., 452
Erman, A., 141, 145
Evreinoff, N., 531
Ewer, M. A., 313, 615

Farnell, L. R., 214
Farquhar, J. N., 124
Ferguson, J. C., 239
Ferguson, W. S., 601
Fletcher, W. J. B., 141
Flore, Joachim de. See De Flore, Joachim
Foerster, W., 613, 619
Forke, A., 139
Foth, M., 253, 273
Franke, A., 148
Frey, F. C., vii
Friedel, E., 581
Froude, 651

Galpin, C., 238, 453
Gardner, E. A., 511
Gardner, P., 312, 313
Garrison, F. H., 204
Gaskell, 86
Gastoué, A., 570, 571
Gaultier, P., 452
Gay, E. F., vii, 223

Gérold, T., 570
Gevaërt, F. A., 552, 557
Ghersi, E., 683
Gibb, E. J. W., 129
Giles, H. A., 125, 126, 127, 139, 148
Gillet, L., 315, 323, 326, 356, 450, 629, 683
Ginsberg, M., 6
Girard, J., 601, 603
Glasenapp, H. S., 124
Golovine, N. N., vii
Gowen, H. H., 111, 113, 124
Graf, T., 301
Granet, M., 63, 125, 128, 139, 148, 149, 243, 280, 535
Gray, C., 203, 206, 539, 569, 571, 577, 579, 580
Gross, O., 84
Grosset, J., 552
Guillon, M. N. S., 633

Haas, R., 582
Hartshorne, E. Y., vii
Hausenstein, W., 237
Hautecoeur, L., 358, 450–52
Hegel, G. W. F., 210, 225
Hekler, A., 293, 302
Helmont, J. B. van. See Van Helmont, J. B.
Herakleitos, 81, 598
Herrick, 86
Herrmann-Brückman, 290
Heyman, G., 84
Hobhouse, L., 6
Homer, 240
Horten, M., 84
Hourticq, L., 322, 325, 327, 329, 350, 356, 365, 465, 521, 523
Hsieh Ho, 265
Hügel, F. von. See Von Hügel, F.
Hughes, R., 651
Hugo, V., 214
Huizinga, J., 315–16, 329, 466, 518, 615, 629
Hulme, E. W., 205
Hunt, R., 84
Husserl, E., 58

Jacob, E., 323
Jacobi, H., 124
James, W., 84, 131
Jenkins, C., 614
Jex-Blake, E., 290, 308
Jitta, J., 273, 305, 322
Jones, W., 552
Jung, C. G., 84

Kaschnitz-Weinberg, G., 310
Keith, B. A., 113, 124
Kempf, B. J., 84
Kimball, F., 510, 511, 512, 513, 514, 515, 516, 519, 520–21, 522
Kirchoff, A., 159–60
Klages, L., 84
Klüver, H., 84
Knowles, D., 131
Koch, M., 613, 619
Kondakov, N. P., 311, 315, 317
Koschwitz, E., 613, 619

Koussevitzky, S., vii
Krauss, H., 406–7
Kretschmer, E., 84
Kretzschmar, H., 582
Krishna, K. B., vii
Kroeber, A. L., 43
Kummer, F., 236
Kurella, H., 84

Labriolle, P. C. de.   See De Labriolle, P. C.
Lagrange, J., 240
Lake, K., 110
Lalo, C., 216, 225, 534, 537, 557, 560, 565, 581
Lamartine, 214
Lang, A., 598
Lange, K., 273, 356
Langfeld, 87
Langlois, V., 613, 619
Lappo-Danilevsky, A., 168
Laprade, V. de.   See De Laprade, V.
Lapshin, I. I., vii, 531
Lawrence, W. W., 615, 616
Lecornu, L., 156
Legge, J., 139, 141, 148
Lenoir, P., 600
Leontieff, V. V., vii
Lesser, A., 43
Lethaby, W. R., 201, 315, 522
Leuba, J. H., 131
Lévy-Bruhl, L., 63
Ligeti, P., 200, 206–7, 253, 343, 348, 525
Lincoln, A., 58
Locke, J., 90
Loret, V., 552
Lorris, G. de.   See De Lorris, G.
Lossky, N. O., vii
Lovejoy, A. O., 130, 167, 347, 452, 644
Lowes, J. L., 236, 262
Loyola, St. Ignatius.   See St. Ignatius Loyola
Luciani, 87
Lucretius, 81
Lunden, W. A., vii

MacDonald, A., 683
Macdonell, A. A., 113, 115, 124
McDougall, W., 84
Mach, E., 29
Machabey, A., 552
Machen, A., 660
Machiavelli, 38
Maillard, P., 589
Mâle, E., 244, 311, 316, 317, 319–20, 322–23, 326, 327–28, 329, 339, 341–43, 345, 466, 523, 623, 629
Malinowski, B., 6, 45–46
Marcel, H., 450, 687
Maritain, J., 283, 315, 325, 365–66, 527, 545
Marston, L. R., 84
Martin, A. von.   See Von Martin, A.
Maspero, H., 125, 148, 276
Maximovitch, E., vii
Mead, M., 6
Mentré, F., 236
Merton, R. K., vii, 156
Metallov, 571
Meung, J. de.   See De Meung, J.

Michel, A., 253, 315, 321, 325, 326, 327, 333, 335, 338–39, 347, 349, 351–52, 354–55, 356–58, 359–61, 363, 516–17, 522
Mickwitz, G., vii
Millar, R., 651
Mironoff, A. M., 311, 312
Monier-Williams, M., 116
Monnier, P., 330, 334
Montalembert, 110
Moore, G. F., 114, 126, 148
Moormon, F. W., 452
Müller, F. Max, 113, 114, 132
Müller-Frienfels, R., 262
Muntz, E., 516

Neumann, C. J., 180
Newton, I., 58, 162–63
Nietzsche, F., 43, 84
Nikolsky, V. A., 314
Nilsson, M. P., 598
Nock, A. D., 131
Nohl, H., 273
Norman, H., 647
Norwood, G., 600

Ogburn, W. F., 201
Okuneff, N. L., vii, 372
Oldenburg, S. S., vii
Ostrouchov, P. A., vii
Ostwald, W., 84

Pareto, V., 38, 63
Parker, E. F., vii
Passarge, W., 237
Paulhan, F., 452
Pauly, A. F., 598
Peers, E. A., 131
Pélagand, F., 552
Petrie, W. M. F., 199–203, 206
Pfuhl, E., 300
Phelps, R. H., vii
Pickard-Cambridge, A. W., 599, 600
Planck, M., 25
Plato, 10, 56, 536, 598, 604
Pliny, 308, 563, 609–10
Plutarch, 564
Poincaré, H., 11, 29, 160
Porter, A. K., 257
Pott, W. S. A., 127
Pottier, E., 300
Pounin, N., 314
Pratt, J. B., 132
Pushkareff, S., vii

Quercy, G., 131

Radcliffe-Brown, A. R., 6, 42–43, 45
Ragozin, Z. J., 113
Ranulf, S., 600
Rapson, E. J., 113, 122
Réau, L., 251, 264, 359, 361, 517
Reicha, A., 584
Reinach, S., 298
Rey, A., 148
Reynaud, L., 634, 644, 660–61

Riazanovsky, V. A., 314
Ricci, C., 347, 349
Richardson, B. E., 294
Rickert, H., 22, 30, 168
Ridder, A. de. See De Ridder, A.
Riegl, A., 273, 306, 310, 347, 349, 525
Riemann, H., 552, 557
Rietsch, H., 225
Robertson, J. G., 613, 619
Roberty, E. de. See De Roberty, E.
Rodenwaldt, G., 290
Rolland, R., 214, 582
Roller, T., 311
Ronsard, P. de, 143
Rosenthal, E., 552
Rosenthal, L., 450
Ross, E. D., 148, 276
Rostovtzeff, M. I., vii
Ruskin, J., 313

St. Augustine, 548, 570, 610
St. Ignatius Loyola, 91, 132
Saintsbury, G., 598, 603, 605, 608–9, 615, 618, 632, 662–65, 687
Sakulin, P. 237
Sapir, E., 6, 39–41
Savitski, P. N., vii
Savonarola, 662
Schäfer, H., 273, 275, 405
Scheffler, K., 408
Scheltema, A. V., 273
Schering, A., 574
Schiller, F. M. S., 84
Schlosser, J., 632
Schmarsow, A., 273, 347, 349, 525
Schmid, W., 598
Schneider, H., 224
Schücking, L. L., 237
Sellers, E., 290, 308
Senart, U., 122
Seneca, 564
Sherrington, 86
Shmitt, F. I., 237
Silberer, H., 131, 615
Sirén, O., 239, 266, 273, 278–81, 454
Smidt, H., 534
Smith, H. L., 236
Smith, K., 156
Smith, T. L., vii
Sorokin, P. A., 5, 17–18, 24, 30, 32, 39, 60, 69, 156, 159, 176, 181, 187, 238, 452, 453, 641, 682
Spangenberg, H., 180
Spaulding, O. L., vii
Spencer, H., x, 534
Spengler, O., 224
Spranger, E., 84
Stählin, O., 598
Starbuck, E. D., 131
Statham, H. H., 257, 510–11, 513, 515, 516, 520, 521, 522, 523, 524, 529
Staudenmaier, 84
Stern, L. W., 84
Stevenson, M. S., 124
Stieve, F., 181

Stravinsky, 577, 592
Strong, A., 306, 308
Struve, P., vii
Strygowski, J., 347, 349
Sydow, E. von. See Von Sydow, E.

Taine, H., 334, 336, 337–38
Tarde, G., 4
Taylor, H. O., 315, 329, 344, 615
Thorndike, E. L., 94
Thurnwald, R., 238
Tieghem, P. van. See Van Tieghem, P.
Tilley, A., 638
Timasheff, N. S., vii
Tolstoi, L., 546
Troeltsch, E., 181
Troubetzkoy, E. N., 314
Tschuproff, A. A., 11, 22, 36
Tucci, G., 683
Tylor, E., 4, 6

Underhill, E., 131, 133
Unger, E., 277
Utitz, E., 253, 273

Valla, L., 636
Van Helmont, J. B., 84
Van Tieghem, P., 645
Venturi, A., 225, 317, 327
Vernon, P. J., 84
Verworn, M., 238, 271
Vico, G. B., x
Vierkandt, A., 273
Villari, P., 637
Vinci, Leonardo da. See Da Vinci, Leonardo
Violleant, 552
Vitry, P., 202, 325, 326
Vogel, W., 181
Vogt, F., 613, 619
Von Below, G., 167
Von Christ, W., 598
Von Hügel, F., 131
Von Martin, A., 637
Von Sydow, E., 238, 271, 453
Vossler, K., 274

Waddell, L. A., 683
Waetzoldt, W., 273
Wagner, P., 570
Waley, A., 239, 279
Wallascheck, V. R., 534
Wallis Budge, E. A. See Budge, E. A. W.
Wallis, W. D., 4, 5, 15
Walters, H. B., 276, 277, 288, 289, 290, 297–98, 300, 304, 305–8, 513–14
Webber, F. R., 314, 519, 615
Wellesz, E., 571, 582
Wells, F. L., 84
Westheim, P., 262
Wheeler, G., 6
Whitehead, A. N., 243
Whitney, L., 634, 644
Wickhoff, F., 306, 308
Wieger, P. L., 125, 127
Wiersma, E., 84

Wieszner, G. G., 236, 525
Wilamowitz-Moellendorff, U. von, 598, 601, 603
Wilpert, M., 311
Wilson, E. B., vii, 158, 186
Wilson, H. H., 112, 115
Winckelmann, 357
Windelbandt, W., 168
Winston, S., 5
Wissler, C., 6, 11, 12, 13
Wissowa, G., 598
Wölfflin, H., 251, 252–53, 273, 330, 332, 343, 347, 348, 408, 525
Woollett, H., 552, 574
Workman, N. B., 110

Worringer, W., 84, 253, 273, 276
Wreszinski, W., 276
Wulf, M. de.   See De Wulf, M.

Xénopol, A. D., 167–68

Young, Kimball, vii

Zadoks, A. H., 273, 305, 310, 322
Zaitzoff, A. A., vii
Ziegenfuss, W., 406
Zimmerman, C. C., vii, 238, 452, 453
Zola, E., 659
Zweig, Stefan, 134

Absolute, category of, 70, 87; in Ideational mentality, 73, 90–94, 114–39, 684; in mysticism, 130–32; nature of, 73, 97, 114–39; reality, 70, 114–39; recurrence, 167, 184–88; union with, 130–34

Absolutely unique process, 173

Absolutistic, ethics, 93–99; mentality, 87, 114–39; truth, 90–91, 98; values, 93, 99, 119–39

Abstract, formula, 22–24; Idealistic art, 259, 293, 323, 511, 679

Abstractions hypostatized in art, 253–54, 343–45, 598, 630–31

Acceleration, as time direction, 157–58; in tempo of art change, 287, 306–8, 352–55, 528–29, 684–86; law of, 685

Accidental, changes, 50–53; congeries, 10–13; factors, 51–52; traits in art, 256, 259, 292, 323, 679

Acephalic art, 251, 527, 650–51

Active, Ideational mentality, 73, 79, 83, 85, 88–99, 134–39; Sensate mentality, 74, 83, 85, 88–99, 139–40

Adaptation, definition of, 69–72; forms of, 72–76

Adjustment, endless in Sensate culture, 71–72, 81–83

Adolescence, in Idealistic art, 291–94; in Sensate art, 299, 300, 334–35

Adultery, frequency of, in literature, 622–24, 626, 636, 638, 656

Adventurer, as a hero in literature, 647

Aesthetic values, 95

Aestheticism, as a trait of Sensate art, 230, 257, 356, 364–66, 544–46, 564–66, 585, 608–12, 665–67. See also *sub* Musical

Age, depicted in art, 291–94, 299–300, 334–35; of certitude, 322

Ages, of gods, heroes, and men, in art, 289–99, 488–89, 499, 514–15, 523–27, 554–59, 575–78, 587, 600, 642–46, 650–51

Agricultural. See Rural

Allegory, and symbolism, 254, 314, 343, 508, 614–15, 629–30; definition of, 254, 344–45; in literature, 598, 614, 620, 625, 630–31; in painting and sculpture, 343–45

Als ob, mentality of, 218–20, 250, 361–64, 388, 654. See also Deceit, Illusionism, Theatricality, Visual

Alternation, in direction of process, 186–88; in theories of art, 224–31, 234–36; of forms of art, 308, 368, 404, 502–6, 672; of pure and purposeful art, 670–71; of Sensate and Ideational art, 678–81, 687; of unification and separation of art from other values, 672. See also Fluctuation, Recurrence

Amateurishness, in art. See Aestheticism

Ancestral portraiture, Chinese, 265–66; European, 322; Greek, 293, 301, 305; Roman, 301, 305–6

Animals, as art subjects, 439, 465–67; proportion of, in painting and sculpture, 465–72

Anonymity, as a trait of Ideational art, 258–59, 296, 323–25, 543–44, 555–56, 561–63, 585, 596, 598, 613, 629

Anthropological theories of culture integration, 4–7, 39–44

Antiquity, topics of, in art, 500–1, 590–91; proportion of, in printing and sculpture, 439–44, 500–1

Apathy, ataraxia, and imperturbability, Ideational, 79, 85, 115–19

Appearance, versus reality, in art, 218–20, 247–48, 251–53, 255, 263, 265, 270, 282–84, 290, 297, 312, 315, 346, 359–63, 368, 388, 398, 507–8, 680; in Buddhism, 114–19; in Christianity, 129; in Hinduism, 114–19; in Ideational and Sensate mentality, 70–71, 75, 80, 88, 90, 97, 114–19, 218–20, 248–51, 361–64, 388, 654; in Jainism, 123; in mysticism, 130–34; in Sufism, 128; in Taoism, 125. See also Illusionism, Reality

Applicability, extent of, of causal law, 29

Archaic, art, 234–35; imitation of, 307, 387, 601, 611; phase of art, 200, 228–29, 234–35

Architectural stage of art, 200, 207, 209, 217

Architecture, fluctuation of forms of, 515–27; Ideational, Idealistic, Sensate forms of, 507–11; order of blossoming among other arts, 200, 207, 209, 211; reaction to Visual, 526–27; revivals in, 523–24

Aristocracy, proportion of, in portraiture, 486; of the rich, 95

Art, and culture mentality, 67–88, 95, 211, 216–20, 227–30, 247–62, 678–88; autonomy of, 670–71, 672; of Assyria, 277, 549–50; of Byzantium, 317–18; of China, 265–66, 277–82, 535, 549–50; of Egypt, 264, 275–77, 535, 549; of India, 282–85, 535, 549; of Islam, 386, 421, 430, 456, 469, 490, 492; sequence of blossoming of various forms of, 200–9, 213–15, 221, 231–34; thematic spectrum of, 438; theories of development of, 223–36; theories of recurrence in, 198–99, 206–16. See also Bourgeoisie in art, Adolescence, Caricature, Catacombs, Complication, Content, Criticism, Free Art, *Genre*, Love in art, Modernism in art, Nudity in art, *Paysage*, Portraiture, Sex in art, Social classes in art, etc.

Art, forms of: architectural, sculptural, *malerisch*, 200–17; cubistic, 263–64, 540, 592; expressionistic, 251, 387–88; formal, 249–50, 387; Idealistic, 255–56; Ideational, Sensate, Mixed, in architecture, 507–10; ideoplastic and physioplastic, 240, 271; impressionistic, 250, 387–88; impure, pure, and purposeful, 543, 668–74; literature, 595–97; music, 531–40; naturalistic, 250, 253, 359–61, 387, 397, 643, 648–49; painting, 243–64; religious and secular, 376–86, 508, 514, 517, 534, 573–79, 598, 612–13; spiritual and Sensate, 409–38; symbolic, 229, 254, 343–45, 508, 614–15, 629–30. See also Architecture, Criticism, Literature, Music, Painting, Sculpture, Visual, etc.

Art appreciation, 230, 257, 356, 364–66, 544–46, 564–66, 585, 608–12, 665–67

Art criticism, 230, 356, 544–46, 564–66, 585, 608–12, 665–67

Artist, anonymity of, 295–96, 323–24, 555, 625; individualism of, 365–66, 544, 562, 601, 658; mentality of, 271–73, 279, 282–84, 324, 559, 617; position of, 302–3, 555, 562, 585, 600–1, 609–11; professionalization of, 544, 559, 562, 600–1, 617, 665, 680–81

As if, mentality of. See *Als ob*

Ascetic, mentality, 73, 79, 83, 85, 88–99, 106, 112–32; and nudity in painting and sculpture, 422–39

Asceticism versus sensuality in literature, 620–24

Aspects of culture, internal and external, 55–57

Association, and portrait, 469–70; between cultural elements, 10–18; between satellites of each type of art, 679–81; of culture, 97–99; of sensatism and genre, 491; of forms of painting with forms of architecture, 517, 528; of literature, 597, 686; of Ideationalism and religious art, 376; of music, 553, 567–68, 593; of sensatism and the secular, 376

Ataraxia. See Apathy

Autonomous self-regulation of social processes, 50–53

Autonomy, of art, 670–71, 672, see also Free art; of social system, 50–53

Baroque, 340, 346–48, 509–10, 525–26, 580–81

Bearers, of culture mentality, 69; of Ideational art, 683

Beat, in process, 174–75. See also Punctuation

Beautification in art, 256, 260, 291–93, 322–24

Beauty, appreciation of, 230–31, see also Aestheticism; Hegelian forms of, 210–12; Idealistic, 255–57, 291, 321–23, 540, 545, 599–600, 618–19, 630

Beauty, Ideational and Sensate, in architecture, 507–10, 517–18; in literature, 595–97, 600–4, 613–15, 633, 659, 668–81; in music, 531–33, 538, 540–41, 559, 587–89; in painting and sculpture, 95, 99, 141, 249–51, 257, 282–84, 325–26, 348, 536–61, 502–3

Becoming, concept of, 153–54; reality of, 73–74, 80–82, 94, 140–43, 247–48, 260–61, 270; specifications of, 154

Behaviorism, visual, 368

Behavioristic, fallacy, 55–57; interpretation of man, 500

Being, as a reality, 73, 80, 93; in Buddhism, 117; in Christianity, 129; in Hinduism; 114; in Jainism, 124; in mysticism, 130; in Taoism, 125; concept of, 153–54; specifications of, 154

Best sellers, 258–60, 262, 299, 304, 365, 585, 658–59

Biography, change in type of, 651; debunking, 651–52

Biological, aspects of mentality, 86–87; interpretation of man, 89, 500, 641, 650–51; needs, 71, 89, 94

Blossoming of art, 215, 263, 286, 290, 321, 542–43; order of various arts, 200, 207, 209, 214–16, 224–28, 230–32, 234

Body, human, in art. See Eroticism, Nudity

Bourgeoisie, in art, 471, 523, 641–42, 644, 651–52; in portraiture, 472–80, 486–89. See Portraiture

Boy in art. See Adolescence

Brahmanism, 108, 112–14, 120–21, 122, 123–24, 135, 282–85

Brahmans. See Brahmanism

Branching variety of linearism, 184

Buddhism, 112, 114–19, 123, 135, 277, 279–80

Byzantine art, 317–18

Caesura in social process, 174–81

Calmness, as a trait of Ideational and Idealistic art, 260, 291, 311, 322; in Ideational mentality, 79, 115–17, 125, 133. See also Being, Static

Caricature in art, 367, 490–91, 587, 641, 648, 650

Carnal needs, 71, 89, 94

Catacombs, art of, 244, 311

Catastrophe, 50–53; as a punctuation of social process, 180

Catholic. See Christian

Causal, and logico-meaningful method, 14–18, 22–32, 368, 505, 681; formula, 31; integration of culture, 10, 14–18, 42; reading of culture, 60

Censorship, as substitute for criticism, 312–14, 544, 550, 554, 565–66, 598–604, 617

Certitude, age of, 322; of logical norms, 62

Chance, congeries, 10–11; factors, 51–52

Change, acceleration of, 287, 306–8, 352–55, 528–29, 684–86; concept of, 153–54; directions of, 157–59; punctuation of, 174; rhythm of, 174–75; specification of, 154; tempo of, 174–75; unit of, 154–55. See also Acceleration, Dynamic, Fluctuation, Process

Chant, Gregorian, 537–39

Chaos, of perceptual world, 22; ways of ordering of perceptional, 22–48

Child in art. See Adolescence, Age

Chinese, art, 265–66, 277–82, 535, 549–50; culture mentality, 125–28, 141–44, 148–50

Christ, representation in art, 255–56, 317–20, 322, 327–28

Christian art, forms of: architecture, 517–18, 520–21; literature, 612–18; music, 537–38, 544, 567–71; painting and sculpture, 309–17, 320–22

Church, architecture, 508, 517–18; symbolism of architecture of, 519–20

Cinema. See Movies

Civilization. See Culture

Classes, social, in literature, 596, 652, 618, 641; in music, 592; in portraiture, 485–88

Classic art, 210, 215, 218–19, 228–29, 234–35

Classification, of art, 249–59; of culture integration, 10–11; of culture mentality, 72–76, 97–99; of direction of process, 157–58; major premises of culture mentality, 70–72; of methods of reading of culture, 57–60; types of processes, 188

Clearness versus unclearness in art, 331–32
Closed versus open in painting and architecture, 331–32
Coalescence of culture elements. See Integration
Code of love, 621
Cognition, of external milieu, 90; of mental processes, 89
Cognitive role of causal and logico-meaningful methods, 22–47
Collective character of Ideational and Idealistic art, 258–59, 296, 323–25, 543–44, 555–56, 561–62, 585, 596–98, 613, 625, 629
Colossalism as a trait of Sensate art, 304, 307, 366, 515–16, 525, 527, 541–42, 560–62, 564, 582–83, 659, 666–67
Column, Doric, Ionic, and others, 510–13
Comedy, 367, 490, 591, 601, 647–49, 653–54; musical, 587, 591
Commercialism in art, 217, 258–60, 262, 299, 304, 365, 542–43, 585, 658–59
Commodity, art as. See Commercialism
Common type of man and event as a topic of art, 89, 260, 298, 308, 338, 367, 485–88, 500, 592, 596, 618, 641–42, 644, 647, 650–53
Community, role of, in art. See Collective
Complexity of technique as a trait of Sensate art. See Complication
Complication of art technique, 229–30, 234, 300, 304, 308, 335, 344–47, 358, 364, 516–18, 522, 527, 541–43, 559–60, 564, 572, 581–83, 584, 586, 593, 653–54, 677
Conceptual reality versus Visual. See Reality, Visual
Confucianism, 148–50. See also Chinese
Congeries of cultural elements, 10–12
Constructivism as art style, 387–88, 399
Content, change of art, 376–84, 438, 440, 455–56, 461, 465, 467, 469, 486, 491, 498, 500, 502–5, 633, 641, 645, 649–50, 652, 655–58; of Ideational and Sensate art, 249–55, 257–58, 263
Control, of self and environment, 83
Convention, revolt against, in literature, 656
Conversion, mystic, 131–32
Corpse in art, 327, 341–43. See also Death, Macabre
Court of love, 572, 621–22
Criminal, as hero in art, 89, 260, 298, 308, 338, 367, 485–88, 500, 592, 596, 618, 641–44, 647, 650–52, 656
Criticism, art, 230, 257, 356, 365–66, 544–46, 564–66, 585, 608–12, 661–68, 675, 676. See sub Musical
Cubism, 263–64, 354, 362–65, 387, 399, 592
Cult of useful, 30, 94
Culture, change of, 48–51, see Change, Content, Dynamic; definition of, 3–5; Ideational, Sensate, and Idealistic, 66–76; internal and external aspects of, 55–57, 69–71; logical reading of, 60–62; major premises of mentality of, 62–66, 69–71; mentality of, 69; methods of reading of, 57–61, 66; methods of study of, 22–34. See also sub Idealistic, Ideational, Logico-meaningful, Mentality, Mixed, Sensate, etc.
Cyclical conception of social processes, 166–67,

184–86, 188. See also Alternation, Fluctuation, Process
Cynical Sensate mentality, 74, 82, 84, 85–87, 90, 93, 97–99, 103, 106, 108, 110, 139–43, 146
Cynics as Ideationalists, 104, 112, 129

Dadaism, 362
Dead, idealized, 322
Death scenes in art, 327, 329, 341–42
Debasing trend in art, 80, 260, 327, 500, 650–52
Decadents, 234–35
Decay, and technique, 468, 584
Deceit in art, 218–20, 248, 251. See also Illusionism
Decline, of heroic in art, 89, 260, 298, 308, 338, 367, 485–86, 500, 592, 618, 649–52; of Idealistic art, 285–87, 326; of Ideational art, 285, 290, 297, 329; of religious topics in art, 383–84; of Sensate art, 310–11, 357, 362–65; of upper classes and clergy in portraiture, 485–88; recurrence of, in art, 224–26, 228–32, 234–36
Delinquent. See Criminal, Pathological
Democracy, as hero in art. See Common type of man
Descriptive method, 45–47, 66
Directions of social process, 157–59
Distribution of types of mentalities, among large cultures, 111–52; among social classes, 103–11
Diversity as trait of Sensate culture and art, 80, 92–93, 230, 258, 260–62, 672, 677. See also Complication
Divine reality, 70–72, 114–18, 129, 131. See also Reality
Divorce in literature, 626. See also Adultery, Sex
Dolor in art, 301, 327–29, 341–43, 463, 589, 629, 657–59
Drama, evolution of, 652
Dramatic, lyric, epic, sequence of, 231–34
Dramatism in Sensate art, 258, 260–62, 300–1, 307, 326, 341–42, 348–49, 356, 361, 368–69, 526, 542, 560, 580–82, 586–87, 588, 654, 657–59
Duration of social process, 157
Duty versus revolt in literature, 620, 622, 624, 627–28, 635, 638–39, 640, 655–57
Dynamic character, of Sensate art, 250–53, 258, 261–62, 298, 300, 341–42, 348, 361, 368–69, 526, 560, 580–82, 586, 588, 658–59; of Sensate mentality, 80–81. See also Process, Time

Eclecticism in art, 28, 230. See also Complication, Impure art
Economic motives in art. See Commercialism
Economic topics in art, frequency of, 626, 641
Economy of cathedral builders, 323
Ecstasy, in art, see Dolor, Dramatic, Theatricality; mystic, 131–33
Education, musical, 585–86
Effeminate art, 346–47, 353–55. See also Aestheticism, Theatricality
Element of culture, 10
Emancipation, of art, 302, 592, 610, see also Free art; of women, reflected in portraiture, 489–91
Emotionality of art. See Dramatism, Dynamic
Emptiness, inner, and technique, 584

Ennobling art, 256, 260, 291–93, 322–24
Epic, heroic, 619, 642–46; sequence of lyric and dramatic, 231–34. See also Romances
Epicurean culture mentality, 73–74, 82, 84–85, 87, 90, 93, 97–99, 103, 106–8, 139–43, 146
Epicureanism in art, 139–43, 146, 409. See also Eroticism, Sensate, Passive
Equilibrium, concept of, 69, 176
Eroticism in art, 139–40, 258, 260, 299, 303, 307, 329, 334, 355, 367, 409–21, 422–28, 498, 535, 556, 588, 602, 621–22, 624, 625, 636, 638–39, 640, 656
Eternal, reality, 79, 97–101; value of, 94
Eternalistic mentality, 73, 80, 93, 124, 125, 130, 153–54, 247
Ethics, absolutistic, 93–99; relativistic, 94–95
Eudaemonism in Sensate art and mentality, 30, 94
Evolution, linear, 81, 183–84
Executives of history, 104
Exotic in art, 588, 602, 647, 649, 657. See also Dramatic, Eroticism
Expressionism in art, 251, 387–88
Extensity of uniformities, 29
External, aspect of culture, 55–56; factor of culture integration, 10–11, 45; nature of causal connections, 25; traits of Sensate and Ideational literature, 614, 630, 659
External milieu, as a factor, 51–52; control of, 83
Externalistic method of explanation, 51
Exteroceptive organs of senses, 86
Extrovert, 84–85

Factor, internal and external, of change, 50–53; method of explanation through main, 45
Fad in art, 258, 261–62
Familistic character of Idealistic and Ideational art, 258–59, 296, 323–25. See also Anonymity, Collective
Fantastic topics, in art, 501–2; proportion of, in painting and sculpture, 439–44, 501–2
Fashion in art, 258, 261–62. See also Acceleration, Alternation, Change, Dynamic
Female sex in portraiture, 489–91. See also Portraiture, Woman
Fluctuation, concept of, 153–54; forms of, 164, 167, 181–87, 188; of forms of art, 308, 368, 404, 502–6, 670–72, 678–81, 687; theories of art, 223–31, 198–99, 206–16
Formal style in art, 249–50, 387. See also Idealistic, Ideational
Formula, causal, logico-meaningful, 31
Free art, 257, 258, 302, 365–66, 544, 555, 562, 585, 592, 600–1, 609–11, 617, 668–74, 680–81
Free artist. See Free art
Functional. See Causal
Futurism, 263–64, 354, 362, 364, 387, 399, 592

Generality of causal laws, 23; logico-meaningful principles of, 23; gradation of, 29–30
Genius and overdevelopment of technique, 584
Genre, as a trait of Sensate art and mentality, 258, 260, 298, 308, 338, 367, 485–88, 500, 592, 596, 618, 641–42, 644, 647, 650–56; proportion of, in music, 587, 591; proportion of, in painting, 439–41, 491–98; satirical and humorous, 498–500; types of, 492–98

Gnostics, 112
God, as a subject in art, 488; as a true reality, 70–72, 114–18, 129, 131
Gregorian chant. See Chant

Happiness, mystic, 131–33; Sensate, 30, 93–94
Hedonism, 30, 94
Hermits, 104
Hero in art, types of, 642–46, 648, 652. See also Common type of man, Criminal Knights
Heroic epics and romances, 488, 619, 642–46
Heuristic value of logico-meaningful method, 33–34
Hieratic style in art, 274
Hindu, art, 282–85, 535, 549; culture mentality, 108, 112–14, 117, 120–22, 123–24, 135, 279–80, 282–85
Hinduism. See Appearance, Brahmanism, Hindu
Historical, narrative, emergence of, 619, 631; topics in music, 591; topics in painting and sculpture, 342, 500–1, 508, 541
History, periods in, 158, 179–81
Hit. See Best sellers, Dynamic, Sensational art
Hypocritical mentality, 74, 82, 84, 87, 90, 93–99, 103, 106, 108, 110, 139–43, 146
Hypostatized abstractions in art, 254, 343, 345, 598, 630–31
Hypothesis, method of verification of, 35–37, 65–66

Icon as a symbol, 314
Iconography, Christian painting as, 314; of Christ, 316, 319, 326, 329, 341; of Madonna, 311, 316, 319–30, 341; of vice and virtue, 345
Iconologia, 345
Idea as integrating principle, 18–19, 23–24. See also Major premises
Idealistic, art, 243–54, 255–62, 507–10, 531–40, 595–97, 618–28, see sub Abstract, Beauty, Calmness, etc.; reality, 79; truth, 89–91; values, 89, 92–99
Idealistic culture mentality, 75; characteristics of, 78–79, 83–100; forms of, 75, 143–44. See also Culture, Mentality, Mixed
Idealization in art, 256–60, 291–93, 322–24
Ideational art, 243–64, 507–10, 531–40, 595–97, see also sub Alternation, Anonymity, Calmness, etc.; pseudo-, 75–76, 150–51; reality, 79; truth, 89–91, values, 92–99
Ideational culture mentality, 73; characteristics of, 78–79, 83–100, 104, 106, 111–39. See also sub Absolute, Active, etc.
Identifiability of unit in process, 176
Identity, law of, 20, 36; mistaken, 36; of meaning, 18–19, 23–24; of recurring processes, 164–67
Illusionism in art, 218, 220, 248, 251, 298, 330–32, 387–88, 508, 525, 541–42, 580–82, 653–55, 657
Illusionistic mentality, 70–71, 75, 80, 88, 90, 97, 114–19, 123, 125, 129, 218–20, 250, 361–64, 388, 654
Imitation, Aristotelian principle of, 566, 605
Imitative waves in art, 234–35, 307, 524–26, 601, 611

Immanent, causation, 50–53; self-regulation, 50–53
Immortals, depicted as mortals, 80, 260, 327, 500, 621–52
Imperative, categoric, 628
Impersonality in art. See Anonymity, Collective
Imperturbability. See Apathy
Impressionism in art, 250, 359–63, 387–88. See also Illusionism
Impure, art, 229–30, 404–5, 543; ideational style, 250; music, 234–36, 542, 560, 581; Sensate style, 253
Incantations, magic, 534–35, 547–48, 554–57
Incoherence in art, 229–30, 359, 404–5. See also Complication
Individualism in art, 259, 298, 304, 338–39, 365–66, 544–45, 561–62, 601–2, 657, 664–65, 680–81
Inferential nature of causality, 25
Inner, aspect of culture, 55–56; character of architecture, 507; character of literature, 612–13, 618–19, 633–34, 655; character of music, 531, 540–41; experience, 91; cognition of, life of mind, 89–91; culture of mentality, 75; traits of types of art, 243–45, 250–55
Integrated culture, types of, 66–67
Integration, key principle of, 40–43, 45, 65–66, 70–76, 190; of culture, forms of, 10–11
Intelligentsia in portraiture, 486–87
Interoceptive receptors, 86–87
Interpretation of culture mentality, methods of, 57–61
Intimate knowledge, 25
Introversion, 84–85
Islamic art, 386, 421, 430, 456, 469, 490, 492

Jainism, 123–24

Key principle of integration, 40–43, 45, 65–66, 70–76, 190
Knights as heroes in literature, 619, 642, 645–46, 652
Knowledge, inferential and intimate, 25; wisdom versus empirical, 90–95, 114–17, 118–19, 127, 129–33. See also Truth

Lag, of music, 578–80, 593; theories of, 200–9, 213–15, 221, 231–34, 240
Landscape, of medieval towns, 518–19. See also Paysage
Laws, causal, 31; logical, 20, 62–64
Limit, principle of, 187–88
Linear, conception of social process, 181–85; forms of the, 181–84; style in painting, 331–33
Literary criticism. See Aestheticism, Censorship, Criticism
Literature, asceticism versus sensuality in, 620; duty versus revolt in, 627, 655–56; economic problems in, 641; hero in, see Hero; of primitive groups, 596–98; order of blossoming among arts, 209; woman in, 622–23
Literature, forms of: allegoric, 614, 620, 630; Ideational and Sensate, 595–96; realistic-naturalistic, 649, 659; religious, 598–99, 612, 618, 633; satirical, 648; secular, 600, 612, 618,

633; symbolic, 614, 630; theatrical, 654. See also Comedy, Tragedy, etc.
Logic, laws of, 20; norms of, 62, 64
Logical reading of culture, 60–62
Logico-meaningful, integration of culture, 10–11, 22; method, 22–39, see Heuristic
Love, in art, 498, 535, 556, 588, 602, 621–22, 624, 625, 636, 638–39, 640, 656, see also Eroticism; in literature, 602, 621–22, 625, 636–38, 656–57
Lyric, epic and dramatic, sequence of, 231–34

Macabre in art, 327, 329, 341–43
Magic incantations, 534–35, 547–48, 554–57
Major premises of culture mentality, 70–72
Male sex in portraiture, 489–90
Malerisch. See Illusionism
Marital relationship in literature, 622–24, 626, 636, 638, 656. See also Adultery, Eroticism
Market and art. See Commercialism
Material value, 95
Materialistic mentality, 70–72, 73–74, 75–98
Meaning as inner aspect of culture, 55, 69
Mechanical integration of culture, 10–14
Mentality, and art, 244–254; as inner aspect of culture, 55, 69; as integrating agency, 23–24; forms of, 72–76; nominalistic, 69–70; satellites of each form of culture, 79–98. See also Als ob, Culture, Epicurean, Illusionistic, Mixed, etc., and sub Ideational, Chinese, Hindu, etc.
Method, causal-functional, 14–18, 22–32; descriptive, 45–47, 66; logico-meaningful, 14–18, 22–32
Methods of reading of culture mentality, 57–61, 66
Milieu, control of, 83
Mind, and logico-meaningful method, 28–29; as inner aspect of culture, 55, 69
Mixed, culture mentality, 74–98, see also Culture, Idealistic, Mixed; style of art, 254–65, 401–24
Mobility. See Acceleration, Change, Dynamic, Fluctuation
Modernism, as a trait of Sensate mentality, 80–81, 234–36, 258, 261–62; in art, see Cubism, Dadaism, Impressionism, Pointilism, Queerness, Surrealism
Morte, nature, 467–69
Movies, 367–68
Multiplicity versus unity, in painting, 331. See also Diversity
Music, commercialization and vulgarization of, 585–86, 589; complication of Sensate, 584; content of, 590–93; crooning in, 589; cubists in, 592; ethos of, 536; inner, 541; order of blossoming among arts, 209, 578–80, 590; pathos and dramatism of, 588–89; phases in development of, 234–35; tonality of, 589
Music, forms of: Idealistic, 540; Ideational and Sensate, 531–34; Oriental, 549; preliterate, 547–48; religious, 534–35, 547–48, 554–57, 567–70; secular, 574–78; state, 550–51; theatrical and nontheatrical, 580. See also Oratorio, Orchestra, Symphonic
Musical, aestheticism, criticism, education, 585–86; comedy, 587; orchestra, size of, 582–83
Mysticism, 129–33. See also sub Absolute, Appearance, Surrender
Mystics, 104

Nations, painting and sculpture of main European, Tables 12–36
Naturalistic style in art, 95, 230, 256, 273, 304, 338–39, 353, 367, 387, 397, 643, 648–49
Nature in art. See Animals, *Nature morte, Paysage*
Nature morte, proportion of, 439–44, 467–69
Needs, material and spiritual, 71; methods of satisfaction of, 72; repression of bodily, 72–73
Nominalistic mentality, 69–70
Norms, ethical, 93–99; validity of logical, 62, 64
Novel, picaresque, 647
Nudity, ascetic and erotic, and their proportion, 422–30; complete and incomplete, 430–38; in art, 303–4, 334–37. 422

Old age in art. See Age
Opera, 578–81, 590–91
Opera buffa, 579–81, 587
Oratorio, proportion of, 580
Orchestra, size of, 582–83
Organs of senses and reality, 70, 75, 88–89, 90–91
Oscillating variety of linearism, 184
Overripe stage of art, 229

Painting, Assyrian, 277; Chinese, 277–82; Egyptian, 275–77; Hindu, 282–85; primitive, 269–74; sequence of blossoming among arts, 200, 207–9; spectrum of the content of, 438–39. See also Animals, Antiquity, Fantastic topics, *Genre, Nature morte, Paysage*, Portraiture
Painting, forms of, 243–47, 249–54; cubistic, 263–64; expressionistic, 398–400; formal, 394–97; Idealistic, 254–55; Ideational-Visual, 386; impressionistic, 388–90; Mixed, 401–4; naturalistic, 397–98; religious and secular, 376–86; spiritual and sensual, 373, 409–22. See also *sub* Allegory
Passive Epicureanism and sensatism, 74. See also Epicureanism
Pathological types as subjects in art, 89, 260, 298, 308, 338, 367, 485–88, 500, 592, 596, 618, 641–42, 647, 650–53, 656
Paysage, content of, 456–61; fluctuation of proportion of, 439–44, 455–56; forms of, 453–54; development correlated with social conditions, 367, 452–53; in music, 591; rural and urban, 461; sunny and gloomy, 463; theories of development of, 448–52
Peace. See Calmness
Perception, of reality, 70; of self, 88–89, 90–91
Periodic processes, 186, 188
Periods in history, 158, 179–81
Personality, and culture, 68, 69; of culture, 29
Pessimism. See Death, Dolor, Macabre
Picaresque novel, 647
Pointilism, 362–63
Portraiture, ancestral, 293, 301, 305–6; as a trait of Sensate art, 90–91, 248, 258; proportion of, in painting and sculpture, 439–44, 455; proportion of male and female sexes in, 489–91; of social classes in, 469–89.
Priesthood and Ideational art, 683–84
Primitivism in art, 234–35, 307, 387, 601, 611
Principle, of immanent self-regulation of social process, 50–53; of limit, 187–88

Process, and space, 156; and time, 156; cognition of mental, 89; creatively recurrent forms of, 186–89; cyclical, 184–86; definition of, 153–54; directions of, 156–61; linear, 181–84; periodical, 186–88; punctuation of, 174–81; recurrent and unique, 161–67, 167–74; rhythm and tempo of, 175; specifications of, 154; unit of, 154–55
Professional unions of musicians in Greece and Rome, 562
Professionalization of art and artists, 544–59, 562, 600–1, 617, 665, 680–81
Proportion in music, 574–78; of theatrical and nontheatrical, 680
Proportion, in painting and sculpture, of animals, 439–44; of expressionistic, 398–400; of fantastic topics, 501–2; of *genre*, 439–44, 491; of Ideational and Visual, 386; of impressionistic, 388–90; of mixed, 401–4; of *nature morte*, 439–44, 469; of *paysage*, 439–44, 455; of portrait, 439–44, 469; of religious and secular, 376–86; of sensual and spiritual, 373, 409–22; of topics of antiquity, 439–44, 500–1
Proportion of types of kings and popes, 106
Pseudo-Ideational mentality, 75–76, 78, 83, 84, 89, 90, 97–99
Punctuation of social processes, 171–84; and periodicity, 186–88
Pure, art, 234–36, 257–58, 668–74; Ideational mentality and style, 77, 249–50, 387; music, 234–36, 542, 581; Visual style, 250
Purposeful art, 668–74

Qualitative direction of social processes, 158
Quantitative direction of social processes, 158
Quantitativism, numerical and verbal, 158
Queerness of modern art, 229–30, 359, 362, 404–5. See also Dadaism, Cubism, Futurism

Reading of culture mentality, methods of, 57–61, 66
Realism in art, various meanings of, 207, 218–19, 249, 592. See also Illusionism
Realistic style, 95, 230, 256, 273, 304, 338–39, 353, 367, 387, 397, 592, 643, 648–49, 659
Reality, forms of true and ultimate, 70, 72–76, 80, 82, 89, 97–99; in Buddhism, 116–18; in Christianity, 129–30; in Hinduism, 114–16; in Jainism, 123; in mysticism, 130–32; in Sufism, 128; in Taoism, 125. See also Becoming, Being, God, and *sub* Perception, etc.
Reality, of cubism, 364–65; of impressionism, 361–63. See also *sub* Absolute
Receptors, interoceptive, 86–87
Recurrence, of forms of art, 308, 368, 404, 502–6, 670–72, 678–81, 687; of theories of art, 198–99, 206–16, 224–31
Recurrence of social processes, 161–67, 168–74; cyclical, 184–86; varyingly creative, 186–89
Relativistic, ethics, 94–95; mentality, 70, 87, 97–99; truth, 89, 90–91; value, 94–95
Religious art, 231, 247, 249, 508, 537–39; Chinese, 279–80; Christian, 309–11, 320–22, 517–21, 537–38, 544, 567–71, 612–18; Egyptian, 510–12; Greek, 289–91, 295, 514, 554–56; Hindu, 282–85

Religious art, proportion of, in music, 574–78; in painting and sculpture, 376–86
Religious mentality, see Ideational mentality
Renaissance, architecture of, 523–25; literature of, 636–37, 645; painting and sculpture of, 326–40
Repression of bodily needs, 72–73
Revelation, as source of truth, 89, 92, 93, 130–33
Revolt, against Visual art, 362–65, 504, 526, 592–93, 661, 667, 687–88
Revolt versus duty in literature, 620, 622, 624, 627–28, 635, 638–40, 655–57
Rhythm, definition of, 175
Romances and epics, heroic, 619, 642–44; pastoral, 646; picaresque, 647
Romanesque architecture, 517, 521
Romantic phase, in art, 210–11; in architecture, 526–28; in literature, 634, 649–51, 657; in music, 213–15, 234, 568, 581, 588; in painting and sculpture, 354–55, 358, 488
Royalty and aristocracy in portraiture, 486
Rural and urban *paysage*, 461

Sacred art, 274. See also Religious art
Satellites of main types of culture, 79, 97–99
Satire as a trait of Sensate art, 260–62, 367, 490–91, 587, 647–50
Sculpture. See Architecture, Painting, Proportion
Secular art, 248, 250, 297–300, 558. See also Religious, Sensate, Visual art
Self-regulation of social process, 50–53
Sensate art, 243–54; style in, 250–54, 263, 507–10, 531–40, 595–97; proportion of, 386. See also *sub* Alternation, Colossalism, etc.
Sensate culture mentality, 73–74; characteristics of, 79–97; form of, 74. See also Cynical, and *sub* Active, Diversity, etc.
Sensate, reality, 90–91; truth, 89–91; values, 92–99
Sensational art, 260, 262. See Dramatism, Dynamic, Eroticism
Senses, exteroceptive organs of, 86; organs of, and reality, 70, 75, 88–89, 90–91
Sensual. See Eroticism
Sentimental. See Dramatism
Separation of art from other values, rhythm of, 671–74
Sequence of blossoming of various arts, theories of, 200–9, 213–15, 221, 231–34
Serenity of Idealistic and Ideational art. See Calmness
Sex in art. See Adultery, Eroticism, Female, Male, Marital relationship
Simplicity of Ideational art, 537–43, 582
Social classes, in literature, 618, 641, 652; in portraiture, 485–88. See also Hero
Social processes. See Alternation, Cyclical, Directions, Fluctuation, Process, etc.
Social system, autonomy of, 50–53; integrated, 48–53; traits of, 48–53
Society. See Social system
Space, as element of process, 154, see Process; complexity of social, 160; social, 157
Spatial direction of process, 158

Spiral variety of linearism, 181–82
Spiritual needs, 71
Spiritualization of reality, 92
Static, character of Idealistic and Ideational art, 260, 291, 311, 322, 684; mentality, 260; reality, see Being
Style, forms of: in architecture, 507–10; in literature, 595–97; in music, 531–40; in painting and sculpture, 243–47, 249–54
Sufism, 128
Superempirical, supersensory reality, 70, 79, 86, 91, 93. See also Reality
Surrealism in painting, 362
Surrender, mystic, 132–33
Symbolism in art, 229, 254, 314, 343–45, 508, 614–15, 629–30, see also Allegory; transcendental, 615
Symphonic music, religious and secular 580; theatrical and nontheatrical, 582
System, integrated social, 48–53

Tactilism, 362
Taoism, 125–28
Technique, as substitute for genius, 584; decay and prominence of, 584; of linear and *malerisch* painting, 331–32
Tempo of social processes, 175; acceleration of, 287, 306–8, 352–55, 528–29, 684–86
Temporalistic mentality, 80–82, 141–43. See also Eternalistic
Theatricality of Sensate art, 218, 220, 248, 251; in architecture, 516, 525, 541; in literature, 653–55, 657; in music, 580–82; in painting and sculpture, 298–300, 330, 359–61, 368, 387–88
Time, and process, 156; blurred in medieval literature, 616; direction of process and, 156–61; overestimation of present, in Sensate mentality, 80–82; role of, in Sensate mentality, 80–81; short-, values, 80–82, 140–43
Tradition versus fashion in art, 258, 261–62
Tragedy, Greek, 599–600
Transcendental reality, see Ideational reality; symbolism, 615
Transitional period, in architecture, 528; in literature, 679–80; in music, 593–94; in painting and sculpture, 403–4, 504
Truth, absolutistic, 90–91, 98; different in different cultures, 70, 89–91; revelation as source of, 89, 92, 93, 130–33. See also Knowledge
Type of heroes in art. See Aristocracy, Common man, Criminal, Hero

Uniformity, formula of, 31
Unilinear variety of linearism, 184
Unit of process, 154–55, 176
Unity of culture elements, causal, 14–18; external, 13; inner or logico-meaningful, 18–22; spatial, 10–11
Unity of Ideational art versus diversity of Sensate art and culture, 80, 92–93, 230, 258, 260–62, 672, 677
Urban and rural *paysage*, 461
Utilitarianism and Sensate culture, 30, 94

Value, absolutistic, 93, 99, 119–39; aesthetic, 95; eternal, 93, 114, 117, 124–25, 130, 153–54, 247; in Ideational and Sensate cultures, 92–99; material, 95; pecuniary, 95; relativistic, 94–95; short-time, 80–82, 140–43

Variety. See Diversity

Varyingly recurrent process, 186–89

Violent character of art. See Dynamic

Vision, different ways of, 331

Visual art, 243–49; characteristics of, 257–66; fluctuation of, 386–406; impure, 253; pure, 250; varieties of, 387. See also Impressionism, Naturalistic, Sensate, Theatricality

Wealth as a value, 95

Wisdom versus empirical knowledge, 90–95, 114–17, 118–19, 127, 129–33

Woman in art, athletic, chaste, covered, 260, 291, 293, 300, 303; emancipation of, reflected in portraiture, 489–91; invasion of, 303; seductive, voluptuous, 260, 299–300, 303, 308. See Female sex